The Bantam
Illustrated World Atlas

The Bantam Illustrated World Atlas

A vivid and informative picture of the Earth

With 74 main and auxiliary maps, approximately 280 color photographs, and over 53,000 listed place names

BANTAM BOOKS

NEW YORK · TORONTO · LONDON · SYDNEY · AUCKLAND

Photo Sources

AeroCamera, Rotterdam: 121
AG Astrophotographie, Neustadt: 11, 15
Anthony-Verlag: 23 (3), 84, 134
Artreference, Frankfurt: 11, 15
Bavaria: 28, 32, 37 (3), 92/93 (7), 181 (3)
Belgisches Verkehrsamt, Düsseldorf: 121
R. Cramm: 32, 37 (7), 92/93, 151, 191
dpa: 56
Esso/David Moore: 22
FPG International/P. Baker: 38
FPG International/David Noble: 39
FPG International/K. Reinhard: 39
FPG International/Keith Gunnar: 41
FPG International/W. Fischer: 45
FPG International/Ron Thomas: 54, 60
FPG International/E. Gebhardt: 54
FPG International/James Blank: 56, 57
FPG International/G. Kufrin: 57
FPG International/Gene Ahrens: 57
FPG International/G. Schwartz: 60
FPG International/Travelpix: 60, 62/63
FPG International/Martin Rogers: 62
FPG International/D. Dietrich: 62/63
FPG International/Frank Gordon: 63
FPG International/P. Beney: 63

FPG International/J. Ranokieu: 64
FPG International/John E. Swedberg: 64
FPG International/Hanson Carroll: 65
FPG International/Peter Gridley: 65 (2)
Michael Friedel: 187
Dr. Georg Gerster: 10, 18/19, 20/21 (2), 40/41 (4), 56 (2), 91, 96/97 (2), 102, 126, 146/147 (2), 156, 164, 168/169 (2), 172/173 (2), 176/177 (3), 180 (2), 185, 187 (2), 193 (2), 196/197
GPA: 107
GPA/Aspect: 22, 186 (2), 196
GPA/Brian Seed: 184/185, 186/187 (5), 192
HB Verlag, Hamburg: 126, 127
Thomas Höpker: 40/41 (3), 54, 60/61 (3), 84, 100 (2), 102, 106/107, 127, 134, 147, 165
U. Hoyer: 92/93 (2)
Huber & Oberländer (Artwork): 97, 159, 165
Interfoto: 32, 37
Irish Tourist Board/Bord Fáilte: 120
Franz Lazi: 19, 28/29, 41, 91, 100 (2), 107 (4), 145, 186, 192
Luftbild Albrecht Brugger: 122
Luftbild Klammet & Aberl: 122, 127, 129
C. Lutze: 123, 152

Magnum/Robert Azzi: 21, 157
Magnum/Micha Bar-Am: 173
Magnum/Bruno Barbey: 146/147 (2), 158, 165
Magnum/Ian Berry: 158
Magnum/Cartière Bresson: 158
Magnum/Réne Burri: 146, 157, 168/169
Magnum/Elliott Erwett: 152
Magnum/Burt Glinn: 41 (2), 153
Magnum/Ernst Haas: 54/55, 196
Magnum/Erich Hartmann: 41, 173
Magnum/Marc Ribaud: 41, 104, 147 (2), 164
Magnum/Schwab: 169
Magnum/H. Sochureic: 147
Magnum/Dennis Stock: 40, 146, 172/173
Magnum/Kryn Tacanis: 44/45 (2)
Mauritius: 118/119 (2), 120, 121, 123, 125 (3), 136/137, 151 (5), 181, 191 (5), 198
B. Michael, Hamburg, 11, 15
Heinz Müller-Brunke: 61, 107, 112, 122, 128/129 (2), 136/137, 146, 186/187 (3)
NASA: 8/9, 11, 12/13
NASA/USIS: 20 (2)
Werner Neumeister: 105, 118, 134/135 (2)
Photri/NASA: 10/11

Erich Reismüller: 18, 40, 90, 96/97 (3), 141, 145, 158/159 (2), 162/163 (2)
Hans Schmied: 18/19, 41 (2), 44, 84/85 (2), 106/107, 127, 136/137 (2), 144, 146/147 (2), 186, 192
Toni Schneiders: 105, 106/107 (7), 112 (2), 122, 128/129, 130/131 (3), 134, 137
Emil Schulthess: 140/141 (2), 152/153 (3)
Schweizer Verkehrsbüro, Frankfurt: 126 (2)
H. Schwenk: 118
H. Steenmans: 92/93 (2), 151
Stern/Max Scheler: 123
Dr. R. Sturm: 191
Manfred Uselmann: 134/135
Wilhelm Wagner (Artwork): 18/19, 20/21, 22/23
Westfälische Volkssternwarte, Recklinghausen: 11, 15
Zefa: 113
Zell am See, Kurverwaltung: 127
Aerial photographs with permission of Reg. Präsidium Stuttgart Nr. 2/4049 3 p. 122
BMfIV Wien Nr. 3702 RAb + B/76 p. 127

THE BANTAM ILLUSTRATED WORLD ATLAS
A Bantam Book/November 1989

All rights reserved.
Copyright © 1989 by RV Reise- und Verkehrsverlag
Berlin · Gütersloh · München · Stuttgart.
No part of this book may be reproduced or transmitted in any form or by any means,
electronic or mechanical, including photocopying, recording, or by any information storage
and retrieval system, without permission in writing from the publisher.
For information address: Bantam Books.

Library of Congress Cataloging-in-Publication Data

Bantam Books (Firm)
  The Bantam illustrated world atlas.

    »Copyright by RV Reise- und Verkehrsverlag« – T.p.
verso.
    Published simultaneously in the U.S. and Canada.
    Includes index.
    1. Atlases. I. Reise- und Verkehrsverlag. II. Title.
III. Title: Illustrated world atlas.
G1021.B225   1989   912   89-675059
  ISBN 0-553-05702-2

Published simultaneously in the United States and Canada

Bantam Books are published by Bantam Books, a division of Bantam Doubleday Dell
Publishing Group, Inc. Its trademark, consisting of the words "Bantam Books" and the
portrayal of a rooster, is registered in U.S. Patent and Trademark Office and in other
countries. Marca Registrada, Bantam Books, 666 Fifth Avenue, New York, New York 10103.

PRINTED IN WEST GERMANY BY MAINPRESSE RICHTERDRUCK WÜRZBURG

0 9 8 7 6 5 4 3 2 1

Contents

Conventional Signs

~~	Constantly water-bearing river		——————	Railroad
-~-	River drying up		————	Main station
~~	Temporarily water-bearing river		————	Branch line
--------	Canal		++++++++	Cable railway
········	Canal under construction		- - - -	Road under construction
~~	Waterfall, rapids		············	Railway ferry
~t~	Dam		⌐--⌐	Tunnel
	Lake with permanent shoreline		——————	Major highway
	Lake with variable or indefinite shoreline		————	Expressway
	Temporary lake		====	Highway under construction
◡	Wells in arid regions		- - - - -	Caravan path, footpath, track
	Swamp, marsh		··············	Ferry
	Salt marsh, dry salt lake		⋈	Pass
	Flood plain		⊕ ✛	Airport
	Mud flats		◄———►	Pipeline or gasline
+ ◯	Reef, coral reef			
	Glacier		▦▦▦▦	State line
	Average ice-pack line in the summer		▦▦▦▦	Boundary of self-governing regions
	Average ice-pack line in the winter		▦▦_ _	Boundaries of subordinate administrative units
	Shelf ice		WASHINGTON	Capital city of a nation
	Sandy desert		Harrisburg / Nachičevan'	Chief places of subordinate administrative units

"in larger scales" applies to Main station / Branch line.
"in larger scales" applies to Expressway / Highway under construction.

	Place			Local section			
						•	Residence, station
⬡	LOS ANGELES	over 1,000,000 inhabitants	✦	L.-A.-HOLLYWOOD		∴	Ruined city
■	BOSTON	500,000–1,000,000 inhabitants	■	B.-DORCHESTER		⚲	Fortress or castle
●	ATLANTA	100,000–500,000 inhabitants	•	A.-BOLTON		⚲	Monastery or church
◎	Malden	50,000–100,000 inhabitants	○	Edgeworth		⚲	Ruin
⊙	Jefferson	10,000–50,000 inhabitants				⊥	Monument
○	Cleveland	under 10,000 inhabitants				⚐	Lighthouse
						◌	National park, wildlife preserve, nature preserve

Conventional Typefaces

CANADA	Independent nation		*MIDDLE WEST* / *Gila Desert* / *Isle Royale*	Landscapes and islands
Texas	Subordinate administrative unit			
(U.S.A.) *(U.S.A.)*	Political or national affiliation		OCEAN / Gulf of Mexico / Mississippi River	Body of water
DENVER / Columbia / *Augusta*	Cities, towns, villages		Cayman Trench	Ocean basin, marine trench, marine ridge, etc.
COAST RANGE / Colorado Plateau	Mountainous region		2789	Elevation, depth in meters
Mt. Shasta	Mountain, cape, pass, glacier		164	Water depth of a lake in meters

Land Elevations and Ocean Depths

1:15,000,000 and smaller	>10000	10000	8000	6000	4000	2000	200	0 Depr. 0	200	500	1000	2000	3000	4000	5000	>5000 m
	>32809	32809	26247	19685	13124	6562	656	0 Depr. 0	656	1640	3281	6562	9843	13124	16405	>16405 ft

1:2,500,000 and 1:5,000,000	>10000	10000	8000	6000	4000	2000	200	0 Depr. 0	100	200	500	1000	2000	3000	4000	5000	>5000 m
	>32809	32809	26247	19685	13124	6562	656	0 Depr. 0	328	656	1640	3281	6562	9843	13124	16405	>16405 ft

1:1,000,000	>200	200	100	40	20	0 Depr. 0	100	200	300	500	700	1000	1500	2000	2500	3000	>3000 m
	>656	656	328	131	66	0 Depr. 0	328	656	984	1640	2297	3281	4921	6562	8202	9843	>9843 ft

Our World Today

Year by year our knowledge of the
planet Earth, the solar system and
the universe grows. Man is reaching
for the stars. Astronauts have set
foot on the Moon and are working in
space. Space probes have landed on
Mars and circled other planets. Mankind is beginning to learn that the
blue planet is home to all and that
our behavior will also influence its future development. The variety of terrain is the distinguishing
characteristic of our globe, and there
are no more uncharted territories on
its face. This atlas presents the fascinating world of today with all its
contrasts. The maps of the continents, with their countries and landscapes, are complemented by vivid
color photographs: the new picture of
the Earth.

The Earth rises: This is the awe-inspiring view seen by astronauts on board *Apollo 11* during the journey to the Moon on July 21, 1969. At the time, Earth was approximately 238,000 miles (384,000 kilometers) away. In the foreground: the Moon's surface.

OUR SMALL EARTH: A BLUE PLANET, A TINY SPHERE AMONG BILLIONS OF STARS AND OTHER BODIES IN THE INFINITE UNIVERSE.

Astronaut Irwin lands on the Moon with Apollo 15.

On July 21, 1969, the American astronaut, Neil Armstrong, as the first man to set foot on the Moon, stepped onto the "Sea of Tranquility" and said: "That's one small step for a man, one giant leap for mankind." (Twelve years earlier, on October 4, 1957, the Russians had put the first satellite, *Sputnik 1,* into orbit around the Earth.) All in all there were six Apollo landings on the Moon; the last one was *Apollo 17,* in December 1972. The twelve astronauts that left their footprints in the Moon dust brought back a total of 30,000 pictures, as well as 20,000 tapes with geophysical data. The secrets of the Moon, Earth's neighbor in the cosmos (its average distance from Earth is 238,000 miles), were solved. In the meantime, other probes are on their way to, or planned for, Mars, Venus, Jupiter and Neptune.

With a burst of flames the giant Saturn-V rocket lifts off from the launch pad at Cape Kennedy. This is how Apollo 11's journey to the Moon began in July 1969. Saturn-V was the means of propulsion for all Moon flights. The rocket was 360 feet (110 meters) tall. Its five thrusters accelerated the first rocket stage to a speed of 24,800 mph (40,000 km/h) within a few minutes. This was necessary to over-come Earth's gravitational pull. The landing sites on the Moon (right) were carefully selected: Today's Moon maps are al-most as complete as maps of the Earth.

Launch of the space shuttle

By landing on the Moon, man took the first step into space. The Moon may also become the starting point for flights to the solar system's more distant planets. If the Moon were used as a base for interplanetary expeditions, a launch would require only one-twentieth of the energy needed to overcome Earth's gravity.

In order to escape Earth's gravitational pull, a speed of approximately 24,800 mph (40,000 km/h) is necessary. This creates enormous physical stress on the astronauts.

This stress is significantly lessened in a spaceship like the space shuttle. In spite of all the technical problems and the tragic disaster on January 28, 1986, this reusable space shuttle will remain America's most important project, at least until the start of the 21st century. This was confirmed when the revitalized shuttle resumed flights in September 1988. Europeans, too, are becoming more actively involved in space flight: In 1979, the first test flight of the booster rocket Ariane took place, and in 1983—in cooperation with NASA—the European space laboratory Spacelab was launched.

Space shuttle during a landing

Giant radio telescope—the communication link to the astronauts

On their flights to investigate our solar system, the cameras of Voyager 1 and Voyager 2 took many photos of distant planets. In early March 1979, Voyager 1 encountered the planet Jupiter and four of its moons: Io, Europa, Ganymede and Callisto (photo far right). The photo of Saturn and its six largest moons was taken in November 1980 (photo right). During Voyager 1's total of 698 orbits around Mars, approximately 7,300 photos were taken of the surface of Mars: They show a barren, reddish rock desert (photo center). The boulder pieces could consist of volcanic minerals.

12

THE SUN AND ITS 9 PLANETS

1. Mercury: Temperatures up to 800°F (425°C) at the equator. Median distance to the Sun is 36 million mi. (58 million km). 2. Venus: Ground temperatures over 800°F (425°C). Its distance to the Sun is 67 million mi. (108 million km). 3. Earth: In an advantageous position in relation to the Sun, 93 million mi. (150 million km) away. 4. Mars: Even at the equator, temperatures are like those in Siberia. Distance to the Sun is approximately 141 million mi. (228 million km). 5. Jupiter: Giant among the planets. Distance to the Sun is 483 million mi. (778 million km). 6. Saturn: Its exterior cloud cover is approximately −360°F (−180°C). Distance to the Sun is 887 million mi. (1.4 billion km). 7. Uranus: Temperatures −340°F (−170°C). Distance to the Sun is 1,783 million mi. (2.9 billion km). 8. Neptune: Covered by a thick layer of ice. The Sun is 2,790 million mi. (4.5 billion km) away. 9. Pluto: The smallest planet is 3,675 million mi. (5.9 billion km) from the Sun.

9

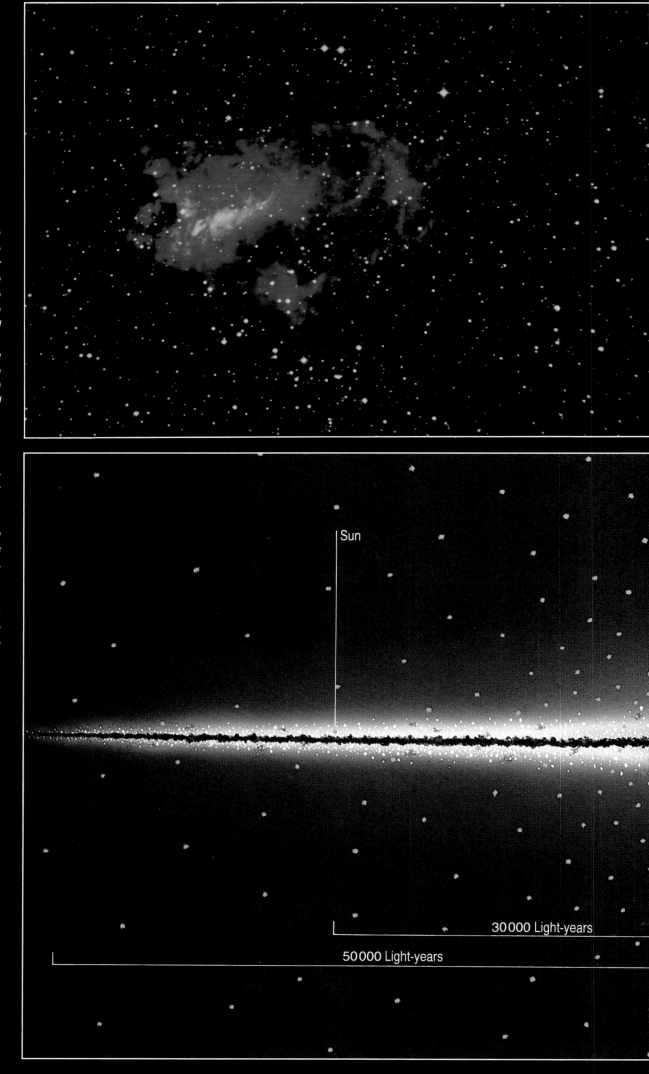

Stars are frequently found in groups, or star clusters. Two of the best-known star clusters can be seen by the unaided eye: Pleiades, also referred to as the "Seven Stars" (photo far right), and Hyades (the "Rain Stars").
These relatively young collections of stars (maximum age 1,000,000,000 years) contain up to several thousand stars.
Significantly older are the spherical star clusters, with 100,000 to 1,000,000 stars. The brightest of spherical star clusters is Omega Centauri (center photo), in the southern sky. Between the stars is the so-called interstellar mass, consisting of dust and gas; it is the raw material of new stars. The Omega nebula in Sagittarius (photo left) is one birthplace of new stars. The bright "young" stars are easily identified.

Sun

30000 Light-years

50000 Light-years

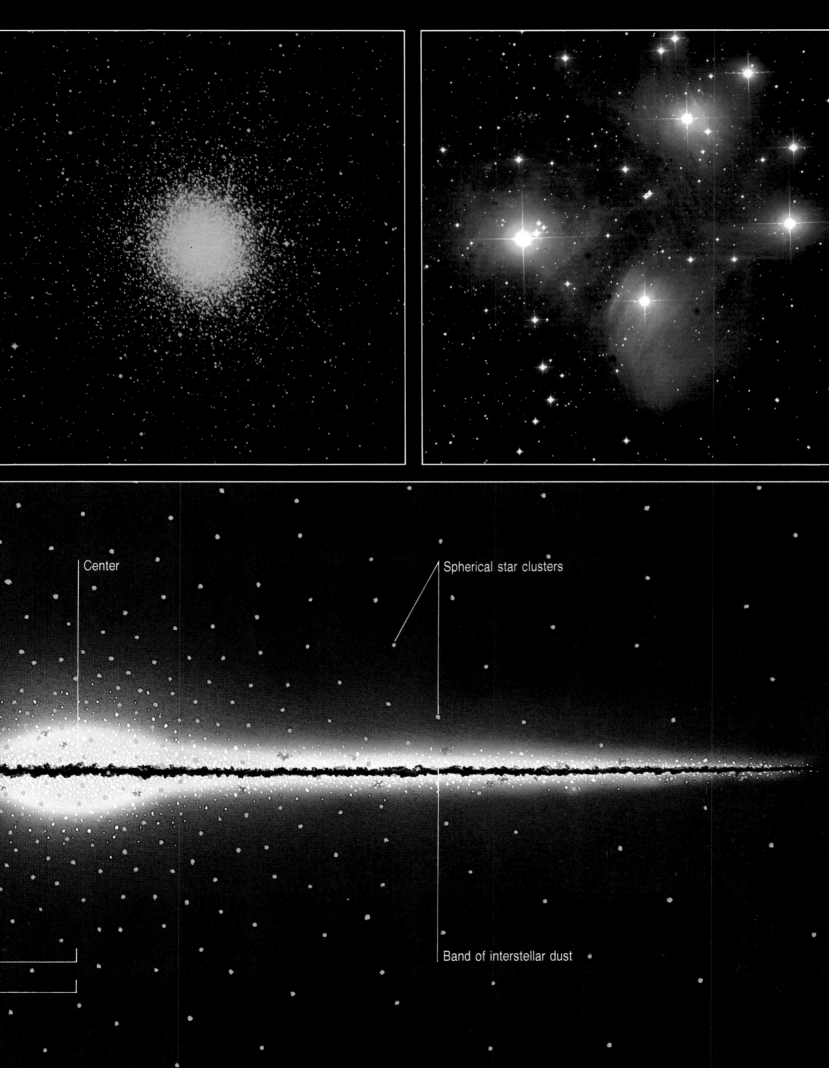

Center

Spherical star clusters

Band of interstellar dust

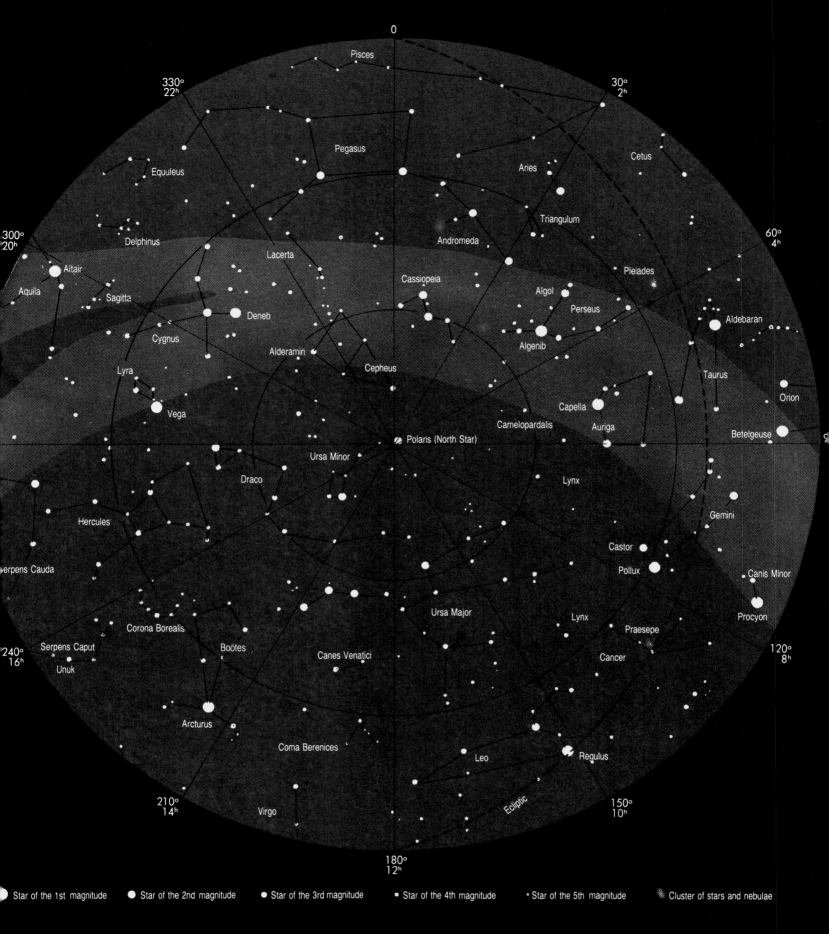

Pisces

330° 22ʰ

0

30° 2ʰ

Cetus

Pegasus

Aries

Equuleus

Triangulum

Andromeda

300° 20ʰ

Delphinus

Lacerta

Pleiades

60° 4ʰ

Altair

Cassiopeia

Algol

Aquila

Sagitta

Deneb

Perseus

Aldebaran

Cygnus

Alderamin

Algenib

Taurus

Lyra

Cepheus

Orion

Vega

Capella

Auriga

Betelgeuse

Polaris (North Star)

Camelopardalis

Ursa Minor

Draco

Lynx

Hercules

Serpens Cauda

Castor

Canis Minor

Pollux

Corona Borealis

Ursa Major

Lynx

Praesepe

Procyon

240° 16ʰ

Serpens Caput

Boötes

Canes Venatici

Cancer

120° 8ʰ

Unuk

Arcturus

Coma Berenices

Leo

Regulus

210° 14ʰ

Virgo

Ecliptic

150° 10ʰ

180° 12ʰ

○ Star of the 1st magnitude   ● Star of the 2nd magnitude   ● Star of the 3rd magnitude   • Star of the 4th magnitude   · Star of the 5th magnitude   ▨ Cluster of stars and nebulae

The naked eye can observe up to 6,000 stars in the star-filled sky. Their brightness observed from Earth separates them into different orders of magnitude. Certain planets appear even brighter than the brightest stars. This is true of Mercury, Venus, Mars and Jupiter. These planets appear brighter than stars because they are much closer to Earth.

Many of the 88 known constellations get their names from Greek mythology.

Other constellations' names have an even older origin. Single stars have Latin, Greek or old Arabic names.

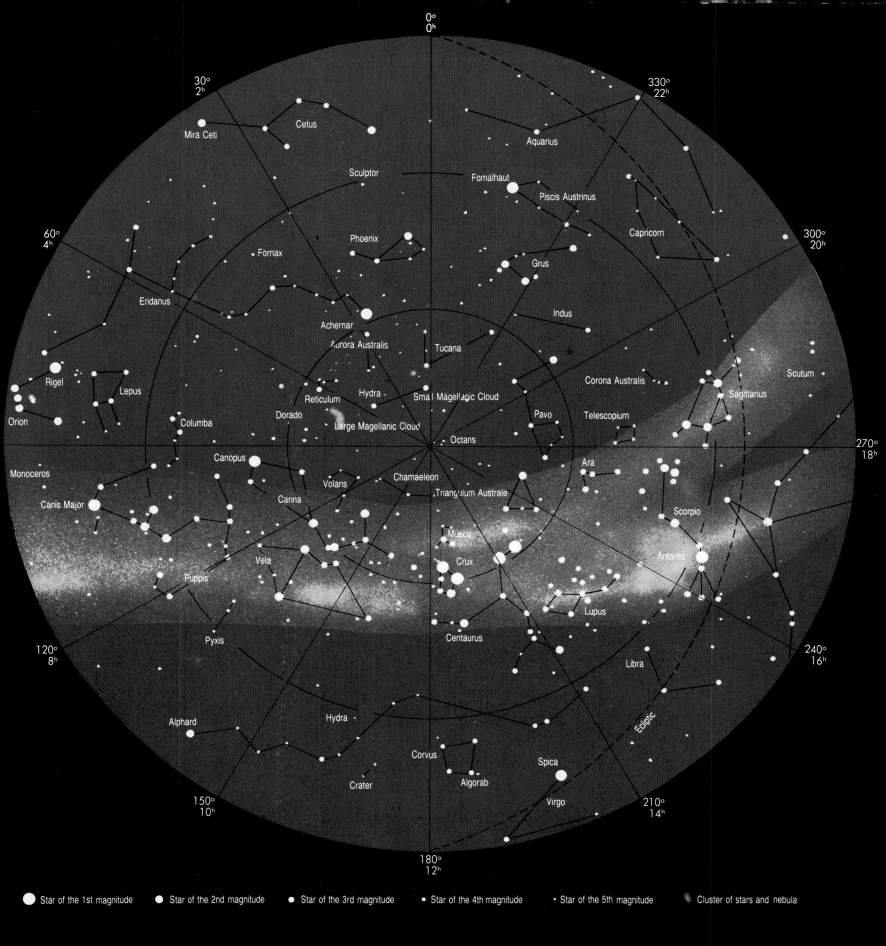

0°
0ʰ

30°
2ʰ

Mira Ceti
Cetus

Sculptor

330°
22ʰ

Aquarius

Fomalhaut
Piscis Austrinus

Capricorn

60°
4ʰ

Fornax

Phoenix

Grus

300°
20ʰ

Eridanus

Achernar
Aurora Australis
Tucana

Indus

Rigel

Lepus

Reticulum
Hydra
Small Magellanic Cloud

Corona Australis

Scutum
Sagittarius

Orion

Columba
Dorado
Large Magellanic Cloud
Octans

Pavo

Telescopium

270°
18ʰ

Monoceros

Canopus

Volans
Chamaeleon
Triangulum Australe

Ara

Canis Major

Carina

Musca
Crux

Scorpio

Antares

Vela
Puppis

Lupus

Pyxis

Centaurus

120°
8ʰ

Libra

240°
16ʰ

Alphard

Hydra

Ecliptic

Corvus
Spica

Crater
Algorab

150°
10ʰ

Virgo

210°
14ʰ

180°
12ʰ

● Star of the 1st magnitude   ● Star of the 2nd magnitude   ● Star of the 3rd magnitude   • Star of the 4th magnitude   · Star of the 5th magnitude   ▨ Cluster of stars and nebula

The appearance of constellations depends on the seasons. For example, in the Mediterranean, Pisces disappears from the night sky when the rainy period (winter) begins.

The maps (above) of the northern and southern skies show the most important stars down to the fifth order of magnitude. The Northern and Southern hemispheres are separated by the celestial equator. The dotted line indicates the ecliptic (zodiac), the zone through which the Sun, Moon and planets move; these celestial bodies can never be found outside of the zodiac.

17

Risen from the turbulent depths of the Earth: the icy, giant mountains of the Himalayas in Asia ... *The Grand Canyon*

FIVE BILLION YEARS AGO THE TURBULENT HISTORY OF EARTH BEGAN

Wherever on Earth a volcano erupts and molten lava brings destruction, wherever the earth trembles and entire cities turn into rubble, a geological fact that is all too easily forgotten is being manifested: Our seemingly tranquil Earth has remained a turbulent planet, just as it was in primordial times.

The illustration below shows the awesome forces at work beneath us.

Earth's crust (2) is composed of large tectonic plates. In continental areas these consist of granite and reach a thickness of up to 24 mi. (40 km). In ocean zones they consist mainly of basalt and are only about 2.5 mi. (4 km) thick. The sedimentary layer (1) is composed of maritime sediments accumulating at the rate of 1–10 millimeters per 1,000 years. These sediments are primarily the remains of dead microorganisms, such as diatoms. When the oceanic plate (2a) is pushed under the continental plate (2b), the sediments are compressed and folded, and mountains (1a), such as the Rocky Mountains, the Andes or the

Himalayas, are created. In the course of this process, tensions and strains occur at the seduction zone (2c), contributing to sea- and earthquakes.

The deep-sea trenches (3) are border zones in which the large plates meet and one plate is pushed under the other. They extend to a depth of 12,000 yards (11,000 meters) below the ocean surface. The deep-sea plateau (4) lies an average of 4,375 yards (4,000 meters) below sea level and consists mainly of sediments. Deep-sea sediments grow no more than 11 yards (10 meters) every million years. No sediments more than 150 million years old have ever been found. Ocean floors are composed of material that is young in

geological terms.

The submerged portion of a continent is called the continental shelf (5). It reaches a depth of 220 yards (200 meters) beneath the ocean's surface and descends farther, as the continental slope (5a), to the deep-sea plateau.

Under the crust of the Earth is the earth mantle. It consists of the upper mantle (6a), approximately 375 mi. (600 km) thick, and the lower mantle (6b), reaching to a depth of 1,800 mi. (2,900 km). Here is where the flows occur that are the main force behind the expansion of the ocean floor and the related continental movements. The schematic representation of the Earth's crust and the earth mantle is extremely condensed.

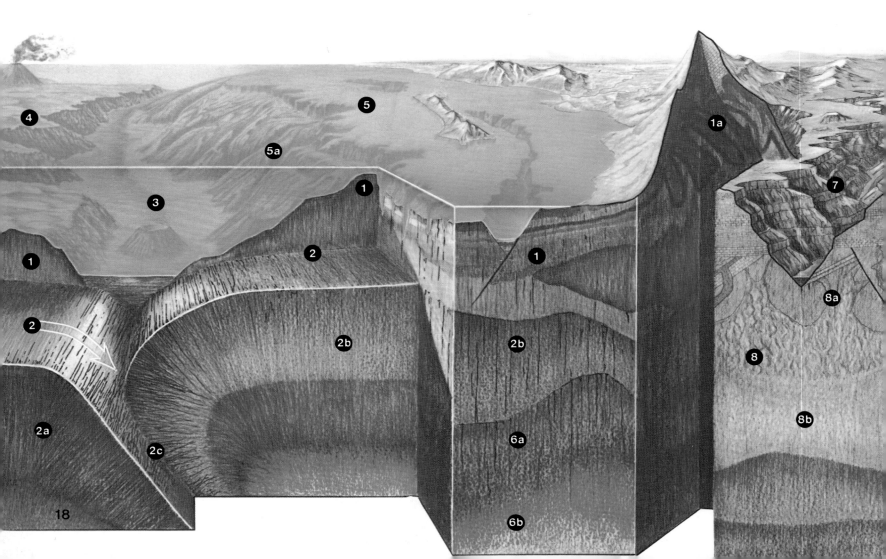

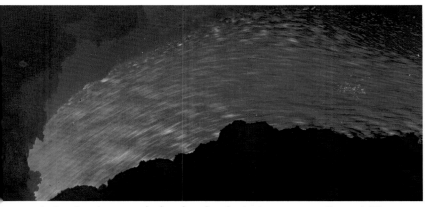

. . red glowing lava and clouds of ash during an eruption of Etna

. . . crater of a dead volcano

. . . hot water of the geysers

The formation of canyons (7) is shown in the example of the Grand Canyon. Here, the Colorado River has dug itself into the rock layers, which were formed over a period of more than a billion years.

At the bottom are minerals, more than 500 million years old, which show traces of a primitive algae believed to be one of the earliest life forms on Earth. The Earth's granite crust (8) is divided into the upper granite crust (8a), with sediments resting on top of it, and a lower crust (8b). Together they build up the continental shelf's thickness to as much as 24 mi. (40 km). The shape of a plain (9)—i.e., the Russian or the North African Plain (Sahara)—was formed from a mountainous terrain, which was planed through

millions of years of erosion.

Lava or cone-shaped shield volcanos (10) are composed of many individual layers of lava. Every eruption produces at least one new layer of lava. Volcanos usually take thousands or even millions of years to form but sometimes take only a few decades, in which time they can reach a height of several hundred yards. Their gaseous emissions (11) contain steam made up of water, chlorine and nitrogen gases. Fluid emissions (12) are usually of relatively liquid lava. Magma pouring forth as lava has a temperature of over 1,800°F (1,000°C). If it flows "quietly," its shape is stringy; if it is ejected violently and irregularly, it is shaped like blocks. Clouds of glow-

ing ash (13) are formed when the lava is so viscous that it blocks the volcano's opening.

The magma, rich in gas and highly compressed, seeks a path through openings on the side of the mountain and escapes in the form of glowing clouds of ash. Magma that does not reach the surface of the Earth either solidifies as dykes, which are sheets of cooled magma projecting through strata of overlying rock (14), or forms lens-shaped subvolcanos, the laccoliths (15), over which dome-shaped knolls are formed (16) on the Earth's surface.

Over the magma chamber (17) are former sedimentary formations (18), which were transformed—that is, metamorphosed—through the heat of earlier volcanos. In the event of a fault eruption (19), basaltic magma comes to the surface through a fissure. Such faults (20) are formed during strong earthquakes. One of the most famous fault lines is the San Andreas fault in California. When ground water that has been heated by volcanic activity is thrust out of the ground, so-called geysers are created (21). In a kind of hydrological cycle the superheated water is released in a hissing and steaming column of water and steam.

19

The American underwater research vessel Sealab II

Researchers can work for weeks in modern underwater laboratories

MOUNTAINS IN THE OCEAN, DESERTS AND OASES, ENERGY FROM SUN AND WATER

Much of the Earth is covered with water; nonetheless, until a few decades ago we knew little of the 70 percent of the Earth's surface that is covered by water. Only after the echo depth sounder was invented following World War I were the secrets of the "submerged landscape" gradually revealed.

A technique developed by oil engineers—the seismic exploration method—also furthered research of the subterranean world. Charges are detonated underwater, generating small seaquake waves on the ocean floor. Their echoes help researchers draw valuable conclusions regarding the Earth's crust (1), sediments (6), continental plate (4), continental shelf (7) and continental slopes (8)—the relief shapes of the ocean floor—as they are described on the two preceding pages.

Of all the landscapes on the ocean floor, the mid-ocean ridge and the mid-ocean trench (2 and 3) are the most intriguing. An extended cartographic survey of the ocean floor by research ships indicates that this ridge, with a length of approximately 40,000 mi. (64,000 km), extends across each ocean. Located at the crest of the ridge is a tremendous trench 8–30 mi. (13–48 km) wide and more than 2,000 feet (600 meters) deep in many places. Along this trench, new ocean floor is constantly being produced by overflowing magma (5). This trench is one of the "seams" between two crust plates that are slowly moving away from each other.

Deserts are among the Earth's largest terrain forms, covering nearly one-seventh of the Earth's surface. Theoretically, every region of the Earth could become a desert if there were no precipitation for a protracted length of time. For example, let's take the Sahara. The Atlas Mountains to the north cause rain to fall on the ocean side (9a) of the range's slopes, while the leeward side facing the interior of the continent has no precipitation (9b). Freshwater lakes (10) frequently can be found in these mountains. The water is transported via pump stations (11) and pipelines (12) to arid regions, where it is used to irrigate the desert ground, and where oases sometimes are created (13): Natural oases are formed where water from water-bearing layers

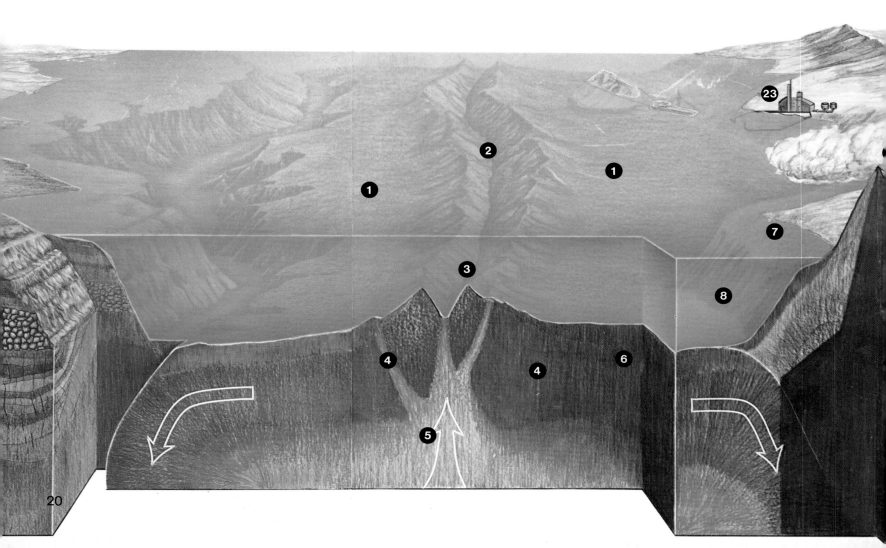

Riches under the desert sand: oil

Water turns deserts into oases

7.7 million sq. mi. (20 mill. sq. km) of the Earth are desert

(16) reaches the surface through a fault plane (14). Water streams down from the mountains and collects in screes (19) at the foot. In deserts, waterways usually end in a dry bed (18) as a wadi, in salt lakes or in brine ponds (22). Artesian wells (15) are a special phenomenon. A water-bearing layer is surrounded both above and below by a waterproof layer (17). If the water-bearing layer is tapped at the deepest area of the depression, water is ejected by its own pressure in a large fountain.

In these desert regions, highlands are carved and mesas (20), or isolated pedestal rocks (21), remain. Frequently the water is also dammed. An example of this is Lake Chad, which has an underground drain. Because of the drain, it did not become a salt lake in the arid desert climate but remained a freshwater lake, the only large lake in this arid region. The result is that cultivated land surrounds Lake Chad. Desalination plants frequently are constructed to obtain fresh water from salt water (23). The fresh water is then pumped many miles to the arid regions. In California, for example, there are plants capable of producing 1,300,000 gallons (5,000,000 liters) of fresh water from ocean water per day. There are also such plants in Kuwait and Israel.

Man has learned to make himself master of Nature's power and re- sources. He has made artificial lakes (24) and directs water through pressure pipes (25) to power-gene- rating plants (26), in which turbines and generators transform the natu- ral power of water into electric ener- gy.

Of all energy sources, the Sun is the one most readily available to man. Modern steam turbines re- quire temperatures between 575°F and 1,000°F (300°C and 600°C). In order to reach such temperatures, sunlight must be concentrated through lenses and mirrors (27,28). Solar energy is still not as economi- cally efficient as other energy sources. Hopefully, in the coming years it will be.

Today, uranium, the fuel of nu- clear energy, has become the most precious of all metals. As it is never found pure and seldom in high con- centrations, enormous amounts of ore must be detected, mined (29,30) and enriched through ex- pensive procedures (31) to obtain even small quantities of the final product. A particular problem of nu- clear energy is the disposal of nu- clear wastes (32): After uranium and plutonium are separated, solu- tions of fission products remain that can no longer be used. Their safe storage is one of the most debated problems of our time. Scientists are still searching for safe solutions.

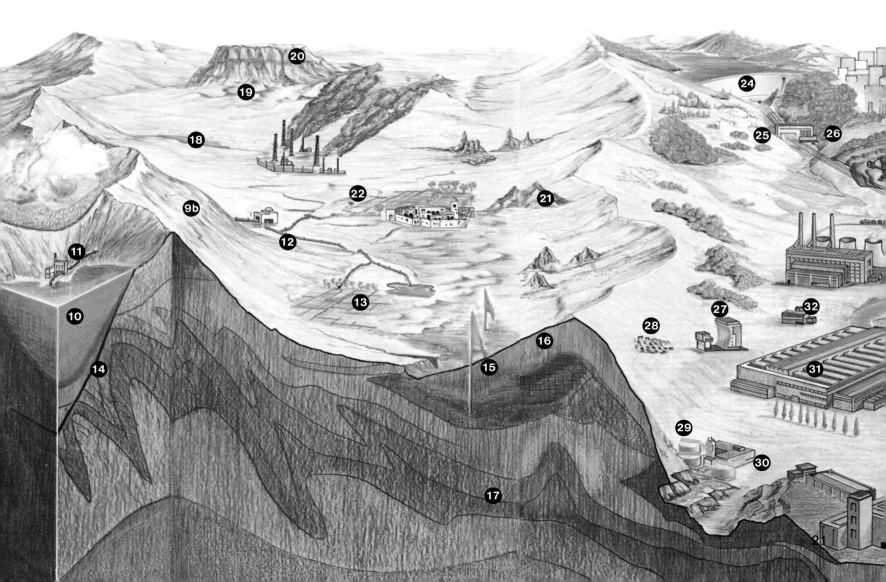

Oil drilling platforms.

Refineries: Heating oil and gasoline are made from crude oil.

RESOURCES BENEATH THE GROUND: A BLESSING, BUT ALSO A DANGER

Immeasurable riches lie in the depths of the Earth and its oceans. The history of mankind is a history of man searching for these riches. Stone-age man already knew that he could make fire with flint. But it was tens of thousands of years before the industrial age dawned, when coal was first used as fuel. Coal mining below ground (1), or strip mining (2), still supplies our number-one energy source and the raw material for the chemical industry. But how was coal created? You have to go back 250 million to 300 million years, for the mineral coal was formed over this period from wood and other plant materials not exposed to air. Vast areas of swampland were covered by primordial forests. Changes in the Earth's crust led to the flooding of these forests, and new swamps were created. The layers of decomposed vegetation hardened and eventually fossilized. The final result was coal. The world's accessible coal reserves are estimated to be about 5,000 billion tons.

Oil, deposited in hollows of sedimentary rock not exposed to air, resulted from the decomposition of organic substances under heat and pressure. Today, drilling rigs extract oil from deserts and the shelf regions of the oceans (3). When stored in tanks and processed in refineries, it becomes "liquid gold" (3,4,5). Nature's energy is also harnessed in tidal-power plants (6). The first large tidal-power plant was put on line in 1966 at the mouth of the La-Rance River near St. Malo, in France. Solar energy is utilized to power steam-generating plants (7,8,9). Residential houses with solar-energy collectors on their roofs (10) are being built now, offering a new prospect for heating and supplying hot water to homes in an environmentally sound manner. Solar heat, however, is still relatively expensive because of the cost of solar-energy collectors in relation to the energy collected. It is hoped that with new, more efficient technology this cost will be reduced. With nuclear-power plants (11,12) a new, if highly debated, age of energy supply has arrived. The most significant difference between a nuclear-power plant and a conventional power plant (13,14) is the energy source. In the case of nu-

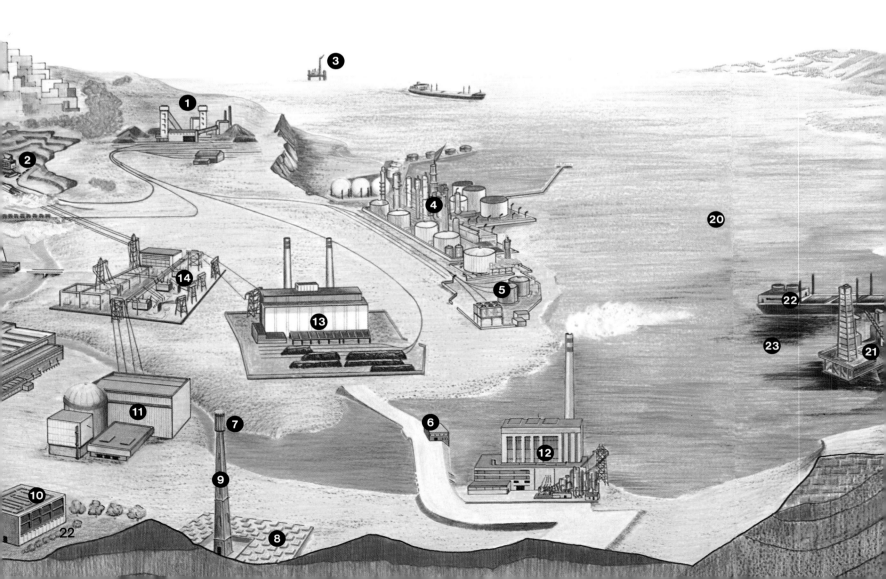

Nuclear energy

Sewage: problems and dangers

Environmental protection: laws for clean air and water

clear power, the energy is generated by nuclear fission of uranium atoms. Through the accompanying strong neutron radiation, the interior components of a nuclear-power plant become highly radioactive. The useful life of a nuclear-power plant is calculated to be 30 to 40 years.

Depletion of forests changes the ground and the climate (15). The rapid growth of the world's population has led to increased use of pesticides and fertilizers in agriculture (16), which disturbs nature's biological balance. Industrialization and expansion of cities pollute air and water (17,18,19). Oil and natural-gas drilling platforms in the sea are

wonders of technology, but during natural disasters they become very dangerous (20,21), just like giant supertankers (22). When they break up or are beached during storms, they release into the ocean gigantic oil spills that drift toward the shore-lines. Used oil is all too often disposed of haphazardly (23,24), contaminating ground water and rivers.

Oil is frequently found in anticline deposits (25) over which natural gas caps (26) form. This is sedimentary rock that is arched. These are called "seal beds" (27) if the oil is surrounded by impermeable rock

formations and cannot flow through the fault. Fissured limestone rock formations (28) are always deposits from shallow oceans.

The effects of both the runoff of pollutants into the ocean and the polluting of landlocked waters through industrial and residential areas (29,30) are seen in the example of a lake (31). Increased eutrophication (overnourishment), usually caused by waste waters from human settlements as well as fertilizers, causes an overabundance of nutrients so that algae rapidly proliferate. By contrast, the natural supply of nutrients from forests and meadows is minor (32,33,34).

There is the danger of a eutro-

phied lake dying; this occurs when the decomposition of organic substances has used up all the oxygen in solution in the lake: All aerobic organisms die, and hydrogen sulfide is formed. The lake turns into sewage (35,36,37). This process occurs in steps: During the summer, algae in the upper layers of heated water produce much oxygen. In the fall these surface algae die, sink to the bottom and are decomposed by bacteria. This decomposition in turn uses up much oxygen.

Air pollution (38) is caused by emissions from industrial plants and traffic and also by heating: hydrocarbons, nitrogen oxides, aerosols and radionuclide gases.

A. = Andorra
ALB. = Albania
AU. = Austria
B. = Belgium
BA. = Bangladesh
BH. = Bhutan
BULG. = Bulgaria
CAM. = Cameroon
CAMB. = Cambodia
CZECH. = Czechoslovakia
DEN. = Denmark
DJ. = Djibouti
DOM. REP. = Dominican Republic

• Cities over 1,000,000 Population
o Cities under 1,000,000 Population
  Shipping trade routes

Scale at the center meridian 1 : 75,000,000   One inch to 1,183 miles

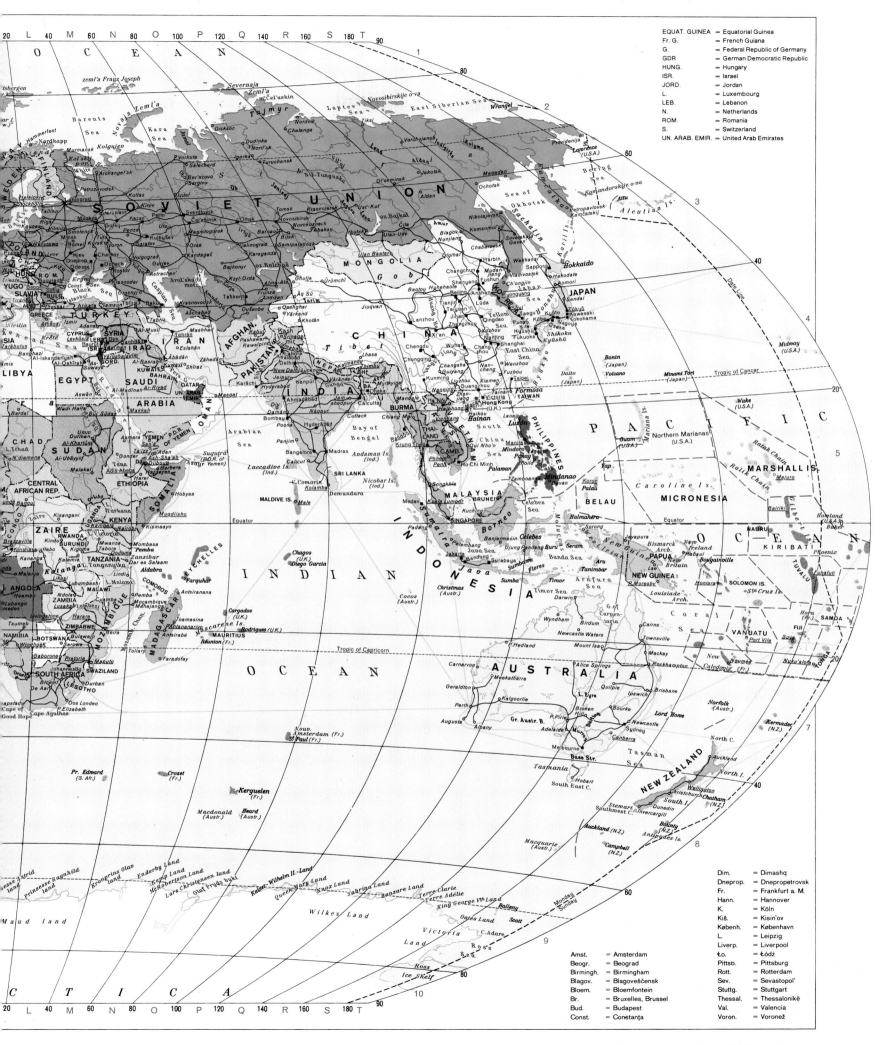

EQUAT. GUINEA	= Equatorial Guinea
Fr. G.	= French Guiana
G.	= Federal Republic of Germany
GDR	= German Democratic Republic
HUNG.	= Hungary
ISR.	= Israel
JORD.	= Jordan
L.	= Luxembourg
LEB.	= Lebanon
N.	= Netherlands
ROM.	= Romania
S.	= Switzerland
UN. ARAB. EMIR.	= United Arab Emirates

Dim.	= Dimashq
Dneprop.	= Dnepropetrovsk
Fr.	= Frankfurt a. M.
Hann.	= Hannover
K.	= Köln
Kiš.	= Kišin'ov
Københ.	= København
L.	= Leipzig
Liverp.	= Liverpool
Ło.	= Łódź
Pittsb.	= Pittsburg
Rott.	= Rotterdam
Sev.	= Sevastopol'
Stuttg.	= Stuttgart
Thessal.	= Thessalonikē
Val.	= Valencia
Voron.	= Voronež

Amst.	= Amsterdam
Beogr.	= Beograd
Birmingh.	= Birmingham
Blagov.	= Blagoveščensk
Bloem.	= Bloemfontein
Br.	= Bruxelles, Brussel
Bud.	= Budapest
Const.	= Constanţa

World, political 25

Scale at the center meridian 1:75,000,000   One inch to 1,183 miles

■ Cities over 1,000,000 Population
○ Cities under 1,000,000 Population

The Arctic has over 400 plant species, among them mosses and lichens, while Antarctica produces only two. Fishing grounds in the phytoplankton-rich waters are numerous and varied. Krill, a luminescent shrimp found in vast swarms around Antarctica, is basic food for whales and numerous bird species. In spite of the ban on whaling by the International Whaling Commission, whalers are still on the loose.

A little less than 100 years ago, man's exploration of storm-swept Antarctica began. The Norwegian Roald Amundsen was the first to reach the South Pole, in December 1911. The Englishman Robert F. Scott was second, in 1912, but weakened and lacking sufficient supplies, he perished during the return trip from the South Pole to the coast. Since then, however, the study of this continent has progressed enormously, and extensive raw-material deposits have been discovered. The ozone hole over Antarctica is making headlines.

After several years of observation by scientists, during which the South Pole's ozone layer—which protects us from the Sun's cancer-causing ultraviolet radiation—constantly diminished, there is now a hole in the ozone layer over Antarctica. The cause, even if not yet absolutely proven, is almost certainly chlorofluorocarbons, which among other things are used as propellant gas for spray cans and as coolant in refrigerators.

More recent studies at the North Pole show that the ozone layer is clearly thinning there, too. These processes are evidence of the reciprocal relationships influencing global climate. In the end, man must suffer the environmental damage he has inflicted on himself. In the United States the use of chlorofluorocarbons as propellant has been prohibited since 1978. Western Europe has not yet prohibited their use.

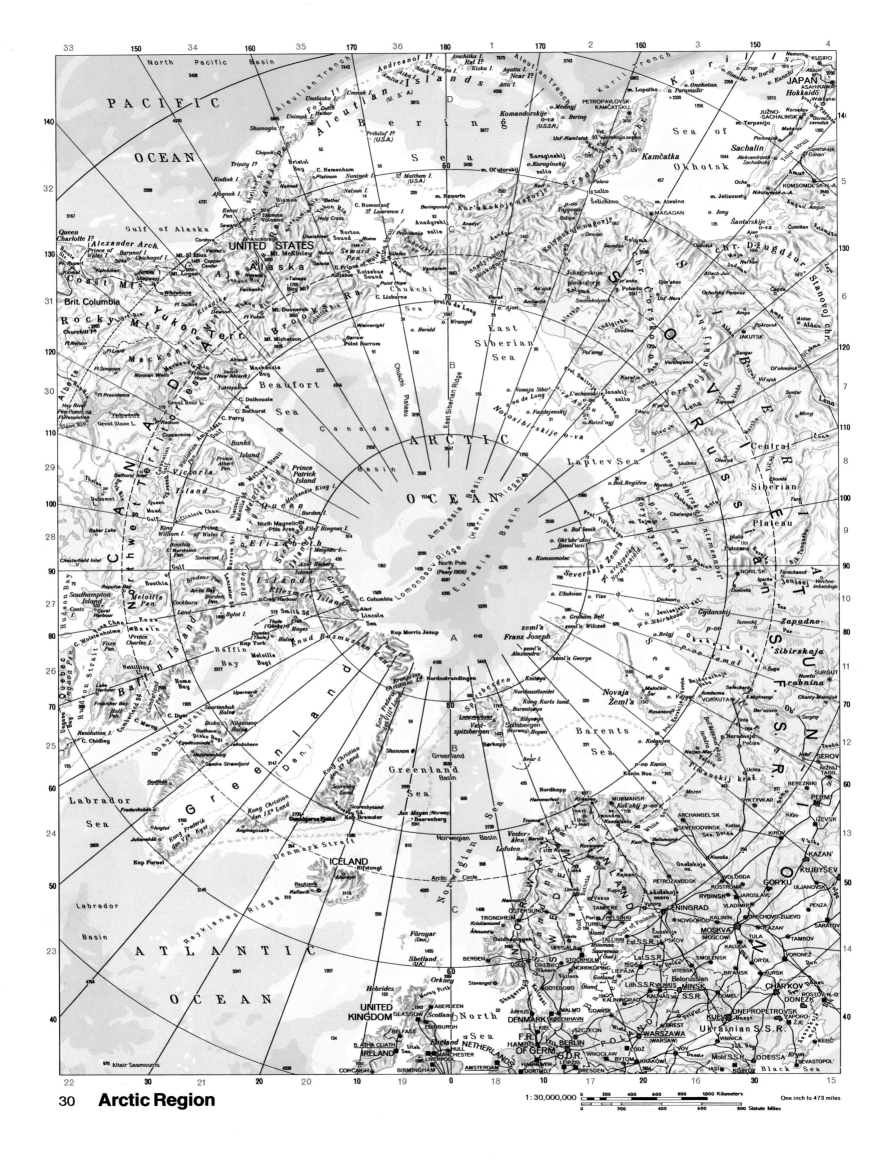

1 : 30,000,000

One inch to 473 miles

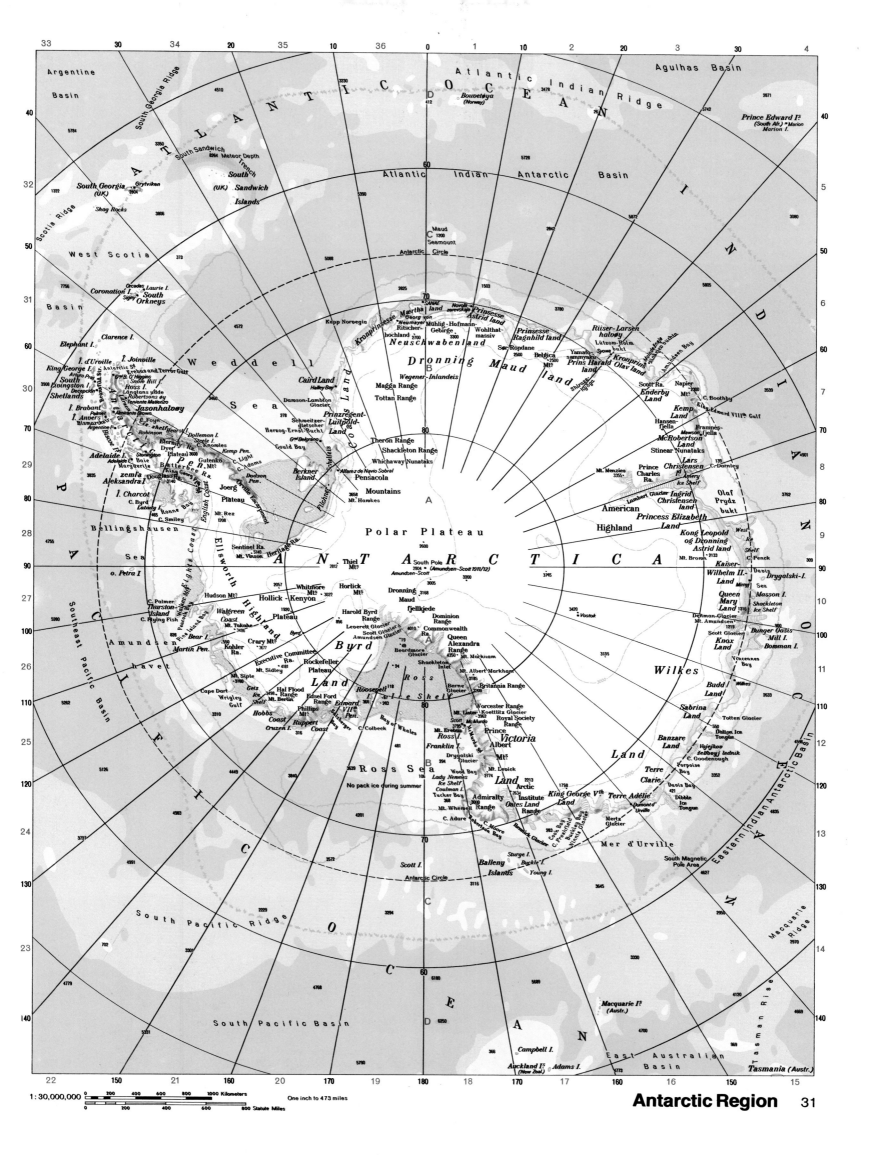

The Arctic region covers 7.3 million sq. mi. (19 million sq. km) of ocean and 4.2 million sq. mi. (11 million sq. km) of land. Antarctica covers 3.2 million sq. mi. (8.3 million sq. km) of land mass and with the islands and shelf ice is about 5.4 million sq. mi. (14 million sq. km).

The most important resources are the coal, gas and oil deposits already being tapped in the Arctic, and gold, tungsten, tin, molybdenum, copper, titanium and silver. While the sovereignty rights seem

The Arctic and Antarctica: icy treasure vaults

clear between the neighboring nations at the North Pole, they are still undetermined in Antarctica. The Antarctica Treaty, signed by 16 nations, allows only the exploration of the continent and prohibits military testing. This treaty has been adhered to in an exemplary manner. Problems are bound to occur when the extraction of resources by one nation continue beyond the expiration of the treaty.

Environmental organizations such as Greenpeace demand the establishment of a "worldpark" in order to preserve the undisturbed ecology. Given the amounts of resources found and not yet found here, it is an unrealistic idea. And yet another pressure on the environment, produced by carbon dioxide, could lead to a long-term melting of the polar ice caps, a change in global climate that would give the saying *après moi, le déluge* new meaning.

1

Photo 1: Fishing boats near the coast of Greenland

Photo 2: Aerial photo on the flight from McMurdo to the South Pole

Photo 3: Eskimo in Greenland

Photo 4: Arctic ice

3

2

4

5

Photo 5: Fishing boats are brought into Thule harbor to protect them from the mighty pack ice

Photo 6: A fish-processing factory on the Faeroe Islands

6

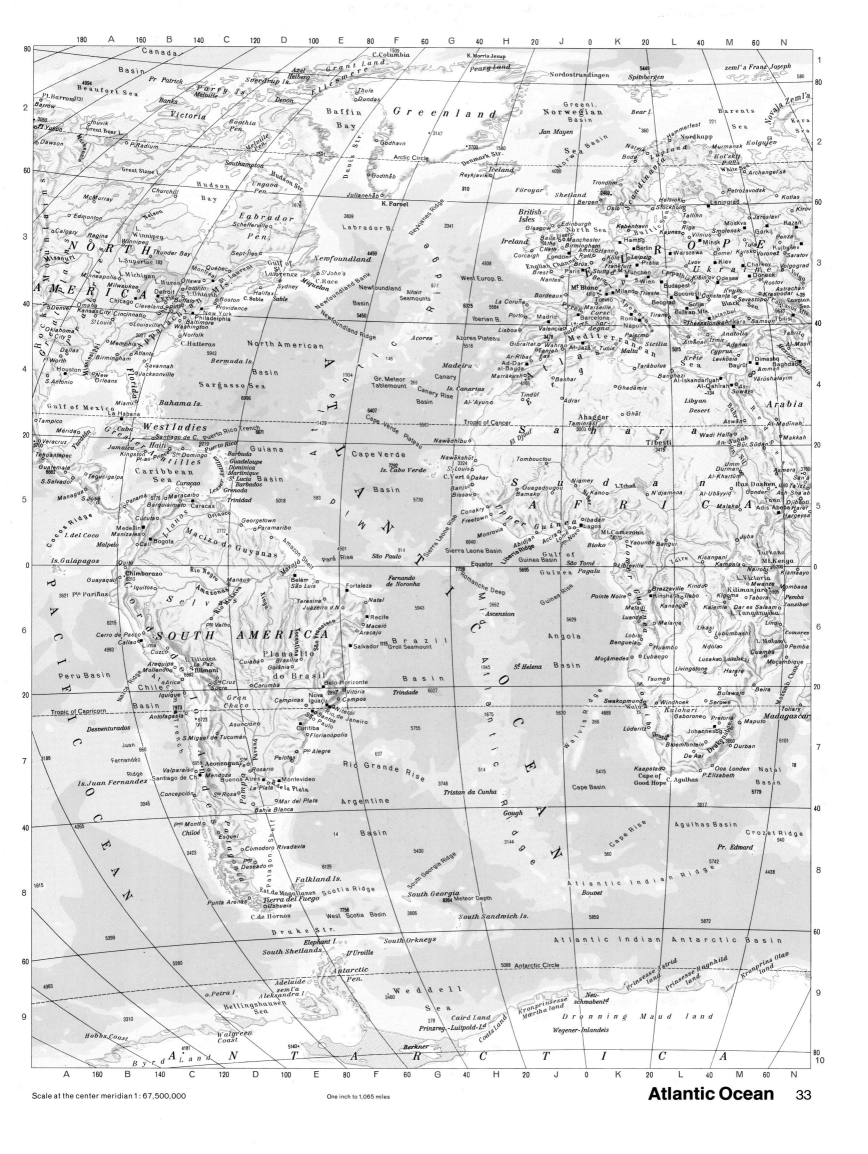

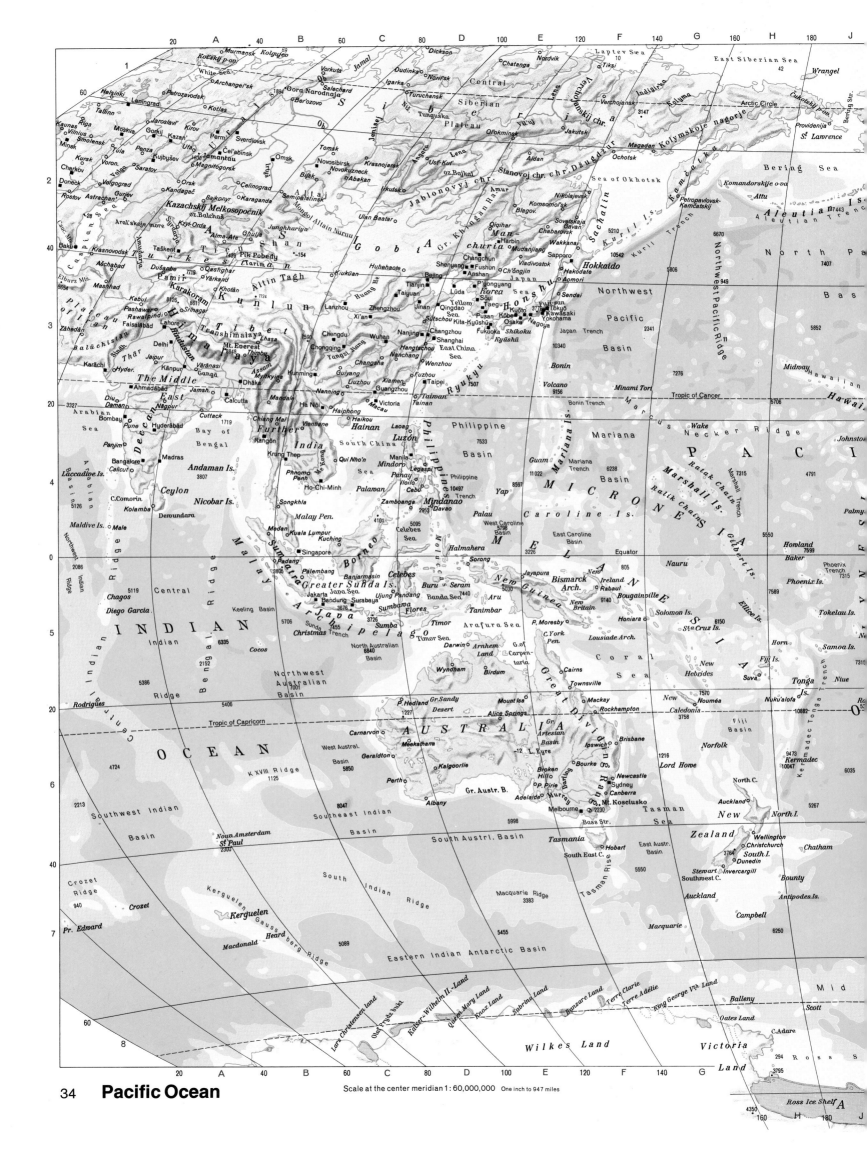

Scale at the center meridian 1 : 60,000,000   One inch to 947 miles

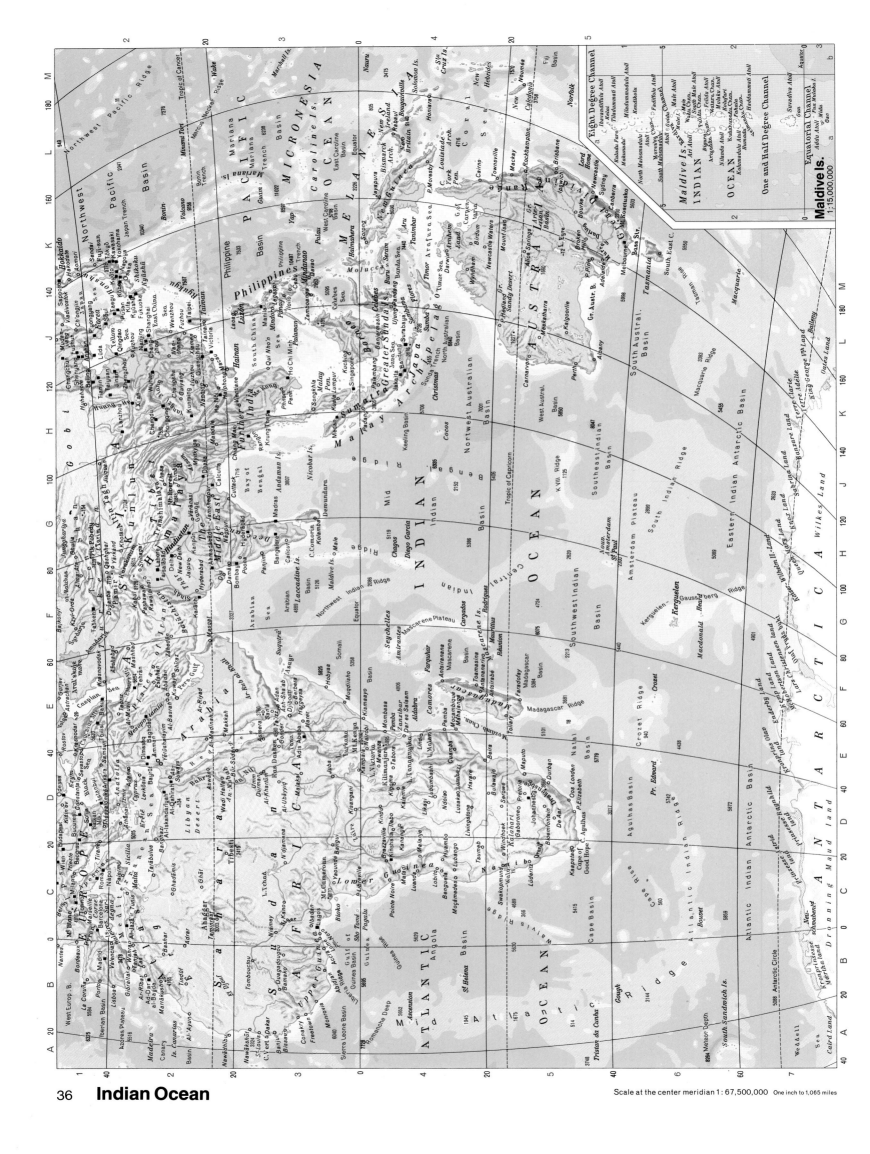

Scale at the center meridian 1 : 67,500,000 One inch to 1,065 miles

Maldive Is. 1:15,000,000

The Atlantic, the Pacific, the Indian and the Arctic Oceans along with the various seas form the continuous body of water that covers almost three-quarters of the Earth.

The special characteristic of ocean water is its salt content, which averages 3.5 percent. Of this, 2.96 percent is regular salt (sodium chloride), while almost all chemical elements can be found in the remaining 0.54 percent.

Various forces cause the movement of ocean water. The regular

Four oceans and numerous seas—they cover 71 percent of the Earth's surface

movement of the tides is caused primarily by the Moon's gravity. Normally, the difference between high and low tides is 2–3 m (6.6–9.8 ft.), but in bays it can be as high as 21 m (69 ft.), as in the Bay of Fundy on Canada's eastern coast. Ocean currents are caused primarily by predominant wind patterns. The southeastern and northeastern trade winds push the surface water against the coast of Central America, where it is deflected and then, as the Gulf Stream, flows along the

North American coast toward Europe. The speed can be up to 21 cm per sec. (about 8 in.). Wind is also the cause of ocean waves, which can reach heights of up to 27 m (about 69 ft.) during winter storms. Variations in the density of water, caused by differences in salt content and varying heating or cooling of the ocean water, lead to layering and mixing of that water. The oceans' deepest point was 11,022 m (36,152 ft.) in the Mariana Trench, located off the Philippines.

1

2

3

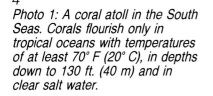

4

Photo 1: A coral atoll in the South Seas. Corals flourish only in tropical oceans with temperatures of at least 70° F (20° C), in depths down to 130 ft. (40 m) and in clear salt water.

Photo 2: The "Lange Anna" ("Tall Anna"), the landmark symbol of Helgoland.

Photo 3: Islands off the Irish coast.

Photo 4: Fishing harbor on the Faeroe islands. Fishing is the basis of life for many peoples.

Photo 5: Surf off the British coast. Wind and waves continually work away at the coastlines, but what is destroyed there is deposited somewhere else.

5

NORTH AMERICA

The third-largest continent in area, North America is bounded on the north by the Arctic Ocean, on the west by the Pacific Ocean and the Bering Sea, and on the east by the Atlantic Ocean, the Gulf of Mexico and the Caribbean Sea. Each of these three photographs represents a unique facet of North America: the pristine beauty of Lake Louise in the Canadian province of Alberta; the skyscrapers of Houston, which seemingly sprout from the coastal flatlands of Texas; and the temple for the Mayan deity Kukulcán at Chichén Itzá, Mexico.

The first human inhabitants of North America were of Asian origin. These first immigrants to the New World crossed over to Alaska from Siberia more than 48,000 years ago. European discovery of North America dates back to the tenth century, when Norsemen reached Greenland and later eastern Canada. Of greater consequence was Christopher Columbus's discovery of the Bahamas in 1492 and his subsequent landings in the West Indies and Central America. Colonies and missionary posts were established following successful English, French and Spanish expeditions. Centuries of immigration by every conceivable ethnic group and nationality earned North America the distinction of being known as the world's "melting pot." Today North America is the fourth-most-populated continent in the world.

North America: This diverse continent boasts glaciers and tropical jungles, deserts and lush valleys, mountains and cities, islands and prairies. It is the melting pot of the entire human race.

Photo 1: U.S.-Americans are extremely proud of their rich and vibrant history. In the Black Hills of South Dakota, the figures of four prominent U.S. American presidents have been sculptured on the side of Mount Rushmore. From left to right are George Washington, Thomas Jefferson, Theodore Roosevelt and Abraham Lincoln. Photo 2: The faithful genuflect in front of the baroque basilica in Guadalupe, site of the sacred shrine for Mexican Catholics. It is believed that the Virgin Mary appeared to an Indian peasant at Guadalupe in 1531 and imprinted her likeness onto his blanket. Photo 3: Vegetation of every variety thrives in California. The combination of sophisticated irrigation systems, an optimal climate and fertile soil helps Californians produce some of the finest grapes, cotton, olives and citrus fruit available. Photo 4: A Sioux Indian, descendant of the original settlers of North America. The Sioux inhabited the Great Plains and western prairies, sustaining themselves first as hunters and later as farmers. Today numbering over 40,000, the Sioux live mostly on reservations in Nebraska, North Dakota, South Dakota and Minnesota. Photo 5: The earliest urban community in North America was Teotihuacan, "City of the Gods." North of Mexico City, this commercial and religious center flourished between A.D. 300 and 900 with a population that at its

2

1

4

3

5

peak reached 250,000. Photo 6: Dynamic Toronto, the largest city in Canada. A provincial capital, Toronto is the financial center of the country and a port of entry on the St. Lawrence Seaway. One of Toronto's many historical buildings and points of interest is its City Hall, a modern structure completed in 1965. Photo 7: Three walruses rest on a drifting ice floe in the Bering Sea. Photo 8: Old Montreal: the dome of the Bonsecours Market. Once the Canadi-

an capital, Montreal has benefited from an extensive restoration. Photo 9: Yellowstone National Park, the first and largest national park in the United States. Located in the Rocky Mountains, Yellowstone features over 10,000 hot springs and 200 active geysers, including Old Faithful. Photo 10: Eskimos inhabit the Arctic coastline from the Bering Sea to Greenland. Photo 11: Pulp and paper mills are often located at the river mouths in eastern Cana-

da. The rivers and tributaries are used to float logs to the mills during the summer, and the river water is also utilized in the papermaking process. Photo 12: San Francisco, a major commercial center on the West Coast, is recognized as one of the most beautiful cities in the world. Photo 13: Wagon wheels, a picket fence and a barn built from rough-hewn timber are reminders of the U.S.'s pioneering heritage. Photo 14: U.S.-Americans love their leisure

time, and enjoy watching and participating in sports. During autumn the American football season is in full swing. Photo 15: Commonly found in Mexico and the southwestern United States, the cactus plant is renowned for its fleshy green stem, sharp spines and delicate flowers. Photo 16: a view from Park Avenue in New York City—the Helmsley Building in front of the Pan Am Building.

6

7

8

9

10

11

12

42   **North America, political**

1 : 30,000,000

One inch to 473 miles

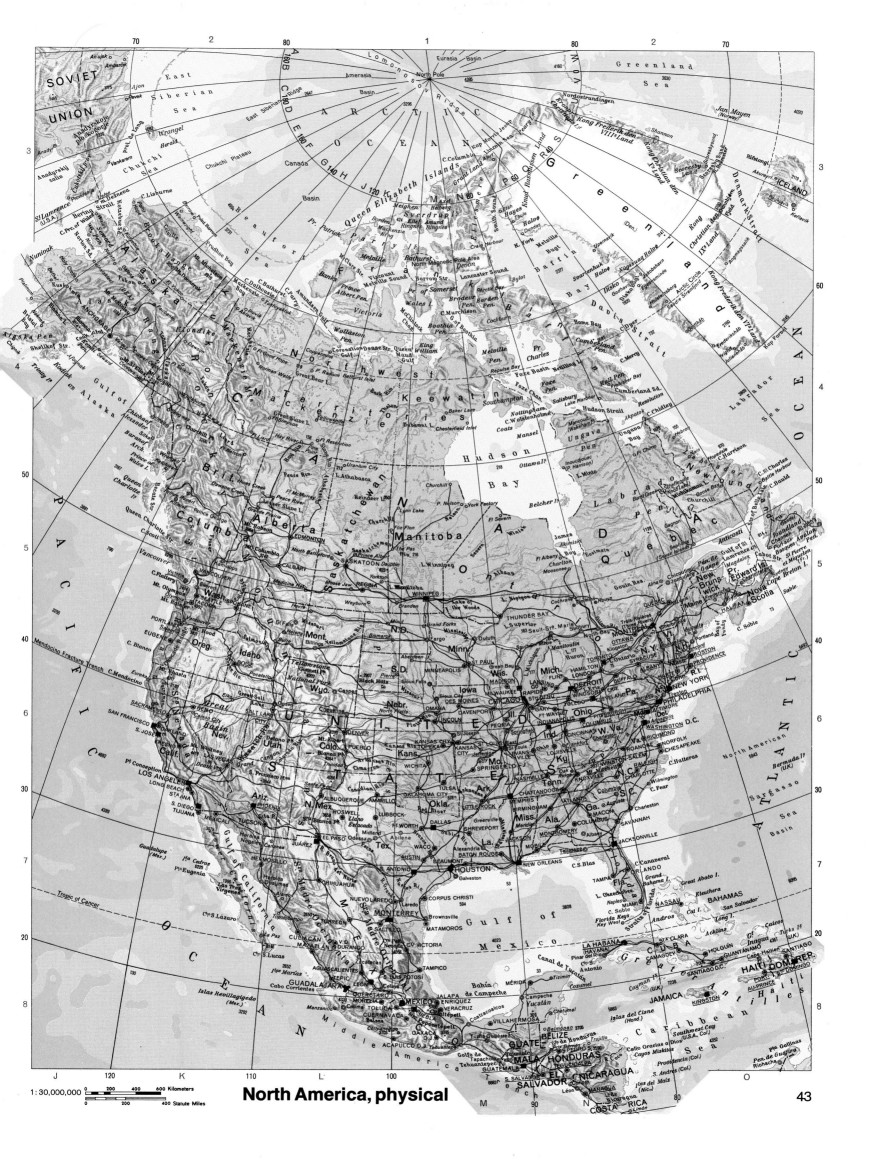

North America, physical

1 : 30,000,000

200   400   600 Kilometers
200   400 Statute Miles

43

The Canadian frontier stretches far and wide, from Newfoundland and the Pacific Ocean to the Yukon Territory bordering Alaska. With a total area of nearly four million square miles (10 million sq. km.), Canada is easily the largest country in the Western Hemisphere, and only the Soviet Union in the Eastern Hemisphere, more than twice the size of Canada, is larger. Except for Alaska, Canada occupies the entire northern half of the North American continent. A transcontinental bor-

Canada: dramatic vistas and bountiful natural resources

der, formed in part by the Great Lakes, divides Canada and the United States.

This large and majestic nation comprises ten provinces—Newfoundland, Nova Scotia, New Brunswick, Prince Edward Island, Quebec, Ontario, Manitoba, Saskatchewan, Alberta and British Columbia—and two territories—the Yukon Territory and the Northwest Territories. The Canadian capital is the city of Ottawa.

Much of Canada is too cold for

large cities and communities to thrive. Arctic and subarctic climates prevail over most of the country, and only the southern portion of Canada has a sufficiently warm growing season to support farming.

Canada, however, continues to be one of the world's leading agricultural exporters. Its chief agricultural products are wheat and other grains, livestock and dairy goods. Fishing and forestry also contribute significantly to the Canadian economy, with most of

the seafood and wood products being exported to other countries. Cod and lobster from the Atlantic Ocean and salmon from the Pacific are particularly abundant.

Among Canada's great wealth of natural resources are minerals. Canada is the world's leading producer of nickel and zinc, and it is the second-largest source of gold, uranium, silver, sulfur and molybdenum ore. Most of Canada's minerals and precious metals are mined in the provinces of Ontario and British Columbia. Also, considerable oil and gas exploration takes place within Canada, and the province of Alberta is a major drilling site for petroleum.

Almost half of Canada's population of 25 million people are of British descent, and nearly a third are of French origin. More than a quarter of a million native Americans live in Canada, along with approximately 16,000 Eskimos. Canada's Eskimos and Indians are descended from the courageous Asian people who first immigrated to North America across the Bering Strait.

The Vikings are purported to have landed in Canada around A.D. 1000. Almost 500 years later, in 1497, John Cabot claimed Canada for England. In 1534 Jacques Cartier did the same for France. Trading posts, settlements and adventurers searching for a Northwest Passage to Asia all aided the British and French efforts at colonizing Canada until 1763, when France relinquished most of its Canadian territories to Great Britain. In the 1850s gold was discovered in British Columbia, and a rush of miners and settlers followed. Thus the Canadian frontier gradually extended westward.

On July 1, 1867, the Dominion of Canada was born and a confederation of the provinces and territories begun. Since then Canada has been an active participant in world affairs. The strong Canadian economy has resulted in a high standard of living for most Canadians.

A peaceful pasture in Waterton Lakes National Park, Alberta. Bison still graze throughout this national park, one of 28 found in Canada (far left).

The wheat-and-corn belt extends across the Canadian prairie provinces, from southern Manitoba and Saskatchewan to Alberta. Successful cultivation of the farm land in this region has contributed to Canada's grain surplus (above).

Vancouver, located in the province of British Columbia, is the largest city in Western Canada. The city's industries include shipbuilding, seafood processing and oil refining. (left)

Quebec remains one of North America's tourist capitals. The charm and customs of the Old World persist in Quebec, where the population is largely French-speaking. Many of the first explorations into the continent were in the province of Quebec; thus it is known as the "Cradle of Canada" (above).

45

1:15,000,000

One inch to 237 miles

Northern North America 47

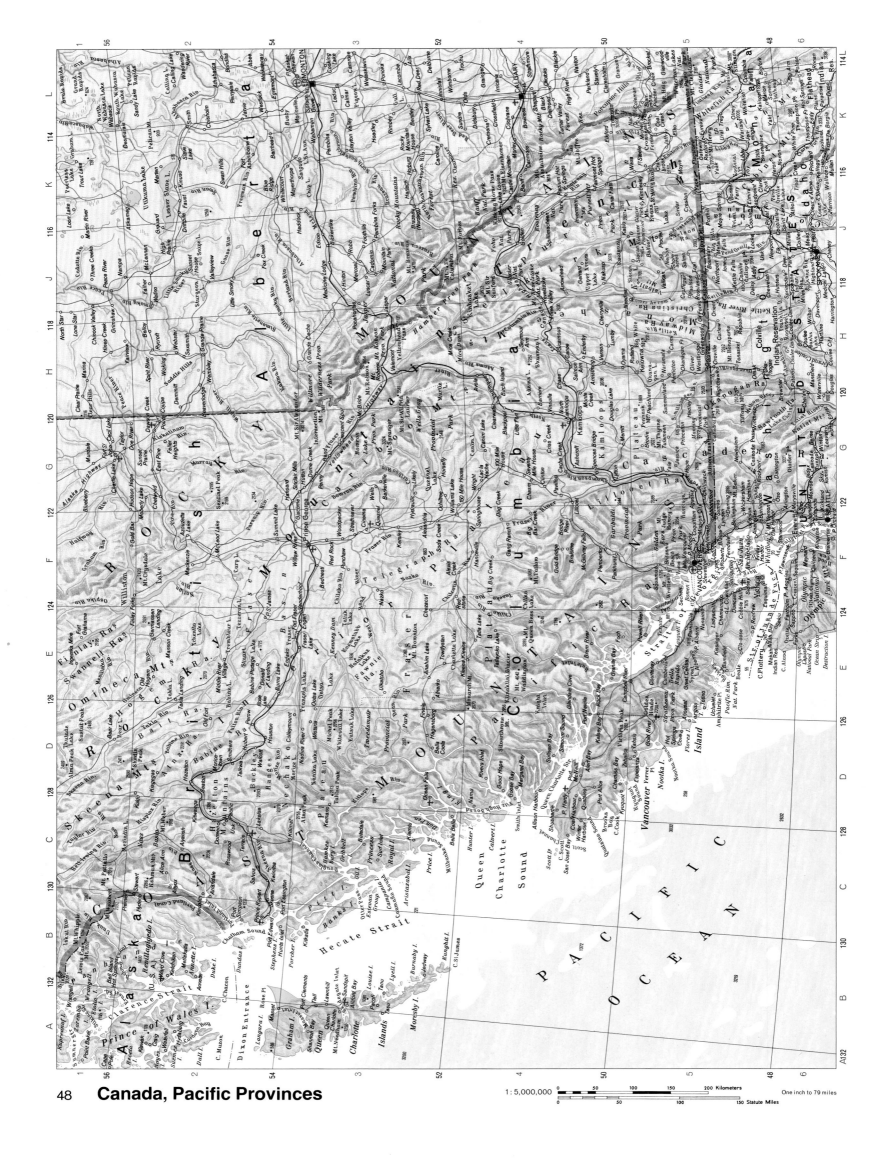

48   **Canada, Pacific Provinces**

1 : 5,000,000

One inch to 79 miles

0   50   100   150   200 Kilometers

0   50   100   150 Statute Miles

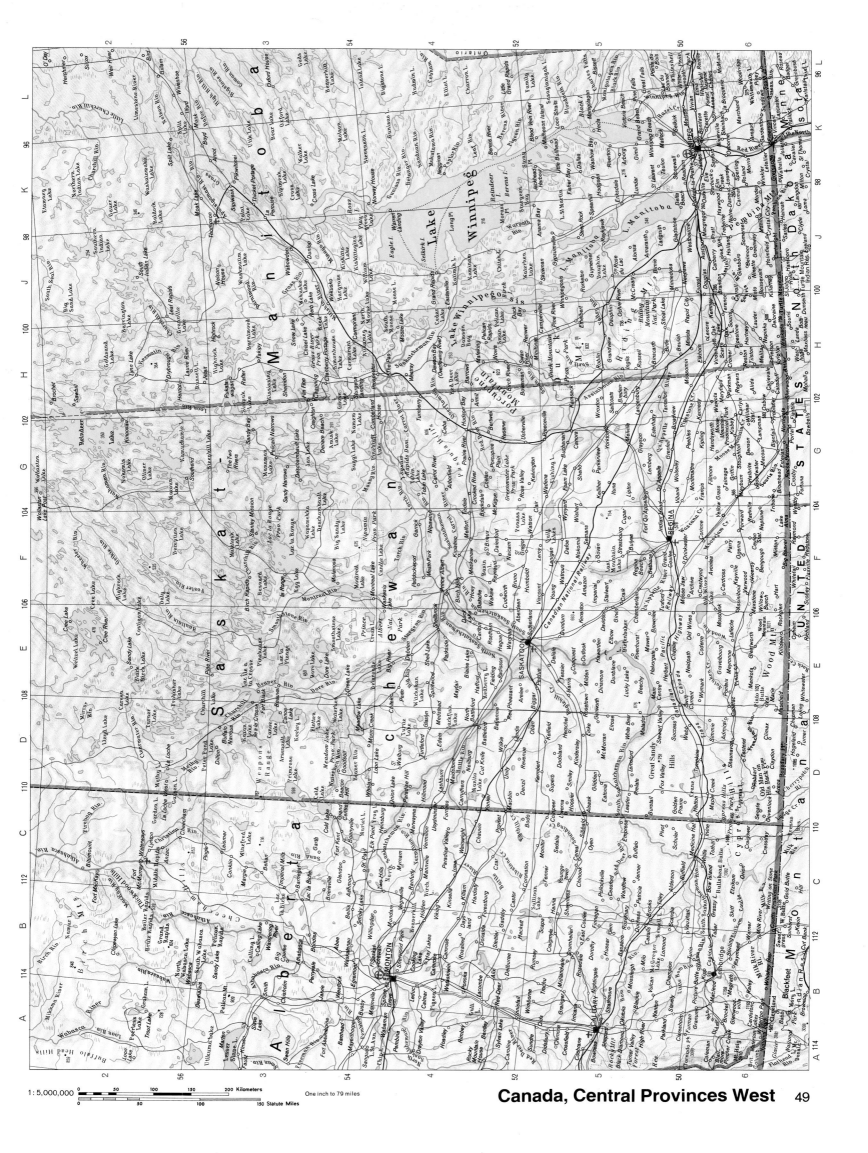

1 : 5,000,000

One inch to 79 miles

50   100   150   200 Kilometers

50   100   150 Statute Miles

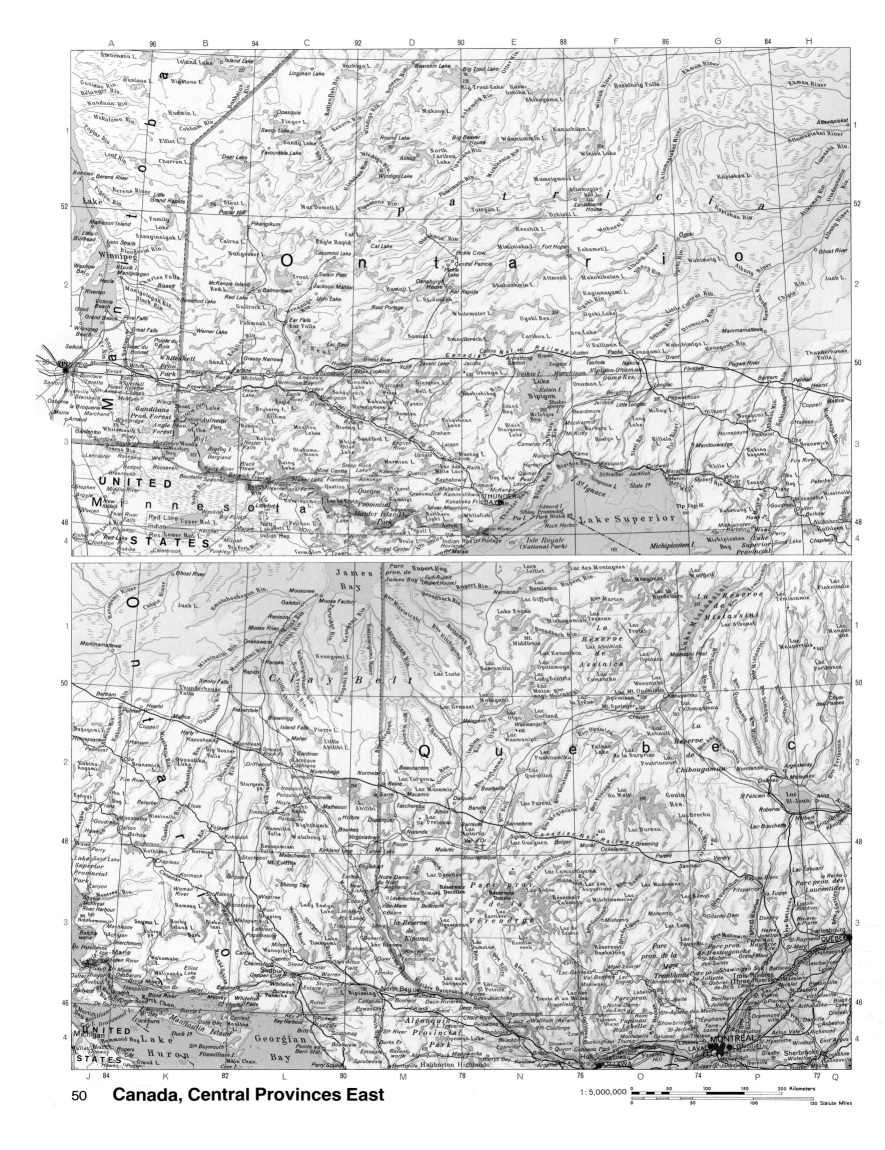

50 **Canada, Central Provinces East**

1 : 5,000,000

0   50   100   150   200 Kilometers

0   50   100   150 Statute Miles

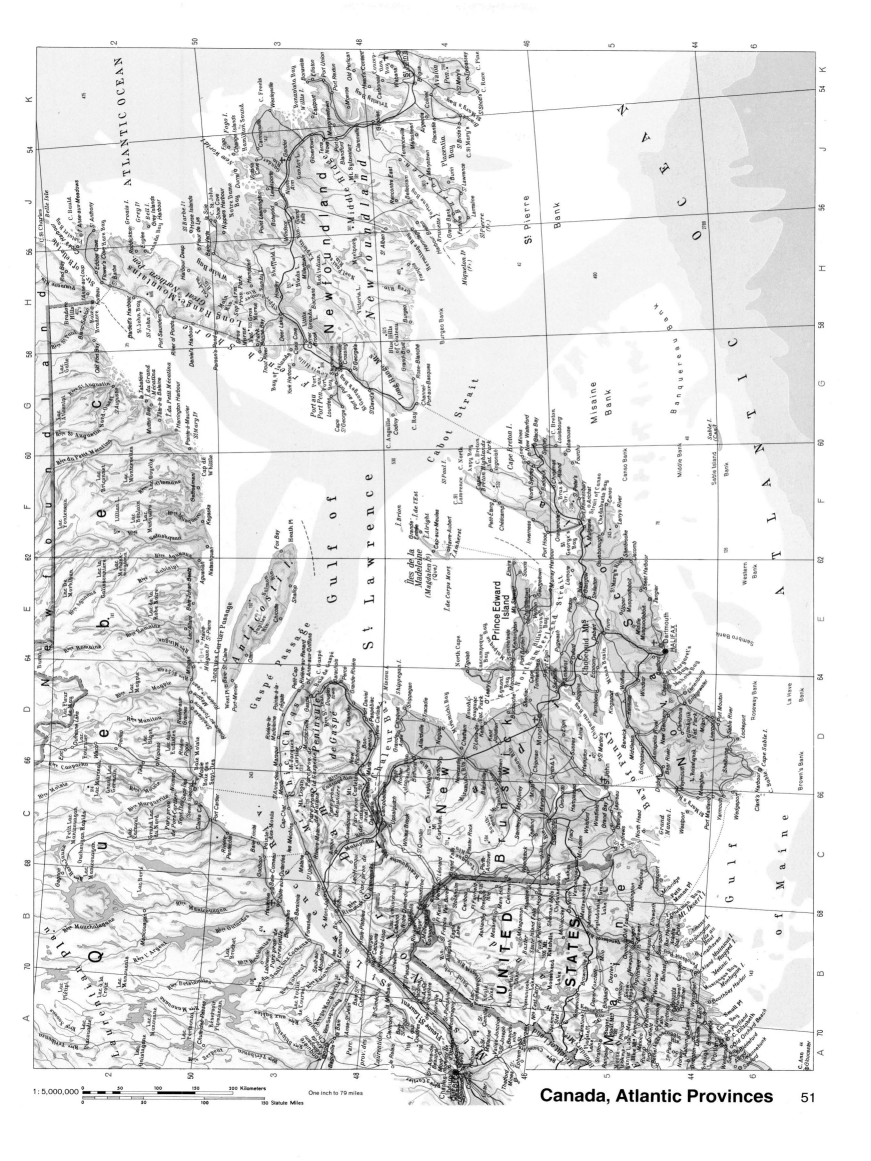

Canada, Atlantic Provinces 51

1 : 5,000,000

One inch to 79 miles

0   50   100   150   200 Kilometers
0   50   100   150 Statute Miles

The legendary West of the United States extends through the huge expanse of land between the Mississippi River and the Pacific Ocean. The Canadian border bounds the United States on the north, while Mexico and the Gulf of Mexico comprise the southern border. Settlement of the Wild West, once the untamed territory of North America, was encouraged by the Gold Rush of 1848 and later by the promise of ample land, as ranchers and farmers swelled the population

USA: the wild west and the treasures of the earth

of trading outposts and small frontier towns.

At first the prospect of acquiring a quick fortune through the discovery of gold stimulated the westward movement across the continent. In the course of time, other precious minerals and metals were discovered as well, and these valuable resources have been systematically mined from the earth. Today, because of the abundance of these natural resources, the United States leads the world in the pro-

duction of natural gas, lead, copper, aluminum, sulfur and uranium. The U.S. ranks second in the production of crude oil, iron ore, silver and zinc.

The most prominent geographical feature of the United States is the Rocky Mountains. These mountains form the Continental Divide, which separates rivers draining into the Atlantic Ocean from those draining into the Pacific. A major barrier to transcontinental travel, the Rocky Mountains stretch more than 3,000 miles from central New

The Sierra Nevada mountain range is heralded for its magnificent scenery. Heavy winter snows in these mountains produce irrigation water for California farms and hydroelectric power for the entire region. Three national parks in this region—Yosemite, Sequoia and Kings Canyon—and many resort areas lure tourists throughout the year (above).

Death Valley is one of the driest and hottest places on Earth. Straddling the California-Nevada borderline, the valley earned its name during the Gold Rush from prospectors who attempted, mistakenly, to cross this desolate region (right).

Mexico to northern Alaska. The highest peak of the Rockies, Mt. Elbert, 14,433 ft. (4,399 m), is located in Colorado.

The Cascade Mountains and the Sierra Nevada mountain range together form the western wall of the highlands in the United States. The Cascades are volcanic, snow-capped mountains, while the Sierra Nevada, also snow-capped, rise to a pinnacle of 14,494 ft. (4,423 m) at Mt. Whitney, the highest peak within the lower 48 contiguous states. Be-

tween the mountain ranges of the western wall and the Rockies are two immense plateaus and two continental basins. The Columbia plateau, northern and volcanic, boasts of rich farm lands and orchards. In contrast is the Colorado plateau, noted for the Grand Canyon and a number of other national parks and Indian reservations.

In the midst of these two plateaus lies the Great Basin, a desert region located mostly in the state of Nevada. Death Valley National Monu-

ment in California, at 282 ft. (86 m) below sea level, is the lowest point not only in the Great Basin but also within the North American continent. Rainfall is infrequent throughout the Great Basin, and because of the extreme aridity, only a few sections of this region can support population centers.

The two major cities in this region are Denver and Salt Lake City. Both of these cities contributed a great deal to the historic and economic development of the American West.

Denver, the financial center of the Rocky Mountain region, is the capital of Colorado. Salt Lake City, the capital of Utah, was founded in 1847 by Brigham Young and became the center of the Mormon religious community.

Reminders of America's Indian and pioneer heritage are found all over the western United States. Today tourism joins manufacturing, raising cattle and farming as a major economic activity of the West.

Golden Gate Bridge, across the Golden Gate strait, which connects San Francisco Bay with the Pacific Ocean. The bridge was built between 1933 and 1937. Its overall length is 9,266 ft. (2,824 m), making it one of the longest bridges in the world (left).

A stark reminder of the Earth's prehistoric past: Monument Valley, which lies across the border between Utah and Arizona. Nearby there is a Navajo Indian reservation renowned both as a tourist attraction and as an arts-and-crafts center. The landscape in Monument Valley is close to 70 million years old. Bizarre sandstone plateaus and monolithic rock structures combine to make Monument Valley one of the most remarkable regions on Earth. Hun-

dreds of Hollywood movies, aptly nicknamed "westerns," have been filmed here (above).

The Midwest is the undeniable heartland of North America. It is the geographic center of the continent, and regionally the Midwest encompasses the area from St. Louis to the foothills of the Appalachians, the cornfields of Iowa and Nebraska to the Dakota prairies. More important, midwestern farms and factories in the United States produce food and consumer goods for the entire world.

The Midwest has some of the richest farming land on Earth and is

USA: the Midwest—crossroads of the continent

particularly renowned for its corn and hogs. Although other crops, such as wheat, oats, alfalfa, soybeans, many vegetables and fruit, are grown here, corn is farmed on almost half of the available land. Most of the corn crop is used to feed cattle, hogs and poultry.

In the past 40 years the American farm has become increasingly mechanized. This mechanization has contributed to the decline of the midwestern rural population, but on the other hand, farms are now oper-

ated more efficiently and produce greater yields. Many farms are owned and operated by large corporations, their expanse of land worth millions of dollars. Most farms, though, are much smaller in scale, and they are proudly handed down within a family from one generation to another. The number of family-owned farms has decreased steadily in recent decades.

North of the cornbelt, near the Great Lakes, dairy farming eclipses corn production; yet manufacturers

A farm in Kansas, typical of the big and small farms that make up much of the landscape, in the farm belt of the American Midwest. This farm produces corn (right).

Mound builders were Native Americans who constructed the mounds in the Midwest, especially in the Mississippi and Ohio River valleys. The mounds were used chiefly as burial places but also as foundations for temples and fortresses. Some mounds date back as far as the beginning of the sixth century (right).

are the chief employers in this region. The Great Lakes—Superior, Michigan, Huron, Ontario and Erie—are all connected to each other by canals, rivers and straits, forming an inland waterway that stretches from Minnesota to New York. Great quantities of iron ore, grain, coal, petroleum and steel are transported on the Great Lakes, except during the winter months. With the opening of the St. Lawrence Seaway in 1959, the Great Lakes became an international shipping route.

Along the shores of the Great Lakes, cities such as Detroit, Cleveland, Buffalo, Chicago, Milwaukee and Toronto became large commercial centers thanks to their access to inexpensive waterway transportation. The construction of railroads throughout the Midwest also helped spur the economic development of these cities. Today Detroit is recognized as the automobile capital of the world.

Chicago, situated on the southern end of Lake Michigan, is an im-mense commercial, financial and industrial city serving primarily the Midwest but also serving as a busy shipping center for all of North America. By 1860 many railways connected Chicago with the rest of the country, and the continent's reliance on lake and canal transportation began to diminish. With the railways, livestock and farm products were transported from over a dozen states to such centers as Chicago, St. Louis and Kansas City for processing and rerouting.

Farm economics helped put many midwestern cities on the map—especially Kansas City, Des Moines, Indianapolis and Omaha. These cities and others, though, benefited greatly from the transportation backbone of the United States—its principal river, the Mississippi. Celebrated by the author Mark Twain, the Mississippi River rises from small streams in northern Minnesota and finally empties into the Gulf of Mexico—down river some 2,350 mi. (3,760 km) later.

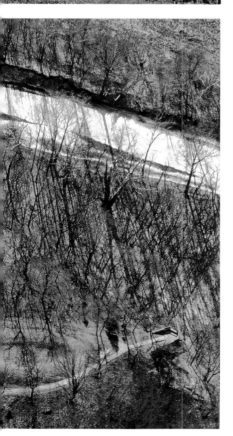

Chicago's reputation as a city with innovative architecture is reinforced by the world's tallest building, the 110-story Sears Tower in the left of this picture (left).

The Great Lakes reach their highest point above sea level—602 ft. (183 m)—at Lake Superior, the world's second-largest lake (left).

Minneapolis, the largest city in Minnesota, produces computers, scientific instruments, flour-mill products and processed foods. It is considered by many to be a model city in the northern Midwest (above).

1:15,000,000

0 100 200 300 400 500 Kilometers

0 100 200 300

400 Statute Miles

One inch to 237 miles

Southern North America 59

To many people, everything seems better in the western United States. The climate is better, the standard of living is better, and the scenery is better. Yet although the West Coast and the Southwest possess huge areas of unique wilderness beauty, most of the population chooses to live and work in cities.

The bold contrast between cities in California illustrates the region's physical diversity. San Diego, southern and sunny, originally grew from Spanish missions. Los An-

The Pacific Coast and the Southwest: remarkable cities, unforgettable landscapes

geles, well known for its casual lifestyle, its beaches and for its key role in the motion-picture industry, is a large, sprawling city. It is entirely different from San Francisco, a charming, cosmopolitan city famous for its street cars and picturesque beauty.

Other notable cities in this region include Las Vegas, Seattle and Spokane, Portland, San Jose and Phoenix. In the past few decades, these cities have all become popular metropolitan areas, as light in-

dustries such as computer manufacturing have attracted millions of new residents.

The western United States, though, is perhaps most famous for its breathtaking scenery. There are the redwood forests north of San Francisco, the Grand Canyon in Arizona, Lake Tahoe in Nevada, Mount Hood in Oregon, as well as Washington's Olympic National Park. All the vacations in a lifetime could not exhaust the multitude of natural wonders to visit.

One of the many moods of the west coast of the United States. Seen here is a fog-enshrouded part of the Oregon coast (top left).

Revenue from hotels, gambling, entertainment and other tourist-oriented industries forms the economic and commercial backbone of Las Vegas (above, left).

The Grand Canyon, one of the natural wonders of the world. This great gorge—over 200 miles (320 km.) long and a mile (1.6 km.) deep—is located in Arizona (top, right).

The Napa Valley in California is world-famous for its wines (right).

60

The Middle Atlantic region of the United States bears a resemblance to New England: The soil is generally poor; the population lives mostly in metropolitan areas; and skilled labor, rather than natural resources, brought the region prosperity.

The Dutch, French and British were the first Europeans to explore and colonize this portion of the Atlantic seaboard. These states—New York, Pennsylvania, New Jersey, Delaware, Maryland and Virginia have maintained or restored

The Mid Atlantic states: North America's historic east coast

many of their historic points of interest. Tourists travel to Philadelphia's Independence Hall, the Maryland State House in Annapolis, and to Williamsburg, Virginia, to learn more about the history of the United States.

A chain of cities forming a megalopolis extends along the Atlantic seaboard from Boston to Richmond, Virginia. The focus of this megalopolis is New York City, trade center of the nation and financial center of the world. Millions of

immigrants to the United States first arrived in New York City, and the Statue of Liberty, which stands in New York Harbor, continues to welcome newcomers with the promise of freedom.

Washington, D.C., the capital of the United States, is almost exclusively a governmental center. Interestingly, not until the 20th century did Washington fully transform itself from a provincial city to a world capital.

The Capitol in Washington, D.C. Its construction began in 1793 on an elevated site that George Washington chose. The edifice as it stands today took many years to build and is the result of enlargements and restorations (above).

Near Wall Street, examples of New York's striking and diversified architecture include the twin towers of the World Trade Center (1973) and, in the foreground, the Woolworth Building (1910) and Saint Paul's Church (1794) (left).

Texas and the southern states have played a unique and vital role in the history of the United States. This region was the site of the first explorations of the New World, it witnessed the refinement of representative government, and it also survived the disastrous defeat of the Civil War. In the 16th century, Texas and the South were sought by the three major trading nations: Spain, England and France. The earliest permanent settlement in this region started at Jamestown in 1607.

Texas and the South: old and new

While France shifted its interest to the Mississippi Valley and the Gulf Coast, Spanish strongholds were established from Florida to present-day South Carolina, and especially in Texas and the Southwest.

Terrain, soil and ease or difficulty of transportation were important factors in shaping the lives of the people here. The settlers of the coastal lowlands had plenty of good farmland and relatively easy access to water transportation. As a result, large-scale farming—plantations—

were developed, and a distinctive cultural and social life also began to prosper. People living in the Appalachian, Blue Ridge or Smoky Mountains, on the other hand, were often isolated in small communities.

Initially, tobacco was the chief crop in the South, and it quickly exhausted the soil, forcing planters to acquire more land. Cotton also depleted the soil, but the invention of the cotton gin made cotton farming wildly profitable. African slave labor contributed enormously to the

Cattle drive near Alpine, Texas. These domestic animals were introduced to the Western world by Christopher Columbus on his second voyage to America. In Texas, wealth was often judged according to the number of cattle a person owned (above).

The Dallas skyline at night. Dallas originated as a cotton market in the 1870s, and later it became the financial and commercial center of the Southwest (above right).

Charleston, South Carolina, is the oldest city in its state and also one of the South's chief seaports. Some of the city's old homes and small, winding streets are particularly charming (below right).

agricultural fortunes won in the South. As cotton planters moved west in search of better soil, cattle and livestock farmers began to move east.

After the United States purchased the Louisiana Territory from the French in 1803, the U.S. and Spain began to disagree over boundaries and immigration restrictions. Thousands of U.S. citizens moved to and settled in Texas when it was under Spanish, and later Mexican, rule. In 1836 Texans fought Mexico for its independence, and in 1845 Texas was admitted to the Union as the 28th state of the United States.

Texas and its neighboring state, Oklahoma, are blessed with vast reserves of gas and oil. Production of crude oil has brought untold material wealth to the Southwest. Financial fortunes helped expand cities such as Dallas, Fort Worth, San Antonio, Tulsa and Oklahoma City. Houston, home of the Johnson Space Center, is one of the fastest-growing metropolitan areas in the United States.

The South still attracts Civil War buffs, outdoor enthusiasts and vacationers, but the South's increasing urbanization has gotten the attention of the business community. A number of well-known corporations have recently relocated their headquarters to the South. The South is now one of the fastest growing regions in the United States. Northerners are attracted by its easy lifestyle and warm, sunny climate. Today in the New South, as in Texas, people are looking forward to continued financial growth and social progress.

The Crescent City: New Orleans. Creole culture dominated New Orleans throughout the 19th century, and the French influence is still seen today. Also, jazz originated in New Orleans during the late 1800s among black musicians (above).

Atlanta, Georgia, is one of the South's leading cities. Its numerous parks are famous for their multitudes of dogwood blossoms during the springtime (below).

63

In 1959 the last two states finally joined the Union: Alaska, nearly one-fifth the size of all the other states put together, and Hawaii, the only one of the 50 states not located on the North American continent. Alaska's vast terrain poses a special challenge to Americans eager to tame this wilderness, and the Hawaiian chain of islands, in the middle of the Pacific Ocean, have become a unique meeting ground for Western and Asian peoples.

Alaska and Hawaii: the frontier states

Hawaii is the only state created entirely by volcanoes. More than a million years ago, a tremendous underwater volcanic eruption created a 1,500-mi.-long (2,400 km) chain of islands. Hawaii's steep, emerald green mountains seem to rise out of the Pacific Ocean. Tourists from all over the world visit Hawaii's tropical rain forests, volcanoes and paradisiacal beaches each year. Honolulu is the state capital.

Alaska is not only the biggest state in the U.S., it is also the least-populated one. Although most of Alaska's Eskimos live in western Alaska, near the Aleutian Islands, a third of Alaska's population lives on the southern coast, close to Anchorage, the state's largest city. Thousands of newcomers arrived in Alaska in 1968 when a major oil field was discovered near Prudhoe Bay. More-reliable air transportation to Alaska has increased the tourist trade.

Hapuna Beach Park on the island of Hawaii. "The Big Island" consists of three massive volcanic mountains that rose from the floor of the Pacific Ocean. Mauna Kea, the largest of these mountains, is 13,796 ft. (4,205 m) above sea level (above).

Alaska abounds with natural wonders. In the Alaska Panhandle, adjacent to British Columbia, the scenic beauty of the mountains and the rugged coastline are augmented by such attractions as the Malaspina Glacier and Glacier Bay National Monument. Juneau, the state capital and a year-round port, is also located in the Panhandle (right).

New England is the name given to the region comprising the six northeastern states of the U.S.: Maine, New Hampshire, Vermont, Massachusetts, Rhode Island and Connecticut. The region supposedly earned its name from British explorers because of its resemblance to the English coast. The soil in New England is poor and rocky, so agriculture was never a major part of the region's economy.

A number of factors—political, economic and religious—contribut-

New England: independence and industry

ed to the settling of New England. In 1620 a group of British religious dissidents known as the Pilgrims established a colony at Plymouth, Massachusetts, and within ten years this colony had prospered and expanded. Today, New Englanders of British ancestry are generally referred to as "Yankees." According to tradition, a Yankee has a penchant for self-government, as well as ingenuity and thrift.

New England was at the center of the events leading up to the Ameri-

can Revolution, as well as the scene for the opening battles between the British army and the American colonists. After the war, manufacturing developed quickly, with the help of Yankee ingenuity, and New England subsequently became fairly industrialized. Long a cultural and educational center for the United States, New England is equally well-known today as a year-round vacation area.

Norwich, Vermont. New England has many picturesque villages and white-steepled churches. Winter brings heavy snows, which usually cover the ground for at least three full months. Dairy farming, evidenced by numerous barns throughout the countryside, has long been the dominant agricultural activity (above).

Mystic, Connecticut, on Long Island Sound, features a re-created 19th-century New England seaport (above right).

Boston is the largest city in New England. It is also one of the great cultural and educational centers of the nation. Its modern-day appearance contrasts wide avenues and colonial alleyways, and features both landmarks of the past and contemporary skyscrapers (right).

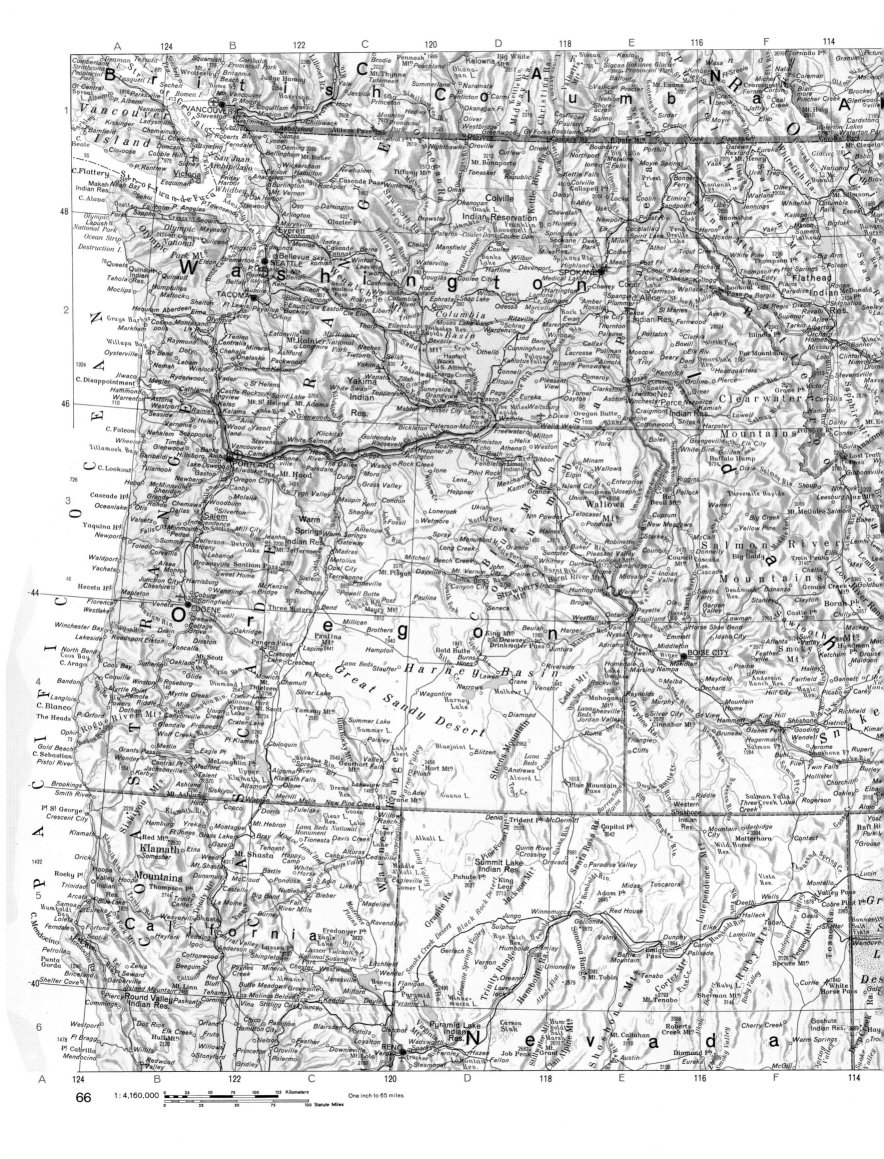

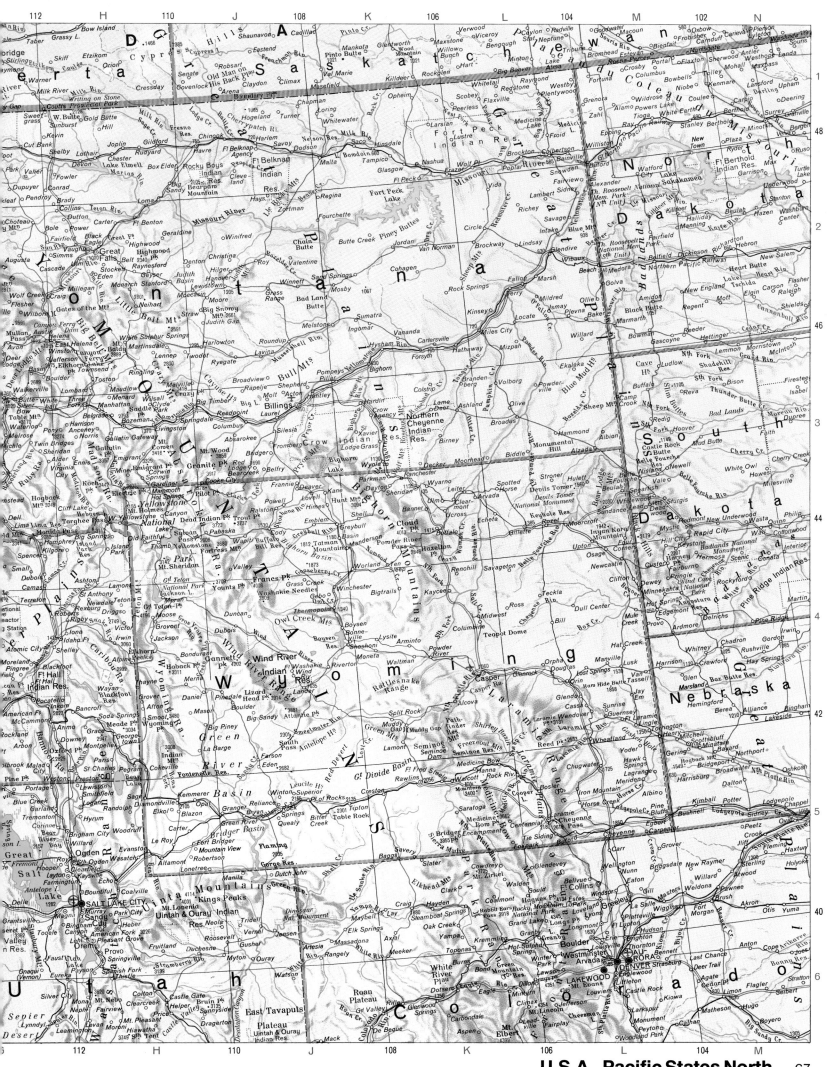

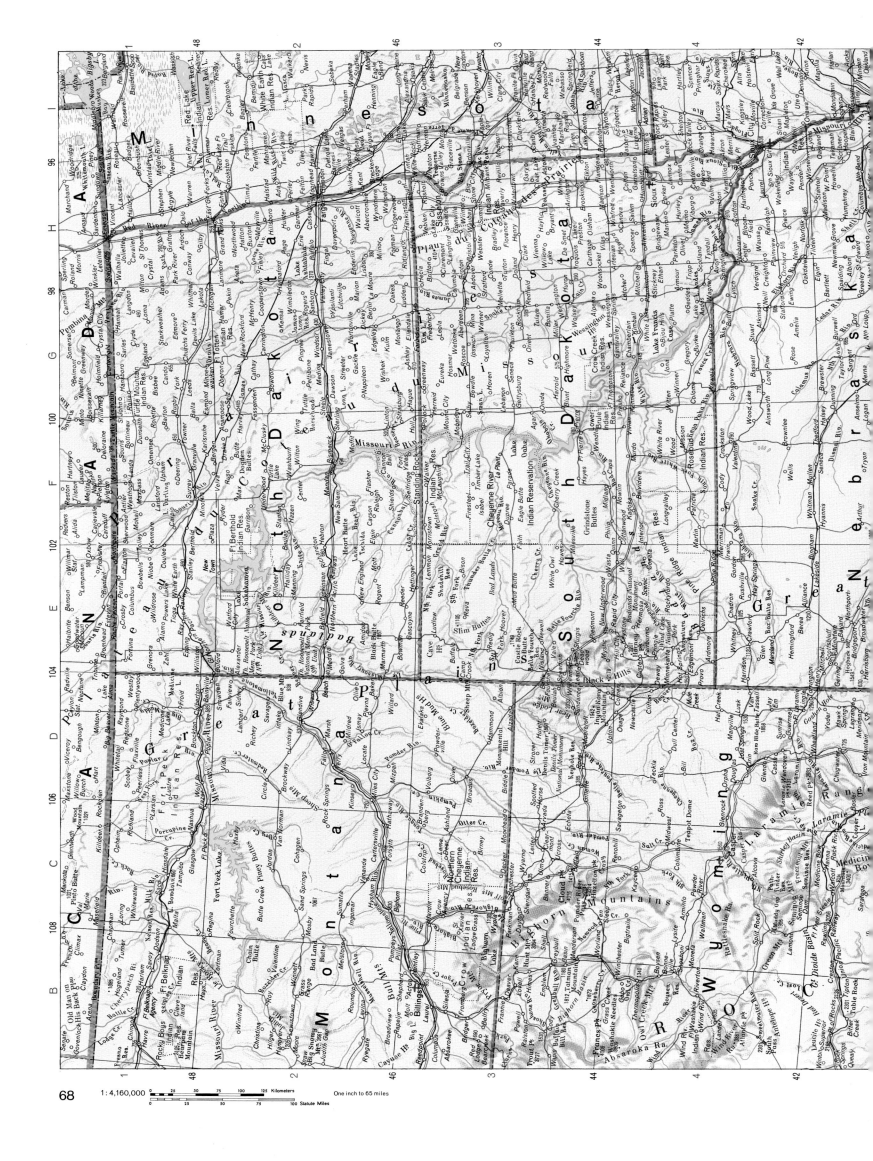

1 : 4,160,000

0   25   50   75   100   125 Kilometers

One inch to 65 miles

0   25   50   75   100 Statute Miles

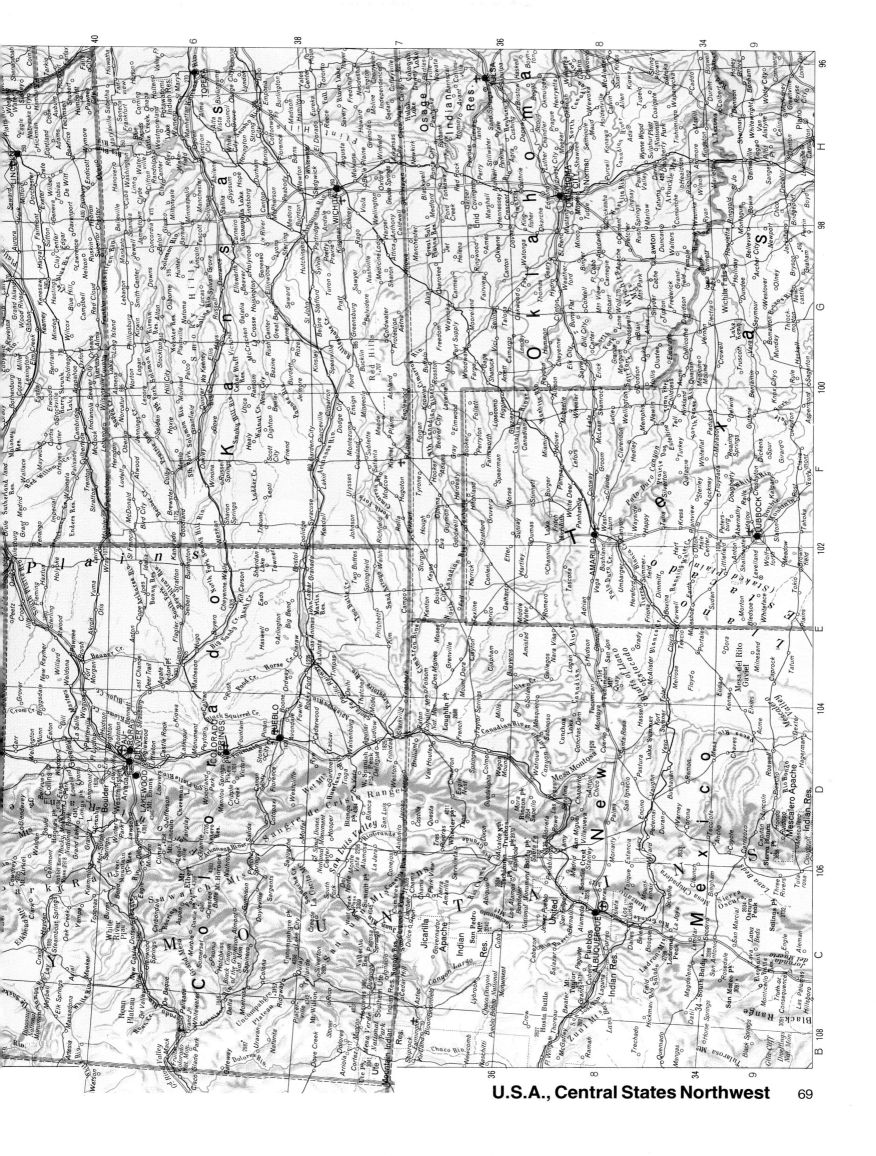

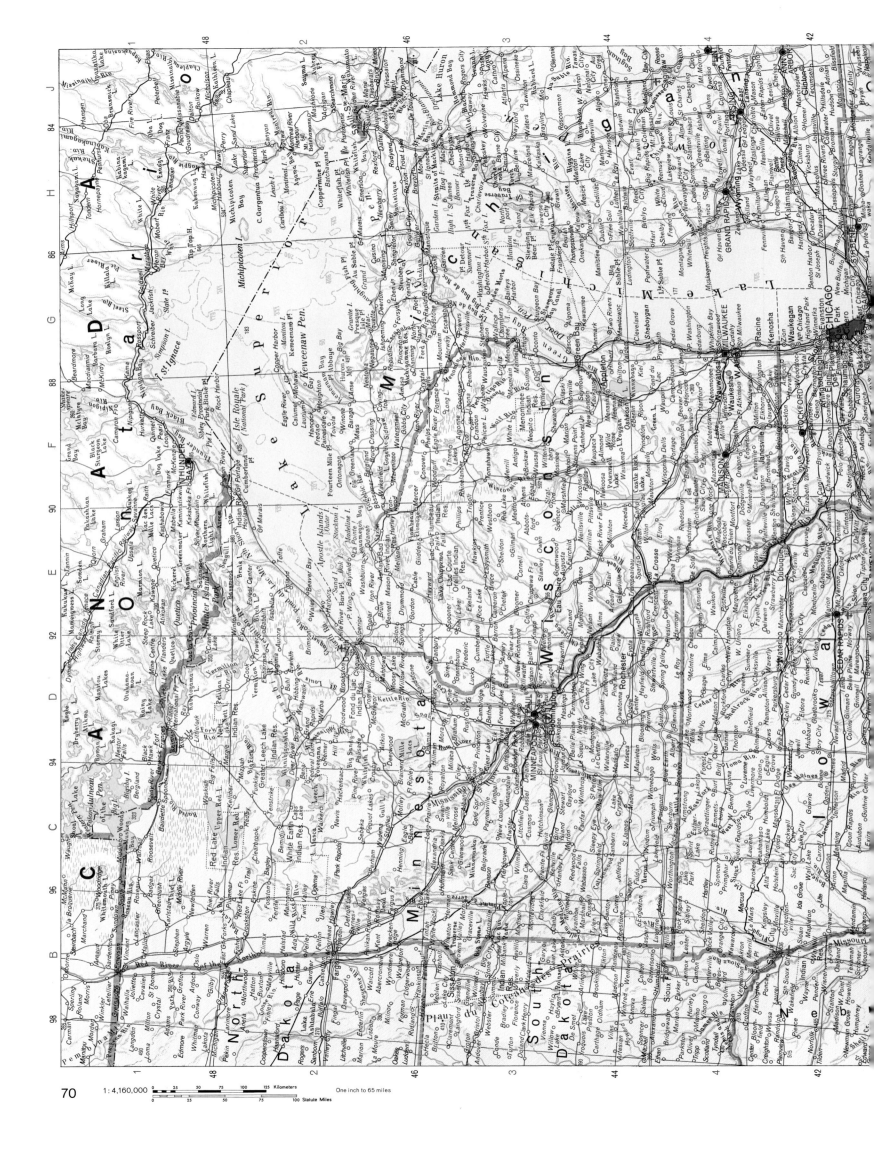

1 : 4,160,000

One inch to 65 miles

0   25   50   75   100   125 Kilometers

0   25   50   75   100 Statute Miles

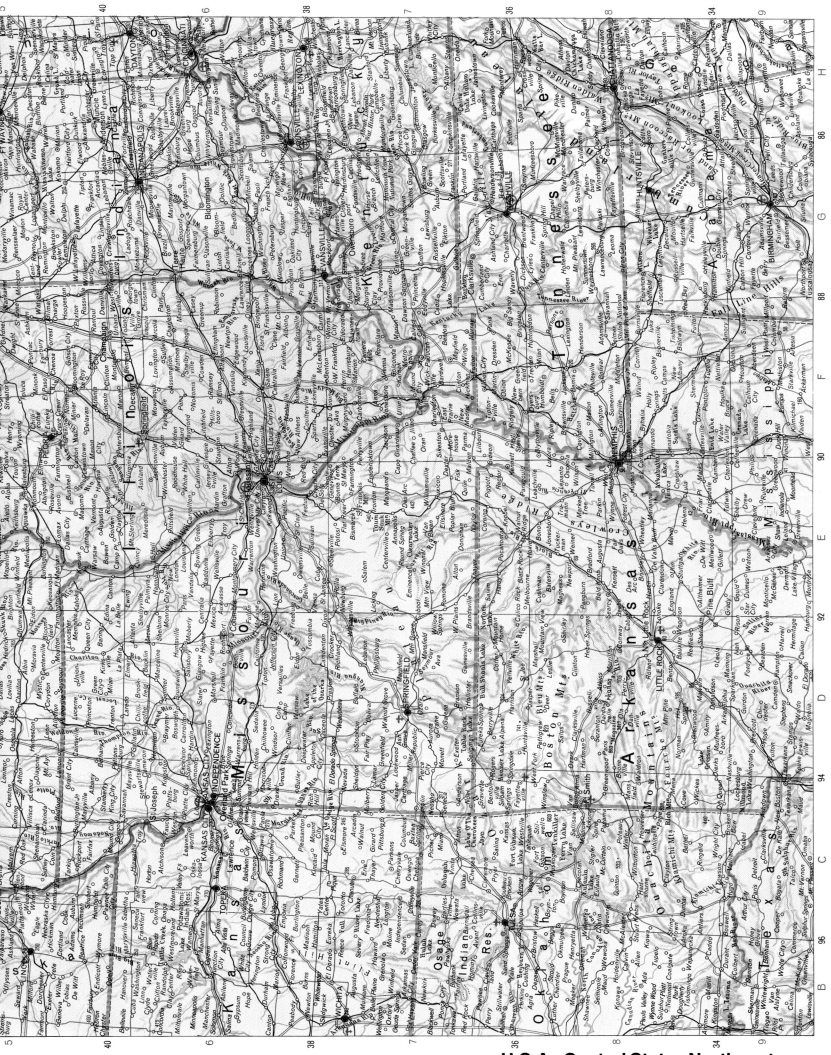

1 : 4,160,000

0   25   50   75   100   125 Kilometers

0   25   50   75   100 Statute Miles

One inch to 65 miles

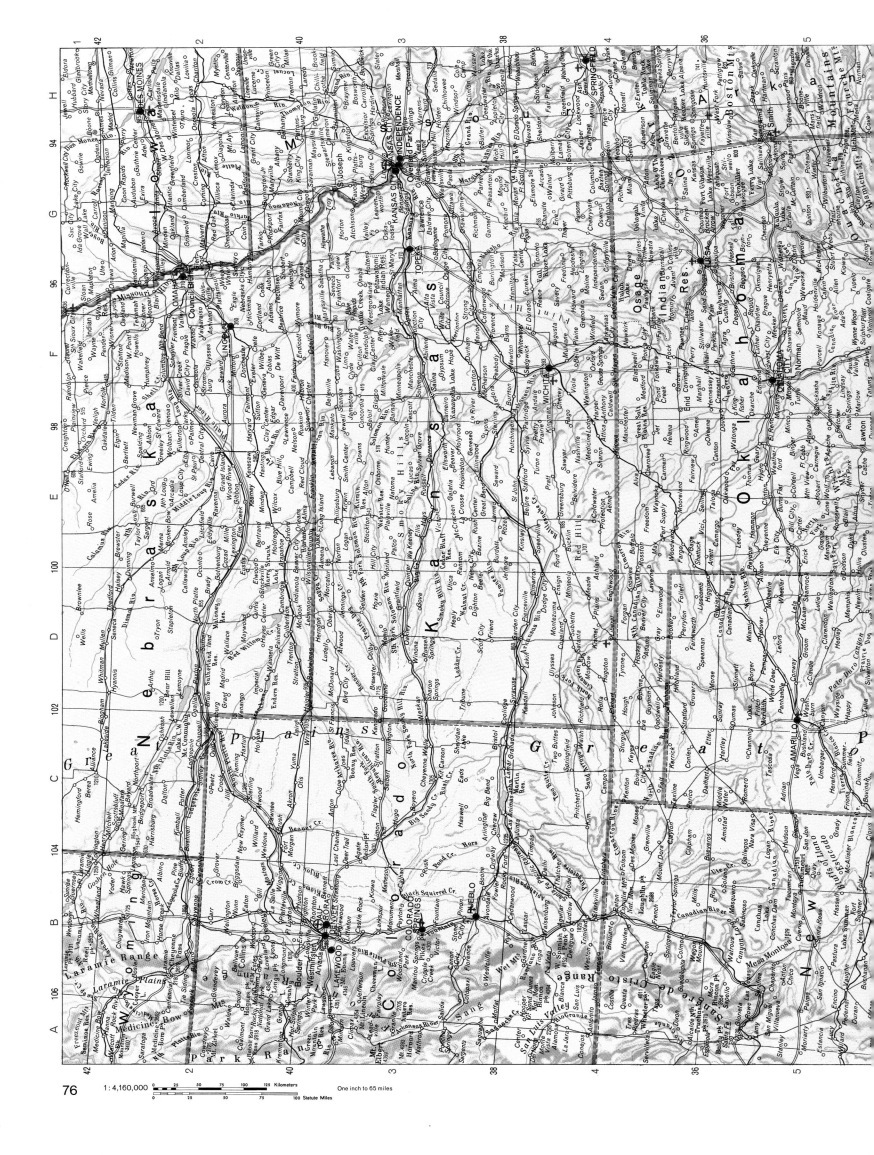

1:4,160,000

25   50   75   100   125 Kilometers

0   25   50   75   100 Statute Miles

One inch to 65 miles

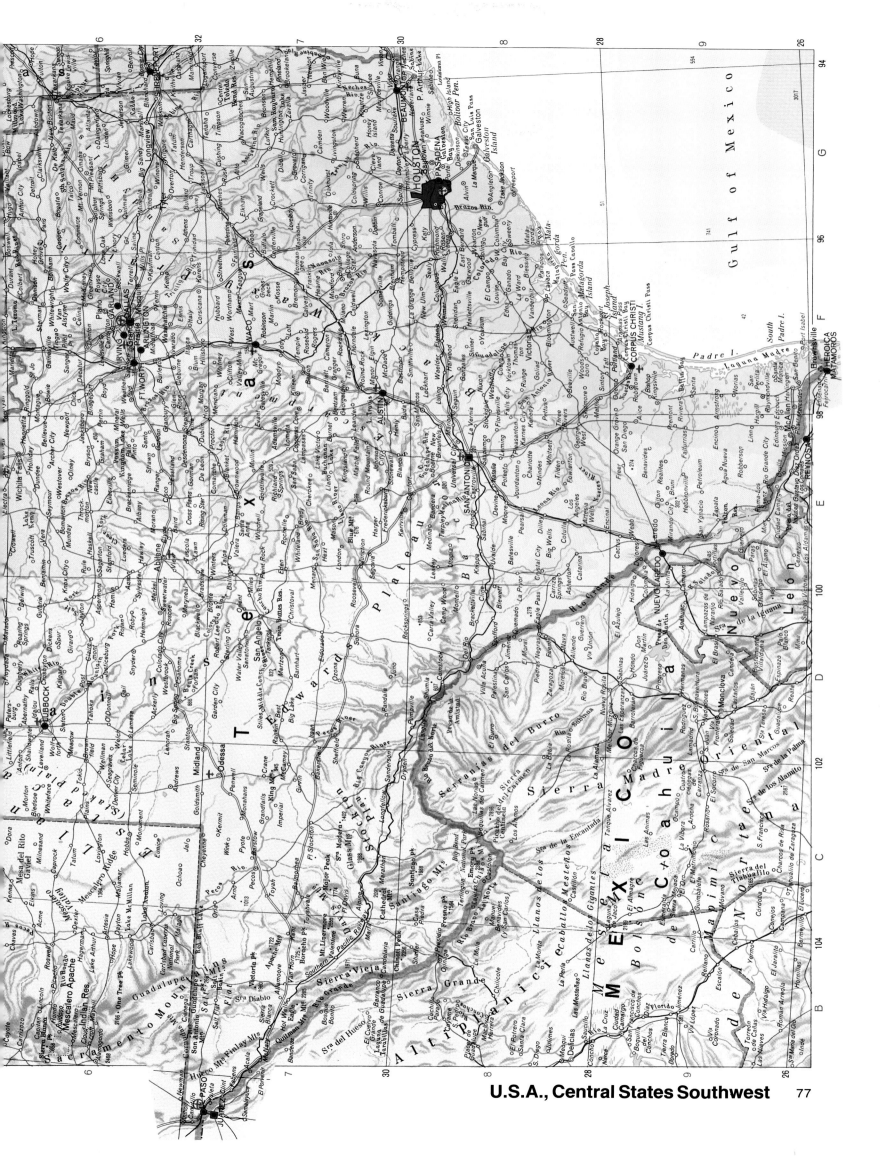

Gulf of Mexico

U.S.A., Central States Southwest 77

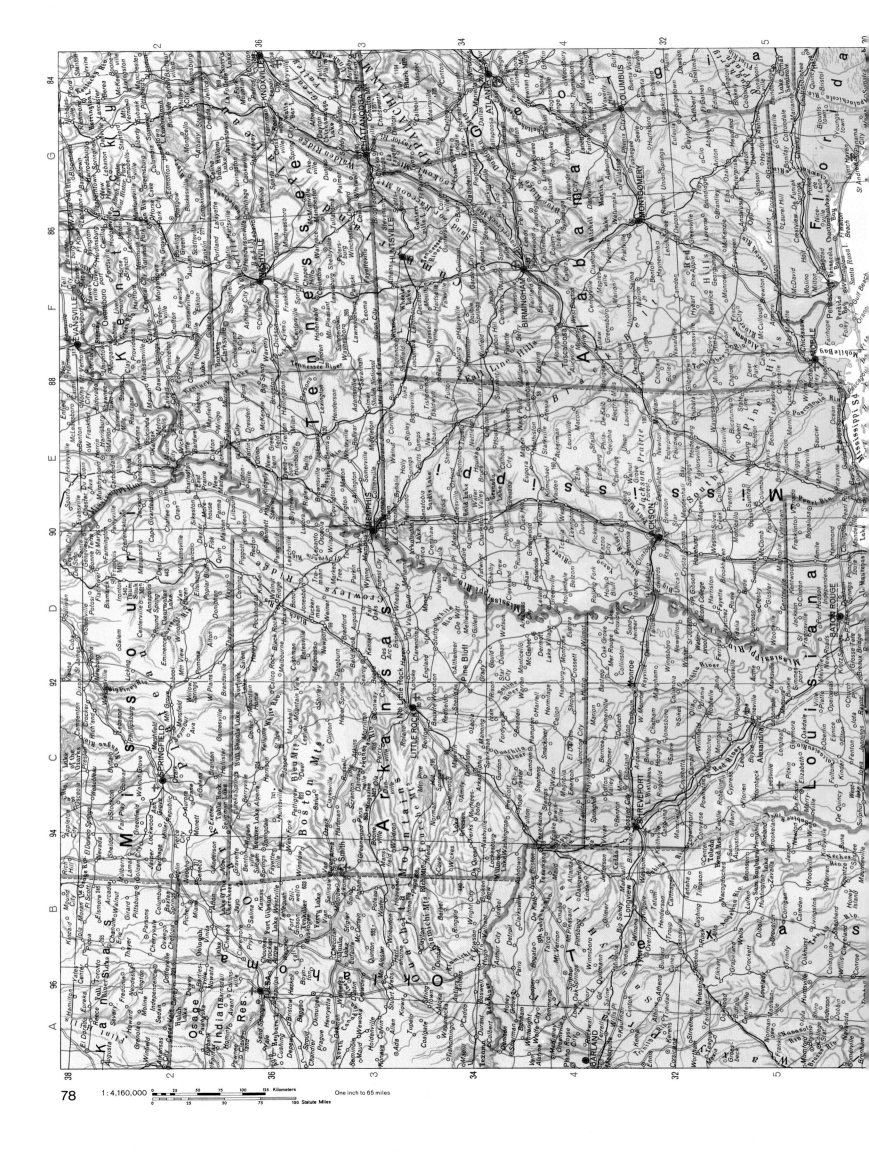

78

1 : 4,160,000

One inch to 65 miles

| 0 | 25 | 50 | 75 | 100 | 125 | Kilometers |

| 0 | 25 | 50 | 75 | 100 Statute Miles |

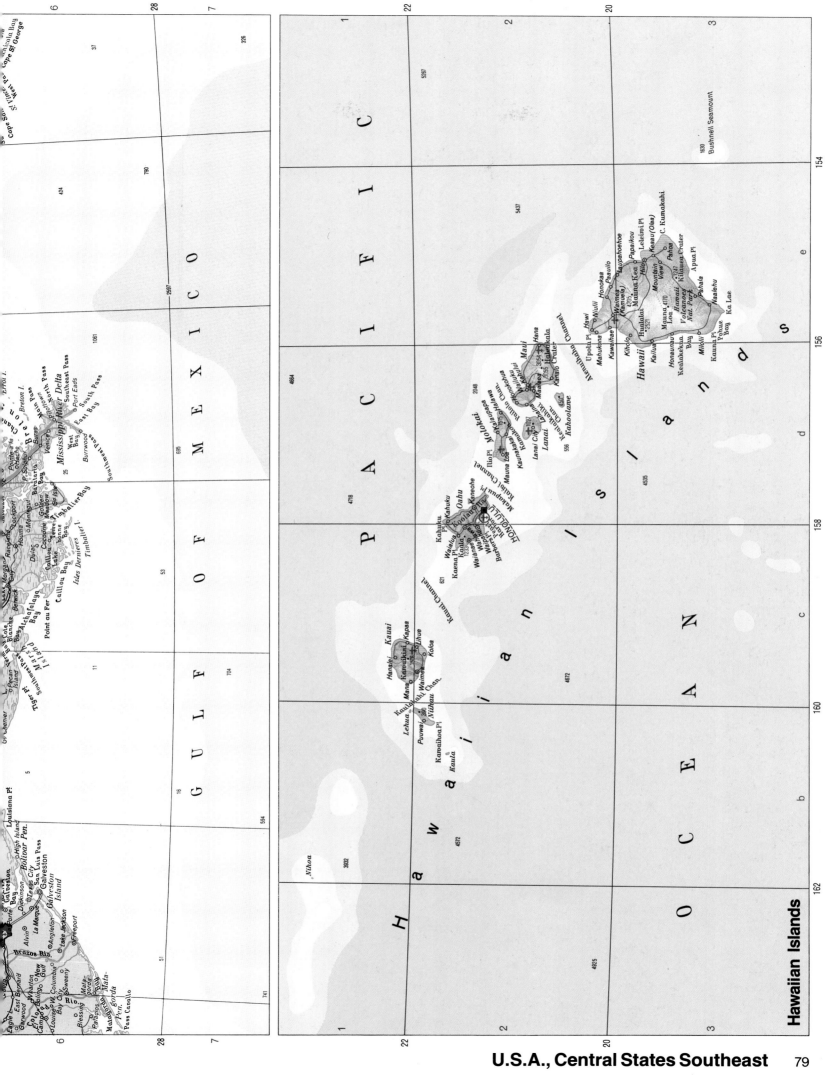

Hawaiian Islands

Florida

82   Montreal · Washington · New York

1:250 000

0   2.5   5   7.5   10 Kilometers

0   2.5   5   7.5 Statute Miles

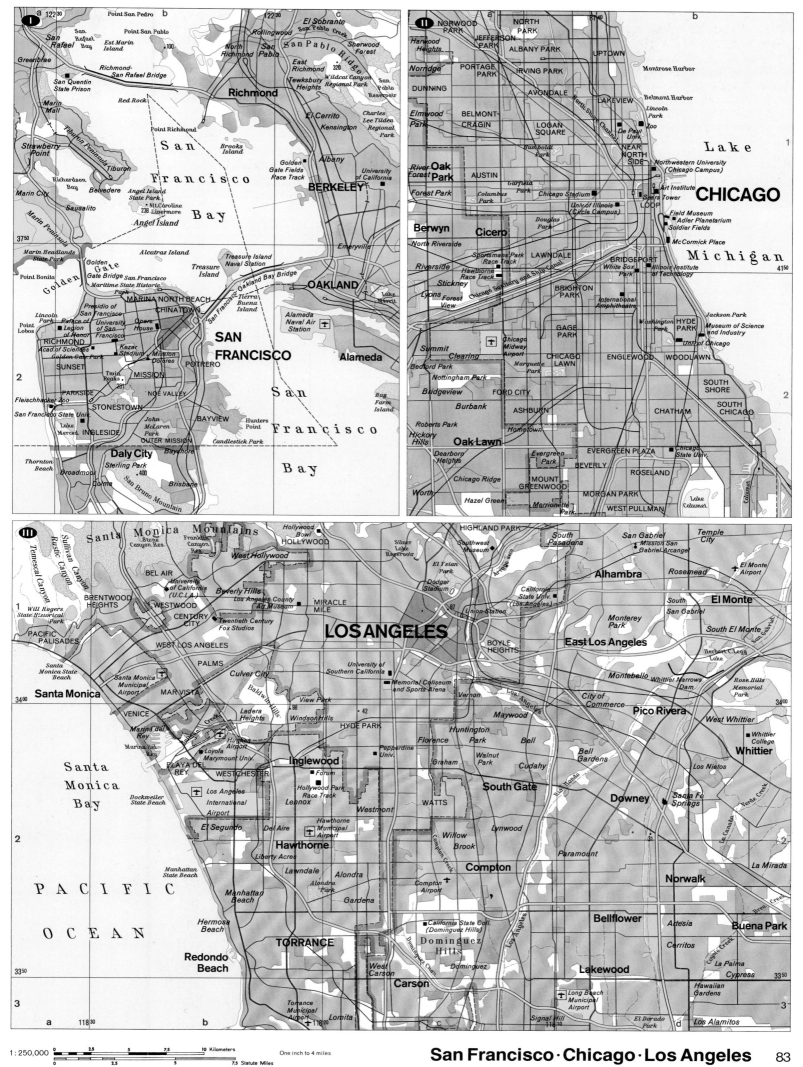

1 : 250,000

0   2.5   5   7.5   10 Kilometers

0   2.5   5   7.5 Statute Miles

One inch to 4 miles

A blazing sun and a wealth of colors; a lush abundance of flowers; rich, dark green agaves and cacti, corn and tobacco fields in warm golden hues of ripeness; the white stone walls of baroque churches; market activity and fiestas; isolated huts with thin smoke columns rising above their slanted roofs—the name "Mexico" conjures an endless succession of colorful images of a country with a rich, albeit still mysterious, history. Mexico's current condition is one of contrasts. In

Mexico: colorful country under a blazing sun, progress and ancient culture.

the agricultural sector, modern, large, globally oriented enterprises confront a multitude of small farmers (*campesinos*), who can barely meet their families' needs. Population growth and urbanization are enormous problems for this nation of 88 million people. Today every fourth Mexican lives in the conglomerate that is Mexico City.

Because of enormous increases in industry and mining operations—especially silver production and crude-oil revenue—the country was

catapulted to the status of a threshold nation during the second half of the 1970s. However, substantial investments in the modernization of the economy and the creation of a contemporary infrastructure have led to a national debt that can hardly be serviced.

The varied and colorful Mexican handicrafts seen in the small markets are important ingredients of international tourism. Of Third World nations, Mexico has been the number-one tourist destination ever

The agave, a high-growing, thorn-protected plant of the amaryllis family, flowers only once in its life (top). The façade of the University of Mexico City is decorated with motifs borrowed from Aztec sources (right).

Mexico's mountains: the central crater of Popocatepetl (above), a view of the state of Oaxaca bordering the Pacific Ocean in the south (right). There, in the mountainous region of the Zapotecs and Mixtecs, a great culture blossomed between 700 B.C. and A.D. 1500. In these mountainous highlands a proud Indian population lives untouched by European culture, which invaded 400 years ago. In addition to Spanish, the Indians speak their many native languages. Because the Zapotecs were pushed out of their old capital of Monte Alban by the Mixtecs, they enthusiastically welcomed the Spaniards as their liberators.

since North Americans and Europeans discovered the fairy-tale-like charm of this country. The nation has focused on this steady stream of visitors, 90 percent of whom are from the United States and Canada, in many ways. Mexican diversity continually provides new and ever-changing impressions that enchant the visitor: the virtually impassable Cordillera Mountains, the fertile highlands, life-threatening, picturesque deserts, tropical beaches with their sometimes mundane re-

sort life. The highland valleys and rugged divides of the mountains on the country's borders, the Sierra Madre Occidental and Oriental, are untouched by modern civilization and are home to an ancient romanticism. Old traditions are rooted here, the origins of which are barely known even to those who practice them. Customs in cult activities performances and daily work routines can be traced back to the times of the flourishing Aztec and Mayan cultures. Today the indigenous

population—the Indians, or the *Indios,* who make up about 9 percent of the population—still speaks the old Aztec and Mayan dialects without being able to understand Spanish, the official national language. Farmers today still weave the same patterns as in days of old, but many are also ingenious technicians and artists, and most certainly patient, untiring workers. Approximately 11,000 excavation sites yield new finds and new scientific insights for archaeologists and historians.

Today Mexico wrestles with low per-capita income and serious inflation problems. Unemployment and underemployment add to the nation's economic woes. Still, there is some hope that progress can be made as crude oil production and a growing tourist industry bring increased revenues to this beautiful but poor country.

1 : 7,500,000

0   50   100   150   200   250 Kilometers

One inch to 119 miles

0   50   100   150

200 Statute Miles

Mexico 87

SOUTH AMERICA

More than 280 million people—whites, blacks, mulattoes and mestizos—live in South America. The social contrasts between rich and poor are blatant, while the differences between landscapes of jungle, desert, mountains and glaciers are equally apparent. Three photos that are typical of its people and landscape: a ranch in Bolivia, an Indian from the south of Chile, and Brazil's tropical rain forest.

This subcontinent displays dimensions of unimaginable scale: The Andes are stretched over 4,700 miles (7,500 km), the longest mountain chain in the world. The largest continuous tropical rain forest surrounds the Amazon. Atacama, in the north of Chile, ranks among the driest deserts in the world. Blacks were shipped to South America as slaves. Whites, *Indios,* blacks, mestizos and mulattoes now form a unique mixture of races and nations. But there are few racial conflicts. Cities grow with breathtaking speed, but so do the slums. A few rich people are masters over huge stretches of land, while millions of propertyless people live hand-to-mouth. No other continent has as much debt as South America.

South America: life full of contrasts

Photo 1: Indians make up a large portion of the South American population. They live mainly in the Andes, the Patagonian south and in the tropical lowlands.

Photo 2: The Brazilian metropolis of Rio de Janeiro presents a different South America. Poverty, slums and open markets where trade is conducted have been crowded out of the city's landscape by high-rise buildings.

Photo 3: Coffee is one of the sub-continent's most significant export goods. After harvest, the laborers dry the coffee, as on a plantation here in Brazil.

Photo 4: In spite of rich oil reserves, most of Venezuela's population continues to live in poverty. The slums of Petare in Caracas, a city of four million inhabitants, are densely packed.

Photo 5: The huts of the Yagua Indians in the Columbian Leticia area on the Amazon are built on stilts.

Photo 6: Once again, Rio de Janeiro: Carnival, with its parades through the streets of Rio and the festively decorated, unrestrained celebrations.

Photo 7: Newly built city centers with grandiose streets frequently give misleading impressions about the living conditions of the majority of inhabitants; here, for example, the Avenida 9 de Julio in Buenos Aires (Argentina).

Photo 8: In Colombia, too, fast-paced progress is for few people. The modern high-rise scenery in Bogota offers little evidence of the

1

2

3

4

5

country's real economic situation.

Photo 9: Argentinian cattle ranching is world famous. Gauchos are branding the sign of their *hacienda* on a cow's hide.

Photo 10: Argentina not only is endless Pampa (grass-covered plain) on which cattle graze but also is the contrasting, colorful play of light of a rainbow over the Iguassu waterfalls on the Brazilian border.

Photo 11: The southernmost portion of Argentina is the Tierra del Fuego National Park. The photo shows the Rio Ovando before snow-covered mountains.

Photo 12: Disputes over the border drawn in Tierra del Fuego existed for many decades. They were finally settled with the help of the Pope. In this, the southernmost part of the subcontinent, an old wooden bridge leads over the Rio Condor into Chile.

Photo 13: The rugged mountains near Aconcagua in the Argentinian Andes.

6

7

9

8

10

11

12

13

1 : 30,000,000

One inch to 473 miles

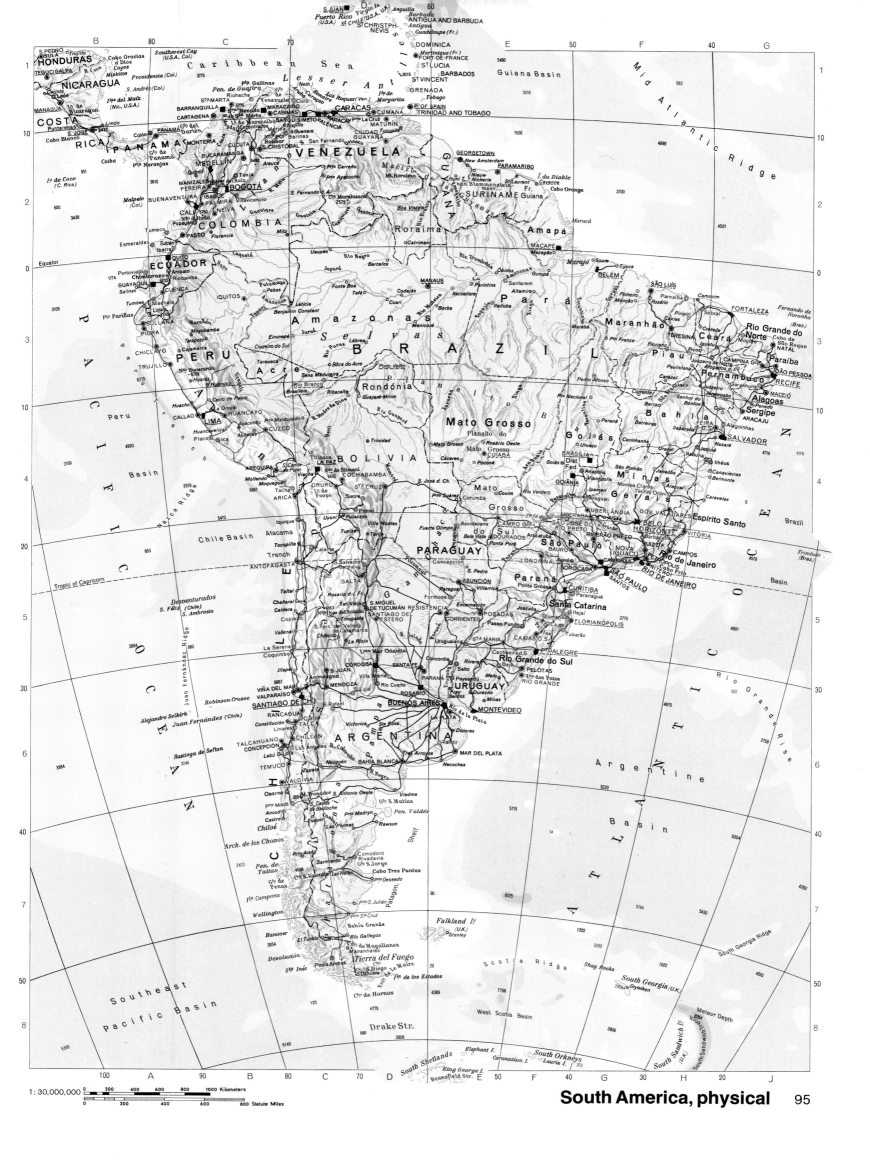

South America, physical   95

A tropical climate covers the north and center of South America down to the Tropic of Capricorn. In addition to the humid, hot regions (Amazon lowlands), there are areas with dry—even drought—periods, as in the northeast of Brazil. In the north of Argentina and Chile the climate is comparable to the north of Mexico, while the south has a climate that is similar to that of North America. South America is characterized by six major regions: the Cordillera de los Andes, the mountain region in

South America: from tropical heat to icy frost

Guyana, the Brazilian mountain and plateau terrain, as well as the three lowland basins of the Orinoco, the Amazon and the Parana. The Cordilleras (or Andes, as the *indios* say) run the entire length of South America in the west, from the Venezuelan coast down to Cape Horn. They are composed of two to three chains, and different altitudes are distinguished (see illustration): tierra caliente (hot country, up to approximately 3,300 ft. [1,000 m]), tierra templada (temperate country,

up to approximately 8,200 ft. [2,500 m]), tierra fria (cool country, over 8,200 ft. [2,500 m]) and tierra helada (frozen country, over 13,000 ft. [4,000 m]). In the central region, the Cordilleras stretch to a width of up to 500 mi. (800 km). America's highest mountain is in the Argentinian Andes: the Aconcagua, 23,034 ft. (7,021 m). Among the most interesting highlands of the world—next to those of Tibet—is the Altiplano, the relatively densely populated highland of Bolivia, of which Peru

The Iguassu waterfalls near the confluence of the Iguassu and the Parana are considered one of South America's premier spectacles. They belong to Brazil and Argentina and consist of some 275 individual falls. Not far from these falls, the world's largest hydroelectric plant was built a few years ago. The Itaipu Lake covers 565 sq. mi. (1,460 sq. km), which is nearly half as big as the great Salt Lake in Utah.

Two different kinds of Andes terrain: a typical highland bog in Peru (above) and the Cordillera de Huayhuash, a mountain chain in the Peruvian Cordillera Occidental (photo right). Highland bogs are found at an altitude between approximately 12,000 ft. (4,000 m) and 15,000 ft. (5,000 m), where hot springs sometime bubble up from the ground. The soil is so rich in minerals that the ponds are rust brown, yellowish or a milky blue, like the creek in the photo. Wildly crevassed glaciers flow into glacier lakes. The vegetation shows that the Cordillera de Huayhuash is made up of tropical mountains. On the right is the Yerupaja, 21,709 ft. (6,618 m). The Indians' villages are at altitudes of up to 12,000 ft. (4,000 m), while their pastures extend even higher. It is surprising how well the Indios have adapted to the thin air found in such altitudes, and they are capable of great physical exertion in pastures and in underground mines.

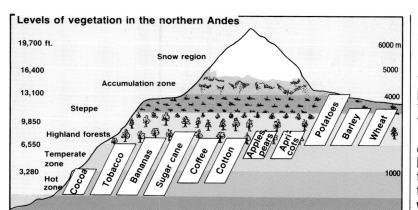

Levels of vegetation in the northern Andes

19,700 ft.   6000 m
       Snow region
16,400   5000
    Accumulation zone
13,100   4000
   Steppe
9,850
  Highland forests
6,550
  Temperate zone
3,280   1000
Hot zone

Cocoa · Tobacco · Bananas · Sugar cane · Coffee · Cotton · Apples pears · Apricots · Potatoes · Barley · Wheat

also shares a part. Barley is planted at altitudes of over 9,000 ft. (3,000 m). The potato was first cultivated here. Indians have adapted to the thin air, and they engage in hard physical labor in mines that sometimes are at an elevation of more than 12,000 ft. (4,000 m).

The Amazon lowland comprises one-third of the subcontinent. The basin of this, the largest river system in the world, is as large as Australia. Through the Casiquiare, which was first written about by Alexander von Humboldt at the beginning of the 19th century, the Orinoco is connected to the Rio Negro and the Amazon. The largest continuous tropical rain forest in the Amazon belongs to those regions and is still primarily undeveloped. Raw-material deposits and the pressure to develop newly cultivated land will continue to change the world's last large "green lung" (oxygen producer), and they may destroy it. The consequences cannot be predicted.

Llamas belong to the group of camels without humps. The Indians use their wool and use them as pack animals. Only at the end of their useful lives are they slaughtered. They graze peacefully at altitudes between 12,000 ft. (4,000 m) and 15,000 ft. (5,000 m), and they eat the tips of the pointy puna grass, as on the Altiplano in Bolivia (photo left).

A coastal desert in the region of the Pisco Valley in Peru: Cotton and corn are grown here, but it is the fortified stretch of dunes that makes irrigated agriculture possible. The dunes can grow up to 60 ft. (20 m) and also can migrate (photo above).

Brazil and Venezuela: countries rich in resources

Brazil, in the northern portion of South America, is the fifth-largest country in the world. Its east-to-west distance is as large as the east-to-west distance of the United States.

Its climate ranges from the tropical Amazon Basin to the cooler south, where there are four seasons, from the vegetation of the tropical rain forests to the grasslands of the south. The Amazon basin is like a giant bowl that narrows toward the Atlantic, with Brazil claiming the largest portion of it. In the always warm temperatures and humid climate, a lush world of plants and animals thrive, producing an almost unimaginable proliferation of life. Away from the large rivers the Amazon Basin is still Indian territory. Brazil, the country of superlatives, the country of the future, is also the developing country with the highest debt. The investment goal of the United States and of Western European countries was the southeast, which became the country's industrial center. With more than ten million inhabitants, São Paulo is Brazil's grand metropolis.

In the impoverished northeast, antiquated agricultural structures dominate; while in the Amazon region—especially in the Sierra dos Carajas—modern, raw-material processing operations are being developed.

The highest waterfall in the world, the Salto del Angel 3,212 ft. (972 m), is located in Venezuela, which is

Large areas of the Amazon are still unexplored. The photo to the left shows the structure of the tropical rain forest, from the low shrubs and bushes to the dense tree canopy to individual jungle giants, which can reach heights of up to 270 ft. (90 m). Many Indian tribes continue to live a Stone Age existence in the dense rain forests of South America.

Rio de Janeiro, two views: The Copacabana Beach is world famous (photo left). During Carnival, when the city is submerged in high spirits for a few days and nights, the differences between rich and poor seem to disappear.

still the richest country in South America. The basis of this wealth is the sale of crude oil and oil products, which comprise about 95 percent of all exports. Other raw-material deposits are in a distant second place. Agriculture can cover only 60 percent of the country's food requirements, livestock farming being the only exception.

Peru: land of the Incas

Peru offers a multitude of landscapes and cultures, from the coast to the mountain chain of the Cordilleras (partially volcanic), which reach altitudes of over 20,000 ft. (6,100 m): Huascaran 22,205 ft. (6,768 m), Yerupaja 21,709 ft. (6,618 m). Peru still shares a portion of the Amazon lowlands in the northeast. The highlands on the border of Bolivia were the Incas' preferred area of settlement; today their former capital city of Cuzco and the legendary Macchu Picchu are Peru's main tourist attractions. It was because of raw-material deposits that the Inca empire was destroyed by the Spanish conquerors. Peru's industry, still based on raw material, today is concentrated on the export of copper, silver, iron ore and crude oil. While its industry remains underdeveloped, Peru is one of the most important fishing nations. Intensive livestock farming (sheep, cattle, goats, alpacas) occurs on large *haciendas*.

Brisk trade on the traditional Indian market of Pisac in the immediate vicinity of Cuzco (large photo above).

Lake Titicaca is located in the southern Andes region of Peru—here with an Uru Indian's reed boat.

Peru's railways are the highest in the world. On the route from Lima to Huancayo, an altitude of 15,885 ft. (4,843 m) at the Ticlio pass (photo above).

Chile, a nation strongly criticized for its political structure, is, along with Paraguay, one of the last South American nations to have a military dictatorship. In 1988, Chile's dictator announced that he would voluntarily leave office in 1990. Because of its north-to-south expansion of 2,650 mi. (4,275 km), Chile shares all climatic zones of the Southern Hemisphere, from the tropical and subtropical climate in the north, a mild winter rain climate in its central portion, to a cool, rainy, subpolar cli-

Chile and Argentina: Latin America's corn belt

mate in Tierra del Fuego.

Separated from Chile by the Cordilleras, Argentina has significantly less precipitation. The fertile soil of the Pampa to the south and west of Buenos Aires is the basis for intensive export-oriented grain farming and equally intensive, and export-oriented, cattle farming. Broad stretches of Patagonia allow for extensive sheep ranching; while in the north, in the Gran Chaco, cotton growing prevails in the former grasslands, which turn into thorn-

bush vegetation toward the west. This type of vegetation is also prominent in western Paraguay. Paraguay and Bolivia are South America's only land-locked nations and rank among its poorest countries. Paraguay, however, because of its participation in the Itaipu hydroelectric plant, has advanced to become Latin America's foremost exporter of electricity. Uruguay, which also generates electricity primarily through hydropower, exports mainly meat and wool.

Probably nowhere on Earth is the contrast between cultivated valley and gray desert as extreme as here: The Atacama, located directly on the Pacific coast in northern Chile on the western slopes of the central Andes, is one of the world's driest deserts. It leads to the highland of Puna de Atacama at 9,800 to 13,000 ft. (3,000 to 4,000 m). Here, borax, saltpeter, silver and copper are mined.

Fernão de Magalhães sought the western sea passage to the Spice Islands in Southeast Asia and in 1519–20 discovered the difficult-to-traverse ocean straits that were named after him (Strait of Magellan). At night he saw the fires of the natives, and so he named this region Tierra del Fuego (photo above). The Tierra del Fuego islands, with their subpolar climate, have a treasure of glaciers, winterlike temperatures and snow-

falls. The Andes continue southward and break into individual island chains, stretching as a submerged mountain chain all the way to Antarctica. Today, crude-oil production is the most important economic activity and has influenced the development of settlements. Tourism is also a significant industry. Ushuaia, in Argentina, is the world's most southern city.

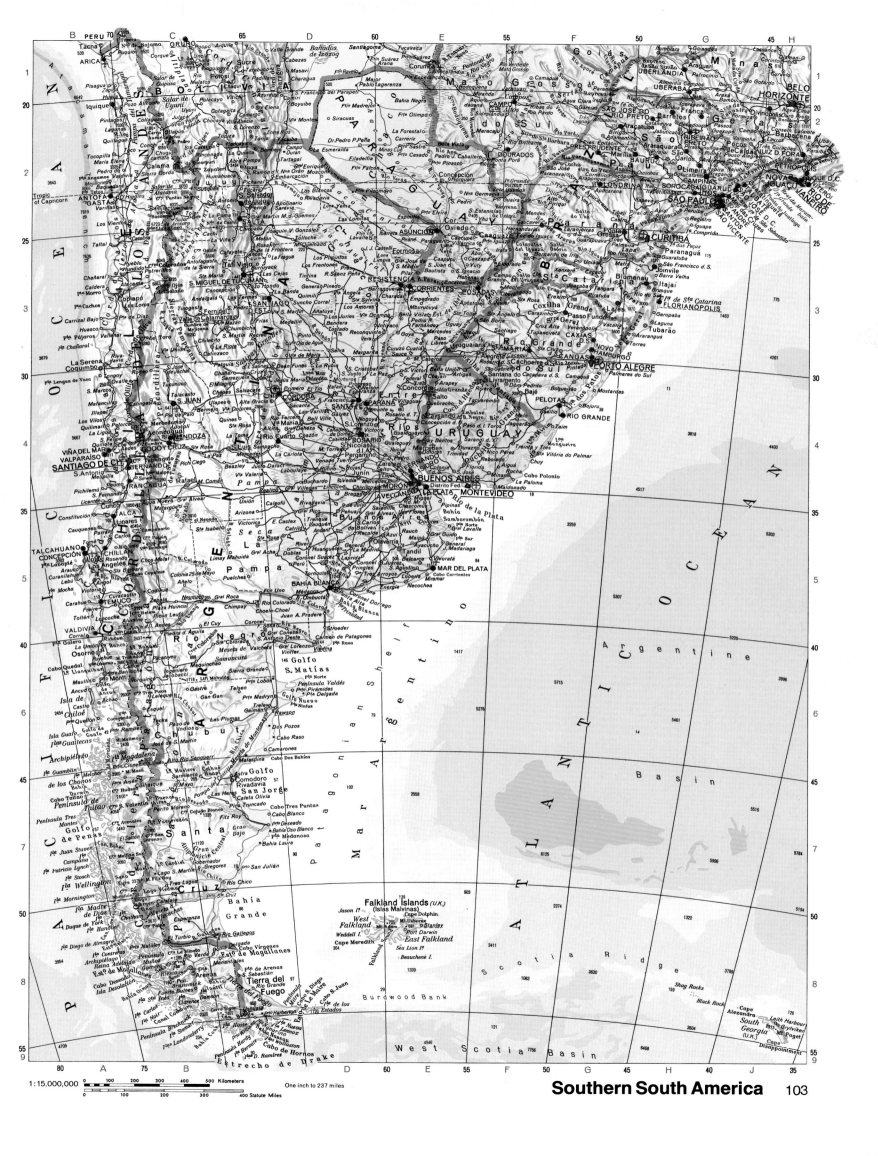

Southern South America 103

1:15,000,000

One inch to 237 miles

EUROPE

It is actually just an appendage of Asia, but it is in the center of Earth's land masses and has richly articulated coastlines. Almost 700 million people live between the Atlantic and the Urals, the Arctic Ocean and the Mediterranean Sea. Three photos represent Europe's innumerable artistic monuments: the Hradčany/St. Vitus' Cathedral in Prague (left); the Palacio de Generalife, with its beautifully designed garden in Granada (photo center); and St. Peters, in Rome (photo right).

"The intellectual center of the world"—this is how the French philosopher Montesquieu referred to Europe. It is inhabited by a mixture of peoples—Celts, Teutons, Romans, Slavs—and ranks among the most densely populated regions of the world. Ideas developed in Europe have shaped the world—ideas like the revelation that the Earth revolves around the Sun and that the Sun is only one star among countless millions of other stars. Europeans traveled to faraway countries as explorers, researchers, missionaries and settlers. European ideas have influenced the history of the world, from Christianity to the Renaissance, to capitalism and communism. The Industrial Revolution began in Europe; and here, too, the first atom was split, the ultimate consequences of which still are not known. It all began in Europe.

Europe has thousands of faces. People and natural forces have shaped the old continent and made it unique. Beauty can be found even in ruins.

Photo 1: Remoteness in Sweden. Gigantic wood floats drift downstream on the Jörnsjörn. Wood is Sweden's precious gold. Photo 2: Pious idyll in front of the majestic mountain scenery of the Watzmann in southeastern Germany near Austria. Nature and church become a unified place of reverence in the Chapel of Mercy of Maria Gern, the destination of many worshippers. Photo 3: High over the Chalcidice peninsula in Greece, on the "holy mountain" Athos, is this self-governing monks republic with twenty cloisters. Photo 4: Time stood still at Groene Rei in the splendid city of Bruges (Brugge) in Belgium. Photo 5: The alpine farmers of Weng in Austria work hard for their daily bread, where cultivation reaches right up to the tree line. The steep and clefted Hochtor mountains reach toward the sky over the fields. Photo 6: The Catherine Palace in the city of Pushkin near Leningrad dates back to a time when Leningrad was still called St. Petersburg and the czars ruled Russia. Photo 7: The small and ancient village of Monreal, West Germany, with its half-timbered buildings lies idyllic in the middle of the Eifel, which has more than 200 volcanic domes. Photo 8: The daring curves of the tent-roof over the Olympic stadium in Munich—one of today's wonders of the world. Photo 9: Bagpipes—the unmistakable sound of Scotland—originated in Asia, but have been known in Europe for more than 2,000 years. Photo 10: Mount Etna, al-

1

2

3

4

5

6

7

most 10,600 ft. (3,265 m) high, looms skyward into the mediterranean sky. It is a volcano that can erupt at any time—as it has many times in the recent past. Photo 11: The Greek theater of Taormina, Sicily, overlooking the bay of Giardini. An earthquake brought about its destruction. Ruins, ocean and shoreline became splendid theatrical scenery. Photo 12: The splendor of an entire era, the era of the sun kings, is reflected by the bridges spanning the Seine River in Paris.

Here, the ostentatious candelabras on the Pont Alexandre. Photo 13: Orient and occident meet in Mostar in the Yugoslavian Hercegowina. Roman legions marched over the ancient stone bridge spanning the Neretva. Photo 14: In a small Paris alley, a former bakery. It was called the golden wheat stalk. Today it is a second-hand market, but still filled with memories of the past. Photo 15: Off the shore of the Atlantic on the Cote Sauvage in Brittany, France, the setting sun enchants

the rugged landscape of the stormy Atlantic coast. Photo 16: The simple life of fishermen, just as it was many centuries ago. After returning home from the catch, the nets are repaired and dried in the sun. Photo 17: A stroll down London's Carnaby Street is unforgettable for its unique richness of contrasts: elegance and curiosity, antiques and modern goods.—Seventeen pictures of Europe out of the thousands that could have been selected instead. Landscape,

history and culture are reflected in each one of them, and in the way and form in which Europe's people live. No other continent on Earth offers such a rich variety. Two thousand years of European history made this possible. And new things are happening every day in old Europe, while it remains as young as ever.

9

10

11

3

3

14

12

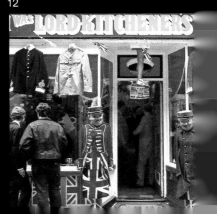

1:15,000,000

One inch to 237 miles

100 200 300 400 500 Kilometers

100   200   300   400 Statute Miles

Administrative units in the Soviet Union:

most 10,600 ft. (3,265 m) high, looms skyward into the mediterranean sky. It is a volcano that can erupt at any time—as it has many times in the recent past. Photo 11: The Greek theater of Taormina, Sicily, overlooking the bay of Giardini. An earthquake brought about its destruction. Ruins, ocean and shoreline became splendid theatrical scenery. Photo 12: The splendor of an entire era, the era of the sun kings, is reflected by the bridges spanning the Seine River in Paris.

Here, the ostentatious candelabras on the Pont Alexandre. Photo 13: Orient and occident meet in Mostar in the Yugoslavian Hercegowina. Roman legions marched over the ancient stone bridge spanning the Neretva. Photo 14: In a small Paris alley, a former bakery. It was called the golden wheat stalk. Today it is a second-hand market, but still filled with memories of the past. Photo 15: Off the shore of the Atlantic on the Cote Sauvage in Brittany, France, the setting sun enchants

the rugged landscape of the stormy Atlantic coast. Photo 16: The simple life of fishermen, just as it was many centuries ago. After returning home from the catch, the nets are repaired and dried in the sun. Photo 17: A stroll down London's Carnaby Street is unforgettable for its unique richness of contrasts: elegance and curiosity, antiques and modern goods.—Seventeen pictures of Europe out of the thousands that could have been selected instead. Landscape,

history and culture are reflected in each one of them, and in the way and form in which Europe's people live. No other continent on Earth offers such a rich variety. Two thousand years of European history made this possible. And new things are happening every day in old Europe, while it remains as young as ever.

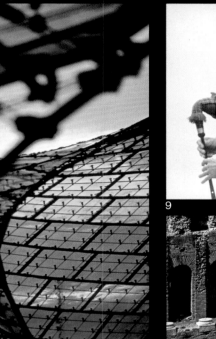

3

9

10

11

3

14

12

1:15,000,000

One inch to 237 miles

Administrative units in the Soviet Union

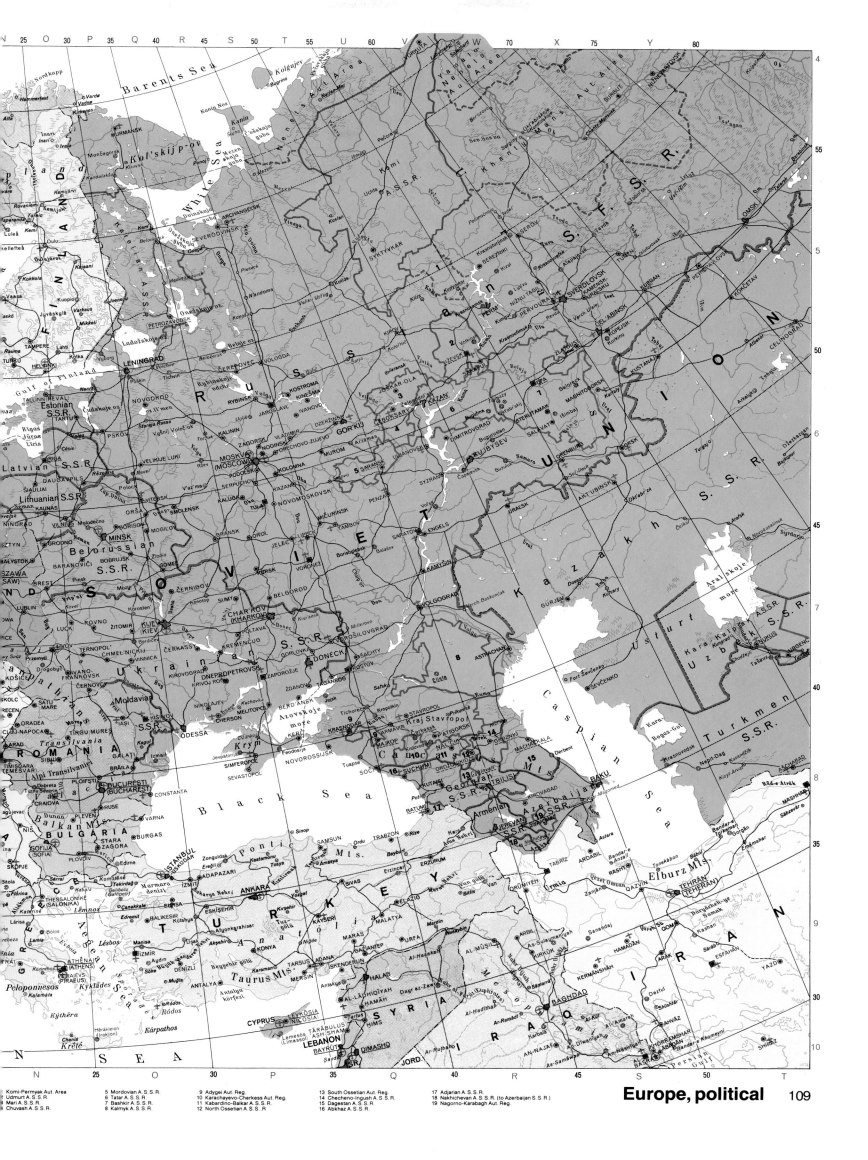

Komi-Permyak Aut. Area
Udmurt A.S.S.R.
Mari A.S.S.R.
Chuvash A.S.S.R.

5 Mordovian A.S.S.R.
6 Tatar A.S.S.R.
7 Bashkir A.S.S.R.
8 Kalmyk A.S.S.R.

9   Adygei Aut. Reg.
10 Karachayevo-Cherkess Aut. Reg.
11 Kabardino-Balkar A.S.S.R.
12 North Ossetian A.S.S.R.

13 South Ossetian Aut. Reg.
14 Checheno-Ingush A.S.S.R.
15 Dagestan A.S.S.R.
16 Abkhaz A.S.S.R.

17 Adjarian A.S.S.R.
18 Nakhichevan A.S.S.R. (to Azerbaijan S.S.R.)
19 Nagorno-Karabagh Aut. Reg.

1:15,000,000

0 100 200 300 400 500 Kilometers

0   100   200   300   400 Statute Miles

One inch to 237 miles

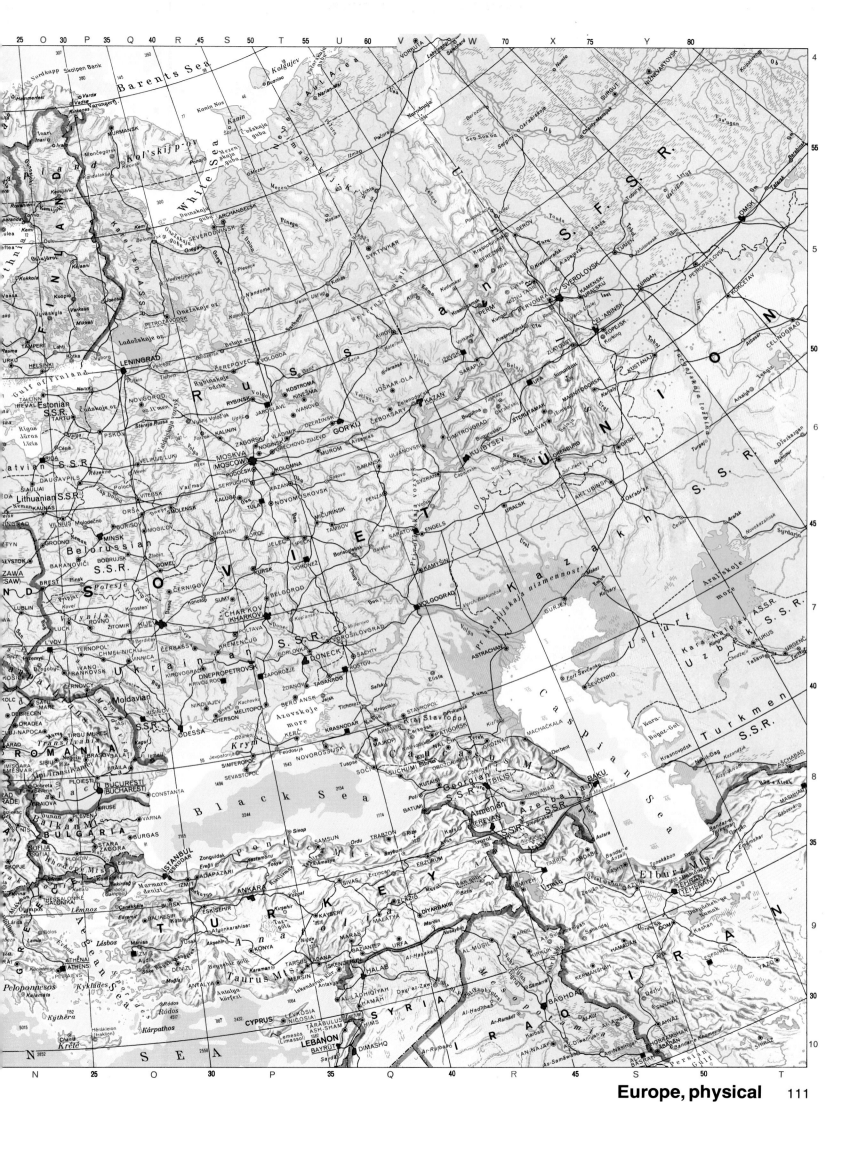

Europe, physical 111

The Scandinavian peninsula comprises Norway, Sweden and northern Finland, but for historical reasons and because of common cultural traditions, Norway, Sweden, Finland, Denmark and Iceland are all counted as Scandinavian countries. A symbolic expression of this is the Scandinavian cross resting on its side, which appears on all of these countries' flags. In terms of geological history, Scandinavian countries share other similarities: The Earth's surface is a typical rem-

Scandinavia: fjords and fjells, forests and lakes, a community of nations linked by a common history

nant of the Ice Age, like the steep fjords in Norway and the drumlins in Sweden, the "thousand lakes" in Finland and the ground and terminal moraines in Denmark. Iceland's landscape is determined by volcanic fire and mighty glacier plateaus. Thanks to the primarily westerly winds and the Gulf Stream, Norway's ports remain ice-free up beyond the Arctic Circle, even in winter, and intensive agriculture is still possible in Denmark and southern Sweden. Grain is still farmed

along the coast of Sweden up to the Arctic Circle.

The landscape, however, is dominated by coniferous forests and the treeless fjell (tundra) with dwarf shrubs, moss and lichens above the tree line. It is found at an altitude of between 1,500 and 3,000 ft. (450 and 900 m) above sea level and in northern Finland reaches almost up to the Arctic Ocean. Only Iceland has no trees. Differences in landscape among the Scandinavian countries result in differences in

The Sogne Fjord is considered the most beautiful of the Norwegian fjords (right). One-hundred-twenty miles (200 km) long, the fjord's rocky cliffs rise steeply and suddenly, sometimes as high as 3,300 ft. (1,000 m). A trip through fjord country is a true adventure.

The Norwegian city of Alesund was formerly a seaport inhabited principally by fishermen and their families. Today the economy is more diverse, but still dependent on the sea (above).

This dreamy little farm in Denmark looks out upon the sea (right). Iceland was formed volcanically. Much of its surface is made up of glaciers, lava deposits, lava desert, geysers and hot springs. This tiny nation in the North Atlantic has a homogeneous population of just under a quarter of a million (opposite page).

economic foundations. Norway is largely a mountainous country with a deeply grooved fjord coastline. Only 3 percent of the country's surface can be used for agricultural purposes, so the population has been dependent upon the ocean for economic activity, engaging in fishing and formerly also in worldwide whaling. Norway ranks as one of the world's leading seafaring nations. In Sweden and Finland, forestry and pasturage are the basic livelihood, as over one-half of both countries is covered by forest. The two countries are also Europe's largest paper producers. The Lapps or Sami, the indigenous Scandinavian population in "Lapland," live on seasonal pasturage between forests and tundra, and the reindeer is their preferred domesticated animal. Thanks to Denmark's favorable climate, agriculture is the most significant economic activity there. On the other hand, an unfavorable climate leaves the Icelanders, who were under Danish sovereignty until 1944, no alternatives other than fishing and sheep raising. The landlocked waters are also valuable, as they not only are rich in fish but also provide opportunities for hydroelectric-power generation. They are also natural transportation routes that are used to float wood from the endless forests to sawmills and cellulose plants.

The iron-ore mines in Kiruna and Gallivare are well known. In Sweden there are additional deposits of lead and copper ores and uranium containing shale deposits. There is considerable mining of copper, nickel, cobalt and chromium in Finland. Of surprising importance is the production of crude oil and natural gas on the shelf off the coast. Successful drilling first occurred in 1966. Of all the Scandinavian countries, Sweden has the most productive industrial structure. The sober and diligent Scandinavians have attained a standard of living that is ranked among the highest in the world.

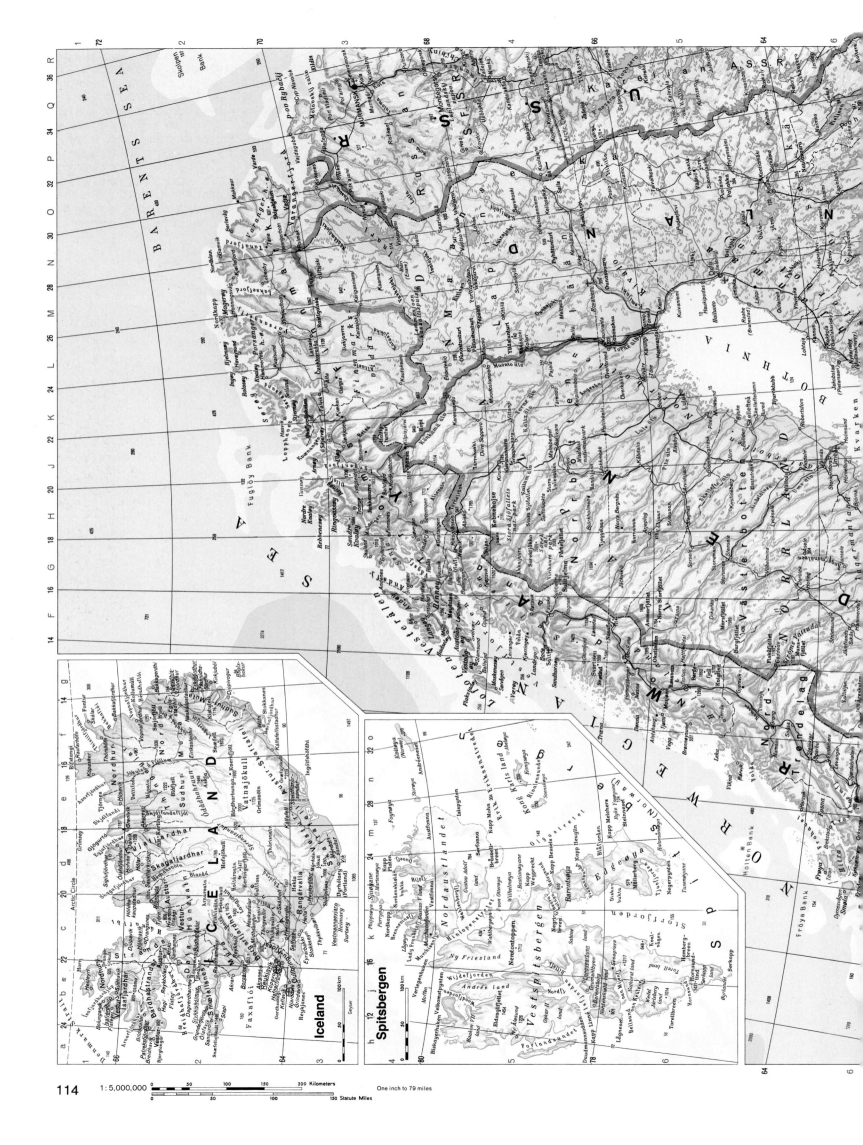

36
34
32
30
28
26
24
22
20
18
16
14

BARENTS SEA

RUSSIAN S.F.S.R.

MURMANSK

F I N M A R K

S V E R I G E

N O R R L A N D

V I N H L A

N O R G E

Iceland

I C E L A N D

Denmark Strait

Arctic Circle

Faxaflói

Reykjavik

Vatnajökull

Hekla

Spitsbergen

Nordaustlandet

Vestspitsbergen

Ny Friesland

Storfjorden

Andrée land

1 : 5,000,000
0   50   100   150   200 Kilometers
0   50   100
150 Statute Miles

One inch to 79 miles

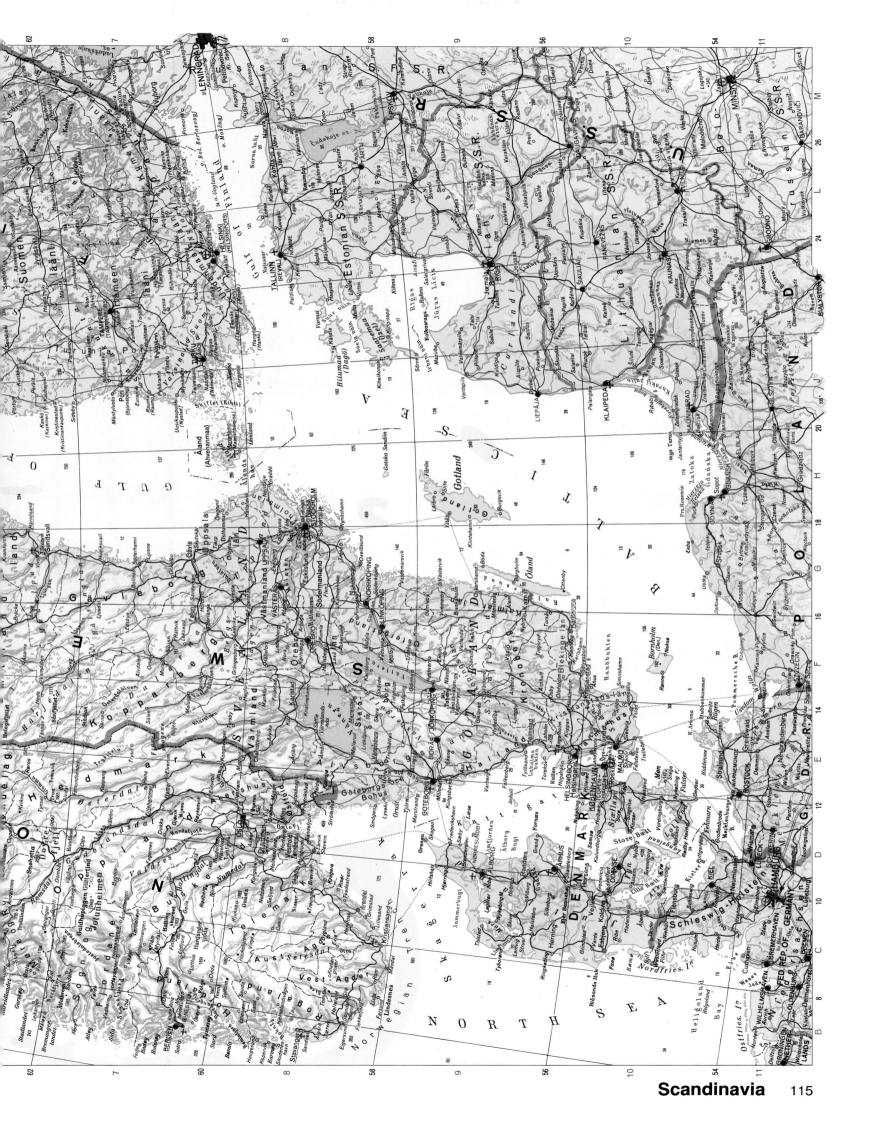

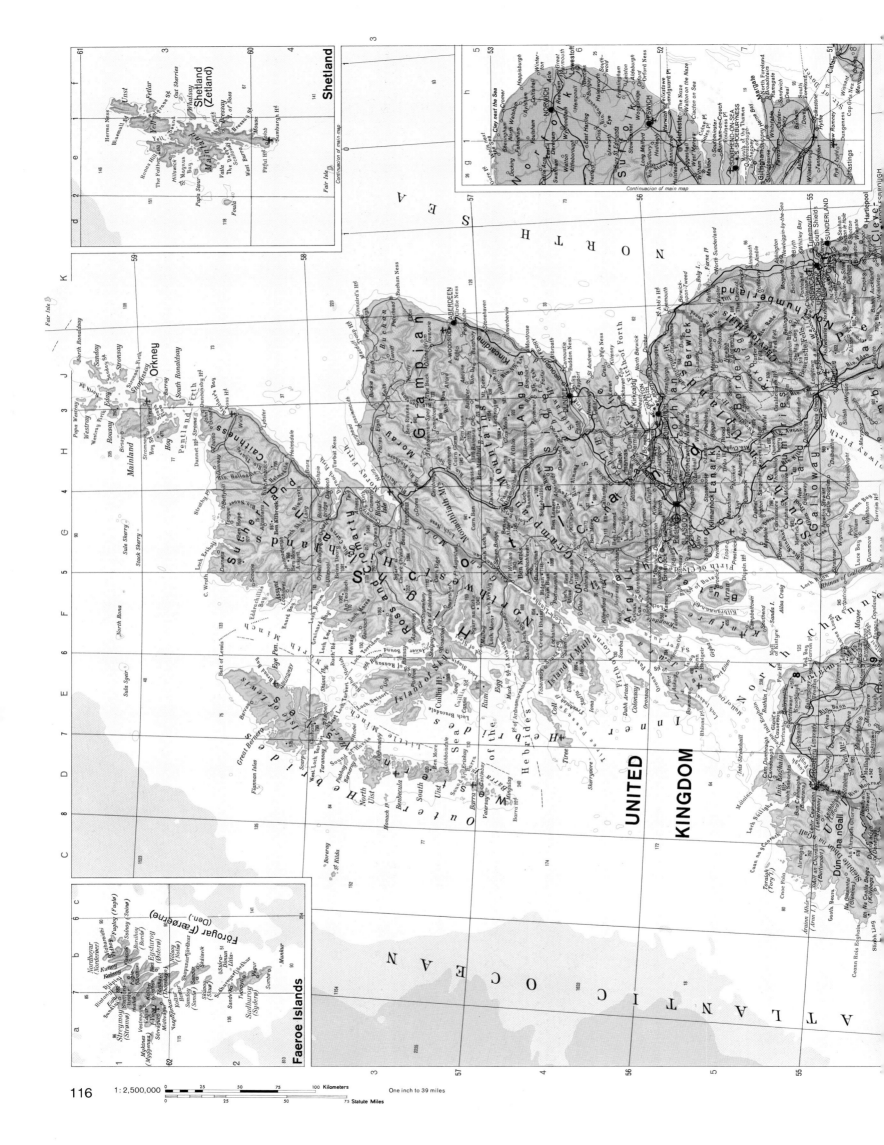

Shetland
(Zetland)

Faeroe Islands

Føroyar (Færøerne)
(Den.)

UNITED

KINGDOM

Orkney

NORTH SEA

ATLANTIC OCEAN

NORWICH

IPSWICH

SOUTHEND-ON-SEA

ABERDEEN

GLASGOW

SUNDERLAND

1 : 2,500,000

0   25   50   75   100 Kilometers

0   25   50   75 Statute Miles

One inch to 39 miles

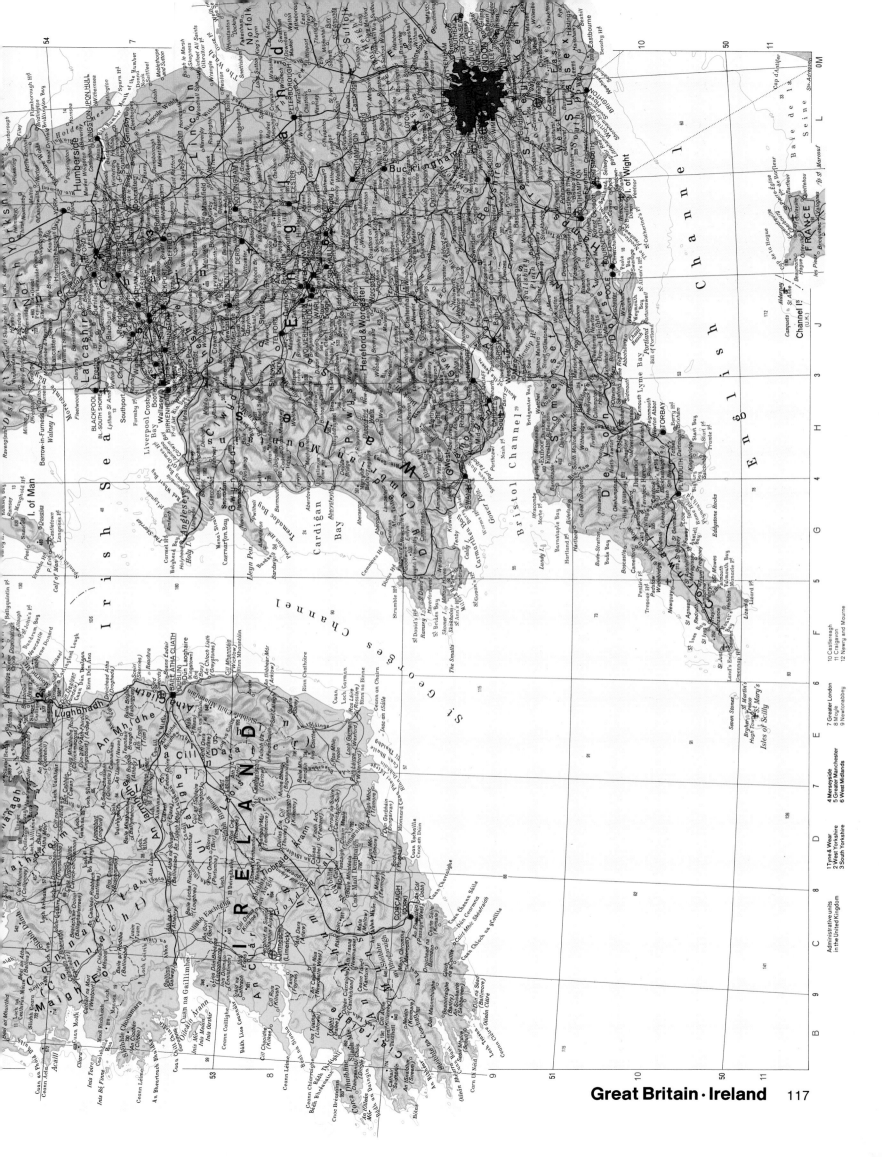

Great Britain · Ireland 117

The British Isles, off to the west of the mainland, are Europe's largest island group. Great Britain and Ireland are the two largest islands. Three dates mark the most significant points in its history. In 1066 the last violent invasion under William the Conqueror took place. From then on the islands developed in "splendid isolation," relatively uninfluenced by the mainland. In 1588 the Spanish Armada was defeated by the British fleet. This marked England's rise to world power. While

Great Britain: kingdom rich in traditions; motherland of the Commonwealth of Nations

the islands had been removed from political power centers and trade before then, the European nations along the Atlantic coast became its focal point when the Spanish and Portuguese Caravels crossed the Atlantic. Thus began the British Empire, one of the largest empires in world history. Since World War II, however, Great Britain has lost its dominant influence abroad, most colonial subjects have fought for and gained their independence, and the empire has become the

nonbinding Commonwealth of Nations. In 1973 Great Britain turned toward the mainland with its entry into the European Economic Community.

The narrowest point between Dover and Calais on the mainland is only about 62 mi. (42 km). Drilling under the English Channel for a railway tunnel (or chunnel) has begun, and Great Britain will be connected to the Continent in 1993.

The ocean is ever-present in Great Britain, where no village is

The Tower Bridge (right), one of London's unmistakable landmarks, in the morning sunshine. The bridge in its current form, with its two 213-ft.-high (65 m) towers, was built in 1894.

Great Britain's coast is quite varied and, with its many different landscapes, is considered among the most beautiful in Europe. There are the fjord coasts in the northwest of Scotland, steep cliffs in the southeast, flat coastlines with sand or gravel beaches in the east and south, and the ria coastlines (flooded river valleys) in the southwest. The southwestern coast of Wales, with the Stack Rocks near Tenby (page 119), is also considered part of the ria coastline.

The city of Bath was built on the site of what was to become England's most famous mineral bath. The elegance of the cityscape is demonstrated by the houses built in the Georgian style. The Royal Crescent was built by John Wood II in the 18th century. Thirty houses are hidden behind the 604-ft.-long (185 m), crescent-shaped facade and the more than 100 Ionic columns (above).

Godskill (right) is only one of the many summer resorts in the style of merry old England on the Isle of Wight, an area of outstanding natural beauty. Poets have sung hymns to the island, and Queen Victoria spent many of her summers there in Osborne House, where she died in 1901.

more than 80 mi. (130 km) away from it. The inhabitants of the predominantly mountainous north —Scotland—and west—Wales— have preserved some of the customs, languages and dress of their Celtic ancestry. England comprises 57 percent of the surface area of Great Britain. Its spine is formed by the Pennines, a flat rolling landscape of hills. The east and south are flatlands with some terraces. The climate is quite oceanic, with mild winters and cool summers.

Portions of the highlands in Scotland and Wales, where desolate bogs and heaths are found, are above the tree line. Farming occurs mainly in the drier southeast. Only 8 percent of the country is covered with forests. Fishing, which was one of the most important economic activities for centuries, has lost significance due to foreign competition and overfishing of the coastal waters.

In the beginning of the 18th century the first industrial society, based on coal and iron ore deposits, was created in central England. Thus the Industrial Revolution, the changing of the world through technology, began. Raw materials for the developing industries came primarily from colonies, which in turn became the markets for the industrial products of the mother nation. Development of crude-oil and natural-gas fields in the North Sea in the 1970s provided a new source of income for the nation. The economic development of recent years benefits primarily southern England, as future-oriented industries such as chemicals, electrotechnics and electronics are growing here.

London, England's capital city, has maintained its position as a center of global commerce in spite of political changes. It has a role in international capital transactions that is second only to that of New York. Heathrow airport has the highest volume of flights in Europe.

Ireland enjoys a distinctly oceanic climate because of the warm Gulf Stream washing up on its shores and predominantly westerly and southwesterly winds. On the southwestern coast there are splendid gardens with subtropical plants. The fishing grounds on the cove-rich coast, and above all, the numerous inland waters, attract sport fishermen from the mainland. The Irish gained their independence only in 1921, after centuries of English domination. In 1949 the nation

Ireland: Eire, the emerald island in the Atlantic

left the Commonwealth as the Republic of Ireland. Irish, a Celtic language, is the nation's second official language, next to English. Only Northern Ireland (formed from a section of Ulster) remains in the United Kingdom; approximately 35 percent of the population is Catholic. The violence in Northern Ireland, and the struggle of some to unite Ireland, continue to this day. The basis of the economy is still agriculture. Ireland's joining the European Common Market has

strengthened the economy. The potato famine of 1845–1848, caused by poor harvests of the basic foodstuff, led to a massive exodus. Ireland became a nation of emigrants. Well into this century the United States was the main destination of these emigrants. To this day there is still a flow of youth to the United States, many of them entering illegally. The population fell from 6.5 million to 2.8 million by 1956. In recent years it has grown to approximately 3.5 million.

The ruins of Clonmacnoise (top) are near Athlone in the center of Ireland. The monastery was the center of intellectual life on the island in the sixth century and remained so for about 1,000 years, even attracting students from the Continent. The high crosses date back to the tenth and eleventh centuries. The Christianizing of Western and Central Europe can be traced back largely to the activities of Irish and Anglo-Saxon traveling monks.

In the gardens of Muckross House near Killarney in the southwest of Ireland, you feel as if you are on the Riviera (center). The park grounds are central to Killarney National Park. Killarney proper is the center of tourism in Ireland. Here, the Ring of Kerry, an approximately 120 mi. (200-km)-long, beautifully scenic road, begins and ends.

The population of the Aran Islands in Galway Bay off the western Irish coast (right) has most faithfully preserved Irish-Gaelic culture and language through the centuries. Much evidence from pre-Christian and early-Christian times can still be found on these remote islands.

In 1947 three nations—Belgium, The Netherlands and Luxembourg—agreed to join as a unified economic region, BE-NE-LUX. Today, strong impulses for the economic unification of Europe are being sent out from these three nations. Brussels is Europe's secret capital city, for it is here that both the commission of the European Economic Community (EEC) and Euratom are based, as is NATO, the North Atlantic Treaty Organization. The EEC's court of justice resides in Luxembourg, and organs of the European Parliament work there, too. The Hague is home to the International Court of Justice, an institution of the UN.

Benelux: two monarchies, one grand duchy; where Europe is most densely populated

With 837 and 1,109 persons per sq. mi. (323 and 428 per sq. km), respectively, Belgium and The Netherlands are Europe's most densely populated nations. In Belgium the landscape rises in the southwest, like giant steps through fertile hills, up to the heavily forested Ardennes. Over one-third of The Netherlands is below sea level. By means of daring dam structures and complicated drainage plants, the Dutch seek to protect themselves from floods. Medieval cities such as Ghent and Bruges were wealthy centers of commerce in the Middle Ages, and Amsterdam was the "Venice of the North," with its rows of houses along the canals. The treasures of Amsterdam's museums are among the most awesome in all of Europe.

The windmills typical of Holland are, for the most part, pump stations regulating the water level of the polders, which lie beneath the ocean's surface (left above). Tulip fields can be found mainly in the triangle formed by the cities of Leiden, Haarlem and Aalsmeer. Flower cultivation is of great significance to the national economy.

The guild houses on the Graslei in Ghent (top right), the capital of Belgian East Flanders, attest to the economic significance of Flanders' cities from the 12th century until the end of the 16th century. The wealth of these cities was based chiefly on the production and trade of cloth.

The "Oosterschelde Dam" (left) was completed in 1986 as an enormous barrier for the delta. It is supposed to protect from spring floods the population centers situated on the mouths of the Rhein, Maas and Schelde rivers.

The Federal Republic of Germany, consisting of ten states, was formed in 1949 out of the 1945 occupation zones of the U.S., France and Great Britain. West Berlin economically and culturally is closely tied to the Federal Republic. This nation was one of the world's first industrialized nations, and with its dense network of freeways and railways, it is Europe's intersection for long-distance traffic. With 642 people per sq. mi. (248 per sq. km), it is one of Europe's most densely populated

The Federal Republic of Germany (West Germany): from the North Sea to the Alps

nations. The Federal Republic also contains very diverse landscapes. The Northern German Plain extends in the countryside south of the North and Baltic seas. The large seaports of Hamburg and Bremen are on the coast, along with many resort towns. The central mountain ranges not only are traversed by roads but also form a network of marked hiking trails. The colorful mosaic of mountain forests is divided by basins, low grounds and valleys. Wine-producing villages dot

the Rhein and Mosel valleys and grape fields, forests and castles cover the hillsides. South of the Main River the Swabian—Bavarian Plateau—begins. If you follow the romantic road from Wurzburg to Füssen, you'll traverse a landscape where tree-covered hills appear amid a colorful succession of open fields and historic villages crowd one another. The southern border is formed by the German Alps. This is Germany's most beloved vacation destination.

The Rhine Valley near Kaub, with the castle ruins of Gutenfels (top). The Pfalzgrafenstein, also known as the Pfalz, was not a residential castle but a customs station in the middle of the Rhine River. The "Michel"—that is, the tower of the St. Michaels Cathedral—is Hamburg's landmark (right). It rises over the Elbe River and the harbor installations of Hamburg, Germany's largest ocean port. It is still about 75 mi. (120 km) to Cuxhaven, at the mouth of the Elbe and the open North Sea. Because of the minor tides of only approximately 7.5 ft., (2.3 m) ships can enter and leave at any time. Because of this, and its modern docking and loading facilities, Hamburg has acquired the reputation of being a "fast harbor." Hamburg is not only a significant economic center but also northern Germany's cultural center.

Tuchersfeld, Franconian Switzerland. The small half-timbered building in the shade is nestled against the limestone rocks. Such bizarre rock formations are frequently found in the Franconian and Suabian Jura Mountains. Half-timbered buildings are evidence of earlier craftsmanship. They are still frequently found in the countryside and small villages throughout Germany.

The other German nation, the German Democratic Republic, comprises the former Soviet occupation zone and, like West Germany, was founded in 1949. East Berlin is its capital city. Both German nations are separated from one another by the GDR's heavily fortified border on its territory, while East and West Berlin are separated by the Wall, one of the world's most inhumane borders. The Communist party exercises all power in this nation through a state-planned economy.

German Democratic Republic (East Germany)

Agriculture, trade and industry are nationalized. The division of Germany was particularly disadvantageous for the GDR, as its industry with its supply of energy, raw materials, processed materials and its transportation network was one unit with the western portion of Germany until 1945. A remarkable reconstruction effort and restructuring of the economy gave the GDR the leading industrial position and highest standard of living of the eastern bloc nations. Machine construction, electronics and chemical products are the economy's main focus. Flatlands and central mountains are the landscape's main elements. Evidence of a common German history, art and culture is present throughout the GDR: At Wartburg, near Eisenach, Martin Luther translated the Bible from Latin into German; the two greatest German poets, Goethe and Schiller, lived in Weimar; Bach composed as cantor in Leipzig and Dresden.

The Semper Operahouse in Dresden (top). It was built in the Renaissance style in 1878, destroyed in 1944 and reopened in 1985.

In the center of East Berlin, the Marx-Engels Bridge, the Palace of the Republic, the cathedral and the television tower set the architectural accents (far left). The Urania world clock in the central traffic junction, the Alexanderplatz, is a meeting point for East Berliners.

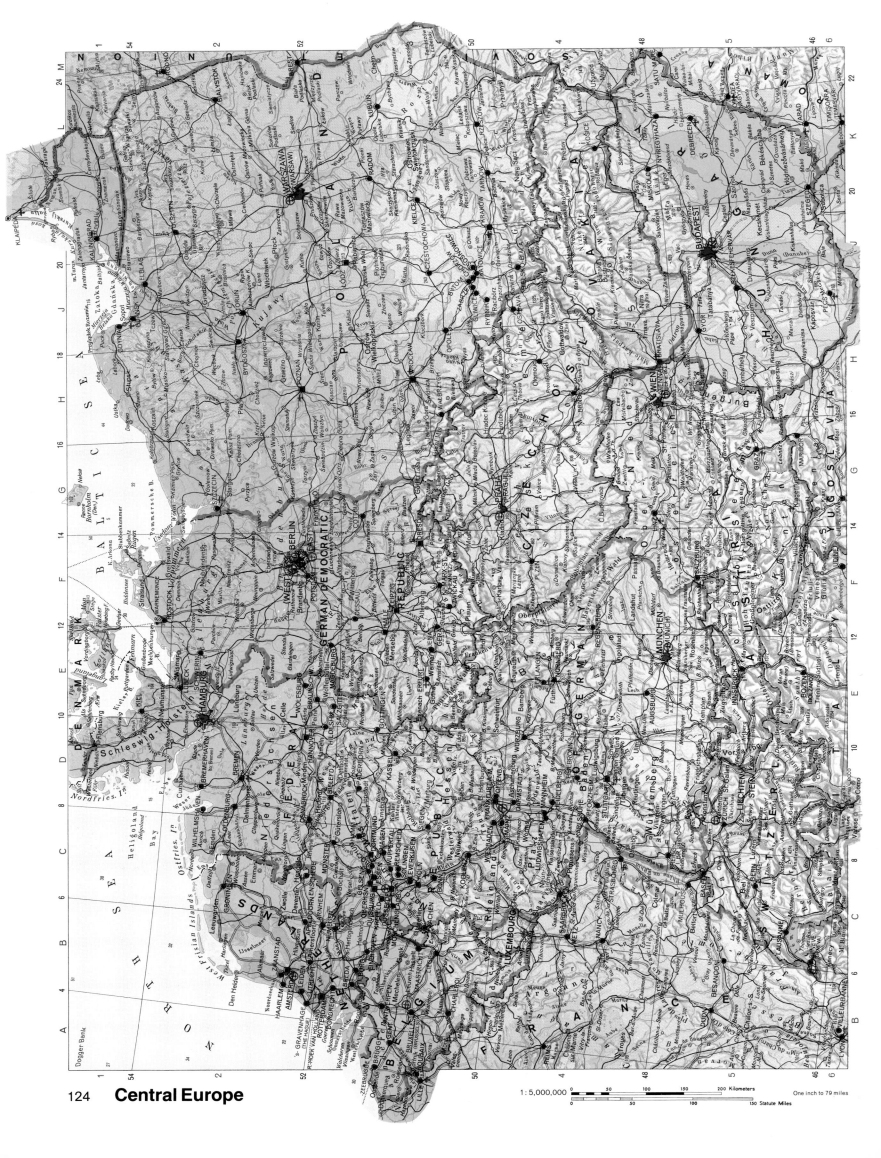

1 : 5,000,000

One inch to 79 miles

Poland, Czechoslovakia and Hungary first appeared on the political map of Europe as independent national entities in 1918. Earlier they had been divided among the superpowers of the 18th and 19th centuries: the Russian Czarist Empire, and Prussia and Austria under the rule of the Hapsburgs. Poland and Czechoslovakia also were the focus of political power struggles between World Wars I and II. After World War II they both came within the Soviet Union's sphere of domi-

Poland, Czechoslovakia and Hungary: between national self-determination and the ideological conformity of socialism

nance, and the Communist party became the sole arbiter of power within these nations. While Czechoslovakia and Hungary essentially retained their borders of 1918, Poland lost a strip of territory approximately 150 mi. (250 km) wide to the Soviet Union and was compensated with German territory in the west up to the Oder-Neisse. Millions of Germans, Poles and Russians were dislodged and resettled. All three nations display characteristics of European nations. In spite of the

political dominance and ideological conformity imposed by the Soviet Union, there are notable differences: In Poland, agriculture is largely privatized and the Catholic church exerts much influence; after the German Democratic Republic, Czechoslovakia is the most industrialized nation of the eastern-bloc countries; Hungary's economy is given the most free reign. The continued goal of these three countries is to retain their national identities, even under Communist rule.

The landmark of Hungary's capital city, Budapest, is the parliament building inaugurated in 1902 (top). It is located in the flat portion of the city called Pest, on the left side of the Danube. On the hills on the right shore is Buda, the portion of Budapest that includes the Castle District.
Karlovy Vary in western Bohemia is one of Europe's best-known and most sought-out mineral baths. Its springs can reach a temperature of 158 ° F, (70 ° C) (left).

Torun, the Polish city founded on the lower Weichsel in the 11th century, is the birthplace of the astronomer Copernicus and still has many historical buildings and fortifications that date back to the Middle Ages.

125

Switzerland, the mountain country in the heart of Europe, kept itself out of Europe's bloody affairs of the 20th century and remained an enviable island of freedom. Its preservation of neutrality and independence extended so far that this nation did not join the United Nations, even though Geneva is the most important location of UN organizations after New York. But this nation has always remained open to trade and traffic and is the bridge between Western and Central Europe and It-

Switzerland: Exemplary nation of tourism, superpower of finances and gold.

aly. The Simplon (railway tunnel, 12.3 mi. [19.8 km]) and the St. Gotthard Pass (railway tunnel, 9.3 mi. [15 km] and motor-vehicle tunnel 10.1 mi. [16.3 km]) are the two most important routes through the mountains. The daring mountain railway routes are masterpieces of engineering, and a ride with the "Glacier Express" between St. Moritz and Zermatt is a special experience. Ever since the British began treating the Alps as Europe's playground more than 100 years ago, Switzer-

land has been a major tourist attraction. Switzerland's living and economic region is the Swiss Plateau, which is spread out before the Alps. The most important cities are found here. While Switzerland does not have an abundance of raw materials, its diligent inhabitants are its greatest asset. Precision mechanical products, specialized machinery and pharmaceuticals are the most significant industries. This small country is a superpower in international monetary affairs.

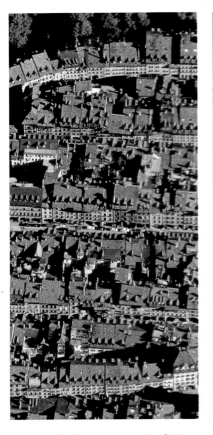

From a bird's-eye view the Old City of Bern, the capital of Switzerland, offers itself as a jewel of urban architecture. Human scale and a feeling of security are also features of the area surrounding the Grossmünster and the Frauenmünster in Zurich (bottom right). In the world of international trade, banking and insurance, this city is considered one of the most important. The three major mountains of the highlands around Bern—the Eiger, Mönch and Jungfrau—rise entrancingly over Interlaken and the Lauterbrunnen Valley (top right). To the left of the Jungfraujoch (center of the photo above), at an altitude of 11,333 ft. (3,470 m), is the highest railway station in Europe. The Matterhorn, 14,692 ft. high (4,499 m) (center below), is one of the most striking mountains on Earth. The dramatic first climb in 1865 initiated the golden age of mountain climbing.

126

Like neighboring Switzerland, approximately 60 percent of Austria consists of mountains. However, the eastern Alps of Austria are not as high and have more valleys, allowing traffic to traverse them more easily; they are also more densely populated than the western Alps. For many in the nation's mountain-region, tourism has become the most important source of income. Among the most important raw materials are the salt deposits in Tyrol and Hallein in the Salzkam-

Austria: International trademark: mountains, lakes and festivals

mergut, as well as the iron ore in Styria. Austria is also an important point on the route between Central Europe and southern and southeastern Europe. Its diplomatic experience and ties date back to the Austro-Hungarian Empire prior to 1918, and its pledge of neutrality made in the 1955 treaty that established its independence, have made it a valued mediator between East and West. The nation has over 7.5 million inhabitants, of whom more than one-fifth live in the capi-

tal city of Vienna. Many buildings remain as evidence of the old monarchy—for example the Hofburg, the former residence of the Hapsburgs; the Schonbrunn palace; and many aristocratic chateaux. Music, ranging from classical to folk, is particularly cherished in Austria. The opera season in Vienna and the festival in Salzburg are international events, and the Vienna Boys Choir are their nation's celebrated ambassadors.

Zell am See (top left), in the state of Salzburg, is an example of why mountains and lakes are particularly attractive destinations for tourists. Zell a.S. has joined Kaprung and Saalbach to become Europe's "sporting region."

Austria is an important transit country. The Brenner Pass is considered one of the most important routes across the Alps from Central to southern Europe. The most daring construction on the Brenner Highway is the Europa Bridge (above), just a few miles south of Innsbruck. It is over 2,700 ft. (827 m) long and spans the Sill Valley at a height of 495 ft. (152 m).

From the Kohlmarkt our view drifts over to the Vienna Hofburg. The Hapsburgs resided in the "Burg," which is how it was referred to until 1918. Today it is the seat of the Austrian chancellor. The vast architectural complex also contains unique collections (far left).

The "Heimatmuseum" in Altenmarkt (left) is an example of wooden architecture in the Alpine region. The tradition of decorating houses with summer flowers is also widespread there.

Framed by the Atlantic and the Mediterranean, the Pyrenees, Alps and Rhine River, France has developed into a nation with a rare sense of its own cultural and political mission in Europe and throughout the world.

The Ile de France region with the capital city Paris, is the heart of the nation. It is France's political, cultural and economic focal point, from which all the main transportation routes radiate. Nine million of the approximately fifty-five million

France: between the Atlantic and the Mediterranean— where living is always fun

French citizens live in greater Paris. In addition to Notre Dame, the Louvre, the Arc de Triomphe and the Eiffel Tower, it is the *savoir vivre* that makes Paris.

France forms a hexagon with sides about 600 mi. (1,000 km) long that extend north–south and west–east. The proximity to the Atlantic and the Mediterranean produces the mild, balanced oceanic climate. Especially favored is the coastal region in the Mediterranean. Dry, warm summers and the beauty of

the coastline between ocean and mountains have made the Côte d'Azur, from St. Tropez to the Italian border, the home of exclusive lifestyles. Monaco, the politically independent principality, is a refuge of international high society. The Mediterranean influence is also present in sun-drenched Provence, where Romans and troubadours, crusaders and popes, have left their traces and where van Gogh and Cézanne painted with passion. On the other side of the Rhone-Saone Val-

Twilight over Paris and sunlight over Provence. At a height of 984 ft. (300 m) the Eiffel Tower was the world's tallest structure until 1931. The ingenious structure— which was built for the 1889 World's Fair—was named after its builder, Gustave Eiffel. The famous tower, with TV transmitter atop, is the sightseeing landmark of France's capital, Paris (above).
The houses of Saint Agnes, in the Maritime Alps, open up to the bright light of Provence (right).

ley the central plateau rises, where in the Auvergne, volcanic domes are strewn about as if by giants. Around Roquefort, the cheese named after this city ripens in rock cellars, the green fungus slowly permeating it. It is made from the milk of the sheep that graze on the barren heights of the central plateau. To the west of the highland, in the Dordogne Valley, lies Lascaux. Here, extraordinary cave paintings of animals, dating back to Neolithic times, were discovered in 1940. On the lower Dordogne and Garonne, around the center of Bordeaux, one finds one of the great wine-producing regions of the world. Similarly, the nearby city of Cognac is famous for its brandy. *"La douce France,"* as the French like to refer to their country, is represented particularly well by the Loire Valley. Fields and forests, gardens and vineyards, simple villages, and cities with steeples line the shores of the Loire, France's longest river. Sumptuous chateaus and mansions remind us of the elegant lifestyles, the intrigues and the high politics of French kings and statesmen.

Agriculture still ranks very high in France. Special cultures of fruit and vegetables, and even lavender for the perfume industry, are not uncommon. Half of all revenue from agriculture can be traced to livestock ranching and associated value-added products like cheese. Next to Italy, France is the largest wine producer in the world, with an average annual production of 74 billion qts. (81 billion ltrs.).

France is a modern, industrialized nation. The sophistication of its technology is seen in the TGV, the high-speed train (160 mph/260 km/h) that travels between Paris and Lyon, and the Rance tidal-power plant on the coast of Brittany. Its garment industry is world famous. Paris fashion sets the pace, and French perfumes and cosmetics are valued luxury items.

Loire castles and the Atlantic coast of Brittany—these are landscapes à la française. A Renaissance masterpiece: Château Chenonceaux, on the Cher. One of the château's wings rests on a five-arch bridge over the river. The watchtower is the remnant of a château from the 15th century (above). The Atlantic coast near Concarneau: This city, in the south of Brittany, is France's biggest port for tuna fishing (photo left).

Nowhere else do the European and African continents come so close to one another than in the south of the Iberian peninsula. They are separated by the only-14-km-wide (8.7 mi.) Strait of Gibraltar. Almost within sight are the Spanish cities of Ceuta and Melilla, on the Moroccan side. But Spain still extends over 620 mi. (1,000 km) further south, for the Canary Islands, which are spread out only 60 to 300 mi. (100–500 km) off the west coast of Northern Africa, still belong to Spain. For over 700

Spain and Portugal: bridge between Europe and Africa

years the Iberian peninsula was part of the Oriental-Islamic world.

From the Atlantic to the Mediterranean, the approximately 275 mi. (440-km)-long Pyrenees separate Spain from France and the rest of Europe. About forty-seven million people live on this peninsula. Politically it is partitioned into Spain, Portugal and the small nation of Andorra, in the Pyrenees. Gibraltar, the 5-sq.-km (1,236-acre) rock in the south of Spain, belongs to Great Britain and has long been a source

of contention between these two nations. "True" Spaniards—that is, Castilian Spaniards—make up 73 percent of the population; 24 percent are Catalan, and 2.5 percent are Basques.

Spanish, Catalan, Basque and Galician are the official national languages. The Mancha, the region where Don Quixote lived his adventures, also belongs to the often completely flat Meseta. In the center of this highland is Madrid. The Escorial, the royal palace to the

Varying rock formations from Spain and Portugal: In Guadix, 37 mi. (60 km) east of Granada, about 5,000 true gypsies live in cave dwellings, the so-called Barrio de Santiago. The chalk white exterior walls of the cuevas contrast with the hues of the desertlike hills. The primitive cave dwellings, which are common in all of Upper Andalusia, are frequently dug in several stories over one another. In the background: the snow-covered Sierra Nevada (photo above). Typical rock blocks on the Atlantic shore of Praia da Roche near Portimao in the Algarve (small photo right).

As far as the eye can reach: olive trees. The Jaen province in Andalusia is home to most of Spain's olive groves. Spain produces more than 500,000 tons of olive oil annually. Jaen is considered the largest olive-growing region not only in Spain but also in the world (photo right).

north, as well as Toledo and Salamanca, still bears much evidence of the era when the Sun never set on the Spanish Empire. The change of seasons keeps the Ebro Basin just as hot and cold as Castile. Its southern counterpart is the Guadalquivir Basin, in Lower Andalusia, which has summer temperatures of up to 113° F (45° C). The barren highlands of Castile, with their wheat farming, extensive cattle, sheep and goat ranching, and Lower Andalusia are Europe's largest olive-growing districts as well as Spain's poorest regions.

The golden edges are the coastal strips along the Atlantic and the Mediterranean. But the nation's economic motor is Catalonia, with its capital city Barcelona, Madrid's rival.

The Costa Brava and the Balearic Islands for many decades have been the favorite vacation destinations for European tourists. To the south is the Levant, a coastal strip where fertile irrigation oases—*huer-*

tas—and tourism form the economic basis. Valencia is the center of orange growing, while near Elche, Europe's unique date-palm forest, which contains about 100,000 trees, can be found.

In the western portion of the Iberian peninsula, Portugal faces the Atlantic Ocean. Its inland border with Spain has hardly changed since the Middle Ages. The country owes its balanced climate—warm winters and cool breezes in the summer—to the ocean. Only the Algarve, the

southernmost coastal strip, is extremely dry, a veritable piece of Africa on European soil. Port wine, aging in oak barrels for years, cork rind and sardines are the nation's most famous export goods. Tourism ranks high in this poorly developed nation. Lisbon is considered one of Europe's most beautiful capitals. In Belem, a western suburb, a monument commemorates such great Portuguese seafarers as Vasco de Gama and Magellan.

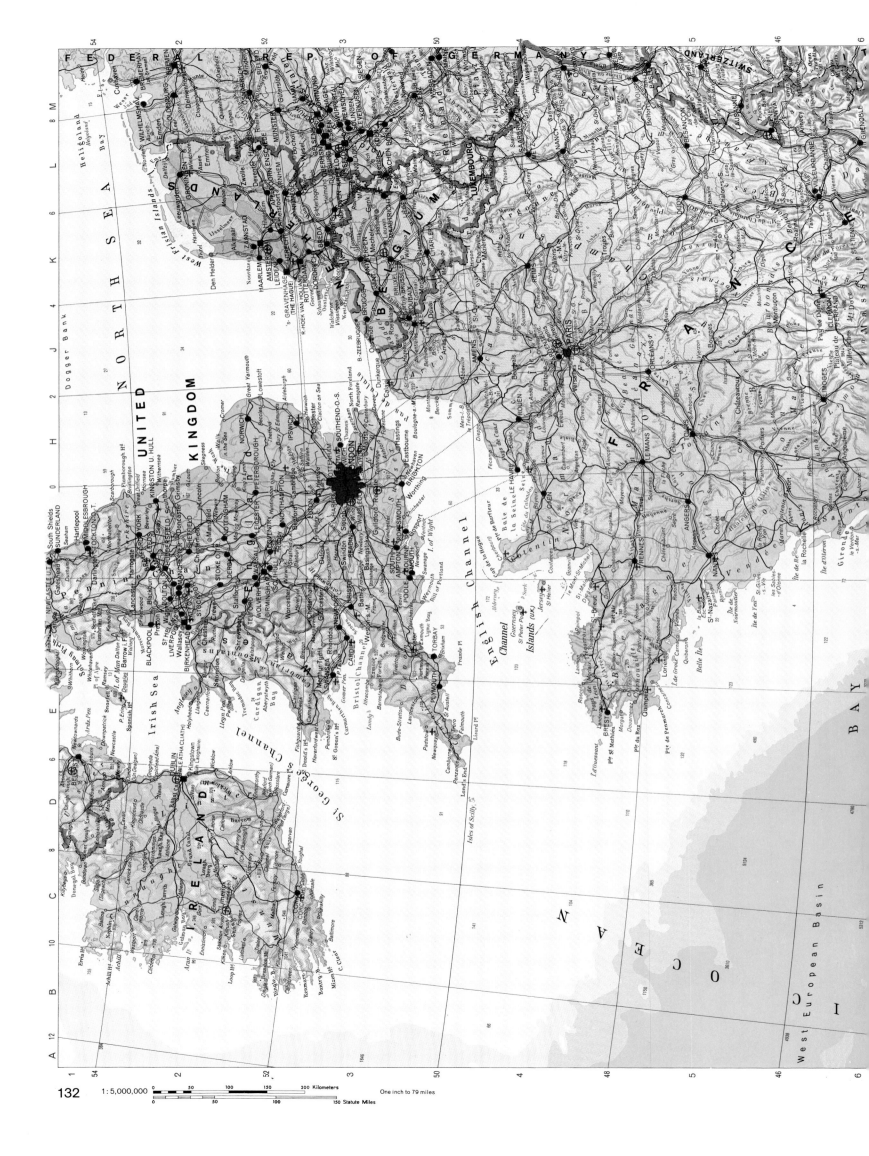

1:5,000,000

| 0 | 50 | 100 | 150 | 200 Kilometers |

One inch to 79 miles

| 0 | 50 | 100 |

150 Statute Miles

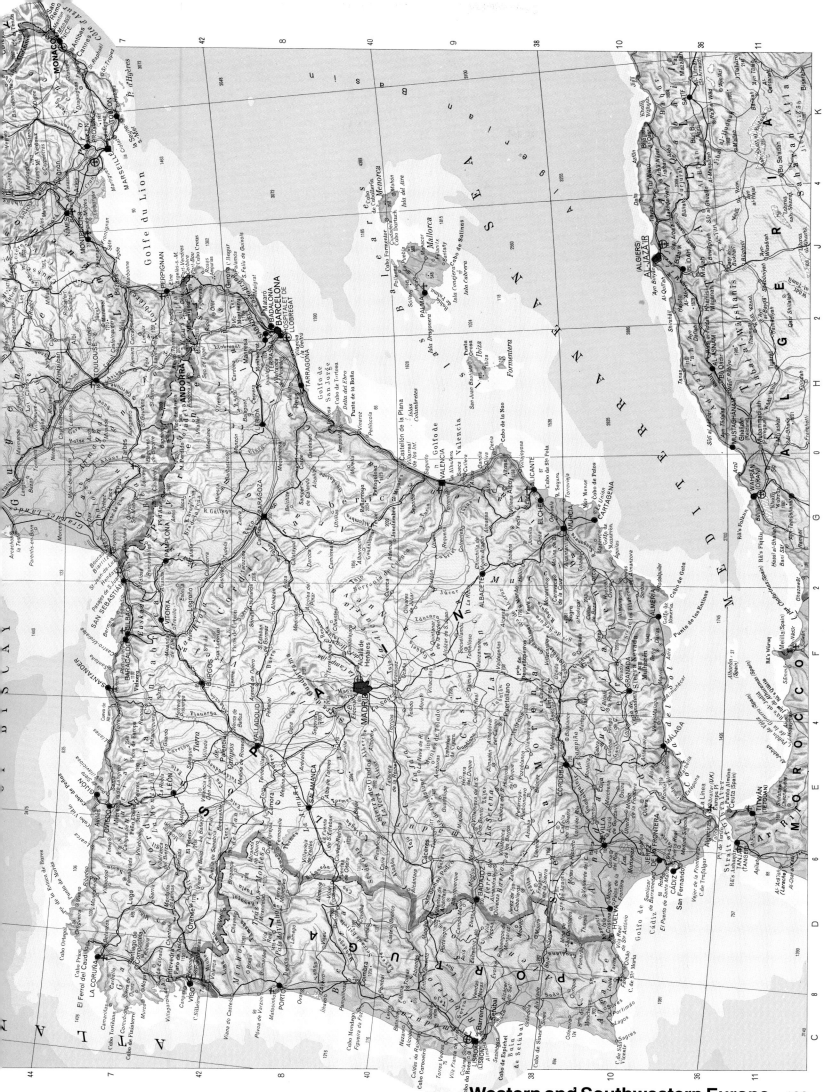

Italy, located in the center of the Mediterranean, for centuries has attracted conquerors, pilgrims, archaeologists, artists and travelers like no other European nation. Italy was Europe's and the rest of the world's link to classical antiquity and Christianity, the foundation of Occidental culture. In Rome—the seat of the Pope—Venice, Florence, Siena and in many other Italian cities, crafts and trade, arts and science, flourished during the Middle Ages and the beginning of the

Italy: rich north, poor south, the cradle of humanity

Renaissance. Few nations in the world have preserved as much of humanity's history in their archaeological sites, monuments, museums and libraries as Italy. For many, the "hazy clearness" (Goethe) of the Mediterranean landscape is just as attractive as the climate, the innumerable beaches and the lively Italian way of life, always focused on beauty and pleasure.

Upper Italy, peninsular Italy and insular Italy are the nation's three major regions. The glaciers in the

western Alps and the bizarre rock towers, crags and alpine meadows of the Dolomites in upper Italy contrast against the completely flat Po Valley. Not only is the Po Valley the richest region in terms of agriculture, but the triangle formed by the cities of Milano, Torino and Genoa also demarcates Italy's industrial heartland, which generates about half the nation's total industrial output.

The Apennines form the spine of the approximately 600 mi. (1,000-

A typical Italian landscape: Ocean and sky seem to melt into each other on the hazy horizon. A pine tree arcs over the seemingly fortified bell towers of the Church of Our Lady of the Annunciation. The village of Maiori hugs the coast and is spread out over the hills. This photo (right) was taken from Ravello, which is famous for its churches of San Giovanni and San Pantaleo.

City view of Siena with the Torre del Mangia (photo above). Colorful market scene in Sicily (center right). Bridge of the St. Angelo and the Castle Santa'Angelo in Rome (photo right). Impressive remains of antique culture near Sirmione: ruins of a villa in the grottoes of Catullus (photo far right).

km)-long and 80 to 150 mi. (130- to 250-km)-wide Italian "boot." Its northern portion, central Italy, is the heart of Italy. A trio of cities—Florence, Siena and Pisa—form the core of its greatest attraction, widely acclaimed Tuscany. Olives, wine and grain are the main agricultural products. This is where Dante wrote the *Divine Comedy* and where the Italian language was created.

Rome, the "Eternal City," marks the approximate border of lower Italy. Lower and insular Italy are the nation's problem regions. Large estates, tenant farming and the limited degree of industrialization are the reasons for the high unemployment in these regions. Heavy emigration to destinations abroad, along with domestic resettlement to the upper Italian industrial centers and Western and Central Europe, are the consequences. Government actions aimed at economic and social restructuring are progressing slowly.

Naples is lower Italy's metropolis. Vesuvius, the only volcano on the European mainland, is a part of lower Italy's landscape. At its foot are the archaeological sites of Pompeii and Herculaneum, which were buried when it erupted in A.D. 79.

Italy is one of the seven big industrial and trading nations of the Western world. Tourism is a significant factor in its trade balance. The cities of Rome, Venice, Florence and Naples above all, are points of attraction for education-minded visitors. Pilgrims visit primarily Rome and Assisi, where St. Francis affirmed the unity of creation in his exalted Canticle of the Sun over 750 years ago. Mass tourism above all seeks out the ocean beaches and water-sports centers on the Adriatic and Riviera and the upper Italian lakes. Because of the completion of freeway construction down to lower Italy, tourism has greatly increased in the South.

The splendid Dolomite Mountains fascinate all those who have experienced them. The steep rock formations are actually the reefs of a primordial ocean (above). The fertile hills stretch into the distance near Aidone on Sicily, the island with a tumultuous history of power and poverty, dedication and hatred (photo left). Its inhabitants today still practice the self-administered justice of blood revenge. The western portion of the island is the heartland of the Mafia, which was once conceived as a self-help organization but then became an international crime syndicate.

The Balkan Peninsula is the easternmost of the three large southern European peninsulas. In the west the Adriatic and Ionian seas wash up on its shores, in the east the Black and Aegean seas. Nowhere in Europe do land and sea commingle as much as in the south of this peninsula, in Greece.

Toward the north the peninsula expands and turns into Central and Eastern Europe, without any distinct natural borders. The Sava River and the lower Danube are

Balkan countries: colorful mixture of peoples where Occident and Orient meet

considered its northern borders.

The name-lending Balkan Mountains are neither the highest nor the most extensive mountain range in the region. The most appropriate name for the peninsula would be the Southeastern European Peninsula. The Dinaric-Hellenic Mountains are made primarily of limestone. The erosion of water-soluble limestone has produced special surface formations, the karst, named after the northern Yugoslavian terrain known as *Kras*.

The karst has sparse vegetation and many large endorheic drainage areas (where surface drainage is not linked to the ocean) and limestone sink holes. Caves are also commonplace. Agriculture is usually possible only in endorheic drainage areas and limestone sink holes, where soil is brought back by floods. Pasturage with goats and sheep is predominant.

Only the coastal areas have a Mediterranean climate, with olive trees, vineyards and citrus trees.

In Thessaly (or Thessalia), central Greece, volcanic rock formations rise out of the ground almost vertically (above).

The ruins of Olympia (right), a classical Greek holy place and sports arena located in the northwestern portion of the Peloponnesus, date back to prehistory. The Olympic games, which unified the otherwise splintered tribes of Greece, were held there for over a millennium, until A.D. 393. In celebration of the modern Olympic Games, the Olympic flame has been ignited in the "holy forest" since 1936 by means of the Sun's rays.

The mountainous interior of the peninsula has a moderate to severe continental climate. In addition to grain and corn farming, specialty cultures are widespread: tobacco in Macedonia, roses in Bulgaria, plums in Yugoslavia, peaches, apricots and currents in Greece.

The variety of ethnic groups and cultures on the Balkan Peninsula also corresponds to the diversity of landscapes found there. This is especially true of the multiethnic nation of Yugoslavia. Ethnic contrasts still produce tension. The Balkan Peninsula is also the bridge between Europe and Asia. Illyrians, the ancestors of the Albanians, Thracians and ancient Greeks pushed into what are now the Balkans from the Danube region. They were later followed by Slavic tribes. The mosques and minarets in the cityscapes of Albania and southern Yugoslavia are remnants of the centuries under the rule of Turkish Sultans, as are the Muslims in Bosnia-Herzogowina, Montenegro and Albania. The Christian Orthodox Church was the preserver of ethnic traditions during the Turkish reign, which explains its influence into the 20th century. Catholicism influenced the northwest until the end of World War I.

Greece, which is exposed to the ocean like no other country of this peninsula, is the birthplace of the Occident. The classical sites are as popular as ever, with Athens and Delphi leading the list, followed by the excavations of the prehistoric high cultures of Knossos on Crete and Mycenae on the Peloponnesus. In a festive celebration the Olympic fire is lit every four years in Olympia. The islands of the Aegean are Greece's poorest region. In recent times tourism has helped improve the standard of living.

The communist nations of Yugoslavia and Bulgaria have developed their sea-resort beaches into welcome currency magnets. Only Albania still surrounds itself with an iron curtain.

Greece and Yugoslavia show off their beauty: The island of Santorin (above) was named Kallisti, "the most beautiful," in antiquity. It is the remaining portion of a volcano. Santorin (traced back to Santa Irini, "the holy Irene") is today again called Thira and is a destination for volcanologists the world over. The island belongs to the Cyclades, which with its 39 islands forms a part of the Aegean Archipelago. The Plitvice Lakes, 16 blue-green lakes, stretch over 4.5 mi. (7.2 km) and are separated by roaring waterfalls. The nature park is 51 mi. (83 km) south of Karlovac and is considered a Yugoslavian rural treasure (top left). Athens: a view of the city and the threatened Acropolis. As in antiquity, Athens is still the economic, intellectual and political center of Greece (photo bottom left).

Southern and Southeastern Europe

1 : 5,000,000

One inch to 79 miles

ASIA: IT COVERS ONE-THIRD OF THE EARTH'S SURFACE AND IS HOME TO NO CONTINENT HAS SO MANY DIFFERENT FACES.

ASIA

The incredible land mass of this continent extends from the Arctic Ocean to the Indian Ocean to the Pacific. Three photos that are representative of Asia: in the Wat Arun, the Temple of the Morning Sun in Bangkok, a porcelain figure (photo right); the giant Himalayas in Nepal (center photo); and the rice fields of Sri Lanka.

It is the giant among continents. Asia covers one-third of the Earth's entire land mass, and three-fifths of the planet's population lives here. The Earth's highest point is in the Himalayas, its deepest point in the Dead Sea. Highly evolved cultures were blossoming in Asia when Europe was still in the Stone Age. The world's great religions—Christianity, Islam, Buddhism and Hinduism—have their roots in Asia. This continent is also in a phase of transition. The industrial age has dawned late in Asia, and it has brought with it severe social problems. Population growth is rapid in some regions, as hundreds of millions of people live in abject poverty.

The Great Plains of European Russia extend from the western border of the USSR between the Black Sea and the Baltic Sea to Romania in the south and Poland in the north. It is separated from the Asiatic portion of the country by the Ural mountain chain, which extends over almost the country's entire north-south length. To the south lies the Ural River and the Caspian Depression—the accepted border between Asia and Europe.

The Soviet Union is rich in natural

USSR: huge area, boundless resources

resources. There are few raw materials in the world that are not found in the USSR—including precious metals and diamonds. Czarist Russia did not have much knowledge of its natural resources. Today, thanks to extensive scientific and technological efforts, this has changed. Formerly an agricultural nation with only a slight degree of technical development, the Soviet Union has become an industrial nation whose production grows year by year. Iron ore, copper, chromi-

um, phosphates, bauxite, coal and brown coal, crude oil and natural gas are extracted in amounts exceeding domestic demand, which permits considerable export.

The two largest industrial centers in European Russia are in the regions around Moscow and the Doneck Basin. Between the Volga and the Urals, drilling rigs stand on one of the world's largest oil fields. The natural-gas deposits in the Volga region are also considerable. Gas pipelines branch out from there to

Harvester-threshers out harvesting the fields (photo right). Grain farming is still the most important form of agriculture in the USSR. Under the Soviet system small parcels of land have given way to large tracts of land. Today the cooperatives in the Black Earth Region of Belgorod have over 3,000 harvester-threshers and 8,000 tractors. Still, the Soviet Union cannot always produce enough grain for domestic consumption. The southern steppe is the actual wheat-growing region. Prior to the Russian Revolution there was hardly any wheat there; barley, oats and rye were dominant.

reach the entire nation. The nation continues to rely in part on electricity generated through nuclear energy even after the reactor catastrophe at Chernobyl. The USSR also uses hydroelectric power, mainly on the Volga. This river, the largest in Europe, is one of the Soviet Union's vital traffic routes. In addition to supplying electrical energy for industry, it also supplies water to the enormous fields on both sides of the river's banks.

The general collectivization of the economy, a feature of the communist political system, of course also applies to agriculture and forestry. Agricultural land is fertile, and the standing growth of forest is almost boundless. Moose still live in the coniferous forests of the Taiga but may not be hunted. The flat land has a very sparse population density, while that of the cities is growing. Moscow, the USSR's most magnificent city and its center, has over ten million inhabitants. Leningrad, formerly St. Petersburg, is second in size and importance. At the same latitude as Greenland's southern tip, it is the most northern of all major cities and is one of the USSR's most important European ports. The artifacts in Leningrad's museums are world famous.

The first steps toward modernization and relaxation of the rigid economic and political systems have been set in motion by the change of power in the Kremlin. Perestroika—"transformation"—and glasnost—"transparency"—have been the slogans since Gorbachev began steering his course of reform. The economy of the USSR, however, must continue to modernize if it is not to fall even further behind Western standards. Freedom of opportunity is at last being discussed. Implementing will not be easy as dramatic changes in thinking are still necessary to accomplish this. Today Western politicians are cautiously optimistic about the Kremlin's disarmament proposals and new openness.

Mighty industrial plants like this one can be found all over the Doneck Basin. Chemical and machine-construction industries have also been established here. However, the heavy industries that developed because of large coal deposits already have been affected by change. Most coal mining has been relocated to much larger deposits in Siberia. The mythical mountains of the Caucasus between the Black and Caspian seas rise from an almost subtropical plain to a glacier region (left).

1:10,000,000

0 100 200 300 400 500 Kilometers

0 100 200 300 Statute Miles

One inch to 158 miles

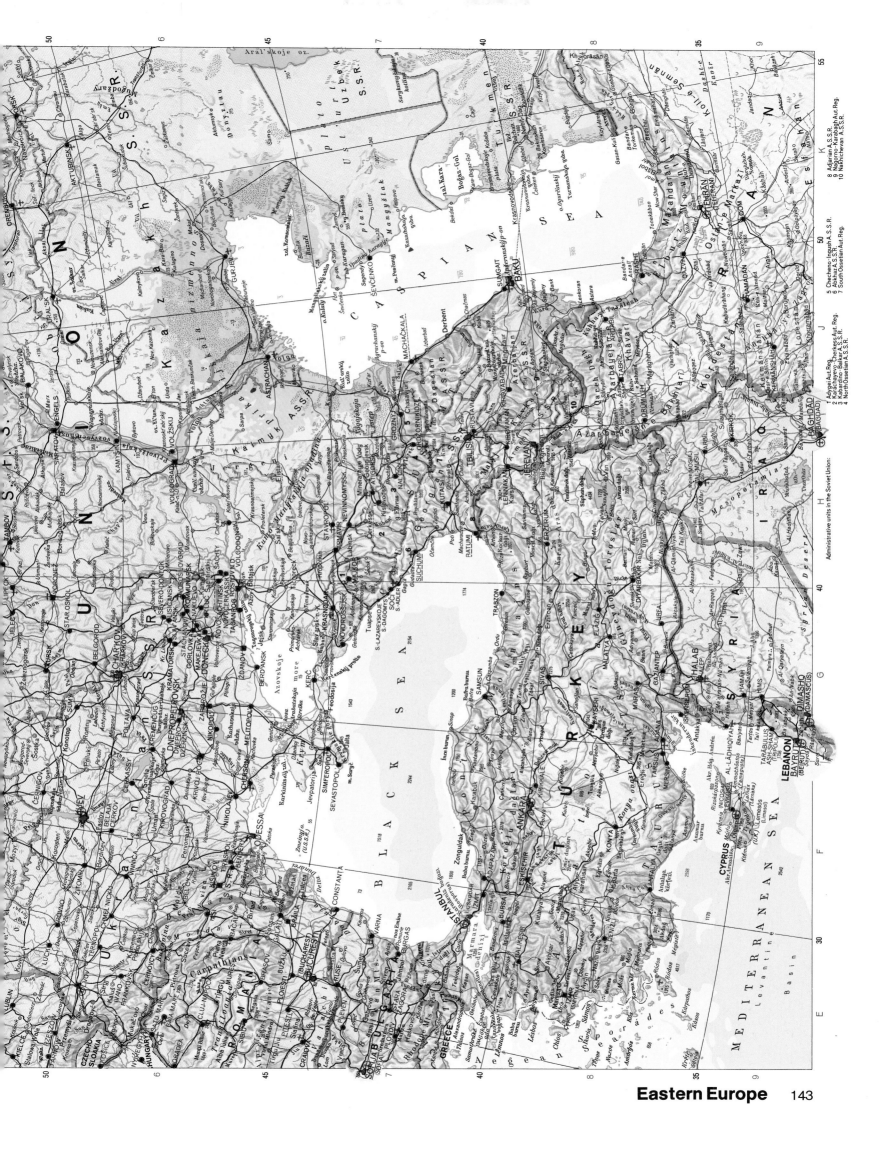

ASIA

The incredible land mass of this continent extends from the Arctic Ocean to the Indian Ocean to the Pacific. Three photos that are representative of Asia: in the Wat Arun, the Temple of the Morning Sun in Bangkok, a porcelain figure (photo right); the giant Himalayas in Nepal (center photo); and the rice fields of Sri Lanka.

t is the giant among continents. Asia covers one-third of the Earth's entire land mass, and three-fifths of the planet's population lives here. The Earth's highest point is in the Himalayas, its deepest point in the Dead Sea. Highly evolved cultures were blossoming in Asia when Europe was still in the Stone Age. The world's great religions— Christianity, Islam, Buddhism and Hinduism— have their roots in Asia. This continent is also in a phase of transition. The industrial age has dawned late in Asia, and it has brought with it severe social problems. Population growth is rapid in some regions, as hundreds of millions of people live in abject poverty.

Asia, the continent with the largest nations, the highest population figures and probably the oldest cultures, deserves the distinction of being the "cradle of humanity."

Photo 1: The young Burmese man, practically a child, wears the yellow-orange robe loosely draped over his shoulder, which distinguishes him as a monk. Photo 2: Thai fishing boats anchor before picturesque lake dwellings in a protected rock cove. Photo 3: The symbol of modern Iran is a daring architectural construction in Teheran: The Shahyad Monument contains the Museum of Persian History. Photo 4: All Buddha images found in the Far East, whether painted or hewn in rock, bear an expression of inner focus turned away from the everyday world. Photo 5: Fuji-san, Japan's holy mountain, is 12,385 ft. (3,776 m) high. Its volcanic peak is covered with snow even in the summer. The last eruption occurred in 1701, but smoke still rises from its crater. Photo 6: Rice harvest in Java. The laborers carry the heavily laden rice baskets from the field. Photo 7: Sea roses on the pond surface of a Japanese garden. The Japanese art of gardening is famous for its harmonious design and dreamy romanticism. Photo 8: The Japanese port city of Nagasaki was almost completely destroyed in 1945 when the second atomic bomb was dropped. The city has been rebuilt, but its inhabitants still suffer the consequences. Photo 9: A Mongolian shepherd on horseback. The vast distances of the Mongolian steppes early on made its inhabitants horseback

1

2

3

4

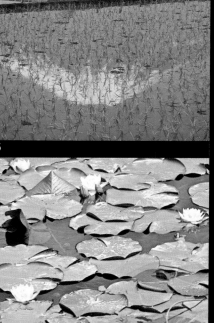

5

6

7

riders. Raising horses, cattle, sheep, goats and camels has been one of their basic occupations. Photo 10: The Chinese junks sailing on the Yangtze in the blue morning mist appear as if a painting has come to life. Their construction and their function as an easy means of transportation have not changed in hundreds of years. Photo 11: In the center of an equal-sided octagon, the gilded Dome of Rock in Jerusalem rests on top of a

cylindrical structure. The exterior walls are decorated with marble and rare Persian faiences. Photo 12: In Konarak on India's east coast near Bhubaneswar, gigantic remains of a sun temple dating from the 13th century stick out of the sand dunes. The temple symbolizes a wagon, with which the Sun is drawn across the sky by seven horses. The 24 wheels, each with a diameter of three meters, represent unsurpassed stone-working skills. Photo 13:

Tankers waiting for their freight in the Persian Gulf. They transport crude oil over the seven seas to the entire world. Photo 14: On the east coast of Malaysia, the process of drying fish is handled simply and unconventionally. The catch is spread out flat on a wooden surface under the burning sun. From time to time the fish are turned over by means of a rake until they are dry enough to be stored. Photo 15: Rubber is made from a precious raw

material: caoutchouc. The method of producing rubber is slowly rendering its source, the gum tree, extinct. The gum trees lose latex, their life's blood, through deep grooves cut into their bark like bleeding wounds. The milky white liquid is caught in wooden containers.

9

11

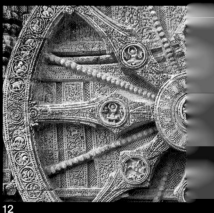

12

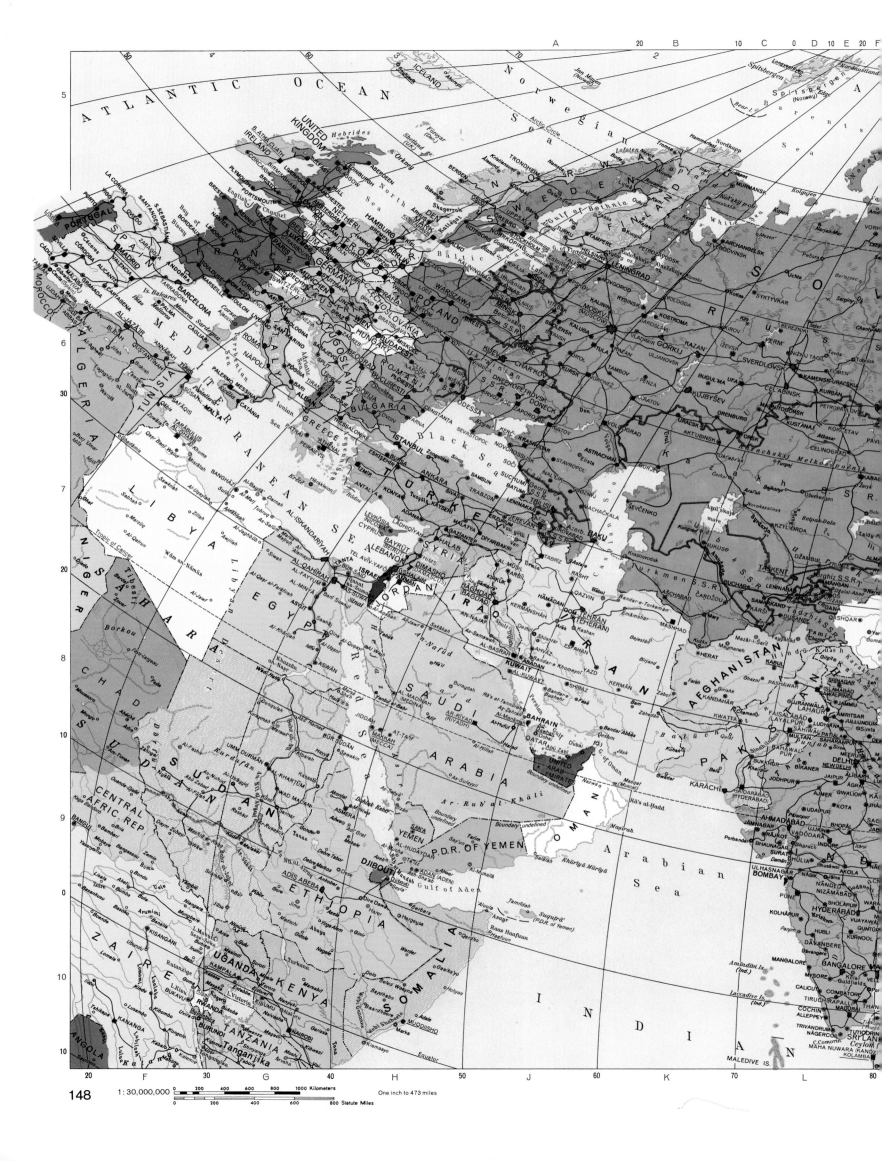

Asia, political 149

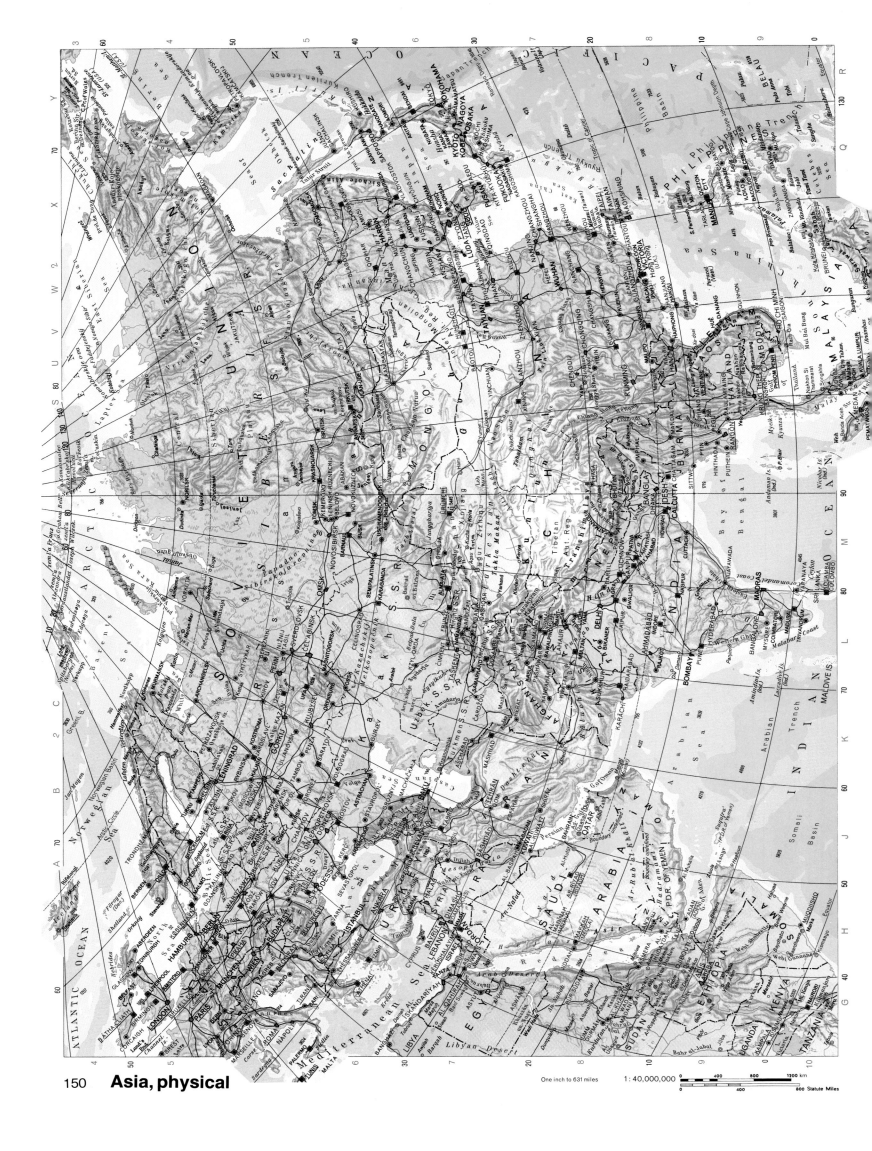

Asia, physical

One inch to 631 miles

1 : 40,000,000

0   400   800   1200 km

0   400   800 Statute Miles

Asia is home to cultures thousands of years old. Large religious communities developed independently in very different regions, thus developing an enormous multiplicity of ethnic groups that cannot be found on any other continent. Northern Siberia is home to the coldest point on Earth, while the Arabian desert ranks among the world's hottest regions. The greatest annual precipitation was measured in the western corner of India. While the entire northern coastline is in the subarc-

Asia: the largest continent on Earth

tic region, the peninsulas and islands of Southeast Asia are in the ever-wet tropics.

Because of various nations' high birthrates, the continent's population is constantly growing. Because of the population explosion, Southeast Asia is faced with enormous social problems: unemployment, malnourishment, illiteracy. Raw-material deposits are spread about very unevenly in Asia. Although many nations are attempting to raise their population's standard of

living through rapid industrialization, this often does not succeed. The main focus of Asian economies is agriculture. Recently, considerable progress was made by expanding cultivated areas, but this effort has not been able to keep pace with the increase in population, and therefore, food supplies are not guaranteed throughout the continent.

Tea is Sri Lanka's (formerly Ceylon) most important export product. As in the highlands of Nuwara Eliya, huge tea plantations cover the country's interior. The photo (far left) shows tea harvesters at work amid tea bushes.

Photo, right: a snake charmer in India.

In Asia, dress is as diverse as religion. In the photo far left: Lama priests in Punakha, Bhutan.

The photo on the right shows Korean girls in traditional costumes.

In Thailand, too, artful robes are manufactured (photo right).

In the rugged mountains of Nepal, efforts to cultivate the meager soil have begun. Large photo left: a Newar porter in Sherpu-Beshi standing in front of a terraced landscape.

The Mongolian People's Republic, where people still live a nomadic existence, has remained largely untouched by industrial influences.

Siberia, in northern Asia, comprises approximately 3.9 million sq. mi. (ten million sq. km) and therefore is still a little larger than the USA, *with Alaska*. The vegetation zones, ranging from permafrost to desert, and the agricultural usage of this area are dictated by the continental climate and the decrease in precipitation toward the east and south. Long, very cold winters produce the Earth's coldest point on the Northern Hemisphere in Ojm'akon, −89.9° F (−67.7° C), on the upper

Siberia: more natural resources than any other region on Earth

course of the Indigirka, and short, hot summers limit the vegetation periods. This is one of the reasons that Siberia was settled much later.

The Trans-Siberian Railroad, built during the reigns of Czars, was the axis of development. The week-long trip from Moscow, through Siberia and down to Beijing, is one of the world's great train rides. During the 1920s and 1930s, the Kusneck Basin on the southeastern border of the West Siberian Plain was developed. Because of rich deposits of

coking coal, the Soviet Union's largest site of iron and steel production grew here. Furthermore, the nearby and extensive raw-material deposits created new industries in previously undeveloped areas such as Norilsk/northern Siberia (nickel and copper), Magadan/the Sea of Okhotsk (mechanical engineering, gold), Surgut on the central Ob (crude oil) and the Yamal Peninsula (natural gas).

Transportation problems encountered in the course of these

Siberian ice, new houses and known technology: Even in the summer, Siberia's northern coast is frequently blocked by pack ice, which makes the economic development of this region very difficult (photo above). In Bratsk on the Angara, one of the world's largest hydroelectric plants was built. Today the old village lies on the bottom of the gigantic reservoir. The approximately 250,000 inhabitants of the new Bratsk live primarily in barracks (photo center). The Trans-Siberian Railroad is the transportation axis along which the development of Siberia took place (photo bottom right).

projects were solved through construction of new routes such as railways (Lena route, BAM), roads, canals and pipelines. The expansion into new industrial zones has led to big changes in the natural landscape: clear-cutting of forests (Taiga), river regulations (Yenisey, Angara), drying of swamps (Siberian Plains), strip mining of coal (Kuzneck). The expansion of the new industrial centers requires the use of water to generate energy, a supply of food and the availability of

labor forces. Gigantic hydroelectric plants continue to be constructed on the Angara and Yenisey, as well as on other Siberian rivers. The Bratsk-Irkutsk project, one of the world's largest hydroelectric power plants, can be seen as a model for the industrialization of Siberia. The reservoir covers 2,100 sq. mi. (5,500 sq. km).

In order to make these new Siberian centers independent of long supply routes for food, agriculture is also promoted in such areas

as Omsk, Novosibirsk and Altay. Since the 1950s, the creation of "new land" has been a special priority. The irrigation of the Kazakh Steppes, undertaken with great effort, has indeed led to an increase in harvests; but at the same time, the water level of the Aral Sea—and the water table in general—has dropped. Forced labor during the "reign" of Stalin guaranteed the manpower for the expansion of the new industries. Today, economic incentives are used to lure manpow-

er; but even with such efforts, the Soviet Union is still experiencing difficulties in settling Siberia at an increased rate. Today, not even 10 percent of the population lives on this half of the Soviet Union's territory.

On a clear day Alaska, across the Bering Strait, is visible from the easternmost tip of Siberia. The International Date Line separates Asia from North America at this point.

The faces of northern Asia: A wide strip of old-growth birch forests is characteristic of the western siberian steppes and the southern edge of the Taiga (photo far left). The Soviet Union is a nation of many ethnic peoples; almost 50 percent of the population is non-Russian. People belonging to small ethnic groups, many of Mongolian origin, like this Buryat from Lake Bajkal, populate northern Asia (photo left). Lake Bajkal is known as "Siberia's holy sea." It is the deepest lake in the world, with a depth of 5,300 ft. (1,620 m). In winter it is covered by an ice layer 3 ft. (1 m) thick. Its unique fauna and abundance of fish are famous, but recently there have been many reports of significant environmental damage (photo above).

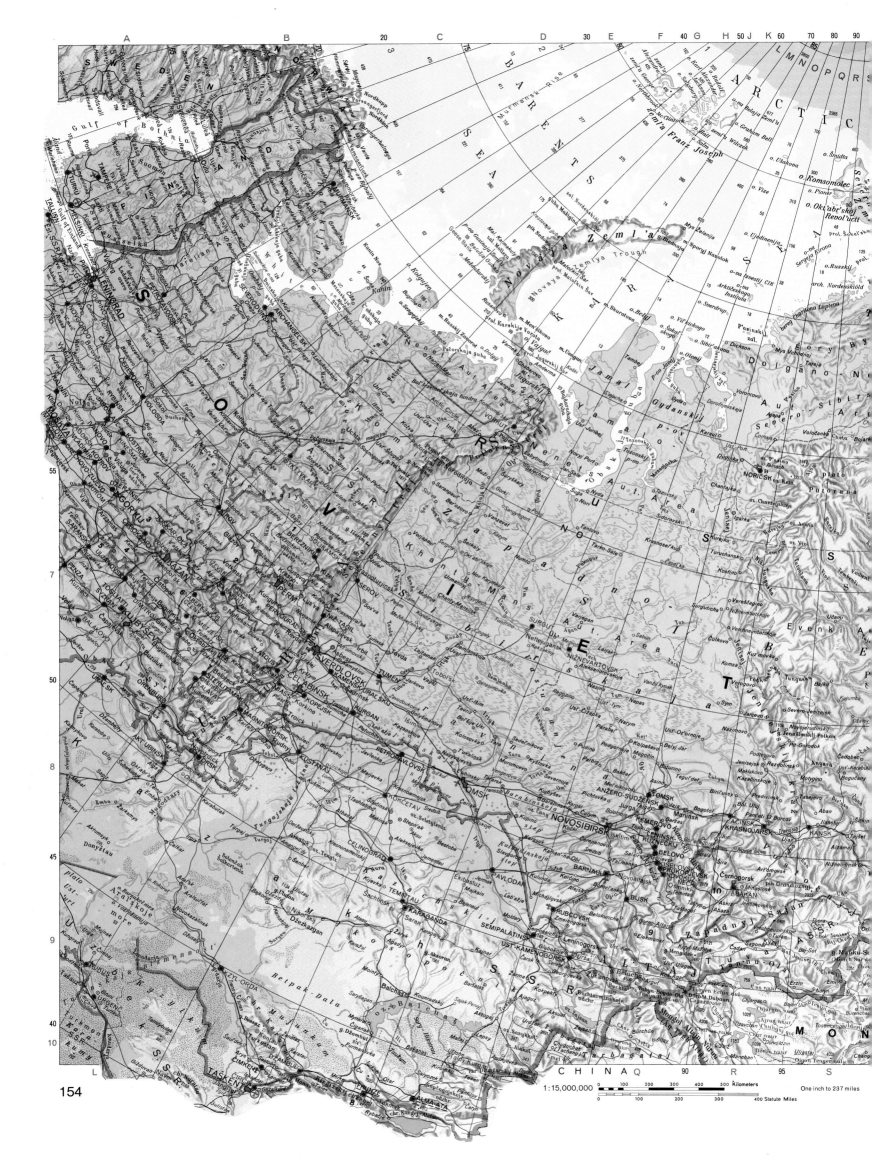

154

1:15,000,000

One inch to 237 miles

Administrative units in the Soviet Union:
1 Komi-Permyak Aut. Area
2 Udmurt A.S.S.R.
3 Mari A.S.S.R.
4 Chuvash A.S.S.R.
5 Mordovian A.S.S.R.
6 Tatar A.S.S.R.
7 Bashkir A.S.S.R.
8 Kirghiz S.S.R.
9 Gorno-Altai Aut. Reg.
10 Khakass Aut. Reg.
11 Ust-Ordynsky-Buryat Aut. Area
12 Aginsky-Buryat Aut. Area
13 Jewish Aut. Reg.

The straits between the Mediterranean and the Black Sea, the Dardanelles and the Bosporus, are like thin seams that have burst and now separate the European continent from the Middle East. Here, at these easily traversed crossing points, exchanges between ancient cultures took place in pre-Christian times in the form of peaceful trade or violent acts of war. Christianity was brought into the world via these routes.

When after centuries ferries

The Middle East: paradise and desert, oil fields and adventure

could no longer accommodate the steady back-and-forth flow of passengers and goods, a dream the rulers of antiquity had never been able to fulfill was finally realized in the early 1970s. One of the world's longest suspension bridges, the Ataturk Bridge, now reaches across the Bosporus with a length of 3,400 ft. (1,040 m). In the meantime, a second one has also been put into service (1988). The mysterious expanse of Asia begins beyond these two bridges.

The majority of peoples live in nonindustrialized "developing nations." The Middle East is caught between progress and tradition. As the years go by, Western civilization and technological progress are advancing along the Mediterranean coasts of Asia Minor, from Israel and Lebanon via Syria and Jordan to the large nations of the Middle East. Iraq, Iran and Saudi Arabia, whose borders meet at the Persian Gulf, are the world's most significant exporters of oil. Vast portions

An aerial photo of the southernmost tip of the Sinai Peninsula. Its sandy tip reaches far into the Red Sea. The varying tones of blue indicate varying depths. In the northeast, in the Gulf of Aqaba, an interesting geological phenomenon appears: The large trench, a morphological barrier, appears as one of the Earth's deepest rifts from the Red Sea, then runs along the Gulf and into the Jordan Valley. However, because of the dry climate, it is not filled with water; much water is diverted from the Jordan River, the only source of water flowing into the Dead Sea. In the last 40 years this has led to a lowering of the water table by 12 ft. (4 m). At 25 percent, the salt content is high.

of what was previously regarded as wasteland—rocks and desert—lie over subterranean oil lakes of enormous magnitude. Their discovery and development have brought these nations long-lasting prosperity and economic power. Their port cities are still dominated by ultramodern refineries, pipelines, glass-and-steel buildings built in exotic architectural styles.

A society steeped in the thought of the Middle Ages has—at least externally—modernized at a pace that is without precedent in world history. It is only the remote, very sparsely populated mountainous areas—for example, the ore-rich Taurus Mountains along Turkey's coastline, or the centrally located mountains in Iran and Afghanistan —that have not been reached by Western civilization as quickly. Climate and terrain form obstacles that are difficult to overcome. Within these areas live frugal mountain people, mostly illiterate. The nomadic tribes of the deserts are also not caught up in the pressures of civilization. Time seems to stand still around their watering holes, which are constantly changing. Here, life is still lived according to ancient laws and traditions.

In the coastal regions and fertile valleys of the interior—especially where irrigation was first developed thousands of years ago, long before in Europe—highly advanced cities like Babylon, Ninive and Ur were founded. In the historic two-river country of the Euphrates and Tigris, fruit growing, along with agriculture and ranching, was modernized; figs, dates and citrus fruits are now valued export items. Wherever the export of agricultural products, raw materials and consumer goods is on the rise, the native population's standard of living is improving. The peoples of the Middle East remain hopeful in spite of unrest and violent confrontations.

Once a Godforsaken area, today the earth on the Persian Gulf has been opened up and continuously pours forth liquid gold: Leaping flames and black clouds of smoke that line the foot of the Zagros Mountains in southern Iran are evidence of burnt-off natural gas, which is still regarded as a waste product generated by the production of crude oil (photo top). An oasis at the foot of the Al-Hajar mountain chain in the Sultanate of Oman displays a lush growth of date palms. Here, the difficult art of canal irrigation has been known since times of old (photo left). A Bedouin village in the Arabian desert. The Bedouins were formerly exclusively nomadic, tent-dwelling camel breeders. Today efforts to settle them have met with mixed success (above).

India, the subcontinent whose natural border with the rest of Asia is formed by the highest mountain formation in the world, the Himalayas, is the most populated nation on Earth after the People's Republic of China. Since its decolonialization in 1947, India has been governed democratically. It ranks among the world's large industrial nations, but its wealth is distributed unevenly. The population is engaged predominantly in agriculture; 75 percent lives in the country.

India: chaos of languages, a system of castes and conflicts between religions

The country's social structure is torn by its system of castes, a chaos of languages and a multiplicity of religions. In addition to 26 main languages there are 200 other splinter groups of languages. Hindus, Buddhists, Moslems, Christians, Jews, Sikhs and Jainas live next to one another, but not always peacefully. Pakistan, which was separated from India in 1947, has become the world's largest Islamic nation.

India's capital is in New Delhi.

There, poverty and wealth can be found side by side. All efforts to industrialize and raise the standard of living remain doubtful, because the predominantly illiterate population has difficulty breaking with traditions and prejudices. Calcutta, which with over nine million inhabitants is India's fastest-growing city, is a prime example of the population's misery: Homeless people sleep, eat, give birth and die on the open street. The poor and the pious find their consolation in Allahabad,

Rice growing in Madras. The young sprouts are planted in the terraced fields that are flooded with 4–8 in. (10–20 cm) of water (top). Delicate, colorful robes and decorative jewelry complete the gracefulness of the thin-boned Indian girls and women (above).

The burial monument of Grand Mogul Humayun was built from red sandstone and white marble and was the model for the Taj Mahal (center). An erotic temple consecrated to the Goddess Shiva, with artful sculptures of embracing lovers (photo right).

an ancient Hindu holy site where the Ganges and the Jumna rivers meet. For them, bathing in the holy waters means absolution from sin and a stronger presence of God.

India's climate is tropical, and the monsoon is of vital importance, for without it there would be drought and starvation: It is caused by the heating of the Asian land masses, which causes air to rise; the heat depression over the country then sucks damp air—the monsoon— from the India Ocean, which brings

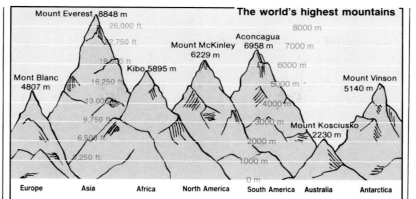

The world's highest mountains

Mount Everest 8848 m	8000 m
26,000 ft.	Aconcagua
22,750 ft.	Mount McKinley 6958 m 7000 m
19,500 ft.	6229 m 6000 m
Kibo 5895 m	Mount Vinson
Mont Blanc 4807 m 16,250 ft.	5000 m 5140 m
13,000 ft.	4000 m
9,750 ft.	3000 m Mount Kosciusko
6,500 ft.	2000 m 2230 m
3,250 ft.	1000 m
	0 m

Europe Asia Africa North America South America Australia Antarctica

the great rains upon which India is so dependent.

Thirty mi. (50 km) off India's southern tip is Sri Lanka, formerly Ceylon. Precious stones are still found in the gravel of its rivers. But the main sources of revenue are the export of tea and textiles, as well as tourism. The 25,325 sq. mi. (65,610-sq.-km) island has about 16 million inhabitants.

Benares, known today as Varanasi, is the final destination of pious pilgrims. Nothing is more desirable for a Hindu than to die here and have the ashes of the burnt body be dispersed into the waters of the Ganges, India's holy river. Wealthy Indians go to some expense for their salvation. During their lifetimes they work to purchase a piece of land on the shores of the holy river. Construction there is becoming more and more dense, and the lucky ones buy what was built by those already deceased; the prices are extremely high. But in the face of death, rupees mean little to those growing old, and residences are purchased at any cost. All this is much cheaper for the poor fellow believers in the slums: During a pilgrimage, they dip into the holy waters as often as possible to be absolved of their sins.

China: Empire of the Center, a country opening itself

The third-largest nation in area on Earth, whose rulers thousands of years ago referred to it as the Empire of the Center or Land of the Rising Sun, is also the world's most populous nation, with over one billion people. Only five percent of the population lives in the western half of the 3,691,000 sq. mi. (9,561,000-sq.-km.) country; 95 percent live in the east and southeast. Even rural areas here are densely populated, in concentrations that otherwise are found only in certain industrial regions of Western Europe and the United States. The majority of the almost fifty cities in China with more than one million inhabitants can also be found here. The very uneven distribution of the population is due to the wide range of natural terrains.

China's northwest, which includes the Gobi Desert, is extremely dry and has a typical continental climate, with cold winters and hot summers. This is the settlement area of traditionally nomadic peoples. The highlands of Tibet, the Roof of the World, with an area of 849 million sq. mi. (2.2 million sq. km) and altitudes of 12,000 to 16,000 ft. (4,000 to 5,000 m), are the world's largest and tallest highlands, but little of them is suitable for agricultural use. The autonomous region of Tibet is 4.6 million sq. mi. (1.2 million sq. km). China's agricultural regions are in the north, northeast and south. In the north, a layer of loess between 33 and 88 yards (30 and 80 meters)—and in

A Saddhu is a holy man who at one time followed a calling to leave behind family and everyday life in order to seek solitude. There he leads the life of a hermit and mendicant friar attempting to unify his own "I" with the world's soul (photo above). The pious Hindus call the world's mightiest mountains, the Himalayas, the "seat of the gods." The word originates from Sanskrit: hima = snow, and alaya = home. The majestic beauty of the moonlit Peak 29, which belongs to the group of the "smaller" 23,000-ft. (7,000 m) mountains, makes the native population's belief seem quite understandable (photo right). At the same time, the Himalayas are Earth's youngest mountains. The fossil layers indicate a Himalayan ocean, Thetys. This was about 60 million years ago.

rain forest is facing destruction.

Sumatra is currently being developed for agriculture by Javanese colonists. Major efforts are under way there to find oil and to develop caoutchouc (rubber) plantations. Singapore has developed into an important meeting point between the Southeast Asian peninsulas and the island world of Indonesia and the Philippines. With breathtaking speed it has become the trade, financial and industrial center of Southeast Asia.

Vietnam has not yet recuperated economically from its civil war. An opening to the West is slowly being sought, since the Soviet-style economic system has not been successful.

Many regions of Southeast Asia were formerly characterized by an early-Indian and later an Islamic influence. They were then colonized and Christianized by the Europeans and also economically influenced by Chinese immigrants. For almost 300 years Indonesia was Dutch, while the Philippines were Spanish until the turn of the century and then administered by the U.S. until 1945. Burma and Malaysia were British colonies; Laos, Vietnam and Cambodia were French. So many different influences over many centuries have created a colorful mixture of people and religions with extraordinary exotic appeal.

Today, Western influences promoted by Japanese and Western media are changing consumer habits and thereby societal structures as well. The authority of the "old ones" is steadily diminishing, and large families are being questioned. Rising individualism, a previously unknown value, is changing Southeast Asian society and paving the way for a Western-style industry consumerism. Despite many serious problems, many believe that Southeast Asia will experience dramatic growth in its standard of living in the coming decades.

Contrasts from Southeast Asia: densely populated high-rise buildings and praying monks. Singapore, with its many apartment complexes, has the standard appearance of a major city (top left), but many people still live on their house boats. About 120,000 monks enjoy privileged positions in Burma. Eighty-five percent of the population is Buddhist (left).

An undesired splendor: water hyacinths on a lagoon of the Philippine island Luzon. Attempts have been made again and again to eradicate this water-born plague, which depletes oxygen in lakes and oceans. Here, fish are caught with arrow-shaped traps.

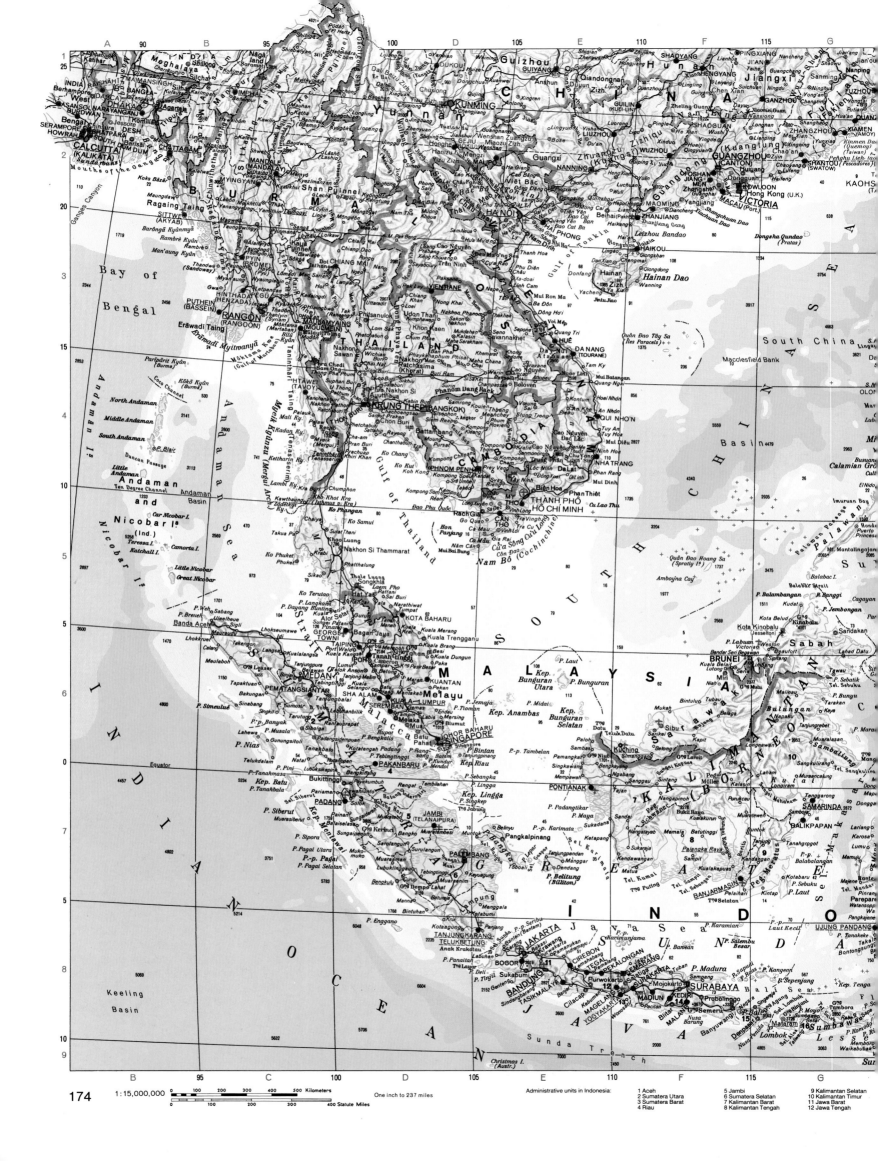

Southeast Asia   175

AUSTRALIA

Located between the Indian and Pacific oceans is this island continent, located entirely in the Southern Hemisphere. It reaches from the tropics all the way to the temperate-climate zone. The three aerial photos show dead trees in the red mud from an alumina plant (photo left); Ayers Rock, referred to as "the largest monolith in the world" (photo center); and a flat island in the Great Barrier Reef (photo right).

Australia is the only continent that is also a unified political entity, excluding Oceania. Long after its discovery in 1616 by the Dutch, it was regarded as a "terrible country, poor and brutal," perfectly suited to be an English penal colony. Only toward the end of the 18th century did free English settlers begin to make their presence known. As large as the U.S. without Alaska, this country has fewer inhabitants than New York State. Over 80 percent of the approximately 16 million inhabitants live on the east and southeastern coasts, while the interior, nearly devoid of people, is hot, dry and host to unpredictable weather. The remaining indigenous Stone Age population, the Aborigines, live here on reservations, and millions of sheep go to pasture here. Valuable and productive ore deposits make this nation an important supplier of

FLORA AND FAUNA. OFF THE COAST IS THE MOST BEAUTIFUL CORAL REEF IN

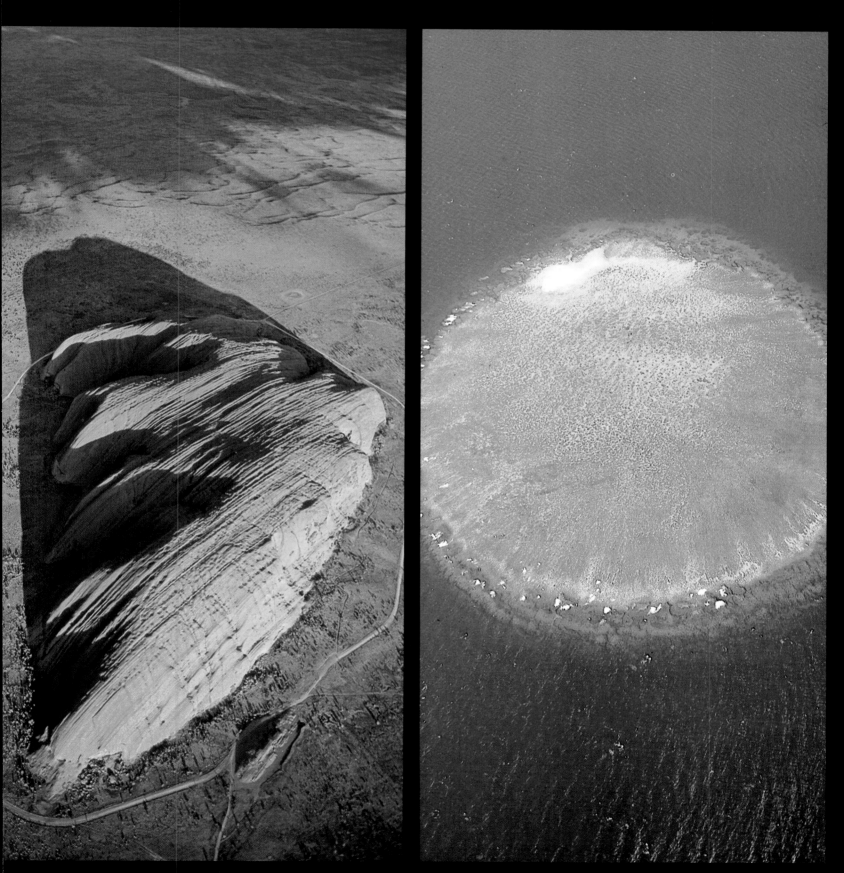

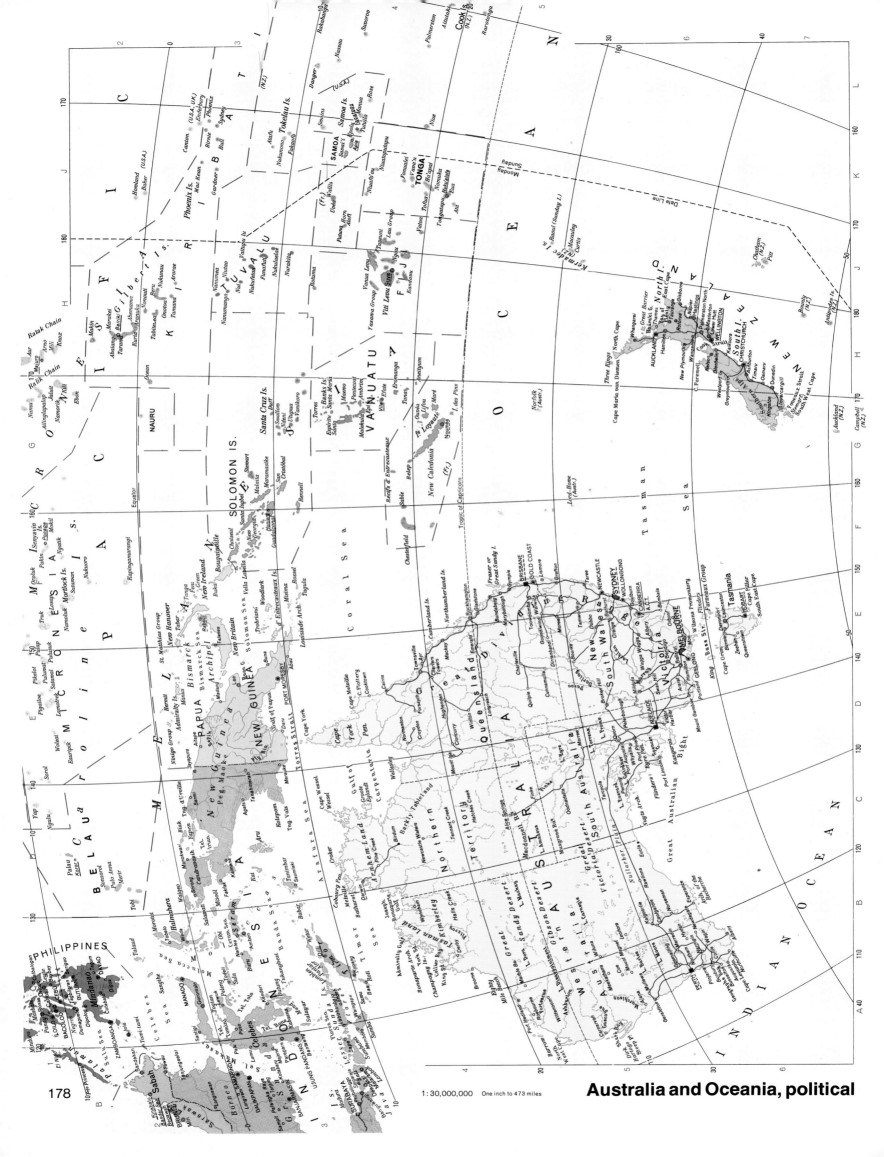

178

1:30,000,000   One inch to 473 miles

Australia and Oceania, political

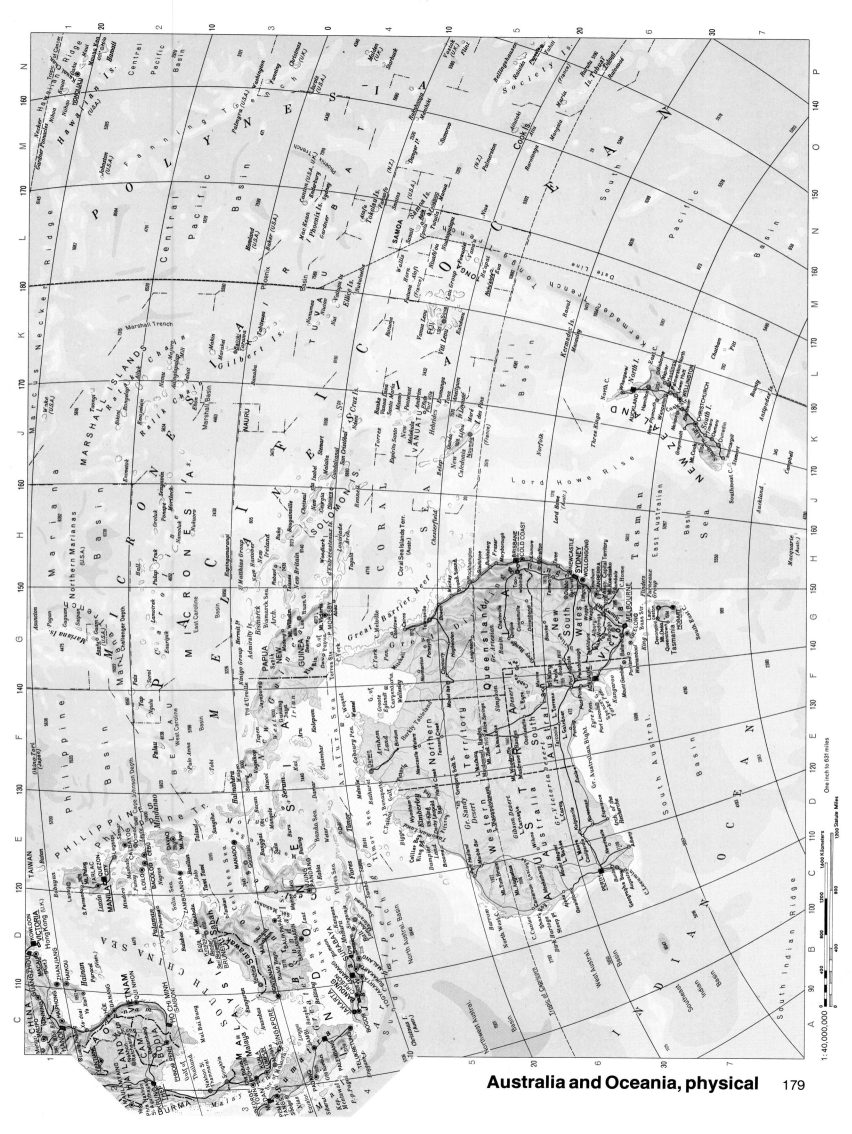

Australia and Oceania, physical

Australia is different. Evidence of just how different are its fauna and flora, among them the koala bear, the kangaroo and eucalyptus (of which there are more than 500 varieties); bushes, trees that grow to be over 330 ft. (100 m), and "wattle" (acacias), with varieties forming the nearly impenetrable scrub, a type of thorn bush. In 1800 there were about 300,000 Aborigines; today there are only about 50,000. These hunters and gatherers have only very meager material posses-

The continent "down under": kangaroos and sheep, an indigenous population and white settlers. Rich in raw materials.

sions but very complex behavior patterns and ritual ceremonies.

"Australia rides on its sheep." Sheep and their wool helped lay the foundation of this country's wealth. Australia today has more than 170 million sheep, and sheep farms that are larger than Luxembourg. Cattle raising is also highly developed. But Australia also refers to itself as "the world's stone quarry," for it is rich in minerals: iron-ore mines are in the Pilbara District, nonferrous heavy-metal mines in New South Wales,

gold fields and deposits of opals and sapphires in western Australia. But there is a shortage of water, and in many areas ground water is tapped in the form of artesian wells (artesian basin). Given the vastness of the country and the unevenly distributed settlements and industrial centers, transportation is a big problem. Off the northeastern shore is the 1,200 mi.-long (2,000 km) Great Barrier Reef. This coral reef is one of the world's natural wonders.

The Sydney Opera House is a symbol of the daring architecture of this "young continent," which in 1988 celebrated the 200th anniversary of its settlement by Europeans. In the background: the 1,700 ft.-long (520 m) port bridge over the fjordlike Port Jackson (photo top).

Among the Aborigines, Australia's indigenous population, there are artists of astonishing expression. Their rock paintings show hunters in skirts, fish, and other symbolic forms that are difficult to decipher (X-ray photo).

New Zealand and Oceania lie spread out over a stretch of the Pacific Ocean that is larger than Africa and Asia together. New Zealand consists of two large and several smaller islands. The capital city of Wellington and the most populous city of Auckland are on the northern island, with a subtropical climate. Lively volcanic activity is registered in the center of the island. The southern island is characterized by high, glaciated mountains and a spectacular fjord coastline in the

New Zealand and Oceania: fjords, volcanoes, South Sea beaches and atolls lost in the vastness of the Pacific Ocean.

southwest. The hills east of the mountains are used for sheep pastures and for wheat cultivation. Among New Zealanders, 3.3 million are of largely British origin; the indigenous Maori population comprises less than 10 percent. New Guinea is off the Australian coast to the north. This island is still almost completely covered by jungle. The population is split into numerous tribal communities with over 700 independent languages! Melanesia is the large island group closest to

Australia and Indonesia. French New Caledonia, with its large nickel deposits, also belongs to Melanesia. Micronesia continues to the north. Hundreds of islands, together barely 1,000 sq. mi. (2,500 sq. km), are spread over 2.7 million sq. mi. (7 million sq. km) of water. The island group between Hawaii and French Polynesia is called Polynesia and contains the dream islands Tahiti and Bora Bora—but also the atomic-testing grounds of the Mururoa atoll.

A Bena native on Papua–New Guinea (top left).

A native couple on a coconut-tree-lined beach on Moorea (French Polynesia) (top right).

Auckland, the largest city in New Zealand, is the "queen city" to New Zealanders and has a mild subtropical climate all year long (top).

Sheep raising, here on the northern island of New Zealand, is one of the nation's most important sources of income. In the background is the beautifully formed volcano dome of the 8,260-ft.-high (2,518-m) Mount Egmont (photo left). Originally 50 percent of the island's surface was covered with forests, today just 15 percent.

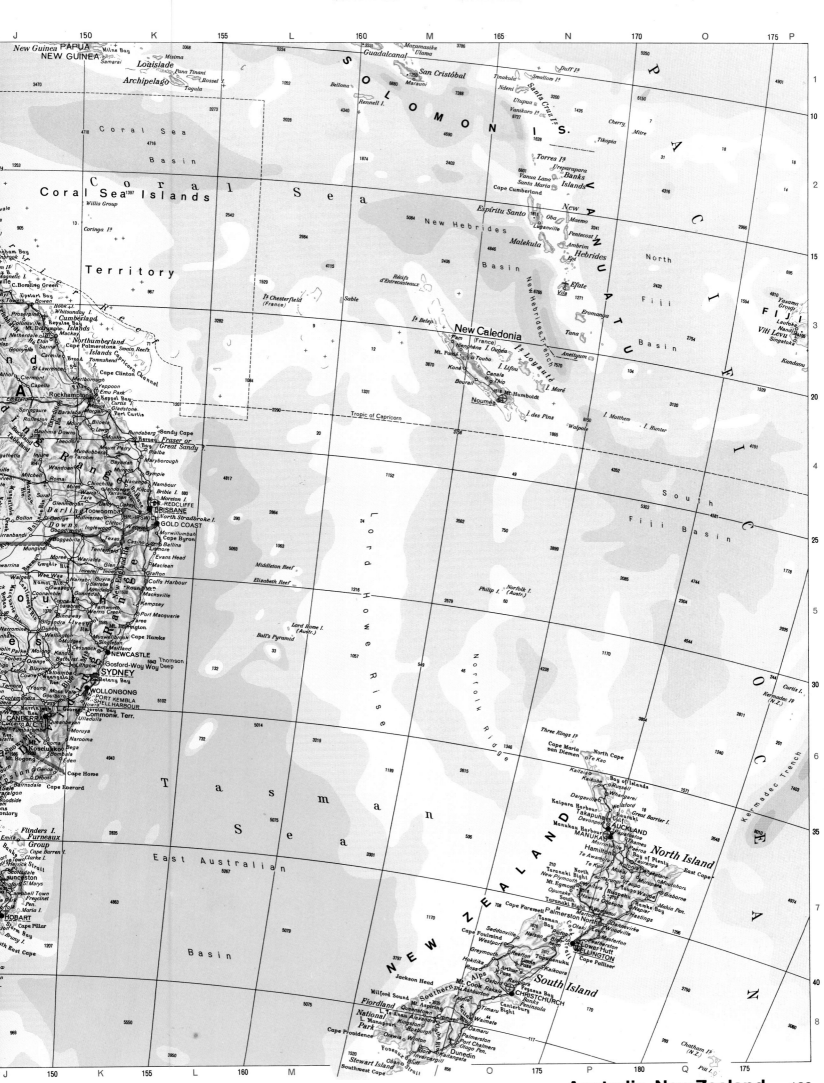

AFRICA

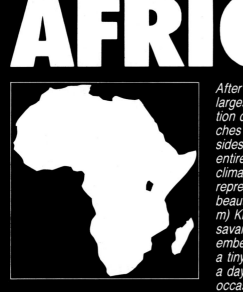

After Asia, Africa is the second-largest continent, with a population of 600 million people. It stretches 5,000 mi. (8,000 km) to both sides of the equator and consists entirely of tropical and subtropical climates. Three photos that are representative: With dreamlike beauty the 19,336-ft. high (5,895 m) Kilimanjaro rises over the savanna (photo left); an oasis, embedded in endless sand dunes, a tiny island of life (photo center); a day in the market in Ghana, an occasion for lively talk (photo right).

Africa: much of the continent is still undeveloped. This is particularly true in the vast area north of South Africa. Light-skinned races live in the North along the Mediterranean Sea: Berbers, Egyptians and Arabs. The living environment of the black tribes starts south of the Sahara, the largest desert in the world. The Sudanese blacks, made up of about 60 tribes, and the Bantu, with about 200 tribes, are considered the true black Africans. Foreign domination and enslavement were the fate of black Africans for many centuries. Only after World War II did most African nations gain their political independence. South Africa, however, remains a bastion of white dominance.

Africa: a continent of tribes, not nations, torn between tradition and the modern age. The seasons are determined not by summer and winter but by rainy seasons and drought.

Photo 1: Not far from an oasis in northern Mauritania these nomads have built their tentlike house out of date-palm leaves; acacia branches serve as a structure. Doom-palm straw mats cover the whole structure. Photo 2: The Pyramids and Sphinx near Gizeh are the essence of ancient Egypt. A camel used as a pack animal in front of them: This photo could have been taken during Roman times. Photo 3: A nomad of the Berber tribe. They are not a unified race and call themselves "Imazighen," that is, the free ones. Photo 4: Tenerife, the largest of the Canary Islands, has rocky coastlines and the dominating, inactive Tide volcano, as well as interesting rock formations formed through wind erosion. Photo 5: The island of Bioko, formerly known as Fernando Poo, lies off the coast of Cameroon in the ever-wet tropics. Photo 6: The pelican belongs to one of the more than 400 different species of waterfowl that can be seen at Lake Nakuru National Park in Kenya. Photo 7: Bushmen and other tribes still live as hunters and gatherers on the level of the Stone Age in the dry savanna and the

1

2

4

5

6

7

thorn-bush steppes of Southwest Africa. Photo 8: The Niger is the most water-rich river in Africa after the Congo. It forms a delta that is half the size of Switzerland. One of its 20 mouths, pictured here, meanders through the impassable mangrove swamps in Nigeria. Photo 9: Green bananas and a parasol in her basket, a child on her arm—a young mother

from Mbini, the mainland portion of Equatorial Guinea, symbolizes daily life there. Photo 10: A market scene in Dar es Salaam, the most important port on the coast of Tanzania. Photo 11: In the dry savannas of the highlands of Adamaoua (Adamawa), in northern Cameroon, the black population lives almost untouched by civilization in simple

straw-thatched round huts. Photo 12: The springs of the blue Nile lie in the area of the 6,002-ft.-high (1,830 m) Lake Tana in northern Ethiopia. A short way from where it flows out of this lake, the Nile, which is referred to here as the Abay, forms large waterfalls. Photo 13: Johannesburg, with 1.7 million inhabitants, is the largest city in South Africa.

It was founded in 1886 in the midst of newly discovered gold-ore deposits. By 1900 it had 100,000 inhabitants, and today it is the republic's economic center. Photo 14 This lioness belongs to the 30,000 big game animals that live in the Ngorongoro Crater Conservation Area. Photo 15: The fields are burned before the sugar-cane harvest.

8

9

11

12

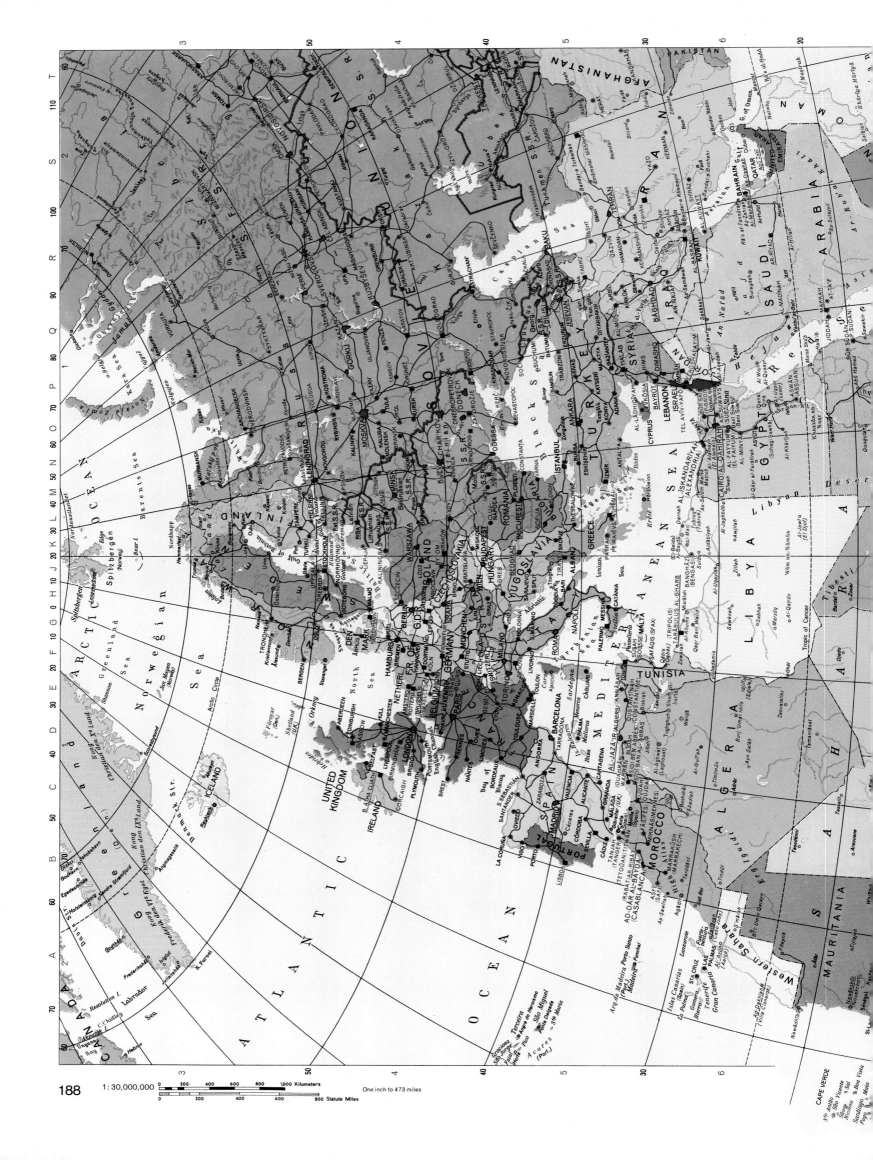

1:30,000,000

| 0 | 200 | 400 | 600 | 800 | 1000 Kilometers |

One inch to 473 miles

| 0 | 200 | 400 | 600 | 800 Statute Miles |

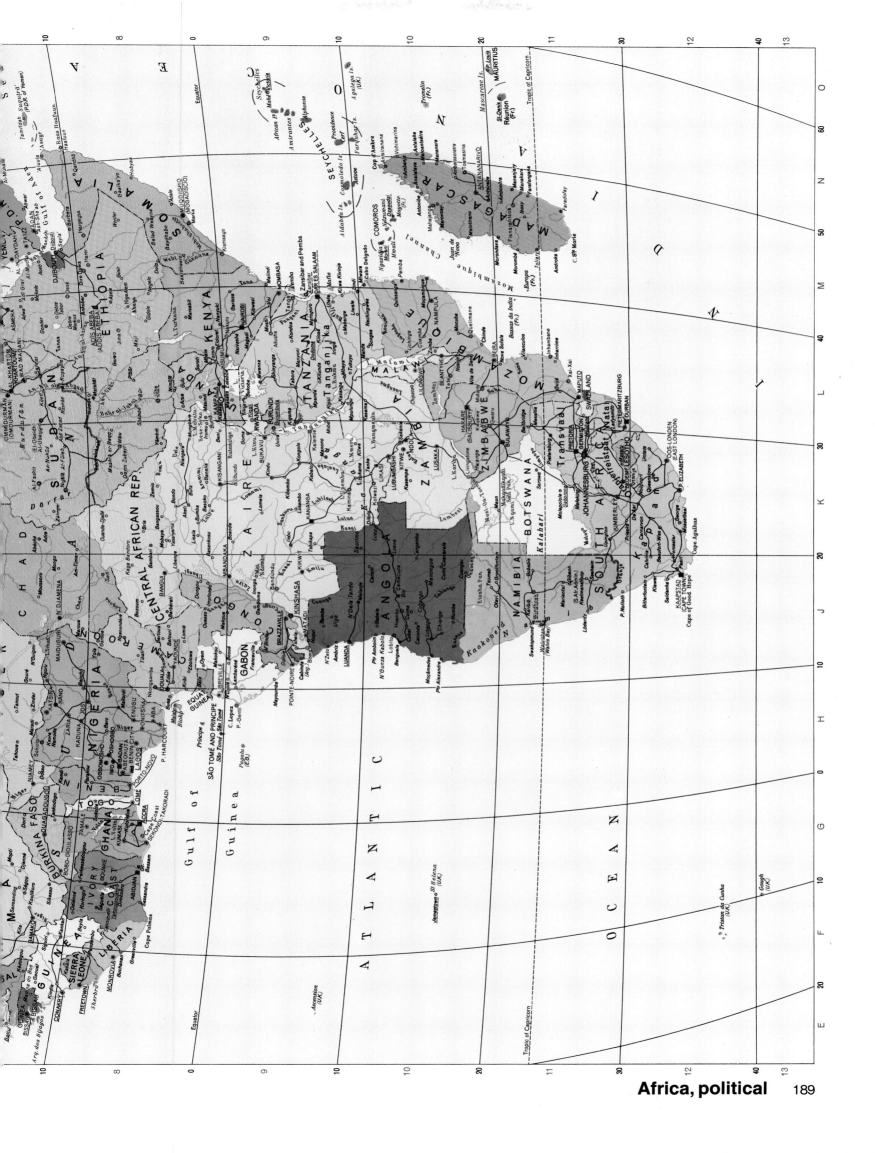

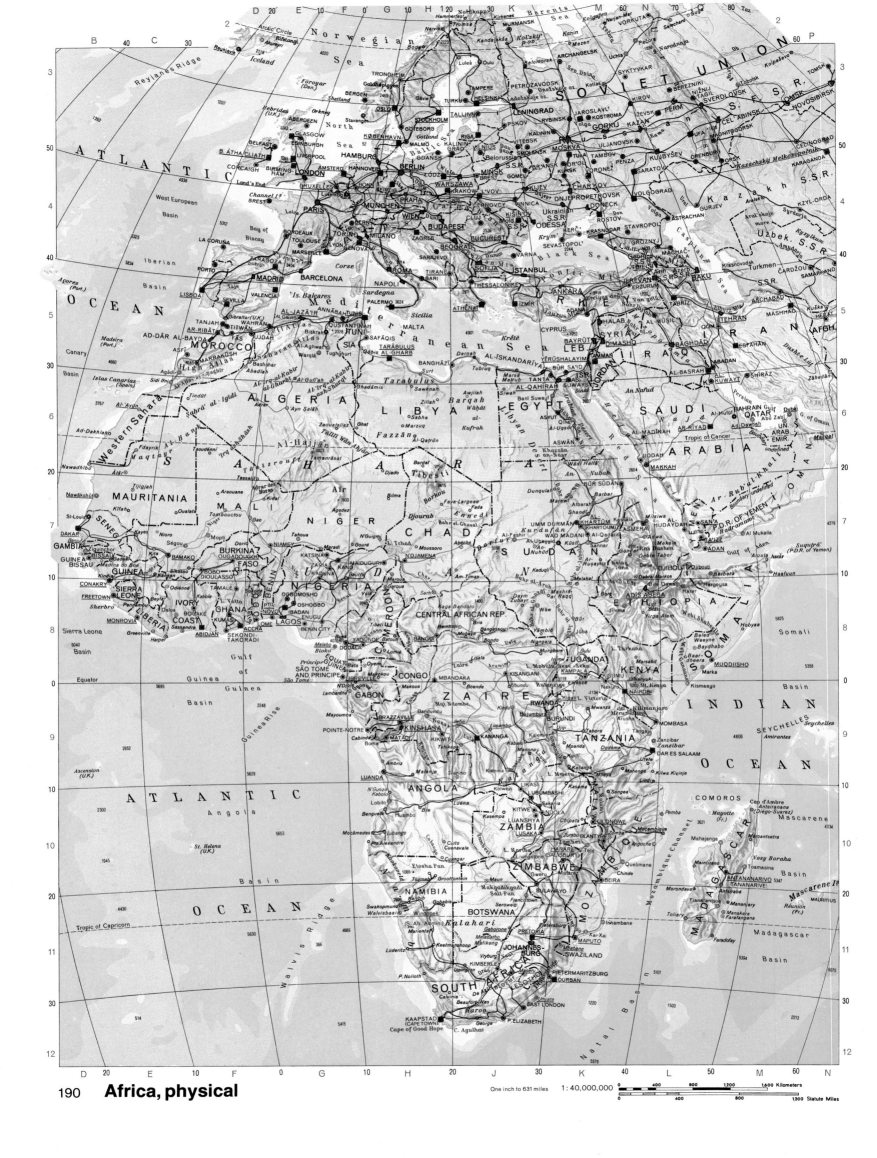

190 **Africa, physical**

One inch to 631 miles 1 : 40,000,000

Three large cultural zones can be distinguished in Africa. The countries bordering the Mediterranean are linked through Islam to the Oriental and Arabic peoples. Ethiopia and portions of Sudan are significantly influenced by Christianity, and the remaining portion of the continent is the domain of independent black-African cultures.

Tribal traditions still frequently conflict with modern government. Another source of strife is the arbitrary borders drawn by former

Africa: government power and tribal traditions in opposition; agriculture and livestock farming as the basis of life.

colonial powers. Rivalries between tribes are frequently based on the ancient struggle between livestock farmers and agricultural farmers. Africa's major dividing line is the Sahara. Light-skinned people—e.g., Berbers and Arabs—live to the north, in "white Africa." "Black Africa" begins south of the Sahara. The most numerous and geographically dispersed races are the Bantus and the Sudanese blacks.

For the vast majority of Africans, agriculture is the basis of life. The

most important export goods are cocoa, sisal, peanuts, oil-bearing fruits and cotton. Only South Africa, Egypt and, to a certain extent, Zimbabwe have a sound industrial structure. Africa is a major producer of gold, diamonds, copper, chromium bauxite, phosphate. The effort to build up raw-material-processing industries is still in its infancy. Improved education and health conditions are critical if this continent is to make significant progress.

1

2

3

4

5

6

7

Photo 1:
A rider with camel in Tunisia—in typical desert costume.
Photo 2:
A Berber woman in the Atlas Mountain region of North Africa.
Photo 3:
The Massai, tall nomadic shepherds, live in the East African highlands of Kenya and Tanzania.
Photo 4:
A Moroccan Berber.

Photo 5:
A warrior of the Zombu tribe in the West African nation of Togo.
Photo 6:
A Ugandan family in their meager field.
Photo 7:
A Poeul woman in the nation of Chad.

191

Nowhere on Earth are climatic and vegetation zones so clearly defined as in North Africa. The regions to the north of the Atlas Mountains, and a stretch along the Mediterranean, still enjoy the favorable winter rains. Here, grain, wine grapes, olives and citrus fruits are cultivated and forests are found. Wherever the annual precipitation falls below 4 in. (100 mm), however, the desert begins.

The Sahara, the largest desert in the world, stretches approximately

North and West Africa: desert, savanna and rain forest—but the desert is growing.

3,700 mi. (6,000 km) from the Atlantic to the Red Sea, and its north-to-south distance is approximately 1,240 mi. (2,000 km). Barren pebbles, boulders and sand surfaces dominate the landscape of the desert. The dramatic temperature differences between night and day burst the stone formations, while the wind, acting like a sandblaster, is the source of significant erosion. Together they create bizarre surface structures. On the sand the temperatures rise to 176° F (80° C),

and in the air it reaches 122° F (50° C). At night, however, temperatures drop to 23° F (-5° C), and in the mountains temperatures as low as 5° F (-15° C) are not unusual. Sandstorms can reach speeds of 60 mi. (100 km) per hour.

Where water can still be reached under the surface, oases are created—green islands in the desert ocean, rest areas along the ancient trade and modern adventure routes. The Nile, with its waters from the highlands of Ethiopia and

Many African women prepare meals similar to the one in the photo: a mash of millet, cassava or yams (top photo). Crocodiles in the Kabelega-National Park at the Victoria Nile sometimes grow up to 23 ft. (7 m) long and can be quite dangerous.

Old Egyptian art: the golden mask of King Tutankhamen, in the British Museum in Cairo. His burial site was discovered in the so-called Valley of the Kings near Luxor (near the city of Qina) and was important for the study of the ancient Egyptian's cult of the dead. Tutankhamen lived in the 14th century B.C.

Contrary to widespread opinion, the desert is not monotonous. Sandy deserts cover only one-fifth of the Sahara's surface; the remaining portion is pebble and boulder desert, Serir and Hammada. The extreme temperature differences between day and night result in bursting rocks, frequently accompanied by a loud bang, leaving sharp-edged fragments. Bizarre rock formations make for a fascinating landscape (top photo).

The highland plateaus of Ethiopia are frequently strewn with farms. The land is cultivated right up to the steep downgrades. Much "Tef," a grain that exists only in Ethiopia and from which bread is baked, is planted here. (photo p. 193 top). Cone-roofed huts are common in many Central African nations. Fences made of reed mats surround the house groups belonging to individual large families (photo p. 193 bottom).

from Lake Victoria, traverses the Sahara and nourishes the largest river oasis in the world: Egypt. Manipulation of the natural rhythms of flooding, and low water levels, endanger the fertility of the soil, which is also in danger of becoming too salty.

To the Arabs the dry savanna on the southern edge of the desert appeared like the shoreline of a new country; hence the name Sahel, which means shoreline in Arabic. The sparse vegetation in the Sahel zone permits only nomadic livestock farming. Overgrazing and population growth, as well as lack of rain, have led to drought and famine in recent years, but firewood frequently is even more expensive than food. Recent research indicates that the desert here is growing by almost 40 sq. mi. (100 sq. km) a day, corresponding to an area the size of Bermuda and Manhattan Island combined. With increasing precipitation, as we move farther from the desert, the dry savanna gradually transforms into the wet savanna, with tall grasslands and rivers bordered by forests. With fewer than six dry months per year, the forest closes in and changes into the always-wet tropical rain forest of the Guinea coast. Agricultural use already has largely displaced the natural vegetation, and the jungle is threatened by the massive clear cutting of wood for export.

The highland of Ethiopia raises itself like a mighty block to 15,000 ft. (4,600 m) above sea level. Years of drought, in conjunction with politically motivated resettlements, have led to chaos in the former empire.

Agriculture and livestock farming are still the basis of North and West African economies. Ivory Coast and Ghana are the world's most important cocoa exporters. The exporting of raw materials is the main source of income for many nations within this area. In Algeria, 75 percent of all exports are based on oil and natural gas; in Nigeria, 90 percent; and in Libya, 98 percent.

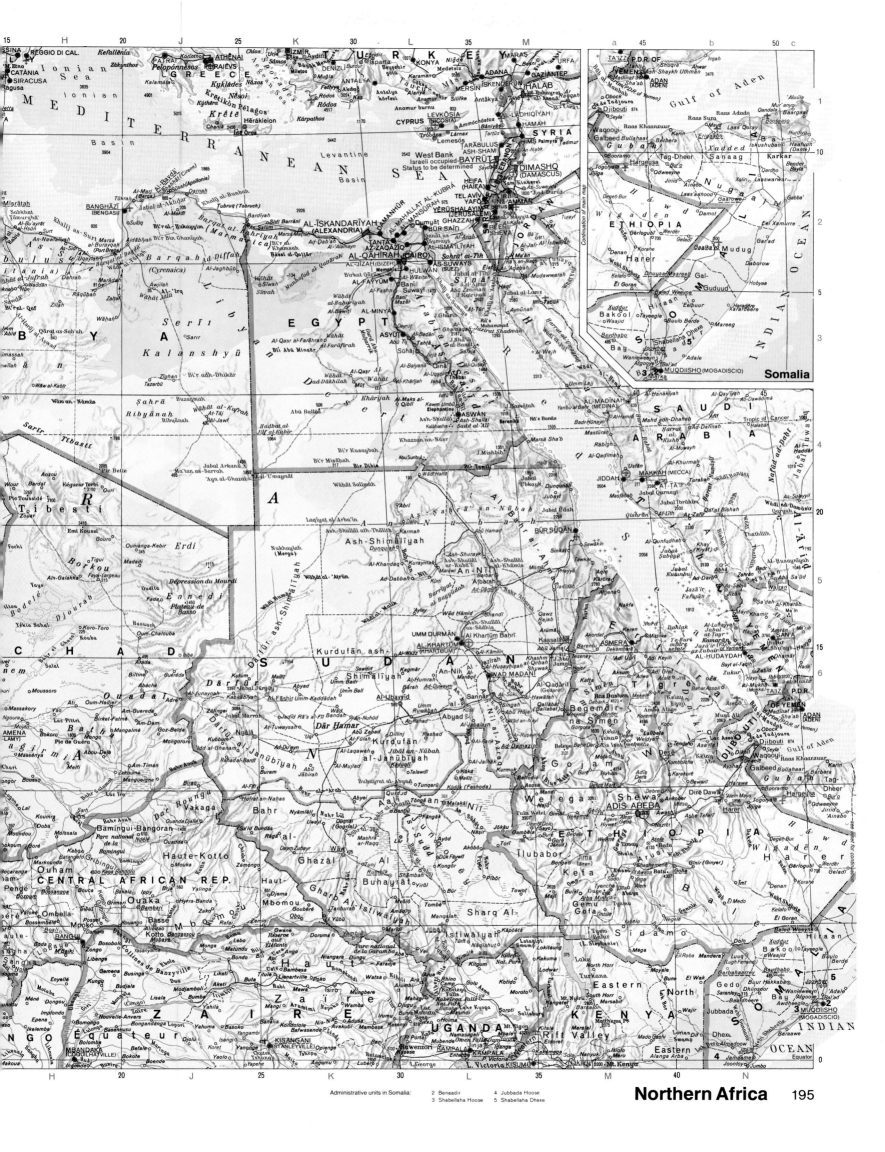

Administrative units in Somalia: 2 Benaadir   4 Jubbada Hoose
                                   3 Shabellaha Hoose 5 Shabellaha Dhexe

Somalia

From the Gulf of Guinea southward, Africa narrows to a wedge shape. Two huge basins, each surrounded by 3,300-to-6,600-ft.-high (1,000-to-2,000-m) rises, occupy Central and southern Africa. These are the Congo (Zaire) and Kalahari basins. Sinking into the East African highlands is the Rift Valley, a system of fault trenches. The Rift Valley is the continuation of the Red Sea trench on the highlands. Mighty volcanoes rise above the steppes of the highlands. The tropical rain forest and

Southern Africa: the world market's premier address for diamonds, gold and nonferrous heavy metals.

the wet savannas of the highlands around the equator are followed to the south by dry forest, bush, grasslands and, finally, desert steppes.

The population of southern Africa is more homogeneous than that of northern Africa, and this region is where the Bantu primarily have spread out. They migrated from the northeast and displaced the indigenous population. Only a few Pygmies have survived in the jungles of Zaire. The bushmen, who do not grow to be taller than 4'6" ft. (1.4

m), were left with the dry-bush-and-thorn savanna of the Kalahari as their only retreat. In spite of their remarkable adaptation to the hostile environment, these hunters and gatherers are doomed to become extinct. On the largest African island, Madagascar, the Indo-Malaysian influence in both people and languages is noticeable.

Southern Africa was apportioned among the European colonial powers—Portugal, England, Belgium, Germany and France—at the end

"Mosi-Oa-Toenja"—"thundering smoke": This is how the Makololo tribe refers to the famous Victoria Falls of the Zambezi River in their image-rich language. The broad, shallow stream falls 360 ft. (110 m) into a perpendicular ravine that is only 165 ft. (50 m) wide. Then it flows on in a zigzag through nine more narrows, formerly waterfalls. Because of the constant water mist, evergreen forests have formed along the banks of the river (photo right).

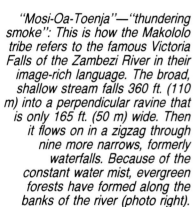

For tribal festivals on Madagascar, splendid old festive robes, sometimes still bearing Malaysian symbols, are worn. Cattle horns play an important role for head adornments (above).

Livestock farming is the basis of life in the arid areas of South Africa. Karacul lambs (right) are the lambs from which Persian-lamb coats are made, using skins of lambs that are no more than three days old.

Johannesburg (photo right) was founded in 1886 in the midst of the world's richest gold fields, the Witwatersrand. It is the largest South African city, with 1.7 million inhabitants and by far the continent's most modern industrial center. Gold mines and heaps of excavated earth stretch from west to east through the city. Separated from the city, which is completely dominated by a white minority, is the satellite city, Soweto, which is inhabited only by blacks.

of the 19th century. In these areas and in East Africa, but also in the drier subtropical regions of South Africa, whose climates were favorable to the Europeans, immigration and settlement by Portuguese, Dutch, British and Germans took place. In the tropical regions, the European settlers started sugarcane, sisal, coffee and tea plantations. In South Africa large farms were developed, cultivating primarily corn and wheat. Cattle and sheep ranching too, are now significant

economically. After World War II the former colonies gained their freedom—some through negotiations, some through bloody unrest.

Only South Africa has remained a bastion of whites. Approximately 4.6 million whites face approximately 18.8 million "nonwhites," of which 15 million are black, almost 3 million are racially mixed people and approximately 800,000 are Asians. Apartheid, or racial segregation in public and private life, is South Africa's state policy. World-

wide protests against the nation that relegates its black majority to second-class status by declaring them politically immature have not brought about much change.

On both sides of the border between Zaire and Zambia, large copper deposits in the copper belt are strip mined. At the *Witwatersrand* near Johannesburg, half of the world's gold and titanium ores are mined. Roughly 30 percent of the diamonds in the world market are from Zaire, and 20 percent from Bo-

tswana and South Africa respectively. Gabon produces manganese and uranium, while nickel and chromium are found in Zimbabwe.

South Africa is the only modern industrialized southern African nation, with modern transportation facilities. Elsewhere in Southern Africa, industry is underdeveloped and transportation systems are rudimentary.

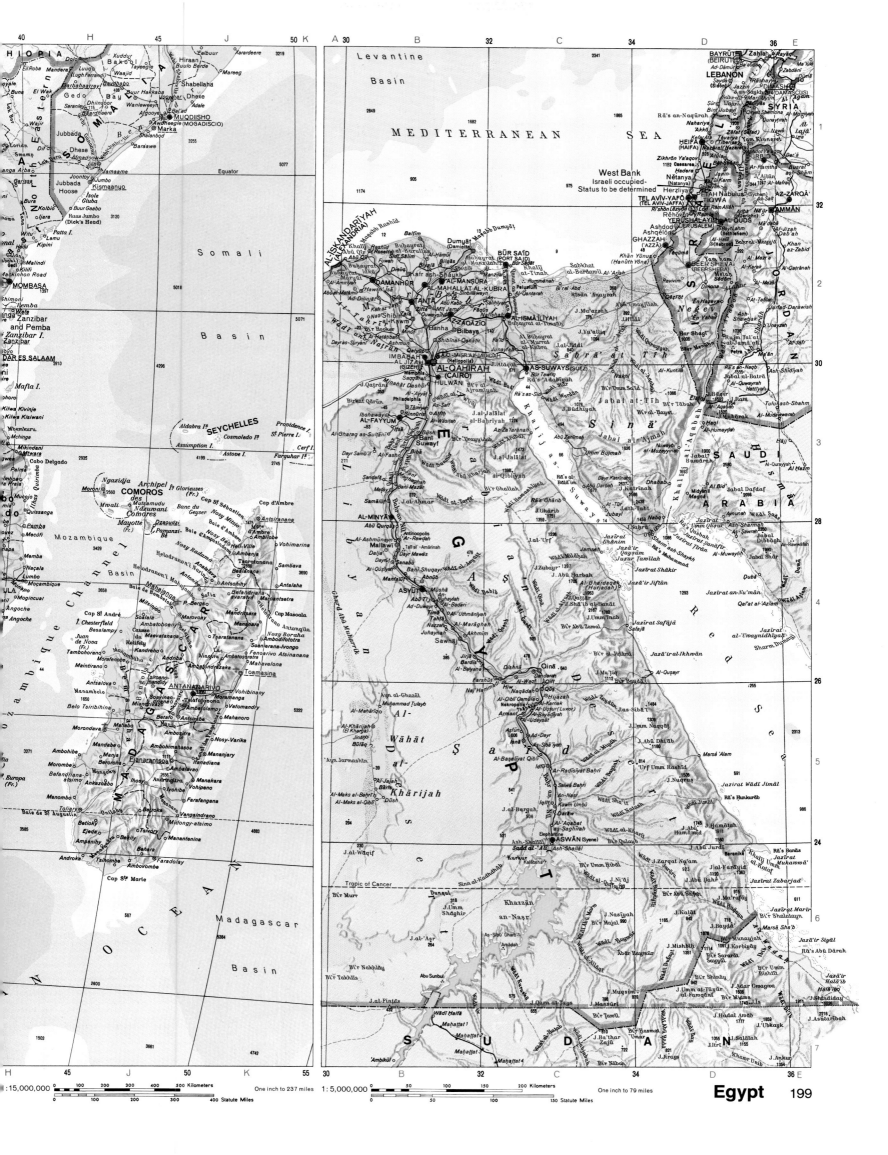

Egypt 199

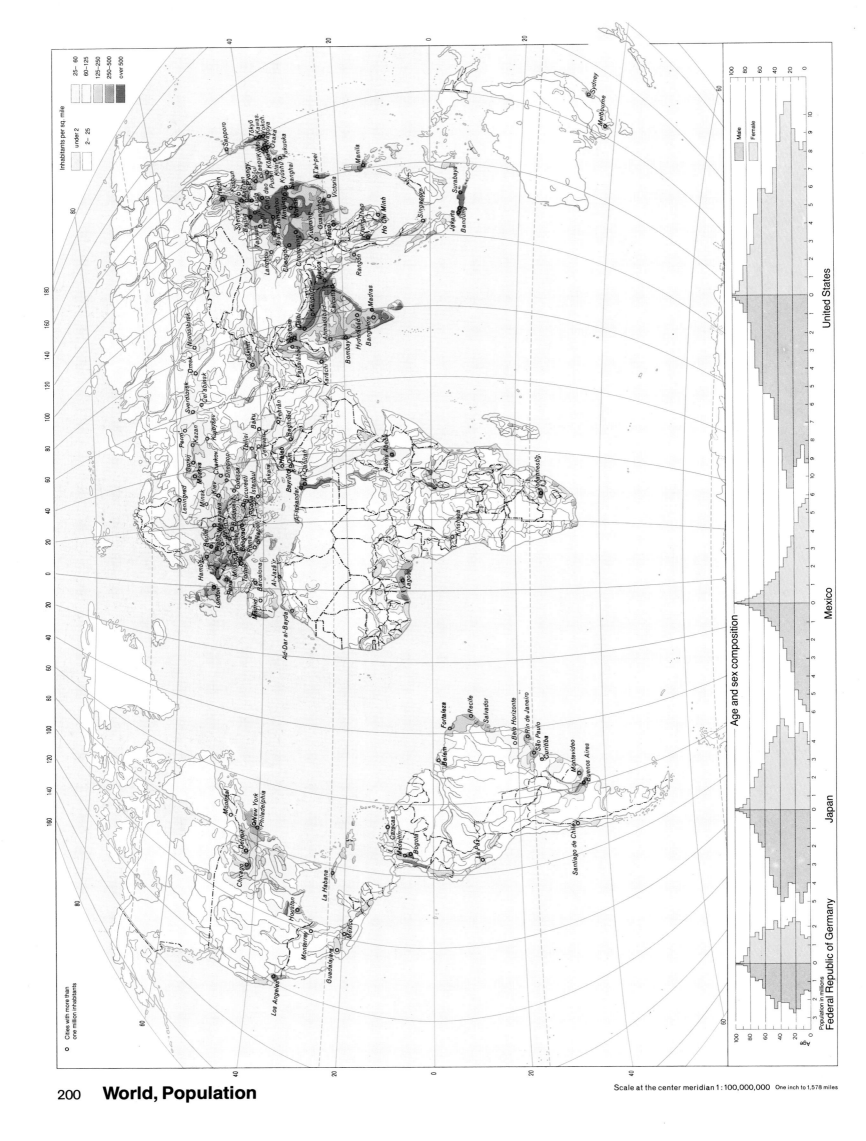

Scale at the center meridian 1 : 100,000,000   One inch to 1,578 miles

Inhabitants per sq. mile

under 2
2– 25
25– 60
60–125
125–250
250–500
over 500

○ Cities with more than one million inhabitants

Age and sex composition

Male
Female

United States

Mexico

Japan

Federal Republic of Germany

Population in millions

Age

Abbreviations of Geographical Names and Terms

General

Bel.	Belyj, -aja -oje,yje	Mal.	Malyj, -aja, -oje	Sred.	Sredne, -ij, -'aja,-eje
Bol.	Bol'šoj, -aja, -oje, ije	Mc	Mac	St.	Sankt
Č.	Český, -á, -é	Nat.	National	S!	Saint
Ea.	East	nat.	national	Sta	Santa
Gd(e)	Grand(e)	Ndo(s)	Nevado(s)	Star.	Staryj, -aja -oje, -yje
Gdes	Grandes	Niž.	Nižnij, -'aja, -eje, -ije	Ste	Sainte
Gr.	Groß, -er, -e, -es	N0	Numero	Sth	South
Gral	General	Nov.	Novo, -yj, -aja -oje	Sto	Santo
G!	Great	Nth	North	Sv.	Sveti, -a, Sväty
Hag.	Hagia	Nva	Nueva	Upp.	Upper
Hág.	Hágios	Nvo	Nuevo	V.	Veliki, -a, -o
Hte	Haute	Pit(e)	Petit(e)	Vel.	Velikij, -aja, -oje
Juž.	Južnyj, -aja, -oje	Pr.	Prince	Vel.'	Vel'ká
		Pres.	Presidente	Verch.	Verchne, -ij, -'aja, -eje, -ije
Kr.	Krasno, -yj, -aja, oje, -yje	Prov.	Provincial	W....	West;
		S....	San	Zap.	Zapadnaja
L.le	Little	Sev.	Severnyj, -aja -oje		

Islands, Landscapes

ad.	adasi	Ie	Isole	o-va	ostrova
Arch.	Archipelago	Ila(s)	Isla(s)	P.	Pulau
arch.	archipelag	(-)In	(-)Inseln, (-inseln)	Pen.	Peninsula
Archip.	Archipiélago			Poj.	Pojezierze
(-)I.	(-)Insel, (-insel)	Is	Islands	p-ov.	poluostrov
I....	Isle	Is.	Îles	P.-p.	Pulau-pulau
....I.	Island	k.	kosa	Res.	Reservation,-e
Î.	Île	Kep.	Kepulauan	Rés.	Réservation
Ia	Ilha	Ld	Land	s.	sima
Ia	Isola	(-)Id(e)	(-)land(e)	Vey	Valley
Ias	Ilhas	Mon.	Monument	y.ad.	yarimada, -si
		o.	ostrov	zapov.	zapovednik

Hydrography

Arr.	Arroio, Arroyo	j.	joki	Rão	Ribeirão
B.	Basin, Bay	Jez.	Jezioro	Rère	Rivière
(-)B.	(-)Bucht, (-bucht)	j:vi	järvi	Res.	Reservoir
Bat.	Batang	Kan.	Kanal; Kanaal	Riba	Ribeira
Can.	Canal	(-)kan.	(-)kanal; -kanaal	Riv.	River
Chan.	Channel	kör.	körfez, -i	-riv.	-rivier
Cr.	Creek	L.	Lago, Lake	...(-)S.	(-)See, (-see)
D.	Danau	Lim.	Limne	Sai	Sungai
Est.	Estero	Lo(a)	Lago(a)	Sd	Sound
Esto	Estrecho	Luna(s)	Laguna(s)	Sei	Sungei
Fj.; -fj.	Fjord; -fjord	n.	nehir, nehri	Sel.	Selat
G.	Gulf	Ou.	Ouèd	Str.	Strait
g.	gawa	oz.	ozero	Tel.	Teluk
Gfe	Golfe	Pass.	Passage	vdchr.	vodochra-nilišče
Gfo	Golfo	prol.	proliv	Wdi	Wadî
gü	gölü	R.	rio	zal.	zaliv

Mountains

A....	Alpes; Alpi	g.	gora	Mts	Monts
...A.	Alpen	Ga	Góra	n.	nos
Aiglle(s)	Aiguille(s)	Geb.	Gebirge	Ndo	Nevado
Akr.	Akrotérion	-geb.	-gebirge	Ör.	Óros
App.	Appennino	Gl.	Glacier	P.,	
Bg.; -bg.	Berg; -berg	Gng	Gunung	Pc(o)	Pic(o)
Bge.; -bge.	Berge; -berge	H.	Hill	Peg.	Pegunungan
Bt	Bukit	h.	hory	per.	pereval
C.	Cape	Hd	Head	Pk(s)	Peak(s)
Cbo	Cabo	Hs	Hills	pla	planina
chr.	chrebet	J.	Jabal	Plau	Plateau
Ci(e)	Col(le)	K.	Kap	ple	planine
Cma	Cima	M.	Monte	pr.	prusmyk
Cno	Corno	m.	mys	Prto	Puerto
Colls	Collines	Mas	Montanhas	Prz.	Przelecz
Cord.	Cordillera	Mgne(s)	Montagne(s)	Pso	Passo
Cpo	Capo	Mt.	Mount	Pt(e)	Point(e)
Cro(s)	Cerro(s)	Mt(i)	Mont(i)	Pta	Punta
Cuch.	Cuchilla	Mtn	Mountain	Pzo	Pizzo
dagl.	daglar, -i	Mts.	Mounts	Ra(s)	Range(s)
Fêt	Forêt	Mts	Mountains	Rca	Rocca

Mountains

Ri.	Ridge	Tng	Tanjung	-w.	-wald
Snia	Serrania	Ván	Volcán	y.	yama
Sra(s)	Sierra(s)	Vol.	Volcano		
Srra	Serra	vozvyš.	vozvyšenn-ost'		

Places

Arr.	Arroio, Arroyo	Hist.	Historical	P.	Port; Pulau
B.	Bad; Ban	-hm.	-heim	Pdg.	Padang
-bg.	-berg	Hqrs.	Headquarters	Ph.	Phum
-bug.	-burg	Hs.	House	Pnte	Puente
-bge.	-berge	-hsn.	-hausen	Prto	Puerto
Bto	Balneario	Hts.	Heights	Pso	Passo
-br(n).	-brück(en)	Jn	Junktion	Pt	Point
Build.	Building	K.	Kuala	Pta	Punta
Cd	Ciudad	-kchn.	-kirchen	Pte	Pointe
Chau	Château	Km	Kilómetro	Pto	Porto
Cle	Castle	Kng	Kampung	R.	Rio
Co.	Country	Kp.	Kompong	Rec.	Recreation
Coll.	College	Kr	Kangkar	S!	Sidi
Cor.	Coronel	-lbn.	-leben	-st.	-stadt
Cr.	Creek	M.	Monte; Mu'o'ng	Stat.	Station
-df.	-dorf	Mem.	Memorial	Tech.	Technical
Eción	Estación	Mgne	Montagne	Univ.	University
-fd	-field	Mt.	Mount	Va	Vila
Frte	Fuerte	Mt(s)	Mont(s)	Vla	Villa
Fs	Falls	Mtn	Mountain	-wd.(e).	-wald(e)
F!(e)	Fort(e)	Mts	Mountains		
Ftin	Fortin	Mus.	Museum		
-gn.	-ingen				

Administration

AK	Alaska	IL	Illinois	OR	Oregon
AL	Alabama	IN	Indiana	PA	Pennsylvania
A(O)	Autonome (Oblast)	Ind.	India	P.D.R.	People's Democratic Republic
AR	Arkansas	Jap.	Japan	Port.	Portugal
Austr.	Australia	KS	Kansas	Reg.	Region
Aut.	Autonomous	KY	Kentucky	Rep.	Republic
AZ	Arizona	LA	Louisiana	RI	Rhode Island
Braz.	Brazil	MA	Massachusetts	S. Afr.	South Africa
CA	California	MD	Maryland	SC	South Carolina
CO	Colorado	ME	Maine		
Col.	Colombia	Mex.	Mexico	SD	South Dakota
C.Rica	Costa Rica	MI	Michigan	S.S.R.	Soviet Socialist Republic
CT	Connecticut	MN	Minnesota		
DC	District of Columbia	MO	Missouri		
		MS	Mississippi	Terr.	Territory, -y, -ies
DE	Delaware	MT	Montana		
Den.	Denmark	NC	North Carolina	TN	Tennessee
Dist.	District	ND	North Dakota	TX	Texas
Ec.	Ecuador	NE	Nebraska	U.K.	United King-dom
E.G.	Equatorial Guinea	Neth.	Netherlands		
		NH	New Hampshire		
Fed.	Federal; Federated	Nic.	Nicaragua	U.S.A.	United States
		NJ	New Jersey	U.S.S.R.	Soviet Union
FL	Florida	NM	New Mexico	UT	Utah
Fr.	France, French	Norw.	Norway	VA	Virginia
GA	Georgia	NV	Nevada	Vietn.	Vietnam
HI	Hawai	NY	New York	VT	Vermont
Hond.	Honduras	N.Z.	New Zealand	WA	Washington
IA	Iowa	OH	Ohio	WI	Wisconsin
ID	Idaho	OK	Oklahoma	WV	West Virginia
				WY	Wyoming

Organizations

ANZUS	Australia-New Zealand-U.S.A. (Tripartite Security Treaty)	NATO	North Atlantic Treaty Organization
ASEAN	Association of South East Asian Nations	OAS	Organization of American States
COMECON	Council of Mutual Economic Aid	OAU	Organization of African Unity
EC	European Community	OPEC	Organization of Petroleum Exporting Countries
EEC	European Economic Community	UNHCR	United Nations High Commissioner for Refugees
EFTA	European Free Trade Association	UNICEF	United Nations Children's Emergency Fund
FAO	Food and Agriculture Organization	UNO	United Nations Organization

Each nation at a glance

Country English name	Country Local name	Capital	Area in sq. km	Area in sq. mi.	Population	Population per sq. km	Population per sq. mi.
AFGHANISTAN	Afghānistān	Kabul	647,497	250,000	18,614,000	29	74
ALBANIA	Shqipëri	Tirana	28,748	11,100	3,022,000	105	272
ALGERIA	Al-Jázá'iriya	Algiers	2,381,741	919,595	22,971,000	10	25
ANDORRA	Andorra	Andorra la Vella	435	175	47,000	104	269
ANGOLA	Angola	Luanda	1,246,700	481,353	8,982,000	7	19
ANTIGUA AND BARBUDA	Antigua and Barbuda	St. John's	442	171	81,000	183	474
ARGENTINA	Argentina	Buenos Aires	2,766,889	1,068,301	31,030,000	11	29
AUSTRALIA	Australia	Canberra	7,686,848	2,967,907	16,133,000	2	5
AUSTRIA	Österreich	Vienna	83,849	32,374	7,573,000	90	234
BAHAMAS	Bahamas	Nassau	13,935	5,380	236,000	17	44
BAHRAIN	Bahrayn	Manama	622	240	412,000	662	1,717
BANGLADESH	Bangladesh	Dhaka	143,998	55,598	112,000,000	699	1,810
BARBADOS	Barbados	Bridgetown	431	166	253,000	587	1,524
BELGIUM	Belgique, België	Brussels	30,513	11,781	9,903,000	325	841
BELIZE	Belize	Belmopan	22,965	8,867	171,000	7	19
BENIN	Bénin	Porto Novo	112,622	43,484	4,040,000	36	93
BHUTAN	Druk-Yul	Thimphu	47,000	18,147	1,447,000	31	80
BOLIVIA	Bolivia	La Paz; Sucre	1,098,581	424,164	6,547,000	6	15
BOTSWANA	Botswana	Gaborone	581,730	224,607	1,130,000	2	5
BRAZIL	Brasil	Brasilia	8,511,965	3,286,487	138,493,000	16	42
BRUNEI	Brunei	Bandar Seri Begawan	5,765	2,226	244,000	42	110
BULGARIA	Bâlgarija	Sofia	110,912	42,823	8,959,000	81	209
BURKINA FASO	Burkina Faso	Ouagadougou	274,200	105,869	6,750,000	25	64
BURMA	Myanmā Naingngandaw	Rangoon	676,552	261,218	39,411,000	58	151
BURUNDI	Burundi	Bujumbura	27,834	10,747	4,852,000	174	451
CAMBODIA	Kampuchéa	Phnom Penh	181,035	69,898	7,492,000	41	107
CAMEROON	Cameroun	Yaoundé	475,442	183,569	10,446,000	22	57
CANADA	Canada	Ottawa	9,976,139	3,851,807	25,591,000	3	7
CAPE VERDE	Cabo Verde	Praia	4,033	1,557	333,000	83	214
CENTRAL AFRICAN REPUBLIC	République Centrafricaine	Bangui	622,984	240,535	2,740,000	4	11
CHAD	Tchad	N'Djamena	1,284,000	495,755	5,139,000	4	10
CHILE	Chile	Santiago de Chile	756,945	292,258	12,466,000	16	43
CHINA	Zhonghua	Beijing	9,560,980	3,691,513	1,069,600,000	110	285
COLOMBIA	Colombia	Bogotá	1,138,914	439,737	29,190,000	26	66
COMOROS	Comoros	Moroni	2,171	838	481,000	222	574
CONGO	Congo	Brazzaville	342,000	132,047	1,787,000	5	14
COSTA RICA	Costa Rica	San José	50,700	19,575	2,666,000	53	136
CUBA	Cuba	Havana	110,861	42,804	10,268,000	93	240
CYPRUS	Kibris, Kypriaki	Nicosia	9,251	3,572	673,000	73	188
CZECHOSLOVAKIA	Ceskoslovenska	Prague	127,869	49,370	15,530,000	121	315
DENMARK	Danmark	Copenhagen	43,069	16,627	5,124,000	119	308
DJIBOUTI	Djibouti	Djibouti	21,783	8,410	456,000	21	54
DOMINICA	Dominica	Roseau	751	290	77,000	103	266
DOMINICAN REPUBLIC	República Dominicana	Santo Domingo	48,734	18,816	6,416,000	132	341
ECUADOR	Ecuador	Quito	283,561	109,483	9,647,000	34	88
EGYPT	Ar-Misr	Cairo	1,001,449	386,661	49,600,000	50	128
EL SALVADOR	El Salvador	San Salvador	21,041	8,124	4,913,000	233	605
EQUATORIAL GUINEA	Guinea Ecuatorial	Malabo	28,051	10,831	401,000	14	37
ETHIOPIA	Ityopya	Addis Ababa	1,221,900	471,778	43,930,000	36	93
FIJI	Fiji	Suva	18,274	7,056	715,000	39	101
FINLAND	Suomi, Finland	Helsinki	337,032	130,129	4,929,000	15	38
FRANCE	France	Paris	547,026	211,208	55,627,000	102	263
GABON	Gabon	Libreville	267,667	103,347	1,171,000	4	11
GAMBIA	Gambia	Banjul	11,295	4,361	662,000	59	143
GERMAN DEMOCRATIC REPUBLIC	Deutsche Demokratische Republik	Berlin (East)	108,333	41,828	16,624,000	153	397
GERMANY, FEDERAL REPUBLIC OF	Bundesrepublik Deutschland	Bonn	248,709	96,027	61,170,000	246	637
GHANA	Ghana	Accra	238,537	92,100	14,045,000	59	152
GREECE	Elliniki Dimokratia	Athens	131,944	50,944	9,966,000	76	196
GRENADA	Grenada	St. George's	344	133	113,000	328	850
GUATEMALA	Guatemala	Guatemala City	108,889	42,042	8,195,000	75	195
GUINEA	République de Guinée	Conakry	245,857	94,926	6,225,000	25	66
GUINEA-BISSAU	Guiné Bissau	Bissau	36,125	13,948	906,000	25	65
GUYANA	Guyana	Georgetown	214,969	83,000	791,000	4	10
HAITI	Haïti	Port-au-Prince	27,750	10,714	5,358,000	193	500
HONDURAS	Honduras	Tegucigalpa	112,088	43,277	4,514,000	40	104
HUNGARY	Magyar Nepköztärasäg	Budapest	93,033	35,920	10,611,000	114	295
ICELAND	Island	Reykjavík	103,000	39,769	241,000	2	6
INDIA	India	New Delhi	3,287,590	1,269,345	833,000,000	233	604
INDONESIA	Indonesia	Jakarta	1,904,569	735,358	187,000,000	88	227
IRAN	Īrān	Teheran	1,648,000	636,296	44,700,000	27	70
IRAQ	Al-'Iraqia	Baghdad	434,924	167,925	16,450,000	38	98
IRELAND	Éire	Dublin	70,284	27,137	3,537,000	50	130
ISRAEL	Medinat Yisrael	Jerusalem	20,770	8,019	4,439,000	214	554
ITALY	Itàlia	Rome	301,225	116,304	57,331,000	190	493
IVORY COAST	Côte d'Ivoire	Yamoussoukro	322,463	124,504	10,165,000	32	82
JAMAICA	Jamaica	Kingston	10,991	4,244	2,372,000	216	559
JAPAN	Nippon	Tokyo	377,708	145,834	122,092,000	323	837
JORDAN	Al-Urduniya	Amman	97,740	37,738	3,656,000	37	97
KENYA	Kenya	Nairobi	582,646	224,961	23,700,000	36	94
KIRIBATI	Kiribati	Bairiki	728	281	65,000	89	231
KOREA, NORTH	Chosŏon	P'yongyang	120,538	46,540	20,883,000	173	449
KOREAN, SOUTH	Taehan Ming'uk	Seoul	98,484	38,025	42,082,000	427	1,107
KUWAIT	Al-Kuwayt	Kuwait	17,818	6,880	1,873,000	105	272
LAOS	Lao	Vientiane	236,800	91,429	4,218,000	18	46
LEBANON	Lubnaniya	Beirut	10,452	4,036	2,707,000	259	671
LESOTHO	Lesotho	Maseru	30,355	11,720	1,559,000	51	133
LIBERIA	Liberia	Monrovia	111,369	43,000	2,221,000	20	52
LIBYA	Lībīyā	Tripoli	1,759,540	679,362	3,742,000	2	6
LIECHTENSTEIN	Liechtenstein	Vaduz	157	61	28,000	178	459
LUXEMBOURG	Luxembourg	Luxembourg	2,586	998	367,000	142	368
MADAGASCAR	Madagascar	Antananarivo	587,041	226,658	10,303,000	18	45
MALAWI	Malawi	Lilongwe	118,484	45,747	7,279,000	61	159

English name	Country Local name	Capital	Area in sq. km	in sq. mi.	Population	Population per sq. km	sq. mi.
MALAYSIA	Malaysia	Kuala Lumpur	329,749	127,317	16,109,000	49	127
MALDIVES	Maldives	Male	298	115	189,000	634	1,643
MALI	Mali	Bamako	1,240,000	478,766	8,438,000	7	18
MALTA	Malta	Valletta	316	122	383,000	1,212	3,139
MARSHALL ISLANDS	Marshall Islands	Majuro	181	70	35,000	193	500
MAURITANIA	Mawrītānīyah	Nouakchott	1,030,700	397,955	1,946,000	2	5
MAURITIUS	Mauritius	Port Louis	2,045	790	1,029,000	503	1,303
MEXICO	México	México City	1,972,547	761,604	88,087,000	41	107
MICRONESIA	Micronesia	Ponape	702	271	88,000	125	325
MONACO	Monaco	Monaco-ville	1.49	0.58	27,000	18,121	46,552
MONGOLIA	Mongol Ard Uls	Ulan Bator	1,565,000	604,250	1,940,000	1	3
MOROCCO	Al-Maghribia	Rabat	446,550	172,414	22,476,000	50	130
MOZAMBIQUE	Moçambique	Maputo	801,590	309,496	14,174,000	18	46
NAURU	Nauru	Yaren	21	8	8,000	381	1,000
NEPAL	Nēpāl	Katmandu	140,797	54,362	17,131,000	122	315
NETHERLANDS	Nederlanden	Amsterdam	40,844	15,770	14,661,000	359	930
NEW ZEALAND	New Zealand	Wellington	268,676	103,736	3,321,000	12	32
NICARAGUA	Nicaragua	Managua	130,000	50,193	3,385,000	26	67
NIGER	Niger	Niamey	1,269,000	489,963	6,698,000	5	14
NIGERIA	Nigeria	Lagos	923,768	356,669	115,152,000	107	276
NORWAY	Norge	Oslo	324,219	125,182	4,169,000	13	33
OMAN	'Umān	Muscat	212,457	82,032	2,000,000	9	24
PAKISTAN	Pākistān	Islamabad	796,095	307,374	110,000,000	125	323
PALAU	Belau	Koror	497	192	15,000	30	78
PANAMA	Panamá	Panama	77,092	29,765	2,227,000	29	75
PAPUA NEW GUINEA	Papua New Guinea	Port Moresby	461,691	178,260	3,400,000	7	19
PARAGUAY	Paraguay	Asunción	406,752	157,048	3,807,000	9	24
PERU	Peru	Lima	1,285,216	496,224	20,207,000	16	41
PHILIPPINES	Pilipinas	Manila	300,000	115,831	56,004,000	187	483
POLAND	Polska	Warsaw	312,677	120,725	37,664,000	120	312
PORTUGAL	Portugal	Lisbon	92,082	35,553	10,289,000	112	289
QATAR	Qatar	Doha	11,000	4,247	335,000	30	79
ROMANIA	România	Bucharest	237,500	91,699	23,177,000	98	253
RWANDA	Rwanda	Kigali	26,338	10,169	6,275,000	238	617
ST. CHRISTOPHER-NEVIS	Saint Christopher-Nevis	Basseterre	261	101	47,000	180	465
ST. LUCIA	Saint Lucia	Castries	616	238	132,000	214	555
ST. VINCENT	Saint Vincent	Kingstown	388	150	105,000	271	700
SAMOA (WESTERN)	Samoa	Apia	2,842	1,097	164,000	58	149
SAN MARINO	San Marino	San Marino	61	24	22,000	361	917
SÃO TOMÉ AND PRINCIPE	São Tomé e Principe	São Tomé	964	372	110,000	114	296
SAUDI ARABIA	Al-'Arabiyat as-Sā'ūdīyah	Riyadh	2,149,690	830,000	13,612,000	6	16
SENEGAL	Sénégal	Dakar	196,192	75,750	6,614,000	34	87
SEYCHELLES	Seychelles	Victoria	280	108	67,000	239	620
SIERRA LEONE	Sierra Leone	Freetown	71,740	27,699	3,670,000	51	132
SINGAPORE	Singapore	Singapore	581	224	2,613,000	4,497	11,665
SOLOMON ISLANDS	Solomon Islands	Honiara	28,446	10,983	281,000	10	26
SOMALIA	Somaliya	Mogadishu	637,657	246,201	4,760,000	7	19
SOUTH AFRICA	Suid-Afrika	Pretoria	1,221,037	471,445	33,221,000	27	70
SOVIET UNION	Sojuz Sovetskich Socialisti'ceskich Respublik	Moscow	22,402,200	8,649,534	284,000,000	13	33
SPAIN	España	Madrid	504,782	194,897	38,853,000	77	199
SRI LANKA	Srī Lanka	Colombo	65,610	25,332	16,117,000	246	636
SUDAN	As-Sūdan	Khartoum	2,505,813	967,499	22,178,000	9	23
SURINAME	Suriname	Paramaribo	163,265	63,037	380,000	2	6
SWAZILAND	Swaziland	Mbabane	17,363	6,704	676,000	39	101
SWEDEN	Sverige	Stockholm	449,964	173,732	8,369,000	19	48
SWITZERLAND	Schweiz, Suisse, Svizzera	Bern	41,293	15,943	6,498,000	157	408
SYRIA	Souriya	Damascus	185,180	71,498	10,612,000	57	148
TAIWAN	Taiwan	Taipeh	35,981	13,892	19,542,000	543	1,407
TANZANIA	Tanzania	Dar-es-Salaam	945,087	364,900	22,462,000	24	62
THAILAND	Muang Thai	Bangkok	514,000	198,456	53,605,000	104	270
TOGO	Togo	Lomé	56,785	21,925	3,052,000	54	139
TONGA	Tonga	Nuku'alofa	699	270	111,000	159	411
TRINIDAD AND TOBAGO	Trinidad and Tobago	Port of Spain	5,128	1,980	1,204,000	235	608
TUNISIA	Tūnisīyah	Tunis	163,610	63,170	7,465,000	46	118
TURKEY	Türkiye	Ankara	780,576	301,382	55,400,000	64	167
TUVALU	Tuvalu	Funafuti	158	61	8,000	51	131
UGANDA	Uganda	Kampala	236,036	91,134	16,018,000	68	176
UNITED ARAB EMIRATES	Al-Imārāt al-'Arabīyath al-Muttahidah	Abu Dhabi	63,600	32,278	1,384,000	17	43
UNITED KINGDOM	Great Britain and Northern Ireland	London	244,046	94,227	56,763,000	233	602
UNITED STATES	United States	Washington, D.C.	9,372,614	3,618,785	247,498,000	26	67
URUGUAY	Uruguay	Montevideo	176,215	68,037	2,982,000	17	44
VANUATU	Vanuatu	Vila	14,763	5,700	143,000	10	25
VATICAN CITY	Città del Vaticano	-	0.44	0.17	1,000	2,273	5,882
VENEZUELA	Venezuela	Caracas	912,050	352,144	17,791,000	20	51
VIETNAM	Viêt Nam	Hanoi	329,556	127,242	60,919,000	185	479
YEMEN (NORTH)	al-Jumhuriyat al-Arabiyah	San'a	195,000	75,290	6,937,000	48	123
YEMEN, PEOPLE'S DEMOCRATIC REPUBLIC OF	Al-Yamaniyah Jumhuriyat Al-Yamaniyah	Aden	332,968	128,560	2,400,000	7	18
YUGOSLAVIA	Jugoslavija	Belgrade	255,804	98,766	23,271,000	91	236
ZAIRE	Zaïre	Kinshasa	2,345,409	905,567	30,850,000	13	34
ZAMBIA	Zambia	Lusaka	752,614	290,586	6,896,000	9	24
ZIMBABWE	Zimbabwe	Harare	390,580	150,804	8,406,000	22	56

Index

The index contains all the names that appear on the metropolitan area, country, regional, and world maps. It is ordered alphabetically. The umlauts ä, ö, and ü have been treated as the letters a, o, and u, and the ligatures æ and œ as ae and oe, while the German ß is alphabetized as ss.

The first number after the name entry indicates the page or double page where the name being looked up is to be found. The letters and numbers after the page reference designate the grid in which the name is located or those grids through which the name extends.

The names that have been abbreviated on the maps are listed unabbreviated in the index. Only with U.S. place names have the official abbreviations been inserted according to common U.S. practice, e.g. Washington, D.C. The alphabetic sequence includes the prefix, e.g. Fort, Saint.

In order to facilitate the search for names consisting of more than one element, these have consistently been given double entries in the index, e.g. Isle of Wight, and Wight, Isle of —; Le Havre, and Havre, Le-.

To a large extent official second forms, language variants, renamings, and other secondary designations are recorded in the index, followed by the names as they appear on the map, e.g. Persia = Iran, Venice = Venézia, Moscow = Moskva.

To differentiate identical names of features located in various countries, motor vehicle nationality letters for the respective countries have been added in brackets following these names. A complete listing of abbreviations is shown below.

A	Austria	H	Hungary	RIM	Mauritania
ADN	People's Democratic Republic of Yemen	HK	Hong Kong	RL	Lebanon
		HV	Burkina Faso	RM	Madagascar
AFG	Afghanistan	I	Italy	RMM	Mali
AL	Albania	IL	Israel	RN	Niger
AND	Andorra	IND	India	RO	Romania
AUS	Australia	IR	Iran	ROK	South Korea
B	Belgium	IRL	Ireland	ROU	Uruguay
BD	Bangladesh	IRQ	Iraq	RP	Philippines
BDS	Barbados	IS	Iceland	RSM	San Marino
BG	Bulgaria	J	Japan	RU	Burundi
BH	Belize	JA	Jamaica	RWA	Rwanda
BOL	Bolivia	JOR	Jordan	S	Sweden
BR	Brazil	K	Cambodia	SD	Swaziland
BRN	Bahrain	KWT	Kuwait	SF	Finland
BRU	Brunei	L	Luxembourg	SGP	Singapore
BS	Bahamas	LAO	Laos	SME	Suriname
BUR	Burma	LAR	Libya	SN	Senegal
C	Cuba	LB	Liberia	SP	Somalia
CDN	Canada	LS	Lesotho	SU	Soviet Union
CH	Switzerland	M	Malta	SUDAN	Sudan
CI	Ivory Coast	MA	Morocco	SY	Seychelles
CL	Sri Lanka	MAL	Malaysia	SYR	Syria
CO	Colombia	MC	Monaco	T	Thailand
CR	Costa Rica	MEX	Mexico	TG	Togo
CS	Czechoslovakia	MS	Mauritius	TJ	China
CY	Cyprus	MW	Malawi	TN	Tunisia
D	Federal Republic of Germany	N	Norway	TR	Turkey
DDR	German Democratic Republic	NA	Netherlands Antilles	TT	Trinidad and Tobago
DK	Denmark	NIC	Nicaragua	USA	United States
DOM	Dominican Republic	NL	Netherlands	V	Vatican City
DY	Benin	NZ	New Zealand	VN	Vietnam
DZ	Algeria	P	Portugal	WAG	Gambia
E	Spain	PA	Panama	WAL	Sierra Leone
EAK	Kenya	PAK	Pakistan	WAN	Nigeria
EAT	Tanzania	PE	Peru	WD	Dominica
EAU	Uganda	PL	Poland	WG	Grenada
EC	Ecuador	PNG	Papua New Guinea	WL	Saint Lucia
ES	El Salvador	PY	Paraguay	WS	Samoa
ET	Egypt	Q	Qatar	WV	Saint Vincent
ETH	Ethiopia	RA	Argentina	Y	Yemen
F	France	RB	Botswana	YU	Yugoslavia
FJI	Fiji	RC	Taiwan	YV	Venezuela
FL	Liechtenstein	RCA	Central African Republic	Z	Zambia
GB	United Kingdom	RCB	Congo	ZA	South Africa
GCA	Guatemala	RCH	Chile	ZRE	Zaire
GH	Ghana	RFC	Cameroon	ZW	Zimbabwe
GR	Greece	RH	Haiti		
GUY	Guyana	RI	Indonesia		

A

Aachen 124 C 3
Aalen 124 E 4
Aalesund = Ålesund 114-115 AB 6
A'alī an-Nīl 194-195 KL 7
Äänekoski 114-115 L 6
Aar, De — 198 D 8
Aarau 124 D 5
Aare 124 D 5
Aavasaksa 114-115 KL 4

Aba [WAN] 194-195 F 7
Aba [ZRE] 198 F 1
Abā ar Rūs, Sabkhat — 160-161 GH 6
Abacaxis, Rio — 98-99 J 7
Abaco Island, Great — 58-59 L 6
Abad 166-167 E 3
Ābādān 160-161 F 4
Ābādeh 160-161 G 4
Abadlah 194-195 D 2
Abaetetuba 98-99 O 5
Abagnar Qi = Xilin Hot 166-167 M 3
Abaí 103 E 3
Abaiang 178 H 2
Abajo Peak 74-75 J 4
Abakan 154-155 R 7
Aban 154-155 S 6
Abancay 98-99 E 7
Abangarit, In — 194-195 F 5
Abā Sa'ūd 160-161 EF 7
Abashiri 166-167 RS 3
Abashiriwan 170-171 d 1-2
Abasiri = Abashiri 166-167 RS 3
Abasolo 86-87 K 7
Abau 174-175 N 9
Abay 194-195 M 6
Abaya 194-195 M 7
Abaza 154-155 R 7
Aba Zangzu Zizhizhou 166-167 J 5
Abbeville 132-133 HJ 3
Abbeville, AL 78-79 G 5
Abbeville, GA 80-81 E 4-5
Abbeville, LA 78-79 CD 5
Abbeville, SC 80-81 E 3
Abbey Peak 182-183 HJ 2
Abbots Bromley 116-117 K 8
Abbotsbury 116-117 J 10
Abbotsford 66-67 BC 1
Abbotsford, WI 70-71 E 3
Abbottabad = Ebuṭṭābād 160-161 L 4
'Abd al Kūrī 160-161 G 8
Abdulino 154-155 J 7
Abe, Kelay — 194-195 N 6
Abéché 194-195 J 6
Abécher = Abéché 194-195 J 6
Abed-Larache, El — = Al-Ādib al-'Arsh 194-195 F 3
Abee 48 L 2
Abeg, In- 194-195 D 4
Abeløya 114-115 n 5
Abemama 178 H 2
Abengourou 194-195 D 7
Åbenrå 114-115 C 10
Abeokuta 194-195 E 7
Aberaeron 116-117 G 8
Abercorn = Mbala 198 F 3
Abercrombie, ND 68-69 H 2
Aberdare 116-117 H 9
Aberdare Mountains 198 G 1-2
Aberdaron 116-117 G 8
Aberdeen, ID 66-67 G 4
Aberdeen, MD 72-73 H 5
Aberdeen, MS 78-79 E 4
Aberdeen, NC 80-81 G 3
Aberdeen, SD 58-59 G 2
Aberdeen, WA 58-59 B 2
Aberdeen [CDN] 49 EF 4
Aberdeen [GB] 116-117 JK 3
Aberdeen [ZA] 198 D 8
Aberdeen Lake 46-47 R 5
Aberdovey 116-117 G 8
Aberfeldy 116-117 GH 4
Aberfoyle 116-117 G 4
Abergavenny 116-117 HJ 9
Abernathy, TX 76-77 D 6
Aberporth 116-117 G 8
Abersychan 116-117 HJ 9
Abert, Lake — 66-67 CD 4
Abertillery 116-117 H 9
Aberystwyth 116-117 G 8
Abez' 154-155 L 4
Abhā 160-161 E 7
Abha Mhór, An — 116-117 C 8
Abiaḍ, Râss el — = Rā's al-Abyaḍ 194-195 FG 1
'Abīd, Umm al- 194-195 H 3
Ābid al-'Arsh, Al- 194-195 F 3
Abidjan 194-195 CD 7
Abijan = Abidjan 194-195 CD 7
Abilene, KS 68-69 H 6
Abilene, TX 58-59 FG 5
Abingdon 116-117 K 9
Abingdon, IL 70-71 E 5
Abingdon, VA 80-81 EF 2
Abingdon = Isla Pinta 98-99 A 4
Abington 116-117 H 5
Abiquiu, NM 76-77 A 4
Abisko 114-115 H 3
Abitibi, Lake — 46-47 UV 8
Abitibi River 46-47 U 7-8
Abkhaz Autonomous Soviet Socialist Republic = 6 ◁ 142-143 7
Abnūb 199 B 4
Abo 170-171 H 1
Åbo = Turku 114-115 K 7
Aboisso 194-195 D 7
Abomé = Abomey 194-195 E 7
Abomey 194-195 E 7
Abong-Mbang 194-195 G 8
Aborigen, pik — 154-155 cd 5
Abou-Deïa 194-195 H 6
Aboyne 116-117 J 3
'Abr, Al — 160-161 F 7
Abraham Bay 52-53 p 6
Abraham Lincoln National Historical Park 70-71 H 7
Abrantes [P] 132-133 CD 9
Abra Pampa 103 CD 2
Abreojos, Punta — 58-59 CD 6
'Abrī 194-195 L 4
Abrolhos, Arquipélago dos — 98-99 M 8
Abruzzi 138-139 EF 4
Absaroka Range 58-59 D 2-E 3
Absarokee, MT 68-69 B 3
Abu 160-161 L 6
Abu, Jabal — 142-143 G 8
Abū al-Maṭāmīr 199 AB 2
Abū 'Aweiqīla = Abū 'Uwayjīlah 199 CD 2
Abū Ballāṣ 194-195 K 4
Abū Ḍahr, Jabal — 199 D 6
Abū Dārah, Rā's — 199 E 6
Abū Darbah 199 C 3
Abū Dhi'āb, Jabal — 199 D 5
Abū Durba = Abū Darbah 199 C 3
Abufari 98-99 G 7
Abū Ġashwah, Rā's — 160-161 G 8
Abū Ḥadd, Wādī — 199 D 7
Abū Ḥamad 194-195 L 5
Abū Ḥamāmīd, Jabal — 199 D 5
Abū Ḥarbah, Jabal — 199 C 4
Abū Hujar 194-195 LM 6
Abuja 194-195 F 7
Abū Jābirah 194-195 K 6
Abū Jamal 194-195 M 5
Abū Jamal, Jabal — 194-195 M 6
Abū Jurdī, Jabal — 199 D 6
Abū Kabīr 199 B 2
Abū Kamāl 160-161 DE 4
Abū Khārga, Wâdî — = Wādī Abū Kharjah 199 BC 3
Abū Kharjah, Wādī — 199 BC 3
Abukuma-sammyaku 170-171 N 4
Abū Marw, Wādī — 199 C 6
Abū Minqār, Bi'r — 194-195 K 3
Abū Muḥarrik, Ghurd — 194-195 KL 3
Abu Mukharik Dunes = Gurd Abu Muḥarik 194-195 KL 3
Abunã 98-99 FG 6
Abunã, Rio — 98-99 F 7
Abunai 98-99 E 5
Abū Qīr 199 B 2
Abū Qīr, Khalīj — 199 B 2
Abū Qurqāṣ 199 B 4
Abū Sa'fah, Bi'r — 199 D 6
Abu Simbil = Abu Sunbul 194-195 L 4
Abū Sinbil = Abu Sunbul 194-195 L 4
Abu Sunbul 194-195 L 4
Abū Tīj 194-195 L 3
Abū 'Uwayjīlah 199 CD 2
Abū Zabad 194-195 K 6
Abū Ẓabī 160-161 G 6
Abū Zanīmah 194-195 L 3
Abū Zawal, Bi'r — 199 C 4
Abū Zenīma = Abū Zanīmah 194-195 L 3
Abyad 194-195 K 6
Abyaḍ, Ar-Rā's al- 194-195 A 4
Abyaḍ, Rā's al- 194-195 FG 1
Abyei 194-195 K 7
Abymes, les — 58-59 O 8
Abyssinia = Ethiopia 194-195 MN 7

Academy of Sciences 83 I ab 2
Acadia National Park 72-73 M 2
Acadie 46-47 XY 8
Acailândia 98-99 P 7
Acaill 116-117 A 7
Acajutla 58-59 HJ 9
Acala, TX 76-77 B 7
Acámbaro 58-59 FG 7
Acampamento Grande 98-99 M 4
Acandí 98-99 D 3
Acapetagua 86-87 O 10
Acaponeta 58-59 EF 7
Acapulco de Juárez 58-59 FG 8
Acapuzal, Serra do — 98-99 MN 5
Acará 98-99 K 5
Acará, Cachoeira — 98-99 J 7
Acaraí, Serra — 98-99 H 4
Acaraú 98-99 LM 5
Acari, Rio — 98-99 J 7-8
Acarigua 98-99 F 3
Acayucan 86-87 N 8-9
Accomac, VA 80-81 J 2
Accra 194-195 DE 7
Accrington 116-117 J 7
Aceh = 1 ◁ 174-175 C 6
Achacachi 98-99 F 8
Achaguas 98-99 F 3
Achaïa 138-139 JK 6
Achalciche 142-143 H 7
Achao 103 B 6
Acharnaí 138-139 K 6
Achegour 194-195 G 5
Achelôos 138-139 J 6
Acheng 166-167 O 2
Acherusia = Zonguldak 160-161 C 2
Achigan 70-71 HJ 2
Achigh Köl 166-167 F 4
Achill Head = Ceann Acla 116-117 A 7
Achill Island = Acaill 116-117 A 7
Achtuba 142-143 J 6
Achtubinsk 142-143 J 6
Achtyrka 142-143 F 5
Acı göl 142-143 EF 8
Ačinsk 154-155 R 6
Acireale 138-139 F 7
Ackerly, TX 76-77 D 6
Ackerman, MS 78-79 E 4
Ackley, IA 70-71 D 4
Acklins Island 58-59 LM 7
Acla, Ceann — 116-117 A 7
Acle 116-117 h 6
Acme, LA 78-79 D 5
Acme, NM 76-77 B 6
Acme, TX 76-77 E 5
Acomayo 98-99 E 7
Aconcagua 103 C 4
Acopiara 98-99 M 6
Açores 26-27 H 4
Acotipa 98-99 L 4
Acoyapa 88-89 D 9
Àcqui Terme 138-139 C 3
Acraman, Lake — 182-183 FG 6
Acre 98-99 EF 6
Acre, Rio — 98-99 F 6
Acri 138-139 G 6
Actatlán de Osorio 86-87 LM 8
Acton 72-73 F 3
Acton, CA 74-75 D 5
Acton, MT 68-69 B 3
Acton Vale 72-73 K 2
Actopan 86-87 KL 6-7
Açú, Rio — = Rio Piranhas 98-99 M 6
Acuña, Villa — 76-77 D 8
Acworth, GA 80-81 D 3

Ada, MN 68-69 H 2
Ada, OH 72-73 E 4
Ada, OK 58-59 G 5
Ada [GH] 194-195 E 7
'Adabīyah, Rā's — 199 C 3
Adado, Raas — 194-195 b 1
Adafir 194-195 BC 5
Adair, Bahía del — 86-87 CD 2
Adairsville, GA 78-79 G 3
Adak, AK 52-53 u 7
Adak Island 30 D 36
Adak Strait 52-53 u 7
Adale 194-195 b 3
Adalia = Antalya 160-161 C 3
Ādam 160-161 H 6
Adam, Monte — = Mount Adam 103 DE 8
Adam, Mount — 103 DE 8
Adama = Nazrēt 194-195 M 7
Adamana, AZ 74-75 HJ 5
Adamantina 98-99 JK 9
Adamaoua 194-195 G 7
Adamaua = Adamaoua 194-195 G 7
Adamello 138-139 D 2
Adamovka 142-143 LM 5
Adam Peak 66-67 E 5
Adams, MA 72-73 K 3
Adams, ND 68-69 GH 1
Adams, NE 68-69 H 5
Adams, NY 72-73 HJ 3
Adams, OK 76-77 D 4
Adams, Cape — 31 B 30-31
Adams, Mount — 58-59 B 2
Adams Island 31 D 17
Adams Lake 48 H 4
Adam's Peak = Samānaḷakanda 160-161 N 9
Adams River 48 H 4
Adamsville, AL 78-79 F 4
Adamsville, TN 78-79 E 3
Adamsville, TX 76-77 E 7
'Adan 160-161 F 8
Adapazarı 160-161 C 2
Adare = Āth Dara 116-117 C 8
Adare, Cape — 31 B 18
Adavale 182-183 HJ 5
Adda 138-139 C 3
Addâr, Râss — = Rā's aṭ-Ṭīb 194-195 G 1
Addis Alem = Alem Gena 194-195 M 7
Addison, NY 72-73 H 3
Addison = Webster Springs, WV 72-73 F 5
Addu Atoll 36 a 3
Addy, WA 66-67 E 1
Adel, GA 80-81 E 5
Adel, IA 70-71 C 5
Adel, OR 66-67 D 4
Adelaide [AUS] 182-183 GH 6-7
Adelaide Island 31 C 29-30
Adelaide Peninsula 46-47 R 4
Adelaide River 182-183 F 2
Adelanto, CA 74-75 E 5
Adélia 98-99 C 8
Adélie, Terre — 31 C 14-15
Adélie Land = Terre Adélie 31 C 14-15
Ademuz 132-133 G 8
Aden, NM 76-77 A 6
Aden = 'Adan 160-161 EF 8
Aden, Gulf of — 160-161 F 8
Adghar = Adrār 194-195 DE 3
Adhar Shahr 142-143 J 8
Adi, Pulau — 174-175 K 7
Adib al-'Arsh, Al- 194-195 F 3
Àdige 138-139 D 3
'Adi Grat 194-195 MN 6
Adi Kaye = Adi Keyih 194-195 MN 6
Adi Keyih 194-195 MN 6
Adin, CA 66-67 C 5
Adirondack Mountains 58-59 M 3
Adīs Abeba 194-195 M 7
Adīs Dera 194-195 M 6
'Adī Ugrī 194-195 M 6
Adıyaman 142-143 G 8
Adjarian Autonomous Soviet Socialist Republic = 8 ◁ 142-143 H 7
Adjuntas, Presa de las — 86-87 LM 6
Adler, Soči- 142-143 G 7
Adler Planetarium 83 II b 1
Admar, Irq — 194-195 F 4
Admiral 49 D 6
Admiralty Gulf 182-183 DE 2
Admiralty Inlet [CDN] 46-47 TU 3
Admiralty Inlet [USA] 66-67 B 1-2
Admiralty Island 46-47 K 6
Admiralty Islands 174-175 N 7
Admiralty Range 31 B 17
Admont 124 G 5
Adonara, Pulau — 174-175 H 8
Ādoni 160-161 M 7
Adour 132-133 G 7
Adra [E] 132-133 F 10
Adramúttion = Edremit 160-161 B 3
Adrār 194-195 DE 3
Adraskan, Däryā-ye — = Hārūt Rōd 160-161 J 4
Adré 194-195 J 6
Adrī 194-195 G 3
Àdria 138-139 E 3
Adrian, MI 70-71 H 5
Adrian, MN 70-71 C 4
Adrian, OR 66-67 E 4
Adrian, TX 76-77 C 5
Adrianopel = Edirne 160-161 B 2
Adriatic Sea 110-111 LM 7
Adua 174-175 J 7
Adua = Adwa 194-195 M 6
Adusa 198 E 1
Aduwa = Adwa 194-195 M 6
Adventure Bank 138-139 DE 7
Adwa 194-195 M 6
Adwick le Street 116-117 KL 7
Adyča 154-155 a 4
Adygei Autonomous Region = 1 ◁ 142-143 H 7
Adž Bogd uul 166-167 GH 3

Aegean Sea 110-111 NO 8
Aegina, Gulf of — = Sarōnikós Kólpos 138-139 K 7
Ærø 114-115 D 10
Aetna, KS 76-77 E 4

Afal, Wādī al- = Wādī al-'Ifāl 199 D 3
Afallah 194-195 B 5
Afántu 138-139 N 7
Afars et Issas = Djibouti 194-195 N 6
Afghānestān 160-161 J 4-L 3
Afgooye 194-195 ab 3
'Afif 160-161 E 6
Afikpo 194-195 F 7
Aflāj, Al — 160-161 F 6
Afmadoow 194-195 N 8
Afogados da Ingàzeira 98-99 M 6
Afognak, AK 52-53 L 7
Afognak Island 46-47 F 6
Afon Teifi 116-117 G 8
Africa 26-27 J-L 5
African Islands 188-189 N 9
Afton, IA 70-71 C 5
Afton, OK 76-77 G 4
Afton, WY 66-67 H 4
Afuá 98-99 J 5
Afyonkarahisar 160-161 C 3

Aga = Aginskoje 154-155 VW 7
Agadem 194-195 G 5
Agades = Agadèz 194-195 F 5
Agadèz 194-195 F 5
Agādīr 194-195 BC 2
Agadyr' 154-155 N 8
Agaie 194-195 F 7
Agalega Islands 188-189 N 10
Agalta, Sierra de — 58-59 J 8-9
Agan 154-155 O 5
Agapa 154-155 Q 3
Agar, SD 68-69 F 3
Agarā = Agra 160-161 M 5
Agartala 160-161 P 6
Agassiz 66-67 BC 1
Agata, ozero — 154-155 R 4
Agate, CO 68-69 E 6
Agathonēsion 138-139 M 7
Agats 174-175 L 8
Agatti Island 160-161 L 8
Agattu Island 30 D 1
Agattu Strait 52-53 p 6
Agawa 70-71 H 2
Agawa Bay 70-71 H 2
Agboville 194-195 D 7
Agdam 142-143 J 7-8
Agde 132-133 J 7
Agen 132-133 H 6
Agere Ḥiywer 194-195 M 7
Āghā Jarī 160-161 FG 4
Aghiyuk Island 52-53 e 1
A'Ghlo, Beinn — 116-117 H 4
Aghwāt, Al- 194-195 E 2
Agiapuk River 52-53 DE 4
Aginskoje 154-155 VW 7
Aginskoye = Aginskoje 154-155 VW 7
Aginsky-Buryat Autonomous Area = 12 ◁ 154-155 V 7
Agnew 182-183 D 5
Agnone 138-139 F 5
Agochi = Aoji 170-171 H 1
Agout 132-133 J 7
Āgra 160-161 M 5
Agra, OK 76-77 F 5
Agrachanskij poluostrov 142-143 J 7
Agrigento 138-139 E 7
Agrihan 148-149 S 8
Agrínion 138-139 J 6
Agrópoli 138-139 F 5
Agrossam 98-99 JK 10
Agryz 154-155 J 6
Agua Brava, Laguna de — 86-87 GH 6
Agua Caliente Indian Reservation 74-75 E 6
Água Clara [BR] 98-99 J 9
Aguadilla 88-89 N 5
Agua Dulce 86-87 NO 8
Agua Fria River 74-75 G 5-6
Aguán, Río — 58-59 J 8
Aguanaval, Río — 86-87 J 5
Aguanish 51 E 2
Agua Nueva 103 BC 4-5
Agua Nueva, TX 76-77 E 9
Aguanus, Rivière — 51 F 2
Agua Prieta 58-59 DE 5
Aguascalientes [MEX, administrative unit] 58-59 F 7
Aguascalientes [MEX, place] 58-59 F 7
Águas Formosas 98-99 L 8
Águeda, Río — 132-133 D 8
Aguila, AZ 74-75 G 6
Aguilar, CO 68-69 D 7
Águilas 132-133 G 10
Aguja, Punta — 98-99 C 6
Agulhas, Cape — 198 D 8
Agulhas Basin 26-27 L 8
Agulhas Negras 98-99 K 9
Agung, Gunung — 174-175 G 8
Agusan 174-175 J 5

Ahaggar = Al-Hajjār 194-195 EF 4
Ahaggar, Tassili Oua n' = Tāsīlī Wān al-Hajjār 194-195 E 5-F 4
Ahar 142-143 J 8
Ahmadābād [IND] 160-161 L 6
Ahmadnagar 160-161 LM 7
Aḥmadpūr Sharqī 160-161 L 5
Aḥmar, Jabal al- 199 B 3
Ahmednagar = Ahmadnagar 160-161 LM 7
Ahogayegua, Sierra de — 58-59 b 2-3
Ahome 86-87 F 5
Ahoskie, NC 80-81 H 2
Ahousat 48 DE 5
Ahtopol 138-139 MN 4
Ahuntsic, Montréal- 82 I b 1
Åhus 114-115 F 10
Ahvāz 160-161 F 4
Ahvenanmaa = Åland 114-115 HJ 7
Aḥwar 160-161 F 8
Ahwaz = Ahvāz 160-161 F 4

Aiaktalik Island 52-53 fg 1
Aiapuá 98-99 GH 7
Aiapuá, Lago — 98-99 G 7
Aibak = Samangān 160-161 K 3
Aibetsu 170-171 c 2
Aichi 170-171 L 5
Aichilik River 52-53 Q 2
Aidin = Aydın 160-161 B 3
Aígina [GR, island] 138-139 K 7
Aígina [GR, place] 138-139 K 7
Aígion 138-139 JK 6
Aigle, l' 132-133 H 4
Aiguá 103 F 4
Aigues-Mortes 132-133 JK 7
Aigun = Aihun 166-167 O 1
Ai He 170-171 E 2
Ai Ho = Ai He 170-171 E 2
Aihsien = Yacheng 166-167 K 8
Aihui 166-167 O 1
Aija 98-99 D 6
Aijal 160-161 P 6
Aikawa 170-171 LM 3
Aiken, SC 58-59 K 5
Aileron 182-183 F 4
Ailigandí 88-89 GH 10
Ailinglapalap 178 G 2
Aillinne, Loch — 116-117 D 6
Ailsa Craig 116-117 F 5
Ailt an Chorráin 116-117 CD 6
Aim 154-155 Z 6
Aimorés 98-99 L 8
Aimorés, Serra dos — 98-99 L 8
Ain 132-133 K 5
'Ain, Wādī al- = Wādī al-'Ayn 160-161 H 6
'Ainabo 194-195 b 2
'Ain al Muqshin, Al — = Al-'Ayn al-Muqshin 160-161 GH 7
Ainaza, Jebel — = Jabal 'Unayzah 160-161 GH 4
Ainaži 142-143 D 4
Aïn-Beïda = 'Ayn Bayḍā' 194-195 F 1
Aïn-ben-Tili = 'Ayn Bin Tīlī 194-195 C 3
Aïn-Galakka 194-195 H 5
Ainninne, Loch — 116-117 D 7
Aïn-Salah = 'Ayn Ṣāliḥ 194-195 E 3
Aïn-Sefra = 'Ayn Ṣafrā 194-195 DE 2
Ainsworth, NE 68-69 FG 4
Aïn-Témouchent = 'Ayn Tamūshanat 194-195 D 1
Aioi 170-171 K 5
Aion Island = ostrov Ajon 154-155 g 4
Aiquile 98-99 F 8
Aïr 194-195 F 5
Air, Point of — 116-117 H 7
Airan Köl = Telijn nuur 166-167 F 2
Airdrie 116-117 H 5
Aire, Isla del — 132-133 K 9
Aireagal 116-117 C 5
Airedale 116-117 J 6-K 7
Air Force Island 46-47 W 4
Airgid, Sléibhte an — 116-117 C 8
Aisch 124 E 4
Aisega 174-175 g 6
Aishihik 46-47 J 5
Aishihik Lake 52-53 T 6
Aisne 132-133 J 4
Aitana 132-133 G 9
Aitape 174-175 M 7
Aitkin, MN 70-71 D 2
Aitutaki 178 K 4
Aiud 138-139 K 2
Aiun, El — = Al-'Ayūn 194-195 B 3
Aix-en-Provence 132-133 KL 7
Aix-la-Chapelle = Aachen 124 C 3
Aix-les-Bains 132-133 KL 6
Aiyansh 48 C 2
Āīzāl = Aijal 160-161 P 6
Aizu-Wakamatsu 166-167 QR 4
Aizu-Wakamatu = Aizu-Wakamatsu 166-167 QR 4

Aj 142-143 L 4
Ajā, Jabal — 160-161 E 5
Ajaccio 138-139 C 5
Ajaguz 154-155 P 8
Ajalpan 86-87 M 8
Ajan [SU, place Pribrežnyj chrebet] 154-155 a 6
Ajan [SU, place Sibirskoje ploskogorje] 154-155 U 6
Ajan [SU, river] 154-155 R 4
Ajana 182-183 BC 5
Ajanka 154-155 g 5
Ajanta Range 160-161 M 6
Ajax Mountain 66-67 G 3
Ajdābiyah 194-195 J 2
Ajedabya = Ajdābiyah 194-195 J 2
Ajigasawa 170-171 MN 2
Ajjer, Tassili n' = Tāsīlī Wan Ahjār 194-195 F 3
Ajkino 142-143 J 3
'Ajmah, Jabal al- 194-195 L 3
'Ajmān 160-161 GH 5
Ajo, AZ 74-75 G 6
Ajo Mountains 74-75 G 6
Ajon, ostrov — 154-155 g 4
Ajrag nuur 166-167 GH 2
'Ajramīyah, Bi'r al- 199 BC 3
Ajtos 138-139 M 4
Aju, Kepulauan — 174-175 K 6

Akabah, Gulf of — = Khalīj al-'Aqabah 194-195 L 3
Akabira 170-171 c 2
Akademii, zaliv — 154-155 a 7
Akaishi-sammyaku 170-171 LM 5
Akalkot 160-161 M 7
Akan ko 170-171 cd 2
Akantarer 194-195 E 5
Akasaki 170-171 J 5
Akashi 170-171 K 5
Akasi = Akashi 170-171 K 5
Äkäsjoki 114-115 KL 4
Akayu 170-171 N 3
Akbulak 142-143 L 5
Akçakale 142-143 G 8
Akchar = Āqshar 194-195 B 4
Akdağ [TR, Taurus Mts.] 160-161 BC 3
Akershus 114-115 D 7-8
Aketi 198 D 1
Akhaia = Achaïa 138-139 JK 6
Akhḍar, Jabal al- [LAR] 194-195 J 2
Akhḍar, Jabal al- [Oman] 160-161 H 6
Akhiok, AK 52-53 f 1
Akhisar 142-143 E 8
Akhmīm 199 BC 4

Akhmīm 205

Aki 170-171 J 6
Akiachak, AK 52-53 FG 6
Akiak, AK 52-53 G 6
Akik = 'Aqiq 194-195 M 5
Akimiski Island 46-47 UV 7
Akita 166-167 QR 4
Akjoujt = Aqjawajat 194-195 B 5
Akkajaure 114-115 G 4
Akka-mori 170-171 N 2
Akkani 52-53 B 4
Akkeshi 170-171 d 2
Akkeshi wan 170-171 d 2
Aklavik 46-47 J 4
Akmal'-Abad = Gižduvan 154-155 L 9
Ak-Mečet' = Kzyl-Orda 154-155 M 9
Akmolinsk = Celinograd 154-155 MN 7
Akō 170-171 K 5
Akōbō 194-195 L 7
Akola 160-161 M 6
Akonolinga 194-195 G 8
Akordat 194-195 M 5
Akpatok Island 46-47 X 5
Akranes 114-115 bc 2
Akrar 114-115 b 2
Akreyri = Akureyri 114-115 de 2
Akrítas, Akrōtérion — 138-139 JK 7
Akron, CO 68-69 E 5
Akron, IA 68-69 H 4
Akron, IN 70-71 GH 5
Akron, OH 58-59 K 3
Akrōtéri 138-139 L 8
Akša 154-155 V 7
Aksaray 142-143 F 8
Akşehir 160-161 C 3
Aks'onovo-Zilovskoje 154-155 VW 7
Aksoran, gora — 154-155 O 8
Aksu [SU] 154-155 N 7
Aksu = Aqsu 166-167 E 3
Aksuat 154-155 P 8
Aksu çay 142-143 F 8
Aksum 194-195 M 6
Aktogaj 154-155 O 8
Akt'ubinsk 154-155 K 7
Aktumsyk 154-155 K 8
Aktyubinsk = Akt'ubinsk 154-155 JK 7
Akulurak, AK 46-47 CD 5
Akune 166-167 OP 5
Akun Island 52-53 o 3
Akure 194-195 F 7
Akureyri 114-115 de 2
Akutan, AK 52-53 o 3
Akutan Island 52-53 no 3
Akutan Pass 52-53 no 3
Akyab = Sittwe 174-175 B 2

Ål 114-115 C 7
Alabama 58-59 J 5
Alabama River 58-59 J 5
Alaca 142-143 FG 7
Alacahöyük 142-143 F 7
Alachua, FL 80-81 b 2
Ālādāgh, Reshteh — 160-161 H 3
Alagadiço 98-99 H 3
Alagnak River 52-53 J 7
Alagoas 98-99 M 6-7
Alagoinhas 98-99 M 7
Alagón 132-133 D 9
Alag Šan Gov' 166-167 J 4
Alaid Island 52-53 pq 6
Alajuela 58-59 K 9-10
Alakanuk, AK 52-53 E 5
Alakol', ozero — 154-155 P 8
Alaktak, AK 52-53 K 1
Alalaú, Rio — 98-99 G 5
'Alamayn, Al- 194-195 K 2
Alameda, CA 74-75 BC 4
Alameda, ID 66-67 G 4
Alameda, NM 76-77 A 5
Alameda, La — 76-77 CD 8
Alameda Naval Air Station 83 I c 2
Alamitos, Sierra de los — 86-87 JK 4
Alamo 86-87 M 7
Alamo, ND 68-69 E 1
Alamo, NV 74-75 F 4
Álamo, El — [MEX, Nuevo León] 76-77 E 9
Alamogordo, NM 58-59 E 5
Alamo Lake 74-75 G 5
Alamo River 74-75 F 6
Alamos 58-59 E 6
Álamos, Los — [MEX] 86-87 J 3
Alamosa, CO 58-59 E 4
Álamos de Peña 76-77 A 7
Åland [SF, administrative unit] 114-115 HJ 7
Åland [SF, island] 114-115 HJ 7
Ålands hav 114-115 H 7-8
Åland Strait = Ålands hav 114-115 H 7-8
Alanga Arba 198 GH 1
Alanga Arba = Hagadera 198 GH 1
Ālanmyō 174-175 C 3
Alanya 160-161 C 3
Alaotra, Lac — 198 J 5
Alapaha, GA 80-81 E 5
Alapaha River 80-81 E 5
Alapajevsk 154-155 L 6
Ālappi = Alleppey 160-161 M 9
Alāq 194-195 B 5
Alaquines 86-87 L 6
Alarcón 132-133 FG 9
Alas, Selat — 174-175 G 8
Alaşehir 142-143 E 8
Alašejev buchta 31 C 5
Alaska 46-47 E-H 4
Alaska, Gulf of — 46-47 G-J 6
Alaska Highway 46-47 H 5
Alaska Peninsula 46-47 DE 6
Alaska Range 46-47 F-H 5
Alàssio 138-139 C 3-4
Alatna, AK 52-53 L 3
Alatna River 52-53 L 3
Alatri 138-139 E 5
Alatyr' [SU, place] 154-155 H 7
Alausí 98-99 D 5
Alava, Cape — 66-67 A 1
Alaverdi 142-143 H 7
Alay, In — 194-195 D 5
Alayunt 142-143 E 8
Alazani 142-143 J 7
Alazeja 154-155 d 3-e 4
Alazejskoje ploskogorje 154-155 c 4
Alba 138-139 C 3
Albacete 132-133 FG 9
Alba de Tormes 132-133 E 8
Alba Iulia 138-139 K 2
Albanel, Lac — 50 P 1
Albania 138-139 J 5
Albano 98-99 K 6
Albany 182-183 C 6-7
Albany, CA 74-75 B 4
Albany, GA 58-59 K 5
Albany, KY 78-79 G 2
Albany, MN 70-71 C 3
Albany, MO 70-71 C 5
Albany, NY 58-59 LM 3
Albany, OR 58-59 B 3
Albany, TX 76-77 E 6
Albany Park, Chicago-, IL 83 II a 1
Albany River 46-47 U 7
Albarracín 132-133 G 8
Albatross Bay 182-183 H 2
Albemarle, NC 80-81 F 3
Albemarle = Isla Isabela 98-99 A 5
Albemarle Sound 80-81 HJ 2
Albenga 138-139 C 3
Alberche 132-133 E 8
Alberga River 182-183 FG 5
Alberni 66-67 A 1
Albert, Lake — 182-183 GH 7
Albert, Parc national — = Parc national Virunga 198 E 1-2
Alberta 46-47 NO 6
Alberta, VA 80-81 H 2
Albertkanaal 132-133 K 3
Albert Lea, MN 58-59 H 3
Albert Markham, Mount — 31 AB 17-15
Alberton, MT 66-67 F 2
Albertson, NY 82 III de 2
Albert Town 88-89 JK 3
Albertville 132-133 L 6
Albertville = Kalemie 198 E 3
Albi 132-133 J 7
Albia, IA 70-71 D 5
Albin, WY 68-69 D 5
Albina 98-99 J 3
Albino 138-139 CD 3
Albion, IL 70-71 F 6
Albion, IN 70-71 H 5
Albion, MI 70-71 H 4
Albion, MT 68-69 D 3
Albion, NE 68-69 GH 5
Albion, NY 72-73 GH 3
Alborán 132-133 F 11
Ålborg 114-115 CD 9
Ålborg Bugt 114-115 D 9
Alborz, Reshteh Kūhhā-ye — 160-161 G 3
Albufera, La — 132-133 GH 9
Albuquerque, NM 58-59 EF 4
Albuquerque, Cayos de — 88-89 F 8
Alburquerque 132-133 D 9
Albury 182-183 J 7
Alcácer do Sal 132-133 C 9
Alcalá de Guadaira 132-133 E 10
Alcalá de Henares 132-133 F 8
Alcalá la Real 132-133 F 10
Alcalde, NM 76-77 AB 4
Álcamo 138-139 E 7
Alcañiz 132-133 G 8
Alcântara [BR] 98-99 L 5
Alcántara [E] 132-133 D 9
Alcantarilla 132-133 G 10
Alcaparra 76-77 AB 7
Alcaraz [E] 132-133 F 9
Alcaraz, Sierra de — 132-133 F 9
Alcarria, La — 132-133 F 8
Alcatraz Island 83 I b 2
Alcázar de San Juan 132-133 F 9
Alcázarquivir = Al-Qṣar al-Kabīr 194-195 C 1
Alcester 116-117 K 8
Alcester Island 174-175 h 6
Alcira [E] 132-133 G 9
Alcira [RA] 103 D 4
Alcoa, TN 80-81 E 3
Alcobaça [BR] 98-99 M 8
Alcobaça [P] 132-133 C 9
Alcolea del Pinar 132-133 FG 8
Alcoota 182-183 F 4
Alcorn College, MS 78-79 D 5
Alcova, WY 68-69 C 4
Alcoy 132-133 G 9
Aldabra Islands 198 J 3
Aldama [MEX, Chihuahua] 86-87 H 3
Aldama [MEX, Tamaulipas] 86-87 LM 6
Aldamas, Los — 76-77 E 9
Aldan [SU, place] 154-155 XY 6
Aldan [SU, river] 154-155 Z 6
Aldan Plateau = Aldanskoje nagorje 154-155 X-Z 6
Aldanskoje nagorje 154-155 X-Z 6
Aldeburgh 116-117 h 6
Alder, MT 66-67 GH 3
Alder, Ben — 116-117 G 4
Alderney 116-117 J 11
Alder Peak 74-75 C 5
Aldershot 116-117 KL 9
Alderson 49 C 5
Aldridge-Brownhils 116-117 K 8
Aledo, IL 70-71 E 5
Aleg = Alaq 194-195 B 5
Alegrete 103 E 3-4
Alegria 98-99 E 6
Alejandra, Cabo — = Cape Alexandra 103 J 8
Alejandro Selkirk 94 A 7
Alejsk 154-155 P 7
Aleknagik, AK 52-53 HJ 7
Aleknagik, Lake — 52-53 H 7
Aleksandra, mys — 154-155 ab 7
Aleksandrov 142-143 GH 4
Aleksandrov Gaj 142-143 J 5
Aleksandrovsk = Belogorsk 154-155 YZ 7
Aleksandrovskoje [SU, Zapadno-Sibirskaja nizmennost'] 154-155 OP 5
Aleksandrovsk-Sachalinskij 154-155 bc 7
Aleksandrów Kujawski 124 J 2
Aleksejevka [SU, Kazachskaja SSR] 154-155 N 7
Aleksejevsk = Svobodnyj 154-155 YZ 7
Aleksinac 138-139 JK 4
Ålem 114-115 G 9
Aleman, NM 76-77 A 6
Alem Gena 194-195 M 7
'Alem Maya 194-195 N 7
Além Paraíba 98-99 L 9
Alençon 132-133 H 4
Alenquer [BR] 98-99 HJ 5
Alentejo 132-133 C 10-D 9
Alenuihaha Channel 174-175 ef 3
Aleppo = Halab 160-161 D 3
Alert 30 A 25
Alerta 98-99 E 7
Alert Bay 48 D 4
Alès 132-133 K 6
Alessàndria 138-139 C 3
Ålesund 114-115 AB 6
Aleutian Islands 30 D 35-1
Aleutian Range 46-47 E 6-F 5
Aleutian Trench 34-35 HJ 2
Aleutka 166-167 T 2
Alevina, mys — 154-155 cd 6
Alexander, ND 68-69 E 2
Alexander, Kap — 46-47 WX 2
Alexander, Point — 182-183 G 2
Alexander Archipelago 46-47 J 6-K 7
Alexanderbaai 198 BC 7
Alexander City, AL 78-79 FG 4
Alexander I[st] Island = zemľa Aleksandra I 31 C 29
Alexandra [NZ] 182-183 N 9
Alexandra, Cape — 103 J 8
Alexandra, zemľa — 154-155 FG 1
Alexandra Fiord 46-47 VW 2
Alexandra land = zemľa Alexandra 154-155 FG 1
Alexandretta = İskenderun 160-161 D 3
Alexandrette = İskenderun 160-161 D 3
Alexandria, IN 70-71 H 5
Alexandria, LA 58-59 H 5
Alexandria, MN 70-71 C 3
Alexandria, SD 68-69 H 4
Alexandria, VA 58-59 L 4
Alexandria [AUS] 182-183 G 3
Alexandria [BR] 98-99 M 6
Alexandria [CDN] 48 F 3
Alexandria [RO] 138-139 L 4
Alexandria [ZA] 198 E 8
Alexandria = Al-Iskandarīyah 194-195 KL 2
Alexandrina, Lake — 182-183 GH 7
Alexandrovsk = Poľarnyj 114-115 P 3
Alexandrúpolis 138-139 L 5
Alexis Creek 48 F 3
Alfambra 132-133 G 8
Alfarez de Navio Sobral 31 A 32-35
Alfatar 138-139 M 4
Alfeiós 138-139 J 7
Alföld 124 J 5-L 4
Alford 116-117 J 3
Ålfotbreen 114-115 A 7
Alfred, ME 72-73 L 3
Alga 154-155 K 8
Ålgård 114-115 A 8
Algarve 132-133 CD 10
Algeciras 132-133 E 10
Algēna 194-195 M 5
Alger, MI 70-71 H 3
Algeria 194-195 D-F 3
Algerian Basin 132-133 J 10-L 8
Alghero 138-139 C 5
Algiers = Al-Jazā'ir 194-195 E 1
Algoabaai 198 E 8
Algoa Bay = Algoabaai 198 E 8
Algodones 74-75 F 6
Algoma, OR 66-67 C 4
Algoma, WI 70-71 G 3
Algona, IA 70-71 CD 4
Algonquin Park 72-73 G 2
Algonquin Provincial Park 46-47 V 8
Alhambra, CA 74-75 DE 5
Alhucemas = Al-Ḥusaymah 194-195 D 1
'Alī, Sadd al- 194-195 L 4
Aliákmon 138-139 JK 5
Ali-Bajramly 142-143 J 8
Alibunar 138-139 J 3
Alicante 132-133 GH 9
Alice, TX 58-59 G 6
Alice, Punta — 138-139 G 6
Alice Arm 48 C 2
Alice Springs 182-183 FG 4
Aliceville, AL 78-79 EF 4
Alicudi 138-139 F 6
Alida 68-69 F 1
Aligar = Alīgarh 160-161 M 5
Alīgarh 160-161 M 5
Alihe 166-167 N 1
Alijos, Rocas — 86-87 C 5
Alima 198 BC 2
Alindao 194-195 J 7-8
Alingsås 114-115 E 9
Alīpur Duār 160-161 M 5
Aliquippa, PA 72-73 F 4
Alisal, CA 74-75 C 4
Alisos, Río — 86-87 E 2
Alitak Bay 52-53 f 1
Aliwal-Noord 198 E 8
Aliwal Suid = Mosselbaai 198 D 8
Alix 48 L 3
Alkali Desert 66-67 EF 5
Alkali Flat 66-67 DE 5
Alkali Lake 66-67 D 5
Alkmaar 132-133 K 2
Allach-Jun' 154-155 a 5
Allada 194-195 E 7
Allagash, ME 72-73 M 1
Allagash River 72-73 M 1
Allāhābād [IND] 160-161 N 5
Allakaket, AK 46-47 F 4
Allamoore, TX 76-77 B 7
Allanmyo = Ālanmyō 174-175 C 3
'Allāqī, Wadī al- 199 C 6
Allardville 51 D 4
Allegan, MI 70-71 H 4
Alleghenies = Allegheny Mountains 58-59 K 4-L 3
Allegheny Mountains 58-59 K 4-L 3
Allegheny Plateau 72-73 F 5
Allegheny River 72-73 G 4
Allen, OK 76-77 F 5
Allen, Mount — 52-53 QR 5
Allendale, SC 80-81 F 4
Allende [MEX, Coahuila] 86-87 K 3
Allende [MEX, León] 86-87 KL 5
Allen Park, MI 72-73 E 3
Allen River 52-53 LM 3
Allentown, PA 58-59 L 3
Alleppey 160-161 M 9
Aller 124 D 2
Allerton, IA 70-71 D 5
Alley Park 82 III d 2
Alliance, NE 58-59 F 3
Alliance, OH 72-73 F 4
Allier 132-133 J 6
Alliford Bay 48 B 3
Alligator Sound 80-81 HJ 3
Allison, IA 70-71 D 4
Allison, TX 76-77 DE 5
Allison Harbour 48 CD 4
Allison Pass 66-67 C 1
Alliston 72-73 G 2
Alloa 116-117 H 4
Allumettes, Île aux — 72-73 H 2
Alma, AR 76-77 G 5
Alma, GA 80-81 E 5
Alma, KS 68-69 H 6
Alma, MI 70-71 H 4
Alma, NE 68-69 G 5
Alma, WI 70-71 E 3
Alma [CDN, New Brunswick] 51 D 5
Alma [CDN, Quebec] 46-47 W 8
Alma, Lake — = Harlan County Reservoir 68-69 G 5-6
Alma-Ata 154-155 O 9
Almada 132-133 C 9
Almadén 132-133 E 9
Almagre, El — 86-87 J 4
Almalyk 160-161 KL 2
Almanor, Lake — 66-67 C 5
Almansa 132-133 G 9
Almanzora 132-133 F 10
Alma Peak 48 D 1
Almazán 132-133 F 8
Almeida 132-133 D 8
Almeidia Campos 98-99 K 8
Almeirim [BR] 98-99 J 5
Almeirim, Serra do — 98-99 M 5
Almena, KS 68-69 G 6
Almenara [BR] 98-99 LM 8
Almendralejo 132-133 D 9
Almería 132-133 F 10
Almería, Golfo de — 132-133 F 10
Al'metjevsk 154-155 J 7
Älmhult 114-115 F 9
Almirante Brown [Antarctica] 31 C 30-31
Almo, ID 66-67 G 4
Almodóvar del Campo 132-133 E 9
Almond, WI 70-71 F 3
Almond, River — 116-117 GH 4
Almont, CO 68-69 C 6
Almonte [CDN] 72-73 H 2
Almorox 132-133 E 8
Almota, WA 66-67 E 2
Almuñécar 132-133 F 10
Alness 116-117 G 3
Alnmouth 116-117 K 5
Alnwick 116-117 K 5
Alo Brasil 98-99 N 10-11
Alofi 174-175 b 1
Aloha, OR 66-67 B 3
Alondra, CA 83 III c 2
Alondra Park 83 III bc 2
Alonsa 49 J 5
Alor, Pulau — 174-175 HJ 8
Álora 132-133 E 10
Alor Setar 174-175 CD 5
Alotau 174-175 NO 9
Aloysius, Mount — 182-183 E 5
Alpena, AR 78-79 C 2
Alpena, MI 58-59 K 2
Alpena, SD 68-69 G 3
Alpercatas, Rio — 98-99 KL 6
Alpes Cottiennes 132-133 G 6
Alpes Graies 132-133 L 6
Alpes Maritimes 132-133 L 6
Alpet e Shqipërisë 138-139 HJ 4
Alpha 182-183 J 4
Alpha, IL 70-71 E 5
Alphonse 188-189 N 9
Alpine, AZ 74-75 J 6
Alpine, ID 66-67 H 4
Alpine, TX 58-59 F 5
Alpi Transilvanici 138-139 KL 3
Alps 138-139 A 3-E 2
Alright, Île — 51 F 4
Alroy Downs 182-183 G 3
Als 114-115 C 10
Alsace 132-133 L 4-5
Alsask 49 D 5
Alsasua 132-133 FG 7
Alsea, OR 66-67 B 3
Alsek River 52-53 T 6-7
Alstahaug 114-115 DE 5
Alston 116-117 J 6
Alta 114-115 K 3
Alta, IA 70-71 C 4
Altaelv 114-115 K 3
Alta Gracia [RA] 103 CD 4
Altagracia [YV] 98-99 E 2
Altair Seamounts 26-27 H 3
Altaj [Mongolia, Altaj] 166-167 H 2
Altaj [Mongolia, Chovd] 166-167 G 2
Altaj [SU] 154-155 PQ 7
Altajn Nuruu = Mongol Altajn nuruu 166-167 F-H 2
Altamaha River 58-59 K 5
Altamira [BR] 98-99 J 5
Altamira [CR] 88-89 DE 9
Altamira, Cueva de — 132-133 EF 7
Altamont, IL 70-71 F 6
Altamont, OR 66-67 BC 4
Altamont, WY 66-67 H 5
Altamura 138-139 G 5
Altamura, Isla — 86-87 F 5
Altanbulag 166-167 K 1-2
Altar 86-87 E 2
Altar, Desierto de — 86-87 D 2-3
Altar, Río — 86-87 E 2
Altar Valley 74-75 H 7
Altata 86-87 FG 5
Alta Vista, KS 68-69 H 6
Altavista, VA 80-81 G 2
Altay 166-167 F 2
Altay = Altaj 154-155 PQ 7
Altdorf 124 D 5
Altenburg 124 F 3
Alter do Chão [BR] 98-99 HJ 5
Altevatn 114-115 H 3
Altheimer, AR 78-79 D 3
Altin Tagh 166-167 EF 4
Altiplanicie Mexicana 58-59 E 5-F 7
Altiplano 98-99 F 8
Altmühl 124 E 4
Altnaharra 116-117 G 2
Alto, TX 76-77 G 7
Alto Anapu, Rio — 98-99 J 5
Alto Garças 98-99 J 8
Alto Longá 98-99 L 6
Alto Molócuè = Molócuè 198 G 5
Alton 116-17 L 9
Alton, IL 58-59 HJ 4
Alton, KS 68-69 G 6
Alton, MO 78-79 D 2
Altoona, PA 58-59 L 3
Alto Parnaíba 98-99 K 6
Alto Piquiri 103 F 2
Alto Río Senguerr 103 BC 6-7
Alturas, CA 66-67 C 5
Altus, OK 58-59 G 5
Altyn Tagh = Altin tagh 166-167 EF 4
Alūksne 142-143 E 4
Aluminé 103 B 5
Alung Gangri 166-167 E 5
'Aluula 194-195 c 1
Alva, FL 80-81 c 3
Alva, OK 76-77 E 4
Alvalade 132-133 C 9-10
Alvand, Kūh-e — 160-161 FG 4
Alvar = Alwar 160-161 M 5
Alvarado 58-59 GH 8
Alvarado, TX 76-77 F 6
Alvarães 98-99 G 5
Álvaro Obregón = Frontera 58-59 H 8
Alvaro Obregón, Presa — 86-87 F 4
Alvdal 114-115 D 6
Älvdalen 114-115 F 7
Alverstone, Mount — 52-53 S 6
Alvesta 114-115 F 9
Alvin, TX 76-77 G 8
Alvord Lake 66-67 D 4
Älvsborgs län 114-115 E 8-9
Älvsbyn 114-115 J 5
Alwar 160-161 M 5
Alys = Kızılırmak 160-161 D 3
Alzada, MT 68-69 D 3
Alzamaj 154-155 S 6

Amada = 'Amādah 199 C 6
Amadabad = Ahmādābād 160-161 L 6
'Amādah 199 C 6
Amadeus, Lake — 182-183 F 4
Amādī 194-195 KL 7
Amadjuak Lake 46-47 W 4-5
Amagasaki 170-171 K 5
Amahai 174-175 J 7
Amak Island 52-53 b 2
Amakusa nada 170-171 G 6
Amakusa-rettō 166-167 O 5
Amakusa syotō = Amakusa-rettō 166-167 O 5
Åmål 114-115 E 8
Amalfi [I] 138-139 F 5
Amaliás 138-139 J 7
Amalyk 154-155 W 6
Amami-guntō 166-167 O 6
Amami-ō-shima 166-167 O 6
Amami-Ō sima = Amami-ō-shima 166-167 O 6
Amandola 138-139 E 4
Amangel'dy 154-155 M 7-8
Amantea 138-139 FG 6
Amapá [BR, Acre] 98-99 D 10
Amapá [BR, Amapá administrative unit] 98-99 J 4
Amapá [BR, Amapá place] 98-99 J 4
Amapari, Rio — 98-99 M 4
Amara 194-195 M 6
'Amarah, Al- 160-161 F 4
Amaramba, Lagoa — = Lagoa Chiuta 198 G 4
Amarante [BR] 98-99 L 6
Amaranth 49 J 5
Amarāvatī = Amrāvati 160-161 M 6
Amargo, CA 74-75 E 5
Amargosa Desert 74-75 E 4
Amargosa Range 74-75 E 4-5
Amargosa River 74-75 E 5
Amari, Laghi — = Al-Buḥayrat al-Murrat al-Kubrá 199 C 2
Amarillo, TX 58-59 F 4
'Amarina, Tel el- = Tall al-'Amārinah 199 B 4
'Amārinah, Tall al- 199 B 4
Amaro Leite 98-99 JK 7
Amarume 170-171 M 3
Amarùsion 138-139 KL 6-7
Amasa, MI 70-71 F 2
Amasya 160-161 D 2
Amatán 86-87 O 9
Amatauraá 98-99 DE 6
Amatignak Island 52-53 t 7
Amatique, Bahía de — 58-59 J 8
Amauã, Lago — 98-99 G 5
Amazon 49 F 5
Amazon = Amazonas 98-99 F-H 5
Amazon, Mouth of the — = Estuário do Rio Amazonas 98-99 JK 4
Amazonas [BR] 98-99 F-H 5
Amazonas, Estuário do Rio — 98-99 JK 4
Amazonas, Rio — [BR] 98-99 HJ 5
Amazonas, Río — [PE] 98-99 E 5
Amazon Shelf 26-27 G 5-6
Amba Alage 194-195 MN 6
Amba Alaji = Amba Alage 194-195 MN 6
Ambājogāi 160-161 M 7
Ambāla 160-161 M 4
Ambalavao 198 J 6
Ambam 194-195 G 8
Ambanja 198 J 4
Ambarčik 154-155 fg 4
Ambaro, Baie d' 198 J 4
Ambato 98-99 D 5
Ambatoboeny 198 J 5
Ambatolampy 198 J 5
Ambatondrazaka 198 J 5
Ambatosoratra 198 J 5
Ambelau, Pulau — 174-175 J 7
Amber, WA 66-67 E 2
Amber Bay 52-53 e 1
Amberg 124 EF 4
Ambergris Cay 58-59 J 8
Ambikāpur 160-161 N 6
'Ambikūl 199 B 7
Ambilobe 198 JK 4

Ambition, Mount — 52-53 W 8
Amble 116-117 K 5
Ambler River 52-53 J 3
Ambodifototra 198 JK 5
Ambohibe 198 H 6
Ambohimahasoa 198 J 6
Amboim = Gabela 198 BC 4
Amboina = Pulau Ambon 174-175 J 7
Amboise 132-133 H 5
Amboland = Ovamboland 198 BC 5
Ambon 174-175 J 7
Ambon, Pulau — 174-175 J 7
Amboseli Game Reserve 198 G 2
Ambositra 198 J 6
Ambovombe 198 J 7
Amboy, CA 74-75 F 5
Amboy, IL 70-71 F 5
Amboyna Cay 174-175 F 5
Ambrakikòs Kólpos 138-139 J 6
Ambre, Cap d' 198 JK 4
Ambre, Montagne d' 198 J 4
Ambridge, PA 72-73 FG 4
Ambrim 182-183 N 3
Ambriz 198 B 3
Ambrizete = N'Zeto 198 B 3
Amchitka, AK 52-53 s 7
Amchitka Island 30 D 1
Amchitka Pass 52-53 t 7
Am-Dam 194-195 J 6
Amderma 154-155 L 4
Ameca 58-59 F 7
Ameca, Río — 86-87 H 7
Amedabad = Ahmadābād 160-161 L 6
Amelia, NE 68-69 G 4
Amelia Court House, VA 80-81 GH 2
Aménas, In — = 'Ayn Umannās 194-195 F 3
Amenia, NY 72-73 K 4
Amer, Grand Lac — = Al-Buḥayrat al-Murrat al-Kubrá 199 C 2
Amerasia Basin 26-27 A-C 1
American Falls, ID 66-67 G 4
American Falls Reservoir 66-67 G 4
American Fork, UT 66-67 H 5
American Highland 31 B 8
American River North Fork 74-75 C 3
Americus, GA 58-59 K 5
Amersfoort [NL] 132-133 K 2
Amery, WI 70-71 D 3
Amery Ice Shelf 31 BC 7-8
Ames, IA 58-59 H 3
Ames, OK 76-77 EF 4
Amesbury 116-117 K 9
Amesbury, MA 72-73 L 3
Amesdale 50 C 2-3
Amfilochía 138-139 J 6
Ámfissa 138-139 K 6
Amga [SU, place] 154-155 Z 5
Amga [SU, river] 154-155 X 6
Amgu 154-155 a 8
Amguema 154-155 k 4
Am-Guereda 194-195 J 6
Amgun' [SU, place] 154-155 a 7
Amgun' [SU, river] 154-155 a 7
Amhara = Amara 194-195 M 6
Amherst 46-47 XY 8
Amherst, MA 72-73 K 3
Amherst, VA 80-81 G 2
Amherst, Île — 51 F 4
Amherst, Mount — 182-183 E 3
Amherstburg 72-73 E 3
Amherst Junction, WI 70-71 F 3
Amiata, Monte — 138-139 D 4
Amidon, ND 68-69 E 2
Amiens 132-133 J 4
Amīndīvi Islands 160-161 L 8
Amino 170-171 K 5
Aminuis 198 C 6
Amirantes 188-189 N 9
'Amīrīyah, Al- 199 AB 2
Amisk Lake 49 G 3
Amisós = Samsun 160-161 D 2
Amistad, NM 76-77 C 5
Amistad, Presa de la — 86-87 JK 3
Amite, LA 78-79 D 5
Amity, AR 78-79 C 3
Amlia Island 30 D 36
Amlwch 116-117 G 7
'Ammān 160-161 D 4
Ammanford 116-117 GH 9
Ammarfjället 114-115 FG 4
Ammerman Mount 52-53 RS 2
Ammersee 124 E 5
Ammóchōstos 160-161 CD 3
Amnok-kang 166-167 O 3
Amnyemachhen Gangri 166-167 HJ 5
Amol 142-143 K 8
Amores, Los — 103 DE 3
Amorgós 138-139 LM 7
Amory, MS 78-79 E 3-4
Amos 46-47 V 8
Amos, CA 74-75 F 6
Amoy = Xiamen 166-167 M 7
Ampanihy 198 H 6
Ampasindava, Baie d' 198 J 4
Ampato, Nevado de — 98-99 E 8
Amphípolis 138-139 K 5
Amphitrite Point 48 DE 5
Amposta 132-133 H 8
Ampthill 116-117 L 8
Ampurias 132-133 J 7
Amqui 51 C 3
Amrāvati 160-161 M 6
Amrawati = Amrāvati 160-161 M 6
Amritsar 160-161 LM 4
Amroha 160-161 M 5
Amsīd, Al- 194-195 B 3
Amsterdam, NY 72-73 JK 3
Amsterdam [NL] 132-133 K 2
Amsterdam Island = Nouvelle Amsterdam 188-189 NO 7
Amsterdam Plateau 26-27 NO 8
Amstetten 124 G 4
Amt'ae-do 170-171 EF 5
Am-Timan 194-195 J 6
Amudarja 160-161 J 2
Amukta Island 52-53 l 4
Amukta Pass 52-53 kl 4
Amuku Mountains 98-99 J 3-4
Amund Ringnes Island 46-47 RS 2
Amundsen, Mount — 31 BC 11
Amundsen Bay 31 C 5
Amundsen Glacier 31 A 23-20
Amundsen Gulf 46-47 L-N 3
Amundsen havet 31 BC 25-26
Amundsen-Scott 31 A
Amur 154-155 Z 8
Amur = Heilong Jiang 166-167 P 2
Amurang 174-175 H 6
Amursk 154-155 a 7
Amurskij zaliv 170-171 H 1

Anabar 154-155 V 3
Anābīb an-Nafṭ 160-161 DE 4
Ana Branch 182-183 H 6
Anabuki 170-171 K 5-6
Anacapa Island 74-75 D 6
Anaconda, MT 58-59 D 2
Anaconda Range 66-67 G 2-3
Anacortes, WA 66-67 B 1
Anacostia, Washington-, DC 82 II b 2
Anacostia Park 82 II b 2
Anacostia River 82 II ab 2
Anadarko, OK 76-77 EF 5
Anadyr' [SU, place] 154-155 j 5
Anadyr' [SU, river] 154-155 hj 5
Anadyrskaja nizmennost' 154-155 j 4-5
Anadyrskij zaliv 154-155 j-l 5
Anadyrskoje ploskogorje 154-155 h 4
Anáfē 138-139 LM 7
Anagni 138-139 E 5
Anaheim, CA 74-75 DE 6
Anahim Lake 48 E 3
Anahuac, TX 76-77 G 8
Anáhuac [MEX, Nuevo León] 86-87 K 4
Anáhuac [MEX, Zacatecas] 86-87 K 5
Anáhuac, Mesa de — 58-59 FG 7-8
Anaiza, Jebel — = Jabal Unayzah 160-161 DE 4
Anajás 98-99 JK 5
Anajás, Ilha — 98-99 N 5
Anajás, Rio — 98-99 N 5
Anak 170-171 E 3
Anakāpalle 160-161 N 7
Anakāpalli = Anakāpalle 160-161 N 7
Anaktuk, AK 52-53 H 1
Anaktuvuk Pass, AK 52-53 KL 2
Anaktuvuk River 52-53 M 2
Analalava 198 J 4
Anamã 98-99 G 5
Anama Bay 49 J 5
Anambas, Kepulauan — 174-175 E 6
Anambra [WAN, administrative unit] 194-195 F 7
Anamoose, ND 68-69 FG 2
Anamosa, IA 70-71 E 4
Anamu, Rio — 98-99 K 4
Anamur 160-161 C 3
Anamur burnu 160-161 C 3
Anan 170-171 K 6
Ananás, Cachoeira — 98-99 M 8
Anantapur 160-161 M 8
Anantnāg 160-161 M 4
Anápolis 98-99 K 8
Anār 160-161 GH 4
Anārak 160-161 G 4
Anārdara 160-161 J 4
Anastasia Island 80-81 c 2
Anatolia 160-161 CD 3
Anatone, WA 66-67 E 2
Añatuya 103 D 3
Anauá, Rio — 98-99 HJ 4
Anavilhanas, Arquipélago dos — 98-99 H 6
Anbyŏn 170-171 F 3
Ancenis 132-133 G 5
Anceny, MT 66-67 H 3
An-ching = Anqing 166-167 M 5
Ancho, NM 76-77 B 6
Anchorage, AK 46-47 FG 5
Anchor Point, AK 52-53 M 7
Anchuras 132-133 E 9
Anclote Keys 80-81 b 2
Ancober = Ankober 194-195 MN 7
Ancona 138-139 E 4
Ancuabe 198 G 4
Ancud 103 B 6
Ancud, Golfo de — 103 B 6
Ancyra = Ankara 160-161 C 3
Anda 166-167 NO 2
Andale, KS 68-69 H 7
Andalgalá 103 C 3
Åndalsnes 114-115 BC 6
Andalucía [E] 132-133 D-F 10
Andalusia, AL 78-79 F 5
Andalusia = Andalucía 132-133 D-F 10
Andaman and Nicobar Islands 160-161 OP 8
Andaman Basin 174-175 BC 4-5
Andamān Dvīp = Andaman Islands 160-161 P 8
Andamanensee 174-175 C 4-5
Andaman Islands 160-161 P 8
Andaman Sea 174-175 C 4-5
Andamooka 182-183 G 6
Andant 103 D 5
Andara 198 D 5
Andelys, les — 132-133 H 4
Andenes 114-115 G 3
Andermatt 124 D 5
Anderson, CA 66-67 BC 5
Anderson, IN 58-59 J 3
Anderson, MO 76-77 G 4
Anderson, SC 58-59 K 5
Anderson, TX 76-77 FG 7
Anderson Ranch Reservoir 66-67 F 4
Anderson River 46-47 L 4
Andes 98-99 D 3
Andes, Cordillera de los — 98-99 E 3-F 9
Andes, Lake — 68-69 G 4
Andes, Los — 103 B 4
Andhra 160-161 M 8-N 7
Andhra Pradesh 160-161 M 8-N 7
Andidanob, Jebel — = Jabal Asūtarībah 199 E 7
Andižan 160-161 L 2
Andizhan = Andižan 160-161 L 2
Andkhoy 160-161 JK 3
Andoas 98-99 D 5
Andong 166-167 O 4
Andong = Dandong 166-167 N 3
Andørja 114-115 GH 3
Andorra 132-133 H 7
Andorra la Vella 132-133 H 7
Andou, Lac — 72-73 H 1
Andover 116-117 K 9
Andover, OH 72-73 F 4
Andover, SD 68-69 GH 3
Andøy 114-115 FG 3
Andra = Āndhra 160-161 M 8-N 7
Andradina 98-99 J 9
Andreafsky = Saint Marys, AK 52-53 F 5
Andreafsky, East Fork — 52-53 FG 5
Andreafsky River 52-53 F 5
Andreanof Islands 30 D 36
Andrēba = Ambatosoratra 198 J 5
Andrée land 114-115 j 5
Andréeneset 114-115 n 4
Andrejevka [SU, Kazachskaja SSR] 154-155 OP 8
Andréville 51 B 4
Andrews, NC 80-81 E 3
Andrews, OR 66-67 D 4
Andrews, SC 80-81 G 4
Andrews, TN 80-81 E 3
Andrews, TX 76-77 C 6
Andrews Air Force Base 82 II b 2
Ándria 138-139 FG 5
Andriba 198 J 5
Andringitra 198 J 6
Androka 198 H 7
Andronica Island 52-53 cd 2
Ándros 138-139 L 7
Androscoggin River 72-73 L 2
Andros Island 58-59 L 7
Andros Town 88-89 H 2
Androth Island 160-161 L 8
Andr'uškino 154-155 de 4
Andsfjord 114-115 G 3
Andújar 132-133 EF 9
Andulo 198 C 4
Anegada 58-59 O 8
Anegada Passage 58-59 O 8
Anêho 194-195 E 7
Aneityum 182-183 N 4
Añelo 103 C 5
Aneta, ND 68-69 GH 2
Aneto, Pico de — 132-133 H 7
Aney 194-195 G 5
An-fu = Linli 166-167 L 6
Angamos, Punta — 103 B 2
Ang-ang-ch'i = Ang'angxi 166-167 N 2
Ang'angxi 166-167 N 2
Angara 154-155 S 6
Angarsk 154-155 T 7
Angarskij kr'až 154-155 S-U 6
Ånge 114-115 F 6
Angel, Salto del — 98-99 G 3
Ángel de la Guarda, Isla — 58-59 D 6
Ángeles, Los — [RCH] 103 B 5
Ängelholm 114-115 E 9
Angelina River 76-77 G 7
Angel Island 83 I b 1
Angel Island State Park 83 I b 1
Angel Provincial Forest 50 B 3
Ångermanälven 114-115 G 5-6
Ångermanland 114-115 GH 6
Angermünde 124 FG 2
Angers 132-133 G 5
Ångesån 114-115 K 4
Angka, Doi — = Doi Inthanon 174-175 C 3
Angkor 174-175 D 4
Anglesey 116-117 G 7
Angleton, TX 76-77 G 8
Angliers 72-73 G 1
Angmagssalik = Angmagssaliq 46-47 de 4
Angmagssaliq 46-47 de 4
Ango 198 E 1
Angoche 198 GH 5
Angoche, Ilhas — 198 GH 5
Angol 103 B 5
Angola 198 CD 4
Angola, IN 70-71 H 5
Angola, NY 72-73 G 3
Angola Basin 26-27 JK 6
Angoon, AK 52-53 U 8
Angoon, AK 52-53 v 8
Angora = Ankara 160-161 C 3
Angostura = Ciudad Bolívar 98-99 G 3
Angostura I, Salto de — 98-99 E 4
Angostura II, Salto de — 98-99 E 4
Angostura Reservoir 68-69 E 4
Angosturas 98-99 E 5
Angoulême 132-133 H 6
Angoumois 132-133 GH 6
Angra do Heroismo 188-189 E 5
Angrapa 124 KL 1
Angra Pequena = Lüderitzbaai 198 BC 7
Angren 160-161 KL 2
Angrenšachtstroj = Angren 160-161 KL 2
Angrigon, Jardin zoologique — 82 I b 2
Anguila = Anguilla 58-59 O 8
Anguilla 58-59 O 8
Anguilla Cays 88-89 G 3
Anguille, Cape — 51 G 4
Angumu 198 E 2
Angus 116-117 HJ 4
Angustora, Presa de la — 86-87 O 9-10
Anholt 114-115 D 9
An-hsi = Anxi 166-167 H 3
An-Huei = Anhui 166-167 M 5
Anhuei = Anhui 166-167 M 5
Anhui 166-167 M 5
Anhumas 98-99 HJ 8
Ani 170-171 N 2-3
Aniaī = Ani 170-171 N 2-3
Aniak, AK 52-53 H 6
Aniakchak Volcano 52-53 de 1
Aniak River 52-53 H 6
Anie, Pic d' 132-133 G 7
Animas, NM 74-75 J 7
Animas, Las — 76-77 C 9
Animas Peak 74-75 J 7
Anina 138-139 JK 3
Anita, AZ 74-75 G 5
Anita, IA 70-71 C 5
Aniuk River 52-53 J 2
Aniva, mys — 154-155 b 8
Aniva, zaliv — 154-155 b 8
Aniva Bay = zaliv Aniva 154-155 b 8
Anjār 160-161 KL 6
Anjou [CDN] 82 I b 1
Anjou [F] 132-133 G 5
Anjou, Les Galleries d' 82 I b 1
Anjou, ostrova — 30 B 4-5
Anjouan = Ndzuwani 198 HJ 4
Anju 166-167 O 4
Ankara 160-161 C 3
Ankaratra 198 J 5
Ankazoabo 198 H 6
An Khe 174-175 E 4
Anking = Anqing 166-167 M 5
Anklam 124 F 2
Ankober 194-195 MN 7
Ankūr, Jabal — 199 DE 7
Anlong 166-167 JK 6
Anlung = Anlong 166-167 JK 6
Anma-do 170-171 E 5
Ann, Cape — 72-73 L 3
Anna, IL 70-71 F 7
Annaba = Annābah 194-195 F 1
Annābah 194-195 F 1
Annai 98-99 H 4
Annalee Heights, VA 82 II a 2
Annam = Trung Bô 174-175 D 3-E 4
Anna Maria Key 80-81 b 3
Annan 116-117 H 6
Annan, River — 116-117 H 5
Annandale, MN 70-71 C 3
Annandale, VA 82 II a 2
Annapolis, MD 58-59 L 4
Annapolis, MO 70-71 E 7
Annapolis Royal 46-47 XY 9
Ann Arbor, MI 58-59 K 3
Annecy 132-133 L 6
Annette, AK 52-53 x 9
Annette Island 52-53 x 9
An Nho'n 174-175 E 4
Anniston, AL 58-59 JK 5
Annobón = Pagalu 188-189 H 9
Annonciation, l' 72-73 J 1
Annotto Bay 88-89 H 5
Anoka, MN 70-71 D 3
Anqing 166-167 M 5
Anṣāb 160-161 F 8
Anṣāb = Niṣāb 160-161 EF 5
Ansbach 124 E 4
Anse-au-Loup, l' 51 H 2
Anse-aux-Griffons, l' 51 DE 3
Anse-aux-Meadows, l' 51 J 2
Anselmo, NE 68-69 FG 5
Anse-Saint-Jean, l' 51 A 3
Anshun 166-167 K 6
Ansley, NE 68-69 G 5
Ansó 132-133 G 7
Anson, TX 76-77 DE 6
Anson Bay 182-183 EF 2
Ansongo 194-195 E 5
Ansonia, CT 72-73 K 4
Ansonville 50 L 2
Ansŏng 170-171 F 4
Ansted, WV 72-73 F 5
Anta [PE] 98-99 E 7
An-ta = Anda 166-167 NO 2
Anta, Cachoeira — [BR, Amazonas] 98-99 H 8
Anta, Cachoeira — [BR, Pará] 98-99 O 7
Antabamba 98-99 E 7
Antakya 160-161 D 3
Antalaha 198 K 4
Antália = Antalya 160-161 C 3
Antalya 160-161 C 3
Antalya körfezi 160-161 C 3
Antananarivo 198 J 5
Antarctica 31 B 28-9
Antarctic Peninsula 31 BC 30-31
Antarctic Sound 31 C 31
Antarktika 31 B 28-9
Antelope, OR 66-67 C 3
Antelope Hills 66-67 J 4
Antelope Island 66-67 G 5
Antelope Range 74-75 E 3
Antequera 132-133 E 10
Antero Reservoir 68-69 CD 6
Anthony, KS 76-77 EF 4
Anthony, NM 76-77 A 7
Anthony Lagoon 182-183 FG 3
Anti Atlas = Al-Aṭlas aṣ-Ṣaghīr 194-195 C 2-3
Antibes 132-133 L 7
Anticosti Island 46-47 Y 8
Antifer, Cap d' 116-117 LM 11
Antigo, WI 70-71 F 3
Antigua 58-59 O 8
Antigua and Barbuda 58-59 OP 8
Antigua Guatemala 58-59 H 9
Antiguo Morelos 86-87 L 6
Antikýthēra 138-139 K 8
Antímēlos 138-139 KL 7
Antimony, UT 74-75 H 3
Antinopolis 199 B 4
Antioch, CA 74-75 C 3-4
Antioch, IL 70-71 F 4
Antioch = Antakya 160-161 D 3
Antioquia [CO, place] 98-99 D 3
Antíparos 138-139 L 7
Antipodes Islands 34-35 HJ 7
Antler, ND 68-69 F 1
Antlers, OK 76-77 G 5
Antofagasta [RCH, place] 103 B 2
Antofagasta de la Sierra 103 C 3
Antón 88-89 F 10
Anton, CO 68-69 E 6
Anton, TX 76-77 C 6
Anton Chico, NM 76-77 B 5
Antongila, Helodrona — 198 JK 5
Antonibe 198 J 4-5
Antônio Lemos 98-99 N 5
Antonito, CO 68-69 CD 7
Anton Lizardo, Punta — 86-87 N 8
Antrim 116-117 E 6
Antrim Mountains 116-117 E 5-F 6
Antsalova 198 H 5
Antsirabé 198 J 5
Antsiranana 198 JK 4
Antsohihy 198 J 4
An Tuc = An Khe 174-175 E 4
Antung = Dandong 166-167 N 3
Antwerp = Antwerpen 132-133 K 3
Antwerpen 132-133 J 3
Anũi 170-171 F 5
An'ujsk 154-155 f 4
An'ujskij chrebet 154-155 fg 4
Anuradhapura = Anurādhapūraya 160-161 MN 9
Anurādhapūraya 160-161 MN 9
Anvers = Antwerpen 132-133 J 3
Anvers, Île — 31 C 30
Anvik, AK 52-53 G 5
Anvik River 52-53 G 5
Anvil Peak 52-53 st 7
Anxi [TJ, Gansu] 166-167 H 3
Anxious Bay 182-183 F 6
Anyang [ROK] 170-171 F 4
Anyang [TJ] 166-167 LM 4
Anyox 48 C 2
Anzá [CO] 98-99 D 3
Anzac 49 C 2
Anzarān, Bi'r — 194-195 B 4
Anžero-Sudžensk 154-155 PQ 6
Anzhero Sudzhensk = Anžero-Sudžensk 154-155 PQ 6
Anzhu = ostrova Anjou 154-155 a-d 2
Ànzio 138-139 E 5

Aoba = Oba 182-183 N 3
Aoga-shima 166-167 Q 5
Aoga sima = Aoga-shima 166-167 Q 5
Aoji 170-171 H 1
Aomen = Macau 166-167 L 7
Aomori 166-167 QR 3
Aonach Urmhumhan 116-117 CD 8
Aonae 170-171 a 2
Aosta 138-139 B 3
Aouk, Bahr — 194-195 HJ 7
Aouker = Āwkār 194-195 BC 5
Aoya 170-171 JK 5
Aozou 194-195 H 4

Apa, Río — 103 E 2
Apache, AZ 74-75 J 7
Apache, OK 76-77 E 5
Apache Mountains 76-77 B 7
Apalachee Bay 58-59 K 6
Apalachicola, FL 78-79 G 6
Apalachicola Bay 78-79 G 6
Apalachicola River 78-79 G 5
Apan 86-87 L 8
Apaporis, Río — 98-99 EF 5
Aparri 174-175 H 3
Apat 46-47 ab 4
Apatity 154-155 EF 4
Apatity 142-143 F 2
Apatzingan de la Constitución 58-59 F 8
Apedia, Rio — 98-99 H 11
Apeldoorn 132-133 KL 2
Apennines 138-139 C 3-G 5
Apex, NC 80-81 G 3
Api [ZRE] 198 E 1
Apia 174-175 c 1
Apiacá, Rio — 98-99 K 9
Apiacás, Serra dos — 98-99 H 6-7
Apiaí 103 G 3
Apiaú, Serra do — 98-99 G 4
Apishapa River 68-69 D 7
Apizaco 86-87 LM 8
Apo, Mount — 174-175 HJ 5
Apodi, Chapada do- 98-99 M 6
Apolda 124 E 3
Apolinario Saravia 103 D 2
Apollonia = Sūsah 194-195 J 2
Apolo 98-99 F 7
Apolyont gölü 142-143 E 7
Aponguao, Río — 98-99 H 3
Apopka, FL 80-81 c 2
Aporé, Rio — 98-99 J 8
Aporema 98-99 N 4
Apostle Islands 58-59 HJ 2
Apóstoles 103 E 3
Apostolovo 142-143 F 6
Apoteri 98-99 H 4
Appalachia, VA 80-81 E 2
Appalachian Mountains 58-59 K 5-N 2
Appennino Abruzese 138-139 E 4-F 5
Appennino Toscano 138-139 D 3-4
Appennino Umbro-Marchigiano 138-139 E 4
Appleby 116-117 J 6
Applecross 116-117 F 3
Appleton, MN 70-71 BC 3
Appleton, WI 58-59 J 3
Appleton City, MO 70-71 CD 6
Appomattox, VA 80-81 G 2
Appozai 160-161 K 4
Approuague 98-99 MN 2
Apšeronsk 142-143 G 7
Apšeronskij poluostrov 142-143 K 7
Apsley Strait 182-183 EF 2
Apua Point 78-79 e 3
Apucarana 103 F 2
Apucarana, Serra de — 103 F 2
Apulia = Púglia 138-139 FG 5
Apure, Río — 98-99 F 3
Apurímac, Río — 98-99 E 7
Apussigamasi River 49 K 3

'Aqabah, Al- [JOR] 160-161 CD 5
'Aqabah, Khalīj al- 160-161 C 5
'Aqabah, Wādī al- 199 CD 2-3
'Aqabat aṣ-Ṣaghīrah, Al- 199 C 5
Āqā Jarī = Āghā Jarī 160-161 FG 4
'Aqeila, el — = Al-'Uqaylah 194-195 H 2
'Aqīq 194-195 M 5
Aqjawajat 194-195 B 5
Aqshār 194-195 B 4
Aqsu [TJ] 166-167 E 3
Aq Tagh Altai = Mongol Altajn Nuruu 166-167 F-H 2
Aquarius Plateau 74-75 H 3-4
Äquatorial-Guinea 194-195 FG 8
Aqueduc 82 I b 2
Aquidauana 98-99 H 9
Aquila, L' 138-139 E 4
Aquiles Serdán 76-77 B 8

Ārā = Arrah 160-161 N 5
'Arab, Baḥr al- 194-195 K 6-7
'Arab, Shaṭṭ al- 160-161 F 4
'Arabah, Wādī — 199 C 3
Arabatskaja Strelka, kosa — 142-143 FG 6
'Arabestān = Khūzestān 160-161 F 4
Arabi, GA 80-81 E 5
Arabia 26-27 LM 4
Arabian Basin 26-27 N 5
Arabian Desert 194-195 L 3-4
Arabian Sea 160-161 JK 7
Arabistan = Khūzestān 160-161 F 4
Araçá, Rio — 98-99 G 4
Aracaju 98-99 M 7
Aracati 98-99 M 5
Araçatuba 98-99 JK 9

Araçatub 207

Araceli = Dumaran Island 174-175 GH 4
Aracena, Sierra de — 132-133 D 10
Arachthós 138-139 J 6
Araçuaí 98-99 L 8
Arad 138-139 J 2
Arada 194-195 J 5-6
Arafura Sea 182-183 FG 2
Arago, Cape — 66-67 A 4
Aragón 132-133 G 7-8
Aragón, Río — 132-133 G 7
Araguacema 98-99 K 6
Araguaçu 98-99 NO 11
Aragua de Barcelona 98-99 G 3
Araguaia, Parque Nacional do — 98-99 NO 10
Araguaia, Rio — 98-99 J 7
Araguaína 98-99 O 8
Araguari 98-99 K 8
Araguari, Rio — [BR, Amapá] 98-99 J 4
Araguatins 98-99 K 6
Arai 170-171 M 4
'Araîch, el — = Al-'Arā'ish 194-195 C 1
Árainnn Mhór 116-117 C 5
Araioses 98-99 L 5
'Arā'ish, Al- 194-195 C 1
Araito = ostrov Altasova 154-155 de 7
'Araiyiḍa, Bîr — = Bi'r 'Urayyiḍah 199 BC 3
Arak [DZ] 194-195 E 3
Arāk [IR] 160-161 F 4
Arakamčečen, ostrov — 154-155 l 5
Arakan = Ragaing Taing 174-175 B 2
Arakan Yoma = Ragaing Yōma 174-175 B 2-3
Arakawa 170-171 M 3
Araks 142-143 J 8
Aral, Lake — = Aral'skoje more 154-155 KL 8-9
Ara Lake 50 F 2
Aral Sea = Aral'skoje more 154-155 KL 8-9
Aral'sk 154-155 L 8
Aral'skoje more 154-155 KL 8-9
Aralsul'fat 154-155 L 8
Aramac 182-183 HJ 4
'Aramah, Al — 160-161 F 5-6
Aramberri 86-87 KL 5
Aranda de Duero 132-133 F 8
Arandas 86-87 J 7
Arandjelovac 138-139 J 3
Aran Island = Árainn Mhór 116-117 C 5
Aran Islands = Oileáin Árann 116-117 B 7
Aranjuez 132-133 F 8-9
Aran Mawddwy 116-117 H 8
Árann, Oileáin — 116-117 B 7
Aransas Pass, TX 76-77 F 9
Aranuka 178 H 2
Arao 170-171 H 6
Araoua, Chaîne d' 98-99 M 3
Araouane 194-195 D 5
Arapahoe, NE 68-69 G 5
Arapari 98-99 O 7
Arapey 103 E 4
Arapiuns, Rio — 98-99 L 6
Arapongas 103 F 2
Araranguá 103 G 3
Araraquara 98-99 K 9
Araras [BR, Pará] 98-99 J 6
Araras [BR, São Paulo] 98-99 K 9
Araras, Cachoeira — 98-99 M 8
Araras, Serra das — [BR, Maranhão] 98-99 P 8
Araras, Serra das — [BR, Mato Grosso] 98-99 J 8
Araras, Serra das — [BR, Paraná] 103 F 2-3
Ararat [AUS] 182-183 H 7
Ararat = Büyük Ağrı dağı 160-161 E 2-3
Arari, Cachoeira do — 98-99 K 5
Arari, Lago — 98-99 O 5
Araripe, Chapada do — 98-99 LM 6
Arariúna = Cachoeira do Arari 98-99 K 5
Aras, Rūd-e — 142-143 HJ 8
Aras nehri 160-161 E 2
Araticu 98-99 O 5
Arato = Shirataka 170-171 MN 3
Arauá, Rio — [BR ◁ Rio Madero] 98-99 H 8
Arauã, Rio — [BR ◁ Rio Purus] 98-99 F 9
Arauan = Araouane 194-195 D 5
Arauca [CO, place] 98-99 E 3
Arauca, Río — 98-99 F 3
Arauco 103 B 5
Aravaipa Valley 74-75 H 6
Ārāvaļā Parvata = Arāvalli Range 160-161 L 6-M 5
Arāvalli Range 160-161 L 6-M 5
Arawa 174-175 j 6
Araxá 98-99 K 8
Arba'in, Lâqiyat al- 194-195 K 4
Arbaj Cheere = Arvajcheer 166-167 J 2
Arba Minch = Arba Minty 194-195 M 7
Arba Minty 194-195 M 7
Arbay Here = Arvajcheer 166-167 J 2
Arbhach, Loch — 116-117 C 6
Arbīl 160-161 E 3
Arboga 114-115 F 8
Arbon, ID 66-67 G 4
Arborfield 49 G 4
Arborg 49 K 5
Arbroath 116-117 J 4
Arbuckle, CA 74-75 B 3
Arbuckle Mountains 76-77 F 5
Arcachon 132-133 G 6
Arcadia, FL 80-81 c 3
Arcadia, IN 70-71 G 5
Arcadia, KS 70-71 C 7
Arcadia, NE 68-69 G 5
Arcadia, TX 78-79 C 4
Arcadia, WI 70-71 E 3
Arcahaie, L' 88-89 K 5
Arcas, Cayos — 86-87 P 7
Arcata, CA 66-67 A 5
Arc Dome 74-75 E 3
Arcelia 86-87 K 8
Archangaj 166-167 J 2
Archangel'sk 154-155 G 5
Archenū, Gebel — = Jabal Arkanū 194-195 J 4
Archer Bay 182-183 H 2
Archer City, TX 76-77 E 6
Archer River 182-183 H 2
Arches National Monument 74-75 J 3
Archive 49 F 5
Arckaringa 182-183 FG 5
Arco 138-139 D 3
Arco, ID 66-67 G 4
Arco, El — 86-87 D 3
Arcola, IL 70-71 F 6
Arctic Bay 46-47 TU 3
Arctic Institute Range 31 B 16
Arctic Ocean 26-27 D-Q 1
Arctic Red River [CDN, place] 46-47 K 4
Arctic Red River [CDN, river] 46-47 K 4
Arctic Village, AK 52-53 OP 2
Arda 138-139 L 5
Ardabīl 160-161 F 3
Ardakān 160-161 G 4
Ardakān = Ardekān 160-161 GH 4
Årdalstangen 114-115 BC 7
Ardar Gwagwa, Jabal — 199 D 6
Ardebil = Ardabīl 160-161 F 3
Ardèche 132-133 K 6
Ardee = Áth Fhirdia 116-117 E 7
Ardekān 160-161 GH 4
Arden, NV 74-75 F 4
Ardennes 132-133 K 4-L 3
Ardennes, Canal des — 132-133 K 4
Ardestān 160-161 G 4
Ardila 132-133 D 9
Ardmore, OK 58-59 G 5
Ardmore, SD 68-69 E 4
Ardnamurchan, Point of — 116-117 E 4
Ardoch, ND 68-69 H 1
Ards 116-117 F 6
Ards Peninsula 116-117 F 6
Ardud 138-139 K 2
Åre 114-115 E 6
Arecibo 58-59 N 8
Areia Branca 98-99 M 5-6
Arelão, Serra do — 98-99 M 5
Arelee 49 E 4
Arena 68-69 B 1
Arena, Point — 74-75 AB 3
Arena de las Ventas, Punta — 86-87 F 5-6
Arenales, Cerro — 103 B 7
Arenas, Cayo — 86-87 P 6
Arenas, Punta de — 103 C 8
Arendal 114-115 C 8
Arequipa [PE, place] 98-99 E 8
Arere 98-99 J 5
Åreskutan 114-115 E 6
Arévalo 132-133 E 8
Arezzo 138-139 DE 4
Argachtach 154-155 d 4
Arga-Muora-Sise, ostrov — 154-155 XY 3
Argelès-sur-Mer 132-133 J 7
Argent, Rivière l' 51 B 2
Argenta 138-139 D 3
Argentan 132-133 GH 4
Argentenay 50 PQ 2
Argenteuil 132-133 J 4
Argentia 46-47 Za 8
Argentina [RA, state] 103 C 7-D 2
Argentine Basin 26-27 GH 7-8
Argentine Islands 31 C 30
Argeş 138-139 M 3
Arghandāb Rōd 160-161 K 4
Argolikós Kólpos 138-139 K 7
Argonne 132-133 K 4
Argonne, WI 70-71 F 3
Árgos 138-139 K 7
Argos, IN 70-71 G 5
Argostólion 138-139 J 6
Arguello, Point — 74-75 C 5
Argun' [SU, river ◁ Amur] 154-155 WX 7
Argungu 194-195 EF 6
Argut 154-155 Q 8
Argyle, MN 68-69 H 1
Argyll 116-117 FG 4
Århus 114-115 D 9
Ariake kai = Ariakeno-umi 170-171 H 6
Ariakeno-umi 170-171 H 6
Ariake-wan = Shibushi-wan 170-171 H 7
Ariano Irpino 138-139 F 5
Ari Atoll 36 a 2
Ariaú 98-99 K 6
Aribinda 194-195 D 6
Arica [CO] 98-99 E 5
Arica [RCH] 103 B 1
Arichat 51 F 5
'Ariḍ, Al- 160-161 F 6-7
Arid, Cape — 182-183 D 6
Ariège 132-133 H 7
Ariel, WA 66-67 B 3
Arikaree River 68-69 E 6
Arikawa 170-171 G 6
Arimã [BR] 98-99 G 6
Arimo, ID 66-67 GH 4
Arimu Mine 98-99 J 1
Arinos 98-99 K 8
Arinos, Rio — 98-99 H 7
Ario de Rosales 86-87 K 8
Arion, IA 70-71 C 5
Aripuanã [BR, landscape] 98-99 J 10
Aripuanã [BR, place] 98-99 J 10
Aripuanã, Rio — 98-99 G 6
Ariquemes 98-99 G 6
Arisaig, Sound of — 116-117 EF 4
'Arīsh, Al- 194-195 L 2
'Arīsh, Wādī al- 199 C 2-3
Arismendi 98-99 F 3
Aristazabal Island 48 C 3
Arita 170-171 K 5
Ariton, AL 78-79 G 5
Arivaca, AZ 74-75 H 7
Ariyaddu Channel 36 a 2
Ariza 132-133 FG 8
Arizaro, Salar de — 103 C 2
Arizona [RA] 103 C 5
Arizona [USA] 58-59 D 5
Arizpe 86-87 E 2
Årjäng 114-115 E 8
Arjeplog 114-115 GH 4
Arjona [CO] 98-99 D 2
Arka 154-155 b 5
Arkabutla Lake 78-79 DE 3
Arkadak 142-143 H 5
Arkadelphia, AR 78-79 C 3
Arkadía 138-139 JK 7
Arkaig, Loch — 116-117 F 4
Arkalyk 154-155 M 7
Arkansas 58-59 H 4
Arkansas City, AR 78-79 D 4
Arkansas City, KS 76-77 F 4
Arkansas River 58-59 F 4
Arkanū, Jabal — 194-195 J 4
Arkell, Mount — 52-53 U 6
Arkenu, Jebel — = Jabal Arkanū 194-195 J 4
Arkhangelsk = Archangel'sk 154-155 G 5
Arklow = An tInbhear Mór 116-117 EF 8
Arkoma, OK 76-77 G 5
Arkona, Kap — 124 F 1
Arktičeskogo Instituta, ostrova — 154-155 OP 2
Arlanzón 132-133 EF 7
Arlberg 124 E 5
Arlee, MT 66-67 F 2
Arles 132-133 K 7
Arlington, CO 68-69 E 6
Arlington, GA 78-79 G 5
Arlington, OR 66-67 CD 3
Arlington, SD 68-69 H 3
Arlington, TN 78-79 E 3
Arlington, TX 76-77 F 6
Arlington, VA 58-59 L 4
Arlington, WA 66-67 BC 1
Arlington Heights, IL 70-71 FG 4
Arlington National Cemetery 82 II a 2
Arlit 194-195 F 5
Arlon 132-133 K 4
Armadale 182-183 C 6
Armagh 116-117 E 6
Armagnac 132-133 GH 7
Arm'anskaja Sovetskaja Socialističeskaja Respublika = Armenian Soviet Socialist Republic 160-161 EF 2-3
Armant 199 C 5
Armavir 142-143 H 7
Armenia [CO] 98-99 D 4
Armenia [SU] 110-111 R 8-S 7
Armenian Soviet Socialist Republic 160-161 EF 2-3
Armentières 132-133 J 3
Armería, Río — 86-87 HJ 8
Armero 98-99 E 4
Armevistês, Akrōtērion — 138-139 M 7
Armidale 182-183 K 6
Arminto, WY 68-69 C 4
Armit 49 GH 4
Armour, SD 68-69 G 4
Arms 70-71 GH 1
Armstead, MT 66-67 G 3
Armstrong, IA 70-71 C 4
Armstrong, TX 76-77 EF 9
Armstrong [CDN] 48 H 4
Armstrong Station 50 E 2
Armuña, La — 132-133 DE 8
Arnarfjördhur 114-115 ab 2
Arnarvatn 114-115 cd 2
Arnas dağı 142-143 H 8
Arnaud 50 A 3
Arnaûtês, Akrotêrion — 142-143 F 8
Årnes 114-115 cd 2
Arnett, OK 76-77 E 4
Arnhem 132-133 KL 2-3
Arnhem, Cape — 182-183 G 2
Arnhem Bay 182-183 G 2
Arnhem Land 182-183 FG 2
Arno, TX 76-77 C 7
Arno [I] 138-139 D 4
Arno [Marshall Islands] 178 H 2
Arnold 116-117 KL 7-8
Arnold, NE 68-69 FG 5
Arnold, PA 72-73 G 4
Arnot 49 K 3
Arnøy 114-115 J 2
Arnprior 72-73 H 2
Arnsberg 124 D 3
Arnstadt 124 E 3
Aroab 198 C 7
Arocha 76-77 C 9
Arōmā = Arūmā 194-195 M 5
Aroostook River 46-47 X 8
Aropuk Lake 52-53 EF 6
Arorae 178 H 3
Aros, Río — 86-87 F 3
Arqa tagh 166-167 FG 4
'Arqūb, Al- 194-195 AB 4
Arrah [IND] 160-161 N 5
Arraias 98-99 K 7
Arraias, Rio — [BR, Mato Grosso] 98-99 L 10-11
Arraias do Araguaia, Rio das — 98-99 N 9-O 8
Arraiján 58-59 b 3
Arran 116-117 F 5
Arrandale 48 C 2
Arras 132-133 J 3
Arrecife 194-195 B 3
Arrée, Monts d' 132-133 EF 4
Arrey, NM 76-77 A 6
Arriaga 58-59 H 8
Arriola, CO 74-75 J 4
Arrochar 116-117 G 4
Arrow, Lough — = Loch Arbhach 116-117 C 6
Arrowhead 48 J 4
Arrow Lake 70-71 EF 1
Arroyo Grande, CA 74-75 CD 5
Arroyo Seco [USA ◁ Colorado River] 74-75 F 6
Arroyo Seco [USA ◁ Los Angeles] 83 III c 1
Arša Nuur = Chagan nuur 166-167 L 3
Arsenault Lake 49 D 3
Arsenjev 154-155 Z 9
Árta 138-139 J 6
Arta, Gulf of — = Ambrakikós Kólpos 138-139 J 6
Arṭāwīyah, Al — 160-161 EF 5
Artemisa 88-89 E 3
Artesia, CA 83 III d 2
Artesia, CO 66-67 J 5
Artesia, MS 78-79 E 4
Artesia, NM 58-59 EF 5
Artesian, SD 68-69 GH 3
Artesia Wells, TX 76-77 E 8
Arthabaska 72-73 KL 1
Arthur 72-73 F 3
Arthur, NE 68-69 F 5
Arthur City, TX 76-77 G 6
Arthur Kill 82 III a 3
Arthur's Pass 182-183 O 8
Arti 142-143 L 4
Artigas [ROU, place] 103 E 4
Art Institute 83 II b 1
Artjärvi 114-115 LM 7
Artois 132-133 J 3
Art'om 154-155 Z 9
Art'omovsk [SU, Rossijskaja SFSR] 154-155 R 7
Art'omovskij [SU ↗ Bodajbo] 154-155 VW 6
Art'omovskij [SU ↗ Sverdlovsk] 154-155 L 6
Artur de Paiva = Capelongo 198 C 4
Artur de Paiva = Cubango 198 C 4
Arturo Prat 31 C 30-31
Artvin 160-161 E 2
Aru 198 F 1
Aru, Kepulauan — 174-175 KL 8
Arua 198 F 1
Aruab 198 C 7
Aruanã 98-99 J 7
Aruba 58-59 N 9
Arumã [BR] 98-99 G 5
Arūmā [Sudan] 194-195 M 5
Arumbi 198 EF 1
Arun 160-161 O 5
Arunachal Pradesh 160-161 P Q 5
Arundel 116-117 L 10
Arunta Desert = Simpson Desert 182-183 G 4-5
Arusha 198 G 2
Arusī 194-195 M 7
Aruwimi 198 E 1
Arvada, CO 68-69 D 6
Arvada, WY 68-69 CD 3
Arvajcheer 166-167 J 2
Arverne, New York-, NY 82 III d 3
Arvida 51 A 3
Arvidsjaur 114-115 H 5
Arvika 114-115 E 8
Arvin, CA 74-75 D 5
Arys' 154-155 M 9
Arzamas 154-155 GH 6
Arzgir 142-143 H 6
Åsa [S] 114-115 E 9
Aša [SU] 142-143 L 4
Asadābād [AFG] 160-161 L 4
Asahi 170-171 N 5
Asahi dake [J, Hokkaidō] 166-167 R 3
Asahi dake [J, Yamagata] 170-171 M 3
Asahigava = Asahikawa 166-167 R 3
Asahi gawa 170-171 J 5
Asahikawa 166-167 R 3
Asalē 194-195 MN 6
Asam 160-161 P 5
Asángaro = Azángaro 98-99 EF7
Asansol 160-161 O 6
Asante = Ashanti 194-195 D 7
Åsarna 114-115 F 6
'Asayr 160-161 G 8
Asayta 194-195 N 6
Asbest 154-155 L 6
Asbestos 72-73 L 2
Asbe Teferī 194-195 N 7
Asbury Park, NJ 72-73 JK 4
Ascensión [BOL] 98-99 G 8
Ascension [GB] 188-189 F 9
Ascensión [MEX] 86-87 FG 2
Ascensión, Bahía de la — 58-59 J 8
Aschabad 160-161 HJ 3
Aschaffenburg 124 D 4
Ascoli-Piceno 138-139 E 4
Aseb 194-195 N 6
Asela 194-195 M 7
Åsele 114-115 G 5
Aselle = Asela 194-195 M 7
Asenovgrad 138-139 L 4-5
Aserraderos 86-87 GH 6
Aşfī 194-195 C 2
Aşfūn 199 C 5
Ashanti 194-195 D 7
Ashbourne 116-117 K 7-8
Ashburn, GA 80-81 E 5
Ashburn, Chicago-, IL 83 II a 2
Ashburton 182-183 O 8
Ashburton River 182-183 C 4
Ashby de la Zouch 116-117 K 8
Ashcroft 48 G 4
Ashdown, AR 76-77 G 6
Asheboro, NC 80-81 FG 3
Asherton, TX 76-77 DE 8
Asheville, NC 58-59 K 4
Asheweig River 50 DE 1
Ashe Yōma 174-175 C 3
Ashford 116-117 M 9
Ashford, AL 78-79 G 5
Ashford, WA 66-67 BC 2
Ash Fork, AZ 74-75 G 5
Ash Grove, MO 78-79 C 2
Ashibetsu 170-171 c 2
Ashikaga 170-171 M 4
Ashington 116-117 K 5
Ashizuri-zaki 170-171 J 6
Ashkhabad = Aschabad 160-161 HJ 3
Ashkum, IL 70-71 FG 5
Ashland, AL 78-79 FG 4
Ashland, IL 70-71 E 6
Ashland, KS 76-77 DE 4
Ashland, KY 58-59 K 4
Ashland, ME 72-73 M 1
Ashland, MT 68-69 CD 3
Ashland, NE 68-69 H 5
Ashland, OH 72-73 EF 4
Ashland, OR 66-67 B 4
Ashland, VA 80-81 H 2
Ashland, WI 58-59 H 2
Ashland, Mount — 66-67 B 4
Ashland City 78-79 F 2
Ashley 70-71 F 6
Ashley, MI 70-71 H 4
Ashley, ND 68-69 G 2
Ashmont 49 C 3
Ashmūn 199 B 2
Ashmūnayn, Al- 199 B 4
Ashshur = Assur 160-161 E 3
Ashtabula, OH 72-73 F 3-4
Ashtabula, Lake — = Baldhill Reservoir 68-69 GH 2
Ashton, ID 66-67 H 3
Ashton, IL 70-71 F 5
Ashuanipi Lake 46-47 X 7
Ashuapmuchuan, Rivière — 50 P 2
Asia 26-27 N-P 3
Asia, Kepulauan — 174-175 K 6
Asike 174-175 LM 8
Asinara 138-139 BC 5
Asinara, Golfo dell' 138-139 C 5
Asi nehri 142-143 G 8
Asino 154-155 PQ 6
'Asīr 160-161 E 7
Asiut = Asyūţ 194-195 L 3
Asker 114-115 D 8
Askersund 114-115 F 8
Askinuk Mountains 52-53 E 6
Askiz 154-155 R 7
Askja 114-115 e 2
Askol'd, ostrov — 170-171 J 1
Asmara = Asmera 194-195 M 5
Asmera 194-195 M 5
Asnām, Al- 194-195 E 1
Asosa 194-195 LM 6
Asotin, WA 66-67 E 2
Aso zan 170-171 H 6
Aspen, CO 68-69 C 6
Aspen Hill, MD 72-73 H 5
Aspermont, TX 76-77 D 6
Aspid, Mount — 52-53 n 4
Aspiring, Mount — 182-183 N 8
Aspromonte 138-139 FG 6
Aspy Bay 51 FG 4
'Aşr, Jabal al- 199 B 6
Assab = Aseb 194-195 N 6
Assad, Buhayrat al- 160-161 D 3
Assaitta = Asaita 194-195 N 6
Assal, Lac — 194-195 N 6
Assale = Asalē 194-195 MN 6
Assam = Asam 160-161 P 5
Assam Hills 160-161 P 5
Assam Himālaya 160-161 OP 5
Assateague Island 72-73 J 5
Assen 132-133 L 2
Assens 114-115 CD 10
Assiniboia 49 F 6
Assiniboine, Mount — 46-47 NO 7
Assiniboine River 46-47 Q 7
Assinica, Lac — 50 O 1
Assinica, la Réserve de — 50 O 1
Assis 98-99 J 9
Assis Brasil 98-99 D 10
Assisi 138-139 E 4
Assiut = Asyūţ 194-195 L 3
Assomption, L' 72-73 K 2
Assuan = Aswān 194-195 L 4
Assumption, IL 70-71 F 6
Assumption Island 198 J 3
Assur 160-161 E 3
Assynt 116-117 F 2
Astakós 138-139 J 6
Astara 142-143 J 8
Astin tagh = Altin tagh 166-167 EF 4
Astley 116-117 J 8
Astorga 132-133 DE 7
Astoria, OR 58-59 B 2
Astoria, SD 68-69 H 3
Astoria, New York-, NY 82 III c 2
Astove Island 198 J 4
Astra 103 C 7
Astrachan' 142-143 J 6
Astrida 198 E 2
Astrolabe Bay 174-175 N 7-8
Asturias 132-133 DE 7
Astypálaia 138-139 LM 7
Asunción [PY] 103 E 3
Asuncion [USA] 148-149 S 8
Asunción, La — 98-99 G 2
Asūtarībah, Jabal — 199 E 7
Aswa 198 F 1
Aswān 194-195 L 4
'Aswân, Sad el — = Sadd al-'Ālī 194-195 L 3
Asyūţ 194-195 L 3
Asyūţī, Wādī al- 199 B 4
Ata 178 J 5
Atacama [RA] 103 BC 3
Atacama, Desierto de — 103 B 3-C 2
Atacama, Salar de — 103 C 2
Atacama Trench 34-35 O 5-6
Atafu 178 J 3
Atakor = Atākūr 194-195 F 4
Atakora [DY, mountains] 194-195 E 6-7
Atakpamé 194-195 E 7
Atākūr 194-195 F 4
Atalaia, Ponta de — 98-99 P 5
Atalanti Channel = Evboïkós Kólpos 138-139 KL 6
Atalaya [PE, place] 98-99 E 7
Ataleia 98-99 L 8
Atami 170-171 M 5
Atanik, AK 52-53 GH 1
Ataniya = Adana 160-161 D 3
Ataouat, Day Nui — 174-175 E 3
Atapupu 174-175 H 8
'Atāqah, Jabal — 199 C 2-3
Āţār 194-195 B 4
Atarque, NM 74-75 J 5
Atascadero, CA 74-75 C 5
Atasta 86-87 O 8
Atasu 154-155 N 8
Ataúba 98-99 H 5
Ataúro, Ilha de — 174-175 J 8
'Aţbarah 194-195 L 5
'Aţbarah, Nahr — 194-195 LM 5
Atbasar 154-155 M 7
Atchafalaya Bay 78-79 D 6
Atchison, KS 70-71 C 6
Atchueelinguk River 52-53 G 5
Atelchu, Rio — 98-99 L 11
Atessa 138-139 F 4-5
Atfārītī 194-195 B 3
Aţfīḩ 199 B 3
Athabasca [CDN, administrative unit] 46-47 O 7
Athabasca [CDN, place] 48 L 2
Athabasca, Lake — 46-47 OP 6
Athabasca River 46-47 O 6
Átha Cliath 116-117 E 7

208 **Araceli**

Athboy = Áth Buidhe 116-117 DE 7
Áth Buidhe 116-117 DE 7
Áth Dara 116-117 C 8
Athena, OR 66-67 D 3
Athēnai 138-139 KL 7
Athenry = Áth na Rí 116-117 C 7
Athens, AL 78-79 F 3
Athens, GA 58-59 K 5
Athens, OH 72-73 E 5
Athens, PA 72-73 H 4
Athens, TN 78-79 G 3
Athens, TX 76-77 FG 6
Athens, WI 70-71 EF 3
Athens = Athēnai 138-139 KL 7
Atherton 182-183 HJ 3
Áth Fhirdia 116-117 E 7
Athi 198 G 2
Áth Í 116-117 DE 8
Athlone = Áth Luain 116-117 CD 7
Áth Luain 116-117 CD 7
Áth na Rí 116-117 C 7
Athol, ID 66-67 E 2
Áthos 138-139 L 5
Áth Trasna 116-117 BC 8
Áth Troim 116-117 E 7
Athy = Áth Í 116-117 DE 8
Ati 194-195 H 6
Atico 98-99 E 8
Aticonipi, Lac — 51 G 2
Atikameg 48 JK 2
Atikameg Lake 49 H 3
Atikameg River 50 H 1-2
Atikins, AR 78-79 C 3
Atikokan 70-71 E 1
Atikup 50 D 1
Atikwa Lake 50 C 3
Atitlán, Volcán — 58-59 H 9
Atka 154-155 d 5
Atka, AK 52-53 j 4
Atka Island 30 D 36
Atka Pass 52-53 j 4-5
Atkarsk 142-143 H 5
Atkinson, NE 68-69 G 4
Atlanta, GA 58-59 K 5
Atlanta, ID 66-67 F 4
Atlanta, IL 70-71 F 5
Atlanta, MI 70-71 HJ 3
Atlanta, MO 70-71 D 6
Atlanta, TX 76-77 G 6
Atlantic, IA 70-71 C 5
Atlantic Beach, NY 82 III d 3
Atlantic City, NJ 58-59 M 4
Atlantic Coastal Plain 58-59 K 5-L 4
Atlantic Indian Antarctic Basin 26-27 J-M 9
Atlantic Indian Ridge 26-27 J-L 8
Atlantic Ocean 26-27 G 4-J 7
Atlantic Peak 68-69 B 4
Aṭlas al-Kabīr, Al- 194-195 CD 2
Aṭlas al-Mutawassiṭ, Al- 194-195 CD 2
Aṭlas aṣ-Ṣaghīr, Al- 194-195 C 2-3
Atlas aṣ-Ṣaḥrā', Al- 194-195 D 2-F 1
Atlasova, ostrov — 154-155 de 7
Atlin 46-47 K 6
Atlin Lake 46-47 K 6
Atlixco 58-59 G 8
Atløy 114-115 A 7
Atmore, AL 78-79 F 5
Atna Peak 48 CD 3
Atna Range 48 D 2
Atnarko 48 E 3
Atoka, OK 76-77 FG 5
Atomic City, ID 66-67 G 4
Atotonilco el Alto 86-87 JK 7
Atouat, Massif d' = Day Nui Ataouat 174-175 E 3
Atoyac, Río — 86-87 L 8
Atoyac de Álvarez 86-87 K 9
Aträk, Rūd-e 160-161 H 3
Aṭrash, Wādī al- 199 C 4
Atrato, Río — 98-99 D 3
Atrek 142-143 K 8
'Aṭrūn, Wāḥāt al- 194-195 K 5
Atsumi 170-171 M 3
Atsumi-hantō 170-171 L 5
Atsunai 170-171 cd 2
Atsuta 170-171 b 2
Atsutoko 170-171 d 2
Attalea = Antalya 160-161 C 3
Attaléia = Antalya 160-161 C 3
Attalla, AL 78-79 F 3-4
Attawapiskat 50 H 1
Attawapiskat Lake 50 F 1
Attawapiskat River 46-47 TU 7
Attica, IN 70-71 G 5
Attica, KS 76-77 E 4
Attica, OH 72-73 E 4
Attleborough 116-117 M 8
Attopeu 174-175 E 3-4
Attopo' = Attopeu 174-175 E 3-4
Attu, AK 52-53 p 6
Attu Island 30 D 1
Attwood Lake 50 E 2
Atūwi, Wād — 194-195 B 4
Atwater, CA 74-75 C 4
Atwater, MN 70-71 C 3
Atwood, CO 68-69 E 5
Atwood, KS 68-69 F 6

Auasbila 88-89 D 7
Auati Paraná, Rio — 98-99 F 5
Aubagne 132-133 K 7
Aube 132-133 K 4
Aubrac, Monts d' 132-133 J 6
Aubrey Falls 50 K 3
Auburn, AL 58-59 J 5
Auburn, CA 74-75 C 3
Auburn, IL 70-71 F 6
Auburn, IN 70-71 H 5
Auburn, KY 78-79 F 2
Auburn, ME 72-73 L 2
Auburn, NE 70-71 BC 5
Auburn, NY 72-73 H 3
Auburn, WA 66-67 B 2
Auburndale, FL 80-81 c 2-3
Auburndale, New York-, NY 82 III d 2
Aucanquilcha, Cerro — 103 C 2
Auch 132-133 H 7
Auchty, Slieve — = Sliabh Eachtgha 116-117 C 7-8
Auckland 182-183 OP 7
Auckland Islands 31 D 17-18
Aude 132-133 J 7
Auden 50 F 2
Audley 116-117 J 7
Audubon, IA 70-71 C 5
Aue 124 F 3
Auenat, Gebel — = Jabal al-'Uwaynāt 194-195 K 4
Auf, Ras el- = Rā's Banās 194-195 M 4
Augathella 182-183 J 5
Aughnacloy 116-117 E 6
Augila = Awjilah 194-195 J 3
Augrabies Falls = Augrabiesval 198 CD 7
Augrabiesval 198 CD 7
Au Gres, MI 70-71 J 3
Augsburg 124 E 4
Augusta, AR 78-79 D 3
Augusta, GA 58-59 K 5
Augusta, IL 70-71 E 5
Augusta, KS 68-69 H 7
Augusta, KY 72-73 DE 5
Augusta, ME 58-59 N 3
Augusta, MT 66-67 G 2
Augusta, WI 70-71 E 3
Augusta [AUS] 182-183 BC 6
Augusta [I] 138-139 F 7
Augustine Island 52-53 L 7
Augustines, Lac des — 72-73 J 1
Augusto Correia 98-99 P 5
Augustów 124 L 2
Augustus, Mount — 182-183 C 4
Augustus Downs 182-183 GH 3
Augustus Island 182-183 D 3
Auk = Bahr Aouk 194-195 HJ 7
Auki 174-175 k 6
Aulander, NC 80-81 H 2
Auld, Lake — 182-183 D 4
Aulneau Peninsula 50 B 3
Aunis 132-133 G 5
Auob 198 C 7
Aur 178 H 2
Aurangābād [IND, Mahārāṣhṭra] 160-161 LM 6-7
Aurélio do Carmo 98-99 P 6
Aurich 124 C 2
Aurignac 132-133 H 7
Aurillac 132-133 J 6
Aurlandsvangen 114-115 B 7
Aurora, AK 52-53 EF 4
Aurora, CO 68-69 D 6
Aurora, IL 58-59 J 3
Aurora, IN 70-71 H 6
Aurora, MN 70-71 DE 2
Aurora, MO 78-79 C 2
Aurora, NC 80-81 H 3
Aurora, NE 68-69 GH 5
Aurora, OH 72-73 D 5
Aurora [CDN] 72-73 G 2-3
Aurora Lodge, AK 52-53 OP 4
Aurukun 182-183 H 2
Aus 198 C 7
Au Sable Point [USA, Lake Huron] 72-73 E 2
Au Sable Point [USA, Lake Superior] 70-71 G 2
Au Sable River 70-71 HJ 3
Ausangate = Nudo Ausangate 98-99 E 7
Ausiait 46-47 Za 4
Aust-Agder 114-115 BC 8
Austfonna 114-115 m 4
Austin 49 J 6
Austin, MN 58-59 H 3
Austin, MT 66-67 GH 2
Austin, NV 74-75 E 3
Austin, OR 66-67 D 3
Austin, TX 58-59 G 5
Austin, Chicago-, IL 83 II a 1
Austin, Lake — 182-183 C 5
Australia 182-183 C-J 4
Australien 182-183 C-J 4
Austria 124 E-G 5
Austur-Bardhastrandar 114-115 bc 2
Austur-Húnavatn 114-115 cd 2
Austur-Skaftafell 114-115 ef 2
Austvågøy 114-115 F 3
Austwell, TX 76-77 F 8
Auteuil 82 I a 1
Autlán de Navarro 58-59 EF 8
Autun 132-133 K 5
Auvergne [AUS] 182-183 EF 3
Auvergne [F] 132-133 J 6
Auxerre 132-133 J 5
Auxvasse, MO 70-71 DE 6
Ava, IL 70-71 F 7
Ava, MO 78-79 C 2
Avadh 160-161 N 5
Avakubi 198 E 1
Avalik River 52-53 H 1
Avalon, CA 74-75 D 6
Avalon, Lake — 76-77 BC 6
Avalon Peninsula 46-47 a 8
Avanavero Dam 98-99 K 2
Avant, OK 76-77 F 4
Avaré 98-99 K 9
Avatanak Island 52-53 o 3-4
Aveiro [BR] 98-99 HJ 5
Aveiro [P] 132-133 C 8
Avellaneda [RA, Buenos Aires] 103 DE 4-5
Avellino 138-139 F 5
Avenal, CA 74-75 CD 4
Averøy 114-115 B 6
Aversa 138-139 EF 5
Avery, ID 66-67 F 2
Aves 88-89 P 7
Avesta 114-115 G 7
Aveyron 132-133 HJ 6
Avezzano 138-139 E 4-5
Aviemore 116-117 H 3
Avignon 132-133 K 7
Ávila [E] 132-133 E 8
Avilés 132-133 DE 7
Avión, Faro de — 132-133 CD 7
Avis 132-133 D 9
Avlije-Ata = Džambul 154-155 MN 9
Avoca 116-117 E 8
Avoca, IA 70-71 C 5
Avola [CDN] 48 H 4
Avola [I] 138-139 F 7
Avon 116-117 J 9
Avon, IL 70-71 E 5
Avon, MT 66-67 G 2
Avon, SD 68-69 GH 4
Avon, Ben — 116-117 H 3
Avon, River — 116-117 J 9
Avondale, AZ 74-75 G 6
Avondale, CO 68-69 D 6
Avondale, Chicago-, IL 83 II b 1
Avon Downs 182-183 G 4
Avonlea 49 F 6
Avon Park, FL 80-81 c 3
Avontuur 198 D 8
Avranches 132-133 G 4

Awadh = Avadh 160-161 N 5
Awādī 194-195 B 4
Awaji-shima 170-171 K 5
'Awānah 194-195 C 5
Awasa [ETH, lake] 194-195 M 7
Awasa [ETH, place] 194-195 M 7
Awash [ETH, place] 194-195 MN 7
Awash [ETH, river] 194-195 M 7
Awa-shima 170-171 M 3
Awaso 194-195 D 7
Awaya 170-171 K 5
Awbārī 194-195 G 3
Awbārī, Ṣaḥrā' — 194-195 G 3
Awdheegle 194-195 N 8
Awe, Loch — 116-117 F 4
Aweil = Uwayl 194-195 K 7
Awjilah 194-195 J 3
Awkār 194-195 BC 5
Awlaytīs, Wād — 194-195 B 3
Awsart 194-195 B 4
Awul 174-175 h 6
Awuna River 52-53 J 2

Axarfjördhur 114-115 e 1
Axel Heiberg Island 46-47 ST 1-2
Axial, CO 68-69 C 5
Axim 194-195 D 8
Axinim 98-99 J 6
Ax-les-Thermes 132-133 HJ 7
Axminster 116-117 J 10
Axochiapán 86-87 L 8

Ayabaca 98-99 CD 5
Ayabe 170-171 K 5
Ayacucho [PE, place] 98-99 E 7
Ayacucho [RA] 103 E 5
Ayagh Qum köl 166-167 F 4
Ayamonte 132-133 D 10
'Ayashī, Jabal — 194-195 CD 2
Ayaviri 98-99 E 7
Ayden, NC 80-81 H 3
Aydın 160-161 B 3
Aydin köl 166-167 F 3
Ayers Rock 182-183 F 5
Ayiyak River 52-53 L 2
'Aylay 194-195 L 5
Aylesbury 116-117 KL 9
Aylmer [CDN, Ontario] 72-73 F 3
Aylmer [CDN, Quebec] 72-73 HJ 2
Aylsham 116-117 h 6
Aylwin 72-73 H 2
'Ayn, Wādī al- 160-161 H 6
'Aynabo 194-195 O 7
'Ayn al-Muqshīn, Al- 160-161 GH 7
'Ayn Azzān 194-195 G 4
'Ayn Qazzān 194-195 EF 5
'Ayn Ṣafrā 194-195 DE 2
'Ayn Ṣāliḥ 194-195 E 3
'Ayn Tādīn 194-195 E 4
'Ayn-Umannās 194-195 F 3
Aynunāh 154-155 D 5
Ayōd 194-195 L 7
Ayr [AUS] 182-183 J 3
Ayr [GB] 116-117 G 5
Ayr, River — 116-117 G 5
Ayre, Piont of — 116-117 G 6
Ayrig Nur = Ajrag nuur 166-167 GH 2
Aysha 194-195 N 6
Ayu Islands = Kepulauan Aju 174-175 K 6
'Ayun, Al- 194-195 B 3
'Ayūn al-'Atrūs 194-195 C 5
Ayutla 86-87 L 9
Ayvalık 142-143 E 8
'Ayyāṭ, Al- 199 B 3

Azafal 194-195 AB 4
Azángaro 98-99 EF 7
Azaoua, In — 194-195 F 4
Azaouad 194-195 D 5
Azaouak 194-195 E 5
Azare 194-195 FG 6
Azawak, Wadi — = Azaouak 194-195 E 5
Azbine 194-195 F 5
Azéfal = Azafal 194-195 AB 4
Azerbaijan Soviet Socialist Republic 142-143 J 7
Azerbaydzhan Soviet Socialist Republic 160-161 F 2
'Azīzīyah, Al- [LAR] 194-195 G 2
Azlam, Wādī — 199 DE 4
'Azmātī, Sabkhat — 194-195 DE 3
Azogues 98-99 D 5
Azores = Açores 188-189 E 5
Azores Plateau 26-27 HJ 4
Azouzetta Lake 48 F 2
Azov 142-143 G 6
Azovskoje more 142-143 G 6
Azroû = Azrū 194-195 CD 2
Azrū 194-195 CD 2
Aztec, AZ 74-75 G 6
Aztec, NM 68-69 BC 7
Azua de Compostela 88-89 L 5
Azuaga 132-133 E 9
Azuero, Península de — 58-59 K 10
Azul [MEX] 86-87 K 4
Azul [RA] 103 E 5
Azul, Cordillera — 98-99 D 6
Azulejo, El — 76-77 D 9
Azuma-yama 170-171 MN 4
Azurduy 98-99 G 8-9
Azza = Ghazzah 160-161 C 4
'Azzān 160-161 F 8
Azzel Matti, Sebkra — = Sabkhat 'Azmātī 194-195 DE 3

B

Baa 174-175 H 9
Ba'an = Batang 166-167 H 6
Baardheere 194-195 N 8
Baargaal 194-195 c 1
Bābā, Bande — 160-161 J 4
Baba burnu [TR, Black Sea] 142-143 F 7
Baba burnu [TR, Ege denizi] 160-161 B 3
Babadag 138-139 N 3
Babadag, gora — 142-143 J 7
Babaeski 142-143 E 7
Baba Hatim 166-167 E 4
Babahoyo 98-99 CD 5
Babajevo 154-155 F 6
Babar, Kepulauan — 174-175 JK 8
Babb, MT 66-67 G 1
Babbage River 52-53 S 2
Babbit, NV 74-75 D 3
Babbitt, MN 70-71 E 2
Babel = Babylon 160-161 EF 4
Bab el Mandeb = Bāb al-Mandab 160-161 E 8
Babelthuap 174-175 KL 5
Babia, La — 76-77 CD 8
Babia Góra 124 J 4
Babícora, Laguna de — 86-87 FG 3
Bābil = Babylon 160-161 EF 4
Babinda 182-183 J 3
Babine Lake 46-47 L 6-7
Babine Portage 48 E 2
Babine Range 46-47 L 6-7
Babine River 48 D 2
Bābol 160-161 G 3
Baboquivari Peak 74-75 H 7
Baboua 194-195 G 7
Babul = Bābol 160-161 G 3
Babuškin 154-155 U 7
Babuškina, zaliv — 154-155 de 6
Babuyan Channel 174-175 H 3
Babuyan Island 174-175 H 3
Babuyan Islands 174-175 H 3
Babylon 160-161 EF 4
Babylon, NY 72-73 K 4
Bacajá, Rio — 98-99 N 7
Bacalar, Laguna de — 86-87 Q 8
Bacamuchi, Río — 86-87 EF 2-3
Bacan, Pulau — 174-175 J 7
Bacău 138-139 M 2
Bắc Bộ 174-175 DE 2
Bacharden 160-161 H 3
Bachchār 194-195 D 2
Bachíniva 86-87 G 3
Bachmač 142-143 F 5
Bachu = Maral Bashi 166-167 D 3-4
Bačka 138-139 H 3
Bačka Palanka 138-139 H 3
Bačka Topola 138-139 HJ 3
Back Bay 80-81 J 2
Back Lick Run 82 II a 2
Back River 46-47 R 4
Backstairs Passage 182-183 G 7
Bac Lio' = Vinh Lo'i 174-175 E 5
Bacolod 174-175 H 4
Bacuit = El Nido 174-175 G 4
Bad', Wādī — 199 C 3
Badajos, Lago — 98-99 G 5
Badajoz 132-133 D 9
Badakhšān 160-161 L 3
Badalona 132-133 J 8
Badanah 160-161 E 4
Badārī, Al- 194-195 L 3
Bad Axe, MI 72-73 E 3
Badāyūn = Budaun 160-161 M 5
Baddeck 51 F 4
Baddūzzah, Rā's al- 194-195 BC 2
Bad Ems 124 C 3
Baden [A] 124 H 4
Baden [CH] 124 D 5
Baden-Baden 124 D 4
Baden-Württemberg 124 D 4
Badgastein 124 F 5
Badger, MN 70-71 BC 1
Bad Hersfeld 124 D 3
Bad Homburg 124 D 3
Badī', Al- [Saudi Arabia] 160-161 F 6
Badīn 160-161 K 6
Badin, NC 80-81 F 3
Badiraguato 86-87 G 5
Bad Ischl 124 F 5
Bad Kissingen 124 E 3
Bad Kreuznach 124 CD 4
Bad Land Butte 68-69 BC 2
Badlands [USA, North Dakota] 58-59 F 2
Badlands [USA, South Dakota] 58-59 F 3
Badlands National Monument 68-69 E 4
Bad Mergentheim 124 DE 4
Bad Nauheim 124 D 3
Bad Neuenahr 124 C 3
Baḍodẽn = Vaḍōdarā 160-161 L 6
Ba Đôn 174-175 E 3
Badong [TJ] 166-167 KL 5
Badr 160-161 E 7
Bad Reichenhall 124 F 5
Badr Ḥunayn 160-161 D 6
Bad River 68-69 F 3
Bad River Indian Reservation 70-71 E 2
Bad Tölz 124 E 5
Badu Danan = Denan 194-195 N 7
Badulla 160-161 N 9
Bad Wildungen 124 D 3
Bafang 194-195 G 7-8
Bafatá 194-195 B 6
Baffin Bay [CDN] 46-47 W-Y 3
Baffin Bay [USA] 76-77 F 9
Baffin Island 46-47 V 3-X 5
Baffin Island National Park 46-47 XY 4
Baffin Land = Baffin Island 46-47 V 3-X 5
Bafia 194-195 G 8
Bafing 194-195 B 6
Bafoulabé 194-195 BC 6
Bafoussam 194-195 G 7
Bāfq 160-161 GH 4
Bafra 142-143 G 7
Bafra burnu 142-143 G 7
Bafwasende 198 E 1
Bagabag Island 174-175 N 7
Bagaço 98-99 E 6
Bāgalakōṭṭē = Bāgalkot 160-161 LM 7
Bāgalkot 160-161 LM 7
Bagalpur = Bhāgalpur 160-161 O 5-6
Bagamojo = Bagamoyo 198 G 3
Bagamoyo 198 G 3
Bagan Jaya 174-175 D 5
Bagdad, AZ 74-75 G 5
Bagdad, FL 78-79 F 5
Bagdād = Baghdād 160-161 EF 4
Bagdarin 154-155 VW 7
Bagenalstown = Muine Bheag 116-117 DE 8
Baggs, WY 68-69 C 5
Baghdād 160-161 EF 4
Baghdādī, Rās — = Rā's Ḥunkurāb 199 D 5
Baghēlkhaṇḍ 160-161 N 6
Bagheria 138-139 E 6
Baghlān 160-161 K 3
Baghrash köl 166-167 F 3
Bagirmi 194-195 H 6
Bagley, MN 70-71 C 2
Bagley Icefield 52-53 QR 6
Bagnères-de-Bigorre 132-133 H 7
Bagnères-de-Luchon 132-133 H 7
Bagoé 194-195 C 6
Bagotville 51 A 3
Bagrationovsk 124 K 1
Baguezane, Monts — 194-195 F 5
Baguio 174-175 H 3
Baguirmi = Bagirmi 194-195 H 6
Bagur, Cabo — 132-133 J 8
Bahama, Canal Viejo de — 58-59 L 7
Bahama Island, Grand — 58-59 L 6
Bahamas 58-59 L 6-M 7
Baharāich = Bahrāich 160-161 N 5
Bahar Assoli 194-195 N 6
Bahar Dar = Bahir Dar 194-195 M 6
Baḥarīyah, Wāḥāt al- 194-195 K 3
Baharu, Kota — 174-175 D 5
Bahāwalpūr 160-161 L 5
Bahia 98-99 LM 7
Bahia = Salvador 98-99 M 7
Bahía, Isla de la — 58-59 J 8
Bahía, Islas de la — 58-59 J 8
Bahía Asunción 86-87 C 4
Bahía Blanca [MEX] 86-87 C 3
Bahía Blanca [RA, bay] 103 D 5
Bahía Blanca [RA, place] 103 D 5
Bahía de Caráquez 98-99 CD 5
Bahía Dulce 86-87 L 9
Bahía Grande 103 C 8
Bahía Laura 103 CD 7
Bahía Negra 103 E 2
Bahía Oso Blanco 103 CD 7
Bahía Solano [CO, place] 98-99 D 3
Bahía Tortugas 86-87 C 4
Bahir Dar 194-195 M 6
Bahrāich 160-161 N 5
Bahrain 160-161 G 5
Baḥr al-Aḥmar, Al- 194-195 L 4-M 5
Baḥr al-Ghazāl [Sudan, administrative unit] 194-195 JK 7
Baḥr al-Ghazāl [Sudan, river] 194-195 KL 7
Bahrampur = Berhampore 160-161 O 6
Bahr Dar Giorgis = Bahir Dar 194-195 M 6
Bahrein = Bahrain 160-161 G 5
Baḥr el Jebel = Baḥr al-Jabal 194-195 L 7
Bahumbelu 174-175 H 7
Bai 166-167 E 3
Baía = Salvador 98-99 M 7
Baía dos Tigres 198 B 5
Baia Mare 138-139 KL 2
Baião 98-99 JK 5
Baia Sprie 138-139 KL 2
Baïbokoum 194-195 H 7
Bai Bung, Mui — 174-175 D 5
Baicheng 166-167 N 2
Baicheng = Bai 166-167 E 3
Baidaratskaya Bay = Bajdarackaja guba 154-155 M 4
Baie, la — 51 A 3
Baie-Johan-Beetz 51 E 2
Baie-Sainte-Catherine 51 AB 2-3
Baie-Sainte-Claire 51 DE 3
Baie-Saint-Paul 51 A 4
Baie-Trinité 51 C 3
Baie Verte 51 HJ 2-3
Baihe [TJ, place] 166-167 KL 5
Baile an Ródhba 116-117 BC 7
Baile Átha Cliath 116-117 EF 7
Baile Brigín 116-117 E 7
Baile Locha Riach 116-117 C 7
Baile Mhathamhna 116-117 D 7
Baile Mhic Anndáin 116-117 DE 8
Baile Mhistéala 116-117 CD 8
Băileşti 138-139 K 3
Baileys Crossroads, VA 82 II a 2
Baileys Harbor, WI 70-71 G 3
Bailique, Ilha — 98-99 O 4
Bailundo 198 C 4
Bainbridge, OH 72-73 E 5
Baindbridge, GA 78-79 G 5
Baing 174-175 H 9
Bain-Tumen = Čojbalsan 166-167 L 2
Bainville, MT 68-69 D 1
Baiqibao = Baiqipu 170-171 D 2
Baiqipu 170-171 D 2
Bā'ir 160-161 D 4
Baird, TX 76-77 E 6
Baird Inlet 52-53 EF 6
Baird Mountains 46-47 DE 4
Bairiki 178 H 2
Bairnsdale 182-183 J 7
Baïse 132-133 H 7
Baitou Shan 170-171 FG 2
Baitou Shan = Changbai Shan 166-167 O 3
Bait Range 48 D 2
Baituchangmen 170-171 CD 2
Baja 124 J 5
Baja California Norte 58-59 CD 6
Baja California Sur 58-59 D 6
Bājah 194-195 F 1
Baján [MEX] 76-77 D 9
Bajan [Mongolia] 166-167 K 2
Bajan Adraga 166-167 KL 2
Bajanaul 154-155 O 7
Bajan Char uuul 166-167 H 5
Bajanchongor 166-167 HJ 2
Bajan Choto 166-167 JK 4
Bajandaj 154-155 U 7
Bajandalaj 166-167 J 3
Bajangol [Mongolia] 166-167 K 2
Bajan Gol [TJ] 166-167 K 3
Bajan Obo 166-167 K 3
Bajan Olgi 166-167 FG 2
Bajan Öndör 166-167 H 3
Bajan Sum = Bajan 166-167 K 2
Bajanteeg 166-167 J 2

Bajantee 209

Bajan Tümen = Čojbalsan 166-167 L 2
Bajan Ulaa = Bajan Uul 166-167 H 2
Bajan Ülegei = Ölgij 166-167 FG 2
Bajan Uul [Mongolia, Dornod] 166-167 L 2
Bajan Uul [Mongolia, Dzavchan] 166-167 H 2
Bajawa 174-175 GH 8
Bajčunas 142-143 K 6
Bajdarackaja guba 154-155 M 4
Baje 103 F 4
Bajío, El — 58-59 F 7
Bajkal, ozero — 154-155 U 7
Bajkal'skij chrebet 154-155 U 6-7
Bajkal'skoje 154-155 UV 6
Bajkit 154-155 S 5
Bajkonyr 154-155 M 8
Bajmak 154-155 K 7
Bajo Baudo 98-99 D 3
Bajram-Ali 160-161 J 3
Bajšint = Chongor 166-167 L 2
Baj-Sot 154-155 S 7
Bajtag Bogd uul 166-167 G 2-3
Bakal 154-155 K 6-7
Bakala 194-195 HJ 7
Bakanas 154-155 O 8-9
Bakčar 154-155 P 6
Bakel [SN] 194-195 B 6
Baker 26-27 T 6
Baker, CA 74-75 E 5
Baker, ID 66-67 G 3
Baker, MT 68-69 D 2
Baker, NV 74-75 FG 3
Baker, OR 58-59 C 3
Baker, Canal — 103 B 7
Baker, Mount — 66-67 C 1
Baker Foreland 46-47 ST 5
Baker Island 52-53 vw 9
Baker Lake [CDN, lake] 46-47 R 5
Baker Lake [CDN, place] 46-47 R 5
Bakersfield, CA 58-59 C 4
Bakersfield, TX 76-77 CD 7
Bakewell 116-117 K 7
Bākhtarī, Āžarbayejān-e — 160-161 EF 3
Bakhtegān, Daryācheh — 160-161 G 5
Bakhuis Gebergte 98-99 K 2
26 Bakinskich Komissarov 142-143 K 8
Bakkafjördhur 114-115 fg 1
Bakkaflói 114-115 f 1
Bakkagerdhi 114-115 g 2
Bakony 124 HJ 5
Bakool 194-195 a 3
Baku 142-143 JK 7
Bakungan 174-175 C 6
Bakwanga = Mbuji-Mayi 198 D 3
B'ala [BG] 138-139 L 4
Bala [CDN] 72-73 G 2
Bala [GB] 116-117 H 8
Bala, Cerros de — 98-99 F 7-8
Balabac Island 174-175 G 5
Balabac Strait 174-175 G 5
Balabaia 198 B 4
Ba'labakk 142-143 G 9
Balabalangan, Pulau-pulau — 174-175 G 7
Balachna 142-143 H 4
Bal'ad [SP] 194-195 b 3
Balad'ok 154-155 Z 7
Balagansk 154-155 T 7
Bālāghāt 160-161 N 6
Balaguer 132-133 H 8
Balā'im, Rā's al- 199 C 3
Balaiselasa 174-175 CD 7
Balaklava [AUS] 182-183 G 6
Balakovo 154-155 HJ 7
Balambangan, Pulau — 174-175 G 5
Balancán de Domínguez 86-87 P 9
Balangan, Kepulauan — = Pulau-pulau Balabalangan 174-175 G 7
Ba Lang An, Mui — = Mui Batangan 174-175 EF 3
Balāngīr 160-161 N 6
Balankanche 86-87 QR 7
B'ala Slatina 138-139 K 4
Balasore 160-161 O 6
Balašov 142-143 H 5
Balaton 124 HJ 5
Balboa 58-59 b 3
Balboa Heights 58-59 b 3
Balbriggan = Baile Brigín 116-117 E 7
Balcarce 103 E 5
Balchaš 154-155 N 8
Balchaš, ozero — 154-155 NO 8
Balčik 138-139 MN 4
Balcones Escarpment 58-59 F 6-G 5
Bald Butte 66-67 D 4
Bald Head 182-183 C 7
Baldhill Reservoir 68-69 GH 2
Bald Knob, AR 78-79 D 3
Bald Knob, WV 80-81 F 2
Bald Mountain 74-75 F 4
Baldock Lake 49 K 2
Baldwin, MI 70-71 H 4
Baldwin, WI 70-71 D 3
Baldwin City, KS 70-71 C 6
Baldwin Hills 83 III b 1-2
Baldwin Peninsula 52-53 F 3
Baldwinsville, NY 72-73 H 3
Baldwyn, MS 78-79 E 3
Baldy, Mount — 66-67 H 2
Baldy Peak [USA, Arizona] 58-59 DE 5
Baldy Peak [USA, New Mexico] 76-77 AB 5
Balē 194-195 N 7-8
Bâle = Basel 124 C 5
Baleares, Islas — 132-133 H 9-K 8
Balearic Islands = Islas Baleares 132-133 H 9-K 8
Balej 154-155 W 7
Bāleshvara = Balasore 160-161 O 6
Balfour [CDN] 66-67 E 1
Balḥāf 160-161 F 8
Bali [RI = 15 ◁] 174-175 F 8
Bali, Pulau — 174-175 FG 8
Balıkesir 160-161 B 3
Balikpapan 174-175 G 7
Balintang Channel 174-175 H 3
Bali Sea 174-175 FG 8
Baljennie 49 DE 4
Balkan Mountains 138-139 K-M 4
Balkh 160-161 K 3
Balkh Āb 160-161 K 3
Balkhash, Lake — = ozero Balchaš 154-155 NO 8
Balla Balla = Mbalabala 198 EF 6
Ballachulish 116-117 FG 4
Balladonia 182-183 D 6
Ballaghaderreen = Bealach an Doirín 116-117 C 7
Ballantrae 116-117 G 5
Ballarat 182-183 H 7
Ballard, Lake — 182-183 D 5
Ballāri = Bellary 160-161 M 7
Ballater 116-117 HJ 3
Ballé 194-195 C 5
Ballenas, Canal de — 86-87 D 3
Balleny Islands 31 C 17
Ballina [AUS] 182-183 K 5
Ballina = Béal an Átha 116-117 B 6
Ballinamore = Béal an Átha Móir 116-117 D 6
Ballinasloe = Béal Átha na Sluagh 116-117 CD 7
Ballinger, TX 76-77 DE 7
Ballinrobe = Baile an Ródhba 116-117 BC 7
Ballona Creek 83 III b 2
Ball's Pyramid 182-183 L 6
Ballstad 114-115 EF 3
Ballycastle 116-117 E 5
Ballyclare 116-117 EF 6
Ballyheige Bay = Cuan Bhaile Uí Thaidhg 116-117 E 8
Ballymahon = Baile Mhathamhna 116-117 D 7
Ballymena 116-117 E 6
Ballymoney 116-117 E 5
Ballyquintin Point 116-117 F 6
Ballyshannon = Béal Átha Seanaigh 116-117 CD 6
Balmertown 50 C 2
Balmoral Castle 116-117 H 3
Balmorhea, TX 76-77 C 7
Balombo 198 B 4
Balonne River 182-183 J 5
Balovale 198 D 4
Balranald 182-183 H 6
Balsas [BR] 98-99 K 6
Balsas [MEX] 86-87 KL 8-9
Balsas, Río — 58-59 F 8
Balsas ó Mezcala, Río — 86-87 KL 8-9
Balsfjord 114-115 HJ 3
Balta, ND 68-69 FG 1
Balta [RO] 138-139 MN 3
Baltic Sea 110-111 L 5-M 4
Baltijsk 124 J 1
Balṭīm 199 B 2
Baltimore, MD 58-59 L 4
Baltimore = Dún na Séad 116-117 B 9
Bāltistān 160-161 M 3-4
Bāltit 160-161 L 3
Balūchestān, Sīstān va — 160-161 H 4-J 5
Balūchistān 160-161 J 5-K 4
Balyanā, Al- 194-195 L 3
Balygyčan 154-155 d 5
Balyul = Nēpāl 160-161 NO 5
Bam 160-161 H 5
Bama 194-195 G 6
Bamaco = Bamako 194-195 C 6
Bamaji Lake 50 D 2
Bamako 194-195 C 6
Bamba [RMM] 194-195 D 5
Bamba [ZRE] 198 C 3
Bambari 194-195 J 7
Bamberg 124 E 4
Bamberg, SC 80-81 F 4
Bambesa 198 E 1
Bambinga 198 C 2
Bambouk 194-195 B 6
Bambuí 98-99 K 8-9
Bamenda 194-195 G 7
Bamfield 66-67 A 1
Bamingui 194-195 HJ 7
Bamingui, Parc national de la — 194-195 HJ 7
Bamingui-Bangoran 194-195 HJ 7
Bāmiyān 160-161 K 4
Bampton 116-117 K 9
Bampūr, Rūd-e 160-161 HJ 5
Ba mTsho 166-167 G 5
Bamum = Foumban 194-195 G 7
Ban, Carn — 116-117 G 3
Baña, Punta de la — 132-133 H 8
Banāder va Jazāyer-e Baḥr-e 'Omān = 6 ◁ 160-161 H 5
Banāder va Jazāyer-e Khalīj-e Fārs = 5 ◁ 160-161 G 5
Banadia 98-99 E 3
Banagher = Beannchar 116-117 D 7
Banalia 198 DE 1
Banana 198 B 3
Bananal, Ilha do — 98-99 J 7
Bananeiras 98-99 M 6
Banat 138-139 J 3
Banatului, Munții — 138-139 JK 3
Banbridge 116-117 E 6
Banbury 116-117 K 8
Banchory 116-117 J 3
Banco, El — 98-99 E 3
Bancroft 72-73 H 2
Bancroft, ID 66-67 H 4
Banda = Sainte-Marie 198 B 2
Banda, Kepulauan — 174-175 J 7
Banda, La — 103 D 3
Banda, Punta — 58-59 C 5
Banda Aceh 174-175 BC 5
Bandama 194-195 CD 7
Bandar [IND] 160-161 N 7
Bandāra = Bandar 160-161 N 7
Bandar 'Abbās 160-161 H 5
Bandar Banhā = Banhā 199 B 2
Bandar-e Anzalī 160-161 FG 3
Bandar-e Būshehr 160-161 G 5
Bandar-e Chāh Bahār 160-161 HJ 5
Bandar-e Khomeynī 160-161 FG 4
Bandar-e Lengeh 160-161 GH 5
Bandar-e Shāh 160-161 G 3
Bandar Maharani = Muar 174-175 D 6
Bandar Penggaram = Batu Pahat 174-175 D 6
Bandar Seri Begawan 174-175 FG 5-6
Banda Sea 174-175 JK 8
Bandawe 198 F 4
Bandeira, Pico da — 98-99 L 9
Bandeirante 98-99 JK 7
Bandelier National Monument 76-77 A 5
Bandera 103 D 3
Bandera, TX 76-77 E 8
Banderas 76-77 B 7
Banderas, Bahía de — 58-59 E 7
Band-e Turkestān = Tirbande Turkestān 160-161 JK 3
Bandiagara 194-195 D 6
Bandırma 160-161 B 2
Bandjarmasin = Banjarmasin 174-175 F 7
Bandjermassin = Banjarmasin 174-175 F 7
Bandon, OR 66-67 A 4
Bandon = Droichead na Bandan 116-117 C 9
Bāndra 160-161 L 7
Bandundu [ZRE, administrative unit] 198 C 2-3
Bandundu [ZRE, place] 198 C 2
Bandung 174-175 E 8
Banes 58-59 L 7
Bañeza, La — 132-133 DE 7
Banff [CDN] 46-47 NO 7
Banff [GB] 116-117 J 3
Banff National Park 46-47 NO 7
Banfora 194-195 D 6
Bangāl Khāṛī = Bay of Bengal 160-161 N-P 7
Bangalore 160-161 M 8
Bangassou 194-195 J 8
Bangassu = Bangassou 194-195 J 8
Bangfou = Bengbu 166-167 M 5
Banggai 174-175 H 7
Banggai, Kepulauan — 174-175 H 7
Banggai, Pulau — 174-175 H 7
Banggala Au = Bay of Bengal 160-161 N-P 7
Banggi, Pulau — 174-175 G 5
Banghāzī 194-195 HJ 2
Bangka, Pulau — 174-175 E 7
Bangka, Selat — 174-175 E 7
Bangkinang 174-175 D 6
Bangko 174-175 D 7
Bangkok = Krung Thep 174-175 D 4
Bangladesh 160-161 OP 6
Bangor, ME 58-59 N 3
Bangor, MI 70-71 G 4
Bangor, PA 72-73 J 4
Bangor [GB, Northern Ireland] 116-117 F 6
Bangor [GB, Wales] 116-117 GH 7
Bangs, TX 76-77 E 7
Bangui [RCA] 194-195 H 8
Bangui [RP] 174-175 GH 3
Bangweulu, Lake — 198 EF 4
Banhā 199 B 2
Baní [DOM] 58-59 M 8
Bani [RMM] 194-195 C 6
Banī, Jabal — 194-195 C 2-3
Banī Abbās 194-195 D 2
Baniara 174-175 NO 8
Banī Mallāl 194-195 C 2
Banī Mazār 194-195 L 3
Banī Shuqayr 199 B 4
Ban Island 52-53 L 7
Banī Suwayf 194-195 L 3
Banī Wanīf 194-195 D 2
Bāniyās [SYR, Al-Lādiqīyah] 160-161 D 3
Banja Luka 138-139 G 3
Banjar 174-175 E 8
Banjarmasin 174-175 F 7
Banjermassin = Banjarmasin 174-175 F 7
Banjo = Banyo 194-195 G 7
Banjul 194-195 A 6
Banjuwangi = Banyuwangi 174-175 F 8
Bank 142-143 J 8
Banka = Pulau Bangka 174-175 E 7
Banka Banka 182-183 F 3
Banks, ID 66-67 E 3
Banks, OR 66-67 B 3
Banksian River 50 B 1
Banks Island [AUS] 182-183 H 2
Banks Island [CDN, British Columbia] 46-47 KL 7
Banks Island [CDN, District of Franklin] 46-47 MN 3
Banks Islands 182-183 N 2
Banks Lake 66-67 D 2
Banks Peninsula 182-183 O 8
Banks Strait 182-183 J 8
Banks Strait = MacClure Strait 46-47 MN 2-3
Banmau 174-175 C 2
Ban Me Thuôt 174-175 E 4
Ban Muang = Pong 174-175 CD 3
Bann, River — 116-117 E 6
Bannack, MT 66-67 G 3
Banner, WY 68-69 C 3
Bannerman Town 88-89 HJ 2
Banning, CA 74-75 E 6
Banningville = Bandundu 198 C 2
Bannockburn [CDN] 72-73 GH 2
Bannockburn [ZW] 198 EF 6
Bannock Range 66-67 G 4
Bannū 160-161 KL 4
Ban Phai 174-175 D 3
Banquereau Bank 51 GH 5
Banská Bystrica 124 J 4
Banská Štiavnica 124 J 4
Bantaeng 174-175 GH 8
Bantam = Banten 174-175 E 8
Banten 174-175 E 8
Bantry = Beanntraighe 116-117 B 9
Bantry Bay = Cuan Baoi 116-117 AB 9
Banyak, Pulau-pulau — 174-175 C 6
Banyak Islands = Pulau-pulau Banyak 174-175 C 6
Banyo 194-195 G 7
Banyuwangi 174-175 F 8
Banzaburō-dake 170-171 M 5
Banzare Land 31 C 13
Banzystad = Yasanyama 198 D 1
Banzyville = Yasanyama 198 D 1
Banzyville, Collines des — 198 D 1
Baoding 166-167 LM 4
Baoi, Cuan — 116-117 AB 9
Baoji 166-167 K 5
Baojing 166-167 K 6
Baoqing 166-167 P 2
Baoshan [TJ, Yunnan] 166-167 HJ 6
Baotou 166-167 KL 3
Baoulé 194-195 C 6
Baoying 166-167 M 5
Baptiste 72-73 GH 2
Ba'qūbah 160-161 EF 4
Baquedano 103 BC 2
Bar [YU] 138-139 H 4
Baraawe 194-195 N 8
Barabinsk 154-155 OP 6
Barabinskaja step' 154-155 O 6-7
Baraboo, WI 70-71 F 4
Baracaldo 132-133 F 7
Barachois 51 DE 3
Baracoa 88-89 J 4
Baraga, MI 70-71 F 2
Bărăganul 138-139 M 3
Bārah 194-195 L 6
Barahī = Barhi 160-161 O 6
Barahona [DOM] 58-59 M 8
Baraka = Barka 194-195 M 5
Baraki [AFG] 160-161 K 4
Baralaba 182-183 JK 4
Bārāmūla 160-161 L 4
Baṛā Nikōbār = Great Nicobar 160-161 P 9
Baṛā Nikōbār = Little Nicobar 160-161 P 9
Baranof, AK 52-53 v 8
Baranof Island 46-47 JK 6
Baranoviči 142-143 E 5
Barão de Grajaú 98-99 L 6
Barataria Bay 78-79 DE 6
Barauaná, Serra — 98-99 H 3-4
Barbacena 98-99 L 9
Barbados 58-59 OP 9
Barbar 194-195 L 5
Barbara Lake 70-71 G 1
Barbastro 132-133 GH 7
Barbers Point 78-79 c 2
Barberton 198 F 7
Barberton, OH 72-73 F 4
Barborá = Berbera 194-195 O 6
Barbosa [CO, Boyacá] 98-99 E 3
Barbourville, KY 72-73 DE 6
Barca = Al-Marj 194-195 J 2
Barca, La — 86-87 J 7
Barcaldine 182-183 HJ 4
Barce = Al-Marj 194-195 J 2
Barcellona Pozzo di Gotto 138-139 F 6
Barcelona [E] 132-133 J 8
Barcelona [YV] 98-99 G 2
Barcelonnette 132-133 L 6
Barcelos [BR] 98-99 G 5
Barchöl Choto = Bar köl 166-167 G 3
Barcoo River 182-183 H 4-5
Barcroft, Lake — 82 II a 2
Bardaï 194-195 H 4
Bardawīl, Sabkhat al- 199 C 2
Barddhmān = Burdwān 160-161 O 6
Bardejov 124 K 4
Bardeliere, Lac la — 50 OP 1
Bárdharbunga 114-115 e 2
Bardīs 199 B 4
Bardīyah 194-195 K 2
Bardon Hill 116-117 K 8
Bardsey 116-117 FG 8
Bardsey Sound 116-117 G 8
Bardstown, KY 70-71 H 7
Barduba 58-59 O 8
Bardwell, KY 78-79 E 2
Bareilly 160-161 MN 5
Barēlī = Bareilly 160-161 MN 5
Barentsburg 114-115 jk 5
Barents Island = Barentsøya 114-115 l 5
Barentsøya 114-115 l 5
Barents Sea 154-155 D-J 2-3
Barentu 194-195 M 5
Barfleur 116-117 K 11
Barfleur, Pointe de — 132-133 G 4
Barga [TJ] 166-167 M 2
Barguzin 154-155 UV 7
Barguzinskij chrebet 154-155 U 7-V 6
Barham 116-117 h 7
Barhampura = Berhampur 160-161 NO 7
Bar Harbor, ME 72-73 M 2
Barhi [IND, Bihār] 160-161 O 6
Bari [I] 138-139 G 5
Bari [SP] 194-195 bc 1
Barillas 86-87 P 10
Bariloche, San Carlos de — 103 B 6
Barīm 160-161 E 8
Barinas [YV, place] 98-99 EF 3
Baring, IA 70-71 D 5
Baring, Cape — 46-47 MN 3
Bārīs 199 B 5
Bariṣāl 160-161 OP 6
Barito 174-175 F 7
Barka [ETH] 194-195 M 5
Barkā' [Oman] 160-161 H 6
Barka = Al-Marj 194-195 J 2
Barkerville 48 G 3
Bark Lake 50 K 3
Barkley, Lake — 78-79 EF 2
Barkley Sound 66-67 A 1
Barkly Tableland 182-183 FG 3
Bar köl [TJ, lake] 166-167 G 3
Bar Köl [TJ, place] 166-167 G 3
Bark Point 70-71 E 2
Bar-le-Duc 132-133 K 4
Barlee, Lake — 182-183 C 5
Barletta 138-139 G 5
Barlovento, Islas de — 58-59 OP 8-9
Bārmēr 160-161 L 5
Barmera 182-183 H 6
Barmouth 116-117 G 8
Barnabus, WV 80-81 EF 2
Barnard, KS 68-69 GH 6
Barnard Castle 116-117 K 6
Barnaul 154-155 P 7
Barnegat 49 C 3
Barnegat Bay 72-73 JK 5
Barne Glacier 31 A 17-18
Barnesville, GA 80-81 DE 4
Barnesville, MN 68-69 H 2
Barnesville, OH 72-73 F 4-5
Barnet, London- 116-117 L 9
Barney Top 74-75 GH 4
Barnhart, TX 76-77 D 7
Barnoldswick 116-117 J 7
Barnsdall, OK 76-77 FG 4
Barnsley 116-117 K 7
Barnstable, MA 72-73 L 4
Barnstaple 116-117 GH 9
Barnstaple Bay 116-117 G 9
Barnwell, SC 80-81 F 4
Baro 194-195 F 7
Baroda = Vadōdarā 160-161 L 6
Barōngā Kyūnmya 174-175 B 3
Barotirê, Reserva Florestal — 98-99 MN 8
Barpeta 160-161 P 5
Barqa = Al-Marj 194-195 J 2
Barqah [LAR] 194-195 J 2
Barqah, Jabal al- 199 C 5
Barqat al-Baḥrīyah 194-195 JK 2
Barqat al-Bayḍā' 194-195 HJ 2-3
Barquisimeto 98-99 EF 2-3
Barra [BR, Bahia] 98-99 L 7
Barra, Sound of — 116-117 D 3
Barraba 182-183 K 6
Barraca da Boca 98-99 MN 5
Barracão do Barreto 98-99 H 6
Barracão São José 98-99 K 9
Barracas [BR] 98-99 F 9
Barra do Bugres 98-99 H 7-8
Barra do Corda 98-99 KL 6
Barra do Garças 98-99 J 8
Barra do São Manuel 98-99 H 6
Barrage 194-195 C 6
Barra Head 116-117 D 4
Barra Islands 116-117 D 3-4
Barranca [PE] 98-99 D 5
Barrancabermeja 98-99 E 3
Barrancas [YV, Monagas] 98-99 G 3
Barranco de Guadalupe 86-87 H 2
Barranqueras 103 DE 3
Barranquilla 98-99 DE 2
Barraute 50 N 2
Barra Velha 103 G 3
Barre, VT 72-73 K 2
Barre, Wilkes —, PA 58-59 L 3
Barreiras 98-99 KL 7
Barreirinha 98-99 H 5
Barreirinhas 98-99 L 5
Barreiro 132-133 C 9
Barreiros 98-99 MN 6
Barren Grounds 46-47 O 4-S 5
Barren Islands 52-53 LM 7
Barrenland = Barren Grounds 46-47 O 4-S 5
Barren Sage Plains 66-67 E 4
Barretos 98-99 K 9
Barrhead [CDN] 48 K 2
Barrie 46-47 UV 9
Barrie Island 50 K 3
Barrière 48 GH 4
Barrington, IL 70-71 F 4
Barrington, Mount — 182-183 K 6
Barrington Lake 49 HJ 2
Barro Colorado, Isla — 58-59 b 2
Barron, WI 70-71 DE 3
Barros, Tierra de — 132-133 D 9
Barroterán 76-77 D 9
Barrow, AK 46-47 E 3
Barrow, Point — 46-47 EF 3
Barrow Creek 182-183 FG 4
Barrow-in-Furness 116-117 H 6
Barrow Island 182-183 BC 4
Barrow River = An Bhearbha 116-117 DE 8
Barrows 49 H 4
Barrow Strait 46-47 RS 3
Barry 116-117 H 9
Barrys Bay 50 N 4
Barsakel mes, ostrov — 154-155 KL 8
Barsaloi 198 G 1
Baršatas 154-155 O 8
Bārshī = Bārsi 160-161 M 7
Bārsi 160-161 M 7
Barstow, CA 58-59 C 4-5
Barstow, TX 76-77 C 7
Bar-sur-Aube 132-133 K 4
Barter Island 52-53 Q 1
Bartibog 51 CD 4
Bartica 98-99 H 3
Bartle, CA 66-67 C 5
Bartlesville, OK 58-59 G 4
Bartlett, NE 68-69 G 5
Bartlett, TX 76-77 F 7
Bartlett's Harbour 51 H 2
Bartolomeu Dias 198 G 6
Barton, ND 68-69 FG 1
Barton-upon-Humber 116-117 L 7
Bartoszyce 124 K 1
Bartow, FL 80-81 bc 3
Barú, Volcán — 58-59 K 10
Baruun Urt 166-167 L 2
Barvas 116-117 E 2
Barville 50 N 2
Barwick 50 BC 3
Barwon River 182-183 J 5
Barwon River = Darling River 182-183 H 6
Barykova, mys — 154-155 jk 5
Barylas 154-155 Z 4
Barzas 154-155 Q 6
Başalīyat Qiblī, Al- 199 C 5
Basankusu 198 CD 1
Basco 166-167 N 7
Basel 124 C 5
Bashi Haixia = Pashih Haihsia 166-167 N 7
Bāshim = Bāsim 160-161 M 5
Bashkir Autonomous Soviet Socialist Republic = 7 ◁ 154-155 K 6
Bash Kurghan = Bash Qurghan 166-167 G 4
Bash Malghun 166-167 F 4
Bash Qurghan 166-167 G 4
Bashshār 194-195 D 2
Basiano 174-175 H 7
Basilan Island 174-175 H 5
Basilan Strait 174-175 H 5
Basilicata 138-139 FG 5
Basílio 103 F 4
Basim 160-161 M 6
Basin, MT 66-67 G 2
Basin, WY 68-69 BC 3
Basin, Rivière — 50 O 3
Basingstocke 116-117 K 9
Basin Lake 49 F 4
Baskatong, Réservoir — 72-73 J 1
Baskineig Falls 50 F 1
Baškirskaja Avtonomnaja Sovetskaja Socialističeskaja Respublika = Bashkir Autonomous Soviet Socialist Republic 154-155 K 7
Basle = Basel 124 C 5

210 **Bajan**

Basoko [ZRE, Haute Zaïre] 198 D 1
Basra = Al-Başrah 160-161 F 4
Başrah, Al- 160-161 F 4
Bassac = Champassak 174-175 DE 4
Bassano 49 B 5
Bassano del Grappa 138-139 D 3
Bassein = Puthein 174-175 B 3
Basse Kotto 194-195 J 7-8
Basse-Terre [Guadeloupe, island] 88-89 PQ 6
Basse-Terre [Guadeloupe, place] 58-59 O 8
Basseterre [Saint Christopher-Nevis] 58-59 O 8
Bassett, NE 68-69 G 4
Bassett, VA 80-81 F 2
Bass Islands 72-73 E 4
Basso, Plateau de — 194-195 J 5
Bass Strait 182-183 HJ 7
Basswood Lake 70-71 E 1
Bastia 138-139 C 4
Bastianøyane 114-115 I 5
Bastogne 132-133 KL 3-4
Bastrop, LA 58-59 H 5
Bastrop, TX 76-77 F 7
Bastuträsk 114-115 HJ 5
Basutoland = Lesotho 198 E 7
Basutos 198 E 5
Bas-Zaïre 198 BC 3
Bata [Equatorial Guinea] 194-195 F 8
Batabanó, Golfo de — 58-59 K 7
Batac 174-175 GH 3
Batagaj 154-155 Za 4
Batagaj-Alyta 154-155 YZ 4
Batajsk 142-143 GH 6
Batāla 160-161 M 4
Batalha [P] 132-133 C 9
Batam, Pulau — 174-175 D 6
Batamaj 154-155 YZ 5
Batang [TJ] 166-167 H 6
Batangafo 194-195 H 7
Batangan, Mui — 174-175 EF 3
Batangas 174-175 H 4
Batan Island 166-167 N 7
Batan Islands 166-167 N 7
Batanta, Pulau — 174-175 JK 7
Batatchatu = Chulaq Aqqan Su 166-167 G 4
Batavia, NY 72-73 GH 3
Batavia, OH 72-73 DE 5
Batavia = Jakarta 174-175 E 8
Batbakkara = Amangel'dy 154-155 M 7
Batchawana 50 J 3
Batchawana, Mount — 70-71 H 2
Batesburg, SC 80-81 F 4
Batesville, AR 78-79 D 3
Batesville, IN 70-71 H 6
Batesville, MS 78-79 E 3
Batesville, OH 72-73 D 5
Batesville, TX 76-77 E 8
Bath 116-117 J 9
Bath, ME 72-73 M 3
Bath, NY 72-73 H 3
Batha 194-195 H 6
B'athar Zajū, Jabal — 199 C 7
Bathurst [AUS] 182-183 JK 6
Bathurst [CDN] 46-47 XY 8
Bathurst = Banjul 194-195 A 6
Bathurst, Cape — 46-47 KL 3
Bathurst Inlet [CDN, bay] 46-47 P 4
Bathurst Inlet [CDN, place] 46-47 P 4
Bathurst Island [AUS] 182-183 EF 2
Bathurst Island [CDN] 46-47 R 2
Batié 194-195 D 6-7
Bāţin, Wādī al- 160-161 F 5
Bāţinah, Al — 160-161 H 6
Batiscan 72-73 K 1
Batiscan, Rivière — 72-73 K 1
Batman 160-161 E 3
Batna = Batnah 194-195 F 1
Batnah 194-195 F 1
Batoche 46-47 PQ 7
Baton Rouge, LA 58-59 H 5
Batouri 194-195 G 8
Battambang 174-175 D 4
Batterbee Range 31 BC 30
Batticaloa = Maḍakalapūwa 160-161 N 9
Battle Creek, MI 58-59 J 3
Battle Creek [USA ◁ Milk River] 68-69 B 1
Battle Creek [USA ◁ Owyhee River] 66-67 E 4
Battle Harbour 46-47 Za 7
Battle Mountain, NV 66-67 E 5
Battle River 46-47 OP 7
Battock, Mount — 116-117 HJ 4
Battonya 124 K 5
Batu 194-195 M 7
Batu, Kepulauan — 174-175 C 7
Batu Arang 174-175 D 6
Batumi 142-143 H 7
Batu Pahat 174-175 D 6
Baturaja 174-175 D 7
Baturi = Batouri 194-195 G 8
Baturino 154-155 Q 6
Baturité 98-99 M 5
Batutinggi 174-175 F 7
Baubau 174-175 H 8
Baucau 174-175 J 8
Bauchi [WAN, place] 194-195 FG 6
Baudette, MN 70-71 C 1
Baudh 160-161 N 6
Baudouinville = Moba 198 E 3
Baudwin 174-175 C 2
Bauhinia 182-183 J 4
Baūl, El — 98-99 F 3
Bauld, Cape — 46-47 Za 7
Baule = Baoulé 194-195 C 6
Baule-Escoublac, la — 132-133 F 5
Baures 98-99 G 7
Bauru 98-99 K 9
Bautzen 124 G 3
Bauxite, AR 78-79 C 3
Bauya 194-195 B 7
Bavaria = Bayern 124 E 4
Bavarian Forest = Bayerischer Wald 124 F 4
Bavispe 86-87 F 2
Bavispe, Río — 86-87 F 2-3
Bavispe, Río de — 74-75 J 7
Bawean, Pulau — 174-175 F 8
Bāwīţī, Al- 194-195 K 3
Bawku 194-195 D 6
Bawlagè 174-175 C 3
Bawtry 116-117 KL 7
Baxten Springs 76-77 G 4
Baxter State Park 72-73 M 1-2
Bay 194-195 a 3
Bayāḍ, Al- [DZ] 194-195 E 2
Bayāḍ, Al- [Saudi Arabia] 160-161 F 6
Bayāḍīyah, Al- 199 C 5
Bay al-Kabīr, Wādī — 194-195 GH 2
Bayamo 58-59 L 7
Bayamón 88-89 N 5
Bayan Tumen = Čojbalsan 166-167 L 2
Bayard, NE 68-69 E 5
Bayas 86-87 H 6
Bayāzeh 142-143 KL 9
Baybay 174-175 HJ 4
Bayboro, NC 80-81 H 3
Bayburt 160-161 E 2
Baychester, New York-, NY 82 III cd 1
Bay City, MI 58-59 K 3
Bay City, TX 76-77 FG 8
Bayḍā', Al- [ADN] 160-161 EF 8
Bayḍā', Al- [LAR] 194-195 J 2
Bayḍā', Bi'r — 199 CD 4
Bayḍā', Jabal — 199 D 6
Baydhabo 194-195 a 3
Bayerischer Wald 124 F 4
Bayern 124 E 4
Bayeux [F] 132-133 G 4
Bay Farm Island 83 I c 2
Bayfield, WI 70-71 E 2
Bayḥān al-Qaṣab 160-161 F 8
Bayingolin Monggol Zizhizhou 166-167 FG 4
Bay Minette, AL 78-79 F 5
Bay Mountains 80-81 E 2
Bayonne 132-133 G 7
Bayonne, NJ 82 III b 3
Bayonne Park 82 III b 2
Bay Port, MI 72-73 E 3
Bayreuth 124 E 4
Bay Ridge, New York-, NY 82 III b 3
Bayrūt 160-161 CD 4
Bays, Lake of — 72-73 G 2
Bay Saint Louis, LA 78-79 E 5
Bayshore, CA 83 I b 2
Bay Shore, NY 72-73 K 4
Bays Mountains 80-81 E 2
Bay Springs, MS 78-79 E 4-5
Bayt al-Faqīh 160-161 E 8
Baytown, TX 58-59 GH 6
Bayview, San Francisco-, CA 83 I b 2
Bayyūdah, Barrīyat al- 194-195 L 5
Bayzaḥ, Wādī — 199 C 5
Baza 132-133 F 10
Bazar Dere 166-167 D 4
Bazard'uzi, gora — 142-143 J 7
Bazaruto, Ilha do — 198 G 6
Bazas 132-133 G 6
Bāzdar 160-161 JK 5
Bazias 138-139 J 3
Bazine, KS 68-69 G 6
Beach, ND 68-69 DE 2
Beachburg 72-73 H 2
Beachport 182-183 G 7
Beachy Head 116-117 M 10
Beacon, NY 72-73 K 4
Beacon Hill [CDN] 49 D 3
Beacon Hill [GB] 116-117 H 8
Beagh, Slieve — 116-117 DE 6
Beagle, Canal — 103 C 8
Beagle Bay 182-183 D 3
Bealach an Doirín 116-117 C 7
Bealanana 198 J 4
Béal an Átha 116-117 B 6
Béal an Átha Móir 116-117 D 6
Béal an Mhuirthid 116-117 B 6
Béal Átha na Sluagh 116-117 CD 7
Béal Átha Seanaigh 116-117 CD 6
Beale, Cape — 48 E 5
Beals Creek 76-77 D 6
Beannchar 116-117 D 7
Beann Éadair 116-117 EF 7
Beanntraighe 116-117 B 9
Beara 174-175 MN 8
Bear Creek 52-53 ST 6
Bearcreek, MT 66-67 J 3
Bearden, AR 78-79 C 4
Beardmore 70-71 G 1
Beardmore Glacier 31 A 20-18
Beardsley, AZ 74-75 G 6
Beardstown, IL 70-71 EF 5
Bear Hill 68-69 F 5
Bear Island 31 B 26
Bear Island = Oileán Bhéarra 116-117 AB 9
Bear Islands = ostrova Medvežji 154-155 f 3
Bear Lake [CDN] 49 KL 3
Bear Lake [CDN, lake] 48 D 1
Bear Lake [CDN, place] 48 D 1
Bear Lake [USA, Idaho, Utah] 58-59 D 3
Bear Lodge Moutains 68-69 D 3
Bear Mount 52-53 QR 2
Béarn [CDN] 72-73 G 1
Béarn [F] 132-133 G 7
Bearpaw, AK 52-53 M 4
Bearpaw Mountain 66-67 J 1
Bear River [CDN] 51 D 5
Bear River [USA] 58-59 D 3
Bear River Bay 66-67 G 5
Bearskin Lake 50 D 1
Beata, Cabo — 88-89 L 6
Beata, Isla — 58-59 M 8
Beatrice 198 F 5
Beatrice, AL 78-79 F 5
Beatrice, NE 58-59 G 3
Beatrice, Cape — 182-183 G 2
Beatty, NV 74-75 E 4
Beattyville 50 N 2
Beattyville, KY 72-73 E 6
Beaucaire 132-133 K 7
Beaucanton 50 M 2
Beauce 132-133 HJ 4
Beauceville 51 A 4
Beauchene Island 103 E 8
Beaufort, NC 80-81 H 3
Beaufort, SC 80-81 F 4
Beaufort Inlet 80-81 H 3
Beaufort Lagoon 52-53 Q 2-R 1
Beaufort Sea 46-47 G-L 3
Beaufort-Wes 198 D 8
Beaufort West = Beaufort-Wes 198 D 8
Beauharnois 72-73 JK 2
Beaujolais 132-133 K 5
Beauly 116-117 G 3
Beaumaris 116-117 GH 7
Beaumont, CA 74-75 E 6
Beaumont, MS 78-79 E 5
Beaumont, TX 58-59 GH 5
Beaumont-Hague 116-117 JK 11
Beaune 132-133 K 5
Beauvais 132-133 HJ 4
Beauval 49 DE 3
Beaver, AK 52-53 O 3
Beaver, KS 68-69 G 6
Beaver, UT 74-75 G 3
Beaver Bay, MN 70-71 E 2
Beaver City, NE 68-69 FG 5
Beaver City, OK 76-77 D 4
Beaver Creek [CDN] 52-53 R 5
Beaver Creek [USA] 52-53 O 3-4
Beaver Creek [USA ◁ Cheyenne River] 68-69 D 4
Beaver Creek [USA ◁ Little Missouri River] 68-69 DE 2
Beaver Creek [USA ◁ Milk River] 66-67 J 1
Beaver Creek [USA ◁ Missouri River] 68-69 F 2
Beaver Creek [USA ◁ Republican River] 68-69 F 6
Beaver Creek [USA ◁ South Platte River] 68-69 E 5-6
Beaver Creek Mountain 78-79 F 4
Beaverdam, VA 80-81 GH 2
Beaver Dam, WI 70-71 F 4
Beaver Falls, PA 72-73 F 4
Beaverhead Range 66-67 G 3
Beaverhead River 66-67 G 3
Beaverhill Lake [CDN, Alberta] 49 BC 4
Beaverhill Lake [CDN, Manitoba] 49 L 3
Beaver Inlet 52-53 no 4
Beaver Island [USA] 70-71 H 3
Beaver Lake 76-77 GH 4
Beaverlodge 48 GH 2
Beaver Mountains 52-53 J 5
Beaver River 46-47 P 7
Beaverton 72-73 G 2
Beāwar 160-161 LM 5
Beazley 103 C 4
Bebedouro 98-99 K 9
Bebra 124 D 3
Becan 86-87 Q 8
Beccles 116-117 h 6
Bečej 138-139 HJ 3
Béchar = Bashshār 194-195 D 2
Becharof Lake 46-47 EF 6
Bechevin Bay 52-53 ab 2
Bechuanaland = Betsjoeanaland 198 D 7
Beckley, WV 58-59 K 4
Beclean 138-139 KL 2
Beda 194-195 M 7
Beddington, ME 72-73 MN 2
Bedele 194-195 M 7
Bedford, IA 70-71 C 5
Bedford, IN 70-71 G 6
Bedford, KY 70-71 H 6
Bedford, PA 72-73 G 4
Bedford, VA 80-81 G 2
Bedford [CDN, Nova Scotia] 51 DE 5
Bedford [CDN, Quebec] 72-73 K 2
Bedford [GB] 116-117 L 8
Bedford Park, IL 83 II a 2
Bedford Park, New York-, NY 82 III c 1
Bedford-Stuyvesant, New York-, NY 82 III c 2
Bēdja = Bājah 194-195 F 1
Bedlington 116-117 K 5
Bednesti 48 F 3
Bedourie 182-183 GH 4
Bedshar 142-143 K 8
Bedworth 116-117 KL 8
Beebe, AR 78-79 CD 3
Beech Creek, OR 66-67 D 3
Beechey Point, AK 52-53 MN 1
Beechy 49 E 5
Beegum, CA 66-67 B 5
Beeler, KS 68-69 FG 6
Beerenberg 30 B 19
Beersheba = Bĕer-Sheva' 160-161 C 4
Bĕer-Sheva' 160-161 C 4
Beeville, TX 58-59 G 6
Befale 198 D 1
Befandriana-atsimo 198 H 6
Befandriana-avavatva 198 J 5
Bega [AUS] 182-183 JK 7
Bega, Canal — 138-139 J 3
Begemdir-na Simen 194-195 M 6
Beggs, OK 76-77 F 5
Begičeva, ostrov — = ostrov Bol'šoj Begičev 154-155 VW 3
Begna 114-115 C 7
Begoritis, Límnē — 138-139 JK 5
Behagle, De — = Laï 194-195 H 7
Behágue, Pointe — 98-99 J 3-4
Behan 49 C 3
Behara 198 J 6
Behbahān 160-161 G 4
Behm Canal 52-53 x 9
Behn, Mount — 182-183 E 3
Bei'an 166-167 O 2
Beibei 166-167 K 6
Beibu Wan 166-167 K 7-8
Beiḍa, Bîr — = Bi'r Bayḍā' 199 CD 4
Beidá', El — = Al-Bayḍā' 194-195 J 2
Beida, Gebel — = Jabal Bayḍā' 199 D 6
Beihai [TJ, Guangxi Zhuangzu Zizhiqu] 166-167 K 7
Beijing 166-167 LM 3-4
Beijingzi 170-171 DE 3
Beipa'a 174-175 N 8
Beipiao 170-171 C 2
Beira [Mozambique] 198 FG 5
Beira [P] 132-133 CD 8
Beiroût = Bayrūt 160-161 CD 4
Beirut = Bayrūt 160-161 CD 4
Beisan = Bēt Sheān 160-161 F 6
Bei Shan 166-167 GH 3
Beishanchengzhen = Caoshi 170-171 E 1
Beitbridge 198 EF 6
Beizaḥ, Wādī — = Wādī Bayzaḥ 199 C 5
Beizhen [TJ, Liaoning] 170-171 C 2
Beja 132-133 D 9-10
Beja = Bājah 194-195 F 1
Bēja = Bājah 194-195 F 1
Bejaïa = Bijāyah 194-195 EF 1
Béjar 132-133 E 8
Bejestān 160-161 H 4
Bekabad 160-161 KL 2
Bekasi 174-175 E 8
Bek-Budi = Karši 160-161 K 3
Bekdaš 160-161 G 2
Békés 124 K 5
Békéscsaba 124 K 5
Bekily 198 J 6
Belā [PAK] 160-161 K 5
Bela Crkva 138-139 J 3
Belaga 174-175 F 6
Belagām = Belgaum 160-161 LM 7
Belaia = Beleye 194-195 b 2-3
Bel Air 132-133 F 4
Bel Air, MD 72-73 H 5
Bel Air, Los Angeles-, CA 83 III b 1
Belaja [SU, river] 154-155 J 6
Belaja Cerkov' 142-143 F 6
Belaja Glina 142-143 H 6
Belaja Zemľa, ostrova — 154-155 L-N 1
Belang 174-175 HJ 6
Bélanger River 50 A 1
Bela Palanka 138-139 K 4
Belau 174-175 KL 5
Bela Vista [BR, Mato Grosso do Sul] 98-99 H 9
Bela Vista [BR, Rondônia] 98-99 G 10
Bela Vista [Mozambique] 198 F 7
Bela Vista, Cachoeira — 98-99 J 5
Bela Vista de Goiás 98-99 K 8
Belawan 174-175 C 6
Belcher Channel 46-47 RS 2
Belcher Islands 46-47 U 6
Belchite 132-133 G 8
Bel'cy 142-143 E 6
Belden, CA 66-67 C 5
Belding, MI 70-71 H 4
Belebej 154-155 J 7
Beled Weeyne 194-195 O 8
Belém [BR, Pará] 98-99 K 5
Belen, NM 58-59 E 5
Belep, Îles — 182-183 M 3
Beleye 194-195 M 6
Belfair, WA 66-67 B 2
Belfast 116-117 EF 6
Belfast, ME 72-73 M 2
Belfast Lough 116-117 F 6
Belfield, ND 68-69 E 2
Belfodio 194-195 LM 6
Belford 116-117 K 5
Belfort 132-133 L 5
Belfry, MT 68-69 B 3
Bélgāñv = Belgaum 160-161 LM 7
Belgaon = Belgaum 160-161 LM 7
Belgaum 160-161 LM 7
Belgica Mountains 31 B 3-4
Belgium 132-133 JK 3
Belgorod 142-143 G 5
Belgorod-Dnestrovskij 142-143 EF 6
Belgrade, MN 70-71 C 3
Belgrade, MT 66-67 H 3
Belgrade = Beograd 138-139 J 3
Belhaven, NC 80-81 H 3
Beli Lom 138-139 LM 4
Belinyu 174-175 E 7
Beli Timok 138-139 K 4
Belitung, Pulau — 174-175 E 7
Belize [BH, place] 58-59 J 8
Belize [BH, state] 58-59 J 8
Belize River 86-87 Q 9
Belkofski, AK 52-53 bc 2
Bel'kovskij, ostrov — 154-155 Za 2
Bell, CA 83 III c 2
Bell, FL 80-81 b 2
Bell, Rivière — 50 N 2
Bella Bella 48 C 3
Bella Coola 46-47 L 7
Bellaire, MI 70-71 H 3
Bellaire, OH 72-73 F 4-5
Bellaire, TX 76-77 G 8
Bellary 160-161 M 7
Bella Unión 103 E 4
Bella Vista [BOL] 98-99 G 8
Bellavista [BR, Amazonas] 98-99 D 6
Bella Vista [RA, Corrientes] 103 E 3
Belle, MO 70-71 E 6
Belleek 116-117 CD 6
Bellefontaine, OH 72-73 E 4
Bellefonte, PA 72-73 GH 4
Belle Fourche, SD 68-69 DE 3
Belle Fourche Reservoir 68-69 E 3
Belle Fourche River 68-69 E 3
Belle Glade, FL 80-81 c 3
Belle Île 132-133 F 5
Belle Isle [CDN] 46-47 Za 7
Belle Isle, Strait of — 46-47 Z 7
Bellemont, AZ 74-75 GH 5
Belleoram 51 J 4
Belle Plaine, IA 70-71 D 5
Belle Plaine, KS 68-69 H 7
Belle Plaine, MN 70-71 D 3
Bellerose, New York-, NY 82 III d 2
Belleterre 72-73 G 1
Belleville, IL 70-71 F 6
Belleville, KS 68-69 H 6
Belleville, NJ 82 III ab 2
Belleville [CDN] 46-47 V 9
Bellevue, IA 70-71 E 4
Bellevue, MI 70-71 H 4
Bellevue, OH 72-73 E 4
Bellevue, TX 76-77 E 6
Bellevue, WA 66-67 BC 2
Bellevue, Washington-, DC 82 II a 2
Bellflower, CA 83 III d 2
Bell Gardens, CA 83 III d 2
Bellin [CDN] 46-47 WX 5
Bellingham 116-117 J 5
Bellingham, WA 66-67 BC 1
Bellingshausen Sea 31 BC 28
Bellinzona 124 D 5
Bell Irving River 48 C 1
Bellis 49 C 3
Bell Island 51 J 2
Bell Island = Wabana 46-47 a 8
Bell Island Hot Springs, AK 52-53 x 8-9
Bell Lake 50 D 3
Bello [CO] 98-99 DE 3
Bello Horizonte = Belo Horizonte 98-99 L 8
Bellona 174-175 j 7
Bellota, CA 74-75 C 3
Bellows Falls, VT 72-73 K 3
Belloy 48 H 2
Bell Peninsula 46-47 U 5
Bells, TN 78-79 E 3
Belluno 138-139 DE 2
Bellville, TX 76-77 F 8
Bel Ville [RA] 103 D 4
Bellvue, CO 68-69 D 5
Belmez 132-133 E 9
Belmond, IA 70-71 D 4
Belmont, NY 72-73 GH 3
Belmont [CDN] 68-69 G 1
Belmont Cragin, Chicago-, IL 83 II a 1
Belmonte [BR] 98-99 M 8
Belmont Harbor 83 II b 1
Belmopan 58-59 J 8
Belmullet = Béal an Mhuirthid 116-117 B 6
Belogorsk [SU, Rossijskaja SFSR] 154-155 YZ 7
Belogorsk [SU, Ukrainskaja SSR] 142-143 FG 6
Belogradčik 138-139 K 4
Belo Horizonte [BR, Minas Gerais] 98-99 L 8
Beloit, KS 68-69 GH 6
Beloit, WI 58-59 J 3
Beloje ozero 154-155 F 5
Belokuricha 154-155 PQ 7
Belo Monte 98-99 N 6
Belomorsk 154-155 EF 5
Belomorsko-Baltijskij kanal 142-143 FG 3
Belo Oriente 98-99 G 11
Belopolje 142-143 F 5
Belopûla 138-139 K 7
Beloreck 154-155 K 7
Belorussian Soviet Socialist Republic 142-143 D-F 5
Belo-Tsiribihina 198 H 5
Bel'ov 142-143 G 5
Belovo 154-155 Q 7
Belozersk 154-155 F 5-6
Belper 116-117 K 7
Belpre, KS 68-69 G 7
Belpre, OH 72-73 F 5
Belsund 114-115 j 6
Belt, MT 66-67 H 2
Belted Range 74-75 E 4
Belton, SC 80-81 E 3
Belton, TX 76-77 F 7
Belucha, gora — 154-155 Q 8
Beluchistan = Balūchistān 160-161 J 5-K 4
Beluga Lake 52-53 M 6
Beluja Guba 154-155 HJ 3
Belvedere, CA 83 I b 1
Belvedere, VA 82 II a 2
Belvidere, IL 70-71 F 4
Belvidere, KS 68-69 G 7
Belvidere, SD 68-69 F 4
Belyj, ostrov — 154-155 MN 3
Belyj Byček = Čagoda 154-155 EF 6
Belyj Jar 154-155 Q 6
Belzoni, MS 78-79 D 4
Bemaraha 198 HJ 5
Bembe 198 BC 3
Bembéréké = Bimbéréké 194-195 E 6
Bement, IL 70-71 F 6
Bemidji, MN 58-59 GH 2
Bemis, TN 78-79 E 3
Bena, MN 70-71 CD 2
Benaadir [SP, administrative unit = 2 ◁] 194-195 O 8
Benaadir [SP, landscape] 194-195 ab 3
Benalla 182-183 J 7
Benares = Vārānasi 160-161 N 5
Benas, Ras — = Rā's Banās 194-195 M 4
Benavente 132-133 DE 7
Benavides, TX 76-77 E 9
Benbecula 116-117 D 3
Bend 48 G 3
Bend, OR 58-59 B 3
Bendel 194-195 F 7
Bendeleben Mountains 52-53 EF 4
Bender Abas = Bandar 'Abbās 160-161 H 5
Bender Bayla 194-195 c 2
Bendery 142-143 EF 6
Bendigo 182-183 HJ 7
Benevento 138-139 F 5
Benfica [BR, Acre] 98-99 C 9
Benfica, Cachoeira — 98-99 L 5
Benga 198 F 5
Bengal, Bay of — 160-161 N-P 7
Bengalian Ridge 26-27 O 5-6
Bengalore = Bangalore 160-161 M 8
Bengalūru = Bangalore 160-161 M 8
Bengasi = Banghāzī 194-195 HJ 2
Bengbu 166-167 M 5
Benge, WA 66-67 D 2
Benghazi = Banghāzī 194-195 HJ 2
Bengkalis, Pulau — 174-175 D 6
Bengkayang 174-175 EF 6
Bengkulu 174-175 D 7
Bengough 68-69 D 1
Benguela 198 B 4
'Ben Guerīr = Bin Gharīr 194-195 C 2
Beni [ZRE] 198 E 1
Beni, Río — 98-99 F 7
Beni-Abbès = Banī Abbās 194-195 D 2
Benicia, CA 74-75 BC 3
Benī Mazār = Banī Mazār 194-195 L 3
'Benī Mellāl = Banī Mallāl 194-195 C 2
Benin 194-195 E 6-7
Bénin = Benin 194-195 E 6-7
Benin, Bight of — 194-195 E 7-8
Benin City 194-195 F 7
Benī Shigeir = Banī Shuqayr 199 B 4
Béni Souef = Banī Suwayf 194-195 L 3
Benī Suêf = Banī Suwayf 194-195 L 3
Benito Juárez 103 DE 5
Benjamim Constant 98-99 EF 5

Benjamim 211

Benjamin, TX 76-77 DE 6
Benjamin Hill 86-87 E 2
Benkelman, NE 68-69 F 5
Benkulen = Bengkulu 174-175 D 7
Bennett 52-53 U 7
Bennett, CO 68-69 D 6
Bennett, WI 70-71 E 2
Bennett, ostrov — 154-155 cd 2
Bennett's Harbour 88-89 J 2
Bennettsville, SC 80-81 G 3
Bennington, VT 72-73 K 3
Bénoué 194-195 G 7
Benqi = Benxi 166-167 N 3
Bensheim 124 D 4
Benson 68-69 E 1
Benson, AZ 74-75 H 7
Benson, MN 70-71 C 3
Bentinck Island 182-183 GH 3
Bentiū 194-195 KL 7
Bentley 48 K 3
Benton, AL 78-79 F 4
Benton, AR 78-79 C 3
Benton, CA 74-75 D 4
Benton, IL 70-71 F 6-7
Benton, KY 78-79 E 2
Benton, LA 78-79 C 4
Benton, WI 70-71 E 4
Benton City, WA 66-67 D 2
Benton Harbor, MI 70-71 G 4
Bentonia, MS 78-79 D 4
Bentonville, AR 76-77 G 4
Benue 194-195 F 7
Benué = Benue 194-195 F 7
Benue Plateau 194-195 F 7
Benwee Head = An Bheann Bhuidhe 116-117 B 6
Benxi 166-167 N 3
Beograd 138-139 J 3
Beppu 170-171 H 6
Bequia 88-89 Q 8
Berat 138-139 H 5
Berau, Teluk — 174-175 K 7
Berau Gulf = Teluk Berau 174-175 K 7
Berber = Barbar 194-195 L 5
Berbera 194-195 b 1
Berbérati 194-195 a 1
Berbice 98-99 J 2-K 3
Berbice River 98-99 JK 3
Berch 166-167 L 2
Berchtesgaden 124 F 5
Berck 132-133 H 3
Berďansk 142-143 G 6
Berdigesťach 154-155 XY 5
Berea, KY 70-71 H 7
Berea, NE 68-69 E 4
Berea, OH 72-73 F 4
Berenda, CA 74-75 CD 4
Berenike 194-195 LM 4
Berens Island 49 K 4
Berens River [CDN, place] 46-47 R 7
Berens River [CDN, river] 46-47 R 7
Beresford, SD 68-69 H 4
Beresford Lake 50 B 2
Beresniki = Berezniki 154-155 JK 6
Beretău 138-139 JK 2
Berezina 142-143 E 5
Berezník 142-143 H 3
Berezniki [SU, Perm'skaja Oblast'] 154-155 JK 6
Bergama 160-161 B 3
Bèrgamo 138-139 CD 3
Bergen, ND 68-69 F 1-2
Bergen [DDR] 124 F 1
Bergen [N] 114-115 A 7
Bergen Beach, New York-, NY 82 III c 3
Bergenfield, NJ 82 III c 1
Bergen Point 82 III b 3
Bergerac 132-133 H 6
Bergland, MI 70-71 F 2
Bergland [CDN] 70-71 C 1
Bergslagen 114-115 F 7-8
Berhampore 160-161 O 6
Berhampur 160-161 NO 7
Berhampur = Berhampore 160-161 O 6
Bering, mys — 154-155 k 5
Bering, ostrov — 154-155 fg 7
Bering Glacier 46-47 H 5
Bering Lake 52-53 P 6
Beringovskij 154-155 j 5
Bering Sea 154-155 k 5-g 6
Bering Strait 46-47 B 5-C 4
Beris = Bārīs 199 B 5
Beristain 86-87 LM 7
Berja 132-133 F 10
Berjozovo = Ber'ozovo 154-155 LM 5
Berkeley, CA 58-59 B 4
Berkner Island 31 B 31-32
Berkovica 138-139 K 4
Berkshire 116-117 KL 9
Berland River 48 J 2
Berlevåg 114-115 N 2
Berlin, MD 72-73 J 5
Berlin, ND 68-69 G 2
Berlin, NH 58-59 M 3
Berlin, WI 70-71 F 4
Berlin [D] 124 FG 2
Berlin, Mount — 31 B 23
Bermejillo 86-87 J 5
Bermejo [BOL] 98-99 G 9
Bermejo [RA] 103 C 4
Bermejo, Río — [RA ◁ Río Paraguay] 103 D 2
Bermeo 132-133 F 7
Bermuda Islands 58-59 NO 5
Bermudas = Bermuda Islands 58-59 NO 5
Bern 124 C 5
Bernalillo, NM 76-77 A 5
Bernardo de Irigoyen 103 F 3
Bernburg 124 EF 3
Berne, IN 70-71 H 5
Berne, WA 66-67 C 2
Berne = Bern 124 C 5
Berner Alpen 124 C 5
Berneray 116-117 D 3
Bernese Alps = Berner Alpen 124 C 5
Bernice, LA 78-79 C 4
Bernier Bay 46-47 ST 3
Bernier Island 182-183 B 4
Bernina 124 D 5
Bĕroia 138-139 JK 5
Beroroha 198 HJ 6
Beroun 124 FG 4
Berounka 124 F 4
Ber'oza 142-143 D 5
Ber'ozovo 154-155 LM 5
Berry 132-133 HJ 5
Berry, AL 78-79 F 4
Berryessa, Lake — 74-75 B 3
Berry Head 116-117 H 10
Berry Islands 88-89 GH 2
Berryville, AR 78-79 C 2
Berryville, VA 72-73 GH 5
Bersabee = Bĕer Shevaʻ 160-161 C 4
Berseba 198 C 7
Bersimis 51 B 3
Berté, Lac — 51 BC 2
Berthierville 72-73 K 1
Berthold, ND 68-69 EF 1
Bertiskos 138-139 K 5
Bertolínia 98-99 L 6
Bertoua 194-195 G 8
Bertraghboy Bay = An Bheartrach Bhuidhe 116-117 AB 7
Bertram 50 G 3
Bertram, TX 76-77 EF 7
Bertrand, NE 68-69 G 5
Bertua = Bertoua 194-195 G 8
Bertwell 49 G 4
Beru 178 H 3
Beruri 98-99 G 5
Berwick, LA 78-79 D 6
Berwick, PA 72-73 H 4
Berwick [CDN] 51 D 5
Berwick [GB] 116-117 J 5
Berwick-upon-Tweed 116-117 JK 5
Berwyn, IL 70-71 FG 5
Berwyn Heights, MD 82 II b 1
Berwyn Mountains 116-117 H 8
Beryl, UT 74-75 G 4
Berytus = Bayrūt 160-161 CD 4
Besalampy 198 H 5
Besançon 132-133 L 5
Besboro Island 52-53 G 4
Beskids = Beskidy 124 JK 4
Beskidy 124 JK 4
Besna Kobila 138-139 K 4
Besnard Lake 49 F 3
Besni 160-161 D 3
Bessa Monteiro 198 B 3
Bessarabija 142-143 E 6
Bessarabka 142-143 E 6
Bessaz gora 154-155 M 9
Bessbrock 116-117 E 6
Bessels, Kapp — 114-115 lm 5
Bessemer, AL 58-59 J 5
Bessemer, MI 70-71 EF 2
Bessemer City, NC 80-81 F 3
Besshi 170-171 J 6
Bessŏky, gora — 160-161 G 2
Best, TX 76-77 D 7
Bestamak 142-143 L 6
Bestobe 154-155 N 7
Bĕţ = Okha 160-161 K 6
Betaf 174-175 L 7
Betafo 198 J 5
Betanzos [E] 132-133 CD 7
Bĕtarĕ-Oya 194-195 G 7
Bethal 198 F 7
Bethanië = Bethanien 198 C 7
Bethanien 198 C 7
Bethany, MO 70-71 CD 5
Bethel, AK 46-47 D 5
Bethel, ME 72-73 L 2
Bethel, MN 70-71 D 3
Bethel, NC 80-81 H 3
Bethel, OH 72-73 DE 5
Bethel, OK 76-77 G 5
Bethel, VT 72-73 K 3
Bethesda, MD 82 II a 1
Bethlehem 198 E 7
Bethlehem, PA 72-73 J 4
Beth Shaan = Bēt Shĕ'ān 160-161 F 6
Bethulie 198 E 8
Bethune [CDN] 49 F 5
Bĕthune [F] 132-133 J 3
Betioky 198 H 6
Betoota 182-183 H 5
Betpak-Dala 154-155 MN 8
Betroka 198 J 6
Bĕt Shĕ'ān 160-161 F 6
Betsiamites 51 B 3
Betsiamites, Rivière — 51 B 3
Betsiboka 198 J 5
Betsie Point 70-71 G 3
Betsjoeanaland 198 D 7
Bette, Pic — 194-195 HJ 4
Bettles, AK 52-53 M 3
Bettles Field = Evansville, AK 52-53 LM 3
Bettyhill 116-117 GH 2
Betvā = Betwa 160-161 M 6
Betwa 160-161 M 6
Beulah 49 H 5
Beulah, MI 70-71 G 3
Beulah, ND 68-69 EF 2
Beulah, OR 66-67 D 4
Beulah, WY 68-69 D 3
Beverley 116-117 L 7
Beverley, Lake — 52-53 H 7
Beverly, MA 72-73 L 3
Beverly, WA 66-67 D 2
Beverly, Chicago-, IL 83 II ab 2
Beverly Hills, CA 83 III b 1
Bewcastle Fells 116-117 J 5
Bewdley 116-117 J 8
Bexhill 116-117 M 10
Bexley, OH 72-73 E 4-5
Beyābān, Kūh-e- 160-161 H 5
Bey el Kebir, Wadi — = Wādī Bey al-Kabīr 194-195 GH 2
Beyla 194-195 C 7
Beyrouth = Bayrūth 160-161 CD 4
Beyşehir gölü 160-161 C 3
Beyt = Okhā 160-161 K 6
Bežeck 142-143 G 4
Beziers 132-133 J 7
Bezwada = Vijayavādā 160-161 N 7

Bhadrakh 160-161 O 6
Bhāgalpur 160-161 O 5-6
Bhaile Uí Thaidhg, Cuan — 116-117 E 8
Bhairab Bāzār 160-161 P 6
Bhamo = Banmau 174-175 C 2
Bhandāra 160-161 MN 6
Bharatpur [IND, Rājasthān] 160-161 M 5
Bharuch 160-161 L 6
Bhāţgāīv = Bhātgaon 160-161 O 5
Bhatgaon 160-161 O 5
Bhatinda 160-161 L 4
Bhātpāra 160-161 O 6
Bhaunagar 160-161 L 6
Bhavānīpāţnā = Bhawānipatna 160-161 N 7
Bhawānipatna 160-161 N 7
Bheann Bhuidhe, An — 116-117 B 6
Bhearbha, An — 116-117 DE 8
Bhéarra, Oileán — 116-117 AB 9
Bheartrach Bhuidhe, An — 116-117 AB 7
Bheigeir, Beinn — 116-117 EF 5
Bhelsā = Vidisha 160-161 M 6
Bhilainagar 160-161 N 6
Bhilsa = Vidisha 160-161 M 6
Bhīma 160-161 M 7
Bhīr 160-161 M 7
Bhivānī = Bhiwāni 160-161 M 5
Bhiwani 160-161 M 5
Bhogaraigh, Sléibhte an — 116-117 BC 8-9
Bhóinn, An — 116-117 E 7
Bhopāl 160-161 M 6
Bhor 160-161 L 7
Bhréanainn, Bádh — 116-117 A 8
Bhubanĕshvara = Bhubaneswar 160-161 O 6
Bhubeneswar 160-161 O 6
Bhuj 160-161 KL 6
Bhusāvaļ = Bhusāwal 160-161 M 6
Bhusāwal 160-161 M 6
Bhutan 160-161 OP 5

Biá, Rio — 98-99 E 7
Bīābān, Kūh-e = Kūh-e Beyābān 160-161 H 5
Biafra 194-195 F 7
Biak, Pulau — 174-175 L 7
Biała Podlaska 124 L 2-3
Białobrzegi 124 K 3
Białogard 124 GH 1-2
Białystok 124 L 2
Biar = Bihār 160-161 NO 6
Biaro, Pulau — 174-175 J 6
Biarritz 132-133 G 7
Biasso = Bissau 194-195 A 6
Bibā 199 B 3
Bibai 170-171 bc 2
Bibala 198 B 4
Biberach 124 D 4
Bic 51 B 3
Bicaner = Bīkaner 160-161 L 5
Bicester 116-117 K 9
Biche, Lac la — 49 BC 3
Bickerdike 48 J 3
Bickerton Island 182-183 G 2
Bickleton, WA 66-67 CD 2
Bicknell, IN 70-71 G 6
Bicknell, UT 74-75 H 3
Biḍ = Bhīr 160-161 M 7
Bid', Al- 199 D 3
Bida 194-195 F 7
Bīdar 160-161 M 7
Bidara = Bīdar 160-161 M 7
Biddeford, ME 58-59 MN 3
Biddle, MT 68-69 D 3
Bidean nam Bian 116-117 F 4
Bideford 116-117 G 9
Bidele Depression = Djourab 194-195 H 5
Bié = Kuito 198 C 4
Bieber, CA 66-67 C 5
Biebrza 124 L 2
Biel 124 C 5
Bielawa 124 H 3
Bielefeld 124 D 2
Biele Karpaty 124 HJ 4
Biella 138-139 BC 3
Bielsko-Biała 124 J 4
Bielsk Podlaski 124 L 2
Bienfait 68-69 E 1
Biên Hoa 174-175 E 4
Bienne = Biel 124 C 5
Bienville, LA 78-79 C 4
Bienville, Lac — 46-47 W 6
Bifuka 170-171 c 1
Big Arm, MT 66-67 FG 2
Big Baldy 66-67 F 3
Big Bar Creek 48 FG 4
Big Bay, MI 70-71 G 2
Big Bay de Noc 70-71 G 3
Big Beaver 68-69 D 1
Big Beaver Falls 50 K 2
Big Beaver House 50 DE 1
Big Bell 182-183 C 5
Big Belt Mountains 66-67 H 2
Big Bend, CA 66-67 C 5
Big Bend, CO 68-69 E 6
Big Bend National Park 58-59 F 6
Big Black River 78-79 D 4
Big Blue River 68-69 H 5-6
Bigbury Bay 116-117 GH 10
Big Canyon River 76-77 CD 7
Big Chino Wash 74-75 G 5
Big Coulee 49 B 3
Big Creek, ID 66-67 F 3
Big Creek [CDN] 48 F 4
Big Creek [USA] 68-69 FG 6
Big Cypress Indian Reservation 80-81 c 3
Big Cypress Swamp 80-81 c 3-4
Big Delta, AK 46-47 GH 5
Big Falls 66-67 E 1
Big Falls, MN 70-71 CD 1
Bigfork, MT 66-67 FG 1
Big Fork River 70-71 CD 2
Biggar [CDN] 46-47 P 7
Biggar [GB] 116-117 H 5
Bigge Island 182-183 DE 2
Biggleswade 116-117 L 8
Biggs, OR 66-67 C 3
Big Hole River 66-67 G 3
Bighorn, MT 68-69 C 2
Bighorn Basin 68-69 B 3
Bighorn Lake 68-69 BC 3
Bighorn Mountains 58-59 E 2-3
Bighorn River 68-69 C 3
Big Island [CDN, Hudson Strait] 46-47 WX 5
Big Island [CDN, Lake of the Woods] 70-71 C 1
Big Koniuji Island 52-53 d 2
Big Lake 68-69 B 3
Big Lake, AK 52-53 N 3
Big Lake, TX 76-77 D 7
Big Lost River 66-67 G 4
Big Muddy Creek 68-69 D 1
Big Muddy River 70-71 F 6-7
Bigot, Lac — 51 D 2
Big Pine, CA 74-75 DE 4
Big Pine Key, FL 80-81 c 4
Big Piney, WY 66-67 HJ 4
Big Piney River 70-71 DE 7
Big Port Walter, AK 52-53 v 8
Biğrān 160-161 G 6
Big Rapids, MI 70-71 H 4
Big River [CDN, place] 49 E 4
Big River [CDN, river] 49 E 4
Big River [USA] 52-53 K 5
Big Sable Point 70-71 G 3
Big Salmon Range 46-47 K 5
Big Salmon River 52-53 U 6
Big Sand Lake 49 J 2
Big Sandy, MT 68-69 AB 1
Big Sandy, TN 78-79 EF 2
Big Sandy, TX 76-77 G 6
Big Sandy, WY 66-67 J 4
Big Sandy Creek 68-69 E 6
Big Sandy Lake [CDN] 49 F 3
Big Sandy Lake [USA] 70-71 D 2
Big Sandy River 74-75 G 5
Bigsby Island 70-71 C 1
Big Sioux River 68-69 H 4
Big Smoky Valley 74-75 E 3
Big Snowy Mountain 68-69 B 2
Big Spring, TX 58-59 F 5
Big Springs, ID 66-67 H 3
Big Squaw Lake = Chandalar, AK 52-53 NO 3
Big Stone City, SD 68-69 H 3
Big Stone Gap, VA 80-81 E 2
Bigstone Lake [CDN] 50 B 1
Big Stone Lake [USA] 68-69 H 3
Bigstone River 49 L 3
Big Sur, CA 74-75 BC 4
Big Timber, MT 66-67 J 3
Bigtrails, WY 68-69 C 4
Big Trout Lake [CDN, lake] 46-47 T 7
Big Trout Lake [CDN, place] 50 E 1
Big Wells, TX 76-77 E 8
Big White Mountain 66-67 D 1
Big Wood River 66-67 F 4
Bihać 138-139 F 3
Bihār [IND, administrative unit] 160-161 NO 6
Bihār [IND, place] 160-161 O 6
Biharamulo 198 F 2
Bihor 138-139 K 2
Bihor, Munţii — 138-139 K 2
Bihoro 170-171 d 2
Bijagós, Arquipélago dos — 194-195 A 6
Bijāpur [IND, Karnataka] 160-161 LM 7
Bijāpura = Bijāpur 160-161 LM 7
Bījār 160-161 F 3
Bij-Chem = Bol'šoj Jenisej 154-155 S 7
Bijie 166-167 K 6
Bījistān = Bejestān 160-161 H 4
Bijnoṛ 160-161 L 5
Bijou Creek 68-69 D 5-6
Bijou Hills, SD 68-69 G 4
Bijrān 160-161 G 6
Bijsk 154-155 Q 7
Bīkaner 160-161 L 5
Bikin [SU, place] 154-155 Za 8
Bikin [SU, river] 154-155 a 8
Bikoro 198 C 2
Bilāspur [IND, Madhya Pradesh] 160-161 N 6
Bilbao 132-133 F 7
Bilbays 199 B 2
Bíldudalur 114-115 ab 2
Bileća 138-139 H 4
Bilecik 142-143 F 7
Bili [ZRE, place] 198 DE 1
Bili [ZRE, river] 198 DE 1
Biliran Island 174-175 H 4
Bill, WY 68-69 D 4
Billefjord 114-115 k 5
Billingborough 116-117 L 8
Billings, MT 58-59 E 2
Billingshurst 116-117 L 9
Billiton = Pulau Belitung 174-175 E 7
Bill Williams River 74-75 FG 5
Bilma 194-195 G 5
Bilma, Grand Erg de — 194-195 G 5
Biloela 182-183 K 4
Bilo gora 138-139 G 2-3
Biloxi, MS 58-59 J 5
Bilqās 199 B 2
Bilqas Qism Auwal = Bilqās 199 B 2
Bilston 116-117 JK 8
Biltine 194-195 J 6
Bilugyn = Bīlū Kyūn 174-175 C 3
Bīlū Kyūn 174-175 C 3
Bimbérekĕ 194-195 E 6
Bimlipatam 160-161 M 7
Binalbagan 174-175 H 4
Bindloe = Isla Marchena 98-99 AB 4
Binga, Mount — 198 F 5
Bin Ganīyah, Bi'r — 194-195 J 2
Bingen 124 C 4
Binger, OK 76-77 E 5
Bingham, ME 72-73 M 2
Bingham, NE 68-69 EF 4
Bingham, NM 76-77 A 6
Bingham Canyon, UT 66-67 GH 5
Binghamton, NY 58-59 LM 3
Bin Gharīr 194-195 C 2
Bingley 116-117 JK 7
Bingo Bay = Hiuchi-nada 170-171 J 5
Bingöl 160-161 E 3
Binjai 174-175 C 6
Binnaway 182-183 JK 6
Binne, Rinn na — 116-117 EF 8
Binscarth 49 H 5
Bintan, Pulau — 174-175 DE 6
Bintuhan 174-175 D 7
Bintulu 174-175 F 6
Binzart 194-195 FG 1
Binzert = Binzart 194-195 FG 1
Bío Bío, Río — 103 B 5
Biograd 138-139 F 4
Bioko 194-195 F 8
Biola, CA 74-75 CD 4
Biorka, AK 52-53 no 4
Biorra 116-117 D 7
Bīr = Bhīr 160-161 M 7
Bira 154-155 Z 8
Birāk 194-195 G 3
Bi'r al-Abd 199 C 2
Bi'r 'Alī 160-161 F 8
Bi'r al-Khamsah 194-195 K 2
Birao 194-195 J 6
Bir Ben Gania = Bi'r Bin Ganīyah 194-195 J 2
Birch Creek 52-53 P 3
Birch Creek, AK 52-53 P 3
Birches, AK 52-53 L 4
Birch Hills 49 F 4
Birch Island [CDN, island] 49 J 4
Birch Island [CDN, place] 48 H 4
Birch Lake [CDN] 49 C 4
Birch Lake [USA] 70-71 E 2
Birch Mountains 46-47 O 6
Birch Rapids 49 EF 3
Birch River [CDN, place] 49 H 4
Birch River [CDN, river] 49 B 2
Bird 49 L 2
Bird Cape 52-53 s 7
Bird City, KS 68-69 F 6
Bird Island 52-53 cd 2
Bird Island, MN 70-71 C 3
Birdsville 182-183 G 5
Birdum 182-183 F 3
Birecik 142-143 G 8
Bīrganj 160-161 NO 5
Birhan 194-195 M 6
Birigui 98-99 J 9
Biril'ussy 154-155 QR 6
Bīrjand 160-161 H 4
Birkenhead 116-117 H 7
Birket-Fatmé 194-195 HJ 6
Bîrlad [RO, place] 138-139 M 2
Bîrlad [RO, river] 138-139 M 2-3
Birma 174-175 BC 2
Birmingham 116-117 K 8
Birmingham, AL 58-59 J 5
Birney, MT 68-69 C 3
Birnie [CDN] 49 J 5
Birnie [Kiribati] 178 J 3
Birnin Kebbi 194-195 EF 6
Birni-n'Konni 194-195 EF 6
Birobidžan 154-155 Z 8
Birr = Biorra 116-117 D 7
Birrindudu 182-183 EF 3
Birsay 116-117 H 1
Birsk 154-155 K 6
Birskij = Obluč'e 154-155 Z 8
Birtavarre 114-115 J 3
Birtle 49 H 5
Bī'r Umm Qarayn 194-195 B 3
Biruni 154-155 L 9
Bir'usa 154-155 S 6
Birxham 116-117 H 10
Biržai 142-143 DE 4
Bisa, Pulau — 174-175 J 7
Bisaliya, El — = Al-Başalīyat Qiblī 199 C 5
Bisbee, AZ 74-75 HJ 7
Bisbee, ND 68-69 G 1
Biscay, Bay of — 110-111 GH 6
Biscayne Bay 80-81 c 4
Biscéglie 138-139 G 5
Bischofshofen 124 F 5
Biscoe Islands 31 C 30
Biscotasing 50 KL 3
Biscra = Biskrah 194-195 F 2
Biševo 138-139 F 4
Bīshah, Wādī — 160-161 E 6-7
Bishenpur 160-161 P 6
Bishop, CA 74-75 D 4
Bishop, TX 76-77 F 9
Bishop Auckland 116-117 JK 6
Bishop's Castle 116-117 HJ 8
Bishop's Stortford 116-117 LM 9
Bishop's Waltham 116-117 KL 10
Bishopville, SC 80-81 F 3
Biskayerhuken 114-115 hj 5
Biskotasi Lake 50 K 3
Biskrah 194-195 F 2
Bisling 174-175 J 5
Bismarck, MO 70-71 E 7
Bismarck, ND 58-59 F 2
Bismarck Archipelago 174-175 gh 5
Bismarckburg = Kasanga 198 F 3
Bismarck Range 174-175 M 7-N 8
Bismarck Sea 174-175 gh 5
Bison, SD 68-69 E 3
Bissagos Islands = Arquipélago dos Bijagós 194-195 A 6
Bissau 194-195 A 6
Bissett 50 B 2
Bistcho Lake 46-47 N 6
Bistineau, Lake — 78-79 C 4
Bistŏnis, Límnē — 138-139 L 5
Bistriţa [RO, place] 138-139 L 2
Bistriţa [RO, river] 138-139 M 2
Bitam 198 B 1
Bitely, MI 70-71 GH 4
Bitlis 160-161 E 3
Bitola 138-139 J 5
Bitonto 138-139 G 5
Bitter Creek 66-67 J 5
Bitter Creek, WY 68-69 B 5
Bitterfeld 124 F 3
Bitterfontein 198 C 8
Bitterroot Range 58-59 C 2-D 3
Bitterroot River 66-67 F 2
Bitumount 49 C 2
Bitung 174-175 J 6
Biu 194-195 G 6
Biviraka 174-175 M 8
Biwa-ko 166-167 Q 4
Biyāḍ, Al- = Al-Bayāḍ 160-161 F 6
Biyalā 199 B 2
Biysk = Bijsk 154-155 Q 7
Bizerta = Binzart 194-195 FG 1
Bizerte = Binzart 194-195 FG 1

Bjargtangar 114-115 a 2
Bjelovar 138-139 G 3
Bjelowo = Belovo 154-155 Q 7
Bjelucha = gora Belucha 154-155 Q 8
Bjorkdale 49 FG 4
Björkholmen 114-115 H 4
Björna 114-115 H 6
Björneborg = Pori 114-115 J 7
Bjuröklubb 114-115 JK 5

Black, AK 52-53 E 5

212 **Benjamin**

Blackall 182-183 HJ 4
Black Bay 70-71 F 1
Black Belt 58-59 J 5
Black Birch Lake 49 E 2
Blackburn 116-117 J 7
Blackburn, Mount — 46-47 H 5
Black Butte 68-69 E 2
Black Canyon 74-75 F 5
Black Canyon of the Gunnison National Monument 68-69 C 6
Black Diamond 48 K 4
Black Diamond, WA 66-67 BC 2
Blackdown Hills 116-117 HJ 10
Black Duck 46-47 ST 6
Black Eagle, MT 66-67 H 2
Blackfeet Indian Reservation 66-67 G 1
Blackfoot, ID 66-67 GH 4
Blackfoot, MT 66-67 G 1
Blackfoot Reservoir 66-67 H 4
Blackfoot River 66-67 G 2
Black Forest = Schwarzwald 124 D 4-5
Black Gobi = Char Gov' 166-167 GH 3
Black Hawk 50 C 3
Black Hills 58-59 F 3
Blackie 48 L 4
Black Island 50 A 2
Black Isle 116-117 G 3
Black Lake [CDN] 72-73 L 1-2
Black Lake [USA] 70-71 HJ 3
Black Lake [USA, Alaska] 52-53 d 1
Blackleaf, MT 66-67 G 1
Black Mesa 74-75 H 4
Black Mountain, NC 80-81 EF 3
Black Mountain [GB] 116-117 H 9
Black Mountain [USA] 78-79 G 3
Black Mountains [GB] 116-117 H 8-9
Black Mountains [USA] 58-59 D 4-5
Black Pine Peak 66-67 G 4
Black Point 52-53 g 1
Blackpool [CDN] 48 G 4
Blackpool [GB] 116-117 H 7
Black Range 76-77 A 6
Black Rapids, AK 52-53 P 5
Black River, MI 72-73 E 4
Black River [CDN] 50 AB 2
Black River [USA ◁ Henderson Bay] 72-73 J 3
Black River [USA ◁ Mississippi River] 70-71 E 3
Black River [USA ◁ Porcupine River] 52-53 Q 3
Black River [USA ◁ Saint Clear River] 72-73 E 3
Black River [USA ◁ Salt River] 74-75 HJ 6
Black River [USA ◁ White River] 78-79 D 2-3
Black River = Sông Đa 174-175 D 2
Black River Falls, WI 70-71 E 3
Black Rock 103 H 8
Black Rock, AR 78-79 D 2
Black Rock, UT 74-75 G 3
Black Rock Desert 58-59 C 3
Blacksburg, VA 80-81 F 2
Black Sea 110-111 PQ 7
Blackshear, GA 80-81 EF 5
Blacksod Bay = Cuan na Fhóid Dhuibh 116-117 AB 6
Black Springs, NM 74-75 J 6
Black Squirrel Creek 68-69 D 6
Blackstone, VA 80-81 GH 2
Black Sturgeon Lake 70-71 F 1
Blackville 51 CD 4
Blackville, SC 80-81 F 4
Blackwater = An Abha Mhór 116-117 C 8
Blackwater, River — 116-117 DE 6
Black Waxy Prairie 58-59 G 5
Blackwell, OK 76-77 F 4
Blackwell, TX 76-77 D 6
Bladensburg, MD 82 II b 1
Bladhma, Sliabh — 116-117 D 7-8
Blaenavon 116-117 HJ 9
Bláfjall 114-115 e 2
Blåfjorden 114-115 lm 5
Blagodarnoje 142-143 H 6
Blagoevgrad 138-139 K 4-5
Blagoveščensk [SU, Bashkir ASSR] 142-143 KL 4
Blagoveščensk [SU, Heilong Jiang] 154-155 YZ 7
Blagoveščenskij proliv 154-155 c 2-d 3
Blagoveshchensk = Blagoveščensk 154-155 YZ 7
Blaine, WA 66-67 B 1
Blaine Lake 49 E 4
Blair, NE 68-69 H 5
Blair, OK 76-77 E 5
Blair, WI 70-71 E 3
Blair Athol 182-183 J 4
Blairgowrie 116-117 H 4
Blairmore 66-67 F 1
Blairsden, CA 74-75 C 3
Blairsville, GA 80-81 DE 3
Blairsville, PA 72-73 G 4
Blakely, GA 78-79 G 5
Blake Point 70-71 F 1
Blanca, CO 68-69 D 7
Blanca Peak 58-59 E 4
Blanchard, LA 76-77 GH 6
Blanche, Lake — [AUS, South Australia] 182-183 GH 5
Blanche, Lake — [AUS, Western Australia] 182-183 D 4
Blanco, TX 76-77 E 7
Blanco Creek 76-77 C 5
Blancos, Los — [RA] 103 D 2
Blanc-Sablon 51 H 2
Blandá 114-115 d 2
Blandford Forum 116-117 JK 10
Blanding, UT 74-75 J 4
Blankaholm 114-115 FG 9
Blanket, TX 76-77 E 7
Blantyre 198 FG 5
Blåvands Huk 114-115 BC 10
Blavet 132-133 F 4-5
Blaydon 116-117 K 6
Blaye 132-133 G 6
Blayney 182-183 J 6
Blaze, Point — 182-183 EF 2
Blazon, WY 66-67 H 5
Blednaja, gora — 154-155 M 2
Bledsoe, TX 76-77 C 6
Blejeşti 138-139 L 3
Blekinge län 114-115 F 9
Blenheim [CDN] 72-73 F 3
Blenheim [NZ] 182-183 O 8
Blessing, TX 76-77 F 8
Bletchley 116-117 L 8-9
Bleu Mountains 78-79 C 3
Blewett, TX 76-77 D 8
Blida = Blīdah 194-195 E 1
Blīdah [DZ, place] 194-195 E 1
Blind River 50 K 3
Bliss, ID 66-67 F 4
Blissfield, MI 72-73 E 4
Blisworth 116-117 L 8
Blitar 174-175 F 8
Blitong = Pulau Belitung 174-175 E 7
Blitta 194-195 E 7
Blitzen, OR 66-67 D 4
Block Island 72-73 L 4
Block Island Sound 72-73 KL 4
Bloddy Foreland = Cnoc Fola 116-117 C 5
Bloemfontein 198 E 7
Blois 132-133 H 5
Blönduós 114-115 cd 2
Blood Vein River [CDN, place] 49 K 5
Bloodvein River [CDN, river] 50 AB 2
Bloody Falls 46-47 NO 4
Bloom, Slieve — = Sliabh Bladhma 116-117 D 7-8
Bloomer, WI 70-71 E 3
Bloomfield, IA 70-71 D 5
Bloomfield, IN 70-71 G 6
Bloomfield, KY 70-71 H 7
Bloomfield, NE 68-69 H 4
Bloomfield, NJ 82 III a 2
Bloomfield, NM 74-75 JK 4
Bloomfield, New York-, NY 82 III ab 3
Blooming Prairie, MN 70-71 D 4
Bloomington, IL 58-59 HJ 3
Bloomington, IN 58-59 J 4
Bloomington, MN 70-71 D 3
Bloomington, TX 76-77 F 8
Bloomsburg, PA 72-73 H 4
Blosseville Kyst 46-47 ef 4
Blossom, mys — 154-155 jk 3
Blountstown, FL 78-79 G 5
Bloxom, VA 80-81 J 2
Blue Bell Knoll 74-75 H 3
Blueberry 48 G 1
Blue Bonnets, Champ de Course — 82 I b 2
Blue Creek, UT 66-67 G 5
Blue Earth, MN 70-71 CD 4
Bluefield, VA 80-81 F 2
Bluefield, WV 80-81 F 2
Bluefields 58-59 K 9
Bluefields, Bahía de — 88-89 E 8
Bluegrass Region 70-71 H 6
Blue Hill, NE 68-69 G 5
Blue Hills of Couteau 51 GH 4
Blue Island, IL 70-71 FG 5
Bluejoint Lake 66-67 D 4
Blue Knob 72-73 G 4
Blue Lake, CA 66-67 B 5
Blue Mountain [USA, Montana] 68-69 DE 2
Blue Mountain [USA, Pennsylvania] 72-73 HJ 4
Blue Mountain Pass 66-67 E 4
Blue Mountains [JA] 58-59 L 8
Blue Mountains [USA, Maine] 72-73 L 2
Blue Mountains [USA, Oregon] 58-59 C 2-3
Blue Mountains [USA, Texas] 76-77 E 7
Blue Mud Bay 182-183 G 2
Blue Mud Hills 68-69 D 3
Bluemull Sound 116-117 ef 3
Blue Nile = An-Nīl al-Azraq 194-195 L 6
Bluenose Lake 46-47 N 4
Blue Rapids, KS 68-69 H 6
Blue Ridge, GA 80-81 D 3
Blue Ridge [CDN] 48 K 2
Blue Ridge [USA, Alabama] 78-79 FG 4
Blue Ridge [USA, New York] 72-73 J 3
Blue Ridge [USA, North Carolina] 58-59 KL 4
Blue River 74-75 J 6
Blue Springs, MO 70-71 CD 6
Blue Stack = An Chruach Ghorm 116-117 CD 6
Bluewater, NM 74-75 JK 5
Bluff 182-183 N 9
Bluff, AK 52-53 F 4
Bluff, UT 74-75 J 4
Bluff, The — 88-89 H 2
Bluffton, IN 72-73 D 4
Bluffton, OH 72-73 E 4
Blufton, IN 70-71 H 5
Blum, TX 76-77 F 6
Blumenau [BR] 103 FG 3
Blumut, Gunung — 174-175 D 6
Blunt, SD 68-69 FG 3
Bly, OR 66-67 C 4
Blying Sound 52-53 N 7
Blyth [CDN] 72-73 F 3
Blyth [GB] 116-117 K 5
Blythe, CA 74-75 F 6
Blytheville, AR 58-59 HJ 4

Bo [WAL] 194-195 B 7
Boaco 88-89 D 8
Boa Esperança [BR, Amazonas] 98-99 G 8
Boa Fé 98-99 B 8
Boa Hora 98-99 G 10
Boakview 72-73 FG 2
Boali 194-195 H 8
Boa Nova [BR, Bahia] 98-99 LM 7
Boa Nova [BR, Pará] 98-99 J 9
Boardman, OR 66-67 D 3
Boa Vista [BR, Acre] 98-99 BC 9
Boa Vista [BR, Amazonas] 98-99 B 7
Boa Vista [BR, Roraima] 98-99 G 4
Boa Vista [Cape Verde] 188-189 E 7
Boaz, AL 78-79 FG 3
Bobbili 160-161 N 7
Bòbbio 138-139 C 3
Bobo-Dioulasso 194-195 D 6
Bobo-Diulasso = Bobo-Dioulasso 194-195 D 6
Bobonong 198 E 6
Bóbr 124 G 3
Bobrof Island 52-53 u 6-7
Bobrujsk 142-143 E 5
Boca, Cachoeira da — 98-99 L 7
Boca, La — 58-59 b 3
Boca del Pao 98-99 FG 3
Boca del Río 86-87 MN 8
Boca do Acre 98-99 F 6
Boca do Jari 98-99 J 5
Boca do Mutum 98-99 DE 7
Boca do Tapauá = Tapauá 98-99 FG 6
Boca Grande, FL 80-81 b 3
Bocaiuva 98-99 L 8
Bocaranga 194-195 H 7
Boca Raton, FL 80-81 cd 3
Bocas 86-87 K 6
Bocas del Toro 88-89 E 10
Bocas del Toro, Archipiélago de — 88-89 EF 10
Bochina 124 K 4
Bocholt 124 C 3
Bochum 124 C 3
Boda [RCA] 194-195 H 8
Böda [S] 114-115 G 9
Bodajbo 154-155 VW 6
Bodega Head 74-75 B 3
Bó Deirge, Loch — 116-117 CD 7
Bodelé 194-195 H 5
Boden 114-115 JK 5
Bodensee 124 D 5
Boderg, Lough — = Loch Bó Deirge 116-117 CD 7
Bodmin 116-117 G 10
Bodmin Moor 116-117 G 10
Bodo [CDN] 49 C 4
Bodø [N] 114-115 EF 4
Bodoquena 98-99 H 8
Bodoquena, Serra — 98-99 H 9
Boekittingi = Bukittinggi 174-175 CD 7
Boende 198 D 2
Boerne, TX 76-77 E 8
Boffa 194-195 B 6
Bó Finne, Inis — 116-117 A 7
Bōfu = Hōfu 170-171 H 5-6
Bogalusa, LA 58-59 HJ 5
Bogandé 194-195 DE 6
Bogan River 182-183 J 6
Bogarnes 114-115 bc 2
Bogata, TX 76-77 G 6
Bogd 166-167 J 2
Bogdanovič 142-143 M 4
Bogdo uul 166-167 FG 3
Boggabilla 182-183 JK 5
Boggeragh Mountains = Sléibhte an Bhogaraigh 116-117 BC 8-9
Boghari = Qasr al-Bukharī 194-195 E 1
Bogia 174-175 MN 7
Bognor Regis 116-117 L 10
Bogo [RP] 174-175 H 4
Bogong, Mount — 182-183 J 7
Bogor 174-175 E 8
Bogorodick 142-143 G 5
Bogoslof Island 52-53 m 4
Bogotá 98-99 E 4
Bogota, NJ 82 III b 1
Bogotol 154-155 Q 6
Bogučany 154-155 S 6
Bo Hai 166-167 M 4
Bohai Haixia 166-167 N 4
Bohemian Forest 124 F 4
Bohemian Forest = Böhmerwald 124 FG 4
Bohemian-Moravian Height = Českomoravská vrchovina 124 GH 4
Bohol 174-175 H 5
Boiaçu 98-99 H 5
Boibeîs, Límnē — 138-139 K 6
Boigu Island 174-175 M 8
Boim 98-99 H 5
Bois, Lac des — 46-47 M 4
Bois Blanc Island 70-71 HJ 3
Boise City, ID 58-59 G 3
Boise City, OK 76-77 C 4
Boise River 66-67 E 4
Bois le Duc = 's-Hertogenbosch 132-133 KL 3
Boissevain 68-69 FG 1
Bojador, Cabo — = Rā's Bujdūr 194-195 AB 3
Bojarka 154-155 S 3
Bojnūrd 160-161 H 3
Bojuru 103 F 4
Boké 194-195 B 6
Boknfjord 114-115 A 8
Bokoro 194-195 H 6
Bokote 198 D 1-2
Bokovskaja 142-143 H 6
Bokungu 198 D 2
Bolaiti 198 DE 2
Bolama 194-195 A 6
Bolān, Kotal — 160-161 K 5
Bolangir = Balāngīr 160-161 N 6
Bolan Pass = Kotal Bolān 160-161 K 5
Bólas 116-117 A 9
Bólbē, Límnē — 138-139 K 6
Bolbec 132-133 H 4
Bole 194-195 D 7
Bole, MT 66-67 GH 2
Boles, ID 66-67 E 3
Bolesławiec 124 GH 3
Bolgatanga 194-195 D 6
Bolger 50 N 2
Bolgrad 142-143 E 6
Boli [TJ] 166-167 P 2
Boliden 114-115 J 5
Boligee, AL 78-79 E 4
Boling, TX 76-77 FG 8
Bolissós 138-139 L 6
Bolivar, MO 70-71 D 7
Bolivar, TN 78-79 E 3
Bolívar [PE] 98-99 D 6
Bolívar, Pico — 98-99 E 3
Bolivar Peninsula 76-77 G 8
Bolivia 98-99 F-H 8
Bolkow [CDN] 70-71 J 1
Bolling Air Force Base 82 II ab 2
Bollnäs 114-115 G 7
Bollon 182-183 J 5
Bolobo 198 C 2
Bologna 138-139 D 3
Bologoje 154-155 EF 6
Bolomba 198 C 1
Bolor = Bāltistān 160-161 M 3-4
Bolo-retto = Penghu Lieh-tao 166-167 M 7
Bólos 138-139 K 6
Bolotnoje 154-155 P 6
Boloven, Cao Nguyên — 174-175 E 3-4
Bol'šaja = Velikaja 154-155 h 5
Bol'šaja Višera 142-143 F 4
Bolsena, Lago di — 138-139 DE 4
Bol'ševik, ostrov — 154-155 T-V 2
Bol'šezemel'skaja tundra 154-155 JK 4
Bolshevik = ostrov Bol'ševik 154-155 T-V 2
Bol'šije Uki 154-155 N 6
Bol'šoj An'uj 154-155 fg 4
Bol'šoj Balchan 142-143 K 8
Bol'šoj Oloj = Oloj 154-155 f 4
Bol'šoj Šantar, ostrov — 154-155 ab 7
Bol'šoj Uluj 154-155 R 6
Bol'sŏj Uzen' 142-143 J 5-6
Bolsover 116-117 K 7
Bolton 116-117 J 7
Bolton, NC 80-81 G 3
Bolu 142-143 F 7
Bolungarvík 114-115 ab 1
Bolus Head = Bólas 116-117 A 9
Bolzano 138-139 D 2
Boma 198 B 3
Boma, Gulf of — = Khalīj al-Bunbah 194-195 JK 2
Bomarton, TX 76-77 E 6
Bómba, Khalig — = Khalīj al-Bunbah 194-195 J 2
Bomba, La — 86-87 C 2
Bombaim = Bombay 160-161 L 7
Bombala 182-183 JK 7
Bombarai 174-175 K 7
Bombay 160-161 L 7
Bombetoka, Baie de — 198 HJ 5
Bom Comércio 98-99 F 6
Bom Despacho 98-99 KL 8
Bom Futuro 98-99 H 10
Bomi Hills 194-195 B 7
Bom Jesus [BR, Piauí] 98-99 L 6
Bom Jesus da Gurguéia, Serra — 98-99 L 6-7
Bom Jesus da Lapa 98-99 L 7
Bømlafjord 114-115 A 8
Bømlo 114-115 A 8
Bomokandi 198 E 1
Bomongo 198 C 1
Bomu 198 D 1
Bon, Cap — = Rā' aṭ-Ṭīh 194-195 G 1
Bona = Annābah 194-195 F 1
Bona, Mount — 52-53 QR 6
Bonaire 58-59 N 9
Bonampak 86-87 P 9
Bonanza 88-89 D 8
Bonanza, ID 66-67 F 3
Bonaparte, Mount — 66-67 D 1
Bonaparte Archipelago 182-183 DE 2
Bonarbridge 116-117 G 3
Bonasila Dome 52-53 G 5
Bonaventura 51 D 3
Bonavista 46-47 a 8
Bonavista Bay 51 K 3
Bond, CO 68-69 C 6
Bondeno 138-139 D 3
Bondiss 48 L 2
Bondo [ZRE] 198 D 1
Bondoc Peninsula 174-175 H 4
Bondoukou 194-195 D 7
Bondurant, WY 66-67 HJ 4
Bône = Annābah 194-195 F 1
Bone = Watampone 174-175 GH 7
Bone, Teluk — 174-175 H 7
Bo'ness 116-117 H 4
Bonfield 72-73 G 1
Bonga 194-195 M 7
Bongandanga 198 D 1
Bongo 198 AB 2
Bongolave 198 J 5
Bongor 194-195 H 6
Bonham, TX 76-77 F 6
Boni, Gulf of — = Teluk Bone 174-175 H 7
Bonifacio 138-139 C 5
Bonifàcio, Bocche di — 138-139 C 5
Bonifay, FL 78-79 G 5
Bonilla, SD 68-69 G 3
Bonin 148-149 RS 7
Bonin Trench 34-35 G 3
Bonita, AZ 74-75 HJ 6
Bonita, Point — 83 I a 2
Bonitas, Las — 98-99 FG 3
Bonn 124 C 3
Bonne Bay 51 H 2
Bonner, MT 66-67 G 2
Bonners Ferry, ID 66-67 E 1
Bonner Springs, KS 70-71 C 6
Bonne Terre, MO 70-71 E 7
Bonneville, OR 66-67 C 3
Bonneville, WY 68-69 BC 4
Bonneville Salt Flats 66-67 G 5
Bonnie Rock 182-183 C 6
Bonny 194-195 F 8
Bonny, Golfe de — 194-195 F 8
Bonny Reservoir 68-69 E 6
Bonnyville 46-47 O 7
Bono, AR 78-79 D 3
Bō-no misaki 170-171 GH 7
Bonthe 194-195 B 7
Bontongssunggu 174-175 G 8
Bon Wier, TX 78-79 C 5
Bookabie 182-183 F 6
Bookaloo 182-183 G 6
Booker, TX 76-77 D 4
Book Plateau = Roan Plateau 68-69 B 6
Booligal 182-183 H 6
Böön Cagaan nuur 166-167 HJ 2
Boone, CO 68-69 D 6
Boone, IA 70-71 CD 4
Boone, NC 80-81 F 2
Booneville, AR 76-77 GH 5
Booneville, KY 72-73 E 6
Booneville, MS 78-79 E 3
Boonville, IN 70-71 G 6
Boonville, MO 70-71 D 6
Boonville, NY 72-73 J 3
Booramo 194-195 a 2
Boosaaso 194-195 bc 1
Boothbay Harbor, ME 72-73 M 3
Boothby, Cape — 31 C 6-7
Boothia, Gulf of — 46-47 ST 3-4
Boothia Isthmus 46-47 S 4
Boothia Peninsula 46-47 RS 3
Bootle 116-117 HJ 7
Booué 198 B 1-2
Boqueirão [BR, Rio Grande do Sul] 103 F 4
Boqueirão, Serra do — [BR, Bahia] 98-99 L 7
Boquilla del Conchos 86-87 H 4
Boquillas del Carmen 86-87 J 3
Bor [YU] 138-139 K 3
Bōr = Būr 194-195 L 7
Bor, Lak — 198 G 1
Boracho Peak 76-77 B 7
Borah Peak 58-59 D 3
Borås 114-115 E 9
Borāzjān 160-161 G 5
Borba [BR] 98-99 H 5
Borborema, Planalto da — 98-99 M 6
Bor Chadyn uul 166-167 EF 3
Bor Choro uul 166-167 E 3
Borcu = Borkou 194-195 H 5
Bordeaux [F] 132-133 G 6
Bordeaux, Montréal- 82 I ab 1
Borden Island 46-47 NO 2
Borden Peninsula 46-47 U 3
Borders 116-117 HJ 5
Bordhoy 116-117 b 1
Bordighera 138-139 BC 4
Bordø = Bordhoy 116-117 b 1
Bordzongijn Gov' 166-167 K 3
Bóreioi Sporádes 138-139 KL 6
Bóreiron Stenón Kerkýras 138-139 HJ 6
Boreray 116-117 C 3
Borgå 114-115 LM 7
Borgarfjardhar 114-115 c 2
Børgefjell 114-115 EF 5
Borger, TX 58-59 F 4
Borgholm 114-115 G 9
Borgne, Lake — 78-79 E 5-6
Borgomanero 138-139 BC 3
Borisoglebsk 142-143 H 5
Borisov 142-143 E 5
Borisova, mys — 154-155 a 6
Borja [PE] 98-99 D 5
Borkhaya Bay = guba Buor-Chaja 154-155 Z 3
Borkou 194-195 H 5
Borku = Borkou 194-195 H 5
Borlänge 114-115 FG 7
Bòrmida 138-139 C 3
Borneo = Kalimantan 174-175 F 7-G 6
Bornholm 114-115 F 10
Borno [WAN] 194-195 G 6
Bornou = Borno 194-195 G 6
Bornu = Borno 194-195 G 6
Borogoncy 154-155 Z 5
B'or'ol'och = Susuman 154-155 cd 5
Boron, CA 74-75 E 5
Boroughbridge 116-117 K 6
Borough Park, New York-, NY 82 III bc 3
Boroviči 154-155 EF 6
Borovľanka 154-155 P 7
Borovskoj 154-155 LM 7
Borroloola 182-183 G 3
Borşa 138-139 L 2
Borščovočnyj chrebet 154-155 W 7
Bortala Monggol Zizhizhou 166-167 E 2-3
Bor Talijn gol 166-167 E 3
Borto 154-155 V 7
Borūjerd 160-161 FG 4
Borusa Strait = proliv Vil'kickogo 154-155 S-U 2
Borz'a 154-155 W 7
Borzya = Borz'a 154-155 W 7
Bosa [I] 138-139 C 5
Bosanska Gradiška 138-139 G 3
Bosanska Krupa 138-139 G 3
Bosanski Novi 138-139 FG 3
Bosanski Petrovac 138-139 G 3
Boscastle 116-117 G 10
Boscobel, WI 70-71 E 4
Bose 166-167 K 7
Boshan 166-167 M 4
Boskamp 98-99 L 1-2
Bosler, WY 68-69 D 5
Bosmanland 198 C 7
Bosna [BG] 138-139 M 4
Bosna [YU] 138-139 GH 3
Bosnia Hercegovina 138-139 GH 3-4
Bosobolo 198 C 1
Bōsō hantō 170-171 N 5
Bosporus = Karadeniz boğazı 160-161 BC 2
Bosque, NM 76-77 A 5
Bosque Bonito 76-77 B 7
Bossangoa 194-195 H 7
Bossembélé 194-195 H 7
Bossier City, LA 58-59 H 5
Bosso 194-195 G 6
Boston 116-117 LM 8
Boston, GA 80-81 E 5
Boston, MA 58-59 MN 3
Boston Mountains 58-59 H 4
Bosveld 198 E 6
Boswell, OK 76-77 G 5-6
Bosworth, MO 70-71 D 6
Botany Bay 182-183 K 6
Botev 138-139 L 4
Bóthar Buidhe, An — 116-117 E 7
Bothnia, Gulf of — 110-111 MN 3
Botlette 198 D 6
Botoşani 138-139 M 2
Botswana 198 DE 6
Botte Donato 138-139 G 6
Bottineau, ND 68-69 F 1
Botucatu 98-99 K 9
Botulu 154-155 W 5
Botwood 51 J 3
Bouaflé 194-195 C 7
Bouaké 194-195 CD 7
Bouar 194-195 H 7
Bouca 194-195 H 7
Boucau 132-133 G 7
Boucherville, Îles de — 82 I bc 1
Boudewijnstad = Moba 198 E 3
Bou Djébéha 194-195 D 5
Bougainville 174-175 j 6
Bougie = Bijāyah 194-195 EF 1

Bougie 213

Bougouni 194-195 C 6
Bougtob = Bū Kutub 194-195 E 2
Bou-Ktoub = Bū Kutub 194-195 E 2
Boulain, Lac — 51 F 2
Boulder 182-183 D 6
Boulder, CO 58-59 EF 3-4
Boulder, MT 66-67 GH 2
Boulder, WY 66-67 HJ 4
Boulder City, NV 58-59 CD 4
Boulder Creek, CA 74-75 B 4
Boulder Dam = Hoover Dam 58-59 D 4
Boulevard Heights, MD 82 II b 2
Boulia 182-183 G 4
Boulogne-sur-Mer 132-133 H 3
Boumba 194-195 H 8
Bouna 194-195 D 7
Bouna, Réserve de Faune de — 194-195 D 7
Boundary, AK 52-53 R 4
Boundary Mountains 72-73 L 2
Boundary Peak 58-59 C 4
Boundary Plateau 66-67 J 1
Bounday, WA 66-67 E 1
Boundiali 194-195 C 7
Boundji 198 C 2
Boundou 194-195 B 6
Bountiful, UT 66-67 H 5
Bounty 34-35 HJ 7
Bourail 182-183 MN 4
Bourbonnais 132-133 J 5
Bourem 194-195 DE 5
Bourg-en-Bresse 132-133 K 5
Bourges 132-133 J 5
Bourgogne 132-133 K 5-6
Bourgogne, Canal de — 132-133 K 5
Bourke 182-183 J 6
Bourkes 50 LM 2
Bourlamaque 50 N 2-3
Bourne 116-117 L 8
Bournemouth 116-117 K 10
Bourton on the Water 116-117 K 9
Bouse, AZ 74-75 FG 6
Bousso 194-195 H 6
Boutilimit = Bū Tilimīt 194-195 B 5
Bouvard, Cape — 182-183 BC 6
Bouvet 26-27 K 8
Bouvetøya 31 D 1
Bovey, MN 70-71 D 2
Bovill, ID 66-67 E 2
Bovina, TX 76-77 C 5
Bowbells, ND 68-69 E 1
Bowdle, SD 68-69 G 3
Bowdoin, Lake — 68-69 C 1
Bowdon, ND 68-69 G 2
Bowen, IL 70-71 E 5
Bowen [AUS] 182-183 J 3-4
Bowen Island 66-67 B 1
Boweyr Ahmad-e Sardsīr va Kohkīlūyeh = 4 ◁ 160-161 G 4
Bowie, AZ 74-75 J 6
Bowie, TX 76-77 F 6
Bow Island 66-67 H 1
Bowling Green, KY 58-59 J 4
Bowling Green, MO 70-71 E 6
Bowling Green, OH 72-73 E 4
Bowling Green, VA 72-73 H 5-6
Bowling Green, Cape — 182-183 J 3
Bowman, ND 68-69 E 2
Bowman Island 31 C 11
Bowmanville 72-73 G 3
Bowmore 116-117 E 5
Bowness 48 K 4
Bowron Lake Provincial Park 48 G 3
Bowron River 48 G 3
Bow Rover 46-47 O 7
Bowsman 49 H 4
Box Butte Reservoir 68-69 E 4
Box Creek 68-69 D 4
Box Elder, MT 68-69 A 1
Boxelder Creek [USA ◁ Little Missouri River] 68-69 D 3
Boxelder Creek [USA ◁ Musselshell River] 68-69 B 2
Bo Xian 166-167 LM 5
Boyce, LA 78-79 C 5
Boyd 49 K 3
Boyd, TX 76-77 F 6
Boydton, VA 80-81 G 2
Boyero, CO 68-69 E 6
Boyer River 70-71 C 4
Boykins, VA 80-81 H 2
Boyle Heights, Los Angeles-, CA 83 III c 1
Boyne City, MI 70-71 H 3
Boyne River = An Bhóinn 116-117 E 7
Boynton, OK 76-77 G 5
Boynton Beach, FL 80-81 cd 3
Boysen, WY 68-69 BC 4
Boysen Reservoir 68-69 B 4
Boyuibe 98-99 G 9
Bozeman, MT 58-59 D 2
Bozen = Bolzano 138-139 D 2
Bozoum 194-195 H 7

Bra 138-139 B 3
Brabant, Île — 31 C 30
Brač [YU] 138-139 G 4
Bracadale, Loch — 116-117 E 3
Bracciano, Lago di — 138-139 DE 4
Bracebridge 72-73 G 2
Bräcke 114-115 F 6
Brackettville, TX 76-77 D 8
Brackley 116-117 KL 8
Braço Menor de Araguia 98-99 JK 7
Brad 138-139 K 2
Brădano 138-139 G 5
Bradda Head 116-117 FG 6
Braddock, Alexandria-, VA 82 II a 2
Bradenton, FL 58-59 K 6
Bradfield 116-117 K 7
Bradford, AR 78-79 D 3
Bradford, PA 72-73 G 4
Bradford [CDN] 72-73 G 2
Bradford [GB] 116-117 K 7
Bradford-on-Avon 116-117 J 9
Bradley, CA 74-75 C 5
Bradley, SD 68-69 H 3
Bradore, Baie — 51 H 2
Bradore Hills 51 H 2
Bradshaw, TX 76-77 DE 6
Brady, MT 66-67 H 1-2
Brady, NE 68-69 F 5
Brady, TX 76-77 E 7
Brady Glacier 52-53 T 7
Braemar 116-117 H 3-4
Braga 132-133 C 8
Bragado 103 D 5
Bragança 132-133 D 8
Bragança [BR, Amazonas] 98-99 D 9
Bragança [BR, Pará] 98-99 K 5
Bragança Paulista 98-99 K 9
Braham, MN 70-71 D 3
Brahestad = Raahe 114-115 L 5
Brāhmani 160-161 O 6
Brahmaputra 160-161 P 5
Brăila 138-139 M 3
Brainerd, MN 58-59 H 2
Braintree 116-117 M 9
Brak = Birāk 194-195 G 3
Bralorne 48 F 4
Bramaputra = Brahmaputra 160-161 P 5
Brampton 72-73 FG 3
Branch 51 JK 4
Branchville, SC 80-81 F 4
Brandberg 198 B 6
Brandenberg, MT 68-69 CD 3
Brandenburg, KY 70-71 G 6-7
Brandenburg [DDR, landscape] 124 FG 2
Brandenburg [DDR, place] 124 F 2
Brandon, FL 80-81 b 3
Brandon, MS 78-79 DE 4
Brandon, VT 72-73 K 3
Brandon [CDN] 46-47 Q 8
Brandon [GB] 116-117 K 6
Brandon Bay = Badh Bhréanainn 116-117 A 8
Brandon Mount = Cnoc Bréanainn 116-117 A 8
Brandsville, MO 78-79 CD 2
Brandywine, MD 72-73 H 5
Branford, FL 80-81 b 1-2
Brang, Kuala — 174-175 D 5-6
Braniewo 124 JK 1
Bransfield Strait 31 C 30-31
Br'ansk 142-143 FG 5
Branson, MO 78-79 C 2
Brantford 72-73 FG 3
Brantley, AL 78-79 FG 5
Brás [BR] 98-99 JK 6
Brásc = Birāk 194-195 G 3
Bras d'Or Lake 46-47 YZ 8
Brasil, El — 76-77 D 9
Brasiléia 98-99 F 7
Brasília 98-99 K 8
Brasília Legal 98-99 H 5
Brașov 138-139 L 3
Bråsvellbreen 114-115 lm 5
Bratislava 124 H 4
Bratsk 154-155 T 6
Bratskoje vodochranilišče 154-155 T 6
Brattieboro, VT 72-73 K 3
Braunau 124 F 4
Braunschweig 124 E 2
Brava 188-189 E 7
Brava = Baraawe 198 H 1
Brawley, CA 58-59 C 5
Bray, CA 66-67 C 5
Bray = Bré 116-117 EF 7
Bray Island 46-47 V 4
Braymer, MO 70-71 D 6
Brazeau 48 J 3
Brazeau, Mount — 48 J 3
Brazeau River 48 K 3
Brazil 98-99 F-M 6
Brazil, IN 70-71 G 6
Brazil Basin 26-27 H 6
Brazilian Plateau = Planalto Brasileiro 98-99 KL 8
Brazos River 58-59 G 5-6
Brazos River, Clear Fork — 76-77 E 6
Brazos River, Salt Fork — 76-77 D 6
Brazza = Brač 138-139 G 4
Brazzaville 198 BC 2
Brčko 138-139 H 3
Brdy 124 FG 4
Bré 116-117 EF 7
Brea Creek 83 III d 2
Bréanainn, Cnoc — 116-117 A 8
Breaux Bridge, LA 78-79 D 5
Brechin [CDN] 72-73 G 2
Brechin [GB] 116-117 J 4
Breckenridge, MN 68-69 H 2
Breckenridge, TX 76-77 E 6
Brecknock, Península — 103 B 8-9
Břeclav 124 H 4
Brecon 116-117 H 9
Brecon Beacons 116-117 H 9
Breda 132-133 K 3
Bredasdorp 198 D 8
Bredenbury 49 H 5
Bredy 154-155 KL 7
Breezy Point, New York-, NY 82 III c 3
Bregalnica 138-139 K 5
Bregenz 124 DE 5
Bregovo 138-139 K 3
Breidhafjördhur 114-115 ab 2
Breidhavik 114-115 a 2
Breidi Fjord = Breidhafjördhur 114-115 ab 2
Brejinho do Nazaré 98-99 K 7
Brekstad 114-115 C 6
Bremangerlandet 114-115 A 7
Bremen 124 D 2
Bremen, GA 78-79 G 4
Bremerhaven 124 D 2
Bremerton, WA 58-59 B 2
Bremond, TX 76-77 F 7
Brem River 48 E 4
Brendon Hils 116-117 H 9
Brenham, TX 76-77 F 7
Brenne 132-133 H 5
Brenner 124 E 5
Brennero = Brenner 124 E 5
Brennevinsfjord 114-115 k 4
Brent 72-73 G 1
Brentwood 116-117 M 9
Brentwood, TN 78-79 F 2-3
Brentwood Heights, Los Angeles-, CA 83 III ab 1
Brèscia 138-139 D 3
Bressanone 138-139 DE 2
Bressay 116-117 ef 3
Bressay Sound 116-117 ef 3
Bresse 132-133 K 5
Bressuire 132-133 G 5
Brest [F] 132-133 E 4
Brest [SU] 142-143 D 5
Bretagne 132-133 F 4-G 5
Breton, Cape — 46-47 Z 8
Breton Island 78-79 E 6
Breton Sound 58-59 J 6
Breueh, Pulau — 174-175 B 5
Brevard, NC 80-81 E 3
Breves 98-99 J 5
Brevik 114-115 C 8
Brevort, MI 70-71 H 2
Brewarrina 182-183 J 5
Brewer, ME 72-73 M 2
Brewster, KS 68-69 F 6
Brewster, NE 68-69 G 5
Brewster, WA 66-67 CD 1
Brewster, Kap — 30 BC 20-21
Brewton, AL 78-79 F 5
Bria 194-195 J 7
Briançon 132-133 L 6
Brian Head 74-75 G 4
Briare 132-133 J 5
Bribie Island 182-183 K 5
Briceland, CA 66-67 AB 5
Bricelyn, MN 70-71 CD 4
Brickaville = Vohibinany 198 JK 5
Briconnet, Lac — 51 F 2
Bricquebec 116-117 K 11
Bridge, ID 66-67 G 4
Bridgeboro, GA 80-81 DE 5
Bridgend 116-117 H 9
Bridgeport, AL 78-79 FG 3
Bridgeport, CA 74-75 D 3
Bridgeport, CT 58-59 M 3
Bridgeport, IL 70-71 FG 6
Bridgeport, NE 68-69 E 5
Bridgeport, TX 76-77 F 6
Bridgeport, Chicago-, IL 83 II b 1
Bridger, MT 68-69 B 3
Bridger Basin 66-67 HJ 5
Bridge River 48 F 4
Bridger Peak 68-69 C 5
Bridgeton, NC 80-81 H 3
Bridgeton, NJ 72-73 J 5
Bridgetown [AUS] 182-183 C 6
Bridgetown [BDS] 58-59 OP 9
Bridgetown [CDN] 51 D 5
Bridgeview, IL 83 II a 2
Bridgewater 51 D 5
Bridgewater, SD 68-69 H 4
Bridgnorth 116-117 J 8
Bridgton, ME 72-73 L 2
Bridgwater 116-117 HJ 9
Bridgwater Bay 116-117 H 9
Bridlington 116-117 LM 6
Bridlington Bay 116-117 LM 6
Bridport 116-117 J 10
Brie 132-133 J 4
Briereville 49 C 3
Brig 124 CD 5
Brigg 116-117 L 7
Briggsdale, CO 68-69 DE 5
Brigham City, UT 58-59 D 3
Brighton, IA 70-71 DE 5
Brighton, MI 70-71 HJ 4
Brighton, NY 72-73 H 3
Brighton [CDN] 72-73 GH 2
Brighton [GB] 116-117 L 10
Brighton Indian Reservation 80-81 c 3
Brighton Park, Chicago-, IL 83 II a 2
Brightwood, Washington-, DC 82 II a 1
Brigthon, CO 68-69 D 5-6
Brigue = Brig 124 CD 5
Brigus 51 K 4
Brijuni 138-139 E 3
Brilliant, NM 76-77 B 4
Brilon 124 D 3
Brimson, MN 70-71 DE 2
Brindakit 154-155 a 5-6
Brindisi 138-139 GH 5
Brinkley, AR 78-79 D 3
Brion, Île — 51 F 4
Brisbane 182-183 K 5
Brisbane, CA 83 I b 2
Brisbane River 182-183 K 5
Bristol, CO 68-69 E 6
Bristol, FL 78-79 G 5
Bristol, RI 72-73 L 4
Bristol, SD 68-69 H 3
Bristol, TN 80-81 E 2
Bristol, VA 58-59 K 4
Bristol [CDN] 72-73 H 2
Bristol [GB] 116-117 J 9
Bristol Bay 46-47 DE 6
Bristol Channel 116-117 GH 9
Bristol Lake 74-75 EF 5
Bristow, OK 76-77 F 5
Britannia Beach 66-67 B 1
Britannia Range 31 AB 15-16
British Columbia 46-47 L 6-N 7
British Isles 110-111 F 5-G 4
British Mountains 46-47 HJ 4
Britstown 198 D 8
Britt 72-73 F 2
Britt, IA 70-71 D 4
Brittany = Bretagne 132-133 F 4-G 5
Britton, SD 68-69 GH 3
Brive-la-Gaillarde 132-133 H 6
Brixen = Bressanone 138-139 DE 2
Brno 124 H 4
Broa, Ensenada de la — 88-89 EF 3
Broach = Bharuch 160-161 L 6
Broadback, Rivière — 50 MN 1
Broad Bay 116-117 E 2
Broadford 116-117 F 3
Broad Law 116-117 H 5
Broadmoor, CA 83 I b 2
Broad Pass, AK 52-53 N 5
Broad River 80-81 F 3
Broad Sound 182-183 JK 4
Broadstairs 116-117 h 7
Broadus, MT 68-69 D 3
Broadview 49 GH 5
Broadview, MT 68-69 B 2
Broadwater, NE 68-69 E 5
Brochet 46-47 Q 6
Brochet, Lac — 51 B 3
Brochu, Lac — 50 OP 2
Brocken 124 E 3
Brocket 48 L 5
Brock Island 46-47 N 2
Brocklyn Marine Park 82 III c 3
Brockman, Mount — 182-183 C 4
Brockport, NY 72-73 GH 3
Brockton, MA 72-73 L 3
Brockton, MT 68-69 D 1
Brockville 46-47 V 9
Brockway, MT 68-69 D 2
Brockway, PA 72-73 G 4
Brodeur Peninsula 46-47 T 3
Brodhead, WI 70-71 F 4
Brodick 116-117 FG 5
Brodie 66-67 C 1
Brodnax, VA 80-81 GH 2
Brodnica 124 J 2
Brody 142-143 E 5
Brogan, OR 66-67 E 3
Brokaw, WI 70-71 F 3
Broken Arrow, OK 76-77 G 4
Broken Bow, NE 68-69 G 5
Broken Bow, OK 76-77 G 5-6
Broken Hill 182-183 H 6
Broken Hill = Kabwe 198 E 4
Brokopondo 98-99 HJ 3
Bromhead 68-69 E 1
Bromley, London- 116-117 LM 9
Bromsgrove 116-117 JK 8
Bromyard 116-117 J 8
Brønderslev 114-115 CD 9
Brønnøysund 114-115 DE 5
Bronson, FL 80-81 b 2
Bronson, MI 70-71 H 5
Bronson, TX 76-77 G 7
Bronte 138-139 F 7
Bronte, TX 76-77 D 7
Bronte Park 182-183 J 8
Bronx, New York-, NY 82 III c 1
Brookeland, TX 76-77 GH 7
Brookfield, MO 70-71 D 6
Brookhaven, MS 78-79 D 5
Brookings, OR 66-67 A 4
Brookings, SD 58-59 G 3
Brookland, Washington-, DC 82 II b 1
Brookline, MA 72-73 L 3
Brooklyn, IA 70-71 D 5
Brooklyn, MS 78-79 E 5
Brooklyn, New York-, NY 82 III bc 3
Brooklyn Park, MN 70-71 D 3
Brookneal, VA 80-81 G 2
Brooks 49 C 5
Brooks, Lake — 52-53 K 7
Brooks, Mount — 52-53 MN 5
Brooks Bay 48 CD 4
Brooks Island 83 I b 1
Brooks Mount 52-53 D 4
Brooks Range 46-47 E-H 4
Brookston, IN 70-71 G 5
Brookston, MN 70-71 D 2
Brooksville, FL 80-81 b 2
Brooksville, KY 72-73 DE 5
Brookton 182-183 C 6
Brookville, IN 70-71 H 6
Brookville, OH 72-73 D 5
Brookville, PA 72-73 G 4
Broom, Loch — 116-117 F 2-3
Broome 182-183 D 3
Broquerie, la — 49 KL 6
Brora 116-117 H 2
Brora, River — 116-117 GH 2
Brosley 116-117 J 8
Brossard 82 I bc 2
Brotas de Macaúbas 98-99 L 7
Brothers, OR 66-67 C 4
Brothers, The — = Jazā'ir al-Ikhwān 199 D 4
Brothers, The — = Samḥah, Darsah 160-161 G 8
Broughty Ferry, Dundee- 116-117 J 4
Brown, Mount — 31 BC 9
Brown Clee Hill 116-117 J 8
Brownfield, TX 76-77 CD 6
Browning, MT 66-67 G 1
Brownlee 49 E 5
Brownlee, NE 68-69 F 4
Brownlow Point 52-53 P 1
Brownrigg 50 L 2
Brown's Bank 51 D 6
Brownstown, IN 70-71 GH 6
Browns Valley, MN 68-69 H 3
Brownsville, OR 66-67 B 3
Brownsville, PA 72-73 FG 4
Brownsville, TN 78-79 E 3
Brownsville, TX 58-59 G 6
Brownsweg 98-99 H 3-4
Brownville Junction, ME 72-73 M 2
Brown Willy 116-117 G 10
Brownwood, TX 58-59 G 5
Broxton, GA 80-81 E 5
Broxtowe 116-117 K 7
Bruay-en-Artois 132-133 J 3
Bruce, MS 78-79 E 3-4
Bruce, WI 70-71 E 3
Bruce, Mount — 182-183 C 4
Bruce Crossing, MI 70-71 F 2
Bruce Mines 70-71 J 2
Bruce Peninsula 72-73 F 2
Bruce Rock 182-183 C 6
Bruceton, TN 78-79 E 2
Bruchsal 124 D 4
Bruck an der Leitha 124 H 4
Bruck an der Mur 124 G 5
Bruges = Brugge 132-133 J 3
Brugge 132-133 J 3
Bruin Peak 74-75 H 3
Bruja, Cerro — 58-59 b 2
Brukkaros, Mount — = Groot Brukkaros 198 C 7
Brule, NE 68-69 F 5
Brule, WI 70-71 E 2
Brule Lake 70-71 E 2
Brule Rapids 48 L 1
Brumado 98-99 L 7
Brundidge, AL 78-79 FG 5
Bruneau, ID 66-67 F 4
Bruneau River 66-67 F 4
Brunei 174-175 F 6
Brunei = Bandar Seri Begawan 174-175 FG 5-6
Brunette Island 51 HJ 4
Bruni, TX 76-77 E 9
Bruno 49 F 4
Brunswick, GA 58-59 K 5
Brunswick, MD 72-73 H 5
Brunswick, ME 72-73 LM 3
Brunswick, MO 70-71 D 6
Brunswick = Braunschweig 124 E 2
Brunswick, Península — 103 B 8
Brunswick Bay 182-183 D 3
Brunswick Lake 70-71 J 1
Bruny Island 182-183 J 8
Brush, CO 68-69 E 5
Brushy Mountains 80-81 F 2-3
Brus Laguna 88-89 DE 7
Brusque 103 G 3
Brussel = Bruxelles 132-133 JK 3
Brussels = Bruxelles 132-133 JK 3
Bruxelles 132-133 JK 3
Bryan, OH 70-71 H 5
Bryan, TX 58-59 G 5
Bryan, WY 66-67 J 5
Bryant, SD 68-69 H 3
Bryce Canyon National Park 74-75 GH 4
Bryher 116-117 E 11
Brykalansk 142-143 KL 2
Bryson, TX 76-77 E 6
Bryson City, NC 80-81 E 3
Bryson City, TN 80-81 E 3
Brzeg 124 H 3

Bṣaiya, Al- = Al-Buṣaīyah 160-161 EF 4

Buake = Bouaké 194-195 CD 7
Buala 174-175 jk 6
Bu'ayrāt al-Ḥsūn, Al- 194-195 H 2
Būbīyan, Jazīrat — 160-161 FG 5
Bucaramanga 98-99 E 3
Bucatunna, MS 78-79 E 5
Buccaneer Archipelago 182-183 D 3
Buchan 116-117 JK 3
Buchanan, MI 70-71 G 5
Buchanan, NM 76-77 B 5
Buchanan, VA 80-81 FG 2
Buchanan [CDN] 49 G 5
Buchanan [LB] 194-195 B 7
Buchanan Lake 76-77 E 7
Buchan Ness 116-117 K 3
Buchans 46-47 Z 8
Buchara 160-161 JK 3
Buchardo 103 D 4
Bucharest = București 138-139 L 3
Buchon, Point — 74-75 C 5
Buchtarma 154-155 Q 8
Buchtarminskoje vodochranilišče 154-155 PQ 8
Buchyn Mangnaj uul 166-167 EF 4-5
Buck, The — 116-117 J 3
Buckeye, AZ 74-75 G 6
Buckfastleigh 116-117 GH 10
Buckhannon, WV 72-73 F 5
Buckhaven 116-117 HJ 4
Buckhorn Lake 72-73 G 2
Buckie 116-117 J 3
Buckingham [CDN] 72-73 J 2
Buckingham [GB, administrative unit] 116-117 L 8-9
Buckingham [GB, place] 116-117 KL 8-9
Buckland, AK 52-53 G 4
Buckland River 52-53 G 4
Buckland Tableland 182-183 J 4-5
Buckleboo 182-183 G 6
Buckle Island 31 C 16-17
Buckley 116-117 HJ 7
Buckley, WA 66-67 BC 2
Buckley Bay 31 C 15-16
Buckley Ranges 48 D 2
Bucklin, KS 68-69 G 7
Bucklin, MO 70-71 D 6
Bucksport, ME 72-73 M 2
Bucovina 138-139 LM 2
Buco Zau 198 B 2
Buctouche 51 D 4
București 138-139 LM 3
Bucyrus, OH 72-73 E 4
Buda, TX 76-77 EF 7
Budapest 124 J 5
Budaun 160-161 M 5
Budd Land 31 C 12
Buddon Ness 116-117 J 4
Bude, MS 78-79 D 5
Bude Bay 116-117 G 10
Bude-Stratton 116-117 G 10
Búdhardalur 114-115 c 2
Būdhīyah, Jabal — 199 C 3
Budjala 198 CD 1
Budva 138-139 H 4
Buea 194-195 F 8
Buena Park, CA 83 III d 2
Buenaventura [CO] 98-99 D 4
Buenaventura [MEX] 86-87 G 3
Buenaventura, Bahía de — 98-99 D 4
Buena Vista, GA 78-79 G 4
Buena Vista, VA 80-81 G 2
Buenavista, San José de — 174-175 H 4
Buena Vista Lake Bed 74-75 D 5
Buenos Aires [PA] 58-59 b 2
Buenos Aires [RA, administrative unit] 103 DE 5
Buenos Aires [RA, place] 103 E 4
Buenos Aires, Lago — 103 B 7
Buen Retiro 58-59 b 3
Bueyeros, NM 76-77 C 4-5
Buffalo 49 C 5
Buffalo, MN 70-71 D 3
Buffalo, MO 70-71 D 7
Buffalo, ND 68-69 H 2
Buffalo, NY 58-59 L 3
Buffalo, OK 76-77 E 4
Buffalo, SD 68-69 E 3
Buffalo, TX 76-77 FG 7
Buffalo, WV 72-73 F 5
Buffalo, WY 68-69 C 3
Buffalo Bill Reservoir 68-69 B 3
Buffalo Head Hills 49 A 2
Buffalo Hump 66-67 F 3
Buffalo Lake 46-47 NO 5
Buffalo Narrows 49 D 3
Buford, GA 80-81 DE 3
Buford, ND 68-69 E 1-2
Buford, WY 68-69 D 5
Buford Reservoir = Lake Sidney Lanier 80-81 DE 3
Bug 124 L 2
Buga 98-99 D 4
Bugant 166-167 K 2
Bugdajli 142-143 KL 8
Bugorkan 154-155 U 5
Bugrino 154-155 H 4
Bugt 166-167 N 2
Bugul'ma 154-155 J 7
Buguruslan 154-155 J 7
Buhăești 138-139 M 2
Buhayrāt, Al- 194-195 KL 7
Buḥayrat al-Abyaḍ 194-195 KL 6
Buhl, ID 66-67 F 4
Buhl, MN 70-71 D 2
Builth Wells 116-117 H 8
Buin [PNG] 174-175 j 6
Buir Nur 166-167 M 2

214 **Bougouni**

Buitenzorg = Bogor 174-175 E 8
Buj 154-155 G 6
Bujalance 132-133 EF 10
Bū Jaydūr, Rā's — 194-195 AB 3
Buji 174-175 M 8
Bujnaksk 142-143 J 7
Bujumbura 198 EF 2
Bukačača 154-155 W 7
Buka Island 174-175 hj 6
Bukama 198 E 3
Bukavu 198 E 2
Bukene 198 F 2
Bukit Besi 174-175 D 6
Bukit Betong 174-175 D 6
Bukittinggi 174-175 CD 7
Bükk 124 K 4-5
Bukoba 198 F 2
Bū Kutub 194-195 E 2
Bula [RI] 174-175 K 7
Bulagan = Bulgan 166-167 J 2
Bulan 174-175 H 4
Būlāq 199 B 5
Bulawayo 198 E 6
Buldir Island 52-53 r 6
Bulford 116-117 K 9
Bulgan [Mongolia, administrative unit = 9 ◁] 166-167 J 2
Bulgan [Mongolia, place Bulgan] 166-167 J 2
Bulgan [Mongolia, place Chovd] 166-167 G 2
Bulgaria 138-139 K-M 4
Buli, Teluk — 174-175 J 6
Bulkī 194-195 M 7
Bullahaar 194-195 a 1
Bullard, TX 76-77 G 6
Bullfinch 182-183 C 6
Bull Mountains 68-69 B 2
Bulloo Downs 182-183 H 5
Bulloo River 182-183 H 5
Bulls Bay 80-81 G 4
Bullshead Butte 49 C 6
Bull Shoals Lake 78-79 C 2
Bulu 174-175 J 6
Buluan 174-175 H 5
Bulukumba 174-175 GH 8
Bulungan 174-175 G 6
Buluntou Hai = Ojorong nuur 166-167 F 2
Bulwell, Nottingham- 116-117 KL 7-8
Bulyea 49 F 5
Bumba [ZRE, Bandundu] 198 C 3
Bumba [ZRE, Équateur] 198 D 1
Bumba = Boumba 194-195 H 8
Buna, TX 78-79 C 5
Buna [EAK] 198 G 1
Buna [PNG] 174-175 N 8
Bunbah, Khalīj al- 194-195 J 2
Bunbury 182-183 BC 6
Buncrana = Bun Crannaighe 116-117 D 5
Bun Crannaighe 116-117 D 5
Bundaberg 182-183 K 4
Bundelkhand 160-161 MN 6
Būndi 160-161 M 5
Bun Dobhráin 116-117 C 6
Bundooma 182-183 FG 4
Bundoran = Bun Dobhráin 116-117 C 6
Bungay 116-117 h 6
Bunge, zemľa — 154-155 b 2-3
Bunger Oasis 31 C 11
Bungo-suidō 166-167 P 5
Bungotakada 170-171 H 6
Bunguran, Pulau — 174-175 E 6
Bunguran Selatan, Kepulauan — 174-175 E 6
Bunguran Utara, Kepulauan — 174-175 E 6
Bunia 198 F 1
Bunker Hill, AK 52-53 E 4
Bunkeya 198 E 4
Bunkie, LA 78-79 CD 5
Bunnell, FL 80-81 c 2
Bunta 174-175 H 7
Buntingford 116-117 LM 9
Buntok 174-175 FG 7
Bunyu, Pulau — 174-175 G 6
Buol 174-175 H 6
Buolkalach 154-155 W 3
Buôn Ma Thuôt = Ban Mê Thuôt 174-175 E 4
Buor-Chaja, guba — 154-155 Z 3
Buor-Chaja, mys — 154-155 Z 3
Buqaliq tagh 166-167 G 4
Buquq 166-167 E 3
Būr 194-195 L 7
Bura 198 GH 2
Bur Acaba = Buur Hakkaba 194-195 N 8
Buram 194-195 K 6
Burao = Bur'o 194-195 O 7
Buras, LA 78-79 E 6
Bur'atskaja Avtonomnaja Sovetskaja Socialističeskaja Respublika = Buryat Autonomous Soviet Socialist Republic 154-155 T 7-V 6
Būr Atyan = Nawādhību 194-195 A 4
Buraydah 160-161 E 5
Buraymī, Al- 160-161 H 6
Burbank, CA 74-75 DE 5
Burbank, IL 83 II a 2
Burbank, OK 76-77 F 4
Burchanbuudaj 166-167 H 2
Burchun 166-167 F 2
Burdeau = Mahdīyah 194-195 E 1
Burdekin River 182-183 J 4
Burdett, KS 68-69 G 6
Burdur 160-161 BC 3
Burdwān 160-161 O 6
Burdwood Bank 103 DE 8
Burē [ETH, Gojam] 194-195 M 6
Bure [ETH, Īlubabor] 194-195 M 7
Bureå 114-115 J 5
Bureau, Lac — 50 O 2
Büreen = Büren 166-167 K 2
Bureinskij chrebet 154-155 Z 7-8
Bureja 154-155 Z 7
Büren [Mongolia] 166-167 K 2
Burenchaan [Mongolia, Chentij] 166-167 L 2
Burenchaan [Mongolia, Chövsgöl] 166-167 H 2
Bürencogt 166-167 L 2
Būr Fu'ād = Būr Sādāt 199 C 2
Burg 124 EF 2
Būr Gābo = Buur Gaabo 198 H 2
Bur Gao = Buur Gaabo 198 H 2
Burgas 138-139 M 4
Burgaski zaliv 138-139 MN 4
Burgaw, NC 80-81 GH 3
Burgenland 124 H 5
Burgeo 51 H 4
Burgeo Bank 51 GH 4
Burgersdorp 198 E 8
Burgess, Mount — 52-53 S 3
Burgess Hill 116-117 L 10
Burgfjället 114-115 F 5
Burghead 116-117 H 3
Burghersdorp = Burgersdrop 198 E 8
Burgh le Marsh 116-117 M 7
Búrgio 138-139 E 7
Burgos 132-133 F 7
Burgsvik 114-115 H 9
Būr Hakkaba 198 H 1
Burhānpur 160-161 M 6
Burias Island 174-175 H 4
Burica, Punta — 58-59 K 10
Burin 51 J 4
Burin Peninsula 46-47 Z 8
Burinšik 142-143 K 6
Buri Ram 174-175 D 3-4
Buriti [BR, Maranhão] 98-99 L 5
Buriti Bravo 98-99 L 6
Buriti dos Lopes 98-99 L 5
Burj al-Ḥaṭṭabah 194-195 F 2
Burj Ban Būl'īd 194-195 E 3
Burjing = Burchun 166-167 F 2
Burj Luṭfī 194-195 F 3-4
Burj 'Umar Idrīs 194-195 EF 3
Burkburnett, TX 76-77 E 5
Burke, SD 68-69 G 4
Burkesville, KY 78-79 G 2
Burketown 182-183 GH 3
Burkeville, VA 80-81 GH 2
Burkina Faso 194-195 D 6
Burks Falls 72-73 G 2
Burleith, Washington-, DC 82 II a 1
Burleson, TX 76-77 F 6
Burley, ID 66-67 G 4
Burlingame, CA 74-75 B 4
Burlingame, KS 70-71 BC 6
Burlington 72-73 G 3
Burlington, CO 68-69 E 6
Burlington, IA 58-59 H 3
Burlington, KS 70-71 BC 6
Burlington, NC 80-81 G 2
Burlington, VT 58-59 M 3
Burlington, WA 66-67 BC 1
Burlington, WI 70-71 F 4
Burlington Junction, MO 70-71 C 5
Burma 174-175 BC 2
Burma = Birma 174-175 BC 2
Burnaby Island 48 B 3
Burnet, TX 76-77 E 7
Burney, CA 66-67 C 5
Burnham-on-Crouch 116-117 gh 7
Burnham on Sea 116-117 J 9
Burnie 182-183 HJ 8
Burnley 116-117 JK 7
Burns, CO 68-69 C 6
Burns, KS 68-69 H 6
Burns, OR 66-67 D 4
Burns Flat, OK 76-77 E 5
Burnside, KY 70-71 H 7
Burns Lake 46-47 LM 7
Burnsville, MS 78-79 E 3
Burnsville, WV 72-73 F 5
Burnt Creek 46-47 X 6-7
Burnt Ground 88-89 J 3
Burnt Lake 51 E 1
Burnt Paw, AK 52-53 QR 3
Burnt River 66-67 DE 3
Burnt River Mountains 66-67 DE 3
Burntwood Lake 49 H 3
Burntwood River 49 J 3
Bur'o 194-195 b 2
Burra 182-183 G 6
Burray 116-117 J 2
Burrinjuck Reservoir 182-183 J 7
Burro, El- 76-77 D 8
Burro, Serranías del — 58-59 F 6
Burrow Head 116-117 G 6
Burrton, KS 68-69 H 6
Burruyacú 103 CD 3
Burrwood, LA 78-79 E 6
Burry Inlet 116-117 G 9
Bursa 160-161 B 2-3
Būr Sādāt 199 C 2
Būr Safāga = Safājah 194-195 L 3
Būr Sa'īd 194-195 L 2
Burstall 49 D 5
Būr Sūdān 194-195 M 5
Burt, IA 70-71 C 4
Būr Tawfīq 199 C 3
Burt Lake 70-71 H 3
Burton Head 116-117 K 6
Burtonport = Ailt an Chorráin 116-117 CD 6
Burton-upon-Trent 116-117 JK 8
Buru, Pulau — 174-175 J 7
Burullus, Buḥayrat al- 199 B 2
Burūm 160-161 F 8
Burundi 198 EF 2
Burun-Šibertuj, gora — 154-155 UV 8
Bururi 198 E 2
Burwash 72-73 F 1
Burwash Landing 52-53 RS 6
Burwell, NE 68-69 G 5
Bury 116-117 J 7
Buryat Autonomous Soviet Socialist Republic 154-155 T 7-V 6
Burye = Burē 194-195 M 6
Bury Saint Edmunds 116-117 MN 8
Busa, Cape — = Akrotḗrion Grambûsa 138-139 K 8
Buṣaīyah, Al- 160-161 EF 4
Busby 48 KL 3
Büs Cagaan Nuur = Böön Cagaan nuur 166-167 HJ 2
Būsh 199 B 3
Būshehr = Bandar-e Būshehr 160-161 G 5
Bushire = Bandar-e Būshehr 160-161 G 5
Bushland, TX 76-77 CD 5
Bushnell 72-73 FG 1
Bushnell, IL 70-71 E 5
Bushnell, NE 68-69 E 5
Bushnell Seamount 78-79 f 3
Businga 198 D 1
Busira 198 C 1-2
Buskerud 114-115 C 7-D 8
Busselton 182-183 BC 6
Bustamante 76-77 D 9
Busto Arsizio 138-139 C 3
Busuanga Island 174-175 G 4
Busuluk = Buzuluk 154-155 J 7
Buta 198 D 1
Bute [GB, administrative unit] 116-117 F 5
Bute [GB, island] 116-117 F 5
Bute, Sound of — 116-117 F 5
Butedale 48 C 3
Bute Inlet 48 E 4
Butha Qi 166-167 N 2
Butiaba 198 F 1
Bū Tilimīt 194-195 B 5
Butler, AL 78-79 E 4
Butler, GA 78-79 G 4
Butler, IN 70-71 H 5
Butler, MO 70-71 C 6
Butler, PA 72-73 G 4
Butsikáki 138-139 J 6
Butte, MT 58-59 D 2
Butte, ND 68-69 F 2
Butte, NE 68-69 G 4
Butte Creek, MT 68-69 C 2
Butte Meadows, CA 66-67 BC 5
Butterworth = Bagan Jaya 174-175 D 5
Butterworth = Gcuwa 198 E 8
Butuan 174-175 HJ 5
Butung, Pulau — 174-175 H 7-8
Buturlinovka 142-143 GH 5
Buulo Berde 194-195 b 3
Buwārah, Jabal — 199 D 3
Buxton 116-117 K 7
Buxton, ND 68-69 H 2
Buxton [GUY] 98-99 JK 1
Buyr Nur = Buir Nur 166-167 M 2
Büyük Ağrı dağı 160-161 E 2-3
Büyük Menderes nehri 160-161 B 3
Buzači 160-161 G 1-2
Buzău [RO, place] 138-139 M 3
Buzău [RO, river] 138-139 M 3
Buzaymah 194-195 J 4
Buzuluk 154-155 J 7
Buzzards Bay 72-73 L 4
Byam Martin Channel 46-47 PQ 2
Byam Martin Island 46-47 Q 2-3
Byāvar = Beāwar 160-161 LM 5
Byawar = Beāwar 160-161 LM 5
Bychawa 124 L 3
Bychov 142-143 EF 5
Bydgoszcz 124 HJ 2
Byely Island = Belyj ostrov 154-155 MN 3
Bygdin 114-115 C 7
Bygland 114-115 BC 8
Byhalia, MS 78-79 E 3
Bykovo 142-143 J 6
Bylot Island 46-47 V 3
Byrd 31 AB 25
Byrd, Cape — 31 C 29
Byrd Land 31 AB 23-22
Byrock 182-183 J 6
Byron, CA 74-75 C 4
Byron, IL 70-71 F 4
Byron, Cape — 182-183 K 5
Byrranga, gory — 154-155 Q 3-V 2
Byske 114-115 J 5
Byssa 154-155 Z 7
Bytom 124 J 3
Bytów 124 H 1
Bzémá = Buzaymah 194-195 J 4
Bzura 124 J 2

C

Caacupé 103 E 3
Caaguazú [PY, place] 103 EF 3
Caaguazú, Cordillera de — 103 E 3
Caála 198 BC 4
Caamaño Sound 48 BC 3
Caapiranga 98-99 H 6
Caapucú 103 E 3
Caatinga 98-99 K 8
Caatingas 98-99 L 7-M 6
Caazapá [PY, place] 103 E 3
Cabaiguán 88-89 G 3
Caballería, Cabo de — 132-133 K 8
Caballococha 98-99 E 5
Caballo Reservoir 76-77 A 6
Caballos Mesteños, Llanos de los — 76-77 BC 8
Cabanatuan 174-175 H 3
Cabano 51 B 4
Cabedelo 98-99 N 6
Cabeza del Buey 132-133 E 9
Cabeza Negra 86-87 HJ 8
Cabezas 98-99 G 8
Cabezon, NM 76-77 A 5
Cabhán, An — 116-116 D 7
Cabimas 98-99 E 2
Cabinda [Angola, administrative unit] 198 B 3
Cabinda [Angola, place] 198 B 3
Cabinet Mountains 66-67 E 1
Cabin John, MD 82 II a 1
Cable, WI 70-71 E 2
Cabo Alto = Cape Dolphin 103 E 8
Cabo Blanco [CR] 58-59 J 10
Cabo Blanco [RA] 103 CD 7
Cabo Branco 98-99 N 6
Cabo Delgado [Mozambique, administrative unit] 198 GH 4
Cabo Delgado [Mozambique, cape] 198 H 4
Cabo Falso [Honduras] 88-89 E 7
Cabo Falso [MEX] 58-59 D 7
Cabo Frio [BR, cape] 98-99 L 9
Cabo Frio [BR, place] 98-99 L 9
Cabonga, Réservoir — 72-73 HJ 1
Cabool, MO 78-79 CD 2
Cabo Pantoja = Pantoja 98-99 DE 5
Cabo Pasado 98-99 C 5
Cabora Bassa 198 F 5
Cabo Raso [RA, place] 103 CD 6
Cabo Raso = Cabo Norte 98-99 K 4
Cabo Rojo [MEX] 58-59 G 7
Cabo Rojo [Puerto Rico] 88-89 N 6
Cabot, AR 78-79 CD 3
Cabot Head 72-73 F 2
Cabot Strait 46-47 YZ 8
Cabo Verde, Islas — 26-27 H 5
Cabra 132-133 E 10
Cabra, Monte — 58-59 b 3
Cabrera 88-89 M 5
Cabrera, Isla — 132-133 J 9
Cabriel 132-133 G 9
Cabrillo, Point — 74-75 AB 3
Cabrón, Cabo — 88-89 M 5
Cabul = Kabul 160-161 K 4
Caçador 103 F 3
Čačak 138-139 J 4
Cacaoui, Lac — 51 C 2
Caçapava do Sul 103 F 4
Càccia, Capo — 138-139 BC 5
Cacequi 103 F 3
Cáceres [BR] 98-99 H 8
Cáceres [CO] 98-99 D 3
Cáceres [E] 132-133 D 9
Cachar [TJ] 166-167 M 3
Cache, OK 76-77 E 5
Cache Creek 48 G 4
Cachegar = Qäshqär 166-167 CD 4
Cachemire = Kashmīr 160-161 LM 4
Cache Peak 66-67 G 4
Cacheu [Guinea Bissau, place] 194-195 A 6
Cachi 103 C 3
Cachi, Nevado de — 103 C 2
Cachimbo, Parque Nacional do — 98-99 K 8-9
Cachimbo, Serra do — 98-99 HJ 6
Cachimo 198 D 3
Cachoeira [BR ↓ Feira de Santana] 98-99 M 7
Cachoeira Alta [BR, Goias] 98-99 NO 7
Cachoeira do Sul 103 F 3-4
Cachoeira Sêca 98-99 L 7
Cachoeiro de Itapemirim 98-99 LM 9
Cachos, Punta — 103 B 3
Caçiporé, Cabo — 98-99 JK 4
Caçiporé, Rio — 98-99 J 4
Cacolo 198 C 3-4
Caconda 198 BC 4
Cactus, TX 76-77 E 9
Cactus Range 74-75 E 4
Caculé 98-99 L 7
Çacuso 198 C 3
Čadan 154-155 R 7
Caddo, OK 76-77 F 5
Caddo Lake 76-77 GH 6
Cadereyta Jiménez 86-87 KL 5
Cader Idris 116-117 H 8
Cadillac, MI 70-71 H 3
Cadillac [CDN] 66-67 JK 1
Cádiz 132-133 D 10
Cadiz, CA 74-75 F 5
Cadiz, KY 78-79 EF 2
Cádiz, Golfo de — 132-133 D 10
Čadobec [SU, place] 154-155 S 6
Čadobec [SU, river] 154-155 S 6
Cadomin 48 J 3
Cadotte River 48 J 1
Caen 132-133 G 4
Caernarfon 116-117 GH 7
Caernarfon Bay 116-117 G 7
Caerphilly 116-117 H 9
Caesarea = Kayseri 160-161 D 3
Caeté, Rio — 98-99 D 9
Caetité 98-99 L 7
Cafayate 103 C 3
Cafta = Kafta 194-195 M 6
Cagaan Cherem = Wanli Changcheng 166-167 K 4
Cagayan de Oro 174-175 HJ 5
Cagayan Islands 174-175 H 5
Cagayan Sulu Island 174-175 GH 5
Čagda 154-155 Z 6
Caggan nuur 166-167 FG 2
Čagil 142-143 L 7
Càgliari 138-139 C 6
Càgliari, Golfo di — 138-139 C 6
Čagoda [SU, place] 154-155 EF 6
Cag Sum = Dzag 166-167 H 2
Caguán, Río — 98-99 E 4
Caguas 58-59 N 8
Cahama 198 BC 5
Cahir = Cathair Dún Iascaigh 116-117 CD 8
Cahirciveen = Cathair Saidhbhín 116-117 AB 9
Cahore Point = Rinn Chathóire 116-117 EF 8
Cahors 132-133 H 6
Cahuapanas 98-99 D 6
Cahuilla Indian Reservation 74-75 E 6
Cahungula = Caungula 198 C 3
Caia [Mozambique] 198 G 5
Caiabi, Cachoeira — 98-99 L 10
Caiabis, Serra dos — 98-99 H 7
Caiambé 98-99 FG 5
Cai Ban, Đao — 174-175 E 2
Caibarién 58-59 L 7
Caicara [YV] 98-99 F 3
Caicos Islands 58-59 M 7
Caicos Passage 58-59 M 7
Cailliġhe, Ceann — 116-117 B 8
Caillou Bay 78-79 D 6
Caillou Lake 78-79 D 6
Caimanero, Laguna del — 86-87 G 6
Caimito 58-59 b 3
Caimito, Río — 58-59 b 3
Cain Creek 68-69 G 3
Cainsville, MO 70-71 D 5
Cairari 98-99 K 5
Caird Land 31 B 33-34
Cairn Mount 52-53 K 6
Cairns 182-183 J 3
Cairns Lake 50 B 2
Cairnsmore 116-117 G 5
Cairo, GA 80-81 D 5
Cairo, IL 58-59 J 4
Cairo, NE 68-69 G 5
Cairo = Al-Qāhira 194-195 KL 2
Caiseal 116-117 D 8
Caisleán a'Bharraigh 116-117 BC 7
Caisleán Nua, An — 116-117 BC 8
Caisleán Riabhach, An — 116-117 C 7
Caistor 116-117 L 7
Caithness 116-117 H 2
Caiundo 198 C 5
Cajabamba 98-99 D 6
Cajamarca [PE, place] 98-99 D 6
Cajapió 98-99 KL 5
Cajatambo 98-99 D 7
Cajdam nuur 166-167 M 2
Cajdamyn nuur, Ich — 166-167 GH 4
Čajek 160-161 L 2
Cajon Pass 74-75 E 5
Cajuás, Ponta dos — 98-99 M 5
Cajueiro [BR, Amazonas] 98-99 C 7
Calabar 194-195 F 7-8
Calabogie 72-73 H 2
Calabozo 98-99 F 3
Calàbria 138-139 FG 6
Calada, CA 74-75 F 5
Calafat 138-139 K 3-4
Calafate 103 B 8
Calagua Islands 174-175 H 4
Calahari = Kalahari Desert 198 CD 6
Calahorra 132-133 G 7
Calais 132-133 H 3
Calais, Pas de — 132-133 HJ 3
Calakmul 86-87 Q 9
Calalaste, Sierra de — 103 C 2-3
Calama [BR] 98-99 G 6
Calama [RCH] 103 C 2
Calamar [CO ↘ Bogotá] 98-99 E 4
Calamian Group 174-175 G 4
Calamus River 68-69 G 4
Calang 174-175 C 6
Calansho Sand Sea = Serīr Kalanshyū 194-195 J 3
Calapan 174-175 H 4
Călăraşi 138-139 M 3
Calatayud 132-133 G 8
Calate = Qalāt 160-161 K 5
Călăţele 138-139 K 2
Calayan Island 174-175 H 3
Calbayog 174-175 HJ 4
Calca 98-99 E 7
Calcanhar, Ponta do — 98-99 M 6-N 5
Calcasieu Lake 78-79 C 6
Calcasieu River 78-79 C 5
Calçoene 98-99 J 4
Calçoene, Rio — 98-99 N 3-4
Calcutta 160-161 O 6
Caldas da Rainha 132-133 C 9
Caldeirão, Ilha do — 98-99 D 7
Caldera 103 B 3
Calder Hall 116-117 H 6
Caldwell, ID 66-67 E 4
Caldwell, KS 76-77 F 4
Caldwell, OH 72-73 F 5
Caldwell, TX 76-77 F 7
Caldy Island 116-117 G 9
Calecute = Calicut 160-161 LM 8
Caledon 198 CD 8
Caledon Bay 182-183 G 2
Caledonia, MN 70-71 E 4
Caledonia [CDN, Nova Scotia] 51 D 5
Caledonia [CDN, Ontario] 72-73 G 3
Caledonian Canal 116-117 F 4-G 3
Caledonrivier 198 E 7-8
Calera, AL 78-79 F 4
Caleta de Vique 58-59 b 3
Caleta Olivia 103 C 7
Caleufú 103 D 5
Calexico, CA 74-75 F 6
Calgary 46-47 O 7
Calhan, CO 68-69 D 6
Calhoun, GA 78-79 G 3
Calhoun, LA 78-79 C 4
Calhoun, TN 80-81 D 3
Calhoun City, MS 78-79 E 4
Calhoun Falls, SC 80-81 E 3
Cali 98-99 D 4
Calico Rock, AR 78-79 CD 2
Calicut 160-161 LM 8
Caliente, CA 74-75 D 5
Caliente, NV 58-59 CD 4
California, MO 70-71 D 6
California [USA, administrative unit] 58-59 B 3-C 5
California [USA, landscape] 42 G 5-H 7
California, Gulf of — 58-59 D 5-E 7
California, University of — [USA, Los Angeles] 83 III b 1
California, University of — [USA, San Francisco] 83 I c 1
California State College 83 III c 2
California State University 83 III c 1
Căliman, Munţii — 138-139 L 2
Calimere, Point — 160-161 MN 8
Călineşti 138-139 L 3
Calingasta 103 BC 4
Calion, AR 78-79 C 4
Calipatria, CA 74-75 F 6
Calispell Peak 66-67 E 1
Calistoga, CA 74-75 B 3
Calkiní 58-59 H 7
Callabonna, Lake — 182-183 G 5
Callafo = Kelafo 194-195 N 7
Callahan, FL 80-81 c 1
Callahan, Mount — 74-75 E 3
Callander [CDN] 72-73 G 1
Callander [GB] 116-117 G 4
Callao 98-99 D 7
Callaway, NE 68-69 FG 5
Calling Lake [CDN, lake] 48 L 2
Calling Lake [CDN, place] 48 L 2
Callison Ranch 52-53 W 7
Calmar 48 L 3
Calmar, IA 70-71 DE 4
Calne 116-117 JK 9
Caloosahatchee River 80-81 c 3
Calotmul 86-87 QR 7
Calstock 116-117 G 10
Caltagirone 138-139 F 7
Caltanissetta 138-139 EF 7
Calulo 198 BC 3-4
Calumet, MI 70-71 F 2
Calumet [CDN] 72-73 J 2
Calumet [USA] 83 II b 2
Calumet, Lake — 83 II b 2
Calva, AZ 74-75 HJ 6
Calvados, Côte du — 132-133 G 4
Calvert, AL 78-79 EF 5
Calvert, TX 76-77 F 7
Calvert City, KY 78-79 E 2
Calvert Island 48 C 4
Calvi 138-139 C 4
Calvin, OK 76-77 F 5
Calvinia 198 CD 8
Camabatela 198 C 3
Camachigama, Lac — 50 NO 3
Camacho [MEX] 86-87 JK 5

Camacho 215

Camacupa 198 C 4
Camagüey 58-59 L 7
Camagüey, Archipiélago de — 58-59 L 7
Camajuaní 88-89 G 3
Camaná 98-99 E 8
Camapuã 98-99 J 8
Camapuã, Sertão de — 98-99 J 8-9
Camaquã 103 F 4
Camararé, Rio — 98-99 J 11
Camargo, OK 76-77 E 4-5
Camargo [BOL] 98-99 FG 9
Camargo [MEX] 58-59 E 6
Camargo, Ciudad — 76-77 E 9
Camargue 132-133 K 7
Camarillo, CA 74-75 D 5
Camariñas 132-133 C 7
Camarón [MEX] 76-77 DE 9
Camarón [PA] 58-59 b 3
Camarón, Cabo — 88-89 D 6
Camarones 103 CD 6
Camas, ID 66-67 G 3
Camas, WA 66-67 B 3
Camas Creek 66-67 GH 3
Camataquí = Villa Abecia 98-99 FG 9
Ca Mâu 174-175 DE 5
Ca Mau = Quan Long 174-175 DE 5
Ca Mau, Mui — = Mui Bai Bung 174-175 D 5
Cambaia = Cambay 160-161 L 6
Cambay 160-161 L 6
Cambay, Gulf of — 160-161 L 6
Cambing = Ilha de Ataúro 174-175 J 8
Cambodia 174-175 DE 4
Camborne 116-117 F 10
Cambrai 132-133 J 3
Cambray, NM 76-77 A 6
Cambria, CA 74-75 C 5
Cambrian Mountains 116-117 G 9-H 7
Cambridge, ID 66-67 E 3
Cambridge, IL 70-71 EF 5
Cambridge, MA 58-59 NM 3
Cambridge, MD 72-73 H 5
Cambridge, MN 70-71 D 3
Cambridge, NE 68-69 F 5
Cambridge, OH 72-73 EF 4
Cambridge [CDN] 72-73 FG 3
Cambridge [GB] 116-117 LM 8
Cambridge [JA] 88-89 H 5
Cambridge Bay 46-47 PQ 4
Cambridge City, IN 70-71 H 6
Cambridge City, OH 72-73 D 5
Cambridge Gulf 182-183 E 2-3
Camden, AL 78-79 F 4-5
Camden, AR 58-59 H 5
Camden, ME 72-73 M 2
Camden, NJ 58-59 LM 4
Camden, SC 80-81 F 3
Camden, TX 76-77 G 7
Camden Bay 52-53 P 1
Camdenton, MO 70-71 D 6-7
Cameia = Lumeje 198 D 4
Camelback Mount 52-53 HJ 5
Camelford 116-117 G 10
Camembert 132-133 H 4
Cameron, AZ 74-75 H 5
Cameron, LA 78-79 C 6
Cameron, MO 70-71 CD 6
Cameron, TX 76-77 F 7
Cameron, WI 70-71 E 3
Cameron, WV 72-73 F 5
Cameron, Tanah-tinggi — 174-175 D 6
Cameron Falls 70-71 F 1
Cameron Run 82 II a 2
Cameroon 194-195 G 8-7
Camerota 138-139 F 5-6
Cameroun, Mont — 194-195 F 8
Cameroun Occidental 194-195 FG 7
Cameroun Oriental 194-195 G 7
Cametá [BR ↙ Belém] 98-99 JK 5
Cametá [BR ↗ Belém] 98-99 P 5
Camiguin Island [RP, Babuyan Channel] 174-175 H 3
Camiguin Island [RP, Mindanao Sea] 174-175 H 5
Camiling 174-175 GH 3
Camilla, GA 80-81 D 5
Camino, CA 74-75 C 3
Caminreal 132-133 G 8
Camira = Camiri 98-99 G 9
Camiranga 98-99 K 5
Camiri 98-99 G 9
Camocim 98-99 L 5
Camooweal 182-183 G 3
Camopi [French Guiana, place] 98-99 M 3
Camopi [French Guiana, river] 98-99 M 3
Camorta Island 160-161 P 9
Camoxilo 198 C 4
Camp 19, AK 52-53 FG 4
Campagna 138-139 F 5
Campagne = Campània 138-139 F 5
Campana [MEX] 76-77 C 9
Campana, Isla — 103 A 7
Campanario, Cerro — 103 BC 5
Campania 138-139 F 5
Campania Island 48 C 3
Campanquiz, Cerros de — 98-99 D 5-6
Campbell, NE 68-69 G 5
Campbell, OH 72-73 F 4
Campbellford 72-73 H 2
Campbell Island 31 D 17
Campbell River 46-47 L 7
Campbellsport, WI 70-71 F 4
Campbellsville, KY 70-71 H 7
Campbellton 46-47 X 8
Campbell Town 182-183 J 8
Campbeltown 116-117 F 5
Camp Crook, SD 68-69 DE 3
Camp Douglas, WI 70-71 EF 4
Campeche 58-59 H 8
Campeche, Bahía de — 58-59 GH 7
Campeche, Gulf of — = Bahía de Campeche 58-59 GH 7
Campeche Bank 58-59 HJ 7
Camperville 49 H 5
Campidano 138-139 C 6
Campiña, La — [E, Andalucia] 132-133 E 10
Campiña del Henares, La — 132-133 F 8
Campina Grande [BR, Amapá] 98-99 MN 6
Campina Grande [BR, Paraíba] 98-99 N 4
Campinas 98-99 K 9
Campli 138-139 E 4
Camp Nelson, CA 74-75 D 4
Campo, CA 74-75 E 6
Campo, CO 76-77 C 4
Campo [RFC, place] 194-195 F 8
Campo [RFC, river] 194-195 G 8
Campobasso 138-139 F 5
Campo Belo 98-99 KL 9
Campo de Diauarum 98-99 J 7
Campo Duran 103 D 2
Campo Grande [BR] 98-99 J 9
Campo Grande [RA] 103 EF 3
Campo Indian Reservation 74-75 E 6
Campo Maior [BR] 98-99 L 5
Campo Maior [P] 132-133 D 9
Campos [BR, landscape] 98-99 L 7
Campos [BR, place] 98-99 L 9
Campos, Tierra de — 132-133 E 7-8
Campos Altos [BR, Mato Grosso] 98-99 HJ 9
Camp Point, IL 70-71 E 5
Camp Springs, MD 82 II b 2
Campti, LA 78-79 C 5
Campton, KY 72-73 E 6
Campton Airport 83 III c 2
Campton Creek 83 III c 2
Camp Verde, AZ 74-75 H 5
Camp Wood, TX 76-77 DE 8
Camrose 46-47 O 7
Camulenba 198 C 3
Canacari, Lago — 98-99 J 6
Canada 46-47 M 5-W 7
Canada Basin 26-27 BC 1-2
Canada Bay 51 HJ 2
Cañada de Gómez 103 D 4
Canadian, TX 76-77 D 5
Canadian Channel = Jacques Cartier Passage 46-47 Y 7-8
Canadian National Railways 46-47 PQ 7
Canadian Pacific Railway 46-47 OP 7
Canadian River 58-59 F 4
Çanakkale 160-161 B 2
Çanakkale boğazı 160-161 B 2-3
Canala 182-183 N 4
Canal de la voie maritime 82 I b 2
Canal de Yucatán 58-59 J 7
Canal du Midi 132-133 HJ 7
Canal Flats 48 JK 4
Canal Número 11 103 E 5
Canamã 98-99 BC 7
Canamari 98-99 C 8
Canandaigua, NY 72-73 H 3
Cananea 58-59 DE 5
Cananor = Cannanore 160-161 LM 8
Cañar [EC, place] 98-99 D 5
Canárias, Ilha das — 98-99 L 5
Canarias, Islas — 194-195 A 3
Canarreos, Archipiélago de los — 58-59 K 7
Canarsie, New York-, NY 82 III c 3
Canary Basin 26-27 HJ 4
Canary Islands = Islas Canarias 194-195 A 3
Canary Rise 26-27 HJ 4
Canastota, NY 72-73 HJ 3
Canastra, Serra da — [BR, Minas Gerais] 98-99 K 9
Canatlán 86-87 H 5
Canaveral, FL 80-81 c 2
Canaveral, Cape — 58-59 KL 6
Canavieiras 98-99 M 8
Cañazas, Sierra de — 88-89 G 10
Canberra 182-183 J 7
Canby, CA 66-67 C 5
Canby, MN 68-69 H 3
Canby, OR 66-67 B 3
Canchenjunga = Gangchhendsönga 160-161 O 5
Candeias, Rio — 98-99 G 9-10
Candela [MEX] 76-77 D 9
Candelaria, TX 76-77 B 7
Candelaria, Río — [MEX] 86-87 P 8
Candi = Maha Nuwara 160-161 N 9
Candia = Hērákleion 138-139 L 8
Cândido Mendes 98-99 KL 5
Candle, AK 52-53 G 4
Candle Lake 49 F 4
Candlestick Park 83 I b 2
Cando, ND 68-69 G 1
Candón 174-175 GH 3
Candravasih 174-175 K 7
Canelos 98-99 D 5
Cañete [PE] 98-99 D 7
Caney, KS 76-77 FG 4
Cangalha, Serra da — [BR, Goiás] 98-99 P 9
Cangallo [PE] 98-99 DE 7
Cangamba 198 C 4
Cangas 132-133 C 7
Cangas de Narcea 132-133 D 7
Cangombe 198 C 4
Canguaretama 98-99 MN 6
Cangxien = Cangzhou 166-167 M 4
Cangzhou 166-167 M 4
Canicatti 138-139 E 7
Canigou, Mont — 132-133 J 7
Canim Lake [CDN, lake] 48 G 4
Canim Lake [CDN, place] 48 G 4
Caninde [BR, Amazonas] 98-99 C 8
Canindé [BR, Ceará] 98-99 M 5
Canisteo, NY 72-73 H 3
Cañitas de Felipe Pescador 86-87 J 6
Çankırı 160-161 C 2
Canmore 48 K 4
Canna 116-117 E 3
Cannae 138-139 G 5
Cannanore 160-161 LM 8
Cannelton, IN 70-71 G 7
Cannes 132-133 L 7
Canning Desert 182-183 D 3
Canning River 52-53 O 2
Cannock 116-117 J 8
Cannon Ball, ND 68-69 F 2
Cannonball River 68-69 F 2
Cannon Falls, MN 70-71 D 3
Cano = Kano 194-195 F 6
Caño, Isla del — 88-89 DE 10
Canoas 103 F 3
Canobie 182-183 H 3
Canoe 48 H 4
Canoeiro, Cachoeiro do — 98-99 OP 10
Canoe Lake [CDN, lake] 49 D 3
Canoe Lake [CDN, place] 49 D 3
Canon City, CO 58-59 EF 4
Caño Quebrado, Río — [PA, Colón] 58-59 a 2
Caño Quebrado, Río — [PA, Panamá] 58-59 b 2-3
Canora 46-47 Q 7
Canouan 88-89 Q 8
Canova, SD 68-69 H 4
Canso 46-47 Y 8
Canso, Strait of — 46-47 YZ 8
Canso Bank 51 F 5
Cansu = Gansu 166-167 G 3-J 4
Canta 98-99 D 7
Cantabrian Mountains = Cordillera Cantábrica 132-133 D-F 7
Cantábrica, Cordillera — 132-133 D-F 7
Canta Galo 98-99 JK 7
Cantal 132-133 J 6
Cantal, Plomb du — 132-133 J 6
Cantaura 98-99 G 3
Canterbury [CDN] 51 C 5
Canterbury [GB] 116-117 h 7
Canterbury Bight 182-183 O 8
Cân Tho' 174-175 E 5
Cantil, CA 74-75 DE 5
Cantilan 174-175 J 5
Cantin, Cap — = Rā's al-Baddūzah 194-195 BC 2
Cantin, Cape — = Rā's Ṭarfāyah 194-195 B 3
Canto do Buriti 98-99 L 6
Canton 178 J 3
Canton, CA 78-79 G 3
Canton, GA 80-81 D 3
Canton, IL 70-71 EF 5
Canton, KS 68-69 H 6
Canton, MA 72-73 L 3
Canton, MO 70-71 E 5
Canton, MS 78-79 DE 4
Canton, NC 80-81 E 3
Canton, NY 72-73 J 2
Canton, OH 58-59 K 3
Canton, OK 76-77 E 4
Canton, PA 72-73 H 4
Canton, SD 68-69 H 4
Canton, TX 76-77 FG 6
Canton = Guangzhou 166-167 LM 7
Cantù 138-139 C 3
Cantwell, AK 52-53 N 5
Canudos [BR, Pará] 98-99 J 8
Canumã 98-99 H 5
Canumã, Rio — 98-99 J 7
Canumã, Rio — = Rio Sucunduri 98-99 H 6
Canuri = Kanouri 194-195 G 6
Canutama 98-99 G 6
Canutillo, TX 76-77 A 7
Canvey Island 116-117 M 9
Čany, ozero — 154-155 O 7
Canyon, TX 76-77 D 5
Canyon, WY 66-67 H 3
Canyon [CDN, Ontario] 70-71 H 2
Canyon [CDN, Yukon Territory] 52-53 T 6
Canyon City, OR 66-67 D 3
Canyon de Chelly National Monument 74-75 J 4-5
Canyon Ferry Dam 66-67 GH 2
Canyon Ferry Reservoir 66-67 H 2
Canyon Largo [USA ← Jicarilla Apache Indian Reservation] 76-77 A 4
Canyon Largo [USA ↑ Mesa Montosa] 76-77 B 5
Canyonville, OR 66-67 B 4
Cao Băng 174-175 F 2
Caolshàile Rua 116-117 AB 7
Caombo 198 C 3
Caopacho, Rivière — 51 C 2
Caorach, Cuan na g- 116-117 CD 5
Caoshi 170-171 E 1
Capa, SD 68-69 F 3
Čapajevo 154-155 J 7
Čapajevsk 154-155 HJ 7
Çapakçur = Bingöl 160-161 E 3
Capana 98-99 D 5
Capanema [BR, Mato Grosso] 98-99 H 7
Capanema [BR, Pará] 98-99 K 5
Capão Bonito 103 G 2
Caparão, Serra do — 98-99 L 8-9
Cap-aux-Meules 51 F 4
Cap Blanc = Ar-Rā's al-Abyaḍ 194-195 A 4
Cap-Chat 51 C 3
Cap-de-la-Madeleine 46-47 W 8
Cape Barren Island 182-183 JK 8
Cape Basin 26-27 K 7
Cape Blanco 58-59 AB 3
Cape Bouqainville 182-183 E 2
Cape Breton Highlands National Park 51 FG 4
Cape Breton Island 46-47 X-Z 8
Cape Charles, VA 80-81 HJ 2
Cape Clear = Ceann Cléire 116-117 B 9
Cape Coast 194-195 D 7
Cape Cod Bay 72-73 L 3-4
Cape Cod Peninsula 58-59 N 3
Cape Coral, FL 80-81 bc 3
Cape Dorset 46-47 VW 5
Cape Fear River 58-59 L 4-5
Cape Girardeau, MO 58-59 HJ 4
Cape Johnson Depth 174-175 J 4
Capella 182-183 J 4
Capelongo 198 C 4
Cape May, NJ 58-59 M 4
Cape May Court House, NJ 72-73 JK 5
Cape Pole, AK 52-53 vw 9
Cape Province = Kaapland 198 DE 8
Cape Rise 26-27 K 8
Cape Sable Island 51 D 6
Cape Saint George [CDN] 51 G 3
Cape Smith 46-47 UV 5
Cape Tormentine 51 DE 4
Cape Town = Kaapstad 198 C 8
Cape Verde 24-25 H 5
Cape Verde = Cap Vert 194-195 A 6
Cape Verde Basin 26-27 GH 4-5
Cape Verde Plateau 26-27 H 4-5
Cape Vincent, NY 72-73 HJ 2
Cape Yakataga, AK 52-53 QR 6
Cape York Peninsula 182-183 H 2
Cap-Haïtien 58-59 M 8
Capibara 98-99 F 4
Capim 98-99 OP 5
Capim, Rio — 98-99 K 5
Capinzal, Cachoeira — 98-99 JK 9
Capitachouahe, Rivière — 50 N 2-3
Capital Territory, Australian — 182-183 J 7
Capitan, NM 76-77 B 6
Capitan Grande Indian Reservation 74-75 E 6
Capitão Cardoso, Rio — 98-99 HJ 10
Capitão Poço 98-99 P 5
Capitol, The — 82 II ab 2
Capitol Heights, MD 82 II b 2
Capitol Hill, Washington-, DC 82 II ab 2
Capitol Peak 66-67 E 5
Capitol Reef National Monument 74-75 H 3
Capivara, Cachoeira — 98-99 J 6
Capiz = Roxas 174-175 H 4
CApodi, Chapada do — 98-99 M 6
Capoeira 98-99 P 7
Capoeiras, Cachoeira das — 98-99 H 6
Cappari = Psérimos 138-139 M 7
Capràia 138-139 CD 4
Capreol 72-73 F 1
Caprera 138-139 C 5
Capri 138-139 EF 5
Capricorn Channel 182-183 K 4
Caprivistrook 198 D 5
Caprock, NM 76-77 C 6
Captiva, FL 80-81 b 3
Càpua 138-139 EF 5
Capulin Mountain National Monument 76-77 BC 4
Capunda 198 C 4
Cap Vert 194-195 A 6
Caquetá, Río — 98-99 E 5
Čara [SU, place] 154-155 W 6
Čara [SU, river] 154-155 W 6
Carabaña 98-99 E 7
Carabaya, Cordillera de — 98-99 GH 7
Carabinamí, Rio — 98-99 G 6
Caracal 138-139 KL 3
Caracaraí 98-99 G 4
Caracaraí, Cachoeira — 98-99 G 4
Caracas 98-99 F 2
Carachi = Karāchī 160-161 K 6
Caracol [BR, Piauí] 98-99 L 6
Caracoles, Punta — 88-89 G 11
Caracórum = Karakoram 160-161 L 3-M 4
Cara Droma Rúisc 116-117 CD 7
Carahue 103 B 5
Carajás, Serra dos — 98-99 J 5-6
Caransebeş 138-139 K 3
Caraquet 51 D 4
Carata 88-89 E 8
Caratasca, Laguna de — 58-59 K 8
Caratinga 98-99 L 8
Caratunk, ME 72-73 LM 2
Carauari 98-99 F 5
Caraúbas [BR, Ceará] 98-99 M 6
Carauna, Serra de — 98-99 H 3
Caravaca de la Cruz 132-133 FG 9
Caravelas 98-99 M 8
Caravelí 98-99 E 8
Carazinho 103 F 3
Carballo 132-133 C 7
Carberry 49 J 6
Carbonara, Capo — 138-139 CD 6
Carbon Creek 52-53 H 2
Carbondale, CO 68-69 C 6
Carbondale, IL 70-71 F 7
Carbondale, PA 72-73 J 4
Carbonear 46-47 a 8
Carbon Hill, AL 78-79 F 4
Carbônia 138-139 C 6
Carcajou Mountains 46-47 L 4-5
Carcar 174-175 H 4-5
Carcassonne 132-133 J 7
Carcross 46-47 K 5
Cardamum Island = Kadmat Island 160-161 L 8
Cárdenas [C] 58-59 K 7
Cárdenas [MEX] 58-59 G 7
Cardiel, Lago — 103 B 7
Cardiff 116-117 H 9
Cardigan 116-117 G 8
Cardigan Bay 116-117 G 8
Cardington, OH 72-73 E 4
Cardona [E] 132-133 H 8
Cardross 49 F 6
Cardston 46-47 O 8
Čardžou 160-161 J 3
Careen Lake 49 DE 2
Carei 138-139 K 2
Careiro 98-99 H 5
Careiro, Ilha do — 98-99 J 6
Carevokokšajsk = Joškar-Ola 154-155 H 6
Carey, ID 66-67 G 4
Carey, OH 72-73 E 4
Carey, Lake — 182-183 D 5
Careysburg 194-195 BC 7
Cargados 26-27 N 6
Carhaix-Plouguer 132-133 F 4
Cariaco 98-99 G 2
Caribana, Punta — 98-99 D 3
Caribbean Basin 58-59 MN 8
Caribbean Sea 58-59 K-N 8
Caribe, Río — 86-87 P 8
Cariboo Mountains 46-47 M 7
Cariboo River 48 G 3
Caribou, AK 52-53 P 4
Caribou, ME 72-73 MN 1
Caribou, Lac — = Rentiersee 46-47 Q 6
Caribou Hide 52-53 XY 8
Caribou Island 70-71 H 2
Caribou Lake 50 E 2
Caribou Mountains 46-47 NO 6
Caribou Range 66-67 H 4
Caribou River 52-53 c 2
Carievale 68-69 F 1
Carinhanha 98-99 L 7
Carinthia = Kärnten 124 FG 5
Caripito 98-99 G 2
Caritianas 98-99 G 9
Carleton 51 C 3
Carleton, Mount — 51 C 4
Carleton Place 72-73 HJ 2
Carlin, NV 66-67 EF 5
Carlinville, IL 70-71 EF 6
Carlisle 116-117 J 6
Carlisle, IA 70-71 D 5
Carlisle, IN 70-71 G 6
Carlisle, KY 72-73 DE 5
Carlisle, PA 72-73 H 4
Carlisle, SC 80-81 F 3
Carlisle Island 52-53 I 4
Carlo, AK 52-53 N 5
Carlos, Isla — 103 B 8
Carlos Chagas 98-99 LM 8
Carlota, La — [RA] 103 D 4
Carlow = Ceatharlach 116-117 DE 8
Carlsbad, CA 74-75 E 6
Carlsbad, NM 58-59 F 5
Carlsbad = Karlovy Vary 124 F 3
Carlsbad Caverns National Park 76-77 B 6
Carlsruhe = Karlsruhe 124 D 4
Carlton, MN 70-71 D 2
Carlton [CDN] 49 E 4
Carlyle 49 GH 6
Carlyle, IL 70-71 F 6
Carmacks 46-47 J 5
Carmagnola 138-139 BC 3
Carman 68-69 GH 1
Carmānia = Kermān 160-161 H 4
Carmanville 51 JK 3
Carmarthen 116-117 G 9
Carmarthen Bay 116-117 G 9
Carmaux 132-133 J 6
Carmel, CA 74-75 BC 4
Carmel Head 116-117 G 7
Carmen, OK 76-77 E 4
Carmen [BR] 98-99 L 11
Carmen, Ciudad del — 58-59 H 8
Carmen, Isla — 58-59 DE 6
Carmen, Isla del — 86-87 OP 8
Carmen, Río del — [MEX] 86-87 D 2-3
Carmen, Sierra del — 86-87 J 3
Carmen de Bolívar, El — 98-99 DE 3
Carmen de Patagones 103 D 6
Carmi 66-67 D 1
Carmi, IL 70-71 F 6
Carmila 182-183 J 4
Carmona [Angola] 198 BC 3
Carmona [E] 132-133 E 10
Carnac 132-133 F 5
Carnamah 182-183 C 5
Carnarvon [AUS] 182-183 B 4
Carnarvon [ZA] 198 D 8
Carnarvon Range 182-183 CD 5
Carnatic 160-161 M 8-9
Carnaubinha 98-99 FG 11
Carn Domhnaigh 116-117 DE 5
Carndonagh = Carn Domhnaigh 116-117 DE 5
Carnduff 68-69 F 1
Carnegie, OK 76-77 E 5
Carnegie, PA 72-73 F 4
Carnegie, Lake — 182-183 D 5
Carneiro, KS 68-69 GH 6
Carnforth 116-117 J 6
Carnic Alps 138-139 E 2
Car Nicobar Island 160-161 P 9
Carnot 194-195 H 8
Carnot Bay 182-183 D 3
Carnoustie 116-117 J 4
Carnsore Point = Ceann an Chairn 116-117 EF 8
Caro, AK 52-53 NO 3
Caro, MI 72-73 E 3
Carole Highlands, MD 82 II b 1
Carolina [BR] 98-99 K 6
Carolina [Puerto Rico] 88-89 O 5
Carolina [ZA] 198 EF 7
Carolina, La — [E] 132-133 F 9
Carolina, North — 58-59 KL 4
Carolina, South — 58-59 K 5
Caroline 48 K 3
Caroline Islands 148-149 RS 9
Caroline Livermore, Mount — 83 I b 1
Carol Springs, FL 80-81 c 3
Caroní, Río — 98-99 G 3
Carora 98-99 EF 2
Carp 72-73 HJ 2
Carp, NV 74-75 F 4
Carpathians 138-139 L 2-M 3
Carpentaria, Gulf of — 182-183 GH 2
Carpenter, WY 68-69 DE 5
Carpentras 132-133 K 6
Carpi 138-139 D 3
Carpina 98-99 M 6
Carpinteria, CA 74-75 D 5
Carpio, ND 68-69 F 1
Carp Lake 48 F 2
Carpolac 182-183 H 7
Carr, CO 68-69 D 5
Carrabelle, FL 78-79 G 6
Carraig Mhachaire Rois 116-117 DE 7
Carraig na Siúre 116-117 D 8
Carrantuohill = Carn Tuathail 116-117 B 9
Carrara 138-139 D 3
Carrbridge 116-117 G 3
Carreria 103 E 2
Carrickfergus 116-117 F 6
Carrickmacross = Carraig Mhachaire Rois 116-117 DE 7
Carrick-on-Shannon = Cara Droma Rúisc 116-117 CD 7
Carrick-on-Suir = Carraig na Siúre 116-117 D 8
Carrière, Lac — 72-73 H 1
Carriers Mills, IL 70-71 F 7
Carrillo 76-77 BC 9
Carrington, ND 68-69 G 2
Carrión 132-133 E 7
Carrizal Bajo 103 B 3
Carrizo Springs, TX 76-77 DE 8
Carrizozo, NM 76-77 B 6
Carroll 49 HJ 6
Carroll, IA 70-71 C 4
Carrollton, GA 78-79 G 4
Carrollton, IL 70-71 E 6
Carrollton, KY 70-71 H 6
Carrollton, MO 70-71 D 6
Carrollton, TX 76-77 F 6
Carron, River — 116-117 G 3
Carrot River [CDN, place] 49 G 4
Carrot River [CDN, river] 49 GH 4

216 **Camacupa**

Carrowmore Lough = Loch na Ceathrun Moire 116-117 B 6
Carruthers 49 D 4
Çarşamba 142-142 G 7
Çarşamba suyu 142-143 G 8
Čaršanga 160-161 K 4
Čarsk 154-155 P 8
Carson, CA 83 III c 3
Carson, ND 68-69 F 2
Carson City, NV 58-59 C 4
Carson Sink 74-75 D 3
Carsonville, MI 72-73 E 3
Carsphairn 116-117 G 5
Cartagena [CO, Bolívar] 98-99 D 2
Cartagena [E] 132-133 G 10
Cartago, CA 74-75 DE 4
Cartago [CO] 98-99 D 4
Cartago [CR] 58-59 K 10
Carta Valley, TX 76-77 D 8
Carter, MT 66-67 H 2
Carter, OK 76-77 E 5
Carter, WY 66-67 H 5
Carteret, NJ 82 III a 3
Carter Fell 116-117 J 5
Cartersville, GA 78-79 G 3
Cartersville, MT 68-69 C 2
Carthage 194-195 G 1
Carthage, IL 70-71 E 5
Carthage, MO 58-59 H 4
Carthage, MS 78-79 E 4
Carthage, NC 80-81 G 3
Carthage, NY 72-73 J 2-3
Carthage, SD 68-69 H 3
Carthage, TN 78-79 G 2
Carthage, TX 76-77 G 6
Carthago 194-195 G 1
Cartier 50 L 3
Cartier Island 182-183 D 2
Cartierville, Aéroport de — 82 I a 1
Cartierville, Montréal- 82 I a 1
Cartum = Al Kharṭūm 194-195 L 5
Cartwright [CDN, Manitoba] 68-69 G 1
Cartwright [CDN, Newfoundland] 46-47 Z 7
Caruaru 98-99 M 6
Carúpano 98-99 G 2
Carutapera 98-99 K 5
Carvalho 98-99 N 6
Carvoeiro 98-99 GH 5
Carvoeiro, Cabo — 132-133 C 9
Cary, NC 80-81 G 3
Čaryn 154-155 OP 9
Čaryš 154-155 P 7
Casablanca = Ad-Dār al-Bayḍā' 194-195 BC 2
Casa de Janos 86-87 F 2
Casadepaga, AK 52-53 EF 4
Casa Grande, AZ 74-75 H 6
Casal di Principe 138-139 EF 5
Casale Monferrato 138-139 C 3
Casalmaggiore 138-139 CD 3
Casanare, Río — 98-99 E 3
Casa Nova 98-99 L 6
Casa Piedra, TX 76-77 BC 8
Casas Grandes, Río — 58-59 E 5-6
Cascadas, Las — 58-59 b 2
Cascade 66-67 DE 1
Cascade, IA 70-71 E 4
Cascade, ID 66-67 EF 3
Cascade, MT 66-67 GH 2
Cascade Head 66-67 A 3
Cascade Pass 66-67 C 1
Cascade Range 58-59 B 2-3
Cascade Reservoir 66-67 EF 3
Cascade Tunnel 66-67 C 2
Cascapédia, Rivière — 51 C 3
Cascavel [BR, Paraná] 103 F 2
Casco, WI 70-71 G 3
Casco Bay 72-73 LM 3
Cascumpeque Bay 51 DE 4
Časel'ka 154-155 P 4-5
Caserta 138-139 F 5
Casetas 132-133 G 8
Caseville, MI 72-73 E 3
Casey, IL 70-71 FG 6
Cashel = Caiseal 116-117 D 8
Cashmere, WA 66-67 C 2
Casilda 103 D 4
Casino 182-183 K 5
Casiquiare, Río — 98-99 F 4
Casma 98-99 D 6
Casmalia, CA 74-75 C 5
Caspe 132-133 GH 8
Casper, WY 58-59 E 3
Casper Range 68-69 C 4
Caspiana, LA 78-79 C 4
Caspian Sea 160-161 F 1-G 3
Casquets 116-117 J 11
Cass, WV 72-73 FG 5
Cassa, WY 68-69 D 4
Cassai = Kasai 198 C 2
Cassai, Rio — 198 CD 4
Cassamba 198 D 4
Cass City, MI 72-73 E 3
Cassel = Kassel 124 D 3
Casselton, ND 68-69 H 2
Cassiar Mountains 46-47 KL 6
Cassils 49 B 5
Cassinga = Kassinga 198 C 5
Cassino [I] 138-139 EF 5
Cass Lake, MN 70-71 C 2
Cassopolis, MI 70-71 GH 5
Cass River 70-71 J 4
Cassville, WI 70-71 E 4
Castaic, CA 74-75 D 5
Castanhal [BR, Amazonas] 98-99 K 6
Castanhal [BR, Pará] 98-99 K 5
Castanheiro 98-99 F 5
Castaños 76-77 D 9
Castejón 132-133 FG 7
Castelfranco Veneto 138-139 DE 3
Castella, CA 66-67 B 5
Castellammare, Golfo di — 138-139 E 6
Castellammare del Golfo 138-139 E 6
Castellammare di Stàbia 138-139 EF 5
Castellana Grotte 138-139 G 5
Castelli = Juan José Castelli 103 DE 3
Castellón de la Plana 132-133 GH 9
Castelnaudary 132-133 HJ 7
Castelo Branco 132-133 D 9
Castelsarrasin 132-133 H 6
Castelvetrano 138-139 E 7
Casterton 182-183 H 7
Castilla la Nueva 132-133 E 9-F 8
Castilla la Vieja 132-133 E 8-F 7
Castilletes 98-99 E 2
Castillo, Pampa del — 103 C 7
Castillo de San Marcos National Monument 80-81 c 1
Castillón 86-87 J 3
Castle Acre 116-117 M 8
Castlebar = Caisleán a'Bharraigh 116-117 BC 7
Castlebay 116-117 D 4
Castle Dale, UT 74-75 H 3
Castle Dome Mountains 74-75 FG 6
Castle Donington 116-117 K 8
Castle Douglas 116-117 GH 6
Castleford 116-117 K 7
Castlegar 66-67 DE 1
Castle Gate, UT 74-75 H 3
Castle Hayne, NC 80-81 H 3
Castleisland = Oileán Ciarraighe 116-117 B 8
Castlemaine 182-183 HJ 7
Castle Mount 52-53 LM 2
Castle Mountain 48 K 4
Castle Peak [USA, Colorado] 68-69 C 6
Castle Peak [USA, Idaho] 66-67 F 3
Castlerea = An Caisleán Riabhach 116-117 C 7
Castlereagh = 10 ◁ 116-117 F 6
Castlereagh Bay 182-183 FG 2
Castlereagh River 182-183 J 6
Castle Rock, CO 68-69 D 6
Castle Rock, WA 66-67 B 2
Castle Rock Butte 68-69 E 3
Castle Rock Lake 70-71 F 4
Castleton Corners, New York-, NY 82 III b 3
Castletown 116-117 G 6
Castle Valley 74-75 H 3
Castolon, TX 76-77 C 8
Castor 49 C 4
Castres 132-133 J 7
Castries 58-59 O 9
Castro [BR] 103 F 2
Castro [RCH] 103 B 6
Castro-Urdiales 132-133 F 7
Castrovillari 138-139 G 6
Castroville, CA 74-75 C 4
Castroville, TX 76-77 E 8
Castrovirreyna 98-99 DE 7
Casuarinenkust 174-175 L 8
Casummit Lake 50 C 2
Caswell, AK 52-53 MN 6
Catacamas 88-89 D 7
Catalina 103 C 3
Catalonia = Cataluña 132-133 H 8-J 9
Cataluña 132-133 H 8-J 7
Catamarca = San Fernando del Valle de Catamarca 103 C 3
Catandica 198 F 5
Catanduanes Island 174-175 HJ 4
Catanduva 98-99 K 9
Catània 138-139 F 7
Catanzaro 138-139 G 6
Cataqueamã 98-99 G 10
Catar = Qaṭar 160-161 G 5
Catarina, TX 76-77 E 8
Catarina, Gebel — = Jabal Katrīnah 194-195 L 3
Catarino, Cachoeira do — 98-99 G 10
Catarman 174-175 HJ 4
Cat Arm River 51 H 2
Catastrophe, Cape — 182-183 F 7-G 6
Catbalogan 174-175 HJ 4
Catemaco 86-87 N 8
Catena Costiera = Coast Mountains 46-47 K 6-M 7
Caterham 116-117 LM 9
Catete 198 B 3
Catete, Rio — 98-99 LM 8
Cathair Dún Iascaigh 116-117 CD 8
Cathair na Mart 116-117 B 7
Cathair Saidhbhín 116-117 AB 9
Cathay, ND 68-69 G 2
Cathedral Mountain 76-77 C 7
Cathedral Peak [USA] 58-59 B 2-3
Cathkin Peak 198 EF 7
Cathlemat, WA 66-67 B 2
Cathro, MI 70-71 J 3
Catiaeum = Kütahya 160-161 BC 3
Catinzaco 103 C 3
Catió 194-195 AB 6
Cat Island [BS] 58-59 L 7
Cat Island [USA] 78-79 E 5
Cativá 58-59 b 2
Cat Lake [CDN, lake] 50 CD 2
Cat Lake [CDN, place] 50 D 2
Catlettsburg, KY 72-73 E 5
Catmandu = Katmāndū 160-161 NO 5
Catoche, Cabo — 58-59 J 7
Catriló 103 D 5
Catrimani 98-99 G 4
Catrimani, Rio — 98-99 G 4
Catskill, NY 72-73 JK 3
Catskill Mountains 72-73 J 3
Cattaraugus, NY 72-73 G 3
Catumbela 198 B 4
Cauaburi, Rio — 98-99 E 4-F 5
Cauaxi, Rio — 98-99 O 7
Cauca, Río — 98-99 E 3
Caucaia 98-99 M 5
Caucasia 98-99 D 3
Caucasus Mountains 160-161 EF 2
Caughnawage 82 I ab 2
Cauldcleuch Head 116-117 HJ 5
Caungula 198 C 3
Caunpore = Kānpur 160-161 MN 5
Čaunskaja guba 154-155 gh 4
Caupolicán 98-99 F 7
Cauquenes 103 B 5
Caura, Río — 98-99 G 3
Caurés, Rio — 98-99 G 5
Causapscal 51 C 3
Causapscal, Parc provincial de — 51 C 3
Causses 132-133 J 6
Cautário, Rio — 98-99 FG 10
Cauterets 132-133 G 7
Caux, Pays de — 132-133 H 4
Cavalcante 98-99 K 7
Cavalier, ND 68-69 H 1
Cavally 194-195 C 7-8
Cavan = An Cabhán 116-117 D 7
Cave Hills 68-69 E 3
Caviana, Ilha — 98-99 K 4
Cavite 174-175 H 4
Cavtat 138-139 GH 4
Cawnpore = Kānpur 160-161 MN 5
Cawood 116-117 K 7
Caxias [BR, Amazonas] 98-99 C 7
Caxias [BR, Maranhão] 98-99 L 5
Caxias do Sul 103 F 3
Caxito 198 B 3
Caxiuana, Baía de — 98-99 J 5
Cayambe [EC, mountain] 98-99 D 5
Cayambe [EC, place] 98-99 D 4
Cayar, Lac — = Ar-R'kīz 194-195 AB 5
Cayenne [French Guiana, administrative unit] 98-99 M 3
Cayenne [French Guiana, place] 98-99 J 3-4
Cayes, Les — 58-59 M 8
Cayey 88-89 N 5
Cayman Brac 58-59 L 8
Cayman Islands 58-59 KL 8
Cayman Trench 58-59 KL 8
Cayo Centro 86-87 R 8
Cayo Nuevo 86-87 O 7
Cay Sal 88-89 F 3
Cayucos, CA 74-75 C 5
Cayuga Lake 72-73 H 3
Cayungo = Nana Candundo 198 D 4
Cayuse Hills 68-69 B 2-3
Cazalla de la Sierra 132-133 E 10
Cazombo 198 D 4
Cchinvali 142-143 H 7
Cé, Loch — 116-117 C 6
Cea 132-133 E 7
Ceachan, Sléibhte na — 116-117 B 9
Ceahlău, Muntele — 138-139 LM 2
Cealla Beaga, Na — 116-117 C 6
Ceanannas 116-117 DE 7
Ceann Sáile 116-117 C 9
Ceann Toirc 116-117 BC 8
Ceará [BR, administrative unit] 98-99 LM 6
Ceará = Fortaleza 98-99 M 5
Ceara, Sliabh — 116-117 B 6
Ceatharlach 116-117 DE 8
Ceathrún Móire, Loch na — 116-117 B 6
Ceba 49 G 4
Ceballos 86-87 HJ 4
Čebarkul 142-143 M 5
Čeboksary 154-155 H 6
Cebú [RP, island] 174-175 H 4
Cebú [RP, place] 174-175 H 4
Cecen Uul 166-167 H 2
Cecerleg 166-167 J 2
Čechov [SU, Sachalin] 154-155 b 8
Cecilia, KY 70-71 GH 7
Cecil Lake 48 GH 1
Cècina 138-139 D 4
Čečujsk 154-155 U 6
Cedar Bluff Reservoir 68-69 G 6
Cedar Breaks National Monument 74-75 G 4
Cedarburg, WI 70-71 FG 4
Cedar City, UT 58-59 D 4
Cedar Creek [USA, North Dakota] 68-69 EF 2
Cedar Creek [USA, Virginia] 72-73 G 5
Cedar Falls, IA 70-71 D 4
Cedar Grove, NJ 82 III a 1
Cedar Grove, WI 70-71 G 4
Cedar Heights, MD 82 II b 2
Cedar Hill, NM 68-69 C 7
Cedar Island [USA, North Carolina] 80-81 H 3
Cedar Island [USA, Virginia] 80-81 J 2
Cedar Key, FL 80-81 b 2
Cedar Lake [CDN] 46-47 Q 7
Cedar Lake [USA] 76-77 C 6
Cedar Mountains [USA, Nevada] 74-75 E 3
Cedar Mountains [USA, Oregon] 66-67 E 4
Cedar Point 68-69 E 6
Cedar Rapids, IA 58-59 H 3
Cedar River [USA ◁ Iowa River] 70-71 E 4-5
Cedar River [USA ◁ Loup River] 68-69 G 5
Cedar Springs, MI 70-71 H 4
Cedartown, GA 78-79 G 3-4
Cedar Vale, KS 76-77 F 4
Cedarville, CA 66-67 C 5
Cedarwood, CO 68-69 D 7
Cedro 98-99 M 6
Cedros, Isla — 58-59 C 6
Ceduna 182-183 F 6
Ceel 166-167 H 2
Cefalù 138-139 F 6
Cega 132-133 E 8
Čegdomyn 154-155 Z 7
Čegitun 52-53 B 3
Cegléd 124 J 5
Ceiba, La — [Honduras] 58-59 J 8
Ceiba, La — [YV] 98-99 E 3
Ceiba Grande 86-87 O 9
Cejas, Las — 103 D 3
Čekanovskogo, kr'až — 154-155 XY 3
Cela = Uaco Cungo 198 C 4
Čel'abinsk 154-155 L 6
Celaya 58-59 F 7
Celebes = Sulawesi 174-175 G 7-H 6
Celebes Sea 174-175 GH 6
Celebessee 174-175 GH 6
Čeleken 160-161 G 3
Celestún 86-87 P 7
Celina, OH 70-71 H 5
Celina, TN 78-79 G 2
Celina, TX 76-77 F 6
Čelinograd 154-155 MN 7
Celje 138-139 F 2
Čelkar 154-155 KL 8
Celle 124 E 2
Celuo = Chira Bazar 166-167 DE 4
Čel'uskin, mys — 154-155 T-V 2
Cement, OK 76-77 EF 5
Cemmaes Head 116-117 G 8
Cenad 138-139 J 2
Cencia = Tyencha 194-195 M 7
Centennial, WY 68-69 CD 5
Center, CO 68-69 C 7
Center, ND 68-69 F 2
Center, NE 68-69 GH 4
Center, TX 76-77 GH 7
Centerfield, UT 74-75 H 3
Centerville, AL 78-79 F 4
Centerville, IA 70-71 D 5
Centerville, MO 70-71 E 7
Centerville, SD 68-69 H 4
Centerville, TN 78-79 F 3
Centerville, TX 76-77 FG 7
Centinela, Picacho del — 58-59 F 6
Central, AK 52-53 P 4
Central, NM 74-75 JK 6
Central [EAK] 198 G 2
Central [GB] 116-117 G 4-H 5
Central [Z] 198 E 4
Central, Plateau — = Cao Nguyên Trung Phân 174-175 E 4
Central African Republic 194-195 HJ 7
Central City, KY 70-71 G 7
Central City, NE 68-69 GH 5
Central Falls, RI 72-73 L 4
Centralia, IL 58-59 J 4
Centralia, MO 70-71 DE 6
Centralia, WA 66-67 B 2
Central Indian Ridge 26-27 N 5-7
Central Intelligence Agency 82 II a 1
Central Karroo = Groot Karoo 198 D 8
Central Mount Stuart 182-183 F 4
Central'nojakutskaja ravnina 154-155 WX 5
Central Pacific Basin 34-35 KL 4
Central Park [USA, New York] 82 III c 2
Central Patricia 50 DE 2
Central Point, OR 66-67 B 4
Central Siberian Plateau 154-155 R-X 4-5
Central Valley, CA 66-67 BC 5
Centreville 51 BC 4
Centreville, MD 72-73 HJ 5
Centreville, MS 78-79 D 5
Century City, Los Angeles-, CA 83 III b 1
Čepca 142-143 K 4
Cephalonia = Kefallēnía 138-139 J 6
Ceram = Seram 174-175 JK 7
Ceram Sea 174-175 J 7
Cerbatana, Serranía de la — 98-99 F 3
Cerbère 132-133 J 7
Cercen = Chārchān 166-167 F 4
Čerdyn 142-143 L 3
Cereal 49 C 5
Čeremchovo 154-155 T 7
Čerepanovo 154-155 P 7
Čerepovec 154-155 F 6
Ceres, CA 74-75 C 4
Ceres [ZA] 198 C 8
Céret 132-133 J 7
Čerevkovo 142-143 J 3
Cerf Island 198 K 3
Cerignola 138-139 F 5
Cerigo = Kýthēra 138-139 K 7
Cerigotto = Antikýthēra 138-139 K 8
Cerillos 86-87 P 8
Čerkassy 142-143 F 6
Čerkessk 142-143 H 7
Čerlak 154-155 N 7
Čern'achovsk 124 K 1
Černatica 138-139 L 4-5
Cernavodă 138-139 MN 3
Černigov 142-143 F 5
Černigovka 154-155 Z 9
Černogorsk 154-155 R 7
Černorečje = Dzeržinsk 154-155 GH 6
Černovcy 142-143 DE 6
Černovskije Kopi, Čita- 154-155 V 7
Černovskoje 142-143 J 4
Černyševskij 154-155 V 5
Černyševskoje 124 KL 1
Cerralvo [MEX, island] 76-77 E 9
Cerralvo [MEX, place] 86-87 KL 4
Cerralvo, Isla — 58-59 E 7
Cerreira Comprida, Cachoeira — 98-99 OP 10
Cerritos 58-59 FG 7
Cerritos, CA 83 III d 2
Cerro, El — 98-99 G 8
Cerro Azul [MEX] 86-87 M 7
Cerro de Pasco 98-99 D 7
Cerro el Nevado [RA, mountain] 103 C 5
Cerro Grande [MEX] 86-87 K 8-9
Cerro las Casitas 58-59 E 7
Cerro Viejo 86-87 DE 2
Čerskij 154-155 f 4
Certaldo 138-139 D 4
Čertež 142-143 L 4
Cervati, Monte — 138-139 F 5
Červen br'ag 138-139 KL 4
Cervera 132-133 H 8
Cervèteri 138-139 E 4
Cèrvia 138-139 E 3
Cesena 138-139 DE 3
Cēsis 142-143 DE 4
Česká Třebova 124 G 4
České Budějovice 124 G 4
České země 124 F-H 4
Českomoravská vrchovina 124 GH 4
Çeşme 142-143 E 8
Cessford 46-47 O 7
Cessnock 182-183 K 6
Cess River 194-195 C 7
Cetinje 138-139 H 4
Çetinkaya 142-143 G 8
Cetraro 138-139 F 6
Ceuta 194-195 CD 1
Cevennes 132-133 JK 6
Ceyhan nehri 142-143 G 8
Ceylon = Srī Laṅkā 160-161 N 9
Ceylon Station 49 F 6
Chaaltyn gol 166-167 GH 4
Cha-am [T] 174-175 CD 4
Chaba 166-167 F 2
Chabar = Bandar-e Chah Bahār 160-161 HJ 5
Chabarovo 154-155 L 4
Chabarovsk 154-155 a 8
Chablis 132-133 J 5
Chachapoyas 98-99 D 6
Chācharān 58-59 K 4
Chačmas 142-143 J 7
Chaco 103 D 3
Chaco Austral 103 DE 3
Chaco Boreal 103 DE 2
Chaco Canyon National Monument 74-75 JK 4-5
Chaco Central 103 D 2-E 3
Chacon, Cape — 52-53 wx 9
Chaco River 74-75 J 4
Chad 194-195 HJ 5
Chad, Lake — = Lac Tchad 194-195 G 6
Chadasan 166-167 J 2
Chadchal = Chatgal 166-167 HJ 1
Chadron, NE 68-69 E 4
Chadum 198 D 5
Chadwick, IL 70-71 F 4
Chadzaar 166-167 G 4
Chaeryŏng 170-171 EF 3
Chaffee, MO 78-79 DE 2
Chagang-do 170-171 EF 2
Chagan nuur 166-167 L 3
Chagford 116-117 H 10
Chagny 132-133 K 5
Chagos 26-27 N 6
Chagres [PA, place] 58-59 b 2
Chagres [PA, river] 58-59 ab 2
Chagres, Brazo del — 58-59 b 2
Chagres, Río — 58-59 bc 2
Chagres Arm = Brazo del Chagres 58-59 b 2
Chagulak Island 52-53 I 4
Chāhār Burjak = Chār Burjak 160-161 J 4
Chahār Maḥāl-e Bakhteyārī = 3 ◁ 160-161 G 4
Chāh Bāhār = Bandar-e Chāh Bahār 160-161 HJ 5
Ch'aho 170-171 G 2
Chaidamu Pendi = Tsaidam 166-167 GH 4
Chailar = Hailar 166-167 M 2
Ch'ail-bong 170-171 F 2
Chai Nat 174-175 D 3
Chain Butte 68-69 B 2
Chairn, Ceann an — 116-117 EF 8
Chaiya 174-175 C 5
Chajarí 103 E 4
Chajdag gol 166-167 EF 3
Chajlar 166-167 M 2
Chajlar = Hailar 166-167 M 2
Chajlar gol = Hailar He 166-167 MN 2
Chajpudyrskaja guba 142-143 LM 2
Chajrchan 166-167 J 2
Chajr'uzovo 154-155 e 6
Chakachamna Lake 52-53 L 6
Chakaktolik, AK 52-53 F 6
Chaka Nor = Chöch nuur 166-167 H 4
Chakhcharān 160-161 K 4
Chakwaktolik, AK 52-53 EF 6
Chala 98-99 E 8
Cha-lan-tun = Yalu 166-167 N 2
Chalatenango 88-89 B 7-8
Chalchuapa 88-89 B 8
Chalchyn gol 166-167 M 2
Chalcidice = Chalkidikē 138-139 K 5
Chaleur Bay 46-47 XY 8
Chalhuanca 98-99 E 7
Cha-ling Hu = Kyaring Tsho 166-167 H 5
Chálkē 138-139 M 7
Chalkidikē 138-139 K 3
Chalkís 138-139 K 6
Chalk River 72-73 H 1-2
Chalkyitsik, AK 52-53 PQ 3
Challapata 98-99 F 8
Challis, ID 66-67 F 3
Chal'mer-Ju 154-155 L 4
Chalmer-Sede = Tazovskij 154-155 OP 4
Châlons-sur-Marne 132-133 JK 4
Chalon-sur-Saône 132-133 K 5
Chalosse 132-133 G 7
Chalturin 154-155 H 6
Cham 124 F 4
Chama, NM 68-69 C 7
Chama, Rio — 76-77 A 4
Chaman 160-161 K 4
Chamba [IND] 160-161 M 4
Chambal [IND ◁ Kālī Sindh] 160-161 M 5-6
Chambal [IND ◁ Yamunā] 160-161 M 5-6
Chambas 88-89 G 3
Chamberlain 49 EF 5
Chamberlain, SD 68-69 G 4
Chamberlain Lake 72-73 M 1
Chamberlain River 182-183 E 3
Chamberlin, Mount — 52-53 P 2
Chambersburg, PA 72-73 GH 4
Chambers Island 70-71 G 3
Chambéry 132-133 K 6
Chambeshi 198 F 4
Chambres Pass = Cumbres Pass 68-69 C 7
Chamdo = Chhamdo 166-167 H 5
Chame 88-89 G 10
Chamela 86-87 H 8
Chami Choto = Hami 166-167 G 3
Chamiss Bay 48 D 4
Chamo, Lake — = Tyamo 194-195 M 7
Chāmpa [IND] 160-161 N 6
Champa [SU] 154-155 X 5
Champagne [CDN] 52-53 TU 6
Champagne [F] 132-133 J 5-K 4
Champagny Islands 182-183 D 3
Champaign, IL 58-59 J 3-4
Champāran = Mōtihārī 160-161 NO 5
Champassak 174-175 DE 4
Champion 49 B 5
Champlain, Lake — 58-59 LM 3
Champlain, Pont — 82 I b 2
Champotón 58-59 H 8
Champotón, Río — 86-87 P 8
Chanāb = Chenāb 160-161 M 4
Chanak Kalessi = Çanakkale 160-161 B 2
Chañar 103 C 4
Chañaral [RCH ↖ Copiapó] 103 B 3
Chañaral, Isla — 103 B 3
Chan Bogd 166-167 K 3
Chancay 98-99 D 7

Chancay 217

Chanch 166-167 J 1
Chan-chiang = Zhanjiang 166-167 L 7
Chanchoengsao 174-175 D 4
Chānda = Chandrapur 160-161 M 7
Chandalar, AK 52-53 NO 3
Chandalar, East Fork — 52-53 P 2
Chandalar, Middle Fork — 52-53 O 2-3
Chandalar, North Fork — 52-53 N 2-3
Chandalar Lake 52-53 NO 3
Chandalar River 46-47 G 4
Chandeleur Islands 58-59 J 6
Chandeleur Sound 78-79 E 5-6
Chandīgarh 160-161 LM 4
Chandler 46-47 Y 8
Chandler, AZ 74-75 H 6
Chandler, OK 76-77 F 5
Chandler Lake 52-53 LM 2
Chandler River 52-53 L 2
Chandless, Rio — 98-99 C 9-10
Chandrapur 160-161 M 7
Chandyga 154-155 a 5
Chang, Ko — [T, Gulf of Thailand] 174-175 D 4
Changai = Shanghai 166-167 N 5
Changaj 166-167 H 2
Changajn Nuruu 166-167 HJ 2
Ch'ang-an = Xi'an 166-167 K 5
Changane, Rio — 198 F 6
Changara 198 F 5
Changbai 170-171 FG 2
Changbai Shan 166-167 O 3
Chang-chia-k'ou = Zhangjiakou 166-167 L 3
Changchih = Changzhi 166-167 L 4
Ch'ang-chih = Changzhi 166-167 L 4
Changchow = Zhangzhou 166-167 M 7
Changchun 166-167 NO 3
Changde 166-167 L 6
Changdu = Chhamdo 166-167 H 5
Change Islands 51 JK 3
Chang-hai = Shanghai 166-167 N 5
Changhang 170-171 F 4-5
Changhowŏn 170-171 F 4
Ch'ang-hsing Tao = Changxing Dao 170-171 C 3
Changhŭng 170-171 F 5
Changhŭng-ni 170-171 FG 2
Chang Jiang [TJ, river ◁ Dong Hai] 166-167 K 5-6
Changji Huizu Zizhizhou 166-167 FG 3
Changjin 170-171 F 2
Changjin-gang 170-171 F 2
Changjin-ho 170-171 F 2
Changjŏn 170-171 G 3
Changkiakow = Zhangjiakou 166-167 L 3
Chang-kuang-ts'ai Ling = Zhangguangcai Ling 166-167 O 2-3
Changnim-ni 170-171 F 3
Ch'angnyŏng 170-171 G 5
Ch'ang-pai = Changbai 170-171 FG 2
Ch'ang-pai Shan = Changbai Shan 166-167 O 3
Chang-san-ying = Zhangsanying 170-171 AB 2
Changsha 166-167 L 6
Changshu 166-167 N 5
Ch'angsŏng = Chongsŏng 170-171 GH 1
Chang Tang = Jang Thang 166-167 E-G 5
Ch'ang-tê = Anyang 166-167 LM 4
Ch'ang-tê = Changde 166-167 L 6
Changteh = Changde 166-167 L 6
Changting 166-167 M 6
Ch'ang-tu = Chhamdo 166-167 H 5
Changtutsung = Chhamdo 166-167 H 5
Ch'angwŏn 170-171 G 5
Changxing Dao [TJ, Liaodong Wan] 170-171 C 3
Changyeh = Zhangye 166-167 J 4
Changyŏn 166-167 NO 4
Changzhi 166-167 L 4
Changzhou 166-167 M 5
Chaniá 138-139 KL 8
Chaniṓn, Kólpos — 138-139 KL 8
Chanka, ozero — 154-155 Z 9
Chankiang = Zhanjiang 166-167 L 7
Chankliut Island 52-53 de 1
Channāb = Chenāb 160-161 M 4
Channel Islands [GB] 116-117 J 11
Channel Islands [USA] 74-75 CD 6
Channel Islands National Monument = Anacapa Island, Santa Barbara Island 74-75 D 6
Channel-Port-aux-Basques 46-47 Z 8
Channing 49 H 3
Channing, MI 70-71 FG 2
Channing, TX 76-77 CD 5
Chanovej 142-143 M 2
Chansi = Shanxi 166-167 L 4
Chantaburi = Chanthaburi 174-175 D 4
Chantada 132-133 CD 7
Chantajka 154-155 PQ 4
Chantajskoje, ozero — 154-155 QR 4
Chantanika River 52-53 O 4
Chan Tengri, pik — 160-161 MN 2
Chanthaburi 174-175 D 4
Chantong = Shandong 166-167 M 4
Chantrey Inlet 46-47 RS 4
Chanty-Mansijsk 154-155 M 5
Chanty-Mansijskij Nacional'nyj Okrug = Khanty-Mansi Autonomous Area 154-155 L-P 5
Chanute, KS 70-71 C 7
Chao'an 166-167 M 7
Chaochow = Chao'an 166-167 M 7
Chao Hu 166-167 M 5
Chao Phraya, Mae Nam — 174-175 CD 3-4
Chaor He 166-167 N 2
Chaotung = Zhaotong 166-167 J 6
Chao-t'ung = Zhaotong 166-167 J 6
Chaoyang [TJ, Guangdong] 166-167 M 7
Chaoyang [TJ, Liaoning] 166-167 MN 3
Ch'ao-yang-chên = Huinan 166-167 O 3
Chapada Diamantina 98-99 L 7
Chapadinha 98-99 L 5
Chapais 50 O 2
Chapala 86-87 J 7
Chapala, Lago de — 58-59 F 7
Chapčeranga 154-155 V 8
Chapel Hill, NC 80-81 G 3
Chapel Hill, TN 78-79 F 3
Chaperito, NM 76-77 B 5
Chapéu, Cachoeira — 98-99 K 7-8
Chapleau 50 H 4
Chapleau River 50 H 3
Chaplin 49 E 5
Chapman, MT 68-69 BC 1
Chappell, NE 68-69 E 5
Chāpra 160-161 N 5
Chaqui 98-99 F 8
Charadai 103 E 3
Charagua 98-99 G 8
Charagua, Cordillera de — 98-99 G 8-9
Char Ajrag 166-167 KL 2
Charaña 98-99 F 8
Charbin = Harbin 166-167 O 2
Chār Burjak 160-161 J 4
Charcas 58-59 F 7
Chārchăn 166-167 F 4
Chārchăn Darya 166-167 F 4
Char Chorin 166-167 J 2
Char Choto 166-167 J 3
Charcos de Figueroa 76-77 CD 9
Charcos de Risa 76-77 C 9
Charcot, Île — 31 C 29
Chard 116-117 HJ 10
Chardon, OH 72-73 F 4
Charente 132-133 G 6
Char Gov' 166-167 GH 3
Chari 194-195 H 6
Chārikār 160-161 K 3-4
Char Irčis 166-167 F 2
Chariton, IA 70-71 D 5
Charitona Lapteva, bereg — 154-155 Q 3-R 2
Chariton River 70-71 D 5-6
Charity 98-99 H 3
Charkhilik = Charqiliq 166-167 F 4
Char'kov 142-143 G 5-6
Charlbury 116-117 K 9
Charleroi 132-133 K 3
Charles, Cape — 58-59 LM 4
Charlesbourg 51 A 4
Charles City, IA 70-71 D 4
Charles Falls 50 B 2
Charles Island 46-47 VW 5
Charles Lee Tilden Regional Park 83 I c 1
Charleston, IL 70-71 FG 6
Charleston, MO 78-79 E 2
Charleston, MS 78-79 DE 3
Charleston, SC 58-59 KL 5
Charleston, TN 78-79 G 3
Charleston, WV 58-59 K 4
Charleston Peak 74-75 F 4
Charlestown, IN 70-71 H 6
Charlestown [Saint Christopher-Nevis] 58-59 O 8
Charlesville 198 D 3
Charleville [AUS] 182-183 J 5
Charleville = Ráth Loirc 116-117 C 8
Charleville-Mézières 132-133 K 4
Charlevoix, MI 70-71 H 3
Charlevoix, Lake — 70-71 H 3
Charley River 52-53 Q 4
Charlie Lake 48 G 1
Charlotte, MI 70-71 H 4
Charlotte, NC 58-59 KL 4-5
Charlotte, TN 78-79 F 2
Charlotte, TX 76-77 E 8
Charlotte Amalie 58-59 O 8
Charlotte Harbor 58-59 K 6
Charlotte Lake 48 E 3
Charlottenberg 114-115 E 8
Charlottesville, VA 58-59 L 4
Charlottetown 46-47 Y 8
Charlottetown = Roseau 58-59 O 8
Charlovka 142-143 G 2
Charlton Island 46-47 UV 7
Charlton Kings 116-117 JK 9
Char Narijn uul 166-167 K 3
Char nuur [Mongolia] 166-167 G 2
Char nuur [TJ] 166-167 H 4
Charny [CDN] 51 A 4
Charolais, Monts du — 132-133 K 5
Charovsk 154-155 G 6
Charqiliq 166-167 F 4
Charron Lake 50 B 1
Charters Towers 182-183 J 3-4
Chartres 132-133 H 4
Char us nuur 166-167 G 2
Chasan 170-171 H 1
Chasavjurt 142-143 J 7
Chascomús 103 E 5
Chase 48 H 4
Chase City, VA 80-81 G 2
Chasm 48 G 4
Chasŏng 170-171 F 2
Chassahowitzka Bay 80-81 b 2
Chašuri 142-143 H 7
Chatanga 154-155 TU 3
Chatan gol 166-167 K 3
Chatangskij zaliv 154-155 UV 3
Chatanika, AK 52-53 O 4
Châteaubriant 132-133 G 5
Château-du-Loir 132-133 H 5
Châteaudun 132-133 H 4
Châteaulin 132-133 EF 4
Châteauroux 132-133 H 5
Château-Thierry 132-133 J 4
Châtellerault 132-133 H 5
Chatfield, MN 70-71 D 4
Chatgal 166-167 HJ 1
Chatham 116-117 M 9
Chatham, AK 52-53 U 8
Chatham, LA 78-79 C 4
Chatham, NY 72-73 K 3
Chatham, VA 80-81 G 2
Chatham [CDN, New Brunswick] 46-47 XY 8
Chatham [CDN, Ontario] 46-47 U 9
Chatham = Isla San Cristóbal 98-99 B 5
Chatham, Chicago-, IL 83 II b 2
Chatham, Isla — 103 B 8
Chatham Islands 182-183 Q 8
Chatham Sound 48 B 2
Chatham Strait 46-47 K 6
Chathóire, Rinn — 116-117 EF 8
Châtillon [I] 138-139 B 3
Châtillon-sur-Seine 132-133 K 5
Chatom, AL 78-79 E 5
Chatsworth 72-73 F 2
Chatsworth, GA 78-79 G 3
Chaṭṭagām 160-161 P 6
Chattahoochee, FL 78-79 G 5
Chattahoochee River 58-59 JK 5
Chattanooga, TN 58-59 J 4
Chattarpur = Chhatarpur 160-161 M 6
Chatteris 116-117 LM 8
Chaudière, Rivière — 51 A 4-5
Châu Đôc = Châu Phu 174-175 E 4
Chauekuktuli Lake 52-53 HJ 6
Chaumont 132-133 K 4
Chaŭn-do 170-171 EF 5
Châu Phu 174-175 E 4
Chautauqua Lake 72-73 G 3
Chauvin 49 C 4
Chaux-de-Fonds, La — 124 C 5
Chavast 160-161 K 2
Chaves, NM 76-77 B 6
Chaves [BR] 98-99 K 5
Chaves [P] 132-133 D 8
Chaves, Isla — = Isla Santa Cruz 98-99 AB 5
Chaviva 98-99 E 4
Chaya = Drayā 166-167 H 5
Ch'a-yü = Dsayul 166-167 H 6
Chazón 103 D 4
Cheadle 116-117 K 8
Cheann Sáile, Cuan — 116-117 C 9
Cheat Mountain 72-73 FG 5
Cheat River 72-73 G 5
Cheb 124 F 3
Chebii, Uáu el — = Wādī Bay al-Kabīr 194-195 GH 2
Cheboksary = Čeboksar 154-155 H 6
Cheboygan, MI 58-59 K 2
Chech, Erg — = Irq ash-Shāsh 194-195 D 3-4
Chechaouène = Shifshawn 194-195 CD 1
Checheno-Ingush Autonomous Soviet Socialist Republic = 5 ◁ 142-143 J 7
Chech'on 170-171 G 4
Checotah, OK 76-77 G 5
Chedabucto Bay 51 F 5
Cheecham 49 C 2
Cheecham Hills 49 B 3-C 2
Cheeching, AK 52-53 E 6
Cheektowaga, NY 72-73 GH 3
Cheepie 182-183 HJ 5
Cheesman Lake 68-69 D 6
Chef, Rivière du — 50 P 1-2
Chefoo = Yantai 166-167 N 4
Chefornak, AK 52-53 E 6
Chefu = Yantai 166-167 N 4
Chegga = Ash-Shaqqāt 194-195 C 3
Chegutu 198 EF 6
Chehalis, WA 66-67 B 2
Chehalis River 66-67 B 2
Cheju 166-167 O 5
Cheju-do 166-167 NO 5
Cheju-haehyŏp 166-167 O 5
Chekiang = Zhejiang 166-167 MN 6
Chela, Serra da — 198 B 5
Chelan 49 G 4
Chelan, WA 66-67 CD 2
Chelan, Lake — 66-67 C 1
Chélia, Djebel — = Jabal Shīlyah 194-195 F 1
Chê-ling Kuan = Zheling Guan 166-167 L 6
Chełm 124 L 3
Chełmińskre, Pojezierze — 124 J 2
Chelmsford [CDN] 50 L 3
Chelmsford [GB] 116-117 M 9
Chełmża 124 J 2
Chelsea, MI 70-71 HJ 4
Chelsea, OK 76-77 G 4
Chelsea, VT 72-73 K 2-3
Cheltenham 116-117 J 9
Cheltenham, PA 72-73 J 4
Chelyabinsk = Čel'abinsk 154-155 L 6
Chemainus 66-67 AB 1
Chemawa, OR 66-67 B 3
Chemba 198 F 5
Chemehuevi Valley Indian Reservation 74-75 F 5
Chemnitz = Karl-Marx-Stadt 124 F 3
Chemulpo = Inch'ŏn 166-167 O 4
Chemult, OR 66-67 C 4
Chenāb 160-161 M 4
Chena Hot Springs, AK 52-53 OP 4
Chena River 52-53 OP 4
Ch'ên-ch'i = Chenxi 166-167 L 6
Chên-chiang = Zhenjiang 166-167 M 5
Ch'ên-chou = Yuanling 166-167 L 6
Chencoyi 86-87 PQ 8
Chenega, AK 52-53 NO 6
Cheney, KS 68-69 H 7
Cheney, WA 66-67 E 2
Chên-fan = Minqin 166-167 J 4
Ch'êng-chiang = Chengjiang 166-167 J 7
Chengde 166-167 M 3
Chengdu 166-167 J 5
Chengjiang 166-167 J 7
Chengkiang = Chengjiang 166-167 J 7
Chengkou 166-167 K 5
Chengmai 166-167 KL 8
Chengteh = Chengde 166-167 M 3
Chengtu = Chengdu 166-167 J 5
Cheng-Xian = Sheng Xian 166-167 N 6
Chengzitan 170-171 D 3
Chên-hsi = Bar Köl 166-167 G 3
Chenik, AK 52-53 KL 7
Chenkiang = Zhenjiang 166-167 M 5
Chennapaṭṭaṇam = Madras 160-161 N 8
Chenoa, IL 70-71 F 5
Chensi = Bar Köl 166-167 G 3
Chensi = Shanxi 166-167 L 4
Chentiin Nuruu 166-167 K 2
Chentij 166-167 L 2
Chenxi 166-167 L 6
Chen Xian 166-167 L 6
Chenyang = Shenyang 166-167 NO 3
Chenyuan = Zhenyuan [TJ, Yunnan] 166-167 J 7
Chên-yüan = Zhenyuan [TJ, Yunnan] 166-167 J 7
Chepes 103 C 4
Chepo 88-89 G 10
Chepstow 116-117 J 9
Chequamegon Bay 70-71 E 2
Cher 132-133 J 5
Cheraw, CO 68-69 E 6
Cheraw, SC 80-81 FG 3
Cherbourg 132-133 G 4
Cherchen = Chārchăn 166-167 F 4
Cheremkhovo = Čeremchovo 154-155 T 7
Cheren = Keren 194-195 M 5
Chergui, Chott ech — = Ash-Shaṭṭ ash-Sharqī 194-195 DE 2
Cheribon = Cirebon 174-175 E 8
Cherlen gol 166-167 KL 2
Cherlen gol = Herlen He 166-167 M 2
Chernabura Island 52-53 d 2
Chernogorsk = Černogorsk 154-155 R 7
Cherokee, IA 70-71 C 4
Cherokee, OK 76-77 E 4
Cherokee, TX 76-77 E 7
Cherokee Lake 80-81 E 2
Cherrapunj = Cherrāpuñji 160-161 P 5
Cherrapunji 160-161 P 5
Cherry 182-183 N 2
Cherry Creek 68-69 E 3
Cherry Creek, NV 74-75 F 3
Cherry Creek, SD 68-69 F 3
Cherrydale, Arlington-, VA 82 II a 2
Cherrypatch Ridge 68-69 B 1
Cherryvale, KS 76-77 G 4
Cherryville 48 H 4
Cherskogo Mountains = chrebet Čorskogo 154-155 a 4-c 5
Cherso = Cres 138-139 F 3
Cherson 142-143 F 6
Chesaning, MI 70-71 HJ 4
Chesapeake, VA 58-59 LM 4
Chesapeake Bay 58-59 L 4
Chesham 116-117 L 9
Cheshire 116-117 J 7
Cheshire, OR 66-67 B 3
Cheshskaya Bay = Čošskaja guba 154-155 H 4
Chesil Beach 116-117 J 10
Chesley 72-73 F 2
Chester, CA 66-67 C 5
Chester, IL 70-71 F 7
Chester, MT 66-67 H 1
Chester, NE 68-69 H 5
Chester, PA 72-73 J 5
Chester, SC 80-81 F 3
Chester [CDN] 51 D 5
Chester [GB] 116-117 J 7
Chesterbrook, VA 82 II a 2
Chesterfield 116-117 K 7
Chesterfield, Île — 198 H 5
Chesterfield, Îles — 182-183 L 3
Chesterfield Inlet [CDN, bay] 46-47 ST 5
Chesterfield Inlet [CDN, place] 46-47 ST 5
Chester-le-Street 116-117 JK 6
Chestertown, MD 72-73 HJ 5
Chesuncook Lake 72-73 LM 1
Cheta [SU, place] 154-155 S 3
Cheta [SU, river] 154-155 S 3
Chetek, WI 70-71 E 3
Chéticamp 51 F 4
Chetlat Island 160-161 L 8
Chetopa, KS 76-77 G 4
Chetumal 58-59 J 8
Chetumal, Bahía de — 58-59 J 8
Chetwynd 48 FG 2
Chevak, AK 52-53 E 6
Cheverly, MD 82 II b 1
Cheviot, The — 116-117 JK 5
Cheviot Hills 116-117 J 5
Chevy Chase, MD 82 II a 1
Chewelah, WA 66-67 DE 1
Cheyenne, OK 76-77 E 5
Cheyenne, TX 76-77 C 7
Cheyenne, WY 58-59 F 3
Cheyenne Pass 68-69 D 5
Cheyenne River 58-59 F 3
Cheyenne River Indian Reservation 68-69 F 3
Cheyenne Wells, CO 68-69 E 6
Chezacut 48 EF 3
Chhamdo 166-167 H 5
Chhaprā = Chāpra 160-161 N 5
Chhārīkār = Chārikār 160-161 K 3-4
Chhatarpur [IND, Madhya Pradesh] 160-161 M 6
Chhattīsgarh 160-161 N 6
Chhergundo 166-167 H 5
Chhergundo Zhou = Yushu Zangzu Zizhizhou 166-167 GH 5
Chhibchang Tsho 166-167 G 5
Chhindvāṛā = Chhindwāra [IND ← Seoni] 160-161 M 6
Chhindwāra [IND ← Seoni] 160-161 M 6
Chhoṭā Andamān = Little Andaman 160-161 P 8
Chhoṭā Nikōbār = Little Nicobar 160-161 P 9
Chhumar 166-167 G 4-5
Chhushul 166-167 FG 6
Chiachi Island 52-53 d 2
Chia-hsing = Jiaxing 166-167 N 5
Chia-i 166-167 MN 7
Chia-li = Lharugö 166-167 G 5
Chia-ling Chiang = Jialing Jiang 166-167 K 5
Chia-mu-szŭ = Jiamusi 166-167 P 2
Chi-an = Ji'an [TJ, Jiangxi] 166-167 LM 6
Chi-an = Ji'an [TJ, Jilin] 170-171 EF 2
Chiang-chou = Xinjiang 166-167 L 4
Chiang Dao 174-175 CD 3
Chiange 198 B 5
Chiang-hsi = Jiangxi 166-167 LM 6
Chiang Khan 174-175 D 3
Chiang Mai 174-175 C 3
Chiang Rai 174-175 CD 3
Chiang-su = Jiangsu 166-167 MN 5
Chiapa, Río — = Rio Grande 58-59 H 8
Chiapas 58-59 H 8
Chiari 138-139 CD 3
Chiarraighe, Ceann — 116-117 AB 8
Chiàvari 138-139 C 3
Chiavenna 138-139 C 2
Chiayi 166-167 MN 7
Chiba 170-171 N 5
Chibabava 198 F 6
Chibemba 198 BC 5
Chibia 198 B 5
Chibinogorsk = Kirovsk 154-155 EF 4
Chibiny 142-143 F 2
Chibougamau 46-47 VW 7-8
Chibougamau, Lac — 50 OP 2
Chibougamau, la Réserve de — 50 OP 2
Chiburi-jima 170-171 J 5
Chibuto 198 F 6
Chica, Costa — 86-87 L 9
Chicacole = Shrīkākulam 160-161 N 7
Chicago, IL 58-59 J 3
Chicago, University of — 83 II b 2
Chicago Campus = Northwestern University 83 II b 1
Chicago Heights, IL 70-71 G 5
Chicago Lawn, Chicago-, IL 83 II a 2
Chicago Midway Airport 83 II a 2
Chicago Ridge, IL 83 II a 2
Chicago Sanitary and Ship Canal 83 II a 1-2
Chicago Stadium 83 II a 1
Chicago State University 83 II b 2
Chicapa, Rio — 198 D 3
Chic-Choqs, Monts — 46-47 X 8
Ch'i-ch = Qiqihar 166-167 N 2
Chichagof, AK 52-53 T 8
Chichagof, Cape — 52-53 HJ 7
Chichagof Island 46-47 J 6
Chichancanab, Laguna — 86-87 Q 8
Chiché, Rio — 98-99 LM 9
Chichén Itzá 58-59 J 7
Chichester 116-117 L 10
Chickaloon, AK 52-53 NO 6
Chickamauga, GA 78-79 G 3
Chickamauga Lake 78-79 G 3
Chickasaw, AL 78-79 EF 5
Chickasha, OK 58-59 G 4-5
Chicken, AK 52-53 QR 4
Chiclayo 98-99 CD 6
Chico, CA 58-59 B 4
Chico, TX 76-77 F 6
Chico, Río — [RA, Chubut] 103 C 6
Chico, Río — [RA, Santa Cruz ◁ Bahía Grande] 103 C 7
Chico, Río — [RA, Santa Cruz ◁ Río Gallegos] 103 C 7
Chico, Río — [YV] 98-99 F 2
Chicoa 198 F 5
Chicoana 103 CD 3
Chicoma Peak = Tschicoma Peak 76-77 AB 4
Chicontepec de Tejeda 86-87 LM 7
Chicopee, MA 72-73 K 3
Chicotte 51 E 3
Chicoutimi 46-47 WX 8
Chidester, AR 78-79 C 4
Chidley, Cape — 46-47 Y 5
Chi-do 170-171 EF 5
Chiefland, FL 80-81 b 2
Chiefs Point 72-73 F 2
Chiehmo = Chārchăn 166-167 F 4
Chiemsee 124 F 5
Chien-ch'ang = Jianchang [TJ → Benxi] 170-171 E 2
Chien-ch'ang = Jianchang [TJ ↙ Jinzhou] 170-171 B 2
Ch'ien-chiang = Qianjiang [TJ, Hubei] 166-167 L 5
Chiengi 198 E 3
Chiengmai = Chiang Mai 174-175 C 3
Chien-Ho = Jian He [TJ, river] 170-171 D 2
Chien-ko = Jiange 166-167 JK 5
Chien-ning = Jian'ou 166-167 M 6
Chien-ou = Jian'ou 166-167 M 6
Chien-p'ing = Jianping 170-171 B 2
Chien-shui = Jianshui 166-167 J 7
Ch'ien-wei = Qianwei 170-171 C 2
Chien-yang = Jianyang [TJ, Sichuan] 166-167 JK 5
Chieti 138-139 F 4
Chifeng 166-167 M 3
Chifre, Serra do — 98-99 L 8
Chiftak, AK 52-53 EF 6
Chiginagak, Mount — 52-53 e 1
Chigmit Mountains 52-53 L 6
Chignecto Bay 51 D 5
Chignik, AK 46-47 E 6
Chignik Lake 52-53 de 1
Chigyŏng 170-171 F 3
Chih-chiang = Zhijiang [TJ, Hunan] 166-167 KL 6
Ch'ih-fêng = Chifeng 166-167 M 3
Chih-fu = Yantai 166-167 N 4
Chihkiang = Zhijiang 166-167 KL 6
Chih-li Wan = Bo Hai 166-167 M 4
Chi-hsi = Jixi 166-167 P 2
Chihuahua 58-59 E 6
Chiingij gol 166-167 GH 2
Chii-san = Chiri-san 170-171 F 5
Chike = Xunke 166-167 O 2
Chikugo 170-171 H 6
Chikuminuk Lake 52-53 HJ 6
Chikwawa 198 FG 5
Chilako River 48 F 3
Chilapa de Alvarez 58-59 G 8
Chilās 160-161 L 3
Chilca 98-99 D 7
Chilcoot, CA 74-75 CD 3
Chilcotin River 48 F 3-4
Childersburg, AL 78-79 F 4
Childress, TX 76-77 DE 5
Chile 103 B 5-C 2
Chile Basin 34-35 O 5-6
Chilecito [RA, La Rioja] 103 C 3
Chilete 98-99 D 6
Chilhowee, MO 70-71 D 6
Chilia, Braţul — 138-139 N 3
Chilibre 58-59 b 2

218 **Chanch**

Chilicote 76-77 B 8
Ch'i-lien Shan = Qilian Shan 166-167 HJ 4
Chilikadrotna River 52-53 K 6
Chilikā Hrada = Chilka Lake 160-161 NO 7
Chililabombwe 198 E 4
Chi-lin = Jilin [TJ, administrative unit] 166-167 N 2-O 3
Chi-lin = Jilin [TJ, place] 166-167 O 3
Chilivani 138-139 C 5
Chilka Lake 160-161 NO 7
Chilko Lake 46-47 M 7
Chill Alaidh, Cuan — 116-117 B 6
Chillán 103 B 5
Chill Chiaráin, Cuan — 116-117 AB 7
Chillicothe, IL 70-71 F 5
Chillicothe, MO 58-59 H 3-4
Chillicothe, OH 58-59 K 4
Chillicothe, TX 76-77 E 5
Chilliwack 66-67 C 1
Chill Mhanntáin, Sléibhte — 116-117 E 7-8
Chillum, MD 82 II b 1
Chilly, ID 66-67 FG 3
Chiloé, Isla de — 103 AB 6
Chilok 154-155 UV 7
Chiloquin, OR 66-67 C 4
Chilpancingo de los Bravos 58-59 G 8
Chiltern Hills 116-117 KL 9
Chilton, WI 70-71 F 3
Chilung 166-167 N 6
Chilwa, Lake — 198 G 5
Chiman 88-89 G 10
Chiman tagh 166-167 FG 4
Chimborazo [EC, mountain] 98-99 D 5
Chimbote 98-99 D 6
Chimkent = Čimkent 154-155 M 9
Chimney Peak = One Tree Peak 76-77 B 6
Chimoio 198 F 5
Chimpay 103 C 5
China [MEX, Campeche] 86-87 P 8
China [MEX, Nuevo Leon] 86-87 L 5
China [TJ] 166-167 E-K 5
China Lake, CA 74-75 E 5
Chinan 170-171 F 5
Chinan = Jinan 166-167 M 4
Ch'in-an = Qin'an 166-167 K 5
Chinandega 58-59 J 9
China Point 74-75 D 6
Chinati Peak 76-77 B 8
Chinatown, San Francisco-, CA 83 I b 2
Chinbo 170-171 G 4
Chincha Alta 98-99 D 7
Chin-ch'êng = Jincheng 166-167 L 4
Chinchilla 182-183 K 5
Chinchilla de Monte-Aragón 132-133 G 9
Chinchorro, Banco — 58-59 J 8
Chinchow = Jinzhou 166-167 N 3
Chincoteague, VA 80-81 J 2
Chincoteague Bay 72-73 J 5
Chinde 198 G 5
Chin-do [ROK, island] 170-171 EF 5
Chindo [ROK, place] 170-171 F 5
Chindwin Myit 174-175 C 1-2
Ching-ch'uan = Yinchuan 166-167 JK 4
Ch'ing Hai = Chöch nuur 166-167 H 4
Chinghai = Qinghai 166-167 GH 4
Ching-ho = Jinghe [TJ, place] 166-167 E 3
Ch'ing-ho-ch'êng = Qinghecheng 170-171 E 2
Ch'ing-ho-mêng = Qinghemen 170-171 C 2
Ching-ku = Jinggu 166-167 J 7
Ching-ning = Jingning 166-167 K 4
Chingola 198 E 4
Ching-po Hu = Jingbo Hu 166-167 O 3
Ching-t'ai = Jingtai 166-167 J 4
Ch'ing-tao = Qingdao 166-167 N 4
Ch'ing-tui-tzŭ = Qingduizi 170-171 D 3
Ching-tung = Jingdong 166-167 J 7
Ch'ing-yang = Qingyang [TJ, Gansu] 166-167 K 4
Ching-yüan = Jingyuan 166-167 JK 4
Ch'ing-yüan = Qingyuan [TJ, Liaoning] 170-171 E 1
Chinhae 170-171 G 5
Chinhae-man 170-171 G 5
Chinhoyi 198 EF 5
Chin-hsien = Jin Xian [TJ, Liaoning ↗ Jinzhou] 170-171 C 2
Chin-hsien = Jin Xian [TJ, Liaoning ↑ Lüda] 166-167 N 4
Chinhsien = Jinzhou 166-167 N 3
Chin-hua = Jinhua 166-167 MN 6
Ch'in-huang-tao = Qinhuangdao 166-167 MN 3-4
Chiniak, Cape — 52-53 LM 8
Chiniak, Cape — 52-53 gh 1
Chi-ning = Jining [TJ, Inner Mongolia Aut. Reg.] 166-167 L 3
Chi-ning = Jining [TJ, Shandong] 166-167 M 4
Chinitna Bay 52-53 L 7
Chinju 166-167 O 4
Chinko 194-195 J 7
Chinle, AZ 74-75 J 4
Chinle Valley 74-75 J 4
Ch'in Ling = Qin Ling 166-167 KL 5
Chin-mên = Kinmen Dao 166-167 M 7
Chinnamp'o = Nampo 166-167 NO 4
Chinon 132-133 H 5
Chinook 49 C 5
Chinook, MT 68-69 B 1
Chinook Valley 48 HJ 1
Chino Valley, AZ 74-75 G 5
Chinquião = Zhenjiang 166-167 M 5
Chinsali 198 F 4
Chin-sha Chiang = Jinsha Jiang 166-167 J 6
Chinsura 160-161 O 6
Chinwangtao = Qinhuangdao 166-167 MN 3-4
Chinwithetha Taing 174-175 B 2
Ch'in-yang = Qinyang 166-167 L 4
Chinyŏng 170-171 G 5
Chiôco 198 F 5
Chioggia 138-139 E 3
Chios [GR, island] 138-139 L 6
Chíos [GR, place] 138-139 M 6
Chipata 198 F 4
Chipewyan Lake 49 B 2
Chipie River 50 GH 2
Chipinge 198 F 6
Chip Lake 48 K 3
Chipley, FL 78-79 G 5
Chipley, GA 78-79 G 4
Chipman 51 D 4
Chiporiro 198 F 5
Chippenham 116-117 JK 9
Chippewa Falls, WI 70-71 E 3
Chippewa Flowage 70-71 E 3
Chippewa Reservoir = Chippewa Flowage 70-71 E 3
Chippewa River [USA, Michigan] 70-71 H 4
Chippewa River [USA, Wisconsin] 70-71 DE 3
Chipping Norton 116-117 K 9
Chipping Sodbury 116-117 JK 9
Chiputneticook Lakes 72-73 MN 2
Chiquimula 58-59 HJ 9
Chiquitos, Llanos de — 98-99 G 8
Chira Bazar 166-167 DE 4
Chiraz = Shīrāz 160-161 G 5
Chiredzi 198 F 6
Chirfa 194-195 G 4
Chiricahua National Monument 74-75 J 6-7
Chiricahua Peak 74-75 J 7
Chirikof Island 46-47 EF 6
Chiriquí 88-89 E 10
Chiriquí, Golfo de — 58-59 K 10
Chiriquí, Laguna de — 58-59 K 9-10
Chiri-san 170-171 F 5
Chiromo 198 G 5
Chirripó Grande, Cerro — 58-59 K 10
Chirundu 198 E 5
Chisamba 198 E 4-5
Chisana, AK 52-53 Q 5
Chisana River 52-53 R 5
Chisec 86-87 P 10
Chisel Lake 46-47 QR 7
Chi-shih Shan = Amnyemachhen Gangri 166-167 HJ 5
Chisholm 48 KL 2
Chishtian Mandi = Chishtiyān Maṇḍī 160-161 L 5
Chishtiyān Maṇḍī 160-161 L 5
Chisimaio = Kismaanyo 198 H 2
Chisos Mountains 76-77 C 8
Chistochina, AK 52-53 PQ 5
Chita = Čita 154-155 V 7
Chitado 198 B 5
Chita-hantō 170-171 L 5
Ch'i-t'ai = Qitai 166-167 FG 3
Chitanana River 52-53 L 4
Chitek 49 DE 4
Chitek Lake 49 J 4
Chitembo 198 C 4
Chitina, AK 52-53 P 6
Chitina River 52-53 Q 6
Chitogarh = Chittaurgarh 160-161 L 6
Chitose 170-171 b 2
Chitradurga 160-161 M 8
Chitrāl 160-161 L 3
Chitré 58-59 K 10
Chittagong = Chāṭṭagām 160-161 P 6
Chittaldurga = Chitradurga 160-161 M 8
Chittaorgarh = Chittaurgarh 160-161 L 6
Chittaurgarh 160-161 L 6
Chittor 160-161 M 8
Chittūru = Chittor 160-161 M 8
Chiuchuan = Jiuquan 166-167 H 4
Chiumbe, Rio — 198 D 3
Chiume 198 D 4-5
Ch'iung-chou Hai-hsia = Qiongzhou Haixia 166-167 KL 7
Chiungshan = Qiongshan 166-167 L 8
Ch'iung-tung = Qionghai 166-167 L 8
Chiuta, Lagoa — 198 G 4
Chiuta, Lake — 198 G 4
Chiva [SU] 154-155 L 9
Chivasso 138-139 B 3
Chivay 98-99 E 8
Chivilcoy 103 DE 4
Chivu 198 F 5
Chiwanda 198 FG 4
Chiweta 198 F 4
Chixoy, Río — 58-59 H 8
Chjargas 166-167 G 2
Chjargas nuur 166-167 GH 2
Chloch Liath, An — 116-117 EF 7
Chloch na gCoillte, Cuan — 116-117 C 9
Chloride, AZ 74-75 F 5
Chmel'nickij 142-143 E 6
Choapas, Las — 86-87 NO 9
Chobe 198 D 5
Chobe National Park 198 DE 5
Chocaya 98-99 F 9
Chocca 98-99 D 7
Chochiang = Charqiliq 166-167 F 4
Choch'iwŏn 170-171 F 4
Chöch nuur 166-167 H 4
Chöch Šili 166-167 G 4
Chöch Šili uul 166-167 FG 4
Chocolate Mountains 74-75 F 6
Chocontá 98-99 E 3
Choctaw, AL 78-79 E 4
Choctawhatchee Bay 78-79 F 5
Choctawhatchee River 78-79 FG 5
Ch'o-do [North Korea] 170-171 E 3-4
Ch'o-do [ROK] 170-171 F 5
Chodžambas 160-161 JK 3
Chodžejli 154-155 K 9
Chodžent = Leninabad 160-161 KL 2-3
Chodzież 124 H 2
Choele-Choel 103 CD 5
Choibalsan = Čojbalsan 166-167 L 2
Choire Chlais, Sgùrr a — 116-117 FG 3
Choiseul 174-175 j 6
Chojna 124 G 2
Chojnice 124 HJ 2
Chōkai-zan 170-171 MN 3
Chōḻamaṇḍala = Coromandel Coast 160-161 N 7-8
Cholame, CA 74-75 CD 5
Chold = Chuld 166-167 K 2-3
Cholet 132-133 G 5
Chŏlla-namdo 170-171 F 5
Chŏlla-pukto 170-171 F 5
Chollerton 116-117 JK 5
Cholm 142-143 F 4
Cholmogory 154-155 G 5
Cholmsk 154-155 b 8
Cholodnoje 142-143 N 3
Cholos nuur 166-167 H 4
Ch'ŏlsan 170-171 E 3
Cholula 86-87 L 8
Choluteca 58-59 J 9
Choma 198 E 5
Chomedey 82 I a 1
Chonamara, Sléibhte — 116-117 AB 7
Ch'ŏnan 170-171 F 4
Chon Buri 174-175 D 4
Chŏnch'ŏn 170-171 F 2
Chone 98-99 CD 5
Ch'ŏng'chŏn-gang 170-171 EF 2-3
Chongdjin = Ch'ŏngjin 166-167 OP 3
Chŏnggŏ-dong 170-171 E 3
Ch'ŏngha 170-171 G 4
Ch'ŏngjin 166-167 OP 3
Chongjin = Ch'ŏngjin 166-167 OP 3
Chŏngju 166-167 O 4
Chongming 166-167 N 5
Chongor 166-167 L 2
Chongor = Bajan Adraga 166-167 KL 2
Chongor Oboo Sum = Bajandalaj 166-167 J 3
Chongor Tagh = Qungur tagh 166-167 D 4
Ch'ŏngp'yŏngch'ŏn 170-171 FG 4
Chongqing 166-167 K 6
Ch'ŏngsan-do 170-171 F 5
Chongshan = Chongzuo 166-167 K 7
Ch'ongsŏktu-ri 170-171 EF 3
Chongsŏng 170-171 GH 1
Chŏngŭp 170-171 F 5
Ch'ŏngyang [ROK] 170-171 F 4
Chongzuo 166-167 K 7
Chŏnju 166-167 O 4
Chonos, Archipiélago de los — 103 AB 6-7
Chonuu 154-155 b 4
Chooloj Gov' 166-167 H 3
Chop'or 142-143 H 5-6
Chor 154-155 Za 8
Chorasan = Khorāsān 160-161 H 3-4
Chôra Sfakíon 138-139 L 8
Chorcaighe, Cuan — 116-117 CD 9
Chordogoj 154-155 W 5
Chor He 166-167 N 2
Chorinsk 154-155 U 7
Chorley 116-117 J 7
Chorog 160-161 L 3
Chorrera, La — [PA] 58-59 b 3
Chorreras, Cerro — 86-87 GH 4
Chŏrwŏn 170-171 F 3
Chŏryŏng-do = Yŏng-do 170-171 G 5
Chorzele 124 K 2
Chorzów 124 J 3
Chosedachard 142-143 L 2
Chŏsen-kaikyō 166-167 O 5
Chōshi 170-171 N 5
Chos-Malal 103 BC 5
Chosŏn-man = Tonghan-man 166-167 O 4
Choszczno 124 GH 2
Chota 98-99 D 6
Chota Nāgpur 160-161 NO 6
Choteau, MT 66-67 G 2
Chotin 142-143 E 6
Chou Shan = Zhoushan Dao 166-167 N 5-6
Chou-shan Ch'ün-tao = Zhoushan Qundao 166-167 N 5
Chouteau, OK 76-77 G 4
Chovd [Mongolia, administrative unit = 3 ◁] 166-167 G 2
Chovd [Mongolia, place] 166-167 G 2
Chovd gol 166-167 G 2
Chövsgöl [Mongolia, administrative unit = 6 ◁] 166-167 J 1
Chövsgöl [Mongolia, place] 166-167 KL 3
Chövsgöl nuur 166-167 J 1
Chowan River 80-81 H 2
Chowchilla, CA 74-75 C 4
Chowiet Island 52-53 e 1
Choybalsan = Čojbalsan 166-167 L 2
Chrisman, IL 70-71 G 6
Christchurch [GB] 116-117 K 10
Christchurch [NZ] 182-183 OP 8
Christian, AK 52-53 P 3
Christiania = Oslo 114-115 D 8
Christian Island 72-73 F 2
Christian River 52-53 P 3
Christiansburg, VA 80-81 FG 2
Christianshåb = Qasigiánguit 46-47 ab 4
Christian Sound 52-53 v 8-9
Christiansted 88-89 OP 6
Christie Bay 46-47 O 5
Christina, MT 68-69 B 2
Christina Range 66-67 D 1
Christina River 49 C 2
Christmas 34-35 K 4
Christmas Creek 182-183 E 3
Christmas Island [AUS] 174-175 E 9
Christmas Island [CDN] 51 F 5
Christmas Mount 52-53 GH 4
Christoval, TX 76-77 D 7
Chromo, CO 68-69 C 7
Chromtau 154-155 K 7
Chruach Ghorm, An — 116-117 CD 6
Chrudim 124 GH 4
Chrysê 138-139 LM 8
Chuang-ho = Zhuanghe 170-171 D 3
Chubb Crater = New Quebec Crater 46-47 VW 5
Chubbuck, CA 74-75 F 5
Chubisgalt = Chövsgöl 166-167 KL 3
Chubsugul = Chövsgöl nuur 166-167 J 1
Chŭbu 170-171 LM 4-5
Chubut 103 BC 6
Chubut, Río — 103 C 6
Chucheng = Zhucheng 166-167 MN 4
Chu-chi = Zhuji 166-167 N 6
Ch'ü-ching = Qujing 166-167 J 6
Ch'ü-chou = Qu Xian 166-167 M 6
Chu-chou = Zhuzhou 166-167 L 6
Chuchow = Zhuzhou 166-167 L 6
Ch'üeh-shan = Queshan 166-167 L 5
Chugach Islands 52-53 M 7
Chugach Mountains 46-47 GH 5
Chuginadak Island 52-53 l 4
Chugoku 170-171 HJ 5
Chūgoku-sammyaku 170-171 JK 5
Chuguchak 166-167 E 2
Chŭgŭchak = Tarbagataj 166-167 EF 2
Chugwater, WY 68-69 D 5
Chuhsien = Qu Xian 166-167 M 6
Ch'u-hsiung = Chuxiong 166-167 J 7
Chü-hua Tao = Juhua Dao 170-171 C 2
Chuilnuk Mountains 52-53 HJ 6
Ch'uja-do 170-171 F 6
Chukchi Peninsula = Čukotskij poluostrov 154-155 kl 4
Chukchi Plateau 30 B 35
Chukchi Sea 30 BC 35-36
Chuki = Zhuji 166-167 N 6
Chukot Autonomous Area 154-155 g-k 4
Chukotskiy, Cape — = mys Čukotskij 154-155 l 5
Chukudu Kraal 198 D 6
Chulaq Aqqan Su 166-167 G 4
Chula Vista, CA 58-59 C 5
Chuld 166-167 K 2-3
Chulga 142-143 L 3
Chulitna, AK 52-53 N 5
Chulitna River 52-53 MN 5
Chü-liu-ho = Juliuhe 170-171 D 1
Chulp'o 170-171 F 5
Chulucanas 98-99 CD 6
Chulumani 98-99 F 8
Chumbicha 103 C 3
Chum Phae 174-175 D 3
Chumphon 174-175 CD 4
Chumsaeng 174-175 D 3
Chumunjin 170-171 G 4
Chuna = Čun'a 154-155 ST 5
Ch'unch'ŏn 166-167 O 4
Chungam-ni 170-171 G 5
Ch'ungch'ŏng-namdo 170-171 F 4
Ch'ungch'ŏng-pukto 170-171 FG 4
Chŭngges 166-167 E 3
Chunghwa 170-171 EF 3
Ch'ungju 170-171 FG 4
Chungking = Chongqing 166-167 K 6
Ch'ung-ming = Chongming 166-167 N 5
Ch'ungmu 170-171 G 5
Chŭngsan 170-171 E 3
Chungshan = Zhongshan 166-167 L 7
Chung-tien = Zhongdian 166-167 HJ 6
Chŭngüj gol 166-167 GH 2
Chung-wei = Zhongwei 166-167 JK 4
Chungyang Shanmo 166-167 N 7
Chunu, Cape — 52-53 u 7
Chunya 198 F 3
Chupadera, Mesa — 76-77 A 5-6
Chuquibamba 98-99 E 8
Chuquicamata 103 C 2
Chuquisaca = Sucre 98-99 FG 8
Chur 124 D 5
Churchill, ID 66-67 FG 4
Churchill [CDN] 46-47 RS 6
Churchill, Cape — 46-47 S 6
Churchill Falls 46-47 XY 7
Churchill Lake 49 DE 2-3
Churchill Peak 46-47 LM 6
Churchill River [CDN ◁ Hamilton Inlet] 46-47 Y 7
Churchill River [CDN ◁ Hudson Bay] 46-47 RS 6
Church Point, LA 78-79 CD 5
Churchs Ferry, ND 68-69 G 1
Churu 160-161 LM 5
Chusei-hokudō = Ch'ungch'ŏng-pukto 170-171 FG 4
Chusei-nandō = Ch'ungch'ŏng-namdo 170-171 F 4
Chu-shan = Zhushan 166-167 KL 5
Chusistan = Khūzestān 160-161 F 4
Chuska Mountains 74-75 J 4-5
Chust 142-143 D 6
Chutag 166-167 J 2
Chute-aux-Outardes 51 BC 3
Chute-des-Passes 51 A 3
Chuučnar 166-167 G 5
Chuŭronjang 170-171 GH 2
Chuvash Autonomous Soviet Socialist Republic = 4 ◁ 154-155 H 6
Chuxiong 166-167 J 7
Chuxiong Yizu Zizhizhou 166-167 J 6
Chuxiong Zizhizhou 166-167 J 6
Chuy 103 F 4
Chu Yang Sin 174-175 E 4
Chužir 154-155 U 7
Chvalynsk 142-143 J 5
Ciarraighe 116-117 B 8-9
Cibit 154-155 Q 7
Cibola, AZ 74-75 F 6
Cibuta 74-75 H 7
Cicero, IL 70-71 G 5
Cícero Dantas 98-99 M 7
Ciche, Sgùrr na — 116-117 F 3
Ciechanów 124 K 2
Ciego de Ávila 58-59 L 7
Ciénaga 98-99 DE 2
Cienega, NM 76-77 B 6
Cienfuegos 58-59 K 7
Cieza 132-133 G 9
Cifuentes 132-133 F 8
Čiganak 154-155 N 8-9
Cihuatlán 86-87 H 8
Čiili 154-155 M 9
Cijara, Embalse de — 132-133 E 9
Cilacap 174-175 E 8
Cill Áirne 116-117 B 8
Cill Chainnigh 116-117 D 8
Cill Chaoidhe 116-117 AB 8
Cill Dalua 116-117 C 8
Cill Dara [IRL, administrative unit] 116-117 E 7-8
Cill Dara [IRL, place] 116-117 E 7
Cill Mhantáin 116-117 EF 7-8
Cill na Sean-rátha 116-117 D 6-7
Cill Ruis 116-117 B 8
Cilo dağı 142-143 H 8
Cima, CA 74-75 F 5
Cimaltepec 58-59 G 8
Cimarron, KS 68-69 FG 7
Cimarron, NM 76-77 B 4
Cimarron River, North Fork — 76-77 D 4
Čimbaj 154-155 KL 9
Čimkent 154-155 M 9
Ciml'ansk 142-143 H 6
Ciml'anskoje vodochranilišče 142-143 H 6
Cimmarron River 58-59 F 4
Cimone, Monte — 138-139 D 3
Cîmpina 138-139 LM 3
Cîmpulung 138-139 L 3
Cîmpulung Moldovenesc 138-139 LM 2
Cinca 132-133 H 8
Cincinnati, OH 58-59 K 4
Cinco de Maio, Cachoeira — 98-99 L 11
Cinder River 52-53 de 1
Cinema 48 FG 3
Cingaly 154-155 MN 5
Cinnabar Mountain 66-67 E 4
Cinta, Serra da — 98-99 K 6
Cintalapa de Figueroa 86-87 NO 9
Cinto, Mont — 138-139 C 4
Cintra = Sintra [BR] 98-99 G 6
Ciotat, la — 132-133 K 7
Čiovo 138-139 G 4
Cipikan 154-155 V 7
Cipó 98-99 M 7
Circel Campus = University of Illinois 83 II ab 1
Circeo, Monte — 138-139 E 5
Čirčik 154-155 M 9
Circle, AK 46-47 H 4
Circle, MT 68-69 D 2
Circle Cliffs 74-75 H 4
Circle Hot Springs, AK 52-53 PQ 4
Circleville, OH 72-73 E 5
Circleville, UT 74-75 G 3
Cirebon 174-175 E 8
Cirenaica = Barqah 194-195 J 2
Cirencester 116-117 JK 9
Cirene = Shaḥḥāt 194-195 J 2
Cirí, Río — 58-59 a 3
Cirò Marina 138-139 G 6
Čirpan 138-139 L 4
Cisa, Passo della — 138-139 CD 3
Cisco, TX 76-77 E 6
Cisco, UT 74-75 J 3
Cisne, IL 70-71 F 6
Cisne, Ilhas del — = Swan Islands 58-59 K 8
Cisneros 98-99 DE 3
Cisterna di Latina 138-139 E 5
Cisternino 138-139 G 5
Čistopol' 154-155 HJ 6
Čita 154-155 V 7
Citadelle, La — 88-89 K 5
Citaré, Rio — 98-99 L 4
Citlaltépetl 58-59 G 8
Citra, FL 80-81 bc 2
Citronelle, AL 78-79 E 5
Citrusdal 198 CD 8
Citrus Height, CA 74-75 C 3
Citrus Heights, CA 58-59 B 4
Cittanova 138-139 FG 6
City Island 82 III d 1
City of Commerce, CA 83 III d 1-2
Ciucaş 138-139 LM 3
Ciudad Altamirano 86-87 K 8
Ciudad Bolívar 98-99 G 3
Ciudad Bolivia 98-99 E 3
Ciudad Camargo = Camargo 58-59 E 6
Ciudad Cancún 86-87 R 7
Ciudad Delicias = Delicias 58-59 E 6
Ciudad del Maíz 86-87 L 6
Ciudadela 132-133 J 8-9
Ciudad Guayana 98-99 G 3
Ciudad Guerrero 86-87 G 3
Ciudad Juárez = Juárez 58-59 E 5
Ciudad Lerdo 58-59 EF 6
Ciudad Linares = Linares 58-59 G 7
Ciudad Mendoza 86-87 M 8
Ciudad Mier 86-87 L 4
Ciudad Ojeda 98-99 E 2-3
Ciudad Pemex 86-87 O 9-P 8
Ciudad Piar 98-99 G 3
Ciudad Real 132-133 EF 9
Ciudad-Rodrigo 132-133 DE 8
Ciudad Serdán 86-87 LM 8
Ciudad Valles 58-59 G 7
Cìvita Castellana 138-139 E 4
Civitanova Marche 138-139 EF 4
Civitavècchia 138-139 D 4
Çivril 142-143 EF 8
Čiža 154-155 G 4
Cizre 160-161 E 3
Čkalov = Orenburg 154-155 JK 7
Clackmannan 116-117 H 4
Clacton on Sea 116-117 h 7
Clain 132-133 H 5
Clair 49 FG 4
Cláir, Abha an — 116-117 BC 7
Claire, Lake — 46-47 O 6
Clairemont, TX 76-77 D 6
Clairton, PA 72-73 FG 4
Clamecy 132-133 J 5
Clan Alpine Mountains 74-75 DE 3
Clanton, AL 78-79 F 4
Clanwilliam 198 C 8
Clapham, NM 76-77 C 4
Clár, An — 116-117 BC 8
Clara = Clárach 116-117 D 7
Clara, River — = Abha an Cláir 116-117 BC 7

Clara 219

Clárach 116-117 D 7
Clara City, MN 70-71 C 3
Clara River 182-183 H 3
Clár Chlainne Mhuiris 116-117 BC 7
Clare, MI 70-71 H 4
Clare [AUS] 182-183 G 6
Clare [GB] 116-117 M 8
Clare = An Clár 116-117 BC 8
Clare = Cliara 116-117 A 7
Claremont, NH 72-73 KL 3
Claremont, SD 68-69 GH 3
Claremore, OK 76-77 G 4
Claremorris = Clár Chlainne Mhuiris 116-117 BC 7
Clarence, Cape — 46-47 S 3
Clarence, Isla — 103 B 8
Clarence Island 31 C 31
Clarence Strait [AUS] 182-183 F 2
Clarence Strait [USA] 52-53 w 8-x 9
Clarendon, AR 78-79 D 3
Clarendon, TX 76-77 D 5
Clarendon, Arlington-, VA 82 II a 2
Clarenville 51 J 3
Claresholm 48 KL 4
Clarinda, IA 70-71 C 5
Clarion, IA 70-71 CD 4
Clarion, PA 72-73 G 4
Clarión, Isla — 86-87 C 8
Clarión Fracture Zone 34-35 KL 4
Clark, CO 68-69 C 5
Clark, SD 68-69 H 3
Clark, Lake — 52-53 K 6
Clarkdale, AZ 74-75 G 5
Clarke City 46-47 X 7
Clarke Island 182-183 J 8
Clarke River 182-183 HJ 3
Clarkfield, MN 70-71 BC 3
Clark Fork, ID 66-67 E 1
Clark Fork River 58-59 CD 2
Clark Hill Lake 80-81 E 4
Clarkia, ID 66-67 EF 2
Clark Mountain 74-75 F 5
Clark Point 72-73 EF 2
Clarks, NE 68-69 GH 5
Clarksburg, WV 58-59 K 4
Clarksdale, MS 58-59 HJ 5
Clarks Fork 68-69 B 3
Clark's Harbour 51 CD 6
Clarks Point, AK 52-53 HJ 7
Clarkston, WA 66-67 E 2
Clarksville, AR 78-79 C 3
Clarksville, IA 70-71 D 4
Clarksville, TN 58-59 J 4
Clarksville, TX 76-77 G 6
Clarksville, VA 80-81 G 2
Claude, TX 76-77 D 5
Claudy 116-117 D 6
Claunch, NM 76-77 AB 5
Claxton, GA 80-81 EF 4
Clay, KY 70-71 G 7
Clay, WV 72-73 F 5
Clay Belt 46-47 T-V 7
Clay Center, KS 68-69 H 6
Clay Center, NE 68-69 GH 5
Claydon 68-69 B 1
Claymont, DE 72-73 J 5
Claypool, AZ 74-75 H 6
Clayton, AL 78-79 G 5
Clayton, GA 80-81 E 3
Clayton, ID 66-67 F 3
Clayton, IL 70-71 E 5
Clayton, MO 70-71 E 6
Clayton, NC 80-81 G 3
Clayton, NM 76-77 C 4
Clayton, NY 72-73 HJ 2
Clayton, OK 76-77 G 5
Clearbrook, MN 70-71 C 2
Clear Creek 52-53 O 4
Clearcreek, UT 74-75 H 3
Cleare, Cape — 52-53 NO 7
Clearfield, PA 72-73 G 4
Clearfield, UT 66-67 GH 5
Clear Hills 46-47 N 6
Clearing, IL 83 II a 2
Clear Island = Oileán Cléire 116-117 B 9
Clear Lake 74-75 B 3
Clear Lake, IA 70-71 D 4
Clear Lake, MN 70-71 D 3
Clear Lake, SD 68-69 H 3
Clear Lake, WI 70-71 DE 3
Clear Lake Reservoir 66-67 C 5
Clearmont, WY 68-69 C 3
Clear Prairie 48 H 1
Clearwater 48 G 4
Clearwater, FL 58-59 C 6
Clearwater Lake [CDN] 46-47 VW 6
Clearwater Lake [USA] 78-79 D 2
Clearwater Mountains 66-67 F 2-3
Clearwater River [CDN ◁ Athabasca River] 49 D 2
Clearwater River [CDN ◁ North Saskatchewan River] 48 K 3-4
Clearwater River [USA] 66-67 E 2
Clearwater River, North Fork — 66-67 F 2
Clearwater River, South Fork — 66-67 F 3
Cleburne, TX 58-59 G 3
Cle Elum, WA 66-67 C 2
Cleethorpes 116-117 LM 7
Cléire, Ceann — 116-117 B 9
Cléire, Oileán — 116-117 B 9
Clen Cove, NY 82 III e 1
Clendenin, WV 72-73 F 5
Cleobury Mortimer 116-117 J 8
Clermont, FL 80-81 bc 2
Clermont [AUS] 182-183 J 4
Clermont [CDN] 51 A 4
Clermont-Ferrand 132-133 J 6
Clevedon 116-117 J 9
Cleveland 116-117 HJ 6
Cleveland, MS 78-79 D 4
Cleveland, MT 68-69 B 1
Cleveland, OH 58-59 K 3
Cleveland, OK 76-77 F 4
Cleveland, TN 58-59 K 4
Cleveland, TX 76-77 G 7
Cleveland, WI 70-71 G 4
Cleveland, Mount — 58-59 D 2
Cleveland Heights, OH 72-73 F 4
Clevelândia do Norte 98-99 N 3
Cleveland Park, Washington-, DC 82 II a 1
Clew Bay = Cuan Modh 116-117 B 7
Clewiston, FL 80-81 c 3
Cley next the Sea 116-117 h 6
Cliara 116-117 A 7
Clifden = An Clochán 116-117 AB 7
Cliff, NM 74-75 J 6
Cliff Lake, MT 66-67 H 3
Cliffs, ID 66-67 E 4
Clifton 182-183 K 5
Clifton, AZ 74-75 J 6
Clifton, KS 68-69 H 6
Clifton, NJ 72-73 J 4
Clifton, TX 76-77 F 7
Clifton, WY 68-69 D 4
Clifton Forge, VA 80-81 G 2
Clifton Hills 182-183 G 5
Climax 68-69 B 1
Climax, CO 68-69 C 6
Climax, GA 78-79 G 5
Climax, MN 68-69 H 2
Clinchco, VA 80-81 E 2
Clinch Mountain 80-81 E 2
Clinch Mountains 80-81 E 2
Clinch River 80-81 E 2
Cline 86-87 KL 3
Cline, TX 76-77 D 8
Clint, TX 76-77 A 7
Clinton, AR 78-79 C 3
Clinton, IA 58-59 H 3
Clinton, IL 70-71 F 5
Clinton, IN 70-71 G 6
Clinton, KY 78-79 E 2
Clinton, LA 78-79 D 5
Clinton, MI 70-71 H 4
Clinton, MO 70-71 D 6
Clinton, MS 78-79 D 4
Clinton, MT 66-67 G 2
Clinton, NC 80-81 G 3
Clinton, OK 76-77 E 5
Clinton, SC 80-81 F 3
Clinton, TN 78-79 GH 2
Clinton, WI 70-71 F 4
Clinton [CDN, British Columbia] 48 G 4
Clinton [CDN, Ontario] 72-73 F 3
Clinton, Cape — 182-183 K 4
Clinton Creek 52-53 R 4
Clintonville, WI 70-71 F 3
Clio, AL 78-79 G 5
Clio, MI 70-71 J 4
Clipperton, Île — 58-59 E 9
Clipperton Fracture Zone 34-35 LM 4
Clisham 116-117 DE 3
Cloates, Point — 182-183 B 4
Clochán, An — 116-117 AB 7
Cloch na gCoillte 116-117 BC 9
Clonakilty = Cloch na gCoillte 116-117 BC 9
Clonakilty Bay = Cuan Cloch na gCoillte 116-117 C 9
Cloncurry 182-183 H 4
Cloncurry River 182-183 H 3
Clonmel = Cluain Meala 116-117 D 8
Clo-oose 66-67 A 1
Cloppenburg 124 CD 2
Cloquet, MN 70-71 D 2
Cloquet River 70-71 DE 2
Cloucester, VA 80-81 H 2
Cloudcroft, NM 76-77 B 6
Cloud Peak 58-59 E 3
Cloudy Mount 52-53 J 5
Clover, VA 80-81 G 2
Cloverdale, CA 74-75 B 3
Cloverdale, NM 74-75 J 7
Cloverport, KY 70-71 G 7
Clovis, CA 74-75 D 4
Clovis, NM 58-59 F 5
Cluain Meala 116-117 D 8
Cluj-Napoca 138-139 KL 2
Clun 116-117 HJ 8
Cluny 132-133 K 5
Clutha River 182-183 N 9
Clwyd 116-117 H 7-8
Clyde 46-47 X 3
Clyde, KS 68-69 H 6
Clyde, ND 68-69 G 1
Clyde, OH 72-73 E 4
Clyde, TX 76-77 E 6
Clyde, Firth of — 116-117 G 5
Clyde, River — 116-117 H 5
Clydebank 116-117 G 5
Clyde Park, MT 66-67 H 3
Clyo, GA 80-81 F 4
Cnossos = Knōssós 138-139 L 8
Coa 132-133 D 8
Coachella, CA 74-75 E 6
Coachella Canal 74-75 EF 6
Coahoma, TX 76-77 D 6
Coahuayutla de Guerrero 86-87 K 8
Coahuila 58-59 F 6
Coalcomán, Sierra de — 86-87 J 8
Coal Creek 66-67 F 1
Coal Creek, AK 52-53 PQ 4
Coaldale 66-67 G 1
Coaldale, NV 74-75 E 3
Coalgate, OK 76-77 F 5
Coal Harbour 48 CD 4
Coalinga, CA 74-75 C 4
Coalmont, CO 68-69 C 5
Coalville 116-117 K 8
Coalville, UT 66-67 H 5
Coamo 88-89 N 5-6
Coari 98-99 G 5
Coari, Lago do — 98-99 G 6-7
Coari, Rio — 98-99 G 5-6
Coast 198 GH 2
Coastal Cordillera = Cordillera de la Costa 103 B 4-5
Coast Mountains 46-47 K 6-M 7
Coast Range 58-59 B 2-C 5
Coatá 98-99 C 8
Coatá, Cachoeira do — 98-99 G 6
Coatbridge 116-117 GH 5
Coatepec 58-59 G 8
Coatesville, PA 72-73 HJ 4
Coaticook 72-73 KL 2
Coats Island 46-47 U 5
Coats Land 31 B 33-34
Coatzacoalcos 58-59 H 8
Cobalt 72-73 G 1
Cobán 58-59 H 8
Cobar 182-183 J 6
Cobble Hill 66-67 AB 1
Cobbo = Kobo 194-195 MN 6
Cobe = Kōbe 166-167 PQ 5
Cobequid Mountains 51 DE 5
Cobh = An Cóf 116-117 C 9
Cobham River 50 B 1
Cobija 98-99 F 7
Coblence = Koblenz 124 C 3
Cobleskill, NY 72-73 J 3
Coboconk 72-73 G 2
Cobourg 72-73 GH 3
Cobourg Peninsula 182-183 F 2
Cobre, NV 66-67 F 5
Cobres, San Antonio de los — 103 C 2
Coburg 124 E 3
Coburg, OR 66-67 B 3
Coburg Island 46-47 V 2
Coca 132-133 E 8
Cocalcomán de Matamoros 86-87 J 8
Cocanada = Kākināda 160-161 N 7
Cochabamba [BOL, place] 98-99 F 8
Cochem 124 C 3
Cochi = Kōchi 166-167 P 5
Cochim = Cochin 160-161 M 9
Cochin 160-161 M 9
Cochinchina = Nam Bô 174-175 DE 5
Cochinos, Bahía de — 88-89 F 3-4
Cochise, AZ 74-75 J 6
Cochran, GA 80-81 E 4
Cochrane [CDN, Alberta] 48 K 4
Cochrane [CDN, Ontario] 46-47 U 8
Cochrane River 46-47 Q 6
Cockburn, Canal — 103 B 8
Cockburn Island 50 K 4
Cockburn Land 46-47 UV 3
Cockermouth 116-117 H 6
Cockeysville, MD 72-73 H 5
Coclé 88-89 F 10
Coco, Cayo — 88-89 G 3
Coco, El — 58-59 b 3
Coco, Isla del — 98-99 B 3
Coco, Río — 58-59 K 9
Côco, Rio do — 98-99 O 9
Cocoa, FL 80-81 c 2
Coco Channel 174-175 B 4
Cocodrie, LA 78-79 D 6
Cocolalla, ID 66-67 E 1
Coconino Plateau 74-75 G 4-5
Cocos [AUS] 26-27 O 6
Cocos = Isla del Coco 98-99 B 3
Coco Solo 58-59 b 2
Cocos Rise 34-35 N 4
Cocula 86-87 HJ 7
Cocuy, El — 98-99 E 3
Cod, Cape — 58-59 N 3
Codajás 98-99 G 5
Codera, Cabo — 98-99 F 2
Coderre 49 E 5
Codihue 103 BC 5
Codó 98-99 L 5
Codroy 51 G 4
Cody, NE 68-69 F 4
Cody, WY 68-69 B 3
Coeli 198 C 4
Coen 182-183 H 2
Coeroeni 98-99 K 3
Coesfeld 124 C 3
Coeur d'Alene, ID 58-59 C 2
Coeur d'Alene Indian Reservation 66-67 E 2
Coeur d'Alene Lake 66-67 E 2
Cóf, An — 116-117 C 9
Coffee Creek 52-53 S 5
Coffeeville, MS 78-79 DE 4
Coffeyville, KS 58-59 G 4
Coffin Bay 182-183 FG 6
Coffin Bay Peninsula 182-183 FG 6
Coffs Harbour 182-183 K 6
Cofrentes 132-133 G 9
Cofu = Kōfu 166-167 Q 4
Cofuini, Rio — 98-99 K 4
Cogealac 138-139 N 3
Coggeshall 116-117 M 9
Cognac 132-133 G 6
Cohagen, MT 68-69 C 2
Cohoes, NY 72-73 K 3
Cohuna 182-183 HJ 7
Cohutta Mountian 78-79 G 3
Coi, Sông = Sông Nhi Ha 174-175 D 2
Coiba, Isla — 58-59 K 10
Coihaique 103 B 7
Coimbatore 160-161 M 8
Coimbra [P] 132-133 C 8
Coín 132-133 E 10
Coin, IA 70-71 C 5
Coipasa, Salar de — 98-99 F 8
Coire = Chur 124 D 5
Coirib, Loch — 116-117 BC 7
Čojbalsan 166-167 L 2
Čojbalsangijn Ajmag = Dornod ◁ 166-167 LM 2
Cojimies 98-99 C 4
Cojudo Blanco, Cerro — 103 BC 7
Cojutepeque 88-89 B 8
Cokato, MN 70-71 C 3
Cokeville, WY 66-67 H 4
Čokurdach 154-155 cd 3
Colac 182-183 H 7
Colapur = Kōlhāpur 160-161 L 7
Cólar = Kōlār Gold Fields 160-161 M 8
Colares 132-133 C 9
Colbeck, Cape — 31 B 20-21
Colbert, OK 76-77 F 6
Colbert, WA 66-67 E 2
Colby, KS 68-69 F 6
Colca, Río — 98-99 E 8
Colchester 116-117 gh 7
Colchester, VT 72-73 K 2
Cold Bay 52-53 b 2
Cold Bay, AK 52-53 b 2
Cold Lake [CDN, lake] 49 D 3
Cold Lake [CDN, place] 49 C 3
Cold Spring, MN 70-71 C 3
Coldspring, TX 76-77 G 7
Coldstream 116-117 J 5
Coldwater 72-73 G 2
Coldwater, KS 76-77 E 4
Coldwater, MI 70-71 H 5
Coldwater, OH 70-71 H 5
Coldwell 70-71 G 1
Colebrook, NH 72-73 L 2
Cole Camp, MO 70-71 D 6
Coleen Mount 52-53 Q 3
Coleen River 52-53 Q 2
Coleford 116-117 J 9
Colégio = Porto Real do Colégio 98-99 M 6-7
Coleman 66-67 F 1
Coleman, MI 70-71 H 4
Coleman, TX 76-77 E 7
Coleman River 182-183 H 2-3
Çölemerik 142-143 H 8
Coleraine 116-117 E 5
Coles, Punta de — 98-99 E 8
Colesburg 198 DE 8
Colesville, CA 74-75 D 3
Colfax, CA 74-75 C 3
Colfax, IA 70-71 D 5
Colfax, LA 78-79 C 5
Colfax, WA 66-67 E 2
Colfax, WI 70-71 E 3
Colgrave Sound 116-117 f 3
Colhué Huapí, Lago — 103 C 7
Colima 58-59 F 8
Colima, Nevado de — 58-59 EF 8
Colinas 98-99 L 6
Colinet 51 K 4
Coll 116-117 E 4
Collaguasi 103 C 2
College, AK 46-47 G 4-5
College Park, GA 80-81 DE 4
College Point, New York-, NY 82 III cd 2
College Station, TX 76-77 F 7
Colles 86-87 L 6
Colleymount 48 D 2
Collie 182-183 C 6
Collier Bay 182-183 D 3
Collierville, TN 78-79 E 3
Collingwood [CDN] 72-73 FG 2
Collins 50 E 2
Collins, IA 70-71 D 5
Collins, MS 78-79 E 5
Collins, MT 66-67 H 2
Collins, Mount — 50 L 3
Collinson Peninsula 46-47 Q 3-4
Collinston, LA 78-79 D 4
Collinsville 182-183 J 4
Collinsville, AL 78-79 FG 3
Collinsville, IL 70-71 F 6
Collinsville, OK 76-77 G 4
Collooney = Cúl Mhuine 116-117 C 6
Colma, CA 83 I b 2
Colmar 132-133 L 4
Colmar Manor, MD 82 II b 1
Colmor, NM 76-77 B 4
Colne 116-117 J 7
Colne Point 116-117 h 7
Colnett, Cabo — 86-87 B 2
Cologne = Köln 124 C 3
Cololo, Nevado — 98-99 F 7
Colomb-Béchar = Bashshār 194-195 D 2
Colômbia [BR] 98-99 K 9
Colombia [CO] 98-99 D-F 4
Colombia [MEX] 76-77 DE 9
Colombo = Koḷamba 160-161 M 9
Colome, SD 68-69 G 4
Colón [C] 58-59 K 7
Colón [PA, administrative unit] 58-59 ab 2
Colón [PA, place] 58-59 b 2
Colón, Archipiélago de — 98-99 AB 5
Colona 182-183 F 6
Colona, CO 68-69 C 6
Colonia del Sacramento 103 E 4
Colonia 25 de Mayo 103 C 5
Colonia Las Heras = Las Heras 103 C 7
Colonial Beach, VA 72-73 H 5
Colonial Heights, VA 80-81 H 2
Colonne, Capo delle — 138-139 G 6
Colonsay 116-117 E 4
Colorada, La — 86-87 EF 3
Colorado [CR] 88-89 E 9
Colorado [USA] 58-59 EF 4
Colorado, Río — [RA, Neuquén Río Negro] 103 D 5
Colorado City, TX 76-77 D 6
Colorado Desert 74-75 EF 6
Colorado National Monument 74-75 J 3
Colorado Plateau 58-59 DE 4
Colorado River [USA ◁ Gulf of California] 58-59 E 4
Colorado River [USA ◁ Gulf of Mexico] 58-59 G 5
Colorado River Aqueduct 74-75 F 5
Colorado River Indian Reservation 74-75 F 6
Colorados, Cerros — [RA] 103 C 6
Colorados, Cerros — [RCH] 103 C 3
Colorado Springs, CO 58-59 F 4
Colotlán 86-87 J 6-7
Colquitt, GA 78-79 G 5
Colstrip, MT 68-69 C 3
Coltishall 116-117 h 6
Colton, SD 68-69 H 4
Colton, UT 74-75 H 3
Columbia, KY 70-71 H 7
Columbia, LA 78-79 CD 4
Columbia, MD 72-73 H 5
Columbia, MO 58-59 H 4
Columbia, MS 78-79 E 5
Columbia, NC 80-81 H 3
Columbia, PA 72-73 H 4
Columbia, SC 58-59 K 5
Columbia, SD 68-69 GH 3
Columbia, TN 78-79 F 3
Columbia, Cape — 30 A 25-26
Columbia, District of — 72-73 H 5
Columbia, Mount — 46-47 N 7
Columbia Basin 66-67 D 2
Columbia City, IN 70-71 H 5
Columbia Falls, MT 66-67 FG 1
Columbia Glacier 52-53 O 6
Columbia Heights, Washington-, DC 82 II a 1
Columbiana, AL 78-79 F 4
Columbia Plateau 58-59 C 2-3
Columbia River 58-59 BC 2
Columbia River, WA 66-67 C 2
Columbine, WY 68-69 C 4
Columbretes, Islas — 132-133 H 9
Columbus, GA 58-59 K 5
Columbus, IN 70-71 H 6
Columbus, KS 76-77 G 4
Columbus, MS 58-59 J 5
Columbus, MT 68-69 B 3
Columbus, ND 68-69 E 1
Columbus, NE 58-59 G 3
Columbus, NM 76-77 A 7
Columbus, OH 58-59 K 3-4
Columbus, TX 76-77 F 8
Columbus, WI 70-71 F 4
Columbus Junction, IA 70-71 E 5
Columbus Park 83 II a 1
Colusa, CA 74-75 BC 3
Colville, WA 66-67 E 1
Colville Bar, AK 52-53 K 2
Colville Indian Reservation 66-67 D 1
Colville River 46-47 EF 4
Colwyn Bay 116-117 H 7
Comácchio 138-139 E 3
Comácchio, Valli di — 138-139 E 3
Comalcalco 86-87 O 8
Comales, Los — 76-77 E 9
Comana 138-139 LM 3
Comanche, OK 76-77 F 5
Comanche, TX 76-77 E 7
Comaraigh, Na — 116-117 D 8
Comayagua 58-59 J 9
Comber 72-73 E 3
Combourg 132-133 G 4
Combs, KY 72-73 E 6
Comeau, Baie — 46-47 X 8
Comencho, Lac — 50 O 1
Comer, GA 80-81 E 3
Comeragh Mountains = Na Comaraigh 116-117 D 8
Comfort, TX 76-77 E 7-8
Comilla = Komillā 160-161 P 6
Comino, Capo — 138-139 CD 5
Comiso 138-139 F 7
Comitán de Domínguez 58-59 H 8
Commerce, GA 80-81 E 3
Commerce, TX 76-77 FG 6
Commewijne 98-99 L 2
Committee Bay 46-47 T 4
Commonwealth Range 31 A
Commonwealth Territory 182-183 K 7
Como 138-139 C 3
Como, Lago di — 138-139 C 2-3
Comodoro Rivadavia 103 C 7
Comoé = Komoe 194-195 D 7
Comondú 86-87 DE 4
Comores, Archipel des — 198 HJ 4
Comorin, Cape — 160-161 M 9
Comoro Islands = Archipel des Comores 198 HJ 4
Comoros 198 HJ 4
Compeer 49 CD 5
Compiègne 132-133 J 4
Compostela 86-87 H 7
Comprida, Cachoeira — = Treze Quedas 98-99 H 4
Comprida, Ilha — [BR, Atlantic Ocean] 103 G 2-3
Comprida, Lago — = Lagoa Nova 98-99 J 4
Compton 116-117 K 9
Compton, CA 74-75 DE 6
Comstock, TX 76-77 D 8
Comundú 86-87 DE 4
Con, Loch — 116-117 BC 6
Čona 154-155 V 5
Conakry 194-195 B 7
Conata, SD 68-69 E 4
Conca = Cuenca 98-99 D 5
Concarneau 132-133 EF 5
Conceição [BR, Mato Grosso] 98-99 H 6
Conceição [BR, Rondônia] 98-99 H 10
Conceição [BR, Roraima] 98-99 H 3
Conceição da Barra 98-99 M 8
Conceição do Araguaia 98-99 JK 6
Concelho = Inhambane 198 G 6
Concepcion, CA 74-75 C 5
Concepción [BOL] 98-99 G 8
Concepción [CO, Putumayo] 98-99 DE 4
Concepción [PY, place] 103 E 2
Concepción [RA, Tucumán] 103 C 3
Concepción [RCH] 103 AB 5
Concepción, Bahía de la — 86-87 E 4
Concepción, Canal — 103 AB 8
Concepción, La — 98-99 E 2
Concepción del Oro 58-59 F 7
Concepción del Uruguay 103 E 4
Conception, Point — 58-59 B 5
Conception Bay 51 K 4
Conchas Dam, NM 76-77 B 5
Conchas Lake 76-77 B 5
Conchi [RCH, Antofagasta] 103 C 2
Concho 76-77 B 9
Concho, AZ 74-75 J 5
Concho River 76-77 DE 7
Conchos, Río — 58-59 EF 6
Concord, CA 74-75 BC 4
Concord, NC 80-81 F 3
Concord, NH 58-59 M 3
Concordia, KS 68-69 GH 6
Concordia, MO 70-71 D 6
Concórdia [BR, Amazonas] 98-99 E 7
Concordia [RA] 103 E 4
Côn Dao 174-175 E 5
Conde 98-99 M 7
Conde, SD 68-69 GH 3
Condobolin 182-183 J 6
Condon, OR 66-67 C 3
Conecuh River 78-79 F 5
Conejera, Isla — 132-133 J 9
Conejos 76-77 C 9
Conejos, CO 68-69 C 7
Conejos River 68-69 C 7
Coney Island 82 III c 3
Confusion Range 74-75 G 3
Congleton 116-117 JK 7
Congo 198 B 2-C 1
Congo = Zaïre 198 D 1
Congress, AZ 74-75 G 5
Congress Heights, Washington-, DC 82 II b 2
Cónia = Konya 160-161 C 3
Coniston [CDN] 72-73 F 1
Coniston [GB] 116-117 H 6
Conjeeveram = Kānchipuram 160-161 MN 8
Conklin 49 C 3
Conlen, TX 76-77 C 4
Conn, Lough — = Loch Con 116-117 BC 6
Connacht = Connachta 116-117 B 6-C 7
Connachta 116-117 B 6-C 7
Conneaut, OH 72-73 F 3-4
Connecticut 58-59 M 3
Connecticut River 72-73 K 3-4
Connell, WA 66-67 D 2
Connellsville, PA 72-73 G 4

220 Clárach

Connemara, Mountains of — = Sléibhte Chonamara 116-117 AB 7
Conner, MT 66-67 FG 3
Conner, Mount — 182-183 F 5
Connersville, IN 70-71 H 6
Connersville, OH 72-73 D 5
Connon, River — 116-117 G 3
Connors 51 B 4
Connors Pass 74-75 F 3
Conover, WI 70-71 F 2
Conquest 49 E 5
Conrad, MT 66-67 H 1
Conroe, TX 76-77 G 7
Conselheiro Lafaiete 98-99 L 9
Consett 116-117 JK 6
Constance = Konstanz 124 D 5
Constance, Lake — = Bodensee 124 D 5
Constância dos Baetas 98-99 G 6
Constanța 138-139 M 3
Constantina = Qusţanţīnah 194-195 F 1
Constantine, Cape — 46-47 DE 6
Constantinople = İstanbul 160-161 BC 2
Constitución 103 B 5
Contact, NV 66-67 F 5
Contamana 98-99 DE 6
Contas, Rio de — 98-99 L 7
Continental, AZ 74-75 H 7
Continental, OH 70-71 H 5
Contoy, Isla — 86-87 R 7
Contratación 98-99 E 3
Contreras, Isla — 103 AB 8
Controller Bay 52-53 P 6
Contwoyto Lake 46-47 OP 4
Converse, LA 78-79 C 5
Conway, AR 78-79 C 3
Conway, ND 68-69 H 1
Conway, NH 72-73 L 3
Conway, SC 80-81 G 4
Conway, TX 76-77 D 5
Conway Bay 116-117 GH 7
Conwy 116-117 H 7
Conyers, GA 80-81 DE 4
Coober Pedy 182-183 F 5
Cook 182-183 F 6
Cook, MN 70-71 D 2
Cook, NE 68-69 H 5
Cook, Bahía — 103 B 9
Cook, Cape — 48 CD 4
Cook, Mount — [NZ] 182-183 NO 8
Cook, Mount — [USA] 52-53 RS 6
Cook Bay 31 C 16
Cooke City, MT 66-67 J 3
Cookeville, TN 78-79 G 2
Cooking Lake 48 L 3
Cook Inlet 46-47 F 5-6
Cook Islands 34-35 K 6
Cooks, MI 70-71 G 3
Cook's Harbour 51 HJ 2
Cookshire 50 Q 4
Cookstown 116-117 DE 6
Cook Strait 182-183 O 8
Cooktown 182-183 HJ 3
Coolgardie 182-183 CD 6
Coolidge, AZ 74-75 H 6
Coolidge, KS 68-69 EF 6
Coolidge Dam 74-75 H 6
Coolin, ID 66-67 E 1
Cooma 182-183 J 7
Coonabarabran 182-183 JK 6
Coonamble 182-183 J 6
Coonana 182-183 D 6
Coondapoor 160-161 L 8
Coongoola 182-183 HJ 5
Coon Rapids, IA 70-71 C 5
Cooper, TX 76-77 G 6
Cooper Creek 182-183 G 5
Cooper Lake 68-69 CD 5
Cooper Landing, AK 52-53 N 6
Cooper's Town 88-89 GH 1
Cooperstown, ND 68-69 GH 2
Cooperstown, NY 72-73 J 3
Coorong, The — 182-183 G 7
Coosa River 78-79 G 3
Coos Bay 66-67 A 4
Coos Bay, OR 58-59 AB 3
Cootamundra 182-183 J 6
Cootehill = An Mhuinchille 116-117 DE 6
Čop 142-143 D 6
Copahue, Paso — 103 BC 5
Copán 58-59 J 9
Copán, Santa Rosa de — 58-59 J 9
Copano Bay 76-77 F 8
Copco, CA 66-67 B 4-5
Cope, CO 68-69 E 6
Copeland, KS 68-69 F 7
Copeland Island 116-117 F 6
Copenhagen = København 114-115 DE 10
Copiapó 103 BC 3
Copparo 138-139 DE 3
Coppell 50 K 2
Coppename 98-99 K 2
Copperas Cove, TX 76-77 EF 7
Copperbelt 198 E 4
Copper Center, AK 46-47 G 5
Copper Cliff 50 L 3
Copper Harbor, MI 70-71 G 2
Coppermine 46-47 N 4
Coppermine Point 70-71 H 2
Coppermine River 46-47 NO 4
Copper River 46-47 GH 5
Copșa Mică 138-139 L 2
Coquet, River — 116-117 J 5
Coquilhatville = Mbandaka 198 C 1-2
Coquille, OR 66-67 AB 4
Coquille River 66-67 AB 4
Coquimbo [RCH, place] 103 B 2
Corabia 138-139 L 4
Coracora 98-99 E 7-8
Coral Gables, FL 58-59 KL 6
Coral Harbour 46-47 U 5
Coral Sea 182-183 K-M 3
Coral Sea Basin 182-183 K 2
Coral Sea Islands Territory 182-183 JK 3
Corantijn 98-99 H 4
Corato 138-139 G 5
Corbeil-Essonnes 132-133 HJ 4
Corbières 132-133 J 7
Corbin 66-67 F 1
Corbin, KY 58-59 K 4
Corby 116-117 L 8
Corcaigh 116-117 C 9
Corcoran, CA 74-75 D 4
Corcovado, Volcán — 103 B 6
Corcubión 132-133 C 7
Cordele, GA 80-81 DE 4
Cordell, OK 76-77 E 5
Cordilheiras, Serra das — 98-99 OP 8
Cordillera Blanca 98-99 D 6
Cordillera Central [BOL] 98-99 F 8-G 9
Cordillera Central [CO] 98-99 D 4-E 3
Cordillera Central [DOM] 58-59 M 8
Cordillera Central [PE] 98-99 D 6
Cordillera Central [RP] 174-175 H 3
Cordillera Iberica 132-133 F 7-G 8
Cordillera Negra 98-99 D 6
Cordillera Occidental [CO] 98-99 D 3-4
Cordillera Occidental [PE] 98-99 D 6-E 8
Cordillera Oriental [BOL] 98-99 FG 8
Cordillera Oriental [CO] 98-99 D 4-E 3
Cordillera Oriental [DOM] 58-59 N 8
Cordillera Oriental [PE] 98-99 D 5-E 7
Cordillera Penibética 132-133 E 9-G 8
Cordillera Real [EC] 98-99 D 5
Córdoba [E] 132-133 E 10
Córdoba [MEX, Durango] 76-77 C 9
Córdoba [MEX, Veracruz] 58-59 G 8
Córdoba [RA] 103 D 4
Córdoba, Sierra de — [RA] 103 C 4-D 3
Córdova 98-99 DE 7
Cordova, AK 46-47 G 5
Cordova, AL 78-79 F 4
Cordova Bay 52-53 w 9
Cordova Peak 52-53 P 6
Core Sound 80-81 H 3
Corfield 182-183 H 4
Corfu = Kérkyra 138-139 H 6
Coria 132-133 D 8-9
Coria del Río 132-133 D 10
Coringa Islands 182-183 K 3
Corinne 49 F 5
Corinne, UT 66-67 G 5
Corinth, MS 78-79 E 3
Corinth = Kórinthos 138-139 K 7
Corinth, Gulf of — = Korinthiakòs Kólpos 138-139 JK 6
Corinto [BR] 98-99 KL 8
Corinto [NIC] 58-59 J 9
Corisco, Isla de — 194-195 F 8
Cork = Corcaigh 116-117 C 9
Cork Harbour = Cuan Chorcaighe 116-117 CD 9
Corleone 138-139 E 7
Corleto Perticara 138-139 FG 5
Çorlu 142-143 E 7
Cormoranes, Rocas — = Shag Rocks 103 H 8
Cormorant 49 HJ 3
Cormorant Lake 49 H 3
Čormoz 142-143 L 4
Čornaja [SU, Nenets Aut. Area] 142-143 L 2
Čornaja [SU, Rossijskaja SFSR] 154-155 Q 3
Cornelia, GA 80-81 E 3
Cornélio Procópio 103 FG 2
Cornell, WI 70-71 E 3
Corner Brook 46-47 Z 8
Corning, AR 78-79 D 2
Corning, CA 74-75 B 3
Corning, IA 70-71 C 5
Corning, KS 70-71 BC 6
Corning, NY 72-73 H 3
Corn Islands = Islas del Maíz 58-59 K 9
Cornouaille 132-133 EF 4
Cornudas Mountains 76-77 B 6-7
Cornwall [BS] 88-89 H 2
Cornwall [CDN] 46-47 VW 8
Cornwall [GB] 116-117 FG 10
Cornwallis Island 46-47 RS 2-3
Cornwall Island 46-47 RS 2
Coro 98-99 EF 2
Coroatá 98-99 L 5
Corocoro 98-99 F 8
Coroico 98-99 F 8
Coromandel Coast 160-161 N 7-8
Corona, CA 74-75 E 6
Corona, NM 76-77 B 5
Coronado, CA 74-75 E 6
Coronado, Bahía de — 58-59 K 10
Coronados, Islas de — 74-75 E 6
Coronation 49 C 4
Coronation Gulf 46-47 OP 4
Coronation Island [Orkney Is.] 31 CD 32
Coronation Island [USA] 52-53 v 9
Coronation Islands 182-183 D 2
Coronel Dorrego 103 DE 5
Coronel Fabriciano 98-99 L 8
Coronel Francisco Sosa 103 CD 5-6
Coronel Galvão = Rio Verde de Mato Grosso 98-99 HJ 8
Coronel Oviedo 98-99 E 2-3
Coronel Pringles 103 D 5
Coronel Suárez 103 D 5
Coronie 98-99 K 2
Coropuna, Nudo — 98-99 E 8
Corozal [BH] 58-59 J 8
Corps Mort, Île de — 51 E 4
Corpus Christi, TX 58-59 G 6
Corpus Christi Bay 76-77 F 9
Corpus Christi Pass 76-77 F 9
Corque 98-99 F 8
Corral [RCH] 103 B 5
Correctionsville, IA 70-71 BC 4
Corregidor Island 174-175 GH 4
Corrente 98-99 KL 7
Corrente, Rio — [BR, Bahia] 98-99 L 7
Correntes [BR, Mato Grosso] 98-99 HJ 8
Correntina 98-99 KL 7
Correo, NM 76-77 A 5
Corrib, Lough — = Loch Coirib 116-117 BC 7
Corrientes, Cabo — [C] 88-89 DE 4
Corrientes, Cabo — [CO] 98-99 D 3
Corrientes, Cabo — [MEX] 58-59 E 7
Corrientes, Cabo — [RA] 103 E 5
Corrigan, TX 76-77 G 7
Corrigin 182-183 C 6
Corry, PA 72-73 G 4
Corse 138-139 C 4
Corse, Cap — 138-139 C 4
Corsham 116-117 J 9
Corsica = Corse 138-139 C 4
Corsicana, TX 58-59 G 5
Čorskogo, chrebet — 154-155 a 4-c 5
Cortazar 86-87 K 7
Corte 138-139 C 4
Cortés [C] 88-89 E 3
Cortez, CO 74-75 J 4
Cortez Mountains 66-67 E 5
Cortina d'Ampezzo 138-139 E 2
Čortkov 142-143 E 6
Cortland, NE 68-69 H 5
Cortland, NY 72-73 HJ 3
Cortona 138-139 D 4
Çoruh = Artvin 160-161 E 2
Çoruh nehri 142-143 H 7
Çorum 160-161 CD 2
Corumbá 98-99 H 8
Corumbá, Rio — 98-99 K 8
Coruña, La — 132-133 C 7
Corunna, MI 70-71 H 4
Corunna = La Coruña 132-133 C 7
Corvallis, MT 66-67 FG 2
Corvallis, OR 58-59 B 3
Corwin, AK 52-53 E 2
Corwin, Cape — 52-53 E 7
Corwin Springs, MT 66-67 H 3
Corydon, IA 70-71 D 5
Corydon, IN 70-71 GH 6
Cos = Kōs 138-139 M 7
Cosala 86-87 G 5
Cosamaloapan 86-87 MN 8
Cosenza 138-139 FG 6
Coshocton, OH 72-73 EF 4
Cosigüina, Punta — 58-59 J 9
Cosigüina, Volcán — 58-59 J 9
Cosmoledo Islands 198 J 3
Cosmopolis, WA 66-67 B 2
Cosmos, MN 70-71 C 3
Cosna River 52-53 M 4
Čošskaja guba 154-155 H 4
Costa, Cordillera de la — [RCH] 103 B 2-3
Costa, Cordillera de la — [YV] 98-99 FG 3
Costa Brava 132-133 J 8
Costa Grande 58-59 F 8
Costa Rica [CR] 58-59 JK 9-10
Costa Rica [MEX, Sinaloa] 86-87 FG 5
Costa Rica [MEX, Sonora] 86-87 D 2
Costera del Golfo, Llanura — 86-87 L-N 5-8
Costera del Pacífico, Llanura — 86-87 E-H 2-7
Costermansville = Bukavu 198 E 2
Costigan Lake 49 EF 2
Costilla, NM 76-77 B 4
Cotabato 174-175 H 5
Cotagaita [BOL] 98-99 F 9
Cotahuasi 98-99 E 8
Cotati, CA 74-75 B 3
Coteau des Prairies, Plateau du — 58-59 G 2-3
Coteau du Missouri, Plateau du — 58-59 FG 2
Côteau-Station 72-73 J 2
Cote Blanche Bay 78-79 D 6
Côte d'Azur 132-133 L 7
Cotentin 132-133 G 4
Côte-Saint-Luc 82 I ab 2
Côte-Visitation, Montréal- 82 I b 1
Cotonou 194-195 E 7
Cotonu = Cotonou 194-195 E 7
Cotopaxi, CO 68-69 D 6
Cotopaxi [EC, mountain] 98-99 D 5
Cotswold Hills 116-117 JK 9
Cottage Grove, OR 66-67 B 4
Cottageville, SC 80-81 F 4
Cottbus 124 G 3
Cotter, AR 78-79 C 2
Cottian Alps = Alpes Cottiennes 132-133 L 6
Cottica 98-99 J 4
Cottingham 116-117 L 7
Cottondale, FL 78-79 G 5
Cotton Valley, LA 78-79 C 4
Cottonwood, AZ 74-75 GH 5
Cottonwood, CA 66-67 B 5
Cottonwood, ID 66-67 E 2
Cottonwood, SD 68-69 F 4
Cottonwood Creek 66-67 B 5
Cottonwood Falls, KS 68-69 H 6
Cottonwood River 70-71 C 3
Cottonwood Wash 74-75 HJ 5
Cotulla, TX 76-77 E 8
Coudersport, PA 72-73 GH 4
Coudres, Île aux — 51 A 4
Coulee, ND 68-69 EF 1
Coulee City, WA 66-67 D 2
Coulee Dam, WA 66-67 D 1-2
Coulman Island 31 B 18
Coulonge, Rivière — 72-73 H 1
Coulterville, IL 70-71 F 6
Council, AK 52-53 F 4
Council, ID 66-67 E 3
Council Bluffs, IA 58-59 GH 3
Council Grove, KS 68-69 H 6
Council Mountain 66-67 E 3
Courantyne River 98-99 K 3
Courtenay [CDN] 46-47 LM 8
Courtmacsherry = Cúirt Mhic Sheafraidh 116-117 C 9
Courtrai = Kortrijk 132-133 J 3
Coushatta, LA 78-79 C 4
Coutances 132-133 G 4
Couto Magalhães 98-99 O 9
Coutts 66-67 H 1
Cove, AR 76-77 G 5
Cove Island 50 KL 4
Coveñas 98-99 D 3
Coventry 116-117 K 8
Covilhã 132-133 D 8
Covington, GA 80-81 E 4
Covington, IN 70-71 G 5
Covington, KY 58-59 JK 4
Covington, LA 78-79 D 5
Covington, MI 70-71 F 2
Covington, OH 70-71 H 5
Covington, OK 76-77 F 4
Covington, TN 78-79 E 3
Covington, VA 80-81 FG 2
Cowal, Lake — 182-183 J 6
Cowan, TN 78-79 FG 3
Cowan, Lake — 182-183 D 6
Cowansville 72-73 K 2
Coward Springs 182-183 G 5
Cowarie 182-183 G 5
Cowden, IL 70-71 F 6
Cowdenbeath 116-117 H 4
Cowdrey, CO 68-69 C 5
Cowen, Mount — 66-67 H 3
Cowes 116-117 K 10
Cowlitz River 66-67 B 2
Cowpen 116-117 K 5
Cowra 182-183 J 6
Coxilha Grande 103 F 3
Coxim 98-99 J 8
Cox River 182-183 FG 3
Cox's Bazar = Koks Bāzār 160-161 P 6
Cox's Cove 51 GH 3
Coyame 86-87 H 3
Coyote, NM 76-77 B 6
Coyote Creek 83 III d 2
Coyotes Indian Reservation, Los — 74-75 E 6
Coyuca de Catalán 86-87 K 8
Cozad, NE 68-69 G 5
Cozumel 58-59 J 7
Cozumel, Isla de — 58-59 J 7
Crab Creek 66-67 D 2
Cradock 198 E 8
Craig, CO 68-69 C 5
Craig, MT 66-67 GH 2
Craigavon = 11 ⊲ 116-117 E 6
Craig Harbour 46-47 UV 2
Craigmont, ID 66-67 E 2
Craigmyle 49 B 5
Craigower 49 CD 6
Craik 49 F 5
Crail 116-117 J 4
Craiova 138-139 K 3
Crakow = Kraków 124 JK 3
Crampel = Ra's al-Mā' 194-195 D 2
Cranberry Portage 49 H 3
Cranbrock 46-47 NO 8
Cranbrook 49 JK 5
Crandon, WI 70-71 F 3
Crane, MO 78-79 C 2
Crane, OR 66-67 D 4
Crane, TX 76-77 C 7
Crane Lake 49 D 5
Crane Lake, MN 70-71 DE 1
Crane Mountain 66-67 CD 4
Cranleigh 116-117 L 9
Cranston, RI 72-73 L 4
Crary Mountains 31 B 25
Crasna [RO, place] 138-139 M 2
Crasna [RO, river] 138-139 K 2
Crater Lake 58-59 B 3
Crater Lake, OR 66-67 BC 4
Crater Lake National Park 66-67 BC 4
Crateús 98-99 LM 6
Crato [BR] 98-99 M 6
Crau 132-133 K 7
Crauford, Cape — 46-47 TU 3
Cravo Norte 98-99 EF 3
Crawford, GA 80-81 E 4
Crawford, NE 68-69 E 4
Crawfordsville, IN 70-71 G 5
Crawfordville, FL 80-81 DE 4
Crawley 116-117 L 9
Crazy Mountains 66-67 H 2-3
Crazy Peak 66-67 HJ 3
Crazy Woman Creek 68-69 C 3
Creach Bheinn 116-117 F 4
Crean Lake 49 E 3
Creciente, Isla — 86-87 DE 5
Crediton 116-117 H 10
Cree, River — 116-117 G 5-6
Creede, CO 68-69 C 7
Creedmoor, NC 80-81 G 2
Creel 86-87 G 4
Cree Lake [CDN, lake] 46-47 P 6
Cree Lake [CDN, place] 49 E 2
Cree River 49 E 2
Crefeld = Krefeld 124 BC 3
Creighton 49 GH 3
Creighton, NE 68-69 GH 4
Creil 132-133 J 4
Crema 138-139 C 3
Cremona [CDN] 49 A 5
Cremona [I] 138-139 CD 3
Crenshaw, MS 78-79 D 3
Crepori, Rio — 98-99 K 7
Crerar 72-73 F 1
Cres [YU, island] 138-139 F 3
Cres [YU, place] 138-139 F 3
Crescent, OK 76-77 F 4-5
Crescent, OR 66-67 C 4
Crescent, Lake — 66-67 B 1
Crescent City, CA 66-67 A 5
Crescent City, FL 80-81 c 2
Crescent Junction, UT 74-75 J 3
Crescent Lake, OR 66-67 C 4
Crescent Spur 48 GH 3
Cresciente, Isla — 86-87 DE 5
Cresco, IA 70-71 DE 4
Cressday 68-69 A 1
Crested Butte, CO 68-69 C 6
Crestline, NV 74-75 F 4
Creston 66-67 E 1
Creston, IA 70-71 C 5
Creston, WY 68-69 BC 5
Crestview, FL 78-79 F 5
Crestwynd 49 F 5
Creswell, OR 66-67 B 4
Crete, NE 68-69 H 5
Crete = Krḗtē 138-139 L 8
Creus, Cabo — 132-133 J 7
Creuse 132-133 H 5
Creusot, le — 132-133 K 5
Creve Coeur, IL 70-71 F 5
Crevice Creek, AK 52-53 LM 3
Crewe 116-117 J 7
Crewe, VA 80-81 G 2
Crewkerne 116-117 J 10
Cribi = Kribi 194-195 F 8
Crichna = Krishna 160-161 M 7
Cricklade 116-117 JK 9
Crikvenica 138-139 F 3
Crillon, Mount — 52-53 T 7
Crillon, mys — 154-155 b 8
Criminosa, Cachoeira — 98-99 HJ 5
Crinan Canal 116-117 F 4
Cripple, AK 52-53 JK 5
Cripple Creek, CO 68-69 D 6
Crișana 138-139 JK 2
Crisfield, MD 72-73 J 5-6
Criss Creek 48 G 4
Cristalândia 98-99 O 10
Cristobal 58-59 b 2
Crișul Alb 138-139 J 2
Crișul Negru 138-139 JK 2
Crivitz, WI 70-71 FG 3
Crna Reka 138-139 J 5
Croatia 138-139 F-H 3
Crocker, MO 70-71 D 7
Crockett, TX 76-77 G 7
Crocodile Islands 182-183 FG 2
Crofton, KY 78-79 F 2
Crofton, NE 68-69 H 4
Croix, Lac à la — 51 A 2
Croix, Lac la — 70-71 DE 1
Croker Island 182-183 F 2
Cromarty 116-117 G 3
Cromarty Firth 116-117 G 3
Cromer [CDN] 49 H 6
Cromer [GB] 116-117 h 6
Cromwell 182-183 NO 8-9
Cromwell, MN 70-71 D 2
Croob, Slieve — 116-117 EF 6
Crook 116-117 K 6
Crook, CO 68-69 E 5
Crooked Creek 66-67 DE 4
Crooked Creek, AK 52-53 QR 4
Crooked Creek, AK 52-53 H 6
Crooked Island 58-59 M 7
Crooked Island Passage 58-59 LM 7
Crooked River [CDN] 49 G 4
Crooked River [USA] 66-67 C 3
Crookes Point 82 III b 3
Crookston, MN 68-69 H 2
Crookston, NE 68-69 F 4
Crooksville, OH 72-73 E 5
Crosby 116-117 H 7
Crosby, MN 70-71 CD 2
Crosby, MS 78-79 D 5
Crosby, ND 68-69 E 1
Crosbyton, TX 76-77 D 6
Cross, Cape — = Kaap Kruis 198 B 6
Cross City, FL 80-81 b 2
Crosse, La —, WI 58-59 H 3
Crossett, AR 78-79 D 4
Cross Fell 116-117 J 6
Crossfield 48 K 4
Cross Lake [CDN, lake] 49 K 3
Cross Lake [CDN, place] 49 K 3
Crossmaglen 116-117 E 6
Crossman Peak 74-75 FG 5
Cross Plains, TX 76-77 E 6
Cross River 194-195 F 7-8
Cross Sound 46-47 J 6
Crossville, TN 78-79 G 3
Croswell, MI 72-73 E 3
Crotone 138-139 G 6
Crow Agency, MT 68-69 C 3
Crowborough 116-117 M 9
Crow Creek 68-69 D 5
Crow Creek Indian Reservation 68-69 G 3
Crowder, OK 76-77 FG 5
Crowell, TX 76-77 E 6
Crow Indian Reservation 68-69 BC 3
Crowland 116-117 LM 8
Crowle 116-117 L 7
Crowley, LA 58-59 H 5-6
Crowley, Lake — 74-75 D 4
Crowleys Ridge 78-79 D 2-3
Crown King, AZ 74-75 G 5
Crown Point, IN 70-71 G 5
Crownpoint, NM 74-75 JK 5
Crown Prince Christian Land = Kronprins Christians Land 30 AB 20-21
Crowsnest Pass 66-67 F 1
Croydon 182-183 H 3
Croydon, London- 116-117 LM 9
Crozet 26-27 M 8
Crozet Ridge 26-27 M 8
Cruachan, Ben — 116-117 FG 4
Crucero, CA 74-75 EF 5
Crucero, Cerro — 86-87 H 7
Cruces 88-89 FG 3
Cruces, Las — 58-59 b 2
Cruces, Las —, NM 58-59 E 5
Cruz, Cabo — 58-59 L 8
Cruz, La — [CR] 88-89 CD 9
Cruz, La — [MEX] 76-77 B 9
Cruz Alta [BR] 103 F 3
Cruz del Eje 103 CD 4
Cruzeiro 98-99 L 9
Cruzeiro do Sul 98-99 E 6
Cruzeiro do Sul, Cachoeira — 98-99 H 10
Cruzen Island 31 B 22-23
Cruz Grande [MEX] 86-87 L 9
Crysdale, Mount — 48 F 2
Crystal, ND 68-69 H 1
Crystal Bay 80-81 b 2
Crystal City 68-69 G 1
Crystal City, MO 70-71 E 6
Crystal City, TX 76-77 E 8
Crystal Falls, MI 70-71 F 2-3
Crystal Lake, IL 70-71 FG 4
Crystal Lake [CDN] 70-71 GH 3
Crystal River, FL 80-81 b 2
Crystal Springs, MS 78-79 D 4-5
Csongrád 124 K 5
Ču 154-155 N 9
Cuajinicuilapa 86-87 L 9
Cuamba 198 G 4
Cuando, Rio — 198 D 5
Cuando-Cubango 198 C 4-D 5
Cuangar 198 C 5
Cuango 198 C 3
Cuango, Rio — 198 C 3
Cuanza Norte 198 BC 3-4
Cuanza Sul 198 BC 3-4
Cu'a Rao 174-175 DE 3
Cuatro Ciénegas de Carranza 86-87 J 4
Cuauhtémoc 58-59 C 6
Cuba 58-59 KL 7
Cuba, KS 68-69 H 6
Cuba, MO 70-71 E 6
Cuba, NM 76-77 A 4
Cubal 198 B 4
Cubango 198 C 4
Cubango, Rio — 198 C 5
Čubartau = Baršatas 154-155 O 8
Cubero, NM 76-77 A 5
Cuchi, Rio — 198 C 4-5
Cuchilla Grande [ROU] 103 EF 4
Cuchillo Parado 76-77 B 8
Cucuí 98-99 F 4

Cucuí 221

Cucumbi 198 C 4
Cucunor = Chöch nuur 166-167 H 4
Cúcuta 98-99 E 3
Cudahy, CA 83 III c 2
Cudahy, WI 70-71 G 4
Cuddalore 160-161 MN 8
Cuddapah 160-161 M 8
Čudovo 154-155 E 6
Čudskoje ozero 154-155 O 6
Cudworth 49 EF 4
Cue 182-183 C 5
Cuello 86-87 Q 8
Cuenca [E] 132-133 FG 8
Cuenca [EC] 98-99 D 5
Cuenca, Serranía de — 132-133 F 8-G 9
Cuencamé de Ceniceros 86-87 J 5
Cuenlum = Kunlun Shan 166-167 D-H 4
Cuernavaca 58-59 FG 8
Cuero, TX 76-77 F 8
Cuervo, NM 76-77 B 5
Cuervo Grande, El — 76-77 B 7
Cuesta Pass 74-75 C 5
Cuevas del Almanzora 132-133 G 10
Cufra, Wāhāt el — = Wāḥāt al-Kufrah 194-195 J 4
Čugujev 142-143 G 6
Cuiabá [BR, Amazonas] 98-99 H 6
Cuiabá [BR, Mato Grosso] 98-99 H 8
Cuiabá, Rio — 98-99 H 8
Cúil an tSúdaire 116-117 D 7
Cuilapa 86-87 P 10
Cuilcagh 116-117 D 6
Cuillin Hills 116-117 E 3
Cuillin Sound 116-117 E 3
Cuilo, Rio — 198 C 3
Cuíma 198 C 4
Cuipo 58-59 a 2
Cúirt Mhic Shéafraidh 116-117 C 9
Cuito, Rio — 198 CD 5
Cuito Cuanavale 198 CD 5
Cuitzeo, Laguna de — 86-87 K 8
Cuiuni, Rio — 98-99 G 5
Čukotskij, mys — 154-155 l 5
Čukotskij Nacional'nyj Okrug = Chukot Autonomous Area 154-155 g-k 4
Čukotskij poluostrov 154-155 kl 4
Culbertson, MT 68-69 D 1
Culbertson, NE 68-69 F 5
Culcairn 182-183 J 7
Culebra [PA] 58-59 b 2
Culebra [Puerto Rico] 88-89 O 5
Culgoa River 182-183 J 5
Culiacán 58-59 E 6-7
Culiacán Rosales = Culiacán 58-59 E 6-7
Culion Island 174-175 G 4
Čulkovo 154-155 Q 5
Cúllar de Baza 132-133 F 10
Cullera 132-133 GH 9
Cullman, AL 78-79 F 3
Cullompton 116-117 H 10
Čul'man 154-155 XY 6
Cúl Mhuine 116-117 C 6
Culpeper, VA 72-73 GH 5
Culuene, Rio — 98-99 J 7
Čuluut gol 166-167 J 2
Culver, Point — 182-183 DE 6
Culver City, CA 83 III b 1
Čulym [SU, place] 154-155 P 6
Čulym [SU, river] 154-155 Q 6
Cum = Qom 160-161 G 4
Cumae 138-139 EF 5
Cumamoto = Kumamoto 166-167 P 5
Cumaná 98-99 G 2
Cumassia = Kumasi 194-195 D 7
Cumberland 66-67 A 1
Cumberland, IA 70-71 C 5
Cumberland, KY 80-81 E 2
Cumberland, MD 58-59 L 4
Cumberland, VA 80-81 GH 2
Cumberland, WI 70-71 DE 3
Cumberland, Cape — 182-183 N 2
Cumberland, Lake — 70-71 H 7
Cumberland City, TN 78-79 F 2
Cumberland House 49 GH 3-4
Cumberland Island 80-81 F 5
Cumberland Islands 182-183 JK 4
Cumberland Peninsula 46-47 XY 4
Cumberland Plateau 58-59 J 5-K 4
Cumberland Point 70-71 F 2
Cumberland River 58-59 J 4
Cumberland Sound [CDN] 46-47 X 4-Y 5
Cumberland Sound [USA] 80-81 c 1
Cumbernauld 116-117 G 5-H 4
Cumbre, Paso de la — 103 BC 4
Cumbres Pass 68-69 C 7
Cumbria 116-117 HJ 6
Cumbrian Mountains 116-117 HJ 6
Čumikan 154-155 Za 7
Cuminá, Rio — 98-99 H 5
Cuminapanema, Rio — 98-99 L 4-5
Cummings, CA 74-75 B 3
Cummins 182-183 G 6
Cumnock 116-117 GH 5
Čuna [SU ◁ Angara] 154-155 S 6
Čun'a [SU ◁ Podkamennaja Tunguska] 154-155 ST 5
Cunani 98-99 J 4
Cunco 103 B 5
Cunene 198 C 5
Cunene, Rio — 198 B 5
Cúneo 138-139 B 3
Cuney, TX 76-77 G 6
Cunnamulla 182-183 HJ 5
Cunningham, WA 66-67 D 2
Cunningham Park [USA, New York] 82 III d 2
Čuokkarašša 114-115 KL 2
Cupar [CDN] 49 F 5
Cupar [GB] 116-117 H 4
Cupica, Golfo de — 98-99 D 3
Cuprum, ID 66-67 E 3
Curaçá [BR, Amazonas] 98-99 G 6
Curaçá [BR, Bahia] 98-99 LM 6
Curaçao 58-59 N 9
Curacautín 103 B 5
Curanilahue 103 B 5
Čurapča 154-155 Z 5
Curaray, Río — 98-99 D 5
Curdistān = Kordestān 160-161 F 3
Curiapo 98-99 G 3
Curicó 103 B 4
Curicuriari, Rio — 98-99 DE 5
Curicuriari, Serra — 98-99 E 5
Curitiba 103 G 3
Curlandia 142-143 D 4
Curlew, WA 66-67 D 1
Curnamona 182-183 GH 6
Currais Novos 98-99 M 6
Curralinho 98-99 NO 5
Currant, NV 74-75 F 3
Current River 78-79 D 2
Currie 182-183 H 7-8
Currie, MN 70-71 C 3
Currie, NV 66-67 F 5
Currituck Sound 80-81 J 2
Curry, AK 52-53 MN 5
Curtea-de-Argeş 138-139 L 3
Curtin Springs 182-183 F 5
Curtis, NE 68-69 F 5
Curtis Island [AUS] 182-183 K 4
Curtis Island [NZ] 182-183 Q 6
Curuá, Ilha — 98-99 NO 4
Curuá, Rio — [BR ◁ Rio Amazonas] 98-99 L 4-5
Curuá, Rio — [BR ◁ Rio Iriri] 98-99 J 6
Curuá do Sul, Rio — 98-99 LM 6
Curuaés, Rio — 98-99 L 9
Curuaí 98-99 H 5
Curuai, Lago Grande do — 98-99 L 6
Curuá Una, Rio — 98-99 L 6
Curuçá 98-99 K 5
Curuçá, Ponta — 98-99 P 5
Curuçá, Rio — 98-99 C 7
Curumu 98-99 N 5
Curunuri, Serra do — 98-99 MN 4
Curup 174-175 D 7
Curuquetê, Rio — 98-99 F 9
Cururú 98-99 G 8
Cururu-Açu, Rio — 98-99 K 9
Cururupu 98-99 L 5
Curuzú Cuatiá 103 E 3
Curva Grande 98-99 K 5
Curvelo 98-99 L 8
Curzola = Korčula 138-139 G 4
Cushing, OK 76-77 F 5
Cushing, TX 76-77 G 7
Cushman, AR 78-79 D 3
Cusino, MI 70-71 G 2
Čusovaja 142-143 L 4
Čusovoj 154-155 K 6
Cusseta, GA 78-79 G 4
Čust 160-161 L 2
Custer, SD 68-69 E 4
Cut Bank, MT 66-67 GH 1
Cutch = Kutch 160-161 K 6
Cutervo 98-99 D 6
Cuthbert, GA 78-79 G 5
Cut Knife 49 D 4
Cutler 50 K 3
Cutler, CA 74-75 D 4
Cutler River 52-53 HJ 3
Cuttack 160-161 NO 6
Cutupí 98-99 G 10
Cutzamala, Río — 86-87 K 8
Cu'u Long, Cu'a Sông — 174-175 E 5
Čuvašskaja Avtonomnaja Sovetskaja Socialističeskaja Respublika = Chuvash Autonomous Soviet Socialist Republic 154-155 H 6
Cuvelai 198 C 5
Cuvier, Cape — 182-183 B 4
Cuvo, Rio — 198 B 4
Cuxhaven 124 D 2
Cuy, El — 103 C 5
Cuyahoga Falls, OH 72-73 F 4
Cuyama River 74-75 C 5
Cuyo Islands 174-175 H 4
Cuyuni River 98-99 G 3
Cuzco [PE, place] 98-99 E 7

C. W. MacConaughy, Lake — 68-69 E 5
Cwmbran 116-117 HJ 9

Cynthiana, KY 72-73 DE 5
Cyp-Navolok 114-115 PQ 3
Cypress, CA 83 III d 2
Cypress, LA 78-79 C 5
Cypress, TX 76-77 FG 8
Cypress Hills 46-47 OP 8
Cypress Hills Provincial Park 49 CD 6
Cypress Lake 66-67 J 1
Cyprus 160-161 C 4
Cyrenaica = Barqah 194-195 J 2
Cyrene = Shaḥḥat 194-195 J 2

Czar 49 C 4
Czechoslovakia 124 F-K 4
Czersk 124 J 2
Częstochowa 124 JK 3

D

Đa, Sông — 174-175 D 2
Ḍab'ah, Aḍ- 194-195 K 2
Dabakala 194-195 D 7
Daba Shan 166-167 KL 5
Dabas nuur 166-167 H 4
Dabat = Debark 194-195 MN 7
Dabbah, Ad- 194-195 KL 5
Dabeiba 98-99 D 3
Dabie Shan [TJ, mountains] 166-167 M 5
Dabola 194-195 B 6
Daborow 194-195 b 2
Dąbrowa Tarnowska 124 K 3
Dabuxun Hu = Dabas nuur 166-167 H 4
Dacaidan = Tagalgan 166-167 H 4
Dacar = Dakar 194-195 A 6
Dacar, Bîr ed — = Bi'r ad-Dhikār 194-195 J 3
Dacca = Ḍhāka [BD, place] 160-161 OP 6
Dachaidan = Tagalgan 166-167 H 4
Dachangshan Dao 170-171 D 3
Dachau 124 E 4
Dachstein 124 F 5
Đac Lăc, Cao Nguyên — 174-175 E 4
Dadanawa 98-99 HJ 3
Dade City, FL 80-81 b 2
Dadeville, AL 78-79 FG 4
Dāḍū 160-161 K 5
Dadu He 166-167 J 5
Daet 174-175 H 4
Dafdaf, Jabal — 199 D 3
Dafīnah, Ad- 160-161 E 6
Dafoe 49 F 5
Dafoe River 49 L 3
Dafter, MI 70-71 H 2
Dagabur = Degeh Bur 194-195 N 7
Dagana 194-195 AB 5
Dagelet = Ullŭng-do 166-167 P 4
Dagestan Autonomous Soviet Socialist Republic 142-143 J 7
Daggett, CA 74-75 E 5
Dagö = Hiiumaa 142-143 D 4
Dagomba 194-195 D 7
Dagomys, Soči- 142-143 G 7
Dagua [PNG] 174-175 M 7
Daguija 170-171 E 1
Dagverdharnes 114-115 b 2
Dāhānu 160-161 L 6-7
Daḥī, Nafūd ad- 160-161 EF 6
Dahlak desēt 194-195 N 5
Dahnā', Ad- 160-161 E 5-F 6
Dahomey = Benin 194-195 E 6-7
Ḍahrah 194-195 H 3
Ḍahr Walātah 194-195 C 5
Dahshûr = Minshāt Dahshūr 199 B 3
Dahushan 170-171 D 2
Daimiel 132-133 F 9
Daingean Uí Chúis 116-117 AB 8
Daingerfield, TX 76-77 G 6
Daingin, Bâdh an — 116-117 A 8-9
Daiō zaki 170-171 L 5
Daipingqiao = Taipingshao 170-171 E 2
Dairbhreach, Loch — 116-117 D 7
Dairen = Lüda-Dalian 166-167 N 4
Dairûṭ = Dayrūṭ 194-195 L 3
Dai-sen 170-171 J 5
Dai-Sengen dake 170-171 ab 3
Daisetta, TX 76-77 G 7
Dais hōji = Kaga 170-171 L 4
Daisy, WA 66-67 DE 1
Daito-jima 166-167 P 6
Daitō-shima 166-167 P 6
Daitō sima = Daitō-shima 166-167 P 6
Dajarra 182-183 G 4
Dakar 194-195 A 6
Daketa 194-195 N 7
Dakhan = Deccan 160-161 M 6-8
Dākhilah, Wāḥāt ad- 194-195 K 3
Dakhlah, Ad- 194-195 A 4
Dakhla Oasis = Wāḥāt ad-Dākhilah 194-195 K 3
Dakka = Ḍhāka 160-161 OP 6
Dakota, North — 58-59 FG 2
Dakota, South — 58-59 FG 3
Dakshin Andamān = South Andamān 160-161 P 8
Dakshin Paṭhār = Deccan 160-161 M 6-8
Dala 114-115 bc 2
Dalaba 194-195 B 6
Dalai 166-167 N 2
Dalai Lama Gangri 166-167 GH 5
Dalai Nur 166-167 M 2
Dalaj Nuur = Hulun Nur 166-167 M 2
Dalälven 114-115 G 7
Dalandzadgad 166-167 JK 3
Dalarna 114-115 EF 7
Da Lat 174-175 E 4
Dālbandīn 160-161 J 5
Dalbeattie 116-117 H 6
Dalby [AUS] 182-183 K 5
Dale 114-115 AB 7
Dale, OR 66-67 D 3
Dale, PA 72-73 G 4
Dalecarlia Reservoir 82 II a 1
Dale Hollow Lake 78-79 G 2
Dalen 114-115 C 8
Dalesford 49 F 4
Dalgaranger, Mount — 182-183 C 5
Dalhart, TX 76-77 C 4
Dalhousie 51 C 3
Dalhousie, Cape — 46-47 KL 3
Dali [TJ, Yunnan] 166-167 HJ 6
Dalian, Lüda- 166-167 N 4
Dalias 132-133 F 10
Dali Baizu Zizhizhou 166-167 HJ 6
Dalies, NM 76-77 A 5
Daling He 170-171 C 2
Daljā' 199 B 4
Ḍalkūt = Kharīfūt 160-161 G 7
Dall, Mount — 52-53 LM 5
Dallas 49 K 5
Dallas, GA 78-79 G 4
Dallas, IA 70-71 D 5
Dallas, OR 66-67 B 3
Dallas, TX 58-59 G 5
Dallas City, IL 70-71 E 5
Dall Island 46-47 K 7
Dall Lake 52-53 F 6
Dall Mount 52-53 N 3
Dallol Bosso 194-195 E 5-6
Dall River 52-53 N 3
Dalmacija 138-139 F 3-H 4
Dalmally 116-117 FG 4
Dalmatia = Dalmacija 138-139 F 3-H 4
Dalmellington 116-117 G 5
Dalnegorsk 154-155 a 9
Dalnerečensk 154-155 Za 8
Dal'nij = Lüda-Dalian 166-167 N 4
Daloa 194-195 C 7
Dalqū 194-195 L 4-5
Dalquier 50 MN 2
Dalry 116-117 G 5
Dalrymple, Mount — 182-183 J 4
Dalton 70-71 HJ 1
Dalton, GA 58-59 JK 5
Dalton, MA 72-73 K 3
Dalton, NE 68-69 E 5
Daltonganj 160-161 N 6
Dalton Ice Tongue 31 C 12-13
Dalton-in-Furness 116-117 HJ 6
Dalvik 114-115 d 2
Dalwhinnie 116-117 GH 4
Daly City, CA 74-75 B 4
Daly Lake 49 F 2
Daly River 182-183 F 2
Daly Waters 182-183 F 3
Damā, Wādī — 199 DE 4
Damān 160-161 L 6
Damanhûr 194-195 L 2
Damão = Damān 160-161 L 6
Damar, Pulau — 174-175 J 8
Damara 194-195 H 8
Damaraland 198 C 6
Damascus, VA 80-81 F 2
Damascus = Dimashq 160-161 D 4
Damaturu 194-195 G 6
Damāvand, Kūh-e — 160-161 G 3
Damazīn, Ad- 194-195 LM 6
Damba 198 BC 3
Dambuki 166-167 S 3-T 2
Dam Dam = South Dum Dum 160-161 OP 6
Dame Marie, Cap — 88-89 J 5
Dāmghān 160-161 GH 3
Damh, Sliabh — 116-117 C 6
Damietta = Dumyāṭ 194-195 L 2
Damietta Mouth = Maṣabb Dumyāṭ 199 BC 2
Dāmīr, Ad- 194-195 L 5
Dammām, Ad- 154-155 FG 5
Dāmodar 160-161 O 6
Damot 194-195 b 2
Dampier 182-183 C 4
Dampier, Selat — 174-175 K 7
Dampier Archipelago 182-183 C 4
Dampier Downs 182-183 D 3
Dampier Land 182-183 D 3
Dan, Kap — 46-47 d 4
Dana, Mount — 74-75 D 4
Đa Năng 174-175 E 3
Danbury, CT 72-73 K 4
Danbury, WI 70-71 D 2-3
Danby Lake 74-75 F 5
Dancharia 132-133 G 7
Dandarah 199 C 4
Dandong 166-167 N 3
Danforth, ME 72-73 MN 2
Danfu 174-175 h 5
Dang 98-99 L 2
Dange, Rio — 198 B 3
Danger 178 K 4
Dang Raek, Phnom — 174-175 DE 4
Dangraek, Phnom — = Phanom Dong Raek 174-175 DE 4
Danguno 194-195 F 6-7
Daniel, WY 66-67 H 4
Daniel's Harbour 51 GH 2
Danilov 154-155 G 6
Danjo-shotō 170-171 G 6
Ḍank 160-161 H 6
Danlí 58-59 J 9
Dannemora, NY 72-73 JK 2
Dannevirke 182-183 P 8
Dan River 80-81 FG 2
Danshui = Tanshui 166-167 N 6
Dansia 98-99 H 4
Dansville, NY 72-73 H 3
Dante, VA 80-81 E 2
Dante = Haafuun 194-195 c 1
Danube = Duna 124 J 5
Danushkodi 160-161 MN 9
Danville 72-73 KL 2
Danville, AR 78-79 C 3
Danville, IL 58-59 J 3
Danville, IN 70-71 G 6
Danville, KY 70-71 H 7
Danville, ME 72-73 L 2-3
Danville, VA 58-59 L 4
Dan Xian 166-167 K 8
Dao-Timni 194-195 G 4
Dapsang = K2 160-161 M 3
Dapupan 174-175 GH 3
Daqing Shan 166-167 L 3
Daqmā', Ad- 160-161 FG 6
Daquan 166-167 H 3
Dārāb 160-161 GH 5
Darabani 138-139 M 1
Darad = Dardistān 160-161 L 3
Darag = Legaspi 174-175 H 4
Daraj 194-195 G 2
Dār al-Bayḍā', Ad- 194-195 BC 2
Darašun = Veršino-Darasunskij 154-155 VW 7
Darau = Darāw 199 C 5
Darāw 199 C 5
Darb, Ad- 160-161 E 7
Darband, Kūh-e — 160-161 H 4
Darbanga = Darbhanga 160-161 O 5
Darbhanga 160-161 O 5
Darbi = Darvi 166-167 G 2
Darby, MT 66-67 FG 2
Darby, Cape — 52-53 F 4
Darby Mountains 52-53 E 4
Darchan 166-167 K 2
Dardanelle, AR 78-79 C 3
Dardanelles = Çanakkale boğazı 160-161 B 2-3
Dardo = Kangding 166-167 J 5-6
Dâr el Beïḍâ', ed — = Ad-Dār al-Bayḍā' 194-195 BC 2
Dar es Salaam 198 GH 3
Dārfūr 194-195 J 6
Dārfūr al-Janūbīyah 194-195 JK 6
Dārfūr ash-Shimālīyah 194-195 J 6-K 5
Dargagā, Jebel ed — = Jabal Ardar Gwagwa 199 D 6
Dargan-Ata 160-161 J 2
Dargaville 182-183 O 7
Dar Hu = Dalaj Nur 166-167 M 3
Darien, GA 80-81 F 5
Darién [PA, landscape] 58-59 L 10
Darien [PA, place] 58-59 b 2
Darien = Lüda-Dalian 166-167 N 4
Darién, Cordillera de — 88-89 D 8
Darién, Golfo del — 98-99 D 3
Darién, Serranía del — 88-89 H 10
Dariganga 166-167 L 2
Darjeeling 160-161 O 5
Dārjiling = Darjeeling 160-161 O 5
Darling, Lake — 68-69 F 1
Darling Downs 182-183 JK 5
Darling Range 182-183 C 6
Darling River 182-183 H 6
Darlington 116-117 K 6
Darlington, SC 80-81 FG 3
Darlington, WI 70-71 EF 4
Darlowo 124 H 1
Darmstadt 124 D 4
Darnah 194-195 J 2
Darnick 182-183 H 6
Darnley, Cape — 31 C 7-8
Daroca 132-133 G 8
Darrington, WA 66-67 C 1
Dar Runga = Dar Rounga 194-195 J 6-7
Darsah 160-161 G 8
Dart, Cape — 31 B 24
Dart, River — 116-117 H 10
Dartmoor Forest 116-117 GH 10
Dartmouth [CDN] 46-47 Y 9
Dartmouth [GB] 116-117 H 10
Dartuch, Cabo — 132-133 J 9
Daru 174-175 M 8
Darūdāb 194-195 M 5
Daruvar 138-139 G 3
Darvaza 160-161 H 2
Darvi 166-167 G 2
Darwešān 160-161 JK 4
Darwin, CA 74-75 E 4
Darwin [AUS] 182-183 F 2
Darwin, Bahía — 103 AB 7
Dāryā-ye 'Omān = Khalīj 'Umān 160-161 HJ 6
Dās 160-161 G 5
Dashen, Ras — 194-195 M 6
Dashiqiao 170-171 D 2
Dasht 160-161 J 5
Dashtīārī = Polān 160-161 J 5
Dassel, MN 70-71 C 3
Dataran Tinggi Cameron = Tanah-tinggi Cameron 174-175 D 6
Date 170-171 b 2
Datia 160-161 M 5
Datil, NM 76-77 A 5
Datiyā = Datia 160-161 M 5
D'atkovo 142-143 FG 5
Datong [TJ, Shanxi] 166-167 L 3
Datong He 166-167 J 4
Datu, Tanjung — 174-175 E 6
Datu, Teluk — 174-175 EF 6
Datu Piang 174-175 H 5
Dau'an = Al-Huraybah 160-161 F 7
Daudmannsodden 114-115 hj 5
Daugava = Severnaja Dvina 154-155 G 5
Daugavpils 142-143 E 4
Daulagiri = Dhaulāgiri 160-161 N 5
Daule, Río — 98-99 CD 5
Dauna Parma = Dawa 194-195 M 7-8
Dauphin 46-47 QR 7
Dauphiné 132-133 KL 6
Dauphin Island 78-79 EF 5
Dauphin Lake 49 J 5
Daurskij chrebet 154-155 V 7
Dautlatābād = Malāyer 160-161 F 4
Davalguiri = Dhaulāgiri 160-161 N 5
Davao 174-175 J 5
Davao Gulf 174-175 J 5
Davenport, AK 52-53 JK 5
Davenport, IA 58-59 H 3
Davenport, ND 68-69 H 2
Davenport, NE 68-69 H 5
Davenport, WA 66-67 D 2
Davenport Downs 182-183 H 4
Davenport Range 182-183 FG 4
Daventry 116-117 KL 8
Davey, Port — 182-183 HJ 8
David 58-59 K 10
David City, NE 68-69 H 5
David-Gorodok 142-143 E 5
Davidof Island 52-53 s 6-7
Davids Island 82 III d 1
Davidson 49 E 5
Davidson, OK 76-77 E 5
Davidson Mountains 46-47 H 4
Davis, CA 74-75 BC 3
Davis, IL 70-71 F 4
Davis, OK 76-77 F 5
Davis, WV 72-73 G 5
Davis Bay 31 C 14
Davis Creek, CA 66-67 C 5
Davis Dam, AZ 74-75 F 5
Davis Mountains 76-77 BC 7
Davis Sea 31 C 10
Davis Strait 46-47 Z 4-5
Davlekanovo 154-155 JK 7
Davos 124 DE 5
Dawa 194-195 M 7-8
Dawādimā, Ad- 160-161 EF 6
Dawangjia Dao 170-171 D 3
Dawanle = Dewelē 194-195 N 6
Dawāsir, Wādī ad- 160-161 EF 6
Dawḥah, Ad- 160-161 G 5
Dawlish 116-117 H 10
Dawson 46-47 J 5
Dawson, GA 78-79 G 5
Dawson, ND 68-69 G 2
Dawson, Isla — 103 BC 8
Dawson Bay [CDN, bay] 49 H 4
Dawson Bay [CDN, place] 49 H 4
Dawson Creek 46-47 M 6
Dawson-Lambton Glacier 31 B 33-34
Dawson Range 46-47 J 5
Dawson Springs, KY 70-71 FG 7
Dawwah 160-161 H 6
Dax 132-133 G 7
Da Xian 166-167 K 5
Daxue Shan 166-167 J 5-6
Day, FL 80-81 b 1
Dayang Bunting, Pulau — 174-175 C 5
Dayang He 170-171 D 2
Daym Zubayr 194-195 K 7
Dayong 166-167 L 6
Dayr, Ad- 199 C 5
Dayr as-Suryānī 199 AB 2
Dayr az-Zawr 160-161 DE 3
Dayr Katrīnah 199 C 3
Dayr Mawās 199 B 4
Dayr Samū'īl 199 B 3
Dayrūṭ 194-195 L 3
Daysland 49 BC 4
Dayton, NM 76-77 B 6
Dayton, NV 74-75 D 3
Dayton, OH 58-59 K 4
Dayton, TN 78-79 G 3
Dayton, TX 76-77 G 7
Dayton, WA 66-67 E 2
Dayton, WY 68-69 C 3
Daytona Beach, FL 58-59 KL 6
Dayu 166-167 L 6
Da Yunhe [TJ, Jiangsu] 166-167 M 5
Dayville, OR 66-67 D 3

Dead Indian Peak 66-67 HJ 3
Dead Lake 70-71 BC 2
Deadman Bay 80-81 b 2

222 **Cucumbi**

Deadman Mount 52-53 NO 5
Deadwood, SD 68-69 E 3
Deadwood Reservoir 66-67 F 3
Deal 116-117 h 7
Deanewood, Washington-, DC 82 II b 2
Deán Funes 103 D 4
Dean River 46-47 L 7
Dearborn, MI 72-73 E 3
Dearborn Heights, IL 83 II a 2
Dearg, Beinn — 116-117 FG 3
Deary, ID 66-67 E 2
Dease Arm 46-47 MN 4
Dease Inlet 52-53 K 1
Dease Lake 46-47 KL 6
Dease Strait 46-47 P 4
Death Valley 58-59 C 4
Death Valley, CA 74-75 E 4
Death Valley National Monument 74-75 E 4-5
Deauville 132-133 GH 4
Deaver, WY 68-69 B 3
Debar 138-139 J 5
Debark 194-195 M 6
Debden 49 E 4
De Beque, CO 68-69 BC 6
Debert 51 E 5
Dębica 124 K 3-4
Dęblin 124 KL 3
Debo, Lac — 194-195 D 5
Deborah, Mount — 52-53 O 5
De Borgia, MT 66-67 F 2
Debra Birhan = Debre Birhan 194-195 MN 7
Debra Marcos = Debre Markos 194-195 M 6
Debre Birhan 194-195 MN 7
Debrecen 124 K 5
Debre Markos 194-195 M 6
Debre Tabor 194-195 M 6
Decamere = Dekemḥarē 194-195 M 5
Decatur, AL 58-59 J 5
Decatur, GA 58-59 K 5
Decatur, IL 58-59 HJ 3-4
Decatur, IN 70-71 H 5
Decatur, MI 70-71 GH 4
Decatur, TX 76-77 F 6
Decazeville 132-133 J 6
Decelles, Lac — 50 M 3
Decelles, Réservoir — 72-73 GH 1
Decepción, Cabo — = Cape Disappointment 103 J 8-9
Deception 31 C 30
Deception Lake 49 F 2
Decherd, TN 78-79 FG 3
Děčín 124 G 3
Decker, MT 68-69 C 3
Declo, ID 66-67 G 4
Decorah, IA 70-71 E 4
Decoto, CA 74-75 BC 4
Décou-Décou, Massif — 98-99 LM 2
Deda 138-139 L 2
Deddington 116-117 K 9
Dedeagach = Alexandrúpolis 138-139 L 5
Dedo, Cerro — 103 B 6
Dédougou 194-195 D 6
Dedza 198 F 4
Dee, River — [GB, England] 116-117 H 7
Dee, River — [GB, Scotland] 116-117 J 3
Deep Creek Range 74-75 G 2-3
Deep River [CDN] 72-73 GH 1
Deep River [USA] 80-81 G 3
Deeps, The — 116-117 e 3
Deepwater, MO 70-71 D 6
Deer, AR 78-79 C 3
Deerfield Beach, FL 80-81 cd 3
Deering, AK 52-53 F 3
Deering, ND 68-69 F 1
Deering, Mount — 182-183 E 5
Deer Island [USA, Pacific Ocean] 52-53 b 2
Deer Lake [CDN, Newfoundland] 51 H 3
Deer Lake [CDN, Ontario] 50 B 1
Deer Lodge, MT 66-67 G 2
Deer Lodge Mountains 66-67 G 2
Deer Lodge Pass 66-67 G 3
Deer Park, AL 78-79 E 5
Deer Park, WA 66-67 E 2
Deer River, MN 70-71 CD 2
Deerton, MI 70-71 G 2
Deer Trail, CO 68-69 DE 6
Deerwood, MN 70-71 D 2
Deeth, NV 66-67 F 5
Deffa, ed — = Aḍ-Ḍiffah 194-195 J 2
Defiance, OH 70-71 H 5
De Funiak Springs, FL 78-79 FG 5
Dêge 166-167 H 5
Degeh Bur 194-195 N 7
Dégelis 51 B 4
Dêgên Zangzu Zizhizhou 166-167 H 6
Deggendorf 124 F 4
Dehlorān 160-161 F 4
Dehna = Ad Dahnā' 160-161 E 5-F 6
Dehna, Ed- = Ad-Dahnā' 160-161 E 5-F 6
Dehong Daizu Zizhizhou 166-167 H 6-7
Dehra Dūn 160-161 M 4
Deir, Ed — = Ad-Dayr 199 C 5
Deir es-Suryânî = Dayr as-Suryānī 199 AB 2
Deir ez Zôr = Dayr az-Zawr 160-161 DE 3
Deirgdheirc, Loch — 116-117 CD 7-8
Deir Katerîna = Dayr Katrīnah 199 C 3
Deir Mawâs = Dayr Mawās 199 B 4
Deir Samweil = Dayr Samū'īl 199 B 3
Dej 138-139 K 2
De Jong, Tanjung — 174-175 L 8
De Kalb, IL 70-71 F 5
De Kalb, MS 78-79 E 4
De Kalb, TX 76-77 G 6
De-Kastri 154-155 ab 7
Dekemḥarē 194-195 M 5
Dekese 198 D 2
Delagoa Bay = Baía do Maputo 198 F 7
Delagua, CO 68-69 D 7
Del Aire, CA 83 III b 2
De Land, FL 80-81 c 2
Delano, CA 74-75 D 5
Delano, MN 70-71 CD 3
Delano Peak 58-59 D 4
Delarof Islands 52-53 t 7
Delaronde Lake 49 E 3-4
Delavan, IL 70-71 F 5
Delavan, WI 70-71 F 4
Delaware 58-59 LM 4
Delaware, OH 72-73 E 4
Delaware Bay 58-59 LM 4
Delaware Lake 72-73 E 4
Delaware Reservoir 72-73 E 4
Delaware River 72-73 J 5
Delburne 48 L 3
Delcambre, LA 78-79 CD 6
Delčevo 138-139 K 4-5
De Leon, TX 76-77 E 6
Delfi = Delphoí 138-139 K 6
Delfzijl 132-133 L 2
Delgerchet 166-167 L 2
Delger mörön 166-167 H 1-2
Delgo = Delqū 194-195 L 4-5
Delhi, CO 68-69 DE 7
Delhi, LA 78-79 D 4
Delhi, NY 72-73 J 3
Delhi [CDN] 72-73 F 3
Delhi [IND] 160-161 M 5
Delhi = Dilli 174-175 J 8
Deli, Pulau — 174-175 DE 8
Delicermak 142-143 F 8
Délices 98-99 J 4
Delicias 58-59 E 6
Delingde 154-155 VW 4
Delisle 49 E 5
Dell, MT 66-67 G 3
Della Rapids 48 DE 5
Delle, UT 66-67 G 5
Del Mar, CA 74-75 E 6
Delmar, IA 70-71 E 4-5
Delmenhorst 124 CD 2
Del Norte, CO 68-69 C 7
de Long, proliv — 154-155 j 3-4
De Long Mountains 46-47 D 4
Deloraine [CDN] 68-69 F 1
Délos 138-139 L 7
Delphi, IN 70-71 G 5
Delphoí 138-139 K 6
Delphos, OH 70-71 H 5
Delray Beach, FL 80-81 cd 3
Del Rio, TX 58-59 F 6
Delta, CO 68-69 B 6
Delta, UT 74-75 G 3
Delta Beach 49 JK 5
Delta Junction, AK 52-53 OP 4
Delta Mendota Canal 74-75 C 4
Delta River 52-53 OP 5
Delvinë 138-139 HJ 6
Delwin, TX 76-77 D 6
Demachi = Tonami 170-171 L 4
Demarcation Point 52-53 RS 2
Demavend = Kūh-e Damāvand 160-161 G 3
Demba 198 D 3
Dembī Dolo 194-195 LM 7
Demchhog 166-167 D 5
Demerara 98-99 J 1-2
Demerara = Georgetown 98-99 H 3
Demerara River 98-99 J 1-2
Deming, WA 66-67 BC 1
Demini, Rio — 98-99 G 4-5
Demjanka 154-155 N 6
Demjanskoje 154-155 MN 6
Demmin 124 F 2
Demmitt 48 H 2
Demopolis, AL 78-79 EF 4
De Morhiban, Lac — 51 E 2
Dempo, Gunung — 174-175 D 7
Demta 174-175 M 7
Denali, AK 52-53 O 5
Denan 194-195 N 7
Denare Beach 49 GH 3
Denau 160-161 K 3
Denbigh 116-117 H 7
Denbigh [CDN] 72-73 H 2
Denbigh, Cape — 52-53 FG 4
Dendang 174-175 E 7
Dengkou = Bajan Gol 166-167 K 3
Denham 182-183 B 5
Denham Springs, LA 78-79 D 5
Denia 132-133 H 9
Denikil 194-195 N 6
Deniliquin 182-183 HJ 7
Denio, OR 66-67 D 5
Denison, IA 70-71 C 4-5
Denison, TX 58-59 G 5
Denison, Mount — 52-53 KL 7
Denizli 160-161 B 3
Denman Glacier 31 BC 10-11
Denman Island 66-67 A 1
Denmark, SC 80-81 F 4
Denmark, WI 70-71 G 3
Denmark [AUS] 182-183 C 6
Denmark [DK] 114-115 CD 10
Denmark Strait 46-47 f 4-e 5
Denpasar 174-175 FG 8
Dent, ID 66-67 E 2
Denton, MD 72-73 HJ 5
Denton, MT 68-69 B 2
Denton, NC 80-81 FG 3
Denton, TX 58-59 G 5
d'Entrecasteaux Islands 174-175 h 6
Denver, CO 58-59 EF 4
Denver City, TX 76-77 C 6
Denzil 49 D 4
Deoghar 160-161 O 6
De Paul University 83 II b 1
Depew, OK 76-77 F 5
Depósito 98-99 H 2
Deqen 166-167 H 6
Deqen Zizhizhou = B ◁ 166-167 H 6
De Queen, AR 76-77 G 5
De Quincy, LA 78-79 C 5
Dera, Lak — 198 H 1
Ḍera Ghāzi Khān 160-161 L 4
Ḍera Ismā'īl Khān 160-161 L 4
Derbent 142-143 J 7
Derby [AUS] 182-183 D 3
Derby [GB] 116-117 K 8
Derg' = Daraj 194-195 G 2
Derg, Lough — = Loch Deirgdheirc 116-117 CD 7-8
De Ridder, LA 78-79 C 5
Derj = Daraj 194-195 G 2
Dermott, AR 78-79 D 4
Derna = Darnah 194-195 J 2
Derravaragh, Lough — = Loch Dairbhreach 116-117 D 7
Derry, NH 72-73 L 3
Derūdēb = Darūdāb 194-195 M 5
Derventa 138-139 G 3
Derwent, River — 116-117 L 6-7
Deržavinskij 154-155 M 7
Desaguadero, Río — [BOL] 98-99 F 8
Des Arc, AR 78-79 D 3
Des Arc, MO 78-79 D 2
Desastre, Cachoeira do — 98-99 J 10
Desbarats 70-71 J 2
Descanso, El — 86-87 B 1
Descanso, Punta — 86-87 B 1
Deschaillons 72-73 KL 1
Deschambault Lake [CDN, lake] 49 FG 3
Deschambault Lake [CDN, place] 49 G 3
Deschutes River 66-67 C 3
Desdemona, TX 76-77 E 6
Desē 194-195 MN 6
Deseado = Puerto Deseado 103 CD 7
Deseado, Cabo — 103 AB 8
Deseado, Río — 103 BC 7
Desemboque, El — 86-87 D 2
Desenzano del Garda 138-139 D 3
Deseret Peak 66-67 G 5
Deseronto 72-73 H 2
Desertas, Ilhas — 194-195 A 2
Desert Center, CA 74-75 F 6
Deserto Salato = Dasht-e Kavīr 160-161 GH 4
Desful = Dezfūl 160-161 F 4
Deshler, OH 72-73 E 4
Deshu 160-161 J 4
Desirade, La — 88-89 Q 6
Desmarais 48 KL 2
De Smet, SD 68-69 H 3
Des Moines, IA 58-59 GH 3
Des Moines, NM 76-77 C 4
Des Moines River 58-59 GH 3
Des Moines River, East Fork — 70-71 C 4
Des Moines River, West Fork — 70-71 C 4
Desna 142-143 F 5
Desolación, Isla — 103 AB 8
Desolation Canyon 74-75 J 3
De Soto, MO 70-71 E 6
De Soto, WI 70-71 E 4
Despeñaperros, Puerto de — 132-133 F 9
Des Plaines, IL 70-71 FG 4
Dessau 124 F 3
Desterrada, Isla — 86-87 Q 6
Destruction Bay 52-53 S 6
Destruction Island 66-67 A 2
Desventurados 94 AB 6
Dete 198 E 5
Detmold 124 D 3
De Tour, MI 70-71 HJ 2-3
Detrital Valley 74-75 F 4-5
Detroit, MI 58-59 K 3
Detroit, TX 76-77 G 6
Detroit Harbor, WI 70-71 G 3
Detroit Lake 66-67 B 3
Detroit Lakes, MN 70-71 BC 2
Detroit River 72-73 E 3-4
Dettifoss 114-115 e 2
Deux-Rivières 72-73 G 1
Deva 138-139 K 3
De Valls Bluff, AR 78-79 D 3
Dévaványa 124 K 5
Deventer 132-133 L 2
Deveron, River — 116-117 HJ 3
Devil Mount 52-53 E 3
Devil's Bridge 116-117 H 8
Devils Elbow 52-53 JK 5
Devils Gate 74-75 D 3
Devil's Hole 110-111 HJ 4
Devils Lake 68-69 G 1
Devils Lake, ND 68-69 G 1
Devils Paw 52-53 UV 7
Devils Playground 74-75 EF 5
Devils Tower 68-69 D 3
Devils Tower National Monument 68-69 D 3
Devin 138-139 L 5
Devine, TX 76-77 E 8
Devizes 116-117 K 9
Devoll 138-139 J 5
Devon 116-117 GH 10
Devon, MT 66-67 H 1
Devon Island 46-47 S-U 2
Devonport [AUS] 182-183 J 8
Devonport [NZ] 182-183 O 7
de Vries, proliv — 166-167 S 2
Dewelē 194-195 N 6
Dewey, OK 76-77 FG 4
Dewey, SD 68-69 DE 4
Dewey Lake 80-81 E 2
De Witt, AR 78-79 D 3
De Witt, IA 70-71 E 5
De Witt, NE 68-69 H 5
Dewsbury 116-117 K 7
Dewundara Tuḍuwa 160-161 N 9
Dexian = Dezhou 166-167 M 4
Dexter, ME 72-73 M 2
Dexter, MO 78-79 DE 2
Dexter, NM 76-77 B 6
Deyālā = Diyālā 160-161 EF 4
Dey Dey, Lake — 182-183 F 5
Dezadeash Lake 52-53 T 6
Dezfūl 160-161 F 4
Dezhou 166-167 M 4
Dežneva, mys — 154-155 lm 4

Dhahab 199 D 3
Dhahran = Aẓ-Ẓahrān 160-161 FG 5
Dhamār 160-161 EF 8
Dhamtari 160-161 N 6
Dhankuta 160-161 O 5
Dhanushkodi 160-161 MN 9
Dhanuṣhkōṭi = Dhanushkodi 160-161 MN 9
Dhaolāgiri = Daulāgiri 160-161 N 5
Dhār 160-161 M 6
Dharamsālā 160-161 M 4
Dhārāvāda = Dhārwār 160-161 LM 7
Dharmsala = Dharamsālā 160-161 M 4
Dharmshala = Dharamsālā 160-161 M 4
Dharoor 194-195 c 1
Dhārvāḍ = Dhārwār 160-161 LM 7
Dhārwār 160-161 LM 7
Dhāt al-Ḥājj = Ḥājj 199 DE 3
Dhāṭ yā Thar = Great Indian Desert 160-161 L 5
Dhaulāgiri 160-161 N 5
Dhāvan'gere = Dāvangere 160-161 M 8
Dhiinsoor 194-195 N 8
Dhikār, Bi'r adh- 194-195 J 3
Dhond 160-161 L 7
Dhorāji 160-161 L 6
Dhrbarī = Dhubri 160-161 OP 5
Dhubri 160-161 OP 5
Dhufar = Ẓufār 160-161 G 7
Dhuibhne, Corca — 116-117 AB 8
Dhulēn = Dhūlia 160-161 L 6
Dhūlia 160-161 L 6
Dhūliyā = Dhūlia 160-161 L 6
Dhún na nGall, Bádh — 116-117 C 6
Dhún na nGall, Sléibhte — 116-117 C 6-D 5
Dhuusa Maareeb 194-195 b 2

Día 138-139 L 8
Diable, Île du — 98-99 J 3
Diablo, Sierra — 76-77 B 7
Diablo Heights 58-59 b 3
Diablo Range 58-59 BC 4
Diagonal, IA 70-71 CD 5
Diamante [RA] 103 DE 4
Diamantina 98-99 L 8
Diamantina River 182-183 H 4
Diamantino [BR ↖ Cuiabá] 98-99 H 7
Diamond, OR 66-67 D 4
Diamond Lake 66-67 B 4
Diamond Peak 74-75 EF 3
Diamondville, WY 66-67 H 5
Diancheng 166-167 L 7
Dian Chi 166-167 J 7
Dianópolis 98-99 K 7
Diapaga 194-195 E 6
Díaz [MEX] 76-77 B 9
Dibaya 198 D 3
Dibbāgh, Jabal — 199 D 4
Dibble Ice Tongue 31 C 14
Dibele, Bena- 198 D 2
Dibella 194-195 G 5
Dibis, Bi'r — 194-195 K 4
Diboll, TX 76-77 G 7
Dibrugarh 160-161 PQ 5
Dibulla 98-99 E 2
Dickens, TX 76-77 D 6
Dickey, ND 68-69 G 2
Dickinson, ND 58-59 F 2
Dickinson, TX 76-77 G 8
Dick's Head = Raas Jumbo 198 H 2
Dickson 154-155 P 3
Dickson, AK 52-53 E 4
Dickson, TN 78-79 F 2-3
Dickson City, PA 72-73 HJ 4
Dickson Harbour = P'asinskij zaliv 154-155 PQ 3
Dicle nehri 142-143 H 8
Didiéni 194-195 C 6
Didsbury 48 K 4
Didymóteichon 138-139 LM 5
Diefenbaker, Lake — 49 E 5
Diego de Amagro, Isla — 103 A 8
Diego Garcia 26-27 N 6
Diego Ramírez, Islas — 103 C 9
Diégo-Suarez = Antsiranana 198 JK 4
Diemensland, Van — = Tasmania 182-183 HJ 8
Điện Biên Phu 174-175 D 2
Diepholz 124 D 2
Dieppe 132-133 H 4
Dierks, AR 76-77 GH 5
Dietrich, ID 66-67 F 4
Dietrich River 52-53 N 3
Diêu, Mui — 174-175 EF 4
Dif 198 H 1
Diffa 194-195 G 6
Ḍiffah, Aḍ- 194-195 J 2
Difícil, El — 98-99 E 3
Digby 51 CD 5
Dighton, KS 68-69 F 6
Digne 132-133 L 6
Digoin 132-133 JK 5
Digos 174-175 J 5
Digul 174-175 M 8
Digura 36 a 2
Dihang 160-161 PQ 5
Dihua = Ürümchi 166-167 F 3
Dīīb, Wādī — 199 DE 6-7
Dijlah, Nahr — 160-161 E 3
Dijlah, Shaṭṭ — 160-161 F 4
Dijon 132-133 K 5
Dikākah, Ad- 160-161 G 7
Dikanäs 114-115 F 5
Dikeman, AK 52-53 J 5
Dikhil 194-195 N 6
Dikoa = Dikwa 194-195 G 6
Díktē Óros 138-139 L 8
Dikwa 194-195 G 6
Dīla 194-195 M 7
Dilam, Ad- 160-161 F 6
Di Linh 174-175 E 4
Dilinjāt, Ad- 199 B 2
Dill City, OK 76-77 E 5
Dilley, TX 76-77 E 8
Dilli 174-175 J 8
Dillī = Delhi 160-161 M 5
Dillia 194-195 G 5-6
Dillingham, AK 46-47 DE 6
Dillinj 194-195 KL 6
Dillon 49 D 3
Dillon, CO 68-69 C 6
Dillon, MT 66-67 G 3
Dillon, SC 80-81 G 3
Dillwyn, VA 80-81 G 2
Dilolo 198 D 4
Dimashq 160-161 D 4
Dimbokro 194-195 D 7
Dime Landing, AK 52-53 FG 4
Dimitrijevskoje = Talas 160-161 L 2
Dimitrovgrad [BG] 138-139 LM 4
Dimitrovgrad [SU] 154-155 HJ 7
Dimmitt, TX 76-77 C 5
Dinagat Island 174-175 J 4
Dinan 132-133 F 4
Dīnār, Kūh-e — 160-161 G 4
Dinara 138-139 G 3-4
Dinard 132-133 F 4
Dinaric Alps = Dinara 138-139 G 3-4
Dinas Head 116-117 FG 8
Dinas-Mawddwy 116-117 H 8
Dindigul 160-161 M 8
Diṇḍukkal = Dindigul 160-161 M 8
Ding 166-167 M 4
Dingle = Daingean Uí Chúis 116-117 AB 8
Dingle Bay = Bádh an Daingin 116-117 A 8-9
Dingle Peninsula = Corca Dhuibhne 116-117 AB 8
Dinguiraye 194-195 BC 6
Dingwall 116-117 G 3
Dingxi 166-167 J 4
Dingxin 166-167 H 3
Dinh, Mui — 174-175 E 4
Dinnebito Wash 74-75 H 5
Dinosaur National Monument 66-67 J 5
Dinsmore 49 E 5
Dinuba, CA 74-75 D 4
Dioïla 194-195 C 6
Diomida, ostrova — 46-47 C 4-5
Diosig 138-139 JK 2
Diouloulou 194-195 A 6
Diourbel 194-195 A 6
Dipolog 174-175 H 5
Dippin Head 116-117 FG 5
Dīr 160-161 L 3
Diradawa = Dirē Dawa 194-195 N 7
Diré 194-195 D 5
Dirē Dawa 194-195 N 7
Dírfys 138-139 KL 6
Dirico 198 D 5
Dirk Hartogs Island 182-183 B 5
Dirkou 194-195 G 5
Dirranbandi 182-183 J 5
Dirty Devil River 74-75 H 3-4
Disappointment, Cape — [Falkland Islands] 103 J 8-9
Disappointment, Cape — [USA] 66-67 A 2
Disappointment, Lake — 182-183 DE 4
Discovery Bay 182-183 GH 7
Discovery Well 182-183 D 4
Dishkakat, AK 52-53 J 5
Dishnā 199 C 4
Dishna River 52-53 J 5
Disko 46-47 a 4
Disko Bugt 46-47 a 4
Diskobukta 114-115 l 6
Dismal River 68-69 F 5
Dismal Swamp 80-81 H 2
Disraëli 72-73 L 2
Diss 116-117 h 6
Disston, OR 66-67 B 4
District Heights, MD 82 II b 2
Distrito Federal [BR] 98-99 K 8
Distrito Federal [MEX] 86-87 L 8
Distrito Federal [RA] 103 E 4
Disūq 199 B 2
Ditton Priors 116-117 J 8
Ditu, Mwene- 198 D 3
Diu 160-161 L 6
Divāṅgiri 160-161 P 5
Diver 72-73 G 1
Divide, MT 66-67 G 3
Divinópolis 98-99 KL 9
Divisa 88-89 F 10
Divisa, Serra da — 98-99 G 9
Divisões, Serra das — 98-99 JK 8
Divisor, Sierra de — 98-99 E 6
Divnoje 142-143 H 6
Dīwānganj 160-161 OP 5
Dīwānīyah, Ad- 160-161 EF 4
Diweir, Ed — = Ad-Duwayr 199 B 4
Dixfield, ME 72-73 L 2
Dixie, ID 66-67 F 3
Dixie, WA 66-67 DE 2
Dixon, CA 74-75 C 3
Dixon, IL 70-71 F 5
Dixon, MO 70-71 DE 6
Dixon, MT 66-67 F 2
Dixon, NM 76-77 B 4
Dixon Entrance 46-47 K 7
Diyālā 160-161 EF 4
Diyālā, Nahr — 160-161 EF 4
Diyarbakır 160-161 DE 3
Dizful = Dezfūl 160-161 F 4

Dja 194-195 G 8
Djado 194-195 G 4
Djado, Plateau du — 194-195 G 4
Djafou, Hassi — = Ḥāssī Jafū 194-195 E 2
Djakarta = Jakarta 174-175 E 8
Djakovica 138-139 J 4
Djakovo 138-139 H 3
Djala 138-139 J 2
Djambala 198 BC 2
Djelfa = Jilfah 194-195 E 2
Djema 194-195 K 7
Djenné 194-195 D 6
Djérém 194-195 G 7
Djerid, Chott el — = Shaṭṭ al-Jarīd 194-195 F 2
Djibhalanta = Uliastaj 166-167 H 2
Djibo 194-195 D 6
Djibouti [Djibouti, place] 194-195 N 6
Djibouti [Djibouti, state] 194-195 N 6
Djibuti = Djibouti 194-195 N 6
Djidda = Jiddah 160-161 D 6
Djidjelli = Jījilī 194-195 F 1
Djilolo = Halmahera 174-175 JK 6
Djirgalanta = Chovd 166-167 G 2
Djokjakarta = Yogyakarta 174-175 EF 8
Djolu 198 D 1
Djouah 198 B 1
Djougou 194-195 E 7
Djourab 194-195 H 5
Djuba = Webi Ganaane 194-195 N 8
Djugu 198 EF 1
Djúpavík 114-115 c 2
Djúpini 116-117 b 1
Djúpivogur 114-115 fg 2
Djurdjura = Jurjurah 194-195 EF 1

Dmitrija Lapteva, proliv — 154-155 a-c 3
Dmitrijevka = Talas 160-161 L 2
Dmitrov 154-155 F 6

Dnepr 142-143 E 6
Dneprodzeržinsk 142-143 F 6

Dneprodz 223

Dneprodzeržinskoje vodochranilišče 142-143 FG 6
Dnepropetrovsk 142-143 FG 6
Dnestr 142-143 E 6
Dno 142-143 EF 4

Doab 160-161 MN 5
Doaktown 51 CD 4
Doba 194-195 H 7
Dobbiaco 138-139 E 2
Dobbin, TX 76-77 G 7
Dobbyn 182-183 GH 3
Doblas 103 D 5
Dobo 174-175 K 8
Doboj 138-139 GH 3
Dobr'anka 142-143 I 4
Dobreta Turnu Severin 138-139 K 3
Dobruja 138-139 M 4-N 3
Doce Ilusão, Cachoeira — 98-99 L 9
Docking 116-117 M 8
Dockweiler State Beach 83 III b 2
Doctor, El — 86-87 C 2
Doctor Pedro P. Peña 103 D 2
Doda Betta 160-161 M 8
Dodecanese = Dōdekánesos 138-139 M 7-8
Dōdekánesos 138-139 M 7-8
Dodge Center, MN 70-71 D 3-4
Dodge City, KS 58-59 FG 4
Dodgeville, WI 70-71 EF 4
Dodoma 198 G 3
Dodsland 49 D 5
Dodson, MT 68-69 BC 1
Dodson, TX 76-77 DE 5
Dodson Peninsula 31 B 30-31
Doe River 48 G 1
Doerun, GA 80-81 E 5
Dofar = Ẓufār 160-161 G 7
Dogai Tshoring 166-167 F 5
Dog Creek 48 FG 4
Dogden Buttes 68-69 F 2
Doger Stadium 83 III c 1
Dogger Bank 110-111 J 4-5
Dog Island 78-79 G 6
Dog Lake [CDN ⤝ Missanabie] 70-71 HJ 1
Dog Lake [CDN ⤝ Thunder Bay] 70-71 F 1
Dōgo 166-167 P 4
Dogondoutchi 194-195 E 6
Dōgo yama 170-171 J 5
Doha = Ad-Dawḥah 160-161 G 5
Doheny 72-73 K 1
Doherty 72-73 E 4
Dois Irmãos, Cachoeira — 98-99 J 9
Dois Irmãos, Serra — 98-99 L 6
Dokka 114-115 D 7
Dokós 138-139 K 7
Doland, SD 68-69 GH 3
Dolbeau 46-47 W 8
Dôle 132-133 K 5
Dolgano-Nenets Autonomous Area 154-155 P-U 3
Dolgellau 116-117 H 8
Dolgij, ostrov — 154-155 K 4
Dolgoi Island 52-53 c 2
Dolhasca 138-139 M 2
Dolinsk 154-155 b 8
Dolinskaja 142-143 F 6
Dolleman Island 31 B 30-31
Dolo 194-195 N 8
Dolomites = Dolomiti 138-139 DE 2
Dolomiti 138-139 DE 2
Doloon Choolojn Gobi = Zaaltajn Gov' 166-167 H 3
Doloon Nuur 166-167 LM 3
Dolores, CO 74-75 J 4
Dolores, TX 76-77 E 9
Dolores [RA] 103 E 5
Dolores [ROU] 103 E 4
Dolores Hidalgo 86-87 K 7
Dolores River 58-59 E 4
Doloroso, MS 78-79 D 5
Dolphin, Cape — 103 E 8
Dolphin and Union Strait 46-47 NO 4
Domazlice 124 F 4
Dombarovskij 154-155 K 7
Dombås 114-115 C 6
Dombe Grande 198 B 4
Dombóvár 124 HJ 5
Dome, AZ 74-75 F 6
Dôme, Puy de — 132-133 J 6
Dome Creek 48 H 3
Dōmēl = Muẓaffarābād 160-161 LM 4
Dome Rock Mountains 74-75 F 6
Domeyko, Cordillera — 103 C 2-3
Domingos Coelho 98-99 HJ 9
Dominguez, CA 83 III c 2
Dominguez Channel 83 III c 2
Dominguez Hills 83 III c 2
Dominica 58-59 O 8
Dominical 88-89 DE 10
Dominican Republic 58-59 MN 7-8
Dominica Passage 88-89 Q 7
Dominion Range 31 A 18-19
Domodòssola 138-139 C 2
Dom Pedrito 103 E 5
Domsjö 114-115 H 6
Domuyo, Volcán — 103 BC 5
Don 142-143 GH 6
Don, River — 116-117 HJ 3
Donaghadee 116-117 F 6
Donald 182-183 H 7

Donalda 49 B 4
Donald Landing 48 E 2
Donaldson, AR 78-79 C 3
Donaldsonville, LA 78-79 D 5
Donalsonville, GA 80-81 E 5
Doña María, Punta — 98-99 D 7
Donau 124 G 4
Donaueschingen 124 D 5
Donauwörth 124 E 4
Don Benito 132-133 E 9
Doncaster 116-117 KL 7
Dondo [Angola] 198 BC 3
Dondo [Mozambique] 198 FG 5
Dondra Head = Dewundara Tuḍuwa 160-161 N 9
Donec 142-143 G 6
Donec 142-143 G 6
Donegal = Dún na nGall [IRL, administrative unit] 116-117 CD 6
Donegal = Dún na nGall [IRL, place] 116-117 CD 6
Donegal Bay = Bádh Dhún na nGall 116-117 C 6
Donegal Mountains = Sléibhte Dhún na nGall 116-117 C 6-D 5
Donga 194-195 G 7
Dongara 182-183 B 5
Dongchuan 166-167 J 6
Đông Đăng 174-175 E 2
Dongfang 166-167 K 8
Donggala 174-175 G 7
Donggou 198 C 1
Dongguan 166-167 LM 7
Đông Ho'i 174-175 E 3
Dongjing Wan = Beibu Wan 166-167 K 7-8
Dongkalang 174-175 GH 6
Dongola = Dunqulah 194-195 KL 5
Dongou 198 C 1
Dong Phaya Yen 174-175 D 3
Dongsha Qundao 166-167 LM 7
Dongsheng 166-167 KL 4
Dongtai 166-167 N 5
Dongting Hu 166-167 L 6
Dongxing 166-167 K 7
Đông Xoai 174-175 EF 2
Doniphan, MO 78-79 D 2
Donjek River 52-53 S 5
Donji Vakuf 138-139 G 3
Don Martín 76-77 D 9
Dønna 114-115 DE 4
Donnacona 51 A 4
Donna Nook 116-117 M 7
Donnely, ID 66-67 EF 3
Donner Pass 58-59 B 4
Donoso 88-89 F 10
Don Peninsula 48 C 3
Donsol 174-175 H 4
Donũsa 138-139 LM 7
Donyztau 154-155 K 8
Donzère 132-133 K 6
Doon, River — 116-117 G 5
Doonerak, Mount — 46-47 FG 4
Doornik = Tournai 132-133 J 3
Door Peninsula 70-71 G 3
Dora, NM 76-77 C 6
Dora, Lake — 182-183 D 4
Dora Báltea 138-139 B 3
Dorada, La — 98-99 E 3
Dorado 76-77 B 9
Dorado, El — AR 58-59 H 5
Dorado, El — [CO] 98-99 E 4
Dorado, El — [YV] 98-99 G 3
Doral 166-167 F 3
Dörböt Dabaan 166-167 FG 2
Dorchester 116-117 J 10
Dorchester, NE 68-69 H 5
Dorchester, Cape — 46-47 V 4
Dordabis 198 C 6
Dordogne 132-133 GH 6
Dordrecht [NL] 132-133 JK 3
Dore 132-133 J 6
Dore, Mont — 132-133 J 6
Doré Lake [CDN, lake] 49 E 3
Doré Lake [CDN, place] 49 E 3
Dore River 49 E 3
Dores 116-117 G 3
Dorgali 138-139 C 5
Dori 194-195 DE 6
Dorion 72-73 J 2
Dornoch 116-117 GH 3
Dornoch Firth 116-117 GH 3
Dornod ◁ 174-175 LM 2
Dornogov 166-167 K 3
Dorohoi 138-139 M 2
Dörööö nuur 166-167 GH 2
Dorotea 114-115 G 5
Dorothy 49 B 5
Dorrance, KS 68-69 G 6
Dorreen 48 C 2
Dorre Island 182-183 B 5
Dorris, CA 66-67 C 5
Dorset 116-117 J 10
Dorset Heights 116-117 J 10
Dortmund 124 CD 3
Dortmund-Ems-Kanal 124 C 2-3
Dorūd 142-143 J 9
Doruma 198 E 1
Dorval 82 I a 2
Dorval, Île de — 82 I a 2
Dörvöldžin 166-167 GH 2

Dorya, Ganale — = Genale 194-195 N 7
Dorylaeum = Eskişehir 160-161 C 2-3
Dos Bahías, Cabo — 103 CD 7
Dos de Mayo 98-99 DE 6
Dos Lagunas 86-87 PQ 9
Dos Pozos 103 CD 6
Dos Rios, CA 74-75 B 3
Dosso 194-195 E 6
Dossor 142-143 K 6
Doswell, VA 80-81 H 2
Dothan, AL 58-59 J 5
Dothan, OR 66-67 B 4
Dot Lake, AK 52-53 PQ 5
Dotsero, CO 68-69 C 6
Doty, WA 66-67 B 2
Doua = Cavally 194-195 C 7-8
Douáb, Rúd-e — = Qareh Sū 160-161 FG 3-4
Douai 132-133 J 3
Douala 194-195 FG 8
Douarnenez 132-133 E 4
Double Mountain Fork 76-77 D 6
Double Peak 52-53 LM 4
Double Springs, AL 78-79 F 3-4
Doubs 132-133 L 5
Doudaogoumen = Yayuan 170-171 P 3
Douentza 194-195 D 6
Dougherty, OK 76-77 F 5
Dougherty, TX 76-77 D 6
Doughty Plain 80-81 DE 5
Douglas, AK 52-53 UV 7
Douglas, AZ 58-59 E 5
Douglas, GA 80-81 E 5
Douglas, WA 66-67 CD 2
Douglas, WY 68-69 D 4
Douglas [CDN] 49 J 6
Douglas [GB] 116-117 G 6
Douglas [ZA] 198 D 7
Douglas, Cape — 52-53 L 7
Douglas, Mount — 52-53 KL 7
Douglas Channel 48 C 3
Douglas Lake [CDN] 48 GH 4
Douglas Lake [USA] 80-81 E 2-3
Douglas Park 83 II a 1
Douglas Point 72-73 EF 2
Douglas Range 31 BC 29-30
Douglastown 51 D 3
Doumé 194-195 G 8
Doumochter, Pass of — 116-117 GH 4
Drumshanbo = Droim Sean-Bhó 116-117 CD 6
Drury Lake 52-53 U 5
Druša = Jabal ad-Durūz 160-161 D 4
Dumfries 116-117 H 5
Dumfries and Galloway 116-117 GH 5
Dumoine, Lac — 72-73 H 1
Dumoine, Rivière — 72-73 H 1
Dumont d'Urville 31 C 14-15
Dumyāṭ 194-195 L 2
Dumyāṭ, Maṣabb — 199 BC 2
Duna [H] 124 J 5
Dunaföldvár 124 J 5
Dunaj [SU] 170-171 J 1
Dunaj, ostrova — 154-155 XY 3
Dunajec 124 K 4
Dún Ána, Rinn — 116-117 EF 7
Dunany Head = Rinn Dún Ána 116-117 EF 7
Dunany Point = Rinn Dún Ána 116-117 EF 7
Dunareä 138-139 M 3
Dún a'Rí 116-117 DE 7
Dunarii, Delta — 138-139 N 3
Dunaüjváros 124 J 5
Dunav 138-139 J 3
Dunbar 116-117 J 4-5
Dunbar, AK 52-53 N 4
Dunbar, OK 76-77 G 5
Dunbar, WV 72-73 F 5
Dunblane [CDN] 49 E 5
Dunblane [GB] 116-117 GH 4
Duncan, AK 52-53 N 4
Duncan, AZ 74-75 J 6
Duncan, OK 58-59 G 5
Duncan, WY 66-67 J 4
Duncan Passage 160-161 P 8
Duncansby Head 116-117 HJ 2
Dún Cearmna 116-117 C 9
Dund Ajmang = Töv ◁ 166-167 K 2
Dundalk, MD 72-73 H 5
Dundalk = Dún Dealgan 116-117 E 6-7
Dundalk Bay = Cuan Dún Dealgan 116-117 EF 7
Dundas 46-47 X 2
Dundas, Lake — 182-183 D 6
Dundas Island 48 B 2
Dundas Peninsula 46-47 O 2-3
Dundas Strait 182-183 F 2
Dún Dealgan 116-117 E 6-7
Dún Dealgan, Cuan — 116-117 EF 7
Dundee, MI 72-73 E 4
Dundee, TX 76-77 E 6
Dundee [GB] 116-117 HJ 4
Dundee [ZA] 198 F 7
Dundgov' 166-167 K 2
Dundrum Bay 116-117 F 6
Dundurn 49 E 5
Dunedin, FL 80-81 b 2
Dunedin 182-183 O 9
Dunfermline 116-117 H 4
Dungannon 116-117 E 6
Dún Garbháin 116-117 D 8
Dungarvan = Dún Garbháin 116-117 D 8

Dung Büree uul 166-167 FG 4-5
Dungeness 116-117 h 8
Dungiven 116-117 E 6
Dungu [ZRE, place] 198 E 1
Dungun, Kuala — 174-175 D 6
Dungunab = Dunqunāb 194-195 M 4
Dunhua 166-167 O 3
Dunhuang 166-167 GH 3
Duniére, Parc provincial de — 51 C 3
Dunkeld 116-117 H 4
Dunkerque 132-133 HJ 3
Dunkery Beacon 116-117 H 9
Dunkirk, IN 70-71 H 5
Dunkirk, NY 72-73 G 3
Dunkirk = Dunkerque 132-133 HJ 3
Dunkwa 194-195 D 7
Dún, Cnoc an — 116-117 D 9
Dún Laoghaire 116-117 EF 7
Dunlap, TN 78-79 G 3
Dunlop 49 J 2
Dunmanway = Dún Maonmhuighe 116-117 B 9
Dún Maonmhuighe 116-117 B 9
Dunmarra 182-183 F 3
Dunmore, PA 72-73 J 4
Dunn, NC 80-81 G 3
Dún na nGall [IRL, administrative unit] 116-117 CD 6
Dún na nGall [IRL, place] 116-117 CD 6
Dún na Séad 116-117 B 9
Dunnellon, FL 80-81 b 2
Dunnet Head 116-117 H 2
Dunning, NE 68-69 FG 5
Dunning, Chicago-, IL 83 II b 1
Dunnville 72-73 FG 3
Dunoon 116-117 FG 5
Dunphy, NV 66-67 E 5
Dunqul 199 B 6
Dunqulah 194-195 KL 5
Dunqunāb 194-195 M 4
Dunreay 116-117 H 2
Duns 116-117 J 5
Dunseith, ND 68-69 F 1
Dunsmuir, CA 66-67 B 5
Dunstable 116-117 L 9
Dunville 182-183 O 9
Du Quoin, IL 70-71 F 6-7
Durack Range 182-183 E 3
Duran, NM 76-77 B 5
Durance 132-133 K 7
Durand, MI 72-73 E 3
Durand, WI 70-71 E 3
Durango, CO 58-59 E 4
Durango [MEX] 58-59 EF 6
Durango, Victoria de — 58-59 F 7
Durant, MS 78-79 DE 4
Durant, OK 58-59 G 5
Durazno [ROU, place] 103 E 4
Durazzo = Durrës 138-139 H 5
Durban 198 F 7
Durga nuur = Dörööö nuur 166-167 GH 2
Durgapur [IND] 160-161 O 6
Durham, KS 68-69 H 6
Durham, NC 58-59 L 4
Durham [CDN] 72-73 F 2
Durham [GB] 116-117 K 6
Durkee, OR 66-67 E 3
Dúrlas Éile 116-117 D 8
Durmitor 138-139 H 4
Durness 116-117 G 2
Duro, Serra do — 98-99 P 10-11
Durrel 51 J 3
Durrës 138-139 H 5
Durt = Chanch 166-167 J 1
D'urt'uli 142-143 K 4
Durūz, Jabal ad- 160-161 D 4
Dušak 160-161 J 3
Dušanbe 160-161 K 3
Dusey River 50 F 2
Dúsh 199 B 5
Du Shan [TJ, mountain] 170-171 B 2
Düsseldorf 124 C 3
Dustin, OK 76-77 FG 5
Dutch Habor 30 D 35
Dutch John, UT 66-67 J 5
Dutton, MT 66-67 H 2
Dutton, Mount — 74-75 G 3-4
Duvan 154-155 K 6
Duved 114-115 E 6
Duvefjord 114-115 I 4
Duvernay 82 I a 1
Duwayd, Ad- 160-161 E 5
Ḍuwayḥin, Dawhat aḍ- 160-161 G 6
Duwaym, Ad- 194-195 L 6
Duwayr, Ad- 199 B 4
Duyun 166-167 K 6
Düzce 142-143 F 7

Dvina, Severnaja — 154-155 G 5
Dvinskaja guba 154-155 F 4-5
Dvorchangaj 166-167 J 2

Embu 198 G 2
Emden 124 C 2
Emei Shan 166-167 J 6
Emel gol 166-167 E 2
Emerald 182-183 J 4
Emerson 68-69 H 1
Emerson, AR 78-79 C 4
Emerson, MI 70-71 H 2
Emery, UT 74-75 H 3
Emeryville, CA 83 I c 1-2
Emesa = Ḥimṣ 160-161 D 4
Emi 154-155 S 7
Emigrant, MT 66-67 H 3
Emigrant Gap, CA 74-75 C 3
Emigrant Pass 66-67 E 5
Emigrant Peak 66-67 H 3
Emigrant Valley 74-75 F 4
Emi Koussi 194-195 H 5
Emi Kusi = Emi Koussi 194-195 H 5
Emìlia-Romagna 138-139 C-E 3
Emine, nos — 138-139 MN 4
Eminence, KY 70-71 H 6
Eminence, MO 78-79 D 2
Emir dağları 142-143 F 8
Emita 182-183 J 7-8
Emmen 132-133 L 2
Emmet 182-183 HJ 4
Emmet, ID 66-67 E 4
Emmetsburg, IA 70-71 C 4
Emory, TX 76-77 G 6
Emory Peak 76-77 C 8
Empalme 58-59 DE 6
Empangeni 198 F 7
Empedrado [RA] 103 E 3
Empire 58-59 b 2
Empire State Building 82 III c 2
Èmpoli 138-139 D 4
Emporia, KS 58-59 G 4
Emporia, VA 80-81 H 2
Emporium, PA 72-73 G 4
Empress 49 C 5
Ems 124 C 2
Emsdale 72-73 G 2
Emu Park 182-183 K 4

Ena 170-171 L 5
Enard Bay 116-117 F 2
Enare = Inari 114-115 M 3
Encampment, WY 68-69 C 5
Encantada, Sierra de la — 76-77 C 8
Encantanda, Sierra de la — 86-87 J 3-4
Encanto 98-99 N 10
Encarnación 103 E 3
Encarnacion de Díaz 86-87 JK 7
Enchi 194-195 D 7
Encinal 86-87 L 3
Encinal, TX 76-77 E 8
Encinitas, CA 74-75 E 6
Encino, NM 76-77 B 5
Encino, TX 76-77 E 9
Encontrados 98-99 E 3
Endako 46-47 LM 7
Endau [MAL] 174-175 D 6
Endeh 174-175 H 8
Enderbury 178 JK 3
Enderby 48 H 4
Enderby Land 31 C 5-6
Endere Langar 166-167 E 4
Enderlin, ND 68-69 H 2
Enders Reservoir 68-69 F 5
Endevour Strait 182-183 H 2
Endicott, NE 68-69 H 5
Endicott, NY 72-73 H 3
Endicott Mountains 46-47 F 4
Endimari, Rio — 98-99 E 9
Ene, Río — 98-99 E 7
Enemutu 98-99 HJ 2
Energía 103 E 5
Enfer, Portes de l' 198 E 3
Enfield, CT 72-73 K 4
Enfield, IL 70-71 F 6
Enfield, NC 80-81 H 2
Enfield = An Bóthar Buidhe 116-117 E 7
Enfield, London- 116-117 L 9
Engadin 124 DE 5
Engano = Pulau Enggano 174-175 D 8
Engaño, Cabo — 88-89 MN 5
Engaru 170-171 c 1
Engelhard, NC 80-81 HJ 3
Engels 142-143 J 5
Engelwood, CO 68-69 D 6
Engen 48 E 3
Enggano, Pulau — 174-175 D 8
England 116-117 J-M 8
England, AR 78-79 D 3
Engle, NM 76-77 A 6
Englee 51 HJ 2
Englehart 50 M 3
Englewood, KS 76-77 DE 4
Englewood, NJ 82 III c 1
Englewood, Chicago-, IL 83 II b 2
Englewood Cliffs, NJ 82 III c 1
English, IN 70-71 G 6
English Bay, AK 52-53 L 7
English Channel 110-111 H 6-J 5
English Channel 116-117 H 11-L 10
English Coast 31 B 29-30
English Company's Islands 182-183 G 2
English River [CDN, place] 70-71 E 1
English River [CDN, river] 50 BC 2
Enid, OK 58-59 G 4
Enid, Mount — 182-183 C 4
Enid Lake 78-79 E 3
Enid Reservoir = Enid Lake 78-79 E 3
Eniwa 170-171 b 2
Enkeldoorn = Chivu 198 F 5
Enken, mys — 154-155 b 6
Enköping 114-115 G 8
Enmelen 154-155 kl 4
Enna 138-139 F 7
Ennadai Lake 46-47 Q 5
Ennedi 194-195 J 5
Ennel, Lough — = Loch Ainninne 116-117 D 7
Enngonia 182-183 HJ 5
En Nikheila 199 B 4
Ennis, MT 66-67 H 3
Ennis, TX 76-77 F 6
Ennis = Inis 116-117 BC 8
Enniscorthy = Inis Coirthe 116-117 E 8
Enniskillen 116-117 D 6
Ennistimon = Inis Díomáin 116-117 BC 8
Enns 124 G 5
Eno 114-115 O 6
Enontekiö 114-115 K 3
Enriquillo 88-89 L 6
Enriquillo, Lago — 88-89 L 5
Enschede 132-133 L 2
Enseada, Cachoeiro — 98-99 J 10
Ensenada [MEX] 58-59 C 5
Ensenada Ferrocarril 76-77 F 10
Enshi 166-167 K 5
Enshih = Enshi 166-167 K 5
Enshū nada 170-171 LM 5
Ensign, KS 68-69 F 7
Entebbe 198 F 1
Entenbühl 124 F 4
Enterprise, AL 78-79 G 5
Enterprise, MS 78-79 E 4
Enterprise, OR 66-67 E 3
Enterprise, UT 74-75 G 4
Entiat, WA 66-67 C 2
Entiat Mountains 66-67 C 1-2
Entiat River 66-67 C 1-2
Entinas, Punta de las — 132-133 F 10
Entrance Island, AK 52-53 V 8
Entrecasteaux, Point d' 182-183 BC 6
Entrecasteaux, Récife d' 182-183 M 3
Entre Rios [BOL] 98-99 G 9
Entre Rios [BR, Amazonas] 98-99 J 7
Entre Rios [BR, Bahia] 98-99 M 7
Entre Rios [BR, Pará] 98-99 LM 7
Entre Ríos [RA] 103 E 4
Entre-Rios = Malemo 198 G 4
Entre Ríos, Cordillera — 58-59 J 9
Entro, AZ 74-75 G 5
Entroncamento [P] 132-133 CD 9
Entronque Huizache 86-87 K 6
Enugu 194-195 F 7
Enumclaw, WA 66-67 C 2
Enurmino 154-155 l 4
Envira 98-99 EF 6
Enyellé 198 C 1
Enz 124 D 4
Enzan 170-171 M 5
Enzeli = Bandare-e Anzalī 160-161 FG 3

Eochaill 116-117 D 8-9
Eochaille, Cuan — 116-117 D 9
Eoghain, Inis — 116-117 D 5
Eòlie o Lìpari, Ìsole — 138-139 F 6

Épeiros 138-139 J 6
Epéna 198 C 1
Épernay 132-133 J 4
Ephraim, UT 74-75 H 3
Ephrata, PA 72-73 H 4
Ephrata, WA 66-67 D 2
Epi 182-183 N 3
Epídauros 138-139 K 7
Epifania = Ḥamāh 160-161 D 3
Épinal 132-133 L 4
Epiphania = Ḥamāh 160-161 D 3
Épiphanie, l' 72-73 K 2
Epira 98-99 H 3
Epirus = Épeiros 138-139 J 6
Epping, ND 68-69 E 1
Epsom 116-117 L 9

Équateur 198 CD 1
Equatoria = Gharb al-Istiwāīyah 194-195 KL 7
Equatorial Channel 36 a 3
Equatorial Guinea 194-195 FG 6
Equeurdreville 116-117 K 11

Eraclea = Ereğli 160-161 C 2
Erakleion = Hērákleion 138-139 L 8
Erāwadī Myit 174-175 C 2
Erāwadī Myitwanyā 174-175 BC 3
Erāwadī Taing 174-175 B 3
Erciyas daği 160-161 D 3
Érd 124 J 5
Erdenecagaan 166-167 LM 2
Erde Plateau = Erdi 194-195 J 5
Erdi 194-195 J 5
Erebus, Mount — 31 B 17-18
Erebus and Terror Gulf 31 C 31
Ereencav 166-167 M 2
Ereen Chabarg 166-167 EF 3
Ereğli [TR, Konya] 142-143 F 8
Ereğli [TR, Zonguldak] 160-161 C 2
Erego 198 G 5
Erenhot = Erlian 166-167 L 3
Erepecu, Lago de — 98-99 H 5
Eresós 138-139 L 6
Erexim 103 F 3
Erfurt 124 E 3
'Erg, el — = Al-'Irq 194-195 J 3
Erg d'Admer = 'Irq Admar 194-195 F 4
Erge-Muora-Sisse, ostrov — = ostrov Arga-Muora-Sise 154-155 XY 3
Ergh, El — = Al-'Irq 194-195 J 3
Erg Ighidi = Ṣaḥrā' al-Igīdi 194-195 CD 3
Er Hai 166-167 J 6
Ērh-ch'iang = Charqiliq 166-167 F 4
Ērh-lien = Erlian 166-167 L 3
Eriboll, Loch — 116-117 G 2
Eric 51 D 2
Ērice 138-139 E 6
Ericht, Loch — 116-117 G 4
Erick, OK 76-77 E 5
Erie, CO 68-69 D 5-6
Erie, IL 70-71 EF 5
Erie, KS 70-71 C 7
Erie, ND 68-69 H 2
Erie, PA 58-59 K 3
Erie, Lake — 58-59 KL 3
Erieau 72-73 F 3
Erie Canal 72-73 G 3
'Erigaabo 194-195 b 1
Erik Eriksenstredet 114-115 m-o 5
Eriksdale 49 JK 5
Erimo misaki = Erimo-saki 166-167 RS 3
Erimo-saki 166-167 RS 3
Erin, TN 78-79 F 2
Erin Dzab = Ereencav 166-167 M 2
Erin Tal 166-167 L 3
Eriskay 116-117 D 3
Eritrea = Ērtira 194-195 M 5-N 6
Erlangen 124 E 4
Erldunda 182-183 F 5
Erlian 166-167 L 3
Ermelo [ZA] 198 EF 7
Erne, River — 116-117 D 6
Erne, River — = An Éirne 116-117 D 7
Ernest Sound 52-53 w 8-9
Erode 160-161 M 8
Eromanga [AUS] 182-183 H 5
Eromanga [Vanuatu] 182-183 NO 3
Erongo 198 C 6
Erqiang = Charqiliq 166-167 F 4
Errigal = Aireagal 116-117 C 5
Erris Head = Ceann Iorruis 116-117 AB 6
Errol, NH 72-73 L 2
Errol Island 78-79 E 6
Ersekë 138-139 J 5
Erskine, MN 70-71 BC 2
Ertira 194-195 M 5-N 6
Ertvågøy 114-115 BC 6
Erwin, NC 80-81 G 3
Erwin, TN 80-81 E 2
Erýmanthos 138-139 JK 7
Erzerum = Erzurum 160-161 E 2-3
Erzgebirge 124 F 3
Erzin 154-155 S 7
Erzincan 160-161 D 3
Erzurum 160-161 E 2-3

Esan-saki 170-171 b 3
Esashi [J ↑ Asahikawa] 170-171 c 1
Esashi [J ← Hakodate] 170-171 ab 3
Esbjerg 114-115 C 10
Esbo = Espoo 114-115 L 7
Escalante, UT 74-75 H 4
Escalante Desert 74-75 G 3-4
Escalante River 74-75 H 4
Escalón 86-87 H 4
Escanaba, MI 58-59 J 2
Escanaba River 70-71 G 2-3
Eschscholtz Bay 52-53 G 3
Eschwege 124 DE 3
Escobal 58-59 ab 2
Escondido, CA 74-75 E 6
Escorial, El — 132-133 EF 8
Escoumins, les — 51 B 3
Escoumins, Rivière — 51 B 3
Escuinapa de Hidalgo 58-59 E 7
Escuintla 58-59 H 9
Escutári = İstanbul-Üsküdar 160-161 BC 2
Esfahan [IR, administrative unit] 142-143 K 9
Eşfahān [IR, place] 160-161 G 4
Eshowe 198 F 7
Esk, River — 116-117 HJ 5
Eska, AK 52-53 N 6
Eskifjördhur 114-115 g 2
Eskilstuna 114-115 G 8
Eskimo Lakes 46-47 K 4
Eskimo Point 46-47 S 5
Eskişehir 160-161 C 2-3
Esla 132-133 E 8
Eslāmābād 160-161 F 4
Eslöv 114-115 E 10
Esmeralda [MEX] 76-77 C 9
Esmeralda, La — [PY] 103 D 2
Esmeraldas [EC, place] 98-99 CD 4
Esmeraldas, Río — 98-99 D 4
Esmond, ND 68-69 G 1
Esna = Isnā 194-195 L 3
Esnagami Lake 50 F 2
Esnagi Lake 70-71 H 1
Espanola 50 L 3
Espanola, NM 76-77 AB 5
Española, Isla — 98-99 B 5
Esparto, CA 74-75 BC 3
Espenberg, AK 52-53 EF 3
Espenberg, Cape — 52-53 F 3
Esperance 182-183 D 6
Esperance Bay 182-183 D 6
Esperanza [CDN] 48 D 5
Esperanza [MEX] 86-87 M 8
Esperanza [RA, Santa Cruz] 103 B 8
Esperanza [RA, Santa Fé] 103 D 4
Esperanza, La — [C] 88-89 DE 3
Esperanza, La — [Honduras] 88-89 BC 7
Esperanzas, Las — 76-77 D 9
Espichel, Cabo de — 132-133 C 9
Espinal 98-99 DE 4
Espinazo 76-77 D 9
Espinhaço, Serra do — 98-99 L 8
Espinillo 103 E 2
Espírito Santo 98-99 L 9-M 8
Espíritu Santo 182-183 MN 3
Espíritu Santo, Bahía del — 86-87 R 8
Espiritu Santo, Isla — 86-87 EF 5
Esplanada 98-99 M 7
Espoo 114-115 L 7
Espungabera 198 F 6
Esqueda 86-87 F 2
Esquel 103 B 6
Esquias 88-89 C 7
Esquimalt 46-47 M 8
Essen 124 C 3
Essendon, Mount — 182-183 D 4
Essequibo 98-99 L 1-3
Essequibo River 98-99 H 4
Essex 116-117 M 9
Essex, CA 74-75 F 5
Essex, MT 66-67 G 1
Essex, VT 72-73 K 2
Essex Junction, VT 72-73 K 2
Esslingen 124 D 4
Esso 154-155 e 6
Est, Île de l' 51 F 4
Estaca de Bares, Punta de la — 132-133 D 6-7
Estación Pichi Ciego = Pichi Ciego 103 C 4
Estación Vanega 86-87 K 6
Estâda, Âbe — 160-161 K 4
Estados, Isla de los — 103 D 8
Estaire 72-73 F 1
Estância 98-99 M 7
Estancia, NM 76-77 AB 5
Este 138-139 D 3
Estelí 58-59 J 9
Estella 132-133 F 7
Estelline, TX 76-77 D 5
Estepona 132-133 E 10
Esterhazy 46-47 Q 7
Estero, FL 80-81 c 3
Estero Bay 74-75 C 5
Estes Park, CO 68-69 D 5
Estevan 46-47 Q 7
Estevan Group 48 BC 3
Estherville, IA 70-71 C 4
Estill, SC 80-81 F 4
Estonian Soviet Socialist Republic 142-143 DE 4
Estor, El — 86-87 Q 10
Estrada, La — 132-133 C 7
Estrela, Serra da — [P] 132-133 CD 8
Estrella, AZ 74-75 G 6
Estrella [MEX] 86-87 C 2
Estrella, Punta — 86-87 C 2
Estrema [BR ↙ Rio Branco] 98-99 C 10
Estremadura 132-133 C 9
Estremoz 132-133 D 9
Estrondo, Serra do — 98-99 K 6

Etadunna 182-183 G 5
Etah 46-47 W 2
Etah = Etāwah 160-161 M 5
Étampes 132-133 HJ 4
Etawney Lake 49 K 2
Eterikan, proliv — 154-155 ab 3
Eternity Range 31 BC 30
Ethan, SD 68-69 GH 4
Ethel, MS 78-79 E 4
Ethelbert 49 H 5
Ethiopia 194-195 MN 7
Etive, Loch — 116-117 F 4
Etivluk River 52-53 J 2
Etna, CA 66-67 B 5
Etna, Monte — 138-139 F 7
Etnesjøen 114-115 AB 8
Etobikoke 72-73 G 3
Étoile du Congo 198 E 4
Etolin, Cape — 52-53 D 6
Etolin Island 52-53 w 8
Etolin Strait 46-47 C 5-6
Eton [AUS] 182-183 J 4
Eton [GB] 116-117 L 9
Etorofu = ostrov Iturup 154-155 c 9
Etosha Game Park 198 C 5
Etosha Pan 198 C 5
Etowah, TN 78-79 G 3
Etrī, Jebel — = Jabal Itrī 199 D 7
Etter, TX 76-77 CD 4
Ettrick 116-117 H 5
Etzatlán 86-87 HJ 7
Etzikom 66-67 H 1
Etzikom Coulée 66-67 GH 1

Eua 178 J 5
Eubank, KY 70-71 H 7
Euboea = Kaì Évboia 138-139 K 6-L 7
Eucla 182-183 E 6
Euclid, OH 72-73 F 4
Euclides da Cunha 98-99 M 7
Eudistes, Lac des — 51 D 2
Eudora, AR 78-79 D 4
Eufaula, AL 78-79 G 5
Eufaula, OK 76-77 G 5
Eufaula Lake, NM 76-77 A 6
Eufaula Reservoir 76-77 G 5
Eugene, OR 58-59 B 3
Eugenia, Punta — 58-59 C 6
Euice, NM 76-77 C 6
Eulo 182-183 J 5
Eunice, LA 78-79 C 5
Eupen 132-133 KL 3
Euphrat = Nahr al-Furāt 160-161 E 4
Euphrates = Nahr al-Furāt 160-161 E 4
Eupora, MS 78-79 E 4
Eurajoki 114-115 J 7
Eurasia Basin 26-27 K-O 1
Eure 132-133 H 4
Eureka, AK 52-53 MN 4
Eureka, CA 58-59 AB 3
Eureka, IL 70-71 F 5
Eureka, KS 68-69 H 7
Eureka, MT 66-67 F 1
Eureka, NV 74-75 EF 3
Eureka, SD 68-69 G 3
Eureka, UT 74-75 G 2-3
Eureka, WA 66-67 D 2
Eureka [CDN] 46-47 T 1
Eureka Roadhouse, AK 52-53 NO 6
Eureka Sound 46-47 TU 2
Eureka Springs, AR 78-79 C 2
Eureupoucigne, Chaîne d' 98-99 M 3
Europa [BR] 98-99 D 8
Europa, Île — 198 H 6
Europa, Picos de — 132-133 E 7
Europa, Point — 132-133 E 10
Europe 26-27 K-M 3
Euskadi [E] 132-133 F 7
Eustis, FL 80-81 c 2
Eustis, NE 68-69 FG 5
Eutaw, AL 78-79 F 4
Eutsuk Lake 48 D 3

Eva, OK 76-77 CD 4
Evans, Lac — 50 N 1
Evans, Mount — [CDN] 48 J 5
Evans, Mount — [USA, Colorado] 68-69 D 6
Evans, Mount — [USA, Montana] 66-67 G 2
Evans Head 182-183 K 5
Evans Strait 46-47 U 5
Evanston, IL 70-71 G 4
Evanston, WY 66-67 H 5
Evansville, AK 52-53 LM 3
Evansville, IL 70-71 F 6
Evansville, IN 58-59 J 4
Evansville, WI 70-71 F 4
Evant, TX 76-77 EF 7
Evart, MI 70-71 H 4
Évboia, Kaì — 138-139 K 6-L 7
Evboïkòs Kólpos 138-139 KL 6
Eveleth, MN 70-71 D 2
Evenki Autonomous Area 154-155 R-T 5
Evensk 154-155 e 5
Everard, Cape — 182-183 JK 7
Everard, Lake — 182-183 F 6
Everard Park 182-183 F 5
Everard Ranges 182-183 F 5
Everest, Mount — = Sagarmatha 166-167 F 6
Everett, GA 80-81 F 5
Everett, WA 58-59 B 2
Everett, Mount — 72-73 K 3
Everglades 58-59 K 6
Everglades, FL 80-81 c 4
Everglades National Park 58-59 K 6
Evergreen, AL 78-79 F 5
Evergreen Park, IL 83 II a 2
Evergreen Plaza, Chicago-, IL 83 II ab 2
Evesham 116-117 K 8
Evinayong 194-195 G 8
Evje 114-115 BC 8
Évora 132-133 CD 9
Évreux 132-133 H 4

Ewan, WA 66-67 E 2
Ewan Lake 52-53 P 5
Ewe, Loch — 116-117 F 3
Ewing, KY 72-73 E 5
Ewing, MO 70-71 E 5-6
Ewing, NE 68-69 G 4
Ewing, VA 80-81 E 2
Ewo 198 BC 2

Exaltación [BOL] 98-99 F 7
Excelsior Mountains 74-75 D 3
Excelsior Springs, MO 70-71 CD 6
Excursion Inlet, AK 52-53 U 7
Exe, River — 116-117 H 10
Executive Committee Range 31 B 24
Exeland, WI 70-71 E 3
Exeter, CA 74-75 D 4
Exeter, MO 78-79 C 2
Exeter, NE 68-69 H 5
Exeter, NH 72-73 L 3
Exeter [CDN] 72-73 F 3
Exeter [GB] 116-117 H 10
Exira, IA 70-71 C 5
Exmoor Forest 116-117 H 9
Exmore, VA 80-81 HJ 2
Exmouth [GB] 116-117 H 10
Exmouth Gulf [AUS, bay] 182-183 B 4
Exmouth Gulf [AUS, place] 182-183 B 4
Expedition Range 182-183 J 4
Exploits River 51 HJ 3
Explorer Mount 52-53 FG 7
Extremadura 132-133 D 9-E 8
Exuma Island, Great — 58-59 L 7
Exuma Sound 58-59 L 7

Eyasi, Lake — 198 FG 2
Eye 116-117 h 6
Eyehill Creek 49 C 4
Eyemouth 116-117 JK 5
Eye Peninsula 116-117 EF 2
Eyjafjardhar 114-115 d 2
Eyjafjördhur 114-115 d 1
Eyl 194-195 b 2
Eynsham 116-117 K 9
Eyota, MN 70-71 D 3-4
Eyrarbakki 114-115 c 3
Eyre 182-183 E 6
Eyre, Lake — 182-183 G 5
Eyre, Seno — 103 B 7
Eyre Peninsula 182-183 G 6
Eysturoy 116-117 b 1

F

Fabens, TX 76-77 AB 7
Fabriano 138-139 E 4
Fachi 194-195 G 5
Fada 194-195 J 5
Fada-n'Gourma 194-195 DE 6
Faddeja, zaliv — 154-155 UV 2
Faddejevskij, ostrov — 154-155 b-d 2
Faddeyev Island = ostrov Faddejevskij 154-155 b-d 2
Fadghâmi 142-143 H 8
Fadiffolu Atoll 36 ab 1
Fadu N'Gurma = Fada-n'Gourma 194-195 DE 6
Faenza 138-139 D 3
Færingehavn 46-47 a 5
Faeroe Iceland Ridge 110-111 FG 3
Færøerne = Föroyar 116-117 b 2
Fafan = Fafen 194-195 N 7
Fafanlap 174-175 K 7
Fafen 194-195 N 7
Făgăraş 138-139 L 3
Fagatoga 174-175 c 1
Fagernes 114-115 C 7
Fagersta 114-115 FG 7-8
Fagibin, Lake — = Lac Faguibine 194-195 CD 5
Faguibine, Lac — 194-195 CD 5
Fagundes [BR, Pará] 98-99 H 6
Fahala 36 a 2
Fahraj 160-161 H 5
Faial 188-189 DE 5
Faʾid 199 C 2
Faijum, El — = Al-Fayyūm 194-195 KL 3
Faing 116-117 B 8
Fairbank, AZ 74-75 H 7
Fairbanks, AK 46-47 G 5
Fairburn, GA 78-79 G 4
Fairburn, SD 68-69 E 4
Fairbury, IL 70-71 F 5
Fairbury, NE 58-59 G 3
Fairchild, WI 70-71 E 3
Fairfax, AL 78-79 G 4
Fairfax, MN 70-71 C 3
Fairfax, MO 70-71 C 5
Fairfax, OK 76-77 F 4
Fairfax, SC 80-81 F 4
Fairfax, SD 68-69 G 4
Fairfield, AL 78-79 F 4
Fairfield, CA 74-75 BC 3
Fairfield, IA 70-71 E 5
Fairfield, ID 66-67 F 4
Fairfield, IL 70-71 F 6
Fairfield, ME 72-73 M 2
Fairfield, MT 66-67 H 2
Fairfield, ND 68-69 E 2
Fairfield, TX 76-77 FG 7
Fairford 116-117 K 9
Fair Head 116-117 E 5
Fairhope, WA 66-67 AB 1
Fairhope, AL 78-79 F 5
Fair Isle 116-117 K 1
Fairlie 182-183 NO 8
Fairmont, MN 70-71 C 4
Fairmont, NC 80-81 G 3

Fairmont, NE 68-69 H 5
Fairmont, WV 72-73 F 5
Fairmont Hot Springs 48 K 4
Fairmount, ND 68-69 H 2-3
Fair Oaks, AR 78-79 D 3
Fairplay, CO 68-69 CD 6
Fair Play, MO 70-71 D 7
Fairport, NY 72-73 H 3
Fairport Harbor, OH 72-73 F 4
Fairview 48 H 1
Fairview, KS 70-71 C 6
Fairview, MT 68-69 D 2
Fairview, OK 76-77 E 4
Fairview, UT 74-75 H 3
Fairway Hills, MD 82 II a 1
Fairway Rock 52-53 C 4
Fairweather, Cape — 52-53 ST 7
Fairweather, Mount — 46-47 J 6
Fais 148-149 S 9
Faisalābād 160-161 L 4
Faith, SD 68-69 EF 3
Faither, The — 116-117 e 3
Faizābād 160-161 N 5
Fajardo 88-89 O 5
Fajr, Wādī — 160-161 D 5
Fakaofo 178 J 3
Fakenham 116-117 M 8
Fakfak 174-175 K 7
Falam = Hpalam 174-175 B 2
Fălciu 138-139 MN 2
Falcon, Cape — 66-67 A 3
Falcone, Capo — 138-139 BC 5
Falcon Island 50 B 3
Falcon Reservoir 58-59 G 6
Falémé 194-195 B 6
Falemé = Falémé 194-195 B 6
Falfurrias, TX 76-77 E 9
Falher 48 J 2
Falkenberg [DDR] 124 F 3
Falkenberg [S] 114-115 DE 9
Falkirk 116-117 H 4
Falkland Islands 103 DE 8
Falkland Sound 103 DE 8
Falkonéra 138-139 KL 7
Falköping 114-115 EF 8
Falkville, AL 78-79 F 3
Fallbrook, CA 74-75 E 6
Fall Line Hills [USA, Alabama] 78-79 E 3
Fall Line Hills [USA, Georgia] 80-81 D-F 4
Fallon, MT 68-69 D 2
Fallon, NV 58-59 C 4
Fall River, MA 58-59 MN 3
Fall River Lake 70-71 BC 7
Fall River Mills, CA 66-67 C 5
Falls Church, VA 82 II a 2
Falls City, NE 70-71 C 5
Falls City, OR 66-67 B 3
Falls City, TX 76-77 EF 8
Falmouth 116-117 FG 10
Falmouth, KY 70-71 H 6
Falmouth, MA 72-73 L 4
Falmouth Bay 116-117 FG 10
False Bay = Valsbaai [ZA, Kaapland] 198 C 8
False Cape 80-81 c 2
False Pass, AK 52-53 ab 2
False Point 160-161 O 6
Falster 114-115 E 10
Falsterbo 114-115 E 10
Faltbush, New York-, NY 82 III c 3
Falterona, Monte — 138-139 DE 4
Fălticeni 138-139 M 2
Falun 114-115 F 7
Famagusta = Ammóchōstos 160-161 CD 3
Family Lake 50 B 2
Fancheng = Xiangfan 166-167 L 5
Fan Foel 116-117 H 9
Fāngāk 194-195 L 7
Fangcheng [TJ, Henan] 166-167 L 5
Fanning 34-35 K 4
Fanning Trench 34-35 J 4-K 5
Fanø [DK] 114-115 C 10
Fano [I] 138-139 E 4
Fan Si Pan 174-175 D 2
Fant, Al- 199 B 3
Fanṭâs, Gebel el — = Jabal al-Finṭās 199 B 6
Fâqûs 199 BC 2
Faraday Seamount Group 110-111 C 5-6
Faradje 198 E 1
Faradofay 198 J 7
Farafangana 198 J 6
Farāfirah, Al-Qaṣr al- 194-195 K 3
Farāfirah, Wāḥāt al- 194-195 K 3
Farāh 160-161 J 4
Farāh Rōd 160-161 J 4
Farallón, Cabo — = Cabo Santa Elena 58-59 J 9
Farallon de Pajaros 148-149 S 7
Farallon Islands 74-75 B 4
Faranah 194-195 BC 6
Farasān, Jazā'ir — 160-161 E 7
Faraulep 174-175 M 5
Farāyid, Jabal al- 199 D 6
Fareham 116-117 KL 10
Farewell, AK 52-53 KL 5
Farewell, MI 72-73 D 3
Farewell, Cape — 182-183 O 8
Farewell, Cape — = Kap Farvel 46-47 c 6
Fargo, GA 80-81 E 5
Fargo, ND 58-59 G 2
Fargo, OK 76-77 E 4
Faribault, MN 70-71 D 3
Fārigh, Wādī al- 194-195 HJ 2-3
Farim 194-195 AB 6
Farina 182-183 G 6
Faringdon 116-117 K 9
Fāris 160-161 G 6
Farlane 50 BC 2
Farmer City, IL 70-71 F 5
Farmersburg, IN 70-71 G 6
Farmerville, LA 78-79 C 4
Farmington, CA 74-75 C 4
Farmington, IA 70-71 DE 5
Farmington, IL 70-71 EF 5
Farmington, ME 72-73 LM 2
Farmington, MN 70-71 D 3
Farmington, MO 70-71 EF 7
Farmington, NM 74-75 J 4
Farmington, UT 66-67 GH 5
Farmville, NC 80-81 H 3
Farmville, VA 80-81 G 2
Farnborough 116-117 L 9
Farne Islands 116-117 K 5
Farnham [CDN] 72-73 K 2
Farnham [GB] 116-117 KL 9
Farnsworth, TX 76-77 D 4
Faro [BR] 98-99 H 5
Faro [P] 132-133 CD 10
Faro [RFC] 194-195 G 7
Faro, Punta di — 138-139 F 6
Fårön 114-115 H 9
Farquhar Islands 198 JK 4
Farrars Creek 182-183 H 4-5
Farrell, PA 72-73 F 4
Far Rockawa, New York-, NY 82 III d 3
Farrukhābād 160-161 M 5
Fārs 160-161 G 4-5
Fársala 138-139 K 6
Farshūṭ 199 BC 4
Farson, WY 66-67 J 4
Farsund 114-115 B 8
Fartak, Rā's — 160-161 G 7
Farvel, Kap — 46-47 c 6
Farwell, MI 70-71 H 4
Farwell, TX 76-77 C 5
Fas 194-195 CD 2
Fasā 160-161 G 5
Fasano 138-139 G 5
Fasham 142-143 K 8
Fāsher, El- = Al-Fāshir 194-195 K 6
Fāshir, Al- 194-195 K 6
Fashn, Al- 194-195 KL 3
Fashoda = Kūdūk 194-195 L 6-7
Fáskrúdhsfjördhur 114-115 fg 2
Fastov 142-143 EF 5
Fatagar, Tanjung — 174-175 K 7
Fatahpur = Fatehpur [IND, Rājasthān] 160-161 L 5
Fatehpur [IND, Rājasthān] 160-161 L 5
Fatḥa, Al- = Al-Fatḥah 160-161 E 3
Father Lake 50 O 2
Fátima 132-133 C 9
Faucett, MO 70-71 C 6
Faucilles, Monts — 132-133 K 5-L 4
Faulkton, SD 68-69 G 3
Făurei 138-139 M 3
Fauro 174-175 j 6
Fauske 114-115 F 4
Faust 48 K 2
Faust, UT 66-67 G 5
Favara 138-139 E 7
Faversham 116-117 gh 7
Favignana 138-139 DE 7
Favourable Lake 50 C 1
Fawnie Range 48 E 3
Fawn River 46-47 T 7
Faxaflói 114-115 b 2
Fay, OK 76-77 E 5
Faya = Largeau 194-195 HJ 5
Fayala 198 C 2
Faya-Largeau 194-195 H 5
Fayḍābād 160-161 KL 3
Fayette, AL 78-79 F 4
Fayette, IA 70-71 E 4
Fayette, MO 70-71 D 6
Fayette, MS 78-79 D 5
Fayetteville, AR 58-59 H 4
Fayetteville, NC 58-59 L 4-5
Fayetteville, OH 72-73 E 5
Fayetteville, TN 78-79 F 3
Fâyid = Fā'id 199 C 2
Fayum, El — = Al-Fayyūm 194-195 KL 3
Fayyūm, Al- 194-195 KL 3
Fayzabad = Faizābād 160-161 N 5
Fazzān 194-195 GH 3
Fdayrik 194-195 B 4
Fear, Cape — 58-59 L 5
Feather Falls, CA 74-75 C 3
Feather River 74-75 C 3
Feather River, North Fork — 74-75 C 2-3
Featherston 182-183 P 8
Featherville, ID 66-67 F 4
Fécamp 132-133 H 4
Federal 103 E 4
Federal Capital Territory = 1 ◁ 194-195 F 7
Federal Capital Territory = Australian Capital Territory 182-183 J 7
Federal Dam, MN 70-71 CD 2
Federick Hills 182-183 G 2
Fedje 114-115 A 7
Fehmarn 124 E 1
Feia, Lagoa — 98-99 L 9
Feijó 98-99 E 6
Feira de Santana 98-99 LM 7
Feisabad = Faizābād 160-161 N 5
Felanitx 132-133 J 9
Feldberg 124 C 5
Feldioara 138-139 L 3
Feldkirch 124 DE 5
Felidu Atoll 36 a 2
Felipe Carillo Puerto 58-59 J 8
Felixtowe 116-117 h 7
Félix U. Gómez 86-87 H 2
Feller Heights 48 G 2
Fellsmere, FL 80-81 c 3
Felt, OK 76-77 C 4
Felton, CA 74-75 B 4
Felton, MN 68-69 H 2
Feltre 138-139 D 2
Femund 114-115 D 6
Femundsenden 114-115 D 7
Fenelon Falls 72-73 G 2
Fénérive = Fenoarivo Atsinanana 198 JK 5
Fengári 138-139 L 5
Fengcheng [TJ, Liaoning] 166-167 N 3
Fêng-chieh = Fengjie 166-167 K 5
Fengdu 166-167 K 5-6
Fengjie 166-167 K 5
Fengkieh = Fengjie 166-167 K 5
Fêng-ming Tao = Fengming Dao 170-171 C 3
Fengming Dao 170-171 C 3
Fengning 166-167 M 3
Fengsien = Feng Xian 166-167 K 5
Fengtu = Fengdu 166-167 K 5-6
Feng Xian [TJ, Shaanxi] 166-167 K 5
Fen He 166-167 L 4
Fên Ho = Fen He 166-167 L 4
Feniak Lake 52-53 HJ 2
Feni Islands 174-175 h 5
Fenner 49 C 5
Fennimore, WI 70-71 E 4
Fennville, MI 70-71 G 4
Fenoarivo Atsinanana 198 JK 5
Fens, The — 116-117 LM 8
Fenshui Ling 170-171 D 2-3
Fenton, LA 78-79 C 5
Fenton, MI 70-71 J 4
Fenyang 166-167 L 4
Feodosija 142-143 G 6-7
Feou-ning = Funing 166-167 MN 5
Fer, Point au — 78-79 D 6
Férai 138-139 M 5
Ferdows 160-161 H 4
Fère, la — 132-133 J 4
Fergana 160-161 L 2-3
Ferganskaja dolina 160-161 L 2
Ferghana = Fergana 160-161 L 2-3
Fergus 72-73 F 3
Fergus Falls, MN 58-59 GH 2
Fergusson Island 174-175 h 6
Ferkéssédougou 194-195 CD 7
Ferlo [SN, landscape] 194-195 AB 5
Fermanagh 116-117 D 6
Fermo 138-139 E 4
Fermoselle 132-133 DE 8
Fermoy = Fir Maighe 116-117 C 8
Fernandina, FL 80-81 c 1
Fernandina, Isla — 98-99 A 4-5
Fernando de Noronha 98-99 N 5
Fernando de Noronha, Ilha — 98-99 N 5
Fernando Póo, Isla de — = Bioko 194-195 F 8
Ferndale, CA 66-67 A 5
Ferndale, WA 66-67 B 1
Fernie 66-67 F 1
Fernley, NV 74-75 D 3
Fernwood, ID 66-67 EF 2
Ferrara 138-139 DE 3
Ferreira Gomes 98-99 J 4
Ferreñafe 98-99 D 6
Ferrer Point 48 D 5
Ferriday, LA 78-79 D 5
Ferris, TX 76-77 F 6
Ferro = Hierro 194-195 A 3
Ferrol, Península de — 98-99 CD 6
Ferrol de Caudillo, El — 132-133 C 7
Ferry, AK 52-53 N 4
Ferryhill 116-117 K 6
Fertile, MN 68-69 H 2
Fes = Fās 194-195 CD 2
Feshi 198 C 3
Fessenden, ND 68-69 FG 2
Festus, MO 70-71 E 6
Feteşti 138-139 M 3
Fethard = Fiodh Ard 116-117 D 8
Fethiye 160-161 B 3
Fetisovo 160-161 G 2
Fetlar 116-117 f 3
Feuerland 103 C 8
Fez = Fas 194-195 CD 2
Fezzan = Fazzān 194-195 GH 3
Ffestiniog 116-117 H 8
Fheoir, An — 116-117 D 8
Fhóid Dhuibh, Cuan an — 116-117 AB 6
Fianarantsoa 198 J 6
Fichtelgebirge 124 EF 3
Fidenza 138-139 D 3
Field 72-73 FG 1
Field, NM 76-77 A 5
Fielding 49 E 4
Field Museum 83 II b 1
Fier 138-139 H 5
Fier, Portile de — 138-139 K 3
Fife 116-117 HJ 4
Fife Ness 116-117 J 4
Fīfī, Al- 194-195 J 6
Figeac 132-133 J 6
Figig = Fijīj 194-195 D 2
Figueira, Cachoeira — 98-99 J 9
Figueira da Foz 132-133 C 8
Figueras 132-133 J 7
Figuîg = Fījīj 194-195 D 2
Fiji 174-175 ab 2
Fiji Basin 34-35 H 6
Fiji Islands 174-175 ab 2
Fījīj 194-195 D 2
Fila = Vila 182-183 N 3
Filabres, Sierra de los — 132-133 F 10
Filadélfia [BR, Goiás] 98-99 K 6
Filadelfia [PY] 103 D 2
Filchner-Schelfeis 31 A 30-B 33
Filer, ID 66-67 F 4
Filey 116-117 L 6
Filiaşi 138-139 K 3
Filiátai 138-139 J 6
Filiatrá 138-139 J 7
Filicudi 138-139 F 6
Filingué 194-195 E 6
Filipevila = Sakīkdah 194-195 F 1
Filippiás 138-139 J 6
Filipstad 114-115 EF 8
Fillmore 49 G 6
Fillmore, CA 74-75 D 5
Fillmore, UT 74-75 G 3
Fimi 198 C 2
Financial District, New York-, NY 82 III bc 3
Finch 72-73 J 2
Findhorn, River — 116-117 H 3
Findlay, OH 58-59 K 3
Finedon 116-117 L 8
Fingal, ND 68-69 H 2
Finger Lake 50 C 1
Finger Lakes 58-59 L 3
Fingoè 198 F 5
Finisterre, Cabo de — 132-133 BC 7
Fink Creek, AK 52-53 F 4
Finke 182-183 FG 5
Finke River 182-183 G 5
Finland 114-115 K 7-M 4
Finland, MN 70-71 E 2
Finland, Gulf of — 110-111 N 4-O 3
Finlay Forks 48 EF 1
Finlay Mountains 76-77 B 7
Finlay Ranges 48 E 1
Finlay River 46-47 LM 6
Finley, ND 68-69 H 2
Finmark 70-71 F 1
Finnegan 49 BC 5
Finnmark 114-115 K 3-N 2
Finnmarksvidda 114-115 KL 3
Finn Mount 52-53 J 6
Finnskogene 114-115 E 7
Finnsnes 114-115 GH 3
Finschhafen 174-175 N 8
Finse 114-115 B 7
Finspång 114-115 FG 8
Finsteraarhorn 124 CD 5
Finsterwalde 124 FG 3
Finṭās, Jabal al- 199 B 6
Fintona 116-117 D 6
Fiodh Ard 116-117 D 8
Fiordland National Park 182-183 N 8-9
Fırat nehri 160-161 D 3
Firebag River 49 C 2
Firebaugh, CA 74-75 C 4
Fire Island 52-53 M 6
Firenze 138-139 D 4
Fire River 70-71 HJ 1
Firesteel, SD 68-69 F 3
Firkessedougou = Ferkéssédougou 194-195 CD 7
Fir Maighe 116-117 C 8
Fīrozābād 160-161 M 5
Firth River 52-53 R 2
Fīrūzābād [IR, Fārs] 160-161 G 5
Firvale 48 DE 3
Fish Creek 52-53 LM 1
Fisher, MN 68-69 H 2
Fisher Bay 49 K 5
Fishermans Island 80-81 J 2
Fisher Strait 46-47 U 5
Fishguard & Goodwick 116-117 G 8-9
Fishing Lake 49 G 5
Fishing Point 80-81 J 2
Fish Lake Valley 74-75 DE 4
Fish River 52-53 F 4
Fisk, MO 78-79 D 2
Fiskåfjället 114-115 F 5
Fiske 49 D 5
Fiskenæsset = Qeqertarssuatsiaq 46-47 a 5
Fiskivötn 114-115 c 2
Fitchburg, MA 72-73 KL 3
Fitful Head 116-117 e 4
Fittri, Lac — 194-195 H 6
Fitzgerald, GA 80-81 E 5
Fitz Hugh Sound 48 D 4
Fitzmaurice River 182-183 EF 2
Fitzpatrick 72-73 K 1
Fitz Roy 103 C 7
Fitz Roy, Monte — 103 B 7
Fitzroy Crossing 182-183 DE 3
Fitzroy River [AUS, Queensland] 182-183 JK 4
Fitzroy River [AUS, Western Australia] 182-183 DE 3
Fitzwilliam Island 50 KL 4
Fitzwilliam Strait 46-47 NO 2
Fiume = Rijeka 138-139 F 3
Five Miles Rapids 66-67 D 2
Fizi 198 E 2
Flå 114-115 C 7
Flagler, CO 68-69 E 6
Flagstaff, AZ 58-59 D 4
Flagstaff Lake 72-73 L 2
Flagstaff Siphaqeni 198 EF 8
Flagstone 66-67 F 1
Flaherty Island 46-47 U 6
Flakstadøy 114-115 E 3
Flåm 114-115 B 7
Flamand = Arak 194-195 E 3
Flambeau Flowage 70-71 E 2
Flamborough Head 116-117 LM 6
Fläming 124 F 2-3
Flaming Gorge Reservoir 66-67 J 5
Flamingo, FL 80-81 c 4
Flamingo, Teluk — 174-175 L 8
Flanders 50 C 3
Flanders = Vlaanderen 132-133 J 3
Flandreau, SD 68-69 H 3
Flanigan, NV 66-67 D 5
Flannan Isles 116-117 D 2
Flasher, ND 68-69 F 2
Flat, AK 52-53 HJ 5
Flatey 114-115 b 2
Flateyri 114-115 ab 1
Flathead Indian Reservation 66-67 FG 2
Flathead Lake 58-59 CD 2
Flathead Mountains = Salish Mountains 66-67 F 1-2
Flathead River 66-67 F 1
Flatonia, TX 76-77 F 8
Flat River, MO 70-71 E 7
Flattery, Cape — [AUS] 182-183 J 2
Flattery, Cape — [USA] 66-67 A 1
Flat Top Mountain 80-81 F 2
Flaxman Island 52-53 P 1
Flaxton, ND 68-69 E 1
Flaxville, MT 68-69 D 1
Flèche, la — 132-133 GH 5
Fleetwood 116-117 H 7
Fleischhacker Zoo 83 II ab 2
Flekkefjord 114-115 AB 8
Fleming, CO 68-69 E 5
Flemingsburg, KY 72-73 E 5
Flen 114-115 G 8
Flensburg 124 DE 1
Flers 132-133 G 4
Flesher, MT 66-67 G 2
Fletcher, OK 76-77 EF 5
Fleur de Lys 51 HJ 2
Fleur de May, Lac — 51 D 2
Flinders Bay 182-183 BC 6
Flinders Island [AUS, Bass Strait] 182-183 J 7
Flinders Island [AUS, Great Australian Bight] 182-183 F 6
Flinders Ranges 182-183 G 6
Flinders River 182-183 H 3-4
Flin Flon 46-47 Q 7
Flint, MI 58-59 K 3
Flint [GB] 116-117 H 7
Flint [island] 34-35 K 6
Flintdale 50 G 2
Flint Hills 68-69 H 6-7
Flint River [USA, Georgia] 78-79 G 5
Flint River [USA, Michigan] 72-73 E 3
Flomaton, AL 78-79 F 5
Floodwood, MN 70-71 D 2
Flora 114-115 A 7
Flora, IL 70-71 F 6
Flora, OR 66-67 E 3
Florala, AL 78-79 F 5
Floral Park, NY 82 III de 2
Floreana 98-99 AB 5
Floreana, Isla — 98-99 A 5
Florence, AL 58-59 J 5
Florence, AZ 74-75 H 6
Florence, CA 83 III c 2
Florence, CO 68-69 D 6
Florence, KS 68-69 H 6
Florence, OR 66-67 A 4
Florence, SC 58-59 L 5
Florence, SD 68-69 H 3
Florence, WI 70-71 F 3
Florence = Firenze 138-139 D 4
Florence Junction, AZ 74-75 H 6
Florencia [CO] 98-99 DE 4
Flores [GB] 58-59 J 8
Flores [RI] 174-175 H 8
Flores, Las — [RA, Buenos Aires] 103 E 5
Florescência 98-99 D 9
Flores Island 48 D 5
Flores Sea 174-175 GH 8
Floressee 174-175 GH 8
Floresta Amazônica 98-99 E-H 6
Floresville, TX 76-77 EF 8
Floriano 98-99 L 6
Floriano Peixoto 98-99 DE 9
Florianópolis 103 G 3
Florida, NM 76-77 A 6
Florida [C] 88-89 GH 4
Florida [ROU, place] 103 E 4
Florida [USA] 58-59 K 5-6
Florida, Cape — 80-81 cd 4
Florida, Straits of — 58-59 K 7-L 6
Florida Bay 58-59 K 7
Florida City, FL 80-81 c 4
Florida Island 174-175 jk 6
Florida Keys 58-59 K 6-7
Florido, Río — 76-77 B 8-9
Florien, LA 78-79 C 5
Flōrina 138-139 J 5
Florissant, MO 70-71 EF 6
Flotten Lake 49 D 3
Flowerpot Island 72-73 F 2
Flower's Cove 51 HJ 2
Flower Station 72-73 H 2
Floyd, NM 76-77 C 5
Floyd, VA 80-81 F 2
Floyd, Mount — 74-75 G 5
Floydada, TX 76-77 D 5-6
Floyd River 70-71 BC 4
Flumendosa 138-139 C 6
Flushing = Vlissingen 132-133 J 3
Flushing, New York-, NY 82 III d 2
Flushing Airport 82 III d 2
Flushing Meadow Park 82 III c 2
Flying Fish, Cape — 31 BC 26
Fly River 174-175 M 8
Foam Lake 49 G 5
Foča [YU] 138-139 H 4
Foch 48 E 4
Fo-chan = Foshan 166-167 L 7
Fochi 194-195 H 5
Focşani 138-139 M 3
Fóggia 138-139 F 5
Fogo [Cape Verde] 188-189 E 7
Fogo [CDN] 51 J 3
Fogo Island 46-47 a 8
Föhr 124 D 1
Foix [F, landscape] 132-133 H 7
Foix [F, place] 132-133 H 7
Fola, Cnoc — 116-117 C 5
Folda [N, Nordland] 114-115 F 4
Folda [N, Nord-Trøndelag] 114-115 D 5
Folégandros 138-139 L 7
Foley, AL 78-79 F 5
Foley, MN 70-71 CD 3
Foleyet 50 K 2
Foley Island 46-47 V 4
Folgefonni 114-115 B 7-8
Folger, AK 52-53 JK 5
Foligno 138-139 E 4
Folkestone 116-117 h 7
Folkston, GA 80-81 E 5
Folldal 114-115 CD 6
Follett, TX 76-77 D 4
Folsom, CA 74-75 C 3
Folsom, NM 76-77 C 4
Folteşti 138-139 MN 3
Fonda, IA 70-71 C 4
Fonda, NY 72-73 J 3
Fond-du-Lac 46-47 PQ 6
Fond du Lac, WI 58-59 J 3
Fond du Lac Indian Reservation 70-71 D 2
Fond du Lac Mountains 70-71 E 2
Fond du Lac River 46-47 Q 6
Fondi 138-139 E 5
Fonsagrada 132-133 D 7
Fonseca, Golfo de — 58-59 J 9
Fontainebleau [F] 132-133 J 4
Fonte Boa 98-99 F 5
Fonteneau, Lac — 51 F 2
Fontenelle Reservoir 66-67 HJ 4
Fontur 114-115 fg 1
Fonualei 174-175 c 2
Foochow = Fengdu 166-167 K 5-6
Foochow = Fujian 166-167 MN 6
Foochow = Fuzhou 166-167 MN 6
Foothills 48 J 3
Foraker, Mount — 46-47 F 5
Forbes 182-183 J 6
Forbes, ND 68-69 G 3
Forbes, Mount — 48 J 4
Ford 116-117 F 4
Ford, KS 68-69 G 7
Ford, KY 70-71 H 7
Ford, Cape — 182-183 E 2
Ford City, CA 74-75 D 5
Ford City, Chicago-, IL 83 II a 2
Førde 114-115 AB 7
Fordingbridge 116-117 K 10
Ford Lake 74-75 F 6
Ford River 70-71 G 2-3
Fords Bridge 182-183 HJ 5
Fordsville, KY 70-71 G 7
Fordyce, AR 78-79 C 4
Forécariah 194-195 B 7
Forel, Mont — 46-47 d 4
Forest, MS 78-79 E 4
Forest, OH 72-73 E 4

Forest 227

Futamata 170-171 L 5
Futaoi-jima 170-171 H 5
Futsing = Fuqing 166-167 MN 6
Futuna 174-175 b 1
Fuwah 199 B 2
Fu Xian [TJ, Liaoning] 166-167 N 4
Fuxian Hu 166-167 J 7
Fuxin 166-167 N 3
Fuyang [TJ, Anhui] 166-167 M 5
Fuyu [TJ, Heilongjiang] 166-167 NO 2
Fuyu [TJ, Jilin] 166-167 NO 2
Fu-yü = Fuyu 166-167 NO 2
Fuyuan 166-167 P 2
Fuzhou [TJ, Fujian] 166-167 MN 6
Fuzhou [TJ, Jianxi] 166-167 M 6
Fuzhoucheng 166-167 N 4

Fyn 114-115 D 10
Fyne, Loch — 116-117 F 4-5
Fyzabad = Faizābād 160-161 N 5

G

Gaalka'yo 194-195 b 2
Gaarowe 194-195 b 2
Gabarouse 51 FG 5
Gabba' 194-195 c 2
Gabbs Valley 74-75 DE 3
Gabbs Valley Range 74-75 DE 3
Gabela [Angola] 198 BC 4
Gaberones = Gaborone 198 DE 6
Gabès = Qābis 194-195 FG 2
Gabes, Gulf of — = Khalīj al-Qabis 194-195 G 2
Gabilan Range 74-75 C 4
Gabon 198 AB 2
Gaborone 198 DE 6
Gabriel Antunes Maciel, Serra — 98-99 G 10-11
Gabrovo 138-139 L 4
Gachsārān 160-161 G 4
Gackle, ND 68-69 G 2
Gacko 138-139 H 4
Gadap = Karāchī 160-161 K 6
Gäddede 114-115 F 5
Gadhra, Loch — 116-117 C 7
Gadīdah, Al- = Al-Jadīdah [MA] 194-195 C 2
Gadrā 160-161 L 5
Gadsby 49 BC 4
Gadsden, AL 58-59 J 5
Găeşti 138-139 L 3
Gaeta 138-139 E 5
Gaeta, Golfo di — 138-139 E 5
Gaf, Bir el — = Bi'r al-Qaf 194-195 H 3
Gaferut 148-149 S 9
Gaffney, SC 80-81 F 3
Gäfle = Gävle 114-115 G 7
Gagarin 142-143 FG 4
Gage, NM 74-75 JK 6
Gage, OK 76-77 E 4
Gage Park, Chicago-, IL 83 II a 2
Gagliano del Capo 138-139 GH 6
Gagnoa 194-195 C 7
Gagnon 46-47 X 7
Gago Coutinho = Lungala N'Guimbo 198 D 4
Gagra 142-143 GH 7
Gaha Mountains = Sléibhte na Ceachan 116-117 B 9
Gahnpa 194-195 C 7
Gaia = Gayā 160-161 NO 5-6
Gaibhlte, Na — 116-117 C 8
Gail 124 F 5
Gail, TX 76-77 D 6
Gaillimh 116-117 B 7
Gaillimhe, Cuan na — 116-117 B 7
Gaima 174-175 M 8
Gaimán 103 C 6
Gainesville, FL 58-59 K 6
Gainesville, GA 58-59 K 5
Gainesville, MO 78-79 C 2
Gainesville, TX 58-59 G 5
Gainsborough 116-117 L 7
Gairdner, Lake — 182-183 G 6
Gairloch 116-117 F 3
Gai Xian 170-171 CD 2
Gajny 154-155 J 5
Gakona, AK 52-53 P 5
Galadi = Geladī 194-195 O 7
Galán, Cerro — 103 C 3
Galana 198 GH 2
Galashiels 116-117 HJ 5
Galaţi 138-139 MN 3
Galatia, KS 68-69 G 6
Galatina 138-139 H 5
Galatz = Galaţi 138-139 MN 3
Galax, VA 80-81 F 2
Galbeed = Waqooyi-Galbeed 194-195 a 1
Galdhøpiggen 114-115 BC 7
Galea 174-175 J 6
Galeana 86-87 G 2
Galena, AK 46-47 E 4-5
Galena, IL 70-71 E 4
Galena, MO 78-79 C 2
Galera, Punta — [EC] 98-99 C 4
Galera, Punta — [RCH] 103 AB 6
Galera Point 58-59 OP 9
Galesburg, IL 58-59 HJ 3
Galesville, WI 70-71 E 3
Galeta, Isla — 58-59 b 2
Galeta Island 58-59 b 2
Galeton 50 L 1
Galeton, PA 72-73 H 4
Gal-Guduud 194-195 b 2-3
Galič [SU, Rossijskaja SFSR] 154-155 G 6
Galicia 132-133 CD 7
Galicja 124 J-L 4
Galilee, Lake — 182-183 HJ 4
Galilee, Sea of — = Yam Kinneret 160-161 D 4
Galineau, Rivière — 72-73 J 1
Galion, OH 72-73 E 4
Galipoli = Gelibolu 160-161 B 2
Galissonnière, Lac la — 51 E 2
Galiuro Mountains 74-75 H 6
Gālla 160-161 MN 9
Gallabat = Qallābāt 194-195 M 6
Galladi = Geladī 194-195 O 7
Gallatin, MO 70-71 D 6
Gallatin, TN 78-79 F 2
Gallatin Gateway, MT 66-67 H 3
Gallatin Peak 66-67 H 3
Gallatin River 66-67 H 3
Gallaudet College 82 II b 2
Galle = Gālla 160-161 MN 9
Galle, Lac — 51 G 2
Gállego, Río — 132-133 G 7
Gallegos, NM 76-77 C 5
Gallegos, Río — 103 BC 8
Galliate 138-139 C 3
Gallina Mountains 76-77 A 5
Gallinas, Punta — 98-99 E 2
Gallipoli 138-139 GH 5
Gallipoli = Gelibolu 160-161 B 2
Gallipolis, OH 72-73 E 5
Gällivare 114-115 J 4
Gallo Mountains 74-75 J 5-6
Galloo Island 72-73 H 3
Galloway, Mull of — 116-117 G 6
Galloway, Rhinns of — 116-117 FG 6
Gallup, NM 58-59 E 4
Galšir 166-167 L 2
Galt, CA 74-75 C 3
Galtee Mountains = Na Gaibhlte 116-117 C 8
Galva, IL 70-71 EF 5
Galveston, TX 58-59 H 6
Galveston Bay 58-59 H 6
Galveston Island 76-77 G 8
Gálvez [RA] 103 D 4
Galway = Gaillimh 116-117 B 7
Galway Bay = Cuan na Gaillimhe 116-117 B 7
Gam, Pulau — 174-175 JK 7
Gamane = Bertoua 194-195 G 8
Gambaga 194-195 D 6
Gambeila = Gambēla 194-195 L 7
Gambēla 194-195 L 7
Gambell, AK 46-47 BC 5
Gambia [WAG, state] 194-195 AB 6
Gambie 194-195 B 6
Gamboa 58-59 b 2
Gamboma 198 C 2
Gambos 198 BC 4
Gamerco, NM 74-75 J 5
Game Reserve Number 1 198 CD 5
Game Reserve Number 2 198 BC 5
Gamhna, Loch — 116-117 D 7
Gamlakarleby = Kokkola 114-115 K 6
Gamleby 114-115 FG 9
Gamova, mys — 170-171 H 1
Gamsah = Jamsah 199 C 4
Gamvik 114-115 N 2
Gan [Maldive Is., island] 36 a 2
Gan [Maldive Is., place] 36 a 3
Gana = Ghana 194-195 DE 7
Ganaane, Webi — 194-195 N 8
Ganado, AZ 74-75 J 5
Ganado, TX 76-77 F 8
Gananoque 72-73 H 2
Ganāveh 160-161 FG 5
Ganchhendzönga = Gangchhendsönga 160-161 O 5
Gand = Gent 132-133 JK 3
Ganda 198 B 4
Gandajika 198 DE 3
Gandak 160-161 NO 5
Gander 46-47 a 8
Gander Lake 51 J 3
Gander River 51 J 3
Gandesa 132-133 H 8
Gandia 132-133 GH 9
Gandilans Provincial Forest 50 B 3
Gangā 160-161 M 5
Ganga, Mouths of the — 160-161 OP 6
Gan Gan 103 C 6
Gangānagar 160-161 LM 5
Gangchhendsönga 160-161 O 5
Ganges = Gangā 160-161 M 5
Ganges Canyon 160-161 O 6-7
Gangou 170-171 B 2
Gangouzhen = Gangou 170-171 B 2
Gang Ranch 48 F 4
Gangthog 160-161 O 5
Gangtö Gangri 166-167 G 6
Gangtok = Gangthog 160-161 O 5
Gangtun 170-171 C 2
Gan He 166-167 N 1
Gan Jiang 166-167 LM 6
Gannan Zangzu Zizhizhou 166-167 J 5
Gannett, ID 66-67 FG 4
Gannett Peak 58-59 E 3
Gannvalley, SD 68-69 G 3-4
Gansu 166-167 G 3-J 4
Ganta = Gahnpa 194-195 C 7
Gantheaume Bay 182-183 B 5
Gan'uškino 142-143 JK 6
Ganxian = Ganzhou 166-167 LM 6
Ganzhou 166-167 LM 6
Gao 194-195 D 5
Gao'an 166-167 LM 6
Gaoligong Shan 166-167 H 6
Gaoqiao = Gaoqiaozhen 170-171 C 2
Gaoqiaozhen 170-171 C 2
Gaotai 166-167 H 4
Gaoth Beara 116-117 C 6
Gaoua 194-195 D 6
Gaoual 194-195 B 6
Gaoxiong = Kaohsiung 166-167 MN 7
Gap 132-133 L 6
Gar, Bir el — = Bi'r al-Qaf 194-195 H 3
Gara, Lough — = Loch Gadhra 116-117 C 7
Garabaldi Provincial Park 48 F 4-5
Garachiné 88-89 GH 10
Gar'ad 194-195 bc 2
Garamba, Parc national de la — 198 EF 1
Garanhuns 98-99 M 6
Gara Samuil 138-139 M 4
Garb, Gebel el — = Jabal Nafusah 194-195 G 2
Garbahaarrey 194-195 N 8
Garber, OK 76-77 F 4
Garberville, CA 66-67 B 5
Garcias 98-99 J 9
Gard 132-133 K 6-7
Garda 138-139 D 3
Garda, Lago di — 138-139 D 3
Gardelegen 124 E 2
Garden, MI 70-71 G 3
Gardena, CA 83 III c 2
Garden City, AL 78-79 F 3
Garden City, KS 58-59 F 4
Garden City, TX 76-77 D 7
Garden Grove, CA 74-75 D 6
Garden Island 70-71 H 3
Garden River 70-71 HJ 2
Gardenton 50 A 3
Garden Valley, ID 66-67 F 3
Gardēz 160-161 K 4
Gardhsskagi 114-115 b 2
Gardiner 50 L 2
Gardiner, ME 72-73 M 2
Gardiner, MT 66-67 H 3
Gardiners Bay 72-73 KL 4
Gardner 178 J 3
Gardner, CO 68-69 D 7
Gardner, IL 70-71 F 5
Gardner, MA 72-73 KL 3
Gardner, ND 68-69 H 2
Gardnerville, NV 74-75 D 3
Gardula-Gidole = Gīdolē 194-195 M 7
Garelochhead 116-117 FG 4
Gareloi Island 52-53 t 6-7
Gare Windsor Forum 82 I b 2
Garfield, NJ 82 III b 1
Garfield Heights, OH 72-73 F 4
Garfield Mountain 66-67 G 3
Garfield Park 83 II a 1
Gargaliánoi 138-139 J 7
Gargano 138-139 FG 5
Gargano, Testa del — 138-139 G 5
Gargantua, Cape — 70-71 H 2
Gargia 114-115 K 3
Garian = Ghayān 194-195 G 2
Garibaldi, OR 66-67 B 3
Garibaldi Provincial Park 66-67 B 1
Garies 198 C 8
Garissa 198 GH 2
Garland, NC 80-81 G 3
Garland, TX 76-77 F 6
Garland, UT 66-67 G 5
Garlingford Lough 116-117 E 6-F 7
Garmashīn, 'Ain — = 'Ayn Jarmashīn 199 B 5
Garmisch-Partenkirchen 124 E 5
Garmsār 142-143 K 8
Garner, IA 70-71 D 4
Garnet, MT 66-67 G 2
Garnett, KS 70-71 C 6
Garomna 116-117 B 7
Garonne 132-133 G 6
Garopaba 103 G 3
Garoua 194-195 G 7
Garretson, SD 68-69 H 4
Garrett, IN 70-71 H 5
Garrick 49 F 4
Garrison, MT 66-67 G 2
Garrison, ND 68-69 F 2
Garron Point 116-117 F 5
Garry Lake 46-47 Q 4
Garson Lake 49 CD 2
Garstang 116-117 J 7
Garston, Liverpool- 116-117 HJ 7
Gartempe 132-133 H 5
Garth 49 C 3
Gartog 166-167 E 5
Gartok = Gartog 166-167 E 5
Garua = Garoua 194-195 G 7
Garway 116-117 J 9
Garwood, TX 76-77 F 8
Gary, IN 58-59 J 3
Gary, SD 68-69 H 3
Garza Garcia 86-87 K 5
Garze 166-167 J 5
Garze Zangzu Zizhizhou 166-167 HJ 5
Garzón [CO] 98-99 DE 4
Gasan-Kuli 160-161 G 3
Gascogne 132-133 GH 7
Gasconade River 70-71 E 6
Gascoyne, ND 68-69 E 2
Gascoyne, Mount — 182-183 C 4
Gascoyne River 182-183 C 5
Gashaka 194-195 G 7
Gasmata 174-175 gh 6
Gaspar, Selat — 174-175 E 7
Gasparilla Island 80-81 b 3
Gaspé 46-47 Y 8
Gaspé, Baie de — 51 DE 3
Gaspé, Cap — 46-47 Y 8
Gaspé, Péninsule de — 46-47 XY 8
Gaspé Passage 46-47 XY 8
Gaspésie, Parc provincial de la — 51 CD 3
Gas-san [J] 170-171 MN 3
Gassaway, WV 72-73 F 5
Gaston, OR 66-67 B 3
Gastonia, NC 58-59 K 4
Gastre 103 C 6
Gašuun Gov' 166-167 G 3
Gašuun nuur 166-167 HJ 3
Gat = Ghat 194-195 G 3
Gata, Cabo de — 132-133 FG 10
Gata, Sierra de — 132-133 D 8
Gatčina 154-155 DE 6
Gate City, VA 80-81 E 2
Gateshead 116-117 K 6
Gates of the Mountains 66-67 H 2
Gatesville, TX 76-77 F 7
Gateway, CO 74-75 J 3
Gateway, MT 66-67 F 1
Gateway, OR 66-67 C 3
Gâtinaïs 132-133 J 4
Gâtine, Hauteurs de — 132-133 G 5
Gatineau 72-73 J 2
Gatineau, Rivière — 72-73 J 1-2
Gatineau Park 72-73 HJ 2
Gatooma = Kadoma 198 E 5
Gatrun, el- = Al-Qaṭrūn 194-195 GH 4
Gatun 58-59 b 2
Gatun, Barrage de — = Presa de Gatún 58-59 ab 2
Gatún, Brazo de — 58-59 b 2
Gatún, Esclusas de — 58-59 b 2
Gatún, Lago de — 58-59 b 2
Gatún, Presa de — 58-59 ab 2
Gatún, Río — 58-59 b 2
Gatun Arm = Brazo de Gatún 58-59 b 2
Gatuncillo 58-59 b 2
Gatuncillo, Río — 58-59 b 2
Gatun Dam = Presa de Gatún 58-59 ab 2
Gatun Lake = Lago de Gatún 58-59 b 2
Gatun Locks = Esclusas de Gatún 58-59 b 2
Gauani = Gewanī 194-195 N 6
Gauer Lake 49 K 2
Gauhati 160-161 P 5
Gaula 114-115 D 6
Gauley Mountain 72-73 F 5
Gaurisankar = Jomotsering 160-161 O 5
Gaurīshankar = Jomotsering 160-161 O 5
Gausta 114-115 C 8
Gausvik 114-115 G 3
Gávdos 138-139 L 8
Gave de Pau 132-133 G 7
Gavins Reservoir = Lewis and Clark Lake 68-69 H 4
Gaviota, CA 74-75 C 5
Gävle 114-115 G 7
Gävleborg 114-115 G 6-7
Gavrilov-Jam 142-143 G 4
Gawler 182-183 G 6
Gawler Ranges 182-183 G 6
Gay, MI 70-71 F 2
Gaya [DY] 194-195 E 6
Gaya [IND] 160-161 NO 5-6
Gaylord, MI 70-71 H 3
Gaylord, MN 70-71 C 3
Gayndah 182-183 K 5
Gaza 198 F 6
Gaza = Ghazzah 160-161 C 4
Gazalkent 154-155 MN 9
Gazelle, CA 66-67 B 5
Gazelle Peninsula 174-175 h 5
Gaziantep 160-161 D 3

Gbarnga 194-195 C 7

Gdańsk 124 J 1
Gdańska, Zatoka — 124 J 1
Gdov 142-143 E 4
Gdynia 124 HJ 1

Gearhart Mountain 66-67 C 4
Geary, OK 76-77 E 5
Geba, Rio de — 194-195 AB 6
Gebe, Pulau — 174-175 J 7
Gebeit = Jubayt 194-195 M 4
Gebo, WY 68-69 B 4
Gedaref = Al-Qadārif 194-195 M 6
Geddes, SD 68-69 G 4
Gedi 198 G 2
Gedid, el — = Sabhah 194-195 G 3
Gediz 142-143 E 8
Gediz çay 142-143 E 8
Gēdo [ETH] 194-195 M 7
Gedo [SP] 194-195 N 8
Gedser 114-115 DE 10
Geelong 182-183 H 7
Geelvink Channel 182-183 B 5
Geese Bank 154-155 GH 3
Geeveston 182-183 J 8
Géfyra 138-139 K 5
Gegeen gol = Gen He 166-167 N 1
Geidam 194-195 G 6
Geikie Island 50 E 2
Geikie River 49 F 2
Geilo 114-115 C 7
Geiranger 114-115 B 6
Geislingen 124 D 4
Geita 198 F 2
Gejiu 166-167 J 7
Gela 138-139 F 7
Geladī 194-195 O 7
Gelendžik 142-143 G 7
Gelib = Jilib 198 H 1
Gelibolu 160-161 B 2
Gelsenkirchen 124 C 3
Gem 49 B 5
Gemas 174-175 D 6
Gemena 198 C 1
Gemona del Friuli 138-139 E 2
Gemsa = Jamsah 199 C 4
Gemu Gofa 194-195 M 7
Genale 194-195 N 7
Geneina, El- = Al-Junaynah 194-195 J 6
General Acha 103 CD 5
General Alvear [RA, Buenos Aires] 103 DE 5
General Alvear [RA, Mendoza] 103 C 4-5
General Belgrano [Antarctica] 31 B 32-33
General Bernardo O'Higgins 31 C 31
General Cepeda 86-87 JK 5
General Conesa [RA, Río Negro] 103 CD 6
General Deheza 103 D 4
General Enrique Mosconi 103 D 2
General Guido 103 E 5
General José de San Martín 103 E 3
General Juan Madariaga 103 E 5
General La Madrid 103 D 5
General Lavalle 103 E 5
General Lorenzo Vintter 103 D 6
General Machado = Camacupa 198 C 4
General Martín Miguel de Güemes 103 CD 2
General Pico 103 D 5
General Pinedo 103 D 3
General Roca 103 C 5
General Santos 174-175 HJ 5
General Toševo 138-139 N 4
General Trías 86-87 GH 3
General Villamil = Playas 98-99 C 5
General Villegas 103 D 4-5
Genesee, ID 66-67 E 2
Genesee River 72-73 GH 3
Geneseo, IL 70-71 E 5
Geneseo, KS 68-69 G 6
Geneseo, NY 72-73 H 3
Geneva, AL 78-79 G 5
Geneva, NE 68-69 H 5
Geneva, NY 72-73 H 3
Geneva, OH 72-73 F 4
Geneva = Genève 124 C 5
Geneva, Lake — = Léman 124 C 5
Genève 124 C 5
Genghiz Khan, Wall of — 166-167 LM 2
Genhe [TJ, place] 166-167 N 1
Gen He [TJ, river] 166-167 N 1
Geničesk 142-143 F 6
Genil 132-133 E 10
Genk 132-133 K 3
Genkai nada 170-171 GH 6
Gennargentu, Monti del — 138-139 C 5-6
Genoa 182-183 J 7
Genoa, IL 70-71 F 4
Genoa, NE 68-69 GH 5
Genoa, WI 70-71 E 4
Genoa = Gènova 138-139 C 3
Gènova 138-139 C 3
Gènova, Golfo di — 138-139 C 4
Genovesa, Isla — 98-99 B 4
Gent 132-133 JK 3
Genteng 174-175 E 8
Genzan = Wŏnsan 166-167 O 4
Geographe Bay 182-183 BC 6
Geographe Channel 182-183 B 4-5
Geok-Tepe 160-161 H 3
George 198 D 8
George, Lake — [AUS] 182-183 JK 7
George, Lake — [EAU] 198 F 2
George, Lake — [USA, Alaska] 52-53 PQ 5
George, Lake — [USA, Florida] 80-81 c 2
George, Lake — [USA, New York] 72-73 K 3
George, zemľa — 154-155 F-H 1
George Gills Range 182-183 F 4
George River [CDN] 46-47 XY 6
George River [USA] 52-53 J 5
Georgetown, CA 74-75 C 3
Georgetown, DE 72-73 J 5
Georgetown, GA 78-79 G 5
Georgetown, ID 66-67 H 4
Georgetown, IL 70-71 G 6
Georgetown, KY 70-71 H 6
Georgetown, OH 72-73 E 5
Georgetown, SC 80-81 G 4
Georgetown, TX 76-77 F 7
Georgetown [AUS, Queensland] 182-183 H 3
George Town [AUS, Tasmania] 182-183 J 8
George Town [BS] 88-89 HJ 3
Georgetown [CDN, Ontario] 72-73 G 3
Georgetown [CDN, Prince Edward I.] 51 E 4
Georgetown [GB] 88-89 F 5
Georgetown [GUY] 98-99 H 3
Georgetown [WV] 88-89 Q 8
George Town = Pinang 174-175 CD 5
Georgetown, Washington-, DC 82 II a 1
Georgetown University 82 II a 2
George Washington Birthplace National Monument 72-73 H 5
George Washington Bridge 82 III c 1
George Washington University 82 II a 2
George West, TX 76-77 E 8
Georgia 58-59 K 5
Georgia, South — 103 J 8
Georgia, Strait of — 46-47 M 8
Georgiana, AL 78-79 F 5
Georgian Bay 46-47 U 8-9
Georgian Soviet Socialist Republic 160-161 EF 2
Georgias del Sur, Islas — = South Georgia 103 J 8
Georgijevka 154-155 P 8
Georgijevsk 142-143 H 7
Georgijevskoje 142-143 HJ 4
Georgina River 182-183 G 4
Georg von Neumayer 31 B 36
Gera 124 EF 3
Gerais, Chapado dos — 98-99 K 8
Geral, Serra — [BR, Rio Grande do Sul ↖ Porto Alegre] 103 F 3
Geral, Serra — [BR, Santa Catarina] 103 F 3
Geral, Serra — = Serra Grande 98-99 P 10
Geraldine, MT 66-67 HJ 2
Geraldton [AUS] 182-183 B 5
Geraldton [CDN] 46-47 T 8
Gerasimovka 154-155 N 6
Gerdine, Mount — 46-47 F 5
Gering, NE 68-69 E 5
Gerlach, NV 66-67 D 5
Gerlachovský štít 124 JK 4
Gērlogubī 194-195 NO 7
German Democratic Republic 124 E-G 2-3
Germansen Landing 48 E 2
Germantown, TN 78-79 E 3
Germany, Federal Republic of — 124 C-F 2-4
Germiston 198 E 7
Gerona 132-133 J 8
Gerrard 48 J 4
Gers 132-133 H 7
Gerstle River 52-53 P 5
Gethsēmani 51 F 2
Gettysburg, PA 72-73 H 5
Gettysburg, SD 68-69 G 3
Getz Ice Shelf 31 B 23-24
Geuda Springs, KS 76-77 F 4
Gevgelija 138-139 K 5
Gewanī 194-195 N 6
Geyik dağı 142-143 F 8
Geyser, MT 66-67 H 2
Geyser, Banc du — 198 J 4
Geysir 114-115 c 2
Gezira, El — = Al-Jazīrah 194-195 L 6

Ghadámes = Ghadāmis 194-195 FG 2-3
Ghadāmis 194-195 FG 2-3
Ghadūn, Wādī — 160-161 G 7
Ghāghara 160-161 N 5
Ghallah, Bi'r — 199 C 3
Ghana 194-195 DE 7
Ghānim, Jazīrat — 199 C 4
Ghanzi 198 D 6
Gharaq as-Sulṭānī, Al- 199 AB 3
Gharb al-Istiwāīyah 194-195 KL 7
Ghardaqah, Al- 194-195 L 3
Ghardāyah 194-195 E 2
Ghārib, Jabal — 194-195 L 3
Gharyān 194-195 G 2
Ghat 194-195 G 3
Ghats, Eastern — 160-161 M 8-N 7

Ghats 229

Ghats, Western — 160-161 L 6-M 8
Ghawdex 138-139 F 7
Ghaydah, Al- [ADN ← Sayhūt] 160-161 FG 7-8
Ghaydah, Al- [ADN ↗ Sayhūt] 160-161 G 7
Ghazāl, 'Ayn al- [ET] 199 B 5
Ghazal, 'Ayn al- [LAR] 194-195 J 4
Ghazawāt 194-195 D1
Ghaz köl 166-167 G 4
Ghazni 160-161 K 4
Ghazzah 160-161 C 4
Ghedo = Gēdo 194-195 M 7
Ghent = Gent 132-133 JK 3
Gheorghe Gheorghiu-Dej 138-139 M 2
Gheorghieni 138-139 LM 2
Gherla 138-139 KL 2
Gherlogubi = Gerlogubī 194-195 NO 7
Ghiedo = Gēdo 194-195 M 7
Ghigner = Gīnīr 194-195 N 7
Ghimbi = Gimbī 194-195 M 7
Ghost River [CDN ↗ Dryden] 50 D 2
Ghost River [CDN ↑ Hearst] 50 H 2
Ghuja 166-167 E 3
Ghurdaqa, El — = Al-Ghardaqah 194-195 L 3
Ghūryān 160-161 J 4

Giannitsá 138-139 K 5
Giannutri 138-139 D 4
Giant Mountains 124 GH 3
Giant's Causeway 116-117 E 5
Gia Rai 174-175 E 5
Giarre 138-139 F 7
Gibara 88-89 HJ 4
Gibbon, NE 68-69 G 5
Gibbon, OR 66-67 D 3
Gibbonsville, ID 66-67 G 3
Gibbs City, MI 70-71 F 2
Gibbs City, WI 70-71 F 2
Gibeil = Jubayl 199 C 3
Gibeon [Namibia, place] 198 C 7
Gibraltar 132-133 E 10
Gibraltar, Strait of — 132-133 DE 11
Gibraltar Point 116-117 M 7
Gibsland, LA 78-79 C 4
Gibson City, IL 70-71 F 5
Gibson Desert 182-183 DE 4
Gidan Mountains = Kolymskij nagorje 154-155 g 4-e 5
Giddings, TX 76-77 F 7
Gideon, MO 78-79 DE 2
Gīdolē 194-195 M 7
Gien 132-133 J 5
Giessen 124 D 3
Giffard, Lac — 50 N 1
Gifu 166-167 Q 4
Giganta, Sierra de la — 58-59 D 6-7
Gigantes, Llanos de los — 86-87 HJ 3
Gigha 116-117 F 5
Giglio 138-139 D 4
Gigüela 132-133 F 9
Gihān, Rās — = Rā's al-Bālā'im 199 C 3
Giheina = Juhaynah 199 B 4
Gihu = Gifu 166-167 Q 4
Gijón 132-133 E 7
Gila Bend, AZ 74-75 G 6
Gila Cliff 74-75 J 6
Gila Cliff Dwellings National Monument 74-75 J 6
Gila Desert 58-59 D 5
Gila Mountains 74-75 J 6
Gīlān 160-161 FG 3
Gilardo Dam 72-73 K 1
Gila River 58-59 D 5
Gila River Indian Reservation 74-75 GH 6
Gilbert, Mount — 52-53 o 3
Gilbert Islands 178 H 2-3
Gilbertown, AL 78-79 E 5
Gilbert River [AUS, place] 182-183 H 3
Gilbert River [AUS, river] 182-183 H 3
Gilbués 98-99 K 6
Gilby, ND 68-69 H 1
Gildford, MT 68-69 A 1
Gilf Kebir Plateau = Haḍbat al-Jilf al-Kabīr 194-195 K 4
Gilgandra 182-183 J 6
Gilgat = Gilgit 160-161 L 3
Gilgit 160-161 L 3
Gil Island 48 C 3
Gill, CO 68-69 D 5
Gillam 46-47 S 6
Gillen, Lake — 182-183 D 5
Gillespie, IL 70-71 EF 6
Gillett, AR 78-79 D 3
Gillett, WI 70-71 F 3
Gillette, WY 68-69 D 3
Gillingham [GB, Kent] 116-117 M 9
Gillingham [GB, Somerset] 116-117 J 9
Gillon Point 52-53 p 6
Gilman, IA 70-71 D 5
Gilman, IL 70-71 FG 5
Gilman, WI 70-71 E 3
Gilmer, TX 76-77 G 6
Gilmore, ID 66-67 G 3
Gilolo = Halmahera 174-175 J 6
Gilroy, CA 74-75 G 4
Giluwe, Mount — 174-175 M 8
Gimbala, Jebel — = Jabal Marrah 194-195 JK 6
Gimbī 194-195 M 7
Gimli 50 A 2
Gimma = Jīma 194-195 M 7
Gimpu 174-175 GH 7
Gineifa = Junayfah 199 C 2
Ginevrabotnen 114-115 kl 5
Gīngiova 138-139 KL 4
Gīnīr 194-195 N 7
Ginyer = Gīnīr 194-195 N 7
Giòia del Colle 138-139 G 5
Giovi, Passo dei — 138-139 C 3
Gippsland 182-183 J 7
Girard, IL 70-71 F 6
Girard, KS 70-71 C 7
Girard, OH 72-73 F 4
Girard, PA 72-73 F 3-4
Girard, TX 76-77 D 6
Girardot 98-99 E 4
Girdle Ness 116-117 JK 3
Girdwood, AK 52-53 N 6
Giren = Jīma 194-195 M 7
Giresun 160-161 D 2
Girge = Jirjā 194-195 L 3
Giri 198 C 1
Giridih 160-161 O 6
Girishk 160-161 J 4
Gironde 132-133 G 6
Girvan 116-117 G 5
Girvas [SU, Rossijskaja SFSR] 114-115 O 4
Girvin 49 EF 5
Girvin, TX 76-77 C 7
Gisasa River 52-53 H 4
Gisborne 182-183 P 7
Giscome 48 FG 2
Gisenyi 198 E 2
Gislaved 114-115 E 9
Gitega 198 EF 2
Giuba = Webi Ganaane 198 H 1
Giuba, Isole — 198 H 2
Giulianova 138-139 EF 4
Giumbo = Jumbo 198 H 2
Giūra 138-139 L 6
Giurgiu 138-139 L 4
Givet 132-133 K 3
Gižduvan 154-155 L 9
Gizeh = Al-Jīzah 194-195 KL 3
Gizhigin Bay = Gižiginskaja guba 154-155 e 5
Gižiga 154-155 f 5
Gižiginskaja guba 154-155 e 5
Gizo 174-175 j 6
Giżycko 124 KL 1

Gjersvik 114-115 E 5
Gjirokastër 138-139 HJ 5
Gjögurtá 114-115 d 1
Gjøvik 114-115 D 7
Gjuhës, Kepi i — 138-139 H 5

Glace Bay 46-47 YZ 8
Glacier Bay 52-53 TU 7
Glacier Bay National Monument 46-47 J 6
Glacier Mount 52-53 QR 4
Glacier National Park [CDN] 48 J 4
Glacier National Park [USA] 58-59 CD 2
Glacier Peak 66-67 C 1
Gladbrook, IA 70-71 D 4
Glade Park, CO 74-75 J 3
Gladstone, MI 70-71 G 3
Gladstone [AUS, Queensland] 182-183 K 4
Gladstone [AUS, South Australia] 182-183 G 6
Gladstone [CDN] 49 J 5
Gladwin, MI 70-71 H 4
Glady, WV 72-73 G 5
Glåma 114-115 b 2
Glamis, CA 74-75 F 6
Glasco, KS 68-69 H 6
Glasgow 116-117 G 5
Glasgow, KY 70-71 H 7
Glasgow, MO 70-71 D 6
Glasgow, MT 68-69 C 1
Glaslyn 49 D 4
Glas Maol 116-117 H 4
Glassboro, NJ 72-73 J 5
Glass Mountains 76-77 C 7
Glastonbury 116-117 J 9
Glauchau 124 F 3
Glazier, TX 76-77 D 4
Glazov 154-155 J 6
Gleanntaí, Na — 116-117 C 6
Gleeson, AZ 74-75 J 7
Gleisdorf 124 GH 5
Glen, NE 68-69 E 4
Glen Afton 72-73 FG 1
Glenboro 49 J 6
Glen Canyon 74-75 H 4
Glencoe, MN 70-71 C 3
Glencoe [CDN] 72-73 F 3
Glendale, AZ 58-59 D 5
Glendale, CA 58-59 C 5
Glendale, NV 74-75 F 4
Glendale, OR 66-67 B 4
Glendale, Washington-, DC 82 II b 2
Glendale Cove 48 E 4
Glendevey, CO 68-69 D 5
Glendive, MT 68-69 D 2
Glendo, WY 68-69 D 4
Glendon 49 C 3
Glenfinnan 116-117 F 4
Glengyle 182-183 GH 4
Glen Innes 182-183 K 5
Glen Lyon, PA 72-73 HJ 4
Glen Mar Park, MD 82 II a 1
Glenmora, LA 78-79 C 5
Glen More 116-117 F 4-G 3
Glenmorgan 182-183 JK 5
Glennallen, AK 52-53 P 5
Glennie, MI 70-71 J 3
Glenns Ferry, ID 66-67 F 4
Glenora 52-53 W 8
Glenore 182-183 H 3
Glen Ridge, NJ 82 III a 2
Glenrio, NM 76-77 C 5
Glenrock, WY 68-69 D 4
Glen Rose, TX 76-77 F 6
Glens Falls, NY 72-73 K 3
Glenties = Na Gleanntaí 116-117 C 6
Glen Trool 116-117 G 5
Glentworth 68-69 C 1
Glenville, MN 70-71 D 4
Glenwood, AR 78-79 C 3
Glenwood, IA 70-71 C 5
Glenwood, MN 70-71 C 3
Glenwood, OR 66-67 B 3
Glenwood, WA 66-67 C 2
Glenwood Springs, CO 68-69 C 6
Glenwoodville 48 L 5
Glidden 49 D 5
Glidden, WI 70-71 E 2
Glide, OR 66-67 B 4
Glina 138-139 G 3
Glittertind 114-115 C 7
Gliwice 124 J 3
Globe, AZ 58-59 D 5
Gloggnitz 124 G 5
Głogów 124 GH 3
Glomfjord 114-115 EF 4
Glomma 114-115 D 7
Glommersträsk 114-115 HJ 5
Glória 98-99 M 6
Gloria, La — [CO] 98-99 E 3
Glorieta, NM 76-77 B 5
Glorieuses, Îles — 198 J 4
Glorioso Islands = Îles Glorieuses 198 J 4
Glossop 116-117 K 7
Gloster, MS 78-79 D 5
Gloucester 116-117 J 9
Gloucester, MA 72-73 L 3
Gloucester City, NJ 72-73 J 5
Glouster, OH 72-73 EF 5
Gloversville, NY 72-73 J 3
Glovertown 51 J 3
Glubokoje [SU, Kazachskaja SSR] 154-155 P 7
Gluchov 142-143 F 5
Glyndon, MN 68-69 H 2

Gmünd 124 G 4
Gmunden 124 FG 5

Gniezno 124 H 2
Gnowangerup 182-183 C 6

Goa 160-161 L 7
Goageb [Namibia, place] 198 C 7
Goaso 194-195 D 7
Goba [ETH] 194-195 N 7
Gobabis 198 C 6
Gobernador Gregores 103 BC 7
Gobi 166-167 H-L 3
Gobō 170-171 K 6
Godalming 116-117 L 9
Godāvari 160-161 N 7
Godāvari Delta 160-161 N 7
Godbout 51 C 3
Goddo 98-99 HJ 4
Goddua = Ghuddawah 194-195 G 3
Goderich 72-73 EF 3
Godfrey's Tank 182-183 E 4
Godhavn = Qeqertarssuq 46-47 Za 4
Godoy Cruz 103 BC 4
Gods Lake [CDN, lake] 46-47 S 7
Gods Lake [CDN, place] 46-47 S 7
Godthåb = Nûk 46-47 a 5
Godwin Austen, Mount — = K2 160-161 M 3
Goede Hoop, De — 98-99 K 2
Goeje Gebergte, De — 98-99 L 3
Goéland, Lac — 50 N 2
Goeree 132-133 J 3
Goffs, CA 74-75 F 5
Gogebic, Lake — 70-71 F 2
Gogebic Range 70-71 EF 2
Goggiam = Gojam 194-195 M 6
Gogra = Ghāghara 160-161 N 5
Gogrial = Qūqriāl 194-195 K 7
Goiana 98-99 MN 6
Goiandira 98-99 K 8
Goiânia 98-99 JK 8
Goiás [BR, administrative unit] 98-99 J 8-K 7
Goiás [BR, place] 98-99 JK 8
Goiatuba 98-99 JK 8
Goidu 36 a 2
Gojam 194-195 M 6
Gojjam = Gojam 194-195 M 6
Gökçe ada 142-143 E 7
Göksun 142-143 G 8
Göksu nehir 160-161 C 3
Gokwe 198 E 5
Gol 114-115 C 7
Golāshkerd 160-161 H 5
Golconda, IL 70-71 F 7
Golconda, NV 66-67 E 5
Gołdap 124 L 1
Gold Bar 48 F 1
Gold Beach, OR 66-67 A 4
Gold Bridge 48 F 4
Goldburg, ID 66-67 G 3
Gold Butte, MT 66-67 H 1
Gold Coast [AUS] 182-183 K 5
Gold Coast [GH] 194-195 DE 8
Gold Creek, AK 52-53 N 5
Golden 48 J 4
Golden, ID 66-67 F 3
Golden, IL 70-71 E 5
Golden City, MO 70-71 C 7
Goldendale, WA 66-67 C 3
Golden Ears Provincial Park 48 F 5
Golden Gate 58-59 B 4
Golden Gate Bridge 83 I b 2
Golden Gate Fields Race Track 83 I bc 1
Golden Gate Park 83 I ab 2
Golden Hinde 48 E 5
Golden Meadow, LA 78-79 D 6
Golden Prairie 49 D 5
Golden Vale 116-117 CD 8
Goldfield, NV 74-75 E 4
Gold Hill, UT 66-67 G 5
Goldküste 194-195 D 8-E 7
Gold Point, NV 74-75 E 4
Gold River 48 D 5
Goldsand Lake 49 H 2
Goldsboro, NC 58-59 L 4-5
Goldsmith, TX 76-77 C 6-7
Goldsworthy, Mount — 182-183 CD 4
Goldthwaite, TX 76-77 E 7
Goléa, El- = Al-Gulī'ah 194-195 E 2
Golec-In'aptuk, gora — = gora In'aptuk 154-155 UV 6
Golec-Longdor, gora — = gora Longdor 154-155 W 6
Golela 198 F 7
Goleniów 124 G 2
Goleta, CA 74-75 D 5
Golfe Nuevo 103 D 6
Golfito 58-59 K 10
Golfo Aranci 138-139 CD 5
Golfo de Santa Clara, El — 86-87 C 2
Golfo Dulce 58-59 K 10
Goliad, TX 76-77 F 8
Golmo 166-167 GH 4
Golodnaja step' = Betpak-Dala 154-155 MN 8
Golog Zangzu Zizhizhou 166-167 HJ 5
Golog Zizhizhou 166-167 HJ 5
Golovnin, AK 52-53 F 4
Golovnin Bay 52-53 F 4
Golovnin Mission, AK 52-53 F 4
Golpāyegān 160-161 G 4
Golspie 116-117 H 3
Golungo Alto 198 B 3
Golva, ND 68-69 E 2
Golyšmanovo 154-155 MN 6
Goma 198 E 2
Gomati 160-161 N 5
Gombe [EAT] 198 F 2
Gombe [WAN] 194-195 G 6
Gomel' 142-143 F 5
Gomera 194-195 A 3
Gomes, Serra do — 98-99 P 9
Gómez Farías 86-87 G 3
Gómez Palacio 58-59 EF 6
Gonābād 160-161 H 4
Gonaïves 58-59 M 8
Gonam [SU, place] 154-155 Z 6
Gonam [SU, river] 154-155 Y 6
Gonâve, Golfe de la — 58-59 M 8
Gonâve, Île de la — 58-59 M 8
Gonbād-e Kavus = Gonbad-e Qābūs 160-161 H 3
Gonbad-e Qābūs 160-161 H 3
Gondar = Gonder 194-195 M 6
Gonder 194-195 M 6
Gongga Shan 166-167 J 6
Gongjiatun = Gangtun 170-171 C 2
Gongoji, Serra do — 98-99 LM 7-8
Gongola 194-195 G 6
Gongyingzi 170-171 BC 2
Gongzhuling = Huaide 166-167 NO 3
Goniądz 124 L 2
Gono-kawa 170-171 J 5
Gonoura 170-171 G 6
Gonzales, CA 74-75 C 4
Gonzales, LA 78-79 D 5
Gonzales, TX 76-77 F 8
González [MEX] 86-87 L 6
Gonzanamá 98-99 D 5
Goobies 51 JK 4
Goodenough, Cape — 31 C 13
Goodenough Island 174-175 gh 6
Good Hope [CDN] 48 D 4
Good Hope, Cape of — 198 C 8
Good Hope, Washington-, DC 82 II b 2
Goodhope Bay 52-53 F 3
Goodhouse 198 C 7
Gooding, ID 66-67 F 4
Goodland, KS 68-69 F 6
Goodman, WI 70-71 F 3
Goodnews, AK 52-53 FG 7
Goodnews Bay 52-53 FG 7
Goodnews River 52-53 G 7
Goodpaster River 52-53 P 4
Goodsoil 49 D 3
Goodwater 68-69 E 1
Goodwell, OK 76-77 CD 4
Goole 116-117 L 7
Goomalling 182-183 C 6
Goona = Guna 160-161 M 6
Goondiwindi 182-183 JK 5
Goonyella 182-183 J 4
Goose Bay [CDN, British Columbia] 48 D 4
Goose Bay [CDN, Newfoundland] 46-47 Y 7
Gooseberry Creek 68-69 B 3-4
Goose Creek 66-67 FG 4
Goose Island 82 II a 2
Goose Lake [CDN] 49 H 3
Goose Lake [USA] 58-59 B 3
Goose River [CDN] 48 J 2
Goose River [USA] 68-69 H 2
Go Quao 174-175 DE 5
Gor'ačegorsk 154-155 Q 6
Gorakhpur = Gorakhpoor 160-161 N 5
Gorakpur = Gorakhpoor 160-161 N 5
Goram Islands = Kepulauan Seram-laut 174-175 K 7
Goran, El — 194-195 N 7
Gordon, AK 52-53 R 2
Gordon, GA 80-81 E 4
Gordon, NE 68-69 E 4
Gordon, TX 76-77 E 6
Gordon, WI 70-71 E 2
Gordon Downs 182-183 E 3
Gordon Lake 49 C 2
Gordons Corner, MD 82 II b 2
Gordonsville, VA 72-73 G 5
Gordonvale 182-183 J 3
Gorē [Chad] 194-195 H 7
Gorē [ETH] 194-195 M 7
Gore [NZ] 182-183 N 9
Gore Bay 50 K 4
Gore Mountain 72-73 L 2
Gore Point [CDN] 52-53 M 7
Gore Point [GB] 116-117 M 7-8
Gorey = Guaire 116-117 E 8
Gorgān 160-161 GH 3
Gorgān, Rūd-e — 160-161 GH 3
Gorgona, Isla — 98-99 D 4
Gorgora 194-195 M 6
Gorizia 138-139 E 3
Gorki [SU, Belorusskaja SSR] 142-143 F 5
Gorki [SU, Rossijskaja SFSR] 154-155 M 4
Gorki = Gor'kij 154-155 GH 6
Gor'kij 154-155 GH 6
Gor'kovskoje vodochranilišče 154-155 GH 6
Görlitz 124 G 3
Gorlovka 142-143 G 6
Gorm, Cairn — 116-117 H 3
Gorman, CA 74-75 D 5
Gorman, TX 76-77 E 6
Gorna Or'ahovica 138-139 LM 4
Gornji Milanovac 138-139 J 3
Gorno-Altai Autonomous Region = 9 ◁ 154-155 Q 7
Gorno-Altajsk 154-155 Q 7
Gorno Badakhshan Autonomous Region 160-161 L 3
Gornozavodsk 154-155 b 8
Gorodok = Zakamensk 154-155 T 7
Goroka 174-175 N 8
Gorom = Gorom-Gorow 194-195 DE 6
Gorom-Gorow 194-195 DE 6
Gorongosa, Serra de — 198 FG 5
Gorontalo 174-175 H 6
Gorrahei = Korahe 194-195 NO 7
Gort = An Gort 116-117 C 7
Gort, An — 116-117 C 7
Gorumna Island = Garomna 116-117 B 7
Goryn' 142-143 E 5
Gorzów Wielkopolski 124 GH 2
Gosen [J] 170-171 M 4
Gosford-Woy Woy 182-183 K 6
Goshen, CA 74-75 D 4
Goshen, IN 70-71 H 5
Goshen, NY 72-73 J 4
Goshen Hole 68-69 D 4-5
Goshogawara 170-171 MN 2
Goshute Indian Reservation 74-75 F 3
Goslar 124 DE 3
Gospić 138-139 F 3
Gosport 116-117 K 10
Gosport, IN 70-71 G 6
Goss, MS 78-79 DE 5
Gostynin 124 J 2
Gosyogahara = Goshogawara 170-171 MN 2
Göta älv 114-115 D 9-E 8
Göta kanal 114-115 EF 8
Götaland 114-115 E-G 9
Göteborg 114-115 D 9
Göteborg och Bohus 114-115 D 8
Gotha 124 E 3
Gothenburg, NE 68-69 FG 5
Gotland [S, administrative unit] 114-115 H 9
Gotland [S, island] 114-115 H 9
Götland = Götaland 114-115 E-G 9
Gotland Deep 110-111 M 4
Gotō-rettō 166-167 O 5
Gotska Sandön 114-115 HJ 8
Gōtsu 170-171 HJ 5
Göttingen 124 DE 3
Gottwaldov [CS] 124 H 4
Goubangzi 170-171 CD 2
Goubéré 194-195 K 7
Goudiry 194-195 B 6
Goudreau 70-71 H 1
Gough 188-189 G 13
Gough, GA 80-81 E 4
Gouin Reservoir 46-47 VW 8
Goulburn 182-183 J 6
Goulburn Islands 182-183 F 2
Gould, AR 78-79 D 4
Gould, CO 68-69 CD 5
Gould Bay 31 B 31-32
Gould City, MI 70-71 GH 2
Goulimīm = Gulimīn 194-195 BC 3
Goundam 194-195 D 5
Gouré 194-195 G 6
Gourma 194-195 E 6
Gourma-Rharous 194-195 D 5
Gouro 194-195 H 5
Gourock 116-117 FG 5
Gouverneur, NY 72-73 J 2
Gouwa 198 E 8
Gōvā = Goa 160-161 L 7
Gov'altaj ◁ 166-167 H 3
Gov'altajn Nuruu 166-167 H 2-J 3
Govan 49 F 5
Gove, KS 68-69 F 6
Govena, mys — 154-155 g 6
Govenlock 68-69 B 1
Governador, NM 76-77 A 4
Governador Valadares 98-99 L 8
Governors Island 82 III b 2
Gowanda, NY 72-73 G 3
Gowan River 49 L 3
Gower Peninsula 116-117 G 9
Gowna, Lough — = Loch Gamhna 116-117 D 7
Gowrie, IA 70-71 C 4
Goya 103 E 3
Goyelle, Lac — 51 F 2
Goz-Beïda 194-195 J 6
Goze Delčev 138-139 KL 5
Gozha Tsho 166-167 E 4
Goz Regeb = Qawz Rajab 194-195 M 5

Graaff-Reinet 198 DE 8
Grā-Canária = Gran Canaria 194-195 A 3
Grace, ID 66-67 H 4
Gracefield 72-73 H 1
Graceville, FL 78-79 G 5
Graceville, MN 68-69 H 3
Gracias 88-89 B 7
Gracias a Dios, Cabo — 58-59 K 8
Graciosa [P] 188-189 DE 5
Gradaús 98-99 J 6
Gradaús, Serra dos — 98-99 JK 6
Gräddö 114-115 H 8
Grady, AR 78-79 D 3
Grady, NM 76-77 C 5
Graettinger, IA 70-71 C 4
Grafton 182-183 K 5
Grafton, IL 70-71 E 6
Grafton, ND 68-69 H 1
Grafton, WV 72-73 FG 5
Graham 70-71 E 1
Graham, CA 83 III c 2
Graham, NC 80-81 G 2-3
Graham, TX 76-77 E 6
Graham, Mount — 58-59 DE 5
Graham Bell, ostrov — 154-155 MN 1
Graham Island 46-47 JK 7
Graham Lake 48 KL 1
Graham Moore, Cape — 46-47 V-X 3
Graham River 48 F 1
Grahamstad = Grahamstown 198 E 8
Grahamstown 198 E 8
Graig, AK 52-53 w 9
Grain Coast 194-195 B 7-C 8
Grainfield, KS 68-69 F 6
Grainger 48 L 4
Grajaú 98-99 K 6
Grajaú, Rio — [BR, Maranhão] 98-99 K 5-6
Grajewo 124 L 2
Grambûsa, Akrōtḗrion — 138-139 K 8
Grámmos 138-139 J 5
Grampian 116-117 HJ 3
Grampian Mountains 116-117 GH 4
Granada, CO 68-69 E 6-7
Granada [E] 132-133 F 10
Granada [NIC] 58-59 JK 9
Gran Altiplanicie Central 103 BC 7
Gran Bajo [RA, Santa Cruz] 103 C 7
Granbori 98-99 L 3
Granbury, TX 76-77 EF 6
Granby 46-47 W 8
Granby, CO 68-69 CD 5
Granby, Lake — 68-69 D 5
Gran Canaria 194-195 AB 3

230 **Ghats**

Gran Chaco 103 D 3-E 2
Grand Ballon 132-133 L 5
Grand Bank 51 HJ 4
Grand Bassa = Buchanan 194-195 B 7
Grand-Bassam 194-195 D 7-8
Grand Bay [CDN, bay] 70-71 F 1
Grand Bay [CDN, place] 51 C 5
Grand Beach 50 A 2
Grand-Bourg 58-59 OP 8
Grand-Bruit 51 G 4
Grand Caicos 88-89 L 4
Grand Canal = Canáil Laighean 116-117 D 7
Grand Canary = Gran Canaria 194-195 AB 3
Grand Canyon 58-59 D 4
Grand Canyon, AZ 74-75 GH 4
Grand Canyon National Monument 74-75 G 4
Grand Canyon National Park 58-59 D 4
Grand Cayman 58-59 KL 8
Grand Centre 49 C 3
Grand Chenier, LA 78-79 C 6
Grand Coulee, WA 66-67 D 2
Grand Coulee [CDN] 49 F 5
Grand Coulee [USA] 66-67 D 2
Grand Coulee Dam 58-59 BC 2
Grand Coulee Equalizing Reservoir = Banks Lake 66-67 D 2
Grande-Anse 51 D 4
Grande Cache 48 H 3
Grande Comore = Ngazidja 198 H 4
Grande Dépression Centrale 198 CD 2
Grande-Entrée 51 F 4
Grande Prairie 46-47 N 6-7
Grande-Rivière 51 DE 3
Grande Ronde, OR 66-67 B 3
Grande Ronde River 66-67 E 2-3
Gran Desierto 58-59 D 5
Grandes Landes 132-133 G 6-7
Grande-Terre 88-89 Q 6
Grandfalls, TX 76-77 C 7
Grand Falls [CDN] 46-47 Za 8
Grand Falls [USA] 74-75 H 5
Grand Falls = Churchill Falls 46-47 XY 7
Grandfather Mountain 80-81 F 2
Grandfield, OK 76-77 E 5
Grand Forks 66-67 D 1
Grand Forks, ND 58-59 G 2
Grand Haven, MI 70-71 G 4
Grandioznyj, pik — 154-155 RS 7
Grand Island, NE 58-59 G 3
Grand Island [USA, Louisiana] 78-79 E 5
Grand Island [USA, Michigan] 70-71 G 2
Grand Island [USA, New York] 72-73 G 3
Grand Isle 72-73 K 2
Grand Isle, LA 78-79 D 6
Grand Junction, CO 58-59 DE 4
Grand Junction, TN 78-79 E 3
Grand Lac du Nord 51 C 2
Grand Lac Germain 51 C 2
Grand-Lahou 194-195 CD 7-8
Grand Lake, CO 68-69 CD 5
Grand Lake [CDN] 51 D 5
Grand Lake [USA, Louisiana] 78-79 D 6
Grand Lake [USA, Maine] 72-73 N 2
Grand Lake [USA, Michigan] 70-71 J 3
Grand Lake [USA, Ohio] 70-71 H 5
Grand Ledge, MI 70-71 H 4
Grand Manan Island 51 C 5
Grand Marais, MI 70-71 GH 2
Grand Marais, MN 70-71 EF 2
Grand Mécatina, Île du — 51 G 2
Grand'Mère 72-73 K 1
Grand Mesa 68-69 C 6
Grândola 132-133 C 9
Grand Paradiso 138-139 B 3
Grand-Popo 194-195 E 7
Grand Portage, MN 70-71 F 2
Grand Portage Indian Reservation 70-71 EF 2
Grand Prairie, TX 76-77 F 6
Grand Rapids, MI 58-59 J 3
Grand Rapids, MN 70-71 D 2
Grand Rapids [CDN, Alberta] 48 L 1
Grand Rapids [CDN, Manitoba] 49 J 4
Grand River [CDN] 72-73 FG 3
Grand River [USA, Michigan] 70-71 GH 4
Grand River [USA, Missouri] 70-71 D 6
Grand River [USA, South Dakota] 58-59 F 2
Grand River, North Fork — 68-69 E 3
Grand River, South Fork — 68-69 E 3
Grand River Valley 74-75 J 3
Grand Saline, TX 76-77 G 6
Grand Sant i 98-99 LM 2
Grand Teton National Park 66-67 H 3-4
Grand Teton Peak 58-59 D 3
Grand Traverse Bay 70-71 H 3
Grand Trunk Pacific Railway = Candian National Railways 46-47 PQ 7
Grand Turk 88-89 L 4
Grand Turk Island 88-89 L 4
Grand Valley, CO 68-69 B 6
Grandview 49 H 5
Grand View, ID 66-67 EF 4
Grandview, MO 70-71 C 6
Grandview, WA 66-67 D 2
Grand Wash Cliffs 74-75 FG 5
Grange 116-117 J 6
Grange, La — 182-183 D 3
Grangemouth 116-117 H 4-5
Granger, TX 76-77 F 7
Granger, WA 66-67 CD 2
Granger, WY 66-67 J 5
Grängesberg 114-115 F 7
Grangeville, ID 66-67 EF 3
Granite, CO 68-69 CD 6
Granite, OK 76-77 E 5
Granite, OR 66-67 D 3
Granite Bay 48 E 4
Granite City, IL 70-71 EF 6
Granite Downs 182-183 F 5
Granite Falls, MN 70-71 C 3
Granite Island [USA, Gulf of Alaska] 52-53 N 7
Granite Island [USA, Lake Superior] 70-71 G 2
Granite Mountains 74-75 F 5
Granite Peak [USA, Montana] 58-59 E 2
Granite Peak [USA, Utah] 66-67 G 5
Granite Range [USA, Alaska] 52-53 QR 6
Granite Range [USA, Nevada] 66-67 D 5
Granites, The — 182-183 F 4
Granite Springs Valley 66-67 D 5
Graniteville, SC 80-81 F 4
Granja 98-99 L 5
Granma 88-89 H 4
Gran Malvina = West Falkland 103 D 8
Gränna 114-115 F 8
Gran Pampa Pelada 98-99 F 9
Gran Rio 98-99 L 3
Gran Sabana, La — 98-99 G 3
Gran San Bernardo 138-139 B 3
Gran Sasso 138-139 E 4
Grant 50 F 2
Grant, FL 80-81 c 3
Grant, MT 66-67 G 3
Grant, NE 68-69 F 5
Grant, Mount — [USA, Clan Alpine Mountains] 74-75 DE 3
Grant, Mount — [USA, Wassuk Range] 74-75 D 3
Grant City, MO 70-71 C 5
Grant Creek, AK 52-53 L 4
Grantham 116-117 L 8
Grant Land 30 A 25-27
Granton, Edinburgh- 116-117 H 5-J 4
Grantown-on-Spey 116-117 H 3
Grant Range 74-75 F 3
Grants, NM 58-59 E 4
Grantsburg, WI 70-71 D 3
Grants Cabin, AK 52-53 M 6
Grantshouse 116-117 J 5
Grants Pass, OR 66-67 B 4
Grantsville, UT 66-67 G 5
Grantsville, WV 72-73 F 5
Granum 66-67 G 1
Granville 132-133 G 4
Granville, ND 68-69 F 1
Granville Lake 49 HJ 2
Grão Pará, Parque Nacional — 98-99 O 6
Grapeland, TX 76-77 G 7
Grass Creek, WY 68-69 B 4
Grasse 132-133 L 7
Grasset, Lac — 50 MN 2
Grass Lake, CA 66-67 B 5
Grass Range, MT 68-69 B 2
Grass River 49 K 2-3
Grass River Provincial Park 49 H 3
Grass Valley, CA 74-75 C 3
Grass Valley, OR 66-67 C 3
Grassy 182-183 H 7-8
Grassy Knob 72-73 F 5-6
Grassy Lake 66-67 H 1
Grassy Narrows 50 C 2
Gratangen 114-115 GH 3
Gravatá 98-99 M 6
Gravelbourg 49 E 6
Gravenhage, 's- 132-133 JK 2
Gravenhurst 72-73 G 2
Grave Peak 66-67 F 2
Gravesend, New York-, NY 82 III c 3
Gravette, AR 76-77 G 4
Gravina di Pùglia 138-139 G 5
Grawn, MI 70-71 H 3
Gray 132-133 K 5
Gray, GA 80-81 E 4
Gray, OK 76-77 D 4
Grayling, AK 52-53 GH 5
Grayling, MI 70-71 H 3
Grays Fork 52-53 QR 3
Grays Harbor 66-67 AB 2
Grayson 49 G 5
Grayson, KY 72-73 E 5
Grays Peak 68-69 CD 6
Grayville, IL 70-71 FG 6
Graz 124 G 5
Gr'azi 142-143 GH 5
Gr'azovec 142-143 GH 4
Grdelica 138-139 JK 4
Great Artesian Basin 182-183 GH 4-5
Great Australian Bight 182-183 E 6-G 7
Great Ayton 116-117 HJ 6
Great Bahama Bank 58-59 L 6-7
Great Barrier Island 182-183 P 7
Great Barrier Reef 182-183 H 2-K 4
Great Basin 58-59 CD 3-4
Great Bay 72-73 J 5
Great Bear Lake 46-47 MN 4
Great Bear River 46-47 LM 4-5
Great Belt = Store Bælt 114-115 D 10
Great Bend, KS 58-59 FG 4
Great Bernera 116-117 DE 2
Great Bitter Lake = Al-Buḥayrat al-Murrat al-Kubrā 199 C 2
Great Blaskets = An tOileán Mór 116-117 A 8
Great Britain 110-111 H 4-5
Great Central 48 E 5
Great Cloche Island 50 KL 3
Great Divide Basin 68-69 BC 4
Great Dividing Range 182-183 H-K 3-7
Great Driffield 116-117 L 6
Great Eastern Erg = Al-ʻIrq al-Kabīr ash-Sharqī 194-195 F 2-3
Greater Antilles 58-59 K 7-N 8
Greater Khingan Range 166-167 M 3-N 1
Greater Leech Lake Indian Reservation 70-71 CD 2
Greater London = 7 ◁ 116-117 L 9
Greater Sunda Islands 174-175 E-H 7-8
Great Falls, MT 58-59 DE 2
Great Falls, SC 80-81 F 3
Great Falls [CDN] 50 AB 2
Great Falls [GUY] 98-99 H 2
Great Falls [USA] 66-67 H 2
Great Guana Cay 88-89 H 2
Great Harwood 116-117 J 7
Great Inagua Island 58-59 M 7
Great Karoo = Groot Karoo 198 D 8
Great Kei = Kepulauan Kai 174-175 K 8
Great Kei River = Groot Keirivier 198 EF 8
Great Kills, New York-, NY 82 III b 3
Great Lake 182-183 J 8
Great Meteor Tablemount 26-27 H 4
Great Namaqua Land = Namaland 198 C 7
Great Natuna = Pulau Bunguran 174-175 E 6
Great Neck, NY 82 III d 2
Great Nicobar 160-161 P 9
Great Northern Pacific Railway 58-59 DE 2
Great Northern Peninsula 46-47 Z 7-8
Great Oasis = Al-Wāḥāt al-Khārīyah 194-195 KL 3-4
Great Ormes Head 116-117 H 7
Great Peconic Bay 72-73 K 4
Great Plains 58-59 E 2-F 5
Great Sacandaga Lake 72-73 JK 3
Great Salt Desert = Dasht-e Kavīr 160-161 GH 3
Great Salt Lake 58-59 D 3
Great Salt Lake Desert 58-59 D 3
Great Salt Plains Reservoir 76-77 EF 4
Great Sand Dunes National Monument 68-69 CD 7
Great Sand Sea = Libysche Wüste 194-195 J 3-L 4
Great Sandy Desert [AUS] 182-183 DE 4
Great Sandy Desert [USA] 58-59 BC 3
Great Sandy Hills 49 D 5
Great Sandy Island 182-183 KL 4-5
Great Shunner Fell 116-117 J 6
Great Slave Lake 46-47 NO 5
Great Smoky Mountains 80-81 E 3
Great Smoky Mountains National Park 80-81 E 3
Great Torrington 116-117 GH 10
Great Valley 80-81 D 3
Great Victoria Desert 182-183 EF 5
Great Wall 166-167 K 4
Great Western Erg = Al-ʻIrq al-Kabīr al-Gharbī 194-195 D 3-E 2
Great Whale River 46-47 VW 6
Great Whernside 116-117 K 6
Great Yarmouth 116-117 h 6
Grebená 138-139 J 5
Grebon, Mont — 194-195 F 4-5
Gredos, Sierra de — 132-133 E 8
Greece 138-139 J 7-L 5
Greeley, CO 58-59 F 3
Greeley, NE 68-69 G 5
Greely Fiord 46-47 UV 1
Green 50 E 2
Green Bay 58-59 J 2-3
Green Bay, WI 58-59 J 3
Greenbelt Park 82 II b 1
Greenbrae, CA 83 I a 1
Greenbrier River 72-73 FG 5
Greenbush, MN 70-71 BC 1
Greencastle, IN 70-71 G 6
Greencastle, PA 72-73 GH 5
Green City, IA 70-71 D 5
Green Cove Springs, FL 80-81 bc 1
Greene, IA 70-71 D 4
Greeneville, TN 80-81 E 2
Greenfield, CA 74-75 C 4
Greenfield, IA 70-71 C 5
Greenfield, IN 70-71 H 6
Greenfield, MA 72-73 K 3
Greenfield, MO 70-71 CD 7
Greenfield, OH 72-73 E 5
Greenfield, TN 78-79 E 2
Greenfield Park 82 I c 2
Greenhorn Mountains 74-75 D 5
Greening 50 O 2
Green Island [AUS] 182-183 J 3
Green Island [USA] 52-53 O 6
Green Islands 174-175 hj 5
Green Lake [CDN] 49 E 3
Green Lake [USA] 70-71 F 4
Greenland 30 BC 23
Greenland, MI 70-71 F 2
Greenland Basin 26-27 JK 2
Greenland Sea 30 B 20-18
Green Lowther 116-117 H 5
Green Mountain Reservoir 68-69 C 6
Green Mountains [USA, Vermont] 72-73 K 2-3
Green Mountains [USA, Wyoming] 68-69 C 4
Greenock 116-117 FG 5
Greenore = Grianphort 116-117 E 6
Greenore Point = Rinn na Binne 116-117 EF 8
Green Pond, SC 80-81 F 4
Greenport, NY 72-73 K 4
Green River, UT 74-75 H 3
Green River, WY 66-67 J 5
Green River [USA, Illinois] 70-71 F 5
Green River [USA, Kentucky] 70-71 G 7
Green River [USA, Wyoming] 58-59 E 3-4
Green River Basin 58-59 DE 3
Greensboro, AL 78-79 F 4
Greensboro, GA 80-81 E 4
Greensboro, NC 58-59 L 4
Greensburg, IN 70-71 H 6
Greensburg, KS 68-69 G 7
Greensburg, KY 70-71 H 7
Greensburg, PA 72-73 G 4
Green Swamp 80-81 G 3
Greenup, IL 70-71 FG 6
Greenup, KY 72-73 E 5
Greenvale 182-183 HJ 3
Greenville 194-195 C 7-8
Greenville, AL 78-79 F 5
Greenville, CA 66-67 C 5
Greenville, FL 80-81 E 5
Greenville, IL 70-71 F 6
Greenville, IN 72-73 D 4
Greenville, KY 70-71 G 7
Greenville, ME 72-73 LM 2
Greenville, MI 70-71 H 4
Greenville, MS 58-59 HJ 5
Greenville, NC 58-59 L 4
Greenville, OH 70-71 H 5
Greenville, PA 72-73 F 4
Greenville, SC 58-59 K 5
Greenville, TX 58-59 GH 5
Greenwater Lake 70-71 E 1
Greenwater Lake Provincial Park 49 G 4
Greenway 68-69 G 1
Greenway, SD 68-69 G 3
Greenwich, OH 72-73 E 4
Greenwich, London- 116-117 LM 9
Greenwich Village, New York-, NY 82 III b 2
Greenwood 66-67 D 1
Greenwood, AR 76-77 GH 5
Greenwood, IN 70-71 GH 6
Greenwood, MS 58-59 HJ 5
Greenwood, SC 58-59 K 5
Greenwood, WI 70-71 E 3
Greer, ID 66-67 EF 2
Greer, SC 80-81 E 3
Greeson, Lake — 78-79 C 3
Gregório, Rio — 98-99 C 8
Gregory, SD 68-69 G 4
Gregory, Lake — 182-183 GH 5
Gregory Downs 182-183 G 3
Gregory Range 182-183 H 3
Gregory River 182-183 G 3
Gregory Salt Lake 182-183 E 3-4
Greifswald 124 F 1
Grein 124 G 4
Greiz 124 EF 3
Gremicha 154-155 F 4
Grenå 114-115 D 9
Grenada 58-59 O 9
Grenada, MS 78-79 E 4
Grenada Lake 78-79 E 4
Grenada Reservoir = Grenada Lake 78-79 E 4
Grenadines 58-59 O 9
Grenen 114-115 D 9
Grenfell [CDN] 49 G 5
Grenivík 114-115 de 2
Grenoble 132-133 KL 6
Grenola, KS 76-77 F 4
Grenora, ND 68-69 E 1
Grenvill, Cape — 182-183 H 2
Grenville, NM 76-77 C 4
Grenville, SD 68-69 H 3
Gretna 68-69 H 1
Gretna, LA 58-59 HJ 6
Gretna Green 116-117 H 5
Grey, De — 182-183 CD 4
Greybull, WY 68-69 BC 3
Greybull River 68-69 B 3
Grey Islands 46-47 Za 7
Grey Islands Harbour 51 J 2
Greylock, Mount — 72-73 K 3
Greymouth 182-183 O 8
Grey Range 182-183 H 5
Grey River 51 H 4
Grey River, De — 182-183 CD 4
Greystones = An Chloch Liath 116-117 EF 7
Greytown = Bluefields 58-59 K 9
Grianphort 116-117 E 6
Gribbell Island 48 C 3
Gribingui 194-195 H 7
Gridley, CA 74-75 C 3
Griekwaland-Wes 198 D 7
Griffin 49 G 6
Griffin, GA 58-59 K 5
Griffin Point 52-53 QR 1
Griffith 182-183 J 6
Grim, Cape — 182-183 H 8
Grimari 194-195 HJ 7
Grimes, CA 74-75 C 3
Grimma 124 F 3
Grimsby [CDN] 72-73 G 3
Grimsby [GB] 116-117 L 7
Grímsey 114-115 d 1
Grimshaw 48 HJ 1
Grimstad 114-115 C 8
Grímsvötn 114-115 e 2
Grindavík 114-115 b 3
Grindsted 114-115 C 10
Grindstone Buttes 68-69 F 3
Grinnell, IA 70-71 D 5
Grinnell Land 46-47 UV 1-2
Grinnell Peninsula 46-47 RS 2
Griqualand West = Griekwaland-Wes 198 D 7
Gris Nez, Cap — 116-117 h 8
Griswold, IA 70-71 C 5
Griva 142-143 K 3
Groais Island 51 J 2
Grodno 142-143 DE 5
Groesbeck, TX 76-77 F 7
Grœtavær 114-115 FG 3
Groix, Île de — 132-133 F 5
Groll Seamount 26-27 H 6
Grong 114-115 E 5
Groningen [NL] 132-133 L 2
Groningen [SME] 98-99 HJ 3
Groom, TX 76-77 D 5
Groot Brukkaros 198 C 7
Groote Eylandt 182-183 G 2
Grootfontein 198 C 5
Groot Keirivier 198 EF 8
Groot Visrivier 198 C 7
Grosa, Punta — 132-133 H 9
Gros Morne [CDN] 51 H 3
Gros-Morne [RH] 88-89 K 5
Gros Morne National Park 46-47 Za 8
Grossenbrode 124 E 1
Grosser Arber 124 F 3
Grosser Beerberg 124 E 3
Grosse Tet, LA 78-79 D 5
Grosseto 138-139 D 4
Grossglockner 124 F 5
Grosvenor, Lake — 52-53 K 7
Gros Ventre River 66-67 H 4
Grotli 114-115 BC 6
Groton, NY 72-73 H 3
Groton, SD 68-69 GH 3
Grottoes, VA 72-73 G 5
Grouard 48 JK 2
Groundhog River 50 K 2
Grouse, ID 66-67 G 4
Grouse Creek, UT 66-67 G 5
Grouse Creek Mountain 66-67 FG 3
Grove City, PA 72-73 FG 4
Grove Hill, AL 78-79 F 5
Groveland, CA 74-75 CD 4
Grover, CO 68-69 DE 5
Grover, WY 66-67 H 4
Grover City, CA 74-75 C 5
Groveton, TX 76-77 G 7
Grovont, WY 66-67 H 4
Growler, AZ 74-75 FG 6
Growler Mountains 74-75 G 6
Groznyj 142-143 HJ 7
Grudovo 138-139 M 4
Grudziądz 124 J 2
Gruinard Bay 116-117 F 3
Grulla, TX 76-77 E 9
Grullo, El — 86-87 H 8
Grumantbyen 114-115 jk 5
Grumo Appula 138-139 G 5
Grünau [Namibia] 198 C 7
Grundarfjördhur 114-115 ab 2
Grundy, VA 80-81 EF 2
Grundy Center, IA 70-71 D 4
Grunidora, Llanos de la — 86-87 JK 5
Gruver, TX 76-77 D 4
Gryfice 124 G 2
Gryllefjord 114-115 G 3
Grymes Hill, New York-, NY 82 III b 3
Grytviken 103 J 8
Guacanayabo, Golfo de — 58-59 L 7
Guachochi 86-87 G 4
Guadalajara [E] 132-133 F 8
Guadalajara [MEX] 58-59 EF 7
Guadalaviar 132-133 G 8
Guadalcanal [Solomon Is.] 174-175 j 6
Guadalcanar Gela = Guadalcanal 174-175 j 6
Guadalete 132-133 DE 10
Guadalimar 132-133 F 9
Guadalope 132-133 G 8
Guadalquivir 132-133 E 10
Guadalupe, CA 74-75 C 5
Guadalupe [E] 132-133 E 9
Guadalupe [MEX ↗ San Luís Potosí] 86-87 KL 6
Guadalupe [MEX ↑ San Luís Potosí] 86-87 K 6
Guadalupe [MEX, Baja California] 86-87 B 2
Guadalupe [MEX, Coahuila] 76-77 D 9
Guadalupe [MEX, Nuevo León] 58-59 FG 6
Guadalupe [MEX, Zacatecas] 86-87 JK 6
Guadalupe, Isla de — 58-59 C 6
Guadalupe, Sierra de — [E] 132-133 E 9
Guadalupe Bravos 86-87 G 2
Guadalupe Mountains [USA → El Paso] 76-77 B 6-7
Guadalupe Peak 58-59 F 5
Guadalupe River 76-77 F 8
Guadalupe Victoria 86-87 J 5
Guadalupe y Calvo 86-87 G 4
Guadalupita, NM 76-77 B 4
Guadarrama, Sierra de — 132-133 EF 8
Guadeloupe 58-59 O 8
Guadeloupe Passage 58-59 O 8
Guadiana 132-133 D 10
Guadiana Menor 132-133 F 10
Guadix 132-133 F 10
Guadur = Gwādar 160-161 J 5
Guafo, Golfo de — 103 B 6
Guafo, Isla — 103 AB 6
Guai 174-175 L 7
Guainía, Río — 98-99 F 4
Guaiquinima, Cerro — 98-99 G 3
Guaíra [BR, Paraná] 103 F 2
Guaire 116-117 E 8
Guaitecas, Islas — 103 AB 6
Guajaba, Cayo — 88-89 H 4
Guajará 98-99 J 7
Guajará-Mirim 98-99 FG 7
Guajira, Península de — 98-99 E 2
Gualala, CA 74-75 B 3
Gualán 86-87 Q 10
Gualaquiza 98-99 D 5
Gualeguay 103 E 4
Gualeguaychú 103 E 4
Gualior = Gwalior 160-161 M 5
Guam 148-149 S 8
Guamá [BR] 98-99 P 5
Guamblin, Isla — 103 A 6
Guamúchil 86-87 FG 5
Guaña 98-99 G 4
Guanahacabibes, Península de — 88-89 D 4
Guanahani = San Salvador 58-59 M 7
Guanaja 88-89 D 6
Guanajutao 58-59 F 7
Guanare 98-99 F 3
Guanarito 98-99 F 3
Guandong Bandao 170-171 C 3
Guane 58-59 K 7
Guang'an 166-167 K 5
Guangchang 166-167 M 6
Guangdong 166-167 L 7
Guanghai 166-167 L 7
Guanghua 166-167 L 5
Guangji 166-167 M 6
Guanglu Dao 170-171 D 3
Guangnan 166-167 JK 7
Guangxi Zhuangzu Zizhiqu 166-167 KL 7
Guangyuan 166-167 K 5
Guangzhou 166-167 LM 7
Guangzhou Wan = Zhanjiang Gang 166-167 L 7
Guano Lake 66-67 D 4
Guanshui 170-171 E 2
Guantánamo 58-59 LM 7-8
Guanyun 166-167 MN 5
Guapí 98-99 D 4
Guápiles 88-89 E 9
Guaporé = Rondônia 98-99 G 7
Guaporé, Rio — [BR ◁ Rio Mamoré] 98-99 G 7
Guaqui 98-99 F 8
Guarabira 98-99 MN 6
Guaranda 98-99 D 5
Guarapuava 103 F 3
Guaratinguetá 98-99 KL 9
Guaratuba 103 G 3
Guarayos, Llanos de — 98-99 G 8
Guarda 132-133 D 8
Guardafui = ʻAsayr 160-161 G 8
Guardo 132-133 E 7
Guarico, Punta — 88-89 JK 4
Guarulhos 98-99 K 9
Guasave 58-59 E 6
Guascama, Punta — 98-99 D 4
Guasdualito 98-99 EF 3
Guasipati 98-99 G 3
Guastalla 138-139 D 3
Guatemala [GCA, place] 58-59 HJ 9
Guatemala [GCA, state] 58-59 HJ 8
Guatemala Basin 34-35 N 4

Guatemal 231

Guaviare, Río — 98-99 F 4
Guaxupé 98-99 K 9
Guayabal [C] 88-89 H 4
Guayama 88-89 N 6
Guayana = Guyana 98-99 H 3-4
Guayaquil 98-99 CD 5
Guayaquil, Golfo de — 98-99 C 5
Guayaramerín 98-99 F 7
Guaymas = Heroica Guaymas 58-59 D 6
Guazapares 86-87 FG 4
Guba 198 E 4
Gubacha 154-155 K 6
Guban 194-195 ab 1
Gubanovo = Vereščagino 154-155 JK 6
Gùbbio 138-139 E 4
Guben 124 G 3
Gučin Us 166-167 J 2
Gūḍalūr = Cuddalore 160-161 MN 8
Gudauta 142-143 GH 7
Gudbrandsdal 114-115 CD 7
Gudenå 114-115 CD 9
Gudermes 142-143 J 7
Gūdūr 160-161 MN 8
Gūḍūru = Gūdūr 160-161 MN 8
Guéckédou 194-195 BC 7
Guéguen, Lac — 50 N 2
Guelma = Qalmah 194-195 F 1
Guelph 46-47 UV 9
Guéné 194-195 E 6
Guéra, Pic de — 194-195 H 6
Guéréda 194-195 J 6
Guéret 132-133 H 5
Guernsey, WY 68-69 D 4
Guerrero [MEX, administrative unit] 58-59 FG 8
Guerrero [MEX, place Coahuila] 76-77 D 8
Guerrero [MEX, place Tamaulipas] 76-77 E 9
Guerrero Negro 86-87 CD 3-4
G'uševo 138-139 K 4
Guettara, Aïn El — 194-195 D 4
Gueydan, LA 78-79 C 5-6
Gugē 194-195 M 7
Gughe = Gugē 194-195 M 7
Guia 98-99 H 8
Guiana Basin 26-27 G 5
Guiana Brasileira 98-99 G-J 4-5
Guiana Highlands = Macizo de las Guyanas 98-99 F 3-J 4
Guichi 166-167 M 5
Guichicovi 86-87 N 9
Guidder = Guider 194-195 G 6-7
Guide 166-167 J 4
Guider 194-195 G 6-7
Guiding 166-167 K 6
Guier, Lac de — 194-195 AB 5
Guiglo 194-195 C 7
Guildford 116-117 L 9
Guilin 166-167 KL 6
Guimarães [BR] 98-99 L 5
Guimarães [P] 132-133 C 8
Guimaras Island 174-175 H 4
Guimbalete 76-77 C 9
Guinan Zhou = Qiannon Zizhizhou 166-167 K 6
Guinea 194-195 B 6-C 7
Guinea, Gulf of — 194-195 C-F 8
Guinea Basin 26-27 J 5
Guinea Bissau 194-195 AB 6
Guinea Rise 26-27 JK 6
Guînes 116-117 h 8
Güines [C] 58-59 K 7
Guingamp 132-133 F 4
Guiones, Punta — 88-89 CD 10
Guiping 166-167 KL 7
Güira de Melena 88-89 E 3
Guiyang [TJ, Guizhou] 166-167 K 6
Guiyang [TJ, Hunan] 166-167 L 6
Guizhou 166-167 JK 6
Gujarāt 160-161 L 6
Gujerat = Gujarāt 160-161 L 6
Gūjrānwāla 160-161 L 4
Gujrāt 160-161 L 4
Gulabarga = Gulburga 160-161 M 7
Gul'ajevo, Archangel'sk- 142-143 H 3
Gul'ajpole 142-143 G 6
Gulbene 142-143 E 4
Gulf Beach, FL 78-79 F 5
Gulf Coastal Plain 58-59 G 6-J 5
Gulfport, FL 80-81 b 3
Gulfport, MS 58-59 J 5
Gulinīm 194-195 BC 3
Gulistan 154-155 M 9
Gulkana, AK 52-53 OP 5
Gullbringu-Kjósar 114-115 b 2-c 3
Gullfoss 114-115 d 2
Gullion, Slieve — 116-117 E 6
Gulliver, MI 70-71 GH 2
Gull Lake [CDN] 48 KL 3
Gull Lake [USA] 70-71 C 2
Gullrock Lake 50 BC 2
Gulrān 160-161 J 3
Gulu 198 F 1
Guma Bazar 166-167 D 4
Gumma 170-171 M 4
Gumti = Gomati 160-161 N 5
Gümüşane 160-161 D 2
Guna 160-161 M 6
Gunabad = Gonābād 160-161 H 4
Gunchū = Iyo 170-171 J 6
Güneydoğu Toroslar 160-161 DE 3
Gungu 198 C 3
Gunisao Lake 50 A 1
Gunisao River 50 A 1
Gunnbjørn Fjeld 46-47 ef 4
Gunnedah 182-183 K 6
Gunnison, CO 58-59 E 4
Gunnison, UT 74-75 H 3
Gunnison Island 66-67 G 5
Gunnison River 68-69 BC 6
Gunt 154-155 L 3
Gūntakal 160-161 M 7
Guntersville, AL 78-79 F 3
Guntersville Lake 78-79 FG 3
Guntūr 160-161 MN 7
Guṁṭūru = Guntūr 160-161 MN 7
Gunungapi, Pulau — 174-175 J 8
Gunungsitoli 174-175 C 6
Gunworth 49 DE 5
Gunzan = Kunsan 166-167 O 4
Gūra = Gūrha 160-161 L 5
Gurage 194-195 M 7
Guraghe = Gurage 194-195 M 7
Gurd Abū Muḥarrik 194-195 KL 3
Gurdāspur 160-161 M 4
Gurdon, AR 78-79 C 4
Gurguéia, Rio — 98-99 L 6
Gūrha 160-161 L 5
Gurjev 142-143 K 6
Gurjevsk 154-155 Q 7
Gurk 124 G 5
Gurma = Gourma 194-195 E 6
Gurskøy 114-115 A 6
Gurudaspur = Gurdāspur 160-161 M 4
Gurun [MAL] 174-175 D 5
Gurupá 98-99 J 5
Gurupá, Ilha Grande de — 98-99 J 5
Gurupi 98-99 O 10
Gurupi, Cabo — 98-99 PQ 5
Gurupi, Rio — 98-99 K 5
Gurupi, Serra do — 98-99 K 5-6
Gurvansajchan 166-167 K 2
Gusau 194-195 F 6
Gus-Chrustal'nyj 142-143 H 4
Gusev 124 L 1
Gushan 170-171 D 3
Gusher, UT 66-67 J 5
Gushi 166-167 M 5
Gusinaja guba 154-155 cd 3
Gusinaja Zeml'a, poluostrov — 154-155 HJ 3
Gustav Adolf land 114-115 l 5
Gustavo Díaz Ordaz 86-87 L 4
Gustavo Sotelo 86-87 D 2
Gustavus, AK 52-53 U 7
Gustav V land 114-115 kl 4
Gustine, CA 74-75 C 4
Güstrow 124 EF 2
Gutaj 154-155 U 7-8
Gutenko Mountains 31 B 30
Gütersloh 124 CD 3
Guthrie, KY 78-79 F 2
Guthrie, OK 76-77 F 5
Guthrie, TX 76-77 D 6
Guthrie Center, IA 70-71 CD 5
Gutiérrez, Tuxtla — 58-59 H 8
Guttenberg, IA 70-71 E 4
Guttenberg, NJ 82 III bc 2
Guulin 166-167 H 2
Guvāhāṭī = Gauhati 160-161 P 5
Guyana 98-99 H 3-4
Guyanas, Macizo de las — 98-99 F 3-J 4
Guyandot River 72-73 EF 5
Guyenne 132-133 G-J 6
Guyi = Miluo 166-167 L 6
Guymon, OK 76-77 D 4
Guynemer 49 J 5
Guyra 182-183 K 6
Guysborough 51 EF 5
Guzmán 86-87 G 2
Guzmán, Ciudad — 58-59 F 8
Guzmán, Laguna de — 86-87 G 2
Gvalior = Gwalior 160-161 M 5
Gvāliyar = Gwalior 160-161 M 5
Gvardejskoje 142-143 F 6
Gwa 174-175 B 3
Gwabegar 182-183 JK 6
Gwādar 160-161 J 5
Gwai 198 E 5
Gwalia 182-183 D 5
Gwalior 160-161 M 5
Gwaliyar = Gwalior 160-161 M 5
Gwanda 198 E 6
Gwane 198 E 1
Gwda 124 H 2
Gweebarra Bay = Gaoth Beara 116-117 C 6
Gwennap Head 116-117 F 10
Gwent 116-117 J 9
Gweru 198 E 5
Gwydir River 182-183 J 5
Gwynedd 116-117 GH 7-8
Gyamda Dsong 166-167 G 5
Gyangtse 166-167 FG 6
Gyáros 138-139 L 7
Gyda 154-155 O 3
Gydanskaja guba 154-155 O 3
Gydanskij poluostrov 154-155 OP 3-4
Gympie 182-183 K 5
Gyöngyös 124 J 5
Győr 124 H 5
Gypsum, KS 68-69 H 6
Gypsumville 49 J 5
Gýtheion 138-139 K 7
Gyula 124 K 5

H

Haafuun 194-195 c 1
Haafuun, Raas — 160-161 G 8
Haag, Den — = 's-Gravenhage 132-133 JK 2
Haakon VII land 114-115 hj 5
Ha'apai 178 J 4
Haapajärvi 114-115 LM 6
Haapamäki 114-115 KL 6
Haapsalu 142-143 D 4
Haardt 124 CD 4
Haarlem [NL] 132-133 JK 2
Habana, La — 58-59 K 7
Habārūt 160-161 G 7
Habay 46-47 N 6
Ḥabīb, Wādī — 199 BC 4
Haboro 170-171 b 1
Hacheim, Bîr — = Bi'r al-Ḥukayyim 194-195 J 2
Hachijō-jima 166-167 Q 5
Hachinohe 166-167 R 3
Hachiōji 170-171 M 5
Hachirō-gata 170-171 MN 3
Hachita, NM 74-75 J 7
Hack, Mount — 182-183 G 6
Hackberry, AZ 74-75 G 5
Hackensack, MN 70-71 CD 2
Hackensack, NJ 82 III b 1
Hackensack River 82 III b 2
Hackett 49 B 4
Hackleburg, AL 78-79 EF 3
Hadal 'Awāb, Jabal — 199 D 7
Haḍbarāh 160-161 H 7
Ḥadd, Rā's al — 160-161 HJ 6
Haddār, Al- 160-161 EF 6
Haddington 116-117 J 5
Haddock 48 J 3
Haddummati Atoll 36 ab 2
Hadejia [WAN, place] 194-195 G 6
Hadejia [WAN, river] 194-195 F 6
Haderslev 114-115 C 10
Ḥadītah, Al- 160-161 F 4
Hadjout = Ḥajut 194-195 E 1
Hadleigh 116-117 gh 6
Hadley Bay 46-47 P 3
Hadong [ROK] 170-171 FG 5
Ha Đông [VN] 174-175 E 2
Hadramaut = Ḥaḍramawt 160-161 F 7
Ḥaḍramaut, Wādī — = Wādī al-Musīlah 160-161 FG 7
Ḥaḍramawt 160-161 F 7
Hadseløy 114-115 EF 3
Hadu 198 GH 2
Ḥaḍūr Shu'ayb 160-161 EF 7
Hadweenzic River 52-53 NO 3
Haedo, Cuchilla de — 103 E 4
Haeju 166-167 O 4
Haeju-man 170-171 E 4
Haemi 170-171 F 4
Haenam 170-171 F 5
Haengyŏng 170-171 GH 1
Ḥafar al- Bāṭin, Al- 160-161 F 5
Ḥaffah 142-143 G 8
Hafford 49 E 4
Hafnarfjördhur 114-115 bc 2
Haft Gel 160-161 FG 4
Hagadera = Alanga Arba 198 GH 1
Hagemeister Strait 52-53 G 7
Hagen 124 C 3
Hagensborg 48 D 3
Hagerman, ID 66-67 F 4
Hagerman, NM 76-77 B 6
Hagermeister Island 46-47 D 6
Hagerstown, MD 72-73 GH 5
Hagersville 72-73 F 3
Hagfors 114-115 EF 7-8
Hagi [IS] 114-115 b 2
Hagi [J] 170-171 H 5
Hagiá 138-139 K 6
Ha Giang 174-175 DE 2
Hágion Óros 138-139 L 5
Hágios Andréa, Akrōtérion — 142-143 FG 8
Hágios Evstrátios 138-139 L 6
Hágios Geṓrgios 138-139 KL 7
Hágios Iōánnēs, Akrōtérion — 138-139 LM 8
Hágios Nikólaos 138-139 LM 8
Hagiwara 170-171 L 5
Hags Head = Ceann Caillighe 116-117 B 8
Hague 49 E 4
Hague, ND 68-69 FG 2
Hague, Cap de la — 132-133 G 4
Hague, The — = 's-Gravenhage 132-133 JK 2
Haguenau 132-133 L 4
Hagues Peak 68-69 CD 5
Hagui = Hagi 170-171 H 5
Hagunia, El — = Al-Haqūniyah 194-195 B 3
Haha 148-149 S 7
Hahnville, LA 78-79 D 6
Hai'an [TJ, Guangdong] 166-167 KL 7
Haibei Zangzu Zizhizhou 166-167 H-J 4
Haicheng 170-171 D 2
Ḥaidarābād 160-161 KL 5
Haiderabad = Hyderābād 160-161 M 7
Haiderbad = Ḥaidarābād 160-161 KL 5
Hai Du'o'ng 174-175 E 2
Haifa = Ḥēfa 160-161 CD 4
Haifeng 166-167 M 7
Haifong = Hai Phong 174-175 E 2
Haig, Mount — 66-67 F 1
Haigler, NE 68-69 F 5-6
Haikang 166-167 KL 7
Haikou 166-167 L 7-8
Haikow = Haikou 166-167 L 7-8
Ḥā'il 160-161 E 5
Hai-la-êrh = Hailar 166-167 M 2
Hailar 166-167 M 2
Hailar He 166-167 MN 2
Hailey, ID 66-67 F 4
Hailong 166-167 O 3
Hailsham 116-117 M 10
Hailun 166-167 O 2
Hailuoto 114-115 L 5
Haimen [TJ, Jiangsu] 166-167 N 5
Haimen [TJ, Zhejiang] 166-167 N 6
Haimur Wells = Ābār Ḥaymūr 199 CD 6
Hainan = Hainan Dao 166-167 KL 8
Hainan Dao 166-167 KL 8
Hainan Strait = Qiongzhou Haixia 166-167 KL 7
Hai-nan Tao = Hainan Dao 166-167 KL 8
Hainan Zangzu Zizhizhou 166-167 H 5-J 4
Hainan Zizhizhou 166-167 K 8
Hainaut 132-133 JK 3
Haines, AK 46-47 JK 6
Haines, OR 66-67 DE 3
Haines City, FL 80-81 c 2
Haines Junction 46-47 J 5
Hai Phong 174-175 E 2
Ḥais = Ḥays 160-161 E 8
Haitan Dao = Pingtan Dao 166-167 MN 6
Haïti 58-59 M 8
Haiti = Hispaniola 58-59 MN 8
Haixi Monggolzu Zangzu Kazakzu Zizhizhou 166-167 GH 4, G 5
Haiyā = Hayyā 194-195 M 5
Haiyang Dao 170-171 D 3
Hai-yang Tao = Haiyang Dao 170-171 D 3
Haizhou 166-167 M 5
Ḥajar, Al- [Oman] 160-161 H 6
Hajdúböszörmény 124 KL 5
Hajiki-saki 170-171 M 3
Ḥajīr, Jabal — 160-161 G 8
Ḥājj 199 DE 3
Ḥajjah 160-161 E 7
Ḥajjār, Al- 194-195 EF 4
Ḥājjīābād 160-161 H 5
Hajnówka 124 L 2
Hajo-do 170-171 F 5
Hajut 194-195 E 1
Hakken san 170-171 KL 5
Hakodate 166-167 R 3
Hakui 170-171 L 4
Haku-san [J ↗ Ōno] 170-171 L 4
Haku-san [J ↓ Ōno] 170-171 L 5
Ḥalab 160-161 D 3
Ḥalabān 160-161 E 6
Hala Hu = Char nuur 166-167 H 4
Ḥalā'ib 194-195 M 4
Ḥalāib, Jazā'ir — 199 E 6
Ḥalāl, Gebel — = Jabal Hilāl 199 CD 2
Halawa, HI 78-79 d 2
Halberstadt 124 E 3
Halbrite 68-69 E 1
Halden 114-115 D 8
Haldensleben 124 E 2
Hale, Mount — 182-183 C 5
Haleakala Crater 174-175 ef 3
Ḥaleb = Ḥalab 160-161 D 3
Hale Center, TX 76-77 CD 5
Halesworth 116-117 h 6
Haleyville, AL 78-79 F 3
Ḥalfīn, Wādī — 160-161 H 6
Hal Flood Range 31 B 23
Halfway Mount 52-53 K 6
Halfway River 48 FG 1
Ḥalī = Khay' 160-161 E 7
Haliburton 72-73 G 2
Haliburton Highlands 50 MN 4
Halifax, VA 80-81 G 2
Halifax [CDN] 46-47 Y 9
Halifax [GB] 116-117 K 7
Halifax Bay 182-183 J 3
Ḥalīl Rūd 160-161 H 5
Halkett, Cape — 52-53 LM 1
Hall 124 E 5
Hall, MT 66-67 G 2
Hall, ostrov — 154-155 KL 1
Halladale, River — 116-117 H 2
Halland 114-115 E 9
Hallandale, FL 80-81 c 4
Halla-san 170-171 F 6
Hallaton 116-117 L 8
Halle 124 EF 3
Halleck, NV 66-67 F 5
Hällefors 114-115 F 8
Hallein 124 F 5
Hallettsville, TX 76-77 F 8
Halley Bay 31 B 33-34
Halliday, ND 68-69 E 2
Hallingdal 114-115 C 7
Hallingskarvet 114-115 BC 7
Hall Lake 46-47 U 4
Hällnäs 114-115 H 5
Hallock, MN 68-69 H 1
Hallowell, ME 72-73 M 2
Hall Peninsula 46-47 X 5
Hallsberg 114-115 F 8
Halls Creek 182-183 E 3
Hallstavik 114-115 H 7-8
Halmahera 174-175 J 6
Halmahera, Laut — 174-175 J 7
Halmeu 138-139 K 2
Halmstad 114-115 E 9
Halmyrós 138-139 K 6
Halonnēsos 138-139 KL 6
Halsey, NE 68-69 F 5
Hälsingland 114-115 F 7-G 6
Halstad, MN 68-69 H 2
Halstead 116-117 M 9
Haltiatunturi 114-115 J 3
Haltwhistle 116-117 J 6
Halvmåneøya 114-115 lm 6
Halvorgate 49 E 5
Hälys = Kızılırmak 160-161 D 3
Hamada 170-171 HJ 5
Hamadān 160-161 F 3-4
Ḥamāh 160-161 D 3
Hamajima 170-171 L 5
Hamamatsu 166-167 Q 5
Hamamatu = Hamamatsu 166-167 Q 5
Hamanaka 170-171 d 2
Hamana ko 170-171 L 5
Hamar 114-115 D 7
Hamar, ND 68-69 G 2
Ḥamar, Dār — 194-195 K 6
Hamas = Ḥamāh 160-161 D 3
Hamasaka 170-171 K 5
Ḥamātah, Jabal — 194-195 LM 4
Hamatonbetu = Hama-Tombetsu 170-171 c 1
Hambergbreen 114-115 k 6
Hamber Provincial Park 46-47 N 7
Hamburg, AR 78-79 CD 4
Hamburg, CA 66-67 B 5
Hamburg, IA 70-71 BC 5
Hamburg, NY 72-73 G 3
Hamburg, PA 72-73 HJ 4
Hamburg [D] 124 E 2
Hamch'ang 170-171 G 4
Ḥamḍ, Wādī al — 160-161 D 5
Ḥamḍah 160-161 E 7
Hämeen lääni 114-115 KL 7
Hämeenlinna 114-115 L 7
Hamelin = Hameln 124 D 2
Hamelin Pool [AUS, bay] 182-183 B 5
Hamelin Pool [AUS, place] 182-183 BC 5
Hameln 124 D 2
Hamersley Range 182-183 C 4
Ham-gang = Namhan-gang 170-171 F 4
Hamgyŏng-namdo 170-171 FG 2-3
Hamgyŏng-pukto 170-171 G 2-H 1
Hamhŭng 166-167 O 3-4
Hami 166-167 G 3
Hamilton, AK 52-53 F 5
Hamilton, AL 78-79 EF 3
Hamilton, KS 68-69 H 6-7
Hamilton, MI 70-71 GH 4
Hamilton, MO 70-71 CD 6
Hamilton, MT 66-67 F 2
Hamilton, NY 72-73 J 3
Hamilton, OH 58-59 K 4
Hamilton, TX 76-77 EF 7
Hamilton, WA 66-67 C 1
Hamilton [AUS] 182-183 H 7
Hamilton [Bermuda Islands] 58-59 O 5
Hamilton [CDN] 46-47 V 9
Hamilton [GB] 116-117 G 5
Hamilton [NZ] 182-183 OP 7
Hamilton, Mount — 74-75 F 3
Hamilton City, CA 74-75 BC 3
Hamilton Inlet 46-47 Z 7
Hamilton River [AUS, Queensland] 182-183 GH 4
Hamilton River [AUS, South Australia] 182-183 FG 5
Hamilton River = Churchill River 46-47 Y 7
Hamilton Sound 51 JK 3
Hamilton Square, NJ 72-73 J 4
Hamina 114-115 M 7
Hamitabad = Isparta 160-161 C 3
Hamlet, NC 80-81 G 3
Hamlin, TX 76-77 D 6
Hamm 124 CD 3
Ḥammāmāt, Khalīj al- 194-195 G 1
Ḥammār, Hawr al- 160-161 F 4
Hammerdal 114-115 F 6
Hammerfest 114-115 KL 2
Hammett, ID 66-67 F 4
Hammon, OK 76-77 E 5
Hammond, IN 58-59 J 3
Hammond, LA 78-79 D 5
Hammond, MT 68-69 D 3
Hammond, OR 66-67 AB 2
Hammond Bay 70-71 HJ 3
Hammonton, NJ 72-73 J 5
Hampden 51 H 3
Hampshire 116-117 K 10-L 9
Hampstead [CDN, New Brunswick] 51 CD 5
Hampstead [CDN, Quebec] 82 I ab 2
Hampton 51 D 5
Hampton, AR 78-79 C 4
Hampton, FL 80-81 bc 2
Hampton, IA 70-71 D 4
Hampton, NH 72-73 L 3
Hampton, OR 66-67 C 4
Hampton, SC 80-81 F 4
Hampton, VA 80-81 H 2
Hampton Tableland 182-183 E 6
Ḥamrā', Al- [Saudi Arabia] 160-161 D 6
Ḥamrā', Al-Ḥammādat al- 194-195 G 2-3
Hamsah, Bi'r al- = Bi'r al-Khamsah 194-195 K 2
Hams Fork 66-67 H 4-5
Ḥāmūl, Al- 199 B 2
Hamun = Daryācheh Sīstān 160-161 HJ 4
Hana, HI 78-79 de 2
Ḥanākīyah, Al — 160-161 E 6
Hanalei, HI 78-79 c 1
Hanamaki 170-171 N 3
Hanang 198 G 2
Hanazura-oki = Sukumo wan 170-171 J 6
Hanceville 48 F 4
Hancheu = Hangzhou 166-167 MN 5
Hancock, MI 70-71 F 2
Hancock, NY 72-73 J 3-4
Handa 170-171 L 5
Handae-ri 170-171 FG 2
Handan 166-167 LM 4
Handaq, Al- = Al-Khandaq 194-195 KL 5
Handeni 198 G 3
Handsworth 49 G 6
Handsworth, Sheffield- 116-117 KL 7
Hanford, CA 74-75 D 4
Hanford Works United States Atomic Energy Commission Reservation 66-67 D 2
Hangai = Changajn nuruu 166-167 HJ 2
Hangchow = Hangzhou 166-167 MN 5
Hang-hsien = Hangzhou 166-167 MN 5
Hängö 114-115 K 8
Hangu 166-167 M 4
Hangzhou 166-167 MN 5
Ḥanīfah, Wādī — 160-161 F 6
Ḥank, Al- 194-195 C 3-4
Hankinson, ND 68-69 H 2-3
Hanko = Hangö 114-115 K 8
Hankou, Wuhan- 166-167 LM 5
Hankow = Wuhan-Hankou 166-167 LM 5
Hanksville, UT 74-75 H 3
Hanku = Hangu 166-167 M 4
Hanley, Stoke on Trend- 116-117 JK 7
Hanley Falls, MN 70-71 C 3
Hann, Mount — 182-183 E 3
Hanna 46-47 O 7
Hanna, WY 68-69 C 5
Hannaford, ND 68-69 GH 2
Hannah, ND 68-69 G 1
Hannibal, MO 58-59 H 3-4
Hannō 170-171 M 5
Hannover 124 D 2
Hanöbukten 114-115 F 10
Ha Nôi 174-175 DE 2
Hanoi = Ha Nôi 174-175 DE 2
Hanover, KS 68-69 H 6
Hanover, MT 68-69 B 2
Hanover, NH 72-73 KL 3
Hanover, PA 72-73 H 5
Hanover, VA 80-81 H 2
Hanover [CDN] 72-73 F 2
Hanover = Hannover 124 D 2
Hanover, Isla — 103 AB 8
Hansard 48 G 2
Hansboro, ND 68-69 G 1
Hansen 70-71 HJ 1
Hansenfjella 31 BC 6
Han Shui 166-167 K 5
Hanson River 182-183 F 4
Hantan = Handan 166-167 LM 4
Hanyang, Wuhan- 166-167 L 5
Hanzhong 166-167 K 5
Haoli = Hegang 166-167 OP 2
Haora = Howrah 160-161 O 6
Haouach 194-195 J 5
Haparanda 114-115 KL 5
Hapch'ŏn 170-171 FG 5
Happisburgh 116-117 h 6
Happy, TX 76-77 D 5
Happy Camp, CA 66-67 C 5
Ḥaql 160-161 CD 5
Ḥaqūnīyah, Al- 194-195 B 3
Ḥaraḍ 160-161 F 6
Haramachi 170-171 N 4
Haranomachi = Haramachi 170-171 N 4

232 Guaviare

Hara nur = Char nuur 166-167 G 2
Hararděre = Xarardeere 194-195 b 3
Harare 198 F 5
Ḥarāsīs, Jiddat al — 160-161 H 6-7
Hara Ulsa nur = Char us nuur 166-167 G 2
Ḥarawa 194-195 N 6-7
Harbin 166-167 O 2
Harbor Beach, MI 72-73 E 3
Harbor Springs, MI 70-71 H 3
Harbour Breton 51 HJ 4
Harbour Deep 51 H 2
Hardangerfjord 114-115 A 8-B 7
Hardangervidda 114-115 BC 7
Hardee, MS 78-79 D 4
Hardeeville, SC 80-81 F 4
Hardesty, OK 76-77 D 4
Hardey River 182-183 C 4
Hardin, IL 70-71 E 6
Hardin, MO 70-71 D 6
Hardin, MT 68-69 C 3
Harding 198 EF 8
Harding Icefield 52-53 MN 6
Hardinsburg, KY 70-71 GH 7
Hardisty 49 C 4
Hardvār = Hardwār 160-161 M 4
Hardwār 160-161 M 4
Hardwick, VT 72-73 K 2
Hardy, AR 78-79 D 2
Hardy, Peninsula — 103 BC 9
Hardy, Río — 74-75 F 6
Hare Bay 51 J 2
Hareidlandet 114-115 A 6
Harer [ETH, administrative unit] 194-195 NO 7
Harer [ETH, place] 194-195 N 7
Hargeisa = Hargeysa 194-195 a 2
Hargeysa 194-195 a 2
Hargill, TX 76-77 EF 9
Hargrave Lake 49 J 3
Hari, Batang — 174-175 D 7
Ḥarīb 160-161 EF 7-8
Haridwar = Hardwār 160-161 M 4
Harima nada 170-171 K 5
Harimgye 170-171 G 4
Harīrōd 160-161 J 4
Härjedalen 114-115 E 6-F 7
Harlan, IA 70-71 C 5
Harlan, KY 80-81 E 2
Harlan County Lake 68-69 G 5-6
Harlech 48 K 3
Harlem, GA 80-81 E 4
Harlem, MT 68-69 B 1
Harlem, New York-, NY 82 III c 2
Harlingen 132-133 K 2
Harlingen, TX 58-59 G 6
Harlow 116-117 M 9
Harlowton, MT 68-69 B 2
Harmanli 138-139 LM 5
Harmony, ME 72-73 M 2
Harmony, MN 70-71 DE 4
Harney Basin 58-59 BC 3
Harney Lake 66-67 D 4
Harney Peak 68-69 E 4
Härnösand 114-115 GH 6
Haro 132-133 F 7
Haro, Cabo — 58-59 D 6
Harold Byrd Range 31 A 25-22
Haro Strait 66-67 B 1
Harper 194-195 C 8
Harper, KS 76-77 EF 4
Harper, OR 66-67 E 4
Harper, TX 76-77 E 7
Harper, Mount — [CDN] 52-53 RS 4
Harper, Mount — [USA] 52-53 PQ 4
Harpers Ferry, WV 72-73 GH 5
Harpster, ID 66-67 F 2-3
Harquahala Mountains 74-75 G 6
Harquahala Plains 74-75 G 6
Ḥarrah, Al — 160-161 D 4
Harrar = Ḥarer 194-195 N 7
Harrawa = Ḥarawa 194-195 N 6-7
Harrell, AR 78-79 C 4
Harricanaw River 46-47 V 7-8
Harriman, TN 78-79 G 3
Harrington, DE 72-73 J 5
Harrington, WA 66-67 DE 2
Harrington Harbour 46-47 Z 7
Harris [CDN] 49 E 5
Harris [GB] 116-117 DE 3
Harris, Sound of — 116-117 DE 3
Harrisburg, IL 70-71 F 7
Harrisburg, NE 68-69 E 5
Harrisburg, OR 66-67 B 3
Harrisburg, PA 58-59 L 3
Harrismith 198 E 7
Harrison, AR 78-79 C 2
Harrison, ID 66-67 E 2
Harrison, MI 70-71 H 3
Harrison, MT 66-67 H 3
Harrison, NE 68-69 E 4
Harrison, NJ 82 III b 2
Harrison, Cape — 46-47 Z 7
Harrison Bay 52-53 LM 1
Harrisonburg, VA 72-73 G 5
Harrison Lake 66-67 BC 1
Harrisonville, MO 70-71 C 6
Harris Ridge = Lomonosov Ridge 30 A
Harriston 72-73 F 3
Harriston, MS 78-79 D 5
Harrisville, MI 72-73 E 2
Harrisville, WV 72-73 F 5
Harrodsburg, KY 70-71 H 7
Harrogate 116-117 K 6-7
Harrold, SD 68-69 G 3
Harrow, London- 116-117 L 9
Harry Strunk Lake 68-69 FG 5
Harstad 114-115 FG 3
Harsvik 114-115 D 5
Hart 68-69 D 1
Hart, MI 70-71 G 4
Hart, TX 76-77 CD 5
Hartenggole He = Chaaltyn gol 166-167 GH 4
Hartford, AL 78-79 G 5
Hartford, CT 58-59 M 3
Hartford, KY 70-71 G 7
Hartford, MI 70-71 G 4
Hartford, WI 70-71 F 4
Hartford City, IN 70-71 H 5
Hartington, NE 68-69 H 4
Hart Island 82 III d 1
Hart-Jaune, Rivière — 51 BC 2
Hartland 116-117 G 10
Hartland Point 116-117 G 9
Hartlebury 116-117 JK 8
Hartlepool 116-117 KL 6
Hartley, IA 70-71 C 4
Hartley, TX 76-77 C 5
Hartley = Chegutu 198 EF 5
Hartline, WA 66-67 D 2
Hartman, AR 78-79 C 3
Hart Mountain 66-67 D 4
Hartney 68-69 F 1
Hartselle, AL 78-79 F 3
Hartshorne, OK 76-77 G 5
Harts Range 182-183 FG 4
Hartsrivier 198 DE 7
Hartsville, SC 80-81 FG 3
Hartsville, TN 78-79 FG 2
Hartwell, GA 80-81 E 3
Hartwell Lake 80-81 E 3
Harty 50 K 2
Harūj al-Aswad, Al- 194-195 H 3
Hārūt Rōd 160-161 J 4
Harvard, CA 74-75 E 5
Harvard, IL 70-71 F 4
Harvard, NE 68-69 GH 5
Harvey 182-183 C 6
Harvey, IL 70-71 G 5
Harvey, ND 68-69 FG 2
Harwell 116-117 K 9
Harwich 116-117 h 7
Harwich, MA 72-73 LM 4
Harwood, TX 76-77 F 8
Harwood Heights, IL 83 II a 1
Haryana 160-161 M 5
Harz 124 E 3
'Hasā', Al — 160-161 F 5
Ḥaṣāḥeīṣa, El — = Al-Ḥuṣayḥiṣah 194-195 L 6
Ḥasakah, Al- 160-161 D 3
Hāsana = Hassan 160-161 M 8
Ḥasb, Shaʿīb — 160-161 E 4
Hasĕtchê, El- = Al-Hasakah 160-161 D 3
Hashimoto 170-171 K 5
Hashun Shamo = Gašuun Gov' 166-167 G 3
Hasib, Sha'ib — = Shaʿīb Ḥasb 160-161 E 4
Haskell, OK 76-77 G 5
Haskell, TX 76-77 E 6
Haskovo 138-139 L 5
Haslemere 116-117 L 9
Ḥasmat 'Umar, Bi'r — 199 CD 7
Hassan 160-161 M 8
Hassayampa River 74-75 G 6
Hassell, NM 76-77 B 5
Hassel Sound 46-47 R 2
Hasselt 132-133 K 3
Ḥāssī ar-Raml 194-195 E 2
Hassi-Inifel = Ḥāssī Īnifil 194-195 E 2-3
Ḥāssī Īnifil 194-195 E 2-3
Ḥāssī Mas'ūd 194-195 F 2
Hassi-Messaoud = Ḥāssī Mas'ūd 194-195 F 2
Hassi-R'Mel = Ḥāssī ar-Raml 194-195 E 2
Hässleholm 114-115 EF 9
Hastings, FL 80-81 c 2
Hastings, MI 70-71 H 4
Hastings, MN 70-71 D 3
Hastings, NE 58-59 G 3
Hastings [GB] 116-117 M 10
Hastings [NZ] 182-183 P 7
Hasvik 114-115 JK 2
Haswell, CO 68-69 E 6
Ḥaṭab, Wādī al- 199 C 7
Hat'ae-do 170-171 E 5
Ḥaṭāṭibah, Al- 199 B 2
Hatch, NM 76-77 A 6
Hatch, UT 74-75 G 4
Hatches Creek 182-183 G 4
Hatchet Bay 88-89 HJ 2
Hatchie River 78-79 E 3
Hat Creek, WY 68-69 D 4
Hațeg 138-139 K 3
Hatfield 116-117 L 9
Hathaway, MT 68-69 CD 2
Hāthras 160-161 M 5
Hatinohe = Hachinohe 166-167 R 3
Hatizyô zima = Hachijō-jima 166-167 Q 5
Ha-tongsan-ni 170-171 F 3
Hatteras, NC 80-81 J 3
Hatteras, Cape — 58-59 LM 4
Hatteras Island 58-59 LM 4
Hattfjelldal 114-115 F 5
Hattiesburg, MS 58-59 J 5
Hatton 46-47 P 7
Hatton, ND 68-69 H 2
Hatvan 124 JK 5
Hat Yai 174-175 D 5
Haud = Ḥāwd 194-195 NO 7
Haugesund 114-115 A 8
Haukadalur 114-115 c 2
Haukeligrend 114-115 B 8
Haukipudas 114-115 L 5
Haukivesi 114-115 N 6-7
Haukivuori 114-115 M 6-7
Haultain River 49 E 2
Ḥaurā = Ḥawrah 160-161 F 7
Ḥāurā = Howrah 160-161 O 6
Ḥaurā, Al — = Al-Ḥawrah 160-161 F 8
Hauraki Gulf 182-183 OP 7
Hausruck 124 F 4
Haute-Kotto 194-195 J 7
Hauterive 51 B 3
Haute-Sangha 194-195 H 8
Hautes Plateaux = Nijād al-'Alī 194-195 D 2-E 1
Haut-Mbomou 194-195 K 7
Haut-Zaïre 198 E 1
Havana, FL 78-79 G 5
Havana, IL 70-71 E 5
Havana, ND 68-69 H 3
Havana = La Habana 58-59 K 7
Havasu Lake 74-75 FG 5
Have Bank, La — 51 D 6
Havel 124 F 2
Havelock 72-73 GH 2
Havelock, NC 80-81 H 3
Haverfordwest 116-117 FG 9
Haverhill 116-117 M 8
Haverhill, MA 72-73 L 3
Haverhill, NH 72-73 KL 3
Haverstraw, NY 72-73 JK 4
Havlíčkův Brod 124 G 4
Havøysund 114-115 L 2
Havre, MT 58-59 DE 2
Havre, le — 132-133 GH 4
Havre-Aubert 51 F 4
Havre de Grace, MD 72-73 HJ 5
Hawai = Hawaii 174-175 ef 4
Hawaii 174-175 ef 4
Hawaiian Gardens, CA 83 III d 3
Hawaiian Islands 174-175 d 3-e 4
Hawaiian Ridge 34-35 JK 3
Hawaii Volcanoes National Park 78-79 e 3
Hawarden, IA 68-69 H 4
Hawarden [CDN] 49 E 5
Hawarden [GB] 116-117 HJ 7
Hawash, Wadi — = Haouach 194-195 J 5
Ḥawashīyah, Wādī — 199 C 3
Ḥawātah, Al- 194-195 LM 6
Ḥāwd 194-195 NO 7
Ḥawḍ, Al- [RIM] 194-195 C 5
Hawera 182-183 OP 7
Hawes 116-117 J 6
Hawesville, KY 70-71 G 7
Hawi, HI 78-79 e 2
Hawick 116-117 J 5
Hawke, Cape — 182-183 K 6
Hawke Bay 182-183 P 7
Hawker 182-183 G 6
Hawkes, Mount — 31 A 32-33
Hawkesbury 72-73 J 2
Hawkesbury Island 48 C 3
Hawkhurst 116-117 M 9
Hawk Inlet, AK 52-53 U 7
Hawkins, WI 70-71 E 3
Hawkinsville, GA 80-81 E 4
Hawk Junction 50 J 2
Hawk Lake 50 C 3
Hawks, MI 70-71 HJ 3
Hawksbill Cay 88-89 H 2
Hawk Springs, WY 68-69 D 5
Hawley, MN 70-71 BC 2
Hawley, TX 76-77 E 6
Ḥawrah 160-161 F 7
Ḥawrah, Al- 160-161 F 8
Ḥawrān, Wādī — 160-161 E 4
Haw River 80-81 G 3
Ḥawsh 'Īsá 199 B 2
Ḥawṭah, Al- = Al-Ḥillah 160-161 F 6
Hawthorn, FL 80-81 bc 2
Hawthorne, CA 83 III b 2
Hawthorne, NV 74-75 D 3
Hawthorne Municipal Airport 83 III bc 2
Hawthorne Race Track 83 II a 1-2
Haxby, MT 68-69 C 2
Haxey 116-117 L 7
Haxtun, CO 68-69 E 5
Hay [AUS] 182-183 HJ 6
Hay [GB] 116-117 H 8
Hay, Mount — 52-53 T 7
Hayang 170-171 G 5
Haycock, AK 52-53 G 4
Hayden, AZ 74-75 H 6
Hayden, CO 68-69 C 5
Hayes, LA 78-79 C 5
Hayes, SD 68-69 F 3
Hayes, Mount — 46-47 G 5
Hayes Center, NE 68-69 F 5
Hayes Glacier 52-53 L 6
Hayes Halvø 46-47 XY 2
Hayes River 46-47 S 6
Hayfield, MN 70-71 D 4
Hayfork, CA 66-67 B 5
Hay Lake = Habay 46-47 N 6
Hay Lakes 49 B 4
Hayle 116-117 F 10
Haylow, GA 80-81 E 5
Ḥaymūr, Ābār — 199 CD 6
Ḥaymūr, Wādī — 199 C 6
Haynesville, LA 78-79 C 4
Hayneville, AL 78-79 F 4
Hay River [AUS] 182-183 G 4
Hay River [CDN, place] 46-47 NO 5
Hay River [CDN, river] 46-47 N 6
Hays 160-161 E 8
Hays, KS 58-59 G 4
Hays, MT 68-69 B 2
Ḥaysī, Bi'r al- — 199 D 3
Hay Springs, NE 68-69 E 4
Haystack Mountain 72-73 K 3
Haystack Peak 74-75 G 3
Hayti, MO 78-79 E 2
Hayti, SD 68-69 H 3
Hayward, CA 74-75 BC 4
Hayward, WI 70-71 E 2
Haywood 49 J 6
Ḥayy, Al- 160-161 F 4
Ḥayyā 194-195 M 5
Hazārān, Kūh-e — = Kūh-e Hezārān 160-161 H 5
Hazard, KY 58-59 K 4
Hazebrouck 132-133 J 3
Hazel Creek River 50 A 2
Hazel Green, IL 83 II a 2
Hazelton Mountains 48 CD 2
Hazelton Peak 68-69 C 3
Hazen, AR 78-79 D 3
Hazen, ND 68-69 F 2
Hazen, NV 74-75 D 3
Hazen Strait 46-47 OP 2
Hazlehurst, GA 80-81 E 5
Hazlehurst, MS 78-79 D 5
Hazleton, PA 72-73 J 4
Hazlett, Lake 182-183 E 4
Ḥazm, Al- 199 E 3
Headland, AL 78-79 G 5
Headquarters, ID 66-67 F 2
Heads, The — 66-67 A 4
Healdsburg, CA 74-75 B 3
Healdton, OK 76-77 F 5
Healy, AK 52-53 N 5
Healy, KS 68-69 F 6
Healy Lake 52-53 P 5
Healy River 52-53 P 4
Heanor 116-117 K 7-8
Heard 26-27 N 8
Hearne, TX 76-77 F 7
Hearst 46-47 U 8
Hearst Island 31 BC 30-31
Heart Butte 68-69 EF 2
Heart Butte Reservoir = Lake Tschida 68-69 EF 2
Heart River 68-69 F 2
Heart's Content 51 K 4
Heath Point 51 F 3
Heavener, OK 76-77 G 5
Hebbronville, TX 76-77 E 9
Hebei 166-167 LM 4
Heber, UT 66-67 H 5
Heber Springs, AR 78-79 C 3
Hebgen Lake 66-67 H 3
Hebo, OR 66-67 AB 3
Hebrides, Sea of the — 116-117 DE 3-4
Hebron, ND 68-69 EF 2
Hebron, NE 68-69 H 5
Hebron [CDN] 46-47 Y 6
Hecate Strait 46-47 K 7
Heceta Head 66-67 A 3
Heceta Island 52-53 vw 9
Hechuan 166-167 JK 5
Hecla 50 A 2
Hecla, SD 68-69 GH 3
Hecla and Griper Bay 46-47 O 2
Hede 114-115 E 6
He Devil Mountain 66-67 E 3
Hedien = Khotan 166-167 DE 4
Hedjas 160-161 D 5-6
Hedley 66-67 CD 1
Hedley, TX 76-77 D 5
Hedmark 114-115 D 6-E 7
Hedrick, IA 70-71 D 5
Heerlen 132-133 KL 3
Hefei 166-167 M 5
Heflin, AL 78-79 G 4
Hegang 166-167 OP 2
Hĕgumenitsa 138-139 J 6
Heian-hokudō = P'yŏngan-pukto 170-171 E 2-3
Heian-nandō = P'yŏngan-namdo 170-171 EF 3
Heide [D] 124 D 1
Heidelberg, MS 78-79 E 5
Heidelberg [D] 124 D 4
Heidoti 98-99 K 2
Ḥeifa 160-161 CD 4
Height of Land 51 A 5
Hei-ho = Aihui 166-167 O 1
Heijo = P'yŏngyang 166-167 NO 4
Heilar He = Chajlar gol 166-167 N 1-2
Heilbronn 124 D 4
Heilongjiang [TJ, administrative unit] 166-167 M-P 2
Heilong Jiang [TJ, river] 166-167 O 1
Hei-lung Chiang = Heilong Jiang 166-167 O 1
Heilung Kiang = Heilong Jiang 166-167 O 1
Heimaey 114-115 c 3
Heine Creek, AK 52-53 N 4
Heinola 114-115 M 7
Heinsburg 49 C 4
Heishan 170-171 CD 2
Ḥeisī, Bīr el- = Bi'r al-Ḥaysī 199 D 3
Hejaz 150 G 7-8
Hejaz = Al-Hijaz 160-161 D 5-6
Hekla 114-115 d 3
Helagsfjället 114-115 E 6
Helder, Den — 132-133 K 2
Helen, Mount — 74-75 E 4
Helena, AR 58-59 H 5
Helena, GA 80-81 E 4
Helena, MT 58-59 D 2
Helena, OK 76-77 E 4
Helendale, CA 74-75 E 5
Helen Reef 174-175 K 6
Helensburgh 116-117 G 4
Heleysund 114-115 l 5
Helgeland 114-115 E 5-F 4
Helgoland 124 C 1
Heligoland = Helgoland 124 C 1
Heligoland Bay 124 C 1
Helikŏn 138-139 K 6
Heliopolis = Al-Qahirah-Miṣr al-Jadīdah 199 BC 2
Helix, OR 66-67 D 3
Hella 114-115 c 3
Helleland 114-115 B 8
Hellepoort = Portes de l'Enfer 198 E 3
Hellín 132-133 G 9
Hell-Ville 198 J 4
Helmand Rōd 160-161 K 4
Helmet Mount 52-53 P 3
Helmond 132-133 KL 3
Helmsdale 116-117 H 2
Helmsdale, River — 116-117 GH 2
Helmsley 116-117 K 6
Helmstedt 124 E 2
Helmville, MT 66-67 G 2
Helong 166-167 O 3
Helper, UT 74-75 H 3
Helsingborg 114-115 DE 9
Helsingfors = Helsinki 114-115 L 7
Helsingør 114-115 DE 9
Helsinki 114-115 L 7
Helska, Mierzeja — 124 J 1
Helston 116-117 F 10
Helvellyn 116-117 H 6
Ḥelwân = Ḥulwān 194-195 L 3
Hemel Hempstead 116-117 L 9
Hemet, CA 74-75 E 6
Hemingford, NE 68-69 E 4
Hemphill, TX 78-79 C 5
Hempnall 116-117 h 6
Hempstead, NY 72-73 K 4
Hempstead, TX 76-77 F 7
Hempstead Harbor 82 III d 1-e 2
Hempstead Lake State Park 82 III de 2
Hemyock 116-117 H 10
Henan 166-167 L 5
Henares 132-133 F 8
Henashi-saki 170-171 M 2
Henbury 182-183 F 4
Henchow = Hengyang 166-167 L 6
Hendaye 132-133 FG 7
Henderson, KY 58-59 J 4
Henderson, NC 80-81 G 2
Henderson, NV 74-75 F 4
Henderson, TN 78-79 E 3
Henderson, TX 76-77 G 6
Henderson Bay 72-73 H 2-3
Hendersonville, NC 80-81 E 3
Hendersonville, TN 78-79 F 2
Hendriktop 98-99 K 2
Heng'ang = Hengyang 166-167 L 6
Heng-chan = Hengyang 166-167 L 6
Heng-chou = Heng Xian 166-167 K 7
Hengduan Shan 166-167 H 6
Hengelo 132-133 L 2
Henghsien = Heng Xian 166-167 K 7
Hengshan [TJ, Hunan] 166-167 L 6
Hengshan = Hengyang 166-167 L 6
Hengshui 166-167 LM 4
Heng Xian 166-167 K 7
Hengyang 166-167 L 6
Henik Lake = South Henik Lake 46-47 R 5
Henley in Arden 116-117 K 8
Henley on Thames 116-117 KL 9
Henlopen, Cape — 72-73 J 5
Henly, TX 76-77 E 7
Hennebont 132-133 F 5
Hennesberget 114-115 E 4
Hennessey, OK 76-77 F 4
Henning, MN 70-71 C 2
Henrietta, TX 76-77 E 6
Henrietta Maria, Cape — 46-47 U 6
Henriette, ostrov — 154-155 ef 2
Henrique de Carvalho = Saurimo 198 D 3
Henry, IL 70-71 F 5
Henry, NE 68-69 DE 4
Henry, SD 68-69 H 3
Henry, Cape — 80-81 J 2
Henry, Mount — 66-67 F 1
Henryetta, OK 76-77 FG 5
Henry Kater Peninsula 46-47 XY 4
Henry Mountains 74-75 H 3-4
Henrys Fork 66-67 H 3-4
Hensall 72-73 F 3
Henson Creek 82 II b 2
Henzada = Hinthāda 174-175 BC 3
Heppner, OR 66-67 D 3
Heppner Junction, OR 66-67 CD 3
Hepu 166-167 K 7
Hepworth 72-73 F 2
Heraclea 138-139 G 5
Heraclea = Ereğli 160-161 C 2
Héradhsflói 114-115 fg 2
Héradhsvötn 114-115 d 2
Hērákleia 138-139 L 7
Hērákleia = Ereğli 160-161 C 2
Hērákleion 138-139 L 8
Herald, ostrov — 30 B 36
Heras, Las — [RA, Santa Cruz] 103 C 7
Herāt 160-161 J 4
Herbert 49 E 5
Herbert C. Legg Lake 83 III d 1
Herbert Island 52-53 l 4
Hérbertville 50 PQ 2
Herb Lake 49 HJ 3
Hercegnovi 138-139 H 4
Herchmer 49 L 2
Heredia 88-89 DE 9
Hereford 116-117 J 8
Hereford, TX 76-77 C 5
Hereford & Worcester 116-117 J 8
Herefoss 114-115 C 8
Hereroland 198 CD 6
Herford 124 D 2
Herington, KS 68-69 H 6
Heri Rud = Harī Rūd 160-161 J 4
Heritage Range 31 B 28-A 29
Herkimer, NY 72-73 J 3
Herlen He 166-167 M 2
Herman, MN 70-71 BC 3
Hermanas 86-87 K 4
Hermanas, NM 74-75 JK 7
Herma Ness 116-117 ef 3
Hermann, MO 70-71 E 6
Hermannsburg [AUS] 182-183 F 4
Hermansverk 114-115 B 7
Hermansville, MI 70-71 G 3
Hermiston, OR 66-67 D 3
Hermitage 51 HJ 4
Hermitage, AR 78-79 C 4
Hermitage Bay 51 H 4
Hermite, Isla — 103 C 9
Hermit Islands 174-175 N 7
Hermleigh, TX 76-77 D 6
Hermosa, SD 68-69 E 4
Hermosa Beach, CA 83 III b 2
Hermosillo 58-59 D 6
Hermúpolis 138-139 L 7
Hernandarias 103 F 3
Hernando, MS 78-79 E 3
Herndon, KS 68-69 F 6
Herne Bay 116-117 h 7
Herning 114-115 C 9
Heroica Alvarado = Alvarado 58-59 GH 8
Heroica Caborca 58-59 D 5
Heroica Cárdenas 86-87 O 8-9
Heroica Guaymas 58-59 D 6
Heroica Matamoros = Matamoros 58-59 G 6
Heroica Nogales 58-59 D 5
Heroica Puebla de Zaragoza = Puebla de Zaragoza 58-59 G 8
Heroica Tlapacoyan 86-87 M 7-8
Heroica Veracruz = Veracruz 58-59 GH 8
Heroica Zitácuaro 86-87 K 8
Heron, MT 66-67 F 1
Heron Bay 70-71 G 1
Heron Lake 70-71 C 4
Hérons, Île aux — 82 I b 2
Herreid, SD 68-69 FG 3
Herrera [E] 132-133 F 7
Herrera [PA] 88-89 F 10
Herrera del Duque 132-133 E 9
Herrera de Pisuerga 132-133 EF 7
Herrick 182-183 J 8
Herrin, IL 70-71 F 7
Herrington Island 72-73 DE 5
Herrington Lake 70-71 H 7
Herriot 49 H 2
Herschel [CDN, island] 52-53 S 2
Herschel [CDN, place] 49 D 5
Herschel Island 46-47 J 3-4
Hertford 116-117 LM 9
Hertford, NC 80-81 H 2
Hertogenbosch, 's- 132-133 KL 3
Hervey Bay 182-183 K 4-5
Hervey-Jonction 72-73 K 1
Herzliya 199 D 1
Herzog-Ernst-Bucht 31 B 32-33
Hesperia, CA 74-75 E 5
Hesperus, CO 68-69 BC 7
Hess Creek 52-53 N 4
Hesse = Hessen 124 D 3

Hesse 233

Hessen 124 D 3
Hessle 116-117 L 7
Hess Mount 52-53 O 5
Hesteyri 114-115 b 1
Hestur 116-117 ab 2
Hettinger, ND 68-69 E 2-3
Hetton le Hole 116-117 K 6
Heuglin, Kapp — 114-115 lm 5
Heves 124 K 5
Hewlett, NY 82 III d 3
Hexham 116-117 J 6
He Xian [TJ, Guangxi Zhuangzu Zizhiqu] 166-167 L 7
Hexigten Qi 166-167 M 3
Hext, TX 76-77 E 7
Heyburn Lake 76-77 F 4-5
Heywood 116-117 J 7
Hezārān, Kūh-e- 160-161 H 5
Heze 166-167 M 4
Hezelton 46-47 L 6

Hialeah, FL 80-81 c 4
Hiawatha, KS 70-71 C 6
Hiawatha, UT 74-75 H 3
Hibbing, MN 58-59 H 2
Hichiro-wan = zaliv Terpenija 154-155 b 8
Hickman, KY 78-79 E 2
Hickman, NE 68-69 H 5
Hickman, NM 74-75 JK 5
Hickman, Mount — 52-53 x 8
Hickory, NC 80-81 F 3
Hickory, Lake — 80-81 F 3
Hickory Hills, IL 83 II a 2
Hicksville, OH 70-71 H 5
Hico, TX 76-77 EF 6
Hidaka 170-171 c 2
Hidaka-sammyaku 170-171 c 2
Hidalgo [MEX, Coahuila] 76-77 DE 9
Hidalgo [MEX, Hidalgo] 58-59 G 7
Hidalgo [MEX, Tamaulipas] 86-87 L 5
Hidalgo, Ciudad — 86-87 K 8
Hidalgo, Salinas de — 86-87 JK 6
Hida sammyaku 170-171 L 4-5
Hiddensee 124 F 1
Hienghène 182-183 MN 4
Hierápetra 138-139 L 8
Hierisós 138-139 KL 5
Hierro 194-195 A 3
Higasiōsaka 170-171 KL 5
Higbee, MO 70-71 D 6
Higgins, TX 76-77 D 4
Higgins Lake 70-71 H 3
High Atlas 194-195 CD 2
High Hill River 49 L 3
High Island 70-71 GH 3
High Island, TX 76-77 GH 8
Highland 116-117 F 3-H 2
Highland, IL 70-71 F 6
Highland, WA 66-67 E 2
Highland Park, IL 70-71 G 4
Highland Park, MI 72-73 E 3
Highland Park, Los Angeles-, CA 83 III c 1
Highland Peak 74-75 F 4
Highley 116-117 J 8
Highmore, SD 68-69 G 3
High Point, NC 58-59 KL 4
High Prairie 46-47 NO 6
High River 48 KL 4
Highrock 49 HJ 3
High Rock Lake 80-81 FG 3
Highrock Lake [CDN, Manitoba] 49 H 3
Highrock Lake [CDN, Saskatchewan] 49 F 2
High Springs, FL 80-81 b 2
High Willhays 116-117 G 10
Highwood, MT 66-67 H 2
Highwood Peak 66-67 H 2
Highworth 116-117 K 9
High Wycombe 116-117 L 9
Hiiumaa 142-143 D 4
Ḥijāz, Al- 160-161 D 5-6
Ḥijāzah 199 C 5
Hijo = Tagum 174-175 J 5
Hikari 170-171 H 6
Hiko, NV 74-75 F 4
Hikone 170-171 L 5
Hiko-san 170-171 H 6
Hilāl, Jabal — 199 CD 2
Hilbert, WI 70-71 FG 3
Hildesheim 124 DE 2
Hilger, MT 68-69 B 2
Hill, MT 66-67 H 1
Hillah, Al- [IRQ] 160-161 E 4
Ḥillah, Al- [Saudi Arabia] 160-161 F 6
Hill City, ID 66-67 F 4
Hill City, KS 68-69 G 6
Hill City, MN 70-71 D 2
Hill City, SD 68-69 E 3-4
Hillcrest Heights, MD 82 II b 2
Hillerød 114-115 DE 10
Hillingdon, London- 116-117 L 9
Hillman, MN 70-71 D 2-3
Hillmond 49 D 4
Hills, MN 68-69 H 4
Hillsboro, GA 80-81 E 4
Hillsboro, IL 70-71 F 6
Hillsboro, NC 80-81 G 2
Hillsboro, ND 68-69 H 2
Hillsboro, NH 72-73 L 3
Hillsboro, NM 76-77 A 6
Hillsboro, OH 72-73 E 5
Hillsboro, OR 66-67 B 3
Hillsboro, TX 76-77 F 6
Hillsboro Canal 80-81 c 3
Hillsborough 116-117 EF 6
Hillsborough Bay 51 E 4
Hillsdale, MI 70-71 H 5
Hillside, AZ 74-75 G 5
Hillside, NJ 82 III a 2
Hillsport 70-71 H 1
Hillston 182-183 HJ 6
Hillsville, VA 80-81 F 2
Hillswick 116-117 e 3
Hillwood, VA 82 II a 2
Hilmänd, Därya-ye- = Helmand Rōd 160-161 K 4
Hilmar, CA 74-75 C 4
Hilo, HI 174-175 ef 4
Hilton Head Island 80-81 F 4
Hilts, CA 66-67 B 5
Hilu-Babor = Īlubabor 194-195 LM 7
Hilversum 132-133 K 2
Himāchal Pradesh 160-161 M 4
Himālaya 160-161 L 4-P 5
Himeji 166-167 P 5
Himes, WY 68-69 B 3
Hime-saki 170-171 M 3
Himezi = Himeji 166-167 P 5
Himi 170-171 L 4
Ḥimṣ 160-161 D 4
Hinai 170-171 N 2
Hinche 88-89 KL 5
Hinchinbrook Entrance 52-53 OP 6
Hinchinbrook Island [AUS] 182-183 J 3
Hinchinbrook Island [USA] 52-53 OP 6
Hinckley, MN 70-71 D 2-3
Hinckley, UT 74-75 G 3
Hindes, TX 76-77 E 8
Hindia, Lautan — 174-175 B 6-D 8
Hinds Lake 51 H 3
Hindūbāgh 160-161 K 4
Hindū Kush 160-161 KL 3
Hindupur 160-161 M 8
Hindupura = Hindupur 160-161 M 8
Hindustan 160-161 M 5-O 6
Hindusthān = Hindustan 160-161 M 5-O 6
Hines, FL 80-81 b 2
Hines, OR 66-67 D 4
Hines Creek 46-47 N 6
Hinesville, GA 80-81 F 5
Hinghwa = Putian 166-167 M 6
Hingjen = Xingren 166-167 K 6
Hingol 160-161 K 5
Hingoli 160-161 M 7
Hinkley 116-117 K 8
Hinkley, CA 74-75 E 5
Hinlopenstretet 114-115 kl 5
Hinna = Īmī 194-195 N 7
Hinnøy 114-115 FG 3
Hinojosa del Duque 132-133 E 9
Hinomi-saki 170-171 J 5
Hinsdale, MT 68-69 C 1
Hinterrhein 124 D 5
Hinthāda 174-175 BC 3
Hinton, WV 80-81 F 2
Hinton [CDN] 46-47 N 7
Hinton [GB] 116-117 K 8
Hipólito 86-87 K 5
Hippo Regius = Annābah 194-195 F 1
Hiraan 194-195 ab 3
Hirado 170-171 G 6
Hirado-shima 170-171 G 6
Hirata 170-171 J 5
Hirato jima = Hirado-shima 170-171 G 6
Hiratori 170-171 c 2
Hirgis Nur = Chjargas nuur 166-167 GH 2
Hîrlău 138-139 M 2
Hirono 170-171 N 4
Hiroo 170-171 c 2
Hirosaki 166-167 QR 3
Hiroshima 166-167 P 5
Hirosima = Hiroshima 166-167 P 5
Hirota-wan 170-171 NO 3
Hirson 132-133 K 4
Hirtshals 114-115 C 9
Hisaka-jima 170-171 G 6
Hisār 160-161 M 5
Ḥiṣār, Kohe — 160-161 K 4
Ḥismā 199 DE 3
Ḥismet ʿUmar, Bīr — = Bi'r Ḥasmat ʿUmar 199 CD 7
Hispaniola 58-59 MN 8
Hissār = Hisār 160-161 M 5
Ḥiṣṣar, Kūh-e- = Kōhe Ḥiṣār 160-161 K 4
Histiaía 138-139 K 6
Hita 170-171 H 6
Hitachi 166-167 R 4
Hitachi-Ōta = Hitati-Ōta 170-171 N 4
Hitati = Hitachi 166-167 R 4
Hitchin 116-117 L 9
Hitchland, TX 76-77 D 4
Hite, UT 74-75 H 4
Hitoyoshi 170-171 H 6
Hitra 114-115 C 6
Hitteren = Hitra 114-115 C 6
Hiuchi-dake 170-171 M 4
Hiuchi-nada 170-171 J 5
Hiw 199 C 4-5
Hiwasa 170-171 K 6

Hjälmaren 114-115 FG 8
Hjälmar Lake = Hjälmaren 114-115 FG 8
Hjelmelandsvågen 114-115 AB 8
Hjelmsøy 114-115 L 2
Hjørring 114-115 C 9

Hkweibûm 174-175 B 2

Hlaingbwè 174-175 C 3
Hluingbwe = Hlaingbwè 174-175 C 3

Ho 194-195 E 7
Hoa Binh 174-175 DE 2
Hoadley 48 K 3
Hoai Nho'n 174-175 E 4
Hoangho = Huang He 166-167 L 4
Hoang Sa, Quân Đao — 174-175 F 5
Hoarusib 198 B 5
Hoback Peak 66-67 H 4
Hobart 182-183 J 8
Hobart, IN 70-71 G 5
Hobart, OK 76-77 E 5
Hobbs, NM 58-59 F 5
Hobbs Coast 31 B 23
Hobe Sound, FL 80-81 cd 3
Hobetsu 170-171 bc 2
Hoboken, NJ 82 III b 2
Hobro 114-115 C 9
Höbsögöl Dalay = Chövsgöl nuur 166-167 J 1
Hobyaa 194-195 b 2
Hochgolling 124 FG 5
Hochow = Hechuan 166-167 K 5-6
Hochwan = Hechuan 166-167 K 5-6
Hoddesdon 116-117 LM 9
Ḥoddua = Ghuddawah 194-195 G 3
Hodeida = Al-Ḥudaidah 160-161 E 8
Ḥôḍein, Wādī — = Wādī Ḥudayn 199 D 6
Hodgdon, ME 72-73 MN 1
Hodge, LA 78-79 C 4
Hodgenville, KY 70-71 GH 7
Hodgson 49 JK 5
Hodh = Al-Ḥawḍ 194-195 C 5
Hódmezővásárhely 124 K 5
Hodna, Chott el — = Ash-Shaṭṭ al-Hudnah 194-195 EF 1
Hodzana River 52-53 N 3
Hoek van Holland, Rotterdam- 132-133 JK 3
Hoengsŏng 170-171 FG 4
Hoeryŏng 170-171 G 1
Hoey 49 F 4
Hoeyang 170-171 F 3
Hof 124 E 3
Höfdhakaupstadhur 114-115 cd 2
Hofei = Hefei 166-167 M 5
Hoffman, MN 70-71 BC 3
Höfn 114-115 f 2
Hofors 114-115 FG 7
Ḥofrat en Naḥās = Ḥufrat an-Naḥās 194-195 JK 7
Hofsjökull 114-115 d 2
Hofsós 114-115 d 2
Hōfu 170-171 H 5-6
Hofuf = Al-Hufūf 160-161 FG 5
Höganäs 114-115 E 9
Hogansville, GA 78-79 G 4
Hogatza River 52-53 K 3
Hogback Mountain [USA, Montana] 66-67 GH 3
Hogback Mountain [USA, Nebraska] 68-69 E 5
Hogeland, MT 68-69 B 1
Hogem Range 48 D 1-E 2
Hog Island [USA, Michigan] 70-71 H 3
Hog Island [USA, Virginia] 80-81 J 2
Hog River, AK 52-53 K 3
Hohe Acht 124 C 3
Hohenwald, TN 78-79 F 3
Hoher Atlas 194-195 CD 2
Hohe Tauern 124 F 5
Hohhot = Huhehaote 166-167 L 3
Hoh-kai = Ohōtsuku-kai 170-171 cd 1
Hoholitna River 52-53 J 6
Ho-hsien = He Xian 166-167 L 7
Hoifung = Haifeng 166-167 M 7
Hoihong = Haikang 166-167 KL 7
Hoima 198 F 1
Hoion = Hai'an 166-167 KL 7
Hoisington, KS 68-69 G 6
Hokitika 182-183 NO 8
Hokkaidō [J, administrative unit] 170-171 bc 2
Hokkaidō [J, island] 166-167 RS 3
Hokuoka = Fukuoka 166-167 OP 5
Hokuriku 170-171 L 5-M 4
Hólar 114-115 d 2
Holbæk 114-115 D 10
Holbox, Isla — 86-87 R 7
Holbrook, AZ 74-75 HJ 5
Holbrook, ID 66-67 G 4
Holden 49 BC 4
Holden, MO 70-71 CD 6
Holden, UT 74-75 G 3
Holdenville, OK 76-77 F 5
Holderness 116-117 L 7
Holdrege, NE 68-69 G 5
Holgate, OH 70-71 HJ 5
Holguín 58-59 L 7
Holikachuk, AK 52-53 H 5
Holitna River 52-53 J 6
Höljes 114-115 E 7
Holland, MI 70-71 GH 4
Holland [CDN] 49 J 6
Hollandale, MS 78-79 D 4
Hollandia = Jayapura 174-175 M 7
Hollick-Kenyon Plateau 31 AB 25-26
Holliday, TX 76-77 E 6
Hollidaysburg, PA 72-73 G 4
Hollis, OK 76-77 E 5
Hollis, New York-, NY 82 III d 2
Hollister, CA 74-75 C 4
Hollister, ID 66-67 F 4
Hollister, MO 78-79 C 2
Hollmann, Cape — 174-175 gh 5
Holly, MI 72-73 E 3
Holly Bluff, MS 78-79 D 4
Holly Hill, FL 80-81 c 2
Holly Hill, SC 80-81 F 4
Holly Ridge, NC 80-81 H 3
Holly Springs, MS 78-79 E 3
Hollywood, FL 58-59 KL 6
Hollywood, Los Angeles-, CA 58-59 BC 5
Hollywood Bowl 83 III b 1
Hollywood Park Race Track 83 III bc 2
Holman Island 46-47 NO 3
Hólmavík 114-115 c 2
Holmes, Mount — 66-67 H 3
Holmes Run 82 II a 2
Holmestrand 114-115 CD 8
Holmfield 68-69 G 1
Holmfirth 116-117 K 7
Holmsund 114-115 J 6
Holo Islands = Sulu Archipelago 174-175 H 5
Holopaw, FL 80-81 c 2
Holroyd River 182-183 H 2
Holsnøy 114-115 A 7
Holstebro 114-115 C 9
Holstein, IA 70-71 C 4
Holsteinsborg = Sisimiut 46-47 Za 4
Holston River 80-81 E 2
Holsworthy 116-117 G 10
Holt, AL 78-79 F 4
Holt, FL 78-79 F 5
Holten, KS 70-71 C 6
Holten Bank 114-115 C 5
Holtville, CA 74-75 F 6
Holtyre 50 LM 2
Holung = Helong 170-171 G 1
Holy Cross, AK 46-47 DE 5
Holy Cross Bay = zaliv Kresta 154-155 k 4
Holyhead 116-117 G 7
Holyhead Bay 116-117 G 7
Holy Island [GB, Irish Sea] 116-117 G 7
Holy Island [GB, North Sea] 116-117 K 5
Holyoke, CO 68-69 E 5
Holyoke, MA 72-73 K 3
Holyrood, KS 68-69 G 6
Holywood 116-117 F 6
Holzminden 124 D 3
Hombori 194-195 D 5
Home, OR 66-67 E 3
Home Bay 46-47 XY 4
Homedale, ID 66-67 E 4
Homer, AK 46-47 F 6
Homer, LA 78-79 C 4
Homer, MI 70-71 H 4
Homer, NY 72-73 H 3
Homerville, GA 80-81 E 5
Homestead 182-183 HJ 4
Homestead, FL 80-81 c 4
Hometown, IL 83 II a 2
Homewood, AL 78-79 F 4
Hominy, OK 76-77 F 4
Homoine 198 FG 6
Homoljske Planine 138-139 J 3
Ḥomra, Al- = Al-Ḥumrah 194-195 L 6
Homra, Hamada el — = Al-Ḥamādat al-Ḥamrā' 194-195 G 2-3
Ḥomṣ = Al-Khums 194-195 GH 2
Ḥomṣ = Ḥimṣ 160-161 D 4
Hon, Cu Lao — = Cu Lao Thu 174-175 EF 4
Honai 170-171 J 6
Honan = Henan 166-167 L 5
Honaunau, HI 78-79 de 3
Honbetsu 170-171 cd 2
Honda 98-99 E 3
Honda Bay 174-175 G 5
Hondo, NM 76-77 B 6
Hondo, TX 76-77 E 8
Hondo [J] 170-171 H 6
Hondo [MEX] 76-77 D 9
Hondo = Honshū 166-167 PQ 4
Honduras 58-59 J 9
Honduras, Cabo de — 58-59 JK 8
Honduras, Golfe de — 58-59 J 8
Honesdale, PA 72-73 J 4
Honey Grove, TX 76-77 FG 6
Honey Island, TX 76-77 G 7
Honey Lake 66-67 C 5
Honfleur 132-133 H 4
Hongch'ŏn 170-171 FG 4
Hong-do 170-171 E 5
Hong He [TJ, Yunnan] 166-167 J 7
Honghe Hanizu Yizu Zizhizhou 166-167 J 7
Honghu [TJ, place] 166-167 L 6
Hongjiang 166-167 KL 6
Hong Kong 166-167 LM 7
Hongluoxian 170-171 C 2
Hongmoxian = Hongluoxian 170-171 C 2
Hongshui He 166-167 K 6-7
Hongsŏng 170-171 F 4
Hongū 170-171 K 6
Hongwŏn 170-171 FG 2-3
Honiara 174-175 jk 6
Honiton 116-117 H 10
Honjo 170-171 MN 3
Honningsvåg 114-115 LM 2
Honokaa, HI 78-79 e 2
Honokohua, HI 78-79 d 2
Honolulu, HI 174-175 e 3
Honshū 166-167 PQ 4
Honsyû = Honshū 166-167 PQ 4
Hood = Isla Española 98-99 B 5
Hood, Mount — 58-59 B 2
Hood Canal 66-67 B 2
Hood Point 182-183 CD 6
Hood River, OR 66-67 C 3
Hooker, OK 76-77 D 4
Hooker, Bi'r — 199 B 2
Hooker Creek 182-183 F 3
Hook Head = Rinn Dubháin 116-117 D 9-E 8
Hook Island 182-183 J 4
Hook of Holland = Rotterdam-Hoek van Holland 132-133 JK 3
Hoonah, AK 46-47 JK 6
Hoopa, CA 66-67 B 5
Hoopa Valley Indian Reservation 66-67 AB 5
Hooper, CO 68-69 D 7
Hooper, NE 68-69 H 5
Hooper, UT 66-67 G 5
Hooper Bay 52-53 DE 6
Hooper Bay, AK 52-53 DE 6
Hoopeston, IL 70-71 G 5
Hoosier 49 CD 5
Hoover, SD 68-69 E 3
Hoover, TX 76-77 D 5
Hoover Dam 58-59 D 4
Hope 66-67 C 1
Hope, AK 52-53 N 6
Hope, AR 58-59 H 5
Hope, AZ 74-75 G 6
Hope, IN 70-71 H 6
Hope, KS 68-69 H 6
Hope, NM 76-77 B 6
Hope, Ben — 116-117 G 2
Hopedale 46-47 YZ 6
Hopeh = Hebei 166-167 LM 4
Hope Island 72-73 F 2
Hopelchén 86-87 PQ 8
Hopen 30 B 16
Hopes Advance, Cape — 46-47 X 5
Hopetoun [AUS, Victoria] 182-183 H 7
Hopetoun [AUS, Western Australia] 182-183 D 6
Hopetown 198 D 7
Hopewell, VA 80-81 H 2
Hopi Indian Reservation 74-75 H 4-5
Hopkins, Lake — 182-183 E 4
Hopkinsville, KY 58-59 J 4
Hopland, CA 74-75 B 3
Hoppo = Hepu 166-167 K 7
Hopu = Hepu 166-167 K 7
Ho-p'u = Hepu 166-167 K 7
Hoquiam, WA 66-67 AB 2
Hōrān, Wādī — = Wādī Ḥawrān 160-161 E 4
Horburg 48 K 3
Hörby 114-115 E 10
Horcasitas 86-87 H 3
Hordaland 114-115 A 8-B 7
Hordio = Hurdiyo 160-161 G 8
Horicon, WI 70-71 F 4
Horlick Mountains 31 A 26-27
Hormoz 160-161 H 5
Hormoz, Tangeh — 160-161 H 5
Hormuz, Strait of — = Tangeh Hormoz 160-161 H 5
Horn [IS] 114-115 bc 1
Horn, Cape — = Cabo de Hornos 103 CD 9
Horn, Îles — 174-175 b 1
Hornafjördhur 114-115 f 2
Hornavan 114-115 GH 4
Hornbeck, LA 78-79 C 5
Horncastle 116-117 L 7
Hörnefors 114-115 H 6
Hornell, NY 72-73 H 3
Hornepayne 50 J 2
Hornillas 76-77 B 9-10
Horn Island 78-79 E 5
Horn Mountains [CDN] 46-47 MN 5
Horn Mountains [USA] 52-53 H 6
Hornos, Cabo de — 103 CD 9
Horn Reefs = Blåvands Huk 114-115 BC 10
Hornsea 116-117 LM 7
Hornsund 114-115 jk 6
Hornsundtind 114-115 k 6
Horobetsu 170-171 b 2
Horonobe 170-171 bc 1
Horqueta 103 E 2
Horse Branch, KY 70-71 G 7
Horse Cave, KY 70-71 H 7
Horse Creek, WY 68-69 D 5
Horse Creek [USA, Colorado] 68-69 E 6
Horse Creek [USA, Wyoming] 68-69 D 5
Horsefly 48 G 3
Horsehead Lake 68-69 FG 2
Horseheads, NY 72-73 H 3
Horse Islands 51 J 2
Horsens 114-115 CD 10
Horseshoe 182-183 C 5
Horse Shoe Bend, ID 66-67 EF 4
Horse Springs, NM 74-75 JK 6
Horsham [AUS] 182-183 H 7
Horsham [GB] 116-117 L 9
Horta [Açores] 188-189 E 5
Horten 114-115 D 8
Horton, KS 70-71 C 6
Horton River 46-47 M 4
Horwood Lake 50 K 3
Hoṣeima, el — = Al-Ḥusaymah 194-195 D 1
Ḥoseināba̅d = Īlām 160-161 F 4
Ḥôsh ʿĪsā = Ḥawsh ʿĪsā 199 B 2
Hosmer, SD 68-69 G 3
Hospitalet de Llobregat 132-133 J 8
Hosta Butte 74-75 JK 5
Hoste, Isla — 103 C 9
Hot 174-175 C 3
Hotan = Khotan 166-167 DE 4
Hotchkiss, CO 68-69 C 6
Hot Creek Valley 74-75 E 3
Hotham Inlet 52-53 FG 3
Hotien = Khotan 166-167 DE 4
Hoting 114-115 G 5
Hot Springs, AR 58-59 H 5
Hot Springs, MT 66-67 F 2
Hot Springs, NC 80-81 E 3
Hot Springs, SD 68-69 E 4
Hot Springs, VA 80-81 G 2
Hot Springs Cove 48 D 5
Hot Sulphur Springs, CO 68-69 CD 5
Hottah Lake 46-47 N 4
Hotte, Massif de la — 88-89 JK 5
Hot Wells, TX 76-77 B 7
Hough, OK 76-77 D 4
Houghton, MI 70-71 F 2
Houghton Lake 70-71 H 3
Houlka, MS 78-79 E 3
Houlton, ME 72-73 MN 1
Houma 166-167 L 4
Houma, LA 58-59 H 6
Houndé 194-195 D 6
Houston 48 D 2
Houston, MS 78-79 E 4
Houston, TX 58-59 G 5-6
Houtman Abrolhos 182-183 B 5
Hove 116-117 L 10
Hoven, SD 68-69 G 3
Hover, WA 66-67 D 2
Hovland, MN 70-71 EF 2
Hovrah = Howrah 160-161 O 6
Howar = Wādī Huwār 194-195 K 5
Howard, KS 68-69 H 7
Howard, SD 68-69 H 3-4
Howard Beach, New York-, NY 82 III cd 3
Howard City, MI 70-71 H 4
Howard University 82 II a 1
Howden 116-117 L 7
Howe, ID 66-67 G 4
Howe, Cape — 182-183 K 7
Howell, MI 70-71 HJ 4
Howells, NE 68-69 H 5
Howes, SD 68-69 E 3
Howe Sound 66-67 B 1
Howick [CDN] 72-73 K 2
Howland 34-35 J 4
Howley 51 H 3
Howrah 160-161 O 6
Howth = Beann Éadair 116-117 EF 7
Hoxie, AR 78-79 D 2-3
Hoxie, KS 68-69 F 6
Hoy 116-117 H 2
Høyanger 114-115 B 7
Hoyle 50 L 2
Hōyokaiko = Bungo-suidō 166-167 P 5
Hoy Sound 116-117 H 2
Höytiäinen 114-115 N 6

Hpā'an 174-175 C 3
Hpalam 174-175 B 2
Hpyū 174-175 C 3

Hradec Králové 124 GH 3
Hrochei La 166-167 DE 5
Hron 124 J 4

Hsay Walad ʿAlī Bābī 194-195 B 5
Hsia-ho = Xiahe 166-167 J 4
Hsia-kuan = Xiaguan 166-167 J 6
Hsia-mên = Xiamen 166-167 M 7
Hsi-an 166-167 K 5
Hsi-an = Xi'an 166-167 K 5
Hsiang-kang = Hong Kong 166-167 LM 7
Hsiang-yang = Xiangyang 166-167 L 5
Hsiang-yang-chên = Xiangyangzhen 170-171 E 1

234 **Hessen**

Hsiao-ch'ang-shan Tao = Xiaochangshan Dao 170-171 D 3
Hsiao-ling Ho = Xiaoling He 170-171 C 2
Hsia-tung = Xiadong 166-167 H 3
Hsi-ch'ang = Xichang [TJ, Sichuan] 166-167 J 6
Hsi Chiang = Xi Jiang 166-167 L 7
Hsi-ch'uan = Xichuan 166-167 L 5
Hsien-hs'ien = Xian Xian 166-167 M 4
Hsien-yang = Xianyang 166-167 K 5
Hsi-fêng-k'ou = Xifengkou 170-171 B 2
Hsi-hsien = She Xian 166-167 M 5-6
Hsi-hsien = Xi Xian [TJ, Shanxi] 166-167 L 4
Hsi-hu = Wusu 166-167 EF 3
Hsi-liao Ho = Xar Moron He 166-167 MN 3
Hsin-chiang = Xinjiang Uygur Zizhiqu 166-167 D-F 3
Hsinchu 166-167 N 6-7
Hsing-ch'êng = Xingcheng 170-171 C 2
Hsing-jên = Xingren 166-167 K 6
Hsing-ning = Xingning 166-167 M 7
Hsin-hai-lien = Haizhou 166-167 M 5
Hsin-hsiang = Xinxiang 166-167 LM 4
Hsin-hua = Xinhua 166-167 L 6
Hsi-ning = Xining 166-167 J 4
Hsin-kao Shan = Yu Shan 166-167 N 7
Hsinking = Changchun 166-167 NO 3
Hsin-liao Ho = Xiliao He 166-167 N 3
Hsin-li-t'un = Xinlitun 170-171 CD 1-2
Hsin-lo = Xinle 166-167 LM 4
Hsin-min = Xinmin 170-171 D 1-2
Hsin-pin = Xinbin 170-171 E 2
Hsin-ts'ai = Xincai 166-167 LM 5
Hsin-tu = Xindu 166-167 L 7
Hsin-yang = Xinyang 166-167 LM 5
Hsi-ta-ch'uan = Xidachuan 170-171 FG 2
Hsüan-hua = Xuanhua 166-167 LM 3
Hsüan-wei = Xuanwei 166-167 J 6
Hsuchang = Xuchang 166-167 L 5
Hsü-chou = Xuzhou 166-167 M 5
Hsûmbârabûm 174-175 C 1
Hsün-hua = Xunhua 166-167 J 4

Htâwei 174-175 C 4

Hua'an 166-167 M 6
Huab 198 B 6
Huacana, La — 86-87 JK 8
Huachi [PE] 98-99 D 5
Huacho 98-99 D 7
Huacrachuco 98-99 D 6
Huagaruancha 98-99 DE 7
Hua-hsien = Hua Xian [TJ, Henan] 166-167 LM 4
Huahua, Río — 88-89 DE 7
Huaiâ-Miço, Rio — 98-99 M 10
Huai'an 166-167 MN 5
Huai-chi = Huaiji 166-167 L 7
Huaide 166-167 NO 3
Huai He 166-167 M 5
Huaiji 166-167 L 7
Huainan 166-167 M 5
Huaining = Anqing 166-167 M 5
Huaiyin 166-167 M 5
Huai-yin = Qingjiang 166-167 M 5
Huajuapan de León 86-87 LM 9
Hualalai 78-79 e 3
Hualian = Hualien 166-167 N 7
Hualien 166-167 N 7
Huallaga, Río — 98-99 D 6
Huallanca 98-99 D 6
Hualpai Indian Reservation 74-75 G 5
Hualpai Mountains 74-75 G 5
Huamantla 86-87 M 8
Huambo [Angola, administrative unit] 198 C 4
Huambo [Angola, place] 198 C 4
Hu'a Mu'o'ng 174-175 D 2-3
Huancabamba 98-99 CD 6
Huancané [PE] 98-99 F 8
Huancavelica [PE, place] 98-99 DE 7
Huancayo 98-99 DE 7
Huanchaca, Serranía de — 98-99 G 7
Huangbai 170-171 F 2
Huang He 166-167 L 4
Huang He = Chatan gol 166-167 K 3
Huang He = Ma Chhu 166-167 J 4
Huangheyan 166-167 H 5
Huang Ho = Chatan gol 166-167 K 3
Huang Ho = Huang He 166-167 L 4
Huang Ho = Ma Chhu 166-167 J 4
Huang-ho-yen = Huangheyan 166-167 H 5
Huang-hsien = Huang Xian 166-167 MN 4
Huanghuadian 170-171 D 2
Huang-hua-tien = Huanghuadian 170-171 D 2
Huangnan Zangzu Zizhizhou 166-167 J 4-5
Huangshi 166-167 LM 5
Huangshijiang = Huangshi 166-167 LM 5
Huang-t'u-liang-tzŭ = Huangtuliangzi 170-171 B 2
Huangtuliangzi 170-171 B 2
Huanguelén 103 D 5
Huang Xian 166-167 MN 4
Huangyuan = Thangkar 166-167 J 4
Huani, Laguna — 88-89 E 7
Huan-jên = Huanren 170-171 E 2
Huanren 170-171 E 2
Huanta 98-99 E 7
Huánuco [PE, place] 98-99 D 6-7
Huapí, Montañas de — 88-89 D 8
Huara 103 BC 1-2
Huaráz 98-99 D 6
Huarmey 98-99 D 7
Huascaran = Nevado Huascaran 98-99 D 6
Huasco 103 B 3
Hua Shan 166-167 L 5
Huatabampo 58-59 DE 6
Huauchinango 58-59 G 7
Huaunta, Laguna — 88-89 E 8
Hua Xian [TJ, Henan] 166-167 LM 4
Ḥubâra, Wâdî — = Wâdî al-Asyûṭî 199 B 4
Hubbaḷi = Hubli 160-161 M 7
Hubbard, IA 70-71 D 4
Hubbard, TX 76-77 F 7
Hubbard, Mount — 46-47 J 5
Hubbard Lake 70-71 HJ 3
Hubei 166-167 KL 5
Hubert 48 D 2
Hubli 160-161 M 7
Huch'ang 170-171 F 2
Hu-chou = Wuxing 166-167 MN 5
Huchuento, Cerro — 58-59 E 7
Hucknall 116-117 KL 7
Ḥudaybû = Ṭamrîdah 160-161 GH 8
Ḥudaydah, Al- 160-161 E 8
Ḥudayn, Wâdî — 199 D 6
Huddersfield 116-117 K 7
Huddur Hadama 198 H 1
Hudiksvall 114-115 G 7
Hudnah, Ash-Shaṭṭ al- 194-195 EF 1
Hudson 50 CD 2
Hudson, CO 68-69 D 5
Hudson, MI 70-71 H 5
Hudson, NM 76-77 C 5
Hudson, NY 72-73 JK 3
Hudson, WI 70-71 D 3
Hudson, Cerro — 103 B 7
Hudson Bay [CDN, bay] 46-47 S-U 5-6
Hudson Bay [CDN, place] 49 GH 4
Hudson Canyon 72-73 KL 5
Hudson Falls, NY 72-73 K 3
Hudson Hope 48 G 1
Hudson Mountains 31 B 27
Hudson River 58-59 M 3
Hudson Strait 46-47 WX 5
Hudwin Lake 50 B 1
Huê 174-175 E 3
Hueco Mountains 76-77 AB 7
Huedin 138-139 K 2
Huehuetenango 86-87 P 10
Huejúcar 86-87 J 6
Huejuquilla el Alto 86-87 HJ 6
Huejutla 86-87 KL 6-7
Huelva 132-133 D 10
Huércal-Overa 132-133 FG 10
Huerfano River 68-69 D 7
Huesca 132-133 G 7
Huéscar 132-133 F 10
Hueso, Sierra del — 76-77 B 7
Huetamo de Núñez 86-87 K 8
Ḥufrat an-Naḥâs 194-195 JK 7
Hufûf, Al- 160-161 FG 5
Huggins Island 52-53 K 4
Hughenden 182-183 H 4
Hughes, AK 52-53 K 3
Hughes, AR 78-79 D 3
Hughes Airport 83 III b 2
Hugh Town 116-117 E 11
Hugo, CO 68-69 E 6
Hugo, OK 76-77 G 5-6
Hugoton, KS 76-77 D 4
Huhehaote 166-167 L 3
Huibplato 198 C 7
Hŭich'ŏn 166-167 O 3
Hui-chou = She Xian 166-167 M 5-6
Huila [Angola, administrative unit] 198 BC 4
Huila [Angola, place] 198 B 5
Huila, Nevado del — 98-99 D 4
Huinan 166-167 O 3
Hui-tsê = Huize 166-167 J 6
Huittinen 114-115 K 7
Hui Xian 166-167 JK 5
Huixtla 58-59 H 8
Huiyang 166-167 LM 7
Huize 166-167 J 6
Ḥukayyim, Bi'r al- 194-195 J 2
Hŭker, Bîr — = Bi'r Hooker 199 B 2
Hŭksan-chedo 170-171 E 5
Hŭksan-jedo = Hŭksan-chedo 170-171 E 5
Hukui = Fukui 166-167 Q 4
Hukuntsi 198 D 6
Hukusima = Fukushima 166-167 R 4
Hulah Lake 76-77 F 4
Hulan 166-167 O 2
Ḥulayfâ' 160-161 E 5
Hulett, WY 68-69 D 3
Hull, IL 70-71 E 6
Hull, ND 68-69 F 2-3
Hull [CDN] 46-47 V 8
Hull [Kiribati] 178 J 3
Hull, River — 116-117 L 6-7
Hull Mountain 74-75 B 3
Hulu 174-175 HJ 6
Huludao 170-171 C 2
Hulun = Hailar 166-167 M 2
Hulun Nur 166-167 M 2
Hulun nuur 166-167 M 2
Hu-lu-tao = Huludao 170-171 C 2
Ḥulwân 194-195 L 3
Huma 166-167 O 1
Humacao 88-89 N 6-O 5
Humadu 36 a 2
Hu-ma-êrh Ho = Huma He 166-167 NO 1
Huma He 166-167 NO 1
Humahuaca 103 C 2
Humaitá [BR] 98-99 G 6
Humansdorp 198 DE 8
Ḥumaydah, Al- 199 D 3
Ḥumaym 160-161 GH 6
Humbe 198 B 5
Humber, Mouth of the — 116-117 LM 7
Humber, River — 116-117 L 7
Humberside 116-117 L 7
Humberto de Campos 98-99 L 5
Humble, TX 76-77 G 7-8
Humboldt, AZ 74-75 GH 5
Humboldt, IA 70-71 C 4
Humboldt, NE 70-71 BC 5
Humboldt, NV 66-67 D 5
Humboldt, SD 68-69 H 4
Humboldt, TN 78-79 E 3
Humboldt [CDN] 46-47 PQ 7
Humboldt, Mount — 182-183 N 4
Humboldt Bay 66-67 A 5
Humboldt Gletscher 46-47 Y 2
Humboldtkette 166-167 H 4
Humboldt Park 83 II a 1
Humboldt Range 66-67 D 5
Humboldt River 58-59 C 3
Humboldt River, North Fork — 66-67 F 5
Humboldt Salt Marsh 74-75 DE 3
Humedad, Isla — 58-59 a 2
Humenné 124 KL 4
Hume Reservoir 182-183 J 7
Humeston, IA 70-71 D 5
Humpata 198 B 5
Humphrey, ID 66-67 GH 3
Humphrey, NE 68-69 H 5
Humphreys, Mount — 74-75 D 4
Humphreys Peak 58-59 D 4
Humptulips, WA 66-67 B 2
Ḥumrah, Al- 194-195 L 6
Hums, Al- = Al-Khums 194-195 GH 2
Hûn 194-195 H 3
Húnaflói 114-115 c 1-2
Hunan 166-167 L 6
Hun Chiang = Hun Jiang 170-171 E 2
Hunchun 166-167 P 3
Hunedoara 138-139 K 3
Hungarian Plain = Alföld 124 J 5-L 4
Hungary 124 H-K 5
Hung-chiang = Hongjiang 166-167 KL 6
Hungerford 116-117 K 9
Hung Ho = Hong He [TJ, Yunnan] 166-167 J 7
Hung Hu = Honghu 166-167 L 6
Hungkiang = Hongjiang 166-167 KL 6
Hŭngnam 166-167 O 4
Hungry = Lima Village, AK 52-53 K 6
Hungry Horse Reservoir 66-67 G 1
Hung-shui Ho = Hongshui He 166-167 K 6-7
Hun He 170-171 D 2
Hun Ho = Hun He 170-171 D 2
Hunish, Rudha — 116-117 E 3
Hunjani 198 F 5
Hunjiang [TJ, place] 170-171 F 2
Hun Jiang [TJ, river] 170-171 E 2
Ḥunkurâb, Râ's — 199 D 5
Hunsrück 124 C 3-4
Hunstanton 116-117 M 8
Hunte 124 D 2
Hunter, KS 68-69 G 6
Hunter, ND 68-69 H 2
Hunter, Île — 182-183 O 4
Hunter Island 48 C 4
Hunter Island Park 70-71 E 1
Hunter Islands 182-183 H 8
Hunters, WA 66-67 DE 1
Hunters Point 83 I b 2
Huntingburg, IN 70-71 G 6
Huntingdon 116-117 L 8
Huntingdon, PA 72-73 GH 4
Huntingdon, TN 78-79 E 2-3
Huntingdon [CDN] 72-73 JK 2
Hunting Island 80-81 F 4
Huntington, IN 70-71 H 5
Huntington, OR 66-67 E 3
Huntington, TX 76-77 G 7
Huntington, UT 74-75 H 3
Huntington, WV 58-59 K 4
Huntington Beach, CA 74-75 DE 6
Huntington Park, CA 83 III c 2
Huntley, MT 68-69 B 3
Huntly 116-117 J 3
Hunt Mountain 68-69 BC 3
Hunts Inlet 48 B 2
Huntsville 72-73 G 2
Huntsville, AL 58-59 J 5
Huntsville, AR 78-79 C 2
Huntsville, MO 70-71 D 6
Huntsville, TX 58-59 GH 5
Hunyung 170-171 H 1
Hunzâ = Bâltit 160-161 L 3
Huon Gulf 174-175 N 8
Huon Peninsula 174-175 N 8
Hupeh = Hubei 166-167 KL 5
Huraybah, Al- 160-161 F 7
Hurd, Cape — 72-73 EF 2
Hurdiyo 194-195 c 1
Hure Qi 166-167 N 3
Huribgah = Khurîbgah 194-195 C 2
Hurjâdah = Al-Ghardaqah 194-195 L 3
Hurkett 70-71 F 1
Hurley, MS 78-79 E 5
Hurley, NM 74-75 J 6
Hurley, SD 68-69 H 4
Hurley, WI 70-71 E 2
Huron, CA 74-75 C 4
Huron, OH 72-73 E 4
Huron, SD 58-59 G 3
Huron, Lake — 58-59 K 2-3
Huron Mountains 70-71 FG 2
Hurricane, UT 74-75 G 4
Hurtsboro, AL 78-79 G 4
Húsavík 114-115 e 1
Ḥuṣayḥiṣah, Al- 194-195 L 6
Ḥusaymah, Al- 194-195 D 4
Ḥusaynîyah, Al- 160-161 EF 7
Huşi 138-139 MN 2
Huskvarna 114-115 F 9
Huslia, AK 52-53 J 4
Huslia River 52-53 J 3
Hussar 49 B 5
Husum 124 D 1
Hutanopan 174-175 CD 6
Hutchinson, KS 58-59 G 4
Hutchinson, MN 70-71 C 3
Hutchinsons Island 80-81 cd 3
Hutch Mountain 74-75 H 5
Huttig, AR 78-79 CD 4
Hutton 48 G 3
Huutokoski 114-115 M 6
Huwâr, Wâdî — 194-195 K 5
Huxley, Mount — 52-53 R 6
Huy 132-133 K 3
Huzhou = Wuxing 166-167 MN 5
Huzi san = Fuji-san 166-167 Q 4-5

Hvalsbakur 114-115 g 2
Hval Sund 46-47 WX 2
Hvalvík 116-117 a 1
Hvammsfjördhur 114-115 bc 2
Hvammstangi 114-115 c 2
Hvar 138-139 G 4
Hveragerdhi 114-115 c 2
Hvítá [IS, Árnes] 114-115 c 2
Hvítá [IS, Mýra] 114-115 c 2
Hvítárvatn 114-115 d 2
Hvolsvöllur 114-115 cd 3

Hwaak-san 170-171 F 3-4
Hwach'ŏn 170-171 F 3
Hwach'ŏn-ni 170-171 FG 3
Hwaian = Huai'an 166-167 MN 5
Hwange 198 E 5
Hwanggan 170-171 FG 4
Hwanghae-namdo 170-171 E 3-4
Hwanghae-pukto 170-171 EF 3
Hwangho = Huang He 166-167 L 4
Hwanghsien = Huang Xian 166-167 MN 4
Hwangju 170-171 EF 3
Hwangyuan = Thangkar 166-167 J 4
Hwap'yŏng 170-171 F 2
Hwasun 170-171 F 5
Hweichow = She Xian 166-167 M 5-6
Hweitseh = Huize 166-167 J 6

Hyannis, NE 68-69 F 4-5
Hyattsville, MD 82 II b 1
Hybart, AL 78-79 F 5
Hybla 72-73 H 2
Hydaburg, AK 52-53 w 9
Hyde 116-117 JK 7
Hyden 182-183 C 6
Hyden, KY 72-73 E 6
Hyde Park, VT 72-73 K 2
Hyde Park, Chicago-, IL 83 II b 2
Hyde Park, Los Angeles-, CA 83 III c 2
Hyder 48 B 2
Hyder, AZ 74-75 G 6
Hyderâbâd 160-161 M 7
Hyderabad = Ḥaidarâbâd 160-161 KL 5
Hýdra 138-139 K 7
Hydraulic 48 FG 3
Hydro, OK 76-77 E 5
Hyères 132-133 L 7
Hyères, Îles d' 132-133 L 7
Hyesanjin 166-167 O 3
Hyland Post 52-53 XY 8
Hyltebruk 114-115 E 9
Hyndman, PA 72-73 G 5
Hyndman Peak 66-67 FG 4
Hyŏgo 170-171 K 5
Hyŏnch'on 170-171 G 2
Hyŏpch'ŏn = Hapch'ŏn 170-171 FG 5
Hypsárion 138-139 L 5
Hyrra-Banda 194-195 J 7
Hyrum, UT 66-67 H 5
Hyrynsalmi 114-115 N 5
Hysham, MT 68-69 C 2
Hythe [GB, Hampshire] 116-117 K 10
Hythe [GB, Kent] 116-117 h 7
Hyûga 170-171 H 6
Hyvinkää 114-115 L 7

I

Iaco, Rio — 98-99 EF 7
Iaçu 98-99 L 7
Ialomiţa 138-139 M 3
Ialu = Yalu Jiang 170-171 EF 2
Iarauarune, Serra — 98-99 HJ 4
Iaripo 98-99 L 4
Iaşi 138-139 M 2
Iauareté 98-99 E 4
Iaundé = Yaoundé 194-195 G 8
Iavello = Yabêlo 194-195 M 7-8

Iba [RP] 174-175 G 3
Ibadan 194-195 E 7
Ibagué 98-99 DE 4
Ibar 138-139 J 4
Ibaraki 170-171 N 4
Ibarra 98-99 D 4
Ibarreta 103 E 3
Ibb 160-161 E 8
Iberá, Esteros del — 103 E 3
Iberian Basin 26-27 HJ 3
Iberville 72-73 K 2
Iberville, Lac d' 46-47 W 6
Ibi [WAN] 194-195 F 7
Ibiá 98-99 J 8
Ibib, Wâdî — 199 D 6
Ibicaraí 98-99 M 7-8
Ibicuí, Rio — 103 E 3
Ibicuy 103 E 4
Ibipetuba 98-99 KL 7
Ibiza [E, island] 132-133 H 9
Ibiza [E, place] 132-133 H 9
Ibjîl 194-195 F 3
Ibo = Sassandra 194-195 C 7
Ibotirama 98-99 L 7
'Ibrâ 160-161 H 6
Ibrâhîm, Jabal — 160-161 E 6
Ibrâhîmîyah, Qanâl al- 199 B 3
'Ibrî 160-161 H 6
Ibshawây 199 B 3
Ibstock 116-117 K 8
Ibu 174-175 J 6
Ibusuki 170-171 H 7

Ica [PE, place] 98-99 D 7
Iča [SU] 154-155 e 6
Içá, Rio — 98-99 F 5
Icabarú 98-99 G 4
Içana 98-99 F 4
Içana, Rio — 98-99 F 4
Icatu 98-99 L 5
İçel = Mersin 160-161 C 3
Iceland 114-115 cd 2
Iceland Basin 110-111 CD 4
Iceland Jan Mayen Ridge 110-111 F 2
Ichang = Yichang 166-167 L 5
Ich Bogd uul 166-167 J 3
Ich Chogosoor 166-167 GH 5
Ichibusa-yama 170-171 H 6
Ichihara 170-171 N 5
Ichikawa 170-171 MN 5
Ichinohe 170-171 N 2
Ichinomya 170-171 L 5
Ichinoseki 166-167 QR 4
Ich'ŏn [North Korea] 170-171 F 3
Ich'ŏn [ROK] 166-167 O 4
Ichow = Linyi 166-167 M 4
Ichun = Yichun [TJ, Heilongjiang] 166-167 O 2
Ichun = Yichun [TJ, Jiangxi] 166-167 LM 6
Ičinskaja sopka = Velikaja Ičinskaja sopka 154-155 e 6
Icoraci 98-99 O 5
Icy Bay 52-53 R 7
Icy Cape 46-47 D 3
Icy Strait 52-53 U 7

Ida, LA 76-77 GH 6
Ida, Mount — = Ídē Óros 138-139 L 8
Idabel, OK 76-77 G 6
Ida Grove, IA 70-71 C 4
Idah 194-195 F 7
Idaho 58-59 C 2-D 3
Idaho City, ID 66-67 F 4
Idaho Falls, ID 58-59 D 3
Idalia, CO 68-69 E 6
Idalou, TX 76-77 D 6
Idanha, OR 66-67 BC 3
Idar-Oberstein 124 C 4
'Idd, Al- 160-161 G 6
'Idd al-Ghanam 194-195 J 6
Idel' 142-143 F 3
Ídē Óros 138-139 L 8
Iderijn gol 166-167 HJ 2
Idfû 194-195 L 4
Idi 174-175 C 5-6
Idiofa 198 C 3
'Idîsât, El — = Al-'Udaysât 199 C 5
Iditarod, AK 52-53 H 5
Iditarod River 52-53 H 5
Idjen, Tanah Tinggi — = Tanahtinggiljen 174-175 r 9-10
Idkû, Buḥayrat — 199 B 2
Idlib 160-161 D 3
Idria, CA 74-75 C 4
Idria = Idrija 138-139 J 5
Idrija 138-139 EF 2
Idylwood, VA 82 II a 2

Ieper 132-133 J 3
Ierapetra = Hierápetra 138-139 L 8
Iesi 138-139 E 4

Ifakara 198 G 3
'Ifâl, Wâdî al- 199 D 3
Ifalik 174-175 MN 5
Ifanadiana 198 J 6
Ife 194-195 EF 7
Iférouane 194-195 F 5
Iffley 182-183 H 3
Iforas, Adrar des — 194-195 E 4-5

Igalula 198 F 3
Iganga 198 F 1
Igarapava 98-99 K 9
Igarapé-Açu 98-99 K 5
Igarapé-Mirim 98-99 K 5
Igarité 98-99 L 7
Igarka 154-155 Q 4
Ighil-Izane = Ghâlizân 194-195 E 1
Ighil M'Goun = Ighil M'Gûn 194-195 C 2
Ighil M'Gûn 194-195 C 2
Igichuk Hill 52-53 FG 3
Igidi, Erg — = Ṣaḥrâ' al-Igîdi 194-195 CD 3
Igiugig, AK 52-53 JK 7
Iglésias 138-139 C 6
Iglesiente 138-139 C 6
'Igma, Gebel el- = Jabal al-'Ajmah 194-195 L 3
Ignace 70-71 E 1
Ignacio, CA 74-75 B 3
Ignacio, CO 68-69 C 7
Igo, CA 66-67 B 5
Igomo 198 F 3
Igra 142-143 K 4
Igrim 154-155 L 5
Iguaçu, Rio — 103 F 3
Igualada 132-133 H 8
Iguala de la Independencia 58-59 G 8
Iguana, Sierra de la — 76-77 D 9
Iguape 103 G 2
Iguatu 98-99 M 6
Iguazú, Cataratas del — 103 F 3
Iguéla 198 A 2
Igvak, Cape — 52-53 f 1

Ihavandiffulu Atoll 36 a 1
Ihosy 198 J 6
I-hsien = Yi Xian [TJ, Liaoning] 170-171 C 2
Ihtiman 138-139 KL 4

Iida 170-171 L 5
Iida = Suzu 170-171 L 4
Iíde-san 170-171 M 4
Iijoki 114-115 LM 5
Iisalmi 114-115 M 6
Iizuka 170-171 H 6

Ijara 198 H 2
Ijjill, Kidyat — 194-195 B 4
IJssel 132-133 KL 2
IJsselmeer 132-133 K 2

Ik 142-143 K 4
Ikaalinen 114-115 K 7
Ikaría 138-139 LM 7
Ikatan, AK 52-53 b 2
Ikeda [J, Hokkaidō] 170-171 c 2
Ikeda [J, Shikoku] 170-171 JK 5-6
Ikeja 194-195 E 7
Ikela 198 D 2
Ikelemba 198 C 1
Ikhîl 'm Goûn = Ighil M'Gûn 194-195 C 2
Ikhwân, Gezir el- = Jazâ'ir al-Ikhwân 199 D 4
Ikhwân, Jazâ'ir al- 199 D 4
Iki 170-171 G 6
Iki suidō 170-171 GH 6
Ikitsuki-shima 170-171 G 6
Ikkerre 194-195 F 7
Ikolik, Cape — 52-53 f 1
Ikoma 198 F 2
Ikonium = Konya 160-161 C 3
Ikopa 198 J 5
Ikpikpuk River 46-47 F 3-4
Ikr'anoje 142-143 J 6
Ikuno 170-171 K 5

Ikuno 235

Ikushumbetsu 170-171 bc 2

Ilagan 174-175 H 3
Ilāhābād = Allahābād 160-161 N 5
Ilak Island 52-53 t 7
Īlām [IR] 160-161 F 4
Īlām va Poshtkuh = 2 ◁ 160-161 F 4
Ilan = Yilan 166-167 OP 2
Ilangali 198 FG 3
Ilanskij 154-155 S 6
Ilaro 194-195 E 7
Ilay, Wādī — 199 D 7
Ilchester 116-117 J 9-10
Ilchuri Alin = Yilehuli Shan 166-167 NO 1
Île à la Crosse 49 D 3
Île à la Crosse, Lac — 49 E 3
Ilebo 198 D 2
Ileckaja Zaščita = Sol'-Ileck 154-155 JK 7
Île-de-France 132-133 HJ 4
Ilek [SU, place] 142-143 K 5
Ilek [SU, river] 142-143 K 5
Île Parisienne 72-73 D 1
Île Royale = Cape Breton Island 46-47 X-Z 8
Ilesha 194-195 EF 7
Îles Marquises 34-35 L 5
Ilford 46-47 RS 6
Ilfracombe 116-117 G 9
Ilha Grande [BR, Amazonas] 98-99 F 5
Ilha Grande [BR, Rio de Janeiro] 98-99 L 9
Ilha Grande = Ilha das Sete Quedas 103 EF 2-3
Ilha Grande ou das Sete Quedas 98-99 HJ 9
Ilha Mexiana 98-99 K 4-5
Ilhas, Cachoeira — 98-99 JK 5
Ilhas Desertas 194-195 A 2
Ílhavo 132-133 C 8
Ilhéus 98-99 M 7
Ilhinha, Cachoeira — 98-99 K 5
Ili [SU] 154-155 O 8
Ili [TJ] 166-167 E 3
Ili = Gulja 166-167 E 3
Iliamna, AK 52-53 K 7
Iliamna Bay 52-53 L 7
Iliamna Lake 46-47 E 6
Iliamna Volcano 46-47 EF 5
Iliff, CO 68-69 E 5
Iligan 174-175 H 5
Ilihuli Shan = Ilchuri Alin 166-167 NO 1
Ilion, NY 72-73 J 3
Ilion = Troia 160-161 B 3
Ilio Point 78-79 d 2
Ilivit Mountains 52-53 G 5
Iljič 154-155 M 9
Iljinskij [SU ↑ Južno-Sachalinsk] 154-155 b 8
Ilkeston 116-117 K 8
Ilkley 116-117 K 7
Illampu, Nevado — 98-99 F 8
Illapel 103 B 4
Illecas 86-87 JK 6
Iller 124 E 4
Illimani, Nevado de — 98-99 F 8
Illinois 58-59 HJ 3
Illinois, University of — 83 II ab 1
Illinois Institut of Technology 83 II b 1
Illinois Peak 66-67 F 2
Illinois River 58-59 HJ 3-4
Illmo, MO 78-79 E 2
Illubabor = Īlubabor 194-195 LM 7
Il'men', ozero — 154-155 E 6
Ilminster 116-117 J 10
Ilnik, AK 52-53 cd 1
Ilo 98-99 E 8
Ilo, Rada de — 98-99 E 8
Iloilo 174-175 H 4
Ilopango, Lago de — 88-89 B 8
Ilorin 194-195 E 7
Il'pyrskij 154-155 f 5-6
Īlubabor 194-195 LM 7
Ilwaco, WA 66-67 AB 2
Ilwaki 174-175 J 8
Iłża 124 K 3

Imabari 170-171 J 5-6
Imabetsu 170-171 N 2
Imabu, Rio — 98-99 K 5
Imagane 170-171 ab 2
Imaichi 170-171 M 4
Imajō 170-171 KL 5
Imandra, ozero — 154-155 E 4
Imari 170-171 GH 6
Imataca, Serranía de — 98-99 G 3
Imatra 114-115 N 7
Imatra vallinkoski 114-115 N 7
Imazu 170-171 KL 5
Imbābah 199 B 2
Imbaimadai 98-99 G 3
Imeri, Serra — 98-99 F 4
Imfal = Imphāl 160-161 P 6
Īmī 194-195 N 7
Imilac 103 C 2
Imja-do 170-171 E 5
Imjin-gang 170-171 F 3
Imlay, NV 66-67 DE 5
Imlay City, MI 72-73 E 3
Immingham 116-117 L 7
Immokalee, FL 80-81 c 3
Immyŏng-dong 170-171 G 2
Imnaha River 66-67 E 3
Imo 194-195 F 7
Ímola 138-139 D 3
Imotski 138-139 G 4
Imperatriz 98-99 K 6
Impèria 138-139 C 4
Imperial, CA 74-75 F 6
Imperial, NE 68-69 F 5
Imperial, TX 76-77 C 7
Imperial [CDN] 49 F 5
Imperial Dam 74-75 F 6
Imperial Mills 49 C 3
Imperial Valley 58-59 CD 5
Impfondo 198 C 1
Imphāl 160-161 P 6
Imp'o 170-171 FG 5
Imuris 86-87 E 2
Imuruan Bay 174-175 G 4
Imuruk Basin 52-53 DE 4
Imuruk Lake 52-53 F 4
Imwŏnjin 170-171 G 4

Ina [J] 170-171 LM 5
In'a [SU, place] 154-155 b 6
In'a [SU, river] 154-155 c 5
Inajá, Rio — 98-99 N 9
Inajá, Serra do — 98-99 N 9
Inanudak Bay 52-53 m 4
Inanwatan 174-175 K 7
Iñapari 98-99 EF 7
In'aptuk, gora — 154-155 UV 6
Inari [SF, lake] 114-115 MN 3
Inari [SF, place] 114-115 M 3
Inaru River 52-53 J 1
Inauini, Rio — 98-99 D 9
Inawashiro 170-171 MN 4
Inawashiro ko 170-171 MN 4
Inbhear Mór, An t- 116-117 EF 8
Inca 132-133 J 9
İnce burun 160-161 C 2
Inchnadamph 116-117 G 2
Inch'ŏn 170-171 F 4
Incoronata = Kornat 138-139 F 4
Incudine, l' 138-139 C 5
Indaal, Loch — 116-117 E 5
Indaor = Indore 160-161 M 6
Indaur = Indore 160-161 M 6
Indé 76-77 B 10
Independence, CA 74-75 D 4
Independence, IA 70-71 E 4
Independence, KS 76-77 FG 4
Independence, LA 78-79 D 5
Independence, MO 58-59 H 4
Independence, OR 66-67 B 3
Independence Mountains 66-67 EF 5
Independence Valley 66-67 F 5
Independencia [MEX] 74-75 F 6
Independencia, Islas — 98-99 D 7
Inderagiri, Batang — 174-175 D 7
Index, WA 66-67 C 2
Index Mount 52-53 PQ 2
India 160-161 L-O 6
India, Bassas da — 198 GH 6
Indiana 58-59 J 3-4
Indiana, PA 72-73 G 4
Indianapolis, IN 58-59 J 4
Indian Head 49 FG 5
Indian Lake [USA, Michigan] 70-71 G 2-3
Indian Lake [USA, Ohio] 72-73 E 4
Indian Mountain 66-67 H 4
Indian Ocean 26-27 N-O 6-7
Indianola, IA 70-71 D 5
Indianola, MS 78-79 D 4
Indianola, NE 68-69 F 5
Indian Peak 74-75 G 3
Indian River [CDN] 50 N 2
Indian River [USA, Alaska] 52-53 KL 4
Indian River [USA, Florida] 58-59 K 6
Indian Springs, NV 74-75 F 4
Indian Springs, VA 82 II a 2
Indian Valley, ID 66-67 E 3
Indiga 154-155 HJ 4
Indigirka 154-155 bc 4
Indio, CA 74-75 E 6
Indio, Río — 58-59 c 2
Índios, Cachoeira dos — 98-99 G 4
Indispensable Strait 174-175 k 6
Indo = Sindh 160-161 L 4
Indonesia 174-175 D-K 7
Indore 160-161 M 6
Indramaiu = Indramayu 174-175 E 8
Indramayu 174-175 E 8
Indrāvati 160-161 N 7
Indre 132-133 H 5
Indre Arna 114-115 AB 7
Indūra = Nizāmābād 160-161 M 7
Indus = Sengge Khamba 166-167 DE 5
Indus = Sindh 160-161 L 4
Indus Canyon 160-161 K 6
İnebolu 142-143 F 7
İnegöl 142-143 E 7-8
Inerie, Gunung — 174-175 H 8
Ineul 138-139 L 2
İnevi 142-143 F 8
In-Ezzane = 'Ayn 'Azzān 194-195 G 4
Infernão, Cachoeira do — 98-99 G 6
Inferninho, Caocheira — 98-99 H 9
Infiernillo, Presa del — 86-87 JK 8
In-Gall 194-195 F 5
Ingende 198 C 2
Ingeniero Jacobacci 103 BC 6
Ingenika Mine 48 E 1
Ingenstrem Rocks 52-53 q 6
Ingersoll 72-73 F 3
Ingham 182-183 J 3
Ingle, CA 74-75 C 4
Inglefield Bredning 46-47 XY 2
Inglefield Land 46-47 XY 2
Ingleside, San Francisco-, CA 83 I b 2
Inglewood 182-183 K 5
Inglewood, CA 74-75 D 6
Inglis 49 H 5
Inglutalik River 52-53 G 4
Ingolf 50 B 3
Ingólfshöfdhi 114-115 ef 3
Ingolstadt 124 EF 4
Ingomar, MT 68-69 C 2
Ingonisch 51 F 4
Ingøy 114-115 KL 2
Ingrid Christensen land 31 BC 8
In Guezzam = 'Ayn Qazzān 194-195 EF 5
Ingulec 142-143 F 6
Inhambane [Mozambique, administrative unit] 198 FG 6
Inhambane [Mozambique, place] 198 G 6
Inhambupe 98-99 M 7
Inhaminga 198 FG 5
Inharrime 198 G 6
Inhung-ni 170-171 F 3
In Iarmhidhe 116-117 D 7
Inírida, Río — 98-99 F 4
Inis 116-117 BC 8
Inis Coirthe 116-117 E 8
Inis Díomáin 116-117 BC 8
Inis Eoghain, Ceann — 116-117 E 5
Inishbofin = Inis Bó Finne 116-117 A 7
Inisheer = Inis Oirthir 116-117 B 7
Inishman = Inis Meáin 116-117 B 7
Inishmore = Inis Mór 116-117 B 7
Inishowen Head = Ceann Inis Eoghain 116-117 E 5
Inishowen Peninsula = Inis Eoghain 116-117 D 5
Inishtrahull Island = Inis Streachaill 116-117 DE 5
Inishturk = Inis Toirc 116-117 A 7
Injune 182-183 J 5
Inkerman 182-183 H 3
Inklin 52-53 V 7
Inklin River 52-53 V 7
Inkom, ID 66-67 GH 4
Inland Lake 52-53 H 3
Inland Sea = Seto-naikai 166-167 P 5
Inn 124 E 5
Inner Hebrides 116-117 E 3-5
Inner Mongolian Autonomous Region 166-167 K 3-M 2
Inner Sound 116-117 F 3
Innisfail [AUS] 182-183 J 3
Innisfail [CDN] 48 L 3
Innoko River 52-53 H 5
Innoshima 170-171 J 5
Innsbruck 124 E 5
Innymnej, gora — 154-155 kl 4
Ino 170-171 J 6
Inomino-misaki 170-171 J 6
Inongo 198 C 2
Inoucdjouac 46-47 V 6
Inowrocław 124 HJ 2
Inquisivi 98-99 F 8
Inscription, Cape — 182-183 B 5
Insein = Inzein 174-175 C 3
Inta 154-155 KL 4
Intake, MT 68-69 D 2
In Tedeini = 'Ayn Tādīn 194-195 E 4
Interamericana, Carretera — 88-89 E 10
Interior, SD 68-69 F 4
Interior Plateau 48 D 2-F 4
Interlaken 124 CD 5
International Amphitheatre 83 II b 2
International Falls, MN 70-71 D 1
Intersection, Mount — 48 G 3
Inthanon, Doi — 174-175 C 3
Intiyaco 103 DE 3
Intracoastal Waterway 78-79 C 6
Inubō saki 170-171 N 5
Inútil, Bahía — 103 BC 8
Inuvik 46-47 K 4
Inveraray 116-117 F 4
Inverbervie 116-117 JK 4
Invercargill 182-183 NO 9
Inverell 182-183 K 5
Inverleigh 182-183 H 3
Invermere 48 J 4
Inverness, FL 80-81 b 2
Inverness [CDN] 51 F 4
Inverness [GB] 116-117 G 3
Invershiel 116-117 F 3
Inverurie 116-117 J 3
Inverway 182-183 EF 3
Investigator Strait 182-183 FG 7
Inwood, NY 82 III d 3
Inyangani 198 F 5
Inyan Kara Mountain 68-69 D 3
Inyokern, CA 74-75 DE 5
Inyo Mountains 74-75 DE 4
Inza [SU, place] 154-155 H 7
Inzein 174-175 C 3
Inzia 198 C 3
Iō 148-149 S 7
Iōánnina 138-139 J 6
Iō-jima 170-171 H 7
Iō-jima = Volcano Islands 148-149 S 7
Iokanga 142-143 G 2
Iola, KS 70-71 C 7
Iola, TX 76-77 FG 7
Iolotan' 160-161 J 3
Iona 116-117 E 4
Iona, ID 66-67 H 4
Iona, SD 68-69 G 4
Ione, CA 74-75 C 3
Ione, OR 66-67 D 3
Ione, WA 66-67 E 1
Ionia, MI 70-71 H 4
Ionian Basin 194-195 HJ 1-2
Ionian Islands 138-139 H 6-J 7
Ionian Sea 110-111 M 8
Ionti = Joontoy 198 H 2
Iony, ostrov — 154-155 b 6
Iorruis, Ceann — 116-117 AB 6
Íos 138-139 L 7
Iosser 142-143 K 3
Iota, LA 78-79 C 5
Iowa 58-59 H 3
Iowa, LA 78-79 C 5
Iowa City, IA 70-71 E 5
Iowa Falls, IA 70-71 D 4
Iowa Park, TX 76-77 E 5-6
Iowa River 70-71 E 5

Ipadu, Cachoeira — 98-99 F 4
Ipameri 98-99 K 8
Iparia 98-99 E 6
Ipatovo 142-143 H 6
Ipel' 124 J 4
Ipewik River 52-53 E 2
Ipiaú 98-99 M 7
Ipin = Yibin 166-167 JK 6
Ipiranga [BR, Amazonas ↗ Benjamin Constant] 98-99 E 5
Ipiranga [BR, Amazonas ↑ Benjamin Constant] 98-99 D 6
Ipixuna 98-99 KL 5
Ipixuna, Rio — [BR ◁ Rio Purus] 98-99 G 6
Ipoh 174-175 D 6
Iporá [BR, Goiás] 98-99 J 8
Ippy 194-195 J 7
Ipsario = Hypsárion 138-139 L 5
Ipswich 116-117 h 6
Ipswich, SD 68-69 G 3
Ipswich, Brisbane- 182-183 K 5
Ipu 98-99 L 5
Ipueiras 98-99 L 5

Iqlīt 199 C 5
Iquique 103 B 2
Iquiri, Rio — 98-99 E 9
Iquitos 98-99 E 5

Iraan, TX 76-77 D 7
Iracema [BR, Acre] 98-99 D 9
Iracema [BR, Amazonas] 98-99 D 8
Iracema [BR, Rondônia] 98-99 H 9
Iracoubo 98-99 J 3
Irago-suidō 170-171 L 5
Irago-zaki 170-171 L 5
Irak 160-161 D-F 4
Irak = Arāk 160-161 F 4
Iraklion = Hērákleion 138-139 L 8
Irala [PY] 103 EF 3
Iran 160-161 F-H 4
Iran, Plateau of — 26-27 MN 4
Īrānshahr 160-161 HJ 5
Irapa 98-99 G 2
Irapuato 58-59 F 7
Irarrarene = Irharharān 194-195 F 3
Irati 103 F 3
Irawadi = Erāwadī Myit 174-175 C 2
Irazú, Volcán — 58-59 K 9
Irbid 160-161 D 4
Irbit 154-155 L 6
Irecê 98-99 L 7
Ireland 116-117 C-E 8
Irene 103 D 5
Irgalem = Yirga 'Alem 194-195 M 7
Irgiz [SU, place] 154-155 L 8
Irgiz [SU, river] 142-143 K 5
Irharharān 194-195 F 3
Irhyang-dong 170-171 GH 2
Iri 170-171 F 4-5
Irian, Teluk — 174-175 KL 7
Iriba 194-195 J 5
Iricoumé, Serra — 98-99 K 4
Iriga 174-175 H 4
Iringa 198 G 3
Iriomote-jima 166-167 N 7
Iriomote zima = Iriomote-jima 166-167 N 7
Iriri, Rio — 98-99 J 5
Irish Sea 116-117 F-H 7
Irituia 98-99 K 5
Irivi Novo, Rio — 98-99 M 9
Irkutsk 154-155 TU 7
Irma 49 C 4
Irmingersee 46-47 d-f 5
Iro, Lac — 194-195 HJ 7
Īrōd = Erode 160-161 M 8
Irona 88-89 D 7
Iron Bridge 50 K 3
Iron City, TN 78-79 F 3
Iron Creek, AK 52-53 E 4
Irondequoit, NY 72-73 H 3
Iron Gate = Porţile de Fier 138-139 K 3
Iron Knob 182-183 G 6
Iron Mountain 74-75 G 4
Iron Mountain, MI 70-71 FG 3
Iron Mountain, WY 68-69 D 5
Iron River, MI 70-71 F 2
Iron River, WI 70-71 E 2
Ironside, OR 66-67 DE 3
Ironton, MO 70-71 E 7
Ironton, OH 72-73 E 5
Ironwood, MI 58-59 HJ 2
Iroquois, SD 68-69 H 3
Iroquois Falls 46-47 U 8
Irō saki 170-171 M 5
'Irq, Al- 194-195 J 3
'Irqah 160-161 F 8
'Irq al-Kabīr al-Gharbī, Al- 194-195 D 3-E 2
'Irq al-Kabīr ash-Sharqī, Al- 194-195 F 2-3
'Irq ash-Shāsh 194-195 D 3-4
Irrawaddy = Erāwadī Myit 174-175 C 2
Irricana 48 L 4
Irtyš 154-155 N 6
Irtyšskoje 154-155 NO 7
Irumu 198 E 1
Irún 132-133 G 7
Iruya 103 CD 2
Irvine 49 CD 6
Irvine 116-117 G 5
Irvine, KY 72-73 E 6
Irving, TX 76-77 F 6
Irving Park, Chicago-, IL 83 II b 1
Irvington, KY 70-71 G 7
Irvington, NJ 82 III a 2
Irwin, ID 66-67 H 4
Irwin, NE 68-69 EF 4
Irwŏl-san 170-171 G 4

Īs, Jabal — 199 D 6
Isabel, SD 68-69 F 3
Isabela 174-175 H 5
Isabela, Isla — 98-99 A 5
Isabela, La — 88-89 FG 3
Isabella, CA 74-75 D 5
Isabella, MN 70-71 E 2
Isabella, Cordillera — 58-59 J 9
Isabella Lake 74-75 D 5
Isachsen 46-47 Q 2
Isachsen, Cape — 46-47 OP 2
Isafjardharjdjúp 114-115 b 1
Isa Fjord = Ísafjardhadjúp 114-115 b 1
Ísafjördhur 114-115 b 1
Isahara = Isahaya 170-171 GH 6
Isahaya 170-171 GH 6
Isangi 198 D 1
Isar 124 F 4
'Isāwīyah, Al- 160-161 D 4
Isāwuwan, 'Irq — 194-195 F 3
Ischia 138-139 E 5
Ise [J] 170-171 L 5
Iseo 138-139 D 3
Isère 132-133 K 6
Isère, Pointe — 98-99 J 3
Išerim, gora — 154-155 K 5
Isèrnia 138-139 F 5
Iset' 154-155 L 6
Ise-wan 170-171 L 5
Iseyin 194-195 E 7
Isezaki 170-171 M 4
Isfahan = Eşfahān 160-161 G 4
İsfendiyar dağları 160-161 CD 2
Isfjorden 114-115 j 5
I-shan = Yishan 166-167 K 7
Isherton 98-99 J 3
Ishibashi 170-171 N 3
Ishigaki-shima 166-167 NO 7
Ishikari 170-171 b 2
Ishikari gawa 170-171 b 2
Ishikari-wan 170-171 b 2
Ishikawa 170-171 L 4
Ishinomaki 170-171 N 3
Ishinomaki wan 170-171 N 3
Ishioka 170-171 N 4
Ishizuchino san 170-171 J 6
Ishpeming, MI 70-71 G 2
Isigaki sima = Ishigaki-shima 166-167 NO 7
Isigny-sur-Mer 132-133 G 4
Isil'kul' 154-155 N 7
Išim [SU, place] 154-155 M 6
Išim [SU, river] 154-155 M 7
Išimbaj 154-155 K 7
Išimskaja step' 154-155 N 6-7
Isiolo 198 G 1
Isiro 198 E 1
Isisford 182-183 H 4
Isispynten 114-115 mn 5
Iskandar 154-155 M 9
Iskandarīyah, Al- 194-195 KL 2
Iskar 138-139 L 4
Iskardū = Skardū 160-161 M 3
İskenderun 160-161 D 3
İskenderun körfezi 142-143 FG 8
İskilip 142-143 F 7
Iskitim 154-155 P 7
Iskushuban 194-195 bc 1
Iskut River 48 B 1
Isla 86-87 N 8
Isla Blanca 86-87 R 7
Isla-Cristina 132-133 D 10
Islāmābād 160-161 L 4
Islāmābād = Anantnāg 160-161 M 4
Islamorada, FL 80-81 c 4
Island City, OR 66-67 E 3
Island Falls 50 L 2
Island Falls, ME 72-73 M 1-2
Island Lagoon 182-183 G 6
Island Lake [CDN, lake] 46-47 RS 7
Island Lake [CDN, place] 50 BC 1
Island Mountain, CA 66-67 B 5
Island Park, ID 66-67 H 3
Island Park Reservoir 66-67 H 3
Island Pond, VT 72-73 KL 2
Islands, Bay of — [CDN] 51 G 3
Islands, Bay of — [NZ] 182-183 OP 7
Isla Nueva 103 C 9
Islay 116-117 E 5
Islay, Sound of — 116-117 EF 5
Isle 132-133 H 6
Isle au Haut 72-73 M 2-3
Isle Royale 58-59 J 2
Isle Royale National Park 70-71 F 2
Isles Dernieres 78-79 D 6
Isleta, NM 76-77 A 5
Isleton, CA 74-75 C 3
Ismailia = Al-Ismā'īlīyah 194-195 L 2
Ismā'īlīyah, Al- 194-195 L 2
Ismay, MT 68-69 D 2
Isnā 194-195 L 3
Isohama = Ōarai 170-171 N 4
Isoka 198 F 4
Ispahān = Eşfahān 160-161 G 4
İsparta 160-161 C 3
Isperih 138-139 M 4
Israel 160-161 CD 4
Israelite Bay 182-183 DE 6
Issano 98-99 H 3
Issaouane, Erg — = 'Irq Isāwuwan 194-195 F 3
Issoudun 132-133 HJ 5
Issyk-Kul', ozero — 166-167 M 3
Istādah, Ab-e- = Ābe Estāda 160-161 K 4
İstanbul 160-161 BC 2
Istmina 98-99 D 3
Isto, Mount — 52-53 Q 2
Istranca dağları 142-143 E 7
Istria 138-139 EF 3
Isvestia Islands = ostrova Izvestij CIK 154-155 OP 2

Itabaianinha 98-99 M 7
Itabaina 98-99 M 6
Itaberaba 98-99 L 7
Itaberaí 98-99 JK 8
Itabuna 98-99 M 7
Itacaiúnas, Rio — 98-99 JK 6
Itacajá 98-99 P 9
Itacaré 98-99 M 7
Itacoatiara 98-99 H 5
Itacolomi, Pico — 98-99 L 9
Itaetê 98-99 L 7
Itaguatins 98-99 K 6
Itaí 103 G 2
Itaipava, Cachoeira — [BR, Rio Araguaia] 98-99 K 6
Itaipava, Cachoeira — [BR, Rio Xingu] 98-99 J 5
Itaituba 98-99 H 5
Itajaí 103 G 3
Itajubá 98-99 K 9
Itajuípe 98-99 LM 7
Itaka 154-155 W 7
Itala = 'Adale 198 J 1
Itálica 132-133 DE 10
Italy 138-139 C 3-F 5
Italy, TX 76-77 F 6
Itambé 98-99 L 8
Itanhauã, Rio — 98-99 F 7
Itany 98-99 J 4
Itaocara 98-99 L 9
Itapaci 98-99 JK 7
Itapagé 98-99 LM 5
Itaparaná, Rio — 98-99 G 8
Itapebi 98-99 M 8
Itapemirim 98-99 LM 9
Itapetinga 98-99 LM 8
Itapetininga 103 G 2
Itapeva 103 G 2
Itapicuru, Rio — [BR, Bahia] 98-99 M 7
Itapicuru, Rio — [BR, Maranhão] 98-99 L 5
Itapicuru, Serra — 98-99 KL 6
Itapicurumirim 98-99 L 5
Itapinima 98-99 H 7
Itapipoca 98-99 M 5
Itapira 98-99 K 9
Itaquaí, Rio — 98-99 C 7
Itaqui 103 E 3
Itārsi 160-161 M 6
Itasca, TX 76-77 F 6
Itasca, Lake — 58-59 G 2
Itatuba 98-99 G 6
Itawa = Etāwah 160-161 M 5
Ithaca, MI 70-71 H 4
Ithaca, NY 58-59 L 3
Ithaca = Ithákē 138-139 J 6
Ithákē 138-139 J 6
Itigi 198 F 3
Itimbiri 198 D 1
Itinga [BR, Maranhão] 98-99 P 7
Itinoseki = Ichinoseki 166-167 QR 4
Itiquira 98-99 J 8

236 **Ikushumb**

Itiquira, Rio — 98-99 H 8
Itiruçu 98-99 L 7
Itiúba 98-99 M 7
Itkillik River 52-53 M 2
'Itmâniya, El- = Al-'Uthmānīyah 199 BC 4
Itō 170-171 M 5
Itoigawa 170-171 L 4
Itoikawa = Itoigawa 170-171 L 4
Itrī, Jabal — 199 D 7
Itsā 199 B 3
Itsjang = Yichang 166-167 L 5
I-tu = Yidu 166-167 M 4
Ituaçu 98-99 L 7
Ituí, Rio — 98-99 E 6
Itula 198 E 2
Itulilik, AK 52-53 J 6
Itumbiara 98-99 K 8
Ituna 49 G 5
Ituni Township 98-99 H 3
Itupiranga 98-99 JK 6
Ituri 198 E 1
Iturup, ostrov — 154-155 c 8
Ituxi, Rio — 98-99 F 6
Itzehoe 124 D 1-2

Iuka, MS 78-79 E 3

Iva, SC 80-81 E 3
Ivaí, Rio — 103 F 2
Ivajlovgrad 138-139 M 5
Ivalo 114-115 M 3
Ivalojoki 114-115 M 3
Ivan, AR 78-79 C 4
Ivanhoe 182-183 H 6
Ivanhoe, MN 70-71 BC 3
Ivanhoe River 50 K 2-3
Ivanof Bay, AK 52-53 cd 2
Ivano-Frankovsk 142-143 DE 6
Ivanovo [SU, Rossijskaja SFSR] 154-155 FG 6
Ivanovo, Voznesensk- = Ivanovo 154-155 FG 6
Ivanuškova 154-155 UV 6
Ivaščenkovo = Čapajevsk 154-155 HJ 7
Ivdel' 154-155 L 5
Ivigtût 46-47 b 5
Ivindo 198 B 1
Ivinheima, Rio — 98-99 J 9
Ivisaruk River 52-53 G 1-2
Iviza = Ibiza 132-133 H 9
Ivohibe 198 J 6
Ivory Coast [RI, landscape] 194-195 CD 8
Ivory Coast [RI, state] 194-195 CD 7
Ivrea 138-139 B 3

Iwadate 170-171 MN 2
Iwaizumi 170-171 NO 3
Iwaki 170-171 N 4
Iwaki yama 170-171 N 2
Iwakuni 170-171 J 5
Iwamizawa 166-167 R 3
Iwanai 170-171 b 2
Iwanowo = Ivanovo 154-155 FG 6
Iwanuma 170-171 N 3
Iwata 170-171 LM 5
Iwate [J, administrative unit] 170-171 N 2-3
Iwate [J, place] 170-171 N 3
Iwate-yama 170-171 N 3
Iwo 194-195 E 7
Iwō-jima = Iō-jima 170-171 H 7
Iwŏn 170-171 G 2

Ixiamas 98-99 F 7
Ixopo 198 EF 8
Ixtayutla 86-87 M 9
Ixtepec 58-59 G 8
Ixtlán del Río 86-87 HJ 7
Ixworth 116-117 gh 6

I-yang = Yiyang [TJ, Hunan] 166-167 L 6
Iyo 170-171 J 6
Iyomishima 170-171 J 6
Iyonada 170-171 HJ 6

Izabal, Lago de — 58-59 HJ 8
Izalco 58-59 H 9
Izamal 86-87 Q 7
Izashiki = Sata 170-171 H 7
Izaviknek River 52-53 F 6
Izberbaš 142-143 J 7
Izembek Bay 52-53 b 2
Iževsk 154-155 J 6
Izhevsk = Iževsk 154-155 J 6
Izigan, Cape — 52-53 n 4
Izkī 160-161 H 6
Ižma [SU, place] 154-155 J 4
Ižma [SU, river] 154-155 J 5
Izmail 142-143 E 6
İzmir 160-161 B 3
İzmit 160-161 BC 2
İznik gölü 142-143 E 7
Izozog, Bañados de — 98-99 G 8
Izúcar de Matamoros 86-87 LM 8
Izu hantō 170-171 M 5
Izuhara 170-171 G 5
Izumi 170-171 H 6
Izumo 170-171 J 5
Izu-shotō 166-167 QR 5
Izu syotō = Izu-shotō 166-167 QR 5
Izvestij CIK, ostrova — 154-155 OP 2

J

Ja = Dja 194-195 G 8
Jaab Lake 50 K 1
Jabal, Baḥr al- 194-195 L 7
Jabalayn, Al- 194-195 L 6
Jabalón 132-133 F 9
Jabalpur 160-161 MN 6
Jabal Ṭāriq, Bughāz — 194-195 CD 1
Jabjabah, Wādī — 199 C 7
Jablanica [AL] 138-139 J 5
Jablanica [BG] 138-139 L 4
Jablanica [YU] 138-139 G 4
Jablunca Pass = Jablunkovsky průsmyk 124 J 4
Jablunkovský průsmyk 124 J 4
Jabung, Tanjung — 174-175 DE 7
Jabuticabal 98-99 K 9
Jaca 132-133 G 7
Jacaré, Rio — [BR, Bahia] 98-99 L 6-7
Jacaré, Travessão — 98-99 O 10
Jacareacanga 98-99 JK 8
Jacarei 98-99 K 9
Jacaretinga 98-99 J 9
Jáchal = San José de Jáchal 103 C 4
Jachhen 166-167 E 5
Jáchymov 124 F 3
Jaciparaná 98-99 G 6
Jaciparana, Rio — 98-99 F 9-10
Jackfish 70-71 G 1
Jackfish Lake 49 DE 4
Jackhead Harbour 49 K 5
Jackman Station, ME 72-73 L 2
Jacksboro, TX 76-77 EF 6
Jackson, AL 78-79 F 5
Jackson, CA 74-75 C 3
Jackson, GA 80-81 DE 4
Jackson, KY 72-73 E 6
Jackson, LA 78-79 D 5
Jackson, MI 58-59 JK 3
Jackson, MN 70-71 C 4
Jackson, MO 70-71 F 7
Jackson, MS 58-59 HJ 5
Jackson, MT 66-67 G 3
Jackson, OH 72-73 E 5
Jackson, TN 58-59 J 4
Jackson, WY 66-67 H 4
Jackson, ostrov — 154-155 H-K 1
Jackson Head 182-183 N 8
Jackson Heights, New York-, NY 82 III c 2
Jackson Lake 66-67 H 4
Jackson Manion 50 CD 2
Jackson Mountains 66-67 D 5
Jackson Park [USA] 83 II b 2
Jackson Prairie 78-79 E 4
Jacksonville, AL 78-79 FG 4
Jacksonville, FL 58-59 KL 5
Jacksonville, IL 70-71 EF 6
Jacksonville, NC 80-81 H 3
Jacksonville, OR 66-67 B 4
Jacksonville, TX 76-77 G 6-7
Jacksonville Beach, FL 80-81 F 5
Jäckvik 114-115 G 4
Jacmel 58-59 M 8
Jacobina 98-99 L 7
Jacob Island 52-53 d 2
Jacob Lake, AZ 74-75 GH 4
Jacobs 50 E 2
Jaconda 86-87 J 8
Jacques Cartier 82 I bc 1
Jacques Cartier, Mount — 51 D 3
Jacques Cartier, Pont — 82 I b 1
Jacques Cartier, Rivière — 51 A 4
Jacques Cartier Passage 46-47 Y 7-8
Jacuípe, Rio — 98-99 LM 7
Jacumba, CA 74-75 EF 6
Jacundá 98-99 K 5
Jacundá, Rio — 98-99 N 6
Jacuzão, Cachoeiro — 98-99 O 8
Jadaf, Wādī al- 160-161 E 4
Jaddī, Wādī — 194-195 E 2
Jade 124 D 2
Jadīda, el — = Al-Jadīdah 194-195 C 2
Jadīdah, Al- [MA] 194-195 G 2
Jadīd Rā's al-Fīl 194-195 K 6
Jado = Jādū 194-195 G 2
Jadotville = Likasi 198 E 4
Jadrin 142-143 J 4
Jādū 194-195 G 2
Jaén [E] 132-133 F 10
Jæren 114-115 A 8
Jaesalmēr = Jaisalmer 160-161 KL 5
Jafa, Tel Avive — = Tel Avīv-Yafō 160-161 C 4
Ja'farābād [IR] 160-161 F 3
Jaffatin = Jazā'ir Jiftūn 199 CD 4
Jaffna = Yāpanaya 160-161 MN 9
Jaffray 66-67 F 1
Jafr, Al- [JOR, place] 160-161 D 4
Jafr, El- = Al-Jafr 160-161 D 4
Jafū, Ḥāssī — 194-195 E 2
Jagdalpur 160-161 N 7
Jaghbūb, Al- 194-195 J 3
Jagodnoje 154-155 cd 5
Jagoe Tsho 166-167 F 5
Jago River 52-53 Q 2
Jagst 124 DE 4
Jagtiāl 160-161 M 7
Jagua, La — 98-99 E 3
Jaguarão 103 F 4
Jaguarari 98-99 LM 7
Jaguaribe, Rio — 98-99 M 6
Jagüé, Río del — 103 C 3
Jagüey Grande 88-89 F 3
Jahrah, Al- 160-161 F 5
Jahrom 160-161 G 5
Jaicós 98-99 L 6
Jailolo 174-175 J 6
Jaipur [IND, Rājasthān] 160-161 M 5
Jaisalmer 160-161 KL 5
Jaja 154-155 Q 6
Jajah, Al- 199 B 5
Jājarm 160-161 H 3
Jajce 138-139 G 3
Jakan, mys — 154-155 j 4
Jakarta 174-175 E 8
Jakobshavn = Jlullssat 46-47 ab 4
Jakobstad 114-115 JK 6
Jakša 154-155 K 5
Jakutsk 154-155 Y 5
Jal, NM 76-77 C 6
Jaladah, Al- 160-161 F 7
Jālālābād = Jalāl Kōt 160-161 KL 4
Jalālat al-Baḥrīyah, Jabal al- 199 BC 3
Jalālat al-Qiblīyah, Jabal al- 199 C 3
Jalāl Kōt 160-161 KL 4
Ja'lan 160-161 H 6
Jalandar = Jullundur 160-161 LM 4
Jalandhar = Jullundur 160-161 LM 4
Jalapa 86-87 Q 10
Jalapa Enríquez 58-59 GH 8
Jalgānv = Jālgaon [IND ← Bhusāwal] 160-161 M 6
Jālgaon [IND ← Bhusāwal] 160-161 M 6
Jalhāk, Al- 194-195 L 6
Jalingo 194-195 G 7
Jalisco 58-59 EF 7
Jālna 160-161 M 7
Jalon, Río — 132-133 G 8
Jalo Oasis = Wāḥāt Jālū 194-195 J 3
Jalostotitlán 86-87 J 7
Jalpa 86-87 J 7
Jalpan 86-87 KL 6-7
Jalta 142-143 F 7
Jaltenango 86-87 O 10
Jalu = Yalu Jiang 170-171 EF 2
Jālū, Wāḥāt — 194-195 J 3
Jaluit 178 G 2
Jamaame 194-195 N 8
Jamaat 166-167 E 2
Jamaica 58-59 L 8
Jamaica, New York-, NY 82 III d 2
Jamaica Bay 82 III cd 3
Jamaica Channel 58-59 L 8
Jamaika 58-59 L 8
Jamakhaṇḍī = Jamkhandi 160-161 LM 7
Jamal, poluostrov — 154-155 MN 3
Jamalo-Neneckij Nacional'nyj Okrug = Yamalo-Nenets Autonomous Area 154-155 M-O 4-5
Jamantau, gora — 154-155 K 7
Jamanxim, Rio — 98-99 H 6
Jamari 98-99 G 9
Jamari, Rio — 98-99 G 6
Jambi [RI, administrative unit = 5 ◁] 174-175 D 7
Jambi [RI, place] 174-175 D 7
Jambol 138-139 M 4
Jambuto 142-143 O 2
Jamdena, Pulau — 174-175 K 8
James Bay 46-47 UV 7
James Bay, Parc provincial de — 50 M 1
James Range 182-183 F 4
James River [USA ◁ Chesapeake Bay] 58-59 L 4
James River [USA ◁ Missouri River] 58-59 G 2
Jamestown, KS 68-69 H 6
Jamestown, KY 70-71 H 7
Jamestown, ND 58-59 G 2
Jamestown, NY 58-59 L 3
Jamestown, OH 72-73 E 5
Jamestown, TN 78-79 G 2
Jamestown [Saint Helena] 188-189 G 10
Jamestown Reservoir 68-69 G 2
Jamkhandi 160-161 LM 7
Jammerbugt 114-115 C 9
Jammu 160-161 LM 4
Jamnā = Yamuna 160-161 MN 5
Jāmnagar 160-161 L 6
Jampol' 142-143 E 6
Jāmpūr 160-161 KL 5
Jamsah 199 C 4
Jämsankoski 114-115 L 7
Jamshedpur 160-161 NO 6
Jamsk 154-155 de 6
Jämtland 114-115 E-G 6
Jämtlands Sikås 114-115 F 6
Jamursba, Tanjung — 174-175 K 7
Jana 154-155 Z 4
Janaperi, Rio — 98-99 G 4
Janaúba 98-99 L 8
Janaucu, Ilha — 98-99 JK 4
Janaul 154-155 JK 6
Jandaq 160-161 GH 4
Jandiatuba, Rio — 98-99 F 5-6
Jandowae 182-183 K 5
Janemale 98-99 L 3
Janesville, CA 66-67 C 5
Janesville, WI 70-71 F 4
Jangarej 154-155 L 4
Jangijul' 154-155 M 9
Jang Thang 166-167 E-G 5
Jangtsekiang = Chang Jiang 166-167 K 5-6
Jan Lake 49 G 3
Jan Mayen 30 B 19-20
Jan Mayen Ridge 110-111 H 1-2
Jannah 194-195 FG 4
Jano-Indigirskaja nizmennost' 154-155 Z-c 3
Jánoshalma 124 J 5
Janskij 154-155 Za 4
Janskij zaliv 154-155 Za 3
Jantarnyj 124 J 1
Jantra 138-139 M 4
J. Antunes, Serra — 98-99 G 10-11
Januária 98-99 KL 8
Jao-ho = Raohe 166-167 P 2
Jaonpur = Jaunpur 160-161 N 5
Jao-yang Ho = Raoyang He 170-171 D 2
Japan 166-167 P 5-R 3
Japan Sea 166-167 P 4-Q 3
Japan Trench 34-35 G 3
Japara 174-175 F 8
Japonskoje more 154-155 a 9
Japurá, Rio — 98-99 F 5
Jara, La — 132-133 E 9
Jarādah 194-195 D 2
Jaraguari 98-99 HJ 8-9
Jaralito, El — 76-77 B 9
Jaransk 154-155 H 6
Jarārah, Wādī — 199 D 6
Jaraucu, Rio — 98-99 M 5-6
Jarbah, Jazīrat — 194-195 G 2
Jarbidge, NV 66-67 F 5
Jarcevo [SU, Jenisej] 154-155 R 5
Jarcevo [SU, Smolenskaja Oblast'] 142-143 F 4
Jardin botanique 82 I b 1
Jardines de la Reina 58-59 L 7
Jarega 142-143 K 3
Jarensk 154-155 H 5
Jari, Rio — 98-99 J 5
Jarīd, Shaṭṭ al- 194-195 F 2
Jarina, Rio — 98-99 M 10
Jarīr, Wādī — 160-161 E 5-6
Jarita, La — 86-87 KL 4
Jarkand = Yarkand 166-167 D 4
Jarkovo 154-155 M 6
Jarmashīn, 'Ayn — 199 B 5
Jarny 132-133 K 4
Jarocin 124 H 2-3
Jarok, ostrov — 154-155 a 3
Jaroslavl' 154-155 FG 6
Jarosław 124 L 3-4
Jaroso, CO 68-69 D 7
Järpen 114-115 E 6
Jarroto 142-143 O 2
Jarrow 116-117 K 6
Jarry, Parc — 82 I b 1
Jar-Sale 154-155 MN 4
Jartum = Al-Kharṭūm 194-195 L 5
Jaru 98-99 G 7
Jaru, Reserva Florestal de — 98-99 GH 9
Jaru, Rio — 98-99 G 10
Järvenpää 114-115 L 7
Jarvie 48 L 2
Jarvis 34-35 J 5
Jāsk 160-161 H 5
Jašma 142-143 H 2
Jasnyj 154-155 Y 7
Jasonhalvøy 31 C 30-31
Jason Islands 103 D 8
Jasonville, IN 70-71 G 6
Jasper, AL 78-79 F 4
Jasper, AR 78-79 C 2-3
Jasper, FL 80-81 b 1
Jasper, GA 78-79 G 3
Jasper, IN 70-71 G 6
Jasper, MN 68-69 H 4
Jasper, MO 76-77 G 4
Jasper, TX 76-77 GH 7
Jasper [CDN, Alberta] 46-47 N 7
Jasper [CDN, Ontario] 72-73 J 2
Jasper National Park 46-47 N 7
Jassy = Iaşi 138-139 M 2
Jastrebac 138-139 J 4
Jászberény 124 JK 5
Jataí [BR ↙ Rio Verde] 98-99 J 8
Jatapu, Rio — 98-99 H 5
Játiva 132-133 G 9
Jatobá 98-99 JK 5
Jat Potī = Kārēz 160-161 K 4
Jaú 98-99 K 9
Jaú, Cachoeira do — 98-99 OP 10
Jaú, Rio — 98-99 G 5
Jauari, Serra — 98-99 M 5
Jauf, Al- = Al-Jawf 160-161 DE 5
Jauf, El — = Al-Jawf 194-195 J 4
Jauja 98-99 DE 7
Jaumave 86-87 L 6
Jaunde = Yaoundé 194-195 G 8
Jaunpur 160-161 N 5
Java 98-99 L 2
Javaés, Serra dos — 98-99 O 10
Java Head = Tanjung Lajar 174-175 DE 8
Javaj, poluostrov — 154-155 NO 3
Javalambre 132-133 G 8
Javari, Cachoeira do — 98-99 LM 5
Javari, Ilha — 98-99 E 5
Javari, Rio — 98-99 E 6
Java Sea 174-175 EF 8
Javhār = Jawhār 160-161 L 7
Javlenka 154-155 M 7
Javor 138-139 HJ 4
Jawa = Java 174-175 EF 8
Jawa Barat = 11 ◁ 174-175 E 8
Jawa Tengah = 12 ◁ 174-175 E 8
Jawa Timur = 14 ◁ 174-175 F 8
Jawf, Al- [LAR] 194-195 J 4
Jawf, Al- [Saudi Arabia] 160-161 DE 5
Jawf, Al- [Y] 160-161 EF 7
Jawhār 160-161 L 7
Jawor 124 H 3
Jaxartes = Syrdarja 160-161 K 2
Jay, OK 76-77 G 4
Jaya, Gunung — 174-175 L 7
Jayapura 174-175 M 7
Jayawijaya, Pegunungan — 174-175 LM 7
Jay Em, WY 68-69 D 4
Jaypur = Jaipur [IND, Rājasthān] 160-161 M 5
Jaypura = Jeypore 160-161 N 7
Jayton, TX 76-77 D 6
Jaza'ir, Al- [DZ] 194-195 E 1
Jazīra, Al- = Arḍ al-Jazīrah 160-161 E 3-F 4
Jazīrah, Al- [Sudan] 194-195 L 6
Jazīrah, Arḍ al- 160-161 E 3-F 4
Jāz Mūreyān, Hāmūn-e — 160-161 H 5

Jbel Târoq, Bôrhâz — = Bughāz Jabal Ṭāriq 194-195 CD 1

Jean, NV 74-75 F 5
Jeanerette, LA 78-79 D 6
Jeanette, ostrov — 154-155 ef 2
Jebba 194-195 E 7
Jebelein, El- = Al-Jabalayn 194-195 L 6
Jeddah = Jiddah 160-161 D 6
Jędrzejów 124 K 3
Jedway 48 B 3
Jefara = Az-Zāwiyah 194-195 G 2
Jeffers, MN 70-71 C 3
Jefferson, CO 68-69 D 6
Jefferson, GA 80-81 E 3
Jefferson, IA 70-71 C 4-5
Jefferson, MT 66-67 GH 2
Jefferson, OH 72-73 F 4
Jefferson, OR 66-67 B 3
Jefferson, TX 76-77 G 6
Jefferson, WI 70-71 F 4
Jefferson, Mount — [USA, Nevada] 74-75 E 3
Jefferson, Mount — [USA, Oregon] 66-67 C 3
Jefferson, Village, VA 82 II a 2
Jefferson City, MO 58-59 H 4
Jefferson City, TN 80-81 E 2
Jefferson Park, Chicago-, IL 83 II a 1
Jeffersonville, GA 80-81 E 4
Jeffersonville, IN 70-71 H 6
Jeffrey Depth 182-183 F 7
Jefremov 142-143 G 5
Jegorjevsk 154-155 FG 6
Jegyrjach 154-155 M 5
Jehlam = Jihlam 160-161 L 4
Jehlum = Jihlam 160-161 L 4
Jehol = Chengde 166-167 M 3
Jejsk 142-143 G 6
Jēkabpils 142-143 E 4
Jekatarinburg = Sverdlovsk 154-155 L 6
Jekaterinovka [SU, Primorskij Kraj] 170-171 J 1
Jekubābād 160-161 K 5
Jekyakarta = Yogyakarta 174-175 EF 8
Jelabuga 142-143 K 4
Jelec 142-143 G 5
Jelenia Góra 124 GH 3
Jelfa = Jilfah 194-195 E 2
Jelgava 142-143 D 4
Jelizavety, mys — 154-155 b 7
Jelizovo [SU, Rossijskaja SFSR] 154-155 e 7
Jellico, TN 78-79 G 2
Jellicoe 50 F 3
Jema = Djema 194-195 K 7
Jemaja, Pulau — 174-175 DE 6
Jemanželinsk 142-143 M 5
Jembongan, Pulau — 174-175 G 5
Jemeck 154-155 G 5
Jemen 160-161 E 7-8
Jementau 154-155 N 7
Jemez Pueblo, NM 76-77 A 5
Jena 124 E 3
Jena, LA 78-79 CD 5
Jenakijevo 142-143 G 6
Jenašimskij Polkan, gora — 154-155 RS 6
Jenisej 154-155 Q 4
Jenisej, Boľšoj — 154-155 S 7
Jenisej, Malyj — 154-155 RS 7
Jenisejsk 154-155 R 6
Jenisejskij kr'až 154-155 R 5-6
Jenisejskij zaliv 154-155 OP 3
Jenkins, KY 80-81 E 2
Jenkins Corner, MD 82 II b 2
Jenkiu = Renqiu 166-167 M 4
Jenner 49 C 5
Jenner, CA 74-75 B 3
Jennings, KS 68-69 F 6
Jennings, LA 78-79 C 5
Jennings, MT 66-67 F 1
Jenny Lind Island 46-47 Q 4
Jensen, UT 66-67 J 5
Jensen Beach, FL 80-81 cd 3
Jens Munk Island 46-47 UV 4
Jens Munks Ø 46-47 cd 5
Jenud = Gorē 194-195 M 7
Jen'uka 154-155 X 6
Jeol = Chengde 166-167 M 3
Jequié 98-99 L 7
Jequitaí 98-99 L 8
Jequitinhonha, Rio — 98-99 L 8
Jerāda = Jarādah 194-195 D 2
Jerantut 174-175 D 6
Jerba = Jazīrat Jarbah 194-195 G 2
Jerbogač'on 154-155 U 5
Jérémie 58-59 M 8
Jeremoabo 98-99 M 6-7
Jerevan 142-143 H 7
Jerez de García Salinas 58-59 F 7
Jerez de la Frontera 132-133 DE 10
Jerez de los Caballeros 132-133 D 9
Jergeni 142-143 H 6
Jericho [AUS] 182-183 J 4
Jermak 154-155 O 7
Jermakovskoje 154-155 R 7
Jerofej Pavlovič 154-155 X 7
Jerome, AZ 74-75 G 5
Jerome, ID 66-67 F 4
Jeropol 154-155 g 4
Jersey City, NJ 58-59 M 3-4
Jersey Shore, PA 72-73 H 4
Jerseyville, IL 70-71 E 6
Jerumenha 98-99 L 6
Jerusalem = Yĕrūshālayim 160-161 CD 4
Jervis Bay 182-183 K 7
Jervois Range 182-183 G 4
Jesenice 138-139 EF 2
Jeseník 124 H 3
Jesil' 154-155 M 7
Jessaur = Jessore 160-161 O 6
Jessej 154-155 T 4
Jesselton = Kota Kinabalu 174-175 FG 5
Jessica 66-67 C 1
Jesso = Hokkaidō 166-167 RS 3
Jessore 160-161 O 6
Jestro, Webi — = Weyb 194-195 N 7
Jesup, GA 80-81 EF 5
Jesup, IA 70-71 DE 4
Jésus, Île — 82 I a 1
Jesús Carranza 86-87 N 9
Jesus Maria [MEX] 86-87 HJ 6
Jesús María [RA] 103 D 4
Jesus María, Boca de — 86-87 M 5
Jet, OK 76-77 E 4
Jetait 49 H 2
Jetmore, KS 68-69 FG 6
Jevpatorija 142-143 F 6
Jewell, IA 70-71 D 4
Jewell, KS 68-69 GH 6
Jewell, Arlington-, VA 82 II a 2
Jewish Autonomous Region = 13 ◁ 154-155 Z 8
Jeypore 160-161 N 7

Jhang Maghiana = Jhang-Maghiyāna 160-161 L 4
Jhang-Maghiyāna 160-161 L 4
Jhānsi 160-161 M 5
Jhārsuguda 160-161 NO 6
Jharsugura = Jhārsuguda 160-161 NO 6
Jhelum = Jihlam 160-161 L 4

Jiali = Lharugö 166-167 G 5
Jiali = Qionghai 166-167 L 8
Jialing Jiang 166-167 K 5
Jiamusi 166-167 P 2
Ji'an [TJ, Jiangxi] 166-167 LM 6
Ji'an [TJ, Jilin] 170-171 EF 2
Jianchang [TJ → Benxi] 170-171 E 2
Jianchang [TJ ← Jinzhou] 170-171 B 2
Jiangdu = Yangzhou 166-167 M 5
Jiange 166-167 JK 5
Jiangling 166-167 L 5
Jiangmen 166-167 L 7
Jiangsu 166-167 MN 5
Jiangxi 166-167 LM 6
Jian He [TJ, river] 170-171 D 2
Jian'ou 166-167 M 6
Jianping 170-171 B 2
Jianshui 166-167 J 7
Jianyang [TJ, Fujian] 166-167 M 6
Jianyang [TJ, Sichuan] 166-167 JK 5
Jiao Xian 166-167 M 4
Jiaozou 166-167 L 4
Jiaxing 166-167 N 5
Jiayi = Chiayi 166-167 MN 7
Jiayuguan 166-167 H 4
Jibhalanta = Uliastaj 166-167 H 2

Jibhalan 237

Kallsoy 116-117 b 1
Kalmar 114-115 G 9
Kalmar län 114-115 FG 9
Kalmarsund 114-115 G 9
Kalmyk Autonomous Soviet Socialist Republic 142-143 HJ 7
Kalmykovo 154-155 J 8
Kaloko 198 E 3
Kalomo 198 E 5
Kalpeni Island 160-161 L 8
Kalskag, AK 52-53 G 6
Kaltag, AK 52-53 H 4
Kaluga 142-143 G 5
Kalulaui = Kahoolawe 174-175 e 3
Kalundborg 114-115 D 10
Kaluš 142-143 D 6
Kalutara 160-161 MN 9
Kálymnos 138-139 M 7
Kama [CDN] 70-71 G 1
Kama [RCB] 198 E 2
Kama [SU, river] 154-155 J 6
Kamae 170-171 HJ 6
Kamaeura = Kamae 170-171 HJ 6
Kamaishi 166-167 R 4
Kamaishi wan 170-171 NO 3
Kamaisi = Kamaishi 166-167 R 4
Kamakou 78-79 d 2
Kamarān 160-161 E 7
Kamar Bay = Ghubbat al-Qamar 160-161 G 7
Kamba [ZRE] 198 D 2
Kambal'naja sopka = Velikaja Kambalnaja sopka 154-155 e 7
Kambalnaja sopka, Velikaja — 154-155 e 7
Kambia 194-195 B 7
Kambing, Pulau — = Ilha de Ataúro 174-175 J 8
Kambove 198 E 4
Kamčatka 154-155 e 6-7
Kamčatskij poluostrov 154-155 fg 6
Kamčatskij zaliv 154-155 f 6
Kamchatka = Kamčatka 154-155 e 6-7
Kamčija 138-139 M 4
Kamela, OR 66-67 D 3
Kamenec-Podol'skij 142-143 E 6
Kamenjak, Rt — 138-139 E 3
Kamenka [SU, Rossijskaja SFSR Mezenskaja guba] 154-155 G 4
Kamenka [SU, Rossijskaja SFSR Penzenskaja Oblast'] 142-143 H 5
Kamen'-na-Obi 154-155 OP 7
Kamennomostskij 142-143 GH 7
Kamenskoje [SU, Rossijskaja SFSR] 154-155 fg 5
Kamensk-Šachtinskij 142-143 GH 6
Kamensk-Ural'skij 154-155 LM 6
Kamenz 124 FG 3
Kameoka 170-171 K 5
Kames 116-117 F 5
Kameshli = Al-Qāmishlīyah 160-161 E 3
Kāmēt 160-161 M 4
Kamiah, ID 66-67 EF 2
Kamień Pomorski 124 G 2
Kamiiso 170-171 b 3
Kamikawa 170-171 c 2
Kami-Koshiki-shima 170-171 G 7
Kāmil, Al- 160-161 H 6
Kamilīn, Al- 194-195 L 5
Kamina 198 DE 3
Kaministikwia 70-71 EF 1
Kaminokuni 170-171 ab 3
Kaminoshima 170-171 G 5
Kaminoyama 170-171 N 3
Kamishak Bay 52-53 KL 7
Kami-Sihoro 170-171 c 2
Kamitsushima 170-171 G 5
Kamiyaku 170-171 H 7
Kāmlīn, El- = Al-Kamilīn 194-195 L 5
Kamliun, Cape — 52-53 e 1
Kamloops 46-47 MN 7
Kamloops Plateau 48 G 4-5
Kammuri yama 170-171 HJ 5
Kamniokan 154-155 V 6
Kamo [J] 170-171 M 4
Kamoa Mountains 98-99 J 4
Kamoenai 170-171 ab 2
Kamortā Drīp = Camorta Island 160-161 P 9
Kamp 124 G 4
Kampala 198 F 1
Kampar 174-175 D 6
Kamp'o 170-171 G 5
Kampo = Campo 194-195 F 8
Kampolombo, Lake — 198 E 4
Kampot 174-175 D 4
Kampuchéa = Kambodscha 174-175 DE 4
Kampung Pasir Besar 174-175 D 6
Kamsack 49 GH 5
Kamskoje vodochranilišče 154-155 K 6
Kamuchawie Lake 49 G 2
Kamuda 98-99 HJ 2
Kamuela = Waimea, HI 78-79 e 2-3
Kamui-misaki 170-171 ab 2
Kamyšin 142-143 HJ 5
Kamyšlov 154-155 L 6
Kan [SU] 154-155 S 6-7
Kanaaupscow River 46-47 VW 7
Kanab, UT 74-75 G 4
Kanab Creek 74-75 G 4
Kanaga Island 52-53 u 6-7
Kanaga Strait 52-53 u 7
Kanagawa 170-171 M 5
Kanaio, HI 78-79 d 2
Kanakanak, AK 52-53 H 7
Kanala = Canala 182-183 N 4
Kananga 198 D 3
Kanarraville, UT 74-75 G 4
Kanaš 154-155 H 6
Kanawha River 72-73 EF 5
Kanazawa 166-167 Q 4
Kanchanaburi 174-175 C 4
Kancheepuram = Kānchipuram 160-161 MN 8
Kanchenjunga = Gangchhendsönga 160-161 O 5
Kānchipuram 160-161 MN 8
Kanchow = Zhangye 166-167 J 4
Kandahār [AFG] 160-161 K 4
Kandal [K, place] 174-175 DE 4
Kandalakša 154-155 EF 4
Kandalakšskaja guba 154-155 EF 4
Kandangan 174-175 FG 7
Kandavu 174-175 a 2
Kandi [DY] 194-195 E 6
Kandik River 52-53 R 4
Kandla 160-161 L 6
Kandos 182-183 JK 6
Kandreho 198 J 5
Kandy = Maha Nuwara 160-161 N 9
Kane, PA 72-73 G 4
Kane, WY 68-69 BC 3
Kane Basin 46-47 WX 2
Kanektok River 52-53 G 7
Kanem 194-195 H 6
Kaneohe, HI 78-79 d 2
Kanevskaja 142-143 G 6
Kaneyama 170-171 M 4
Kang 198 D 6
Kangar 174-175 D 5
Kangaroo Island 182-183 G 7
Kangaruma 98-99 J 2
Kangding 166-167 J 5-6
Kangean, Pulau — 174-175 G 8
Kangerdlugssuaq [Greenland, bay] 46-47 ef 4
Kangerdlugssuaq [Greenland, place] 46-47 ab 4
Kangetet 198 G 1
Kanggye 166-167 O 3
Kanggyŏng 170-171 F 4
Kanghwa 170-171 F 4
Kanghwa-do 170-171 EF 4
Kanghwa-man 170-171 E 4
Kangik, AK 52-53 GH 1
Kangjin 170-171 F 5
Kangnŭng 170-171 G 4
Kango 198 B 1
Kangsar, Kuala — 174-175 CD 6
Kangsŏ 170-171 E 3
Kan Ho = Gan He 166-167 N 1
Kaniama 198 DE 3
Kaniapiskau Lake 46-47 W 7
Kaniapiskau River 46-47 X 6
Kaniet Islands 174-175 N 7
Kanin, poluostrov — 154-155 GH 4
Kanin Nos [SU, cape] 154-155 G 4
Kanin Nos [SU, place] 142-143 H 2
Kanita 170-171 N 2
Kankakee, IL 58-59 J 3
Kankakee River 70-71 G 5
Kankan 194-195 C 6
Kankō = Hamhŭng 166-167 O 3-4
Kankō = Hŭngnam 166-167 O 4
Kankossa = Kankūssah 194-195 B 5
Kan-kou-chên = Gango 170-171 B 2
Kankūssah 194-195 B 5
Kankyō-hokudō = Hamgyŏng-pukto 170-171 G 2-H 1
Kankyō-nandō = Hamgyŏng-namdo 170-171 FG 2-3
Kannanūr = Cannanore 160-161 LM 8
Kannapolis, NC 80-81 F 3
Kannus 114-115 K 6
Kano [WAN, place] 194-195 F 6
Kanoji 170-171 J 5
Kanopolis Lake 68-69 H 6
Kanorado, KS 68-69 EF 6
Kanosh, UT 74-75 G 3
Kanouri 194-195 G 6
Kanoya 170-171 H 7
Kānpur 160-161 MN 5
Kansas 58-59 FG 4
Kansas, OK 76-77 G 4
Kansas City, KS 58-59 GH 4
Kansas City, MO 58-59 H 4
Kansas River 58-59 G 4
Kansk 154-155 S 6
Kansŏng 170-171 G 3
Kansu = Gansu 166-167 G 3-J 4
Kantalahti = Kandalakša 154-155 EF 4
Kantara = Al-Qanṭarah 199 C 2
Kantchari 194-195 E 6
Kantishna, AK 52-53 M 5
Kantishna River 52-53 M 4
Kantō 170-171 MN 4
Kantō sammyaku 170-171 M 4-5
Kanturk = Ceann Toirc 116-117 BC 8
Kanuchuan Lake 50 EF 1
Kanuku Mountains 98-99 J 3
Kanuma 170-171 M 4
Kanuri = Kanouri 194-195 G 6
Kanuti River 52-53 L 3
Kanyākumārī Antarīp = Cape Comorin 160-161 M 9
Kanye 198 DE 6-7
Kao-an = Gao'an 166-167 LM 6
Kaohsiung 166-167 MN 7
Kaokoveld 198 B 5-6
Kaolack 194-195 A 6
Kaolak River 52-53 G 2
Kaolan = Lanzhou 166-167 JK 4
Kao-li-kung Shan = Gaoligong Shan 166-167 H 6
Kaosiung = Kaohsiung 166-167 MN 7
Kaotai = Gaotai 166-167 H 4
Kaouar 194-195 G 5
Kapaa, HI 78-79 c 1
Kap'a-do 170-171 F 6
Kapagere 174-175 N 8-9
Kapanga 198 D 3
Kapčagajskoje vodochranilišče 160-161 O 9
Kapela 138-139 F 3
Kapfenberg 124 G 5
Kapingamarangi 178 F 2
Kapiri Mposhi 198 E 4
Kapiskau Lake 50 G 1
Kapiskau River 50 G 1-2
Kapit 174-175 F 6
Kaplan, LA 78-79 C 5-6
Kāpōētā 194-195 L 8
Kapona 198 E 3
Kapos 124 J 5
Kaposvár 124 HJ 5
K'appesel'ga 142-143 F 3
Kapsan 170-171 FG 2
Kapsukas 142-143 D 5
Kapuas, Sungai — [RI, Kalimantan Barat] 174-175 F 6
Kapuskasing 46-47 U 8
Kapuskasing River 50 FG 3
Kapustin Jar 142-143 J 6
Kara 154-155 LM 4
Kara Bau 142-143 K 6
Karabekaul 160-161 JK 3
Kara-Bogaz-Gol 142-143 K 7
Kara-Bogaz-Gol, zaliv — 160-161 G 2
Karabük 160-161 C 2
Karabutak 154-155 L 8
Karachayevo-Cherkess Autonomous Region = 2 ◁ 142-143 H 7
Karāchī 160-161 K 6
Kara deniz 160-161 B-D 2
Karadeniz boğazı 160-161 BC 2
Karafuto = Sachalin 154-155 b 7-8
Karagajly 154-155 NO 8
Karaganda 154-155 NO 8
Karagije, Vpadina — 142-143 K 7
Karaginskij, ostrov — 154-155 fg 6
Karaginskij zaliv 154-155 fg 6
Karagoua 194-195 G 6
Karahallı 160-161 C 3
Kāraikkāl = Kārikāl 160-161 MN 8
Karaj 160-161 G 3
Karak, Al- 160-161 D 4
Kara-Kalpak Autonomous Soviet Socialist Republic 108-109 UV 7
Karakelong, Pulau — 174-175 J 6
Karakoram 160-161 L 3-M 4
Karakoram Pass = Qaramurun davan 160-161 MN 3
Karakorē 194-195 MN 6
Karakorum = Char Chorin 166-167 J 2
Karaköse 160-161 E 3
Karakumskij kanal 160-161 J 3
Karakumy 160-161 HJ 3
Karam = Karin 194-195 O 6
Karaman 160-161 C 3
Karamian, Pulau — 174-175 F 8
Karanambo 98-99 J 3
Karas, Pulau — 174-175 K 7
Karasberge, Groot — 198 C 7
Karasburg 198 C 7
Kara Sea 154-155 L 3-Q 2
Kara Shar = Qara Shahr 166-167 F 3
Kara Shar = Qara Shahr 166-167 F 3
Karasjok 114-115 L 3
Karasjokka 114-115 L 3
Karas Mountains, Great — = Groot Karasberge 198 C 7
Kara Strait = proliv Karskije Vorota 154-155 J-L 3
Karasu-Aras dağları 160-161 E 2-3
Karasuk 154-155 O 7
Karatau 154-155 N 9
Karatau, chrebet — 154-155 MN 9
Karatobe 154-155 J 8
Karatsu 170-171 G 6
Karaul 154-155 P 3
Karaussa Nor = Char us nuur 166-167 G 2
Karažal 154-155 N 8
Karbalā' 160-161 E 4
Karcag 124 K 5
Kardeljevo 138-139 G 4
Kardítsa 138-139 JK 6
Kardiva Channel 36 a 1-2
Kărdžali 138-139 L 5
Kareeberge 198 D 8
Kareima = Kuraymah 194-195 L 5
Karelia 142-143 EF 3
Karelian Autonomous Soviet Socialist Republic 154-155 E 4-5
Karel'skaja Avtonomnaja Sovetskaja Socialističeskaja Respublika = Karelian Autonomous Soviet Socialist Republic 154-155 E 4-5
Karelstad = Charlesville 198 D 3
Karema 198 F 3
Karen = Karin Pyinnei 174-175 C 3
Karenni = Karin Pyinnei 174-175 C 3
Karesuando 114-115 JK 3
Karet = Qārrāt 194-195 C 4
Kārēz 160-161 K 4
Kargat 154-155 P 6
Kargopol' 154-155 F 5
Karhula 114-115 M 7
Kariba, Lake — 198 E 5
Kariba Dam 198 E 5
Kariba Gorge 198 EF 5
Kariba-yama 170-171 ab 2
Karibib 198 C 6
Karigasniemi 114-115 LM 3
Kārikāl 160-161 MN 8
Karima = Kuraymah 194-195 L 5
Karimata, Pulau-pulau — 174-175 E 7
Karimata, Selat — 174-175 E 7
Karimon Java Islands = Pulau-pulau Karimunjawa 174-175 EF 8
Karimunjawa, Pulau-pulau — 174-175 EF 8
Karin 194-195 O 6
Karin Pyinnei 174-175 C 3
Karis 114-115 KL 7-8
Karisimbi, Mont — 198 E 2
Kariya 170-171 L 5
Karjaa = Karis 114-115 KL 8
Karjepolje 142-143 H 2
Karkar 194-195 b 2
Karkar Island 174-175 N 7
Karkinitskij zaliv 142-143 F 6
Karkkila 114-115 KL 7
Karkūk = Kirkūk 160-161 EF 3
Karl Alexander, ostrov — 154-155 H-K 1
Karl-Marx-Stadt 124 F 3
Karlobag 138-139 F 3
Karlovac 138-139 F 3
Karlovy Vary 124 F 3
Karlsborg 114-115 F 8
Karlshamn 114-115 F 9
Karlskoga 114-115 F 8
Karlskrona 114-115 FG 9
Karlsruhe 124 D 4
Karlsruhe, ND 68-69 F 1
Karlstad 114-115 EF 8
Karlstad, MN 68-69 H 1
Karluk, AK 52-53 K 8
Karluk Lake 52-53 f 1
Karmah 194-195 L 5
Karmøy 114-115 A 8
Karnak, IL 70-71 F 7
Karnak, Al- 199 C 5
Karnāl 160-161 M 5
Karnataka 160-161 M 7-8
Karnes City, TX 76-77 EF 8
Karnobat 138-139 M 4
Kärnten 124 FG 5
Karnūlu = Kurnool 160-161 M 7
Karoi 198 E 5
Karonga 198 F 3
Karoo, Groot — 198 D 8
Karoo, Klein — 198 D 8
Kārōra 194-195 M 5
Karosa 174-175 G 7
Kárpathos [GR, island] 138-139 M 8
Kárpathos [GR, place] 138-139 M 8
Karpenésion 138-139 JK 6
Karpinsk = Krasnoturjinsk 154-155 L 5-6
Karrats Fjord 46-47 Za 3
Kars 160-161 E 2
Karsakpaj 154-155 M 8
Karsantı 160-161 F 4
Kārši 160-161 K 3
Karskije Vorota, proliv — 154-155 J-L 3
Kartabu 98-99 J 1
Kartaly 154-155 KL 7
Karumba 182-183 H 3
Kārūn, Rūd-e — 160-161 FG 4
Karungi 114-115 K 4-5
Karviná 124 J 4
Kārwār 160-161 L 8
Karyai 138-139 KL 5
Kaş 160-161 BC 3
Kasa = Ui-do 170-171 E 5
Kasabonika Lake 50 E 1
Kasai [ZRE] 198 C 2
Kasai-Occidental 198 CD 2-3
Kasai-Oriental 198 DE 2-3
Kasaji 198 D 4
Kasama 198 F 4
Kasan = Kazan' 154-155 HJ 6
Kasane 198 DE 5
Kasanga 198 F 3
Kasaoka 170-171 J 5
Kasatochi Island 52-53 j 4
Kasba Lake 46-47 Q 5
Kaseda 170-171 H 7
Kasegaluk Lagoon 52-53 EF 2
Kasempa 198 DE 4
Kasenga 198 E 4
Kasenyi 198 EF 1
Kasese 198 EF 1
Kashabowie 70-71 EF 1
Kāshān 160-161 G 4
Kashega, AK 52-53 n 4
Kashegelok, AK 52-53 J 6
Kashgar = Qashqar 166-167 CD 4
Kashghariya 166-167 DE 4
Kashi 166-167 D 4
Kashi = Qāshqār 166-167 CD 4
Kashima 170-171 GH 6
Kashing = Jiaxing 166-167 N 5
Kashishibog Lake 50 E 3
Kashiwazaki 170-171 LM 4
Kāshmar 160-161 H 3-4
Kashmīr 160-161 LM 4
Kashmīr, Jammu and — 160-161 LM 3-4
Kashmor 160-161 O 5
Kashqar = Qāshqār 166-167 CD 4
Kash Rūd = Khāsh Rōd 160-161 J 4
Kasigluk, AK 52-53 F 6
Kasilof, AK 52-53 M 6
Kasimov 154-155 G 7
Kašin 142-143 G 4
Kašira 142-143 G 5
Kasirota = Pulau Kasiruta 174-175 J 7
Kasiruta, Pulau — 174-175 J 7
Kasivobara = Severo-Kuril'sk 154-155 de 7
Kaskaskia River 70-71 F 6
Kaskinen = Kaskö 114-115 J 6
Kaskö 114-115 J 6
Kaslo 48 J 5
Kasongo 198 E 2
Kásos 138-139 M 8
Kassai = Kasai 198 C 2
Kassalā 194-195 M 5
Kassándra 138-139 K 5-6
Kassel 124 D 3
Kasserine = Al-Qasrayn 194-195 F 1-2
Kastamonu 160-161 CD 2
Kastamum = Kastamonu 160-161 CD 2
Kasteli Selianou = Palaiochṓra 138-139 KL 8
Kastéllion 138-139 K 8
Kastoría 138-139 J 5
Kastornoje 142-143 G 5
Kasulu 198 F 2
Kasumiga ura 170-171 N 5
Kasungu 198 F 4
Kasur = Qaṣūr 160-161 L 4
Kataba 198 DE 5
Katahdin, Mount — 58-59 MN 2
Kaṭaka = Cuttack 160-161 NO 6
Katakturuk River 52-53 P 2
Katakumba 198 D 3
Katalla, AK 52-53 P 6
Katami sammyaku 170-171 c 1-2
Katanga 154-155 T 5-6
Katanga = Shaba 198 DE 3
Katangli 154-155 b 7
Katanning 182-183 C 6
Katav-Ivanovsk 154-155 K 7
Katāwāz 160-161 K 4
Katchal Island 160-161 P 9
Katchall Island 174-175 B 5
Kateel River 52-53 H 4
Katenga 198 E 3
Katerîna, Gebel — = Jabal Katrīnah 194-195 L 3
Katerinē 138-139 K 5
Kates Needle 46-47 KL 6
Katete 198 F 4
Kathā 174-175 C 2
Katherina, Gebel — = Jabal Katrīnah 194-195 L 3
Katherine 182-183 F 2
Kāthiāwār 160-161 K 6
Kathlambagebirge = Drakensberge 198 E 8-F 7
Kathleen Lake 70-71 J 2
Kathleen Lakes 52-53 T 6
Kati 194-195 C 6
Katif, El- = Al-Qaṭīf 160-161 F 5
Katihār 160-161 O 5
Katimik Lake 49 J 4
Katiola 194-195 CD 7
Katmai, Mount — 46-47 F 6
Katmai Bay 52-53 K 8
Katmai National Monument 46-47 EF 6
Kātmāndu 160-161 NO 5
Káto Achaïa 138-139 J 6
Katomba 182-183 JK 6
Katoomba = Blue Mountains 182-183 JK 6
Katowice 124 J 3
Katrīnah, Jabal — 194-195 L 3
Katrineholm 114-115 G 8
Katsina 194-195 F 6
Katsina Ala [WAN, place] 194-195 F 7
Katsuda 170-171 N 4
Katsumoto 170-171 G 6
Katsuura 170-171 N 5
Katsuyama 170-171 L 4
Katta = Katsuta 170-171 N 4
Kattakurgan 160-161 K 2-3
Kattegat 114-115 D 9
Katy, TX 76-77 G 8
Kau, Teluk — 174-175 J 6
Kauai 174-175 e 3
Kauai Channel 174-175 e 3
Kaufbeuren 124 E 5
Kaufman, TX 76-77 FG 6
Kauhajoki 114-115 JK 6
Kaukauna, WI 70-71 F 3
Kaukauveld 198 D 5
Kaula 78-79 b 2
Kaulakahi Channel 78-79 b 1-c 2
Kauliranta 114-115 KL 4
Kaulun = Kowloon 166-167 LM 7
Kaunakakai, HI 78-79 d 2
Kauna Point 78-79 de 3
Kaunas 142-143 D 4-5
Kaura Namoda 194-195 F 6
Kautokeino 114-115 KL 3
Kavajë 138-139 H 5
Kavalga Island 52-53 t 7
Kaval'kan 154-155 a 6
Kavaratti 160-161 L 8
Kavaratti Island 160-161 L 8
Kavardhā = Kawardha 160-161 N 6
Kavarna 138-139 N 4
Kavieng 174-175 h 5
Kavik River 52-53 O 2
Kavīr, Dasht-e — 160-161 GH 4
Kavīr-e Khorāsān = Dasht-e Kavīr 160-161 GH 4
Kavīr-e Lūt 154-155 J 5
Kavīr-e Namak-e Mīghān 160-161 H 4
Kaw 98-99 J 4
Kawagoe 170-171 M 5
Kawaguchi 170-171 MN 4-5
Kawaharada = Sawata 170-171 M 3-4
Kawaihae, HI 174-175 e 3
Kawaihoa Point 78-79 b 2
Kawaikini 78-79 c 1
Kawamata 170-171 N 4
Kawambwa 198 EF 3
Kawanoe 170-171 J 5-6
Kawardha 160-161 N 6
Kawasaki 166-167 QR 4
Kawashiri-misaki 170-171 H 5
Kawene 70-71 E 1
Kawich Range 74-75 E 3-4
Kawimbe 198 F 3
Kawinaw Lake 49 J 4
Kawlin 174-175 C 2
Kawm Umbū 194-195 L 4
Kawnipi Lake 70-71 E 1
Kawn Ken = Khon Kaen 174-175 D 3
Kawthaung 174-175 C 4
Kaya [HV] 194-195 D 6
Kaya [J] 170-171 K 5
Kaya [RI] 174-175 G 6
Kayak Island 46-47 H 6
Kayambi 198 F 3
Kayā Pyinnei 174-175 C 3
Kaya-san 170-171 G 5
Kaycee, WY 68-69 C 4
Kayenta, AZ 74-75 H 4
Kayes 194-195 B 6
Kayhaydi 194-195 B 5
Kayoa, Pulau — 174-175 J 6
Kay Point 52-53 S 2
Kayser Gebergte 98-99 K 3
Kayseri 160-161 D 3
Kaysville, UT 66-67 GH 5
Kayuagung 174-175 DE 7
Kayville 49 F 6
Kazachskaja guba 142-143 K 7
Kazachskaja Sovetskaja Socialističeskaja Respublika = Kazakh Soviet Socialist Republic 154-155 J-P 8
Kazachskij Melkosopočnik 154-155 M-P 7-8
Kazachstan = Aksaj 154-155 J 7
Kazačinskoje [SU, Jenisej] 154-155 R 6
Kazačinskoje [SU, Kirenga] 154-155 U 6
Kazačje 154-155 a 3
Kazakh Soviet Socialist Republic 154-155 J-P 8
Kazakhstan 110-111 T-V 6
Kazakhstan = Kazakh Soviet Socialist Republic 154-155 J-P 8
Kazakh Uplands = Kazachskij Melkosopočnik 154-155 M-P 7-8
Kazamoto = Katsumoto 170-171 G 6
Kazan' [SU, Tatarskaja ASSR] 154-155 HJ 6
Kazandžik 160-161 GH 3
Kazanlak 138-139 L 4
Kazan Lake 49 D 3
Kazan-rettō = Volcano Islands 148-149 RS 7
Kazan River 46-47 Q 5
Kazanskoje [SU, Zapadno-Sibirskaja nizmennost'] 154-155 M 6
Kazatin 142-143 E 6
Kazbek, gora — 142-143 H 7
Kāzerūn 160-161 G 5
Kazi-Magomed 142-143 J 7
Kazincbarcika 124 K 4
Kazumba 198 D 3
Kazungula 198 E 5
Kazvin = Qazvīn 160-161 FG 3

Kazvin 239

Kazym [SU, place] 154-155 M 5
Kazym [SU, river] 142-143 N 3

Kbīr Kūh 160-161 F 4

Kea 138-139 L 7
Keaau, HI 78-79 e 3
Keady 116-117 E 6
Kealaikahiki Channel 78-79 d 2
Kealakekua Bay 78-79 de 3
Keams Canyon, AZ 74-75 H 5
Kearney, NE 58-59 G 3
Kearny, NJ 82 III b 2
Kebâng 160-161 PQ 5
Kebbi = Sokoto 194-195 EF 6
Kébémer 194-195 A 5
Kebkābiya = Kabkābīyah 194-195 J 6
Kebnekajse 114-115 H 4
Kebumen 174-175 E 8
Kecskemét 124 J 5
Keddie, CA 74-75 C 2-3
Kedia d'Idjil = Kidyat Ijjill 194-195 B 4
Kediri 174-175 F 8
Kédougou 194-195 B 6
Keele Peak 46-47 KL 5
Keeler, CA 74-75 E 4
Keele River 46-47 L 5
Keeley Lake 49 D 3
Keeling Basin 26-27 OP 6
Keelung = Chilung 166-167 N 6
Keen, Mount — 116-117 J 4
Keene, NH 72-73 K 3
Keeseville, NY 72-73 K 2
Keetmanshoop 198 C 7
Keewatin 50 B 3
Keewatin, District of — 46-47 RS 4-5
Keewatin River 49 H 2
Keezhik Lake 50 E 2
Kefa 194-195 M 7
Kefallēnía 138-139 J 6
Kéfalos 138-139 M 7
Kefamenanu 174-175 HJ 8
Kéfisiá 138-139 KL 6
Keflavík 114-115 b 2-3
Kegaska 51 F 2
Kégueur Terbi 194-195 H 4
Kehl 124 CD 4
Keighley 116-117 K 7
Kei Islands = Kepulauan Kai 174-175 K 8
Keiki-dō = Kyŏnggi-do 170-171 F 4
Keishō-hokudō = Kyŏngsang-pukto 170-171 G 4
Keishō-nandō = Kyŏngsang-namdo 170-171 FG 5
Keitele 114-115 LM 6
Keith [AUS] 182-183 GH 7
Keith [GB] 116-117 J 3
Keith Arm 46-47 M 4
Keithsburg, IL 70-71 E 5
Keithville, LA 76-77 GH 6
Kejimkujik National Park 51 D 5
Kejvy 142-143 G 2
Kelafo 194-195 N 7
Kelfield 49 D 5
Kelford, NC 80-81 H 2
Kelifely, Causse du — 198 HJ 5
Kelil'vun, gora — 154-155 g 4
Kelkit çayı 142-143 G 7
Kellé 198 B 1-2
Keller Lake 46-47 M 5
Kellett, Cape — 46-47 L 3
Kelleys Island 72-73 E 4
Kelleys Islands 72-73 E 4
Kelliher 49 G 5
Kelliher, MN 70-71 C 1-2
Kellogg, ID 66-67 EF 2
Kelloselkä 114-115 N 4
Kells = Ceanannas 116-117 DE 7
Kelly, Mount — 52-53 EF 2
Kelly River 52-53 F 2
Kélo 194-195 H 7
Kelowna 46-47 N 7-8
Kelsey Bay 48 D 4
Kelso, CA 74-75 F 5
Kelso, WA 66-67 B 2
Kelso [GB] 116-117 J 5
Kelso [ZA] 198 F 8
Kelton Pass 66-67 G 5
Kelulun He = Herlen He 166-167 M 2
Kelvin, AZ 74-75 H 6
Kelvington 49 G 4
Kelvin Island 50 E 3
Kem' [SU, place] 154-155 E 4
Kemā 166-167 H 6
Kê-Macina 194-195 C 6
Kemanai = Towada 170-171 N 2
Kembalpūr 160-161 L 4
Kembolcha 194-195 MN 6
Kemerovo 154-155 PQ 6
Kemi 114-115 L 5
Kemijärvi [SF, lake] 114-115 MN 4
Kemijärvi [SF, place] 114-115 M 4
Kemijoki 114-115 L 4-5
Kemijoki = Kem' 154-155 E 4
Kemmerer, WY 66-67 H 5
Kemnay 49 H 6
Kémo-Gribingui 194-195 H 7
Kemp, TX 76-77 F 6
Kemp, Lake — 76-77 E 6
Kemp Land 31 C 6
Kemp Peninsula 31 B 31
Kempsey 182-183 K 6
Kempston 116-117 L 8
Kempt, Lac — 72-73 JK 1
Kempten 124 E 5
Kemptville 72-73 HJ 2
Kena = Qinā 194-195 L 3
Kenai, AK 46-47 F 5
Kenai Lake 52-53 N 6
Kenai Mountains 46-47 F 6-G 5
Kenai Peninsula 46-47 FG 5
Kenamo 46-47 L 7
Kenansville, FL 80-81 c 3
Kenaston 49 EF 5
Kenbridge, VA 80-81 GH 2
Kendal 116-117 J 6
Kendall, KS 68-69 F 7
Kendallville, IN 70-71 H 5
Kendari 174-175 H 7
Kendawangan 174-175 F 7
Kendikolu 36 a 1
Kēndrāpaḍā = Kendrāpāra 160-161 O 6
Kendrāpāra 160-161 O 6
Kendrick, ID 66-67 E 2
Kenedy, TX 76-77 EF 8
Kenema 194-195 B 7
Kenesaw, NE 68-69 G 5
Kenge 198 C 2
Kengtung = Kyöngdôn 174-175 CD 2
Kenhardt 198 D 7
Kenia 198 G 1
Kenibuna Lake 52-53 L 6
Kéniéba 194-195 B 6
Kenilworth 116-117 K 8
Kenitra = Al-Q'nitrah 194-195 C 2
Kenmare, ND 68-69 EF 1
Kenmare = Neidín 116-117 B 9
Kenmare River = An Ribhéar 116-117 AB 9
Kenmore, NY 72-73 G 3
Kenna, NM 76-77 BC 6
Kennebec, SC 68-69 FG 4
Kennebec River 72-73 LM 2
Kennebunk, ME 72-73 L 3
Kennedy 49 GH 5
Kennedy, Mount — 46-47 J 5
Kennedy Channel 46-47 WX 1-2
Kenner, LA 78-79 D 5-6
Kennett, MO 78-79 DE 2
Kennewick, WA 66-67 D 2
Kenney Dam 46-47 M 7
Kennicott, AK 52-53 Q 6
Kénogami 51 A 3
Kenogami River 50 G 2
Kenogamissi Falls 50 L 2-3
Keno Hill 46-47 JK 5
Kenonisca, Lac — 50 NO 1
Kenora 46-47 S 8
Kenosha, WI 58-59 J 3
Kenova, WV 72-73 E 5
Kensal, ND 68-69 G 2
Kensett, AR 78-79 D 3
Kensington 51 E 4
Kensington, CA 83 I c 1
Kensington, New York-, NY 82 III c 3
Kent 116-117 M 9
Kent, MN 68-69 H 2
Kent, OH 72-73 F 4
Kent, OR 66-67 C 3
Kent, TX 76-77 B 7
Kent, WA 66-67 B 2
Kent, Washington-, DC 82 II a 1
Kentau 154-155 M 9
Kent Junction 51 D 4
Kentland, IN 70-71 G 5
Kenton, OH 72-73 E 4
Kenton, OK 76-77 C 4
Kent Peninsula 46-47 P 4
Kentucky 58-59 JK 4
Kentucky Lake 58-59 J 4
Kentucky River 70-71 H 6
Kent Village, MD 82 II b 1
Kentville 51 D 5
Kentwood, LA 78-79 D 5
Kenya 198 GH 1
Kenya, Mount — 198 G 1-2
Keokuk, IA 58-59 H 3
Keosauqua, IA 70-71 E 5
Kępno 124 J 3
Keppel Bay 182-183 K 4
Kerala 160-161 M 8-9
Kerang 182-183 H 7
Kerasūs = Giresun 160-161 D 2
Kerava 114-115 L 7
Kerbi = Poliny-Osipenko 154-155 a 7
Kerby, OR 66-67 B 4
Kerč 142-143 G 6
Kerčel 142-143 M 4
Kerčenskij proliv 142-143 G 6-7
Kerema 174-175 N 8
Keren 194-195 M 5
Kerens, TX 76-77 F 6
Kerga 142-143 J 3
Kerguelen 26-27 N 8
Kerguelen-Gaussberg Ridge 26-27 N 8-O 9
Kerinci, Gunung — 174-175 D 7
Keriske 154-155 Z 4
Keriya 166-167 E 4
Keriya Darya 166-167 E 4
Kerkenah Island = Juzur Qarqannah 194-195 G 2
Kerkenna, Îles — = Jazur Qarqannah 194-195 G 2
Kerkhoven, MN 70-71 C 3
Kerki 160-161 K 3
Kérkyra [GR, island] 138-139 H 6
Kérkyra [GR, place] 138-139 H 6
Kerling 114-115 de 2
Kerlingarfjöll 114-115 d 2
Kerma = Karmah 194-195 L 5
Kermadec Islands 182-183 PQ 6
Kermadec Tonga Trench 34-35 J 5-6
Kermān 160-161 H 4
Kerman, CA 74-75 CD 4
Kermānshāh 160-161 F 4
Kermānshāhān = 1 ◁ 160-161 F 4
Kerme körfezi 142-143 E 8
Kermit, TX 76-77 C 7
Kern River 74-75 D 5
Kernville, CA 74-75 D 5
Kérouané 194-195 C 7
Kerrick, TX 76-77 C 4
Kerrobert 49 D 4-5
Kerrville, TX 76-77 E 7
Kerry = Ciarraighe 116-117 B 8-9
Kerry Head = Ceann Chiarraighe 116-117 AB 8
Kershaw, SC 80-81 F 3
Kersley 48 F 3
Kerulen = Cherlen gol 166-167 L 2
Kesagami Lake 50 L 1
Kesagami River 50 LM 1
Keşan 142-143 E 7
Kesennuma 170-171 NO 3
Kesh 116-117 D 6
Keshan 166-167 O 2
Keski-Suomen lääni 114-115 L 6
Kestenga 114-115 OP 5
Kesten'ga 154-155 E 4
Keswick 116-117 HJ 6
Keszthely 124 H 5
Ket' 154-155 P 6
Keta 194-195 E 7
Keta, ozero — 154-155 QR 4
Ketapang [RI, Kalimantan] 174-175 EF 7
Ketchikan, AK 46-47 K 6
Ketchum, ID 66-67 F 4
Kete Krachi 194-195 DE 7
Ketik River 52-53 H 2
Ketok Mount 52-53 J 7
Kętrzyn 124 K 1-2
Kettering 116-117 L 8
Kettering, OH 72-73 DE 5
Kettharin Kyûn 174-175 C 4
Kettle Falls, WA 66-67 DE 1
Kettle Point 72-73 EF 3
Kettle River [CDN] 66-67 D 1
Kettle River [USA] 70-71 D 2
Kettle River Range 66-67 D 1
Kevin, MT 66-67 H 1
Kevir = Kavīr-e Namak-e Mīghān 160-161 GH 4
Kew 88-89 KL 4
Kewanee, IL 70-71 F 5
Kewaunee, WI 70-71 G 3
Keweenaw Bay 70-71 FG 2
Keweenaw Peninsula 58-59 J 2
Keweenaw Point 70-71 G 2
Keweigek 98-99 H 2
Kewir = Kavīr-e Namak-e Mīghān 160-161 GH 4
Kexholm = Priozʼorsk 154-155 DE 5
Key, Lough — = Loch Cé 116-117 C 6
Keyaluvik, AK 52-53 E 6
Keya Paha River 68-69 FG 4
Keyes, OK 76-77 C 4
Key Harbour 72-73 F 2
Keyhole Reservoir 68-69 D 3
Key Junction 72-73 F 2
Key Largo 80-81 cd 4
Key Largo, FL 80-81 c 4
Keyser, WV 72-73 G 5
Keystone, SD 68-69 E 4
Keysville, VA 80-81 G 2
Key West, FL 58-59 K 7
Kezar Stadium 83 I b 2
Kežma 154-155 T 6
Kežmarok 124 K 4

Kgun Lake 52-53 EF 6

Khaanzuur, Raas — 194-195 ab 1
Khabarovsk = Chabarovsk 154-155 a 8
Khabir, Zab al- 142-143 H 8
Khābūr, Nahr al- 160-161 E 3
Khābūrah, Al- 160-161 H 6
Khaibar = Shurayf 160-161 D 5
Khaibar, Kotal — 160-161 L 4
Khaīj as-Sintirā', Al- 194-195 A 4
Khairābād 160-161 N 5
Khairpūr [PAK, Punjab] 160-161 K 5
Khakass Autonomous Region = 10 ◁ 154-155 R 7
Khaliq tau 166-167 E 3
Khalki = Chálkē 138-139 M 7
Khalūf, Al- 160-161 H 6
Kham 166-167 H 5
Khamāsīn, Al- 160-161 EF 6
Khambat = Cambay 160-161 L 6
Khambhāt = Cambay 160-161 L 6
Khambhāt nī Khāḍī = Gulf of Cambay 160-161 L 6
Khamir 160-161 E 7
Khāmis, Ash-Shallāl al- 194-195 L 5
Khampa Dsong 166-167 F 6
Khamsa, Bi'r el- = Bi'r al-Khamsah 194-195 K 2
Khamsha, Bi'r al- 194-195 K 2
Khandaq, Al- 194-195 KL 5
Khandaq, El- = Al-Khandaq 194-195 KL 5
Khaṅḍavā = Khandwa 160-161 M 6
Khandwa 160-161 M 6
Khangai = Changajn nuruu 166-167 HJ 2
Khania = Chaniá 138-139 KL 8
Khanion Bay = Kólpos Chaniōn 138-139 KL 8
Khāniqīn 160-161 F 4
Khānpūr [PAK, Sindh] 160-161 KL 5
Khanshalah 194-195 F 1
Khantan = Kuantan 174-175 D 6
Khanty-Mansi Autonomous Area 154-155 L-P 5
Khanty-Mansiysk = Chanty-Mansijsk 154-155 M 5
Khān Yūnūs 199 CD 2
Khanzi 198 D 6
Khanzi = Ghanzi 198 D 6
Khānzūr, Ras — = Raas Khaanzuur 194-195 ab 1
Kharāb, Al- 160-161 EF 7
Kharagpur [IND, West Bengal] 160-161 O 6
Kharan Kalat = Khārān Qalāt 160-161 K 5
Khārān Qalāt 160-161 K 5
Kharaz, Jabal — 160-161 E 8
Kharbin = Harbin 166-167 O 2
Khārga, El- = Al-Khārījah 194-195 L 3
Khārga, Wâhât el- = Al-Wāḥāt al-Khārījah 194-195 KL 3-4
Kharīfūt 160-161 G 7
Khārījah, Al- 194-195 L 3
Khārījah, Al-Wāḥāt al- 194-195 KL 3-4
Kharīṭ, Wādī al- 199 CD 5
Kharīṭ, Wâdī el- = Wādī al-Kharīṭ 199 CD 5
Kharj, Al- 160-161 F 6
Khārk, Jazīreh-ye — 160-161 FG 5
Kharkov = Char'kov 142-143 G 5
Khartoum = Al-Kharṭum 194-195 L 5
Khartoum North = Al-Kharṭūm Baḥrī 194-195 L 5
Kharṭūm, Al- 194-195 L 5
Khartūm Baḥri, Al- 194-195 L 5
Kharṭūm Baḥrī, El- = Al-Kharṭūm Baḥrī 194-195 L 5
Khaṣab, Al- 160-161 H 5
Khashm al-Qirbah 194-195 LM 6
Khāsh Rōd 160-161 J 4
Khaṭāṭba, El- = Al-Haṭāṭibah 199 B 2
Khaṭṭ, Wād al- 194-195 B 3
Khāvarī, Āzarbāyejān-e- 160-161 EF 3
Khawr al-Fakkān 160-161 H 5
Khawr Rūrī 160-161 G 7
Khay' 160-161 E 7
Khaybar, Ḥarrat — 160-161 DE 5
Khazhung Tsho 166-167 F 5
Khemarat 174-175 DE 3
Khem Belder = Kyzyl 154-155 R 7
Khenachich, El — 194-195 D 4
Khenachich, Oglat — 194-195 D 4
Khenchela = Khanshalah 194-195 F 1
Khentei Nuruu = Chentin nuruu 166-167 K 2
Khios = Chíos 138-139 L 6
Khīrābād = Khairābād 160-161 N 5
Khirr, Wādī al- 160-161 E 4
Khobdo = Chovd 166-167 G 2
Khobso Gol = Chövsgöl nuur 166-167 J 1
Khökh Nuur = Chöch nuur 166-167 H 4
Khomas Highland = Khomasplato 198 C 6
Khomasplato 198 C 6
Khomeyn 142-143 JK 9
Khong Sedone 174-175 E 3
Khon Kaen 174-175 D 3
Khor 142-143 L 9
Khorāsān 160-161 H 3-4
Khorāsān, Kavīr-e — = Kavīr-e Namak-e Mīghān 160-161 H 4
Khorat = Nakhon Ratchasima 174-175 D 3-4
Khorramābād [IR, Lorestān] 160-161 FG 4
Khorramshahr 160-161 F 4
Khotan 166-167 DE 4
Khotan darya 166-167 E 3-4
Khotol Mount 52-53 J 4
Khourîbga = Khurībgah 194-195 C 2
Khuff 160-161 E 6
Khükhe Noor = Chöch nuur 166-167 H 4
Khums, Al- 194-195 GH 2
Khurasan = Khorāsān 160-161 H 3-4
Khurayṣ 160-161 F 5
Khurībgah 194-195 C 2
Khūrīyā Mūrīyā, Jazā'ir — 160-161 H 7
Khurmah, Al- 160-161 E 6
Khushāb 160-161 L 4
Khūzdār 160-161 K 5
Khūzestān 160-161 F 4
Khuzistan = Khuzestan 160-161 F 4
Khvāf 160-161 J 4
Khvostof Island 52-53 s 6
Khvoy 160-161 EF 3
Khwāf = Khvāf 160-161 J 4
Khyber Pass = Kotal Khāibar 160-161 L 4
Khyetentshering 166-167 G 5

Kiambi 198 E 3
Kiamichi Mountains 76-77 G 5
Kiamichi River 76-77 G 5-6
Kiamusze = Jiamusi 166-167 P 2
Kian = Ji'an 166-167 LM 6
Kiana, AK 52-53 G 3
Kiangning = Nanjing 166-167 M 5
Kiangsi = Jiangxi 166-167 LM 6
Kiangsu = Jiangsu 166-167 MN 5
Kiantajärvi 114-115 N 5
Kiaohsien = Jiao Xian 166-167 M 4
Kiawah Island 80-81 FG 4
Kiayukwan = Jiuquan 166-167 H 4
Kibaha = Bagamoyo 198 G 3
Kibali 198 EF 1
Kibamba 198 E 2
Kibangou 198 B 2
Kibau 198 FG 3
Kibaya 198 G 3
Kiberege 198 G 3
Kibombo 198 E 2
Kibondo 198 F 2
Kibungu 198 F 2
Kibwezi 198 G 2
Kičevo 138-139 J 5
Kichčik 154-155 de 7
Kicking Horse Pass 46-47 NO 7
Kidal 194-195 E 5
Kidatu 198 G 3
Kidderminster 116-117 JK 8
Kidepo National Park 198 F 1
Kidira 194-195 B 6
Kidsgrove 116-117 J 7
Kidston 182-183 H 3
Kidwelly 116-117 G 9
Kiel 124 E 1
Kiel, WI 70-71 F 4
Kiel Canal = Nord-Ostsee-Kanal 124 D 1-2
Kielce 124 K 3
Kieler Bucht 124 E 1
Kiên Hung = Go Quao 174-175 DE 5
Kienning = Jian'ou 166-167 M 6
Kienshui = Jianshui 166-167 J 7
Kierunavaara 114-115 J 4
Kiestinki = Kesten'ga 154-155 E 4
Kieta 174-175 j 6
Kīfah 194-195 B 5
Kiffa = Kīfah 194-195 B 5
Kigali 198 F 2
Kigalik River 52-53 K 2
Kigluaik Mountains 52-53 DE 4
Kigoma 198 E 2
Kiha = Kwiha 194-195 MN 6
Kiholo, HI 78-79 e 3
Kihti = Skiftet 114-115 J 7
Kii hantō 166-167 Q 5
Kii sammyaku 170-171 KL 5-6
Kii-suidō 166-167 PQ 5
Kijang 170-171 G 5
Kijev 142-143 F 5
Kijevka [SU, Kazachskaja SSSR] 154-155 N 7
Kijevka [SU, Rossijskaja SFSR] 170-171 J 1
Kijevskoje vodochranilišče 142-143 F 5
Kijik, AK 52-53 K 6
Kikiakrorak River 52-53 L 2
Kikinda 138-139 J 3
Kikonai 170-171 B 3
Kikori 174-175 M 8
Kikwit 198 C 3
Kil 114-115 E 8
Kilambé, Cerro — 88-89 CD 8
Kilauea Crater 174-175 ef 4
Kilbrannan Sound 116-117 F 5
Kilbuck Mountains 46-47 E 5-D 6
Kilchu 170-171 G 2
Kilcoy 182-183 K 5
Kildare = Cill Dara [IRL, administrative unit] 116-117 E 7-8
Kildare = Cill Dara [IRL, place] 116-117 E 7
Kil'din 142-143 FG 2
Kildinstroj 114-115 PQ 3
Kildonan 198 F 5
Kilgore, ID 66-67 GH 3
Kilgore, TX 76-77 G 6
Kili 178 G 2
Kilifi 198 GH 2
Kiligwa River 52-53 H 2
Kilimanjaro [EAT, administrative unit] 198 G 2
Kilimanjaro [EAT, mountain] 198 G 2
Kilimatinde 198 FG 3
Kilin = Jilin 166-167 N 2-O 3
Kilis 142-143 G 8
Kiliuda Bay 52-53 g 1
Kilkee = Cill Chaoidhe 116-117 AB 8
Kilkeel 116-117 EF 6
Kilkenny = Cill Chainnigh 116-117 D 8
Kilkieran Bay = Cuan Chill Chiarain 116-117 AB 7
Kilkis 138-139 K 5
Killala Bay = Cuan Chill Alaidh 116-117 B 6
Killala Lake 70-71 G 1
Killaloe = Cill Dalua 116-117 C 8
Killam 49 C 4
Killarney [CDN] 68-69 FG 1
Killarney = Cill Áirne 116-117 B 8
Killary Harbour = Caolshàile Rua 116-117 AB 7
Killashandra = Cill na Sean-rátha 116-117 D 6-7
Killdeer 68-69 C 1
Killdeer, ND 68-69 E 2
Killdeer Mountains 68-69 E 2
Killeen, TX 76-77 F 7
Killiecrankie, Pass of — 116-117 H 4
Killik River 52-53 KL 2
Killin 116-117 G 4
Killinek Island 46-47 Y 5
Killington Peak 72-73 K 3
Killough 116-117 F 6
Kill van Kull 82 III b 3
Killybegs = Na Cealla Beaga 116-117 C 6
Kilmarnock 116-117 G 5
Kilmelfort 116-117 F 4
Kil'mez 142-143 K 4
Kilmichael, MS 78-79 E 4
Kilombero 198 G 3
Ki-long = Chilung 166-167 N 6
Kilosa 198 G 3
Kilossa = Kilosa 198 G 3
Kilpisjärvi 114-115 J 3
Kilrea 116-117 E 6
Kilrenny 116-117 J 4
Kilrush = Cill Ruis 116-117 B 8
Kilsyth 116-117 G 4-5
Kiltān Island 160-161 L 8
Kilwa 198 E 3
Kilwa Kisiwani 198 GH 3
Kilwa-Kissiwni = Kilwa Kisiwani 198 GH 3
Kilwa Kivinje 198 GH 3
Kilwa-Kiwindje = Kilwa Kivinje 198 GH 3
Kim, CO 68-69 E 7
Kimaam 174-175 L 8
Kimama, ID 66-67 G 4
Kimasozero 114-115 O 5
Kimball, MN 70-71 C 3
Kimball, NE 68-69 E 5
Kimball, SD 68-69 G 4
Kimball, Mount — 52-53 PQ 5
Kimbe 174-175 gh 6
Kimbe Bay 174-175 h 6
Kimberley [AUS] 182-183 E 3
Kimberley [CDN] 46-47 NO 8
Kimberley [ZA] 198 DE 7
Kimberly, NV 74-75 F 3
Kimchaek 166-167 OP 3
Kimch'ŏn 166-167 O 4
Kimje 170-171 F 5
Kimkang = Chengmai 166-167 KL 8
Kimōlos 138-139 L 7
Kimpoku san 170-171 LM 3
Kimry 154-155 F 6
Kimuenza 198 C 2
Kinabalu, Gunung — 174-175 G 5
Kinak Bay 52-53 F 7
Kinaskan Lake 52-53 WX 8
Kinbasket Lake 48 HJ 4
Kinbrace 116-117 H 2
Kincaid, KS 70-71 C 6
Kincardine [CDN] 72-73 F 2
Kincardine [GB] 116-117 J 3-4
Kinchinjunga = Gangchhendsönga 160-161 O 5
Kincolith 48 BC 2
Kinder, LA 78-79 C 5
Kindersley 46-47 P 7
Kindia 194-195 B 6
Kindu 198 E 2
Kinel' 154-155 J 7
Kinešma 154-155 G 6
King and Queen Court House, VA 80-81 H 2
King Charles Land = Kong Karlsland 114-115 mn 5
Kingchow = Jiangling 166-167 L 5
King Christian IX Land = Kong Christian den IX[e] Land 30 C 22
Kingchwan = Jingchuan 166-167 K 4
King City, CA 74-75 C 4
King City, MO 70-71 C 5
King Cove, AK 52-53 bc 2
King Edward VIIIth Gulf 31 C 6-7
King Edward VIIth Land = Edward VIIth Peninsula 31 B 21-22
King Edward VIIth Plateau = Dronning Maud fjellkjede 31 A
Kingfisher, OK 76-77 F 5
King Frederik VIII Land = Kong Frederik den VIII[s] Land 30 B 21
King Frederik VI Land = Kong Frederik den VI[s] Kyst 30 C 23

240 **Kazym**

King George Island 31 CD 30-31
King George Sound 182-183 CD 7
King George VIth Sound 31 B 29-30
King George Vth Land 31 BC 15-16
King Hill, ID 66-67 F 4
Kingisepp 142-143 D 4
King Island [AUS] 182-183 H 7
King Island [CDN] 48 D 3
King Island [USA] 52-53 C 4
King Island = Kadan Kyûn 174-175 C 4
Kingku = Jinggu 166-167 J 7
King Lear 66-67 D 5
King Leopold Ranges 182-183 DE 3
Kingman, AZ 74-75 FG 5
Kingman, KS 68-69 GH 7
King Mountain [USA, Oregon] 66-67 D 4
King Mountain [USA, Texas] 76-77 C 7
Kingoonya 182-183 G 6
King Oscar Land 46-47 TU 2
King Salmon, AK 52-53 JK 7
King Salmon River [CDN ◁ Egegik Bay] 52-53 J 7
King Salmon River [CDN ◁ Nushagak River] 52-53 HJ 6
Kingsbridge 116-117 H 10
Kings Canyon National Park 74-75 D 4
Kingsclere 116-117 KL 9
Kingscote 182-183 G 7
Kingscourt = Dún a'Rí 116-117 DE 7
Kingsland, GA 80-81 F 5
Kingsland, TX 76-77 E 7
Kingsley, IA 70-71 BC 4
King's Lynn 116-117 M 8
Kings Mountain, NC 80-81 F 3
King Sound 182-183 D 3
Kings Peaks 58-59 DE 3
Kings Point, NY 82 III d 2
Kingsport 51 D 5
Kingsport, TN 80-81 E 2
Kings River 74-75 CD 4
Kingston, MO 70-71 C 6
Kingston, NY 72-73 JK 4
Kingston, OK 76-77 F 5-6
Kingston, PA 72-73 HJ 4
Kingston, WA 66-67 B 2
Kingston [CDN] 46-47 Y 9
Kingston [JA] 58-59 L 8
Kingston [NZ] 182-183 N 9
Kingston Peak 74-75 EF 5
Kingston SE 182-183 G 7
Kingston upon Hull 116-117 LM 7
Kingston upon Thames, London- 116-117 L 9
Kingstown [West Indies] 58-59 O 9
Kingstown = Dún Laoghaire 116-117 EF 7
Kingstree, SC 80-81 G 4
Kingsville, TX 58-59 G 6
Kingussie 116-117 GH 3
King William Island 46-47 R 4
King William's Town 198 E 8
Kingwood, WV 72-73 G 5
Kingyang = Qingyang 166-167 K 4
Kingyuan = Yishan 166-167 K 7
Kinhwa = Jinhua 166-167 MN 6
Kinibalu = Mount Kinabalu 174-175 G 5
Kinistino 49 F 4
Kinkala 198 B 2
Kinkazan tō 170-171 NO 3
Kinlochleven 116-117 FG 4
Kinmen = Kinmen Dao 166-167 M 7
Kinmen Dao 166-167 M 7
Kinmount 72-73 G 2
Kinmundy, IL 70-71 F 6
Kinnaird's Head 116-117 K 3
Kinneret, Yam — 160-161 D 4
Kino kawa 170-171 K 5
Kinomoto = Kumano 170-171 L 6
Kinoosao 49 GH 2
Kinosaki 170-171 K 5
Kinross 116-117 H 4
Kinsale = Ceann Sáile 116-117 C 9
Kinsale Harbour = Cuan Cheann Sáile 116-117 C 9
Kinsella 49 BC 4
Kinsey, MT 68-69 D 2
Kinshasa 198 C 2
Kinsien = Jin Xian 166-167 N 4
Kinsley, KS 68-69 G 7
Kinston, NC 58-59 L 4
Kintampo 194-195 D 7
Kintap 174-175 G 7
Kin-tcheou = Jinzhou 166-167 N 3
Kintyre 116-117 F 5
Kintyre, Mull of — 116-117 F 5
Kinuso 48 K 2
Kiokluk Mount 52-53 HJ 6
Kiokluk Mountains 52-53 H 6
Kioshan = Queshan 166-167 L 5
Kiosk 72-73 G 1
Kioto = Kyōto 166-167 PQ 4
Kiowa, CO 68-69 D 6
Kiowa, KS 76-77 E 4
Kiowa, OK 76-77 FG 5
Kiowa Creek 68-69 D 5-6
Kipawa 72-73 G 1
Kipawa, Lac — 72-73 G 1
Kipawa, la Reserve de — 72-73 G 1
Kipembawe 198 F 3
Kipili 198 F 3
Kipini 198 H 2
Kipling 49 G 5
Kipnuk, AK 52-53 EF 7
Kipp 66-67 G 1
Kiptopeke, VA 80-81 J 2
Kipushi 198 E 4
Kirakira 174-175 k 7
Kirbyville, TX 76-77 GH 7
Kirenga 154-155 U 6
Kirensk 154-155 U 6
Kirghiz Soviet Socialist Republic 160-161 LM 2
Kirgis Nor = Chjargas nuur 166-167 GH 2
Kirgiz Kizilsu Zizhizhou 166-167 CD 3-4
Kirgizskaja Sovetskaja Socialističeskaja Respublika = Kirghiz Soviet Socialist Republic 160-161 LM 2
Kirgizskij chrebet 160-161 LM 2
Kiri 198 C 2
Kiribati 24-25 S 6
Kırıkkale 160-161 C 2-3
Kirillov 154-155 F 6
Kirin = Jilin [TJ, administrative unit] 166-167 N 2-O 3
Kirin = Jilin [TJ, place] 166-167 O 3
Kirin-do 170-171 E 4
Kirishima-yama 170-171 H 7
Kirit = Jiriid 194-195 O 7
Kiriwina Islands = Trobriand Islands 174-175 h 6
Kirkburton 116-117 K 7
Kirkby in Ashfield 116-117 K 7
Kirkby Lonsdale 116-117 J 6
Kirkby Stephen 116-117 JK 6
Kirkcaldy 116-117 HJ 4
Kirkcudbright 116-117 GH 6
Kirkenes 114-115 O 3
Kirkintilloch 116-117 G 5
Kirkjuból 114-115 g 2
Kirkland, TX 76-77 D 5
Kirkland Lake 46-47 U 8
Kırklareli 160-161 B 2
Kirksville, MO 58-59 H 3
Kirkūk 160-161 EF 3
Kirkwall 116-117 HJ 2
Kirkwood 198 DE 8
Kirkwood, MO 70-71 E 6
Kirman = Kermān 160-161 H 4
Kirov [SU, Kalužskaja Oblast'] 142-143 F 5
Kirov [SU, Kirovskaja Oblast'] 154-155 HJ 6
Kirovabad 142-143 J 7
Kirovakan 142-143 HJ 7
Kirovograd 142-143 F 6
Kirovsk [SU, Rossijskaja SFSR ↓ Murmansk] 154-155 EF 4
Kirovskij [SU, Kazachskaja SSR] 154-155 O 9
Kirovskij [SU, Rossijskaja SFSR ↖ Petropavlovsk-Kamčatskij] 154-155 de 7
Kirriemuir 116-117 H 4
Kirs 154-155 J 6
Kırşehir 160-161 C 3
Kīrthar, Koh — 160-161 K 5
Kirthar Range = Koh Kīrthar 160-161 K 5
Kirtland, NM 74-75 J 4
Kiruna 114-115 HJ 4
Kiruru 174-175 KL 7
Kirwin, KS 68-69 G 6
Kirwin Reservoir 68-69 G 6
Kiryū 170-171 M 4
Kisa 114-115 F 8-9
Kisakata 170-171 M 3
Kisale, Lac — 198 E 3
Kisangani 198 E 1
Kisangire 198 G 3
Kisar, Pulau — 174-175 J 8
Kisaralik River 52-53 G 6
Kisarawe 198 G 3
Kisarazu 170-171 MN 5
Kisbey 49 G 6
Kisel'ovsk 154-155 Q 7
Kisen = Hŭich'ŏn 166-167 O 3
Kisengwa 198 E 3
Kisenyi = Gisenyi 198 E 2
Kisgegas 48 D 2
Kīsh, Jazīreh-ye — 160-161 G 5
Kishb, Ḥarrat al- 160-161 E 6
Kishikas River 50 CD 1
Kishiwada 170-171 K 5
Kishm = Qeshm [IR, landscape] 160-161 H 5
Kishm = Qeshm [IR, place] 160-161 H 5
Kisii 198 F 2
Kišin'ov 142-143 E 6
Kiska Island 30 D 1
Kiskatinaw River 48 G 2
Kiska Volcano 52-53 r 6
Kiskittogisu Lake 49 J 3
Kiskitto Lake 49 J 3
Kiskunfélegyháza 124 JK 5
Kiskunhalas 124 J 5
Kislovodsk 142-143 H 7
Kismaanyo 198 H 2
Kismayu = Kismaanyo 198 H 2
Kismet, KS 76-77 D 4
Kiso gawa 170-171 L 5
Kiso sammyaku 170-171 L 5
Kispiox River 48 C 2
Kisreka 114-115 O 5
Kissangire = Kisangire 198 G 3
Kissaraing Island = Kettharin Kyûn 174-175 C 4
Kissenje = Gisenyi 198 E 2
Kissenji = Gisenyi 198 E 2
Kisserawe = Kisarawe 198 G 3
Kissidougou 194-195 BC 7
Kissimmee, FL 80-81 c 2
Kissimmee, Lake — 80-81 c 2-3
Kissimmee River 80-81 c 3
Kissinger 66-67 A 1
Kississing Lake 49 H 3
Kistna = Krishna 160-161 M 7
Kistufell 114-115 f 2
Kisumu 198 FG 2
Kisvárda 124 KL 4
Kita 194-195 C 6
Kita Daitō-jima 166-167 P 6
Kita-Daitō zima = Kita-Daitō-jima 166-167 P 6
Kitagō 170-171 H 7
Kitai = Qitai 166-167 FG 3
Kita-Ibaraki 170-171 N 4
Kita Iwojima = Kita-lo 148-149 S 7
Kitakami 170-171 N 3
Kitakami gawa 166-167 R 4
Kitakami kōti 170-171 N 2-3
Kitakata 170-171 MN 4
Kita-Kyūshū 166-167 OP 5
Kita-Kyûsyû = Kita-Kyūshū 166-167 OP 5
Kitale 198 G 1
Kita lo 148-149 S 7
Kitami 166-167 R 3
Kita ura 170-171 N 4
Kitčan 154-155 Y 5
Kit Carson, CO 68-69 E 6
Kitchener 46-47 U 9
Kitchigama, Rivière — 50 M 1
Kitee 114-115 O 6
Kitega = Gitega 198 EF 2
Kitgum 198 F 1
Kitimat 46-47 L 7
Kitinen 114-115 LM 3
Kitkatla 48 B 3
Kitlope River 48 D 3
Kitsuki 170-171 H 6
Kittanning, PA 72-73 G 4
Kittery, ME 72-73 L 3
Kitthareng = Kettharin Kyûn 174-175 C 4
Kittilä 114-115 L 4
Kitty Hawk, NC 80-81 J 2
Kitui 198 G 2
Kitunda 198 F 3
Kitwanga 48 C 2
Kitwe 198 E 4
Kitzbühel 124 EF 5
Kitzingen 124 E 4
Kiuchuan = Jiuquan 166-167 H 4
Kiukiang = Jiujiang 166-167 M 6
Kiunga 174-175 M 8
Kiung-chow = Qiongshan 166-167 L 8
Kiungchow Hai-hsia = Qiongzhou Haixia 166-167 KL 7
Kiuruvesi 114-115 M 6
Kiushiu = Kyūshū 166-167 P 5
Kivalina, AK 52-53 E 3
Kivalina River 52-53 E 2-3
Kivalo 114-115 L 5-M 4
Kivu 198 E 2
Kivu, Lac — 198 EF 2
Kiwalik, AK 52-53 FG 3
Kiyāt = Khay' 160-161 E 7
Kizel 154-155 K 6
Kizema 142-143 HJ 3
Kızılırmak 160-161 D 3
Kizil Khoto = Kyzyl 154-155 R 7
Kizil Orda = Kzyl-Orda 154-155 M 9
Kizilsu Kirgiz Zizhizhou 166-167 C 4-D 3
Kizl'ar 142-143 J 7
Kizl'arskij zaliv 142-143 J 7
Kizyl-Arvat 160-161 H 3
Kizyl-Atrek 160-161 G 3

Kjækan 114-115 K 3
Kjerringøy 114-115 EF 4
Kjøllefjord 114-115 MN 2
Kjøpsvik 114-115 G 3

Kladno 124 FG 3
Kladovo 138-139 K 3
Klagenfurt 124 G 5
Klaipėda 142-143 CD 4
Klaksvík 116-117 b 1
Klamath, CA 66-67 A 5
Klamath Falls, OR 58-59 B 3
Klamath Mountains 58-59 B 3
Klamath River 58-59 B 3
Klamono 174-175 K 7
Klappan River 52-53 X 8
Klapper = Pulau Deli 174-175 DE 8
Klarälven 114-115 E 7
Klatovy 124 F 4
Klaver = Klawer 198 C 8
Klawer 198 C 8
Klawock, AK 52-53 w 9
Klay = Bomi Hills 194-195 B 7
Kl'az'ma 142-143 H 4
Kleena Kleene 48 E 3
Klemtu 48 C 3
Klerksdorp 198 E 7
Klery Creek, AK 52-53 GH 3
Kleve 124 BC 3
Klibreck, Ben — 116-117 G 2
Klickitat, WA 66-67 C 3
Klickitat River 66-67 C 2-3
Klin 154-155 F 6
Klinaklini Glacier 48 E 4
Klincy 142-143 F 5
Klínovec 124 F 3
Klintehamn 114-115 GH 9
Klippan 114-115 E 9
Klippebjergene = Rocky Mountains 46-47 L 5-P 9
Klippiga bergen = Rocky Mountains 46-47 L 5-P 9
Kłodzko 124 H 3
Klondike 46-47 HJ 5
Klosterneuburg 124 GH 4
Klotz, Mount — 52-53 R 4
Kluane 52-53 ST 6
Kluane Lake 46-47 J 5
Kluane National Park 52-53 RS 6
Kl'učevskaja sopka = Velikaja Kl'učevskaja sopka 154-155 f 6
Kl'uči 154-155 f 6
Kluczbork 124 HJ 3
Klukwan, AK 52-53 U 7
Klutina Lake 52-53 OP 6

Knabengruver 114-115 B 8
Knapdale 116-117 F 4-5
Knapp, WI 70-71 DE 3
Knaresborough 116-117 K 6-7
Knewstubb Lake 48 E 3
Kneža 138-139 L 4
Knife River 68-69 EF 2
Knife River, MN 70-71 DE 2
Knight Inlet 48 E 4
Knight Island 52-53 N 6
Knighton 116-117 H 8
Knin 138-139 FG 3
Knippa, TX 76-77 E 8
Knjaževac 138-139 K 4
Knobel, AR 78-79 D 2
Knob Lake = Schefferville 46-47 X 7
Knockadoon Head = Cnoc an Dúin 116-117 D 9
Knocklayd 116-117 E 5
Knockmealdown Mountains = Cnoc Maol Domhnaigh 116-117 CD 8
Knolls, UT 66-67 G 5
Knōssós 138-139 L 8
Knottingley 116-117 KL 7
Knowles, OK 76-77 DE 4
Knowles, Cape — 31 B 30-31
Knox 178 H 2
Knox, IN 70-71 G 5
Knox City, TX 76-77 DE 6
Knox Land 31 C 11
Knoxville, IA 70-71 D 5
Knoxville, TN 58-59 K 4
Knud Rasmussen Land 30 B 25-A 21
Knutsford 116-117 J 7
Knysna 198 D 8

Ko, gora — 154-155 a 8
Kob'aj 154-155 Y 5
Kobakof Bay 52-53 j 4-5
Kobayashi 170-171 H 6-7
Kobdo = Chovd 166-167 G 2
Kōbe 166-167 PQ 5
København 114-115 DE 10
Koblenz 124 C 3
Kobo 194-195 MN 6
Kobrin 142-143 D 5
Kobroör, Pulau — 174-175 KL 8
Kobrur = Pulau Kobroör 174-175 KL 8
Kobuk, AK 52-53 J 3
Kobuk River 46-47 E 4
Kočani 138-139 K 5
Kočečum 154-155 ST 4
Kočevje 138-139 F 3
Kochana = Kočani 138-139 K 5
Kŏch'ang 170-171 F 5
Kochchi-Kaṇayannūr = Cochin 160-161 M 9
Kōchi 166-167 P 5
Koch Island 46-47 V 4
Ko-chiu = Gejiu 166-167 J 7
Kochow = Maoming 166-167 L 7
Koch Peak 66-67 H 3
Kochtel = Kohtla 154-155 D 6
Kočki 154-155 P 7
Kodiak, AK 46-47 F 6
Kodiak Island 46-47 F 6
Kōdikkarai Antarip = Point Calimere 160-161 MN 8
Kodima 142-143 H 3
Kodino 154-155 F 5
Kodok = Kūdūk 194-195 L 6-7
Kodomari-misaki 170-171 MN 2
Koes 198 C 7
Koesan 170-171 FG 4
Koettlitz Glacier 31 B 15-16
Kofa Mountains 74-75 FG 6
Kofiau, Pulau — 174-175 JK 7
Koforidua 194-195 DE 7
Kōfu 166-167 Q 4
Koga 170-171 M 4
Kogane-saki = Henashi-saki 170-171 M 2
Køge 114-115 DE 10
Kōgen-dō = Kangwŏn-do 170-171 F 3-G 4
Kogoluktuk River 52-53 J 3
Kogota 170-171 N 3
Kogrukluk River 52-53 H 6
Kŏgŭm-do 170-171 F 5
Kogunsan-kundo 170-171 EF 5
Kohāṭ 160-161 L 4
Kohīma 160-161 P 5
Koh Kong 174-175 D 4
Kohler Range 31 B 25
Kohtla-Järve 154-155 D 6
Kōhu = Kōfu 166-167 Q 4
Koide 170-171 M 4
Koitere 114-115 O 6
Kŏje 170-171 G 5
Kŏje-do 170-171 G 5
Kojgorodok 154-155 HJ 5
Kojp, gora — 142-143 L 3
Kōkai = Kanggye 166-167 O 3
Kōkai-hokudō = Hwanghae-pukto 170-171 EF 3
Kōkai-nandō = Hwanghae-namdo 170-171 E 3-4
Kokand 160-161 L 2-3
Kokanee Glacier Provincial Park 66-67 E 1
Kokaral, ostrov — 154-155 L 8
Kokčetav 154-155 MN 7
Kŏk-dong = Irhyang-dong 170-171 GH 2
Kokechik Bay 52-53 D 6
Kokemäenjoki 114-115 JK 7
Kokiu = Gejiu 166-167 J 7
Kok-Jangak 160-161 L 2
Kokkola 114-115 K 6
Kokoda 174-175 N 8
Kōkō Kyûn 174-175 B 4
Kokolik River 52-53 G 2
Kokomo, IN 58-59 JK 3
Kokonau 174-175 L 7
Koko Noor = Chöch nuur 166-167 H 4
Koko Nor = Chöch nuur 166-167 H 4
Kokonselkä 114-115 N 7
Koko Shili = Chöch Šili uul 166-167 FG 4
Kokpekty 154-155 P 8
Kokrines, AK 52-53 K 4
Kokrines Hills 52-53 KL 4
Kokšaal-Tau, chrebet — 160-161 M 2
Koksan 170-171 F 3
Koks Bāzār 160-161 P 6
Kök shal 166-167 D 3
Koksoak River 46-47 X 6
Koksŏng 170-171 F 5
Kokubo = Kokubu 170-171 H 7
Kokubu 170-171 H 7
Kokwok River 52-53 HJ 7
Kōl = Alīgarh 160-161 M 5
Kola [SU, place] 154-155 E 4
Kola [SU, river] 114-115 P 3
Kola, Pulau — 174-175 KL 8
Kolaka 174-175 H 7
Koḷamba 160-161 MN 9
Kolār 160-161 M 8
Kolār Gold Fields 160-161 M 8
Kolari 114-115 KL 4
Kōlāru = Kolār 160-161 M 8
Kolašin 138-139 H 4
Kolbio 198 H 2
Kolbuszowa 124 KL 3
Kol'čugino = Leninsk-Kuzneckij 154-155 Q 6-7
Kolda 194-195 B 6
Kolding 114-115 C 10
Kole 198 D 2
Kolepom, Pulau — 174-175 L 8
Kolguev Island = ostrov Kolgujev 154-155 GH 4
Kolgujev, ostrov — 154-155 GH 4
Kolhāpur [IND, Mahārāshtra] 160-161 L 7
Koli 114-115 N 6
Koliganek, AK 52-53 J 7
Kolín 124 G 3-4
Kollafjördhur 116-117 ab 1
Kōllam = Quilon 160-161 M 9
Kollumúli 114-115 fg 2
Köln 124 C 3
Kolno 124 K 2
Koło 124 J 2
Koloa, HI 78-79 c 2
Kołobrzeg 124 GH 1
Kologriv 154-155 G 6
Kolokani 194-195 C 6
Kolombangara 174-175 j 6
Kolombo = Koḷamba 160-161 MN 9
Kolomna 142-143 GH 4
Kolonodale 174-175 H 7
Kolosovka 154-155 N 6
Kolpaševo 154-155 P 6
Kol'skij poluostrov 154-155 EF 4
Koltur 116-117 ab 2
Kolufuri 36 a 2
Kolumadulu Channel 36 a 2
Kolwezi 198 DE 4
Kolyma 154-155 de 4
Kolymskaja nizmennost' 154-155 de 4
Kolymskoje nagorje 154-155 e 4-f 5
Kom 138-139 K 4
Komadugu Gana 194-195 G 6
Komadugu Yobe 194-195 G 6
Komaga-dake 170-171 b 2
Komagane 170-171 LM 5
Komaga take 170-171 M 4
K'o-mai = Kemä 166-167 H 6
Komandorskije ostrova 154-155 f 6-g 7
Komárom 124 J 5
Komatipoort 198 F 7
Komatsu 170-171 L 4
Komatsujima = Komatsushima 170-171 K 5-6
Komatsushima 170-171 K 5-6
Kombe, Katako- 198 D 2
Kombol = Kompot 174-175 H 6
Kombolcha = Kembolcha 194-195 MN 6
Komi Autonomous Soviet Socialist Republic 154-155 JK 5
Komi Avtonomnaja Sovetskaja Socialističeskaja Respublika = Komi Autonomous Soviet Socialist Republic 154-155 JK 5
Komīllā 160-161 P 6
Komi-Permyak Autonomous Area = 1 ◁ 154-155 J 6
Kommunarsk 142-143 GH 6
Kommunizma, pik — 160-161 L 3
Komodo, Pulau — 174-175 G 8
Komoe 194-195 D 7
Kôm Ombô = Kawm Umbū 194-195 L 4
Komono 198 B 2
Komoran, Pulau — 174-175 L 8
Komoro 170-171 M 4
Komotēnē 138-139 L 5
Kompong Cham 174-175 E 4
Kompong Chhnang 174-175 D 4
Kompong Kleang 174-175 DE 4
Kompong Som 174-175 D 4
Kompong Speu 174-175 D 4
Kompong Thom 174-175 DE 4
Kompot 174-175 H 6
Komsa 154-155 Q 5
Komsomolec 154-155 L 7
Komsomolec, ostrov — 154-155 P-R 1
Komsomolec, zaliv — 160-161 G 1
Komsomolets = ostrov Komsomolec 154-155 P-R 2
Komsomol'skij [SU, Kalmyckaja ASSR] 142-143 KL 6
Komsomol'skij [SU, Neneckij NO] 154-155 KL 4
Komsomol'sk-na-Amure 154-155 a 7
Komsomol'skoj Pravdy, ostrova — 154-155 U-W 2
Kŏmun-do 170-171 F 5
Komusan 170-171 G 1
Kona 194-195 D 6
Konakovo 142-143 G 4
Konawa, OK 76-77 F 5
Koncha = Kontcha 194-195 G 7
Konche darya 166-167 F 3
Konda 154-155 M 6
Kondiaronk, Lac — 72-73 H 1
Kondinskoje = Okt'abr'skoje 154-155 M 5
Kondirskoje 154-155 M 6
Kondoa 198 G 2
Kondolole 198 E 1
Kondopoga 154-155 EF 5
Koné 182-183 M 4
Konec-Kovdozero 114-115 O 4
Koness River 52-53 P 2
Kong, Mae Nam — 174-175 D 3
Kong, Mê — 174-175 E 4
Kongakut River 52-53 QR 2
Kong Christian den IXs Land 46-47 de 4
Kong Christian den Xs Land 30 B 21-22
Kong Frederik den VIIIs Land 30 B 21
Kong Frederik den VIs Kyst 46-47 c 5
Kongju 170-171 F 4
Kong Karls land 114-115 mn 5
Kong Leopold og Dronning Astrid land 31 BC 9
Kongolo 198 E 3
Kongōr 194-195 L 7
Kongpo 166-167 G 6
Kongsberg 114-115 C 8
Kongsøya 114-115 n 5
Kongsvinger 114-115 DE 7
Kongwa 198 G 3
Kŏnha-dong 170-171 F 2
Koni, poluostrov — 154-155 d 6
Konin 124 J 2
Konjic 138-139 GH 4
Könkämä älv 114-115 J 3
Konken = Khon Kaen 174-175 D 3
Konkiep = Goageb 198 C 7
Konna = Kona 194-195 D 6
Konoša 154-155 G 5
Konotop 142-143 F 5
Konšakovskij Kamen 142-143 L 4
Konstanz 124 D 5
Kontagora 194-195 F 6
Kontcha 194-195 G 7
Kontiomäki 114-115 N 5
Kontrashibuna Lake 52-53 KL 6

Kontrash 241

Kontum 174-175 E 4
Konya 160-161 C 3
Konya ovası 142-143 F 8
Kookynie 182-183 D 5
Koolau Range 78-79 cd 2
Koosharem, UT 74-75 H 3
Kootenai = Kootenay 46-47 N 8
Kootenai Falls 66-67 F 1
Kootenai River 58-59 C 2
Kootenay 46-47 N 8
Kootenay Lake 48 J 4-5
Kootenay National Park 48 J 4
Kootenay River 66-67 E 1
Kopaonik 138-139 J 4
Kópasker 114-115 ef 1
Kópavogur 114-115 bc 2
Kopejsk 154-155 L 6-7
Koper 138-139 EF 3
Kopervik 114-115 A 8
Kopeysk = Kopejsk 154-155 L 6-7
Köping 114-115 FG 8
Koppang 114-115 D 7
Kopparberg 114-115 EF 7
Koppeh Dāgh 160-161 HJ 3
Kopperå 114-115 D 6
Koprivnica 138-139 G 2
Köprülü = Tito Veles 138-139 JK 5
Korab 138-139 J 5
Korahe 194-195 NO 7
Kor'akskaja sopka = Velikaja Kor'akskaja sopka 154-155 ef 7
Kor'akskoje nagorje 154-155 j-f 5
Koram = Korem 194-195 M 6
Korapun 174-175 h 6
Korarou, Lac — 194-195 D 5
Korat = Nakhon Ratchasima 174-175 D 3-4
Kor'ažma 142-143 J 3
Korbiyāy, Jabal — 199 D 6
Korbu, Gunung — 174-175 D 5-6
Korçë 138-139 J 5
Korčino 154-155 P 7
Korčula 138-139 G 4
Kordestān 160-161 D 3
Kordofān = Kurdufān al-Janūbīyah 194-195 KL 6
Korea Bay = Sŏhan-man 166-167 NO 4
Korea Strait = Chōsen-kaikyō 166-167 O 4-5
Korein = Al-Kuwayt 160-161 F 5
Korem 194-195 M 6
Koret 198 D 1
Korf 154-155 g 5
Korhogo 194-195 C 7
Korinthiakòs Kólpos 138-139 JK 6
Kórinthos 138-139 K 7
Kőrishegy 124 HJ 5
Kōriyama 166-167 QR 4
Korkino 154-155 L 7
Korkodon 154-155 de 5
Korla 166-167 F 3
Kormack 50 K 3
Kornat 138-139 F 4
Kornsjø 114-115 DE 8
Koro [FJI] 174-175 a 2
Korogwe 198 G 3
Koromo = Toyota 170-171 L 5
Korōneia, Límnē — 138-139 K 5
Koror 174-175 KL 5
Körös 124 K 5
Koro Sea 174-175 ab 2
Korosko = Wādī Kuruskū 199 C 6
Korosten' 142-143 E 5
Koro-Toro 194-195 H 5
Korovin Island 52-53 cd 2
Korovinski, AK 52-53 j 4
Korovin Volcano 52-53 jk 4
Korpilombolo 114-115 JK 4
Korppoo 114-115 JK 7
Korsakov 154-155 b 8
Korsør 114-115 D 10
Kŏrtī = Kūrtī 194-195 L 5
Kortrijk 132-133 J 3
Koryak Autonomous Area 154-155 g 5-e 6
Kōs [GR, island] 138-139 M 7
Kōs [GR, place] 138-139 M 7
Kosa 142-143 KL 4
Košaba 142-143 K 7
Koš-Agač 154-155 Q 7-8
Kosaka 170-171 N 2
Kō-saki 170-171 G 5
Koščagyl 160-161 G 1
Koscian 124 H 2
Kościerzyna 124 HJ 1
Kosciusko, MS 78-79 E 4
Kosciusko, Mount — 182-183 J 7
Kosciusko Island 52-53 vw 9
Köse dağı 142-143 G 7
K'o-shan = Keshan 166-167 O 2
K'o-shih = Qāshqār 166-167 CD 4
Koshiki-rettō 170-171 G 7
Kōshū = Kwangju 166-167 O 4
Kōsī = Aruṇ 160-161 O 5
Kōsī = Sapt Kosi 160-161 O 5
Kosī, Sūn — 160-161 O 5
Košice 124 K 4
Kosju 154-155 KL 4
Koški [SU] 154-155 M 3
Koslan 154-155 H 5
Kosmos, WA 66-67 BC 2
Koso Gol = Chövsgöl nuur 166-167 J 1
Kosŏng [North Korea] 166-167 O 4
Kŏsŏng [ROK] 170-171 G 5
Kosŏng-ni 170-171 F 6
Kosovo 138-139 J 4
Kosovo polje 138-139 J 4
Kosovska Mitrovica 138-139 J 4
Kosse, TX 76-77 F 7
Kōsti = Kūstī 194-195 L 6
Kostino [SU ↓ Igarka] 154-155 Q 4
Kostroma [SU, place] 154-155 G 6
Kostrzyn 124 G 2
Koszalin 124 H 1
Kőszeg 124 H 5
Kota [IND] 160-161 M 5
Kotaagung 174-175 D 8
Kotabaru 174-175 G 7
Kotabaru = Jayapura 174-175 M 7
Kota Belud 174-175 G 5
Kotabumi 174-175 DE 7
Kotah = Kota 160-161 M 5
Kota Kinabalu 174-175 FG 5
Kota Kota 198 F 4
Kotamobagu 174-175 HJ 6
Kotatengah 174-175 D 6
Kotel 138-139 M 4
Kotel'nič 154-155 H 6
Kotel'nikovo 142-143 H 6
Kotel'nyj, ostrov — 154-155 Za 2-3
Kotido 198 F 1
Kotka 114-115 M 7
Kotlas 154-155 H 5
Kotlik, AK 52-53 F 5
Kotolnoi Island = Kotel'nyj ostrov 154-155 Za 2
Kotooka 170-171 N 2
Kotor 138-139 H 4
Kotor Varoš 138-139 G 3
Kotovsk [SU, Rossijskaja SFSR] 142-143 H 5
Kotovsk [SU, Ukrainskaja SSR] 142-143 EF 6
Koṭrī [PAK] 160-161 K 5
Kottagūdem 160-161 N 7
Kotto 194-195 J 7
Kotuj 154-155 T 3
Kotujkan 154-155 U 3
Kotzebue, AK 46-47 D 4
Kotzebue Sound 46-47 CD 4
Kouango 194-195 HJ 7
Kouba 194-195 H 5
Kouchibouguac National Park 51 D 4
Koudougou 194-195 D 6
Koufra, Oasis de — = Wāḥāt al-Kufrah 194-195 J 4
Kougarok Mount 52-53 E 4
Kouilou 198 B 2
Koukdjuak River 46-47 W 4
Koula-Moutou 198 B 2
Koulen 174-175 DE 4
Koulikoro 194-195 C 6
Koumass = Kumasi 194-195 D 7
Koumra 194-195 H 7
Koungheul 194-195 B 6
Kounradskij 154-155 O 8
Kountze, TX 76-77 G 7
Kou-pang-tzŭ = Goubangzi 170-171 CD 2
Koupéla 194-195 D 6
Kourou 98-99 J 3
Kouroussa 194-195 BC 6
Koutiala 194-195 C 6
Kouvola 114-115 M 7
Kouyou 198 BC 2
Kovdor 154-155 DE 4
Kovdozero 114-115 OP 4
Kovel' 142-143 D 5
Kovero 114-115 O 6
Kovik 46-47 V 5
Kovrov 154-155 G 6
Kowloon 166-167 LM 7
Kowŏn 166-167 O 4
Kōyampattūr = Coimbatore 160-161 M 8
Kōyikōṭa = Calicut 160-161 LM 8
Koyuk, AK 52-53 G 4
Koyuk River 52-53 FG 4
Koyukuk, AK 52-53 HJ 4
Koyukuk, Middle Fork — 52-53 M 3
Koyukuk, North Fork — 52-53 M 3
Koyukuk, South Fork — 52-53 M 3
Koyukuk Island 52-53 J 4
Koyukuk River 46-47 EF 4
Kozáně 138-139 J 5
Kozara 138-139 G 3
Kožle 124 HJ 3
Kozloduj 138-139 K 4
Koz'mino [SU ↘ Nachodka] 170-171 J 1
Koz'modemjansk 142-143 J 4
Kōzu-shima 170-171 M 5
Kožva 154-155 K 4

Kpalimé 194-195 E 7
Kpandu 194-195 DE 7

Kra, Isthmus of — = Kho Kot Kra 174-175 CD 4
Kra, Kho Khot — 174-175 CD 4
Krabi 174-175 C 5
Kra Buri 174-175 C 4
Kragerø 114-115 C 8
Kragujevac 138-139 J 3
Krai, Kuala — 174-175 D 5
Krakatao = Anak Krakatau 174-175 DE 8
Krakatau, Anak — 174-175 DE 8
Kraków 124 JK 3
Kralendijk 58-59 N 9
Kraljevo 138-139 J 4
Kramatorsk 142-143 G 6
Kramfors 114-115 G 6
Kranídion 138-139 K 7
Kranj 138-139 F 2
Krapina 138-139 FG 2
Kras 138-139 EF 3
Krasavino 154-155 GH 5
Kraskino 170-171 H 1
Kraśnik 124 KL 3
Krasnoarmejsk [SU, Kazachskaja SSR] 154-155 MN 7
Krasnoarmejsk [SU, Saratovskaja Oblast'] 142-143 HJ 5
Krasnoarmejskij 142-143 H 6
Krasnodar 142-143 G 6
Krasnograd 142-143 G 6
Krasnogvardejsk 160-161 K 3
Krasnogvardejsk = Gatčina 154-155 DE 6
Krasnoj Armii, proliv — 154-155 ST 1
Krasnojarsk 154-155 R 6
Krasnoje 142-143 H 4
Krasnokamensk 154-155 W 7-8
Krasnokamsk 154-155 K 6
Krasnonamenskij 154-155 M 7
Krasnookt'abr'skij 142-143 HJ 6
Krasnosel'kup 154-155 OP 4
Krasnoturjinsk 154-155 L 5-6
Krasnoufimsk 154-155 K 6
Krasnoural'sk 154-155 L 6
Krasnousolskij 142-143 L 5
Krasnovišersk 154-155 K 5
Krasnovodsk 160-161 G 2-3
Krasnovodskaja guba 142-143 K 8
Krasnovodskoje plato 160-161 G 2
Krasnoyarsk = Krasnojarsk 154-155 R 6
Krasnyj = Možga 154-155 J 6
Krasnyj Čikoj 154-155 UV 7
Krasnyj Jar 142-143 J 6
Krasnyj Liman 142-143 G 6
Krasnyj Luč 142-143 G 6
Krasnystaw 124 L 3
Kratié 174-175 E 4
Kraulshavn = Nûgssuaq 46-47 YZ 3
Krawang 174-175 E 8
Krebs, OK 76-77 G 5
Krečetovo 142-143 G 3
Krefeld 124 BC 3
Krekatok Island 52-53 D 5
Kremenčug 142-143 FG 6
Kremenčugskoje vodochranilišče 142-143 F 6
Kremmling, CO 68-69 C 5
Kremnica 124 J 4
Krems 124 G 4
Krenachich, El — = El Khenachich 194-195 D 4
Krenachich, Oglat — = Oglat Khenachich 194-195 D 4
Krenitzin Islands 52-53 no 3
Kress, TX 76-77 D 5
Kresta, zaliv — 154-155 k 4
Krestcy 142-143 F 4
Krestovaja guba 154-155 H-K 3
Krestovyj, pereval — 142-143 HJ 7
Krĕtĕ 138-139 L 8
Kribi 194-195 F 8
Kričev 142-143 F 5
KXVIII Ridge 26-27 O 7
Kriós, Akrōtḗrion — 138-139 K 8
Krishna 160-161 M 7
Krishna Delta 160-161 N 7
Kristiansand 114-115 BC 8
Kristianstad 114-115 F 9-10
Kristianstads län 114-115 E 9-F 10
Kristiansund 114-115 B 6
Kristiinankaupunki = Kristinestad 114-115 J 6
Kristineberg 114-115 H 5
Kristinehamn 114-115 EF 8
Kristinestad 114-115 J 6
Kriva Palanka 138-139 JK 4
Krivoj Rog 142-143 F 6
Križevci [YU, Bilo gora] 138-139 G 2
Krk 138-139 F 3
Krnov 124 HJ 3
Krohnwodoke = Nyaake 194-195 C 8
Kroksfjardharnes 114-115 c 2
Kronoberg 114-115 EF 9
Kronockaja sopka = Velikaja Kronockaja sopka 154-155 ef 7
Kronockij, mys — 154-155 f 7
Kronockij zaliv 154-155 f 7
Kronoki 154-155 f 7
Kronprins Christians Land 30 AB 20-21
Kronprinsesse Mærtha land 31 B 35-1
Kronprins Frederiks Bjerge 46-47 de 4
Kronprins Olav land 31 C 5
Kroonstad 198 E 7
Kropotkin 142-143 H 6
Krosno 124 K 4
Krosno Odrzańskie 124 G 2-3
Krotoszyn 124 H 3
Krotz Springs, LA 78-79 D 5
Kruger National Park 198 F 6-7
Krugersdorp 198 E 7
Krugloi Point 52-53 pq 6
Krui 174-175 D 8
Kruis, Kaap — 198 B 6
Krujë 138-139 HJ 5
Krusenstern, Cape — 52-53 EF 3
Kruševac 138-139 J 4
Kruševo 138-139 J 5
Kruzof Island 52-53 v 8
Krym' 142-143 F 6
Krymsk 142-143 G 7
Krymskije gory 142-143 F 7
Krynica 124 K 4
Krzyż 124 H 2

Ksar-el-Boukhari = Qaṣr al-Bukharī 194-195 E 1
Ksar el Kebir = Al-Qaṣr al-Kabīr 194-195 C 1
Ksar es Seghir = Al-Qaṣr aṣ-Ṣaghīr 194-195 D 2
Ksar es Souk = Al-Qaṣr as-Sūq 194-195 K 2
Ksenjevka 154-155 WX 7
Kshwan Mountain 48 C 2
Ksyl-Orda = Kzyl-Orda 154-155 M 8-9

Ktēma 142-143 F 9

Kuala Belait 174-175 F 6
Kualakapuas 174-175 F 7
Kualalangsa 174-175 C 6
Kuala Lumpur 174-175 D 6
Kuala Trengganu 174-175 DE 5
Kuancheng 170-171 B 2
Kuandang 174-175 H 6
Kuandian 170-171 E 2
Kuang-an = Guang'an 166-167 K 5
Kuang-ch'ang = Guangchang 166-167 M 6
Kuangchou = Guangzhou 166-167 L 7
Kuang-chou Wan = Zhanjiang Gang 166-167 L 7
Kuang-hai = Guanghai 166-167 L 7
Kuang-hsi = Guangxi Zhuangzu Zizhiqu 166-167 KL 7
Kuang-hsin = Shangrao 166-167 M 6
Kuang-lu Tao = Guanglu Dao 170-171 D 3
Kuang-nan = Guangnan 166-167 JK 7
Kuango = Kwango 198 C 2-3
Kuangsi = Guangxi Zhuangzu Zizhiqu 166-167 KL 7
Kuangtung = Guangdong 166-167 L 7
Kuang-yüan = Guangyuan 166-167 K 5
Kuantan 174-175 D 6
Kuantan, Batang — = Batang Inderagiri 174-175 D 7
K'uan-tien = Kuandian 170-171 E 2
Kuan-tung Pan-tao = Guandong Bandao 170-171 C 3
Kuan-yün = Guanyun 166-167 MN 5
Kuba [C] 58-59 KL 7
Kuba [SU] 142-143 J 7
Kuban' 142-143 G 6
Kubango = Rio Cubango 198 C 5
Kubbum 194-195 J 6
Kubokawa 170-171 J 6
Kučevo 138-139 J 3
Kucha 166-167 E 3
Kuche = Kucha 166-167 E 3
Kuchengtze = Qitai 166-167 FG 3
Kuching 174-175 F 6
Kuchinoerabu-jima 170-171 GH 7
Kuchino-shima 170-171 G 7
Kudahuvadu Channel 36 a 2
Kudamatsu 170-171 H 5-6
Kudat 174-175 G 5
Kuḍḍlā = Kandla 160-161 L 6
Kudiakof Islands 52-53 b 2
Kudō = Taisei 170-171 ab 2
Kudobin Islands 52-53 c 1
Kūdūk 194-195 L 6-7
Kudymkar 154-155 JK 6
Kuei-ch'ih = Guichi 166-167 M 5
Kueichou = Guizhou 166-167 JK 6
Kuei-lin = Guilin 166-167 KL 6
Kuei-p'ing = Guiping 166-167 KL 7
Kuei-tê = Guide 166-167 J 4
Kuei-ting = Guiding 166-167 K 6
Kuei-yang = Guiyang [TJ, Guizhou] 166-167 K 6
Kuei-yang = Guiyang [TJ, Hunan] 166-167 L 6
Kuerhlei = Korla 166-167 F 3
Kufra = Wāḥāt al-Kufrah 194-195 J 4
Kufrah, Wāḥāt al- 194-195 J 4
Kufra Oasis = Wāḥāt al-Kufrah 194-195 J 4
Kufstein 124 F 5
Kugrua River 52-53 H 1
Kugruk River 52-53 F 4
Kugururok River 52-53 G 2
Kūhak 160-161 J 5
Kuhmo 114-115 NO 5
Kuito 198 C 4
Kuitozero 114-115 O 5
Kuiu Island 46-47 K 6
Kuivaniemi 114-115 L 5
Kuja 154-155 G 4
Kujang-dong 170-171 EF 3
Kujawy 124 J 2
Kujbyšev [SU, Kujbyševskaja Oblast'] 154-155 HJ 7
Kujbyšev [SU, Om'] 154-155 O 6
Kujbyševka-Vostočnaja = Belogorsk 154-155 YZ 7
Kujbyševskoje vodochranilišče 154-155 HJ 7
Kuji 166-167 R 3
Kujto, ozero — 154-155 E 5
Kujulik Bay 52-53 e 1
Kujumba 154-155 S 5
Kujū-san 170-171 H 6
Kuk 52-53 H 1
Kukaklek Lake 52-53 K 7
Kukarka = Sovetsk 154-155 H 6
Kukatush 50 KL 2
Kukawa 194-195 G 6
Kuke 198 D 6
Kukpowruk River 52-53 F 2
Kukpuk River 52-53 DE 2
Kukukus Lake 70-71 E 1
Kuku Noor = Chöch nuur 166-167 H 4
Kula [BG] 138-139 K 4
Kula [YU] 138-139 H 3
Kul'ab 160-161 K 3
Kulagino 142-143 K 6
Kulaly, ostrov — 142-143 J 7
Kulambangra = Kolombangara 174-175 j 6
Kular, chrebet — 154-155 Z 4
Kulaura 160-161 P 6
Kuldja = Gulja 166-167 E 3
Kuldo 48 CD 2
Kulebaki 142-143 H 4
Kulgera 182-183 F 5
Kulha Gangri 166-167 G 6
Kulhakangri = Kulha Gangri 166-167 G 6
Kulik, Lake — [USA ↑ Kuskokwim River] 52-53 G 6
Kulik, Lake — [USA ↓ Kuskokwim River] 52-53 H 7
Kulikoro = Koulikoro 194-195 C 6
Kulja = Ghulja 166-167 E 3
Kullen 114-115 E 9
Kulm, ND 68-69 G 2
Kulmbach 124 E 3
Kul'sary 154-155 J 8
Kultuk 154-155 T 7
Kulu 142-143 F 8
Kuludu Faro 36 a 1
Kulukak Bay 52-53 H 7
Kulumadau 174-175 h 6
Kulunda 154-155 OP 7
Kulundinskaja step' 154-155 O 7
Kum = Qom 160-161 G 4
Kuma [J] 170-171 J 6
Kuma [SU] 142-143 J 6-7
Kumagaya 170-171 M 4
Kumai, Teluk — 174-175 F 7
Kumaishi 170-171 ab 2
Kumaka 98-99 J 3
Kumakahi, Cape — 78-79 e 3
Kumamba, Pulau-pulau — 174-175 LM 7
Kumamoto 166-167 P 5
Kumano 170-171 L 6
Kumano-nada 170-171 L 5-6
Kumanovo 138-139 JK 4
Kumasi 194-195 D 7
Kumaun 160-161 M 4
Kumba 194-195 F 8
Kumbakale 174-175 j 6
Kumbakonam 160-161 MN 8
Kumbe 174-175 LM 8
Kŭmch'on 170-171 F 3
Kŭmch'ŏn = Kimch'ŏn 166-167 O 4
Kumertau 154-155 K 7
Kŭm-gang 170-171 F 4
Kŭmgang-san 170-171 FG 3
Kŭmhwa 170-171 F 3
Kumini-dake 170-171 H 6
Kŭmje = Kimje 170-171 F 5
Kumla 114-115 F 8
Kŭmnyŏng 170-171 F 6
Kŭmo-do 170-171 FG 5
Kumo-Manyčskaja vpadina 142-143 HJ 6
Kumon Range = Kŭmûn Taungdan 174-175 C 1
Kumphawapi 174-175 D 3
Kŭmsan 170-171 F 4
Kumul = Hami 166-167 G 3
Kŭmûn Taungdan 174-175 C 1
Kuna River 52-53 J 2
Kunašir, ostrov — 154-155 c 9
Kuṇḍāpura = Condapoor 160-161 L 8
Kundelungu 198 E 3-4
Kundiawa 174-175 M 8
Kundur, Pulau — 174-175 D 6
Kunduz 160-161 K 3
Kunene 198 B 5
Kungej-Alatau, chrebet — 154-155 O 9
Kunghit Island 48 B 3
Kungok River 52-53 H 1
Kungrad 154-155 K 9
Kungsbacka 114-115 DE 9
Kungu 198 C 1
Kungur 154-155 K 6
Kung-ying-tsŭ = Gongyingzi 170-171 BC 2
Kunie = Île des Pins 182-183 N 4
Kŭnlôn 174-175 C 2
Kunlun Shan 166-167 D-H 4
Kunming 166-167 J 6
Kunovat 142-143 N 3
Kunoy 116-117 b 1
Kunsan 166-167 O 4
Kunsan-man 170-171 F 5
Kuntillā, Al- 199 D 3
K'ŭnyŏnp'yŏng-do = Tae-yŏnp'yŏng-do 170-171 E 4
Kuolajarvi 142-143 EF 2
Kuopio 114-115 M 6
Kupa 138-139 FG 3
Kupang 174-175 H 9
Kup'ansk 142-143 G 6
Kuparuk River 52-53 N 1-2
Kupino 154-155 O 7
Kupreanof Island 46-47 K 6
Kupreanof Point 52-53 d 2
Kupreanof Strait 52-53 KL 7
Kura 142-143 H 7
Kurahashi-jima 170-171 J 5
Kurashiki 170-171 J 5
Kuraymah 194-195 L 5
Kurayoshi 170-171 JK 5
Kurchahan Hu = Chagan nuur 166-167 L 3
Kurdistan = Kordestān 160-161 F 3
Kurdufān al-Janūbīyah 194-195 KL 6
Kurdufān ash-Shimālīyah 194-195 KL 5-6
Kure [J] 166-167 P 5
Kurejka [SU, place] 154-155 PQ 4
Kurejka [SU, river] 154-155 QR 4
Kurgan 154-155 M 6
Kurganinsk 142-143 GH 6-7
Kurgan-T'ube 160-161 KL 3
Kuria 178 H 2
Kuria Muria Island = Jazā'ir Khūrīyā Mūrīyā 160-161 H 7
Kurikka 114-115 JK 6
Kurikoma yama 170-171 N 3
Kuril Islands 166-167 S 3-T 2
Kuril'sk 154-155 c 8
Kuril'skije ostrova 166-167 S 3-T 2
Kuril Trench 34-35 GH 2
Kurkur 199 C 6
Kurle = Korla 166-167 F 3
Kurleja 154-155 WX 7
Kurmuk 194-195 L 6
Kurnool 160-161 M 7
Kurobe 170-171 L 4
Kuroishi 170-171 N 2
Kuromatsunai 170-171 b 2
Kurosawajiri = Kitakami 170-171 N 3
Kuro-shima 170-171 G 7
Kursk 142-143 G 5
Kurskaja kosa 124 K 1
Kurskij zaliv 124 K 1
Kuršumlija 138-139 J 4
Kūrtī 194-195 L 5
Kuruman 198 D 7
Kurume [J, Kyūshū] 170-171 H 6
Kurumkan 154-155 V 7
Kurunegala 160-161 MN 9
Kurun-Ur'ach 154-155 a 6
Kurupa Lake 52-53 KL 2
Kurupa River 52-53 K 2
Kurupukari 98-99 H 4
Kuruskū, Wādī — 199 C 6
Kuryongp'o 170-171 G 5
Kusakaki-shima 170-171 G 7
Kusatsu 170-171 KL 5
Kusawa Lake 52-53 T 6
Kusawa River 52-53 T 6
Kusaybah, Bi'r — 194-195 K 4
Kušč'ovskaja 142-143 GH 6
Kus gölü 142-143 E 7
Ku-shan = Gushan 170-171 D 3
Kushih = Gushi 166-167 M 5
Kushikino 170-171 GH 7
Kushima 170-171 H 7
Kushimoto 170-171 K 6
Kushiro 166-167 RS 3
Kushtaka Lake 52-53 PQ 6
Kushui 166-167 G 3
Kusilvak Mount 52-53 EF 6
Kusiro = Kushiro 166-167 RS 3
Kuška 160-161 J 3
Kuskokwim, North Fork — 52-53 KL 5
Kuskokwim, South Fork — 52-53 KL 5
Kuskokwim Bay 46-47 D 6
Kuskokwim Mountains 46-47 EF 5
Kuskokwim River 46-47 DE 5
Kušmurun 154-155 LM 7
Kusnezk = Kuzneck 154-155 H 7
Kusŏng 170-171 E 2-3
Kustanaj 154-155 LM 7
Kustatan, AK 52-53 M 6
K'ustendil 138-139 K 4
Küstenkanal 124 CD 2
Kūstī 194-195 L 6
Kusu 170-171 H 6
Kušum 142-143 K 5

242 **Kontum**

K'us'ur 154-155 Y 3
Kušva 154-155 K 6
Kūt, Al — 160-161 F 4
Kut, Ko — 174-175 D 4
Kütahya 160-161 BC 3
Kutai 174-175 G 6
Kutaisi 142-143 H 7
Kut-al-Imara = Al-Kūt 160-161 F 4
Kutaradja = Banda Aceh 174-175 BC 5
Kutch 160-161 K 6
Kutch, Gulf of — 160-161 KL 6
Kutch, Rann of — 160-161 KL 6
Kutchan 170-171 b 2
Kutcharo-ko 170-171 d 2
Kutina 138-139 G 3
Kutno 124 J 2
Kutsing = Qujing 166-167 J 6
Kutu 198 C 2
Kutum 194-195 J 6
Kutunbul, Jabal — 160-161 E 7
Kutuzof, Cape — 52-53 c 1
Kuusamo 114-115 N 5
Kuusankoski 114-115 M 7
Kuvandyk 154-155 K 7
Kuwaima Falls 98-99 H 1-2
Kuwait 160-161 F 5
Kuwana 170-171 L 5
Kuwayt, Al- 160-161 F 5
Kuyuwini River 98-99 J 3
Kuzitrin River 52-53 EF 4
Kuz'movka 154-155 QR 5
Kuzneck 154-155 H 7
Kuzneckij Alatau 154-155 Q 6-7
Kuzneck-Sibirskij = Novokuzneck 154-155 Q 7
Kuznetsk = Kuzneck 154-155 H 7
Kuzomen' 154-155 F 4

Kvænangen 114-115 J 2
Kvaløy 114-115 KL 2
Kvalsund 114-115 KL 2
Kvalvågen 114-115 k 6
Kvarken 114-115 J 6
Kvarner 138-139 F 3
Kvarnerič 138-139 F 3
Kverkfjöll 114-115 ef 2
Kvichak, AK 52-53 J 7
Kvichak Bay 52-53 J 7
Kvichak River 52-53 J 7
Kvigtind 114-115 EF 5
Kvikne 114-115 D 6
Kvitøya 114-115 no 4

Kwa 198 C 2
Kwakhanai 198 D 6
Kwakoegron 98-99 L 2
Kwakwani 98-99 JK 2
Kwamouth 198 C 2
Kwangan = Guang'an 166-167 K 5
Kwangchang = Guangchang 166-167 M 6
Kwangch'on 170-171 F 4
Kwangchow = Guangzhou 166-167 L 7
Kwanghua = Guanghua 166-167 L 5
Kwangju 166-167 O 4
Kwango 198 C 2-3
Kwangsi = Guangxi Zhuangzu Zizhiqu 166-167 KL 7
Kwangtung = Guangdong 166-167 L 7
Kwangyuan = Guangyuan 166-167 K 5
Kwanmo-bong 170-171 G 2
Kwanto = Kantō 170-171 MN 4
Kwanyun = Guanyun 166-167 MN 5
Kwanza 198 C 3-4
Kwanza, Rio — 198 B 3
Kwara 194-195 E 6-F 7
Kwataboahegan River 50 KL 1
Kwatta 160-161 K 4
Kwazulu 198 F 7
Kweiang = Guiyang 166-167 K 6
Kweichih = Guichi 166-167 M 5
Kweichow = Fengjie 166-167 K 5
Kweichow = Guizhou 166-167 JK 6
Kweichu = Guiyang 166-167 K 6
Kweilin = Guilin 166-167 KL 6
Kweiping = Guiping 166-167 KL 7
Kweiteh = Shangqiu 166-167 LM 5
Kweiyang = Guiyang 166-167 K 6
Kwekwe 198 E 5
Kwenge 198 C 3
Kwenlun = Kunlun Shan 166-167 D-H 4
Kwesang-bong 170-171 G 2
Kwethluk, AK 46-47 DE 5
Kwethluk River 52-53 G 6
Kwidzyn 124 J 2
Kwigillingok, AK 46-47 D 6
Kwigluk Island 52-53 E 7
Kwiguk, AK 52-53 E 5
Kwiha 194-195 MN 6
Kwikpak, AK 52-53 E 5
Kwilu 198 C 2
Kwinana 182-183 BC 6
Kwinhagak = Quinhagak, AK 52-53 FG 7
Kwinitsa 48 C 2
Kwonghoi = Guanghai 166-167 L 7

Kyaiktō 174-175 C 3
Kyancutta 182-183 G 6
Kyaring Tsho [TJ, Qinghai] 166-167 H 5
Kyaring Tsho [TJ, Xizang Zizhiqu] 166-167 F 5
Kyaukhsī 174-175 C 2
Kyaukse = Kyaukhsī 174-175 C 2
Kyebang-san 170-171 G 4
Kyezīmanzan 174-175 C 2
Kyle of Lochalsh 116-117 F 3
Kyllēnē 138-139 J 7
Kýmē 138-139 L 6
Kymen lääni 114-115 MN 7
Kymijoki 114-115 M 7
Kynuna 182-183 H 4
Kyoga, Lake — 198 F 1
Kyogami, Cape — = Kyōga-saki 170-171 K 5
Kyōga-saki 170-171 K 5
Kyŏmip'o = Songnim 166-167 O 4
Kyŏngan-ni 170-171 F 4
Kyŏngdŏn 174-175 CD 2
Kyŏnggi-do 170-171 F 4
Kyonghŭng 170-171 H 1
Kyŏngju 166-167 OP 4
Kyŏngnyŏlbi-yŏlto 170-171 E 4
Kyŏngsan 170-171 G 5
Kyŏngsang-pukto 170-171 G 4
Kyŏngsan-namdo 170-171 FG 5
Kyŏngsŏng 170-171 GH 2
Kyŏngsŏng = Sŏul 166-167 O 4
Kyŏngwŏn 170-171 H 1
Kyōto 166-167 PQ 4
Kyparissia 138-139 J 7
Kyparissiakòs Kólpos 138-139 J 7
Kyrá Panagía 138-139 KL 6
Kyrēneia 142-143 F 8
Kyrksæterøra 114-115 C 6
Kyrkslätt 114-115 L 7
Kyrönjoki 114-115 K 6
Kyštovka 154-155 O 6
Kyštym 154-155 L 6
Kýthēra 138-139 K 7
Kythēron, Stenòn — 138-139 K 7-8
Kýthnos 138-139 L 7
Kytyl-Žura 154-155 Y 5
Kyūgōk 174-175 C 2
Kyuguot Sound 48 D 5
Kyuquot 48 D 4
Kyūshū 166-167 P 5
Kyushu Ridge 166-167 P 6-Q 7
Kyūshū sammyaku 170-171 H 6
Kyūsyū = Kyūshū 166-167 P 5
Kyzyl 154-155 R 7
Kyzyl-Kija 160-161 L 2-3
Kyzylkum 154-155 LM 9
Kyzyl-Mažalyk 154-155 QR 7
Kyzylsu 160-161 L 3

Kzyl-Orda 154-155 M 9

L

Laa 124 H 4
Laas'aanood 194-195 b 2
Laas Qoray 194-195 b 1
Laaswarwar 194-195 bc 2
La Barge, WY 66-67 HJ 4
Labbezanga 194-195 E 5-6
Labe [CS] 124 G 3
Labé [Guinea] 194-195 B 6
Labelle 72-73 J 1
La Belle, FL 80-81 c 3
La Belle, MO 70-71 DE 5
Laberge, Lake — 52-53 U 6
Labin 138-139 F 3
Labinsk 142-143 H 7
Labis 174-175 D 6
La Blanquilla, Isla — 98-99 G 2
La Boquilla, Presa — 86-87 GH 4
Labota 174-175 H 7
Laboulaye 103 D 4
Labrador, Coast of — 46-47 YZ 6-7
Labrador Basin 26-27 G 3
Labrador City 46-47 X 7
Labrador Peninsula 46-47 V 6-Y 7
Labrador Sea 46-47 Y-a 5-6
Lábrea 98-99 G 6
Labrieville 51 B 3
Labuan, Pulau — 174-175 FG 5
Labuha 174-175 J 7
Labuhan 174-175 E 8
Labuhanbajo 174-175 GH 8
Labuhanbilik 174-175 CD 6
Labytnangi 154-155 M 4
Lača, ozero — 142-143 G 3
Lac-Allard 51 E 2
La Canada Verde Creek 83 III d 2
Lac-Bouchette 50 P 2
Laccadive Islands 160-161 L 9
Lac Courte Oreilles Indian Reservation 70-71 E 3
Lac des Mille Lacs 70-71 EF 1
Lac du Bonnet 50 AB 2
Lac du Flambeau Indian Reservation 70-71 E 2-3
Lac-Édouard 50 PQ 3
Lacepede Islands 182-183 D 3
Lacey, WA 66-67 B 2
Lac-Frontiere 51 A 4
Lac-Gatineau 72-73 HJ 1
Lachine 72-73 JK 2
Lachine, Canal — 82 I b 2
Lachine, Rapides de — 82 I b 2
Lachlan River 182-183 HJ 6
Lac-Humqui 51 C 3
Lachute 72-73 JK 2
Lackawanna, NY 72-73 G 3
Lac La Biche [CDN, place] 49 C 3
Lac la Hache 48 G 4
Lac la Ronge Provincial Park 49 F 3
Lac Long 72-73 J 1
Lacolle 72-73 K 2
Lacombe 46-47 O 7
Laconia, NH 72-73 L 3
Lacoochee, FL 80-81 b 2
Lacq 132-133 G 7
Lac qui Parle 68-69 H 3
La Crescent, MN 70-71 E 4
La Crosse, KS 68-69 G 6
Lacrosse, WA 66-67 E 2
Lac-Saguay 72-73 J 1
Lac Seul [CDN, place] 50 C 2
Ladākh 160-161 M 4
Ladākh Range 160-161 M 3-4
Ladder Creek 68-69 F 6
Laddonia, MO 70-71 E 6
Ladera Heights, CA 83 III b 2
Lādhiqīyah, Al- 160-161 CD 3
Ladiqiya, El — = Al-Lādhiqīyah 160-161 CD 3
Ladismith 198 D 8
Ladner 66-67 B 1
Ladoga, IN 70-71 G 6
Ladoga, Lake — = Ladožskoje ozero 154-155 E 5
Ladožskoje ozero 154-155 E 5
Ladrones Peak 76-77 A 5
Ladron Mountains 76-77 A 5
Ladue River 52-53 R 5
Lady Beatrix, Lac — 50 N 1
Ladybrand 198 E 7
Lady Evelyn Lake 72-73 F 1
Lady Franklinfjord 114-115 k 4
Lady Newnes Ice Shelf 31 B 18-17
Ladysmith, WI 70-71 E 3
Ladysmith [CDN] 66-67 AB 1
Ladysmith [ZA] 198 EF 7
Lae [PNG] 174-175 N 8
La Encantada, Cerro de — 58-59 C 5
Lærdalsøyri 114-115 BC 7
Læsø 114-115 D 9
Lafayette, AL 78-79 G 4
La Fayette, GA 78-79 G 3
Lafayette, IN 58-59 J 3
Lafayette, LA 58-59 H 5-6
Lafayette, TN 78-79 FG 2
Lafia 194-195 F 7
Lafiagi 194-195 EF 7
Laflamme, Rivière — 50 N 2
Laflèche [CDN, Quebec] 82 I c 2
Laflèche [CDN, Saskatchewan] 49 E 6
La Follette, TN 78-79 G 2
Lafontaine, Parc — 82 I b 1
Laforest 50 L 3
Lagan 114-115 E 9
Lagarfljót 114-115 f 2
La Garita Mountains 68-69 C 6-7
Lagarterito 58-59 b 2
Lagarto = Palmas Bellas 58-59 a 2
Lågen 114-115 CD 7
Laghouat = Al-Aghwāt 194-195 E 2
Lågneset 114-115 j 6
Lago Argentino 103 B 8
Lagodei, El- = Qardho 160-161 F 9
Lago Maggiore 138-139 C 2-3
Lagonegro 138-139 FG 5
Lago Novo 98-99 J 4
Lagos [P] 132-133 C 10
Lagos [WAN] 194-195 E 7
Lagosa 198 EF 3
Lagos de Moreno 58-59 F 7
Lagosta = Lastovo 138-139 G 4
Lagowa, El — = Al-Laqawah 194-195 K 6
Lågøya 114-115 k 4
La Grande, OR 66-67 D 3
La Grange, GA 58-59 JK 5
Lagrange, IN 70-71 H 5
La Grange, KY 70-71 H 6
La Grange, NC 80-81 H 3
La Grange, TX 76-77 F 7-8
Lagrange, WY 68-69 D 5
La Guardia Airport 82 III c 2
Laguna, NM 76-77 A 5
Laguna [BR] 103 G 3
Laguna, Ilha da — 98-99 N 5
Laguna, La — [PA ↑ Panamá] 58-59 b 2
Laguna, La — [PA ← Panamá] 58-59 b 3
Laguna Beach, CA 74-75 DE 6
Laguna Dam 74-75 FG 6
Laguna de Jaco 76-77 C 9
Laguna Mountains 74-75 E 6
Lagunas [PE] 98-99 DE 6
Lagunas [RCH] 103 BC 2
Laguna Superior 58-59 H 8
Laguna Yema 103 D 2
Lahad Datu 174-175 G 5-6
Lahaina, HI 78-79 d 2
Laham [RI] 174-175 G 6
Lahat 174-175 D 7
Lāhaur 160-161 L 4
Lahewa 174-175 C 6
Laḥij 160-161 EF 8
Lāhījān 160-161 FG 3
Lahn 124 D 3
Laholm 114-115 E 9
Laholms bukten 114-115 E 9
Lahontan Reservoir 74-75 D 3
Lahore = Lāhaur 160-161 L 4
Lahti 114-115 LM 7
Laï 194-195 H 7
Lai Châu 174-175 D 2
Laighean, Canáil — 116-117 D 7
Laighin 116-117 DE 7-8
Lai Hka = Lechā 174-175 C 2
Lailā = Laylā 160-161 F 6
Laingsburg 198 CD 8
Laipo = Lipu 166-167 KL 7
Laird, CO 68-69 E 5
Lairg 116-117 G 2
Laiyuan 166-167 LM 4
Lai-yüan = Laiyuan 166-167 LM 4
La Jara, CO 68-69 CD 7
Laje, Cachoeira da — 98-99 L 5
Lajeado, Cachoeira do — 98-99 H 10
Lajes [BR, Rio Grande do Norte] 98-99 M 6
Lajes [BR, Santa Catarina] 103 F 3
Lajitas, TX 76-77 C 8
Lajkovac 138-139 HJ 3
La Jolla, CA 74-75 E 6
La Joya, NM 76-77 A 5
Lajtamak 154-155 M 6
La Junta, CO 58-59 F 4
Lake, WY 66-67 H 3
Lake, The — 88-89 K 4
Lake Alma 68-69 D 1
Lake Andes, SD 68-69 G 4
Lake Arthur, LA 78-79 C 5
Lake Arthur, NM 76-77 B 6
Lake Benton, MN 70-71 BC 3
Lake Butler, FL 80-81 b 1
Lake Cargelligo 182-183 J 6
Lake Charles, LA 58-59 H 5
Lake City, CO 68-69 C 6
Lake City, FL 80-81 b 1
Lake City, IA 70-71 C 4
Lake City, MI 70-71 H 3
Lake City, MN 70-71 D 3
Lake City, SC 80-81 G 4
Lake City, SD 68-69 H 3
Lake Cormorant, MS 78-79 DE 3
Lake Cowichan 66-67 AB 1
Lake Crystal, MN 70-71 C 3
Lake District 116-117 HJ 6
Lakefield, MN 70-71 C 4
Lakefield [AUS] 182-183 H 2-3
Lake Geneva, WI 70-71 F 4
Lake George, NY 72-73 JK 3
Lake Grace 182-183 C 6
Lake Harbour 46-47 WX 5
Lake Havasu City, AZ 74-75 FG 5
Lake Jackson, TX 76-77 G 8
Lake King 182-183 CD 6
Lakeland, FL 58-59 K 6
Lakeland, GA 80-81 E 5
Lake Louise [CDN] 48 JK 4
Lakelse 48 C 2
Lake Mead National Recreation Area 74-75 FG 4
Lake Mills, IA 70-71 D 4
Lake Mills, WI 70-71 F 4
Lake Minchumina, AK 52-53 L 5
Lake Odessa, MI 70-71 H 4
Lake Oswego, OR 66-67 B 3
Lake Park, IA 70-71 C 4
Lake Placid, FL 80-81 c 3
Lake Placid, NY 58-59 M 3
Lake Pleasant, NY 72-73 J 3
Lakeport, CA 74-75 B 3
Lake Preston, SD 68-69 H 3
Lake Providence, LA 78-79 D 4
Lake Range 66-67 D 5
Lakeside, AZ 74-75 J 5
Lakeside, NE 68-69 E 4
Lakeside, OR 66-67 A 4
Lakeside, UT 66-67 G 5
Lakeside, VA 80-81 H 2
Lake Sidney Lanier 80-81 DE 3
Lake Sinclair 80-81 E 4
Lake Superior Provincial Park 50 G 4
Lake Toxaway, NC 80-81 E 3
Lake Victor, TX 76-77 E 7
Lakeview, MI 70-71 H 4
Lakeview, OR 66-67 C 4
Lakeview, Chicago-, IL 83 II ab 1
Lake Village, AR 78-79 D 4
Lake Wales, FL 80-81 c 3
Lakewood, CA 83 III d 2
Lakewood, CO 68-69 D 6
Lakewood, NJ 72-73 J 4
Lakewood, NM 76-77 B 6
Lakewood, NY 72-73 G 3
Lakewood, OH 72-73 EF 4
Lake Worth, FL 58-59 KL 6
Lakhadsweep 160-161 L 8
Lakhnaū = Lucknow 160-161 MN 5
Lakin, KS 68-69 F 7
Lakonia, Gulf of — = Lakōnikòs Kólpos 138-139 K 7
Lakōnikòs Kólpos 138-139 K 7
Lakota, IA 70-71 CD 4
Lakota, ND 68-69 G 1
Laksefjord 114-115 M 2
Lakselv 114-115 L 2
Lakṣhadvīp = Lakshadweep 160-161 L 8
Lalaua 198 G 4
Lalībela 194-195 M 6
La Luz, NM 76-77 AB 6
Lamadrid [MEX] 76-77 D 9
Lamaline 51 J 4
Lamar, CO 68-69 E 6
Lamar, MO 70-71 C 7
La Marque, TX 76-77 G 8
Lambaréné 198 B 2
Lambasa 174-175 a 2
Lambayeque [PE, place] 98-99 CD 6
Lambay Island = Reachra 116-117 F 7
Lambert, MS 78-79 DE 3
Lambert, MT 68-69 D 2
Lambert Glacier 31 B 8
Lambi Kyûn 174-175 C 4
Lambourn 116-117 K 9
Lambton, Cape — 46-47 M 3
Lāmding = Lumding 160-161 P 5
Lamé 194-195 G 7
Lame Deer, MT 68-69 C 3
Lamego 132-133 D 8
La Mesa, CA 74-75 E 6
La Mesa, NM 76-77 A 6
Lamesa, TX 76-77 D 6
Lamèzia Terme 138-139 FG 6
Lamía 138-139 K 6
L'amin 154-155 N 5
La Mirada, CA 83 III d 2
Lammermuir Hills 116-117 J 5
Lamo = Lamu 198 H 2
Lamoille, NV 66-67 F 5
La Moine, CA 66-67 B 5
Lamona, WA 66-67 D 2
Lamon Bay 174-175 H 4
Lamond, Washington-, DC 82 II a 1
Lamoni, IA 70-71 CD 5
Lamont, CA 74-75 D 5
Lamont, ID 66-67 H 3-4
Lamont, WY 68-69 C 4
Lamotrek 174-175 N 5
La Moure, ND 68-69 GH 2
Lampa [PE] 98-99 EF 8
Lampang 174-175 C 3
Lampasas, TX 76-77 E 7
Lampazos de Naranjo 86-87 K 4
Lampedusa 138-139 E 8
Lampedusa, Ìsola — 194-195 G 1
Lampeter 116-117 G 8
Lampi Island = Lambi Kyûn 174-175 C 4
Lampman 68-69 E 1
Lampung 174-175 DE 7
Lamu [EAK] 198 H 2
Lamy, NM 76-77 B 5
Lanai 174-175 e 3
Lanai City, HI 78-79 d 2
Lanao, Lake — 174-175 HJ 5
Lanark [GB, administrative unit] 116-117 GH 5
Lanark [GB, place] 116-117 H 5
Lancang Jiang 166-167 HJ 7
Lancashire 116-117 J 7
Lancaster 116-117 J 6
Lancaster, CA 74-75 DE 5
Lancaster, IA 70-71 D 5
Lancaster, KY 70-71 H 7
Lancaster, MN 68-69 H 1
Lancaster, NH 72-73 L 2
Lancaster, OH 72-73 E 5
Lancaster, PA 72-73 HJ 4
Lancaster, SC 80-81 F 3
Lancaster, WI 70-71 E 4
Lancaster Sound 46-47 TU 3
Lancheu = Lanzhou 166-167 JK 4
Lanchou = Lanzhou 166-167 JK 4
Lanchow = Lanzhou 166-167 JK 4
Lanciano 138-139 F 4
Lancun 166-167 N 4
Landa, ND 68-69 F 1
Landau 124 D 4
Landeck 124 E 5
Landego 114-115 EF 4
Lander, WY 68-69 B 4
Landerneau 132-133 E 4
Lander River 182-183 F 4
Landguard Point 116-117 h 7
Landis 49 D 4
Landover Hills, MD 82 II b 1
Landrum, SC 80-81 E 3
Landsberg am Lech 124 E 4
Land's End [CDN] 46-47 LM 2
Land's End [GB] 116-117 F 10
Landshut 124 F 4
Landskrona 114-115 E 10
Lanett, AL 78-79 G 4
Langara Island 48 A 2
Langchhen Khamba 166-167 DE 5
Langchung = Langzhong 166-167 JK 5
Langdon, ND 68-69 G 1
Langdon, Washington-, DC 82 II b 1
Langeland 114-115 D 10
Langenburg 49 GH 5
Langford, SD 68-69 H 3
Langholm 116-117 HJ 5
Langjökull 114-115 cd 2
Langkawi, Pulau — 174-175 C 5
Langley, VA 82 II a 1
Langlois, OR 66-67 A 4
Langness Point 116-117 G 6
Langon 132-133 G 6
Langøy 114-115 F 3
Langres 132-133 K 5
Langres, Plateau de — 132-133 K 5
Langruth 49 J 5
Langsa 174-175 C 6
Lang Shan = Char Narijn uul 166-167 K 3
Lang So'n 174-175 E 2
Langtans udde 31 C 31
Langtry, TX 76-77 D 8
Languedoc 132-133 J 7-K 6
Langzhong 166-167 JK 5
Lan Hsü 166-167 N 7
Laniel 72-73 G 1
Lanigan 49 F 5
Lanín, Volcán — 103 B 5
Lannion 132-133 F 4
Lansdale, PA 72-73 J 4
Lansdowne House 50 F 1
L'Anse, MI 70-71 F 2
Lansford, ND 68-69 F 1
Lansing, IA 70-71 E 4
Lansing, MI 58-59 K 3
Lan-ts'ang Chiang = Lancang Jiang 166-167 HJ 7
Lan-ts'un = Lancun 166-167 N 4
Lanusei 138-139 C 6
Lanzarote 194-195 B 3
Lanzhou 166-167 JK 4
Laoag 174-175 GH 3
Laodicea = Al-Lādhiqīyah 160-161 CD 3
Laoha He 170-171 B 2
Lao-ha Ho = Laoha He 170-171 B 2
Laohekou = Guanghua 166-167 L 5
Laohokow = Guanghua 166-167 L 5
Laohushan 170-171 BC 2
Laoi, An — 116-117 BC 9
Laoigh, Beinn — 116-117 FG 4
Laoighis = Laois 116-117 D 7-8
Laois 116-117 D 7-8
Lao Kay 174-175 D 2
Laon 132-133 J 4
Laona, WI 70-71 F 3
Laora 174-175 H 7
Laos 174-175 D 2-3
Laoshan 166-167 N 4
Lao-t'ieh-shan-hsi Chiao = Laotieshanxi Jiao 170-171 C 3
Lapa 103 FG 3
La Palma, CA 83 III d 2
La Panza Range 74-75 CD 5
La Paz, Bahía de — 58-59 DE 7
Lapeer, MI 72-73 E 3
La Pérouse, proliv — 154-155 b 8
La Pérouse Strait = proliv la Pérouse 166-167 R 2
Lapine, OR 66-67 C 4
Lapin lääni 114-115 L-N 4
Lapinlahti 114-115 MN 6
Laplace, LA 78-79 D 5
Lapland 114-115 F 5-N 3
Laplandskij zapovednik 114-115 OP 4
La Plant, ND 68-69 F 3
La Plant, SD 68-69 F 3
La Plata, IA 70-71 D 5
La Plata, MD 72-73 H 5
La Plata, MO 70-71 D 5
La Pointe, WI 70-71 E 2
La Porte, IN 70-71 G 5
Laporte, PA 72-73 H 4
La Porte, TX 76-77 G 8
La Porte City, IA 70-71 DE 4
Lapovo 138-139 J 3
Lappajärvi 114-115 KL 6
Lappeenranta 114-115 N 7
Lappi 114-115 L 5
Laprida [RA, Buenos Aires] 103 D 5
La Pryor, TX 76-77 DE 8
Lapteva Strait = proliv Dmitrija Lapteva 154-155 a-c 3
Laptev Sea 154-155 V 2-Z 3
Lapua 114-115 K 6
Lapush, WA 66-67 A 2
Łapy 124 L 2
Laqawah, Al- 194-195 K 6
Lār 160-161 G 5
Larache = Al-'Arā'ish 194-195 C 1
Laramie, WY 58-59 EF 3
Laramie Peak 68-69 D 4
Laramie Plains 68-69 D 4-5
Laramie Range 58-59 E 3
Laramie River 68-69 D 4-5
Laranjal 98-99 K 7
Laranjeiras do Sul 103 F 3
Larantuka 174-175 H 8
Larat, Pulau — 174-175 K 8
Lärbro 114-115 H 9
Larch River 46-47 W 6
Larder Lake 50 M 2
Laredo, IA 70-71 D 5-6
Laredo, TX 58-59 G 6
Lārestān 160-161 GH 5
Largeau = Faya-Largeau 194-195 H 5
Largo Remo, Isla — 58-59 b 2
Largo Remo Island 58-59 b 2
Largs 116-117 G 5
Lariang 174-175 G 7
Larimore, ND 68-69 GH 2
Larino 138-139 F 5
Lárisa 138-139 K 6
Laristan = Lārestān 160-161 GH 5

Laristan 243

Likati 198 D 1
Likely 48 G 3
Likely, CA 66-67 C 5
Likiang = Lijiang 166-167 J 6
Likoma Island 198 FG 4
Likoto 198 D 2
Likouala [RCB ⊲ Sangha] 198 C 1
Likouala [RCB ⊲ Zaïre] 198 C 1
Likuala = Likouala [RCB ⊲ Sangha] 198 C 1
Likuala = Likouala [RCB ⊲ Zaïre] 198 C 1
Likupang 174-175 J 6
Liland 114-115 G 3
Lilbourn, MO 78-79 E 2
Lille 132-133 J 3
Lille Bælt 114-115 CD 10
Lille-Ballangen 114-115 G 3
Lillehammer 114-115 D 7
Lillesand 114-115 C 8
Lillestrøm 114-115 D 7-8
Lillian Lake 51 F 2
Lillooet 48 FG 4
Lillooet Range 48 F 4-G 5
Lilongwe [MW, place] 198 F 4
Lim 138-139 H 4
Lima, MT 66-67 G 3
Lima, OH 58-59 K 3
Lima [P] 132-133 C 8
Lima [PE, place] 98-99 D 7
Lima = Dsayul 166-167 H 6
Lima, La — 88-89 B 7
Limão, Cachoeira do — 98-99 J 6
Lima Reservoir 66-67 GH 3
Limasol = Lemesós 160-161 C 4
Limassol = Lemesós 160-161 C 4
Limavady 116-117 E 5
Lima Village, AK 52-53 K 6
Limay, Río — 103 C 5
Limay Mahuida 103 C 5
Limbang 174-175 FG 6
Limburg 124 D 3
Limchow = Hepu 166-167 K 7
Limeira 98-99 K 9
Limerick = Luimneach 116-117 C 8
Limestone River 49 L 2
Limfjorden 114-115 D 9
Limia 132-133 C 8-D 7
Li Miao Zhou = Hainan Zangzu Zizhizhou 166-167 K 8
Limin = Thásos 138-139 L 5
Liminka 114-115 L 5
Limkong = Lianjiang 166-167 KL 7
Limmen Bight 182-183 G 2
Límnē 138-139 K 6
Limoges [CDN] 72-73 J 2
Limoges [F] 132-133 H 6
Limón 58-59 K 9-10
Limon, CO 68-69 E 6
Limón, Bahía — 58-59 b 2
Limon Bay 58-59 b 2
Limousin 132-133 HJ 6
Limoux 132-133 J 7
Limpia, Laguna — [RA ↖ Resistencia] 103 DE 3
Limpopo 198 E 6
Lin 138-139 J 5
Linan = Jianshui 166-167 J 7
Linares [CO] 98-99 D 4
Linares [E] 132-133 F 9
Linares [MEX] 58-59 G 7
Linares [RCH] 103 B 5
Lincang 166-167 HJ 7
Lin-chiang = Linjiang [TJ, Jilin] 166-167 O 3
Lin-ch'ing = Linqing 166-167 M 4
Linchow = Hepu 166-167 K 7
Linchuan = Fuzhou 166-167 MN 6
Lincoln, CA 74-75 C 3
Lincoln, IL 70-71 F 5
Lincoln, KS 68-69 G 6
Lincoln, ME 72-73 M 2
Lincoln, NE 58-59 G 3
Lincoln, NH 72-73 KL 2
Lincoln, NM 76-77 B 6
Lincoln [GB, administrative unit] 116-117 LM 7
Lincoln [GB, place] 116-117 L 7
Lincoln [RA] 103 D 4
Lincoln Center 82 III c 2
Lincoln City, IN 70-71 G 6
Lincolnia Heights, VA 82 II a 2
Lincoln Memorial 82 II a 2
Lincoln Museum 82 II ab 2
Lincoln Park, MI 72-73 E 3
Lincoln Park [USA, Chicago] 83 II b 1
Lincoln Park [USA, New York] 82 III b 2
Lincoln Park [USA, San Francisco] 83 I ab 2
Lincoln Sea 30 A 24-25
Lincolnton, NC 80-81 F 3
Lincoln Wolds 116-117 LM 7
Lind, WA 66-67 D 2
Lindale, GA 78-79 G 3
Lindale, TX 76-77 G 6
Lindau [D] 124 D 5
Linde [SU] 154-155 X 4
Linden, AL 78-79 F 4
Linden, IN 70-71 G 5
Linden, NJ 82 III a 3
Linden, TN 78-79 F 3
Linden, TX 76-77 G 6
Linden Airport 82 III a 3
Lindesberg 114-115 F 8
Lindesnes 114-115 B 9
Lindi [EAT] 198 G 3-4
Lindi [ZRE] 198 E 1
Lindian 166-167 NO 2
Líndos 138-139 N 7
Lindsay 72-73 G 2
Lindsay, CA 74-75 D 4
Lindsay, MT 68-69 D 2
Lindsay, OK 76-77 F 5
Lindsborg, KS 68-69 H 6
Linea, La — 132-133 E 10
Lineville, AL 78-79 G 4
Lineville, IA 70-71 D 5
Linfen 166-167 L 4
Lingao 166-167 K 8
Lingayen Gulf 174-175 GH 3
Linge [BUR] 174-175 C 2
Lingeh = Bandar-e Lengeh 160-161 GH 5
Lingen 124 C 2
Lingfield 116-117 LM 9
Lingga, Kepulauan — 174-175 DE 7
Lingga, Pulau — 174-175 DE 7
Lingle, WY 68-69 D 4
Lingling 166-167 L 6
Lingman Lake 50 C 1
Lingmar 166-167 F 5-6
Linguère 194-195 AB 5
Lingyuan 170-171 B 2
Ling-yüan = Lingyuan 170-171 B 2
Lingyun 166-167 K 7
Linhai 166-167 N 6
Linhares 98-99 LM 8
Linh Cam 174-175 E 3
Linhe 166-167 K 3
Lin-ho = Linhe 166-167 K 3
Lin-hsi = Linxi 166-167 M 3
Lin-hsia = Linxia 166-167 J 4
Lini = Linyi [TJ ↗ Xuzhou] 166-167 M 4
Linjiang [TJ, Jilin] 166-167 O 3
Linköping 114-115 FG 8
Linkou 166-167 OP 2
Linkow = Linkou 166-167 OP 2
Linli 166-167 L 6
Linlithgow 116-117 H 5
Linn, KS 68-69 H 6
Linn, MO 70-71 E 6
Linn, TX 76-77 E 9
Linn, Mount — 66-67 B 5
Linné, Kapp — 114-115 j 5
Linnhe, Loch — 116-117 F 4
Linosa 138-139 E 8
Linosa, Ìsola — 194-195 G 1
Linqing 166-167 M 4
Lins 98-99 JK 9
Linsia = Linxia 166-167 J 4
Linsin = Linxia 166-167 J 4
Lintan 166-167 J 5
Lintao 166-167 J 4
Lintien = Lindian 166-167 NO 2
Linton, IN 70-71 G 6
Linton, ND 68-69 FG 2
Linton-Jonction 72-73 KL 1
Lintsing = Linqing 166-167 M 4
Linxi 166-167 M 3
Linxia 166-167 J 4
Linxia Huizu Zizhizhou 166-167 J 4
Linyanti 198 D 5
Linyi [TJ, Shandong ↗ Xuzhou] 166-167 M 4
Linyu = Shanhaiguan 170-171 BC 2
Linz 124 FG 4
Lion, Golf du — 132-133 JK 7
Lions, Gulf of — = Golfe du Lion 132-133 JK 7
Lions Head 72-73 F 2
Lios Bún Bheárna 116-117 BC 7
Lios Ceannúir, Bádh — 116-117 B 8
Lios Mor 116-117 D 8
Lios Tuathail 116-117 B 8
Liouesso 198 BC 1
Lípari 138-139 F 6
Lipari Islands = Ìsole Eòlie o Lípari 138-139 F 6
Lipeck 142-143 G 5
Lípez, Cordillera de — 98-99 F 9
Lipin Bor 142-143 G 3
Liping 166-167 K 6
Lipljan 138-139 J 4
Lipno 124 J 2
Lipova 138-139 J 2
Lippe 124 C 3
Lippstadt 124 D 3
Lipscomb, TX 76-77 D 4
Lipton 49 G 5
Lipu 166-167 KL 7
Lira 198 F 1
Liranga 198 C 2
Lisala 198 D 1
Lisboa 132-133 C 9
Lisbon, ND 68-69 H 2
Lisbon, OH 72-73 F 4
Lisbon = Lisboa 132-133 C 9
Lisbon, Rock of — = Cabo da Roca 132-133 C 9
Lisburn 116-117 E 6
Lisburne, Cape — 46-47 C 4
Liscannor Bay = Bádh Lios Ceannúir 116-117 B 8
Liscomb 51 F 5
Lisdoonvarna = Lios Dún Bheárna 116-117 BC 7
Lishi 166-167 L 4
Lishih = Lishi 166-167 L 4
Lishui [TJ, Zhejiang] 166-167 MN 6
Lisičansk 142-143 G 6
Lisieux 132-133 H 4
Liskeard 116-117 G 10
Lisle, NY 72-73 HJ 3
Lismore [AUS] 182-183 K 5
Lismore [CDN] 51 E 5
Lismore = Lios Mór 116-117 D 8
Lista 114-115 B 8
Lister, Mount — 31 B 17
Listowel [CDN] 72-73 F 3
Listowel = Lios Tuathail 116-117 B 8
Litan 166-167 J 5
Litang 166-167 K 7
Litchfield, CA 66-67 CD 5
Litchfield, IL 70-71 F 6
Litchfield, MN 70-71 C 3
Litchfield, NE 68-69 G 5
Litchville, ND 68-69 G 2
Līth, Al- 160-161 E 6
Lithgow 182-183 K 6
Lithuanian Soviet Socialist Republic 142-143 DE 4
Litinon, Cape — = Akrōtḗrion Lídinon 138-139 L 8
Litke 154-155 ab 7
Lítla Dímun 116-117 b 2
Litóchōron 138-139 K 5
Litoměřice 124 G 3
Litomyšl 124 GH 4
Litovko 154-155 Za 8
Little Abaco Island 88-89 GH 1
Little Abitibi Lake 50 L 2
Little Abitibi River 50 L 1-2
Little Andaman 160-161 P 8
Little Bay de Noc 70-71 G 3
Little Belt = Lille Bælt 114-115 CD 10
Little Belt Mountains 66-67 H 2
Little Bighorn River 68-69 C 3
Little Black River 52-53 Q 3
Little Blue River 68-69 G 5
Little Bow River 49 B 5
Little Bullhead 50 A 2
Little Carpathians = Male Karpaty 124 H 4
Little Cayman 58-59 KL 8
Little Churchill River 49 L 2
Little Colorado River 58-59 DE 5
Little Current 50 KL 4
Little Current River 50 FG 2
Little Falls, MN 70-71 C 2-3
Little Falls, NJ 82 III a 1
Little Falls, NY 72-73 J 3
Little Falls Dam 82 II a 1
Littlefield, AZ 74-75 G 4
Littlefield, TX 76-77 CD 6
Littlefork, MN 70-71 D 1
Little Fork River 70-71 D 1
Little Fort 48 G 4
Little Grande Lake 51 H 3
Little Grand Rapids 50 B 1
Littlehampton 116-117 L 10
Little Humboldt River 66-67 E 5
Little Inagua Island 88-89 K 4
Little Kiska Island 52-53 rs 7
Little Koniuji Island 52-53 d 2
Little Lake, CA 74-75 E 5
Little Longlac 50 F 3
Little Mecatina River 46-47 YZ 7
Little Melozitna River 52-53 L 4
Little Minch 116-117 DE 3
Little Missouri River 68-69 E 2
Little Neck Bay 82 III d 2
Little Nicobar 160-161 P 9
Little Osage River 70-71 C 7
Little Pee Dee River 80-81 G 3-4
Littleport 116-117 M 8
Little Powder River 68-69 D 3
Little River, KS 68-69 GH 6
Little Rock, AR 58-59 H 5
Littlerock, CA 74-75 DE 5
Little Rock, WA 66-67 B 2
Little Rock Mountains 66-67 J 1-2
Little Rocky Mountains 68-69 B 1-2
Little Sable Point 70-71 G 4
Little Salmon Lake 52-53 U 5
Little Sanke River 68-69 B 5
Little Sioux River 70-71 C 4
Little Sitkin Island 52-53 s 7
Little Smoky 48 J 2
Little Smoky River 48 J 2
Little Smoky Valley 74-75 F 3
Little Snake River 66-67 J 5
Littleton, CO 68-69 D 6
Littleton, NC 80-81 GH 2
Littleton, NH 72-73 L 2
Little Traverse Bay 70-71 H 3
Little Valley, NY 72-73 G 3
Little Wood River 66-67 FG 4
Liu-chia-tzŭ = Liujiazi 170-171 C 2
Liuchow = Liuzhou 166-167 K 7
Liuhe [TJ, Jilin] 170-171 E 1
Liu-ho = Liuhe [TJ, Jilin] 170-171 E 1
Liujiazi 170-171 C 2
Liurbao 170-171 D 2
Liuwa Plain 198 D 4
Liuzhou 166-167 K 7
Livengood, AK 52-53 N 4
Live Oak, FL 80-81 b 1
Livermore, CA 74-75 C 4
Livermore, IA 70-71 CD 4
Livermore, KY 70-71 G 7
Livermore, Mount — 58-59 F 5
Livermore Falls, ME 72-73 LM 2
Liverpool [CDN] 51 D 5-6
Liverpool [GB] 116-117 J 7
Liverpool Bay [CDN] 46-47 L 3-4
Liverpool Bay [GB] 116-117 H 7
Liverpool Range 182-183 JK 6
Livingston, AL 78-79 EF 4
Livingston, KY 72-73 DE 6
Livingston, MT 66-67 H 3
Livingston, TN 78-79 G 2
Livingston, TX 76-77 G 7
Livingstone 198 E 5
Livingstone Creek 52-53 UV 6
Livingstone Memorial 198 F 4
Livingstone Mountains 198 F 3-4
Livingstonia = Chiweta 198 F 4
Livingston Island 31 CD 30
Livno 138-139 G 4
Livny 142-143 G 5
Livonia, MI 72-73 E 3
Livorno 138-139 CD 4
Liwale 198 G 3
Lǐ Yūbū 194-195 K 7
Lizard 116-117 F 11
Lizarda 98-99 K 6
Lizard Head Peak 66-67 J 4
Lizard Point 116-117 F 11
Ljubljana 138-139 F 2
Ljungan 114-115 G 6
Ljungby 114-115 E 9
Ljusdal 114-115 FG 7
Ljusnan 114-115 F 6-7
Ljusne 114-115 G 7
Llamellín 98-99 D 6
Llandaff, Cardiff- 116-117 HJ 9
Llandeilo 116-117 GH 9
Llandovery 116-117 H 8-9
Llandrindod Wells 116-117 H 8
Llandudno 116-117 H 7
Llanelli 116-117 G 9
Llanes 132-133 E 7
Llanfairfechan 116-117 H 7
Llangefni 116-117 G 7
Llangollen 116-117 HJ 8
Llangynog 116-117 H 8
Llannon 116-117 GH 9
Llano, TX 76-77 E 7
Llano Estacado 58-59 F 5
Llano Estacado, Bluffs of — 76-77 C 5
Llano River 76-77 E 7
Llanquihue, Lago — 103 B 6
Llanrwst 116-117 H 7
Llantrisant 116-117 H 9
Llata 98-99 D 6
Llera de Canales 86-87 L 6
Llerena 132-133 DE 9
Lleyn Peninsula 116-117 FG 8
Llobregat 132-133 H 8
Llorena, Punta — = Punta San Pedro 58-59 K 10
Lloron, Cerro — 86-87 H 7
Lloyd Bay 182-183 H 2
Lloyd Lake 49 D 2
Lloydminster 46-47 OP 7
Llullaillaco, Volcán — 103 C 2-3
Loa, UT 74-75 H 3
Loa, Río — 103 BC 2
Loanda = Luanda 198 B 3
Loange 198 D 2-3
Loango 198 B 2
Lobatse 198 DE 7
Lobaye 194-195 H 8
Lobería [RA, Buenos Aires] 103 E 5
Lobito 198 B 4
Lob nuur 166-167 G 3
Lobos, Cayo — 86-87 R 8
Lobos, Point — 83 I a 2
Lobstick Lake 46-47 Y 7
Lobva 142-143 LM 4
Locate, MT 68-69 D 2
Lochaline 116-117 F 4
Lochboisdale 116-117 DE 3
Loche, La — 46-47 P 6
Loche West, La — 49 CD 2
Loch Garman 116-117 E 8
Loch Garman, Cuan — 116-117 EF 8
Lochgilphead 116-117 F 4
Lo-ch'ing = Yueqing 166-167 N 6
Lochinver 116-117 F 2
Lochmaddy 116-117 DE 3
Lochnagar 116-117 H 4
Lochsa River 66-67 F 2
Lochy, Loch — 116-117 G 4
Lockeport 51 D 6
Lockerbie 116-117 H 5
Lockes, NV 74-75 F 3
Lockesburg, AR 76-77 GH 6
Lockhart, AL 78-79 F 5
Lockhart, TX 76-77 F 8
Lock Haven, PA 72-73 H 4
Lockney, TX 76-77 D 5
Lockport, LA 78-79 D 6
Lockport, NY 72-73 G 3
Lockwood, MO 76-77 GH 4
Lôc Ninh 174-175 E 4
Locri 138-139 G 6
Locust Creek 70-71 D 5
Lodejnoje Pole 142-143 FG 3
Lodge, Mount — 52-53 T 7
Lodge Creek 68-69 B 1
Lodge Grass, MT 68-69 C 3
Lodgepole, NE 68-69 E 5
Lodgepole Creek 68-69 D 5
Lodi 138-139 C 3
Lodi, CA 74-75 C 3
Lodi, NJ 82 III b 1
Lodi, WI 70-71 F 4
Lødingen 114-115 F 3
Lodja 198 D 2
Lodwar 198 G 1
Łódź 124 J 3
Loei 174-175 D 3
Loffa River 194-195 B 7
Lofoten 114-115 E 3-4
Lofoten Basin 110-111 JK 1
Lofthus 114-115 B 7
Lofty Range, Mount — 182-183 G 6
Logan, IA 70-71 BC 5
Logan, KS 68-69 G 6
Logan, NE 68-69 F 5
Logan, NM 76-77 C 5
Logan, OH 72-73 E 5
Logan, UT 58-59 D 3
Logan, WV 80-81 EF 2
Logan, Mount — [CDN, Quebec] 51 C 3
Logan, Mount — [CDN, Yukon Territory] 46-47 HJ 5
Logandale, NV 74-75 F 4
Logan Glacier 52-53 RS 6
Logan Island 50 E 2
Logan Mountains 46-47 L 5
Logansport, IN 58-59 J 3
Logansport, LA 78-79 C 5
Logan Square, Chicago-, IL 83 II a 1
Loge, Rio — 198 B 3
Log na Coille 116-117 E 7-8
Logone 194-195 H 7
Logroño [E] 132-133 F 7
Løgstør 114-115 C 9
Lohārdaga 160-161 N 6
Lōhārdaggā = Lohārdaga 160-161 N 6
Lōhit = Luhit 160-161 Q 5
Lohja 114-115 KL 7
Lohtaja 114-115 K 5
Loibl 124 G 5
Loikaw = Lûykau 174-175 C 3
Loimaa 114-115 K 7
Loir 132-133 G 5
Loire 132-133 H 5
Loja [E] 132-133 E 10
Loja [EC, place] 98-99 D 5
Loji 174-175 J 7
Lo-jung = Luorong 166-167 K 7
Lokan tekojärvi 114-115 MN 3
Lokitaung 198 FG 1
Lokka 114-115 MN 4
Lokoja 194-195 F 7
Lokolo 198 CD 2
Loks Land 46-47 Y 5
Lōl, Nahr — = Nahr Lūl 194-195 K 7
Lola, Mount — 74-75 C 3
Loleta, CA 66-67 A 5
Lolland 114-115 D 10
Lolo 198 B 2
Lolo, MT 66-67 F 2
Lolobau 174-175 h 5
Loloda 174-175 J 6
Lom [BG] 138-139 K 4
Lom [RFC] 194-195 G 7
Loma, MT 66-67 H 1-2
Loma, ND 68-69 G 1
Loma Bonita 86-87 MN 8-9
Lomadi 174-175 C 3
Lomami 198 DE 2
Loma Mountains 194-195 B 7
Lomas [PE] 98-99 E 8
Lomax, IL 70-71 E 5
Lombard, MT 66-67 H 2
Lombarda, Serra — 98-99 J 4
Lombardia 138-139 C 3-D 2
Lombardy = Lombardia 138-139 C 3-D 2
Lomblem = Pulau Lomblen 174-175 H 8
Lomblen, Pulau — 174-175 H 8
Lombok, Pulau — 174-175 G 8
Lombok, Selat — 174-175 G 8
Lomé 194-195 E 7
Lomela [ZRE, place] 198 D 2
Lomela [ZRE, river] 198 D 2
Lometa, TX 76-77 E 7
Lomié 194-195 G 8
Lomita, CA 83 III c 3
Lomitas, Las — 103 D 2
Lomond 49 B 5
Lomond, Ben — 116-117 G 4
Lomond, Loch — 116-117 G 4
Lomonosov 142-143 E 4
Lomonosov Ridge 30 A
Lomonosovskij 154-155 M 7
Lompoc, CA 74-75 C 5
Lom Sak 174-175 D 3
Łomża 124 L 2
Loncoche 103 B 5
London, KY 72-73 DE 6
London, OH 72-73 E 5
London, TX 76-77 E 7
London [CDN] 46-47 UV 9
London [GB] 116-117 LM 9
Londonderry 116-117 DE 5-6
Londonderry, Cape — 182-183 E 2
Londonderry, Islas — 103 B 9
Londrina 103 FG 2
Lone Mountain 74-75 E 4
Lone Oak, TX 76-77 FG 6
Lone Pine, CA 74-75 DE 4
Lonerock, OR 66-67 D 3
Lone Rock, WI 70-71 EF 4
Lone Star 48 HJ 1
Lonetree, WY 66-67 H 5
Lone Wolf, OK 76-77 E 5
Long, AK 52-53 K 4
Long, ostrova de — 154-155 c-e 2
Longa [Angola] 198 C 4
Long Bay [USA] 58-59 L 5
Long Beach, CA 58-59 BC 5
Long Beach, NY 82 III d 3
Long Beach Municipal Airport 83 III d 3
Longboat Key 80-81 b 3
Long Branch, NJ 72-73 JK 4
Long Cay 88-89 J 3
Longchuan [TJ, Dehong Daizu Zizhizhou] 166-167 H 7
Long Creek, OR 66-67 D 3
Longdor, gora — 154-155 W 6
Long Eaton 116-117 K 8
Long Eddy, NY 72-73 J 4
Longfellow, TX 76-77 C 7
Longford [AUS] 182-183 J 8
Longford = Longphort 116-117 D 7
Longhua 166-167 M 3
Longiram 174-175 G 6-7
Long Island, KS 68-69 G 6
Long Island [BS] 58-59 LM 7
Long Island [CDN] 46-47 UV 7
Long Island [PNG] 174-175 N 7-8
Long Island [USA, New York] 58-59 M 3-4
Long Island City, New York-, NY 82 III c 2
Long Island Sound 72-73 K 4
Longjing 170-171 G 1
Longlac 50 F 3
Long Lake, WI 70-71 F 3
Long Lake [CDN, Ontario] 70-71 G 1
Long Lake [CDN, Yukon Territory] 52-53 T 6
Long Lake [USA, Alaska] 52-53 K 6
Long Lake [USA, Michigan] 70-71 J 3
Long Lake [USA, North Dakota] 68-69 G 2
Longleaf, LA 78-79 C 5
Longling 166-167 H 7
Long Melford 116-117 MN 8
Longmire, WA 66-67 C 2
Longmont, CO 68-69 D 5
Long Mountain 116-117 HJ 8
Longnan 166-167 LM 7
Longnawan 174-175 FG 6
Longphort 116-117 D 7
Long Pine, NE 68-69 G 4
Long Point [CDN, Lake Winnipeg] 49 J 4
Long Point [CDN, Ontario] 72-73 FG 3
Long Point Bay 72-73 FG 3
Long Prairie, MN 70-71 C 2-3
Longqi = Zhangzhou 166-167 M 7
Longquan 166-167 M 6
Long Range Mountains 46-47 Z 7-8
Longreach 182-183 H 4
Longs Peak 58-59 E 3
Long Sutton 116-117 M 8
Longton, KS 76-77 FG 4
Longton, Stoke on Trent- 116-117 JK 8
Longtown [GB, Hereford & Worcester] 116-117 HJ 9
Longtown [GB, Northumberland] 116-117 J 5
Longueuil 72-73 K 2
Longvalley, SD 68-69 F 4
Long Valley [USA, California] 74-75 D 4
Long Valley [USA, Nevada] 66-67 D 5
Longview, TX 58-59 GH 5
Longview, WA 58-59 B 2
Longxi 166-167 J 4-5
Long Xuyên 174-175 DE 4
Longyearbyen 114-115 jk 5
Longyou 166-167 M 6
Longzhen 166-167 O 2
Lonja 138-139 G 3
Lonoke, AR 78-79 CD 3
Lønsdal 114-115 F 4
Lons-le-Saunier 132-133 K 5
Lontra 98-99 N 7
Looe 116-117 G 10
Loogootee, IN 70-71 G 6
Lookout, Cape — [USA, North Carolina] 58-59 L 5
Lookout, Cape — [USA, Oregon] 66-67 A 3
Lookout Mount 52-53 H 5
Lookout Mountain 66-67 E 3
Lookout Mountains [USA, Alabama] 78-79 G 3
Lookout Mountains [USA, Washington] 66-67 BC 2
Lookout Pass 66-67 F 2
Lookout Ridge 52-53 HJ 2
Lookwood Hills 52-53 JK 3
Loon 70-71 F 1
Loongana 182-183 E 6

Loongana 245

Loon Lake [CDN, Alberta] 48 K 1
Loon Lake [CDN, Saskatchewan] 49 D 4
Loon River [CDN, Alberta] 49 A 2
Loon River [CDN, Manitoba] 49 H 2
Loon Straits 50 A 2
Loop, Chicago-, IL 83 II b 1
Loop Head = Ceann Léime 116-117 AB 8
Lopatina, gora — 154-155 b 7
Lopatino = Volžsk 154-155 H 6
Lop Buri 174-175 D 4
Lopez, Cap — 198 A 2
Loping = Leping 166-167 M 6
Lop Noor = Lob nuur 166-167 G 3
Lop Nor = Lob nuur 166-167 G 3
Lopori 198 D 1
Lopphavet 114-115 JK 2
Lopp Lagoon 52-53 D 3-4
Lopt'uga 142-143 J 3
Lopydino 142-143 K 3
Lōra, Hāmūn-e — 160-161 JK 5
Lora Creek 182-183 FG 5
Lora del Río 132-133 E 10
Lorain, OH 58-59 K 3
Loralai = Lorālāy 160-161 K 4
Lorālāy 160-161 K 4
Lorca 132-133 G 10
Lord Howe Island 182-183 LM 6
Lord Howe Islands = Ontong Java Islands 174-175 j 6
Lord Howe Rise 182-183 M 5-7
Lord Mayor Bay 46-47 ST 4
Lordsburg, NM 74-75 J 6
Lorena 98-99 KL 9
Lorengau 174-175 N 7
Lorestān 160-161 F 4
Loreto [BOL] 98-99 G 8
Loreto [BR, Amazonas] 98-99 F 5
Loreto [BR, Maranhão] 98-99 K 6
Loreto [CO] 98-99 EF 5
Loreto [MEX, Baja California Norte] 58-59 D 6
Loreto [MEX, Zacatecas] 86-87 JK 6
Lorette 49 K 6
Lorian Swamp 198 GH 1
Lorica 98-99 D 3
Lorient 132-133 F 5
Lorimor, IA 70-71 C 5
Loring, MT 68-69 C 1
Loris, SC 80-81 G 3
Lorne, Firth of — 116-117 EF 4
Loro 98-99 F 4
Loros, Los — 103 BC 3
Lörrach 124 C 5
Lorraine 132-133 KL 4
Los Alamitos, CA 83 III d 3
Los Alamos, CA 74-75 C 5
Los Alamos, NM 58-59 E 4
Los Angeles 83 III c 2
Los Angeles, CA 58-59 BC 5
Los Angeles, TX 76-77 E 8
Los Ángeles, Bahía de — 86-87 CD 3
Los Angeles Aqueduct 74-75 DE 5
Los Angeles County Art Museum 83 III b 1
Los Angeles International Airport 83 III b 2
Losap 178 F 2
Los Banos, CA 74-75 C 4
Los Gatos, CA 74-75 C 4
Lošinj 138-139 F 3
Los Lunas, NM 76-77 A 5
Los Molinos, CA 66-67 BC 5
Los Monjes, Islas — 98-99 EF 2
Los Nietos, CA 83 III d 2
Los Reyes de Salgado 86-87 J 8
Los Roques, Islas — 98-99 F 2
Lossiemouth 116-117 HJ 3
Lost Creek 68-69 B 4
Los Testigos, Islas — 98-99 G 2
Lost Hills, CA 74-75 D 5
Lost River, AK 52-53 D 4
Lost River Range 66-67 FG 3
Lost Springs, WY 68-69 D 4
Lost Trail Pass 66-67 G 3
Lot [F] 132-133 H 6
Lota 103 B 5
Lotagipi Swamp 198 FG 1
Lothair, MT 66-67 H 1
Lothian 116-117 HJ 5
Lotmozero 114-115 NO 3
Lott, TX 76-77 F 7
Lotta 142-143 EF 2
Loubomo 198 B 2
Louchi 154-155 E 4
Loudéac 132-133 F 4
Loudonville, OH 72-73 EF 4
Louellen, KY 80-81 E 2
Louga 194-195 A 5
Loughborough 116-117 KL 8
Lougheed Island 46-47 PQ 2
Loughrea = Baile Locha Riach 116-117 C 7
Louisa, VA 72-73 GH 5
Louisbourg 46-47 Z 8
Louisburg, NC 80-81 G 2
Louise, TX 76-77 F 8
Louise, Lake — 52-53 O 5
Louise Island 48 B 3
Louiseville 72-73 K 1
Louisiade Archipelago 174-175 h 7
Louisiana 58-59 H 5
Louisiana, MO 70-71 E 6
Louisiana Point 76-77 GH 8
Louis Trichardt 198 EF 6
Louisville, CO 68-69 D 6
Louisville, GA 80-81 E 4
Louisville, IL 70-71 F 6
Louisville, KY 58-59 JK 4
Louisville, MS 78-79 E 4
Louisville, NE 68-69 H 5
Loulan = Loulanyiyi 166-167 F 3
Loulanyiyi 166-167 F 3
Loulé 132-133 C 10
Loup City, NE 68-69 G 5
Loup River 58-59 G 3
Lourdes [CDN] 51 G 3
Lourdes [F] 132-133 G 7
Lourenço 98-99 N 3
Lourenço Marques = Maputo 198 F 7
Lourenço Marques, Baía de — = Baía do Maputo 198 F 7
Lousia, KY 72-73 E 5
Louth [AUS] 182-183 HJ 6
Louth [GB] 116-117 LM 7
Louth = Lughbhadh 116-117 E 6-7
Louvain = Leuven 132-133 K 3
Louviers 132-133 H 4
Louviers, CO 68-69 D 6
Lovászi 124 H 5
Lovat' 142-143 F 4
Loveč 138-139 L 4
Lovelady, TX 76-77 G 7
Loveland, CO 68-69 D 5
Loveland, OH 70-71 H 6
Lovell, WY 68-69 B 3
Lovelock, NV 66-67 D 5
Lovenia, Mount — 66-67 H 5
Loverna 49 CD 5
Loviisa = Lovisa 114-115 M 7
Lovilia, IA 70-71 D 5
Loving, NM 76-77 BC 6
Lovingston, VA 80-81 G 2
Lovington, IL 70-71 F 6
Lovington, NM 76-77 C 6
Lovisa 114-115 M 7
Lovľa 142-143 JK 4
Lovozero 142-143 G 2
Lóvua 198 D 4
Low 72-73 HJ 2
Low, Cape — 46-47 T 5
Lowa 198 E 2
Low Cape 52-53 f 1
Lowell, ID 66-67 F 2
Lowell, IN 70-71 G 5
Lowell, MA 58-59 M 3
Lowell, MI 70-71 H 4
Lowell, OR 66-67 B 4
Lower Arrow Lake 66-67 D 1
Lower Austria = Niederösterreich 124 F-H 4
Lower Bay 82 III b 3
Lower Brule Indian Reservation 68-69 F 3
Lower California 86-87 B 2-E 5
Lower California = Baja California 58-59 C 5-D 7
Lower Egypt = Miṣr-Baḥrī 199 BC 2
Lower Guinea 26-27 K 5-6
Lower Hutt 182-183 OP 8
Lower Kalskag, AK 52-53 G 6
Lower Laberge 52-53 U 6
Lower Lake 66-67 CD 5
Lower Lake, CA 74-75 B 3
Lower Lough Erne 116-117 D 6
Lower Peninsula 58-59 JK 3
Lower Red Lake 70-71 C 2
Lower Saxony = Niedersachsen 124 C-E 2
Lower Tonsina, AK 52-53 PQ 6
Lower Tunguska = Nižn'aja Tunguska 154-155 Q 4-R 5
Lowestoft 116-117 h 6
Łowicz 124 J 2
Lowlands 116-117 H 5-J 4
Lowman, ID 66-67 F 3
Lowville, NY 72-73 J 3
Loyalton, CA 74-75 C 3
Loyalton, SD 68-69 G 3
Loyalty Islands = Îles Loyauté 182-183 N 4
Loyang = Luoyang 166-167 L 5
Loyauté, Îles — 182-183 N 4
Loyola Marymount University 83 III b 2
Lozère 132-133 J 6
Loznica 138-139 H 3
Lozva 142-143 M 3-4

Luacano 198 D 4
Luachimo 198 D 3
Luala 198 E 3
Lualaba 198 E 3
Luama 198 E 2
Lu'an 166-167 M 5
Luanda 198 B 3
Luando, Rio — 198 C 4
Luang, Khao — [T ← Nakhon Si Thammarat] 174-175 CD 5
Luang, Thale — 174-175 D 5
Luanginga, Rio — 198 D 4
Lu'ang Prabang 174-175 D 3
Luangue, Rio — 198 C 3
Luangwa 198 F 4
Luangwa Valley Game Reserve 198 F 4
Lua Nova 98-99 K 7
Luanping 166-167 M 3
Luanshya 198 E 4
Luan Xian 166-167 M 4
Luapula 198 E 4
Luarca 132-133 D 7
Luau 198 D 4
Lubaantun 86-87 Q 9
Lubań [PL] 124 G 3
Lubang Islands 174-175 G 4
Lubango 198 B 4
Lubbock, TX 58-59 F 5
L'ubča 142-143 E 5
Lübeck 124 E 2
Lubefu [ZRE, place] 198 D 2
Lubefu [ZRE, river] 198 D 2
L'ubercy 142-143 G 4
Lubero 198 E 2
Lubilash 198 D 3
Lubin 124 H 3
L'ubinskij 154-155 N 6
Lublin 124 L 3
Lubliniec 124 J 3
Lubny 142-143 F 5-6
L'ubotin 142-143 G 6
Lubudi [ZRE, place] 198 E 3
Lubudi [ZRE, river] 198 DE 3
Lubuklinggau 174-175 D 7
Lubuksikaping 174-175 CD 6
Lubumbashi 198 E 4
Lubutu 198 E 2
Lucania, Mount — 46-47 HJ 5
Lucas, IA 70-71 D 5
Lucas, KS 68-69 G 6
Lucas, Punta — = Cape Meredith 103 D 8
Lucas Channel = Main Channel 50 L 4
Lucca 138-139 D 4
Lucea 88-89 G 5
Luce Bay 116-117 G 6
Lucedale, MS 78-79 E 5
Lucena [E] 132-133 E 10
Lucena [RP] 174-175 H 4
Lučenec 124 J 4
Lucera 138-139 F 5
Lucerne, IA 70-71 D 5
Lucerne = Luzern 124 CD 5
Lucerne, Lake — = Vierwaldstätter See 124 D 5
Lucerne Lake 74-75 E 5
Lucerne Valley, CA 74-75 E 5
Lucero, El — [MEX] 76-77 C 10
Lu-chou = Hefei 166-167 M 5
Luchow = Lu Xian 166-167 K 6
Luchuan 166-167 KL 7
Luchwan = Luchuan 166-167 KL 7
Lucia, CA 74-75 C 4
Luciara 98-99 N 10
Lucie 98-99 K 3
Lucie, Lac — 50 M 1
Lucin, UT 66-67 G 5
Lucipara, Pulau-pulau — 174-175 J 8
Lucira 198 B 4
Luck 142-143 DE 5
Luck, WI 70-71 D 3
Luckenwalde 124 F 2
Lucknow [CDN] 72-73 F 3
Lucknow [IND] 160-161 MN 5
Lucky Lake 49 E 5
Lucrecia, Cabo — 88-89 J 4
Lucy, NM 76-77 B 5
Lüda [TJ] 166-167 N 4
Ludden, ND 68-69 G 2
Ludell, KS 68-69 F 6
Lüderitz [Namibia] 198 BC 7
Lüderitzbaai 198 BC 7
Ludgate 72-73 F 2
Ludhiāna 160-161 M 4
Ludhiyānā = Ludhiāna 160-161 M 4
Ludington, MI 70-71 G 4
L'udinovo 142-143 F 5
Ludlow 116-117 J 8
Ludlow, CA 74-75 EF 5
Ludlow, CO 68-69 D 7
Ludlow, SD 68-69 E 3
Ludogorie 138-139 M 4
Ludowici, GA 80-81 F 5
Luduş 138-139 KL 2
Ludvika 114-115 F 7
Ludwigsburg 124 D 4
Ludwigshafen 124 CD 4
Ludwigslust 124 E 2
Luebo 198 D 3
Lueders, TX 76-77 E 6
Luembe, Rio — 198 D 3
Luena 198 D 4
Luena, Rio — 198 D 4
Luena Flats 198 D 4
Lufeng 166-167 M 7
Lufira 198 E 3-4
Lufkin, TX 58-59 H 5
Luga [SU, place] 154-155 D 6
Luga [SU, river] 154-155 D 6
Lugano 124 D 5
Luganville 182-183 N 3
Lugela 198 G 5
Lugenda, Rio — 198 G 4
Lughbhadh 116-117 E 6-7
Lugh Ferrandi = Luuq 194-195 N 8
Lugnaquillia = Log na Coille 116-117 E 7-8
Lugo [E] 132-133 D 7
Lugo [I] 138-139 D 3
Lugoj 138-139 JK 3
Luḥayyah, Al- 160-161 E 7
Luhit 160-161 Q 5
Luhsien = Lu Xian 166-167 K 6
Luiana, Rio — 198 D 5
Luichow = Haikang 166-167 KL 7
Luichow Peninsula = Leizhou Bandao 166-167 L 7
Luik = Liège 132-133 K 3
Luilaka 198 D 2
Luimneach 116-117 C 8
Luirojoki 114-115 M 4
Luís Correira 98-99 L 5
Luishia 198 E 4
Luiza 198 D 3
Luján [RA, Buenos Aires] 103 E 4
Lujenda = Rio Lugenda 198 G 4
Lujiapuzi 170-171 D 2
Lukanga Swamp 198 E 4
Lukašek 154-155 Z 7
Lukenie 198 C 2
Lukenie Supérieure, Plateau de la — 198 D 2
Lukfung = Lufeng 166-167 M 7
Lukolela 198 C 2
Lukovit 138-139 L 4
Łuków 124 L 3
Lukuga 198 E 3
Lūl, Nahr — 194-195 K 7
Lula, MS 78-79 D 3
Luleå 114-115 JK 5
Lule älv 114-115 J 4-5
Luling, TX 76-77 F 8
Lulonga 198 C 1
Lulua 198 D 3
Luluabourg = Kananga 198 D 3
Lumbala 198 D 4
Lumber River 80-81 G 3
Lumberton, MS 78-79 E 5
Lumberton, NC 58-59 L 5
Lumberton, NM 68-69 C 7
Lumbo 198 H 4-5
Lumby 48 H 4
Lumding 160-161 P 5
Lumege = Cameia 198 D 4
Lumeje 198 D 4
Lüm Fiord = Limfjorden 114-115 D 9
Lumpkin, GA 78-79 G 4
Lumu 174-175 G 7
Lumut 174-175 D 5
Lün 166-167 K 2
Luna, NM 74-75 J 6
Lund 114-115 E 10
Lund, NV 74-75 F 3
Lund, UT 74-75 G 3-4
Lunda 198 CD 3
Lunda, Kasongo- 198 C 3
Lundar 49 K 5
Lundazi [Z, place] 198 F 4
Lundi [ZW, place] 198 F 6
Lundi [ZW, river] 198 F 6
Lundy Island 116-117 G 9
Lüneburg 124 E 2
Lüneburger Heide 124 DE 2
Luneburg Heath = Lüneburger Heide 124 DE 2
Lunenburg 46-47 Y 9
Lunéville 132-133 L 4
Lunga [Z] 198 E 4
Lunga = Dugi Otok 138-139 F 4
Lunga Game Reserve 198 DE 4
Lungala N'Guimbo 198 CD 4
Lung-chên = Longzhen 166-167 O 2
Lung-chiang = Qiqihar 166-167 N 2
Lung-ching-ts'un = Longjing 170-171 G 1
Lung-chuan = Suichuan 166-167 L 6
Lung-hsi = Longxi 166-167 J 4-5
Lung-hua = Longhua 170-171 AB 2
Lungki = Zhangzhou 166-167 M 7
Lunglē = Lungleh 160-161 P 6
Lungleh 160-161 P 6
Lungling = Longling 166-167 H 7
Lung-nan = Longnan 166-167 LM 7
Lungsi = Longxi 166-167 J 4-5
Lungué-Bungo, Rio — 198 D 4
Lungyu = Longyou 166-167 M 6
Lūni [IND, river] 160-161 L 5
Luninec 142-143 E 5
Lunsemfwa 198 EF 4
Luntai = Buquq 166-167 E 3
Luorong 166-167 K 7
Luoyang 166-167 L 5
Luozi 198 B 2
Łupkowska, Przełęcz — 124 L 4
Luputa 198 D 3
Luray, VA 72-73 G 5
Lurgan 116-117 E 6
Lúrio, Rio — 198 GH 4
Luristan = Lorestān 160-161 F 4
Lusaka 198 E 5
Lusambo 198 D 2
Luscar 48 J 3
Lusenga Flats 198 E 3
Lu Shan [TJ, Jiangxi] 166-167 M 6
Lushnjë 138-139 H 5
Lushoto 198 G 2
Lüshun, Lüda- 166-167 MN 4
Lusien = Lu Xian 166-167 K 6
Lusk, WY 68-69 D 4
Luso = Moxico 198 CD 4
Lussino = Lošinj 138-139 F 3
Lustre, MT 68-69 D 1
Lūṭ, Dasht-e — 160-161 H 4
Lutcher, LA 78-79 D 5-6
Luther, MI 70-71 H 3
Luther, OK 76-77 F 5
Lutie, TX 76-77 D 5
Luton 116-117 L 9
Lutong 174-175 F 6
Lutterworth 116-117 KL 8
Lützow-Holm bukt 31 C 4-5
Luuq 194-195 N 8
Luverne, AL 78-79 F 5
Luverne, IA 70-71 CD 4
Luverne, MN 68-69 H 4
Luvua 198 E 3
Luwegu 198 G 3
Luwingu 198 F 4
Luwu 174-175 GH 7
Luwuk 174-175 H 7
Luxembourg [L, place] 132-133 KL 4
Luxembourg [L, state] 132-133 KL 4
Lu Xian 166-167 K 6
Luxico, Rio — 198 CD 3
Luxor = Al-Uqṣur 194-195 L 3
Luxora, AR 78-79 DE 3
Lüyang 170-171 C 2
Lüykau 174-175 C 3
Lüylin 174-175 C 2
Luz [BR] 98-99 K 8
Luza [SU, place] 154-155 H 5
Luza [SU, river] 142-143 J 3
Luzern 124 CD 5
Luzón 174-175 H 3
Luzón Strait 174-175 H 2

L'vov 142-143 D 5

Lwanhsien = Luan Xian 166-167 M 4

Lyallpur = Faisalābād 160-161 L 4
Lybrook, NM 76-77 A 4
Lybster 116-117 H 2
Lycksele 114-115 H 5
Lydd 116-117 g 8
Lydell Wash 74-75 G 4
Lydenburg 198 EF 7
Lydford 116-117 G 10
Lydney 116-117 J 9
Lyell Island 48 B 3
Lyle, MN 70-71 D 4
Lyle, WA 66-67 C 3
Lyles, TN 78-79 F 3
Lyleton 68-69 F 1
Lyme Bay 116-117 HJ 10
Lyme Regis 116-117 HJ 10
Lymington 116-117 K 10
Lynas, Point — 116-117 G 7
Lynbrook, NY 82 III de 3
Lynch, KY 80-81 E 2
Lynch, NE 68-69 G 4
Lynchburg, VA 58-59 L 4
Lynches River 80-81 FG 3
Lynden, WA 66-67 B 1
Lyndon, KS 70-71 C 6
Lyndonville, VT 72-73 KL 2
Lyngenfjord 114-115 J 2-3
Lyngseiden 114-115 HJ 3
Lynhurst, NJ 82 III b 2
Lynn, IN 70-71 H 5
Lynn, MA 72-73 L 3
Lynn Canal 52-53 U 7
Lynndyl, UT 74-75 G 3
Lynn Haven, FL 78-79 G 5
Lynn Lake 46-47 Q 6
Lynton [CDN] 49 C 2
Lynton [GB] 116-117 H 9
Lynwood, CA 83 III c 2
Lyon 132-133 K 6
Lyon Park, Arlington-, VA 82 II a 2
Lyons, CO 68-69 D 5
Lyons, GA 80-81 E 4
Lyons, IL 83 II a 2
Lyons, KS 68-69 GH 6
Lyons, NE 68-69 H 5
Lyons, NY 72-73 H 3
Lyons = Lyon 132-133 K 6
Lyons River 182-183 C 4
Lysá hora 124 J 4
Lysekil 114-115 D 8
Lysite, WY 68-69 C 4
Lyskovo 154-155 GH 6
Łyso gory 124 K 3
Lyster 51 A 4
Lys'va 154-155 K 6
Lyswa = Lys'va 154-155 K 6
Lytham Saint Anne's 116-117 HJ 7
Lytton [CDN, British Columbia] 48 G 4
Lytton [CDN, Quebec] 72-73 HJ 1

M

Mā, Wād al- 194-195 C 4
Ma'abūs = Tazarbū 194-195 J 3
Maalaea, HI 78-79 d 2
Ma'ān [JOR] 160-161 D 4
Ma'anīyah, Al- 160-161 E 4
Maanselkä 114-115 L 3-N 4
Maarianhamina = Mariehamn 114-115 HJ 7
Ma'arrat an-Nu'mān 142-143 G 8
Maas 132-133 K 3
Maastricht 132-133 K 3
Ma'azzah, Jabal — 199 C 2
Mababe Depression 198 D 5
Mabalane 198 F 6
Mabang Gangri 166-167 DE 5
Mabaruma 98-99 H 3
Mabella 70-71 EF 1
Maben, MS 78-79 E 4
Mablethorpe and Sutton 116-117 M 7
Mabrouk 194-195 D 5
Mabruck = Mabrouk 194-195 D 5
Mabton, WA 66-67 CD 2
Mabuki 198 F 2
Mača 154-155 W 6
Macá, Monte — 103 B 7
Macacos, Ilha dos — 98-99 N 5
MacAdam 51 C 5
Macaé 98-99 L 9
MacAlester, OK 58-59 GH 5
MacAlister, NM 76-77 C 5
MacAllen, TX 58-59 G 6
MacAlpine Lake 46-47 PQ 4
Macamic 50 M 2
Macamic, Lac — 50 M 2
Macao = Macau 166-167 L 7
Macao, El — 88-89 M 5
Macapá [BR, Amapá] 98-99 J 4
Macapá [BR, Amazonas] 98-99 E 9
Macaquara, Cachoeira — 98-99 M 4
Macará 98-99 CD 5
Maçaranduba, Cachoeira — 98-99 J 4-5
Macarani 98-99 LM 8
MacArthur, OH 72-73 E 5
MacArthur River 182-183 G 3
Macas 98-99 D 5
Macassar = Ujung Pandang 174-175 G 8
Macau [BR] 98-99 M 5-6
Macau [Macau] 166-167 L 7
Macauã, Rio — 98-99 D 9
Macaúba 98-99 J 7
Macauley 178 J 6
Macayari 98-99 E 4
Macaza, Rivière — 72-73 J 1-2
MacBee, SC 80-81 F 3
MacBride 48 GH 3
MacCall, ID 66-67 EF 3
MacCamey, TX 76-77 C 7
MacCammon, ID 66-67 G 4
MacCarthy, AK 52-53 Q 6
Macchu Picchu 98-99 E 7
MacClellanville, SC 80-81 G 4
Macclenny, FL 80-81 b 1
Macclesfield 116-117 JK 7
Macclesfield Bank 174-175 FG 3
MacClintock, ostrov — 154-155 H-K 1
MacClintock Channel 46-47 Q 3
MacCloud, CA 66-67 BC 5
Maccluer, Teluk — = Teluk Berau 174-175 K 7
MacClure, PA 72-73 H 4
MacClure Strait 46-47 MN 2-3
MacClusky, ND 68-69 F 2
MacColl, SC 80-81 G 3
MacComb, MS 58-59 H 5
MacConnellsburg, PA 72-73 GH 5
MacConnelsville, OH 72-73 F 5
MacCook, NE 58-59 F 3
MacCormick, SC 80-81 EF 4
MacCormick Place 83 II b 1
MacCracken, KS 68-69 G 6
MacCreary 49 J 5
MacCullough, AL 78-79 F 5
MacCurtain, OK 76-77 G 5
MacDade, TX 76-77 F 7
MacDavid, FL 78-79 F 5
MacDermitt, NV 66-67 DE 5
Macdhui, Ben — 116-117 H 3
Macdiarmid 70-71 FG 1
MacDonald 26-27 N 8
MacDonald, KS 68-69 F 6
Macdonald, Lake — [AUS] 182-183 E 4
MacDonald, Lake — [CDN] 66-67 FG 1
MacDonald Peak 66-67 G 2
Macdonnell Ranges 182-183 F 4
MacDonough, GA 80-81 DE 4
MacDouall Peak 182-183 F 5
MacDougall Sound 46-47 R 2-3
MacDowell Lake 50 C 1
MacDowell Peak 74-75 GH 6
Macduff 116-117 J 3
Macedonia 138-139 JK 5
Maceió 98-99 MN 6
Macenta 194-195 C 7
Macerata 138-139 E 4
Macfarlane, Lake — 182-183 G 6
MacGaffey, NM 74-75 J 5
MacGehee, AR 78-79 D 4
MacGill, NV 74-75 F 3
MacGillivray Falls 48 F 4
MacGill University 82 I b 1
MacGivney 51 C 4
MacGrath, AK 46-47 EF 5
MacGrath, MN 70-71 D 2
Macgregor 49 J 6
MacGregor, MN 70-71 D 2
MacGregor, TX 76-77 F 7
MacGregor Lake 49 B 5

MacGuire, Mount — 66-67 F 3
Machachi 98-99 D 5
Machačkala 142-143 J 7
Machado, Serra do — [BR, Amazonas] 98-99 H 8-9
Machaila 198 F 6
Machakos 198 G 2
Machala 98-99 CD 5
Machambet 142-143 K 6
Machaneng 198 E 6
Machanga 198 G 6
Macharadze 142-143 H 7
Machattie, Lake — 182-183 GH 4
Machaze 198 F 6
MacHenry, ND 68-69 G 2
Ma Chha 166-167 HJ 5
Machhalīpaṭṭaṇam = Bandar 160-161 N 7
Ma Chhu [TJ] 166-167 J 4
Machias, ME 72-73 N 2
Machiques 98-99 E 2-3
Machynlleth 116-117 H 8
Macia [Mozambique] 198 F 7
Macias Nguema = Bioko 194-195 F 8
Măcin 138-139 N 3
Macina 194-195 CD 6
MacIntire, IA 70-71 D 4
MacIntosh 50 C 3
MacIntosh, SD 68-69 F 3
MacIntyre Bay 70-71 F 1
Mack, CO 74-75 J 3
MacKague 49 FG 4
Mackay 182-183 J 4
Mackay, ID 66-67 G 4
Mackay, Lake — 182-183 E 4
MacKay Lake [CDN, Northwest Territories] 46-47 O 5
MacKay Lake [CDN, Ontario] 70-71 G 1
MacKay River 49 BC 2
Mac Kean 178 J 3
MacKee, KY 72-73 DE 6
MacKeesport, PA 58-59 KL 3
MacKenzie, AL 78-79 F 5
MacKenzie, TN 78-79 E 2
Mackenzie [CDN, British Columbia] 48 F 2
MacKenzie [CDN, Ontario] 70-71 F 1
Mackenzie [GUY] 98-99 H 3
Mackenzie, District of — 46-47 L-P 5
Mackenzie Bay 46-47 J 4
MacKenzie Bridge, OR 66-67 BC 3
Mackenzie Highway 46-47 N 6
Mackenzie Island 50 BC 2
Mackenzie King Island 46-47 OP 2
Mackenzie Mountains 46-47 J 4-L 5
Mackenzie River 46-47 KL 4
Mackinac, Straits of — 70-71 H 3
Mackinaw City, MI 70-71 H 3
Mackinaw River 70-71 F 5
MacKinlay 182-183 H 4
MacKinley, Mount — 46-47 F 5
MacKinley Park, AK 52-53 N 5
MacKinney, TX 76-77 F 6
Mackinnon Road 198 GH 2
MacKirdy 70-71 FG 1
MacKittrick, CA 74-75 D 5
Macklin 49 D 4
Macksville 182-183 K 6
Maclaren River 52-53 O 5
MacLaughlin, SD 68-69 F 3
MacLean, TX 76-77 D 5
Maclean [AUS] 182-183 K 5
MacLean [USA] 82 II a 1
MacLeansboro, IL 70-71 F 6
Maclear 198 E 8
MacLennan 46-47 N 6
Macleod 66-67 G 1
MacLeod, Lake — 182-183 B 4
MacLeod Bay 46-47 OP 5
MacLeod Lake 48 F 2
MacLeod River 48 J 3-K 2
MacLoughlin Peak 66-67 B 4
Maclovio Herrera 86-87 H 3
MacMechen, WV 72-73 F 5
MacMillan, Lake — 76-77 BC 6
Macmillan River 52-53 U 5
MacMinnville, OR 66-67 B 3
MacMinnville, TN 78-79 FG 3
MacMorran 49 D 5
MacMunn 49 L 6
MacMurdo 31 B 16-17
MacMurdo Sound 31 B 17
MacNary, AZ 74-75 J 5
MacNary, TX 76-77 B 7
MacNeill, MS 78-79 E 5
Macoa, Serra — 98-99 JK 4
Macomb, IL 70-71 E 5
Macomia 198 GH 4
Macon, GA 58-59 K 5
Macon, MO 70-71 D 6
Macon, MS 78-79 E 4
Mâcon [F] 132-133 K 5
Macondo 198 D 4
Macorís, San Francisco de — 58-59 MN 8
Macorís, San Pedro de — 58-59 N 8
Macoun 68-69 E 1
Macoun Lake 49 G 2
Macouria 98-99 M 2
MacPherson, KS 68-69 H 6
Macquarie Harbour 182-183 HJ 8
Macquarie Islands 31 D 16
Macquarie Ridge 26-27 Q 8
Macquarie River 182-183 J 6
MacRae 52-53 U 6
MacRae, GA 80-81 E 4
MacRoberts, KY 80-81 E 2
MacRobertson Land 31 BC 6-7
Macroom = Magh Chromtha 116-117 C 9
MacTavish Arm 46-47 N 4
MacTier 72-73 FG 2
Macuçaua 98-99 C 8
Macumba 182-183 G 5
Macusani 98-99 E 7
Macuspana 86-87 O 9
Macúzari, Presa — 86-87 F 4
MacVivar Arm 46-47 MN 4-5
Madadi 194-195 J 5
Madagascar 198 H 6-J 5
Madagascar Basin 26-27 M 7
Madagascar Ridge 26-27 M 7
Madā'in Ṣāliḥ 160-161 D 5
Maḍakalapūwa 160-161 N 9
Madama 194-195 G 4
Madan 138-139 L 5
Madang 174-175 N 8
Madanīyīn 194-195 FG 2
Madaoua 194-195 F 6
Madawaska [CDN, New Brunswick] 51 B 4
Madawaska [CDN, Ontario] 72-73 GH 2
Madawaska River 72-73 H 2
Maddalena 138-139 C 5
Madden, Lago — 58-59 b 2
Madden, Presa de — 58-59 b 2
Madden Dam = Presa de Madden 58-59 b 2
Madden Lake = Lago Madden 58-59 b 2
Madeira 194-195 A 2
Madeira = Arquipélago da Madeira 194-195 A 2
Madeira, Arquipélago da — 194-195 A 2
Madeira, Rio — 98-99 G 6
Madeirinha, Rio — 98-99 H 9
Madeleine, Îles de la — 46-47 Y 8
Madeley 116-117 J 8
Madelia, MN 70-71 C 3-4
Madeline, CA 66-67 C 5
Madeline Island 70-71 E 2
Madeline Plains 66-67 C 5
Madera 58-59 E 6
Madera, CA 74-75 CD 4
Madera, Sierra — 76-77 C 7
Madera, Sierra de la — 86-87 F 2-3
Madero, Ciudad — 58-59 G 7
Madhya Andamān = Middle Andaman 160-161 P 8
Madhya Pradesh 160-161 MN 6
Madidi, Río — 98-99 F 7
Madill, OK 76-77 F 5
Madimba 198 C 2-3
Madina do Boé 194-195 B 6
Madīnah, Al- [Saudi Arabia] 160-161 DE 6
Madīnat ash-Sha'ab 160-161 EF 8
Madingou 198 B 2
Madison, FL 80-81 b 1
Madison, GA 80-81 E 4
Madison, IN 70-71 H 6
Madison, KS 68-69 H 6
Madison, ME 72-73 LM 2
Madison, MN 70-71 BC 3
Madison, NE 68-69 H 5
Madison, SD 68-69 H 3
Madison, WI 58-59 HJ 3
Madison, WV 72-73 F 5
Madison Range 66-67 H 3
Madison River 66-67 H 3
Madison Square Garden 82 III c 2
Madisonville, KY 70-71 FG 7
Madisonville, TX 76-77 G 7
Madiun 174-175 F 8
Madjerda, Quèd — = Wad Majradah 194-195 F 1
Madley 116-117 J 8
Madley, Mount — 182-183 D 4
Madoc 72-73 H 2
Mado Gashi 198 G 1
Madonie 138-139 EF 7
Madrakah, Rā's al- 160-161 H 7
Madras 160-161 N 8
Madras, OR 66-67 C 3
Madrās = Tamil Nadu 160-161 M 8-9
Madrasta = Madrās 160-161 N 8
Madre, Laguna — 58-59 G 6-7
Madre, Sierra — [MEX] 58-59 H 8
Madre, Sierra — [RP] 174-175 H 3
Madre de Dios [PE, place] 98-99 EF 7
Madre de Dios, Isla — 103 A 8
Madre de Dios, Río — 98-99 F 7
Madrid, IA 70-71 D 5
Madrid, NE 68-69 F 5
Madrid, NM 76-77 AB 5
Madrid [E] 132-133 EF 8
Mad River 66-67 B 5
Madrona, Sierra — 132-133 EF 9
Madruba, Lago — 98-99 J 6
Madura 182-183 E 6
Madura = Madurai 160-161 M 9
Madura = Pulau Madura 174-175 F 8
Madura, Pulau — 174-175 F 8
Madurai 160-161 M 9
Maē = Mahe 160-161 M 8
Maebashi 170-171 M 4
Mae Nam Khong 174-175 D 3
Maengbu-san 170-171 F 2
Mae Sai 174-175 CD 2
Mae Sariang 174-175 C 3
Maesteg 116-117 H 9
Maestra, Sierra — 58-59 L 7-8
Maevatanana 198 J 5
Maewo 182-183 N 3
Mafeking [CDN] 49 H 4
Mafeking = Mmabatho 198 DE 7
Mafia Island 198 GH 3
Mafra [BR] 103 FG 3
Mafupa 198 E 4
Magadan 154-155 CD 6
Magadi 198 G 2
Magadoxo = Muqdiisho 194-195 O 8
Magallanes, Estrecho de — 103 AB 8
Maganguė 98-99 E 3
Magaria 194-195 F 6
Magazine Mountain 78-79 C 3
Magburaka 194-195 B 7
Magdagači 154-155 Y 7
Magdalena, NM 76-77 A 5
Magdalena [BOL] 98-99 G 7
Magdalena [MEX, Baja California Sur] 86-87 DE 4
Magdalena, Bahía — 58-59 D 7
Magdalena, Isla — 103 B 6
Magdalena, Llano de la — 58-59 D 6-7
Magdalena, Río — [CO] 98-99 E 2-3
Magdalena, Río — [MEX] 58-59 D 5
Magdalen Islands = Îles de la Madeleine 46-47 Y 8
Magdeburg 124 E 2
Magee, MS 78-79 DE 5
Magee, Island — 116-117 F 6
Mageik, Mount — 52-53 K 7
Magelang 174-175 EF 8
Magerøy 114-115 M 2
Magga Range 31 B 35-36
Maghāghah 199 B 3
Maghayrā', Al- 160-161 G 6
Magh Chromtha 116-117 C 9
Maghera 116-117 E 6
Magherafelt 116-117 E 6
Magi = Maji 194-195 M 7
Magic Reservoir 66-67 F 4
Mãglie 138-139 H 5
Magna, UT 66-67 GH 5
Magnesia = Manisa 160-161 B 3
Magness, AR 78-79 D 3
Magnetic Island 182-183 J 3
Magnitogorsk 154-155 KL 7
Magnolia, AR 78-79 C 4
Magnolia, MS 78-79 D 5
Magnor 114-115 DE 7-8
Māgoė 198 F 5
Magog 72-73 KL 2
Magpie 51 D 2
Magpie, Lac — 51 D 2
Magpie, Rivière — 51 D 2
Magpie River 70-71 H 1
Magrath 66-67 G 1
Magreb = Al-Maghrib 194-195 C 3-D 2
Maguari, Cabo — 98-99 K 4-5
Magude 198 F 6-7
Magwe 174-175 BC 2
Mahābād 160-161 F 3
Mahābhārat Lekh 160-161 NO 5
Mahabo 198 HJ 6
Maha Chana Chai 174-175 DE 3
Mahagi 198 F 1
Mahaicony 98-99 H 3
Mahajamba, Helodranon'i — 198 J 4-5
Mahajanga 198 J 5
Mahakam, Sungai — 174-175 G 6-7
Mahalapye 198 E 6
Maḥallat al-Kubra, Al- 194-195 L 2
Mahānadi 160-161 N 6
Mahānadi Delta 160-161 O 7
Mahanoro 198 J 5
Maha Nuwara 160-161 N 9
Mahārāshtra [IND, landscape] 160-161 M 7
Maḥāriq, Al- 199 B 5
Maha Sarakham 174-175 D 3
Maḥaṭṭat 1 199 B 7
Maḥaṭṭat 2 199 BC 7
Maḥaṭṭat 3 199 BC 7
Maḥaṭṭat 4 199 C 7
Mahawa 160-161 M 9
Mahd adh-Dhahab 160-161 E 6
Mahdia 98-99 H 3
Mahdīyah, Al- 194-195 G 1
Mahe [IND] 160-161 M 8
Mahé [Seychelles] 188-189 N 9
Mahé Archipelago = Seychelles 26-27 MN 6
Mahendra Parvata = Eastern Ghats 160-161 M 8-N 7
Mahenge 198 G 3
Maher 50 L 2
Mahēsāṇā = Mehsāna 160-161 L 6
Maheson Island 50 A 2
Māhī = Mahe 160-161 M 8
Mahia, El — 194-195 D 4
Mahia Peninsula 182-183 P 7
Mahnomen, MN 70-71 BC 2
Maho = Mahawa 160-161 M 9
Mahogany Mountain 66-67 E 4
Mahón [F] 132-133 K 9
Mahone Bay 51 DE 5
Mahtowa, MN 70-71 D 2
Mahukona, HI 78-79 de 2
Maiaú, Ponta — 98-99 P 5
Maicasagi, Lac — 50 N 1
Maicasagi, Rivière — 50 NO 1
Maichaila 198 F 6
Maicuru, Rio — 98-99 J 5
Maiden Newton 116-117 J 10
Maidī = Maydī 160-161 E 7
Maidstone [CDN] 49 D 4
Maidstone [GB] 116-117 M 9
Maiduguri 194-195 G 6
Maiella 138-139 F 4
Maigaiti = Marqat Bazar 166-167 D 4
Maigh Eo 116-117 B 6-7
Maigualida, Serranía de — 98-99 F 3-G 4
Maijdī 160-161 P 6
Mai-kai-t'i = Marqat Bazar 166-167 D 4
Maiko 198 E 1-2
Maiko, Parc national de — 198 E 2
Maikoor, Pulau — 174-175 K 8
Maimacheng = Altanbulag 166-167 K 1-2
Maimansingh 160-161 OP 5-6
Main [D] 124 D 4
Ma'in [Y] 160-161 EF 7
Main Barrier Range 182-183 H 6
Main Centre 49 E 5
Main Channel 50 L 4
Mai Ndombe 198 C 2
Maine [F] 132-133 GH 4
Maine [USA] 58-59 MN 2
Maine, Gulf of — 58-59 N 3
Maīnė-Soroa 194-195 G 6
Mainland [GB, Orkney] 116-117 H 1
Mainland [GB, Shetland] 116-117 e 3
Main Pass 78-79 E 6
Main River 51 H 3
Maintirano 198 H 5
Mainz 124 D 3-4
Maio 188-189 E 7
Maipo, Volcán — 103 C 4
Maipú [RA, Buenos Aires] 103 E 5
Maipures 98-99 F 3
Maiquetía 98-99 F 2
Maisí, Cabo — 58-59 M 7
Maisonneuve, Parc de — 82 I b 1
Maisūru = Mysore 160-161 M 8
Mait = Mayd 160-161 F 8
Maitland 182-183 K 6
Maitland, Lake — 182-183 D 5
Maíz, Islas del — 58-59 K 9
Maizuru 166-167 Q 4
Maja 154-155 Za 6
Majagual 98-99 E 3
Majal, Bi'r — 199 C 6
Majari, Rio — 98-99 H 3
Majene 174-175 G 7
Majevica 138-139 H 3
Maji 194-195 M 7
Maji Moto 198 F 3
Majja 154-155 Z 5
Majkain 154-155 O 7
Majkop 142-143 GH 7
Majma'ah 160-161 F 5
Majn 154-155 h 5
Majngy-Pil'gyn = Mejnypil'gyno 154-155 j 5
Majoli 98-99 H 4
Majorca = Mallorca 132-133 J 9
Major Pablo Lagerenza 103 DE 1
Major Peak 76-77 C 7
Majradah, Wad — 194-195 F 1
Majunga = Mahajanga 198 J 5
Majuriã 98-99 F 8
Majuro 178 H 2
Makah Indian Reservation 66-67 A 1
Makale = Mekele 194-195 MN 7
Makalle = Mekelē 194-195 M 6
Makapuu Point 78-79 d 2
Makarov 154-155 b 8
Makarska 138-139 G 4
Makasar = Ujung Pandang 174-175 G 8
Makasar, Selat — 174-175 G 6-7
Makassar = Ujung Pandang 174-175 G 8
Makassar Strait = Selat Makasar 174-175 G 6-7
Makat 154-155 J 8
Makedonía 138-139 JK 5
Makedonija 138-139 B-D 4
Makejevka 142-143 G 6
Make-jima 170-171 H 7
Makeni 194-195 B 7
Makgadikgadi Salt Pan 198 DE 6
Makian, Pulau — 174-175 J 6
Makīlī, Al- 194-195 J 2
Makin 178 H 2
Makinsk 154-155 MN 7
Makinson Inlet 46-47 UV 2
M'akit 154-155 d 5
Makka = Makkah 160-161 DE 6
Makkah 160-161 DE 6
Makkaur 114-115 O 2
Maklakovo 154-155 R 6
Makó 124 K 5
Makokibatan Lake 50 F 2
Makokou 198 B 1
Makoop Lake 50 D 1
Makoua 198 BC 1-2
Makounda = Markounda 194-195 H 7
Makran = Mokrān 160-161 HJ 5
Makrāna 160-161 L 5
Makrónēsos 138-139 L 7
Maks al-Baḥrī, Al- 199 AB 5
Maks al-Qiblī, Al- 194-195 L 4
Maks el-Bahârî = Al-Maks al-Baḥrī 199 AB 5
Makteir = Maqṭayr 194-195 BC 4
Maku 142-143 H 8
Makumbi 198 CD 3
Makunudu 36 a 1
Makurazaki 170-171 GH 7
Makurdi 194-195 F 7
Makushin, AK 52-53 n 4
Makushin Bay 52-53 n 4
Makushin Volcano 52-53 n 4
Mala 116-117 C 8
Mala = Malaita 174-175 k 6
Malabar Coast 160-161 L 8-M 9
Malabo 194-195 F 8
Malacca = Malaiische Halbinsel 174-175 C 5-D 6
Malacca, Strait of — 174-175 C 5-D 6
Malad City, ID 66-67 G 4
Maladeta 132-133 H 7
Malaga, NM 76-77 B 6
Málaga [CO] 98-99 E 3
Málaga [E] 132-133 E 10
Malagarasi [EAT, river] 198 F 2
Malaija = Melayu 174-175 D 6
Málainn 116-117 D 5
Malaita 174-175 k 6
Malaja Ob' 154-155 M 5-L 4
Malaja Višera 154-155 E 6
Malakāl 194-195 L 7
Mālākaṇḍ 160-161 L 4
Mala Krsna 138-139 J 3
Malalaling 198 D 7
Malang 174-175 F 8
Malange 198 C 3
Malangen 114-115 H 3
Mälaren 114-115 G 8
Malargüe 103 C 5
Mälar Lake = Mälaren 114-115 G 8
Malartic 46-47 V 8
Malartic, Lac — 50 N 2
Malaspina 103 C 6-7
Malaspina Glacier 46-47 H 5-6
Malatia = Malatya 160-161 D 3
Malatosh Lake 49 F 3
Malatya 160-161 D 3
Malavi = Malawi 198 FG 4
Malawi 198 FG 4
Malawi, Lake — 198 F 4
Malayagiri 160-161 O 6
Malayalam Coast = Malabar Coast 160-161 L 8-M 9
Malaya Parvata = Eastern Ghats 160-161 M 8-N 7
Malay Archipelago 26-27 O 5-Q 6
Malāyer 160-161 F 4
Malay Peninsula 174-175 C 5-D 6
Malaysia 174-175 D-F 6
Malayu = Melayu 174-175 D 6
Malbaie, la — 51 AB 4
Malbon 182-183 H 4
Malbork 124 J 1-2
Malcèsine 138-139 D 3
Malcolm River 52-53 RS 2
Malden 34-35 K 5
Malden, MA 72-73 L 3
Malden, MO 78-79 DE 2
Maldive Islands 36 F 3
Maldon 116-117 M 9
Maldonado [ROU, place] 103 F 4
Maldonado, Punta — 58-59 FG 8
Male [Maldive Is.] 24-25 N 5
Male, Lac du — 50 O 2
Maléas, Akrōtērion — 138-139 K 7
Male Atoll 36 a 2
Mālēgāňv = Mālegaon 160-161 LM 6
Mālegaon 160-161 LM 6
Male Island 36 a 2
Male Karpaty 124 H 4
Malekula 182-183 N 3
Malela 198 E 2
Malemo 198 G 4
Malen'ga 142-143 G 3
Malepeque Bay 51 E 4
Malghīr, Shaṭṭ — 194-195 F 2
Malgrat 132-133 J 8
Malheur Lake 66-67 D 4
Malheur River 66-67 E 4
Mali [RMM] 194-195 C 6-D 5
Malije Derbety 142-143 HJ 6
Malik, Wādī al- 194-195 KL 5
Mali Kyûn 174-175 C 4
Malin 142-143 E 5
Malin, OR 66-67 C 4
Malinaltepec 86-87 L 9
Malinau 174-175 G 6
Malindi 198 H 2
Malines = Mechelen 132-133 K 3
Malin Head = Málainn 116-117 D 5
Malipo 166-167 J 7
Malita 174-175 HJ 5
Maljamar, NM 76-77 C 6
Małkinia Górna 124 L 2
Mallaig 116-117 F 3-4
Mallakastër 138-139 HJ 5
Mallapunyah 182-183 G 3
Mallawī 199 B 4
Mallès Venosta 138-139 D 2
Mallicolo = Malekula 182-183 N 3
Mallīt 194-195 K 6
Mallorca 132-133 J 9
Mallow = Mala 116-117 C 8
Malmberget 114-115 J 4
Malmedy 132-133 L 3
Malmesbury [GB] 116-117 JK 9
Malmesbury [ZA] 198 C 8
Malmö 114-115 E 10
Malmöhus 114-115 E 9-10
Malmyž 142-143 JK 4
Maloca 98-99 H 4
Maloca Macu 98-99 G 3
Malojaroslavec 142-143 FG 4
Maloje Karmakuly 154-155 HJ 3
Malombe, Lake — 198 G 4
Malone, NY 72-73 J 2
Maloney Reservoir 68-69 F 5
Malonga 198 D 4
Måløy 114-115 A 7
Malpas 116-117 J 7-8
Malpelo, Isla — 98-99 C 4
Malta, ID 66-67 G 4
Malta, MT 68-69 C 1
Malta [M] 138-139 EF 8
Maltahöhe 198 C 6
Malton 116-117 L 6
Malu 174-175 k 6
Maluku <| 174-175 J 7
Malumba 198 E 2
Malumteken 174-175 h 5
Malung 114-115 E 7
Malūṭ 194-195 L 6
Mālvan 160-161 L 7
Malvern 116-117 J 8
Malvern, AR 78-79 C 3
Malvern, IA 70-71 C 5
Malvérnia 198 F 6
Mālwa 160-161 M 6
Malyj Kavkaz 142-143 HJ 7
Malyj L'achovskij, ostrov — 154-155 bc 3
Malyj Tajmyr, ostrov — 154-155 UV 2
Malyj Uzen' 142-143 J 6
Mama 154-155 V 6
Mamasa 174-175 G 7
Mambasa 198 E 1
Mamberamo 174-175 L 7
Mambere = Carnot 194-195 H 8
Mambone = Nova Mambone 198 G 6
Mameigwess Lake 50 EF 1
Mamfe 194-195 F 7
Māmī, Rā's — 160-161 GH 8
Mammamattawa 50 G 2
Mammola 138-139 G 6
Mammoth, AZ 74-75 H 6
Mammoth Cave National Park 70-71 G 7
Mammoth Hot Springs, WY 66-67 H 3
Mamoneiras, Serra das — 98-99 P 7-8
Mamonovo 124 JK 1
Mamoré, Río — 98-99 FG 7-8
Mamou 194-195 B 6
Mampawah 174-175 E 6
Mampi = Sepopa 198 D 5
Mampong 194-195 D 7
Mamry, Jezioro — 124 K 1
Mamuíra, Cachoeira — 98-99 P 6
Mamuju 174-175 G 7
Mamuru, Rio — 98-99 K 6
Man [CI] 194-195 C 7
Man, Calf of — 116-117 FG 6
Man, Isle of — 116-117 GH 6
Mana, HI 78-79 c 1
Mana [French Guiana, place] 98-99 J 3
Mana [French Guiana, river] 98-99 M 2
Manaas 166-167 F 3
Manacapuru 98-99 G 5
Manacle Point 116-117 FG 10
Manacor 132-133 J 9
Manado 174-175 H 6
Managua 58-59 J 9
Managua, Lago de — 58-59 J 9
Manakara 198 J 6
Manāmah, Al- 160-161 G 5
Manambaho 198 HJ 5
Manambolo 198 H 5
Manam Island 174-175 N 7
Manamo, Caño — 98-99 G 3
Mananara [RM, place] 198 J 5
Mananara [RM, river] 198 J 6
Mananjary 198 J 6
Manantenina 198 J 6
Manantiales 103 BC 8
Manapouri, Lake — 182-183 N 9
Manāqil, Al- 194-195 L 6
Manār, Jabal al- 160-161 EF 8
Manas, gora — 154-155 N 9
Mānasārovar = Mapham Tsho 166-167 E 5

Mānasāro 247

Manasquan, NY 72-73 JK 4
Manatí [Puerto Rico] 88-89 N 5
Manaus 98-99 H 5
Man'auung Kyûn 174-175 B 3
Manawan Lake 49 G 3
Mancelona, MI 70-71 H 3
Mancha, La — 132-133 F 9
Manchan 166-167 G 2
Manchester 116-117 JK 7
Manchester, CT 72-73 K 4
Manchester, GA 78-79 G 4
Manchester, IA 70-71 E 4
Manchester, KS 68-69 H 6
Manchester, KY 72-73 DE 6
Manchester, MI 70-71 H 4
Manchester, NH 58-59 MN 3
Manchester, OK 76-77 EF 4
Manchester, TN 78-79 FG 3
Manchester, VT 72-73 K 3
Manchouli = Manzhouli 166-167 M 2
Manchuria 166-167 N-P 2
Manchuria = Manzhou 166-167 N-P 2
Máncora 98-99 C 5
Máncora = Puerto Máncora 98-99 C 5
Mancos, CO 74-75 J 4
Mand, Rūd-e- = Rūd-e Mond 160-161 G 5
Manda [EAT, Iringa] 198 FG 4
Mandab, Bāb al- 160-161 E 8
Mandabe 198 H 6
Mandal [Mongolia] 166-167 K 2
Mandal [N] 114-115 B 8-9
Mandalay = Mandale 174-175 C 2
Mandalgov' 166-167 JK 2
Mandalī 142-143 HJ 9
Mandal Ovoo 166-167 JK 3
Mandan, ND 68-69 F 2
Mandaon 174-175 H 4
Mandar 174-175 G 7
Mandar, Teluk — 174-175 G 7
Mandara, Monts — 194-195 G 6-7
Mândas 138-139 C 6
Mandasor 160-161 LM 6
Māndavī = Māndvi 160-161 K 6
Mandeb, Bab al- = Bāb al-Mandab 160-161 E 8
Manderson, WY 68-69 BC 3
Mandeville 88-89 GH 5
Mandeville, LA 78-79 DE 5
Mandi 160-161 M 4
Mandidzudzure 198 F 5-6
Mandimba 198 G 4
Manding 194-195 C 6
Mandioli, Pulau — 174-175 J 7
Mandla 160-161 N 6
Mandritsara 198 J 5
Mandsaur 160-161 LM 6
Mandsaur = Mandsaor 160-161 LM 6
Mandui = Māndvi 160-161 K 6
Mandurah 182-183 BC 6
Mandùria 138-139 G 5
Māndvi [IND, Gujarāt ↙ Bhuj] 160-161 K 6
Manfalūṭ 199 B 4
Manfredònia 138-139 FG 5
Manfredònia, Golfo di — 138-139 FG 5
Manga [BR] 98-99 L 7
Manga [RN] 194-195 G 6
Man'niyah, Al — = Al-Ma'anīyah 160-161 E 4
Mangabeiras, Chapada das — 98-99 K 6-L 7
Mangai 198 C 2
Mangalia 138-139 N 4
Mangalmé 194-195 HJ 6
Mangalore 160-161 L 8
Mangaḷūru = Mangalore 160-161 L 8
Mangas, NM 74-75 J 5
Mangeni, Hamada — 194-195 G 4
Manggar 174-175 E 7
Manggyŏng-dong 170-171 GH 1
Mangham, LA 78-79 CD 4
Mangi 198 E 1
Mangkalihat, Tanjung — 174-175 GH 6
Manglares, Cabo — 98-99 CD 4
Mango 194-195 E 6
Mangoche 198 G 4
Mangoky 198 H 6
Mangole, Pulau — 174-175 J 7
Mangoli = Pulau Mangole 174-175 J 7
Mangrove, Punta — 58-59 F 8
Manguari 98-99 D 5
Mangueigne 194-195 J 6
Mangueira, Lagoa — 103 F 4
Mangui 166-167 O 1
Manguinho, Ponta do — 98-99 M 7
Mangum, OK 76-77 E 5
Mangyai 166-167 G 4
Mangyšlak, plato — 160-161 G 2
Mangyšlakskij zaliv 142-143 JK 6-7
Manhasset, NY 82 III d 2
Manhattan, KS 58-59 G 4
Manhattan, MT 66-67 H 3
Manhattan, NV 74-75 E 3
Manhattan Beach, CA 74-75 D 6
Manhattan State Beach 83 III b 2
Manhatten, New York-, NY 82 III bc 2
Manhuaçu 98-99 L 9
Maní [CO] 98-99 E 4
Mani [TJ] 166-167 F 5
Mania 198 J 6
Maniamba 198 FG 4
Manica [Mozambique, administrative unit] 198 5-6 F
Manica [Mozambique, place] 198 F 5
Manicaland 198 F 5
Maniçauá-Miçu, Rio — 98-99 LM 10
Manicoré 98-99 G 6
Manicoré, Rio — 98-99 H 8
Manicouagan 51 B 2
Manicouagan, Lac — 51 BC 2
Manicouagan, Rivière — 46-47 X 7-8
Manigotagan 50 AB 2
Manigotagan River 50 AB 2
Manihiki 34-35 JK 5
Manika, Plateau de la — 198 E 3-4
Manila 174-175 H 3-4
Manila, UT 66-67 HJ 5
Manila Bay 174-175 GH 4
Manilla, IA 70-71 C 5
Manimba, Masi- 198 C 2
Manipur [IND, administrative unit] 160-161 P 5-6
Manipur = Imphāl 160-161 P 6
Manisa 160-161 B 3
Manislee River 72-73 D 2
Manistee, MI 70-71 G 3
Manistee River 70-71 H 3
Manistique, MI 70-71 GH 2
Manistique Lake 70-71 H 2
Manitoba 46-47 Q-S 6
Manitoba, Lake — 46-47 R 7
Manito Lake 49 D 4
Manitou 68-69 G 1
Manitou, Rivière — 51 D 2
Manitou Island 70-71 G 2
Manitou Islands 70-71 G 3
Manitou Lake 50 L 4
Manitou Lakes 50 C 3
Manitou Lakes 70-71 D 1
Manitoulin Island 46-47 U 8
Manitou Springs, CO 68-69 D 6
Manitouwadge 46-47 T 8
Manitowoc, WI 58-59 J 3
Manītsoq 46-47 Za 4
Maniwaki 46-47 V 8
Manizales 98-99 D 3
Manja 198 H 6
Manjacaze 198 F 6-7
Manjimup 182-183 C 6
Mānjra 160-161 M 7
Mankato, KS 68-69 GH 6
Mankato, MN 58-59 H 3
Mankono 194-195 C 7
Mankota 68-69 C 1
Mankoya 198 D 4
Manley Hot Springs, AK 52-53 M 4
Manly, IA 70-71 D 4
Manna 174-175 D 7
Mannar, Gulf of — 160-161 M 9
Mannār Khārī = Gulf of Mannar 160-161 M 9
Mannheim 124 D 4
Manning, AR 78-79 C 3
Manning, IA 70-71 C 5
Manning, ND 68-69 E 2
Manning, SC 80-81 FG 4
Manning Provincial Park 66-67 C 1
Mannington, WV 72-73 F 5
Manningtree 116-117 gh 7
Man'niyah, Al — = Al-Ma'anīyah 160-161 E 4
Mannville 49 C 4
Manoa [BR] 98-99 F 9
Manokotak, AK 52-53 H 7
Manokwari 174-175 K 7
Manombo 198 H 6
Manono 198 E 3
Manor, TX 76-77 F 7
Manorhaven, NY 82 III d 1
Manouane, Lac — [CDN ↑ Québec] 51 A 2
Manouane, Lac — [CDN ← Québec] 72-73 J 1
Manouane, Rivière — 51 A 2-3
Manouanis, Lac — 51 AB 2
Manp'ojin 170-171 F 2
Manqalah 194-195 L 7
Manresa 132-133 HJ 8
Mans, le — 132-133 H 4-5
Mansa [ZRE] 198 E 4
Mansalar = Pulau Musala 174-175 C 6
Mansaya = Masaya 58-59 J 9
Mansel Island 46-47 U 5
Manseriche, Pongo de — 98-99 D 5
Mansfield 116-117 KL 7
Mansfield, AR 76-77 G 5
Mansfield, LA 78-79 C 4
Mansfield, MO 78-79 C 2
Mansfield, OH 58-59 K 3
Mansfield, PA 72-73 H 4
Mansfield, WA 66-67 D 2
Manso, Rio — 98-99 J 7-8
Manson, IA 70-71 C 4
Manson Creek 48 E 2
Mansura, LA 78-79 C 5
Manşūrah, Al- [ET] 194-195 L 2
Manta 98-99 C 5
Manta, Bahía de — 98-99 C 5
Mantalingajan, Mount — 174-175 G 5
Mantaro, Río — 98-99 E 7
Mante, Ciudad — 58-59 G 7
Manteca, CA 74-75 C 4
Manteco, El — 98-99 G 3
Manteo, NC 80-81 J 3
Mantes-la-Jolie 132-133 H 4
Manti, UT 74-75 H 3
Mantiqueira, Serra da — 98-99 KL 9
Manto 88-89 C 7
Manton, MI 70-71 H 3
Mantova 138-139 D 3
Mänttä 114-115 L 6
Mantua = Mantova 138-139 D 3
Manturovo 142-143 HJ 4
Mäntyharju 114-115 M 7
Mäntyluoto 114-115 J 7
Manū 98-99 E 7
Manua 178 K 4
Manuan 72-73 J 1
Manuel 86-87 LM 6
Manuel Alves, Rio — 98-99 OP 10
Manuel Benavides 86-87 HJ 3
Manuelito, NM 74-75 J 5
Manuel Jorge, Cachoeira — 98-99 LM 7
Manuel Urbano 98-99 CD 9
Manuelzinho 98-99 HJ 6
Manuk, Pulau — 174-175 K 8
Manukau 182-183 OP 7
Manukau Harbour 182-183 O 7
Manus 174-175 N 7
Manville, WY 68-69 D 4
Many, LA 78-79 C 5
Manyara, Lake — 198 G 2
Manyč 142-143 H 6
Manyoni 198 F 3
Manzai 160-161 KL 4
Manzanares [E, place] 132-133 F 9
Manzanares [E, river] 132-133 F 8
Manzanillo [C] 58-59 L 7
Manzanillo [MEX] 58-59 EF 8
Manzanillo, Punta — 58-59 L 9-10
Manzano Mountains 76-77 A 5
Manzhouli 166-167 M 2
Manzilah, Al- 199 BC 2
Manzilah, Buḥayrat al- 199 BC 2
Manzini 198 F 7
Manzovka 154-155 Z 9
Mao 194-195 H 6
Maoka = Cholmsk 154-155 b 8
Maoke, Pegunungan — 174-175 LM 7
Maol Domhnaigh, Cnoc — 116-117 CD 8
Maol Riabhach 116-117 B 7
Maoming 166-167 L 7
Mapaga 174-175 G 7
Mapai 198 F 6
Mapastepec 86-87 O 10
Mapham Tsho 166-167 E 5
Mapham Yumtsho = Mapham Tsho 166-167 E 5
Mapi 174-175 L 8
Mapia, Kepulauan — 174-175 KL 6
Mapichi, Serranía de — 98-99 F 3-4
Mapimí 86-87 HJ 5
Mapimi, Bolsón de — 58-59 F 6
Ma-p'ing = Liuzhou 166-167 K 7
Mapinhane 198 FG 6
Mapire 98-99 G 3
Mapireme 98-99 LM 4
Mapiripan, Salto — 98-99 E 4
Maple Creek 49 D 6
Maplesville, AL 78-79 F 4
Mapleton, IA 70-71 BC 4
Mapleton, MN 70-71 D 4
Mapleton, OR 66-67 AB 3
Mapoon 182-183 H 2
Mappi = Mapi 174-175 L 8
Maprik 174-175 M 7
Mapuera, Rio — 98-99 H 5
Mapulau, Rio — 98-99 G 3-4
Maputo [Mozambique, place] 198 F 7
Maputo, Baía do — 198 F 7
Ma'qalā' 160-161 F 5
Maqinchao 103 C 6
Maqnā 199 D 3
Maqṭayr 194-195 BC 4
Maquan He = Tsangpo 166-167 EF 6
Maquela do Zombo 198 BC 3
Maqueze 198 F 6
Maquoketa, IA 70-71 E 4
Maquoketa River 70-71 E 4
Mar, Serra do — 103 G 2-3
Mara [EAT, administrative unit] 198 FG 2
Mara [EAT, river] 198 F 2
Mara [GUY] 98-99 K 1-2
Maraã 98-99 F 5
Marabá 98-99 K 6
Marabitanas 98-99 F 4
Maracá 98-99 N 3
Maracá, Ilha — 98-99 G 4
Maracá, Ilha de — 98-99 JK 4
Maraca, Rio — 98-99 N 5
Maracaibo 98-99 E 2
Maracaibo, Lago de — 98-99 E 2-3
Maracaju 98-99 H 9
Maracaju, Serra de — 98-99 H 9-J 8
Maracanã [BR, Pará] 98-99 K 5
Maracanaquará, Planalto — 98-99 M 5
Maracay 98-99 F 2
Marādah 194-195 H 3
Maradi 194-195 F 6
Ma'rafāy, Jabal — 199 D 6
Mara Game Reserve 198 FG 2
Marāghah, Al- 199 B 4
Marāgheh 160-161 F 3
Marahuaca, Cerro — 98-99 FG 4
Marais des Cygnes River 70-71 C 6
Marajó, Baía de — 98-99 K 4-5
Marajó, Ilha de — 98-99 JK 5
Marakei 178 H 2
Maralal 198 G 1
Maral Bashi 166-167 D 3-4
Maralinga 182-183 F 6
Maramasike 174-175 k 6
Maramba = Livingstone 198 E 5
Marambaia, Restinga da — 98-99 L 9
Marampa 194-195 B 7
Maran [MAL] 174-175 D 6
Marana, AZ 74-75 H 6
Maranboy 182-183 F 2
Marandellas = Marondera 198 F 5
Maranguape 98-99 M 5
Maranhão 98-99 KL 5-6
Maranoa River 182-183 J 5
Marañón, Río — 98-99 DE 5
Marapanim 98-99 P 5
Marapi, Rio — 98-99 K 4
Mar Argentino 103 D 7-E 5
Maraş 160-161 D 3
Mărăşeşti 138-139 M 3
Maratha = Mahārāshtra [IND, administrative unit] 160-161 L 7-M 6
Maratha = Mahārāshtra [IND, landscape] 160-161 M 7
Marathon, FL 80-81 c 4
Marathon, TX 76-77 C 7
Marathon [CDN] 46-47 T 8
Marathón [GR] 138-139 KL 6
Maratua, Pulau — 174-175 G 6
Marauiá, Rio — 98-99 F 4-5
Marauni 174-175 k 7
Marawī 194-195 L 5
Mar'ayt 160-161 G 7
Marbella 132-133 E 10
Marble, CO 68-69 C 6
Marble Bar 182-183 CD 4
Marble Canyon, AZ 74-75 H 4
Marble Falls, TX 76-77 E 7
Marble Gorge 74-75 H 4
Marble Hall 198 E 7
Marburg 124 D 3
Marcali 124 H 5
Marcaria 138-139 D 3
Marceau, Lac — 51 CD 2
Marceline, MO 70-71 D 6
Marcelino 98-99 F 5
Marcellus, MI 70-71 H 4
Marcellus, WA 66-67 D 2
March 116-117 LM 8
Marcha [SU, place] 154-155 X 5
Marcha [SU, river] 154-155 W 5
Marchand [CDN] 68-69 H 1
Marche [F] 132-133 HJ 5
Marche [I] 138-139 E 4
Marchena 132-133 E 10
Marchena, Isla — 98-99 AB 4
Mar Chiquita, Laguna — 103 D 4
Marcoule 132-133 K 6
Marcus, IA 70-71 BC 4
Marcus = Minami Tori 34-35 G 3
Marcus Baker, Mount — 46-47 G 5
Marcus Island = Minami Tori 34-35 G 3
Marcus Necker Ridge 34-35 G 3-J 4
Marcy, Mount — 72-73 JK 2
Mardān 160-161 L 4
Mar del Plata 103 E 5
Marden 116-117 M 9
Mardin 160-161 E 3
Maré, Île — 182-183 N 4
Mare, Muntele — 138-139 K 2
Marebe = Mā'rib 160-161 F 7
Maree, Loch — 116-117 F 3
Mareeba 182-183 HJ 3
Mareeg 194-195 b 3
Maremma 138-139 D 4
Maréna 194-195 B 6
Marengo, IA 70-71 D 5
Marengo, IN 70-71 G 6
Marengo, WA 66-67 DE 2
Marengo = Ḥajut 194-195 E 1
Marenisco, MI 70-71 F 2
Marèttimo 138-139 DE 7
Marfa, TX 76-77 B 7
Marfa', Al- = Al-Maghayrā' 160-161 G 6
Marg, Dasht-e — 160-161 J 4
Margaret Bay 48 D 4
Margarita 103 D 3
Margarita, Isla de — 98-99 G 2
Margate 116-117 h 7
Margeride, Monts de la — 132-133 J 6
Margherita = Jamaame 198 H 1
Margherita, Lake — = Abaya 194-195 M 7
Margie 49 C 3
Margie, MN 70-71 D 1
Margilan 160-161 L 2
Margoh, Dasht-e — = Dasht-e Marg 160-161 J 4
Marguerite, Baie — 31 C 29-30
Marguerite, Rivière — 51 C 2
Maria [CDN] 51 D 3
María Chiquita 58-59 b 2
María Cleofas, Isla — 86-87 G 7
María Elena 103 BC 2
María Enrique, Altos de — 58-59 bc 2
Maria Island [AUS, Northern Territory] 182-183 G 2
Maria Island [AUS, Tasmania] 182-183 J 8
María Madre, Isla — 58-59 E 7
María Magdalena, Isla — 58-59 E 7
Mariana Islands 148-149 S 7-8
Marianao 58-59 K 7
Mariana Trench 34-35 G 4
Marianna, AR 78-79 D 3
Marianna, FL 78-79 G 5
Mariano Machado = Ganda 198 B 4
Mariánské Lázně 124 F 4
Marías, Islas — 58-59 E 7
Marias Pass 58-59 D 2
Marias River 66-67 H 1
Mari Autonomous Soviet Socialist Republic = 3 ◁ 154-155 H 6
Maria van Diemen, Cape — 182-183 O 6
Maria Velha, Cachoeira — 98-99 K 7
Mariazell 124 G 5
Mā'rib 160-161 F 7
Maribor 138-139 F 2
Marica [BG, place] 138-139 LM 4
Marica [BG, river] 138-139 L 4
Maricopa, AZ 74-75 G 6
Maricopa, CA 74-75 D 5
Maricopa Indian Reservation 74-75 G 6
Maricourt 46-47 W 5
Marīdī 194-195 KL 8
Marié, Rio — 98-99 F 5
Marie-Galante 58-59 OP 8
Mariehamn 114-115 HJ 7
Mariental 198 C 6
Mariestad 114-115 E 8
Marietta, GA 58-59 K 5
Marietta, OH 72-73 F 5
Marietta, OK 76-77 F 6
Marieville 72-73 K 2
Marigot [Anguilla] 88-89 P 5
Marigot [WD] 88-89 Q 7
Mariinsk 154-155 Q 6
Marii Prončiščevoj, buchta — 154-155 VW 2
Marijskaja Avtonomnaja Sovetskaja Socialističeskaja Respublika = Mari Autonomous Soviet Socialist Republic 154-155 H 6
Marília 98-99 JK 9
Marina 48 H 1
Marina, Île — = Espíritu Santo 182-183 MN 3
Marina del Rey 83 III b 2
Marina del Rey, CA 83 III b 2
Marina di Gioiosa Iònica 138-139 G 6
Marina North Beach, San Francisco-, CA 83 I b 2
Marin City, CA 83 I a 1
Marinduque Island 174-175 H 4
Marine City, MI 72-73 E 3
Mariners Harbor, New York-, NY 82 III ab 3
Marinette, WI 58-59 J 2
Maringa [ZRE] 198 D 1
Marin Headlands State Park 83 I ab 2
Marin Mall, CA 83 I ab 1
Marin Peninsula 83 I a 1-b 2
Marion 31 E 4
Marion, AL 78-79 F 4
Marion, IA 70-71 E 4
Marion, IL 70-71 F 7
Marion, IN 70-71 H 5
Marion, KS 68-69 H 6
Marion, KY 70-71 F 7
Marion, LA 78-79 C 4
Marion, MI 70-71 H 3
Marion, MT 66-67 F 1
Marion, NC 80-81 EF 3
Marion, ND 68-69 G 2
Marion, OH 72-73 E 4
Marion, SC 80-81 G 3
Marion, SD 68-69 H 4
Marion, TX 76-77 EF 8
Marion, VA 80-81 F 2
Marion, WI 70-71 F 3
Marion, Lake — 80-81 F 4
Marion Island 31 E 4
Marion Junction, AL 78-79 F 4
Maripa 98-99 FG 3
Maripasoula 98-99 J 4
Mariposa, CA 74-75 D 4
Marīr, Jazīrat — 199 DE 6
Marismas, Las — 132-133 D 10
Maritime Alps = Alpes Maritimes 132-133 L 6
Maritsa = Marica 138-139 L 4
Mārīyah, Al- 160-161 G 6
Marj, Al- 194-195 J 2
Marjan = Wāza Khwā 160-161 K 4
Marjevka 154-155 M 7
Marka [SP] 194-195 NO 8
Markazī, Ostān-e — 160-161 E 3-F 4
Markdale 72-73 F 2
Marked Tree, AR 78-79 D 3
Market Deeping 116-117 L 8
Market Drayton 116-117 J 8
Market Harborough 116-117 KL 8
Market Rasen 116-117 L 7
Market Weighton 116-117 L 7
Markha = Marcha 154-155 W 5
Markham 72-73 G 3
Markham, WA 66-67 AB 2
Markham, Mount — 31 A 15-16
Markkēri = Mercāra 160-161 M 8
Markleeville, CA 74-75 CD 3
Markounda 194-195 H 7
Markovo [SU, Čukotskij NO] 154-155 gh 5
Marks, MS 78-79 D 3
Marksville, LA 78-79 CD 5
Marktredwitz 124 EF 3-4
Marlborough [AUS] 182-183 JK 4
Marlbourough [GB] 116-117 K 9
Marlette, MI 72-73 E 3
Marlin, TX 76-77 F 7
Marlinton, WV 72-73 FG 5
Marlow 116-117 L 9
Marlow, OK 76-77 F 5
Marlow Heights, MD 82 II b 2
Marmagao 160-161 L 7
Marmande 132-133 H 6
Marmara adası 160-161 B 2
Marmara denizi 160-161 B 2
Marmarica = Barqat al-Baḥrīyah 194-195 JK 2
Marmaris 142-143 E 8
Marmarth, ND 68-69 E 2
Marmelão, Cachoeira — 98-99 KL 7
Marmelos, Rio dos — 98-99 G 6
Mar Menor 132-133 G 10
Marmet, WV 72-73 F 5
Marmion Lake 70-71 E 1
Marmolada 138-139 DE 2
Marmot Bay 52-53 L 7-8
Marmot Island 52-53 M 7
Mar Muerto 86-87 NO 9
Marne 132-133 JK 4
Marne au Rhin, Canal de la — 132-133 K 4
Maroa, IL 70-71 F 5
Maroantsétra 198 JK 5
Marocco, IN 70-71 G 5
Marokko 194-195 C 3-D 2
Marondera 198 F 5
Maroni 98-99 J 3-4
Maros [RI] 174-175 GH 7-8
Marosvasarhely = Tîrgu Mureş 138-139 L 2
Maroua 194-195 G 6
Marouini 98-99 LM 3
Marovoay 198 J 5
Marowijne [SME, administrative unit] 98-99 L 2-3
Marowijne [SME, river] 98-99 J 3-4
Marqat Bazar 166-167 D 4
Marquand, MO 70-71 E 7
Marquesas Keys 80-81 b 4
Marquette, IA 70-71 E 4
Marquette, MI 58-59 J 2
Marquette Park 83 II a 2
Marquise 116-117 h 8
Marrah, Jabal — 194-195 JK 6
Marrâkech = Marrākush 194-195 C 2
Marrakesh = Marrākush 194-195 C 2
Marrākush 194-195 C 2
Marrawah 182-183 H 8
Marree 182-183 G 5
Marromeu 198 G 5
Marrupa 198 G 4
Marsá 'Alam 199 D 5
Marsá al-Burayqah 194-195 HJ 2
Marsabit 198 G 1
Marsala 138-139 E 7
Marsá Sha'b 194-195 M 4
Marsa Sūsa = Sūsah 194-195 J 2
Marseille 132-133 K 7
Marseilles, IL 70-71 F 5
Marseilles = Marseille 132-133 K 7
Marsfjället 114-115 F 5
Marsh, MT 68-69 D 2
Marshall, AK 52-53 FG 6
Marshall, AR 78-79 C 3
Marshall, IL 70-71 FG 6
Marshall, MI 70-71 H 4
Marshall, MN 70-71 BC 3
Marshall, MO 70-71 D 6
Marshall, NC 80-81 E 3
Marshall, OK 76-77 F 4
Marshall, TX 58-59 H 5
Marshall, Mount — 72-73 G 5
Marshall Basin 179 J 3
Marshall Islands 34-35 H 4
Marshalltown, IA 70-71 D 4
Marshall Trench 34-35 H 4
Marshfield, MO 78-79 C 2
Marshfield, WI 70-71 EF 3
Marshfield = Coos Bay, OR 58-59 AB 3
Marsh Harbour 88-89 H 1
Mars Hill, ME 72-73 MN 1
Marsh Island 78-79 CD 6
Marsing, ID 66-67 E 4
Marsland, NE 68-69 E 4
Marsqui 51 D 3
Marstrand 114-115 D 9
Mart, TX 76-77 F 7
Martaban = Môktama 174-175 C 3

248 **Manasqua**

Marten 48 K 2
Marten, Rivière — 50 O 1
Martensdale, IA 70-71 D 5
Martensøya 114-115 I 4
Martha's Vineyard 58-59 MN 3
Martí 88-89 H 4
Martigny 124 C 5
Martigues 132-133 K 7
Martim Vaz, Ilhas — 98-99 O 9
Martin 124 J 4
Martin, SD 68-69 EF 4
Martin, TN 78-79 E 2
Martínez de la Torre 86-87 M 7
Martinique 58-59 OP 9
Martinique Passage 88-89 Q 7
Martin Lake 78-79 FG 4
Martin Peninsula 31 B 25-26
Martin Point 46-47 H 3
Martin River 48 JK 1
Martinsburg, WV 72-73 GH 5
Martinsdale, MT 66-67 H 2
Martins Ferry, OH 72-73 F 4
Martinsville, IN 70-71 G 6
Martinsville, VA 80-81 G 2
Martock 116-117 J 10
Marton 182-183 OP 8
Martos 132-133 EF 10
Martre, Lac la — 46-47 MN 5
Martuk 154-155 K 7
Marua = Maroua 194-195 G 6
Maruai 98-99 H 3
Marudi Mountains 98-99 J 3
Marugame 170-171 J 5
Marui 174-175 M 7
Maruim 98-99 M 7
Marungu 198 EF 3
Marvão 132-133 D 9
Mārvāṛ = Mārwār [IND, landscape] 160-161 L 5
Mārvāṛ = Mārwār [IND, place] 160-161 L 5
Marvel, AR 78-79 D 3
Marvine, Mount — 74-75 H 3
Mar Vista, Los Angeles-, CA 83 III b 1
Mārwār [IND, landscape] 160-161 L 5
Mārwār [IND, place] 160-161 L 5
Marwayne 49 CD 4
Marx 142-143 J 5
Mary 160-161 J 3
Maryborough [AUS, Queensland] 182-183 K 5
Maryborough [AUS, Victoria] 182-183 HJ 7
Maryborough = Port Laoise 116-117 D 7
Maryfield 49 GH 6
Mary Kathleen 182-183 GH 4
Maryland [USA] 58-59 L 4
Maryneal, TX 76-77 D 6
Maryport 116-117 H 6
Mary Rvier 182-183 F 2
Marystown 51 J 4
Marysvale, UT 74-75 GH 3
Marysville 51 C 4-5
Marysville, KS 68-69 H 6
Marysville, OH 72-73 E 4
Marysville, WA 66-67 BC 1
Maryūṭ, Buḥayrat — 199 AB 2
Maryvale 182-183 HJ 3
Maryville, CA 74-75 C 3
Maryville, MO 70-71 C 5
Maryville, TN 80-81 DE 3
Marzo, Cabo — 98-99 D 3
Marzūq 194-195 G 3
Marzūq, Ṣaḥrā' — 194-195 G 3-4
Masai Steppe 198 G 2
Masaka 198 F 2
Masampo = Masan 166-167 O 4-5
Masan 166-167 O 4-5
Masandam, Rā's — 160-161 H 5
Masardis, ME 72-73 M 1
Masasi 198 G 4
Masavi 98-99 G 8
Masaya 58-59 J 9
Masbat = Masbate 174-175 H 4
Masbate 174-175 H 4
Mascara = Mū'askar 194-195 E 1
Mascarene Basin 26-27 M 6
Mascarene Islands 188-189 N 10-11
Mascarene Plateau 26-27 MN 6
Masefield 68-69 C 1
Maseru 198 E 7
Mashala 198 D 2-3
Mashhad 160-161 HJ 3
Mashike 170-171 b 2
Māshkel, Hāmūn-i — 160-161 J 5
Mashkode 70-71 HJ 2
Mashonaland North 198 EF 5
Mashonaland South 198 EF 5
Mashrā' ar-Raqq 194-195 K 7
Mashraqī Bangāl 160-161 O 5-P 6
Mashū-ko 170-171 d 2
Mašigina, guba — 154-155 HJ 3
Masīlah, Wādī al- 160-161 F 7
Masin 174-175 L 8
Masindi 198 F 1
Maṣīrah, Jazīrat al- 160-161 HJ 6
Maṣīrah, Khalij al- 160-161 H 6-7
Masjed Soleymān 160-161 FG 4
Mask, Lough — = Loch Measca 116-117 B 7
Masoala, Cap — 198 K 5
Mason, MI 70-71 H 4
Mason, TN 78-79 E 3
Mason, TX 76-77 E 7
Mason, WI 70-71 E 2
Mason, WY 66-67 HJ 4
Mason City, IA 58-59 H 3
Mason City, IL 70-71 F 5
Masonville, VA 82 II a 2
Maspeth, New York-, NY 82 III c 2
Masqaṭ 160-161 H 6
Maṣr el-Gedīda = Al-Qahīrah-Miṣr al-Jadīdah 199 B 2
Mass, MI 70-71 F 2
Massa 138-139 D 3
Massachusetts 58-59 M 3
Massachusetts Bay 58-59 MN 3
Massadona, CO 68-69 B 5
Massakori = Massakory 194-195 H 6
Massakory 194-195 H 6
Massa Marittima 138-139 D 4
Massangena 198 F 6
Massango 198 C 3
Massasi = Masasi 198 G 4
Massaua = Mitsiwa 194-195 MN 5
Massawa = Mitsawa 194-195 MN 5
Massena, NY 72-73 J 2
Massénya 194-195 H 6
Masset 46-47 K 7
Masset Inlet 48 A 3
Massey 50 KL 3
Massif Central 132-133 J 6
Massillon, OH 72-73 F 4
Massina = Macina 194-195 CD 6
Massinga 198 G 6
Masson 72-73 J 2
Masson Island 31 C 10
Mastabah 160-161 D 6
Masters, CO 68-69 D 5
Masterton 182-183 P 8
Mastiogouche, Parc provincial de — 50 P 3
Mastung 160-161 K 5
Mastūrah 160-161 D 6
Masuda 170-171 H 5
Masuria = Pojezierze Mazurskie 124 K 2-L 1
Maṣyāf 142-143 G 8-9
Mataban, Cape — = Akrōtērion Taínaron 138-139 K 7
Matabeleland 198 E 5-6
Matachewan 50 L 3
Mata da Corda, Serra da — 98-99 K 8
Matadi 198 B 3
Matador 49 DE 5
Matador, TX 76-77 D 5-6
Matagalpa 58-59 J 9
Matagami 46-47 V 8
Matagami, Lac — 50 N 2
Matagamon, ME 72-73 M 1
Matagorda, TX 76-77 G 8
Matagorda Bay 58-59 GH 6
Matagorda Island 58-59 G 6
Matagorda Peninsula 76-77 FG 8
Maṭāi = Maṭāy 199 B 3
Mataj 154-155 O 8
Matala 198 C 4
Matam 194-195 B 5
Matamatá, Cachoeira — 98-99 HJ 8
Matamoros [MEX, Coahuila] 58-59 F 6
Matamoros [MEX, Tamaulipas] 58-59 G 6
Matancillas 103 B 4
Matane 46-47 X 8
Matane, Parc provincial de — 51 C 3
Matanuska, AK 52-53 MN 6
Matanuska River 52-53 NO 6
Matanzas 58-59 K 7
Matão, Serra do — 98-99 J 6
Matapalo, Cabo — 58-59 K 10
Matapédia, Rivière — 51 C 3
Mataporquera 132-133 E 7
Mātara [CL] 160-161 N 9
Mataram 174-175 G 8
Matarani 98-99 E 8
Mataranka [AUS] 182-183 F 2
Mataró 132-133 J 8
Matatiele 198 E 8
Maṭāy 199 B 3
Mategua 98-99 G 7
Matehuala 58-59 F 7
Matera 138-139 G 5
Mátészalka 124 KL 4-5
Matetsi 198 E 5
Māṭeur = Māṭir 194-195 FG 1
Mather, CA 74-75 D 4
Matheson 50 L 2
Matheson, CO 68-69 E 6
Mathews, VA 80-81 H 2
Mathis, TX 76-77 EF 8
Mathiston, MS 78-79 E 4
Mathura 160-161 M 5
Mati 174-175 J 5
Matías Hernández 58-59 bc 2
Matías Romero 86-87 N 9
Matimbuka 198 G 4
Matinenda Lake 50 K 3
Matinicus Island 72-73 M 3
Māṭir 194-195 FG 1
Matlock, WA 66-67 B 2
Matlock [CDN] 49 K 5
Matlock [GB] 116-117 K 7
Matochkin Shar = proliv Matočkin Šar 154-155 KL 3
Matočkin Šar 154-155 KL 3
Matočkin Šar, proliv — 154-155 KL 3
Mato Grosso [BR, Acre] 98-99 C 9
Mato Grosso [BR, Mato Grosso administrative unit] 98-99 HJ 7
Mato Grosso [BR, Mato Grosso place] 98-99 H 7-8
Mato Grosso, Planalto do — 98-99 HJ 7
Mato Grosso do Sul 98-99 HJ 8-9
Matope 198 FG 5
Matopo Hills 198 E 6
Matosinhos [P] 132-133 C 8
Matoury 98-99 M 2
Mátra 124 JK 5
Matra = Mathurā 160-161 M 5
Maṭraḥ 160-161 H 6
Matrimonio, El — 76-77 C 9
Maṭrûḥ = Marsá Maṭrūḥ 194-195 K 2
Maṭrūḥ, Marsá — 194-195 K 2
Matsue 166-167 P 4
Matsumae 170-171 ab 3
Matsumoto 170-171 LM 4
Matsunami = Suzu 170-171 L 4
Matsusaka 170-171 KL 5
Matsu Tao 166-167 MN 6
Matsuwa = Matua 148-149 T 5
Matsuyama 170-171 J 6
Mattagami River 46-47 U 7-8
Mattamuskeet Lake 80-81 HJ 3
Mattawa 72-73 G 1
Mattawamkeag, ME 72-73 MN 2
Mattawin, Rivière — 72-73 K 1
Matterhorn [USA] 66-67 F 5
Matthew, Île — 182-183 O 4
Matthews Peak 198 G 1
Matthew Town 88-89 JK 4
Maṭṭī, Sabkhat — 160-161 G 6
Mattice 50 H 3
Matto Grosso = Mato Grosso 98-99 HJ 7
Matua [RI] 174-175 F 7
Matua [SU] 148-149 T 5
Matucana 98-99 D 7
Matue = Matsue 166-167 P 4
Matuku 174-175 ab 2
Matumoto = Matsumoto 166-167 Q 4
Matūn 160-161 KL 4
Matundu 198 D 1
Matura = Mathurā 160-161 M 5
Maturín 98-99 G 2-3
Maturucá 98-99 H 2
Matuyama = Matsuyama 166-167 P 5
Maúa [Mozambique] 198 G 4
Maubeuge 132-133 JK 3
Mauchline 116-117 G 5
Maud, OK 76-77 F 5
Maud, TX 76-77 G 6
Maudlow, MT 66-67 H 2
Maud Seamount 31 C 1
Maués 98-99 H 5
Maués-Açu, Rio — 98-99 H 5
Maughold Head 116-117 GH 6
Mauhan 174-175 C 2
Maui 174-175 e 3
Maulamyaing 174-175 C 3
Maullín 103 B 6
Maumee, OH 72-73 DE 4
Maumee River 70-71 H 5
Maumere 174-175 H 8
Maun [RB] 198 D 5
Mauna Kea 174-175 e 4
Mauna Loa 174-175 e 4
Mauna Loa, HI 78-79 d 2
Mauneluk River 52-53 K 3
Maungdaw 174-175 B 2
Maunoir, Lac — 46-47 M 4
Maupertuis, Lac — 50 PQ 1
Maupin, OR 66-67 C 3
Maurepas, Lake — 78-79 D 5
Maurice, Lake — 182-183 EF 5
Mauriceville, TX 76-77 GH 7
Mauricie, Parc national — 50 P 3
Mauritania 194-195 BC 4
Mauritius 24-25 MN 7
Maury Mountains 66-67 C 3
Mauston, WI 70-71 EF 4
Mautong 174-175 H 6
Mava 174-175 M 8
Mavago 198 G 4
Mavinga 198 CD 5
Mawa 198 E 1
Mawer 49 E 5
Mawhun = Mauhan 174-175 C 2
Mawson 31 C 7
Max, ND 68-69 F 2
Maxbass, ND 68-69 F 1
Maxcanú 86-87 P 7
Maxstone 68-69 CD 1
Maxville 72-73 J 2
Maxville, MT 66-67 G 2
Maxwell, CA 74-75 B 3
May, ID 66-67 G 3
May, OK 76-77 E 4
Maya, Pulau — 174-175 E 7
Mayaguana Island 58-59 M 7
Mayagüez 58-59 N 8
Mayama 198 BC 2
Maya Mountains 58-59 J 8
Mayang-do 170-171 G 2-3
Mayapán 58-59 J 7
Mayari 88-89 HJ 4
Maybell, CO 68-69 B 5
Maybole 116-117 G 5
Mayd 194-195 b 1
Maydena 182-183 J 8
Maydī 160-161 E 7
Mayence = Mainz 124 D 3-4
Mayenne [F, place] 132-133 G 4
Mayenne [F, river] 132-133 G 4-5
Mayer, AZ 74-75 G 5
Mayerthorpe 48 K 3
Mayesville, SC 80-81 F 3-4
Mayfair 49 E 4
Mayfield, ID 66-67 F 4
Mayfield, KY 78-79 E 2
Mayhill, NM 76-77 B 6
Maymaneh 160-161 JK 3
Maymyo = Memyō 174-175 C 2
Maynard, WA 66-67 B 2
Maynas 98-99 DE 5
Mayo, FL 80-81 b 1-2
Mayo = Maigh Eo 116-117 B 6-7
Mayodan, NC 80-81 FG 2
Mayo Landing 46-47 JK 5
Mayor, El — 74-75 F 6
Mayotte 198 H 4
Mayoumba 198 AB 2
May Point, Cape — 72-73 J 5
Mayrhofen 124 EF 5
Maysville, KY 72-73 E 5
Maysville, MO 70-71 C 6
Maysville, NC 80-81 H 3
Maytown 182-183 HJ 3
Mayu, Pulau — 174-175 J 6
Mayunga 198 E 2
Mayville, ND 68-69 H 2
Mayville, NY 72-73 G 3
Maywood, CA 83 III c 2
Maywood, NE 68-69 F 5
Maywood, NJ 82 III b 1
Mayyit, Baḥr al- 160-161 D 4
Mazabuka 198 E 5
Mazagan = Al-Jadīdah 194-195 C 2
Mazagão 98-99 J 5
Mazáka = Kayseri 160-161 D 3
Mazamet 132-133 J 7
Mazan = Villa Mazán 103 C 3
Māzandarān 160-161 GH 3
Mazara del Vallo 138-139 DE 7
Mazār-i-Sharīf 160-161 K 3
Mazarrón 132-133 G 10
Mazarrón, Golfo de — 132-133 G 10
Mazar tagh 166-167 D 4
Mazaruni River 98-99 HJ 1
Mazatenango 58-59 H 9
Mazatlán 58-59 E 7
Mazatzal Peak 74-75 H 5
Mažeikiai 142-143 D 4
Mazhafah, Jabal — = Jabal Buwārah 199 D 3
Mazomanie, WI 70-71 F 4
Mazurskie, Pojezierze — 124 K 2-L 1

Mbabane 198 F 7
M'Baiki 194-195 H 8
Mbala 198 F 3
Mbalabala 198 EF 6
Mbale 198 F 1
M'Balmayo 194-195 G 8
Mbandaka 198 C 1-2
Mbanga 194-195 FG 8
Mbanza Congo 198 B 3
Mbanza Ngungu 198 B 2-3
Mbarara 198 F 2
Mbari 194-195 J 7
M'Bé 198 C 2
Mbemkuru 198 GH 3
Mbeya [EAT, place] 198 F 3
M'Bigou 198 B 2
Mbin 194-195 F 8
M'Binda 198 B 2
Mbini [Equatorial Guinea, administrative unit] 194-195 G 8
Mbizi 198 F 6
Mbomou 194-195 J 7-8
M'Bour 194-195 A 6
Mbud 194-195 B 5
Mbuji-Mayi 198 D 3
Mburucuyá 103 E 3

Mcensk 142-143 G 5
Mchinga 198 GH 3
Mchinji 198 F 4
M'Clintok 52-53 U 6

Meacham, OR 66-67 D 3
Mead, WA 66-67 E 2
Mead, Lake — 58-59 D 4
Meade, KS 68-69 F 7
Meade Peak 66-67 H 4
Meade River 52-53 J 1
Meade River, AK 52-53 J 1
Meadow, TX 76-77 CD 6
Meadow Lake 46-47 P 7
Meadow Lake Provincial Park 49 D 3
Meadow Valley Range 74-75 F 4
Meadow Valley Wash 74-75 F 4
Meadville, PA 72-73 FG 4
Meaford 72-73 F 2
Meáin, Inis — 116-117 B 7
Mealy Mountains 46-47 Z 7
Mearim, Rio — 98-99 L 5
Measca, Loch — 116-117 B 7
Meath = Mhíde 116-117 E 7
Meath Park 49 F 4
Meat Mount 52-53 G 2
Meaux 132-133 J 4
Mebote 198 F 6
Mebreije, Rio — = Rio M'Bridge 198 B 3
Mebridege, Rio — 198 B 3
Meca = Makkah 160-161 DE 6
Mecca, CA 74-75 EF 6
Mecca = Makkah 160-161 DE 6
Mechanicsburg, PA 72-73 H 4
Mechanicville, NY 72-73 K 3
Meched = Mashhad 160-161 HJ 3
Mechelen 132-133 K 3
Méchéria = Mīshrīyah 194-195 DE 2
Méchins, les — 51 C 3
Mechlin = Mechelen 132-133 K 3
Mecklenburg 124 EF 2
Mecklenburger Bucht 124 EF 1
Mecsek 124 J 5
Mecúfi 198 H 4
Mecula 198 G 4
Medan 174-175 C 6
Médanos [RA, Buenos Aires place] 103 D 5
Medanosa, Punta — 103 CD 7
Medaryville, IN 70-71 G 5
Medellín [CO] 98-99 D 3
Medellín [RA] 103 D 3
Medelpad 114-115 FG 6
Medenīn = Madanīyīn 194-195 FG 2
Medetsiz 160-161 C 3
Medford, MA 72-73 L 3
Medford, OK 76-77 F 4
Medford, OR 58-59 B 3
Medford, WI 70-71 EF 3
Medfra, AK 52-53 K 5
Medgidia 138-139 N 3
Mediano 132-133 H 7
Mediapolis, IA 70-71 E 5
Mediaş 138-139 L 2
Medical Lake, WA 66-67 DE 2
Medicanceli 132-133 F 8
Medicine Bow, WY 68-69 C 5
Medicine Bow Mountains 68-69 CD 5
Medicine Bow Peak 58-59 EF 3
Medicine Bow River 68-69 CD 5
Medicine Hat 46-47 O 7
Medicine Lake 68-69 DE 1
Medicine Lake, MT 68-69 D 1
Medicine Lodge 48 J 3
Medicine Lodge, KS 76-77 EF 4
Medicine Mound, TX 76-77 E 5
Medina, ND 68-69 G 2
Medina, TX 76-77 E 8
Medina = Al-Madīnah 160-161 DE 6
Medina del Campo 132-133 E 8
Medina de Rioseco 132-133 E 8
Medina River 76-77 E 8
Medina-Sidonia 132-133 DE 10
Medinīpur = Midnapore 160-161 O 6
Mediterranean Sea 110-111 J 8-O 9
Mednogorsk 154-155 K 7
Mednyj, ostrov — 30 D 2
Médoc 132-133 G 6
Medora, KS 68-69 H 6
Medora, ND 68-69 E 2
Medstead 49 DE 4
Medvedica 142-143 H 5-6
Medvežij, ostrova — 154-155 f 3
Medvežjegorsk 154-155 EF 5
Meekatharra 182-183 C 5
Meeker, CO 68-69 C 5
Meeker, OK 76-77 F 5
Meelpaeg Lake 51 H 3
Meerut 160-161 M 5
Mēga [ETH] 194-195 M 8
Mega [RI] 174-175 K 7
Megálē Préspa, Límnē — 138-139 J 5
Megalópolis 138-139 JK 7
Megálo Sofráno 138-139 M 7
Mégantic 72-73 L 2
Mégara 138-139 K 6-7
Meghalaya 160-161 P 5
Megion 154-155 O 5
Mégiscane, Rivière — 50 NO 2
Megler, WA 66-67 B 2
Megrega 154-155 E 5
Mehadia 138-139 K 3
Mehdia = Mahdīyah 194-195 E 1
Meherrin River 80-81 H 2
Mehsāna 160-161 L 6
Meia Ponte, Rio — 98-99 K 8
Meighen Island 46-47 RS 1
Meihekou = Shanchengzhen 170-171 EF 1
Meikhtīlā 174-175 BC 2
Meiktila = Meikhtīlā 174-175 BC 2
Meilghe, Loch — 116-117 C 6
Meiling Guan = Xiaomei Guan 166-167 LM 6
Meiningen 124 E 3
Meissen 124 F 3
Mei Xian 166-167 M 7
Mejicana, Cumbre de — 103 C 3
Mejillones 103 B 2
Mejnypil'gyno 154-155 j 5
Mekambo 198 B 1
Mekelē 194-195 M 6
Mekerrhane, Sebkra — = Sabkhat Mukrān 194-195 E 3
Meknès = Miknās 194-195 C 2
Mekong, Mouths of the — = Cu'a Sông Cu'u Long 174-175 E 5
Mekongga, Gunung — 174-175 H 7
Mekoryuk, AK 52-53 D 6
Mekran = Mokrān 160-161 HJ 5
Mékrou 194-195 E 6
Melaka [MAL, place] 174-175 D 6
Melaka, Selat — 174-175 CD 6
Melanesia 34-35 F 4-H 5
Mělas 138-139 L 7
Melayu 174-175 D 6
Melba, ID 66-67 E 4
Melbourn 116-117 LM 8
Melbourne, AR 78-79 D 2-3
Melbourne, FL 80-81 c 2
Melbourne [AUS] 182-183 H 7
Melbourne [GB] 116-117 K 8
Melbu 114-115 F 3
Melchers, Kapp — 114-115 m 6
Melchor, Isla — 103 AB 7
Melchor de Mencos 86-87 Q 9
Melchor Múzquiz 58-59 F 6
Meldrim, GA 80-81 F 4
Meldrum Bay 50 K 3
Meleda = Mljet 138-139 G 4
Melenki 142-143 H 4
Melfi [Chad] 194-195 H 6
Melfi [I] 138-139 F 5
Melfort 46-47 Q 7
Melik, Wadi el — = Wādī al-Malik 194-195 KL 5
Melilia = Melilla 194-195 D 1
Melilla 194-195 D 1
Melimoyu, Monte — 103 B 6
Melinde = Malindi 198 H 2
Melipilla 103 B 4
Melita 68-69 F 1
Melitene = Malatya 160-161 D 3
Melito di Porto Salvo 138-139 FG 7
Melitopol' 142-143 FG 6
Melk 124 G 4
Melksham 116-117 JK 9
Mellen, WI 70-71 E 2
Mellerud 114-115 E 8
Mellette, SD 68-69 G 3
Mellīṭ = Mallīṭ 194-195 K 6
Mellizo Sur, Cerro — 103 B 7
Mellwood, AR 78-79 D 3
Mělník 124 G 3
Mel'nikovo [SU ← Tomsk] 154-155 P 6
Melo [ROU] 103 F 4
Melozitna River 52-53 KL 4
Melrhir, Chott — = Shaṭṭ Malghīr 194-195 F 2
Melrose 116-117 J 5
Melrose, MN 70-71 C 3
Melrose, MT 66-67 G 3
Melrose, NM 76-77 C 5
Melrose, New York-, Ny 82 III c 2
Melsetter = Mandidzudzure 198 F 5-6
Melstone, MT 68-69 BC 2
Meltaus 114-115 L 4
Melton Mowbray 116-117 L 8
Melun 132-133 J 4
Melunga 198 C 5
Melūṭ = Malūṭ 194-195 L 6
Melvaig 116-117 F 3
Melville 49 G 5
Melville, LA 78-79 D 5
Melville, MT 66-67 HJ 2
Melville, Cape — 182-183 HJ 2
Melville, Lake — 46-47 YZ 7
Melville Bay 182-183 G 2
Melville Bugt 46-47 X-Z 2
Melville Hills 46-47 M 4
Melville Island [AUS] 182-183 F 2
Melville Island [CDN] 46-47 N-P 2
Melville Peninsula 46-47 U 4
Melville Sound = Viscount Melville Sound 46-47 O-Q 3
Melvin, Lough — = Loch Meilghe 116-117 C 6
Memala 174-175 F 7
Memba 198 H 4
Memboro 174-175 G 8
Memmingen 124 DE 5
Memorial Coliseum and Sports Arena 83 III c 1
Memphis 194-195 L 3
Memphis, IA 70-71 D 5
Memphis, TN 58-59 HJ 4
Memphis, TX 76-77 D 5
Memphremagog, Lac — 72-73 KL 2
Memuro 170-171 c 2
Memyō 174-175 C 2
Mena, AR 76-77 G 5
Menado = Manado 174-175 H 6
Menai Strait 116-117 G 7
Ménaka 194-195 E 5
Menam = Mae Nam Chao Phraya 174-175 CD 3-4
Menan Khong 174-175 D 3
Menarandra 198 HJ 6-7
Menard, MT 66-67 H 3
Menard, TX 76-77 DE 7
Menasha, WI 70-71 F 3
Menaskwagama, Lac — 51 EF 2
Mende 132-133 J 6
Mendenhall, MS 78-79 E 4-5
Mendenhall, Cape — 52-53 DE 7
Mendez [EC] 98-99 D 5
Méndez [MEX] 86-87 L 5

Méndez 249

Mirandela 132-133 D 8
Mirando City, TX 76-77 E 9
Mirândola 138-139 D 3
Mirapinima 98-99 G 5
Mirbāṭ 160-161 GH 7
Mirêar, Gezîret — = Jazīrat Marīr 199 DE 6
Mirebalais 88-89 KL 5
Mirfield 116-117 K 7
Mirgorod 142-143 F 5-6
Miri 174-175 F 6
Mirim, Lagoa — 103 F 4
Miriti 98-99 H 6
Miriti, Cachoeira — 98-99 J 8
Mīrjāveh 160-161 J 5
Mirnyj [Antarctica] 31 C 10
Mirnyj [SU] 154-155 V 5
Mirror River 49 D 2
Miryang 170-171 G 5
Mirzāpur 160-161 N 5-6
Mis, Sliabh — 116-117 B 8
Misāḥah, Bi'r — 194-195 K 4
Misaine Bank 51 G 5
Misantla 86-87 M 8
Miscouche 51 DE 4
Miscou Island 51 DE 4
Mish, Slieve — = Sliabh Mis 116-117 B 8
Mish'āb, Al- 160-161 F 5
Mishagomish, Lac — 50 NO 1
Mishan 166-167 P 2
Mishawaka, IN 70-71 GH 5
Mishbīh, Jabal — 194-195 L 4
Misheguk Mountain 52-53 G 2
Mi-shima 170-171 H 5
Mishomis 72-73 J 1
Misima 174-175 h 7
Misión, La — 74-75 E 6
Misiones [RA] 103 EF 3
Miskito, Cayos — 58-59 K 9
Miskito Cays = Cayos Miskitos 58-59 K 9
Miskolc 124 K 4
Mismār 194-195 M 5
Misol = Pulau Misoöl 174-175 K 7
Misoöl, Pulau — 174-175 K 7
Misore = Mysore 160-161 M 8
Miṣr, Al- 194-195 KL 3
Misrātah 194-195 H 2
Miṣr-Baḥrī 199 BC 2
Miṣr el-Gedīda = Al-Qāhirah-Miṣr al-Jadīdah 199 BC 2
Misriç 142-143 H 8
Missanabie 70-71 HJ 1
Missinaibi Lake 70-71 J 1
Missinaibi River 46-47 U 7
Mission, SD 68-69 F 4
Mission, TX 76-77 E 9
Mission, San Francisco-, CA 83 I b 2
Mission City 66-67 B 1
Mission Dolores 83 I b 2
Mission San Gabriel Arcangel 83 III d 1
Missippinewa Lake 70-71 GH 5
Missicabi, Rivière — 50 M 1
Mississauga 72-73 G 3
Mississippi 58-59 J 5
Mississippi River 58-59 H 3
Mississippi River Delta 58-59 J 6
Mississippi Sound 78-79 E 5
Missolonghi = Mesolóngion 138-139 J 6
Missoula, MT 58-59 D 2
Missouri 58-59 H 3-4
Missouri River 58-59 G 3
Missouri Valley, IA 70-71 BC 5
Mistassibi, Rivière — 50 P 2
Mistassini 50 PQ 2
Mistassini, Lake — 46-47 W 7
Mistassini, la Réserve de — 50 P 1
Mistassini, Rivière — 50 P 2
Mistassini Post 50 OP 1
Mistelbach 124 H 4
Misumi 170-171 H 6
Misurāta = Misrātah 194-195 H 2
Mita, Punta de — 58-59 E 7
Mitai 170-171 H 6
Mitchell, IN 70-71 G 6
Mitchell, NE 68-69 E 5
Mitchell, OR 66-67 CD 3
Mitchell, SD 58-59 G 3
Mitchell [AUS] 182-183 J 5
Mitchell [CDN] 72-73 F 3
Mitchell, Mount — 58-59 K 4
Mitchell Lake 78-79 F 4
Mitchell River [AUS, place] 182-183 H 3
Mitchell River [AUS, river] 182-183 H 3
Mitchelstown = Baile Mhistéala 116-117 CD 8
Mitchinamecus, Lac — 72-73 J 1
Mithrāu 160-161 KL 5
Mitilini = Mytilēnē 138-139 M 6
Mi'tiq, Gebel — = Jabal Mu'tiq 199 C 4
Mitishto River 49 HJ 3
Mīt Jamr 199 B 2
Mitla 86-87 M 9
Mitlawī, Al- 194-195 F 2
Mitliktavik, AK 52-53 G 1
Mito 166-167 R 4
Mitre 182-183 O 2
Mitre, Península — 103 CD 8
Mitrofania Island 52-53 d 2
Mitsinjo 198 J 5
Mitsio, Nosy — 198 J 4
Mitšiwa 194-195 MN 5
Mitsuke 170-171 M 4
Mitsumata 170-171 c 2
Mitsushima 170-171 G 5
Mittellandkanal 124 CD 2
Mitú 98-99 EF 4
Mitumba, Chaîne des — 198 E 3-4
Mitumba, Monts — 198 E 2
Mitwaba 198 E 3
Mitzic 198 B 1
Mitzusawa 166-167 QR 4
Miyagi 170-171 N 3
Miyāh, Wādī — 194-195 EF 2
Miyāh, Wādī al- 199 C 5
Miyāh, Wādī al- = Wādī Jarīr 160-161 E 5-6
Miya kawa 170-171 L 5
Miyake-jima 166-167 QR 5
Miyake zima = Miyake-jima 166-167 QR 5
Miyako 170-171 N 3
Miyako-jima 166-167 O 7
Miyakonojō 166-167 P 5
Miyakonozyō = Miyakonojō 166-167 P 5
Miyako wan 170-171 NO 3
Miyako zima = Miyako-jima 166-167 O 7
Mīyāneh = Meyāneh 160-161 F 3
Miyanoura = Kamiyaku 170-171 H 7
Miyānwālī 160-161 L 4
Miyazaki 166-167 P 5
Miyazu 170-171 K 5
Miyet, Baḥr el- = Baḥr al-Mayyit 160-161 D 4
Miyoshi 170-171 J 5
Mizdah 194-195 G 2
Mizen Head = Carn Uí Néid 116-117 AB 9
Mizil 138-139 M 3
Mizoram 160-161 P 6
Mizpah, MN 70-71 CD 2
Mizpah, MT 68-69 D 2
Mizque 98-99 FG 8
Mizusawa 166-167 QR 4
Mjölby 114-115 F 8
Mjøsa 114-115 D 7
Mkhili = Al-Makīlī 194-195 J 2
Mladá Boleslav 124 G 3
Mladenovac 138-139 J 3
Mława 124 K 2
Mljet 138-139 G 4
Mmabatho 198 DE 7
Moa [C] 88-89 J 4
Moa, Pulau — 174-175 J 8
Moab, UT 74-75 J 3
Moak Lake 49 K 2-3
Moala 174-175 a 2
Moamba 198 F 7
Moapa, NV 74-75 F 4
Moba [ZRE] 198 E 3
Mobaye 194-195 J 8
Mobeetie, TX 76-77 D 5
Moberly, MO 58-59 H 4
Moberly Lake 48 FG 2
Mobert 70-71 H 1
Mobile, AL 58-59 J 5
Mobile Bay 58-59 J 5
Mobridge, SD 68-69 FG 3
Mobutu-Sese-Seko, Lac — 198 F 1
Moca = Al-Mukhā 160-161 E 8
Mocajuba 98-99 K 5
Moçambique [Mozambique, place] 198 H 4-5
Moçambique [Mozambique, state] 198 F 6-G 4
Moçambique, Canal de — 198 H 6-4
Moçâmedes 198 B 5
Moccasin, MT 68-69 AB 2
Mocha = Al-Mukhā 160-161 E 8
Mocha, Isla — 103 B 5
Mochis, Los — 58-59 E 6
Möch Sar'dag uul 166-167 HJ 1
Mochudi 198 E 6
Mocidade, Serra da — 98-99 GH 4
Mocímboa da Praia 198 GH 4
Mocksville, NC 80-81 F 3
Moclips, WA 66-67 A 2
Mocó, Rio — 98-99 E 6
Mocoa 98-99 D 4
Moções, Rio — 98-99 O 5
Moçoró 98-99 M 6
Moctezuma 86-87 F 3
Moctezuma, Río — 86-87 F 2-3
Mocuba 198 G 5
Modane 132-133 L 6
Model, CO 68-69 DE 7
Módena 138-139 D 3
Modena, UT 74-75 FG 4
Modesto, CA 58-59 BC 4
Modh, Cuan — 116-117 B 7
Módica 138-139 F 7
Modjamboli 198 D 1
Modoc Lava Bed 66-67 C 5
Modriča 138-139 H 3
Moel Sych 116-117 H 8
Moengo 98-99 J 3
Möen Island = Møn 114-115 E 10
Moenkopi Wash 74-75 H 4
Moe-Yallourn 182-183 J 7
Moffat 116-117 H 5
Moffat, CO 68-69 D 6-7
Moffen 114-115 j 4
Moffett, Mount — 52-53 u 6-7
Moffit, ND 68-69 F 2
Mogadiscio = Muqdiisho 194-195 O 8
Mogadishu = Muqdiisho 194-195 O 8
Mogador = Aṣ-Ṣawīrah 194-195 BC 2
Mogalakwenarivier 198 E 6
Mogami gawa 170-171 MN 3
Mogdy 154-155 Z 7
Moghān, Dasht-e — 160-161 F 3
Mogil'ov 142-143 F 5
Mogil'ov-Podol'skij 142-143 E 6
Mogincual 198 H 5
Mogoča [SU, place] 154-155 WX 7
Mogočin 154-155 P 6
Mogollon Mountains 74-75 J 6
Mogollon Rim 74-75 H 5
Mogororo = Mongororo 194-195 J 6
Mogotón, Cerro — 88-89 C 8
Moguer 132-133 D 10
Mogzon 154-155 V 7
Mohács 124 J 6
Mohall, ND 68-69 F 1
Mohammadia = Muḥammadīyah 194-195 DE 1
Mohammed, Ras — = Rā's Muḥammad 194-195 LM 4
Moḥammerah = Khorramshar 160-161 F 4
Mohawk, AZ 74-75 G 6
Mohawk, MI 70-71 FG 2
Mohawk River 72-73 J 3
Mohe 166-167 N 1
Mohéli = Mwali 198 H 4
Mohican, Cape — 46-47 C 5
Mohilla = Mwali 198 H 4
Mohn, Kapp — 114-115 m 5
Mo-ho = Mohe 166-167 N 1
Mohon Peak 74-75 G 5
Mohoro 198 G 3
Mointy 154-155 N 8
Mo i Rana 114-115 F 4
Moira River 72-73 H 2
Moisie 51 CD 2
Moisie, Baie — 51 D 2
Moisie, Rivière — 46-47 X 7
Moissac 132-133 H 6
Moïssala 194-195 H 7
Mojave, CA 74-75 DE 5
Mojave Desert 58-59 C 4
Mojave River 74-75 E 5
Moji das Cruzes 98-99 KL 9
Mojjero 154-155 T 4
Mojo, Pulau — 174-175 G 8
Mojokerto 174-175 F 8
Moju 98-99 L 6
Mōka 170-171 MN 4
Mokai 182-183 P 7
Mokambo 198 E 4
Mokane, MO 70-71 DE 6
Mokelumne Aqueduct River 74-75 C 3-4
Mokil 178 F 2
Mokolo 194-195 G 6
Mokp'o 166-167 O 5
Mokrān 160-161 HJ 5
Môktama 174-175 C 3
Môktama Kwe 174-175 C 3
Moktok-to = Kyŏngnyŏlbi-yŏlto 170-171 E 4
Mola di Bari 138-139 G 5
Molalla, OR 66-67 B 3
Molango 86-87 L 7
Molanosa 49 F 3
Molat 138-139 F 3
Mold 116-117 H 7
Moldary 154-155 O 7
Moldavia 138-139 M 2-3
Moldavian Soviet Socialist Republic 142-143 E 6
Molde 114-115 B 6
Moldova 138-139 M 2
Moldoviţa 138-139 L 2
Molepolole 198 DE 6
Molfetta 138-139 G 5
Molina de Segura 132-133 G 9
Moline, IL 58-59 HJ 3
Moline, KS 76-77 F 4
Molino, FL 78-79 F 5
Moliro 198 EF 3
Molise 138-139 F 5
Mollendo 98-99 E 8
Mollera, zaliv — 154-155 HJ 3
Mölndal 114-115 DE 9
Molócue 198 G 5
Molodečno 142-143 E 5
Molodežnaja 31 C 5
Molodogvardejcev 154-155 N 7
Molokai 174-175 e 3
Moloma 142-143 J 4
Molong 182-183 J 6
Molopo 198 D 7
Molotovsk = Nolinsk 154-155 HJ 6
Molotovsk = Severodvinsk 154-155 FG 5
Moloundou 194-195 H 8
Molson 49 K 5
Molson Lake 49 K 3
Molt, MT 68-69 B 3
Molu, Pulau — 174-175 K 8
Moluccas 174-175 J 6-7
Molucca Sea 174-175 HJ 7
Molundu = Moloundou 194-195 H 8
Moma [Mozambique] 198 G 5
Moma [SU] 154-155 bc 4
Mombasa 198 GH 2
Mombetsu 166-167 R 3
Mombongo 198 D 1
Momboyo 198 C 2
Momčilgrad 138-139 L 5
Momence, IL 70-71 G 5
Mōminābād = Ambājogāi 160-161 M 7
Momskij chrebet 154-155 b 4-c 5
Møn 114-115 E 10
Mona 58-59 N 8
Mona, UT 74-75 GH 3
Mona, Canal de la — 58-59 N 8
Móna, Punta — 88-89 E 10
Monach Islands 116-117 CD 3
Monaco [MC, place] 132-133 L 7
Monaco [MC, state] 132-133 L 7
Monadhliath Mountains 116-117 GH 3
Monaghan = Muineachán 116-117 DE 6
Monahans, TX 58-59 F 5
Monango, ND 68-69 G 2
Monapo 198 H 4-5
Monarch, MT 66-67 H 2
Monarch Mount 48 E 4
Monashee Mountains 46-47 N 7
Monastir = Bitola 138-139 J 5
Monbetsu 170-171 bc 2
Monča Guba = Mončegorsk 154-155 DE 4
Monção [BR] 98-99 K 5
Mončegorsk 154-155 DE 4
Mönchchaan 166-167 L 2
Mönch Chajrchan uul 166-167 FG 2
Mönchengladbach 124 BC 3
Monchique, Serra de — 132-133 C 10
Moncks Corner, SC 80-81 FG 4
Monclova 58-59 F 6
Moncton 46-47 XY 8
Mond, Rūd-e — 160-161 G 5
Mondamin, IA 70-71 BC 5
Mondego 132-133 CD 8
Mondego, Cabo — 132-133 C 8
Mondoñedo 132-133 D 7
Mondovì 138-139 BC 3
Mondovi, WI 70-71 E 3
Mondragon 132-133 K 6
Moné Lávras 138-139 L 5
Monembasia 138-139 K 7
Moneron, ostrov — 154-155 b 8
Monessen, PA 72-73 G 4
Monet 50 O 2
Moneta, VA 80-81 G 2
Moneta, WY 68-69 C 4
Monett, MO 78-79 C 2
Moneymore 116-117 E 6
Monfalcone 138-139 E 3
Monforte de Lemos 132-133 D 7
Monga [ZRE] 198 D 1
Mongala 198 CD 1
Mongalla = Manqalah 194-195 L 7
Möngbyat 174-175 CD 2
Möngdôn 174-175 C 2
Monger, Lake — 182-183 C 5
Monggŭmp'o-ri 170-171 E 3
Monghyr 160-161 O 5
Mongo [Chad] 194-195 H 6
Mongol Altajn Nuruu 166-167 F-H 2
Mongolia 166-167 H-L 2
Mongororo 194-195 J 6
Möng Tun = Möngdôn 174-175 C 2
Mongu 198 D 5
Monhegan Island 72-73 M 3
Moniaive 116-117 GH 5
Monico, WI 70-71 F 3
Monida Pass 66-67 GH 3
Monilla = Mwali 198 H 4
Monitor 49 C 5
Monitor Range 74-75 E 3
Monkoto 198 D 2
Monmouth 116-117 J 9
Monmouth, IL 70-71 E 5
Monmouth, OR 66-67 B 3
Mono 194-195 E 7
Mono, Punta del — 88-89 E 9
Mono Island 174-175 j 6
Mono Lake 58-59 C 4
Monomoy Point 72-73 M 4
Monon, IN 70-71 G 5
Monópoli 138-139 G 5
Monor 124 J 5
Monqalla = Manqalah 194-195 L 7
Monreale 138-139 E 6
Monroe 51 K 3
Monroe, GA 80-81 DE 4
Monroe, LA 58-59 H 5
Monroe, MI 72-73 E 3-4
Monroe, NC 80-81 F 3
Monroe, OR 66-67 B 3
Monroe, UT 74-75 GH 3
Monroe, VA 80-81 G 2
Monroe, WA 66-67 C 2
Monroe, WI 70-71 F 4
Monroe City, MO 70-71 DE 6
Monroeville, AL 78-79 F 5
Monroeville, IN 70-71 H 5
Monrovia 194-195 B 7
Mons 132-133 J 3
Monsélice 138-139 DE 3
Monserrate, Isla — 86-87 E 5
Mönsterås 114-115 FG 9
Montagnana 138-139 D 3
Montagnes, Lac des — 50 O 1
Montagne Tremblante, Parc procincial de la — 46-47 VW 8
Montague, CA 66-67 B 5
Montague, MI 70-71 G 4
Montague, TX 76-77 EF 6
Montague Island 46-47 G 6
Montague Strait 52-53 N 7-M 6
Montain View, WY 66-67 HJ 5
Montana 58-59 DE 2
Montana, AK 52-53 MN 5
Montaña, La — [E] 132-133 DE 7
Montaña, La — [PE] 98-99 E 5-6
Montargis 132-133 J 5
Montauban 132-133 H 6
Montauk, NY 72-73 L 4
Montauk Point 72-73 L 4
Montbard 132-133 K 5
Montbéliard 132-133 L 5
Mont Blanc 132-133 L 6
Montbrison 132-133 K 6
Montceau-les-Mines 132-133 K 5
Mont Cenis, Col du — 132-133 L 6
Montcevelles, Lac — 51 FG 2
Montclair, NJ 82 III a 2
Mont-de-Marsan 132-133 GH 7
Monteagudo [RA] 103 F 3
Monte Albán 58-59 G 8
Monte Alegre [BR, Pará] 98-99 J 5
Monte Azul 98-99 L 8
Montebello 72-73 J 2
Montebello, CA 83 III d 1
Montebello Islands 182-183 BC 4
Montebu = Mombetsu 166-167 R 3
Monte Caseros 103 E 4
Montecatini Terme 138-139 D 4
Monte Comán 103 C 4
Monte Creek 48 GH 4
Montecristo [I] 138-139 D 4
Montefiascone 138-139 DE 4
Montego Bay 58-59 L 8
Montegut, LA 78-79 D 6
Montejinni 182-183 F 3
Montélimar 132-133 K 6
Monte Lirio 58-59 b 2
Montell, TX 76-77 D 8
Montello, NV 66-67 F 5
Montello, WI 70-71 F 4
Montemayor, Meseta de — 103 C 6-7
Montemorelos 58-59 G 6
Montenegro [YU] 138-139 H 4
Monte Plata 88-89 LM 5
Montepuez [Mozambique, place] 198 GH 4
Montepulciano 138-139 D 4
Monte Quemado 103 D 3
Monterey, CA 58-59 B 4
Monterey, TN 78-79 G 2
Monterey, VA 72-73 G 5
Monterey Bay 58-59 B 4
Monterey Park, CA 83 III d 1
Montería 98-99 D 3
Montero 98-99 G 8
Monte Rosa 138-139 BC 2-3
Monterrey [MEX] 58-59 FG 6
Montesano, WA 66-67 B 2
Monte Sant'Angelo 138-139 FG 5
Monte Santo 98-99 M 7
Montes Claros 98-99 KL 8
Monte Torres 103 D 4
Montevideo 103 EF 4-5
Montevideo, MN 70-71 BC 3
Monte Vista, CO 68-69 C 7
Montezuma, GA 80-81 DE 4
Montezuma, IA 70-71 D 5
Montezuma, IN 70-71 G 6
Montezuma, KS 68-69 F 7
Montezuma Castle National Monument 74-75 H 5
Montfort 132-133 FG 4
Montfort, WI 70-71 E 4
Montgomery 116-117 HJ 8
Montgomery, AL 58-59 J 5
Montgomery, LA 78-79 C 5
Montgomery, MN 70-71 D 3
Montgomery, WV 72-73 F 5
Montgomery = Sāhīwāl 160-161 L 4
Montgomery City, MO 70-71 E 6
Montgomery Pass 74-75 D 3
Monticello, AR 78-79 D 4
Monticello, FL 80-81 E 5
Monticello, GA 80-81 E 4
Monticello, IA 70-71 E 4
Monticello, IL 70-71 F 5
Monticello, IN 70-71 G 5
Monticello, KY 78-79 G 2
Monticello, MS 78-79 DE 5
Monticello, NM 76-77 A 6
Monticello, NY 72-73 J 4
Monticello, UT 58-59 DE 4
Monticello Reservoir = Lake Berryessa 74-75 B 3
Montijo 132-133 D 9
Montijo, Golfo de — 88-89 F 11
Montilla 132-133 E 10
Mont-Joli 51 B 3
Mont-Laurier 46-47 V 8
Montluçon 132-133 J 5
Montmagny [CDN] 51 AB 4
Montmartre 49 G 5
Montmorency [CDN] 51 A 4
Montmorillon 132-133 H 5
Monto 182-183 K 4
Montoro 132-133 E 9
Montoya, NM 76-77 B 5
Montpelier, ID 66-67 H 4
Montpelier, OH 70-71 H 5
Montpelier, VT 58-59 M 3
Montpellier 132-133 JK 7
Mont Perry 182-183 K 5
Montréal [CDN] 46-47 VW 8
Montréal, Île de — 82 I a 2-b 1
Montréal, Université de — 82 I b 1
Montréal International Airport 82 I a 2
Montreal Island 70-71 H 2
Montreal Lake [CDN, lake] 49 F 3
Montreal Lake [CDN, place] 49 F 3
Montréal-Nord 82 I b 1
Montréal-Ouest 82 I ab 2
Montreal River [CDN ◁ Lake Superior] 70-71 HJ 2
Montreal River [CDN ◁ North Saskatchewan River] 49 F 3
Montreal River [CDN ◁ Ottawa River] 72-73 FG 1
Montreal River Harbour 70-71 H 2
Montreuil [F → Berck] 132-133 H 3
Montreuil [F → Paris] 132-133 J 4
Montreux 124 C 5
Montrose 116-117 J 4
Montrose, AR 78-79 D 4
Montrose, CO 58-59 E 4
Montrose, PA 72-73 J 4
Montrose Harbor 83 II b 1
Montross, VA 72-73 H 5
Mont Royal [CDN, mountain] 82 I b 1
Mont-Royal [CDN, place] 82 I ab 1
Mont Royal, Parc du — 82 I b 1
Mont Royal Tunnel 82 I b 1
Mont-Saint-Michel, le — 132-133 FG 4
Montseny 132-133 J 8
Montserrat [E] 132-133 H 8
Montserrat [West Indies] 58-59 O 8
Montsinéry 98-99 J 4
Mont Tremblant Provincial Park = Parc provincial de la Montagne Tremblante 46-47 VW 8
Mont Wright 46-47 X 7
Monument, CO 68-69 D 6
Monument, NM 76-77 C 6
Monument, OR 66-67 D 3
Monumental Hill 68-69 D 3
Monument Mount 52-53 FG 4
Monument Valley 74-75 H 4
Monza 138-139 C 3
Monze 198 E 5
Monzón [E] 132-133 H 8
Moody, TX 76-77 F 7
Mookhorn 80-81 J 2
Moonbeam 50 KL 2
Moonda Lake 182-183 H 5
Moon National Monument, Craters of the — 66-67 G 4
Moonta 182-183 G 6
Moora 182-183 C 6
Moorcroft, WY 68-69 D 3
Moore, ID 66-67 G 4
Moore, MT 68-69 B 2
Moore, OK 76-77 F 5
Moore, TX 76-77 E 8
Moore, Cape — 31 BC 17
Moore, Lake — 182-183 C 5
Moore Creek, AK 52-53 J 5
Mooreland, OK 76-77 E 4
Mooresville, IN 70-71 G 6
Mooresville, NC 80-81 F 3
Moorhead, MN 58-59 G 2
Moorhead, MS 78-79 D 4
Moorhead, MT 68-69 CD 3
Moose, WY 66-67 H 4
Moose Factory 50 LM 1
Moosehead Lake 72-73 M 2
Mooseheart Mount 52-53 M 4
Moose Jaw 46-47 P 7
Moosejaw Creek 49 F 6
Moose Lake, MN 70-71 D 2
Moose Lake [CDN, lake] 46-47 R 7
Moose Lake [CDN, place] 49 HJ 4
Mooselookmeguntic Lake 72-73 L 2
Moose Mountain Creek 49 G 6
Moose Mountain Provincial Park 49 G 6
Moose Pass, AK 52-53 N 6
Moose River [CDN, place] 50 L 1
Moose River [CDN, river] 46-47 U 7
Moosomin 49 H 5
Moosonee 46-47 U 7
Mopeia 198 G 5
Mopipi 198 DE 6
Moppo = Mokp'o 166-167 O 5
Mopti 194-195 D 6
Moquegua [PE, place] 98-99 E 8
Moqur 160-161 K 4
Mór, Inis — 116-117 B 7
Mora, MN 70-71 D 3
Mora, NM 76-77 B 5

Mora [E] 132-133 EF 9
Mora [RFC] 194-195 G 6
Mora [S] 114-115 F 7
Morača 138-139 H 4
Morādābād 160-161 MN 5
Morafenobe 198 H 5
Moral, El — 76-77 D 8
Moraleda, Canal de — 103 B 6-7
Moramanga 198 J 5
Moran, KS 70-71 C 7
Moran, MI 70-71 H 2-3
Moran, TX 76-77 E 6
Moran, WY 66-67 H 4
Morant Point 88-89 HJ 6
Morar, Loch — 116-117 F 4
Morás, Punta de — 132-133 D 6-7
Morass Point 49 J 4
Moratalla 132-133 FG 9
Morava [CS] 124 H 4
Morava [YU] 138-139 J 3
Moravia, IA 70-71 D 5
Morawa 182-183 C 5
Morawhanna 98-99 H 3
Moray 116-117 H 3
Moray Firth 116-117 GH 3
Morcenx 132-133 G 6
Morden 68-69 GH 1
Mordovian Autonomous Soviet Socialist Republic = 5 ◁ 154-155 H 7
Mordovskaja Avtonomnaja Sovetskaja Socialističeskaja Respublika = Mordovian Autonomous Soviet Socialist Republic 154-155 H 7
More, Ben — [GB, Grampian Mountains] 116-117 G 4
More, Ben — [GB, Island of Mull] 116-117 EF 4
More, Ben — [GB, Outer Hebrides] 116-117 D 3
Morea = Pelopónnēsos 138-139 JK 7
More Assynt, Ben — 116-117 G 2
Moreau River 68-69 F 3
Moreau River, North Fork — 68-69 E 3
Moreau River, South Fork — 68-69 E 3
Morecambe Bay 116-117 H 7-J 6
Morecambe & Heysham 116-117 J 6
Moree 182-183 J 5
Morehead, KY 72-73 E 5
Morehead City, NC 80-81 H 3
Morehouse, MO 78-79 E 2
Moreland, ID 66-67 G 4
Morelia 58-59 F 8
Morella [AUS] 182-183 H 4
Morella [E] 132-133 GH 8
Morelos [MEX, administrative unit] 58-59 G 8
Morelos [MEX, place Coahuila] 76-77 D 8
Morelos [MEX, place Zacatecas] 86-87 J 6
Morenci, AZ 74-75 J 6
Morenci, MI 70-71 H 5
Moreno [BR] 98-99 M 6
Møre og Romsdal 114-115 BC 6
Morerú, Rio — 98-99 J 10
Moresby Channel 36 a 1
Moresby Island 46-47 K 7
Mores Isle 88-89 GH 1
Moreton 182-183 H 2
Moretonhampstead 116-117 H 10
Moreton in Marsh 116-117 K 8-9
Moreton Island 182-183 K 5
Mórfu 142-143 F 8
Morgan 182-183 GH 6
Morgan, TX 76-77 F 6
Morgan City, LA 78-79 D 6
Morganfield, KY 70-71 G 7
Morgan Hill, CA 74-75 C 4
Morgan Park, Chicago-, IL 83 II ab 2
Morganton, NC 80-81 F 3
Morgantown, IN 70-71 G 6
Morgantown, KY 70-71 G 7
Morgantown, WV 72-73 FG 5
Morgat 132-133 E 4
Mori [J] 170-171 b 2
Mori [RI] 174-175 H 7
Mori = Kusu 170-171 H 6
Moriah, Mount — 74-75 FG 3
Moriarty, NM 76-77 AB 5
Morice Lake 48 D 2
Morice River 48 D 2
Moricetown 48 D 2
Morin Creek 49 D 3-4
Morinville 48 KL 3
Morioka 166-167 R 4
Morita, La — 76-77 B 8
Morizane = Yamakuni 170-171 H 6
Morjärv 114-115 K 4
Morkoka 154-155 V 4
Morlaix 132-133 F 4
Morland, KS 68-69 FG 6
Morley 48 K 4
Mormon Range 74-75 F 4
Morningside, MD 82 II b 2
Mornington, Isla — 103 A 7
Mornington Island 182-183 G 3
Moro, OR 66-67 C 3
Morobe 174-175 N 8
Morocco 194-195 C 3-D 2
Morogoro 198 G 3
Moro Gulf 174-175 H 5
Morokwen = Morokweng 198 D 7
Morokweng 198 D 7
Moroleón 86-87 K 7
Morombe 198 H 6
Morón [C] 58-59 L 7
Mörön [Mongolia] 166-167 J 2
Morón [RA] 103 E 4
Morona, Río — 98-99 D 5
Morondava 198 H 6
Morón de la Frontera 132-133 E 10
Moroni 198 H 4
Moroni, UT 74-75 H 3
Mörönus 166-167 G 5
Morotai, Pulau — 174-175 J 6
Moroto [EAU, place] 198 F 1
Morozovsk 142-143 H 6
Morpeth 116-117 K 5
Morrilton, AR 78-79 C 3
Morrinsville 182-183 OP 7
Morris 50 A 3
Morris, IL 70-71 F 5
Morris, MN 70-71 BC 3
Morrisburg 72-73 J 2
Morris Jesup, Kap — 30 A 19-23
Morrison, IL 70-71 EF 5
Morristown, SD 68-69 EF 3
Morristown, TN 58-59 K 4
Morro Grande 98-99 HJ 5
Morros [BR, Maranhão] 98-99 L 5
Morrosquillo, Golfo de — 98-99 D 2-3
Morrumbala 198 G 5
Morrumbene 198 G 6
Mors 114-115 C 9
Moršansk 142-143 H 5
Morse, TX 76-77 D 4
Mortandade, Cachoeira — 98-99 P 8
Mortara 138-139 C 3
Morte Point 116-117 G 9
Morteros 103 D 4
Mortlock Islands 178 F 2
Morton, MN 70-71 C 3
Morton, TX 76-77 C 6
M'ortvij Kultuk 142-143 K 6
Moruya 182-183 K 7
Morvan 132-133 K 5
Morven 182-183 J 5
Morwell 182-183 J 7
Morzhovoi Bay 52-53 b 2
Moržovec, ostrov — 154-155 GH 4
Mosby, MT 68-69 C 2
Moscovo = Moskva [SU, place] 154-155 F 6
Moscow, ID 58-59 C 2
Moscow, KS 68-69 F 7
Moscow = Moskva 154-155 F 6
Mosel 124 C 4
Moselle 132-133 L 4
Mosera = Jazirat al-Maṣīrah 160-161 H 6
Mosera Bay = Khalīj al-Maṣīrah 160-161 H 6-7
Moses, NM 76-77 C 4
Moses Lake 66-67 D 2
Moses Lake, WA 66-67 D 2
Moses Point, AK 52-53 F 4
Moshi [EAT] 198 G 2
Mosinee, WI 70-71 F 3
Mosi-Oa-Toenja 198 DE 5
Mosjøen 114-115 E 5
Moskal'vo 154-155 b 7
Moskenesøy 114-115 EF 4
Moskva [SU, place] 154-155 F 6
Moskva [SU, river] 142-143 G 4
Mosonmagyaróvár 124 HJ 5
Mosquera 98-99 D 4
Mosquero, NM 76-77 BC 5
Mosquitia 58-59 K 8
Mosquito Lagoon 80-81 c 2
Mosquitos, Costa de — 58-59 K 9
Mosquitos, Golfe de los — 58-59 K 10
Moss 114-115 D 8
Mossaka 198 C 2
Mossbank 49 EF 6
Mosselbaai 198 D 8
Mossendjo 198 B 2
Mossi 194-195 D 6
Mossleigh 49 B 5
Mossman 182-183 HJ 3
Moss Point, MS 78-79 E 5
Moss Town 88-89 J 2
Mossul = Al-Mūṣil 160-161 E 3
Moss Vale 182-183 JK 6
Mossy River 49 G 3
Most 124 F 3
Mostaganem = Mustaghānam 194-195 DE 1
Mostar 138-139 GH 4
Mostardas 103 D 4
Mostyn 116-117 H 7
Mosul = Al-Mūṣil 160-161 E 3
Mosūlp'o 170-171 EF 6
Moṭa 194-195 M 6
Motaba 198 C 1
Motagua, Río — 86-87 Q 10
Motala 114-115 F 8
Mother Goose Lake 52-53 e 1
Motherwell and Wishaw 116-117 H 5
Motīhāri 160-161 NO 5
Motley, MN 70-71 C 2
Motoichiba = Fuji 170-171 M 5
Motomiya 170-171 N 4
Motovskij zaliv 114-115 PQ 3
Motril 132-133 F 10
Mott, ND 68-69 E 2
Mottinger, WA 66-67 D 2-3
Motul de Felipe Carillo Puerto 58-59 J 7
Motygino 154-155 RS 6
Motyklejka 154-155 c 6
Mouchalagane, Rivière — 51 B 2
Mouila 198 B 2
Mouka 194-195 J 7
Moulamein 182-183 HJ 6-7
Moulamein Creek 182-183 HJ 7
Mould Bay 46-47 MN 2
Moulins 132-133 J 5
Moulmein = Maulamyaing 174-175 C 3
Mouloûya, Ouèd — = Wād Mūlūyā 194-195 D 2
Moulton, AL 78-79 F 3
Moulton, IA 70-71 D 5
Moultrie, GA 58-59 K 5
Moultrie, Lake — 80-81 F 4
Mound City, IL 70-71 F 7
Mound City, KS 70-71 C 6
Mound City, MO 70-71 C 5
Mound City, SD 68-69 FG 3
Moundou 194-195 H 7
Moundsville, WV 72-73 F 5
Moundville, AL 78-79 F 4
Moung 174-175 D 4
Mountain, WI 70-71 F 3
Mountainair, NM 76-77 A 5
Mountain Ash 116-117 H 9
Mountain City, NV 66-67 F 5
Mountain City, TN 80-81 EF 2
Mountain Grove, MO 78-79 C 2
Mountain Home, AR 78-79 C 2
Mountain Home, ID 66-67 F 4
Mountain Park 48 J 3
Mountain Park, OK 76-77 E 5
Mountain Pine, AR 78-79 C 3
Mountain View, AR 78-79 CD 3
Mountain View, HI 78-79 e 3
Mountain View, MO 78-79 D 2
Mountain View, OK 76-77 E 5
Mountain Village, AK 46-47 D 5
Mount Airy, NC 80-81 F 2
Mount Ayr, IA 70-71 CD 5
Mount Barker 182-183 C 6
Mount Carmel, IL 70-71 FG 6
Mount Carmel, PA 72-73 H 4
Mount Carmel, UT 74-75 G 4
Mount Caroll, IL 70-71 EF 4
Mount Darwin 198 F 5
Mount Desert Island 72-73 MN 2
Mount Dora, FL 80-81 c 2
Mount Dora, NM 76-77 C 4
Mount Douglas [AUS] 182-183 J 4
Mount Edgecumbe, AK 52-53 v 8
Mount Elbert 58-59 E 4
Mount Elliot = Selwyn 182-183 H 4
Mount Forest 72-73 F 2-3
Mount Gambier 182-183 GH 7
Mount Garnet 182-183 HJ 3
Mount Gilead, OH 72-73 E 4
Mount Greenwood, Chicago-, IL 83 II a 2
Mount Hagen 174-175 M 8
Mount Harvard 68-69 C 6
Mount Hebron, CA 66-67 BC 5
Mount Holly, NJ 72-73 J 4-5
Mount Hope, WV 80-81 F 2
Mount Hope [AUS, South Australia] 182-183 FG 6
Mount Horeb, WI 70-71 F 4
Mount Isa 182-183 G 4
Mount Lavinia, Dehiwala- 160-161 M 9
Mount Lincoln 68-69 CD 6
Mount MacKinley National Park 46-47 FG 5
Mount Magnet 182-183 C 5
Mount Manara 182-183 H 6
Mount Morgan 182-183 K 4
Mount Morris, MI 70-71 HJ 4
Mount Morris, NY 72-73 H 3
Mount Mulligan 182-183 H 3
Mount Olive, NC 80-81 G 3
Mount Pleasant 80-81 G 2
Mount Pleasant, IA 70-71 E 5
Mount Pleasant, MI 70-71 H 4
Mount Pleasant, TN 78-79 F 3
Mount Pleasant, TX 76-77 G 6
Mount Pleasant, UT 74-75 H 3
Mount Rainier, MD 82 II b 1
Mount Rainier National Park 66-67 C 2
Mount Revelstoke National Park 48 HJ 4
Mount Riley, NM 76-77 A 7
Mount Robson [CDN, place] 48 H 3
Mount Robson Provincial Park 48 H 3
Mount's Bay 116-117 F 10
Mount Shasta, CA 66-67 B 5
Mount Snowy 72-73 J 3
Mount Sterling, IL 70-71 E 6
Mount Stewart 51 E 4
Mount Swan 182-183 G 4
Mount Tom Price 182-183 C 4
Mount Union, PA 72-73 H 4
Mount Vernon, GA 80-81 E 4
Mount Vernon, IA 70-71 E 5
Mount Vernon, IL 58-59 J 4
Mount Vernon, IN 70-71 FG 7
Mount Vernon, KY 70-71 H 7
Mount Vernon, NY 72-73 K 4
Mount Vernon, OH 72-73 E 4
Mount Vernon, OR 66-67 D 3
Mount Vernon, TX 76-77 G 6
Mount Vernon, WA 66-67 BC 1
Mount Victory, OH 72-73 E 4
Mount Willoughby 182-183 F 5
Mount Wilson 68-69 BC 7
Mount Zirkel 68-69 C 5
Moura [AUS] 182-183 JK 4
Moura [BR] 98-99 G 5
Moura [P] 132-133 D 9
Mourão 132-133 D 9
Mourdi, Dépression du — 194-195 J 5
Mourdiah 194-195 C 6
Mourne, River — 116-117 D 6
Mourne Mountains 116-117 EF 6
Mousa 116-117 ef 4
Moussoro 194-195 H 6
Moutiers 132-133 L 6
Moutohora 182-183 P 7
Moutong = Mautong 174-175 H 6
Moutsamoudou = Mutsamudu 198 HJ 4
Móvano 76-77 C 9
Moville, IA 70-71 BC 4
Mowasi 98-99 J 2
Moweaqua, IL 70-71 F 6
Mowich, OR 66-67 BC 4
Mowming = Maoming 166-167 L 7
Moxico 198 CD 4
Moy 116-117 G 3
Moyale 198 G 1
Moyamba 194-195 B 7
Moyie 66-67 F 1
Moyie Springs, ID 66-67 E 1
Moyle = 8 ◁ 116-117 E 5
Moyne, La — 82 I c 1
Moyo = Pulau Moyo 174-175 G 8
Moyobamba 98-99 D 6
Moyock, NC 80-81 HJ 2
Møysalen 114-115 FG 3
Moyto 194-195 H 6
Mozambique 198 F 6-G 4
Mozambique = Moçambique [Mozambique, place] 198 H 4-5
Mozambique = Moçambique [Mozambique, state] 198 F 6-G 4
Mozambique Basin 198 H 4
Mozambique Channel 198 H 4-6
Mozdok 142-143 H 7
Možga 154-155 J 6
Mozyr' 142-143 E 5

Mpanda 198 F 3
Mpepo 198 F 4
Mpika 198 F 4
Mporokoso 198 EF 3
M'Pouya 198 C 2
Mpulungu 198 F 3
Mpurakasese 198 G 4

M'rāītī, Al- 194-195 C 4
Mrayyah, Al- 194-195 C 5
Mreïti, El — = Al-M'rāītī 194-195 C 4
M. R. Gomez, Presa — 86-87 L 4

Msagali 198 G 3
Msta [SU, river] 154-155 E 6

Mtakuja 198 F 3
Mtwara 198 H 4

Mu'o'ng Khoua 174-175 D 2
Mualama 198 G 5
Muan 170-171 F 5
Muar 174-175 D 6
Muaraaman 174-175 D 7
Muaraancalung 174-175 G 6
Muaraenim 174-175 D 7
Muaralasan 174-175 G 6
Muarasiberut 174-175 C 7
Muaratebo 174-175 D 7
Muaratembesi 174-175 D 7
Muarateweh 174-175 FG 7
Mū'askar 194-195 E 1
Mubende 198 F 1
Mubi 194-195 G 6
Mucajaí, Rio — 98-99 G 4
Mucajaí, Serra do — 98-99 G 4
Muck 116-117 E 4
Mučkapskij 142-143 H 5
Mucojo 198 H 4
Muconda 198 D 4
Mucucuaú, Rio — 98-99 H 4
Mucuim, Rio — 98-99 F 8
Mucuri 98-99 M 8
Mucuri, Rio — 98-99 L 8
Mucuripe, Ponta de — 98-99 M 5
Mucusso 198 D 5
Mudanjiang 166-167 OP 3
Mudawwarah, Al- 160-161 D 5
Mud Butte, SD 68-69 E 3
Muddo Gashi = Mado Gashi 198 G 1
Muddusnationalpark 114-115 J 4
Muddy Creek 74-75 H 3
Muddy Gap 68-69 C 4
Muddy Gap, WY 66-67 K 4
Muddy Peak 74-75 F 4
Mudgee 182-183 JK 6
Mudīriyat el Istwā'ya = Al-Istiwā'īyah 194-195 K-M 7
Mudīriyat esh Shimāliya = Ash-Shimālīyah 194-195 KL 5
Mud Lake 74-75 E 4
Mudôn 174-175 C 3
Mŭdros 138-139 L 6
Mudug 194-195 b 2
Muecate 198 G 4
Mueda 198 G 4
Mufulira 198 E 4
Mugi 170-171 K 6
Múgica 86-87 JK 8
Mugila, Monts — 198 E 3
Muğla 160-161 B 3
Mugodžary 154-155 K 8
Mugodzharskie Mountains = Mugodžary 154-155 K 8
Muḥammad, Rā's — 194-195 LM 4
Muḥammad Ṭulayb 199 B 5
Muhammed, Ras — = Rā's Muḥammad 194-195 LM 4
Muhembo 198 D 5
Muhinga = Muyinga 198 EF 2
Mühldorf 124 F 4
Mühlhausen 124 E 3
Mühlig-Hoffmann-Gebirge 31 B 1-2
Muileann Cearr, An — 116-117 DE 7
Muineachán 116-117 DE 6
Muine Bheag 116-117 DE 8
Muir Glacier 52-53 T 7
Muirkirk 116-117 GH 5
Muja 154-155 W 6
Mujeres, Isla — 86-87 R 7
Mujezerskij 154-155 E 5
Mujlad, Al — 194-195 K 6
Mujnak 154-155 K 9
Muju 170-171 F 4
Mujunkum 154-155 MN 9
Muka = Mouka 194-195 J 7
Mukačovo 142-143 D 6
Mukah 174-175 F 6
Mukallā, Al- 160-161 FG 8
Mukawa 170-171 b 2
Mukawwa', Jazīrat — 199 DE 6
Mukdahan 174-175 D 3
Mukden = Shenyang 166-167 NO 3
Mukhā, Al- 160-161 E 8
Mukinbudin 182-183 C 6
Mukomuko 174-175 D 7
Mukrān, Sabkhat — 194-195 E 3
Mukry 160-161 K 3
Mukumbi = Makumbi 198 D 3
Mukutawa River 50 A 1
Mula, La — 76-77 B 8
Mulainagiri 160-161 LM 8
Mulaku Atoll 36 a 2
Mulan 166-167 O 2
Mulanje 198 G 5
Mulanje, Mount — 198 G 5
Mulata 98-99 LM 5
Mŭlayit Taung 174-175 C 3
Mulberry, KS 70-71 C 7
Mulchatna River 52-53 JK 6
Muldoon, ID 66-67 G 4
Muldrow, OK 76-77 G 5
Mule Creek, NM 74-75 J 6
Mule Creek, WY 68-69 D 4
Mulegé 86-87 DE 4
Muleshoe, TX 76-77 C 5
Mulgrave 51 F 5
Mulgrave Hills 52-53 F 3
Mulgrave Island 182-183 H 2
Mulgubi 170-171 G 2
Mulhacén 132-133 F 10
Mulhall, OK 76-77 F 4
Mulhouse 132-133 L 5
Muli = Vysokogornyj 154-155 ab 7
Mull, Island of — 116-117 EF 4
Mull, Sound of — 116-117 EF 4
Mullaghcarn 116-117 DE 6
Mullan, ID 66-67 EF 2
Mullan Pass 58-59 D 2
Mullen, NE 68-69 F 4
Mullens, WV 80-81 F 2
Müller, Pegunungan — 174-175 F 6
Müllerberg 114-115 l 6
Mullet Lake 70-71 H 3
Mullewa 182-183 C 5
Mulligan River 182-183 G 4-5
Mullin, TX 76-77 E 7
Mullingar = An Muileann Cearr 116-117 DE 7
Mullins, SC 80-81 G 3
Mulobezi 198 DE 5
Multān 160-161 L 4
Mulu, Gunung — 174-175 FG 6
Mulula, Wed — = Wād Mūlūyā 194-195 D 2
Mūlūyā, Wād — 194-195 D 2
Mulvane, KS 68-69 H 7
Mulymja 154-155 LM 5
Mumbai = Bombay 160-161 L 7
Mumbwa 198 E 5
Mumeng 174-175 N 8
Mumford, TX 76-77 F 7
Mumra 142-143 J 6
Mumtrak = Coodnews, AK 52-53 FG 7
Mun, Mae Nam — 174-175 D 3
Muna [MEX] 86-87 Q 7
Muna [SU] 154-155 W 4
Muna, Pulau — 174-175 H 8
Munasarowar Lake = Mapham Tsho 166-167 E 5
Munayjah, Bi'r — 199 D 6
München 124 EF 4
Munch'ŏn 170-171 F 3
Muncie, IN 58-59 JK 3
Mundare 49 BC 4
Munday, TX 76-77 E 6
Münden 124 D 3
Mundiwindi 182-183 CD 4
Mundo, Río — 132-133 F 9
Mundrabilla 182-183 E 6
Mundubbera 182-183 JK 5
Mundurucânia, Reserva Florestal — 98-99 JK 8
Munfordville, KY 70-71 H 7
Mungallala Creek 182-183 J 5
Mungana 182-183 H 3
Mungari 198 F 5
Mungbere 198 E 1
Mungĕr = Monghyr 160-161 O 5
Mungindi 182-183 J 5
Munhango 198 C 4
Munich = München 124 EF 4
Munising, MI 70-71 G 2
Munk 49 L 3
Munkfors 114-115 EF 8
Munksund 114-115 JK 5
Munkur 116-117 b 2
Muñoz Gamero, Península — 103 B 8
Munsan 170-171 F 4
Munsfjället 114-115 F 5
Münster [D] 124 C 2-3
Munster = An Mhumha 116-117 BC 8
Munte 174-175 G 6
Muntok 174-175 DE 7
Muodoslompolo 114-115 K 4
Muong Kwa = Mu'o'ng Khoua 174-175 D 2
Mu'o'ng Pak Beng 174-175 D 2-3
Muong Plateau = Cao Nguyên Trung Phân 174-175 E 4
Mu'o'ng Sen, Deo — 174-175 DE 3
Muonio 114-115 KL 4
Muonio älv 114-115 K 4
Mup'yŏng-ni = Chŏnch'ŏn 170-171 F 2
Muqayshit 160-161 G 6
Muqayyar, Al- = Ur 160-161 F 4
Muqsim, Jabal — 199 CD 6
Muqur = Moqur 160-161 K 4
Mur 124 FG 5
Mura 138-139 FG 2
Murādābād = Morādābād 160-161 MN 5
Murakami 170-171 M 3
Murallón, Cerro — 103 B 7
Murang'a 198 G 2
Mur'anyo 194-195 bc 1
Muraši 154-155 H 6
Murat dağı 160-161 B 3
Murat nehri 160-161 E 3
Murauaú, Rio — 98-99 H 4
Muravera 138-139 CD 6
Murayama 170-171 N 3
Murchison, Cape — 46-47 S 3
Murchison Falls = Kabelega Falls 198 F 1
Murchison Falls National Park = Kabelega Falls National Park 198 F 1
Murchisonfjord 114-115 k 4-5
Murchisonfjorden 114-115 kl 4
Murchison Island 50 EF 2
Murchison River 182-183 C 5
Murcia [E, landscape] 132-133 G 9-10
Murcia [E, place] 132-133 G 9-10
Murdale 48 G 1
Murdo, SD 68-69 F 4
Murdochville 46-47 XY 8
Murdock, FL 80-81 b 3
Mureş 138-139 K 2-3
Murfreesboro, AR 78-79 C 3
Murfreesboro, NC 80-81 H 2
Murfreesboro, TN 58-59 J 4
Murgab [SU, place] 160-161 L 3
Murgab [SU, river] 160-161 J 3
Murge 138-139 G 5
Murghāb rōd 160-161 JK 3-4
Murgon 182-183 K 5
Muriaé 98-99 L 9
Muriel Lake 49 C 3
Müritz 124 F 2
Murmansk 154-155 EF 4
Murmanskij bereg 142-143 G 2
Murmansk Rise 154-155 EF 2
Murmaši 154-155 E 4
Muro, Capo di — 138-139 C 5
Muro Lucano 138-139 FG 5
Murom 154-155 G 6
Muromcevo 154-155 O 6
Muroran 166-167 R 3
Muros 132-133 C 7
Muroto 170-171 JK 6
Muroto zaki 170-171 K 6
Murphy, ID 66-67 E 4
Murphy, NC 78-79 G 3
Murphy, TN 80-81 D 3
Murphysboro, IL 70-71 F 7
Murr, Bi'r — 199 B 6
Murrat al-Kubrā, Al-Buḥayrat al- 199 C 2

Murrat el-Kubrâ, Buḥeirat el — = Al-
Buḥayrat al-Murrat al-Kubrâ
199 C 2
Murray, KY 78-79 E 2
Murray, Lake — [PNG] 174-175 M 8
Murray, Lake — [USA] 80-81 F 3
Murray Fracture Zone 34-35 KL 3
Murray Harbour 51 EF 5
Murray River [AUS] 182-183 H 6-7
Murray River [CDN] 48 G 2
Murrumbidgee River 182-183 HJ 6
Murtle Lake 48 H 3
Murupara 182-183 P 7
Murupu 98-99 G 4
Murvārā = Murwāra 160-161 N 6
Murwāra 160-161 N 6
Murwillumbah 182-183 K 5
Murzūq = Marzūq 194-195 G 3
Mürzzuschlag 124 G 5
Muş 160-161 E 3
Muşa Ali 194-195 N 6
Musala 138-139 K 4
Musala, Pulau — 174-175 C 6
Musan 166-167 OP 3
Mūsa Qal'a 160-161 JK 4
Musayʿīd 160-161 G 5-6
Muscat = Masqaṭ 160-161 HJ 6
Muscatine, IA 70-71 E 5
Muscoda, WI 70-71 E 4
Muscongus Bay 72-73 M 3
Musgrave 182-183 H 2
Musgrave Ranges 182-183 F 5
Musgravetown 51 JK 3
Mūshā 199 B 4
Mushie 198 C 2
Musi, Sungai — 174-175 D 7
Mūşil, Al- 160-161 E 3
Musinia Peak 74-75 H 3
Muskat = Masqaṭ 160-161 H 6
Muskeg Bay 70-71 C 1
Muskeg Lake 70-71 EF 1
Muskegon, MI 58-59 J 3
Muskegon Heights, MI 70-71 G 4
Muskegon River 70-71 GH 4
Muskingum River 72-73 EF 5
Muskogee, OK 58-59 GH 4
Muskoka, Lake — 72-73 G 2
Musmār = Mismār 194-195 M 5
Musoma 198 F 2
Musquaro, Lac — 51 F 2
Musquaro, Rivière — 51 F 2
Mussali, Mount — = Muşa Ali
194-195 N 6
Mussau 174-175 N 7
Musselburgh 116-117 HJ 5
Musselshell River 58-59 E 2
Mussende 198 C 4
Mussuma 198 D 4
Mustaghānam 194-195 DE 1
Mustang, OK 76-77 EF 5
Mustang Island 76-77 F 9
Musters, Lago — 103 BC 7
Mustique 88-89 Q 8
Mustvee 142-143 E 4
Musu-dan 170-171 GH 2
Muswellbrook 182-183 K 6
Mût [ET] 194-195 K 3
Mutankiang = Mudanjiang
166-167 OP 3
Mutare 198 F 5
Muʿtiq, Jabal — 199 C 4
Mutis, Gunung — 174-175 H 8
Mutsamudu 198 HJ 4
Mutshatsha 198 D 4
Mutsu 170-171 N 2
Mutsu-wan 170-171 N 2
Mutton Bay 51 G 2
Muttra = Mathurā 160-161 M 5
Mutum, Rio — 98-99 D 7
Mututi, Ilha — 98-99 N 5
Muwayḥ, Al- 160-161 E 6
Muwayliḥ, Al- 199 D 4
Muxima 198 B 3
Muyinga 198 EF 2
Muyumba 198 E 3
Muẓaffarābād 160-161 LM 4
Muẓaffargaṛh 160-161 L 4-5
Muzaffarnagar 160-161 M 5
Muzaffarpur 160-161 NO 5
Muži 154-155 L 4
Muzon, Cape — 52-53 w 9
Muz tagh 166-167 E 4
Muz tagh ata 166-167 D 4

Mvōlō 194-195 KL 7
Mvuma 198 F 5

Mwali 198 H 4
Mwanza [EAT] 198 F 2
Mwanza [ZRE] 198 E 3
Mwaya 198 F 3
Mweelrea = Maol Riabhach
116-117 B 7
Mweka 198 D 2
Mwenga 198 E 2
Mweru, Lake — 198 E 3
Mweru Swamp 198 E 3
Mwinilunga 198 DE 4

Myan'aung 174-175 BC 3
Myeik 174-175 C 4
Myeik Kyûnzu 174-175 C 4
Myggenæs = Mykines 116-117 a 1
Myingyan 174-175 BC 2
Myitkyīnā 174-175 C 1
Mykėnai 138-139 K 7
Mykines 116-117 a 1
Mýkonos 138-139 L 7
Myla 142-143 K 2
Mymensingh = Maimansingh
160-161 OP 6
Mynämäki 114-115 JK 7
Mynaral 154-155 N 8
Mynydd Bach 116-117 GH 8
Mynydd Prescelly 116-117 G 9
Myohyang-sanmaek 170-171 E 3-F 2
Myōkō-zan 170-171 LM 4
Myŏngch'ŏn 170-171 GH 2
Mýra 114-115 c 2
Myrdal 114-115 B 7
Mýrdalsjökull 114-115 d 3
Mýrdalssandur 114-115 d 3
Myre 114-115 F 3
Mýrina 138-139 L 6
Myrnam 49 C 4
Myrthle 72-73 G 2
Myrtle Beach, SC 80-81 G 4
Myrtle Creek, OR 66-67 B 4
Myrtle Point, OR 66-67 AB 4
Mysen 114-115 D 8
Myślenice 124 JK 4
mys Lopatka 30 D 3
Mysovsk = Babuškin 154-155 U 7
Mystic, IA 70-71 D 5
Mystic, SD 68-69 E 3
Mys Vchodnoj 154-155 QR 3
Mys Želanija 154-155 MN 2
My Tho 174-175 E 4
Mytilēnē 138-139 M 6
Myton, UT 66-67 HJ 5
Mývatn 114-115 e 2

Mziha 198 G 3
Mzimba 198 F 4

N

Naab 124 F 4
Na'ăg, Gebel — = Jabal Ni'āj
199 C 6
Naalehu, HI 78-79 e 3
Naantali 114-115 JK 7
Naas = Nås 116-117 E 7
Näätämöjoki 114-115 MN 3
Naauwpoort = Noupoort 198 DE 8
Nābah, Bi'r — 199 C 7
Nabč 166-167 G 4
Nabesna, AK 52-53 Q 5
Nabesna Glacier 52-53 Q 5
Nâbeul = Nābul 194-195 G 1
Nabire 174-175 L 7
Nabīsar 160-161 KL 5-6
Nabisipi, Rivière — 51 E 2
Nabk, An- [SYR] 160-161 D 4
Nabq 199 D 3
Nābul 194-195 G 1
Naçala 198 H 4
Nacfa = Nakfa 194-195 M 5
Naches, WA 66-67 C 2
Načičevan' 142-143 J 8
Nachingwea 198 GH 4
Nachodka 154-155 Z 9
Nachrači = Kondirskoje
154-155 M 6
Nacimiento Mountains 76-77 A 4-5
Nacka 114-115 H 8
Naco 86-87 EF 2
Naco, AZ 74-75 HJ 7
Nacogdoches, TX 76-77 G 7
Nacozari de García 58-59 DE 5
Nadadores 76-77 D 9
Nādendal = Naantali 114-115 JK 7
Nadeždinsk = Serov 154-155 L 6
Nadiād 160-161 L 6
Nadina River 48 D 3
Nadjaf, An- = An-Najaf 160-161 E 4
Nadjd = Najd 160-161 E 5-6
Nădlac 138-139 J 2
Nadoa = Dan Xian 166-167 K 8
Nadqān 160-161 G 6
Nadvoicy 142-143 F 3
Nadym 142-143 O 2
Næstved 114-115 DE 10
Nafada 194-195 G 6
Nafīshah 199 BC 2
Nafūd, An- 160-161 E 5
Nafusah, Jabal — 194-195 G 2
Naga 174-175 H 4
Nagagami Lake 70-71 H 1
Nagahama [J, Ehime] 170-171 J 6
Nagahama [J, Shiga] 170-171 L 5
Nagai 170-171 MN 3
Nagai Island 52-53 cd 2
Nāgāland 160-161 P 5
Nagano 166-167 Q 4
Naganohara 170-171 M 4
Nagaoka 166-167 Q 4
Nāgaor = Nāgaur 160-161 L 5
Nāgapattinam 160-161 MN 8
Nagā Pradesh = Nāgāland
160-161 P 5
Nagara gawa 170-171 L 5
Nagar Aveli = Dādra and Nagar
Haveli 160-161 L 6
Nagar Haveli, Dadra and —
160-161 L 6
Nāgarkōyil = Nāgercoil 160-161 M 9
Nagar Pārkar 160-161 KL 6
Nagasaki 166-167 O 5
Naga-shima [J, island] 170-171 GH 6
Nagashima [J, place] 170-171 L 5
Nagato 170-171 H 5
Nāgaur 160-161 L 5
Nag Chhu 166-167 G 5
Nagchhu Dsong 166-167 G 5
Nagchhukha = Nagchhu Dsong
166-167 G 5
Nāgercoil 160-161 M 9
Nāgishōt = Nāqīshūt 194-195 L 8
Nagorno-Karabagh Autonomous
Region = 9 ◁ 142-143 J 7-8
Nagornyj 154-155 Y 6
Nagoya 166-167 Q 4
Nāgpur 160-161 M 6
Naguun Mörön 166-167 NO 1-2
Nagykanizsa 124 H 5
Nagykőrös 124 JK 5
Nagyvárad = Oradea 138-139 JK 2
Naha 166-167 O 6
Nahanni National Park 46-47 LM 5
Nahari 170-171 JK 6
Nahlin River 52-53 W 7
Nahuel Huapí, Lago — 103 B 6
Nahunta, GA 80-81 EF 5
Naica 76-77 B 9
Naicam 49 F 4
Nailsworth 116-117 JK 9
Nain [CDN] 46-47 Y 6
Nāʾīn [IR] 160-161 G 4
Naindi 174-175 a 2
Naini Tal 160-161 M 5
Nain Singh Range = Nganglong
Gangri 166-167 E 5
Nairn 116-117 H 3
Nairn, River — 116-117 GH 3
Nairobi 198 G 2
Naivasha 198 G 2
Najaf, An- 160-161 E 4
Najafābād 160-161 G 4
Najd 160-161 E 5-6
Naj' Ḥammādī 199 BC 4-5
Najin 166-167 P 3
Najran 160-161 E 7
Naju 170-171 F 5
Naka = Io 148-149 S 7
Nakadōri-shima 170-171 G 6
Naka gawa 170-171 K 6
Nakajō 170-171 M 3
Nakaminato 170-171 N 4
Nakamura 170-171 J 6
Nakamura = Sōma 170-171 N 4
Nakano 170-171 M 4
Nakano-shima 170-171 J 4
Nakano-umi 170-171 J 5
Nakasato 170-171 N 2
Nakatane 170-171 H 7
Nakatsu 170-171 H 6
Nakatsukawa 170-171 L 5
Nakatsukawa = Nakatsugawa
170-171 L 5
Nakatu 170-171 H 6
Nakchamik Island 52-53 e 1
Naked Island 52-53 O 6
Nakfa 194-195 M 5
Nakhichevan Autonomous Soviet
Socialist Republic = 10 ◁
142-143 J 8
Nakhl 199 C 3
Nakhlāy, Bi'r — 199 B 6
Nakhon Lampang = Lampang
174-175 C 3
Nakhon Pathom 174-175 CD 4
Nakhon Phanom 174-175 D 3
Nakhon Ratchasima 174-175 D 3-4
Nakhon Sawan 174-175 CD 3
Nakhon Si Thammarat 174-175 CD 5
Nakina 46-47 T 7
Nakło nad Notecią 124 H 2
Naknek, AK 46-47 E 6
Naknek Lake 52-53 JK 7
Nakskov 114-115 D 10
Naktong-gang 170-171 G 5
Nakuru 198 G 2
Nakusp 48 J 4
Nāl 160-161 K 5
Nalajch 166-167 K 2
Nal'čik 142-143 H 7
Nālūt 194-195 G 2
Namacurra 198 G 5
Na'mah, An- 194-195 C 5
Namak, Daryācheh — 160-161 G 4
Namakwaland 198 C 7
Namakzār-e Khwāf 160-161 HJ 4
Namaland 198 C 7
Na'mān, Jazīrat an — = Jazīrat an-
Nu'mān 199 D 4
Namanga 198 G 2
Namangan 160-161 L 2
Namanyere 198 F 3
Namapa 198 GH 4
Namarrói 198 G 5
Namasagali 198 F 1
Namatanai 174-175 h 5
Nam Bô 174-175 DE 5
Nambour 182-183 K 5
Năm Căn 174-175 D 5
Nam Chon Yai = Kra Buri
174-175 C 4
Namch'ŏnjŏm 170-171 F 3
Namcy 154-155 Y 5
Nam Đinh 174-175 E 2-3
Namerikawa 170-171 L 4
Nametil 198 GH 5
Namew Lake 49 G 3
Nam-gang 170-171 F 3
Namhae-do 170-171 G 5
Namhan-gang 170-171 F 4
Namhoi = Foshan 166-167 L 7
Namib = Namibwoestyn 198 B 5-C 7
Namib Desert = Namibwoestyn
198 B 5-C 7
Namibia 198 C 6
Namib-Naukluft Park 198 BC 6
Namibwoestyn 198 B 5-C 7
Namjabarba Ri 166-167 H 6
Namlea 174-175 J 7
Namling Dsong 166-167 FG 6
Namoi River 182-183 J 6
Namoluk 178 F 2
Namorik 178 G 2
Namous, Ouèd en — = Wādī an-
Nāmus 194-195 D 2
Nampa 48 J 1
Nampa, ID 58-59 C 3
Nampala 194-195 C 5
Nampo 166-167 NO 4
Namp'ot'ae-san 170-171 G 2
Nampula 198 GH 5
Namsen 114-115 E 5
Namsi 170-171 E 3
Namsos 114-115 DE 5
Nam Tsho 166-167 G 5
Namu [CDN] 48 D 4
Namu [Micronesia] 178 G 2
Namuli, Serra — 198 G 5
Namuling Zong = Namling Dsong
166-167 FG 6
Namur 132-133 K 3
Namur Lake 49 B 2
Nāmūs, Wādī an- 194-195 D 2
Nāmūs, Waw an- 194-195 H 4
Namutoni 198 C 5
Namwala 198 E 5
Namwŏn 170-171 F 5
Nan 174-175 D 3
Nan, Mae Nam — 174-175 D 3
Nana Candungo 198 D 4
Nanae 170-171 b 3
Nanafalia, AL 78-79 F 4
Nanaimo 46-47 M 8
Nanam 170-171 GH 2
Nana-Mambéré 194-195 GH 7
Nanango 182-183 K 5
Nanao [J] 170-171 L 4
Nanao wan 170-171 L 4
Nanay, Río — 98-99 E 5
Nancha 166-167 O 2
Nanchang 166-167 LM 6
Nanchang = Nanchong
166-167 JK 5
Nancheng 166-167 M 6
Nan-ching = Nanjing [TJ, Jiangsu]
166-167 M 5
Nanchino = Nanjing 166-167 M 5
Nanchong 166-167 JK 5
Nanchung = Nanchong
166-167 JK 5
Nancy 132-133 L 4
Nanda Devi 160-161 MN 4
Nandan 170-171 K 5
Nānded 160-161 M 7
Nandeir = Nānded 160-161 M 7
Nandi [FJI] 174-175 a 2
N'andoma 154-155 G 5
Nanduan River 50 A 1
Nandurbār 160-161 L 6
Nandyāl 160-161 M 7
Nanga-Eboko 194-195 G 8
Nan-gang = Nam-gang 170-171 F 3
Nangā Parbat 160-161 LM 3-4
Nangapinoh 174-175 F 7
Nang'-ch'ien = Nangqian
166-167 H 5
Nangnim-sanmaek 170-171 F 2
Nangqian 166-167 H 5
Nan Hai 166-167 L 8-M 7
Nanhai = Foshan 166-167 L 7
Nan-hsiung = Nanxiong
166-167 LM 6
Nanika Lake 48 D 3
Nanjing [TJ, Jiangsu] 166-167 M 5
Nankhu 166-167 G 3
Nanking = Nanjing 166-167 M 5
Nankoku 170-171 JK 6
Nanlaoye Ling 170-171 E 2-F 1
Nan Ling [TJ, mountains]
166-167 L 6-7
Nanling [TJ, place] 166-167 M 5
Nanning 166-167 K 7
Nannup 182-183 C 6
Nanpan Jiang 166-167 JK 7
Nanping [TJ, Fujian] 166-167 M 6
Nanping [TJ, Hubei] 166-167 L 6
Nansei Islands = Nansei-shotō
166-167 N 7-O 6
Nansei-shotō 166-167 NO 6-7
Nansei syotō = Nansei-shotō
166-167 NO 6-7
Nansen Sound 46-47 ST 1
Nan Shan 166-167 HJ 4
Nansio 198 F 2
Nantai-san 170-171 M 4
Nan-tch'ang = Nanchang
166-167 LM 6
Nan-tch'eng = Nancheng
166-167 M 6
Nan-tch'ong = Nanchong
166-167 JK 5
Nantes 132-133 G 5
Nanticoke, PA 72-73 HJ 4
Nanton 48 L 4
Nantong 166-167 N 5
Nantsang = Nanchang
166-167 LM 6
Nantucket, MA 72-73 LM 4
Nantucket Island 58-59 N 3
Nantucket Sound 72-73 L 4
Nantung = Nantong 166-167 N 5
Nantwich 116-117 J 7
Nanty Glo, PA 72-73 G 4
Nanumanga 178 H 3
Nanumea 178 H 3
Nanuque 98-99 LM 8
Nanushuk River 52-53 M 2
Nanxiong 166-167 LM 6
Nanyang 166-167 L 5
Nanyi = Nancha 166-167 O 2
Nanyuki 198 G 1
Nanzheng = Hanzhong 166-167 K 5
Nao, Cabo de la — 132-133 H 9
Naoconane Lake 46-47 W 7
Naoetsu 170-171 LM 4
Naōgata = Nōgata 170-171 H 6
Naoli He 166-167 P 2
Nao-li Ho = Naoli He 166-167 P 2
Naos, Isla — 58-59 bc 3
Napa, CA 74-75 B 3
Napaimiut, AK 52-53 H 6
Napakiak, AK 52-53 FG 6
Napaku 174-175 G 6
Napan 174-175 L 7
Napanee 72-73 H 2
Napas 154-155 P 6
Napaseudut 30
Nape 174-175 DE 3
Napier [NZ] 182-183 P 7
Napier, Mount — 182-183 EF 3
Napier Mountains 31 C 6
Napinka 68-69 F 1
Naples, FL 58-59 K 6
Naples, NY 72-73 H 3
Naples = Nàpoli 138-139 EF 5
Naples, Gulf of — = Golfo di Nàpoli
138-139 E 5
Napo, Río — 98-99 E 5
Napoleon, ND 68-69 G 2
Napoleon, OH 70-71 HJ 5
Napoleonville, LA 78-79 D 5-6
Nàpoli 138-139 E 5
Nàpoli, Golfo di — 138-139 EF 5
Nappanee, IN 70-71 GH 5
Naqâda = Naqādah 199 C 5
Naqādah 199 C 5
Nāqīshūt 194-195 L 8
Nara [J] 170-171 KL 5
Nārā [PAK] 160-161 K 5
Nara [RMM] 194-195 C 5
Naracoorte 182-183 GH 7
Naramata 66-67 D 1
Naranjas, Punta — 98-99 C 3
Narathiwat 174-175 DE 5
Nara Visa, NM 76-77 C 5
Narāyanganj 160-161 OP 6
Narbadā = Narmada 160-161 LM 6
Narberth 116-117 G 9
Narbonne 132-133 J 7
Nardò 138-139 GH 5
Narembeen 182-183 C 6
Narew 124 K 2
Nārī 160-161 K 5
Narinda, Helodranon'i — 198 J 4
Narjan-Mar 154-155 JK 4
Narmada 160-161 LM 6
Narodnaja, gora — 154-155 L 5
Naro-Fominsk 142-143 FG 4
Narok 198 G 2
Narooma 182-183 JK 7
Narrabri 182-183 JK 6
Narragansett Bay 72-73 L 4
Narrandera 182-183 J 6
Narrogin 182-183 C 6
Narromine 182-183 J 6
Narrows, OR 66-67 D 4
Narrows, VA 80-81 F 2
Narrows, The — 82 III b 3
Narssaq 46-47 bc 5
Narssarssuaq 46-47 bc 5
Narugo 170-171 N 3
Naru-shima 170-171 G 6
Naruto 170-171 K 5
Narva [SU, place] 154-155 D 6
Narvik 114-115 G 3
Narwa = Narva 154-155 D 6
Narym 154-155 P 6
Naryn [SU, Kirgizskaja SSR place]
160-161 M 2
Naryn [SU, Kirgizskaja SSR river]
160-161 L 2
Naryn [SU, Rossijskaja SFSR]
154-155 S 7
Naryn = Taš-Kumyr 160-161 L 2
Narynkol 160-161 MN 2
Nås 116-117 E 7
Nasafjell 114-115 F 4
Nasarawa [WAN, Plateau]
194-195 F 7
Năsăud 138-139 L 2
Naschitti, NM 74-75 J 4
Nash Harbor, AK 52-53 D 6
Nāshik = Nāsik 160-161 L 6-7
Nash Point 116-117 H 9
Nashua, MT 68-69 C 1
Nashua, NH 72-73 L 3
Nashville, AR 76-77 GH 5
Nashville, GA 80-81 E 5
Nashville, IL 70-71 F 6
Nashville, KS 68-69 G 7
Nashville, MI 70-71 H 4
Nashville, TN 58-59 J 4
Nashville Basin 78-79 F 2
Nashwauk, MN 70-71 D 2
Našice 138-139 H 3
Näsijärvi 114-115 KL 7
Nāsik 160-161 L 6-7
Nāşir 194-195 L 7
Nasir, Jabal an- 194-195 F 4
Nāsiriyah, An- 160-161 F 4
Nasīyah, Jabal — 199 C 6
Nasondoye 198 DE 4
Naşr 199 B 2
Naşr, An- 199 C 5
Naşr, Hazzān an- 199 C 6
Naşr, Khazzan an- 194-195 L 4
Nassarawa = Nasarawa
194-195 F 7
Nassau [BS] 58-59 L 6
Nassau [island] 34-35 J 5
Nassau, Bahía — 103 C 9
Nassau Sound 80-81 c 1
Nass Basin 48 C 2
Nässjö 114-115 F 9
Nass River 46-47 L 6-7
Nastapoka Islands 46-47 V 6
Nata 198 E 6
Na-ta = Dan Xian 166-167 K 8
Natagaima 98-99 DE 4
Natal [BR, Amazonas] 98-99 D 7
Natal [BR, Rio Grande do Norte]
98-99 MN 6
Natal [CDN] 66-67 F 1
Natal [RI] 174-175 C 6
Natal [ZA] 198 EF 7
Natal Basin 26-27 LM 7
Natalia, TX 76-77 E 8
Natalkuz Lake 48 E 3
Natal Ridge 198 G 8
Natash, Wādī — 199 CD 5
Natashquan 51 EF 2
Natashquan River 46-47 Y 7
Natchez, MS 58-59 H 5
Natchitoches, LA 58-59 H 5
Nathorst land 114-115 jk 6
Nathrop, CO 68-69 C 6
Nation, AK 52-53 QR 4
National Arboretum 82 II b 2
National City, CA 74-75 E 6
National City, MI 70-71 HJ 3
National Park 80-81 E 3
National Reactor Testing Station
66-67 G 4
National Zoological Park 82 II ab 1
Nation River [CDN] 48 F 2
Nation River [USA] 52-53 R 4
Natitingou 194-195 E 6
Natividade 98-99 K 7
Natoma, KS 68-69 G 6
Nātong Dsong 166-167 G 6
Natron, Lake — 198 G 2
Natrun, Bir el — = Wāhât al-'Aṭrūn
194-195 K 5
Naṭrūn, Wādī an- 199 AB 2
Natrun Lakes = Wādī an-Naṭrūn
199 AB 2
Natuna Islands = Kepulauan
Bunguran Utara 174-175 E 6
Natural Bridges National Monument
74-75 HJ 4
Naturaliste, Cape — 182-183 B 6
Naturita, CO 74-75 J 3
Nauja Vileika, Vilnius- 142-143 DE 5
Naulavaraa 114-115 N 6
Naulila 198 BC 5
Nauru 34-35 H 5
Nāusa 138-139 JK 5
Nauški 154-155 U 7
Nauta 98-99 E 5
Nautla 86-87 M 7
Nauvo 114-115 JK 7
Nava [MEX] 76-77 D 8
Nava de Ricomalillo, La —
132-133 E 9
Navajo, AZ 74-75 J 5
Navajo Indian Reservation 74-75 HJ 4
Navajo Mountain 74-75 H 4
Navajo Reservoir 68-69 C 7
Naval Air Station [USA, New York]
82 III c 3
Naval Observatory 82 II a 1
Navan = An Uaimh 116-117 DE 7
Navangar = Jāmnagar 160-161 L 6
Navarin, mys — 154-155 jk 5
Navarino, Isla — 103 C 9
Navarra 132-133 G 7
Navarre = Navarra 132-133 G 7
Navasota, TX 76-77 FG 7
Navasota River 76-77 F 7
Navassa Island 58-59 LM 8
Navenby 116-117 L 7
Naver, River — 116-117 G 2
Navia 132-133 D 7

Navia 253

Navoi 154-155 M 9
Navoj 160-161 K 2
Navojoa 58-59 E 6
Navolato 58-59 E 7
Návpaktos 138-139 JK 6
Návplion 138-139 K 7
Navrongo 194-195 D 6
Navy Board Inlet 46-47 U 3
Navy Town, AK 52-53 p 6
Nawa = Naha 166-167 O 6
Nawābshāh 160-161 K 5
Nawādhību 194-195 A 4
Nawākshūt 194-195 A 5
Nawari = Nahari 170-171 JK 6
Nawāṣīf, Ḥarrat — 160-161 E 6
Nawfalīyah, An- 194-195 H 2
Naws, Rā's — 160-161 H 7
Náxos [GR, island] 138-139 L 7
Náxos [GR, place] 138-139 L 7
Naxos [I] 138-139 F 7
Nayarit 58-59 EF 7
Nāy Band [IR, Banāder va Jazāyer-e Khalīj-e Fārs] 160-161 G 5
Nāy Band [IR, Khorāsān] 160-161 H 4
Nāy Band, Ra's-e — 160-161 G 5
Naylor, MO 78-79 D 2
Nayoro 170-171 c 1
Nayoro = Gornozavodsk 154-155 b 8
Nazan Bay 52-53 jk 4
Nazaré [BR, Amapá] 98-99 N 4
Nazaré [BR, Amazonas] 98-99 F 4
Nazaré [BR, Bahia] 98-99 M 7
Nazaré [BR, Pará] 98-99 M 8
Nazaré [P] 132-133 C 9
Nazas, Río — 86-87 H 5
Nazca 98-99 DE 7
Nazca Ridge 34-35 N 6-O 5
Naze, The — 116-117 h 7
Naze, The — = Lindesnes 114-115 B 9
N'azepetrovsk 142-143 LM 4
Nazija 142-143 F 4
Nazilli 142-143 E 8
Nazimovo 154-155 QR 6
Nazina 154-155 OP 5-6
Nazko 48 F 3
Nazko River 48 F 3
Nazrēt 194-195 M 7
Nazwá 160-161 H 6
Nazyvajevsk 154-155 N 6
Nazzah 199 B 4

N'daghāmshah, Sabkhat — 194-195 AB 5
Ndai 174-175 k 6
Ndalatando 198 BC 3
N'Dali 194-195 E 7
Ndélé 194-195 J 7
N'Dendé 198 B 2
Ndeni 174-175 l 7
N'djamena 194-195 GH 6
N'Djolé [RFC] 198 AB 2
Ndola 198 E 4
Ndzuwani 198 HJ 4

Neagh, Lough — 116-117 E 6
Neah Bay, WA 66-67 A 1
Neale, Lake — 182-183 F 4
Neales 182-183 G 5
Neápolis [GR, Grámmos] 138-139 J 5
Neápolis [GR, Pelopónnēsos] 138-139 K 7
Near Islands 30 D 1
Near North Side, Chicago-, IL 83 II b 1
Neath 116-117 H 9
Nebek, En — = An-Nabk 160-161 D 4
Nebine Creek 182-183 J 5
Nebit-Dag 160-161 GH 3
Neblina, Pico da — 98-99 FG 4
Neblina, Pico de — 98-99 F 4
Nebo, Mount — 74-75 H 3
Nebraska 58-59 FG 3
Nebraska City, NE 70-71 BC 5
Nebrodie, Monti — 138-139 F 7
Necadah, WI 70-71 E 3
Nechako Plateau 46-47 L 7
Neches, TX 76-77 G 7
Neches River 76-77 G 7
Neckar 124 D 4
Necochea 103 E 5
Nederland, TX 76-77 G 8
Nederlandse Antillen 88-89 M 8
Neebish Island 70-71 H 2
Needham, Mount — 48 A 3
Needle Peak 74-75 E 5
Needles 48 HJ 4-5
Needles, CA 74-75 F 5
Needles, The — 116-117 K 10
Neenah, WI 70-71 F 3
Neepawa 46-47 R 7
Nefoussa, Djebel — = Jabal Nafusah 194-195 G 2
Neftejugansk 154-155 NO 5
Nefud = An-Nafūd 160-161 E 5
Nefud, En — = An-Nafūd 160-161 E 5
Negade = Naqādah 199 C 5
Negapatam = Nāgapattinam 160-161 MN 8
Negara 174-175 FG 8
Negaunee, MI 70-71 G 2
Negelē 194-195 MN 7
Negerpynten 114-115 l 6
Negginan 49 K 4
Neggio = Nejo 194-195 M 7
Neghilli = Negelē 194-195 MN 7
Negoiu 138-139 L 3
Negombo = Migamuwa 160-161 M 9
Negotin 138-139 K 3
Negribreen 114-115 k 5
Negros 174-175 H 5
Negru Vodă 138-139 N 4
Neguac 51 D 4
Nehalem, OR 66-67 B 3
Nehbandān 160-161 HJ 4
Nehe 166-167 NO 2
Neiafu 174-175 c 2
Nei-chiang = Neijiang 166-167 JK 6
Neidín 116-117 B 9
Neidpath 49 E 5
Néifin 116-117 B 6
Neihart, MT 66-67 H 2
Neijiang 166-167 JK 6
Neikiang = Neijiang 166-167 JK 6
Neilburg 49 D 4
Neillsville, WI 70-71 E 3
Neisse 124 G 3
Neiva 98-99 DE 4
Neja 154-155 G 6
Nejd = Najd 160-161 E 5-6
Nejo 194-195 M 7
Nejto 142-143 NO 1-2
Nekemtē 194-195 M 7
Nekoosa, WI 70-71 F 3
Nekropolis 199 C 5
Neksø 114-115 F 10
Nelidovo 142-143 F 4
Neligh, NE 68-69 GH 4
Nel'kan 154-155 Za 6
Nellore 160-161 MN 8
Nellūru = Nellore 160-161 MN 8
Nel'ma 154-155 ab 8
Nelson, AZ 74-75 G 5
Nelson, CA 74-75 C 3
Nelson, NE 68-69 G 5
Nelson, WI 70-71 E 3
Nelson [CDN] 46-47 N 8
Nelson [GB] 116-117 J 7
Nelson [NZ, place] 182-183 O 8
Nelson [RA] 103 DE 4
Nelson, Estrecho — 103 AB 8
Nelson Forks 46-47 M 6
Nelson House 49 J 3
Nelson Island 46-47 C 5
Nelson Reservoir 68-69 BC 1
Nelson River 46-47 RS 6
Nelsonville, OH 72-73 E 5
Nelspruit 198 F 7
Nemah, WA 66-67 B 2
Neman 142-143 D 4
Nemira, Muntele — 138-139 M 2
Nemiscau 50 N 1
Nemiscau, Lac — 50 N 1
Nemours = Ghazawat 194-195 D 1
Nemuro 166-167 S 3
Nemuro-kaikyō 170-171 d 1-2
Nemuro wan 170-171 d 2
Nemurs = Ghazawāt 194-195 D 2
Nenagh = Aonach Urmhumhan 116-117 CD 8
Nenana, AK 46-47 FG 5
Nenana River 52-53 N 4-5
Nenets Autonomous Area 154-155 J-L 4
Nenjiang [TJ, place] 166-167 O 2
Nen Jiang [TJ, river] 166-167 N 2
Nen Jiang = Naguun Mörön 166-167 NO 1-2
Nenusa, Pulau-pulau — 174-175 J 6
Neodesha, KS 70-71 BC 7
Neoga, IL 70-71 F 6
Neola, UT 66-67 H 5
Neopit, WI 70-71 F 3
Neosho, MO 76-77 G 4
Neosho River 58-59 G 4
Nepa 154-155 U 6
Nepal 160-161 NO 5
Nephi, UT 74-75 GH 3
Nephin = Néifin 116-117 B 6
Nepisiguit River 51 CD 4
Nepoko 198 E 1
Neponsit, New York-, NY 82 III c 3
Neptune 49 FG 6
Nérac 132-133 H 6
Neragon Island 52-53 D 6
Nerbudda = Narmada 160-161 LM 6
Nerča 154-155 W 7
Nerčinsk 154-155 W 7
Nerčinskij Zavod 154-155 W 7
Nerechta 142-143 H 4
Neretva 138-139 H 4
Neriquinha = N'Riquinha 198 D 5
Nerka, Lake — 52-53 H 7
Ñermete, Punta — 98-99 C 6
Nerojka, gora — 154-155 KL 5
Nerskoje ploskogorje 154-155 c 5
Nes, Föroyar 116-117 b 1
Nes' [SU] 142-143 HJ 2
Nesebăr 138-139 MN 4
Neškan 52-53 A 3
Neskaupstadhur 114-115 fg 2
Nesna 114-115 E 4
Ness, Loch — 116-117 G 3
Ness City, KS 68-69 FG 6
Nesselrode, Mount — 52-53 UV 7
Nestaocano, Rivière — 50 P 1-2
Nestor Falls 70-71 D 1
Nestoria, MI 70-71 FG 2
Nêstos 138-139 L 5
Nesttun, Bergen- 114-115 AB 7
Netherdale 182-183 J 4
Netherlands 132-133 J 3-L 2
Nettilling Lake 46-47 W 4
Nett Lake 70-71 D 1
Nett Lake Indian Reservation 70-71 D 1-2
Nettleton, MS 78-79 E 3
Netzahualcóyotl, Ciudad — 86-87 L 8
Netzahualcóyotl, Presa — 86-87 O 9
Neubrandenburg 124 F 2
Neuchâtel 124 C 5
Neuchâtel, Lac de — 124 C 5
Neufchâteau [B] 132-133 K 4
Neufchateau [F] 132-133 KL 4
Neufchâtel-en-Bray 132-133 H 4
Neumarkt 124 E 4
Neumünster 124 DE 1
Neunkirchen [A] 124 H 5
Neunkirchen [D] 124 C 4
Neuquén [RA, place] 103 C 5
Neuruppin 124 F 2
Neuschwabenland 31 B 36-2
Neuse River 80-81 H 3
Neusiedler See 124 H 5
Neustrelitz 124 F 2
Neutral Zone 160-161 F 5
Neu-Ulm 124 E 4
Neuwied 124 CD 3
Neva 142-143 F 4
Nevada 58-59 CD 4
Nevada, IA 70-71 D 4-5
Nevada, MO 70-71 C 7
Nevada City, CA 74-75 C 3
Nevado, Cerro El — 98-99 E 4
Nevado, Sierra del — 103 C 5
Nevado Huascaran 98-99 D 6
Neve, Serra da — 198 B 4
Nevel' 142-143 EF 4
Never 154-155 XY 7
Nevers 132-133 J 5
Nevin 116-117 G 8
Nevinnomyssk 142-143 H 7
Nevis 58-59 O 8
Nevis, MN 70-71 C 2
Nevis, Ben — 116-117 FG 4
Nevjansk 154-155 KL 6
Nevşehir 160-161 C 3
Newala 198 G 4
New Albany, IN 58-59 J 4
New Albany, MS 78-79 E 3
New Alexandria, VA 82 II a 2
New Amsterdam 98-99 H 3
Newark, DE 72-73 J 5
Newark, NJ 58-59 M 3
Newark, NY 72-73 H 3
Newark, OH 72-73 E 4
Newark Airport 82 III a 2
Newark Bay 82 III b 2
Newark upon Trent 116-117 L 7
New Athens, IL 70-71 F 6
Newaygo, MI 70-71 H 4
New Bedford, MA 58-59 MN 3
Newberg, OR 66-67 B 3
New Bern, NC 58-59 L 4
Newbern, TN 78-79 E 2
Newberry, CA 74-75 E 5
Newberry, MI 70-71 H 2
Newberry, SC 80-81 F 3
Newbiggin-by-the-Sea 116-117 KL 5
New Bosten, OH 72-73 E 5
New Boston, IL 70-71 E 5
New Boston, OH 72-73 E 5
New Boston, TX 76-77 G 6
New Braunfels, TX 58-59 G 6
New Brighton, New York-, NY 82 III b 3
New Britain 174-175 gh 6
New Britain, CT 72-73 K 4
New Britain Bougainville Trench 174-175 h 6
New Brunswick 46-47 X 8
New Brunswick, NJ 72-73 J 4
New Buffalo, MI 70-71 G 5
Newburg, MO 70-71 E 7
Newburgh, NY 72-73 J 4
Newburgh [CDN] 72-73 H 2
Newburgh [GB] 116-117 HJ 4
Newbury 116-117 K 9
Newburyport, MA 72-73 L 3
Newby Bridge 116-117 J 6
New Caledonia 182-183 MN 3
New Carlisle 51 D 3
New Carrollton, MD 82 II b 1
Newcastel 51 CD 4
Newcastel Creek 182-183 F 3
New Castile = Castilla la Nueva 132-133 E 9-F 8
New Castle, CO 68-69 C 6
New Castle, IN 70-71 H 5-6
New Castle, OH 72-73 D 5
New Castle, PA 72-73 F 4
Newcastle, TX 76-77 E 6
Newcastle, VA 80-81 F 2
Newcastle, WY 68-69 D 4
Newcastle [AUS] 182-183 K 6
Newcastle [GB] 116-117 F 6
Newcastle [ZA] 198 EF 7
Newcastle Bay 182-183 H 2
Newcastle Emlyn 116-117 G 8-9
Newcastleton 116-117 J 5
Newcastle under Lyme 116-117 J 7-8
Newcastle upon Tyne 116-117 JK 5-6
Newcastle Waters 182-183 F 3
Newcastle West = An Caisleán Nua 116-117 BC 8
Newcomb, NM 74-75 J 4
Newcomerstown, OH 72-73 F 4
Newdale, ID 66-67 H 4
Newdegate 182-183 CD 6
New Delhi 160-161 M 5
New Dorp, New York-, NY 82 III b 3
Newell, SD 68-69 E 3
Newell Lake 49 BC 5
Newellton, LA 78-79 D 4
New England, ND 68-69 E 2
New England [USA] 58-59 M 3-N 2
New England Range 182-183 K 5-6
Newenham, Cape — 46-47 D 6
Newent 116-117 J 9
Newfane, VT 72-73 K 3
Newfolden, MN 70-71 BC 1
New Forest 116-117 K 10
Newfoundland [CDN, administrative unit] 46-47 Y 6-Z 8
Newfoundland [CDN, island] 46-47 Za 8
Newfoundland Bank 26-27 G 3
Newfoundland Basin 26-27 GH 3
Newfoundland Ridge 26-27 G 3-H 4
New Galloway 116-117 G 5
New Georgia 174-175 j 6
New Georgia Group 174-175 j 6
New Georgia Sound = The Slot 174-175 j 6
New Germany 51 D 5
New Glasgow 46-47 Y 8
New Glatz, MD 82 II a 2
New Guinea 174-175 L 7-M 8
New Guinea Rise 174-175 M 5-6
Newgulf, TX 76-77 G 8
Newhalem, WA 66-67 C 1
Newhalen, AK 52-53 K 7
Newhall, CA 74-75 D 5
New Hamilton, AK 52-53 F 5
New Hampshire 58-59 M 3
New Hampton, IA 70-71 DE 4
New Hanover [PNG] 174-175 gh 5
New Harmony, IN 70-71 G 6
Newhaven 116-117 LM 10
New Haven, CT 58-59 M 3
New Haven, IN 70-71 H 5
New Haven, KY 70-71 H 7
New Hebrides 182-183 NO 2-3
New Hebrides Basin 182-183 MN 2
New Hebrides Trench 182-183 N 2-3
New Hyde Park, NY 82 III de 2
New Iberia, LA 58-59 H 5-6
New Ireland 174-175 h 5
New Jersey 58-59 M 3
New Kensington, PA 72-73 G 4
Newkirk, OK 76-77 F 4
New Knockhock, AK 52-53 E 5
New Lexington, OH 72-73 EF 5
Newlin, TX 76-77 D 5
New Liskeard 46-47 UV 8
New London, CT 72-73 KL 4
New London, MN 70-71 C 3
New London, MO 70-71 E 6
New London, WI 70-71 F 3
New Madrid, MO 78-79 E 2
Newman, CA 74-75 C 4
Newman, NM 76-77 AB 6
Newman Grove, NE 68-69 GH 5
Newmarket [CDN] 72-73 G 2
Newmarket [GB] 116-117 M 8
Newmarket = Áth Trasna 116-117 BC 8
New Martinsville, WV 72-73 F 5
New Meadows, ID 66-67 E 3
New Mecklenburg = New Ireland 174-175 h 5
New Mexico 58-59 EF 5
Newnan, GA 78-79 G 4
Newnham 116-117 J 9
New Norfolk 182-183 J 8
New Orleans, LA 58-59 HJ 5-6
New Philadelphia, OH 72-73 F 4
New Philippines = Caroline Islands 148-149 RS 9
New Pine Creek, OR 66-67 C 4
New Plymouth 182-183 O 7
New Pomerania = New Britain 174-175 gh 6
Newport, AR 78-79 D 3
Newport, KY 58-59 K 4
Newport, ME 72-73 M 2
Newport, NH 72-73 KL 3
Newport, OR 66-67 A 3
Newport, RI 72-73 L 4
Newport, TN 80-81 E 2-3
Newport, TX 76-77 EF 6
Newport, VT 72-73 KL 2
Newport, WA 66-67 E 1
Newport [GB, Buckingham] 116-117 KL 8
Newport [GB, Gwent] 116-117 J 9
Newport [GB, I. of Wight] 116-117 K 10
Newport [GB, Salop] 116-117 J 8
Newport News, VA 58-59 L 4
New Port Richey, FL 80-81 b 2
New Providence Island 58-59 L 6-7
Newquay 116-117 F 10
New Quebec 46-47 V-X 6
New Quebec Crater 46-47 VW 5
New Radnor 116-117 HJ 8
New Raymer, CO 68-69 E 5
New Richmond 51 D 3
New Richmond, WI 70-71 DE 3
New River 98-99 JK 3
New Roads, LA 78-79 D 5
New Rochelle, NY 72-73 K 4
New Rockford, ND 68-69 G 2
New Romney 116-117 gh 8
New Ross = Ros Mhic Treoin 116-117 E 8
Newry 116-117 E 6
Newry and Mourne = 12 ◁ 116-117 E 6
New Salem, ND 68-69 F 2
New Sharon, IA 70-71 D 5
New Siberia = ostrov Novaja Sibir' 154-155 de 3
New Siberian Islands = Novosibirskije ostrova 154-155 Z-f 2
New Smyrna Beach, FL 80-81 c 2
New South Wales 182-183 H-K 6
New Stuyahok, AK 52-53 J 7
Newton, AL 78-79 G 5
Newton, IA 70-71 D 5
Newton, IL 70-71 F 6
Newton, KS 58-59 G 4
Newton, MA 72-73 L 3
Newton, MS 78-79 E 4
Newton, NC 80-81 F 3
Newton, NJ 72-73 J 4
Newton, TX 78-79 C 5
Newtonabbey = 9 ◁ 116-117 F 6
Newton Abbot 116-117 H 10
Newton Falls, NY 72-73 J 2
Newton South Boswells 116-117 J 5
Newton Stewart 116-117 G 6
Newtontoppen 114-115 k 5
Newtown 116-117 H 8
New Town, ND 68-69 E 1-2
Newtownards 116-117 F 6
Newtown Butler 116-117 D 6
Newtown Stewart 116-117 D 6
New Ulm, MN 70-71 C 3
New Ulm, TX 76-77 F 8
New Underwood, SD 68-69 E 3
New Waterford 51 FG 4
New Westminster 46-47 MN 8
New World Island 51 J 3
New York 58-59 LM 3
New York, NY 58-59 M 3-4
New York Mountains 74-75 F 5
New Zealand 182-183 N 8-O 7
Neyed = Najd 160-161 E 5-6
Neyrīz 160-161 G 5
Neyshābūr 160-161 H 3
Nezametnyj = Aldan 154-155 XY 6
Nežin 142-143 F 5
Nezperce, ID 66-67 EF 2
Nez Perce Indian Reservation 66-67 EF 2

Ngabang 174-175 EF 6
Ngamdo Tsonag Tsho 166-167 G 5
Ngami, Lake — 198 D 6
Nganghouei = Anhui 166-167 M 5
Nganglaring Tso = Ngangla Ringtsho 166-167 EF 5
Nganglong Gangri 166-167 E 5
Ngangtha Ringtsho 166-167 EF 5
Ngangtse Tsho 166-167 F 5
Ngan-yang = Anyang 166-167 LM 4
Ngao 174-175 CD 3
Ngaoundéré 194-195 G 7
Ngatik 178 F 2
Ngau 174-175 a 2
Ngaumdere = Ngaoundéré 194-195 G 7
Ngaundere = Ngaoundéré 194-195 G 7
Ngazidja 198 H 4
Ngiro, Ewaso — 198 G 2
Ngiva 198 C 5
Ngoc Linh 174-175 E 3
Ngoko 198 C 1
Ngong 198 G 2
Ngoring Tsho 166-167 H 4-5
Ngorongoro Crater 198 FG 2
N'Gounié 198 B 2
Ngoura 194-195 H 6
Ngouri 194-195 H 6
N'Gourti 194-195 G 5
Ngoywa 198 F 3
N'Guigmi 194-195 G 6
Ngulu 174-175 L 5
Ngunza 198 B 4
N'Guri = Ngouri 194-195 H 6
Nguru 194-195 G 6

Nhambiquara 98-99 J 11
Nhamundá 98-99 K 6
Nhamundá, Rio — 98-99 K 5
Nha Trang 174-175 EF 4
Nhecolândia 98-99 H 8
Nhi Ha, Sông — 174-175 D 2
Nhill 182-183 H 7

Niafounké 194-195 D 5
Niagara Falls 58-59 KL 3
Niagara Falls, NY 58-59 L 3
Niagara River 72-73 G 3
Niah 174-175 F 6
Ni'āj, Jabal — 199 C 6
Niamey 194-195 E 6
Niangara 198 E 1
Niangua River 70-71 D 7
Nia-Nia 198 E 1
Nianqingtanggula Shan = Nyanchhenthanglha 166-167 G 5-6
Nias, Pulau — 174-175 C 6
Niassa 198 G 4
Niassa = Malawi 198 FG 4
Niassa, Lago — = Lake Malawi 198 F 4
Nibāk 160-161 G 6
Nibe 114-115 C 9
Niblinto 103 B 5
Nicaragua 58-59 JK 9
Nicaragua, Lago de — 58-59 JK 9
Nicaro 58-59 L 7
Nice 132-133 L 7
Niceville, FL 78-79 F 5
Nichinan 170-171 H 7
Nicholasville, KY 70-71 H 7
Nicholl's Town 88-89 GH 2
Nicholson [AUS] 182-183 E 3
Nicholson [CDN] 70-71 J 1-2
Nicholson River 182-183 G 3
Nickel Lake 50 C 3
Nickerie [GUY, administrative unit] 98-99 K 2-3
Nickerie [GUY, river] 98-99 K 2
Nickol Bay 182-183 C 4
Nicman 51 CD 2
Nicobar Islands 160-161 P 9
Nicolás, Canal — 58-59 KL 7
Nicolet 72-73 K 1
Nicomedia = İzmit 160-161 BC 2
Nico Pérez 103 EF 4
Nicosia 138-139 F 7
Nicosia = Levkōsía 160-161 C 3
Nicoya 58-59 J 9
Nicoya, Golfo de — 58-59 J 9
Nicoya, Península de — 58-59 J 9-10
Nida 124 K 3
Nī Dillī = New Delhi 160-161 M 5
Nido, El — 174-175 G 4
Niebüll 124 D 1
Niedere Tauern 124 FG 5
Niederösterreich 124 GH 4
Niedersachsen 124 C-E 2
Nienburg 124 D 2
Nienchentangla = Nyanchhenthanglha 166-167 F 6-G 5
Nieuw Amsterdam [SME] 98-99 HJ 3
Nieuw-Antwerpen = Nouvelle-Anvers 198 CD 1
Nieuw Nickerie 98-99 H 3
Nieuwoudtville 198 C 8
Nieves = Nevis 58-59 O 8
Nieves, Las — 76-77 B 9
Nifīsha = Nafīshah 199 C 2
Niğde 160-161 CD 3
Niger [RN, administrative unit] 194-195 F 7
Niger [RN, river] 194-195 E 6
Niger [RN, state] 194-195 FG 5
Nîger = Niger 194-195 FG 5
Nigeria 194-195 E-G 7
Nighthawk, WA 66-67 D 1
Nighthawk Lake 50 L 2
Nightingale 49 B 5
Nigisaktuvik River 52-53 H 1
Nigrita 138-139 K 5
Nigtmute, AK 52-53 E 6
Nigu River 52-53 JK 2
Nihoa 78-79 b 1
Nihonmatsu = Nihommatsu 170-171 N 4
Niigata 166-167 Q 4
Niihama 170-171 J 5-6
Niihau 174-175 de 3
Niimi 170-171 J 5
Nii-shima 170-171 M 5
Niitsu 170-171 M 4
Nijād al-'Alī 194-195 D 2-E 1
Nijamābād = Nizāmābād 160-161 M 7
Nijmegen 132-133 KL 3
Nikabuna Lakes 52-53 JK 6
Nikel' 154-155 E 4
Nikēphorion = Ar-Raqqah 160-161 DE 3
Nikhaib, An- = Nukhayb 160-161 E 4
Nikishka Numero 2, AK 52-53 M 6
Nikito-Ivdel'skoje = Ivdel' 154-155 L 5
Nikki 194-195 E 6-7
Nikolai, AK 52-53 KL 5
Nikolajev 142-143 F 6
Nikolajevsk = Pugačov 154-155 HJ 7
Nikolajevskij 142-143 J 5
Nikolajevsk-na-Amure 154-155 b 7
Nikol'sk [SU, Severnyje uvaly] 154-155 H 6
Nikolski, AK 52-53 m 4
Nikol'skij 154-155 M 8
Nikol'skoje [SU, Komandorskije ostrova] 154-155 fg 6
Nikomēdeia = İzmit 160-161 BC 2
Nikopol' 142-143 F 6

254 **Navoi**

Nikopol [BG] 138-139 L 4
Nikosia = Levkōsia 160-161 C 3
Nikšić 138-139 H 4
Nīl, An- 194-195 L 5
Nīl, Baḥr an- 194-195 L 3-4
Nila, Pulau — 174-175 JK 8
Nīlagiri = Nīlgiri Hills 160-161 M 8
Nīl al-Abyaḍ, An- 194-195 L 6
Nīl al-Azraq, An- [Sudan, administrative unit] 194-195 L 6
Nīl al-Azraq, An- [Sudan, river] 194-195 L 6
Niland, CA 74-75 F 6
Nilandu Atoll 36 a 2
Nile = Bahr an-Nīl 194-195 L 3-4
Nile, Albert — 198 F 1
Niles, MI 70-71 G 5
Niles, OH 72-73 F 4
Nilo 98-99 B 9
Nimba, Mont — 194-195 C 7
Nîmes 132-133 JK 7
Nimiuktuk River 52-53 H 2
Nimnyrskij 154-155 Y 6
Nimrod, MT 66-67 G 2
Nimūlē 194-195 L 8
Nine Degree Channel 160-161 L 9
Ninette 68-69 G 1
Nineve = Ninive 160-161 E 3
Ninfas, Punta — 103 D 6
Ning'an 166-167 OP 3
Ningbo 166-167 N 6
Ningcheng 170-171 B 2
Ningde 166-167 M 6
Ningdu 166-167 M 6
Ningguo 166-167 M 5
Ninghsia, Autonomes Gebiet 166-167 H 3-K 4
Ning-hsiang = Ningxiang 166-167 L 6
Ninghsien = Ning Xian 166-167 K 4
Ninghua 166-167 M 6
Ninghwa = Ninghua 166-167 M 6
Ning-po = Ningbo 166-167 N 6
Ningsia = Ningxia 166-167 H 3-K 4
Ningsia Autonomous Region 166-167 JK 3-4
Ningteh = Ningde 166-167 M 6
Ninguta = Ning'an 166-167 OP 3
Ningxia 166-167 H 3-K 4
Ningxia Huizu Zizhiqu 166-167 JK 3-4
Ning Xian 166-167 K 4
Ningxiang 166-167 L 6
Ninh Giang 174-175 E 2
Ninh Hoa [VN ↑ Nha Trang] 174-175 EF 4
Ninigo Group 174-175 M 7
Ninilchik, AK 52-53 M 6
Ninive 160-161 E 3
Ninjintangla Shan = Nyanchhenthanglha 166-167 G 5-6
Ninnis Glacier 31 C 16-15
Ninua = Ninive 160-161 E 3
Niobe, ND 68-69 E 1
Niobrara, NE 68-69 GH 4
Niobrara River 58-59 F 3
Niokolo-Koba, Parc National du — 194-195 B 6
Nioro-du-Rip 194-195 A 6
Nioro du Sahel 194-195 C 5
Niort 132-133 G 5
Nipawin 46-47 Q 7
Nipawin Provincial Park 49 F 3
Nipe, Bahía de — 88-89 J 4
Nipigon 46-47 T 8
Nipigon, Lake — 46-47 ST 8
Nipigon Bay 70-71 FG 1
Nipigon-Onaman Game Reserve 50 F 2-3
Nipigon River 70-71 F 1
Nipissing, Lake — 46-47 UV 8
Nipisso 51 D 2
Nippers Harbour 51 J 3
Nipton, CA 74-75 F 5
Niquelândia 98-99 K 7
Niquero 88-89 GH 4
Nirasaki 170-171 M 5
Niriz, Däryacheh i — = Daryācheh Bakhtegān 160-161 G 5
Niš 138-139 JK 4
Nişāb 160-161 E 5
Niṣāb, An — = Anṣāb 160-161 F 8
Nišava 138-139 K 4
Niscemi 138-139 F 7
Nishinomiya 170-171 K 5
Nishinoomote 170-171 H 7
Nishino shima 170-171 J 4
Nishio 170-171 L 5
Nishisonoki hantō 170-171 G 6
Nishiyama 170-171 M 4
Nishlik Lake 52-53 H 6
Nishtawn 160-161 G 7
Nishtūn = Nishtawn 160-161 G 7
Nísia-Floresta 98-99 MN 6
Nisibin = Nusaybin 160-161 E 3
Nisibis = Nusaybin 160-161 E 3
Nisko 124 KL 3
Nisland, SD 68-69 E 3
Nisling Range 52-53 S 5-T 6
Nisling River 52-53 S 5
Nissan 114-115 E 9
Nisser 114-115 C 8
Nisutlin Plateau 46-47 K 5
Nísyros 138-139 M 7
Niterói 98-99 L 9
Nith, River — 116-117 H 5
Nitra 124 J 4
Nitro, WV 72-73 F 5
Niuafo'ou 174-175 b 2
Niuatoputapu 174-175 c 2
Niue 34-35 J 5
Niulii, HI 78-79 e 2
Niut, Gunung — 174-175 E 6
Niutao 178 H 3
Niva 114-115 P 4
Nivernais 132-133 J 5
Niverville 49 K 6
Nivskij 154-155 E 4
Nixon, TX 76-77 F 8
Niya Bazar 166-167 E 4
Nizāmābād 160-161 M 7
Nizamghāṭ 160-161 Q 5
Nizām Sāgar 160-161 M 7
Nizhne Ilimsk = Nižne-Ilimsk 154-155 T 6
Nizhni Tagil = Nižnij Tagil 154-155 KL 6
Nizhniy Novgorod = Gor'kij 154-155 GH 6
Nizina, AK 52-53 Q 6
Nizina River 52-53 Q 6
Nízke Tatry 124 JK 4
Nizki Island 52-53 pq 6
Nizkij, mys — 154-155 hj 5
Nižn'aja Kamenka 142-143 JK 2
Nižn'aja Peša 154-155 H 4
Nižn'aja Tunguska 154-155 TU 5
Nižn'aja Tura 154-155 K 6
Nižneangarsk 154-155 UV 6
Nižneilimsk 154-155 T 6
Nižneimbatskoje 154-155 QR 5
Nižnekamsk 154-155 J 7
Nižneleninskoje 154-155 Z 8
Nižneudinsk 154-155 S 7
Nižnevartovsk 154-155 O 5
Nižnije Sergi 142-143 L 4
Nižnij Lomov 142-143 H 5
Nižnij Novgorod = Gor'kij 154-155 GH 6
Nižnij Tagil 154-155 KL 6
Njala = Mono 194-195 E 7
Njardhvík 114-115 b 3
Njassa = Lake Malawi 198 F 4
Njombe [EAT, place] 198 FG 3
Njombe [EAT, river] 198 F 3
Nkata Bay = Nkhata Bay 198 F 4
Nkhata Bay 198 F 4
Nkiōna 138-139 K 6
Nkongsamba 194-195 FG 8
Noanama 98-99 D 4
Noatak, AK 46-47 D 4
Noatak River 46-47 DE 4
Nobeoka 166-167 P 5
Noblesville, IN 70-71 GH 5
Nodaway River 70-71 C 5
Noel, MO 76-77 G 4
Noel Paul's River 51 H 3
Noe Valley, San Francisco-, CA 83 I b 2
Nófilia, en — = An-Nawfalīyah 194-195 H 2
Nogajskaja step' 142-143 J 7
Nogal = Nugal 160-161 F 9
Nogales, AZ 58-59 D 5
Nogamut, AK 52-53 HJ 6
Nogat 124 J 1
Nōgata 170-171 H 6
Noginsk 142-143 G 4
Nogoyá 103 DE 4
Noheji 170-171 N 2
Noir, Isla — 103 B 8
Noirmoutier, Île de — 132-133 F 5
Nojima-saki 170-171 MN 5
Nojon 166-167 J 3
Nokia 114-115 K 7
Nok Kuṇḍī 160-161 J 5
Nokomis 49 F 5
Nokomis, IL 70-71 F 6
Nokomis Lake 49 G 2
Nola [RCA] 194-195 H 8
Nolan, AK 52-53 M 3
Nolinsk 154-155 HJ 6
Nolsø = Nólsoy 116-117 b 2
Nólsoy 116-117 b 2
Nomamisaki 170-171 GH 7
Nome, AK 46-47 C 5
Nome, Cape — 52-53 E 4
No-min Ho = Nuomin He 166-167 N 2
Nomo-saki 170-171 G 6
Nomuka 178 J 5
Nondalton, AK 52-53 K 6
Nong'an 166-167 NO 3
Nong Khai 174-175 D 3
Nongoma 198 F 7
Nonni = Nen Jiang 166-167 O 1-2
Nonoava 86-87 G 4
Nonouti 178 H 3
Nonsan 170-171 F 4
Nonvianuk Lake 52-53 K 7
Noordzeekanaal 132-133 K 2
Noormarkku 114-115 JK 7
Noorvik, AK 46-47 DE 4
Nootka Island 46-47 L 8
Nootka Sound 48 D 5
Noqui 198 B 3
Nora [ETH] 194-195 MN 5
Nora [S] 114-115 F 8
Noranda 50 M 2
Norcatur, KS 68-69 F 6
Nórcia 138-139 E 4
Norcross, GA 78-79 G 4
Nordaustlandet 114-115 k-m 5
Nordcross, GA 80-81 D 4
Nordegg = Brazeau 48 J 3
Norden 124 C 2
Nordenskiöld, archipelag — 154-155 RS 2
Nordenskiöld, zaliv — 154-155 JK 2
Nordenskiøldbukta 114-115 l 4
Nordenskiøld land 114-115 jk 6
Nordenskiold River 52-53 T 6
Norderøer = Nordhoyar 116-117 b 1
Nordfjord 114-115 AB 7
Nordfjorden 114-115 j 5
Nordfriesische Inseln 124 D 1
Nordhausen 124 E 3
Nordhorn 124 C 2
Nordhoyar 116-117 b 1
Nordhur-Ísafjardhar 114-115 b 1-2
Nordhur-Múla 114-115 f 2
Nordhur-Thingeyjar 114-115 ef 1-2
Nordkapp [N] 114-115 LM 2
Nordkapp [Svalbard] 114-115 k 4
Nordkinn 114-115 MN 2
Nordkjosbotn 114-115 HJ 3
Nordland 114-115 E 5-G 3
Nördlingen 124 E 4
Nordostrundingen 30 A 18-20
Nord-Ostsee-Kanal 124 D 1-2
Nordre Kvaløy 114-115 H 2
Nordre Strømfjord 46-47 a 4
Nordrhein-Westfalen 124 CD 3
Nord-Trøndelag 114-115 DE 5
Nordvik 154-155 V 3
Nore 114-115 C 7
Nore River = An Fheoir 116-117 D 8
Norfolk 116-117 gh 6
Norfolk, NE 58-59 G 3
Norfolk, VA 58-59 LM 4
Norfolk Island 182-183 N 5
Norfolk Lake 78-79 CD 2
Norfolk Ridge 182-183 N 6-O 7
Norheimsund 114-115 AB 7
Nori 154-155 N 4
Norias, TX 76-77 F 9
Norias, Las — 76-77 C 8
Norikura dake 170-171 L 4
Noril'sk 154-155 Q 4
Norische Alpen 124 FG 5
Norlina, NC 80-81 G 2
Normal, IL 70-71 F 5
Norman, AR 78-79 C 3
Norman, OK 58-59 G 4
Normanby 116-117 KL 6
Normanby Island 174-175 h 7
Normandie 132-133 GH 4
Normandin 50 P 2
Normandy = Normandie 132-133 GH 4
Normangee, TX 76-77 F 7
Norman River 182-183 H 3
Normanton 182-183 H 3
Norman Wells 46-47 KL 4
Normetal 50 M 2
Nornalup 182-183 C 6-7
Norquinco 103 B 6
Norra Bergnäs 114-115 H 4
Norra Storfjället 114-115 FG 5
Norrbotten [S, administrative unit] 114-115 G-K 4
Norrbotten [S, landscape] 114-115 J 5-K 4
Norrembega 50 L 2
Nørresundby, Ålborg- 114-115 CD 9
Norridge, IL 83 II a 1
Norris, MT 66-67 H 3
Norris Arm 51 J 3
Norris City, IL 70-71 F 7
Norris Lake 78-79 GH 2
Norristown, PA 72-73 J 4
Norrköping 114-115 G 8
Norrland 114-115 F-J 5
Norrtälje 114-115 H 8
Norseman 182-183 D 6
Norsk 154-155 Y 7
Norte, Cabo — 98-99 K 4
Norte, Canal do — 98-99 JK 4
Norte, Serra do — 98-99 H 7
North, SC 80-81 F 4
North, Cape — 46-47 YZ 8
North Adams, MA 72-73 K 3
North Albanian Alps = Alpet e Shiqërise 138-139 HJ 4
Northallerton 116-117 K 6
Northam [AUS] 182-183 C 6
Northam [ZA] 198 E 7
North America 26-27 DE 3
North American Basin 26-27 FG 4
Northampton, MA 72-73 K 3
Northampton [AUS] 182-183 B 5
Northampton [GB] 116-117 L 8
North Andaman 160-161 P 8
North Arlington, NJ 82 III b 2
North Arm 46-47 NO 5
North Augusta, SC 80-81 EF 4
North Australian Basin 26-27 P 6
North Baltimore, OH 72-73 E 4
North Banda Basin 174-175 HJ 7
North Battleford 46-47 P 7
North Bay 46-47 UV 8
North Belcher Islands 46-47 U 6
North Bend, NE 68-69 H 5
North Bend, OR 66-67 A 4
North Bend, WA 66-67 C 2
North Bergen, NJ 82 III b 2
North Berwick 116-117 J 4
Northbrook, ostrov — 154-155 GH 2
North Burton 116-117 L 6
North Caicos 88-89 L 4
North Canadian River 58-59 FG 4
North Cape [CDN] 51 E 4
North Cape [NZ] 182-183 O 6
North Cape [USA] 52-53 jk 4
North Cape = Nordkapp 114-115 LM 2
North Caribou Lake 46-47 ST 7
North Channel [CDN] 46-47 U 8
North Channel [GB] 116-117 E 5-F 6
North Charleston, SC 80-81 G 4
North Chicago, IL 70-71 G 4
Northcliffe 182-183 C 6
North Creek, NY 72-73 JK 3
North Downs 116-117 LM 9
North East, PA 72-73 FG 3
Northeast Branch 82 II b 1
Northeast Cape [USA] 52-53 CD 5
North East Carry, ME 72-73 LM 2
North Eastern 198 H 1-2
North-East Island = Nordaustlandet 114-115 k-m 5
Northeast Providence Channel 58-59 L 6
Northeim 124 DE 3
Northern [Z] 198 E 3-F 4
Northern Cheyenne Indian Reservation 68-69 C 3
Northern Indian Lake 49 K 2
Northern Ireland 116-117 D-F 6
Northern Light Lake 70-71 E 1
Northern Marianas 179 GH 2
Northern Pacific Railway 58-59 EF 2
Northern Province = Ash-Shimālīyah 194-195 KL 5
Northern Sporades = Bóreioi Sporádes 138-139 KL 6
Northern Territory 182-183 FG 3-4
North Esk, River — 116-117 J 4
Northfield, MN 70-71 D 3
Northfield, VT 72-73 K 2
North Fiji Basin 182-183 O 2
North Foreland 116-117 h 7-8
North Fork, CA 74-75 D 4
North Fork, ID 66-67 FG 3
North Fork Mountain 72-73 G 5
North Fox Island 70-71 H 3
North French River 50 L 1-2
North Frisian Islands = Nordfriesische Inseln 124 D 1
Northgate 68-69 EF 1
North Head [CDN] 51 C 5
North Horr 198 G 1
North Island [NZ] 182-183 P 7
North Island [USA] 80-81 G 4
North Islands 78-79 E 6
North Judson, IN 70-71 G 5
North Kamloops 48 GH 4
North Korea 166-167 O 3-4
Northland, MI 70-71 G 2
North Land = Severnaja Zeml'a 154-155 ST 1-2
North Laramie River 68-69 D 4
North Las Vegas, NV 74-75 F 4
Northleach 116-117 K 9
North Little Rock, AR 58-59 H 4-5
North Loup, NE 68-69 G 5
North Loup River 68-69 G 5
North Magnetic Pole 46-47 Q 3
North Magnetic Pole Area 30 B 29
North Malosmadulu Atoll 36 a 1
North Manchester, IN 70-71 H 5
North Miami, FL 80-81 cd 4
North Minch 116-117 E 3-F 2
North Moose Lake 49 HJ 3
North Natuna Islands = Kepulauan Bunguran Utara 174-175 E 6
North Negril Point 88-89 G 5
North New River Canal 80-81 c 3
North Ossetian Autonomous Soviet Socialist Republic = 4 ◁ 142-143 H 7
North Pacific Basin 34-35 H-K 2-3
North Pageh = Pulau Pagai Utara 174-175 C 7
North Palisade 58-59 C 4
North Park, Chicago-, IL 83 II a 1
North Pass 58-59 J 6
North Pease River 76-77 D 5
North Platte, NE 58-59 F 3
North Platte River 58-59 F 3
North Point [USA] 72-73 E 2
North Pole, AK 52-53 O 4
Northport, AL 78-79 F 4
Northport, MI 70-71 H 3
Northport, NE 68-69 E 5
Northport, WA 66-67 E 1
North Powder, OR 66-67 DE 3
North Range 70-71 DE 2
North Rhine-Westphalia = Nordrhein-Westfalen 124 CD 3
North Richmond, CA 83 I b 1
North Riverside, IL 83 II a 1
North Rona 116-117 F 1
North Ronaldsay 116-117 JK 1
North Santiam River 66-67 B 3
North Saskatchewan River 46-47 OP 7
North Sea 110-111 J 4
North Sea Channel = Noordzeekanaal 132-133 K 2
North Share Channel 83 II ab 1
North Shore Range 70-71 E 1-2
North Slape 52-53 G-N 2
North Sound 116-117 J 1
North Star 48 HJ 1
North Stradbroke Island 182-183 K 5
North Stratford, NH 72-73 L 2
North Sunderland 116-117 K 5
North Sydney 51 F 4
North Taranaki Bight 182-183 O 7
North Tawton 116-117 H 10
North Thompson River 48 G 4-H 3
North Tonawanda, NY 72-73 G 3
North Truchas Peak 58-59 E 4
North Tyne, River — 116-117 J 5
North Uist 116-117 D 3
Northumberland 116-117 J 6-K 5
Northumberland Islands 182-183 JK 4
Northumberland Strait 46-47 Y 8
North Umpqua River 66-67 B 4
North Valleystream, NY 82 III de 2
North Vancouver 66-67 B 1
North Vernon, IN 70-71 H 6
North Wabasca Lake 48 L 1
North Walsham 116-117 h 6
Northway, AK 52-53 QR 5
Northway Junction, AK 52-53 R 5
Northwest Australian Basin 26-27 OP 6
Northwest Branch 82 II b 1
North West Cape 182-183 B 4
North Western 198 DE 4
Northwestern University 83 II b 1
North-West-Frontier 154-155 L 3-4
Northwest Highlands 116-117 F 4-G 2
Northwest Indian Ridge 26-27 N 5-6
Northwest Pacific Basin 34-35 G 3
Northwest Pacific Ridge 34-35 H 2-3
Northwest Passage 46-47 J-L 3
Northwest Territories 46-47 M-U 4
Northwich 116-117 J 7
North Wilkesboro, NC 80-81 F 2
Northwood, IA 70-71 D 4
Northwood, ND 68-69 H 2
North York 72-73 G 3
North York Moors 116-117 KL 6
North Yorkshire 116-117 J-L 6
Norton 116-117 L 6
Norton, KS 68-69 G 6
Norton, VA 80-81 E 2
Norton Bay 52-53 FG 4
Norton Point 82 III b 3
Norton Sound 46-47 D 5
Nortonville, ND 68-69 G 2
Norvegia, Kapp — 31 B 34-35
Norwalk, CA 83 III d 2
Norwalk, CT 72-73 K 4
Norwalk, MI 70-71 GH 3
Norwalk, OH 72-73 E 4
Norway 114-115 C 8-L 2
Norway, IA 70-71 DE 5
Norway, ME 72-73 L 2
Norway, MI 70-71 G 3
Norway House 46-47 R 7
Norwegian Basin 26-27 JK 2
Norwegian Bay 46-47 ST 2
Norwegian Sea 110-111 F-K 2
Norwegian Trench 110-111 K 4
Norwich, CT 72-73 KL 4
Norwich, NY 72-73 J 3
Norwich [CDN] 72-73 F 3
Norwich [GB] 116-117 h 6
Norwood, MN 70-71 CD 3
Norwood, NC 80-81 F 3
Norwood, NY 72-73 J 2
Norwood, OH 70-71 H 6
Norwood Park, Chicago-, IL 83 II a 1
Noshiro 166-167 QR 3
Nosiro = Noshiro 166-167 QR 3
Noss, Isle of — 116-117 f 3
Noss Head 116-117 HJ 2
Nossob 198 C 6
Nosy-Bé 198 J 4
Nosy Boraha 198 K 5
Nosy-Varika 198 J 6
Nota 142-143 EF 2
Notch Peak 74-75 G 3
Noteć 124 G 2
Noto [I] 138-139 F 7
Noto [J] 170-171 L 4
Notodden 114-115 C 8
Noto hantō 166-167 Q 4
Noto-jima 170-171 L 4
Notoro-ko 170-171 d 1
Notre Dame, Monts — 46-47 WX 8
Notre Dame Bay 46-47 Z 8-a 7
Notre-Dame-des-Lourdes 49 JK 6
Notre-Dame-des-Victoires, Montréal- 82 I b 1
Notre-Dame-du-Lac 51 BC 4
Notre-Dame-du-Laus 72-73 J 1
Notre Dame du Nord 50 M 3
Nottawasaga Bay 72-73 F 2
Nottaway River 46-47 V 7
Nottingham 116-117 KL 8
Nottingham Island 46-47 VW 5
Nottingham Park, IL 83 II a 2
Nottoway River 80-81 H 2
Notuken Creek 49 E 6
Nouadhibou = Nawādhību 194-195 A 4
Nouakchott = Nawākshūt 194-195 A 5
Nouméa 182-183 N 4
Noupoort 198 DE 8
Nouvelle Amsterdam 26-27 NO 7
Nouvelle-Anvers 198 CD 1
Nova Aripuanã 98-99 H 9
Novabad 160-161 L 3
Nova Chaves = Muconda 198 D 4
Nova Cruz 98-99 MN 6
Nova Freixo = Cuamba 198 G 4
Nova Gaia 198 C 3-4
Nova Goa = Panjim 160-161 L 7
Nova Gradiška 138-139 GH 3
Nova Iguaçu 98-99 L 9
Novaja Buchara = Kagan 160-161 J 3
Novaja Kazanka 142-143 J 6
Novaja L'al'a 142-143 M 4
Novaja Pis'm'anka = Leninogorsk 154-155 J 7
Novaja Sibir', ostrov — 154-155 de 3
Novaja Zeml'a 154-155 J 3-L 2
Nova Lamego 194-195 B 6
Nova Lima 98-99 L 8-9
Nova Lisboa = Huambo 198 C 4
Nova Lusitânia 198 F 5
Nova Mambone 198 G 6
Novanninskij 142-143 H 5
Nova Olinda [BR, Pará] 98-99 N 8
Nova Olinda do Norte 98-99 J 6
Novara 138-139 C 3
Nova Scotia 46-47 X 9-Y 8
Nova Sofala 198 FG 6
Novato, CA 74-75 B 3
Nova Vida 98-99 G 10
Novaya Zemlya = Novaja Zeml'a 154-155 J 3-L 2
Novaya Zemlya Trough 154-155 K 3-L 2
Nova Zagora 138-139 LM 4
Nové Zámky 124 J 4
Novgorod 154-155 E 6
Novgorod-Severskij 142-143 F 5
Novi Bečej 138-139 J 3
Novigrad 138-139 E 3
Novi Pazar [BG] 138-139 M 4
Novi Pazar [YU] 138-139 J 4
Novi Sad 138-139 HJ 3
Novo Acôrdo 98-99 P 9-10
Novoaleksandrovskaja 142-143 H 6
Novoaltajsk 154-155 PQ 7
Novobogatinskoje 142-143 K 6
Novočerkassk 142-143 GH 6
Novograd-Volynskij 142-143 E 5
Novogrudok 142-143 E 5
Novo Hamburgo 103 FG 3
Novojerudinskij 154-155 RS 6
Novokazalinsk 154-155 L 8
Novokujbyševsk 142-143 JK 5
Novokuzneck 154-155 Q 7
Novolazarevskaja 31 B 1
Novo-Mariinsk = Anadyr' 154-155 j 5
Novo Mesto 138-139 F 3
Novomoskovsk 142-143 GH 5
Novonikolajevsk = Novosibirsk 154-155 P 6-7
Novo Redondo = N'Gunza Kabolo 198 B 4
Novorossijsk 142-143 G 7
Novošachtinsk 142-143 GH 6
Novosibirsk 154-155 P 6-7
Novosibirskije ostrova 154-155 Z-f 2
Novosokol'niki 142-143 EF 4
Novos'olovo 154-155 R 6
Novotroick 154-155 K 7
Novo-Troickij Promysel = Balej 154-155 W 7
Novoukrainka 142-143 F 6
Novo-Urgenč = Urgenč 154-155 L 9
Novouzensk 142-143 J 5
Novozybkov 142-143 F 5
Novra 49 H 4
Novska 138-139 G 3
Novyj Bor 142-143 K 2
Novyj Bug 142-143 F 6
Novyje Karymkary 154-155 MN 5
Novyj Margelan = Fergana 160-161 L 2-3
Novyj Port 154-155 MN 4
Nowa Sól 124 G 3
Nowata, OK 76-77 G 4
Nowbarān 142-143 JK 8
Nowe 124 J 2
Nowgorod = Novgorod 154-155 E 6
Nowitna River 52-53 K 4
Nowlin, SD 68-69 F 3-4
Nowood Creek 68-69 C 3-4
Nowra 182-183 K 6
Now Shar 142-143 K 8
Nowy Korczyn 124 K 3
Nowy Sącz 124 K 4
Nowy Targ 124 K 4
Noxon, MT 66-67 F 1-2
Noya 132-133 C 7
Noyes Island 52-53 vw 9
Noyon 132-133 J 4

Noyon 255

N'Riquinha = Lumbala 198 D 5

Nsanje 198 G 5
Nsukka 194-195 F 7

Ntcheu 198 FG 4

Nuanetsi = Mwenezi 198 EF 6
Nubah, An- 194-195 K-M 4-5
Nūbah, Aş-Şaḥrā' an- 194-195 LM 4
Nūbah, Jibāl an- 194-195 KL 6
Nubian Desert = Aş-Şaḥrā' an-Nūbah 194-195 LM 4
Nubieber, CA 66-67 C 5
Nūbiya = An-Nubah 194-195 K-M 4-5
Nu Chiang = Nag Chhu 166-167 G 5
Nudo Ausangate 98-99 E 7
Nueces River 58-59 G 6
Nueltin Lake 46-47 R 5
Nueva Antioquia 98-99 EF 3
Nueva Casas Grandes 58-59 E 5
Nueva Germania 103 E 2
Nueva Gerona 88-89 E 3-4
Nueva Ocotepeque 88-89 B 7
Nueva Orán, San Ramón de la — 103 CD 2
Nueva Providencia 58-59 b 2
Nueva Rosita 58-59 F 6
Nueva San Salvador 58-59 HJ 9
Nueve de Julio [RA, Buenos Aires] 103 D 5
Nuevitas 88-89 H 4
Nuevo Chagres 58-59 ab 2
Nuevo Emperador 58-59 b 2
Nuevo Laredo 58-59 FG 6
Nuevo León 58-59 F 7-G 6
Nuevo Padilla 86-87 L 6
Nuevo Rocafuerte 98-99 D 5
Nuevo San Juan 58-59 b 2
Nugaal 194-195 b 2
Nugruş, Gebel — = Jabal Nuqruş 199 D 5
Nûgssuaq 46-47 YZ 3
Nûgssuaq Halvø 46-47 a 3
Nuguria Islands 174-175 hj 5
Nuhaylah, An- 199 B 4
Nuhūd, An- 194-195 K 6
Nuhurowa = Pulau Kai Kecil 174-175 K 8
Nuhu Rowa = Pulau Kai Kecil 174-175 K 8
Nuhu Tjut = Pulau Kai Besar 174-175 K 8
Nuhu Yut = Pulau Kai Besar 174-175 K 8
Nui 178 H 3
Nui Đeo 174-175 E 2
N'uja [SU, place] 154-155 W 5
N'uja [SU, river] 154-155 V 5
Nu Jiang = Nag Chhu 166-167 G 5
Nujiang Lisuzu Zizhizhou 166-167 H 6
Nûk 46-47 a 5
Nuka Island 52-53 M 7
Nuka River 52-53 H 2
Nukhayb 160-161 E 4
Nukhaylah 194-195 K 5
Nukheila, Bîr — = Nukhaylah 194-195 K 5
Nuku'alofa 178 J 5
Nukufetau 178 H 3
Nukulaelae 178 H 3
Nukumanu Islands 174-175 jk 5
Nukunau 178 H 3
Nukunono 178 J 3
Nukuoro 178 F 2
Nukus 154-155 KL 9
N'ukža 154-155 X 6-7
Nulato, AK 46-47 E 5
Nulato River 52-53 H 4
Nullagine 182-183 D 4
Nullarbor 182-183 EF 6
Nullarbor Plain 182-183 EF 6
Nuluk River 52-53 D 4
Num, Mios — 174-175 KL 7
Numakunai = Iwate 170-171 N 3
Numan 194-195 G 7
Nu'mān, Jazīrat an- 199 D 4
Numancia 132-133 F 8
Numata [J, Gunma] 170-171 M 4
Numata [J, Hokkaidō] 170-171 bc 2
Numazu 170-171 M 5
Numedal 114-115 C 7-8
Numeia = Nouméa 182-183 N 4
Numero 1 Station = Maḥaṭṭat 1 199 B 7
Numero 2 Station = Maḥaṭṭat 2 199 BC 7
Numero 3 Station = Maḥaṭṭat 3 199 BC 7
Numero 4 Station = Maḥaṭṭat 4 199 C 7
Numfoor, Pulau — 174-175 KL 7
Numto 154-155 MN 5
Nunachuak, AK 52-53 J 7
Nunapitchuk, AK 52-53 F 6
Nunavakanuk River 52-53 E 5-6
Nunavak Anukslak Lake 52-53 FG 6
Nunavakpok Lake 52-53 F 6
Nunavaugaluk, Lake — 52-53 H 7
Nun Chiang = Nen Jiang 166-167 O 1-2
Nuneaton 116-117 K 8
Nungan = Nong'an 166-167 NO 3
Nungesser Lake 50 BC 2
Nungo 198 G 4
Nunica, MI 70-71 GH 4
Nunivak Island 46-47 C 6
Nunn, CO 68-69 D 5
Nunyamo 52-53 BC 4
Nuomin He 166-167 N 2
Nuoro 138-139 C 5
Nuqruş, Jabal — 199 D 5
Nura 154-155 N 7
Nurakita 178 H 4
Nuratau, chrebet — 154-155 M 9
N'urba 154-155 W 5
Nuremburg = Nürnberg 124 E 4
Nūrestān 160-161 KL 3-4
Nurmes 114-115 N 6
Nürnberg 124 E 4
Nusa Tenggara Barat = 16 ◁ 174-175 G 8
Nusa Tenggara Timur = 17 ◁ 174-175 H 8
Nusaybin 160-161 E 3
Nushagak Bay 52-53 H 7
Nushagak Peninsula 52-53 H 7
Nushagak River 46-47 E 5-6
Nu Shan 166-167 H 6
Nūshkī 160-161 K 5
Nutak 46-47 Y 6
Nutley, NJ 82 III b 2
Nutrias = Puerto de Nutrias 98-99 EF 3
Nutt, NM 76-77 A 6
Nutzotin Mountains 46-47 H 5
Nuwara Eliya 160-161 N 9
Nuwaybi' al-Muzayyinah 199 D 3
Nuweiba' = Nuwaybi' al-Muzayyinah 199 D 3
Nuyakuk Lake 52-53 H 7
Nuyakuk River 52-53 HJ 7
Nuyts Archipelago 182-183 F 6

Nxai Pan National Park 198 DE 5

Nyaake 194-195 C 8
Nyac, AK 52-53 GH 6
Nya Chhu = Yalong Jiang 166-167 HJ 5
Nyahanga 198 F 2
Nyakahanga 198 F 2
Nyâlâ 194-195 J 6
Ny Ålesund 114-115 hj 5
Nyamandhlovu 198 E 5
Nyambiti 198 F 2
Nyâmlêll 194-195 K 7
Nyamtumbu 198 G 4
Nyanchhenthanglha [TJ, mountains] 166-167 F 6-G 5
Nyanchhenthanglha [TJ, pass] 166-167 G 5-6
Nyanda 198 F 5
Nyanga 198 B 2
Nyanza [EAK] 198 F 1-2
Nyasa = Lake Malawi 198 F 4
Nyasameer = Lake Malawi 198 F 4
Nyaunglebin 174-175 C 3
Nyborg 114-115 D 10
Nybro 114-115 F 9
Nyda 154-155 N 4
Nyenchentanglha = Nyanchhenthanglha 166-167 F 6-G 5
Nyeri [EAK] 198 G 2
Ny Friesland 114-115 k 5
Nyika Plateau 198 F 3-4
Nyírbátor 124 KL 5
Nyíregyháza 124 K 5
Nyiro, Uoso — = Ewaso Ngiro 198 G 2
Nyiru, Mount — 198 G 1
Nyitra = Nitra 124 J 4
Nykarleby 114-115 K 6
Nykøbing Falster 114-115 DE 10
Nykøbing Mors 114-115 C 9
Nykøbing Sjælland 114-115 D 9-10
Nyköping 114-115 G 8
Nyland = Uusimaa 114-115 KL 7
Nylstroom 198 E 6
Nymburk 124 G 3
Nynäshamn 114-115 GH 8
Nyngan 182-183 J 6
Nyong 194-195 G 8
Nyonga 198 F 3
Nyrud 114-115 N 3
Nysa 124 H 3
Nysa Kłodzka 124 H 3
Nyslott = Savonlinna 114-115 N 7
Nyssa, OR 66-67 E 4
Nystad = Uusikaupunki 114-115 J 7
Nytva 154-155 JK 6
Nyūdō-saki 170-171 M 2
Nyunzu 198 E 3

Nzega 198 F 2
N'Zérékoré 194-195 C 7
N'Zeto 198 B 3

O

Oa, Mull of — 116-117 E 5
Oahe, Lake — 58-59 F 2
Oahu 174-175 e 3
Oakbank 182-183 H 6
Oak City, UT 74-75 G 3
Oak Creek, CO 68-69 C 5
Oakdale, CA 74-75 C 4
Oakdale, LA 78-79 C 5
Oakdale, NE 68-69 GH 4
Oakes, ND 68-69 G 2
Oakey 182-183 K 5
Oak Grove, LA 78-79 D 4
Oakham 116-117 L 8
Oakharbor, OH 72-73 E 4
Oak Harbor, WA 66-67 B 1
Oak Hill, FL 80-81 c 2
Oak Hill, WV 72-73 F 5-6
Oakhurst, TX 76-77 G 7
Oak Island 70-71 E 2
Oak Lake [CDN, lake] 49 H 6
Oak Lake [CDN, place] 49 H 6
Oakland, CA 58-59 B 4
Oakland, IA 70-71 C 5
Oakland, MD 72-73 G 5
Oakland, NE 68-69 H 5
Oakland, OR 66-67 B 4
Oakland City, IN 70-71 G 6
Oak Lawn, IL 70-71 FG 5
Oaklawn, MD 82 II b 2
Oakley, ID 66-67 FG 4
Oakley, KS 68-69 F 6
Oakover River 182-183 D 4
Oak Park, IL 70-71 G 5
Oakridge, OR 66-67 B 4
Oak Ridge, TN 58-59 K 4
Oakville [CDN, Manitoba] 49 JK 6
Oakville [CDN, Ontario] 72-73 G 3
Oakwood, OK 76-77 E 5
Oakwood, TX 76-77 FG 7
Oakwood, New York-, NY 82 III b 3
Oamaru 182-183 O 9
Ōarai 170-171 N 4
Oasis, CA 74-75 DE 4
Oasis, NV 66-67 F 5
Oates Land 31 B 16-17
Oatman, AZ 74-75 F 5
Oaxaca 58-59 G 8

Ob' 154-155 NO 5
Ob, Gulf of — = Obskaja guba 154-155 N 3-4
Oba [CDN] 70-71 HJ 1
Oba [Vanuatu] 182-183 N 3
Oba Lake 70-71 H 1
Obama 170-171 K 5
Oban [CDN] 49 D 4
Oban [GB] 116-117 F 4
Oban [NZ] 182-183 N 9
Obara = Ōchi 170-171 J 5
Obdorsk = Salechard 154-155 M 4
Obeidh, El- = Al-Ubayyiḍ 194-195 KL 6
Oberá 103 F 3
Oberhausen 124 C 3
Oberlin, KS 68-69 F 6
Oberlin, LA 78-79 C 5
Oberon, ND 68-69 G 2
Oberösterreich 124 F-H 4
Oberpfälzer Wald 124 F 4
Oberstdorf 124 E 5
Obervolta 194-195 DE 6
Obetz, OH 72-73 E 5
Obi, Pulau — 174-175 J 7
Óbidos [BR] 98-99 HJ 5
Obihiro 166-167 R 3
Obion, TN 78-79 E 2
Objačevo 154-155 H 5
Obkeik, Jebel — = Jabal 'Ubkayk 194-195 M 4
Oblačnaja, gora — 154-155 Za 9
Oblučje 154-155 Z 8
Obo 194-195 K 7
Obock 194-195 N 6
Obojan 142-143 G 5
Obok = Obock 194-195 N 6
Obonai = Tazawako 170-171 N 3
Obonga Lake 50 E 2
Oboz'orskij 142-143 H 3
Obra 124 G 2
Obrayeri 88-89 DE 7
Obregón, Ciudad — 58-59 DE 6
Obrenovac 138-139 HJ 3
Obrian Peak = Trident Peak 66-67 D 5
Obrovac 138-139 F 3
Obščij Syrt 154-155 H-K 7
Obskaja guba 154-155 N 3-4
Obuasi 194-195 D 7
Obuchi = Rokkasho 170-171 N 2

Ocala, FL 58-59 K 6
Očamčire 142-143 H 7
Ocampo [MEX, Chihuahua] 86-87 F 3
Ocampo [MEX, Tamaulipas] 86-87 L 6
Ocaña [CO] 98-99 E 3
Ocaña [E] 132-133 F 9
Ocean 178 GH 3
Ocean City, MD 72-73 J 5
Ocean City, NJ 72-73 J 5
Ocean Falls 46-47 L 7
Oceanlake, OR 66-67 AB 3
Oceanside, CA 58-59 C 5
Ocean Springs, MS 78-79 E 5
Ocean Strip 66-67 A 2
Ocha 154-155 b 7
Öchë 138-139 L 6
Ochiai = Dolinsk 154-155 b 8
Ochil Hills 116-117 H 4
Ochiltree 48 FG 3
Ochoa, NM 76-77 C 6
Ochogbo = Oshogbo 194-195 EF 7
Öch'ŏng-do 170-171 E 4
Och'onjang 170-171 G 2
Ochota 154-155 b 5
Ochotsk 154-155 b 6
Ochotskij Perevoz 154-155 a 5
Ochre River 49 HJ 5
Ocilla, GA 80-81 E 5
Ockelbo 114-115 G 7
Ocmulgee National Monument 80-81 E 4
Ocmulgee River 80-81 E 4-5
Oconee River 80-81 E 4
Oconto, NE 68-69 FG 5
Oconto, WI 70-71 G 3
Oconto Falls, WI 70-71 FG 3
Oconto River 70-71 F 3
Ocotal 88-89 C 8
Ocotlán 58-59 F 7
Ocracoke Island 80-81 J 3
Octave, Rivière — 50 M 2
Octeville 116-117 K 11
October Revolution Island = ostrov Okt'abr'skoj Revol'ucii 154-155 Q-S 2
Oculi 88-89 D 7

Oda [GH] 194-195 D 7
Ōda [J] 170-171 J 5
'Ōda, Jebel — = Jabal Ūdah 194-195 M 4
Ódáđhahraun 114-115 e 2
Ōdaejin 170-171 GH 2
Odanah, WI 70-71 E 2
Ōdate 170-171 N 2
Odawara 170-171 M 5
O'Day 49 L 2
Odda 114-115 B 7
Oddur = Huddur Hadama 198 H 1
Odell, NE 68-69 H 5
Odem, TX 76-77 F 9
Odemira 132-133 C 10
Ödemis 142-143 E 8
Odendaalsrus 198 E 7
Odense 114-115 D 10
Odenwald 124 D 4
Oder 124 G 2
Oderzo 138-139 E 3
Odessa 142-143 F 6
Odessa, TX 58-59 F 5
Odessa, WA 66-67 D 2
Odienné 194-195 C 7
Odin, IL 70-71 F 6
Odiongan 174-175 H 4
Ōdomari = Korsakov 154-155 b 8
O'Donnell, TX 76-77 D 6
Odorheiul Secuiesc 138-139 L 2
Odra 124 H 3
Odum, GA 80-81 E 5
Odweeyne 194-195 b 2
Odzala 198 BC 1

Oelrichs, SD 68-69 E 4
Oelwein, IA 70-71 E 4
Oenpelli Mission 182-183 F 2
Oe-raro-do 170-171 F 5
Oeyŏn-do 170-171 F 4

O'Fallon Creek 68-69 D 2
Ofani, Gulf of — = Kólpos Orfánu 138-139 KL 5
Ofanto 138-139 F 5
Offenbach 124 D 3
Offenburg 124 CD 4
Ofooué 198 B 2
Ofotfjord 114-115 G 3
Ōfunato 170-171 NO 3

Oga 170-171 M 3
Ōgada 170-171 J 6
Ogaden = Wigadēn 194-195 NO 7
Oga hantō 170-171 M 3
Ōgaki 170-171 L 5
Ogallala, NE 68-69 EF 5
Ogasawara-guntō = Bonin 148-149 RS 7
Ogascanan, Lac — 72-73 GH 1
Ogashi 170-171 N 3
Ogashi tōge 170-171 MN 3
Ōgawara 170-171 N 2
Ogawara ko 170-171 N 2
Ogbomosho 194-195 E 7
Ogden, IA 70-71 C 4
Ogden, KS 68-69 H 6
Ogden, UT 58-59 D 3
Ogden, Mount — 52-53 V 7
Ogdensburg, NY 58-59 LM 3
Ogeechee River 80-81 EF 4
Ogema 49 F 6
Ogema, MN 70-71 BC 2
Ogi 170-171 M 4
Ogida = Hinai 170-171 N 2
Ogilby, CA 74-75 F 6
Ogilvie Mountains 46-47 J 4-5
Oglala Strait 52-53 s 7
Oglesby, IL 70-71 F 5
Ōglio 138-139 CD 3
Ogliuga Island 52-53 t 7
Ognon 132-133 KL 5
Ogoja 194-195 F 7
Ogoki 50 G 2
Ogoki Lake 50 F 2
Ogoki Reservoir 50 E 2
Ogoki River 46-47 T 7
Ogon'ok 154-155 ab 6
Ogooué 198 B 2
Ogr = 'Uqr 194-195 K 6
Ogué = Ogooué 198 B 2
Ogulin 138-139 F 3
Ogun 194-195 E 7
Ogurčinskij, ostrov — 160-161 G 3

Ohakune 182-183 P 7
Ōhara 170-171 N 5
Ōhasama 170-171 N 3
Ōhata 170-171 N 2
Ohazama 170-171 N 3
O'Higgins [RCH, place] 103 BC 2
Ohio 58-59 K 3
Ohio River 58-59 J 4
Ohogamiut, AK 52-53 G 6
Ohopoho 198 B 5
Ohōtuku-kai 170-171 cd 1
Ohře 124 G 3
Ohrid 138-139 J 5
Ohridsko Ezero 138-139 J 5
Ohuam 194-195 H 7
Ōhunato 170-171 NO 3

Oiapoque 98-99 J 4
Oiapoque, Rio — 98-99 J 4
Ōi gawa 170-171 M 5
Oil Bay 52-53 L 7
Oil City, PA 58-59 L 3
Oildale, CA 74-75 D 5
Oileán Ciarraighe 116-117 B 8
Oileán Mór, An t- 116-117 A 8
Oilton, TX 76-77 E 9
Oio = Oyo 194-195 E 7
Oir, Beinn an — 116-117 EF 5
Oirthir, Inis — 116-117 B 7
Oise 132-133 J 4
Ōita 170-171 H 6

Ojai, CA 74-75 D 5
Ojem = Oyem 194-195 G 8
Ojika-shima 170-171 G 6
Ojinaga 58-59 EF 6
Ojiya 170-171 M 4
Ojm'akon 154-155 b 5
Ojm'akonskoje nagorje 154-155 b 5
Ojocaliente 86-87 J 6
Ojo de Agua = Villa Ojo de Agua 103 D 3
Ojo de Laguna 86-87 G 3
Ojo de Liebre, Laguna — 86-87 CD 4
Öjöngö Nuur = Ojorong nuur 166-167 F 2
Ojorong nuur 166-167 F 2
Ojos del Salado, Nevado — 103 C 3
Ojrot-Tura = Gorno-Altajsk 154-155 Q 7
Ojtal = Merke 154-155 N 9

Oka [SU ◁ Bratskoje vodochranilišče] 154-155 T 7
Oka [SU ◁ Volga] 154-155 G 6
Okaba 174-175 L 8
Okahandja 198 C 6
Okaloacoochee Slough 80-81 c 3
Okanagan Falls 66-67 D 1
Okanagan Lake 46-47 MN 8
Okano 198 B 1
Okanogan, WA 66-67 D 1
Okanogan Range 66-67 CD 1
Okanogan River 66-67 D 1
Okarche, OK 76-77 F 5
Okaukuejo 198 C 5
Okavango 198 C 5
Okavango Basin 198 D 5
Ōkawara = Ōgawara 170-171 N 3-4
Okaya 170-171 LM 4
Okayama 166-167 P 5
Okazaki 170-171 L 5
Okeechobee, FL 80-81 c 3
Okeechobee, Lake — 58-59 K 6
Okeene, OK 76-77 E 4
Okefenokee Swamp 58-59 K 5
Okehampton 116-117 GH 10
Okemah, OK 76-77 F 5
Okene 194-195 F 7
Oketo 170-171 c 2
Okha 160-161 K 6
Okhotsk = Ochotsk 154-155 b 6
Okhotsk, Sea of — 154-155 b-d 6-7
Okhrid = Ohrid 138-139 J 5
Okhrid Lake = Ohridsko Ezero 138-139 J 5
Oki 166-167 P 4
Okinawa 166-167 O 6
Okinawa-guntō 166-167 O 6
Okino Daitō-jima 166-167 P 7
Okino-Daitō zima = Okino-Daitō-jima 166-167 P 7
Okino-shima 170-171 J 6
Okino-Tori-shima 166-167 Q 7
Okino-Tori sima = Okino-Tori-shima 166-167 Q 7
Okkang-dong 170-171 E 2
Oklahoma 58-59 G 4
Oklahoma City, OK 58-59 G 4
Okmok Volcano 52-53 m 4
Okmulgee, OK 76-77 FG 5
Okobojo Creek 68-69 F 3
Okokmilaga River 52-53 L 2
Okolona, MS 78-79 E 3-4
Okombahe 198 BC 6
Okoppe 170-171 c 1
Okotoks 48 L 4
Okoyo 198 BC 2
Okpilak River 52-53 PQ 2
Oksenof, Cape — 52-53 a 2
Øksfjordjøkelen 114-115 JK 2
Oksovskij 142-143 G 3
Okstindan 114-115 F 5
Okt'abr'sk [SU, Kazachskaja SSR] 154-155 K 8
Okt'abr'skaja magistral' 142-143 F 4
Okt'abr'skij [SU, Rossijskaja SFSR Baškirskaja ASSR] 154-155 JK 7
Okt'abr'skij [SU, Rossijskaja SFSR chrebet Džagdy] 154-155 Y 7
Okt'abr'skoje [SU, Chanty-Mansijskij NO] 154-155 M 5
Okt'abr'skoj Revol'ucii, ostrov — 154-155 Q-S 2
Oktember'an 142-143 H 7
Ōkuchi 170-171 H 6
Okujiri-shima 170-171 a 2
Okulovka 142-143 F 4
Okushiri = Okujiri-shima 170-171 a 2

Ola, AR 78-79 C 3
Ola, ID 66-67 E 3
Ola [SU, Rossijskaja SFSR] 154-155 d 6
Olaa = Keaau, HI 78-79 e 3
Olaf Prydz bukt 31 C 8
Ólafsfjörđhur 114-115 d 1
Ólafsvík 114-115 ab 2
Olancha Peak 74-75 D 4
Öland 114-115 G 9
Olanga 114-115 NO 4
Olary 182-183 GH 6
Olathe, KS 70-71 C 6
Olavarría 103 DE 5
Ólbia 138-139 C 5
Ol'chon, ostrov — 154-155 U 7
Ol'chovskij = Art'omovsk 154-155 R 7
Olcott, NY 72-73 G 3
Old Castile = Castilla la Vieja 132-133 E 8-F 7
Oldcastle = An Sean-chaisleán 116-117 D 7
Old Chitambo = Livingstone Memorial 198 F 4
Old Crow 46-47 J 4
Old Crow River 52-53 RS 2
Oldeani [EAT, mountain] 198 FG 2
Oldeani [EAT, place] 198 G 2
Oldenburg 124 CD 2
Old Faithful, WY 66-67 H 3
Old Ford Bay 51 GH 2
Old Forge, NY 72-73 J 3
Old Fort 48 D 2
Old Gumbiro 198 G 3-4
Oldham 116-117 JK 7
Oldham, SD 68-69 H 3
Old Harbor, AK 52-53 fg 1
Old Head of Kinsale = Dún Cearmna 116-117 C 9
Old Hogem 48 E 2
Old John Lake 52-53 P 2
Old Man on His Back Plateau 68-69 B 1
Oldman River 49 B 6
Oldmeldrum 116-117 J 3
Old Orchard Beach, ME 72-73 LM 3
Old Perlican 51 K 3
Old Rampart, AK 52-53 QR 3
Olds 48 KL 4
Old Town, ME 72-73 M 2
Old Wives 49 E 5
Old Wives Lake 49 F 5-6
Old Woman Mountains 74-75 F 5
Old Woman River 52-53 GH 5
Öldzijt 166-167 J 2
Olean, NY 72-73 G 3
O'Leary 51 D 4
Olecko 124 L 1
Ölegey = Ölgij 166-167 FG 2
Olene, OR 66-67 C 4
Olenegorsk 142-143 FG 2
Olenek = Olen'ok 154-155 X 3
Olenij, ostrov — 154-155 O 3
Olen'ok [SU, place] 154-155 V 4
Olen'ok [SU, river] 154-155 X 3
Olen'okskij zaliv 154-155 WX 3
Oléron, Île d' 132-133 G 6
Oleśnica 124 H 3
Ol'ga 154-155 a 9
Olga, Lac — 50 N 2
Olga, Mount — 182-183 EF 5
Olga Bay 52-53 f 1
Olgastretet 114-115 m 5
Ölgij 166-167 FG 2
Olhão 132-133 D 10
Olib 138-139 F 3
Olifantsrivier [Namibia] 198 C 6-7
Olifantsrivier [ZA, Transvaal] 198 F 6
Oliktot Point 52-53 N 1
Olimarao 174-175 MN 5
Olinalá 86-87 L 9
Olinda 98-99 N 6
O-Ling Hu = Ngoring Tsho 166-167 H 4-5
Olio 182-183 H 4
Oliva 132-133 GH 9
Oliva, Cordillera de — 103 BC 3
Olivares de Júcar 132-133 F 9
Olive, MT 68-69 D 3

256 N'Riquin

Olive Hill, KY 72-73 E 5
Olivenza 132-133 D 9
Oliver 66-67 D 1
Oliver Lake 49 G 2
Olivet, MI 68-69 H 4
Olivia, MN 70-71 C 3
Olkusz 124 J 3
Olla, LA 78-79 C 5
Ollagüe 103 C 2
Ollas Arriba 58-59 b 3
Ollerton 116-117 KL 7
Ollie, MT 68-69 D 2
Ollita, Cordillera de — 103 B 4
Olmos [PE] 98-99 CD 6
Olney 116-117 L 8
Olney, IL 70-71 FG 6
Olney, MT 66-67 F 1
Olney, TX 76-77 E 6
Olofström 114-115 F 9
Oloj 154-155 f 4
Ol'okma 154-155 X 5-6
Ol'okminsk 154-155 WX 5
Ol'okminskij stanovik
154-155 W 7-X 6
Ol'okmo-Čarskoje ploskogorje
154-155 WX 6
Olomane, Rivière — 51 F 2
Olomouc 124 H 4
Ölön = Lün 166-167 K 2
Olongapo 174-175 GH 4
Oloron-Sainte-Marie 132-133 G 7
Olot 132-133 J 7
Olov'annaja 154-155 W 7
Öls nuur 166-167 G 4
Olsztyn 124 K 2
Olt 138-139 L 3
Olten 124 C 5
Oltenița 138-139 M 3
Olteț 138-139 KL 3
Olton, TX 76-77 C 5
Olustee, OK 76-77 E 5
Ol'utorskij, mys — 154-155 h 6
Ol'utorskij poluostrov 154-155 h 5
Ol'utorskij zaliv 154-155 g 5-6
Olvera 132-133 E 10
Olympia, WA 58-59 B 2
Olympia [GR] 138-139 J 7
Olympic Mountains 66-67 AB 2
Olympic National Park 66-67 A 2
Ólympos [GR, mountain]
138-139 K 5-6
Ólympos [GR, place] 138-139 M 8
Olympus, Mount — 66-67 B 2
Olyphant, PA 72-73 J 4
Olyutorski Bay = Ol'utorskij zaliv
154-155 g 5-6

Om' 154-155 O 6
Ōma 170-171 N 2
Ōmachi 170-171 L 4
Omae-zaki 170-171 M 5
Ōmagari 170-171 N 3
Om Ager = Om Hajer 194-195 M 6
Omagh 116-117 D 6
Omaha, NE 58-59 G 3
Omaha, TX 76-77 G 6
Omak, WA 66-67 D 1
Omak Lake 66-67 D 1
Oman 160-161 H 6-7
Oman, Gulf of — 160-161 HJ 6
Omar, WV 80-81 E 2
Omaruru 198 C 6
Ōma-saki 170-171 N 2
Omatako, Omuramba — 198 C 5-6
Omate 98-99 E 8
Ombella-Mpoko 194-195 H 7-8
Ombepera 198 B 5
Omboué 198 A 2
Ombrone 138-139 D 4
Ombu = Umbu 166-167 F 5
Ombuctá 103 D 5
Omčak 154-155 c 5
Omdurmān = Umm Durmān
194-195 L 5
O-mei Shan = Emei Shan
166-167 J 6
Omemee, ND 68-69 F 1
Omer, MI 70-71 HJ 3
Ometepe, Isla de — 58-59 J 9
Omgon, mys — 154-155 e 6
Om Hajer 194-195 M 6
Ōminato 170-171 N 2
Omineca Mountains 46-47 LM 6
Omineca River 48 D 1-E 2
Omiš 138-139 G 4
Ōmi-shima 170-171 H 5
Ōmiya 170-171 M 4-5
Ommaney, Cape — 52-53 v 8
Ommanney Bay 46-47 Q 3
Ömnödelger 166-167 KL 2
Ömnögov' ◁ 166-167 K 3
Omo [ETH] 194-195 M 7
Omo Bottego = Omo 194-195 M 7
Omoloj 154-155 Z 3
Omolon [SU, place] 154-155 e 5
Omolon [SU, river] 154-155 e 4-f 5
Ōmon 170-171 J 5
Omono-gawa 170-171 N 3
Omsk 154-155 N 7
Omsukčan 154-155 de 5
Ōmu 166-167 R 3
Omul 138-139 L 3
Ōmura 170-171 G 6
Ōmura wan 170-171 G 6
Omuta 166-167 OP 5
Omutninsk 154-155 J 6

Ona, FL 80-81 bc 3
Onaga, KS 70-71 BC 6
Onagawa 170-171 N 3
Onahama = Iwaki 170-171 N 4
Onakawana 50 KL 1
Onalaska, WA 66-67 B 2
Onaman Lake 50 F 3
Onamia, MN 70-71 D 2
Onancock, VA 80-81 HJ 2
Onangué, Lac — 198 AB 2
Onaping Lake 50 L 3
Onaqui, UT 66-67 G 5
Onarga, IL 70-71 FG 5
Onawa, IA 70-71 BC 4
Onaway, MI 70-71 HJ 3
Onças, Ilha das — 98-99 K 6
Onças, Serra das — 98-99 H 9-10
Onch'on-ni = Onyang 170-171 F 4
Oncócua 198 B 5
Ondangua 198 C 5
Ondo 194-195 EF 7
Öndörchaan 166-167 L 2
Öndör Han = Öndörchaan
166-167 L 2
Ondor Khan = Öndörchaan
166-167 L 2
One and Half Degree Channel 36 a 2
Onega [SU, place] 154-155 F 5
Onega [SU, river] 154-155 F 5
Onega, Lake — = Onežkoje ozero
154-155 EF 5
Onega Bay = Onežkaja guba
154-155 F 4-5
Oneida, NY 72-73 J 3
Oneida, TN 78-79 G 2
Oneida Lake 72-73 HJ 3
O'Neill, NE 68-69 G 4
Onekama, MI 70-71 G 3
Onekotan, ostrov — 30 E 3
Oneonta, AL 78-79 F 4
Oneonta, NY 72-73 J 3
One Tree Peak 76-77 B 6
Onežskaja guba 154-155 F 5
Onežskij poluostrov 154-155 F 5
Onežskoje ozero 154-155 EF 5
Ongerup 182-183 C 6
Ongijn gol 166-167 J 2
Ongjin 166-167 NO 4
Ongole 160-161 MN 7
Ôñgūlu = Ongole 160-161 MN 7
Onib, Khōr — = Khawr Unib 199 D 7
Onida, SD 68-69 FG 3
Onilahy 198 HJ 6
Onion Lake 49 D 4
Onistagane, Lac — 51 A 2
Onitsha 194-195 F 7
Onjŏng 170-171 EF 2
Onjŏng-ni 170-171 E 3
Ōno [J, Fukui] 170-171 L 5
Onoda 170-171 H 5-6
Onomichi 170-171 J 5
Onon gol 166-167 L 2
Onotoa 178 H 3
Onslow 182-183 C 4
Onslow Bay 58-59 L 5
Onsong 170-171 GH 1
Ontake san 170-171 L 5
Ontario 46-47 S 7-V 8
Ontario, CA 74-75 E 5
Ontario, OR 66-67 E 3
Ontario, Lake — 58-59 L 3
Ontario Peninsula 46-47 UV 9
Ontonagon, MI 70-71 F 2
Ontong Java Islands 174-175 j 6
Onverwacht 98-99 H 3

Oodnadatta 182-183 G 5
Ooldea 182-183 F 6
Oolitic, IN 70-71 G 6
Oologah Lake 76-77 G 4
Ooratippra 182-183 G 4
Oos-Londen 198 E 8
Oostende 132-133 J 3
Oosterschelde 132-133 JK 3
Ootsa Lake [CDN, lake] 48 E 3
Ootsa Lake [CDN, place] 48 E 3

Opal, WY 66-67 H 5
Opala [SU] 154-155 e 7
Opala [ZRE] 198 D 2
Opal City, OR 66-67 C 3
Oparino 154-155 H 6
Opasatika Lake 50 K 2
Opasatika River 50 K 2
Opasquia 50 C 1
Opataka, Lac — 50 O 1
Opatawaga, Lac — 50 N 1
Opatija 138-139 EF 3
Opava 124 H 4
Opawica, Rivière — 50 O 2
Opazatika Lake 70-71 J 1
Opelika, AL 78-79 G 4
Opelousas, LA 78-79 CD 5
Opémisca, Lac — 50 O 1
Opémisca, Mont — 50 O 1-2
Opeongo Lake 72-73 GH 2
Opera House [USA] 83 I b 2
Opheim, MT 68-69 C 1
Ophir, AK 46-47 E 5
Ophir, OR 66-67 A 4
Ophira 199 D 4
Ophthalmia Range 182-183 CD 4
Opienge 198 E 1
Opočka 142-143 E 4
Opole 124 HJ 3
Opole Lubelskie 124 KL 3
Oporto = Porto 132-133 C 8
Opp, AL 78-79 F 5
Oppa gawa 170-171 N 3
Oppdal 114-115 C 6
Oppeid 114-115 F 3
Oppland 114-115 C 6-D 7
Optima, OK 76-77 D 4
Opunake 182-183 O 7

'Oqr = 'Uqr 194-195 K 6
Oquawka, IL 70-71 E 5

Or, Côte d' 132-133 K 5
'Or, Wâdî — = Wādī Ur 199 B 6-7
Oradea 138-139 JK 2
Öræfajökull 114-115 e 2
Orahovica 138-139 GH 3
Or'ahovo 138-139 KL 4
Oraibi, AZ 74-75 H 5
Oran, MO 78-79 E 2
Orán = San Ramón de la Nueva Orán
103 CD 2
Oran = Wahrān 194-195 D 1
Orange, CA 74-75 E 6
Orange, NJ 82 III a 2
Orange, TX 58-59 H 5
Orange, VA 72-73 GH 5
Orange [AUS] 182-183 J 6
Orange [F] 132-133 K 6
Orange = Oranje-Vrystaat 198 E 7
Orange, Cabo — 98-99 J 4
Orange Beach, AL 78-79 F 5
Orangeburg, SC 58-59 K 5
Orange City, IA 70-71 BC 4
Orange Cliffs 74-75 H 3
Orangedale 51 F 5
Orange Free State = Oranje-Vrystaat
198 E 7
Orange Grove, TX 76-77 EF 9
Orange Park, FL 80-81 bc 1
Orange River = Oranjerivier [ZA, river]
198 D 7
Orangeville 72-73 FG 3
Orange Walk Town 86-87 Q 8-9
Orango, Ilha de — 194-195 A 6
Orani [RP] 174-175 GH 4
Oranje = Oranjerivier 198 BC 7
Oranje Gebergte 98-99 HJ 4
Oranje Gebergte = Pegunungan
Jayawijaya 174-175 LM 7
Oranjerivier [ZA, river] 198 D 7
Oranjestad 58-59 NM 9
Oranje-Vrystaat 198 E 7
Orawia 182-183 N 9
Orbetello 138-139 D 4
Orbost 182-183 J 7
Örbyhus 114-115 G 7
Orca, AK 52-53 P 6
Orca Bay 52-53 OP 6
Orcadas 31 CD 32
Orchard, ID 66-67 EF 4
Orchard, NE 68-69 GH 4
Orchard Homes, MT 66-67 F 2
Orchila, Isla — 98-99 F 2
Orchómenos 138-139 K 6
Orchon gol 166-167 J 2
Ord, NE 68-69 G 5
Ördene 166-167 L 3
Orderville, UT 74-75 G 4
Ordi, el — = Dunqulah
194-195 KL 5
Ord Mountain 74-75 E 5
Ordos 166-167 K 4
Ord River 182-183 E 3
Ordu 160-161 D 2
Ordway, CO 68-69 E 6
Ordžonikidze 142-143 HJ 7
Orealla 98-99 H 3
Oreana, NV 66-67 D 5
Örebro [S, administrative unit]
114-115 F 8
Örebro [S, place] 114-115 F 8
Oregon 58-59 BC 3
Oregon, IL 70-71 F 4-5
Oregon, MO 70-71 C 5-6
Oregon, WI 70-71 F 4
Oregon Butte 66-67 E 2
Oregon City, OR 66-67 B 3
Oregon Inlet 80-81 J 3
Öregrund 114-115 H 7
Orekhovo-Zuyevo = Orechovo-Zujevo
154-155 FG 6
Orem, UT 66-67 H 5
Ore Mountains = Erzgebirge 124 F 3
Orenburg 154-155 JK 7
Orense [E] 132-133 D 7
Öresund 114-115 E 10
Orfa = Urfa 160-161 D 3
Orfánu, Kólpos — 138-139 KL 5
Orford 116-117 h 6
Orford Ness 116-117 h 6
Organ Pipe Cactus National
Monument 58-59 D 5
Orick, CA 66-67 A 5
Orient, SD 68-69 G 3
Orient, TX 76-77 D 7
Orient, WA 66-67 D 1
Oriental 86-87 M 8
Oriental, NC 80-81 H 3
Oriente [BR, Acre] 98-99 CD 9
Oriente [C] 58-59 LM 7
Orihuela 132-133 G 9
Orillia 46-47 V 9
Orin, WY 68-69 D 4
Orinduik 98-99 HJ 2
Orinoco, Delta del — 98-99 G 3
Orinoco, Llanos del — 98-99 E 4-F 3
Orinoco, Río — 98-99 F 3
Orion 66-67 H 1
Orion, IL 70-71 E 5
Orissa 160-161 N 7-O 6
Oristano 138-139 C 6
Orivesi [SF, lake] 114-115 N 6
Orivesi [SF, place] 114-115 L 7
Oriximiná 98-99 H 5
Orizaba 58-59 G 8
Orizaba, Pico de — 86-87 M 8
Orizaba, Pico de — = Citlaltépetl
58-59 G 8
Orkanger 114-115 C 6
Orkney 116-117 J 2
Orla, TX 76-77 BC 7
Orland, CA 74-75 B 3
Orlando, FL 58-59 K 6
Orléanais 132-133 HJ 4-5
Orléans 132-133 HJ 5
Orleans, NE 68-69 G 5
Orléans, Île d' 51 A 4
Orléansville = Al-Asnām
194-195 E 1
Orlik 154-155 S 7
Orlinga 154-155 U 6
Orlov = Chalturin 154-155 H 6
Ormārā 160-161 JK 5
Ormoc 174-175 HJ 4
Ormond Beach, FL 80-81 c 2
Ormsby 72-73 GH 2
Ormuz, Strait of — = Tangeh
Hormoz 160-161 H 5
Orne 132-133 G 4
Örnsköldsvik 114-115 H 6
Oro, El — [MEX, Coahuila] 76-77 C 9
Oro, El — [MEX, México] 86-87 K 8
Oročen 154-155 Y 6
Orocué 98-99 E 4
Orodara 194-195 CD 6
Orofino, ID 66-67 EF 2
Orogrande, NM 76-77 AB 6
Or'ol 142-143 G 5
Oroluk 178 F 2
Oromocto 51 C 5
Orongo gol 166-167 F 2
Orono, ME 72-73 M 2
Oronoque 98-99 H 4
Oronoque River 98-99 K 3-4
Oronsay 116-117 E 4
Oronsay Passage 116-117 E 5-F 4
Orope 98-99 E 3
Oroquieta 174-175 H 5
Oro-ri 170-171 F 2
Oros 98-99 M 6
Orosei 138-139 C 5
Orosháza 124 K 5
Orosi, Volcán — 58-59 JK 9
Orotukan 154-155 d 5
Orovada, NV 66-67 DE 5
Oroville, CA 74-75 C 3
Oroville, WA 66-67 D 1
Oroya, La — 98-99 D 7
Orpha, WY 68-69 D 4
Orr, MN 70-71 D 1
Orrville, OH 72-73 F 4
Orsa [S] 114-115 F 7
Orša [SU] 142-143 EF 5
Orsk 154-155 K 7
Orșova 138-139 K 3
Ørsta 114-115 AB 6
Ortegal, Cabo — 132-133 CD 7
Orthez 132-133 G 7
Ortigueira 132-133 CD 7
Orting, WA 66-67 BC 2
Ortler = Ortles 138-139 D 2
Ortles 138-139 D 2
Ortona 138-139 F 4
Ortonville, MN 68-69 H 3
Orūmīyeh 160-161 E 3
Orūmīyeh, Daryācheh-ye —
160-161 E 3
Oruro [BOL, place] 98-99 F 8
Orust 114-115 D 8
Orvieto 138-139 DE 4
Orville Escarpment 31 B 29-30

Oš [SU] 160-161 L 2
Osa 142-143 L 4
Osa, Península de — 58-59 JK 10
Osage, IA 70-71 D 4
Osage, WY 68-69 D 4
Osage City, KS 70-71 BC 6
Osage Indian Reservation 76-77 F 4
Osage River 58-59 H 4
Ōsaka 166-167 Q 5
Ōsaka wan 170-171 K 5
Osakis, MN 70-71 C 3
Osâm 138-139 L 4
Osan 170-171 F 4
Ošarovo 154-155 S 5
Osawatomie, KS 70-71 C 6
Osborne 49 K 6
Osborne, KS 68-69 G 6
Osborne, Cerro — = Mount Usborne
103 E 8
Osby 114-115 EF 9
Osceola, AR 78-79 DE 3
Osceola, IA 70-71 D 5
Osceola, MO 70-71 D 6
Osceola, NE 68-69 H 5
Osceola, WI 70-71 D 3
Oscoda, MI 72-73 E 2
Oscura, Sierra — 76-77 A 6
Oscura Peak 76-77 A 6
Ösel = Saaremaa 142-143 D 4
Ōse-zaki 170-171 G 6
Osgood, IN 70-71 H 6
Oshamambe 170-171 b 2
Oshawa 46-47 V 9
Ō-shima [J, Hokkaidō] 170-171 a 3
Ō-shima [J, Nagasaki] 170-171 G 6
Ō-shima [J, Sizuoka] 170-171 M 5
Ō-shima [J, Wakayama] 170-171 KL 6
Oshima hantō 166-167 Q 3
Oshkosh, NE 68-69 E 5
Oshkosh, WI 58-59 HJ 3
Oshogbo 194-195 EF 7
Oshwe 198 CD 2
Osijek 138-139 H 3
Osima hantō = Oshima-hantō
166-167 QR 3
Osinniki 154-155 Q 7
Oskaloosa, IA 58-59 H 3
Oskaloosa, KS 70-71 C 6
Oskar II land 114-115 j 5
Oskarshamn 114-115 G 9
Oskelaneo 50 O 2
Oslo 114-115 D 8
Oslo, MN 68-69 H 1
Oslofjord 114-115 D 8
Osnabrück 124 D 2
Osnaburgh House 50 D 2
Oso, WA 66-67 C 1
Osogovski Planini 138-139 K 4
Osório, Salto — 103 F 3
Osório Fonseca 98-99 JK 6
Osorno [RCH] 103 B 6
Osorno, Volcán — 103 B 6
Osowiec 124 L 2
Osoyoos 66-67 D 1
Osøyra 114-115 A 7
Ospika River 48 F 1
Ossa 138-139 K 6
Ossa, Mount — 182-183 J 8
Ossabaw Island 80-81 F 5
Osseo, WI 70-71 E 3
Ossidinge = Mamfé 194-195 F 7
Ossineke, MI 70-71 J 3
Ossining, NY 72-73 K 4
Ossipee, NH 72-73 L 3
Ossora 154-155 f 6
Ostaškov 142-143 F 4
Oste 124 D 2
Ostend = Oostende 132-133 J 3
Österbotten = Pohjanmaa
114-115 K 6-M 5
Österdalälven 114-115 E 7
Østerdalen 114-115 D 7
Östergötland 114-115 F 8-9
Østerø = Eysturoy 116-117 b 1
Östersund 114-115 F 6
Østfold 114-115 D 8
Ostfriesische Inseln 124 C 2
Östhammar 114-115 GH 7
Ostia Antica, Roma- 138-139 DE 5
Ostrava 124 J 4
Ostróda 124 JK 2
Ostrołęka 124 KL 2
Ostrov [CS] 124 H 4-5
Ostrov [SU] 142-143 E 4
Ostrowiec Świętokrzyski 124 KL 3
Ostrów Mazowiecka 124 KL 2
Ostrów Wielkopolski 124 HJ 3
Osttirol 124 F 5
Ostuni 138-139 G 5
O'Sullivan Lake 50 F 2
O'Sullivan Reservoir = Potholes
Reservoir 66-67 D 2
Osum 138-139 J 5
Osumi Channel = Ōsumi-kaikyō
166-167 P 5
Ōsumi-kaikyō 166-167 P 5
Ōsumi-shotō 166-167 OP 5
Ōsumisyotō = Ōsumi-shotō
166-167 OP 5
Osuna 132-133 E 10
Oswego, KS 76-77 G 4
Oswego, NY 58-59 L 3
Oswego = Lake Oswego, OR
66-67 B 3
Oswestry 116-117 HJ 8
Oświęcim 124 J 3-4

Ōta 170-171 M 4
Ōta = Mino-Kamo 170-171 L 5
Otadaonanis River 50 H 1
Otago Peninsula 182-183 O 9
Ōtahara = Ōtawara 170-171 N 4
Ōtake 170-171 HJ 5
Otaki 182-183 OP 8
Ōtakine yama 170-171 N 4
Otar 154-155 O 9
Otare, Cerro — 98-99 E 4
Otaru 166-167 QR 3
Otaru-wan = Ishikari-wan
170-171 b 2
Otatal, Cerro — 86-87 E 3
Otavalo 98-99 D 4
Otavi 198 C 5
Otawi = Otavi 198 C 5
Oteros, Río — 86-87 F 4
Otgon Tenger uul 166-167 H 2
O'The Cherokees, Lake — 76-77 G 4
Othello, WA 66-67 D 2
Othōnoí 138-139 H 6
Óthrys 138-139 K 6
Oti 194-195 E 7
Otis, CO 68-69 E 5
Otis, OR 66-67 B 3
Otish Mountains 46-47 W 7
Otjekondo 198 C 5
Otjiwarongo 198 C 6
Otley 116-117 K 7
Otobe 170-171 b 2-3
Otofuke 170-171 c 2
Otoineppu 170-171 c 1
Otoskwin River 50 D 2
Otpor = Zabajkal'sk 154-155 W 8
Otra 114-115 B 8
Ótranto 138-139 H 5
Ótranto, Canale d' 138-139 H 5-6
Otsego, MI 70-71 GH 4
Ōtsu [J, Hokkaidō] 170-171 c 2
Ōtsu [J, Shiga] 170-171 KL 5
Ōtsuchi 170-171 NO 3
Otta 114-115 C 7
Ottawa 46-47 V 8
Ottawa, IL 70-71 F 5
Ottawa, KS 70-71 C 6
Ottawa, OH 70-71 HJ 5
Ottawa Islands 46-47 U 6
Ottawa River 46-47 V 8
Ottenby 114-115 G 9
Otter 51 E 3
Otter, Peaks of — 80-81 G 2
Otter Creek 68-69 C 3
Otter Creek, FL 80-81 b 2
Otterie Saint Mary 116-117 HJ 10
Otter Lake 72-73 G 2
Otter Lake, MI 72-73 E 3
Otter Passage 48 BC 3
Otter River 50 E 1
Ottumwa, IA 58-59 H 3
Otukamamoan Lake 50 C 3
Oturkpo 194-195 F 7
Otuzco 98-99 D 6
Otway, Bahía — 103 AB 8
Otway, Cape — 182-183 H 7
Otway, Seno — 103 B 8
Otwock 124 K 2
Ötztaler Alpen 124 E 5

Ouachita Mountains 58-59 GH 5
Ouachita River 58-59 H 5
Ouadaï 194-195 HJ 6
Ouadda 194-195 J 7
Ouagadougou 194-195 D 6
Ouahigouya 194-195 D 6
Ouahran = Wahrān 194-195 D 2
Ouaka 194-195 J 7
Oualata = Walātah 194-195 C 5
Oua n'Ahaggar, Tassili — = Tāsīlī
Wān al-Hajjār 194-195 E 5-F 4
Ouanary 98-99 MN 2
Ouanda Djallé 194-195 J 7
Ouango = Kouango 194-195 HJ 7
Ouangolodougou 194-195 C 7
Ouareau, Rivière — 72-73 JK 1
Ouargla = Warqlā 194-195 F 2
Ouasiemsca, Rivière — 50 P 2
Ouataouais, Rivière — 50 NO 3
Oubangui 198 C 1
Ouchougan Rapids 51 C 2
Oudtshoorn 198 D 8
Oued, El- = Al-Wād 194-195 F 2
Oued Zem = Wād Zam 194-195 C 2
Oueïta 194-195 J 5
Ouémé [DY, river] 194-195 E 7
Ouessant, Île d' 132-133 E 4
Ouesso 198 C 1
Ouezzân = Wazzān 194-195 C 2
Oughter, Lough — = Loch Uachtair
116-117 D 6
Ouham-Pendé 194-195 H 7
Ouidah 194-195 E 7
Ouina 194-195 G 7
Oulainen 114-115 L 5
Oulu 114-115 LM 5
Oulujärvi 114-115 M 5
Oulujoki 114-115 M 5
Oum-Chalouba 194-195 J 5
Oum ed Drouss, Sebka — = Sabkhat
Umm ad-Durūs 194-195 B 4
Oum er Rbia, Ouèd — = Wād Umm
ar-Rabīyah 194-195 C 2
Oum-Hadjer 194-195 H 6
Oumm el Drouss, Sebkha — =
Sabkhat Umm ad-Durūs
194-195 B 4
Ounasjoki 114-115 L 4
Ounastunturi 114-115 KL 3
Ounasvaara 114-115 LM 4
Oundle 116-117 L 8
Ounianga-Kebir 194-195 J 5
Oupu 166-167 O 1
Ouray, CO 68-69 C 6-7
Ouray, UT 66-67 J 5
Ourém 98-99 K 5
Ouri 194-195 H 4
Ourinhos 98-99 K 9
Ourique 132-133 C 10
Ouro Preto [BR, Minas Gerais]
98-99 L 9
Ouro Preto [BR, Pará] 98-99 LM 7
Ouro Preto, Rio — 98-99 F 10

Ouro 257

Parkin, AR 78-79 D 3
Parkland 48 KL 4
Parklawn, VA 82 II a 2
Parkman 49 H 6
Parkman, WY 68-69 C 3
Park Range 58-59 E 3-4
Park Rapids, MN 70-71 C 2
Park Ridge, IL 70-71 FG 4
Park River 68-69 H 1
Park River, ND 68-69 H 1
Parkside 49 E 4
Parkside, San Fransisco-, CA 83 I b 2
Parkston, SD 68-69 GH 4
Parksville 66-67 A 1
Park Valley, UT 66-67 G 5
Park View, NM 76-77 A 4
Parlākimidi 160-161 NO 7
Parma 138-139 D 3
Parma, ID 66-67 E 4
Parma, MO 78-79 E 2
Parma, OH 72-73 F 4
Parnaguá 98-99 L 7
Parnaíba 98-99 L 5
Parnaíba, Rio — 98-99 L 5
Parnassós 138-139 K 6
Párnēs 138-139 K 6
Párnōn 138-139 K 7
Pärnu 142-143 D 4
Paromaj 154-155 b 7
Paroo Channel 182-183 H 6
Páros 138-139 L 7
Parowan, UT 74-75 G 4
Parr, SC 80-81 F 3
Parral 103 B 5
Parral, Hidalgo del — 58-59 EF 6
Parramore Island 80-81 J 2
Parras de la Fuente 58-59 F 6
Parrett, River — 116-117 J 9
Parrita 88-89 D 10
Parrsboro 51 D 5
Parry 49 F 6
Parry, Cape — 46-47 M 3
Parry Bay 46-47 U 4
Parry Island 72-73 F 2
Parry Islands 46-47 M-R 2
Parrygya 114-115 kl 4
Parry Sound 50 L 4
Parsa = Persepolis 160-161 G 5
Parsnip River 46-47 M 6-7
Parsons, KS 58-59 G 4
Parsons, TN 78-79 E 3
Parsons, WV 72-73 G 5
Parson's Pond 51 GH 2-3
Parta Jebel 138-139 J 3
Pårtefjället 114-115 GH 4
Parthenay 132-133 GH 5
Partinico 138-139 E 6
Partizansk 154-155 Z 9
Partridge, KS 68-69 GH 7
Partridge River 50 L 1
Paru, Rio — [BR] 98-99 J 5
Paru de Este, Río — 98-99 L 3-4
Paru de Oeste, Rio — 98-99 L 3-4
Pārvatī = Pārbati 160-161 M 5
Pārvatīpurom 160-161 N 7
Pasadena, CA 58-59 C 5
Pasadena, TX 58-59 GH 6
Pasáiste, An — 116-117 C 9
Pasaje 98-99 D 5
Pasajes de San Juan 132-133 FG 7
Pascagama, Rivière — 50 O 2
Pascagoula, MS 58-59 J 5
Pascagoula River 78-79 E 5
Paşcani 138-139 M 2
Pasco, WA 66-67 D 2
Pasewalk 124 FG 2
Pashāwar 160-161 KL 4
Pashchimī Bangāl = West Bengal 160-161 O 6
Pashid Haihsia 166-167 N 7
P'asina 154-155 QR 3
P'asino, ozero — 154-155 QR 4
P'asinskij zaliv 154-155 PQ 3
Pasión, Río — 86-87 PQ 9
Pasir Besar = Kampung Pasir Besar 174-175 D 6
Paska 50 F 2
Paskenta, CA 74-75 B 3
Pasley, Cape — 182-183 D 6
Pašman [YU] 138-139 F 4
Pasnī 160-161 J 5
Paso, El — 98-99 E 3
Paso Caballos 86-87 PQ 9
Paso de Indios 103 BC 6
Paso de los Libres 103 E 3
Paso de los Toros 103 EF 4
Paso Robles, CA 74-75 C 5
Paspébiac 51 D 3
Pasquia Hills 49 G 4
Passage West = An Pasáiste 116-117 C 9
Passaic, NJ 82 III b 1
Passau 124 F 4
Pass Cavallo 76-77 FG 8
Pàssero, Capo — 138-139 F 7
Passo Fundo 103 F 3
Passos 98-99 K 9
Pastaza, Río — 98-99 D 5
Pasto 98-99 D 4
Pastol Bay 52-53 F 5
Pastora Peak 74-75 J 4
Pastura, NM 76-77 B 5
Pasvikelv 114-115 NO 3
Patagonia 103 B 8-C 6
Patagonia, AZ 74-75 H 7
Patagonian Cordillera = Cordillera Patagónica 103 B 8-5
Patagonian Shelf 26-27 FG 8
Patagónica, Cordillera — 103 B 8-5
Pātan [Nepal] 160-161 NO 5
Patana = Pattani 174-175 D 5
Patane = Pattani 174-175 D 5
Patang = Batang 166-167 H 6
Patargān, Daqq-e — 160-161 J 4
Patauá, Cachoeira — 98-99 HJ 9
Patchogue, NY 72-73 K 4
Pateley Bridge 116-117 JK 6
Paternò 138-139 F 7
Pateros, WA 66-67 D 1-2
Paterson, NJ 72-73 J 4
Paterson, WA 66-67 D 2-3
Pathfinder Reservoir 68-69 C 4
Pathum Thani 174-175 CD 4
Patía, Río — 98-99 D 4
Patiāla 160-161 M 4
Patience Well 182-183 E 4
P'atigorsk 142-143 H 7
Paṭiyālā = Patiāla 160-161 M 4
Pátmos 138-139 M 7
Patna 160-161 O 5
Patomskoje nagorje 154-155 V 6-W 6
Patos [BR, Paraíba] 98-99 M 6
Patos, Lagoa dos — 103 F 4
Patos, Laguna de — 86-87 GH 2
Patquía 103 C 4
Pátrai 138-139 J 6
Patraïkós Kólpos 138-139 J 6-7
Patras = Pátrai 138-139 JK 6
Patras, Gulf of — = Patraïkós Kólpos 138-139 J 6-7
Patreksfjördhur 114-115 ab 2
Patricia, SD 68-69 F 4
Patricia [CDN, landscape] 46-47 S-U 7
Patricia [CDN, place] 49 C 5
Patricio Lynch, Isla — 103 A 7
Patrington 116-117 LM 7
Patrocínio 98-99 K 8
Patta Island 198 H 2
Pattani 174-175 D 5
Patten, ME 72-73 M 2
Patterson, CA 74-75 C 4
Patterson, GA 80-81 E 5
Patti 138-139 F 6
Pattiá 98-99 D 4
Patton, PA 72-73 G 4
Pattonsburg, MO 70-71 CD 5
Pattullo, Mount — 48 C 1
Patu 98-99 M 6
Patuca, Punta — 58-59 K 8
Patuca, Río — 58-59 J 9-K 8
Patung = Badong 166-167 KL 5
Pátzcuaro, Lago de — 86-87 JK 8
Pau 132-133 G 7
Pau d'Arco 98-99 K 6
Pauillac 132-133 G 6
Pauini 98-99 E 8
Pauini, Rio — [BR ◁ Rio Purus] 98-99 D 8-9
Pauini, Rio — [BR ◁ Rio Unini] 98-99 G 5-6
Paulding, MS 78-79 E 4
Paulding, OH 70-71 H 5
Paulina, OR 66-67 D 3
Paulina Mountains 66-67 C 4
Paulis = Isiro 198 E 1
Paul Island [USA] 52-53 d 2
Paulista [BR, Pernambuco] 98-99 MN 6
Paulista [BR, Zona litigiosa] 98-99 L 8
Paulistana 98-99 L 6
Paulo Afonso, Cachoeira de — 98-99 M 6
Paulson 66-67 DE 1
Pauls Valley, OK 76-77 F 5
Paungde = Paungdī 174-175 BC 3
Paungdī 174-175 BC 3
Pavant Mountains 74-75 G 3
Pavia 138-139 C 3
Pavillon 48 G 4
Pavino 142-143 J 4
Pavlodar 154-155 O 7
Pavlof Bay 52-53 c 2
Pavlof Harbor, AK 52-53 bc 2
Pavlof Islands 52-53 c 2
Pavlof Volcano 52-53 b 2
Pavlovac 138-139 G 3
Pavlovo 142-143 H 4
Pavlovskaja 142-143 GH 6
Pavo, GA 80-81 E 5
Pavullo nel Frignano 138-139 D 3
Pavuvu = Russell Islands 174-175 j 6
Pawhuska, OK 76-77 F 4
Pawleys Island, SC 80-81 G 4
Pawnee, CO 68-69 E 5
Pawnee, OK 76-77 F 4
Pawnee City, NE 70-71 BC 5
Pawnee River 68-69 FG 6
Paw Paw, MI 70-71 GH 4
Pawtucket, RI 72-73 L 4
Páxoi 138-139 J 6
Paxson, AK 52-53 OP 5
Paxson Lake 52-53 OP 5
Paxton, IL 70-71 FG 5
Paxton, NE 68-69 F 5
Payakumbuh 174-175 D 7
Payette, ID 66-67 E 3
Payette River 66-67 E 3-4
Payette River, North Fork — 66-67 E 3
Payne, OH 70-71 H 5
Payne Bay = Bellin 46-47 WX 5
Payne Lake 46-47 W 6
Payne River 46-47 W 6
Paynes Creek, CA 66-67 BC 5
Paynesville, MN 70-71 C 3
Paysandú [ROU, place] 103 E 4
Payson, AZ 74-75 H 5
Payson, UT 66-67 GH 5
Payún, Cerro — 103 BC 5
Paz, La — [BOL, place] 98-99 F 8
Paz, La — [Honduras] 88-89 C 7
Paz, La — [MEX, Baja California Sur] 58-59 DE 7
Paz, La — [MEX, San Luis Potosí] 86-87 K 6
Paz, La — [RA, Entre Ríos] 103 DE 4
Paz, La — [RA, Mendoza] 103 C 4
Pazardžik 138-139 KL 4
Pažn'a 142-143 L 3
Pčinja 138-139 J 4-5
Peabody, KS 68-69 H 6
Peace River [CDN, place] 46-47 N 6
Peace River [CDN, river] 46-47 MN 6
Peachland 66-67 CD 1
Peach Springs, AZ 74-75 G 5
Peacock Bay 31 B 26-27
Peaima Falls 98-99 H 1
Peak District 116-117 K 7
Peak Hill [AUS, Western Australia] 182-183 C 5
Peale, Mount — 58-59 DE 4
Pearce, AZ 74-75 J 7
Peard Bay 52-53 H 1
Pearl 70-71 F 1
Pearl Harbor 174-175 e 3
Pearl River 58-59 H 5
Pearl River, LA 78-79 DE 5
Pearsall, TX 76-77 E 8
Pearson, GA 80-81 E 5
Peary Channel 46-47 R 2
Peary Land 30 A 21-23
Pebane 198 G 5
Pebas 98-99 E 5
Peć 138-139 J 4
Pecan Island, LA 78-79 C 6
Peças, Ilha das — 103 G 3
Pecatonica River 70-71 F 4
Pečenga [SU, place] 154-155 E 4
Pechabun = Phetchabun 174-175 CD 3
Pechawar = Pashāwar 160-161 KL 4
Pechora Bay = Pečorskaja guba 154-155 JK 4
Pečora [SU, place] 154-155 K 4
Pečora [SU, river] 154-155 K 5
Pecoraro, Monte — 138-139 FG 6
Pečorskaja guba 154-155 JK 4
Pečorskaja magistral' 154-155 JK 5
Pecos, TX 58-59 F 5
Pecos River 58-59 F 5
Pécs 124 HJ 5
Pedasí 88-89 FG 11
Pedee, OR 66-67 B 3
Pedernal, NM 76-77 B 5
Pedernales [DOM] 88-89 L 5-6
Pedernales [EC] 98-99 CD 4
Pedernales [YV] 98-99 G 3
Pederneira, Cachoeira — 98-99 FG 6
Pedra Azul 98-99 L 8
Pedra de Amolar 98-99 P 10
Pedra Sêca, Cachoeira da — 98-99 M 9
Pedras Negras 98-99 G 7
Pedras Negras, Reserva Florestal — 98-99 G 11
Pedregal [PA] 58-59 c 2
Pedreiras 98-99 KL 5
Pedrera, La — 98-99 EF 5
Pedro, Point — = Pēduru Tuḍuwa 160-161 N 9
Pedro Afonso 98-99 K 6
Pedro Bay, AK 52-53 K 7
Pedro Cays 58-59 L 8
Pedro de Valdivia 103 BC 2
Pedro II 98-99 L 5
Pedro Juan Caballero 103 E 2
Pedro Miguel 58-59 b 2
Pedro Miguel, Esclusas de — 58-59 b 2
Pedro Miguel Locks = Esclusas de Pedro Miguel 58-59 b 2
Pedro R. Fernández 103 E 3
Pedro Totolapan 86-87 MN 9
Pēduru Tuḍuwa [CL, cape] 160-161 N 9
Peebinga 182-183 H 6
Peebles, OH 72-73 E 5
Peebles [CDN] 49 G 5
Peebles [GB] 116-117 H 5
Pee Dee River 58-59 L 5
Peek, mys — 52-53 C 4
Peekskill, NY 72-73 K 4
Peel 116-117 G 6
Peel Fell 116-117 J 5
Peel River 46-47 JK 4
Peel Sound 46-47 R 3
Peene 124 F 2
Peera Peera Poolanna Lake 182-183 G 5
Peerless, MT 68-69 D 1
Peerless Lake 48 K 1
Peetz, CO 68-69 E 5
Pegasus Bay 182-183 O 8
Pegram, ID 66-67 H 4
Pègū 174-175 C 3
Pehpei = Beipei 166-167 K 6
Pehuajó 103 D 5
Peian = Bei'an 166-167 O 2
Pei-chên = Beizhen 170-171 C 2
Pei-hai = Beihai 166-167 K 7
P'ei-hsien = Pei Xian 166-167 M 5
Peine 124 E 2
Pei-ngan = Bei'an 166-167 O 2
Peipei = Beipei 166-167 K 6
Pei-p'iao = Beipiao 170-171 C 2
Peiping = Beijing 166-167 LM 3-4
Peipsi Lake = Čudskoje ozero 154-155 D 6
Peiraiévs 138-139 K 7
Peirce, Cape — 52-53 FG 7
Pei Shan = Bei Shan 166-167 GH 3
Peixe 98-99 K 7
Peixes, Rio dos — 98-99 K 10
Pei Xian [TJ ↖ Xuzhou] 166-167 M 5
Pekalongan 174-175 EF 8
Pekan 174-175 D 6
Pekin, IL 70-71 F 5
Pekin, IN 70-71 GH 6
Pekin, ND 68-69 G 2
Peking = Beijing 166-167 LM 4
Pekul'nej, chrebet — 154-155 hj 4
Pelagosa = Palagruža 138-139 G 4
Pelahatchie, MS 78-79 E 4
Pelaihari 174-175 F 7
Peleaga 138-139 K 3
Peleduj 154-155 V 6
Pelée, Montagne — 58-59 O 8
Pelee Island 72-73 E 4
Pelee Point 72-73 E 4
Pelēnaïon 138-139 LM 6
Peleng, Pulau — 174-175 H 7
Pelham, GA 80-81 D 5
Pelham Bay Park 82 III d 1
Pelham Manor, NY 82 III d 1
Pelican, AK 52-53 TU 8
Pelican Lake, WI 70-71 F 3
Pelican Lake [CDN] 49 H 4
Pelican Lake [USA] 70-71 D 1
Pelican Mountains 48 KL 2
Pelican Narrows 49 G 3
Pelican Rapids [CDN, Alberta] 48 L 2
Pelican Rapids [CDN, Saskatchewan] 49 H 4
Pelikan Rapids, MN 68-69 H 2
Pēlion 138-139 K 6
Pelješac 138-139 G 4
Pelkosenniemi 114-115 MN 4
Pella, IA 70-71 D 5
Pell City, AL 78-79 FG 4
Pello 114-115 L 4
Pellston, MI 70-71 H 3
Pelly Bay 46-47 S 4
Pelly Crossing 52-53 T 5
Pelly Mountains 46-47 K 5
Pelly River 46-47 K 5
Peloncillo Mountains 74-75 J 6
Pelopónnēsos 138-139 JK 7
Peloritani, Monti — 138-139 F 6-7
Pelotas 103 F 4
Pelotas, Rio — 103 F 3
Pelusium 199 C 2
Pelusium, Bay of — = Khalīj aṭ-Ṭīnah 199 C 2
Pelvoux 132-133 L 6
Pelym [SU, place] 154-155 L 6
Pelym [SU, river] 154-155 L 5
Pemadumcook Lake 72-73 M 2
Pemalang 174-175 EF 8
Pematangsiantar 174-175 C 6
Pemba [EAT] 198 GH 3
Pemba [Mozambique] 198 H 4
Pemba [Z] 198 E 5
Pemberton [AUS] 182-183 C 6
Pemberton [CDN] 48 F 4
Pembina 46-47 NO 7
Pembina Forks 48 JK 3
Pembina Mountains 68-69 G 1
Pembina River 48 K 3
Pembine, WI 70-71 FG 3
Pembroke, GA 80-81 F 4
Pembroke [CDN] 58-59 L 2
Pembroke [GB] 116-117 FG 9
Peña, Sierra de la — 132-133 G 7
Penablanca, NM 76-77 AB 5
Peñafiel 132-133 EF 8
Peñagolosa 132-133 G 8
Peña Negra, Punta — 98-99 C 5
Peña Nevada, Cerro — 58-59 FG 7
Penang = George Town 174-175 CD 5
Peñarroya 132-133 G 8
Peñarroya-Pueblonuevo 132-133 E 9
Penarth 116-117 H 9
Peñas, Cabo de — 132-133 E 7
Penas, Golfo de — 103 AB 7
Peñas, Punta — 98-99 G 2
Penawawa, WA 66-67 E 2
Penck, Cape — 31 C 9
Pendembu 194-195 B 7
Pender, NE 68-69 H 4
Pender Bay 182-183 D 3
Pendjab = Punjab [IND] 160-161 LM 4
Pendjab = Punjab [PAK] 160-161 L 4
Pendleton, OR 58-59 C 2
Pend Oreille Lake 66-67 E 1-2
Pend Oreille River 66-67 E 1
Pendroy, MT 66-67 GH 1
Pendžikent 160-161 K 3
Pēneiós 138-139 K 6
Penetanguishene 72-73 FG 2
Penganga 160-161 M 7
Penge [ZRE, Kasai-Oriental] 198 DE 3
Penghu Liedao = Penghu Lieh-tao 166-167 M 7
Penghu Lieh-tao 166-167 M 7
Penglai 166-167 N 4
Pengra Pass 66-67 BC 4
Pengze 166-167 M 6
Penhall 50 H 3
Penhurst 70-71 H 1
Penicuik 116-117 H 5
Penida, Nusa — 174-175 FG 8
Peñíscola 132-133 H 8
Penistone 116-117 K 7
Penitente, Serra do — 98-99 K 6
Pénjamo 86-87 K 7
Penki = Benxi 166-167 N 3
Penkilan Head 116-117 G 8
Penmarch, Pointe de — 132-133 E 5
Penn 49 E 4
Pennask Mountain 66-67 C 1
Penne 138-139 EF 4
Penn Hills, PA 72-73 G 4
Pennine Chain 116-117 J 6-K 7
Pennsylvania 58-59 KL 3
Penny 48 G 3
Penn Yan, NY 72-73 H 3
Penny Highland 46-47 X 4
Penny Strait 46-47 R 2
Penobscot Bay 72-73 M 2
Penobscot River 72-73 M 2
Penong 182-183 F 6
Penonomé 88-89 F 10
Penrith 116-117 J 6
Penryn 116-117 F 10
Pensa = Penza 154-155 GH 7
Pensacola, FL 58-59 J 5
Pensacola Bay 78-79 F 5
Pensacola Mountains 31 A 33-34
Pentagon 82 II a 2
Pentecost Island 182-183 N 3
Penticton 46-47 N 8
Pentire Point 116-117 FG 10
Pentland Firth 116-117 HJ 2
Pentwater, MI 70-71 G 4
Penwell, TX 76-77 C 7
Pen-y-Ghent 116-117 J 6
Penyu, Pulau-pulau — 174-175 J 8
Penza 154-155 GH 7
Penzance 116-117 F 10
Penžina 154-155 g 5
Penžinskaja guba 154-155 f 5
Peoples Creek 68-69 B 1
Peoria, AZ 74-75 G 6
Peoria, IL 58-59 HJ 3
Peotillos 86-87 K 6
Peotone, IL 70-71 G 5
Pepel 194-195 B 7
Pepin, WI 70-71 D 3
Pepperdine University 83 III c 2
Pequeni, Río — 58-59 bc 2
Pequizeiro 98-99 O 9
Pequop Mountains 66-67 F 5
Pequot Lakes, MN 70-71 C 2
Perälä 114-115 JK 6
Percé 51 DE 3
Perche 132-133 H 4
Percival Lakes 182-183 DE 4
Perdido, Monte — 132-133 GH 7
Perdido Bay 78-79 F 5
Perdue 49 E 4
Pereguete, Río — 58-59 b 3
Pereira 98-99 D 4
Pereira, Cachoeira — 98-99 KL 7
Pereira, Cachoeiro — 98-99 H 5
Pereira d'Eça = N'Giva 198 C 5
Pereirinha 98-99 K 9
Perekop 142-143 F 6
Perelik 138-139 L 5
Peremul Par 160-161 L 8
Perenosa Bay 52-53 LM 7
Pereslavl'-Zalesskij 142-143 G 4
Perevoz [SU ↗ Bodajbo] 154-155 W 6
Pérez, Isla — 86-87 PQ 6
Pergamino 103 D 4
Perham, MN 70-71 C 2
Perhonjoki 114-115 KL 6
Peribonca, Lac — 51 A 2
Péribonca, Rivière — 46-47 W 7-8
Perico 103 CD 2
Perico, TX 76-77 C 4
Pericos 86-87 G 5
Périgord 132-133 H 6
Perigoso, Canal — 98-99 K 4
Périgueux 132-133 H 6
Perija, Sierra de — 98-99 E 2-3
Peril Strait 52-53 U 8
Perim Island = Barīm 160-161 E 8
Periquito, Cachoeira do — 98-99 G 6
Perito Moreno 103 BC 7
Peritos, Cachoeira — 98-99 GH 9
Perkins, OK 76-77 F 4-5
Perla, La — 86-87 HJ 3
Perlas, Archipiélago de las — 58-59 KL 10
Perlas, Laguna de — 88-89 E 8
Perlas, Las — 88-89 E 8
Perlas, Punta de — 58-59 K 9
Perley, MN 68-69 H 2
Perlis, Kuala — 174-175 CD 5
Perm' 154-155 K 6
Permé 88-89 H 10
Permskoje = Komsomol'sk-na-Amure 154-155 a 7
Pernambuco 98-99 LM 6
Pernambuco = Recife 98-99 N 6
Pernik 138-139 K 4
Péronne 132-133 J 4
Peron Peninsula 182-183 B 5
Perouse, La — 49 K 3
Perovsk = Kzyl-Orda 154-155 M 9
Perow 48 D 2
Perpignan 132-133 J 7
Perrégaux = Muḥammadīyah 194-195 DE 1
Perrin, TX 76-77 EF 6
Perrine, FL 80-81 c 4
Perris, CA 74-75 E 6
Perry 70-71 H 2
Perry, FL 80-81 b 1
Perry, GA 80-81 E 4
Perry, IA 70-71 CD 5
Perry, NY 72-73 GH 3
Perry, OK 76-77 F 4
Perry Island 52-53 O 6
Perrysburg, OH 72-73 E 4
Perryton, TX 76-77 D 4
Perryvale 48 L 2
Perryville, AK 52-53 d 2
Perryville, AR 78-79 C 3
Perryville, MO 70-71 EF 7
Persepolis 160-161 G 5
Perseverancia 98-99 G 7
Pershore 116-117 JK 8
Persia = Iran 160-161 F-H 4
Persian Gulf 160-161 FG 5
Perth [AUS, Western Australia] 182-183 BC 6
Perth [CDN] 72-73 H 2
Perth [GB] 116-117 H 4
Perth Amboy, NJ 72-73 J 4
Perth-Andover 51 C 4
Peru, IL 70-71 F 5
Peru, IN 70-71 GH 5
Peru [PE] 98-99 D 5-E 7
Perú [RA] 103 D 5
Peru Basin 34-35 N 5
Peru Chile Trench 98-99 C 6-D 7
Perùgia 138-139 E 4
Peruíbe 103 G 2
Pervomajsk 142-143 EF 6
Pervoural'sk 154-155 KL 6
Pervyj Kuril'skij proliv 154-155 de 7
Perzhinsk, Gulf of — = zaliv Šelechova 154-155 e 5-6
Pèsaro 138-139 E 4
Pesca, La — 86-87 M 6
Pescada, Ponta da — 98-99 NO 3
Pescadero, CA 74-75 B 4
Pescadores = Penghu Lieh-tao 166-167 M 7
Pesčanyj, mys — 142-143 K 7
Pesčanyj, ostrov — 154-155 WX 3
Pescara 138-139 F 4
Pèschici 138-139 FG 5
Peshawar = Pashāwar 160-161 KL 4
Peshtigo, WI 70-71 G 3
Peshtigo River 70-71 F 3
Peshwar = Pashāwar 160-161 KL 4
Peštera 138-139 KL 4
Petacalco, Bahía — 86-87 JK 9
Petaliōn, Kólpos — 138-139 L 7
Petaluma, CA 74-75 B 3
Petatlán 86-87 K 9
Petauke 198 F 4
Petawana 72-73 H 2
Petén, El — 58-59 H 8
Petén Itzá, Lago — 86-87 Q 9
Petenwell Lake 70-71 F 3
Petenwell Reservoir = Petenwell Lake 70-71 F 3
Peterbell 70-71 J 1
Peterborough, NH 72-73 KL 3
Peterborough [AUS, South Australia] 182-183 GH 6
Peterborough [CDN] 46-47 V 9
Peterborough [GB] 116-117 LM 8
Peterculter 116-117 JK 3
Peterhead 116-117 JK 3
Peter I^st Island = ostrov Petra I 31 C 27
Petermann Ranges 182-183 E 4-F 5
Peter Pond Lake 46-47 P 6
Petersburg, AK 46-47 K 6
Petersburg, IL 70-71 F 5
Petersburg, IN 70-71 G 6
Petersburg, TN 78-79 F 3
Petersburg, TX 76-77 D 6
Petersburg, VA 58-59 L 4
Petersburg, WV 72-73 G 5
Petersburg = Leningrad 154-155 E 5-6
Peters Creek, AK 52-53 M 5
Petersfield 116-117 KL 9-10
Peter's Mine 98-99 J 1
Petersville, AK 52-53 M 5
Petilia Policastro 138-139 G 6
Petit Bois Island 78-79 E 5-6
Petit-Cap 51 DE 3

Petit 259

Petit-Étang 51 F 4
Petit-Goâve 88-89 K 5
Petitjean = Sīdī Qāsim 194-195 CD 2
Petit Lac Manicouagan 51 C 2
Petit Manan Point 72-73 N 2
Petit Mécatina, Île du — 51 G 2
Petit Mécatina, Rivière du — 51 FG 2
Petitot River 46-47 M 5-6
Petit-Rocher 51 CD 4
Peto 58-59 J 7
Petorca 103 B 4
Petoskey, MI 70-71 H 3
Petra, ostrova — 154-155 VW 2
Petra I, ostrov — 31 C 27
Petra Velikogo, zaliv — 154-155 Z 9
Petre, Point — 72-73 H 3
Petrel Bank 52-53 st 6
Petrič 138-139 K 5
Petrified Forest National Monument 74-75 J 5
Pétriou = Chachoengsao 174-175 D 4
Petroaleksandrovsk = Turtkul' 154-155 L 9
Petrograd = Leningrad 154-155 E 5-6
Petrolândia 98-99 M 6
Petrólea 98-99 E 3
Petroleum, TX 76-77 E 9
Petrolia 72-73 E 3
Petrolia, CA 66-67 A 5
Petrolina [BR, Amazonas] 98-99 E 6
Petrolina [BR, Pernambuco] 98-99 L 6
Petropavlovka 154-155 TU 7
Petropavlovsk 154-155 MN 7
Petropavlovsk-Kamčatskij 154-155 ef 7
Petropavlovsk-Kamchatskiy = Petropavlovsk-Kamčatskij 154-155 ef 7
Petrópolis 98-99 L 9
Petros, TN 78-79 G 2
Petroşeni 138-139 K 3
Petroskoi = Petrozavodsk 154-155 EF 5
Petrovaradin 138-139 HJ 3
Petrovka [SU, Vladivostok] 170-171 J 1
Petrovsk 142-143 J 5
Petrovskij Zavod = Petrovsk-Zabajkal'skij 154-155 U 7
Petrovsk-Zabajkal'skij 154-155 U 7
Petrozavodsk 154-155 EF 5
Petrun 142-143 LM 2
Pettibone, ND 68-69 G 2
Pettigrew, AR 78-79 C 3
Pettus, TX 76-77 EF 8
Petuchovo 154-155 M 6
Peumo 103 B 4
Pevek 154-155 gh 4
Pewsey 116-117 K 9
Peyton, CO 68-69 D 6
Peza 142-143 J 2
Pézenas 132-133 J 7

Pfaffenhofen 124 E 4
Pfarrkirchen 124 F 4
Pforzheim 124 D 4

Phalodi 160-161 L 5
Phaltan 160-161 LM 7
Phangan, Ko — 174-175 CD 5
Phanggong Tsho 166-167 DE 5
Phan Rang 174-175 EF 4
Phan Thiet 174-175 E 4
Pharr, TX 76-77 E 9
Phatthalung 174-175 D 5
Phaykkhaphum Phisai 174-175 D 3
Phelps, WI 70-71 F 2-3
Phelps Corner, MD 82 II b 2
Phelps Lake 80-81 H 3
Phenix City, AL 58-59 J 5
Phetchabun 174-175 CD 3
Phetchaburi 174-175 CD 4
Philadelphia, MS 78-79 E 4
Philadelphia, PA 58-59 LM 3-4
Philadelphia [ET] 199 B 3
Philip, SD 68-69 F 3
Philip Island 182-183 N 5
Philipp, MS 78-79 DE 4
Philippe-Thomas = Al-Mittawī 194-195 F 2
Philippeville 132-133 K 3
Philippeville = Sakīkdah 194-195 F 1
Philippi, WV 72-73 FG 5
Philippi, Lake — 182-183 G 4
Philippiada = Filippiás 138-139 J 6
Philippines 174-175 H 3-J 5
Philippopolis = Plovdiv 138-139 L 4
Philipsburg, MT 66-67 G 2
Philipsburg, PA 72-73 G 4
Philip Smith Mountains 46-47 GH 4
Phillips, ME 72-73 L 2
Phillips, WI 70-71 E 3
Phillipsburg, KS 68-69 G 6
Phillipsburg, MO 70-71 D 7
Phillipsburg, NJ 72-73 J 4
Phillips Mountains 31 B 22-23
Philo, CA 74-75 B 3
Phippsøya 114-115 kl 4
Phitsanulok 174-175 D 3
Phnom Penh 174-175 D 4
Pho, Laem — 174-175 D 5
Phoenix 178 JK 3
Phoenix, AZ 58-59 D 5
Phoenix Basin 179 KL 4
Phoenix Islands 34-35 J 5
Phoenix Trench 34-35 J 5
Phoenixville, PA 72-73 HJ 4
Phong Saly 174-175 D 2
Phort Láirge, Cuan — 116-117 D 9-E 8
Phosphate Hill 182-183 GH 4
Phra Chedi Sam Ong 174-175 C 3-4
Phra Nakhon Si Ayutthaya 174-175 D 4
Phu Diên Châu 174-175 E 3
Phuket 174-175 C 5
Phuket, Ko — 174-175 C 5
Phu Ly 174-175 E 2
Phum Rovieng 174-175 E 4
Phunakha 160-161 OP 5
Phu Quôc, Đao — 174-175 D 4
Phu Tho 174-175 DE 2

Piacá 98-99 K 6
Piacenza 138-139 C 3
Piacouadie, Lac — 51 A 2
Pialba 182-183 K 5
Piangil 182-183 H 7
Pianosa, Ìsola — 138-139 D 4
Piara-Açu 98-99 M 9
Piaseczno 124 K 2
Piatra 138-139 L 3
Piatra-Neamţ 138-139 M 2
Piauí 98-99 L 6
Piauí, Rio — 98-99 L 6
Piave 138-139 E 2
Piaxtla, Punta — 86-87 G 6
Piaxtla, Río — 86-87 G 6
Piazza Armerina 138-139 F 7
Pībōr 194-195 L 7
Pībōr, Nahr — 194-195 L 7
Picabo, ID 66-67 F 4
Picacho, AZ 74-75 H 6
Picacho, CA 74-75 F 6
Picacho, NM 76-77 B 6
Picados, Cerro dos 86-87 CD 3
Picardie 132-133 HJ 4
Picayune, MS 78-79 E 5
Pichanal 103 CD 2
Picher, OK 76-77 G 4
Pichi Ciego 103 C 4
Pichieh = Bijie 166-167 K 6
Pichilemú 103 B 4
Pichtovka 154-155 P 6
Pickens, MS 78-79 DE 4
Pickens, SC 80-81 E 3
Pickerel 72-73 F 2
Pickerel Lake 70-71 E 1
Pickering 116-117 L 6
Pickle Crow 46-47 ST 7
Pickle Lake 50 D 2
Pico 188-189 E 5
Pico, El — 98-99 G 8
Pico Rivera, CA 83 III d 2
Picos 98-99 L 6
Pico Truncado 103 C 7
Pic River 70-71 G 1
Picton [CDN] 72-73 H 2-3
Picton [NZ] 182-183 O 8
Pictou 51 E 5
Picture Butte 66-67 G 1
Picuí 98-99 M 6
Picún Leufú 103 BC 5
Pidurutalāgala 160-161 N 9
Piedad Cavadas, La — 86-87 JK 7
Pie de Palo 103 C 4
Piedmont 58-59 K 5-L 4
Piedmont, AL 78-79 G 4
Piedmont, SC 80-81 E 3
Piedmont, SD 68-69 E 3
Piedmont, WV 72-73 G 5
Piedra del Águila 103 BC 6
Piedras 98-99 CD 5
Piedras, Río — 58-59 b 2
Piedras, Río de las — 98-99 E 7
Piedras Negras 58-59 F 6
Pie Island 70-71 F 1
Pieksämäki 114-115 M 6
Pielinen 114-115 N 6
Piemonte 138-139 BC 3
Pierce, ID 66-67 F 2
Pierce, NE 68-69 H 4
Pierce City, MO 76-77 GH 4
Pierceville, KS 68-69 F 7
Piercy, CA 74-75 B 3
Pierre, SD 58-59 F 3
Pierre Lake 50 L 2
Pierreville 72-73 K 1
Pierson 68-69 F 1
Pierson, FL 80-81 c 2
Piešťany 124 HJ 4
Pietarsaari = Jakobstad 114-115 JK 6
Pietermaritzburg 198 F 7
Pietersburg 198 E 6
Pietrasanta 138-139 CD 4
Pietrosul [RO ↙ Borşa] 138-139 L 2
Pietrosul [RO ↙ Vatra Dornei] 138-139 L 2
Pieux, les — 116-117 JK 11
Pigailoe 174-175 N 5
Pigeon, MI 72-73 E 3
Pigeon Bay 72-73 E 4
Pigeon Lake 49 L 3
Pigeon Point 74-75 B 4
Pigeon River [CDN, place] 70-71 F 1
Pigeon River [CDN, river] 50 A 1
Piggott, AR 78-79 D 2
Pigŭm-do 170-171 E 5
Pihtipudas 114-115 LM 6
Pihyŏn 170-171 E 2
Piippola 114-115 LM 5
Pija, Sierra de — 58-59 J 8
Pikangikum 50 C 2
Pikelot 174-175 N 5
Pikes Peak 58-59 F 4
Piketberg 198 C 8
Piketon, OH 72-73 E 5
Pikeville, KY 80-81 E 2
Pikeville, TN 78-79 G 3
Pikmiktalik, AK 52-53 FG 5
Pikou 170-171 D 3
Pikwitonei 49 K 3
Piła [PL] 124 H 2
Pilão Arcado 98-99 L 7
Pilar [PY] 103 E 3
Pilas Group 174-175 H 5
Pilawa 124 K 3
Pilcaniyeu 103 BC 6
Pilcomayo, Rio — [BR] 103 D 2
Pile Bay, AK 52-53 L 7
Pilgrim Springs, AK 52-53 EF 4
Pil'gyn 154-155 jk 4
Pilica 124 K 3
Pillar, Cape — 182-183 J 8
Pilões, Cachoeira dos — 98-99 OP 9
Pilot Mountain, NC 80-81 F 2
Pilot Peak [USA, Absaroka Range] 66-67 HJ 3
Pilot Peak [USA, Gabbs Valley Range] 74-75 E 3
Pilot Peak [USA, Toano Range] 66-67 FG 5
Pilot Point, AK 52-53 HJ 8
Pilot Point, TX 76-77 F 6
Pilot Rock, OR 66-67 D 3
Pilot Station, AK 52-53 F 6
Pilottown, LA 78-79 E 6
Pim 154-155 N 5
Pimba 182-183 G 6
Pimenta Bueno 98-99 G 7
Pimental 98-99 J 7
Pimmit Hills, VA 82 II a 2
Pimmit Run 82 II a 1-2
Piña [PA] 58-59 a 2
Pinacate, Cerro del — 86-87 D 2
Pinaleno Mountains 74-75 HJ 6
Pinamelayan 174-175 H 4
Pinar del Río 58-59 K 7
Pincher Creek 66-67 FG 1
Pinckneyville, IL 70-71 F 6
Pinconning, MI 70-71 HJ 4
Pîncota 138-139 J 2
Pindaré, Rio — 98-99 K 5
Pindobal 98-99 O 6
Píndos Óros 138-139 J 5-6
Pindus = Píndos Óros 138-139 J 5-6
Pine, ID 66-67 F 4
Pine, Cape — 51 K 4
Pine Apple, AL 78-79 F 5
Pine Bluff, AR 58-59 H 5
Pinebluff Lake 49 G 3-4
Pine Bluffs, WY 68-69 D 5
Pine City, MN 70-71 D 3
Pine City, WA 66-67 E 2
Pine Creek [AUS] 182-183 F 2
Pine Creek [USA] 66-67 E 5
Pinedale, WY 66-67 J 4
Pine Falls 50 AB 2
Pine Forest Mountains 66-67 D 5
Pinega 154-155 H 5
Pine Hills 58-59 J 5
Pinehouse Lake 49 E 3
Pineimuta River 50 DE 1
Pine Island 80-81 b 3
Pine Island, MN 70-71 D 3
Pine Island Bay 31 B 26
Pine Islands 80-81 c 4
Pineland, TX 76-77 GH 7
Pine Mountain [USA, Georgia] 78-79 G 4
Pine Mountain [USA, Kentucky] 80-81 DE 2
Pine Point 46-47 O 5
Pine Ridge 68-69 C 2-3
Pine Ridge, SD 68-69 E 4
Pine Ridge Indian Reservation 68-69 EF 4
Pine River, MN 70-71 CD 2
Pine River [CDN, place Manitoba] 49 HJ 5
Pine River [CDN, place Saskatchewan] 49 E 2
Pine River [CDN, river] 48 FG 2
Pinerolo 138-139 B 3
Pine Valley Mountains 74-75 G 4
Pineville, KY 72-73 E 6
Pineville, LA 78-79 C 5
Piney [CDN] 70-71 BC 1
Piney Buttes 68-69 C 2
Ping, Mae Nam — 174-175 C 3
P'ing-ch'üan = Pingquan 170-171 B 2
Pingdong = Pingtung 166-167 N 7
P'ing-hsiang = Pingxiang 166-167 L 6
P'ing-hsien = Pingxiang 166-167 K 7
Pingle [CDN] 49 C 3
Pingle [TJ] 166-167 L 7
P'ing-leang = Pingliang 166-167 K 4
Pingliang 166-167 K 4
Pingliang = Pingtung 166-167 N 7
Pinglo = Pingle 166-167 L 7
P'ing-lo = Pingluo 166-167 K 4
Pingluo 166-167 K 4
Pingquan 170-171 B 2
Pingree, ID 66-67 G 4
Pingree, ND 68-69 G 2
Pingrup 182-183 C 6
Pingsiang = Pingxiang 166-167 L 6
Pingtan Dao 166-167 MN 6
Pingtung 166-167 N 7
Pingurbek Island 52-53 E 7
Pingwu 166-167 J 5
Pingxiang [TJ, Guangxi Zhuangzu Zizhiqu] 166-167 K 7
Pingxiang [TJ, Jiangxi] 166-167 L 6
Pinhal 98-99 K 9
Pinheiro 98-99 KL 5
Pinhuã, Rio — 98-99 F 8
Pini, Pulau — 174-175 C 6
Pinjarra 182-183 C 6
Pinkiang = Harbin 166-167 O 2
Pinnacles National Monument 74-75 C 4
Pinnaroo 182-183 H 7
Pinon, CO 68-69 D 6
Pinon, NM 76-77 B 6
Pinón, Monte — 58-59 b 2
Pinos, Mount — 74-75 D 5
Pinos, Point — 74-75 BC 4
Pino Suárez, Tenosique de — 58-59 H 8
Pinrang 174-175 G 7
Pins, Îles de — 182-183 N 4
Pins, Pointe aux — 72-73 F 3
Pinsk 142-143 E 5
Pinta, Isla — 98-99 A 4
Pintada [BR, Rio Grande do Sul] 103 F 4
Pintados 103 BC 2
Pinto [RA] 103 D 3
Pinto Butte 49 E 6
Pinto Creek 66-67 K 1
Pinware River 51 H 1-2
Pioche, NV 74-75 F 4
Piombino 138-139 D 4
Pioneer Island = ostrov Pioner 154-155 QR 2
Pioneer Mountains 66-67 G 3
Pioner, ostrov — 154-155 QR 2
Pionki 124 K 3
Piorini, Lago — 98-99 G 5
Piorini, Rio — 98-99 G 5
Piotrków Trybunalski 124 J 3
Pipérion 138-139 L 6
Pipestone 49 H 6
Pipestone, MN 70-71 BC 3
Pipestone Creek 49 GH 5
Pipestone River 50 DE 1
Pipinas 103 E 5
Pipmuacan, Rėservoir — 51 A 3
Piqua, KS 70-71 C 7
Piqua, OH 70-71 H 5
Piquetberg = Piketberg 198 C 8
Piquiri, Rio — 103 F 2
Pira, Salto de — 88-89 D 8
Piracanjuba 98-99 JK 8
Piracuruca 98-99 L 5
Piraeus = Peiraiévs 138-139 K 7
Piraí do Sul 103 G 2
Pirajuí 98-99 K 9
Piran 138-139 E 3
Piranė 103 E 3
Piranga, Serra da — 98-99 MN 6
Piranhas 98-99 M 6
Piranhas, Cachoeira das — 98-99 HJ 10
Piranhas, Rio — [BR, Goiás ◁ Rio Grande do Norte] 98-99 O 9
Piranhas, Rio — [BR, Rio Grande do Norte] 98-99 M 6
Pirapora 98-99 L 8
Pirarara, Cachoeira — 98-99 KL 5
Pirassununga 98-99 K 9
Pir'atin 142-143 F 5
Piratuba 103 F 3
Pirin 138-139 K 5
Piripiri 98-99 L 5
Pirmasens 124 C 4
Pirna 124 F 3
Piro-bong 170-171 G 3
Pirot 138-139 K 4
Pirpintos, Los — 103 D 3
Pirtleville, AZ 74-75 J 7
Piru 174-175 J 7
Pisa 138-139 D 4
Pisagua 103 B 1
Pisco 98-99 D 7
Pisco, Bahía de — 98-99 D 7
Písek 124 G 4
Pisgah, Mount — 66-67 C 3
Pishan = Guma Bazar 166-167 D 4
P'i-shan = Guma Bazar 166-167 D 4
Pisoridorp 98-99 L 3
Pispek = Frunze 154-155 NO 9
Pisticci 138-139 G 5
Pistòia 138-139 D 3-4
Pistolet Bay 51 J 2
Pistol River, OR 66-67 A 4
Pisuerga 132-133 E 7
Pisz 124 K 2
Pita 194-195 B 6
Pitcairn 34-35 L 6
Piteå 114-115 J 5
Pite älv 114-115 HJ 5
Piteşti 138-139 L 3
Pit-Gorodok 154-155 RS 6
Pithara 182-183 C 6
Piti, Cerro — 103 C 2
Pitigliano 138-139 D 4
Pitk'ajarvi 114-115 NO 3
Pitkin, LA 78-79 C 5
Pitlochry 116-117 H 4
Pitman River 52-53 XY 7
Pitmega River 52-53 E 2
Pit River 66-67 BC 5
Pitssville, WI 70-71 EF 3
Pitt Island [CDN] 46-47 KL 7
Pitt Island [NZ] 182-183 Q 8
Pittsboro, NC 80-81 G 3
Pittsburg, CA 74-75 C 3
Pittsburg, KS 58-59 H 4
Pittsburg, KY 80-81 D 2
Pittsburg, TX 76-77 G 6
Pittsburgh, PA 58-59 KL 3
Pittsfield, IL 70-71 E 6
Pittsfield, MA 72-73 K 3
Pittsfield, ME 72-73 M 2
Pittston, PA 72-73 J 4
P'i-tzŭ-wo = Pikou 170-171 D 3
Piuka = Bifuka 170-171 c 1
Piura [PE, place] 98-99 CD 6
Piute Peak 74-75 D 5
Piva 138-139 H 4
Pivka 138-139 F 3
Pivot 49 C 5
Pixuna, Rio — 98-99 G 8
Pizzo 138-139 G 6

Pjagina, poluostrov — 154-155 de 6

Place Bonaventure 82 I b 2
Place des Artes 82 I b 1
Place Metropolitaine Centre 82 I b 1
Placentia 51 J 4
Placentia Bay 46-47 Za 8
Placer de Guadalupe 86-87 H 3
Placerville, CA 74-75 C 3
Placerville, CO 68-69 B 6-7
Placetas 58-59 L 7
Place Versailles 82 I b 1
Plácido de Castro 98-99 F 7
Plain City, OH 72-73 E 4
Plains, GA 78-79 G 4-5
Plains, KS 76-77 D 4
Plains, MT 66-67 F 2
Plains, TX 76-77 C 6
Plainview, MN 70-71 DE 3
Plainview, NE 68-69 GH 4
Plainview, TX 58-59 F 5
Plainville, KS 68-69 G 6
Plainwell, MI 70-71 H 4
Plana Cays 88-89 K 3
Planada, CA 74-75 CD 4
Planaltina 98-99 K 8
Planalto Brasileiro 98-99 KL 8
Plankinton, SD 68-69 G 4
Plano, TX 76-77 F 6
Plantation, FL 80-81 c 3
Plant City, FL 80-81 b 2-3
Plaquemine, LA 78-79 D 5
Plasencia 132-133 D 8
Plast 154-155 L 7
Plaster City, CA 74-75 EF 6
Plaster Rock 51 C 4
Plastun 154-155 a 9
Plata, Isla de la — 98-99 C 5
Plata, La — [CO] 98-99 D 4
Plata, La — [RA] 103 E 5
Plata, Río de la — 103 EF 5
Plate, River — = Río de la Plata 103 E 4-F 5
Platen, Kapp — 114-115 lm 4
Platinum, AK 46-47 D 6
Platte, SD 68-69 G 4
Platte City, MO 70-71 C 6
Platte River [USA, Missouri, Iowa] 70-71 C 5
Platte River [USA, Nebraska] 58-59 FG 3
Platteville, CO 68-69 D 5
Platteville, WI 70-71 E 4
Platt National Park 76-77 F 5
Plattsburg, MO 70-71 C 6
Plattsburgh, NY 58-59 LM 3
Plattsmouth, NE 70-71 BC 5
Plauen 124 F 3
Playa del Carmen 86-87 R 7
Playa de Rey, Los Angeles-, CA 83 III b 2
Playa Larga 88-89 F 3
Playas 98-99 C 5
Playa Vicente 86-87 N 9
Playgreen Lake 49 J 3-4
Plaza, ND 68-69 F 1
Plaza Huincul 103 BC 5
Pleasant Grove, UT 66-67 H 5
Pleasant Hill, MO 70-71 C 6
Pleasanton, KS 70-71 C 6
Pleasanton, TX 76-77 E 8
Pleasant Valley, OR 66-67 E 3
Pleasant View, WA 66-67 DE 2
Pleasantville, NJ 72-73 JK 5
Pleiku 174-175 E 4
Pleniţa 138-139 K 3
Plenty, Bay of — 182-183 P 7
Plentywood, MT 68-69 D 1
Pleseck 154-155 G 5
Plessisville 72-73 KL 1
Pleszew 124 HJ 3
Plétipi, Lac — 51 A 2
Pleven 138-139 L 4
Plevna, MT 68-69 D 2
Plevskoj 142-143 M 4
Plitvice 138-139 F 3
Plitvička Jezera 138-139 FG 3
Pljevlja 138-139 H 4
Płock 124 JK 2
Ploieşti 138-139 LM 3
Plonge, Lac la — 49 E 3
Plovdiv 138-139 L 4
Plover Islands 52-53 K 1
Plumas, Las — 103 C 6
Plummer, ID 66-67 E 2
Plummer, MN 70-71 BC 2
Plummer, Mount — 52-53 GH 6
Plumtree 198 E 6
Plush, OR 66-67 D 4
Plymouth, CA 74-75 C 3
Plymouth, IN 70-71 GH 5
Plymouth, MA 72-73 L 4
Plymouth, NC 80-81 H 3
Plymouth, NH 72-73 KL 3
Plymouth, PA 72-73 HJ 4
Plymouth, WI 70-71 FG 4
Plymouth [GB] 116-117 GH 10
Plymouth [West Indies] 88-89 P 6
Plymouth Sound 116-117 G 10
Plynlimon Fawr 116-117 GH 8
Plzeň 124 F 4

Pnom Penh = Phnom Penh 174-175 D 4

Pô [HV] 194-195 D 6
Po [I] 138-139 D 3
Pobé 194-195 E 7
Pobeda, gora — 154-155 c 4
Pobedino 154-155 b 8
Pobedy, pik — 160-161 MN 2
Pocahontas 48 HJ 3
Pocahontas, AR 78-79 D 2
Pocahontas, IA 70-71 C 4
Pocão, Salto — 98-99 L 5
Pocatello, ID 58-59 D 3
P'och'ŏn 170-171 F 4
Pochutla 86-87 M 10
Pochval'nyj 154-155 cd 4
Pocklington 116-117 L 7
Pocklington Reef 174-175 j 7
Poções 98-99 LM 7
Pocomoke City, MD 72-73 J 5
Pocomoke Sound 80-81 HJ 2
Poconé 98-99 H 8
Poços de Caldas 98-99 K 9
Podborovje 142-143 FG 4
Podgorica = Titograd 138-139 H 4
Podgornoje 154-155 P 6
Podkamennaja Tunguska 154-155 R 5
Podkova 138-139 L 5
Podol'sk 142-143 G 4
Podor 194-195 AB 5
Podporožje 154-155 EF 5
Podravska Slatina 138-139 GH 3
Podtesovo 154-155 R 6
Po-êrh-t'a-la Chou = Bortala Monggol Zizhizhou 166-167 E 2-3
Pofadder 198 CD 7
Pogamasing 50 L 3
Poggibonsi 138-139 D 4
Pogibi 154-155 b 7
Pogromni Volcano 52-53 a 2
Pogyndeno 154-155 fg 4
P'oha-dong 170-171 GH 2
Po Hai = Bo Hai 166-167 M 4
Pohai, Gulf of — = Bohai Haixia 166-167 N 4
Po-hai Hai-hsia = Bohai Haixia 166-167 N 4
P'ohang 166-167 OP 4
Pohjanmaa 114-115 K 6-M 5
Pohjois-Karjalan lääni 114-115 N 6
Pohsien = Bo Xian 166-167 LM 5
Pohue Bay 78-79 e 3
Poinsett, Lake — 68-69 H 3
Point Abbaye 70-71 FG 2
Point Arena, CA 74-75 AB 3
Point Baker, AK 52-53 w 8
Point Detour 70-71 G 3
Pointe-à-la-Fregate 51 D 3
Pointe a la Hache, LA 78-79 E 6
Pointe-à-Maurier 51 G 2
Pointe-à-Pitre 58-59 O 8
Pointe au Baril Station 72-73 F 2
Pointe Aux Barques 72-73 E 2
Pointe-des-Monts 51 C 3
Pointe du Bois 50 B 2
Pointe-Noire 198 B 2
Point Harbor, NC 80-81 J 2
Point Lake 46-47 O 4
Point Lay, AK 52-53 EF 2
Point Leamington 51 J 3
Point Marion, PA 72-73 G 5
Point of Rocks, WY 68-69 B 5
Point Pleasant, NJ 72-73 JK 4
Point Pleasant, WV 72-73 EF 5
Point Roberts, WA 66-67 B 1
Poisson Blanc, Lac — 72-73 J 1-2
Poitevin, Marais — 132-133 G 5
Poitiers 132-133 H 5

260 Petit

Poitou 132-133 GH 5
Poivre, Côte du — = Malabar Coast 160-161 L 8-M 9
Poix 132-133 HJ 4
Pojarkovo 154-155 Y 8
Pokegama Lake 70-71 CD 2
Pokhara 160-161 N 5
Poko 198 E 1
Poko Mount 52-53 F 2
Pokrovsk 154-155 Y 5
Pokrovsk-Ural'skij 154-155 K 5
Polacca Wash 74-75 H 5
Pola de Siero 132-133 E 7
Polān [IR] 160-161 J 5
Poland 124 H-L 3
Pol'arnyj [SU, Indigirka] 154-155 c 3
Pol'arnyj [SU, Tuloma] 142-143 F 2
Polar Plateau 31 A 31-6
Polatli 160-161 C 3
Polcirkeln 114-115 J 4
Polesje 142-143 D-F 5
Polessk 124 K 1
Põlgyo 170-171 F 5
Poli 194-195 G 7
Poli = Boli 166-167 P 2
Policastro, Golfo di — 138-139 F 5-6
Polillo Islands 174-175 H 3-4
Poliny Osipenko 154-155 a 7
Pólis 142-143 F 8-9
Polk, PA 72-73 FG 4
Poll an Phúca 116-117 E 7
Pollaphuca Reservior = Poll an Phúca 116-117 E 7
Pollensa 132-133 J 9
Pollino 138-139 G 5-6
Pollock, ID 66-67 E 3
Pollock, LA 78-79 C 5
Pollock, SD 68-69 FG 3
Pollockville 49 C 5
Polmak 114-115 N 2
Polo, IL 70-71 F 5
Polock 142-143 E 4
Pologi 142-143 G 6
Polonio, Cabo — 103 F 4
Polousnyj kr'až 154-155 bc 4
Polson, MT 66-67 FG 2
Poltava 142-143 F 6
Poltorack = Ašchabad 160-161 HJ 3
Poluj [SU, place] 154-155 MN 4
Poluj [SU, river] 154-155 M 4
Polunočnoje 154-155 L 5
Polýaigos 138-139 L 7
Polýchnitos 138-139 LM 6
Polýgyros 138-139 K 5
Polynesia 34-35 J 4-5
Poma, La — 103 C 2
Pomarão 132-133 D 10
Pomasi, Cerro de — 98-99 E 8
Pombal [BR] 98-99 M 6
Pombal [P] 132-133 C 9
Pombetsu = Honbetsu 170-171 cd 2
Pomerania 124 G 2-H 1
Pomeranian Bay = Pommersche Bucht 124 FG 1
Pomeroy, OH 72-73 EF 5
Pomeroy, WA 66-67 E 2
Pomme de Terre River 70-71 C 2-3
Pommersche Bucht 124 FG 1
Pomona, CA 74-75 E 5-6
Pomona, KS 70-71 C 6
Pomona, MO 78-79 D 2
Pomorie 138-139 MN 4
Pompano Beach, FL 80-81 cd 3
Pompeji 138-139 F 5
Pompeys Pillar, MT 66-67 JK 2
Pomut 142-143 N 3
Ponape 178 F 2
Ponass Lake 49 F 4
Ponca, NE 68-69 H 4
Ponca City, OK 58-59 G 4
Ponca Creek 68-69 G 4
Ponce 58-59 N 8
Ponce de Leon, FL 78-79 FG 5
Ponce de Leon Bay 80-81 c 4
Poncha Springs, CO 68-69 C 6
Ponchatoula, LA 78-79 D 5
Pond Creek 68-69 E 6
Pond Creek, OK 76-77 F 4
Pondicheri = Pondicherry 160-161 MN 8
Pondicherry 160-161 MN 8
Pond Inlet [CDN, bay] 46-47 VW 3
Pond Inlet [CDN, place] 46-47 V 3
Pondo Dsong 166-167 G 5
Pondosa, CA 66-67 C 5
Pondosa, OR 66-67 E 3
Ponferrada 132-133 D 7
Pong 174-175 CD 3
Pongnim-ni = Põlgyo 170-171 F 5
Pongola [ZA, river] 198 F 7
Ponoj [SU, place] 154-155 FG 4
Ponoj [SU, river] 142-143 G 2
Ponoka 48 L 3
Ponta Albina 198 B 5
Ponta Alta do Norte 98-99 P 10
Ponta Delgada 188-189 E 5
Ponta de Pedras 98-99 JK 5
Ponta Grossa [BR, Amapá] 98-99 K 4
Ponta Grossa [BR, Paraná] 103 F 3
Ponta Negra = Pointe-Noire 198 B 2
Ponta Porã 98-99 HJ 9
Pontarlier 132-133 KL 5
Pontchartrain, Lake — 58-59 HJ 5
Ponte de Pedra [BR ↖ Diamantino] 98-99 H 7
Ponteix 49 E 6
Ponteland 116-117 K 5
Ponte-Leccia 138-139 C 4
Ponte Nova 98-99 L 9
Pontes-e-Lacerda 98-99 H 8
Pontevedra 132-133 C 7
Ponthierville = Ubundu 198 DE 2
Pontiac, IL 70-71 F 5
Pontiac, MI 58-59 K 3
Pontianak 174-175 E 7
Pontic Mountains 160-161 C-E 2
Pontivy 132-133 F 4
Pontoise 132-133 HJ 4
Pontotoc, MS 78-79 E 3
Pontrêmoli 138-139 CD 3
Pontrilas 116-117 J 9
Pont-Viau 82 I a 1
Pontypool 116-117 H 9
Pontypridd 116-117 H 9
Pony, MT 66-67 GH 3
Ponza 138-139 E 5
Ponziane, Ísole — 138-139 E 5
Poole 116-117 JK 10
Poole Bay 116-117 K 10
Pool Malebo 198 C 2
Poona = Pune 160-161 L 7
Pooncarie 182-183 H 6
Poopó 98-99 F 8
Poopó, Lago de — 98-99 F 8
Poorman, AK 52-53 K 4
Popa = Pulau Kofiau 174-175 JK 7
Popayán 98-99 D 4
Popeys Pillar, MT 68-69 BC 2
Popigaj 154-155 UV 3
Poplar, MT 68-69 D 1
Poplar, WI 70-71 E 2
Poplar Bluff, MO 58-59 H 4
Poplar Hill 50 B 1
Poplar River [CDN] 50 A 1
Poplar River [USA] 68-69 D 1
Poplar River, West Fork — 68-69 CD 1
Poplarville, MS 78-79 E 5
Popocatépetl 58-59 G 8
Popof Island 52-53 cd 2
Popokabaka 198 C 3
Popondetta 174-175 N 8
Popovo 138-139 M 4
Poprad [CS, place] 124 K 4
Poprad [CS, river] 124 K 4
Põpsõngp'o 170-171 F 5
Poptun 86-87 Q 9
Porāli 160-161 K 5
Porangatu 98-99 K 7
Porbandar 160-161 K 6
Porbunder = Porbandar 160-161 K 6
Porcher Island 48 B 3
Porchov 142-143 E 4
Porcupine, AK 52-53 T 7
Porcupine Creek 68-69 C 1
Porcupine Creek, AK 52-53 M 3
Porcupine Hills 48 K 4-5
Porcupine Mountain 46-47 Q 7
Porcupine Plain 49 G 4
Porcupine River 46-47 H 4
Pordenone 138-139 E 2-3
Pore 98-99 E 3
Pori 114-115 J 7
Porjus 114-115 HJ 4
Porlamar 98-99 G 2
Pornic 132-133 F 5
Poronajsk 154-155 b 8
Poroshiri-dake 170-171 c 2
Porosozero 142-143 F 3
Porpoise Bay 31 C 13
Porquis Junction 50 L 2
Porsangerfjord 114-115 LM 2
Porsangerhalvøya 114-115 L 2
Porsgrunn 114-115 CD 8
Porsuk çayı 142-143 F 8
Portachuelo 98-99 G 8
Portadown 116-117 E 6
Portaferry 116-117 F 6
Portage, AK 52-53 N 6
Portage, UT 66-67 G 5
Portage, WI 70-71 F 4
Portage-la-Prairie 46-47 R 8
Portage Park, Chicago-, IL 83 II b 1
Portal, ND 68-69 E 1
Port Alberni 46-47 LM 8
Port Albert [CDN] 72-73 EF 3
Portalegre 132-133 D 9
Portales, NM 58-59 F 5
Port Alexander, AK 52-53 v 8
Port Alfred 198 E 8
Port Alice 48 D 4
Port Allegany, PA 72-73 GH 4
Port Allen, LA 78-79 D 5
Port Angeles, WA 66-67 B 1
Port Antonio 58-59 L 8
Portarlington = Cúil an tSúdaire 116-117 D 7
Port Armstrong, AK 52-53 v 8
Port Arthur, TX 58-59 H 6
Port Arthur = Lüda-Lüshun 166-167 MN 4
Port Ashton, AK 52-53 N 6
Port Askaig 116-117 E 5
Port Augusta 182-183 G 6
Port au Port 51 G 3
Port au Port Bay 51 G 3
Port au Port Peninsula 51 G 3
Port-au-Prince 58-59 M 8
Port Austin, MI 72-73 E 2
Port-Bergé 198 J 5
Port Blair 160-161 P 8
Port Blandford 51 J 3
Port Borden 51 E 4
Port-Bou 132-133 J 7
Port Brega = Marsá al-Burayqah 194-195 H 2
Port Burwell [CDN, Ontario] 72-73 F 3
Port Burwell [CDN, Quebec] 46-47 XY 5
Port Cartier 46-47 X 7
Port-Cartier-Sept-Îles, Parc provincial de — 51 C 2
Port Chalmers 182-183 O 9
Port Chilkoot 52-53 U 7
Port Clarence 52-53 D 4
Port Clements 48 AB 3
Port Clinton, OH 72-73 E 4
Port Colborne 72-73 G 3
Port Coquitlam 66-67 B 1
Port Curtis 182-183 K 4
Port Daniel 51 D 3
Port Darwin 103 E 8
Port-de-Paix 88-89 K 5
Port Dunford = Buur Gaabo 198 H 2
Port Eads, LA 78-79 E 6
Porte des Morts 70-71 G 3
Port Edward [CDN] 48 B 2
Portel [BR] 98-99 J 5
Port Elgin [CDN, New Brunswick] 51 DE 4-5
Port Elgin [CDN, Ontario] 72-73 F 2
Port Elizabeth 198 E 8
Port Ellen 116-117 EF 5
Porterdale, GA 80-81 DE 4
Port Erin 116-117 G 6
Porterville 198 CD 8
Porterville, CA 74-75 D 4-5
Portes de l'Enfer 198 E 3
Port Essington 46-47 KL 7
Port-Étienne = Nawādhību 194-195 A 4
Port Fairy 182-183 H 7
Port-Francqui = Ilebo 198 D 2
Port Fu'ad = Būr Sādāt 199 C 2
Port-Gentil 198 A 2
Port Gibson, MS 78-79 D 5
Port Glasgow 116-117 G 5
Port Graham, AK 52-53 M 7
Port Harcourt 194-195 F 8
Port Hardy 46-47 L 7
Port Harrison = Inoucdjouac 46-47 V 6
Port Hawkesbury 51 F 5
Porthcawl 116-117 H 9
Port Hedland 182-183 C 4
Port Heiden 52-53 d 1
Port Heiden, AK 52-53 de 1
Port Henry, NY 72-73 K 2-3
Port Herald = Nsanje 198 G 5
Porthill, ID 66-67 E 1
Porthmadog 116-117 G 8
Port Hood 51 F 4
Port Hope 72-73 G 2-3
Port Hope, MI 72-73 E 3
Port Hudson, LA 78-79 D 5
Port Hueneme, CA 74-75 D 5
Port Huron, MI 58-59 K 3
Portimão 132-133 C 10
Port Isabel, TX 76-77 F 9
Portishead 116-117 J 9
Port Jefferson, NY 72-73 K 4
Port Jervis, NY 72-73 J 4
Port Keats 182-183 EF 2
Port Kembla, Wollongong- 182-183 K 6
Port Kenny 182-183 F 6
Port Lairge 116-117 DE 8
Portland, IN 70-71 H 5
Portland, ME 58-59 MN 3
Portland, MI 70-71 H 4
Portland, OR 58-59 B 2
Portland, TN 78-79 F 2
Portland, TX 76-77 F 9
Portland [AUS, Victoria] 182-183 H 7
Portland [CDN] 72-73 HJ 2
Portland [GB] 116-117 J 10
Portland = Dyrhólaey 114-115 d 3
Portland, Bill of — 116-117 J 10
Portland Canal 52-53 x 9
Portland Inlet 52-53 xy 9
Portland Point 88-89 H 6
Portland Promontory 46-47 UV 6
Port Laoise 116-117 D 7
Port Lavaca, TX 76-77 F 8
Port Lincoln 182-183 FG 6
Port Lions, AK 52-53 KL 8
Port Loko 194-195 B 7
Port Louis [MS] 188-189 N 11
Port-Lyautey = Al-Q'nitrah 194-195 C 2
Port MacNeill 48 D 4
Port Maitland 51 C 5-6
Port Maria 88-89 H 5
Port Mayaca, FL 80-81 c 3
Port-Menier 51 D 3
Port Moller 52-53 c 1-2
Port Moller, AK 52-53 cd 1
Port Moody 66-67 B 1
Port Moresby 174-175 N 8
Port Mouton 51 D 6
Port Musgrave 182-183 H 2
Portnacroish 116-117 F 4
Port Natal = Durban 198 F 7
Port Neches, TX 78-79 C 6
Port Nellie Juan, AK 52-53 NO 6
Port Nelson [BS] 88-89 J 3
Port Nelson [CDN, bay] 46-47 S 6
Port Nelson [CDN, place] 46-47 S 6
Portneuf, Rivière — 51 AB 3
Port Neville 48 DE 4
Port Nolloth 198 C 7
Port Norris, NJ 72-73 J 5
Porto [P] 132-133 C 8
Porto Acre 98-99 F 6
Porto Alegre [BR, Pará] 98-99 M 7
Porto Alegre [BR, Rio Grando do Sul] 103 FG 4
Porto Alexandre 198 B 5
Porto Alexandre, Parque National de — 198 B 5
Porto Amboim 198 B 4
Porto Amélia = Pemba 198 H 4
Porto Artur 98-99 HJ 7
Portobello, Edinburgh- 116-117 HJ 5
Portobelo [PA] 58-59 b 1
Porto Bicentenário 98-99 G 10
Port O'Brien, AK 52-53 KL 8
Porto Caneco 98-99 HJ 7
Porto Conceição 98-99 H 8
Porto de Más 98-99 H 8
Porto de Mós [BR] 98-99 J 5
Porto do Lontra 98-99 M 7
Porto dos Gaúchos 98-99 K 10
Porto Empêdocle 138-139 E 7
Portoferrâio 138-139 CD 4
Porto Franco 98-99 K 6
Port of Spain 58-59 O 9
Porto Grande 98-99 N 4
Portogruaro 138-139 E 3
Port Okha = Okha 160-161 K 6
Portola, CA 74-75 C 3
Pörtom 114-115 J 6
Porto Mau 98-99 E 7
Porto Mendes 103 F 2
Port Omna 116-117 CD 7
Porto Nacional 98-99 K 7
Porto Novo [DY] 194-195 E 7
Porto Poet 98-99 L 4
Port Orchard, WA 66-67 B 2
Porto Real do Colégio 98-99 M 6-7
Port Orford, OR 66-67 A 4
Porto Rico 98-99 B 8
Porto Rubim 98-99 C 9
Porto Santana 98-99 J 5
Porto Santo 194-195 AB 2
Porto São José 103 F 2
Porto Seguro 98-99 M 8
Porto Seguro, Cachoeira — 98-99 MN 8
Porto Tolle 138-139 E 3
Porto Tôrres 138-139 C 5
Porto União 103 F 3
Porto-Vecchio 138-139 C 5
Porto Velho 98-99 G 6
Portoviejo 98-99 C 5
Porto Walter 98-99 E 6
Portpatrick 116-117 F 6
Port Phillip Bay 182-183 H 7
Port Pirie 182-183 G 6
Port Radium 46-47 NO 4
Port Reading, NJ 82 III a 3
Portree 116-117 E 3
Port Renfrew 66-67 AB 1
Port Rexton 51 K 3
Port Richmond, New York-, NY 82 III b 3
Port Rowan 72-73 F 3
Port Royal = Annapolis Royal 46-47 XY 9
Port Royal Sound 80-81 F 4
Portrush 116-117 E 5
Port Safâga = Safâjah 194-195 L 3
Port Safety, AK 52-53 E 4
Port Said = Būr Saʿīd 194-195 L 2
Port Saint Joe, FL 78-79 G 6
Port Saunders 51 H 2
Port Shepstone 198 F 8
Port Simpson 48 BC 2
Portsmouth, NH 58-59 MN 3
Portsmouth, OH 58-59 K 4
Portsmouth, VA 58-59 L 4
Portsmouth [GB] 116-117 KL 10
Portsmouth [West Indies] 88-89 PQ 7
Port Stanley 72-73 F 3
Port Stanley = Stanley 103 E 8
Portstewart 116-117 E 5
Port Sūdān = Būr Sūdān 194-195 M 5
Port Sulphur, LA 78-79 E 6
Port Talbot 116-117 H 9
Port Tewfik = Būr Tawfīq 199 C 3
Porttipahdan tekojärvi 114-115 LM 3-4
Port Townsend, WA 66-67 B 1
Portugal 132-133 C 10-D 8
Portugalete 132-133 F 7
Portugália = Luachimo 198 D 3
Portugues, El — 98-99 D 6
Portuguesa, Río — 98-99 F 3
Portumna = Port Omna 116-117 CD 7
Port Union 51 K 3
Port-Vendres 132-133 J 7
Port Victoria [EUA] 198 F 1-2
Port Vladimir 142-143 FG 2
Port Washington, NY 82 III d 2
Port Washington, WI 70-71 G 4
Port Weld 174-175 CD 6
Port Wells 52-53 NO 6
Port William 116-117 G 6
Port Wing, WI 70-71 E 2
Porvenir, El — [MEX] 76-77 AB 7
Porvoo = Borgå 114-115 LM 7
Posadas [RA] 103 E 3
Posen, MI 70-71 J 3
Poshan = Boshan 166-167 M 4
Posio 114-115 N 4
Posjet 154-155 Z 9
Poso 174-175 H 7
Posŏng 166-167 O 5
Posse 98-99 K 7
Possum Kingdom Reservoir 76-77 E 6
Post, OR 66-67 C 3
Post, TX 76-77 D 6
Post Falls, ID 66-67 E 2
Postmasburg 198 D 7
Pôsto Indígena 98-99 H 5
Postojna 138-139 F 3
Poston, AZ 74-75 F 5
Postville, IA 70-71 E 4
Potawatomi Indian Reservation 70-71 BC 6
Potchefstroom 198 E 7
Poteau, OK 76-77 G 5
Poteet, TX 76-77 E 8
Potenza 138-139 F 5
Potgietersrus 198 E 6
Pothea = Kálymnos 138-139 M 7
Potholes Reservoir 66-67 D 2
Poti 142-143 HJ 7
Potiskum 194-195 G 6
Potlatch, ID 66-67 E 2
Pot Mountain 66-67 F 2
Potomac River 72-73 H 5
Potomac River, South Branch — 72-73 G 5
Potosi, MO 70-71 E 7
Potosí [BOL, place] 98-99 F 8
Potosí, El — 86-87 K 5
Potossí, El — 86-87 K 5
Potrerillos [Honduras] 86-87 R 10
Potrerillos [RCH] 103 C 3
Potrero, El — 76-77 B 8
Potrero, San Francisco-, CA 83 I b 2
Põtsamaa 142-143 E 4
Potsdam 124 F 2
Potsdam, NY 72-73 J 2
Potter, NE 68-69 E 5
Potts Camps, MS 78-79 E 3
Pottstown, PA 72-73 J 4
Pottsville, PA 72-73 H 4
Pottuvil = Potuvil 160-161 N 7
Potuvil 160-161 N 7
Pouce Coupe 48 GH 2
Poughkeepsie, NY 58-59 LM 3
Poulin de Courval, Lac — 51 AB 3
Poŭn 170-171 F 4
Pouso 98-99 H 11
Pouso Alegre [BR, Mato Grosso] 98-99 H 7
Pouso Alegre [BR, Minas Gerais] 98-99 K 9
Poutrincourt, Lac — 50 O 2
Póvoa de Varzim 132-133 C 8
Povorino 142-143 H 5
Povungnituk 46-47 V 6
Powassan 72-73 G 1
Powder River, WY 68-69 C 4
Powder River [USA, Montana] 58-59 E 2
Powder River [USA, Oregon] 66-67 E 3
Powder River, North Fork — 68-69 C 4
Powder River, South Fork — 68-69 C 4
Powder River Pass 68-69 C 3
Powderville, MT 68-69 D 3
Powell, WY 68-69 B 3
Powell, Lake — 58-59 D 4
Powell Butte, OR 66-67 C 3
Powell Creek 182-183 FG 3
Powell Islands = South Orkneys 31 C 32
Powell River 46-47 M 8
Power, MT 66-67 H 2
Powers, MI 70-71 G 3
Powers, OR 66-67 AB 4
Powers Lake, ND 68-69 E 1
Powhatan, LA 78-79 C 5
Powys 116-117 H 8
Poxoréu 98-99 J 8
Poyang Hu 166-167 M 6
Poygan, Lake — 70-71 F 3
Požarevac 138-139 J 3
Poza Rica 58-59 G 7
Požeg 142-143 KL 3
Poznań 124 H 2
Pozo, El — 86-87 F 2
Pozo Almonte 103 C 2
Pozoblanco 132-133 E 9
Pozo Hondo [RA] 103 D 3
Pozzallo 138-139 F 7
Pozzuoli 138-139 EF 5
Pra [WG] 194-195 D 7
Prachuap Khiri Khan 174-175 CD 4
Praděd 124 H 3
Prades 132-133 J 7
Prades Thai = Muang Thai 174-175 CD 3
Prado [BR] 98-99 M 8
Prague, NE 68-69 H 5
Prague, OK 76-77 F 5
Prague = Praha 124 G 3
Praha 124 G 3
Praia 188-189 E 7
Praião, Cachoeira do — 98-99 K 8
Prainha [BR, Amazonas] 98-99 G 6
Prainha [BR, Pará] 98-99 J 5
Prairie, ID 66-67 F 4
Prairie, La — 82 I bc 2
Prairie City, OR 66-67 D 3
Prairie Dog Creek 68-69 F 6
Prairie Dog Town Fork 76-77 DE 5
Prairie du Chien, WI 70-71 E 4
Prairie River 49 G 4
Prairies 46-47 Q 7-R 9
Prairies, Rivière des — 82 I ab 1
Pran Buri 174-175 CD 4
Prānhita 160-161 MN 7
Praskoveja 142-143 HJ 7
Prasonēsion, Akrōtērion — 138-139 MN 8
Prata [BR, Pará] 98-99 K 5
Prata, Rio — 98-99 P 9
Pratas = Dongsha Qundao 166-167 LM 7
Prato 138-139 D 4
Pratt 49 J 6
Pratt, KS 68-69 G 7
Prattville, AL 78-79 F 4
Prawle Point 116-117 H 10
Prêbeza 138-139 J 6
Precordillera 103 C 3-4
Predivinsk 154-155 R 6
Preeceville 49 G 4-5
Pregol'a 124 K 1
Preissac, Lac — 50 M 2
Prelate 49 D 5
Premier 52-53 y 8
Premio 51 D 2
Premont, TX 76-77 EF 9
Premuda 138-139 F 3
Prentice, WI 70-71 EF 3
Prentiss, MS 78-79 E 5
Prenzlau 124 FG 2
Přerov 124 H 4
Prescott 72-73 J 2
Prescott, AR 78-79 C 4
Prescott, AZ 58-59 D 5
Prescott, WI 70-71 D 3
Presho, SD 68-69 FG 4
Presidencia Roque Sáenz Peña 103 D 3
Presidente Aleman, Presa — 86-87 M 8
Presidente Dutra 98-99 L 6
Presidente Epitácio 98-99 J 9
Presidente Hermes 98-99 G 7
Presidente Prudente 98-99 J 9
Presidio, TX 58-59 F 6
Prešov 124 K 4
Prespa Lake = Prespansko jezero 138-139 J 5
Prespansko Ezero 138-139 J 5
Presque Isle, ME 58-59 N 2
Presque Isle Point 70-71 G 2
Press Lake 50 D 3
Prestea 194-195 D 7
Presteigne 116-117 HJ 8
Preston, CA 74-75 B 3
Preston, ID 66-67 H 4
Preston, MN 70-71 DE 4
Preston, MO 70-71 D 7
Preston [AUS] 182-183 C 4
Preston [GB] 116-117 J 7
Prestonsburg, KY 80-81 E 2
Prestwick 116-117 G 5
Preto, Rio — [BR ◁ Rio Grande] 98-99 K 7
Preto, Rio — [BR ◁ Rio Madeira] 98-99 G 9
Preto, Rio — [BR ◁ Rio Negro] 98-99 F 4
Preto, Rio — [BR ◁ Rio Paracatu] 98-99 K 8
Preto do Igapó-Açu, Rio — 98-99 H 7
Pretoria 198 E 7
Pretty Prairie, KS 68-69 GH 7
Preveza = Prébeza 138-139 J 6
Préville 82 I c 2
Prey Veng 174-175 E 4
Priargunsk 154-155 WX 7
Pribilof Islands 30 D 35-36
Příbram 124 G 4
Pribrežnyj chrebet 154-155 Za 6
Price 51 B 3
Price, UT 58-59 D 4
Price Island 48 C 3
Price River 74-75 H 3
Prichard, AL 58-59 J 5
Prichard, ID 66-67 EF 2
Priego de Córdoba 132-133 E 10
Prieska 198 D 7
Priest Lake 66-67 E 1
Priest Rapids Reservoir 66-67 CD 2
Priest River, ID 66-67 E 1
Prijedor 138-139 G 3
Prikaspijskaja nizmennost' 142-143 JK 6
Prikumsk 142-143 H 7

Prikumsk 261

Prilep 138-139 J 5
Priluki 142-143 F 5
Primeira Cachoeira 98-99 J 5
Primghar, IA 70-71 C 4
Primorskij chrebet 154-155 TU 7
Primorsko-Achtarsk 142-143 G 6
Primrose Lake 49 D 3
Primrose River 52-53 U 6
Prince Albert 46-47 P 7
Prince Albert Mountains 31 B 16-17
Prince Albert National Park 46-47 P 7
Prince Albert Peninsula 46-47 NO 3
Prince Albert Sound 46-47 NO 3
Prince Alfred, Cape — 46-47 KL 3
Prince Charles Island 46-47 V 4
Prince Charles Range 31 B 7
Prince Edward Bay 72-73 H 2-3
Prince Edward Island 46-47 Y 8
Prince Edward Islands 31 E 4
Prince Edward Peninsula 72-73 H 2-3
Prince Frederick, MD 72-73 H 5
Prince George 46-47 M 7
Prince Gustav Adolf Sea 46-47 P 2
Prince Island = Pulau Panaitan 174-175 DE 8
Prince of Wales, Cape — 46-47 C 4-5
Prince of Wales Island [AUS] 182-183 H 2
Prince of Wales Island [CDN] 46-47 QR 3
Prince of Wales Island [USA] 46-47 JK 6
Prince of Wales Island = Wales Island 46-47 T 4
Prince of Wales Strait 46-47 N 3
Prince Patrick Island 46-47 M 2
Prince Regent Inlet 46-47 ST 3
Prince Regent Luitpold Land = Prinzregent-Luitpold-Land 31 B 33-34
Prince Rupert 46-47 KL 7
Princes Bay, New York-, NY 82 III a 3
Princess Anne, MD 72-73 J 5
Princess Astrid Land = Princesse Astrid land 31 B 1-2
Princess Charlotte Bay 182-183 H 2
Princess Elizabeth Land 31 BC 8-9
Princess Royal Island 46-47 L 7
Princeton 66-67 C 1
Princeton, CA 74-75 BC 3
Princeton, IA 70-71 D 5
Princeton, IL 70-71 F 5
Princeton, IN 70-71 G 6
Princeton, KY 78-79 F 2
Princeton, MI 70-71 G 2
Princeton, MN 70-71 D 3
Princeton, NJ 72-73 J 4
Princeton, WI 70-71 F 4
Princeton, WV 80-81 F 2
Princetown 116-117 H 10
Prince William Sound 46-47 G 5
Príncipe, Ilha do — 194-195 F 8
Príncipe da Baira 98-99 G 7
Príncipe da Beira 98-99 G 7
Prineville, OR 66-67 C 3
Pringle, SD 68-69 E 4
Prins Christian Sund 46-47 c 5-d 6
Prinsesse Astrid land 31 B 1-2
Prinsesse Ragnhild land 31 B 3
Prins Harald land 31 B 4-C 5
Prinzapolca [NIC, place] 88-89 E 8
Prinzapolca [NIC, river] 88-89 D 8
Prinzregent-Luitpold-Land 31 B 33-34
Prior, Cabo — 132-133 C 7
Priozersk = Prioz'orsk 154-155 DE 5
Prioz'orsk 154-155 DE 5
Prip'at 142-143 EF 5
Priština 138-139 J 4
Pritchett, CO 68-69 E 7
Privas 132-133 K 6
Priverno 138-139 E 5
Prividencia, Isla de — 98-99 C 2
Privolžskaja vozvyšennosť 142-143 H 6-J 5
Prizren 138-139 J 4
Probolinggo 174-175 F 8
Prochladnyj 142-143 H 7
Procter 48 J 5
Proctor, TX 76-77 E 6-7
Proddattūru = Proddatūr 160-161 M 8
Proddatūr 160-161 M 8
Professor Dr. Ir. W. J. van Blommesteinmeer 98-99 H 4
Progreso [MEX, Coahuila] 76-77 D 9
Progreso [MEX, Yucatán] 58-59 J 7
Progreso [RA] 103 D 4
Progreso, El — [GCA] 86-87 P 10
Progreso, El — [Honduras] 58-59 J 8
Prokopjevsk 154-155 Q 7
Prokopyevsk = Prokopjevsk 154-155 Q 7
Prokuplje 138-139 J 4
Proletarsk 142-143 H 6
Prome = Pyin 174-175 C 3
Promyslovka 170-171 J 1
Prončiščeva, bereg — 154-155 UV 2-3
Propriá 98-99 M 7
Propriano 138-139 C 5
Proserpine 182-183 J 4
Prosna 124 J 3
Prospect, OR 66-67 B 4
Prospector 49 H 3-4
Prospect Point 82 III d 1
Prospekt Park 82 III c 3
Prosser, WA 66-67 D 2
Prostějov 124 H 4
Protection, KS 76-77 E 4
Provadija 138-139 M 4
Provence 132-133 K 7-L 6
Providence, KY 70-71 G 7
Providence, RI 58-59 MN 3
Providence, Cape — [NZ] 182-183 MN 9
Providence, Cape — [USA] 52-53 ef 1
Providence Island 198 JK 3
Providence Mountains 74-75 F 5
Providencia 58-59 KL 9
Providência, Serra da — 98-99 H 10
Providenciales Island 88-89 K 4
Providenija 154-155 kl 5
Provincetown, MA 72-73 LM 3
Provins 132-133 J 4
Provo, SD 68-69 E 4
Provo, UT 58-59 D 3
Provost 46-47 O 7
Prudenville, MI 70-71 H 3
Prudhoe Bay [CDN, bay] 52-53 NO 1
Prudhoe Bay [CDN, place] 46-47 G 3
Prudhoe Land 46-47 XY 2
Prüm 124 C 3
Prūsa = Bursa 160-161 B 2-3
Pruszków 124 K 2
Prut' 142-143 E 6
Pruth 138-139 N 3
Pryor, OK 76-77 G 4
Pryor Creek 68-69 B 3
Pryor Mountains 68-69 B 3
Przemyśl 124 L 4
Prževal'sk 160-161 M 2
Przeworsk 124 L 3
Psará 138-139 L 6
Psérimos 138-139 M 7
Pskov 142-143 E 4
Ps'ol 142-143 F 6
Pszczyna 124 J 3-4
Ptolemaïs 138-139 J 5
Ptuj 138-139 FG 2
Puale Bay 52-53 K 8
Pucallpa 98-99 E 6
Pucarani 98-99 F 8
Puchang Hai = Lob nuur 166-167 G 3
Pucheng [TJ, Fujian] 166-167 M 6
Pucheng [TJ, Shaanxi] 166-167 KL 4-5
Puchi = Puqi 166-167 L 6
Puck 124 J 1
Pūdão 174-175 C 1
Pudasjärvi 114-115 M 5
Puding, Cape — = Tanjung Puting 174-175 F 7
Pudino 154-155 OP 6
Pudož 154-155 F 5
Puebla [MEX, administrative unit] 86-87 LM 8
Puebla [MEX, place] 58-59 G 8
Puebla, La — 132-133 J 9
Puebla de Sanabria 132-133 D 7
Pueblo, CO 58-59 F 4
Pueblo Bonito, NM 74-75 JK 5
Pueblo Hundido 103 BC 3
Pueblo Nuevo [PA] 58-59 b 2-3
Pueblo Nuevo [YV] 98-99 F 2
Pueblo Valley 74-75 HJ 6
Pueblo Viejo [CO] 98-99 F 4
Puelches 103 C 5
Puenteáreas 132-133 CD 7
Puente de Ixtla 86-87 L 8
Puerco, Rio — 76-77 A 5
Puerco River 74-75 J 5
Puercos, Morro de — 88-89 FG 11
Pu-êrh-ching = Burchun 166-167 F 2
Puerto Acosta 98-99 F 8
Puerto Aisén 103 B 7
Puerto Alegre [BOL] 98-99 G 7
Puerto Alfonso 98-99 E 5
Puerto Ángel 86-87 MN 10
Puerto Argentina 98-99 E 4
Puerto Armuelles 58-59 K 10
Puerto Asís 98-99 D 4
Puerto Ayacucho 98-99 F 3
Puerto Baquerizo 98-99 B 5
Puerto Barrios 58-59 HJ 8
Puerto Berrío 98-99 E 3
Puerto Caballas 98-99 D 7
Puerto Cabello 98-99 F 2
Puerto Cabezas 58-59 K 9
Puerto Carreño 98-99 F 3
Puerto Casado 103 E 2
Puerto Castilla 88-89 CD 6
Puerto Chicama 98-99 CD 6
Puerto Cisnes 103 B 6-7
Puertocitos 86-87 C 2
Puerto Cortés [CR] 88-89 DE 10
Puerto Cortés [Honduras] 58-59 J 8
Puerto Cumarebo 98-99 F 2
Puerto de Chorrera 58-59 b 3
Puerto de Lobos 74-75 G 7
Puerto del Rosario 194-195 B 3
Puerto de Nutrias 98-99 EF 3
Puerto de Santa Maria, El — 132-133 D 10
Puerto Deseado 103 CD 7
Puerto Elvira 103 E 2
Puerto Escondido [MEX] 86-87 LM 10
Puerto Esperidião 98-99 H 8
Puerto Estrella 98-99 E 2
Puerto Frey 98-99 G 7
Puerto Grether 98-99 FG 8
Puerto Harberton 103 C 8
Puerto Heath 98-99 F 7
Puerto Iguazú 103 EF 3
Puerto Isabel 98-99 H 8
Puerto Juárez 58-59 J 7
Puerto La Cruz 98-99 G 2
Puerto Leguízamo 98-99 E 5
Puerto Lempira 88-89 DE 7
Puerto Libertad 86-87 D 3
Puertollano 132-133 EF 9
Puerto Lobos [MEX] 86-87 D 2
Puerto Lobos [RA] 103 C 6
Puerto Madero 86-87 O 10
Puerto Madryn 103 C 6
Puerto Maldonado 98-99 EF 7
Puerto Manatí 88-89 H 4
Puerto México = Coatzacoalcos 58-59 H 8
Puerto Montt 103 B 6
Puerto Natales 103 B 8
Puerto Nuevo [CO] 98-99 F 3
Puerto Ordaz, Ciudad Guayana- 98-99 G 3
Puerto Padre 88-89 HJ 4
Puerto Páez 98-99 F 3
Puerto Peñasco 86-87 CD 2
Puerto Pilón 58-59 b 2
Puerto Pinasco 103 E 2
Puerto Pirámides 103 D 6
Puerto Píritu 98-99 FG 2-3
Puerto Pizarro 98-99 E 5
Puerto Plata 58-59 M 8
Puerto Portillo 98-99 E 6
Puerto Potrero 88-89 CD 9
Puerto Prado 98-99 DE 7
Puerto Princesa 174-175 G 5
Puerto Quellón 103 B 6
Puerto Quellón = Quellón 103 B 6
Puerto Ramírez 103 B 6
Puerto Real 132-133 DE 10
Puerto Rico [BOL] 98-99 F 7
Puerto Rico [Puerto Rico] 58-59 N 8
Puerto Rico Trench 26-27 FG 4
Puerto Rondón 98-99 E 3
Puerto San Julián 103 C 7
Puerto Santa Cruz 103 C 8
Puerto Santa Cruz = Santa Cruz 103 C 8
Puerto Sastre 103 E 2
Puerto Suárez 98-99 H 8
Puerto Supe 98-99 D 7
Puerto Tejada 98-99 D 4
Puerto Trinidad 58-59 b 3
Puerto Vallarta 86-87 H 7
Puerto Victoria [PE] 98-99 DE 6
Puerto Wilches 98-99 E 3
Puerto Williams 103 C 9
Pueyrredón, Lago — 103 B 7
Pugačov 154-155 HJ 7
Pūgal 160-161 L 5
Puget Sound 66-67 B 2
Pùglia 138-139 FG 5
Pugwash 46-47 Y 8
Pujehun 194-195 B 7
Pujŏn-ho 170-171 FG 2
Puka Puka 34-35 L 5
Pukatawagan 49 H 3
Pukchin 170-171 E 2
Pukch'ŏng 166-167 O 3
Puket = Ko Phuket 174-175 C 5
Pukhan-gang 170-171 F 3-4
Puksa 142-143 H 3
Puksubæk-san = Ch'ail-bong 170-171 F 2
Pula 138-139 E 3
Pulacayo 98-99 F 9
Pulandian = Xinjin 170-171 CD 3
Pulantien = Xinjin 170-171 CD 3
Pulap 174-175 N 5
Pular, Volcán — 103 C 2
Pulaski, NY 72-73 HJ 3
Pulaski, TN 78-79 F 3
Pulaski, VA 80-81 F 2
Pulaski, WI 70-71 F 3
Puławy 124 L 3
Puli = Tash Qurghan 166-167 D 4
Pullmann, WA 66-67 E 2
Pulo Anna 174-175 K 6
Pulog, Mount — 174-175 H 3
Pulozero 114-115 PQ 3
Púlpito, Punta — 86-87 E 4
Pułtusk 124 K 2
Pu-lun-t'o Hai = Ojorong nuur 166-167 F 2
Pulusuk 174-175 NO 5
Puluwat 174-175 NO 5
Pumpkin Creek 68-69 D 3
Pumpville, TX 76-77 D 8
Puná [EC] 98-99 CD 5
Puna = Pune 160-161 L 7
Puná, Isla — 98-99 C 5
Puna Argentina 103 C 2-3
Punākha = Phunakha 160-161 OP 5
Punata 98-99 F 8
Punchaw 48 F 3
Pune 160-161 L 7
Puṇē = Pune 160-161 L 7
P'ungnam-ni 170-171 F 5
P'ungnyu-ri 170-171 F 2
P'ungsan 170-171 FG 2
Punia 198 E 2
Punjab [IND] 160-161 LM 4
Punjab [PAK] 160-161 L 4
Puno = San Carlos de Puno 98-99 EF 8
Punta Alta 103 D 5
Punta Arenas [RCH, place] 103 BC 8
Punta Baja [MEX, Baja California Norte] 58-59 C 5
Punta Baja [MEX, Sonora] 86-87 DE 3
Punta Baja [YV] 98-99 G 3
Punta de Díaz 103 BC 3
Punta Delgada [RA, place] 103 D 6
Punta Delgada [RCH] 103 C 8
Punta Gorda, FL 80-81 bc 3
Punta Gorda [BH] 58-59 J 8
Punta Gorda [NIC] 88-89 E 7
Punta Mala 58-59 L 10
Punta Morro 103 B 3
Punta Negra [PE] 98-99 C 6
Punta Norte 103 D 6
Punta Norte del Cabo San Antonio 103 E 5
Punta Pequeña 86-87 D 4
Punta Rasa 103 D 6
Puntarenas 58-59 K 9-10
Punta Rosa 86-87 EF 4
Puntas Negras, Cerro — 103 C 2
Punta Sur del Cabo San Antonio 103 E 5
Puntilla, La — 98-99 C 5
Punuk Islands 52-53 C 5
Punxsutawney, PA 72-73 G 4
Punyu = Guangzhou 166-167 LM 7
Puolanka 114-115 MN 5
Pup'yŏng-dong 170-171 G 2
Puqi 166-167 L 6
Puquio 98-99 E 7
Puquios [RCH ↗ Arica] 103 C 1
Pur 154-155 O 4
Purcell, OK 76-77 F 5
Purcell Mount 52-53 J 3
Purcell Mountains 46-47 N 7-8
Purcell Mountains Provincial Park 48 JK 4
Purgatoire River 68-69 DE 7
Purgatory, AK 52-53 N 3
Puri 160-161 O 7
Purísima, La — 86-87 DE 4
Purnea 160-161 O 5
Purniyā = Purnea 160-161 O 5
Pursat 174-175 D 4
Purukcau 174-175 F 7
Purūlia 160-161 O 6
Puruliyā = Purūlia 160-161 O 6
Purus, Rio — 98-99 F 6
Purvis, MS 78-79 E 5
Purwakarta 174-175 E 8
Purwaredja = Purworejo 174-175 EF 8
Purwokerto 174-175 EF 8
Purworejo 174-175 EF 8
Puryŏng 170-171 GH 1-2
Pusan 166-167 OP 4
Puškin 154-155 DE 6
Puškino 142-143 J 5
Puskitamika, Lac — 50 N 2
Püspökladány 124 K 5
Putao = Pūdão 174-175 C 1
Put'atina, ostrov — 170-171 J 1
Puthein 174-175 B 3
Putian 166-167 M 6
Putien = Putian 166-167 M 6
Puting, Tanjung — 174-175 F 7
Putla de Guerrero 86-87 M 9
Putorana, plato — 154-155 RS 4
Puttalam = Puttalama 160-161 M 9
Puttalama 160-161 M 9
Puttgarden 124 E 1
Puttuchcheri = Pondicherry 160-161 MN 8
Putumayo [CO, place] 98-99 D 4-5
Putumayo, Río — 98-99 E 5
Putuskum = Potiskum 194-195 G 6
Puulavesi 114-115 M 7
Puuwai, HI 78-79 b 2
Puxico, MO 78-79 D 2
Puy, le — 132-133 J 6
Puyallup, WA 66-67 B 2
Puyehue [RCH, place] 103 B 6
Puyo 98-99 D 5
Pwani 198 G 3
Pweto 198 E 3
Pwllheli 116-117 G 8
Pye Islands 52-53 MN 7
Pyhäjärvi 114-115 L 6
Pyhäjoki 114-115 L 5-6
Pyhäranta 114-115 JK 7
Pyhätunturi 114-115 M 4
Pyin 174-175 C 3
Pyinmanā 174-175 C 3
Pýlos 138-139 J 7
Pymatuning Reservoir 72-73 F 4
Pyŏktong 170-171 E 2
Pyŏngam-ni 170-171 F 5
P'yŏngan-namdo 170-171 EF 3
P'yŏngan-pukto 170-171 E 2-3
P'yŏngch'ang 170-171 G 4
P'yŏnggang 170-171 F 3
Pyŏnggok-tong 170-171 G 4
P'yŏnghae 170-171 G 4
P'yŏngnamjin 170-171 F 2
P'yŏngt'aek 170-171 F 4
P'yŏngyang 166-167 NO 4
Pyote, TX 76-77 C 7
Pyramid, NV 66-67 D 5
Pyramid Lake 58-59 C 3
Pyramid Lake Indian Reservation 74-75 D 3
Pyrenees 132-133 G-J 7
Pyre Peak 52-53 k 4
Pyrgion 138-139 LM 6
Pýrgos [GR, Pelopónnēsos] 138-139 J 7
Pýrgos [GR, Sámos] 138-139 M 7
Pyrzyce 124 G 2
Pyšma 142-143 M 4
Pytalovo 142-143 E 4
Pyu = Hpyū 174-175 C 3

Q

Qa'āmiyāt, Al- 160-161 F 7
Qābes = Qābis 194-195 FG 2
Qābis 194-195 FG 2
Qābis, Khalīj al- 194-195 G 2
Qabīt, Wādī — = Wādī Qitbīt 160-161 G 7
Qabr Hūd 160-161 FG 7
Qadārif, Al- 194-195 M 6
Qadīmah, Al- 160-161 DE 6
Qā'en 160-161 H 4
Qaf, Bi'r al- 194-195 H 3
Qafṣah 194-195 F 2
Qāhirah, Al- 194-195 KL 2
Qāhirah-Miṣr al-Jadīdah, Al- 199 BC 2
Qairouān, El — = Al-Qayrawān 194-195 FG 1
Qairwan = Al-Qayrawān 194-195 FG 1
Qaisā = Qaysā' 160-161 G 8
Qal'ah, Al- 194-195 F 1
Qal'āh-ye Shaharak = Shaharak 160-161 J 4
Qal'a-i-Bist 160-161 JK 4
Qal'a-i-Naw 160-161 J 3-4
Qal'a-i-Shahar 160-161 K 3
Qalāt 160-161 K 5
Qal'at al-'Azlam 199 D 4
Qal'at al-'Uwainīd = Qal'at al-'Azlam 199 D 4
Qal'at Bishah 160-161 E 6-7
Qalb ar-Rīshāt 194-195 B 4
Qalībīyah 194-195 G 1
Qallābāt 194-195 M 6
Qalmah 194-195 F 1
Qaltat Zammūr 194-195 B 3
Qalyūb 199 B 2
Qamar, Ghubbat al- 160-161 G 7
Qamar, Jabal al- 160-161 G 7
Qāmishlīyah, Al- 160-161 E 3
Qânâq 46-47 WX 2
Qandahār = Kandahār 160-161 K 4
Qandala 194-195 b 1
Qanṭarah, Al- [ET] 199 C 2
Qaqortoq 46-47 b 5
Qara Dong 166-167 E 4
Qaramai 166-167 EF 2
Qaramurun davan 154-155 MN 3
Qara Qash Darya 166-167 D 4
Qara Qorām = Karakoram 160-161 L 3-M 4
Qara Shahr 166-167 F 3
Qardho 194-195 b 2
Qareh Dāgh 160-161 F 3
Qarghaliq 166-167 D 4
Qarliq Tagh 166-167 GH 3
Qarn at-Tays, Jabal — 199 C 6
Qarnayt, Jabal — 160-161 E 6
Qarqannah, Jazur — 194-195 G 2
Qārrāt Ṣaḥrā' al-Igīdi 194-195 C 4-D 3
Qārūn, Birkat — 194-195 KL 3
Qaryah 160-161 E 7
Qaryatayn, Al- 142-143 G 9
Qaṣab = Al-Khaṣab 160-161 H 5
Qaṣab, Wādī — 199 C 4
Qaṣbah, Rā's — 199 D 3-4
Qāshqār 166-167 CD 4
Qāshqār daryā 166-167 CD 4
Qasigiánguit 46-47 ab 4
Qaṣīm, Al- 160-161 E 5
Qaṣr, Al- [ET] 194-195 K 3
Qasr al-Bukhari 194-195 E 1
Qaṣrayn, Al- 194-195 F 1-2
Qaṣr Banī Walīd 194-195 G 2
Qaṣr-e Shīrīn 142-143 J 9
Qaṣṣerîn, El — = Al-Qaṣrayn 194-195 F 1-2
Qaṣūr 160-161 L 4
Qāsvīn = Qazvīn 160-161 FG 3
Qatar 160-161 G 5
Qaṭīf, Al- 160-161 F 5
Qaṭrānī, Jabal — 199 B 3
Qaṭrūn, Al- 194-195 GH 4
Qaṭṭār, Ḥāssī al- 194-195 K 2
Qaṭṭār, Jabal — 199 C 4
Qattara Depression = Munhafaḍ al-Qaṭṭarah 194-195 K 2-3
Qaṭṭārah, Munhafaḍ al- 194-195 K 2-3
Qawz Rajab 194-195 M 5
Qay'īyah, Al- 160-161 E 6
Qayrawān, Al- 194-195 FG 1
Qaysā' 160-161 G 8
Qayṣūhmah, Al- 160-161 F 5
Qaysūm, Jazā'ir — 199 CD 4
Qazvīn 160-161 FG 3
Qedhāref, El- = Al-Qaḍārif 194-195 M 6
Qeisûm, Gezir — = Jazā'ir Qaysūm 199 CD 4
Qelībia = Qalībiyah 194-195 G 1
Qenâ = Qinā 194-195 L 3
Qenâ, Wâdî — = Wādī Qinā 199 C 4
Qenîtra, el — = Al-Q'nitrah 194-195 C 2
Qeqertarssuatsiaq 46-47 a 5
Qeqertarssuq 46-47 Za 4
Qeshm 160-161 H 5
Qeshm = Jazīreh Qeshm 160-161 H 5
Qeshm, Jazīreh- 160-161 H 5
Qezel Owzan, Rūd-e — 160-161 F 3
Qiandongnan Zizhizhou 166-167 K 6
Qianjiang [TJ, Hubei] 166-167 L 5
Qianjiang [TJ, Sichuan] 166-167 K 6
Qiannon Zizhizhou 166-167 K 6
Qian Shan [TJ, mountains] 170-171 D 2-3
Qianwei 170-171 C 2
Qiblī Qamūlā, Al- 199 C 5
Qiduqou 166-167 GH 5
Qiemo = Chārchān 166-167 F 4
Qift 199 C 4-5
Qil'a Safeḍ 160-161 J 5
Qilian Shan 166-167 HJ 4
Qilin Hu = Seling Tsho 166-167 FG 5
Qinā 194-195 L 3
Qinā, Wādī — 199 C 4
Qin'an 166-167 K 5
Qing'an 166-167 O 2
Qingcheng = Qing'an 166-167 O 2
Qingdao 166-167 N 4
Qingduizi 170-171 D 3
Qinghai 166-167 GH 4
Qing Hai = Chöch nuur 166-167 H 4
Qinghecheng 170-171 E 2
Qinghemen 170-171 C 2
Qingjiang [TJ, Jiangsu] 166-167 M 5
Qingjiang [TJ, Jiangxi] 166-167 M 6
Qinglong 170-171 B 2
Qinglong He 170-171 B 2
Qingshuitai 170-171 DE 1
Qingyang [TJ, Gansu] 166-167 K 4
Qingyuan [TJ, Guangdong] 166-167 L 7
Qingyuan [TJ, Liaoning] 170-171 E 1
Qingyuan = Baoding 166-167 LM 4
Qin He 166-167 L 4
Qinhuangdao 166-167 MN 3-4
Qin Ling 166-167 KL 5
Qinyang 166-167 L 4
Qinzhou 166-167 K 7
Qionghai 166-167 L 8
Qiongshan 166-167 L 8
Qiongzhou Haixia 166-167 KL 7
Qiqihar 166-167 N 2
Qiraiya, Wâdî — = Wādī Qurayyah 199 D 2
Qishm = Qeshm [IR, island] 160-161 H 5
Qishm = Qeshm [IR, place] 160-161 H 5
Qishn 160-161 G 7
Qishrān 160-161 D 6
Qitai 166-167 FG 3
Qitbīt, Wādī — 160-161 G 7
Qizan = Jīzān 160-161 E 7
Qizil Uzun = Rūd-e Qezel Owzan 160-161 F 3
Q'nitrah, Al- 194-195 C 2
Qom 160-161 G 4
Qomul = Hami 166-167 G 3
Qoqriāl = Qūqriāl 194-195 K 7
Qoseir, El- = Al-Quṣayr 194-195 L 3
Qoṭūr 160-161 E 3
Qôz Regeb = Qawz Rajab 194-195 M 5
Qṣar al-Kabīr, Al- 194-195 C 1
Qṣar as-Sūq = Ar-Rashidīyah 194-195 D 2
Quabbin Reservoir 72-73 K 3
Quainton 116-117 KL 9
Quakenbrück 124 CD 2
Quakertown, PA 72-73 J 4
Quanah, TX 76-77 E 5
Quân Đao Tây Sa 174-175 EF 3
Quangbinh = Đông Ho'i 174-175 E 3
Quang Ngai 174-175 EF 3-4
Quang Tri 174-175 E 3
Quang Yên 174-175 E 2
Quantico, VA 72-73 H 5
Quantock Hills 116-117 HJ 9
Quanxian = Quanzhou 166-167 KL 6
Quanzhou [TJ, Fujian] 166-167 MN 6-7

262 Prilep

Quanzhou [TJ, Guangxi Zhuangzu Zizhiqu] 166-167 KL 6
Qu'Appelle 49 G 5
Qu'Appelle River 46-47 Q 7
Quarnaro, Gulf of — = Kvarner 138-139 F 3
Quartu Sant'Elena 138-139 C 6
Quartzsite, AZ 74-75 FG 6
Quatsino 48 D 4
Quatsino Sound 48 CD 4
Quay, NM 76-77 C 5
Qùchàn 160-161 H 3
Qũchghàr 160-161 F 3
Quealy, WY 66-67 J 5
Queanbeyan 182-183 JK 7
Quebec [CDN, administrative unit] 46-47 V-Y 7
Québec [CDN, place] 46-47 W 8
Quebracho 103 E 4
Quebra Pote 98-99 K 5
Quedal, Cabo — 103 AB 6
Quedlinburg 124 E 3
Queen Alexandra Range 31 A 17-15
Queen Bess, Mount — 48 E 4
Queen Charlotte 46-47 K 7
Queen Charlotte Islands 46-47 K 7
Queen Charlotte Sound 46-47 KL 7
Queen Charlotte Strait 46-47 L 7
Queen Elizabeth Islands 46-47 N-V 2
Queen Elizabeth National Park = Ruwenzori National Park 198 EF 2
Queen Mary, Mount — 52-53 S 6
Queen Mary Coast = Queen Mary Land 31 C 10
Queen Mary Land 31 C 10
Queen Maud Gulf 46-47 Q 4
Queen Maud Land = Dronning Maud land 31 B 36-4
Queen Maud's Range = Dronning Maud fjellkjede 31 A
Queens, New York-, NY 82 III cd 2
Queensberry 116-117 H 5
Queensborough-in-Sheppey 116-117 gh 7
Queensland 182-183 GJ-J 4
Queenstown [AUS] 182-183 HJ 8
Queenstown [NZ] 182-183 N 8
Queenstown [ZA] 198 E 8
Queenstown = An Cóf 116-117 C 9
Queens Village, New-York, NY 82 III d 2
Queets, WA 66-67 A 2
Queimada, Ilha — 98-99 N 5
Quela 198 C 3
Quelimane 198 G 5
Quelpart = Cheju-do 166-167 NO 5
Quemada, La — 86-87 J 6
Quemado, NM 74-75 J 5
Quemado, TX 76-77 D 8
Quemoy = Kinmen Dao 166-167 M 7
Quenn City, IA 70-71 D 5
Que Que = Kwekwe 198 E 5
Queras, Rio — 58-59 a 3
Quercy 132-133 H 6
Querero, Cachoeira — 98-99 K 4-5
Querétaro 58-59 FG 7
Quesada 132-133 F 10
Queshan 166-167 L 5
Quesnel 46-47 M 7
Quesnel Lake 48 G 3
Questa, NM 76-77 B 4
Quetico 70-71 E 1
Quetico Lake 50 CD 3
Quetico Provincial Park 70-71 E 1
Quetta = Kwatta 160-161 K 4
Quettehou 116-117 K 11
Quévillon, Lac — 50 N 2
Quezaltenango 58-59 H 9
Quezon City 174-175 H 4
Quffah, Wàdî al- 199 C 6
Quiaca, La — 103 CD 2
Quiansu = Jiangsu 166-167 LM 6
Quibala 198 BC 4
Quibaxe 198 B 3
Quibdó 98-99 D 3
Quibell 50 C 2-3
Quiberon 132-133 F 5
Quijotoa, AZ 74-75 GH 6
Quilcene, WA 66-67 B 2
Quilengues 198 BC 4
Quilimari 103 B 4
Quillacollo 98-99 F 8
Quill Lakes 46-47 Q 7
Quillota 103 B 4
Quilon 160-161 M 9
Quilpie 182-183 H 5
Quimet 76-77 F 1
Quimilí 103 D 3
Quimper 132-133 E 4-5
Quimperle 132-133 F 5
Quinault, WA 66-67 B 2
Quinault Indian Reservation 66-67 AB 2
Quince Mil 98-99 EF 7
Quincy, CA 74-75 C 3
Quincy, FL 78-79 G 5
Quincy, IL 58-59 H 4
Quincy, MA 72-73 L 3
Quincy, WA 66-67 D 2

Quindage 198 B 3
Quines 103 C 4
Quinhagak, AK 52-53 FG 7
Qui Nho'n 174-175 EF 4
Quinn, SD 68-69 EF 3
Quinn River 66-67 E 5
Quinn River Crossing, NV 66-67 DE 5
Quintanar de la Orden 132-133 F 9
Quintana Roo 58-59 J 7-8
Quinter, KS 68-69 FG 6
Quinton, OK 76-77 G 5
Quiongdong = Quionghai 166-167 L 8
Quirigua 86-87 Q 10
Quirima 198 C 4
Quirimba, Ilhas — 198 H 4
Quissanga 198 H 4
Quissico 198 FG 6
Quitaque, TX 76-77 D 5
Quitman, GA 80-81 E 5
Quitman, MS 78-79 E 4
Quitman, TX 76-77 G 6
Quitman Mountains 76-77 B 7
Quito 98-99 D 5
Quixadá [BR, Ceará] 98-99 M 5
Quixada [BR, Rondônia] 98-99 G 10
Quixeramobim 98-99 M 5-6
Qujiang = Shaoguan 166-167 L 6-7
Qujing 166-167 J 6
Qûlàshgird = Golàshkerd 160-161 H 5
Qulayb, Bi'r — 199 CD 5
Quleib, Bîr — = Bi'r Qulayb 199 CD 5
Raichûr 160-161 M 7
Raidat aş Şai'ar = Raydat aş-Şay'ar 160-161 F 7
Raidestós = Tekirdağ 160-161 B 2
Raigarh 160-161 N 6
Railroad Pass 74-75 E 3
Railroad Valley 74-75 F 3-4
Rainbow Bridge National Monument 74-75 H 4
Rainier, OR 66-67 B 2
Rainier, Mount — 58-59 BC 2
Rainy Lake [CDN] 50 C 3
Rainy Lake [USA] 58-59 H 2
Rainy Pass Lodge, AK 52-53 L 5
Rainy River 50 B 3
Raipur [IND, Madhya Pradesh] 160-161 N 6
Raith 70-71 F 1
Rajada 98-99 L 6
Rajahmundry 160-161 N 7
Rajakoski 114-115 N 3
Râjamahêndri = Rajahmundry 160-161 N 7
Rajang [RI, river] 174-175 F 6
Râjapâlaiyam = Râjapâlaiyam 160-161 M 9
Râjapâlayam = Râjapâlaiyam 160-161 M 9
Râjasthân 160-161 LM 5
Rajchichinsk 154-155 YZ 8
Rajeputana = Râjasthân 160-161 LM 5
Râjkot 160-161 L 6
Rajputana = Râjasthân 160-161 LM 5
Râjputânâ = Râjasthân 160-161 LM 5
Râjshâhî 160-161 O 6
Rakahanga 178 K 4
Rakaia 182-183 O 8
Rakasdal 166-167 E 5
Rakata = Anak Krakatau 174-175 DE 8
Rakhshân 160-161 JK 5
Rakiura = Stewart Island 182-183 N 9
Rakops 198 D 6
Rakovnik 124 F 3
Raksakiny 154-155 NO 5
Rakvere 142-143 E 4
Raleigh 50 DE 3
Raleigh, NC 58-59 L 4
Raleigh, ND 68-69 F 2
Raleigh Bay 80-81 HJ 3
Raley 66-67 G 1
Ralik Chain 34-35 H 4
Ralls, TX 76-77 D 6
Ralston, WY 68-69 B 3
Rama 88-89 D 8
Ramadi, Ar- 160-161 E 4
Ramah 46-47 Y 6
Ramah, NM 74-75 J 5
Ramalho, Serra do — 98-99 KL 7
Raman 142-143 D 6
Ramapo Deep 166-167 R 5
Rambi 174-175 b 2
Rambré 174-175 B 3
Rambré Kyûn 174-175 B 3
Rame Head 116-117 FG 10
Ramer, AL 78-79 F 4
Ramon, NM 76-77 B 5
Ramona, CA 74-75 E 6
Ramos 98-99 M 5
Ramos Arizpe 86-87 K 5
Rampart, AK 52-53 M 4
Rampur [IND, Uttar Pradesh → Morâdâbâd] 160-161 MN 5
Ramree = Rambré 174-175 B 3
Ramree Island = Rambré Kyûn 174-175 B 3
Ramsay 50 KL 3

Rae 46-47 NO 5
Râe Bareli 160-161 N 5
Raeford, NC 80-81 G 3
Rae Isthmus 46-47 T 4
Rae Strait 46-47 RS 4
Rafaela 103 D 4
Rafael del Encanto 98-99 E 5
Rafai 194-195 J 7-8
Rafhah 160-161 E 5
Rafsanján 160-161 H 4
Rafter 49 H 3
Raft River 66-67 G 4
Raft River Mountains 66-67 G 5
Râgâ [Sudan] 194-195 K 7
Ragged Island 72-73 M 3
Ragged Island Range 88-89 J 3
Ragland, AL 78-79 FG 4
Rago, KS 68-69 GH 7
Rago = Pag 138-139 F 3
Ragozino 154-155 O 6
Ragunda 114-115 H 6
Ragusa 138-139 F 7
Ragusa = Dubrovnik 138-139 GH 4
Raha 174-175 H 7
Rahad, Ar- 194-195 L 6
Rahad, Nahr ar- 194-195 L 6
Rahad al-Bardî 194-195 J 6
Rahaeng = Tak 174-175 C 3
Rahat, Ḥarrat — 160-161 DE 6
Rahway River 82 III a 3
Raiàât, Wàdî — = Wàdî Rayâytît 199 D 6
Ramsay Lake 50 K 3
Ramseur, NC 80-81 G 3
Ramsey, IL 70-71 F 6
Ramsey [GB, England] 116-117 L 8
Ramsey [GB, I. of Man] 116-117 G 6
Ramsey Bay 116-117 G 6
Ramsey Island 116-117 F 9
Ramsgate 116-117 h 7
Ramu River 174-175 N 8
Ramuro, Rio — 98-99 L 11
Raŋ, Môṭuṇ — = Rann of Kutch 160-161 KL 6
Rancagua 103 BC 4
Ranchester, WY 68-69 C 3
Rânchi 160-161 O 6
Ranco, Lago — 103 B 6
Randazzo 138-139 F 7
Randers 114-115 CD 9
Randijaur 114-115 HJ 4
Randolph, KS 68-69 H 6
Randolph, NE 68-69 H 4
Randolph, UT 66-67 H 5
Randolph, WI 70-71 F 4
Randsburg, CA 74-75 DE 5
Randsfjord 114-115 D 7
Rânêbanûra = Rânîbennur 160-161 M 8
Rânêbanûru = Rânîbennur 160-161 M 8
Ranenburg = Rânîbennur 160-161 M 8
Ranfurly 45 C 4
Rangârvalla 114-115 cd 3
Rangeley, ME 72-73 L 2
Rangely, CO 66-67 J 5
Ranger, TX 76-77 E 6
Ranger Lake = Saymo Lake 70-71 J 2
Rangiora 182-183 O 8
Rangôn 174-175 BC 3
Rangoon = Rangôn 174-175 BC 3
Rangsang, Pulau — 174-175 D 6
Rangun = Rangôn 174-175 BC 3
Rânîbennur 160-161 M 8
Ranier, MN 70-71 D 1
Rank, Ar- 194-195 L 6
Rankin, TX 76-77 D 7
Rankins Springs 182-183 J 6
Rannoch, Loch — 116-117 G 4
Ransom, KS 68-69 FG 6
Rantauprapat 174-175 CD 6
Rantekombala, Gunung — 174-175 GH 7
Rantoul, IL 70-71 FG 5
Ranyah, Wàdî — 160-161 E 6
Raohe 166-167 P 2
Raoui, Erg er — = 'Irq ar-Rawî 194-195 D 3
Raouping, Rio — 98-99 L 11
Rapa 34-35 K 6
Rapallo 138-139 C 3
Rapelje, MT 68-69 B 2-3
Raper, Cape — 46-47 XY 4
Rapid City, SD 58-59 F 3
Rapide-Blanc 72-73 K 1
Rapides-des-Joachims 72-73 H 1
Rapid River, MI 70-71 G 2-3
Rapid River [USA, Alaska] 52-53 R 3
Rapid River [USA, Minnesota] 70-71 C 1
Rapids 50 KL 1
Rappahannock River 80-81 H 2
Râpti [IND] 160-161 N 5
Raqqah, Ar- 160-161 DE 3
Râqûbah 194-195 K 3
Râypur = Raipur [IND, Madhya Pradesh] 160-161 N 6
Ray River 52-53 M 4
Rayville, LA 78-79 CD 4
Raz, Pointe du — 132-133 E 4
R'azan' 142-143 GH 5
Razdel'naja 142-143 F 6
Razdolinsk 154-155 R 6
Razelm, Lacul — 138-139 N 3
Razgrad 138-139 M 4
R'azsk 142-143 H 5

Rathlin Island 116-117 E 5
Râth Loirc 116-117 C 8
Ratisbon = Regensburg 124 EF 4
Râtische Alpen 124 DE 5
Rat Island 52-53 s 7
Rat Islands 30 D 1
Ratlâm 160-161 LM 6
Ratmanova, ostrov — 52-53 BC 4
Ratnâgiri 160-161 L 7
Raton, NM 58-59 F 4
Rat Rapids 50 DE 2
Rattlesnake Creek 68-69 G 7
Rattlesnake Range 68-69 C 4
Rättvik 114-115 F 7
Ratz, Mount — 52-53 VW 8
Raualpindi = Râwalpindî 160-161 L 4
Rauch 103 E 5
Raudales 86-87 O 9
Raudhamelur 114-115 bc 2
Raufarhöfn 114-115 f 1
Rauma 114-115 J 7
Raumo = Rauma 114-115 J 7
Raunds 116-117 L 8
Raurkela 160-161 NO 6
Rausu 170-171 d 1-2
Ravalli, MT 66-67 F 2
Ravalpindi = Râwalpindî 160-161 L 4
Râvar 160-161 H 4
Rava-Russkaja 142-143 DE 5
Ravendale, CA 66-67 CD 5
Ravenglass 116-117 H 6
Ravenna 138-139 E 3
Ravenna, NE 68-69 G 5
Ravenna, OH 72-73 F 4
Ravensburg 124 D 5
Ravenshoe 182-183 HJ 3
Ravensworth 72-73 G 2
Ravensworth, VA 82 II a 2
Ravenwood, VA 82 II a 2
Râwalpindî 160-161 L 4
Rawa Mazowiecka 124 K 3
Rawdah, Ar- 199 B 4
Raw Hide Butte 68-69 D 4
Rawî, 'Irq ar- 194-195 D 3
Rawicz 124 H 3
Rawlinna 182-183 E 6
Rawlins, WY 58-59 E 3
Rawlinson Range 182-183 E 4-5
Rawmarsh 116-117 K 7
Rawson [RA, Chubut] 103 CD 6
Rawtenstall 116-117 JK 7
Rawwâfah, Ar- 199 E 4
Ray, MN 70-71 D 1
Ray, ND 68-69 E 1
Ray, Cape — 46-47 Z 8
Raya, Bukit — 174-175 F 7
Raya, Isla — 88-89 FG 11
Râyachûru = Raichûr 160-161 M 7
Rayâytît, Wàdî — 199 D 6
Râay Barêli = Râe Bareli 160-161 N 5
Raydat aş-Şay'ar 160-161 F 7
Râygaŗh = Raigarh 160-161 N 6
Rayne, LA 78-79 C 5
Raynesford, MT 66-67 H 2
Ray Mountains 46-47 F 4
Rayong 174-175 D 4
Râypur = Raipur [IND, Madhya Pradesh] 160-161 N 6

Reboly 142-143 F 3
Rebun-jima 166-167 QR 2
Recalde 103 D 5
Recherche, Archipelago of the — 182-183 D 6
Rechô Taung 174-175 C 4
Recht — 160-161 FG 3
Rečica 142-143 EF 5
Recife 98-99 N 6
Reconquista 103 DE 3
Recreo [RA, La Rioja] 103 CD 3
Rector, AR 78-79 D 2
Reģa'iyeh = Orûmiyeh 160-161 EF 3
Reģa'iyeh, Daryâcheh — = Daryâcheh-ye Orûmîyeh 160-161 F 3
Red Bank, NJ 72-73 J 4
Red Bay, TN 78-79 EF 3
Red Bay [CDN] 51 H 2
Red Bay [GB] 116-117 E 4
Redberry Lake 49 E 4
Red Bluff, CA 58-59 B 3
Red Bluff Lake 76-77 BC 7
Red Bluff Reservoir = Red Bluff Lake 76-77 BC 7
Red Bud, IL 70-71 EF 6
Red Butte 74-75 GH 5
Redby, MN 70-71 C 2
Redcliffe, Brisbane- 182-183 K 5
Red Cloud, NE 68-69 G 5
Redd City, MI 70-71 H 4
Red Deer 46-47 O 7
Red Deer Lake 49 H 4
Red Deer River 46-47 O 7
Red Desert 68-69 B 4-5
Red Devil, AK 52-53 J 6
Reddick, FL 80-81 b 2
Redding, CA 58-59 B 3
Reddit 50 B 3
Redditch 116-117 JK 8
Redd Peak 68-69 D 4
Rede, River — 116-117 J 5
Redeyef, Er — = Ar-R'dayif 194-195 F 2
Redfield, AR 78-79 C 3
Redfield, SD 68-69 G 3
Red Hill 182-183 HJ 7
Red Hills [USA, Alabama] 58-59 J 5
Red Hills [USA, Kansas] 68-69 G 7
Red House, NV 66-67 E 5
Redig, SD 68-69 E 3
Red Indian Lake 51 H 3
Red Lake [CDN, lake] 50 B 2
Red Lake [CDN, place] 46-47 S 7
Red Lake [USA] 58-59 G 2
Red Lake Falls, MN 70-71 BC 3
Red Lake Indian Reservation 70-71 C 1-2
Red Lake River 68-69 H 1-2
Redlands, CA 74-75 E 5-6
Red Lion, PA 72-73 H 4
Red Lodge, MT 68-69 B 3
Redmond, OR 66-67 C 3
Redmond, WA 66-67 B 2
Red Mountain, CA 74-75 E 5
Red Mountain [USA, California] 66-67 B 5
Red Mountain [USA, Montana] 66-67 G 2
Rednitz 124 E 4
Red Oak, IA 70-71 C 5
Redon 132-133 F 5
Redonda, Ponta — 98-99 M 5
Redondela 132-133 C 7
Redondo, Pico — 98-99 G 3
Redondo Beach, CA 74-75 D 6
Redoubt Volcano 52-53 L 6
Red Pheasant 49 DE 4
Red River 58-59 H 5
Red River = Sông Nhi Ha 174-175 D 2
Red River, North Fork — 76-77 E 5
Red River, Salt Fork — 76-77 E 5
Red River of the North 58-59 G 2
Redrock, AZ 74-75 H 6
Redrock, NM 74-75 J 6
Red Rock, OK 76-77 F 4
Red Rock [CDN] 48 F 3
Red Rock [USA] 83 I b 1
Red Rock Point 182-183 E 6
Redruth 116-117 E 10
Red Sandstone Desert = Ad-Dahnâ' 160-161 E 5-F 6
Red Sea 160-161 D 5-E 7
Red Springs, NC 80-81 G 3
Redstone 48 F 3
Redstone, MT 68-69 D 1
Red Tank 58-59 b 2
Redvers 68-69 F 1
Redwater Creek 68-69 D 2
Red Wharf Bay 116-117 GH 7
Redwick 116-117 J 9
Red Willow Creek 68-69 F 5
Red Wing, MN 70-71 D 3
Redwood City, CA 74-75 B 4
Redwood Falls, MN 70-71 C 3
Redwood Valley, CA 74-75 B 3
Ree, Lough — = Loch Ríbh 116-117 D 7
Reece, KS 68-69 H 7
Reed City, MI 72-73 D 3
Reeder, ND 68-69 E 2
Reedham 116-117 h 6
Reed Lake 49 H 3
Reedley, CA 74-75 D 4

Reedpoint, MT 68-69 B 3
Reedsburg, WI 70-71 EF 4
Reedsport, OR 66-67 AB 4
Reefton 182-183 O 8
Reese, MI 70-71 J 4
Reese River 74-75 E 3
Reform, AL 78-79 EF 4
Refugio, TX 76-77 F 8
Regen 124 F 4
Regência 98-99 M 8
Regência, Ponta de — 98-99 M 8
Regensburg 124 EF 4
Regent, ND 68-69 E 2
Reggane = Rijān 194-195 E 3
Règgio di Calàbria 138-139 FG 6
Règgio nell'Emìlia 138-139 D 3
Regina, MT 68-69 C 2
Regina [CDN] 46-47 Q 7
Régina [French Guiana] 98-99 J 4
Regina Beach 49 F 5
Registan = Rīgestān 160-161 JK 4
Registro 103 G 2
Regocijo 86-87 H 6
Regresso, Cachoeira — 98-99 HJ 5
Reguengos de Monsaraz 132-133 D 9
Reh 166-167 M 3
Rehoboth 198 C 6
Rehoboth Beach, DE 72-73 J 5
Reichle, MT 66-67 G 3
Reid 182-183 E 6
Reidsville, NC 80-81 G 2
Reigate 116-117 LM 9
Reihoku 170-171 GH 6
Reims 132-133 JK 4
Reina Adelaida, Archipiélago — 103 AB 8
Reinbeck, IA 70-71 D 4
Reindeer Island 49 K 4
Reindeer Lake 46-47 Q 6
Reindeer Station, AK 52-53 GH 3
Reine, la — 50 M 2
Reinosa 132-133 E 7
Reinøy 114-115 H 2-3
Reisa 114-115 J 3
Relais, le — 51 A 4
Relalhuleu 86-87 OP 10
Relem, Cerro — 103 B 5
Reliance, SD 68-69 G 4
Reliance, WY 66-67 J 5
Relizane = Ghālizān 194-195 E 1
Rellano 76-77 B 9
Remansão 98-99 JK 5
Remanso 98-99 L 6
Remanso Grande 98-99 DE 10
Remarkable, Mount — 182-183 G 6
Remédios [BR, Fernando de Noronha] 98-99 N 5
Remer, MN 70-71 D 2
Remeshk 160-161 H 5
Remington, IN 70-71 G 5
Remington, VA 72-73 H 5
Rémire 98-99 J 3-4
Remiremont 132-133 KL 4
Remote, OR 66-67 B 4
Rems 124 D 4
Remscheid 124 C 3
Remsen, NY 72-73 J 3
Remus, MI 70-71 H 4
Rena 114-115 D 7
Renascença 98-99 F 5
Rencontre East 51 J 4
Rendova Island 174-175 j 6
Rendsburg 124 DE 1
Rēnēia 138-139 L 7
Renfrew [CDN] 72-73 H 2
Renfrew [GB] 116-117 G 5
Rengat 174-175 D 7
Reni 142-143 E 6
Renison 50 L 1
Renk = Al-Rank 194-195 L 6
Renmark 182-183 H 6
Rennell Island 174-175 k 7
Rennes 132-133 G 4
Rennick Glacier 31 C 16-17
Rennie 49 L 6
Reno, ID 66-67 G 3
Reno, NV 58-59 C 4
Reno [I] 138-139 DE 3
Reno, El —, OK 58-59 G 4
Renohill, WY 68-69 C 4
Renoville, CA 74-75 EF 5
Renovo, PA 72-73 H 4
Renqiu 166-167 M 4
Rensselaer, IN 70-71 G 5
Rensselaer, NY 72-73 JK 3
Renton, WA 66-67 B 2
Renville, MN 70-71 C 3
Renwer 49 H 4
Reo 174-175 H 8
Repartição 98-99 K 7
Repartimento 98-99 K 6
Repartimento, Rio — 98-99 E 7
Repartimento, Serra — 98-99 E 7
Repton 116-117 K 8
Republic, MI 70-71 G 2
Republic, MO 78-79 C 2
Republic, WA 66-67 D 1
Republican River 58-59 G 3
Republican River, South Fork — 68-69 E 6
Repulse Bay [AUS] 182-183 JK 4
Repulse Bay [CDN, bay] 46-47 T 4
Repulse Bay [CDN, place] 46-47 TU 4
Repunshiri = Rebun-jima 170-171 b 1
Reqiang = Charqiliq 166-167 F 4
Requena [E] 132-133 G 9
Requena [PE] 98-99 E 6
Resa'iya = Orūmīyeh 160-161 EF 3
Reschenpass 124 E 5
Reserve 49 G 4
Reserve, NM 74-75 J 6
Resht = Rasht 160-161 FG 3
Resistencia 103 DE 3
Reşiţa 138-139 J 3
Resolute 46-47 S 3
Resolution Island 46-47 Y 5
Restigouche River 51 C 4
Restinga de Sefton 94 AB 7
Reston 68-69 F 1
Rethel 132-133 K 4
Réthymnon 138-139 L 8
Retimo = Réthymnon 138-139 L 8
Reus 132-133 H 8
Reuss 124 D 5
Reutlingen 124 D 4
Reva, SD 68-69 E 3
Revā = Narmada 160-161 LM 6
Revda [SU, Srednij Ural] 154-155 KL 6
Revelation Mountains 52-53 KL 6
Revelstoke 46-47 N 7
Revenue 49 D 4
Revillagigedo, Islas — 86-87 C-E 8
Revillagigedo, Islas de — 58-59 D 8
Revillagigedo Island 46-47 KL 6
Revillo, SD 68-69 H 3
Revoil-Beni-Ounif = Banī Wanīf 194-195 D 2
Rewā = Narmada 160-161 LM 6
Rewa River 98-99 J 3
Rewda = Revda 154-155 KL 6
Rex, AK 52-53 N 4
Rex, Mount — 31 B 29
Rexburg, ID 66-67 H 4
Rexford, MI 70-71 H 2
Rexford, MT 66-67 F 1
Rexton, MI 70-71 H 2
Rey, Isla del — 58-59 L 10
Reydon, OK 76-77 E 5
Reyes, Point — 74-75 B 3-4
Reykhólar 114-115 b 2
Reykholt 114-115 c 2
Reykjanes 114-115 b 3
Reykjanes Ridge 26-27 H 2-3
Reykjavík [CDN] 49 J 5
Reykjavík [IS] 114-115 bc 2
Reynaud 49 F 4
Reynolds, ID 66-67 E 4
Reynolds, IN 70-71 G 5
Reynolds Range 182-183 F 4
Reynoldsville, PA 72-73 G 4
Reynosa 58-59 G 6
Rezā'iyeh = Orūmīyeh 160-161 EF 3
Rēzekne 142-143 E 4
Rhaetian Alps = Rätische Alpen 124 DE 5
Rhayader 116-117 H 8
Rheims = Reims 132-133 JK 4
Rhein 124 C 3
Rheine 124 C 2
Rheinland-Pfalz 124 CD 3-4
Rhine = Rhein 124 C 3
Rhinelander, WI 70-71 F 3
Rhineland-Palatinate = Rheinland-Pfalz 124 C 3-4
Rhinns Point 116-117 E 5
Rhino Camp 198 F 1
Rhode Island [USA, administrative unit] 58-59 MN 3
Rhode Island [USA, island] 72-73 L 4
Rhodes = Ródos 138-139 N 7
Rhodope Mountains 138-139 KL 5
Rhön 124 DE 3
Rhondda 116-117 H 9
Rhone [CH] 124 C 5
Rhône [F] 132-133 K 6
Rhône au Rhin, Canal du — 132-133 L 4-5
Rhyddhywel 116-117 H 8
Rhyl 116-117 H 7
Rhymney 116-117 H 9
Riachão 98-99 K 6
Riad, Er — = Ar-Riyāḍ 160-161 F 6
Riāng 160-161 P 5
Riau, Kepulauan — 174-175 DE 6
Ribadeo 132-133 D 7
Ribas do Rio Pardo 98-99 J 9
Ribaṭ, Ar- 194-195 C 2
Ribatejo 132-133 C 9
Ribauè 198 G 4-5
Ribe 114-115 C 10
Ribeira [P] 132-133 C 7
Ribeirão [BR, Pernambuco] 98-99 MN 6
Ribeirão [BR, Rondônia] 98-99 FG 7
Ribeirão Preto 98-99 K 9
Ribeiro Gonçalves 98-99 KL 6
Riberalta 98-99 F 7
Rìbh, Loch — 116-117 D 7
Ribhéar, An — 116-117 AB 9
Rib Lake 72-73 FG 1
Rib Lake, WI 70-71 EF 3
Ribstone Creek 49 C 4
Ribyānah 194-195 J 4
Ribyānah, Ṣaḥrā' — 194-195 J 4
Ricardo Flores Magón 86-87 GH 2-3
Riccione 138-139 E 3-4
Rice, CA 74-75 F 5
Riceboro, GA 80-81 F 5
Rice Lake 72-73 GH 2
Rice Lake, WI 70-71 E 3
Richard's Bay 198 F 7
Richardson, AK 52-53 OP 4
Richardson Bay 83 I ab 1
Richardson Mountains 46-47 J 4
Richardton, ND 68-69 EF 2
Richelieu, Rivière — 72-73 K 1-2
Richey, MT 68-69 D 2
Richfield, ID 66-67 FG 4
Richfield, KS 68-69 F 7
Richfield, MN 70-71 D 3
Richfield, UT 74-75 GH 3
Richford, VT 72-73 K 2
Richgrove, CA 74-75 D 5
Rich Hill, MO 70-71 C 6
Richland, GA 78-79 G 4
Richland, MO 70-71 D 7
Richland, MT 68-69 C 1
Richland, WA 58-59 C 2
Richland Balsam 80-81 E 3
Richland Center, WI 70-71 EF 4
Richlands, VA 80-81 F 2
Richland Springs, TX 76-77 E 7
Richmond, CA 58-59 B 4
Richmond, IN 58-59 JK 3-4
Richmond, KS 70-71 C 6
Richmond, KY 70-71 H 7
Richmond, MO 70-71 CD 6
Richmond, TX 76-77 FG 8
Richmond, VA 58-59 L 4
Richmond [AUS] 182-183 H 4
Richmond [CDN] 72-73 KL 2
Richmond [GB] 116-117 K 6
Richmond [ZA, Kaapland] 198 D 8
Richmond [ZA, Natal] 198 F 7-8
Richmond, New York-, NY 82 III ab 4
Richmond, Point — 83 I b 1
Richmond, San Francisco-, CA 83 I ab 2
Richmond Gulf 46-47 V 6
Richmond Hill, GA 80-81 F 5
Richmond-San Rafael Bridge 83 I b 1
Richmond Valley, New York-, NY 82 III a 3
Rich Mountain 76-77 G 5
Richton, MS 78-79 E 5
Richwood, OH 72-73 E 4
Richwood, WV 72-73 F 5
Rico, CO 68-69 BC 7
Ridder = Leninogorsk 154-155 P 7
Riddle, ID 66-67 EF 4
Riddle, OR 66-67 B 4
Rideau Lake 72-73 H 2
Ridgecrest, CA 74-75 E 5
Ridgefield, NJ 82 III c 1-2
Ridgefield Park, NJ 82 III b 1
Ridgeland, SC 80-81 F 4
Ridgely, TN 78-79 E 2
Ridgetown 72-73 F 3
Ridgeway, SC 80-81 F 3
Ridgewood, New York-, NY 82 III c 2
Ridgway, CO 68-69 BC 6
Ridgway, PA 72-73 G 4
Riding Mountain 49 HJ 5
Riding Mountain National Park 46-47 Q 7
Ridīsiya, Er- = Ar-Radīsīyat Baḥrī 199 C 5
Riesa 124 F 3
Riesco, Isla — 103 B 8
Riesi 138-139 F 7
Rietfontein 198 D 7
Rieth, OR 66-67 D 3
Rieti 138-139 E 4
Rīf = Ar-Rīf 194-195 CD 1-2
Rīf, Ar- [MA, mountains] 194-195 CD 1-2
Rifle, CO 68-69 D 6
Rifstangi 114-115 ef 1
Rift Valley 198 G 1
Riga 142-143 D 4
Rīgas Jūras Līcis 142-143 D 4
Rigby, ID 66-67 H 4
Rīgestān 160-161 JK 4
Riggins, ID 66-67 E 3
Rigo 174-175 N 8
Rigolet 46-47 Z 7
Riihimäki 114-115 L 7
Riiser-Larsen halvøy 31 C 4-5
Rijān 194-195 E 3
Rijeka 138-139 F 3
Rijpfjord 114-115 l 4
Rikers Island 82 III c 2
Rikeze = Zhigatse 166-167 F 6
Rikorda, ostrov — 170-171 H 1
Riksgränsen 114-115 GH 3
Rikubetsu 170-171 c 2
Rikuzen-Takada 170-171 NO 3
Rila 138-139 K 4-5
Riley, KS 68-69 H 6
Rimah, Wādī ar- 160-161 E 5
Rimāl, Ar- = Ar-Rub' al-Khālī 160-161 F 7-G 6
Rimbey 48 K 3
Rimini 138-139 E 3
Rîmnicu Sărat 138-139 M 3
Rîmnicu Vîlcea 138-139 L 3
Rimouski 46-47 X 8
Rimouski, Parc provincial des — 51 BC 3-4
Rimouski, Rivière — 51 B 3
Rim Rocky Mountains 66-67 C 4
Rincon, NM 76-77 A 6
Rinconada 103 C 2
Rincón de Romos 86-87 J 6
Rincon Peak 76-77 B 5
Rin'gang = Riāng 160-161 P 5
Ringerike-Hønefoss 114-115 CD 7
Ringgold, LA 78-79 C 4
Ringgold, TX 76-77 F 6
Ringkøbing 114-115 BC 9
Ringling, MT 66-67 H 2
Ringling, OK 76-77 F 5
Ringold, OK 76-77 G 5
Ringvassøy 114-115 H 3
Ringwood 116-117 K 10
Ringwood, OK 76-77 E 4
Riñihue [RCH, place] 103 B 5-6
Rinja, Pulau — 174-175 G 8
Rinjani, Gunung — 174-175 G 8
Rinnes, Ben — 116-117 H 3
Río Abajo 58-59 bc 2
Riobamba 98-99 D 5
Rio Blanco [BR] 98-99 G 7
Rio Branco [BR, Acre] 98-99 D 9
Rio Branco [BR, Amazonas] 98-99 F 6
Rio Branco [BR, Rio Branco] 98-99 G 4-5
Rio Branco [BR, Rondônia] 98-99 F 9-G 10
Río Bravo 76-77 D 8
Río Bravo, Ciudad — 86-87 LM 5
Río Bravo del Norte 58-59 E 5-F 6
Río Caribe [MEX] 86-87 P 8
Río Chico [RA, Santa Cruz place] 103 C 7
Rio Claro [BR, Goiás ◁ Rio Araguaia] 98-99 J 8
Rio Claro [BR, Goiás ◁ Rio Paranaíba] 98-99 J 8
Rio Claro [TT] 58-59 O 9
Rio Colorado [BOL] 98-99 GH 11
Río Colorado [MEX] 58-59 CD 5
Río Colorado [RA, La Pampa] 103 C 5
Río Colorado [RA, Río Negro] 103 CD 5
Rio Corrente [BR, Bahia] 98-99 L 7
Río Cuarto [RA, place] 103 D 4
Rio de Janeiro [BR, administrative unit] 98-99 LM 9
Rio de Janeiro [BR, place] 98-99 L 9
Rio do Sul 103 G 3
Rio Ferro 98-99 L 11
Rio Formoso [BR, Goiás] 98-99 O 10
Rio Grande [BOL, river] 98-99 G 8
Rio Grande [BR, Minas Gerais] 98-99 K 8-9
Rio Grande [BR, Rio Grande do Sul] 103 F 4
Río Grande [MEX] 58-59 H 8
Río Grande [NIC, place] 88-89 E 8
Río Grande [NIC, river] 58-59 JK 9
Río Grande [RA, Tierra del Fuego place] 103 C 8
Rio Grande [USA, Colorado] 76-77 AB 4
Rio Grande [USA, Texas] 58-59 FG 6
Río Grande, Ciudad — 86-87 J 6
Rio Grande City, TX 76-77 E 9
Río Grande de Santiago 58-59 F 7
Rio Grande do Norte 98-99 M 6
Rio Grande do Norte = Natal 98-99 MN 6
Rio Grande do Sul 103 F 3-4
Rio Grande Rise 26-27 GH 7
Ríohacha 98-99 E 2
Río Hato 88-89 FG 10
Rio Hondo [USA, California] 83 III cd 2
Rio Hondo [USA, New Mexico] 76-77 B 6
Rioja [PE] 98-99 D 6
Rioja, La — [E] 132-133 F 7
Rioja, La — [RA, place] 103 C 3
Río Lagartos 86-87 QR 7
Rio Largo 98-99 MN 6
Río Mayo [RA, place] 103 BC 7
Río Mulatos 98-99 F 8
Río Muni = Mbini 194-195 G 8
Rio Negro [BR, Amazonas] 98-99 G 5
Rio Negro [BR, Mato Grosso] 98-99 H 8
Rio Negro [BR, Paraná place] 103 F 3
Río Negro [RA, Río Negro administrative unit] 103 C 6
Río Negro [RA, Río Negro river] 103 D 5-6
Río Negro [ROU, river] 103 EF 4
Río Negro, Embalse del — 103 E 4
Rio Negro, Pantanal do — 98-99 H 8
Rio Pardo [BR, Bahia] 98-99 L 8
Rio Pardo [BR, Mato Grosso] 98-99 J 9
Rio Pardo de Minas 98-99 L 8
Rio Perdido [BR, Goiás] 98-99 P 9
Río Primero [RA, place] 103 D 4
Rio Real 98-99 M 7
Río Seco [MEX] 86-87 E 2
Rio Solimões 98-99 F 5
Río Sonora 58-59 D 6
Ríosucio 98-99 D 3
Río Tercero [RA, place] 103 D 4
Riouw Archipel = Kepulauan Riau 174-175 DE 6
Rio Verde [BR, Goiás ◁ Rio Paranaíba] 98-99 J 8
Rio Verde [BR, Goiás place] 98-99 J 8
Rio Verde [BR, Mato Grosso ◁ Rio Paraná] 98-99 J 9
Rio Verde [BR, Mato Grosso ◁ Rio Teles Pires] 98-99 H 7
Río Verde [MEX, Oaxaca] 58-59 G 8
Rioverde [MEX, San Luis Potosí place] 86-87 KL 7
Río Verde [MEX, San Luis Potosí river] 86-87 L 7
Río Verde [PY] 103 E 2
Río Verde [RCH] 103 B 8
Rio Verde de Mato Grosso 98-99 HJ 8
Rio Vermelho [BR, Goiás] 98-99 P 8-9
Rio Vermelho [BR, Pará] 98-99 O 7-8
Riozinho [BR, Amazonas place] 98-99 E 9
Riozinho [BR, Amazonas river] 98-99 E 6
Riparia, WA 66-67 DE 2
Ripley, CA 74-75 F 6
Ripley, MS 78-79 E 3
Ripley, NY 72-73 G 3
Ripley, TN 78-79 E 3
Ripley, WV 72-73 F 5
Ripoll 132-133 J 7
Ripon, WI 70-71 F 4
Ripon [CDN] 72-73 J 2
Ripon [GB] 116-117 K 6
Ripple Mountain 66-67 E 1
Rīsām 'Anayzah 199 C 2
Rīsānī, Ar- 194-195 D 2
Risasi 198 E 2
Risca 116-117 H 9
Rishiri suidō 170-171 b 1
Rishiri tō 166-167 QR 2
Rising Star, TX 76-77 E 6
Rising Sun, IN 70-71 H 6
Rising Sun, OH 72-73 D 5
Risiri 170-171 b 1
Risle 132-133 H 4
Rison, AR 78-79 CD 4
Risør 114-115 C 8
Ristikent 114-115 O 3
Rito Gaviel, Mesa del — 76-77 C 6
Ritscherhochland 31 B 36
Ritter, Mount — 58-59 C 4
Rittman, OH 72-73 EF 4
Rittman,, OH 72-73 EF 4
Ritzville, WA 66-67 D 2
Riukiu = Ryūkyū 166-167 N 7-O 6
Riva [I] 138-139 D 3
Rivadavia [RA, Buenos Aires] 103 D 5
Rivadavia [RA, Salta] 103 D 2
Rivadavia [RCH] 103 B 3
Rivalensundet 114-115 mn 5
Rivaliza 98-99 B 8
Rivas [NIC] 88-89 CD 9
Rivera [RA] 103 D 5
Rivera [ROU, place] 103 E 4
Riverbank, CA 74-75 C 4
River Cess 194-195 BC 7
Riverdale, CA 74-75 D 4
Riverdale, New York-, NY 82 III c 1
River Falls, WI 70-71 D 3
River Forest 83 II a 1
Riverhead, NY 72-73 K 4
Riverhurst 49 E 5
Riverina 182-183 HJ 6-7
River Niger, Mouths of the — 194-195 F 7-8
River of Ponds 51 GH 2
Rivers 194-195 F 7-8
Riversdal 198 D 8
Riversdale = Riversdal 198 D 8
Riverside, CA 58-59 C 5
Riverside, IL 83 II a 1
Riverside, OR 66-67 DE 4
Rivers Inlet 48 D 4
Riverton, WY 68-69 B 4
Riverton [AUS] 182-183 G 6
Riverton [CDN] 50 A 2
Riviera, TX 76-77 EF 9
Riviera Beach, FL 80-81 cd 3
Rivière-à-Pierre 72-73 KL 1
Rivière-au-Renard 51 DE 3
Rivière-au-Tonnerre 51 D 2-3
Rivière-aux-Graines 51 D 2
Rivière-Bleue 51 B 4
Rivière-du-Loup 46-47 WX 8
Rivière-la-Madelaine 51 D 3
Rivière-Matane 51 C 3
Rivière Noire 72-73 H 1
Rivière-Pentecôte 51 C 3
Rivière-Pigou 51 D 2
Rivière-Saint-Jean [CDN, place] 51 D 2-3
Rivière-Verte 51 BC 4
Rivoli 138-139 B 3
Rivtangi 116-117 ab 1
Rivungo 198 D 5
Riyad = Ar-Riyāḍ 160-161 F 6
Riyāḍ, Ar- 160-161 F 6
Riyadh = Ar-Riyāḍ 160-161 F 6
Rize 160-161 E 2
Rizokárpason 142-143 F 8
Rizzuto, Cabo — 138-139 G 6
Rjukan 114-115 C 8
R'kīz, Ar- 194-195 AB 5
R'kīz, Lac — = Ar-R'kīz 194-195 AB 5
Roachdale, IN 70-71 G 6
Road Town 88-89 O 5
Roald Amundsen Sea = Amundsen havet 31 BC 25-26
Roan Cliffs 74-75 J 3
Roan Creek 68-69 B 6
Roanne 132-133 K 5
Roanoke, AL 78-79 G 4
Roanoke, VA 58-59 KL 4
Roanoke Island 80-81 J 3
Roanoke Rapids, NC 80-81 H 2
Roanoke River 58-59 L 4
Roan Plateau 68-69 B 6
Roaring Fork 68-69 C 6
Roaring Springs, TX 76-77 D 6
Roaringwater Bay = Loch Trasna 116-117 B 9
Roatán, Isla de — 58-59 J 8
Roba el Khali = Ar-Rub' al-Hālī 160-161 F 7-G 6
Robalo 88-89 E 10
Robb 48 J 3
Robberson, TX 76-77 E 9
Robbinsdale, MN 70-71 D 3
Robeline, LA 78-79 C 5
Robe Noir, Lac de la — 51 E 2
Roberta, GA 80-81 DE 4
Robert Lee, TX 76-77 D 7
Roberts, ID 66-67 GH 4
Roberts Creek Mountain 74-75 E 3
Robertsfors 114-115 J 5
Roberts Mount 52-53 E 7
Robertson, WY 66-67 HJ 5
Robertson Bay 31 BC 17-18
Robertsons øy 31 C 31
Roberts Park, IL 83 II a 2
Robertsport 194-195 B 7
Roberval 46-47 W 8
Robinette, OR 66-67 E 3
Robin Hood's Bay 116-117 L 6
Robinson 52-53 U 6
Robinson, IL 70-71 G 6
Robinson, TX 76-77 F 7
Robinson Crusoe 94 AB 7
Robinson Island 31 C 30
Robinson Mountains 52-53 QR 6
Robinson Ranges 182-183 C 5
Robinson River 182-183 G 3
Robinvale 182-183 H 6
Robla, La — 132-133 E 7
Roblin 49 H 5
Robsart 68-69 B 1
Robson, Mount — 46-47 N 7
Robstown, TX 76-77 F 9
Roby, TX 76-77 D 6
Roca, Cabo da — 132-133 C 9
Roçadas = Xangongo 198 C 5
Roçalgate = Rās al Ḥadd 160-161 HJ 6
Rocamadour 132-133 HJ 6
Roca Partida 86-87 D 8
Rocas, Atol das — 98-99 N 5
Rocas Negras = Black Rock 103 H 8
Rocha [ROU, place] 103 F 4
Rochdale 116-117 J 7
Rochefort 132-133 G 5-6
Rochelle, IL 70-71 F 5
Rochelle, LA 78-79 C 5
Rochelle, TX 76-77 E 7
Rochelle, la — 132-133 G 7
Roche-Percée 68-69 E 1
Rocheport, MO 70-71 D 6
Rochester 116-117 M 9
Rochester, IN 70-71 GH 5
Rochester, MI 72-73 E 3
Rochester, MN 58-59 H 3
Rochester, NH 72-73 L 3
Rochester, NY 58-59 L 3
Roche-sur-Yon, la — 132-133 G 5
Rock, MI 70-71 G 2
Rockall 110-111 EF 4
Rockall Plateau 110-111 E 4
Rockaway Beach 82 III cd 3
Rockaway Inlet 82 III c 3
Rockaway Point 82 III c 3
Rock Bay 48 E 4
Rock Creek, OR 66-67 CD 3
Rock Creek [USA ◁ Clark Fork River] 66-67 G 2
Rock Creek [USA ◁ Milk River] 68-69 C 1
Rock Creek [USA ◁ Potomac River] 82 II a 1
Rock Creek Park 82 II a 1
Rockdale, TX 76-77 F 7
Rockefeller Center 82 III bc 2
Rockefeller Plateau 31 AB 23-24
Rock Falls, IL 70-71 F 5
Rockford, IA 70-71 D 4
Rockford, IL 58-59 HJ 3
Rockford, OH 70-71 H 5
Rockglen 68-69 CD 1
Rockham, SD 68-69 G 3
Rockhampton 182-183 JK 4
Rock Harbor, MI 70-71 FG 1
Rock Hill, SC 58-59 K 4-5
Rockingham 182-183 BC 6
Rockingham, NC 80-81 FG 3
Rockingham Bay 182-183 J 3
Rock Island, IL 58-59 HJ 3

264 **Reedpoin**

Rock Island, WA 66-67 CD 2
Rock Lake 66-67 E 2
Rockland, ID 66-67 G 4
Rockland, ME 72-73 M 2-3
Rocklands Reservoir 182-183 H 7
Rockmart, GA 78-79 G 3
Rockport, IN 70-71 G 7
Rockport, MO 70-71 C 5
Rockport, TX 76-77 F 8
Rockport, WA 66-67 C 1
Rock Rapids, IA 70-71 BC 4
Rock River, WY 68-69 CD 5
Rock River [USA, Illinois] 70-71 F 4-5
Rock River [USA, Minnesota] 68-69 H 4
Rocksprings 86-87 KL 2-3
Rock Springs, AZ 74-75 GH 5
Rock Springs, MT 68-69 CD 2
Rocksprings, TX 76-77 D 7
Rock Springs, WY 58-59 E 3
Rockstone 98-99 H 3
Rockton, IL 70-71 F 4
Rock Valley, IA 70-71 BC 4
Rockville, IN 70-71 G 6
Rockville, MD 72-73 H 5
Rockville, OR 66-67 E 4
Rockwall, TX 76-77 F 6
Rockway Park, New York-, NY 82 III c 3
Rockwell City, IA 70-71 C 4
Rockwood, PA 72-73 G 5
Rockwood, TN 78-79 G 3
Rocky Boys Indian Reservation 68-69 B 1
Rocky Ford, CO 68-69 DE 6
Rockyford, SD 68-69 E 4
Rocky Island Lake 50 K 3
Rocky Mount, NC 80-81 H 2-3
Rocky Mount, VA 80-81 G 2
Rocky Mountain 66-67 G 2
Rocky Mountain House 48 K 3
Rocky Mountain National Park 58-59 EF 3
Rocky Mountains 46-47 L 5-P 9
Rocky Mountains Forest Reserve 48 JK 3-4
Rocky Mountain Trench 46-47 L 6-N 7
Rocky Point [USA, Alaska] 52-53 F 4
Rocky Point [USA, California] 66-67 A 5
Rôḍâ, Er- = Ar-Rawḍah 199 B 4
Roda, la — 132-133 F 9
Rodalquilar 132-133 FG 10
Rødberg 114-115 C 7
Rødby Havn 114-115 D 10
Roddickton 51 HJ 2
Rodel 116-117 E 3
Rodeo 103 BC 4
Rodeo, NM 74-75 J 7
Rodez 132-133 J 6
Rodney 72-73 F 3
Rodney, Cape — 52-53 D 4
Ródos [GR, island] 138-139 N 7
Ródos [GR, place] 138-139 N 7
Rodosto = Tekirdağ 160-161 B 2
Rodovia Perimetral Norte 98-99 G 4
Rodrigues [BR] 98-99 B 8
Rodrigues [Mascarene Islands] 26-27 N 6-7
Rodríguez 76-77 D 9
Roebourne 182-183 C 4
Roebuck Bay 182-183 D 3
Roermond 132-133 K 3
Roeselare 132-133 J 3
Roe's Welcome Sound 46-47 T 4-5
Rogačov 142-143 EF 5
Rogagua, Lago — 98-99 F 7
Rogaland 114-115 B 8
Rogers, AR 76-77 GH 4
Rogers, ND 68-69 G 2
Rogers, TX 76-77 F 7
Rogers City, MI 70-71 J 3
Rogerson, ID 66-67 F 4
Rogersville, TN 80-81 E 2
Rognan 114-115 F 4
Rogoaguado, Lago — 98-99 F 7
Rogue River 66-67 A 4
Rogue River Mountains 66-67 AB 4
Roha-Lalibela = Lalibela 194-195 M 6
Rohan 132-133 F 4
Rohault, Lac — 50 O 2
Rohrī 160-161 K 5
Rohtak 160-161 M 5
Rois Eoghain, Ceann — 116-117 BC 6
Rojas 103 D 4
Rokkasho 170-171 N 2
Rokugō-saki = Suzu misaki 170-171 L 4
Roland 68-69 H 1
Roland, AR 78-79 C 3
Rolette, ND 68-69 FG 1
Rolfe, IA 70-71 C 4
Rolla 114-115 G 3
Rolla, KS 76-77 D 4
Rolla, MO 58-59 H 4
Rolla, ND 68-69 G 1
Rolleston 182-183 J 4
Rolleville 88-89 H 3
Rolling Fork, MS 78-79 D 4
Rollingwood, CA 83 I bc 1
Rolvsøy 114-115 K 2
Rom [N] 114-115 B 8
Roma [AUS] 182-183 J 5
Roma [I] 138-139 E 5
Romain, Cape — 80-81 G 4
Romaine, Rivière — 46-47 Y 7
Roma-Los Saenz, TX 76-77 E 9
Roman 138-139 M 2
Romana, La — 58-59 J 8
Román Arreola 76-77 B 9
Romanche Deep 26-27 J 6
Romang, Pulau — 174-175 J 8
Români = Rummānah 199 C 2
Romania 138-139 K-M 2
Romano, Cape — 80-81 bc 4
Romano, Cayo — 58-59 L 7
Romanovka [SU, Bur'atskaja ASSR] 154-155 V 7
Romans-sur-Isère 132-133 K 6
Roman Wall 116-117 J 5-6
Romanzof, Cape — 46-47 C 5
Romanzof Mountains 52-53 PQ 2
Romblon 174-175 H 4
Rome, GA 58-59 J 5
Rome, NY 58-59 LM 3
Rome, OR 66-67 E 4
Rome = Roma 138-139 E 5
Romeo, MI 72-73 E 3
Romero, TX 76-77 C 5
Romilly-sur-Seine 132-133 J 4
Romney, WV 72-73 G 5
Romny 142-143 F 5
Rømø 114-115 C 10
Romsdal 114-115 BC 6
Romsdalfjord 114-115 B 6
Romsey 116-117 K 10
Ronan, MT 66-67 FG 2
Ronas Hill 116-117 e 3
Roncador, Serra do — 98-99 J 7
Roncador Reef 174-175 j 6
Roncesvalles [E] 132-133 G 7
Ronceverte, WV 80-81 F 2
Ronda 132-133 E 10
Rondane 114-115 C 7
Rondôn = Puerto Rondón 98-99 E 3
Rondon, Pico — 98-99 G 4
Rondônia [BR, administrative unit] 98-99 G 7
Rondônia [BR, place] 98-99 G 7
Rondonópolis 98-99 HJ 8
Ronge, la — 46-47 P 6
Ronge, Lac la — 46-47 Q 6
Ron Ma, Mui — 174-175 E 3
Rønne 114-115 F 10
Ronne Bay 31 B 29
Ronneby 114-115 F 9
Ronne Entrance = Ronne Bay 31 B 29
Roodhouse, IL 70-71 EF 6
Roof Butte 74-75 J 4
Roosendaal en Nispen 132-133 K 3
Roosevelt, MN 70-71 C 1
Roosevelt, OK 76-77 E 5
Roosevelt, TX 76-77 DE 7
Roosevelt, UT 66-67 HJ 5
Roosevelt, WA 66-67 C 3
Roosevelt, Rio — 98-99 G 6-7
Roosevelt Island 31 AB 20-21
Rootok Island 52-53 o 3-4
Root Portage 50 D 2
Root River 70-71 DE 4
Roper River 182-183 F 2
Roper River Mission 182-183 FG 2
Roper Valley 182-183 F 2-3
Ropi 114-115 J 3
Ropley 116-117 KL 9
Roquefort-sur-Soulzon 132-133 J 7
Roraima 98-99 GH 4
Roraima, Mount — 98-99 G 3
Rorketon 49 J 5
Røros 114-115 D 6
Rørvik 114-115 D 5
Rosa 198 F 3
Rosalia, WA 66-67 E 2
Rosalind 49 B 4
Rosamond, CA 74-75 D 5
Rosamond Lake 74-75 DE 5
Rosa Morada 86-87 H 6
Rosário [BR] 98-99 L 5
Rosario [MEX, Coahuila] 76-77 C 9
Rosario [MEX, Durango] 86-87 H 4
Rosario [MEX, Sinaloa] 86-87 GH 6
Rosario [RA, Santa Fe] 103 DE 4
Rosario de Arriba 86-87 C 2-3
Rosario de la Frontera 103 D 3
Rosario del Tala 103 E 4
Rosário do Sul 103 EF 4
Rosário Oeste 98-99 HJ 7
Rosario Villa Ocampo 86-87 H 4
Rosarito [MEX, Baja California Norte ↑ Santo Domingo] 86-87 CD 3
Rosarito [MEX, Baja California Norte ↓ Tijuana] 74-75 E 6
Rosarito [MEX, Baja California Sur] 86-87 E 4
Rosas [E] 132-133 J 7
Roscoe, NY 72-73 J 4
Roscoe, SD 68-69 G 3
Roscoe, TX 76-77 D 6
Roscoff 132-133 EF 4
Ros Comáin 116-117 C 7
Roscommon, MI 70-71 H 3
Roscommon = Ros Comáin 116-117 C 7
Ros Cré 116-117 D 8
Roscrea = Ros Cré 116-117 D 8
Rose 178 K 4
Rose, NE 68-69 G 4
Roseau 58-59 O 8
Roseau, MN 70-71 BC 1
Roseau River 70-71 BC 1
Roseberry River 50 C 1
Rosebery 182-183 HJ 8
Rose-Blanche 51 G 4
Roseboro, NC 80-81 G 3
Rosebud, TX 76-77 F 7
Rosebud Creek 68-69 C 3
Rosebud Indian Reservation 68-69 F 4
Rosebud Mountains 68-69 C 3
Roseburg, OR 66-67 B 4
Rosecroft Raceway 82 II b 2
Rosedale 49 B 5
Rosedale, NM 76-77 A 6
Rose Hills Memorial Park 83 III d 1
Roşeireş, Er- = Ar-Ruşayriş 194-195 LM 6
Rose Lake 48 DE 2
Roseland, Chicago-, IL 83 II b 2
Rosemary 49 BC 5
Rosemead, CA 83 III d 1
Rosenberg, TX 76-77 FG 8
Rosenheim 124 EF 5
Rose Point 48 AB 2
Rose River 182-183 G 2
Roses 88-89 J 3
Rosetown 46-47 P 7
Rosetta = Rashīd 199 B 2
Rosetta Mouth = Maṣabb Rashīd 199 B 2
Rosette = Rashīd 199 B 2
Rose Valley 49 G 4
Roseville, IL 70-71 E 5
Roseville, MI 72-73 E 3
Roseway Bank 51 D 6
Rosholt, SD 68-69 H 3
Rosholt, WI 70-71 F 3
Rosiclare, IL 70-71 F 7
Rosignano Marittimo 138-139 CD 4
Rosignol 98-99 H 3
Roşiori-de-Vede 138-139 L 3-4
Rosita, La — 86-87 K 3
Roskilde 114-115 E 10
Ros Láire 116-117 E 8
Roslavl' 142-143 F 5
Roslyn, WA 66-67 C 2
Roslyn Lake 70-71 G 1
Ros Mhic Treoin 116-117 E 8
Ross 182-183 O 8
Ross, WY 68-69 D 4
Ross and Cromarty 116-117 FG 3
Rossano 138-139 G 6
Rossan Point = Ceann Rois Eoghain 116-117 BC 6
Rossel Island 174-175 hi 7
Ross Ice Shelf 31 AB 20-17
Rossignol, Lake 51 D 5
Rossijskaja Sovetskaja Federativnaja Socialističeskaja Respublika = Russian Soviet Federated Socialist Republic 154-155 I-g 4
Ross Island [Antarctica, Ross Sea] 31 B 17-18
Ross Island [Antarctica, Weddell Sea] 31 C 31
Ross Island [CDN] 46-47 R 7
Rossland 66-67 DE 1
Rosslare = Ros Láire 116-117 E 8
Rosslyn, Arlington-, VA 82 II a 2
Rosso 194-195 A 5
Ross-on-Wye 116-117 J 9
Rossoš 142-143 GH 5
Rossport 70-71 G 1
Ross River 46-47 K 5
Ross Sea 31 B 20-18
Rosston, OK 76-77 E 4
Røssvatn 114-115 E 5
Røssvik 114-115 FG 4
Rossville 182-183 HJ 3
Rossville, GA 78-79 G 3
Rossville, IL 70-71 G 5
Rossville, New York-, NY 82 III a 3
Rosswood 48 C 2
Rosthern 49 E 4
Rostock 124 F 1
Rostov 154-155 FG 6
Rostov-na-Donu 142-143 GH 6
Roswell, NM 58-59 F 5
Rota 132-133 D 10
Rotan, TX 76-77 D 6
Rothaargebirge 124 D 3
Rothbury 116-117 K 5
Rothenburg 124 DE 4
Rotherham 116-117 KL 7
Rothesay 116-117 FG 5
Rothsay, MN 70-71 BC 2
Rothwell 116-117 KL 8
Roti, Pulau — 174-175 H 9
Roto 182-183 J 6
Rotondo, Mont — 138-139 C 4
Rotorua 182-183 P 7
Rottenfish River 50 C 1
Rotterdam 132-133 JK 3
Rotti = Pulau Roti 174-175 H 9
Rotuma 178 H 4
Roubaix 132-133 J 3
Rouen 132-133 H 4
Roulers = Roeselare 132-133 J 3
Round Lake 50 D 1
Round Mountain 182-183 K 6
Round Mountain, NV 74-75 E 3
Round Mountain, TX 76-77 E 7
Round Rock, TX 76-77 F 7
Round Spring, MO 78-79 D 2
Roundup, MT 68-69 B 2
Round Valley Indian Reservation 74-75 B 3
Rounga, Dar — 194-195 J 6-7
Roura 98-99 MN 2
Rousay 116-117 H 1
Rouses Point, NY 72-73 K 2
Roussillon 132-133 J 7
Rouyn 46-47 V 8
Rovaniemi 114-115 L 4
Rovdino 142-143 H 3
Rover, Mount — 52-53 R 3
Rovereto 138-139 D 3
Rovigo 138-139 D 3
Rovinj 138-139 E 3
Rovno 142-143 E 5
Rovuma, Rio — 198 G 4
Rowan Lake 50 C 3
Rowe, NM 76-77 B 5
Rowley Island 46-47 UV 4
Rowley Shoals 182-183 C 3
Rowuma = Rio Rovuma 198 G 4
Rox, NV 74-75 F 4
Roxas 174-175 H 4
Roxboro, NC 80-81 G 2
Roxburgh [GB] 116-117 J 5
Roxburgh [NZ] 182-183 N 9
Roxie, MS 78-79 D 5
Roy, MT 68-69 B 2
Roy, NM 76-77 B 5
Roy, UT 66-67 G 5
Royal Canal = Canail na Midhe 116-117 E 7
Royal Center, IN 70-71 G 5
Royal Leamington Spa 116-117 K 8
Royal Society Range 31 B 15-16
Royalton, MN 70-71 CD 3
Royal Turnbridge Wells 116-117 M 9
Royan 132-133 G 6
Roy Hill 182-183 CD 4
Røykenvik 114-115 D 7
Royse City, TX 76-77 F 6
Royston 116-117 LM 8
Royston, GA 80-81 E 3
Royton 116-117 JK 7
Rozel, KS 68-69 G 6
Rozendo 98-99 G 3
Rozet, WY 68-69 D 3
Rozewie, Przylądek — 124 J 1
Rožňava 124 K 4
Roztocze 124 L 3

Rtiščevo 142-143 H 5

Ruacana Falls 198 BC 5
Ruaha, Great — 198 G 3
Ruanda = Rwanda 198 EF 2
Ruapehu 182-183 P 7
Rubāʿī, Ash-Shallāl ar 194-195 L 5
Rub' al-Khālī = Ar-Rub'al-Khālī 160-161 F 7-G 6
Rub' al-Khālī, Ar- 160-161 F 7-G 6
Rubcovsk 154-155 P 7
Rubesibe 170-171 c 2
Rubi 198 D 1
Rubia, La — 103 D 4
Rubtsovsk = Rubcovsk 154-155 P 7
Ruby, AK 46-47 EF 5
Ruby Lake 66-67 F 5
Ruby Mountains 66-67 F 5
Ruby Range [CDN] 52-53 ST 6
Ruby Range [USA] 66-67 G 3
Ruby Valley 66-67 F 5
Ruchlovo = Skovorodino 154-155 XY 7
Rudnaja Pristan' 154-155 a 9
Rudnyj 154-155 L 7
Rudog 166-167 D 5
Rudolf, ostrov — 154-155 JK 1
Rudyard, MI 70-71 H 2
Rudyard, MT 66-67 H 1
Ruel 50 L 3
Ruffec 132-133 GH 5
Rufiji 198 G 3
Rufino 103 D 4
Rufisque 194-195 A 5-6
Rufunsa 198 EF 5
Rugao 166-167 N 5
Rugby 116-117 K 8
Rugby, ND 68-69 FG 1
Rugeley 116-117 JK 8
Rügen 124 FG 1
Rugozero 142-143 F 3
Ruhr 124 D 3
Ruidoso, NM 76-77 B 6
Ruijin 166-167 M 6
Rūi Khāf = Khvāf 160-161 J 4
Ruivo, Pico — 194-195 A 2
Ruíz 86-87 H 7
Ruiz, Nevado del — 98-99 DE 4
Rūjiena 142-143 DE 4
Rukas Tal Lake = Rakasdal 166-167 E 5
Ruki 198 C 1-2
Rukwa 198 F 3
Rukwa, Lake — 198 F 3
Rule, TX 76-77 E 6
Ruleville, MS 78-79 D 4
Rum 116-117 E 4
Ruma 138-139 H 3
Rumāh, Ar- 160-161 F 5
Rumahui 174-175 k 7
Rumbalara 182-183 FG 5
Rumberpon, Pulau — 174-175 KL 7
Rumbīk 194-195 K 7
Rum Cay 58-59 M 7
Rumelija 138-139 LM 4
Rumford, ME 72-73 L 2
Rum Jungle 182-183 F 2
Rummānah 199 C 2
Rumoe = Rumoi 170-171 b 2
Rumoi 166-167 R 3
Rumorosa 74-75 EF 6
Rum River 70-71 D 3
Rumsey 49 B 5
Rumula 182-183 HJ 3
Runcorn 116-117 J 7
Rundu 198 C 5
Runge, TX 76-77 F 8
Rungwa [EAT, place] 198 F 3
Rungwe Mount 198 F 3
Running Water Creek 76-77 CD 5
Runton Range 182-183 D 4
Ruo Shui 166-167 HJ 3
Ruoxi 166-167 M 6
Rupat, Pulau — 174-175 D 6
Rupert, ID 66-67 G 4
Rupert Bay 50 M 1
Rupert House = Fort Rupert 46-47 V 7
Rupert River 46-47 VW 7
Ruppert Coast 31 B 21-22
Rūrkalā = Raurkela 160-161 NO 5
Rurrenabaque 98-99 F 7
Rusanovo 154-155 JK 3
Rusape 198 F 5
Ruşayriş, Ar- 194-195 LM 6
Ruse 138-139 LM 4
Ruşetu 138-139 M 3
Rush, CO 68-69 DE 6
Rush Center, KS 68-69 G 6
Rush City, MN 70-71 D 3
Rush Creek 68-69 E 6
Rushden 116-117 L 8
Rushford, MN 70-71 E 4
Rush Springs, OK 76-77 EF 5
Rushville, IL 70-71 E 5
Rushville, IN 70-71 H 6
Rushville, NE 68-69 E 4
Rusk, TX 76-77 G 7
Ruskin, NE 68-69 GH 5
Ruskington 116-117 L 7
Ruso, ND 68-69 F 2
Russas 98-99 M 5
Russell, KS 68-69 G 6
Russell, MN 70-71 BC 3
Russell [CDN] 49 H 5
Russell [NZ] 182-183 OP 7
Russell, Mount — 52-53 LM 5
Russell Fiord 52-53 S 7
Russell Island 46-47 R 3
Russell Islands 174-175 j 6
Russell Lake 49 H 2
Russell Range 182-183 D 6
Russell Springs, KS 68-69 F 6
Russellville, AL 78-79 F 3
Russellville, AR 78-79 C 3
Russellville, KY 78-79 F 2
Russel Springs, KS 68-69 F 6
Russenes 114-115 L 2
Russian Mission, AK 52-53 G 6
Russian River 74-75 B 3
Russian Soviet Federated Socialist Republic 154-155 L-g 4
Russisi = Ruzizi 198 E 2
Russkij, ostrov — [SU, Japan Sea] 154-155 Z 9
Russkij, ostrov — [SU, Kara Sea] 154-155 RS 2
Russkij Zavorot, mys — 154-155 JK 4
Rustāq, Ar- 160-161 H 6
Rustavi 142-143 HJ 7
Rustenburg 198 E 7
Rustic Canyon 83 III a 1
Ruston, LA 58-59 H 5
Rūṣū = Al-Quwārib 194-195 A 5
Rutana 198 EF 2
Rutanzig 198 E 2
Ruṭbah, Ar- [IRQ] 160-161 DE 4
Ruth, NV 74-75 F 3
Rutherford, NJ 82 III b 2
Rutherfordton, NC 80-81 F 3
Rutherglen 116-117 GH 5
Ruth Glacier 52-53 M 5
Ruthin 116-117 H 7
Ruthven, IA 70-71 C 4
Rutland 48 H 5
Rutland, ND 68-69 H 2
Rutland, VT 58-59 M 3
Rutshuru 198 E 2
Rutter 72-73 F 1
Ruvo di Púglia 138-139 G 5
Ruvu [EAT, river] 198 G 3
Ruvu = Pangani 198 G 2
Ruvuma [EAT, administrative unit] 198 G 4
Ruwenzori 198 F 1
Ruwenzori National Park 198 EF 2
Ruwu = Pangani 198 G 2
Ruzajevka 154-155 GH 7
Ruzizi 198 E 2
Ružomberok 124 J 4
Rwanda 198 EF 2

Ryan, OK 76-77 F 5
Ryan, Loch — 116-117 F 5-6
Ryanggang-do 170-171 FG 2
Rybačij 124 K 1
Rybačij, poluostrov — 154-155 EF 4
Rybačje 154-155 NO 9
Rybinsk 154-155 F 6
Rybinskoje vodochranilišče 154-155 FG 6
Rybinsk Reservoir = Rybinskoje vodochranilišče 154-155 F 6
Rybnica 142-143 E 6
Rybnik 124 J 3
Rycroft 48 H 2
Ryde 116-117 K 10
Ryder, ND 68-69 F 2
Ryder's Hill 116-117 GH 10
Ryderwood, WA 66-67 B 2
Rye 116-117 M 10
Rye, CO 68-69 D 7
Ryegate, MT 68-69 B 2
Rye Patch Reservoir 66-67 D 5
Ryke Yseøyane 114-115 m 6
Ryōtsu 170-171 M 3
Rypin 124 J 2
Ryūkyū 166-167 N 7-O 6
Ryukyu Trench 166-167 P 6-R 7

Rzeszów 124 KL 3
Ržev 142-143 FG 4

S

Sá [BR] 98-99 L 8
Saale 124 E 3
Saalfeld 124 E 3
Saar 124 C 4
Saarbrücken 124 C 4
Saaremaa 142-143 D 4
Saarijärvi 114-115 L 6
Saariselkä 114-115 MN 3
Saarland 124 C 4
Saarlouis 124 C 4
Saba [West Indies] 58-59 O 8
Sabaa, Gebel es — = Qārat as-Sab'ah 194-195 H 3
Šabac 138-139 H 3
Sabadell 132-133 J 8
Sabae 170-171 KL 5
Sabah 174-175 G 5
Sab'ah, Qārat as- 194-195 H 3
Sabak, Cape — 52-53 pq 6
Sabaki = Galana 198 GH 2
Sabalān, Kuhha-ye — 142-143 J 8
Sabana, Archipiélago de — 58-59 KL 7
Sabana de la Mar 88-89 M 5
Sabanalarga [CO, Atlántico] 98-99 DE 2
Sabancuy 86-87 P 8
Sabang [RI, Aceh] 174-175 C 5
Sābari 160-161 N 7
Ṣabāyā, Jabal — 160-161 E 7
Sabetha, KS 70-71 BC 6
Sabhah 194-195 G 3
Sabi 198 F 6
Sabina, OH 72-73 E 5
Sabinal, TX 76-77 E 8
Sabinal, Cayo — 88-89 H 4
Sabinas 58-59 F 6
Sabinas, Río — 86-87 JK 3
Sabinas Hidalgo 58-59 F 6
Sabine, TX 76-77 GH 8
Sabine Lake 78-79 C 6
Sabine land 114-115 k 5
Sabine Peninsula 46-47 OP 2
Sabine River 58-59 H 5
Sabini, Monti — 138-139 E 4
Sabinoso, NM 76-77 B 5
Sabioncello = Pelješac 138-139 G 4
Sable 182-183 M 3
Sable, Cape — [CDN] 46-47 XY 9
Sable, Cape — [USA] 58-59 K 6
Sable Island [CDN] 46-47 Z 9
Sable Island [PNG] 174-175 hj 5
Sable Island Bank 51 F 5-6
Sable River 51 D 6
Sables, River aux — 50 K 3
Sables, Rivière aux — 51 A 3
Sables-d'Olonne, les — 132-133 FG 5
Sabrina Land 31 C 12-13
Sabun 154-155 P 5
Ṣabyā, Aṣ- 160-161 E 7
Sābzawār = Shīndand 160-161 J 4
Sabzevār 160-161 H 3
Sacaba 98-99 F 8
Sacaca 98-99 F 8
Sacajawea Peak 66-67 E 3
Sacanta 103 D 4
Sac City, IA 70-71 C 4
Sachalin 154-155 b 7-8
Sachalinskij zaliv 154-155 b 7
Sach'ang-ni 170-171 F 2
Sacharvan 142-143 KL 2
Sachigo Lake 50 CD 1
Sachigo River 46-47 S 6-7
Šachrisabz 160-161 K 3
Sachsen 124 FG 3

Sachsen 265

Šachtinsk 154-155 N 8
Šachty 142-143 H 6
Šachunja 154-155 GH 6
Šack 142-143 H 5
Sackets Harbor, NY 72-73 HJ 3
Sackville 51 DE 5
Saco, ME 72-73 L 3
Saco, MT 68-69 C 1
Sacramento, CA 58-59 B 4
Sacramento, Pampa del — 98-99 D 6
Sacramento Mountains 58-59 EF 5
Sacramento River 58-59 B 3-4
Sacramento Valley 58-59 B 3-4
Sac River 70-71 D 6
Ṣa'dah 160-161 E 7
Sada-misaki 170-171 HJ 6
Sadani 198 G 3
Saddle Brook, NJ 82 III b 1
Saddle Hills 48 H 2
Saddle Mountain 66-67 G 4
Saddle Mountains 66-67 CD 2
Saddle Peak 66-67 H 3
Sa Đec 174-175 E 4
Sâdhis, Ash-Shallāl as- 194-195 L 5
Sadiya 160-161 Q 5
Sadlerochit River 52-53 P 2
Sado [J] 166-167 Q 4
Sado [P] 132-133 C 10
Ṣadr, Wādī — 199 D 3
Šadrinsk 154-155 LM 6
Sæby 114-115 D 9
Saeki = Saiki 170-171 HJ 6
Safad = Ẓefat 160-161 D 4
Safājā 194-195 L 3
Safājā, Jazīrat — 199 D 4
Safaji Island = Jazīrat Safājah 199 D 4
Ṣafāqis 194-195 FG 2
Ṣafār 160-161 J 4
Safed Kōh 160-161 JK 4
Ṣaff, Aṣ- 199 B 3
Saffānīyah 160-161 F 5
Saffi = Aṣfī 194-195 C 2
Säffle 114-115 E 8
Safford, AZ 74-75 J 6
Saffron Walden 116-117 M 8
Safi = Aṣfī 194-195 C 2
Säfid Kuh = Safed Kōh 160-161 JK 4
Saga 166-167 P 5
Sagae 170-171 MN 3
Sagaing = Sitkaing 174-175 D 2
Sagaing = Sitkaing Taing 174-175 B 2-C 1
Sagami nada 166-167 Q 4-R 5
Saganoga Lake 70-71 E 1
Saganoseki 170-171 HJ 6
Sāgar [IND, Mahārāshtra] 160-161 M 6
Sagara 170-171 M 5
Saga-ri 170-171 F 5
Sagarmatha 166-167 F 6
Sagavanirktok River 46-47 G 3-4
Sage, WY 66-67 H 5
Sage Creek 68-69 A 1
Sagerton, TX 76-77 E 6
Sage Zong = Sakha Dsong 166-167 F 6
Saghir, Zab as- 142-143 H 8
Ṣaghrū', Jabal — 194-195 C 2
Sagigik Island 52-53 k 5
Saginaw, MI 58-59 K 3
Saginaw, TX 76-77 F 6
Saginaw Bay 58-59 K 3
Sagiz 154-155 JK 8
Šagonar 154-155 R 7
Sagra 132-133 F 10
Sagra, La — 132-133 EF 8
Sagres 132-133 C 10
Saguache, CO 68-69 CD 6
Saguache Creek 68-69 C 6-7
Sagua la Grande 88-89 FG 3
Saguaro National Monument 74-75 H 6
Saguenay, Rivière — 46-47 WX 8
Sagunto 132-133 GH 9
Sahagún 132-133 E 7
Sahand, Kūh-e — 142-143 J 8
Sahara 194-195 C-K 4
Saharan Atlas 194-195 D 2-F 1
Sahāranpur 160-161 M 4
Sahara Well 182-183 D 4
Saharunpore = Sahāranpur 160-161 M 4
Ṣahbā', Wādī aṣ- 160-161 F 6
Ṣahel = Sāḥil 194-195 BC 5
Ṣaḥḥāt = Shaḥḥāt 194-195 J 2
Ṣāḥil 194-195 BC 5
Sāhīwāl 160-161 L 4
Ṣaḥrā, Jabal — 199 CD 4
Sahuaripa 86-87 F 3
Sahuarita, AZ 74-75 H 7
Sahuayo 58-59 F 7-8
Sahuayo de José María Morelos 86-87 J 7-8
Sahyādri = Western Ghats 160-161 L 6-M 8
Saibai Island 174-175 M 8
Sai Buri 174-175 D 5
Saiburi = Alor Setar 174-175 CD 5
Ṣa'īd, Aṣ- 194-195 L 3-4
Saïd, Es- = Aṣ-Ṣa'īd 194-195 L 3-4
Ṣaïdā = Ṣaydā [RL] 160-161 CD 4
Sa'īdābād = Sīrjān 160-161 H 5
Saidaiji 170-171 JK 5
Sa'īd Bundās 194-195 JK 7
Saigō 170-171 J 4
Saigon = Thàn Phô Hô Chí Minh 174-175 E 4
Saiḥūt = Sayḥūt 160-161 G 7
Saijo 170-171 J 6
Saikai National Park = Gotō-rettō 170-171 G 6
Saiki 170-171 HJ 6
Sàile, Inse an t- 116-117 E 8
Šaim 154-155 L 5
Saima 170-171 E 2
Saimaa 114-115 MN 7
Sai-ma-chi = Saima 170-171 E 2
Sainjang 170-171 E 3
Saint Abbs' Head 116-117 JK 5
Saint Agnes 116-117 F 10
Saint Albans, VT 72-73 K 3
Saint Albans, WV 72-73 EF 5
Saint Alban's [CDN] 51 H 4
Saint Albans [GB] 116-117 L 9
Saint Albans, New York-, NY 82 III d 2
Saint Alban's Head 116-117 JK 10
Saint-Amand-Mont-Rond 132-133 J 5
Saint-André, Cap — 198 H 5
Saint Andrew, FL 78-79 FG 5
Saint Andrew Bay 78-79 FG 6
Saint Andrew Point 78-79 FG 6
Saint Andrews, SC 80-81 FG 4
Saint Andrews [CDN] 51 C 5
Saint Andrews [GB] 116-117 J 4
Saint Ann, Lake — 48 K 3
Saint Anne 116-117 J 11
Saint Anne, IL 70-71 FG 5
Saint Ann's Bay 88-89 H 5
Saint Ann's Head 116-117 F 9
Saint Anthony 46-47 Za 7
Saint Anthony, ID 66-67 H 4
Saint Antonio = Vila Real de Santo Antônio 132-133 D 10
Saint Augustin 51 G 2
Saint Augustin, Baie de — 198 H 6
Saint-Augustin, Rivière — 51 G 2
Saint-Augustine, FL 58-59 KL 6
Saint-Augustin Nord-Ouest, Rivière — 51 G 2
Saint Austell 116-117 FG 10
Saint Austell Bay 116-117 G 10
Saint-Avold 132-133 L 4
Saint Barbe 51 H 2
Saint Barbe Islands 51 J 2
Saint Barthélemy 58-59 O 8
Saint Blazey 116-117 G 10
Saint-Boniface 46-47 R 8
Saint Boniface Down 116-117 K 10
Saint Bride's 51 J 4
Saint Brides Bay 116-117 F 9
Saint-Brieuc 132-133 F 4
Saint Brieux 49 F 4
Saint-Camille 51 A 4
Saint Catharines 46-47 UV 9
Saint Catherines Island 80-81 F 5
Saint Catherine's Point 116-117 K 10
Saint Charles, ID 66-67 H 4
Saint Charles, MI 70-71 H 4
Saint Charles, MO 58-59 H 4
Saint Charles, Cape — 46-47 Za 7
Saint Christopher-Nevis 58-59 O 8
Saint Clair, MI 72-73 E 3
Saint Clair, MO 70-71 E 6
Saint Clair, Lake — 46-47 U 9
Saint Clair River 72-73 E 3
Saint Clairsville, OH 72-73 F 4
Saint Cloud, FL 80-81 c 2
Saint Cloud, MN 58-59 H 2
Saint Croix 58-59 O 8
Saint Croix Falls, WI 70-71 D 3
Saint Croix River 70-71 D 2-3
Saint David Islands = Kepulauan Mapia 174-175 KL 6
Saint David's [CDN] 51 G 3
Saint David's [GB] 116-117 FG 9
Saint David's Head 116-117 F 9
Saint-Denis [F] 132-133 J 4
Saint-Denis [Réunion] 188-189 N 11
Saint-Dié 132-133 L 4
Saint-Dizier 132-133 K 4
Sainte-Adresse 116-117 LM 11
Sainte-Agathe-des-Monts 46-47 VW 8
Sainte-Anne-de-Beaupré 51 A 4
Sainte-Anne-de-la-Pocatière 51 AB 4
Sainte-Anne-des-Chênes 49 KL 6
Sainte-Anne-des-Monts 51 CD 3
Sainte-Catherine-d'Alexandrie 82 I b 2
Saint Edward, NE 68-69 GH 5
Sainte Genevieve, MO 70-71 E 6-7
Sainte Helène, Île de — 82 I b 1
Saint Elias, Cape — 52-53 P 7
Saint Elias, Mount — 46-47 H 5
Saint Elias Mountains 46-47 J 5-6
Saint-Élie 98-99 J 3-4
Saint Elmo, IL 70-71 F 6
Sainte-Louis, Lac — 82 I a 2
Sainte Marguerite, Rivière — 51 A 3
Sainte-Marie [CDN] 72-73 L 1
Sainte-Marie [Gabon] 198 B 2
Sainte-Marie [Martinique] 58-59 O 9
Sainte-Marie, Cap — 198 J 7
Sainte-Marie, Île — = Nosy Boraha 198 K 5
Saint-Ephrem 51 A 4
Sainte-Rose 88-89 PQ 6
Sainte Rose du Lac 49 J 5
Saintes 132-133 G 6
Saintes, Îles des — 88-89 PQ 7
Sainte-Thérèse 72-73 JK 2
Saint-Étienne 132-133 JK 6
Saint-Félicien 50 P 2
Saint-Flour 132-133 J 6
Saint Francis, KS 68-69 EF 6
Saint Francis, ME 72-73 M 1
Saint Francis River 58-59 H 4
Saint Francisville, IL 70-71 FG 6
Saint Francisville, LA 78-79 D 5
Saint François, Lac — 72-73 L 2
Saint François, Rivière — 72-73 K 1-2
Saint François Mountains 70-71 E 7
Saint-Gabriel-de-Brandon 72-73 K 1
Saint Gall = Sankt Gallen 124 D 5
Saint-Gaudens 132-133 H 7
Saint George, GA 80-81 E 5
Saint George, SC 80-81 F 4
Saint George, UT 74-75 G 4
Saint George [AUS] 182-183 J 5
Saint George [CDN] 51 C 5
Saint George, Cape — 78-79 G 5
Saint George, Point — 66-67 A 5
Saint George Island 78-79 G 6
Saint George's [CDN, Newfoundland] 51 G 3
Saint-Georges [CDN, Quebec] 51 A 4
Saint-Georges [French Guiana] 98-99 J 4
Saint George's [WG] 58-59 O 9
Saint George's Bay [CDN, Newfoundland] 51 G 3
Saint George's Bay [CDN, Nova Scotia] 51 F 5
Saint George's Channel [GB] 116-117 E 9-F 8
Saint George's Channel [PNG] 174-175 h 5-6
Saint-Georges-de-Cacouna 51 B 4
Saint George Sound 78-79 G 6
Saint Germans 116-117 G 10
Saint-Gilles-sur-Vie 132-133 FG 5
Saint-Girons 132-133 H 7
Saint Govan's Head 116-117 FG 9
Saint Gregor 49 F 4
Saint Helena 188-189 G 10
Saint Helena, CA 74-75 B 3
Saint Helena Bay = Sint Helenabaai 198 C 8
Saint Helena Range 74-75 B 3
Saint Helena Sound 80-81 FG 4
Saint Helens 116-117 J 7
Saint Helens, OR 66-67 B 3
Saint Helens, WA 66-67 B 2
Saint Helens, Mount — 66-67 BC 2
Saint-Hyacinthe 46-47 W 8
Saint Ignace, MI 70-71 H 3
Saint-Ignace, Île — 70-71 FG 1
Saint Ignatius, MT 66-67 FG 2
Saint Isidore = Laverlochère 72-73 G 1
Saint Ives [GB, Cambridge] 116-117 LM 8
Saint Ives [GB, Cornwall] 116-117 F 10
Saint Ives Bay 116-117 F 10
Saint James 49 K 6
Saint James, MI 70-71 H 3
Saint James, MN 70-71 C 3-4
Saint James, MO 70-71 E 6-7
Saint James, Cape — 46-47 K 7
Saint-Jean 46-47 W 8
Saint-Jean, Lac — 46-47 W 8
Saint-Jean, Rivière — [CDN, Pen. de Gaspé] 51 D 3
Saint-Jean, Rivière — [CDN, Quebec] 51 D 2
Saint-Jean-de-Luz 132-133 FG 7
Saint-Jérôme 72-73 JK 2
Saint Jo, TX 76-77 F 6
Saint Joe, AR 78-79 C 2
Saint Joe River 66-67 E 2
Saint John, KS 68-69 G 6-7
Saint John, ND 68-69 FG 1
Saint John [CDN] 46-47 X 8
Saint John [West Indies] 88-89 O 5
Saint John, Cape — 51 J 3
Saint John, Lake — = Lac Saint Jean 46-47 W 8
Saint John Bay 51 H 2
Saint John Islands 51 F 3
Saint John River 46-47 X 8
Saint Johns, AZ 74-75 J 5
Saint Johns, MI 70-71 H 4
Saint John's [CDN] 46-47 a 8
Saint John's [West Indies] 58-59 O 8
Saint Johns = Saint-Jean 46-47 W 8
Saint Johnsbury, VT 72-73 K 2
Saint John's Point 116-117 F 6
Saint Johns River 80-81 c 1-2
Saint-Joseph 51 A 4
Saint Joseph, LA 78-79 D 5
Saint Joseph, MI 70-71 G 4
Saint Joseph, MO 58-59 GH 4
Saint Joseph, Lake — 46-47 ST 7
Saint Joseph Bay 78-79 G 6
Saint-Joseph-d'Alma = Alma 46-47 W 8
Saint Joseph Island [CDN] 70-71 HJ 2
Saint Joseph Island [USA] 76-77 F 8-9
Saint Joseph Point 78-79 G 6
Saint-Jovite 72-73 J 1
Saint-Junien 132-133 H 6
Saint Just 116-117 F 10
Saint Kilda 116-117 C 3
Saint-Lambert [CDN] 72-73 K 2
Saint Laurent [CDN, place] 49 K 5
Saint-Laurent [CDN, river] 82 I a 1-2
Saint-Laurent, Fleuve — 46-47 W 8-9
Saint-Laurent, Golfe du — = Gulf of Saint Lawrence 46-47 Y 8
Saint-Laurent-du-Maroni 98-99 LM 2-3
Saint Lawrence [AUS] 182-183 J 4
Saint Lawrence [CDN] 51 J 4
Saint Lawrence, Cape — 51 F 4
Saint Lawrence, Gulf of — 46-47 Y 8
Saint Lawrence Island 46-47 BC 5
Saint Lawrence River 46-47 X 8
Saint-Léonard [CDN ↑ Montréal] 82 I b 1
Saint-Léonard [CDN ↗ Montréal] 72-73 KL 1
Saint-Léonard [CDN → Québec] 51 C 4
Saint-Lô 132-133 G 4
Saint-Louis 194-195 A 5
Saint Louis, MI 70-71 H 4
Saint Louis, MO 58-59 H 4
Saint-Louis-de-Kent 51 D 4
Saint Louis Park, MN 70-71 D 3
Saint Louis River 70-71 D 2
Saint Lucia 58-59 O 9
Saint Lucia, Lake — = Sint Luciameer 198 F 7
Saint Lucia Channel 88-89 Q 7
Saint Magnus Bay 116-117 e 3
Saint-Malachie 51 A 4
Saint-Malo 132-133 FG 4
Saint-Marc [CDN] 72-73 K 1
Saint-Marc [RH] 88-89 K 5
Saint Marcouf, Îles — 116-117 LM 11
Saint Margaret's Bay 51 DE 5
Saint Maries, ID 66-67 E 2
Saint Marks, FL 80-81 D 5
Saint Martin [island] 58-59 O 8
Saint Martin, Lake — 49 JK 5
Saint Martin Bay 70-71 H 2-3
Saint Martin's [CDN] 51 D 5
Saint Martin's [GB] 116-117 E 11
Saint Martins Bay 72-73 D 1-2
Saint Mary Islands 51 G 2
Saint Mary Lake 66-67 G 1
Saint Mary Peak 182-183 G 6
Saint Mary River 48 JK 5
Saint Marys, AK 52-53 F 5
Saint Marys, GA 80-81 F 5
Saint Marys, KS 70-71 BC 6
Saint Marys, MO 70-71 EF 7
Saint Marys, OH 70-71 H 5
Saint Marys, PA 72-73 G 4
Saint Marys, WV 72-73 F 5
Saint Marys [AUS] 182-183 J 8
Saint Mary's [CDN, Newfoundland] 51 K 4
Saint Mary's [CDN, Ontario] 72-73 F 3
Saint Mary's [GB] 116-117 E 11
Saint Mary's, Cape — 51 J 4
Saint Mary's Bay [CDN, Newfoundland] 51 JK 4
Saint Mary's Bay [CDN, Nova Scotia] 51 CD 5
Saint Mary's River [CDN] 51 E 5
Saint Marys River [USA] 58-59 K 2
Saint Mathieu, Pointe — 132-133 E 4
Saint Matthew 154-155 I 5
Saint Matthew Island 46-47 B 5
Saint Matthew Island = Zādetkyī Kyûn 174-175 C 5
Saint Matthews, SC 80-81 F 4
Saint Matthias Group 174-175 NO 7
Saint-Maurice, Rivière — 46-47 W 8
Saint Mawes 116-117 FG 10
Saint Michael, AK 46-47 D 5
Saint Michael = São Miguel 188-189 E 5
Saint Michaels, AZ 74-75 J 5
Saint-Michel, Montréal- 82 I b 1
Saint-Michel-des-Saints 72-73 K 1
Saint-Nazaire 132-133 F 5
Saint Neots 116-117 L 8
Saint-Omer 132-133 HJ 3
Saintonge 132-133 G 6
Saint-Pacôme 51 AB 4
Saint-Pamphile 51 AB 4
Saint Paris, OH 70-71 HJ 5
Saint-Pascal 51 B 4
Saint Patrice, Lac — 72-73 H 1
Saint Paul, MN 58-59 H 2
Saint Paul, NE 68-69 G 5
Saint Paul, VT 80-81 E 2
Saint Paul [CDN] 46-47 O 7
Saint Paul [Saint Paul] 26-27 NO 7
Saint-Paul, Rivière — 51 H 2
Saint Paul Island 51 F 4
Saint Paul River 194-195 BC 7
Saint Pauls, NC 80-81 G 3
Saint Peter, MN 70-71 CD 3
Saint Peter's 51 F 5
Saint Petersburg, FL 58-59 K 6
Saint Petersburg = Leningrad 154-155 E 5-6
Saint-Pierre 82 I b 2
Saint-Pierre, Havre- 46-47 Y 7
Saint-Pierre, Lac — 72-73 K 1
Saint Pierre Bank 51 HJ 5-6
Saint-Pierre-Église 116-117 K 11
Saint Pierre Island 198 JK 3
Saint-Quentin [CDN] 51 C 4
Saint-Quentin [F] 132-133 J 4
Saint-Raphaël 132-133 L 7
Saint-Raymond 72-73 KL 1
Saint Regis, MT 66-67 F 2
Saint-Rémi 72-73 J 1-2
Saint-Romuald 51 A 4
Saint-Sebastien, Cap — 198 J 4
Saint Shott's 51 K 4
Saint-Siméon 51 AB 4
Saint Simons Island 80-81 F 5
Saint Simons Island, GA 80-81 F 5
Saint Stephens, SC 80-81 G 4
Saint Terese, AK 52-53 U 7
Saint Thomas, ND 68-69 H 1
Saint Thomas [CDN] 72-73 F 3
Saint Thomas [West Indies] 58-59 NO 8
Saint-Tite 72-73 K 1
Saint-Tropez 132-133 L 7
Saint-Ulric 51 C 3
Saint Vincent, MN 68-69 H 1
Saint Vincent [WV] 58-59 O 9
Saint Vincent = São Vicente 188-189 E 7
Saint Vincent, Gulf — 182-183 G 6-7
Saint-Vincent-de-Paul 82 I ab 1
Saint Vincent Island 78-79 G 6
Saint Vincent Passage 88-89 Q 7
Saint Walburg 49 D 4
Saint Xavier, MT 68-69 C 3
Saio = Dembī Dolo 194-195 LM 7
Saishū = Cheju-do 170-171 F 6
Saitama 170-171 M 4
Saito 170-171 H 6
Sai'wun = Say'ūn 160-161 F 7
Sajak Pervyj 154-155 O 8
Sajama, Nevado de — 98-99 F 8
Sajan, Vostočnyj — 154-155 R 6-T 7
Sajan, Zapadnyj — 154-155 Q-S 7
Saji-dong 170-171 G 2
Sajmak 160-161 L 3
Sajnšand 166-167 KL 3
Sajo 124 K 4
Sajram nuur 166-167 DE 3
Sakai 166-167 Q 5
Sakaide 170-171 JK 5
Sakaiminato 170-171 J 5
Sakākah 160-161 E 4-5
Sakakawea, Lake — 58-59 F 2
Sakamachi = Arakawa 170-171 M 3
Sakami Lake 46-47 V 7
Sakania 198 E 4
Sakarya = Adapazarı 160-161 C 2
Sakarya nehri 160-161 C 2
Sakata 166-167 Q 4
Sakawa 170-171 J 6
Sakchu 170-171 E 2
Saketa 174-175 J 7
Sakha Dsong 166-167 F 6
Sakhalin = ostrov Sachalin 154-155 b 7-8
Sakhalin, Gulf of — = Sachalinskij zaliv 154-155 b 7
Saki 142-143 F 6
Sakīkdah 194-195 F 1
Sakinohama 170-171 K 6
Sakishima-guntō 166-167 NO 7
Sakisima guntō = Sakishima-guntō 166-167 NO 7
Sakkane, Erg in — 194-195 D 4
Sakon Nakhon 174-175 B 3
Sakonnet Point 72-73 L 4
Sakovlevskoje = Privolžsk 154-155 N 5
Sakrivier [ZA, place] 198 CD 8
Sal [Cape Verde] 188-189 E 7
Sal [SU] 142-143 H 6
Sala 114-115 G 8
Sala Consilina 138-139 F 5
Salada, Laguna — [MEX] 86-87 C 1
Saladillo [RA, Buenos Aires] 103 DE 5
Salado, Río — [MEX] 86-87 L 4
Salado, Río — [RA, Santa Fe] 103 D 3
Salado, Rio — [USA] 76-77 A 5
Salado, Valle del — 58-59 F 7
Salaga 194-195 D 7
Salah, In- = 'Ayn Ṣāliḥ 194-195 E 3
Salair 154-155 PQ 7
Salairskij kr'až 154-155 PQ 7
Salajar = Pulau Kabia 174-175 H 8
Salal 194-195 H 6
Ṣalālah 160-161 G 7
Salālah, Jabal — 199 D 7
Salamá 86-87 P 10
Salamanca, NY 72-73 G 3
Salamanca [E] 132-133 E 8
Salamanca [MEX] 86-87 K 7
Salamat, Bahr — 194-195 H 6-7
Salamaua 174-175 N 8
Salamis 138-139 K 7
Salamīyah 142-143 G 8-9
Salang = Ko Phuket 174-175 C 5
Salatan, Cape — = Tanjung Selatan 174-175 F 7
Salatiga 174-175 F 8
Salavat [SU] 154-155 K 7
Salaverry 98-99 D 6
Salawati, Pulau — 174-175 K 7
Salayar, Pulau — 174-175 H 8
Sala y Gómez 34-35 M 6
Salazar, NM 76-77 A 5
Salazar = N'Dala Tando 198 BC 3
Salcha River 52-53 P 4
Salcombe 116-117 H 10
Saldanha [ZA] 198 C 8
Sale [AUS] 182-183 J 7
Sale [GB] 116-117 J 7
Salé = Slā' 194-195 C 2
Salebabu, Pulau — 174-175 J 6
Salechard 154-155 M 4
Saleh, Teluk — 174-175 G 8
Sālehābād 142-143 J 8-9
Salekhard = Salechard 154-155 M 4
Salem, AR 78-79 D 2
Salem, FL 80-81 b 2
Salem, IL 70-71 F 6
Salem, IN 70-71 GH 6
Salem, MA 72-73 L 3
Salem, MO 70-71 E 7
Salem, NJ 72-73 J 5
Salem, OH 72-73 F 4
Salem, OR 58-59 B 2
Salem, SD 68-69 H 4
Salem, VA 80-81 F 2
Salem, WV 72-73 F 5
Salem [IND] 160-161 M 8
Salem, Winston-, NC 58-59 KL 4
Salembu Besar, Pulau — 174-175 FG 8
Salemi 138-139 E 7
Salen [GB] 116-117 F 4
Sälen [S] 114-115 E 7
Salentina 138-139 GH 5
Salerno 138-139 F 5
Salerno, Golfo di — 138-139 F 5
Sales Point 116-117 gh 7
Salford 116-117 J 7
Salgótarjan 124 J 4
Salgueiro 98-99 M 6
Salibabu Islands = Kepulauan Talaud 174-175 J 6
Salida, CO 58-59 E 4
Ṣalīf, Aṣ- 160-161 E 7
Ṣāliḥīyah, Aṣ- [ET] 199 BC 2
Salihli 142-143 E 8
Sálima 198 FG 4
Ṣalīmah, Wāḥāt — 194-195 K 4
Salina, KS 58-59 G 4
Salina, OK 76-77 G 4
Salina, UT 74-75 H 3
Salina, Ìsola — 138-139 F 6
Salina Cruz 58-59 G 8
Salinas, CA 58-59 B 4
Salinas [BR] 98-99 L 8
Salinas [EC] 98-99 C 5
Salinas [MEX] 86-87 H 8
Salinas, Cabo de — 132-133 J 9
Salinas, Punta de — 98-99 D 7
Salinas Grandes [RA ↖ Córdoba] 103 C 4-D 3
Salinas Peak 76-77 A 6
Salinas River 74-75 C 4-5
Salinas Victoria 76-77 DE 9
Saline, LA 78-79 C 4
Saline River [USA, Arkansas] 78-79 CD 4
Saline River [USA, Kansas] 68-69 G 6
Saline Valley 74-75 E 4
Salinópolis 98-99 K 4-5
Salisbury 116-117 K 9
Salisbury, CT 72-73 K 3-4
Salisbury, MD 58-59 LM 4
Salisbury, MO 70-71 D 6
Salisbury, NC 58-59 KL 4
Salisbury = Harare 198 F 5
Salisbury, Lake — 198 FG 1
Salisbury, Mount — 52-53 O 2
Salisbury, ostrov — 154-155 HJ 1
Salisbury Island 46-47 VW 5
Salisbury Plain 116-117 JK 9
Salish Mountains 66-67 F 1-2
Šaljany 142-143 J 8
Šalkar 142-143 K 5
Šalkar, ozero — 142-143 K 5
Salkum, WA 66-67 B 2
Salla 114-115 N 4
Salle, La — [CDN, Montréal] 82 I b 2
Salley, SC 80-81 F 4
Sallisaw, OK 76-77 G 5
Sallyana 160-161 N 5
Salm, ostrov — 154-155 KL 2
Salmah, Jabal — 160-161 E 5
Salmi 154-155 E 5
Salmo 66-67 E 1
Salmon, ID 66-67 FG 3
Salmon Arm 48 H 4
Salmon Falls 66-67 F 4
Salmon Falls Creek 66-67 F 4
Salmon Falls Creek Lake 66-67 F 4
Salmon Fork 52-53 R 3
Salmon Gums 182-183 D 6
Salmon River [CDN, Acadie] 51 D 4
Salmon River [CDN, Anticosti I.] 51 E 3
Salmon River [USA, Alaska] 52-53 H 3
Salmon River [USA, Idaho] 58-59 CD 2
Salmon River, Middle Fork — 66-67 F 3
Salmon River, South Fork — 66-67 F 3
Salmon River Mountains 58-59 C 3-D 2

266 **Šachtins**

Salmon Village, AK 52-53 QR 3
Salo 114-115 K 7
Salonga 198 D 2
Salonga Nord, Parc national de la — 198 D 2
Salonga Sud, Parc national de la — 198 D 2
Salonika = Thessaloníkē 138-139 K 5
Salonika, Gulf of — = Thermaïkòs Kólpos 138-139 K 5-6
Salonta 138-139 JK 2
Salop 116-117 J 8
Salor 132-133 D 9
Salpausselkä 114-115 L-O 7
Salsacate 103 CD 4
Sal'sk 142-143 H 6
Salso 138-139 E 7
Salsomaggiore Terme 138-139 C 3
Salta [RA, place] 103 CD 2
Saltash 116-117 G 10
Salt Basin 76-77 B 7
Saltcoats [CDN] 49 GH 5
Saltcoats [GB] 116-117 G 5
Salt Creek 68-69 C 4
Saltee Islands = Inse an tSáile 116-117 E 8
Salten 114-115 F 4-G 3
Saltfjord 114-115 EF 4
Salt Flat 76-77 B 7
Salt Flat, TX 58-59 EF 5
Saltfleet 116-117 M 7
Saltillo 58-59 FG 6
Salt Lake, NM 74-75 J 5
Salt Lake City, UT 58-59 D 3
Salt Lakes 182-183 CD 5
Salt Lick, KY 72-73 E 5
Salt Marsh = Lake MacLeod 182-183 B 4
Salto [RA] 103 DE 4
Salto [ROU, place] 103 E 4
Salto, El — 58-59 E 7
Salto da Divisa 98-99 LM 8
Salto Grande, Embalse — 103 E 4
Saltoluokta 114-115 H 4
Salton, CA 74-75 F 6
Saltón, El — 103 B 7
Salton Sea 58-59 CD 5
Salt River [USA, Arizona] 58-59 D 5
Salt River [USA, Kentucky] 70-71 H 6-7
Salt River [USA, Missouri] 70-71 E 6
Salt River Indian Reservation 74-75 H 6
Saltspring Island 66-67 B 1
Saltville, VA 80-81 F 2
Saluda, SC 80-81 EF 3
Saluen 166-167 H 6
Salūm, As- 194-195 K 2
Salus, AR 78-79 C 3
Salut, Îles du — 98-99 MN 2
Saluzzo 138-139 B 3
Salvador 98-99 M 7
Salvador, El — [ES] 58-59 J 9
Salvador, Lake — 78-79 D 6
Salvatierra [MEX] 86-87 K 7
Salvus 48 C 2
Salwá Baḥrī 199 C 5
Salween = Thanlwin Myit 174-175 C 2-3
Salyānā = Sallyana 160-161 N 5
Salyersville, KY 72-73 E 6
Salzach 124 F 4-5
Salzbrunn 198 C 6
Salzburg [A, administrative unit] 124 F 5
Salzburg [A, place] 124 F 5
Salzgitter 124 E 2-3
Salzwedel 124 E 2
Sam 142-143 L 6
Sama de Langreo 132-133 E 7
Samalayuca 76-77 A 7
Samalga Island 52-53 m 4
Samālūṭ 199 B 3
Samaná, Bahía de — 58-59 N 8
Samaná, Cabo — 88-89 M 5
Samana Cay 88-89 K 3
Samānajakanda 160-161 N 9
Samangān 160-161 K 3
Samani 166-167 R 3
Samaqua, Rivière — 50 P 1-2
Samar 174-175 J 4
Samara [SU, Rossijskaja SFSR] 154-155 J 7
Samara = Kujbyšev 154-155 HJ 7
Samarai 174-175 gh 7
Samarga 154-155 ab 8
Samarinda 174-175 G 7
Samarkand 160-161 K 3
Samarkand = Temirtau 154-155 N 7
Sāmarrā' 160-161 E 4
Samāwah, As- 160-161 EF 4
Sambala 198 D 3
Sambaliung 174-175 G 6
Sambalpore = Sambalpur 160-161 N 6
Sambalpur [IND, Orissa] 160-161 N 6
Sambas 174-175 E 6
Sambava 198 K 4
Sambhal 160-161 M 5
Sambia 198 E 5-F 4
Samboja 174-175 G 7
Sambongi = Towada 170-171 N 2
Sambor [K] 174-175 E 4
Sambor [SU] 142-143 D 6
Samborombón, Bahía — 103 E 5
Sambre 132-133 K 3
Sambro Bank 51 E 6
Samch'ŏk 166-167 OP 4
Samch'ŏnp'o 170-171 FG 5
Sam Creek, AK 52-53 Q 4
Samdŭng 170-171 F 3
Same [EAT] 198 G 2
Samḥah 160-161 G 8
Samīm, Umm as- 160-161 H 6
Samnagjin 170-171 G 5
Sam Neua 174-175 D 2
Samoa 174-175 c 1
Samoa, CA 66-67 A 5
Samoa Islands 174-175 c 1
Samora = Zamora de Hidalgo 58-59 F 7-8
Sámos [GR, island] 138-139 M 7
Sámos [GR, place] 138-139 M 7
Samosir, Pulau — 174-175 C 6
Samothrákē 138-139 L 5
Sampacho 103 CD 4
Sampang 174-175 F 8
Samper de Calanda 132-133 G 8
Sampit 174-175 F 7
Sampit, Teluk — 174-175 F 7
Sam Rayburn Lake 76-77 G 7
Samrong 174-175 D 4
Samsø 114-115 D 10
Samson, AL 78-79 FG 5
Samsu 170-171 G 2
Samsun 160-161 D 2
Samtredia 142-143 H 7
Samuel, Cachoeira do — 98-99 G 9
Samuel, Mount — 182-183 F 3
Samui, Ko — 174-175 D 5
Samur 142-143 J 7
Samut Prakan 174-175 D 4
San [PL] 124 L 3
San [RMM] 194-195 CD 6
Sanā [ADN] 160-161 FG 7
Ṣan'ā' [Y] 160-161 EF 7
Sana [YU] 138-139 G 3
Sanaag 194-195 b 2
Ṣanabū 199 B 4
SANAE 31 b 36-1
Ṣanāfir, Jazīrat — 199 D 4
Sanaga 194-195 G 8
San Agustín [RA, Buenos Aires] 103 E 5
San Agustin, Cape — 174-175 J 5
Sanak Island 52-53 b 2
Sanām, As- 160-161 G 6
San Ambrosio 94 B 6
Sanana = Pulau Sulabesi 174-175 J 7
Sanandaj 160-161 F 3
San Andreas, CA 74-75 C 3
San Andrés [CO, island] 58-59 KL 9
San Andres Mountains 58-59 E 5
San Andrés Tuxtla 58-59 GH 8
San Andrés y Providencia 88-89 F 8-9
San Angel 98-99 E 2-3
San Angelo, TX 58-59 FG 5
San Anselmo, CA 74-75 B 4
San Antonio, NM 76-77 A 6
San Antonio, TX 58-59 G 6
San Antonio [RCH] 103 B 4
San Antonio, Cabo — [C] 58-59 K 7
San Antonio, Sierra de — 86-87 E 2-3
San Antonio Bay 76-77 F 8
San Antonio de Caparo 98-99 E 3
San Antonio Mountain 76-77 B 7
San Antonio Oeste 103 CD 6
San Antonio Peak 74-75 E 5
San Antonio River 76-77 F 8
San Ardo, CA 74-75 C 4
Sanatorium, TX 76-77 D 7
San Augustine, TX 76-77 GH 7
Sanāw 160-161 G 7
Sanbalpur = Sambalpur 160-161 N 6
San Benedetto del Tronto 138-139 EF 4
San Benedicto, Isla — 58-59 DE 8
San Benito, TX 58-59 G 6
San Benito, Isla — 86-87 BC 3
San Benito Mountain 74-75 C 4
San Bernardino, CA 58-59 CD 5
San Bernardino Mountains 74-75 E 5
San Bernardo [RCH] 103 BC 4
San Blas [MEX] 86-87 F 4
San Blas, Archipiélago de — 88-89 GH 10
San Blas, Bahía de — 86-87 H 7
San Blas, Cape — 58-59 J 6
San Blas, Cordillera de — 58-59 L 10
San Blas, Punta — 58-59 L 10
San Borja 98-99 F 7
San Borja, Sierra de — 86-87 D 3
Sanborn, MN 70-71 C 3
Sanborn, ND 68-69 G 2
San Bruno Mountain 83 I b 2
San Buenaventura [MEX] 86-87 JK 4
San Buenaventura = Ventura, CA 74-75 D 5
San Carlos, AZ 74-75 H 6
San Carlos [MEX, Baja California Sur] 86-87 DE 5
San Carlos [MEX, Tamaulipas] 86-87 L 5
San Carlos [NIC] 88-89 D 9
San Carlos [RCH] 103 B 5
San Carlos [RP, Luzón] 174-175 GH 3
San Carlos [RP, Negros] 174-175 H 4
San Carlos [YV, Cojedes] 98-99 F 3
San Carlos, Bahía — 86-87 D 3-4
San Carlos, Estrecho de — = Falkland Sound 103 DE 8
San Carlos, Mesa de — 86-87 C 3
San Carlos, Punta — 86-87 C 3
San Carlos Bay 80-81 bc 3
San Carlos de Bolívar 103 D 5
San Carlos de Puno 98-99 EF 8
San Carlos de Río Negro 98-99 F 4
San Carlos de Zulia 98-99 E 3
San Carlos Indian Reservation 74-75 HJ 6
San Carlos Lake 74-75 H 6
San Clemente, CA 74-75 E 6
San Clemente Island 58-59 BC 5
San Cristóbal [CO, Amazonas] 98-99 E 5
San Cristóbal [PA] 88-89 F 10
San Cristóbal [RA] 103 D 4
San Cristóbal [Solomon Is.] 174-175 k 7
San Cristóbal [YV] 98-99 E 3
San Cristóbal, Isla — 98-99 B 5
San Cristóbal de las Casas 58-59 H 8
San Cristobal Wash 74-75 G 6
San Cristoval = San Cristóbal 174-175 k 7
Sancti-Spíritus [C] 58-59 L 7
Sand 114-115 AB 8
Ṣandafā' 199 B 3
Sandai 174-175 F 7
Sanda Island 116-117 F 5
Sandakan 174-175 G 5
Sandalwood Island = Sumba 174-175 G 9
Sandane 114-115 AB 7
Sandanski 138-139 K 5
Sand Arroyo 68-69 E 7
Sanday 116-117 J 1
Sanday Sound 116-117 J 1
Sandefjord 114-115 D 8
Sanders, AZ 74-75 J 5
Sanderson, TX 76-77 C 7
Sandersville, GA 80-81 E 4
Sandfontein [Namibia → Gobabis] 198 CD 6
Sandford Lake 70-71 E 1
Sandhornøy 114-115 EF 4
Sandia 98-99 F 7
Sandia Crest 76-77 AB 5
Sandia Peak = Sandia Crest 76-77 AB 5
San Diego 76-77 B 8
San Diego, CA 58-59 C 5
San Diego, TX 76-77 E 9
San Diego, Cabo — 103 CD 8
San Diego Aqueduct 74-75 E 6
San Diego de la Unión 86-87 K 7
Sand Island 70-71 E 2
Sand Islands 52-53 DE 5
Sand Key 80-81 b 3
Sand Lake [CDN, lake] 50 B 2
Sand Lake [CDN, place] 70-71 H 2
Sand Mountains 58-59 J 5
Sandnes 114-115 A 8
Sandø = Sandoy 116-117 ab 2
Sandoa 198 D 3
Sandomierz 124 K 3
San Donà di Piave 138-139 E 3
Sandover River 182-183 FG 4
Sandoway = Thandwe 174-175 B 3
Sandown-Shanklin 116-117 KL 10
Sandoy 116-117 ab 2
Sand Point, AK 52-53 c 2
Sandpoint, ID 66-67 E 1
Sandringham 182-183 G 4
Sand River 49 C 3
Sandspit 48 B 3
Sand Springs, MT 68-69 C 2
Sand Springs, OK 76-77 F 4
Sandstone 182-183 C 5
Sandstone, MN 70-71 D 2
Sand Tank Mountains 74-75 G 6
Sandur 116-117 b 2
Sandur [IS] 114-115 ab 2
Sandusky, MI 72-73 E 3
Sandusky, OH 72-73 E 4
Sandusky Bay 72-73 E 4
Sandveld [Namibia] 198 CD 6
Sandvík 116-117 ab 2
Sandviken 114-115 G 7
Sandwich 116-117 h 7
Sandwich, IL 70-71 F 5
Sandy 116-117 L 8
Sandy, NV 74-75 F 5
Sandy Bay 49 G 3
Sandybeach Lake 50 CD 3
Sandy Cape [AUS, Queensland] 182-183 K 4
Sandy City, UT 58-59 D 3
Sandy Creek [USA, Wyoming] 66-67 J 4-5
Sandy Desert = Ar-Rub' al-Hālī 160-161 F 7-G 6
Sandy Hills 58-59 GH 5
Sandy Hook 72-73 K 4
Sandy Hook, KY 72-73 E 5-6
Sandy Key 80-81 c 4
Sandy Lake [CDN, lake Newfoundland] 51 H 3
Sandy Lake [CDN, lake Ontario] 46-47 S 7
Sandy Lake [CDN, place Alberta] 48 L 2
Sandy Lake [CDN, place Ontario] 50 C 1
Sandy Lake [CDN, place Saskatchewan] 49 E 2
Sandy Narrows 49 G 3
Sandy Ridge 80-81 E 2
Sandy River 66-67 BC 3
San Estanislao 103 E 2
San Esteban de Gormaz 132-133 F 8
San Felipe, NM 76-77 A 5
San Felipe [CO] 98-99 F 4
San Felipe [MEX, Baja California Norte] 86-87 C 2
San Felipe [MEX, Guanajuato] 86-87 K 7
San Felipe [RCH] 103 B 4
San Felipe [YV] 98-99 F 2
San Felipe de Puerto Plata = Puerto Plata 58-59 M 8
San Feliu de Guixols 132-133 J 8
San Félix [RCH] 94 A 6
San Fernando, CA 74-75 D 5
San Fernando [E] 132-133 D 10
San Fernando [MEX] 86-87 LM 5
San Fernando [RA] 103 E 4
San Fernando [RCH] 103 B 4
San Fernando [RP ↖ Baguio] 174-175 GH 3
San Fernando [RP ↖ Manila] 174-175 H 3
San Fernando [TT] 58-59 L 9
San Fernando [YV] 98-99 F 3
San Fernando, Río — [MEX] 86-87 LM 5
San Fernando de Atabapo 98-99 F 4
San Fernando del Valle de Catamarca 103 C 3
Sånfjället 114-115 E 6
Sanford 49 K 6
Sanford, FL 58-59 K 6
Sanford, ME 72-73 L 3
Sanford, NC 80-81 G 3
Sanford, Mount — 52-53 Q 5
San Francisco, CA 58-59 AB 4
San Francisco [ES] 88-89 BC 8
San Francisco [MEX, Coahuila] 76-77 C 9
San Francisco [MEX, Sonora] 86-87 D 2
San Francisco [RA] 103 D 4
San Francisco, Presedio of — 83 I b 2
San Francisco, University of — 83 I b 2
San Francisco Bay 74-75 B 4
San Francisco de Conchos 76-77 B 9
San Francisco de la Caleta 58-59 bc 3
San Francisco del Oro 58-59 E 6
San Francisco del Parapetí 98-99 G 8-9
San Francisco del Rincón 86-87 JK 7
San Francisco Maritime State Historic Park 83 I b 2
San Francisco-Oakland Bay Bridge 83 I bc 2
San Francisco Peaks 74-75 GH 5
San Francisco Plateau 58-59 D 4-E 5
San Francisco River 74-75 J 6
San Francisco Solano, Punta — 98-99 D 3
San Francisco State University 83 I ab 2
Sangā 174-175 C 2
Sanga = Sangha 198 C 1-2
San Gabriel, CA 83 III d 1
San Gabriel [EC] 98-99 D 4
San Gabriel Mountains 74-75 DE 5
Sangagchhö Ling 166-167 G 6
Šangaly 142-143 H 3
Sangamon River 70-71 EF 5
Sangar 154-155 Y 5
Sangários = Sakarya nehri 160-161 C 2
Sangay 98-99 D 5
Sangeang, Pulau — 174-175 GH 8
Sanger, CA 74-75 D 4
Sanger, TX 76-77 F 6
San Germán [Puerto Rico] 88-89 N 5-6
Sanggau 174-175 F 6
Sangha 198 C 1-2
Sangihe, Kepulauan — 174-175 J 6
Sangihe, Pulau — 174-175 J 6
Sang-i Māsha 160-161 K 4
San Giovanni in Persiceto 138-139 D 3
Sangju 170-171 G 4
Sangkulirang 174-175 G 6
Sangkulirang, Teluk — 174-175 G 6
Sāngli 160-161 LM 7
Sangmélima 194-195 G 8
Sangonera, Río — 132-133 G 10
San Gorgonio Mountain 74-75 E 5
Sangre de Cristo Range 58-59 E 4
Sangre Grande 58-59 OP 9
Sangsues, Lac aux — 72-73 GH 1
Sangudo 48 K 3
Sangue, Cachoeira do — 98-99 L 7
Sangue, Rio do — 98-99 H 7
Sangymgort 154-155 M 5
San Hipólito 86-87 CD 4
Sanibel Island 80-81 b 3
San Ignacio, NM 76-77 B 5
San Ignacio [BOL ↗ La Paz] 98-99 F 7
San Ignacio [BOL ↗ Santa Cruz] 98-99 G 8
San Ignacio [MEX] 86-87 D 4
San Ignacio [PY] 103 E 3
San Ignacio, Laguna — 86-87 D 4
San Isidro [RA] 103 E 4
Sanitatas 198 B 5
San Jacinto, CA 74-75 E 6
San Jacinto Mountains 74-75 E 6
San Javier [BOL, Santa Cruz] 98-99 G 8
San Javier [RA, Misiones] 103 EF 3
San Jerónimo, Serranía de — 98-99 D 3
Sanjō 170-171 M 4
San Joaquín [BOL] 98-99 FG 7
San Joaquin River 58-59 BC 4
San Joaquin Valley 58-59 BC 4
San Jon, NM 76-77 C 5
San Jorge [NIC] 88-89 CD 9
San Jorge, Bahía de — 86-87 D 2
San Jorge, Golfo — 103 CD 7
San Jorge, Golfo de — 132-133 H 8
San Jose, CA 58-59 B 4
San José [CR] 58-59 K 9-10
San José [GCA] 58-59 H 9
San José [PA] 58-59 b 3
San José [ROU, place] 103 E 4
San José [RP] 174-175 H 3
San José, Isla — [MEX] 58-59 DE 6
San José, Isla — [PA] 88-89 G 10
San José, Isla — = Weddell Island 103 D 8
San José de Chiquitos 98-99 G 8
San José de Jáchal 103 C 4
San Jose de las Raíces 86-87 KL 5
San José de las Salinas 103 CD 4
San José del Cabo 58-59 E 7
San José del Guaviare 98-99 E 4
San José de Ocuné 98-99 E 4
San Josef Bay 48 C 4
San Jose River 74-75 JK 5
San Juan [DOM] 88-89 L 5
San Juan [MEX] 76-77 D 9
San Juan [PE] 98-99 DE 8
San Juan [Puerto Rico] 58-59 N 8
San Juan [RA, place] 103 C 4
San Juan, Cabo — [Equatorial Guinea] 194-195 F 8
San Juan, Cabo — [RA] 103 D 8
San Juan, Río — [MEX] 86-87 L 5
San Juan, Río — [NIC] 58-59 K 9
San Juan Archipelago 66-67 B 1
San Juan Bautista [E] 132-133 H 9
San Juan Bautista [PY] 103 E 3
San Juan Bautista = Villahermosa 58-59 H 8
San Juan Bautista Tuxtepec 86-87 M 9-10
San Juan de Guadalupe 86-87 J 5
San Juan de Guía, Cabo de — 98-99 DE 2
San Juan del Norte 88-89 E 9
San Juan del Norte = Bluefields 58-59 K 9
San Juan del Norte, Bahía de — 58-59 K 9
San Juan de los Lagos 86-87 J 7
San Juan de los Morros 98-99 F 3
San Juan del Río 86-87 KL 7
San Juan del Sur 88-89 CD 9
San Juanico, Isla — 86-87 G 7
San Juan Mountains 58-59 E 4
San Juan Quiotepec 86-87 MN 9
San Juan River 58-59 E 4
San Justo [RA, Santa Fe] 103 D 4
Sankisen 170-171 cd 2
Sankt Gallen 124 D 5
Sankt Gotthard 124 D 5
Sankt Michel = Mikkeli 114-115 MN 7
Sankt Moritz 124 DE 5
Sankt Pölten 124 G 4
Sankuru 198 D 2
San Lázaro, Cabo — 58-59 D 7
San Lázaro, Sierra — 86-87 EF 6
San Lázaro, Sierra de — 86-87 E 5-F 6
San Lorenzo [BOL ↙ Riberalta] 98-99 F 7
San Lorenzo [BOL ↑ Tarija] 98-99 FG 9
San Lorenzo [EC] 98-99 D 4
San Lorenzo [MEX, Veracruz] 86-87 N 9
San Lorenzo [RA, Santa Fe] 103 D 4
San Lorenzo [YV, Zulia] 98-99 E 3
San Lorenzo, Cabo de — 98-99 C 5
San Lorenzo, Cerro — 103 B 7
San Lorenzo, Isla — [MEX] 86-87 D 3
San Lorenzo, Isla — [PE] 98-99 D 7
San Lorenzo, Río — 86-87 G 5
San Lorenzo, Sierra de — 132-133 F 7
Sanlúcar de Barrameda 132-133 D 10
San Lucas, CA 74-75 C 4
San Lucas [MEX] 86-87 F 6
San Lucas, Cabo — 58-59 E 7
San Luis, CO 68-69 D 7
San Luis [C] 88-89 J 4
San Luis [GCA] 86-87 Q 9
San Luis [RA, place] 103 C 4
San Luis, Sierra de — [YV] 98-99 EF 2
San Luis de la Paz 86-87 KL 7
San Luis Gonzaga 86-87 C 3
San Luis Obispo, CA 58-59 B 4
San Luis Obispo Bay 74-75 C 5
San Luis Pass 76-77 G 8
San Luis Potosí 58-59 FG 7
San Luis Río Colorado 86-87 C 1
San Luis Valley 68-69 CD 7
San Manuel, AZ 74-75 H 6
San Marcial, NM 76-77 A 6
San Marco, Capo — 138-139 BC 6
San Marcos, TX 58-59 G 6
San Marcos [GCA] 86-87 OP 10
San Marcos [MEX] 86-87 L 9
San Marcos [RCH] 103 B 4
San Marcos, Isla — 86-87 DE 4
San Marcos, Sierra de — 76-77 CD 9
San Marino [RSM, place] 138-139 E 4
San Marino [RSM, state] 138-139 E 4
San Martín [BOL] 98-99 G 7-8
San Martín [RA, La Rioja] 103 C 3
San Martín, Lago — 103 B 7
San Martin, Río — 98-99 G 8
San Mateo, CA 58-59 B 4
San Mateo Ixtatán 86-87 P 10
San Mateo Peak 58-59 E 5
San Matías 103 H 8
San Matías, Golfo — 103 D 6
Sanmaur 50 OP 3
San-mên-hsia = Sanmenxia 166-167 L 5
Sanmenxia 166-167 L 5
San Miguel, AZ 74-75 H 7
San Miguel, CA 74-75 C 5
San Miguel, NM 76-77 B 5
San Miguel [ES] 58-59 J 9
San Miguel, Golfo de — 88-89 G 10
San Miguel, Río — [BOL] 98-99 G 7-8
San Miguel, Río — [MEX, Chihuahua] 86-87 G 4
San Miguel, Río — [MEX, Sonora] 86-87 E 2
San Miguel de Allende 86-87 KL 7
San Miguel de Huachi 98-99 F 8
San Miguel del Monte 103 E 5
San Miguel Island 74-75 C 5
San Miguelito [NIC] 88-89 D 9
San Miguelito [PA] 58-59 bc 3
San Miguel River 74-75 JK 3
Sannār 194-195 L 6
San Narciso 174-175 GH 3
San Nicolás de los Arroyos 103 D 4
San Nicolas de los Garzas 86-87 KL 5
San Nicolas Island 58-59 BC 5
Sannikova, proliv — 154-155 ab 3
Sanniquellie 194-195 C 7
Sannohe 170-171 N 2
Sannūr, Wādī — 199 B 3
Sanok 124 L 4
San Pablo, CA 83 I bc 1
San Pablo [RP] 174-175 H 4
San Pablo, Point — 83 I b 1
San Pablo, Punta — 86-87 C 4
San Pablo Bay 74-75 B 3
San Pablo Creek 83 I c 1
San Pablo Huitzo 86-87 M 9
San Pablo Reservoir 83 I c 1
San Pablo Ridge 83 I c 1
San Pedro [BOL, Santa Cruz ↗ Santa Cruz] 98-99 G 8
San Pedro [BOL, Santa Cruz ↑ Trinidad] 98-99 G 7
San Pedro [MEX, Baja California Sur] 86-87 E 6
San Pedro [MEX, Chihuahua] 76-77 B 8
San Pedro [MEX, Durango] 76-77 AB 9
San Pedro [PY, place] 103 E 2
San Pedro [RA, Buenos Aires] 103 E 4
San Pedro [RA, Santiago del Estero] 103 C 3
San Pedro, Point — 83 I b 1
San Pedro, Punta — [CR] 58-59 K 10
San Pedro, Río — [GCA] 86-87 P 9
San Pedro, Río — [MEX, river ◁ Pacific Ocean] 86-87 H 6
San Pedro, Río — [MEX, river ◁ Río Conchos] 86-87 GH 4
San Pedro, Sierra de — 132-133 D 9
San Pedro, Volcán — 98-99 F 9
San Pedro Channel 74-75 D 6
San Pedro de la Cueva 86-87 F 3
San Pedro de las Colonias 58-59 F 6
San Pedro Mártir, Sierra — 58-59 CD 5
San Pedro Mártir, Sierra de — 86-87 C 2
San Pedro Mountain 76-77 A 4
San Pedro River 74-75 H 6
San Pedro Sula 58-59 J 8
San Pedro Taviche 86-87 M 9
San Perlita, TX 76-77 F 9
San Pietro [I] 138-139 BC 6
San Quentin State Prison 83 I ab 1
Sanquhar 116-117 GH 5
San Quintín 86-87 BC 2

San Quintin, Bahía de — 86-87 BC 2
San Quintin, Cabo — 58-59 C 5
San Rafael, CA 58-59 B 4
San Rafael [RA] 103 C 4
San Rafael, Bahía de — 86-87 D 3
San Rafael Bay 83 I b 1
San Rafael del Encanto 98-99 E 5
San Rafael Mountains 74-75 CD 5
San Rafael River 74-75 H 3
San Rafael Swell 74-75 H 3
San Ramón [NIC] 88-89 D 7
San Remo 138-139 BC 4
San Román, Cabo — 98-99 EF 2
San Rosendo 103 B 5
San Saba, TX 76-77 E 7
San Saba River 76-77 E 7
San Salvador [BS] 58-59 M 7
San Salvador [ES] 58-59 HJ 9
San Salvador, Isla — 98-99 A 5
Sansanding 194-195 CD 6
Sansanné-Mango = Mango 194-195 E 6
San Sebastián [E] 132-133 FG 7
San Sebastián [RA] 103 C 8
San Sebastian, Isla — 86-87 DE 3
San Sebastián de la Gomera 194-195 A 3
San Severo 138-139 F 5
San Silvestre [YV] 98-99 EF 3
San Simeon, CA 74-75 C 5
San Simon, AZ 74-75 J 6
Sansing = Yilan 166-167 OP 2
Santa Ana, CA 58-59 C 5
Santa Ana [BOL ↖ Trinidad] 98-99 F 7
Santa Ana [CO, Guainía] 98-99 F 4
Santa Ana [ES] 58-59 HJ 9
Santa Ana [MEX] 58-59 D 5
Santa Ana Mountains 74-75 E 6
Santa Anna, TX 76-77 E 7
Santa Barbara, CA 58-59 BC 5
Santa Bárbara [Honduras] 88-89 BC 7
Santa Bárbara [MEX] 58-59 E 6
Santa Bárbara [RCH] 103 B 5
Santa Bárbara [YV ↙ Maturín] 98-99 G 3
Santa Bárbara [YV → San Cristóbal] 98-99 E 3
Santa Bárbara [YV → San Fernando de Atabapo] 98-99 F 4
Santa Bárbara, Serra de — 98-99 J 9
Santa Barbara Channel 74-75 CD 5
Santa Barbara Island 74-75 D 6
Santa Catalina [RA, Jujuy] 103 C 2
Santa Catalina = Catalina 103 C 3
Santa Catalina, Gulf of — 74-75 DE 6
Santa Catalina, Isla — 86-87 EF 5
Santa Catalina Island 58-59 BC 5
Santa Catarina 103 FG 3
Santa Catarina, Ilha de — 103 G 3
Santa Catarina, Valle de — 74-75 EF 7
Santa Catarina de Tepehuanes 86-87 H 5
Santa Clara, CA 58-59 B 4
Santa Clara [C] 58-59 KL 7
Santa Clara [CO] 98-99 EF 5
Santa Clara [MEX, Chihuahua] 76-77 B 8
Santa Clara [MEX, Durango] 86-87 J 5
Santa Comba = Cela 198 C 4
Santa Cruz, CA 58-59 B 4
Santa Cruz [BOL, place] 98-99 G 8
Santa Cruz [BR, Amazonas ↙ Benjamin Constant] 98-99 BC 7
Santa Cruz [BR, Amazonas ↗ Benjamin Constant] 98-99 D 6
Santa Cruz [BR, Rio Grande do Norte] 98-99 M 6
Santa Cruz [CR] 88-89 CD 9
Santa Cruz [MEX] 86-87 E 2
Santa Cruz [RA, Santa Cruz] 103 BC 7
Santa Cruz, Isla — [EC] 98-99 AB 5
Santa Cruz, Isla — [MEX] 86-87 E 5
Santa Cruz Cabrália 98-99 M 8
Santa Cruz de Barahona = Barahona 58-59 M 8
Santa Cruz de la Palma 194-195 A 3
Santa Cruz del Quiché 86-87 P 10
Santa Cruz del Sur 88-89 GH 4
Santa Cruz de Tenerife 194-195 A 3
Santa Cruz do Sul 103 F 3
Santa Cruz Island 58-59 BC 5
Santa Cruz Islands 174-175 l 7
Santa Cruz Mountains 74-75 BC 4
Santa Cruz River 74-75 H 6
Santa Elena [BOL] 98-99 G 9
Santa Elena [PE] 98-99 E 5
Santa Elena, Cabo — 58-59 J 9
Santa Elena de Uairén 98-99 G 4
Santa Fe, NM 58-59 E 4
Santa Fé [C] 88-89 E 4
Santa Fe [RA, place] 103 D 4
Santa Fé do Sul 98-99 J 9
Santa Fe Pacific Railway 58-59 F 4
Santa Fe Springs, CA 83 III d 2
Santa Filomena 98-99 K 6
Santa Genoveva = Cerro las Casitas 58-59 E 7
Santa Helena [BR, Maranhão] 98-99 K 5
Santa Helena [BR, Pará] 98-99 H 5-6
Santai 166-167 JK 5
Santa Inês [BR, Bahia] 98-99 LM 7
Santa Inés, Isla — 103 B 8
Santa Isabel [RA, La Pampa] 103 C 5
Santa Isabel [Solomon Is.] 174-175 jk 6
Santa Isabel = Malabo 194-195 F 8
Santa Isabel, Cachoeira de — 98-99 OP 8
Santa Isabel, Ilha Grande de — 98-99 L 5
Santa Isabel do Araguaia 98-99 K 6
Santa Isabel do Morro 98-99 J 7
Santa Lucía, Sierra de — 86-87 D 4
Santa Lucia Range 74-75 C 4-5
Santaluz [BR, Bahia] 98-99 M 7
Santa Luzia [BR, Rondônia] 98-99 G 9
Santa Magdalena, Isla — 86-87 D 5
Santa Margarita, CA 74-75 C 5
Santa Margarita, Isla — 58-59 D 7
Santa Margherita Ligure 138-139 C 3
Santa Maria, CA 58-59 B 5
Santa Maria [Açores] 188-189 E 5
Santa Maria [BR, Amazonas] 98-99 H 5
Santa Maria [BR, Rio Grande do Sul] 103 EF 3
Santa Maria [PE, Loreto] 98-99 E 5
Santa Maria [RA] 103 C 3
Santa Maria [Vanuatu] 182-183 N 2
Santa María, Bahía de — 86-87 F 5
Santa María, Boca — 86-87 M 5
Santa Maria, Cabo de — 132-133 CD 10
Santa Maria, Cabo de — = Cap Sainte-Marie 198 J 7
Santa María, Lugana de — 86-87 G 2
Santa María, Punta — [MEX] 86-87 F 5
Santa María, Río — [MEX ◁ Laguna de Santa María] 86-87 G 2-3
Santa María, Río — [MEX ◁ Río Tamuín] 86-87 K 7
Santa Maria das Barreiras 98-99 JK 6
Santa María de Ipire 98-99 F 3
Santa María del Oro 86-87 GH 5
Santa Maria di Leuca, Capo — 138-139 H 6
Santa Maria do Pará 98-99 P 5
Santa Maria Otaes 86-87 GH 5
Santa Marta [CO] 98-99 DE 2
Santa Marta, Sierra Nevada de — 98-99 E 2
Santa Maura = Levkás 138-139 J 6
Santa Monica, CA 58-59 BC 5
Santa Monica, TX 76-77 F 9
Santa Monica Bay 83 III ab 2
Santa Monica Mountains 83 III ab 1
Santa Monica Municipal Airport 83 III b 1
Santa Monica State Beach 83 III a 1
Santana 98-99 L 7
Santana, Coxilha da — 103 E 3-F 4
Santana, Ilha de — 98-99 L 5
Santana do Araguaia 98-99 NO 9
Santana do Livramento 103 EF 4
Santander [CO, Cauca] 98-99 D 4
Santander [E] 132-133 F 7
Santander Jiménez 86-87 LM 5
Sant'Antioco [I, island] 138-139 BC 6
Sant'Antioco [I, place] 138-139 BC 6
Santaņy 132-133 J 9
Santa Paula, CA 74-75 D 5
Santa Pola, Cabo de — 132-133 GH 9
Santarém [BR] 98-99 J 5
Santarem [P] 132-133 C 9
Santaren Channel 58-59 L 7
Santa Rita, NM 74-75 J 6
Santa Rita [BR, Amazonas] 98-99 C 8
Santa Rita [BR, Paraíba] 98-99 MN 6
Santa Rita [YV, Zulia] 98-99 E 2
Santa Rita do Araguaia 98-99 J 8
Santa Rito do Weil 98-99 F 5
Santa Rosa, CA 58-59 B 4
Santa Rosa, NM 76-77 B 5
Santa Rosa [BOL, Beni ↘ Riberalta] 98-99 F 7
Santa Rosa [BR, Acre] 98-99 EF 6
Santa Rosa [BR, Rio Grande do Sul] 103 F 3
Santa Rosa [BR, Rondônia] 98-99 GH 10
Santa Rosa [CO, Guainía] 98-99 EF 4
Santa Rosa [PE] 98-99 E 5
Santa Rosa [RA, La Pampa] 103 CD 5
Santa Rosa [RA, Mendoza] 103 c 4
Santa Rosa [RA, San Luis] 103 C 4
Santa Rosa del Palmar 98-99 G 8
Santa Rosa Island [USA, California] 58-59 B 5
Santa Rosa Island [USA, Florida] 78-79 F 5
Santa Rosalia [MEX, Baja California Norte] 86-87 C 3
Santa Rosalía [MEX, Baja California Sur] 58-59 D 6
Santa Rosalia de las Cuevas 86-87 G 3-4
Santa Rosalilia 86-87 C 3
Santa Rosa Range 66-67 E 5
Santa Rosa Wash 74-75 GH 6
Šantarskije ostrova 154-155 a 6-7
Santa Sylvina 103 DE 3
Santa Tecla = Nueva San Salvador 58-59 HJ 9
Santa Teresa [MEX] 76-77 D 9
Santa Teresa, Cachoeira — 98-99 G 9-10
Santa União 98-99 O 10
Santa Vitória do Palmar 103 F 4
Santa Ynez, CA 74-75 CD 5
Santee River 80-81 G 4
San Telmo, Punta — 86-87 HJ 8
Sant'Eufèmia, Golfo di — 138-139 FG 6
Santiago [BR] 103 EF 3
Santiago [Cape Verde] 188-189 E 7
Santiago [DOM] 58-59 M 7
Santiago [MEX] 86-87 F 6
Santiago [PA] 58-59 K 10
Santiago, Cerro — 88-89 EF 10
Santiago de Chile 103 B 4
Santiago de Chuco 98-99 D 6
Santiago de Cuba 58-59 L 7-8
Santiago del Estero [RA, place] 103 CD 3
Santiago di Compostela 132-133 CD 7
Santiago Ixcuintla 58-59 EF 7
Santiago Jamiltepec 86-87 LM 9
Santiagoma 98-99 H 8
Santiago Mountains 76-77 C 7-8
Santiago Papasquiaro 58-59 EF 6-7
Santiago Peak 76-77 C 8
Santiaguillo, Laguna de — 86-87 H 5
Santiam Pass 66-67 BC 3
San Tiburcio 86-87 K 5
Santigi 174-175 H 6
Santo, TX 76-77 E 6
Santo Amaro 98-99 M 7
Santo André 98-99 K 9
Santo André = Isla de San Andrés 58-59 KL 9
Santo Ângelo 103 EF 3
Santo Antão 188-189 E 7
Santo Antônio [BR, Pará] 98-99 O 6
Santo Antônio [São Tomé and Príncipe] 194-195 F 8
Santo Antônio, Cachoeira — [BR, Rio Madeira] 98-99 FG 6
Santo Antônio, Cachoeira — [BR, Rio Roosevelt] 98-99 HJ 9
Santo Antônio de Jesus 98-99 LM 7
Santo Antônio do Içá 98-99 DE 6
Santo Antônio do Zaire = Soyo 198 B 3
Santo Corazón 98-99 H 8
Santo Domingo [DOM] 58-59 MN 8
Santo Domingo [MEX, Baja California Norte] 86-87 CD 3
Santo Domingo [MEX, Baja California Sur] 86-87 DE 5
Santo Domingo [MEX, San Luis Potosí] 86-87 K 6
Santo Domingo [NIC] 88-89 D 8
Santo Domingo, Río — [MEX] 58-59 G 8
Santo Domingo de Guzmán = Santo Domingo 58-59 MN 8
Santoña 132-133 F 7
Santorinē = Thēra 138-139 L 7
Santos 98-99 K 9
Santos, Los — 88-89 F 11
Santos Dumont [BR, Amazonas] 98-99 D 8
Santo Tomás [MEX] 86-87 B 2
Santo Tomás [PE] 98-99 E 7
Santo Tomás de Castilla 88-89 B 7
Santo Tomé [RA, Corrientes] 103 E 3
Sanup Plateau 74-75 G 5
San Valentín, Cerro — 103 B 7
San Vicente [ES] 58-59 J 9
San Víctor 103 E 4
San Vito, Capo — 138-139 E 6
San Xavier Indian Reservation 74-75 H 6-7
Sanya = Ya Xian 166-167 KL 8
San Yanaro 98-99 EF 4
San Ygnacio, TX 76-77 E 9
San Ysidro, CA 74-75 E 6
Sanza Pombo 198 C 3
São Benedito, Rio — 98-99 KL 9
São Bernardo 98-99 L 5
São Borja 103 EF 3
São Caetano do Odivelas 98-99 OP 5
São Carlos [BR, Rondônia] 98-99 G 9
São Carlos [BR, São Paulo] 98-99 K 9
São Domingos [Guinea Bissau] 194-195 A 6
São Felipe 98-99 H 3
São Felix [BR, Mato Grosso] 98-99 N 10
São Félix do Xingu 98-99 J 6
São Fernando 98-99 F 7
São Filipe 98-99 M 7
São Francisco, Cachoeira — 98-99 LM 7
São Francisco, Rio — [BR ◁ Atlantic Ocean] 98-99 LM 6
São Francisco do Sul 103 G 3
São Gabriel 103 EF 4
São Gotardo 98-99 KL 8
São Jerónimo, Serra de — 98-99 J 8
São João [BR, Amazonas] 98-99 E 5
São João, Ilhas de — 98-99 L 5
São João, Serra de — [BR, Amazonas] 98-99 GH 9
São João de Araguaia 98-99 O 7
São João do Piauí 98-99 L 6
São Joaquim [BR, Amazonas] 98-99 E 4-5
São Jorge 188-189 DE 5
São José [BR, Mato Grosso] 98-99 M 10
São José do Anauá 98-99 H 4
São José do Rio Preto [BR, São Paulo] 98-99 JK 9
São José dos Campos 98-99 KL 9
São Lucas, Cachoeira de — 98-99 J 9
São Luís 98-99 L 5
São Luís de Cacianã 98-99 F 8
São Manuel, Rio — 98-99 K 9
São Marcos, Baía de — 98-99 L 5
São Mateus [BR, Espírito Santo] 98-99 M 8
São Mateus [BR, Pará] 98-99 O 7
São Miguel [Açores] 188-189 E 5
São Miguel dos Macacos 98-99 N 5
São Miguel do Tapuio 98-99 L 6
Saona, Isla — 58-59 N 8
Saône 132-133 K 5
São Nicolau 188-189 E 7
São Paulo [BR, administrative unit] 98-99 JK 9
São Paulo [BR, island] 24-25 H 5
São Paulo [BR, place Acre] 98-99 BC 9
São Paulo [BR, place Amazonas] 98-99 B 8
São Paulo de Olivença 98-99 F 5
São Pedro [BR, Amazonas ↘ Benjamin Constant] 98-99 D 7
São Pedro [BR, Amazonas ↗ Benjamin Constant] 98-99 D 6
São Pedro [BR, Rondônia] 98-99 GH 9
São Pedro de Viseu 98-99 NO 6
São Raimundo Nonato 98-99 L 6
São Romão [BR, Amazonas] 98-99 F 6
São Romão [BR, Minas Gerais] 98-99 KL 8
São Roque, Cabo de — 98-99 MN 6
São Salvador [BR, Acre] 98-99 B 8
São Sebastião [BR, Pará] 98-99 M 7
São Sebastião, Ilha de — 98-99 KL 9
São Sebastião, Ponta — 198 G 6
São Sebastião do Boa Vista 98-99 O 5
São Simão, Represa de — 98-99 JK 8
São Tiago 98-99 K 5
São Tomé [São Tomé and Príncipe] 194-195 F 8
São Tomé, Cabo de — 98-99 LM 9
São Tomé, Ilha — 194-195 F 8-9
São Tomé and Principe 194-195 F 8
Şaouīra, eş — = Aş-Şawīrah 194-195 BC 2
Saoura, Ouèd — = Wādī as-Sāwrah 194-195 D 2-3
São Vicente [BR, São Paulo] 98-99 K 9
São Vicente [Cape Verde] 188-189 E 7
São Vicente, Cabo de — 132-133 C 10
Sápai 138-139 L 5
Sapateiro, Cachoeira do — 98-99 H 5
Sape [RI] 174-175 G 8
Sapele 194-195 EF 7
Sapello, NM 76-77 B 5
Sapelo Island 80-81 F 5
Sapiéntza 138-139 J 7
Sapinero, CO 68-69 C 6
Saposoa 98-99 D 6
Sappa Creek 68-69 F 6
Sapphire Mountains 66-67 G 2-3
Sappho, WA 66-67 AB 1
Sapporo 166-167 QR 3
Sapri 138-139 F 5
Sapt Kosi 160-161 O 5
Sapudi, Pulau — 174-175 FG 8
Sapulpa, OK 58-59 G 4
Saqasiq, Es- = Az-Zaqaziq 194-195 KL 2
Saqīyat al-Ḥamrā' 194-195 B 3
Şaqqārah 199 B 3
Saqqez 160-161 F 3
Sarāb [IR, Āžarbayejān-e Khāvarī] 142-143 J 8
Sarab [IR, Eşfahān] 142-143 K 9
Saraburi 174-175 D 4
Sarafutsu 170-171 c 1
Saragossa = Zaragoza 132-133 G 8
Saraguro 98-99 D 5
Sarajevo 138-139 H 4
Sarala 154-155 Q 7
Saramacca 98-99 KL 2
Saramaṭī 160-161 P 5
Saran' [SU, Kazachskaja SSR] 154-155 N 8
Sāran = Chhaprā 160-161 N 5
Sarana Bay 52-53 p 6
Saranac Lake, NY 72-73 J 2
Sarandë 138-139 HJ 6
Sarandí del Yí 103 EF 4
Sarangani Bay 174-175 HJ 5
Sarangani Islands 174-175 HJ 5
Saranlay 194-195 N 8
Saranpaul' 154-155 L 5
Saransk 154-155 GH 7
Sarånta Ekklēsíes = Kırklareli 160-161 B 2
Saranzal, Cachoeira — 98-99 H 8
Sarapul 154-155 J 6
Sarapul'skoje 154-155 a 8
Sararāt Sayyāl, Bi'r — 199 D 6
Sarasota, FL 58-59 K 6
Saratoga, WY 68-69 C 5
Saratoga Springs, NY 58-59 M 3
Saratov 142-143 HJ 5
Saratovskoje vodochranilišče 142-143 J 5
Sarāvān 160-161 J 5
Saravane 174-175 E 3
Sarawak 174-175 F 6
Sarayū = Ghāghara 160-161 N 5
Sardalas 194-195 G 3
Sardārshahar = Sardārshahr 160-161 L 5
Sardārshahr 160-161 L 5
Sardegna 138-139 C 5
Sardes 142-143 E 8
Sardinia, OH 72-73 E 5
Sardinia = Sardegna 138-139 C 5
Sardis, GA 80-81 EF 4
Sardis, MS 78-79 E 3
Sardis Lake 78-79 E 3
Sardis Reservoir = Sardis Lake 78-79 E 3
Sarek nationalpark 114-115 GH 4
Sarektjåkko 114-115 G 4
Sarepul 160-161 K 3
Sargasso Sea 58-59 N-P 6
Sargent, NE 68-69 G 5
Sargent Icefield 52-53 N 6
Sargents, CO 68-69 C 6
Sargho, Djebel — = Jabal Şaghrū' 194-195 C 2
Sargoda = Sargodhā 160-161 L 4
Sargodhā 160-161 L 4
Sarh 194-195 H 7
Sarhade Wākhān 160-161 L 3
Şarhrō', Jbel — = Jabal Şaghrū' 194-195 C 2
Sārī 160-161 G 3
Sariá 138-139 M 8
Sarıkamış 142-143 H 7
Sarikei 174-175 F 6
Sarina 182-183 J 4
Sarıoğlan 142-143 G 8
Sarir 194-195 J 3
Sarita, TX 76-77 F 9
Sarī Tappah 142-143 H 8
Sariwŏn 166-167 O 4
Šarja 154-155 H 6
Sarjū = Ghāghara 160-161 N 5
Sarlat 132-133 H 6
Sarles, ND 68-69 G 1
Šārmāsag 138-139 K 2
Sarmi 174-175 L 7
Sarmiento 103 BC 7
Sär mörön 166-167 MN 3
Särna 114-115 E 7
Sarnia 46-47 U 9
Sarny 142-143 E 5
Sarolangun 174-175 D 7
Saroma-ko 170-171 c 1
Saronikòs Kólpos 138-139 K 7
Sarpa 142-143 J 6
Šar Planina 138-139 J 4-5
Sarpsborg 114-115 D 8
Sarrah, Ma'tan as- 194-195 J 4
Sarre, la — 46-47 V 8
Sarrebourg 132-133 L 4
Sarreguemines 132-133 L 4
Sarria 132-133 D 7
Sarro, Djebel — = Jabal Şaghrū 194-195 C 2
Šar Süm = Altay 166-167 F 2
Sartang 154-155 Z 4
Sartène 138-139 C 5
Sarthe 132-133 G 5
Saruhan = Manisa 160-161 B 2
Saruyama-zaki 170-171 L 4
Saryč, mys — 142-143 F 7
Sary-Išikotrau 154-155 O 8
Sarykamyšskaja kotlina 142-143 L 7
Šaryngol 166-167 K 2
Saryozek 154-155 O 9
Saryšagan 154-155 N 8
Sarysu 154-155 M 8
Sarytaš [SU, Kazachskaja SSR] 142-143 K 7
Sary-Taš [SU, Tadžikskaja SSR] 160-161 L 3
Sásabe 86-87 E 2
Sasaginnigak Lake 50 AB 2
Sasebo 166-167 O 5
Saskatchewan 46-47 PQ 6-7
Saskatchewan River 46-47 Q 7
Saskatoon 46-47 P 7
Saskylach 154-155 VW 3
Sasmik, Cape — 52-53 u 7
Sasovo 142-143 H 5
Saspamco, TX 76-77 E 8
Sassafras Mountain 80-81 E 3
Sassandra [CI, place] 194-195 C 7-8
Sassandra [CI, river] 194-195 C 7
Sàssari 138-139 C 5
Sassnitz 124 FG 1
Sastobe 154-155 MN 9
Sasykkol', ozero — 154-155 P 8
Sata 170-171 H 7
Satadougou 194-195 B 6
Satakunta 114-115 JK 7
Sata-misaki 166-167 OP 5
Satanta, KS 68-69 F 7
Sātāra 160-161 L 7
Satawal 174-175 N 5
Satawan 178 F 2
Satevó 86-87 G 3-4
Saţīf 194-195 F 1
Satilla River 80-81 F 5
Satipo 98-99 DE 7
Satka 154-155 KL 6
Satlaj 160-161 L 4
Satlaj = Langchhen Khamba 166-167 DE 5
Såtleg = Satlaj 160-161 L 4
Sátoraljaújhely 124 K 4
Sātpura Range 160-161 L-N 6
Satsuma-hantō 170-171 GH 7
Sattahip 174-175 D 4
Saţţāt 194-195 C 2
Satu Mare 138-139 K 2
Saturnina, Rio — 98-99 J 11
Sauce [RA] 103 E 3-4
Sauce, El — 88-89 C 8
Saucier, MS 78-79 E 5
Saucillo 86-87 H 3-4
Saucito 86-87 K 4
Sauda 114-115 B 8
Sauda, Jebel el — = Jabal a Sawdā' 194-195 GH 3
Sauda, Jebel el — = Jabal as-Sawdā' 194-195 GH 3
Saudade, Cachoeira da — 98-99 M 8
Saúde 98-99 L 7
Saudhárkrókur 114-115 d 2
Saudi Arabia 160-161 D 5-F 6
Saudi Kingdom = Saudi Arabia 160-161 D 5-F 6
Saugeen Peninsula = Bruce Peninsula 72-73 F 2
Saugeen River 72-73 F 2
Saugerties, NY 72-73 JK 3
Saugor = Sāgar 160-161 M 6
Sāūjbolāgh = Mahābād 160-161 F 3
Sauk Centre, MN 70-71 C 3
Sauk City, WI 70-71 EF 4
Saukira Bay = Dawḥat as-Sawqirah 160-161 H 7
Saukorem 174-175 K 7
Sauk Rapids, MN 70-71 CD 3
Saül 98-99 J 4
Šaul'der 154-155 M 9
Sault-au-Mouton 51 B 3
Sault-au-Recollet, Montréal- 82 I b 1
Sault aux Cochons, Rivière du — 51 B 3
Sault-Sainte-Marie 46-47 U 8
Sault Sainte Marie, MI 58-59 JK 2
Saumlaki 174-175 K 8
Saumur 132-133 G 5
Şauqirah, Ghubbat — = Dawḥat as-Sawqirah 160-161 H 7
Saura, Wed — = Wādī as-Sāwrah 194-195 D 2-3
Saurāshtra 160-161 KL 6
Saurimo 198 D 3
Sausalito, CA 74-75 B 4
Sautar 198 C 4
Sauz, El — 86-87 G 3
Sauzal, El — 74-75 E 7
Sava [YU] 138-139 J 3
Savage, MT 68-69 D 2
Savageton, WY 68-69 CD 4
Savai'i 174-175 c 1
Savalou 194-195 E 7
Savane, Rivière — 51 A 2
Savanna, IL 70-71 E 4
Savannah, GA 58-59 KL 5
Savannah, MO 70-71 C 6
Savannah, TN 78-79 EF 3
Savannah Beach, GA 80-81 F 4
Savannah River 58-59 K 5
Savannakhet 174-175 DE 3
Savanna-la-Mar 88-89 G 5
Savanne 70-71 EF 1
Savant Lake [CDN, lake] 50 D 2
Savant Lake [CDN, place] 50 D 2
Savari = Sābarī 160-161 N 7
Savé [DY] 194-195 E 7
Save [F] 132-133 H 7
Save, Rio — 198 F 6
Sāveh 160-161 G 3-4
Savery, WY 68-69 C 5
Savigliano 138-139 BC 3
Savo 114-115 M 6-7
Savoie 132-133 L 5-6
Sāvojbolāgh = Mahābād 160-161 F 3
Savona 138-139 C 3
Savonlinna 114-115 N 7
Savoy, MT 68-69 B 1
Sävsjö 114-115 F 9
Savu = Pulau Sawu 174-175 H 9
Savukoski 114-115 N 4
Savu Sea 174-175 H 8
Sawahlunto 174-175 D 7
Sawākin 194-195 M 5
Sawara 170-171 N 5
Sawata 170-171 M 3-4
Sawatch Mountains 58-59 E 4
Sawazaki-bana 170-171 LM 4
Sawbill 49 H 2
Sawdā', Jabal as- 194-195 GH 3

Sawdirī 194-195 K 6
Şawīrah, Aş- 194-195 BC 2
Sawknah 194-195 GH 3
Sawqirah 160-161 H 7
Sawqirah, Dawḥat as- 160-161 H 7
Şawrah, Aş- 199 D 4
Sāwrah, Wādī as- 194-195 D 2-3
Sawtooth Mount 52-53 MN 4
Sawtooth Mountains 66-67 FG 3
Sawtooth Range 66-67 C 1-2
Sawu, Pulau — 174-175 H 9
Sawyer, KS 68-69 G 7
Saxilby 116-117 L 7
Saxon, WI 70-71 E 2
Saxony = Sachsen 124 F 3
Saxton, PA 72-73 GH 4
Say 194-195 E 6
Sayaboury 174-175 D 3
Şaydā [RL] 160-161 CD 4
Sayḥūt 160-161 G 7
Saymo Lake 70-71 J 2
Sayn Shanda = Sajnšand 166-167 KL 3
Sayo = Dembī Dolo 194-195 LM 7
Şayq, Wādī — 160-161 F 8
Sayre, OK 76-77 E 5
Sayre, PA 72-73 H 4
Sayula 86-87 HJ 8
Say'ūn 160-161 F 7
Sazanit 138-139 H 5

S'bū', Wād — 194-195 CD 2

Scafell Pike 116-117 H 6
Scalby 116-117 L 6
Scalford 116-117 KL 8
Scalloway 116-117 e 3
Scalpay 116-117 F 3
Scammon Bay 52-53 E 5-6
Scammon Bay, AK 52-53 E 6
Scandia 49 BC 5
Scandia, KS 68-69 H 6
Scandinavia 110-111 K 4-N 1
Scapa 49 B 5
Scapa Flow 116-117 HJ 2
Scappoose, OR 66-67 B 3
Scarba 116-117 F 4
Scarborough [GB] 116-117 L 6
Scarborough [TT] 58-59 OP 9
Scarp 116-117 D 2
Scarpanto = Kárpathos 138-139 M 8
Scarth 49 H 6
Ščeglovsk = Kemerovo 154-155 PQ 6
Sceirí 116-117 EF 7
Scenic, SD 68-69 E 4
Scerpeddi, Punta — 138-139 C 6
Schaffhausen 124 D 5
Schaumburg, IL 70-71 F 5
Schebschi Mountains 194-195 G 7
Schefferville 46-47 X 7
Schelde 132-133 J 3
Schell Creek Range 74-75 F 3
Schenectady, NY 58-59 LM 3
Schiehallion 116-117 GH 4
Schíza 138-139 J 7
Schleswig 124 DE 1
Schleswig-Holstein 124 D 1-E 2
Schlüchtern 124 DE 3
Schmidt Island = ostrov Šmidta 154-155 QR 1
Scholle, NM 76-77 A 5
Schouwen 132-133 J 3
Schrag, WA 66-67 D 2
Schreiber 70-71 G 1
Schuckmannsburg 198 D 5
Schuler 49 C 5
Schull = Scoil Mhuire 116-117 B 9
Schurz, NV 74-75 D 3
Schuyler, NE 68-69 H 5
Schwabach 124 E 4
Schwäbische Alb 124 D 5-E 4
Schwäbisch Gmünd 124 DE 4
Schwäbisch Hall 124 DE 4
Schwandorf 124 F 4
Schwaner, Pegunungan — 174-175 F 7
Schwarze Elster 124 FG 3
Schwarzwald 124 D 4-5
Schwatka Mountains 46-47 EF 4
Schweinfurt 124 E 3
Schweitzergletscher 31 B 32-33
Schweizer Land 46-47 d 4
Schwerin 124 E 2
Schwyz 124 D 5
Sciacca 138-139 E 7
Scicli 138-139 F 7
Scie, la — 51 J 2
Science and Industry, Museum of — 83 II b 2
Scilly, Isles of — 116-117 E 11
Sciobairín, An — 116-117 B 9
Scioto River 72-73 E 5
Scipio, UT 74-75 G 3
Scobey, MT 68-69 D 1
Scoil Mhuire 116-117 B 9
Scoresby Land 30 B 21
Scoresby Sund [Greenland, bay] 30 B 20-21
Scoresbysund [Greenland, place] 30 B 20-21
Scotia, CA 66-67 AB 5
Scotia Ridge 26-27 G 8
Scotland 116-117 F 3-H 5
Scotland, SD 68-69 GH 4
Scotland Neck, NC 80-81 H 2
Scotstown 72-73 L 2
Scott 31 B 17-18
Scott, Cape — 46-47 L 7
Scott, Mount — [USA → Crater Lake] 58-59 B 3
Scott, Mount — [USA ↓ Pengra Pass] 66-67 BC 4
Scott Channel 48 C 4
Scott City, KS 68-69 F 6
Scott Glacier [Antarctica, Dronning Maud fjellkjede] 31 A 21-23
Scott Glacier [Antarctica, Knox Land] 31 C 11
Scottie Creek Lodge, AK 52-53 R 5
Scott Inlet 46-47 WX 3
Scott Island 31 C 19
Scott Islands 48 C 4
Scott Range 31 C 5-6
Scott Reef 182-183 D 2
Scott Run 82 II a 1
Scottsbluff, NE 58-59 F 3
Scottsboro, AL 78-79 FG 3
Scottsburg, IN 70-71 GH 6
Scottsdale 182-183 J 8
Scotts Head 88-89 Q 7
Scottsville, KY 78-79 F 2
Scottsville, VA 80-81 G 2
Scottville, MI 70-71 GH 4
Scourie 116-117 FG 2
Scranton, AR 78-79 C 3
Scranton, PA 58-59 LM 3
Scribner, NE 68-69 H 5
Ščuč'a 142-143 N 2
Ščučinsk 154-155 MN 7
Scunthorpe 116-117 L 7
Scutari = İstanbul-Üsküdar 160-161 BC 2
Scutari = Shkodër 138-139 H 4
Scutari, Lake — = Skadarsko jezero 138-139 H 4

Seadrift, TX 76-77 F 8
Seaford 116-117 LM 10
Seaford, DE 72-73 J 5
Seagraves, TX 76-77 C 6
Seagull Lake 70-71 E 1
Seaham 116-117 K 6
Sea Islands 58-59 K 5
Seal Cape 52-53 d 1
Seale, AL 78-79 G 4
Sea Lion Islands 103 E 8
Seal Islands 52-53 d 1
Seal River 46-47 R 6
Sealy, TX 76-77 F 8
Sean-chaisleán, An — 116-117 D 7
Searchlight, NV 74-75 F 5
Searchmont 70-71 HJ 2
Searcy, AR 78-79 CD 3
Searles Lake 74-75 E 5
Searsport, ME 72-73 M 2
Sears Tower 83 II b 1
Seaside, CA 74-75 C 4
Seaside, OR 66-67 B 3
Seaside Park, NJ 72-73 JK 5
Seaton [CDN] 48 D 2
Seaton [GB] 116-117 H 10
Seat Plesant, MD 82 II b 2
Seattle, WA 58-59 B 2
Sebá', Gebel es- = Qārat as-Sab'ah 194-195 H 3
Sebago Lake 72-73 L 3
Sebangan, Teluk — 174-175 F 7
Sebangka, Pulau — 174-175 DE 6
Sebastian, FL 80-81 c 3
Sebastian, Cape — 66-67 A 4
Sebastián Vizcaíno, Bahía — 58-59 CD 6
Sebastopol, CA 74-75 B 3
Sebatik, Pulau — 174-175 G 6
Sebeka, MN 70-71 C 2
Sebeş 138-139 K 2-3
Sebes Körös 124 K 5
Sebewaing, MI 72-73 E 3
Sebḥa = Sabhah 194-195 G 3
Sebree, KY 70-71 G 7
Sebring, FL 80-81 c 3
Sebta = Ceuta 194-195 CD 1
Sebuku, Pulau — 174-175 G 7
Sebuku, Teluk — 174-175 G 6
Seburi-yama 170-171 H 6
Secaucus, NJ 82 III b 2
Secen Chaan = Öndörchaan 166-167 L 2
Sechelt 66-67 AB 1
Sechuan = Sichuan 166-167 J 5-6
Sechura 98-99 C 6
Sechura, Bahía de — 98-99 C 6
Secunderābād 160-161 M 7
Sedalia 49 C 5
Sedalia, MO 70-71 D 6
Sedan, KS 76-77 F 4
Sedan [AUS] 182-183 G 6
Sedan [F] 132-133 K 4
Sedanka Island 52-53 no 4
Seddonville 182-183 O 8
Sedel'nikovo 154-155 O 6
Sedgwick, KS 68-69 H 7
Sédhiou 194-195 AB 6
Šedok 142-143 H 7
Sedona, AZ 74-75 H 5
Sedova, pik — 154-155 J 3
Seechelt Peninsula 66-67 AB 1
Seeheim [Namibia] 198 C 7
Seeis 198 C 6
Seeley Lake, MT 66-67 G 2
Sefadu 194-195 B 7
Segendy 142-143 K 7
Segesta 138-139 E 7
Segeža 154-155 EF 5
Segguedim = Séguédine 194-195 G 4
Sego, UT 74-75 J 3
Segorbe 132-133 G 9
Ségou 194-195 C 6
Šegovary 142-143 H 3
Segovia, TX 76-77 E 7
Segovia [E] 132-133 E 8
Segovia, Río — = Río Coco 58-59 K 9
Segozero 142-143 F 3
Segré 132-133 G 5
Segre, Río — 132-133 H 8
Segu = Ségou 194-195 C 6
Seguam Island 52-53 kl 4
Seguam Pass 52-53 k 4
Séguédine 194-195 G 4
Séguéla 194-195 C 7
Seguin, TX 58-59 G 6
Seguine Point 82 III a 3
Segula Island 52-53 s 6
Segura, Río — 132-133 G 9
Segura, Sierra de — 132-133 F 9-10
Seibal 86-87 P 9
Seibert, CO 68-69 E 6
Seiland 114-115 K 2
Seiling, OK 76-77 E 4
Seinäjoki 114-115 K 6
Seine 132-133 H 4
Seine, Baie de la — 132-133 G 4
Seishin = Ch'ŏngjin 166-167 OP 3
Seishū = Ch'ŏngju 166-167 O 4
Seistan = Sīstān 160-161 J 4
Seiyit, Sarārāt — = Bi'r Sarārāt Sayyāl 199 D 6
Sejm 142-143 F 5
Sejmčan 154-155 d 5
Sejny 124 L 1
Seke 198 F 2
Sekenke 198 F 2
Šeki 142-143 J 7
Sekiu, WA 66-67 A 1
Sekondi-Takoradi 194-195 D 7-8
Šelagskij, mys — 154-155 gh 3
Selah, WA 66-67 C 2
Sēlam = Salem 160-161 M 8
Selangor, Kuala — 174-175 D 6
Selaru, Pulau — 174-175 K 8
Selatan, Tanjung — 174-175 F 7
Selawik, AK 46-47 DE 4
Selawik Lake 46-47 DE 4
Selawik River 52-53 H 3
Selbu 114-115 D 6
Selby 116-117 K 7
Selby, SD 68-69 FG 3
Selden, KS 68-69 F 6
Seldovia, AK 46-47 F 6
Selemdža 154-155 YZ 7
Selenge [Mongolia, administrative unit = 11 ◁] 166-167 K 2
Selenge [Mongolia, place] 166-167 J 2
Selenge mörön 166-167 J 2
Selenn'ach 154-155 a 4
Selenodolsk = Zelenodol'sk 154-155 HJ 6
Sélestat 132-133 L 4
Seletyteniz, ozero — 154-155 N 7
Seleucia = Silifke 160-161 C 3
Selévkeia = Silifke 160-161 C 3
Selfoss 114-115 c 3
Selfridge, ND 68-69 F 2
Šelichova, zaliv — 154-155 e 5-6
Seliger, ozero — 142-143 F 4
Seligman, AZ 74-75 G 5
Seligman, MO 78-79 C 2
Selīma, Wāḥat es — = Wāḥāt Şalīmah 194-195 K 4
Seling Tsho 166-167 FG 5
Selinus 138-139 E 7
Seliphug Gonpa 166-167 E 5
Seljord 114-115 C 8
Selkirk [CDN] 46-47 R 7
Selkirk [GB] 116-117 HJ 5
Selkirk Island 49 J 4
Selkirk Mountains 46-47 N 7-8
Selle, la — 88-89 KL 5
Selleck, WA 66-67 C 2
Sells, AZ 74-75 H 7
Selma, AL 58-59 J 5
Selma, CA 74-75 D 4
Selma, NC 80-81 G 3
Selmer, TN 78-79 E 3
Selous Game Reserve 198 G 3
Selsey 116-117 L 10
Selukwe 198 F 5
Selva 103 D 3
Selvagens, Ilhas — 194-195 A 2
Selvas 95 DE 3
Selway River 66-67 F 2
Selwyn 182-183 H 4
Selwyn Mountains 46-47 KL 5
Selwyn Range 182-183 GH 4
Selz, ND 68-69 G 2
Seman 138-139 H 5
Semans 49 F 5
Semarang 174-175 F 8
Semau, Pulau — 174-175 H 9
Sembodja = Samboja 174-175 G 7
Semeru, Gunung — 174-175 F 8
Semeuluë, Pulau — 174-175 BC 6
Semeyen = Simēn 194-195 M 6
Semidi Islands 52-53 e 1-2
Seminoe Dam, WY 68-69 C 4
Seminoe Mountains 68-69 C 4
Seminoe Reservoir 68-69 C 4
Seminole, OK 76-77 F 5
Seminole, TX 76-77 C 6
Seminole, Lake — 78-79 G 5
Semipalatinsk 154-155 OP 7
Semirara Islands 174-175 H 4
Semisopochnoi Island 52-53 st 6
Semka = Sangā 174-175 C 2
Semmering 124 GH 5
Semnān 160-161 G 3
Semnan, Koll-e — 160-161 GH 3
Semois 132-133 K 4
Šemonaicha 154-155 P 7
Sem'onov 142-143 H 4
Senador Pompeu 98-99 LM 6
Sena Madureira 98-99 F 6
Senanga 198 D 5
Senate 68-69 B 1
Senatobia, MS 78-79 E 3
Šenber 154-155 M 8
Sendai [J, Kagoshima] 170-171 GH 7
Sendai [J, Miyagi] 166-167 R 4
Sene 194-195 D 7
Seneca, KS 68-69 H 6
Seneca, MO 76-77 G 4
Seneca, NE 68-69 F 4-5
Seneca, OR 66-67 D 3
Seneca, SC 80-81 E 3
Seneca, SD 68-69 G 3
Seneca Falls, NY 72-73 H 3
Seneca Lake 72-73 H 3
Sénégal [SN, river] 194-195 B 5
Sénégal [SN, state] 194-195 AB 6
Senegal = Sénégal 194-195 AB 6
Seney, MI 70-71 H 2
Sengejskij, ostrov — 154-155 HJ 4
Sengge Khamba 166-167 DE 5
Sengilej 142-143 J 5
Sengwe 198 E 5
Senhor do Bonfim 98-99 L 7
Senigàllia 138-139 E 4
Senj 138-139 F 3
Senja 114-115 G 3
Senkaku-shotō 166-167 N 6
Senkaku syotō = Senkaku-shotō 166-167 N 6
Šenkursk 154-155 G 5
Senlis 132-133 J 4
Senmonorom 174-175 E 4
Sennār = Sannār 194-195 L 6
Sennen 116-117 F 10
Senneterre 50 N 2
Seno 174-175 DE 3
Senoia, GA 78-79 G 4
Sens 132-133 J 4
Senta 138-139 HJ 3
Sentery 198 E 3
Sentinel, AZ 74-75 G 6
Sentinel Peak 48 G 2
Sentinel Range 31 B 28
Sento-Sé 98-99 L 6
Senyavin Islands 178 F 2
Seo de Urgel 132-133 H 7
Seoni 160-161 M 6
Seoul = Sŏul 166-167 O 4
Separ, NM 74-75 J 6
Separation Well 182-183 D 4
Sepatini, Rio — 98-99 E 9-F 8
Sepenjang, Pulau — 174-175 G 8
Šepetovka 142-143 E 5
Sepik River 174-175 M 7
Sepone 174-175 E 3
Sepopa 198 D 5
Sep'o-ri 170-171 F 3
Sept-Îles 46-47 X 7-8
Sept-Îles, Baie des — 51 CD 2-3
Sequim, WA 66-67 B 1
Sequoia National Park 58-59 C 4
Serachs 160-161 J 3
Serafina, NM 76-77 B 5
Seram [RI] 174-175 JK 7
Seram-laut, Kepulauan — 174-175 K 7
Serampore 160-161 O 6
Seramsee 174-175 JK 7
Serang 174-175 E 8
Serang = Seram 174-175 JK 7
Serbia 138-139 H 3-J 4
Serdce Kamen', mys — 52-53 BC 3
Serdēles = Sardalas 194-195 G 3
Serdobsk 142-143 HJ 5
Serebr'ansk 154-155 P 8
Seremban 174-175 D 6
Serena, La — [E] 132-133 E 9
Serena, La — [RCH] 103 B 3
Serengeti National Park 198 FG 2
Serenje 198 F 4
Serenli = Saranley 198 H 1
Sereno, Rio — 98-99 P 8
Sergeja Kirova, ostrova — 154-155 QR 2
Sergijev = Zagorsk 154-155 F 6
Serginy 154-155 LM 5
Sergipe 98-99 M 7
Seria 174-175 F 6
Seribu, Pulau-pulau — 174-175 E 7-8
Sérifos 138-139 L 7
Seringa, Serra da — 98-99 J 6
Šerkaly 154-155 M 5
Šerlovaja gora 154-155 W 7
Sermata, Pulau — 174-175 J 8
Sermilik 46-47 d 4
Serov 154-155 L 6
Serowe 198 E 6
Serpa 132-133 D 10
Serpa Pinto = Menongue 198 C 4
Serpeddì, Punta — 138-139 C 6
Serpent, Rivière — 51 A 2-3
Serpentine Hot Springs, AK 52-53 EF 4
Serpiente, Boca de la — 98-99 G 2-3
Serpuchov 142-143 G 5
Serra Azul [BR, mountains] 98-99 L 5
Serra do Navio 98-99 M 4
Serra Geral de Goiás 98-99 K 7
Serra Grande [BR, Goiás] 98-99 OP 7
Serra Grande [BR, Rondônia] 98-99 H 9-10
Serra Grande ou de Carauna 98-99 H 3
Sérrai 138-139 K 5
Serra Negra [BR, Goiás] 98-99 P 10
Serra Talhada 98-99 M 6
Serrezuela 103 C 4
Serrinha [BR ↑ Feira de Santana] 98-99 M 7
Sertânia 98-99 M 6
Sertão 98-99 L 7-M 6
Serua, Pulau — 174-175 K 8
Serule 198 E 6
Servilleta, NM 76-77 AB 4
Serxü 166-167 H 5
Sešan 52-53 B 3
Sese Islands 198 F 2
Sesepe 174-175 J 7
Sesfontein 198 B 5
Sesheke 198 DE 5
Sesimbra 132-133 C 9
Sessa Aurunca 138-139 EF 5
Sestroreck 154-155 DE 5
Setana 166-167 Q 3
Sète 132-133 J 7
Sētēia 138-139 M 8
Sete Quedas, Salto das — [BR, Rio Teles Pires] 98-99 H 6
Setermoen 114-115 H 3
Setesdal 114-115 B 8
Sétif = Saṭīf 194-195 F 1
Seto 170-171 L 5
Seto-naikai 166-167 P 5
Settât = Saṭṭāt 194-195 C 2
Setté Cama 198 A 2
Sette-Daban, chrebet — 154-155 a 5
Settle 116-117 J 6
Setúbal 132-133 C 9
Setúbal, Baía de — 132-133 C 9
Seul = Sŏul 166-167 O 4
Seul, Lac — 46-47 S 7
Sevan 142-143 H 7
Sevan, ozero — 142-143 J 7
Sevastopol' 142-143 F 7
Ševčenko 142-143 JK 7
Seven Emus 182-183 G 3
Seven Islands = Sept-Îles 46-47 X 7-8
Sevenoaks 116-117 M 9
Seven Stones 116-117 E 10
Seventy Mile House 48 G 4
Severn, Mouth of the — 116-117 HJ 9
Severn, River — 116-117 J 8-9
Severnaja 154-155 QR 4
Severnaja Semlja = Severnaja Zeml'a 154-155 ST 1-2
Severnaja Sos'va 154-155 L 5
Severnaja Zeml'a 154-155 ST 1-2
Severnaya Zemlya = Severnaja Zeml'a 154-155 ST 1-2
Severnoje [SU ↑ Kujbyšev] 154-155 O 6
Severn River 46-47 T 6-7
Severnyj 154-155 LM 4
Severnyj čink = Donyztau 154-155 K 8
Severnyje uvaly 154-155 HJ 5-6
Severnyj Ledovityj okean 154-155 J-c 1
Severo-Bajkal'skoje nagorje 154-155 UV 6
Severo-Doneck 142-143 GH 6
Severodvinsk 154-155 FG 5
Severo-Jenisejsk 154-155 RS 5
Severo-Kuril'sk 154-155 de 7
Severo-Sibirskaja nizmennost' 154-155 P-X 3
Severouralsk 142-143 LM 3
Severy, KS 68-69 H 7
Sevier Desert 74-75 G 3
Sevier Lake 74-75 G 3
Sevier River 58-59 D 4
Sevier River, East Fork — 74-75 GH 4
Sevierville 80-81 E 3
Sevierville, TN 80-81 E 3
Sevilla 132-133 E 10
Sevlievo 138-139 L 4
Sèvre 132-133 G 5
Sevsib 154-155 M 6
Sewa 194-195 B 7
Seward, AK 46-47 G 5-6
Seward, KS 68-69 G 6
Seward, NE 68-69 H 5
Seward Glacier 52-53 R 6
Seward Peninsula 46-47 CD 4
Sewell, Lake — = Canyon Ferry Reservoir 66-67 H 2
Sexsmith 48 H 2
Seybaplaya 86-87 P 8
Seychelles 198 J 3
Seydhisfjördhur 114-115 fg 2
Seyhan = Adana 160-161 D 3
Seyhan nehri 160-161 D 3
Seyla' 194-195 N 6
Seymour, IA 70-71 D 5
Seymour, IN 58-59 JK 4
Seymour, MO 78-79 C 2
Seymour, TX 76-77 E 6
Seymour, WI 70-71 F 3
Seymour Arm 48 H 4
Seyne-sur-Mer, la — 132-133 K 7
Sezze 138-139 E 5

Sfax = Şafāqis 194-195 FG 2
Sfîntu Gheorghe 138-139 LM 3
Sfîntu Gheorghe, Braţul — 138-139 N 3

Sha Alam 174-175 D 6
Shaanxi 166-167 K 4-5
Shaba 198 DE 3
Shabani = Zvishavane 198 F 6
Shabbona, IL 70-71 F 5
Shabeelle, Webi — 194-195 N 8
Shabellaha Dhexe = 5 ◁ 194-195 b 3
Shabellaha Hoose = 3 ◁ 194-195 N 8
Shabēlle, Webi — = Wabī Shebelē 194-195 N 7
Shabunda 198 E 2
Shabuskwia Lake 50 E 2
Shabwah 160-161 F 7
Shackleton Ice Shelf 31 C 10
Shackleton Inlet 31 A 19-17
Shackleton Range 31 A 35-1
Shadehill Reservoir 68-69 E 3
Shafter, CA 74-75 D 5
Shafter, NV 66-67 F 5
Shafter, TX 76-77 B 8
Shaftesbury 116-117 J 9-10
Shageluk, AK 52-53 H 5
Shag Rocks 103 H 8
Shaguotun 170-171 C 2
Shāhābād [IND, Maisūru] 160-161 M 7
Shaḥāmbī, Jabal — 194-195 F 1-2
Shaḥan, Wādī — = Wādī Shiḥan 160-161 G 7
Shaharak 160-161 J 4
Shahdād 160-161 H 4
Shahdād, Namakzār-e — 160-161 H 4
Shāhī 160-161 G 3
Shahidulla Mazar 166-167 D 4
Shāhjahānpur 160-161 MN 5
Shāhpura [IND, Rājasthān] 160-161 L 5
Shahr-e Bābak 160-161 GH 4
Shahredā 160-161 G 4
Shahr-e Kord 160-161 G 4
Shāhrūd [IR, place] 160-161 GH 3
Shāh Rūd [IR, river] 142-143 K 8
Shā'ib al-Banāt, Jabal — 194-195 L 3
Sha'īt, Wādī — 199 C 5
Shajianzi 170-171 E 2
Shakespeare Island 70-71 F 1
Shakh yar 166-167 E 3
Shaki 194-195 E 7
Shakīr, Jazīrat — 194-195 LM 3
Shakopee, MN 70-71 D 3
Shakotan misaki 170-171 b 2
Shaktoolik, AK 52-53 G 4
Shaktoolik River 52-53 G 4
Shāl 142-143 J 8
Shala 194-195 M 7
Shalanbod 194-195 N 8
Shallāl, Ash- [ET, place] 194-195 L 3
Shallāl, Ash- [ET, river] 194-195 L 3
Shallop 51 E 3
Shallotte, NC 80-81 G 3-4
Shallowater, TX 76-77 CD 6
Shāmbah 194-195 L 7
Shammar, Jabal — 160-161 E 5
Shamo = Gobi 166-167 H-K 3
Shamokin, PA 72-73 H 4
Shamrock, FL 80-81 b 2
Shamrock, TX 76-77 DE 5
Shamva 198 F 5
Shanchengzhen 170-171 EF 1
Shandan 166-167 J 4
Shandī 194-195 L 5
Shandish, MI 72-73 DE 3
Shandong 166-167 M 4
Shandong Bandao 166-167 MN 4
Shangani 198 E 5
Shangbangcheng 170-171 B 2
Shang-chia-ho = Shangjiahe 170-171 E 2
Shang-ch'iu = Shangqiu 166-167 LM 5
Shangchuan Dao 166-167 L 7
Shangcigang = Beijingzi 170-171 DE 3
Shanghai 166-167 N 5

Shanghai 269

Shanghang 166-167 M 6-7
Shanghsien = Shang Xian 166-167 KL 5
Shangjao = Shangrao 166-167 M 6
Shangjiahe 170-171 E 2
Shangkiu = Shangqiu 166-167 LM 5
Shangqiu 166-167 LM 5
Shangrao 166-167 M 6
Shang Xian 166-167 KL 5
Shangzhi 166-167 O 2
Shanhaiguan 166-167 MN 3
Shan-hai-kuan = Shanhaiguan 170-171 BC 2
Shan-hsi = Shaanxi 166-167 L 4-5
Shaniko, OR 66-67 C 3
Shankiu = Shangqiu 166-167 LM 5
Shannon, Mouth of the — = Béal na Sionna 116-117 AB 8
Shannon Airport = Aerphort na Sionna 116-117 C 8
Shannon Bay 48 A 3
Shannon Ø 30 B 20
Shannon River = An tSionna 116-117 CD 7
Shannontown, SC 80-81 FG 4
Shan Pyinnei 174-175 C 2
Shanshan 166-167 G 3
Shansi = Shanxi 166-167 L 4
Shan-tan = Shandan 166-167 J 4
Shantar Islands = Šantarskije ostrova 154-155 a 6
Shantou 166-167 M 7
Shantow = Shantou 166-167 M 7
Shantung = Shandong 166-167 M 4
Shanxi 166-167 L 4
Shanyin 166-167 L 4
Shaoguan 166-167 L 6-7
Shaohsing = Shaoxing 166-167 N 5-6
Shaol Lake 70-71 C 1
Shaotze = Wan Xian 166-167 K 5
Shaowu 166-167 M 6
Shaoxing 166-167 N 5-6
Shaoyang 166-167 L 6
Shapinsay 116-117 J 1-2
Shaqqāt, Ash- 194-195 C 3
Shaqrā' 160-161 F 5
Shār, Jabal — [Saudi Arabia] 199 D 4
Sharafkhāneh 142-143 HJ 8
Sharbithāt, Rā's ash- 160-161 H 7
Sharbot Lake 72-73 H 2
Shari 170-171 d 2
Shari = Chari 194-195 H 6
Shari-dake 170-171 d 2
Shāriqah, Ash- 160-161 GH 5
Sharja = Ash-Shāriqah 160-161 GH 5
Shark Bay 182-183 B 5
Sharmah, Ash- 199 D 3-4
Sharmah, Wādī ash- = Wādī Ṣadr 199 D 3
Sharm ash-Shaykh 199 D 4
Shar Mörön = Chatan gol 166-167 K 3
Sharon, KS 76-77 E 4
Sharon, PA 58-59 KL 3
Sharon Springs, KS 68-69 F 6
Sharq al-Istiwā'īyah 194-195 L 7-8
Sharqī, Ash-Shaṭṭ ash- 194-195 DE 2
Shashamanna = Shashemene 194-195 M 7
Shashemenē 194-195 M 7
Shashi 166-167 L 5-6
Shasta, Mount — 58-59 B 3
Shasta Lake 66-67 B 5
Shattuck, OK 76-77 E 4
Shau = Wādī Huwār 194-195 K 5
Shaunavon 66-67 J 1
Shaviovik River 52-53 O 2
Shaw, MS 78-79 D 4
Shawano, WI 70-71 F 3
Shawatun = Shaguotun 170-171 C 2
Shawbridge 72-73 J 2
Shawinigan Sud 46-47 W 8
Shaw Island 52-53 L 7
Shawnee, OK 58-59 G 4
Shawneetown, IL 70-71 F 7
Shaw River 182-183 C 4
Shawville 72-73 H 2
Sha Xian 166-167 M 6
Shaykh 'Uthmān, Ash- 160-161 EF 8
Shayōg = Shyog 160-161 M 3-4
Shcherbakov = Rybinsk 154-155 F 6
Shea 98-99 H 4
Sheaville, OR 66-67 E 4
Shebelē, Wabī — 194-195 N 7
Sheboygan, WI 58-59 J 3
Shediac 51 D 4
Shedin Peak 48 D 2
Sheduan Island = Jazirat Shadwān 194-195 LM 3
Sheelin, Lough — = Loch Síleann 116-117 D 7
Sheenborough 72-73 H 1-2
Sheenjek River 46-47 H 4
Sheep Creek 68-69 CD 4
Sheep Haven = Cuan na gCaorach 116-117 CD 5
Sheep Mountain 68-69 D 3
Sheep Mountains 68-69 CD 2
Sheep Peak 74-75 F 4
Sheep Range 74-75 F 4
Sheepshead Bay, New York-, NY 82 III c 3
Sheerness 49 C 5
Sheet Harbour 51 EF 5
Sheffield 116-117 K 7
Sheffield, AL 78-79 EF 3
Sheffield, IA 70-71 D 4
Sheffield, TX 76-77 CD 7
Sheffield Lake 51 H 3
Shefoo = Yantai 166-167 N 4
Sheho 49 G 5
Shê-hsien = She Xian [TJ, Anhui] 166-167 M 5-6
Sheikh, Sharm esh- = Sharm ash-Shayh 199 D 4
Sheikh Othman = Ash-Shaykh 'Uthmān 160-161 E 8
Shekak River 70-71 H 1
Shekhar Dsong 166-167 F 6
Shekiak River 50 G 3
Sheklukshuk Range 52-53 J 3
Shelbina, MO 70-71 D 6
Shelburne [CDN, Nova Scotia] 51 D 6
Shelburne [CDN, Ontario] 72-73 FG 2
Shelburne Bay 182-183 H 2
Shelby, MI 70-71 G 4
Shelby, MS 78-79 D 4
Shelby, MT 66-67 H 1
Shelby, NC 58-59 K 4
Shelby, OH 72-73 E 4
Shelbyville, IL 70-71 F 6
Shelbyville, IN 70-71 H 6
Shelbyville, KY 70-71 H 6
Shelbyville, MO 70-71 DE 6
Shelbyville, TN 78-79 F 3
Sheldon, IA 70-71 BC 4
Sheldon, MO 70-71 C 7
Sheldon, WI 70-71 E 3
Sheldons Point, AK 52-53 DE 5
Sheldrake 51 D 2
Shelikof Strait 46-47 EF 6
Shell, WY 68-69 C 3
Shell Beach, LA 78-79 E 6
Shellbrook 49 EF 4
Shell Creek [USA, Colorado] 66-67 J 5
Shell Creek [USA, Nebraska] 68-69 H 5
Shelley, ID 66-67 GH 4
Shellharbour, Wollongong- 182-183 K 6
Shell Lake 49 E 4
Shell Lake, WI 70-71 E 3
Shellman, GA 78-79 G 5
Shell River 49 H 5
Shellrock River 70-71 D 4
Shelter Cove, CA 66-67 A 5
Shelton, WA 66-67 B 2
Shemichi Islands 52-53 pq 6
Shemya Island 52-53 q 6
Shenandoah, IA 70-71 C 5
Shenandoah, PA 72-73 HJ 4
Shenandoah, VA 72-73 G 5
Shenandoah Mountains 72-73 G 5
Shenandoah National Park 72-73 GH 5
Shenandoah River 72-73 GH 5
Shendam 194-195 FG 7
Shendī = Shandī 194-195 L 5
Sheng Xian 166-167 N 6
Shenmu 166-167 L 4
Shensa Dsong 166-167 FG 5
Shensi = Shaanxi 166-167 K 4-5
Shenton, Mount — 182-183 D 5
Shenyang 166-167 NO 3
Sheopuri = Shivpuri 160-161 M 5
Shepard 48 KL 4
Shepherd, MT 68-69 B 2-3
Shepherd, TX 76-77 G 7
Shepparton 182-183 HJ 7
Sheppey, Isle of — 116-117 gh 5
Shepton Mallet 116-117 J 9
Sherborne 116-117 J 10
Sherbro Island 194-195 B 7
Sherbrooke [CDN, Nova Scotia] 51 F 5
Sherbrooke [CDN, Quebec] 46-47 W 8
Sherburn, MN 70-71 C 4
Shereik = Ash-Shurayk 194-195 L 5
Sheridan, AR 78-79 C 3
Sheridan, MT 66-67 GH 3
Sheridan, OR 66-67 B 3
Sheridan, TX 76-77 F 8
Sheridan, WY 58-59 E 3
Sheridan, Mount — 66-67 H 3
Sheridan Lake, CO 68-69 E 6
Sheringham 116-117 gh 6
Sherman, MS 78-79 E 3
Sherman, TX 58-59 G 5
Sherman Inlet 46-47 R 4
Sherman Mills, ME 72-73 MN 2
Sherman Mountain 66-67 EF 5
Sherridon 46-47 Q 6
Sherwood, ND 68-69 F 1
Sherwood Forest, CA 83 I c 1
Sherwood Park 49 B 4
Sheshalik, AK 52-53 F 3
Sheslay 52-53 W 7
Sheslay River 52-53 V 7
Shetland 116-117 f 3
Shewa 194-195 M 7
She Xian [TJ, Anhui] 166-167 M 5-6
Sheyenne River 68-69 H 2
Shiant Islands 116-117 E 3
Shibām 160-161 F 7
Shibarghān 160-161 K 3
Shibata 170-171 M 4
Shibecha 170-171 d 2
Shibetsu [J ↑ Asahikawa] 170-171 c 1
Shibetsu [J ↖ Nemuro] 170-171 d 2
Shibetsu, Naka- 170-171 d 2
Shībigā 174-175 C 1
Shībīn al-Kawn 199 B 2
Shībīn al-Qanāṭir 199 B 2
Shib Kūh 160-161 G 5
Shibogama Lake 50 EF 1
Shibukawa 170-171 M 4
Shibushi 170-171 H 7
Shibushi-wan 170-171 H 7
Shibutami = Tamayama 170-171 N 3
Shicheng Dao 170-171 D 3
Shickshock, Monts — = Monts Chic-Choqs 46-47 X 8
Shidād, Umm ash- = Sabkhat Abā ar-Rūs 160-161 G-H 6
Shiel, Loch — 116-117 F 4
Shields, ND 68-69 F 2
Shifshawn 194-195 CD 1
Shiga 170-171 KL 5
Shigatse = Zhigatse 166-167 F 6
Shiḥan, Wādī — 160-161 G 7
Shih-ch'êng Tao = Shicheng Dao 170-171 D 3
Shih-ch'ien = Shiqian 166-167 K 6
Shih-ch'ü = Serxü 166-167 H 5
Shihchuan = Shiquan 166-167 K 5
Shihnan = Enshi 166-167 K 5
Shih-p'ing = Shiping 166-167 J 7
Shiḥr, Ash- 160-161 F 8
Shihtsien = Shiqian 166-167 K 6
Shijiazhuang 166-167 L 4
Shikārpūr [PAK] 160-161 K 5
Shikhartse = Zhigatse 166-167 F 6
Shikine-chima 170-171 M 5
Shikoku 166-167 P 5
Shikoku sammyaku 170-171 JK 6
Shikotan-tō 166-167 S 3
Shikotsu-ko 170-171 b 2
Shilaong = Shillong 160-161 P 5
Shilchar = Silchar 160-161 P 6
Shildon 116-117 K 6
Shilif 194-195 E 1
Shilka = Šilka 154-155 W 7
Shillelagh = Síol Éalaigh 116-117 E 8
Shillington, PA 72-73 HJ 4
Shillong 160-161 P 5
Shiloguṛī = Siliguri 160-161 O 5
Shiloh National Military Park and Cemetery 78-79 EF 3
Shilong = Shajianzi 170-171 E 2
Shīlyah, Jabal — 194-195 F 1
Shimabara 170-171 H 6
Shimabara hantō 170-171 H 6
Shimada 170-171 M 5
Shima-hantō 170-171 L 5
Shimālīyah, Ash- 194-195 KL 5
Shimane 170-171 HJ 5
Shimen = Shijiazhuang 166-167 LM 4
Shimizu 166-167 Q 4-5
Shimizu = Tosashimizu 170-171 J 6
Shimlā = Simla 160-161 M 4
Shimminato 170-171 L 4
Shimo = Kyūshū 166-167 P 5
Shimoda 170-171 M 5
Shimodate 170-171 MN 4
Shimoga 160-161 LM 8
Shimokita-hantō 166-167 R 3
Shimo-Koshiki-chima 170-171 G 7
Shimoni 198 GH 2
Shimonoseki 166-167 P 5
Shimono-shima 170-171 G 5
Shimoyaku = Yaku 170-171 H 7
Shimushiru = ostrov Simušir 154-155 d 8
Shimushu = ostrov Šumšu 154-155 e 7
Shin, Loch — 116-117 G 2
Shinano gawa 170-171 M 4
Shināṣ 160-161 H 6
Shināy, Bi'r — 199 D 6
Shinbwīyan 174-175 C 1
Shīndand 160-161 J 4
Shindidāy, Jabal — 199 E 6
Shiner, TX 76-77 F 8
Shingbwiyang = Shinbwīyan 174-175 C 1
Shingishu = Sinŭiju 166-167 NO 3
Shingleton, MI 70-71 G 2
Shingletown, CA 66-67 C 5
Shingu 170-171 KL 6
Shining Tree 50 L 3
Shinjiang = Xinjiang Uyghur Zizhiqu 166-167 D-G 3
Shinji-ko 170-171 J 5
Shinjō 166-167 QR 4
Shinko = Chinko 194-195 J 7
Shinkolobwe 198 E 4
Shin-nan = Enshi 166-167 K 5
Shinnston, WV 72-73 F 5
Shinqīṭi 194-195 B 4
Shinshān, Sabkhat — 194-195 B 4
Shinshū = Chinju 166-167 O 4
Shinyanga 198 F 2
Shiobara 170-171 MN 4
Shiogama 170-171 N 3
Shionomi, Cape — = Shiono-misaki 170-171 K 6
Shiono-misaki 170-171 K 6
Shioya-misaki 170-171 N 4
Shiping 166-167 J 7
Ship Island 78-79 E 5
Shipley 116-117 K 7
Shippegan 51 D 4
Shippegan Island 51 DE 4
Shippensburg, PA 72-73 GH 4
Shiprock, NW 74-75 J 4
Shipshaw, Rivière — 51 A 3
Shipston on Stour 116-117 K 8
Shiqian 166-167 K 6
Shiqq, Ḥāssī — 194-195 B 3
Shiquan 166-167 K 5
Shiquan He = Sengge Khamba 166-167 DE 5
Shirahama 170-171 K 6
Shirakami-saki 170-171 MN 2
Shirakawa 170-171 N 4
Shirane-san 170-171 LM 5
Shiranuka 170-171 cd 2
Shiraoi 170-171 b 2
Shirataka 170-171 MN 3
Shīrāz 160-161 G 5
Shiraze-hyōga 31 B 4-5
Shirbīn 199 B 2
Shire 198 FG 5
Shiretoko hantō 170-171 d 1-2
Shiretoko-misaki 170-171 d 1
Shiritoru = Makarov 154-155 b 8
Shiriya-saki 170-171 N 2
Shirley, AR 78-79 C 3
Shirley Basin 68-69 C 4
Shiro, TX 76-77 G 7
Shiroishi 170-171 N 3-4
Shirotori 170-171 L 5
Shishaldin Volcano 52-53 a 2
Shishikui 170-171 K 6
Shishmaref, AK 46-47 CD 4
Shishmaref Inlet 52-53 DE 3
Shitai 166-167 M 5
Shivālak Pahāṛiyān = Siwālik Range 160-161 M 4-N 5
Shivamagga = Shimoga 160-161 LM 8
Shivpuri 160-161 M 5
Shivwits Indian Reservation 74-75 FG 4
Shivwits Plateau 74-75 G 4
Shizukawa 170-171 N 3
Shizunai 170-171 c 2
Shizuoka 170-171 LM 5
Shkodër 138-139 H 4
Shkumbin 138-139 H 5
Shligigh, Cuan — 116-117 C 6
Shmidt Island = ostrov Šmidta 154-155 QR 1
Shoa = Shewa 194-195 M 7
Shoal Lake [CDN, lake] 50 B 3
Shoal Lake [CDN, place] 49 H 5
Shoals, IN 70-71 G 6
Shōbara 170-171 J 5
Shōdo-shima 170-171 K 5
Shodu 166-167 H 5
Shoeburyness, Southend on Sea- 116-117 gh 7
Shoe Cove 51 J 3
Shokalsky Strait = proliv Šokal'skogo 154-155 RS 2
Shokambetsu-dake 170-171 b 2
Shokotsu 170-171 c 1
Sholāpur 160-161 M 7
Shorāpur 160-161 M 7
Shoreacres 66-67 E 1
Shoreham-by-Sea 116-117 L 10
Shorewood, WI 70-71 G 4
Shortland Island 174-175 hj 6
Shoshone, CA 74-75 EF 5
Shoshone, ID 66-67 F 4
Shoshone Falls 66-67 FG 4
Shoshone Mountain 74-75 E 4
Shoshone Mountains 58-59 C 3-4
Shoshone River 68-69 B 3
Shoshoni, WY 68-69 BC 4
Shott el Jerid = Shaṭṭ al-Jarīd 194-195 F 2
Shotton 116-117 K 6
Shotts, Plateau of the — = At-Tall 194-195 D 2-E 1
Shoulder Mount 52-53 Q 3
Shoup, ID 66-67 F 3
Showak = Shuwak 194-195 M 6
Show Low, AZ 74-75 H 5
Shreveport, LA 58-59 H 5
Shrewsbury 116-117 HJ 8
Shrīkākulam = Srīkākulam 160-161 M 7
Shrīrāmpur = Serampore 160-161 O 6
Shrīrangam = Srīrangam 160-161 M 8
Shrīvardhan = Srīvardhan 160-161 L 7
Shuangcheng 166-167 NO 2
Shuang-ch'êng = Shuangcheng 166-167 NO 2
Shuangliao 166-167 N 3
Shubert, NE 70-71 BC 5
Shublik Mountains 52-53 P 2
Shubuta, MS 78-79 E 5
Shufu = Qāshqār 166-167 CD 4
Shugra = Shuqrā 160-161 F 8
Shuifeng Supong Hu = Supung Hu 170-171 E 2
Shuikou 166-167 M 6
Shullsburg, WI 70-71 EF 4
Shumagin Islands 46-47 DE 6
Shuman House, AK 52-53 PQ 3
Shumla 86-87 K 3
Shumla, TX 76-77 D 8
Shumlūl, Ash- = Ma'qalā' 160-161 F 5
Shungnak, AK 46-47 EF 4
Shungnak River 52-53 J 3
Shunking = Nanchong 166-167 JK 5
Shunsen = Ch'unch'ŏn 166-167 O 4
Shunteh = Xingtai 166-167 L 4
Shuqrā' 160-161 F 8
Shurayf 160-161 D 5
Shurayk, Ash- 194-195 L 5
Shurugwi 198 EF 5
Shushartie 48 CD 4
Shūshtar 160-161 F 4
Shuswap Lake 48 H 4
Shuwak 194-195 M 6
Shuyak Island 52-53 LM 7
Shuyak Strait 52-53 L 7
Shuyang 166-167 M 5
Shuzenji 170-171 M 5
Shwangcheng = Shuangcheng 166-167 NO 2
Shwangliao = Liaoyuan 166-167 NO 3
Shwebō 174-175 C 2
Shyog 160-161 M 3-4
Shyopur = Shivpuri 160-161 M 5

Siakwan = Xiaguan 166-167 J 6
Sialcote = Siyālkoṭ 160-161 LM 4
Sialkot = Siyālkoṭ 160-161 LM 4
Siam = Thailand 174-175 CD 3
Sian = Xi'an 166-167 K 5
Siangfan = Fangcheng 166-167 L 5
Siangtan = Xiangtan 166-167 L 6
Siangyang = Xiangyang 166-167 L 5
Siao Hingan Ling = Xiao Hinggan Ling 166-167 O 1-P 2
Siargao Island 174-175 J 4-5
Siau, Pulau — 174-175 J 6
Šiauliai 142-143 D 4
Sibā'i, Jabal as- 199 CD 5
Sibā'īyah, As- 199 C 5
Sibaj 154-155 K 7
Sibbald 49 C 5
Šibenik 138-139 FG 4
Siberia 154-155 O-X 5
Siberut, Pulau — 174-175 C 7
Siberut, Selat — 174-175 C 7
Sibī 160-161 K 5
Sibir'akova, ostrov — 154-155 OP 3
Sibirien 154-155 N-W 5
Sibiti [RCA] 198 B 2
Sibiu 138-139 KL 3
Sibley, IA 70-71 BC 4
Sibley Provincial Park 70-71 F 1
Sibolga 174-175 C 6
Sibu 174-175 F 6
Sibū 'Gharb, As- 199 C 6
Sibutu Group 174-175 G 6
Sibuyan Island 174-175 H 4
Sibuyan Sea 174-175 H 4
Sibyŏn-ni 170-171 F 3
Sicamous 48 H 4
Sicasica 98-99 F 8
Sicasso = Sikasso 194-195 C 6
Sichang = Xichang 166-167 J 6
Sichota-Alin = Sichotė-Alin' 154-155 a 8-Z 9
Sichotė-Alin' 154-155 a 8-Z 9
Šichrany = Kanaš 154-155 H 6
Sichuan 166-167 J 5-6
Sichwan = Xichuan 166-167 L 5
Sicilia 138-139 EF 7
Sicily = Sicilia 138-139 EF 7
Sico, Río — 88-89 D 7
Sicuani 98-99 E 7
Sīdamo 194-195 MN 8
Sidamo-Borana = Sīdamo 194-195 MN 8
Sidaogou 170-171 F 2
Sideby 114-115 J 6
Sidērókastron 138-139 K 5
Síderos, Akrōtērion — 138-139 M 8
Sīdī Ban al-'Abbas 194-195 DE 1
Sīdī Barrānī 194-195 K 2
Sidi-bel-Abbès = Sīdī Ban al-'Abbas 194-195 DE 1
Sīdī Ifnī 194-195 B 3
Sīdī Mirwān 194-195 JK 1
Sīdī Qāsim 194-195 CD 2
Sīdī Sālim 199 B 2
Sidlaw Hills 116-117 HJ 4
Sidley, Mount — 31 B 24
Sidmouth 116-117 H 10
Sidnaw, MI 70-71 F 2
Sidney 66-67 B 1
Sidney, IA 70-71 C 5
Sidney, MT 68-69 D 2
Sidney, NE 68-69 E 5
Sidney, NY 70-71 F 3
Sidney, OH 72-73 D 4
Sidr, As- 194-195 H 2
Sidr, Wādī — 199 C 3
Sidra = As-Surt 194-195 H 2-3
Sidra, Khalīg — = Khalīj as-Surt 194-195 H 2
Sidrolândia 98-99 HJ 9
Siedlce 124 L 2
Sieg 124 C 3
Siegen 124 D 3
Siemiatycze 124 L 2
Siem Reap 174-175 D 4
Siena 138-139 D 4
Sienyang = Xianyang 166-167 K 5
Sieradz 124 J 3
Sierpc 124 JK 2
Sierra Blanca, TX 76-77 B 7
Sierra Blanca Peak 58-59 E 5
Sierra Colorada 103 C 6
Sierra de Outes 132-133 C 7
Sierra Gorda 103 C 2
Sierra Grande [MEX] 86-87 H 3
Sierra Grande [RA, Río Negro place] 103 C 6
Sierra Leone 194-195 B 7
Sierra Leone Basin 26-27 HJ 5
Sierra Leone Rise 26-27 HJ 5
Sierra Madre [USA] 68-69 C 5
Sierra Madre del Sur 58-59 FG 8
Sierra Madre Mountains 74-75 CD 5
Sierra Madre Occidental 58-59 E 5-F 7
Sierra Madre Oriental 58-59 F 6-G 7
Sierra Mochada 86-87 HJ 4
Sierra Mojada 86-87 J 4
Sierra Morena 132-133 D 10-E 9
Sierra Nevada [E] 132-133 F 10
Sierra Nevada [USA] 58-59 BC 4
Sierra Pinta 74-75 G 6
Sierra Sabinas = Sierra de la Iguana 76-77 D 9
Sierras Pampeanas 103 C 3
Sierra Vieja 76-77 B 7
Siesta Key 80-81 b 3
Sífnos 138-139 L 7
Sifton Pass 46-47 LM 6
Sig 142-143 F 2
Sighetul Marmației 138-139 KL 2
Sighișoara 138-139 L 2
Sighty Crag 116-117 J 5
Sigli 174-175 C 5
Siglufjördhur 114-115 d 1
Signai 50 N 2
Signal Hill 83 III cd 3
Signal Peak 74-75 FG 6
Signy 31 C 32
Sigourney, IA 70-71 DE 5
Sigtuna 114-115 GH 8
Siguiri 194-195 C 6
Sigurd, UT 74-75 H 3
Sihsien = She Xian 166-167 M 5-6
Sihsien = Xi Xian [TJ, Shanxi] 166-167 L 4
Siilinjärvi 114-115 M 6
Siinai = Sīnā' 194-195 L 3
Siirt 160-161 E 3
Sijerdijelach Jur'ach = Batamaj 154-155 YZ 5
Sijiazi = Laohushan 170-171 BC 2
Sikandarābād = Secunderābād 160-161 M 7
Sikao 174-175 C 5
Sikasso 194-195 C 6
Sikes, LA 78-79 C 4
Sikeston, MO 78-79 E 2
Sikhim = Sikkim 160-161 O 5
Sikhiu 174-175 D 4
Sikhota Alin = Sichotė-Alin' 154-155 a 8-Z 9
Siking = Xi'an 166-167 K 5
Síkinos 138-139 L 7
Sikkim 160-161 O 5
Sikoku = Shikoku 166-167 P 5
Sikotan tō = Shikotan-tō 166-167 S 3
Sikt'ach 154-155 X 4
Siktyakh = Sikt'ach 154-155 X 4
Sikyṓn 138-139 K 7
Sil 132-133 D 7
Sila, La — 138-139 G 6
Silao 86-87 K 7
Silasjaure 114-115 G 3-4
Silcox 49 L 2
Síleann, Loch — 116-117 D 7
Silencio 86-87 K 3
Siler City, NC 80-81 G 3
Silesia 124 GH 3
Silesia, MT 68-69 B 3
Silifke = Silifke 160-161 C 3
Silgarhi Doti 160-161 N 5
Silhaṭ 160-161 P 5-6
Silifke 160-161 C 3
Siligir 154-155 V 4
Silīguri 160-161 O 5
Silistra 138-139 M 3
Siljan 114-115 F 7
Šilka 154-155 W 7
Šilkan 154-155 c 6
Silkeborg 114-115 C 9
Silleiro, Cabo — 132-133 C 7
Silloth 116-117 H 6
Sillyŏng 170-171 G 4
Siloam Springs, AR 76-77 G 4
Silsbee, TX 76-77 GH 7
Siltou 194-195 H 5
Siluria, AL 78-79 F 4
Silva, Ilha da — 98-99 F 5
Silva Porto = Bié 198 C 4
Silverbell, AZ 74-75 H 6
Silverbow, MT 66-67 G 2-3
Silver City 58-59 b 2
Silver City, ID 66-67 E 4
Silver City, NM 58-59 E 5

270 **Shanghan**

Silver City, UT 74-75 G 3
Silver Creek 66-67 D 4
Silver Creek, MS 78-79 DE 5
Silver Creek, NE 68-69 H 5
Silver Creek, NY 72-73 G 3
Silver Lake, CA 74-75 EF 5
Silver Lake, OR 66-67 C 4
Silver Lake Reservoir 83 III c 1
Silvermine Mountains = Sléibhte an Airgid 116-117 C 8
Silver Mountain 70-71 EF 1
Silverpeak, NV 74-75 E 4
Silver Peak Range 74-75 E 4
Silverthrone Mount 48 D 4
Silverton 182-183 H 6
Silverton, CO 68-69 C 7
Silverton, OR 66-67 B 3
Silverton, TX 76-77 D 5
Silves [BR] 98-99 J 6
Silves [P] 132-133 C 10
Silvies River 66-67 D 4
Silwa Baḥarī = Salwá Baḥrī 199 C 5
Šimanggang 174-175 F 6
Šimanovsk 154-155 Y 7
Simao 166-167 J 7
Simard, Lac — 72-73 G 1
Simbillâwein, Es- = As-Sinbillâwayn 199 BC 2
Simbirsk = Ujanovsk 154-155 H 7
Simcoe 72-73 FG 3
Simcoe, Lake — 46-47 V 9
Simēn 194-195 M 6
Simeonof Island 52-53 d 2
Simferopol' 142-143 F 7
Simḥām, Jabal as- 160-161 GH 7
Similkameen River 66-67 CD 1
Simingan = Samangān 160-161 K 3
Simití 98-99 E 3
Simi Valley, CA 74-75 D 5
Simizu = Shimizu 166-167 Q 4-5
Simla 160-161 M 4
Simmesport, LA 78-79 CD 5
Simmie 49 D 6
Simms, MT 66-67 GH 2
Simnij bereg 142-143 H 2
Simokita hantō = Shimokita-hantō 166-167 R 3
Simola 114-115 MN 7
Simonette River 48 HJ 2
Simonhouse Lake 49 H 3
Simonoseki = Shimonoseki 166-167 P 5
Simonstad 198 C 8
Simonstown = Simonstad 198 C 8
Simoom Sound 48 D 4
Simplício Mendes 98-99 L 6
Simplon 124 CD 5
Simpson, Cape — 52-53 KL 1
Simpson Desert 182-183 G 4-5
Simpson Island 70-71 G 1
Simpson Islands 46-47 O 5
Simpson Peninsula 46-47 T 4
Simpson Strait 46-47 R 4
Simrishamn 114-115 F 10
Simular = Pulau Simeulue 174-175 BC 6
Simušir, ostrov — 166-167 T 2
Sīnā' [ET] 194-195 L 3
Sinabang 174-175 C 6
Sinadhapo = Dhuusa Maareeb 194-195 b 2
Sinai = Sīnā' 194-195 L 3
Sinaloa 58-59 E 6-7
Sinaloa, Río — 86-87 FG 4-5
Sinan 166-167 K 6
Sinanju 170-171 E 3
Sinaru, AK 52-53 HJ 1
Sinaúen = Sīnāwan 194-195 G 2
Sīnāwan 194-195 G 2
Sinbillâwayn, As- 199 BC 2
Sincelejo 98-99 DE 3
Sinch'ang 170-171 G 2
Sinch'ang-ni 170-171 F 3
Sincheng = Xingren 166-167 K 6
Sinch'ŏn 170-171 E 3
Sinclair Mills 48 G 2
Sinclair's Bay 116-117 HJ 2
Sind 160-161 M 5
Sind = Sindh 160-161 K 5
Sinda = Sindh 160-161 K 5
Sindangbarang 174-175 E 8
Sindelfingen 124 D 4
Sindh 160-161 K 5
Sindhu = Sindh 160-161 L 4
Sin-do 170-171 DE 3
Šindy = Sajmak 160-161 L 3
Sinel'nikovo 142-143 G 6
Sines 132-133 C 10
Sines, Cabo de — 132-133 C 10
Singah 194-195 L 6
Si-ngan = Xi'an 166-167 K 5
Singapore 174-175 DE 6
Singapore, Strait of — 174-175 DE 6
Singapur 174-175 DE 6
Singaraja 174-175 G 8
Singatoka 174-175 a 2
Sing Buri 174-175 D 3-4
Singen 124 D 5
Singida 198 F 2
Singkawang 174-175 E 6
Singkep, Pulau — 174-175 DE 7
Singkil 174-175 C 6
Singleton 182-183 K 6
Singleton, Mount — 182-183 F 4
Singora = Songkhla 174-175 D 5
Sin'gosan 170-171 F 3
Singtai = Xingtai 166-167 L 4
Sin'gye 170-171 F 3
Siṅhbhūm = Singhbhūm 160-161 NO 6
Sin-hiang = Xinxiang 166-167 LM 4
Sinhsien = Xin Xian 166-167 L 4
Sining = Xining 166-167 J 4
Siniscola 138-139 CD 5
Sinjai 174-175 GH 8
Sinjār, Jabal — 142-143 H 8
Sin-kalp'ajin 170-171 F 2
Sinkāt 194-195 M 5
Sinkiang = Xinjiang 166-167 L 4
Sinkiang = Xinjiang Uygur Zizhiqu 166-167 G 3
Sinlo = Xinle 166-167 LM 4
Sinmak 170-171 F 3
Sinmi-do 170-171 E 3
Sinmin = Xinmin 170-171 D 1-2
Sinnamary [French Guiana, place] 98-99 J 3
Sinnamary [French Guiana, river] 98-99 M 2
Sinneh = Sanandaj 160-161 F 3
Sinnhabhūm = Singhbhūm 160-161 NO 6
Sinnūris 199 B 3
Sinnyŏng = Sillyŏng 170-171 G 4
Sinoe = Greenville 194-195 C 7-8
Sinola = Chinhoyi 198 EF 5
Sinop 160-161 D 2
Sinope = Sinop 160-161 D 2
Sinp'o 166-167 O 3-4
Sinquim = Xi'an 166-167 K 5
Sinsiang = Xinxiang 166-167 LM 4
Sintang 174-175 F 6
Sint Eustatius 58-59 O 8
Sint Helenabaai 198 C 8
Sint Luciameer 198 F 7
Sinton, TX 76-77 F 8
Sintra [BR] 98-99 G 6
Sintra [P] 132-133 C 9
Sintsai = Xincai 166-167 LM 5
Sinuk, AK 52-53 D 4
Sinuk River 52-53 DE 4
Sinwŏn-ni 170-171 E 3
Sinyang = Xinyang 166-167 LM 5
Sinzyô = Shinjō 166-167 QR 4
Siò 124 J 5
Síol Éalaigh 116-117 E 8
Sioma 198 D 5
Sion [CH] 124 C 5
Sionna, Aerphort an — 116-117 C 8
Sionna, An t- 116-117 CD 7
Sionna, Béal na — 116-117 AB 8
Sioux City, IA 58-59 GH 3
Sioux Falls, SD 58-59 G 3
Sioux Lookout 46-47 S 7
Sioux Rapids, IA 70-71 C 4
Šipaliwini 98-99 K 3
Šipčenski prohod 138-139 LM 4
Siphageni 198 EF 8
Siping 166-167 N 3
Sipitang 174-175 G 5-6
Sipiwesk 49 K 3
Sipiwesk Lake 49 K 3
Siple, Mount — 31 B 24
Sipolilo = Chiporiro 198 F 5
Sipora, Pulau — 174-175 C 7
Sip Sông Châu Thai 174-175 D 2
Sipura, Pulau — = Pulau Sipora 174-175 C 7
Siquijor Island 174-175 H 5
Siquisique 98-99 F 2
Sira [N, place] 114-115 B 8
Sira [N, river] 114-115 B 8
Šira [SU] 154-155 QR 7
Siracuas 103 D 2
Siracusa 138-139 F 7
Sir Alexander, Mount — 48 GH 2
Sirdar 66-67 E 1
Sir Edward Pellew Group 182-183 G 3
Siren, WI 70-71 D 3
Siret [RO, place] 138-139 M 2
Siret [RO, river] 138-139 M 3
Sirḥān, Wādī as — 160-161 D 4
Sirirskaja ravnina 154-155 L-P 5-6
Sir James MacBrien, Mount — 46-47 KL 5
Sīrjān 160-161 H 5
Sirr, Nafūd as- 160-161 E 5-F 6
Sirsa 160-161 LM 5
Sir Sanford, Mount — 48 J 4
Sirte = Khalīj as-Surt 194-195 H 2
Sirte, Gulf of — = Khalīj as-Surt 194-195 H 2
Sir Thomas, Mount — 182-183 EF 5
Sirtica = As-Surt 194-195 H 2-3
Sir Wilfrid Laurier, Mount — 48 GH 3
Sisak 138-139 G 3
Si Sa Ket 174-175 D 3-4
Sisal 86-87 P 7
Sishen 198 D 7
Sisimiut 46-47 Za 4
Sisipuk Lake 49 H 3
Siskiyou, OR 66-67 B 4
Siskiyou Mountains 66-67 B 4-5
Sisophon 174-175 D 4
Sisseton, SD 68-69 H 3
Sisseton Indian Reservation 68-69 H 3
Sīstān 160-161 J 4
Sīstān, Daryācheh — 160-161 HJ 4
Sisteron 132-133 K 6
Sisters, OR 66-67 C 3
Sithōnia 138-139 K 5-6
Sítio da Abadia 98-99 K 7
Sitka, AK 46-47 J 6
Sitkaing 174-175 C 2
Sitkaing Taing 174-175 B 2-C 1
Sitkalidak Island 52-53 g 1
Sitkinak Island 52-53 g 1
Sitkinak Strait 52-53 fg 1
Šitkino 154-155 S 6
Sittingbourne 116-117 M 9
Sittwe 174-175 B 2
Siúir, An t- 116-117 D 8
Siunī = Seoni 160-161 M 6
Siuslaw River 66-67 B 4
Siut = Asyūṭ 194-195 L 3
Sivaki 154-155 Y 7
Sīvand 160-161 G 4
Sivas 160-161 D 3
Sivaš, ozero — 142-143 F 6
Siverek 142-143 G 8
Sivučij, mys — 154-155 fg 6
Sīwah 194-195 K 3
Sīwah, Wāḥāt — 194-195 K 3
Siwālik Range 160-161 M 4-N 5
Siwni = Seoni 160-161 M 6
Sixtymile 52-53 RS 4
Siyāl, Jazā'ir — 199 E 6
Siyālkoṭ 160-161 LM 4

Sjælland 114-115 DE 10
Sjöbo 114-115 EF 10
Sjøvegan 114-115 GH 3
Sjuøyane 114-115 l 4

Skadarsko jezero 138-139 H 4
Skagafjardhar 114-115 d 2
Skagafjördhur 114-115 c 1-d 2
Skagen 114-115 D 9
Skagens Horn = Grenen 114-115 D 9
Skagerrak 114-115 B 9-D 8
Skagit River 66-67 C 1
Skagway, AK 46-47 JK 6
Skaland 114-115 G 3
Skálar 114-115 f 1
Skalavík 116-117 b 2
Skálholt 114-115 cd 2
Skalistyi Golec, gora — 154-155 WX 6
Skanderborg 114-115 CD 9
Skåne 114-115 E 10
Skanör 114-115 E 10
Skara 114-115 E 8
Skaraborg 114-115 EF 8
Skardū 160-161 M 3
Skarżysko-Kamienna 124 K 3
Skaw, The — = Grenen 114-115 D 9
Skead 72-73 F 1
Skeena 48 BC 2
Skeena Mountains 46-47 L 6
Skeena River 46-47 L 6
Skegness 116-117 M 7
Skeidharársandur 114-115 e 3
Skeldon 98-99 K 2
Skellefteå 114-115 J 5
Skellefte älv 114-115 H 5
Skelleftehamn 114-115 JK 5
Skene 114-115 E 9
Skerries = Sceirí 116-117 EF 7
Skerries, The — 116-117 G 7
Skerryvore 116-117 D 4
Ski 114-115 D 8
Skíathos 138-139 K 6
Skibbereen = An Sciobairín 116-117 B 9
Skidaway Island 80-81 F 5
Skidegate Inlet 48 AB 3
Skidmore, TX 76-77 EF 8
Skien 114-115 C 8
Skierniewice 124 K 3
Skiff 66-67 H 1
Skiftet 114-115 J 7
Skikda = Sakīkdah 194-195 F 1
Skilak Lake 52-53 M 6
Skipskjølen 114-115 NO 2
Skipton 116-117 J 7
Skive 114-115 C 9
Skjalfandafljót 114-115 e 2
Skjálfandi 114-115 e 1
Skjervøy 114-115 J 2
Skjold 114-115 H 3
Sklad 154-155 X 3
Skobelev = Fergana 160-161 L 2-3
Skógafoss 114-115 cd 3
Skokholm 116-117 F 9
Skokie, IL 70-71 FG 4
Skolpen Bank 110-111 OP 1
Skomer Island 116-117 F 9
Skönvik 114-115 G 6
Skópelos 138-139 K 6
Skopin 142-143 G 5
Skopje 138-139 J 4-5
Skoplje = Skopje 138-139 J 4-5
Skopunarfjördhur 116-117 b 2
Skövde 114-115 EF 8
Skovorodino 154-155 XY 7
Skowhegan, ME 72-73 M 2
Skownan 49 J 5
Skudeneshavn 114-115 A 8
Skukuza 198 F 7
Skull Valley, AZ 74-75 G 5
Skull Valley Indian Reservation 66-67 G 5
Skunk River 70-71 DE 5
Skuø = Skúvoy 116-117 ab 2
Skuratova, mys — 154-155 LM 3
Skutari, İstanbul- = İstanbul-Üsküdar 160-161 BC 2
Skutskär 114-115 GH 7
Skúvoy 116-117 ab 2
Skwentna, AK 52-53 M 6
Skwentna River 52-53 LM 6
Skwierzyna 124 G 2
Skye, Island of — 116-117 EF 3
Skykomish, WA 66-67 C 2
Skyring, Seno — 103 B 8
Skyrópula 138-139 KL 6
Skýros 138-139 L 6

Slā' 194-195 C 2
Slættaratindur 116-117 ab 1
Slagelse 114-115 D 10
Slagnäs 114-115 H 5
Sláinge, An t- 116-117 E 8
Slana, AK 52-53 PQ 5
Slancy 114-115 N 8
Slaney River = An tSláinge 116-117 E 8
Slănic 138-139 L 3
Slapin, Loch — 116-117 E 3
Slate Islands 70-71 G 1
Slater, CO 68-69 C 5
Slater, MO 70-71 D 6
Slatina 138-139 L 3
Slaton, TX 76-77 D 6
Slatoust = Zlatoust 154-155 K 6
Slav'anka 170-171 H 1
Slav'ansk 142-143 G 6
Slav'ansk-na-Kubani 142-143 G 6
Slave Coast 194-195 E 7
Slave Lake 48 K 2
Slave River 46-47 O 5-6
Slavgorod [SU, Rossijskaja SFSR] 154-155 O 7
Slavkov u Brna 124 H 4
Slavonija 138-139 GH 3
Slavonska Požega 138-139 GH 3
Slavonski Brod 138-139 GH 3
Sławno 124 H 1
Slayton, MN 70-71 BC 3
Sleaford 116-117 L 7-8
Sleat, Sound of — 116-117 F 3-4
Sledge Island 52-53 D 4
Sleeping Bear Point 70-71 G 3
Sleepy Eye, MN 70-71 C 3
Sleetmute, AK 46-47 E 5
Slidell, LA 78-79 E 5
Slide Mountain 72-73 J 3
Sliema 138-139 F 8
Slieve Car = Sliabh Ceara 116-117 B 6
Sligeach 116-117 C 6
Sligo = Sligeach 116-117 C 6
Sligo Bay = Cuan Shligigh 116-117 C 6
Sligo Branch 82 II ab 3
Slim Buttes 68-69 E 3
Slite 114-115 H 9
Sliten = Zlītan 194-195 GH 2
Sliven 138-139 M 4
Slivnica 138-139 K 4
Sloan, IA 68-69 H 4
Slobodčikovo 142-143 J 3
Slobodskoj 154-155 HJ 6
Slobozia 138-139 M 3
Slocan 66-67 E 1
Slocan Lake 66-67 E 1
Sloko River 52-53 V 7
Slonim 142-143 E 5
Slot, The — 174-175 j 6
Slough 116-117 L 9
Slovenia 138-139 F 3-G 2
Slovenské rudohorie 124 JK 4
Sluck 142-143 E 5
Sl'ud'anka 154-155 T 7
Slunj 138-139 F 3
Słupsk 124 H 1
Slyne Head = Ceann Léime 116-117 A 7

Smackover, AR 78-79 C 4
Småland 114-115 EF 9
Small, ID 66-67 G 3
Small Point 72-73 M 3
Smalls, The — 116-117 F 9
S'marah 194-195 B 3
Smederevo 138-139 J 3
Smela 142-143 F 6
Smeru = Gunung Semeru 174-175 F 8
Smethport, PA 72-73 G 4
Smethwick 116-117 JK 8
Šmidta, ostrov — 154-155 QR 1
Smiley 49 D 5
Smiley, Cape — 31 B 29
Smiltene 142-143 E 4
Smith [CDN] 46-47 O 6-7
Smith Arm 46-47 M 4
Smith Bay 52-53 KL 1
Smith Center, KS 68-69 G 6
Smithers 46-47 L 7
Smithfield, NC 80-81 G 3
Smithfield, UT 66-67 H 5
Smithfield, VA 80-81 H 2
Smith Inlet 48 CD 4
Smith Island [CDN] 46-47 V 5
Smith Island [USA] 80-81 H 4
Smith River 66-67 H 2
Smith River, CA 66-67 A 5
Smiths Creek Valley 74-75 E 3
Smith's Falls 46-47 V 9
Smiths Ferry, ID 66-67 EF 3
Smiths Grove, KY 70-71 G 7
Smith Sound 46-47 W 2
Smithton 182-183 HJ 8
Smithville, GA 80-81 DE 5
Smithville, TN 78-79 G 2
Smithville, TX 76-77 F 7-8
Smjörfjöll 114-115 f 2
Smögen 114-115 D 8
Smoke Creek Desert 66-67 D 5
Smoky Falls 50 K 1
Smoky Hill River 58-59 FG 4
Smoky Hill River, North Fork — 68-69 EF 6
Smoky Hills 68-69 G 6
Smoky Lake 49 BC 3
Smoky Mountains 66-67 F 4
Smoky River 46-47 N 7
Smøla 114-115 B 6
Smol'an 138-139 L 5
Smolensk 142-143 F 5
Smólikas 138-139 J 5
Smoot, WY 66-67 H 4
Smooth Rock Falls 50 L 2
Smoothrock Lake 50 DE 2
Smoothstone Lake 49 E 3
Smoothstone River 49 E 3
Smyrna, TN 78-79 F 2-3
Smyrna = İzmir 160-161 B 3

Snaefell [GB] 116-117 G 6
Snæfell [IS] 114-115 f 2
Snæfellsjökull 114-115 ab 2
Snæfellsnes 114-115 b 2
Snag 46-47 HJ 5
Snaght, Slieve — = Sliabh Sneachta 116-117 D 5
Snaidhm, An t- 116-117 AB 9
Snaith 116-117 KL 7
Snake Creek [USA, Nebraska] 68-69 F 4
Snake Creek [USA, South Dakota] 68-69 G 3
Snake Range 74-75 F 3
Snake River [USA ◁ Columbia River] 58-59 C 2
Snake River [USA ◁ Croix River] 70-71 D 2-3
Snake River Canyon 66-67 E 3
Snake River Plains 58-59 D 3
Snake Valley 74-75 G 3
Snåsa 114-115 E 5
Sneachta, Sliabh — 116-117 D 5
Sneem = An tSnaidhm 116-117 AB 9
Snettisham 116-117 M 8
Śniardwy, Jezioro — 124 K 2
Sniežka 124 GH 3
Snigir'ovka 142-143 F 6
Snipe Lake 48 J 2
Snizort, Loch — 116-117 E 3
Snodland 116-117 M 9
Snøhetta 114-115 C 6
Snohomish, WA 66-67 BC 2
Snoqualmie Pass 66-67 C 2
Snota 114-115 C 6
Snøtind 114-115 E 4
Snowden, MT 68-69 D 1-2
Snowdon 116-117 G 7
Snowdrift 46-47 OP 5
Snowflake, AZ 74-75 H 5
Snow Hill, MD 72-73 J 5
Snow Hill Island 31 C 31
Snow Lake 49 H 3
Snow Road 72-73 H 2
Snowshoe Peak 66-67 F 1
Snowville, UT 66-67 G 5
Snowy Mountains 182-183 J 7
Snug Corner 88-89 K 3
Snyder, OK 76-77 E 5
Snyder, TX 58-59 F 5

Soalala 198 HJ 5
Soanierana-Ivongo 198 JK 5
Soan-kundo 170-171 F 5
Soap Lake, WA 66-67 D 2
Soasiu 174-175 J 6
Soavinandriana 198 J 5
Soay 116-117 E 3
Sobaek-sanmaek 170-171 F 5-G 4
Sōbāṭ, Nahr — = As-Sūbāṭ 194-195 L 7
Sobolevo 154-155 e 7
Sobo-zan 170-171 H 6
Sobozo 194-195 GH 4
Sobradinho [BR, Pará] 98-99 K 7
Sobrado [BR] 98-99 J 6
Sobral [BR, Ceará] 98-99 L 5
Socha 98-99 E 3
Sochaczew 124 K 2
Soche = Yarkand 166-167 D 4
Sŏch'ŏn 170-171 E 4
Sochor, gora — 154-155 TU 7
Soči 142-143 G 7
Society Islands 34-35 K 5
Socompa, Volcán — 103 C 2
Socorro, NM 76-77 A 5-6
Socorro [CO] 98-99 E 3
Socorro, El — [MEX] 76-77 C 9
Socorro, Isla — 58-59 DE 8
Socoto = Sokoto 194-195 EF 6
Socotra = Suquṭrā' 160-161 G 8
Socuéllamos 132-133 F 9
Sódá, Gebel es — = Jabal as-Sawdā' 194-195 GH 3
Soda Creek 48 F 3
Soda Lake 74-75 F 5
Sodankylä 114-115 LM 4
Soda Springs, ID 66-67 H 4
Soddu = Sodo 194-195 M 7
Soddy, TN 78-79 G 3
Söderhamn 114-115 G 7
Söderköping 114-115 G 8
Södermanland 114-115 G 8
Södertälje 114-115 GH 8
Sōdirī = Sawdirī 194-195 K 6
Sodo 194-195 M 7
Sodus, NY 72-73 H 3
Soekmekaar 198 E 6
Soest 124 D 3
Sœurs, Île des — 82 I b 2
Sofala, Baía de — 198 FG 6
Sofala, Manica e — 198 F 5-6
Sofia 198 J 5
Sofia = Sofija 138-139 K 4
Sofija 138-139 K 4
Sofijsk 154-155 Z 7
Sofporog 114-115 O 5
Sogamoso 98-99 E 3
Sogndalstrand 114-115 B 8
Sognefjord 114-115 AB 7
Sogn og Fjordane 114-115 AB 7
Sogwip'o 170-171 F 6
Sôhâg = Sawhāj 194-195 L 3
Soham 116-117 M 8
Sŏhan-man 166-167 NO 4
Sohano 174-175 h 6
Sohar = Ṣuḥār 160-161 H 6
So-hŭksan-do 170-171 E 5
Soissons 132-133 J 4
Sŏja 170-171 J 5
S'ojacha [SU, place] 154-155 N 3
S'ojacha [SU, river] 142-143 NO 1
Šojna [SU] 154-155 G 4
Sŏjosŏn-man = Sŏhan-man 166-167 NO 4
Šokal'skogo, ostrov — 154-155 NO 3
Šokal'skogo, proliv — 154-155 RS 2
Söke 160-161 B 3
Sokhna = Sawknah 194-195 GH 3
Sokodé 194-195 E 7
Sokol 154-155 G 6
Sokółka 124 L 2
Sokolo 194-195 C 6
Sokołów Podlaski 124 L 2
Sokoto [WAN, place] 194-195 EF 6
Sokoto [WAN, river] 194-195 E 6
Sokotra = Suquṭrā' 160-161 G 8
Sŏkpā 174-175 C 3
Sŏk-to 170-171 E 3
Sol, Costa del — 132-133 EF 10
Sola de Vega 86-87 M 9
Solai 198 G 1-2
Solano, NM 76-77 BC 5
Sōlāpur = Sholāpur 160-161 M 7
Soldedad 98-99 DE 2
Soldier Fields 83 II b 1
Soldotna, AK 52-53 M 6
Soledad, CA 74-75 C 4
Soledad [MEX] 76-77 D 9
Soledad [YV] 98-99 G 3
Soledad, Isla — = East Falkland 103 E 8
Soledad Díez Gutiérrez 86-87 K 6
Soledade [BR, Amazonas] 98-99 D 8
Soledade [BR, Roraima] 98-99 H 3
Soledade, Cachoeira — 98-99 LM 7
Solent, The — 116-117 K 10
Solesmes 132-133 G 5
Soleure = Solothurn 124 C 5
Solfonn 114-115 B 8
Solihull 116-117 K 8
Solikamsk 154-155 K 6
Sol'-Ileck 154-155 JK 7
Solimões, Rio — 98-99 G 5
Solingen 124 C 3
Sollefteå 114-115 G 6
Sóller 132-133 J 9
Sollum = As-Salûm 194-195 K 2
Sol-lun = Solon 166-167 N 2
Solna 114-115 GH 8
Solo = Surakarta 174-175 F 8
Sologne 132-133 HJ 5
Šologoncy 154-155 VW 4
Solok 174-175 D 7
Sololá 86-87 P 10
Solomon, AK 52-53 E 4
Solomon, KS 68-69 H 6
Solomon Islands [archipelago] 174-175 h 6-k 7
Solomon Islands [Solomon Is., state] 174-175 kl 7
Solomon River 68-69 GH 6
Solomon River, North Fork — 68-69 FG 6
Solomon River, South Fork — 68-69 F 6
Solomons Basin 174-175 h 6
Solomon Sea 174-175 hj 6
Solon, IA 70-71 E 5

Solon 271

Solončak Šalkarteniz 154-155 L 8
Solong Cheer = Sulan Cheer 166-167 K 3
Solon Springs, WI 70-71 DE 2
Solor, Pulau — 174-175 H 8
Solothurn 124 C 5
Soloveckije ostrova 154-155 F 4
Šolta 138-139 G 4
Soltānābād = Arāk 160-161 F 4
Soltau 124 DE 2
Soluch = Sulūq 194-195 J 2
Solun 166-167 N 2
Soluq = Sulūq 194-195 J 2
Solvay, NY 72-73 H 3
Sölvesborg 114-115 F 9
Sol'vyčegodsk 154-155 H 5
Solway Firth 116-117 H 6
Solwezi 198 E 4
Sōma [J] 170-171 N 4
Soma [TR] 142-143 E 8
Somabhula 198 E 5
Somalia 194-195 N 8-O 7
Somali Basin 26-27 M 5-6
Sombor 138-139 H 3
Sombrerete 86-87 J 6
Sombrero 88-89 P 5
Sombrero, El — [YV] 98-99 F 3
Şomcuta Mare 138-139 K 2
Somero 114-115 K 7
Somers, MT 66-67 F 1
Somerset, CO 68-69 C 6
Somerset, KY 70-71 H 7
Somerset, PA 72-73 G 4-5
Somerset [AUS] 182-183 H 2
Somerset [CDN] 68-69 G 1
Somerset [GB] 116-117 HJ 9
Somerset East = Somerset-Oos 198 DE 8
Somerset Island 46-47 S 3
Somerset-Oos 198 DE 8
Somersworth, NH 72-73 L 3
Somerton, AZ 74-75 F 6
Somerville, MA 72-73 L 3
Somerville, NJ 72-73 J 4
Somerville, TN 78-79 E 3
Somerville, TX 76-77 F 7
Someş 138-139 K 2
Somesbar, CA 66-67 B 5
Somme 132-133 H 3
Sommerset, MD 82 II a 1
Somuncurá, Meseta de — 103 C 6
Son [IND] 160-161 N 6
Sona 88-89 F 11
Sŏnch'ŏn 170-171 E 3
Sønderborg 114-115 CD 10
Sondershausen 124 E 3
Sondheimer, LA 78-79 D 4
Søndre Kvaløy 114-115 GH 3
Søndre Strømfjord 46-47 a 4
Søndre Strømfjord = Kangerdlugssuaq 46-47 ab 4
Sondrio 138-139 CD 2
Sŏngch'on 170-171 F 3
Songea 198 G 4
Songhua Hu 166-167 O 3
Songhua Jiang 166-167 O 2
Sŏnghwan 170-171 F 4
Songjiang 166-167 N 5
Songjiangzhen 170-171 F 1
Sŏngjin = Kim Chak 166-167 OP 3
Songjŏng-ni 170-171 F 5
Songkhla 174-175 D 5
Songkla = Songkhla 174-175 D 5
Sŏngnae-ri = Inhung-ni 170-171 F 3
Songnim 166-167 O 4
Songo 198 BC 3
Songpan 166-167 J 5
Sonhāt 160-161 N 6
Sonkovo 154-155 F 6
Sonmiani = Sonmiyānī 160-161 K 5
Sonmiyāni 160-161 K 5
Sonmiyānī, Khalīj — 160-161 J 6-K 5
Sonneberg 124 E 3
Sono, Rio do — [BR, Goiás] 98-99 K 6-7
Sonoita 86-87 D 2
Sonoma, CA 74-75 B 3
Sonoma Range 66-67 E 5
Sonora 58-59 DE 6
Sonora, AZ 74-75 H 6
Sonora, CA 74-75 C 3-4
Sonora, TX 76-77 D 7
Sonora Peak 74-75 D 3
Sonsón 98-99 DE 3
Sonsonate 58-59 HJ 9
Sonsorol 174-175 K 5
Soperton, GA 80-81 E 4
Sŏp'o-ri 170-171 FG 2
Sopot 124 J 1
Sopron 124 H 5
Sop's Arm Provincial Park 51 H 3
Sor 132-133 C 9
Sora 138-139 E 5
Sŏrak-san 170-171 G 3
Sōrath = Jūnāgaḍh 160-161 KL 6
Sorbas 132-133 FG 10
Sörd 116-117 E 7
Sorel 46-47 W 8
Sorell, Cape — 182-183 HJ 8
Soren Arwa = Selat Yapen 174-175 L 7
Sørfonna 114-115 lm 5
Sòrgono 138-139 C 5
Sörhād = Sarhade Wākhān 160-161 L 3
Soria 132-133 F 8
Sørkapp 114-115 k 6
Sørkapp land 114-115 k 6
Sørkjosen 114-115 J 3
Sorø [DK] 114-115 D 10
Sorocaba 103 G 2
Soročinsk 154-155 J 7
Soroka = Belomorsk 154-155 EF 5
Sorol 174-175 M 5
Sorong 174-175 K 7
Soroti 198 F 1
Sørøy 114-115 K 2
Sørøysund 114-115 K 2
Sorraia 132-133 C 9
Sør-Randane 31 B 2-3
Sorrento 138-139 F 5
Sorsele 114-115 G 5
Sør-Shetland = South Shetlands 31 C 30
Sorsogon 174-175 HJ 4
Sortavala 154-155 E 5
Sorte Gobi = Char Gov' 166-167 GH 3
Sortland 114-115 F 3
Sør-Trøndelag 114-115 CD 6
Sørvågen 114-115 E 4
Sörvágur 116-117 a 1
Sōsan 170-171 F 4
Soscumica, Lac — 50 N 1
Sosnogorsk 154-155 JK 5
Sosnovka 142-143 H 5
Sosnovo-Oz'orskoje 154-155 V 7
Sosnowiec 124 J 3
Šostka 142-143 F 5
Sōsura 170-171 H 1
Sos'va [SU ↘ Serov] 154-155 L 6
Sos'va [SU, Chanty-Mansijskij NO] 154-155 L 5
So-tch'ê = Yarkand 166-167 D 4
Sotério, Rio — 98-99 F 10
Sotkamo 114-115 N 5
Sotra 114-115 A 7
Souanké 198 B 1
Soubré 194-195 C 7
Soudan 182-183 G 4
Soufrière 58-59 O 9
Souillac 132-133 H 6
Souk-Ahras = Sūq Ahrās 194-195 F 1
Sŏul 166-167 O 4
Sound, The — = Öresund 114-115 E 10
Sounding Creek 49 C 5
Soundview, New York-, NY 82 III c 2
Sources, Mont aux — 198 E 7
Soure [BR] 98-99 K 5
Souris, ND 68-69 F 1
Souris [CDN, Manitoba] 49 H 6
Souris [CDN, Prince Edward I.] 51 E 4
Souris River 46-47 Q 8
Sourlake, TX 76-77 G 7
Sousa 98-99 M 6
Sousse = Sūsah 194-195 G 1
South Africa 198 D-F 7
South Alligator River 182-183 F 2
Southam 116-117 K 8
South America 26-27 FG 6
Southampton, NY 72-73 KL 4
Southampton [CDN] 72-73 F 2
Southampton [GB] 116-117 KL 10
Southampton Island 46-47 TU 5
South Andaman 160-161 P 8
South Aulatsivik Island 46-47 YZ 6
South Australia 182-183 E-G 5-6
South Australian Basin 26-27 PQ 8
South Baldy 76-77 A 5-6
South Banda Basin 174-175 J 8
South Baymouth 50 K 4
South Beach, New York-, NY 82 III b 3
South Bend, IN 58-59 JK 3
South Bend, WA 66-67 B 2
South Boston, VA 80-81 G 2
South Brent 116-117 GH 10
South Brooklyn, New York-, NY 82 III bc 2
South Charleston, OH 72-73 E 5
South Charleston, WV 72-73 EF 5
South Chicago, Chicago-, IL 83 II b 2
South China Basin 174-175 FG 3-4
South China Sea 166-167 L 8-M 7
South Downs 116-117 LM 10
South Dum Dum 160-161 OP 6
South East Cape 182-183 J 8
Southeast Indian Basin 26-27 OP 7
Southeast Pacific Basin 34-35 MN 7-8
Southeast Pass 78-79 E 6
South El Monte, CA 83 III d 1
Southend [CDN] 46-47 PQ 6
Southend [GB] 116-117 F 5
Southend-on-Sea 116-117 M 9
Southern [Z] 198 E 5
Southern Alps 182-183 NO 8
Southern California, University of — 83 III c 1
Southern Cross 182-183 CD 6
Southern Indian Lake 46-47 R 6
Southern Pacific Railway 58-59 EF 5
Southern Pine Hills = Pine Hills 58-59 J 5
Southern Pines, NC 80-81 G 3
Southern Sierra Madre = Sierra Madre del Sur 58-59 FG 8
Southern Uplands 116-117 G-J 5
Southern Ute Indian Reservation 68-69 BC 7
South Esk, River — 116-117 HJ 4
South Fiji Basin 182-183 OP 4-5
South Foreland 116-117 h 7
South Fork, CO 68-69 C 7
South Fork Flathead River 66-67 G 2
South Fork Mountains 66-67 B 5
South Fork Owyhee River 66-67 E 4-5
South Fox Island 70-71 GH 3
South Gate, CA 74-75 DE 6
South Georgia Ridge 26-27 H 8
South Glamorgan 116-117 H 9
South Grand River 70-71 CD 6
South Haven, KS 76-77 F 4
South Haven, MI 70-71 G 4
South Henik Lake 46-47 R 5
South Hill, VA 80-81 G 2
South Honshu Ridge 166-167 R 5-6
South Horr 198 G 1
South Indian Lake [CDN, place] 49 J 2
South Indian Ridge 26-27 OP 8
South Island 182-183 OP 8
South Junction 70-71 BC 1
South Kirkby 116-117 KL 7
South Korea 166-167 OP 4
South Lawn, MD 82 II b 2
South Loup River 68-69 FG 5
Southmag 72-73 FG 2
South Magnetic Pole Area 31 C 14-15
South Male Atoll 36 ab 2
South Malosmadulu Atoll 36 a 1-2
South Milwaukee, WI 70-71 G 4
Southminster 116-117 M 9
South Molton 116-117 H 9-10
South Moose Lake 49 H 4
South Mountain 72-73 H 4-5
South Nahanni River 46-47 LM 5
South Natuna Islands = Kepulauan Bunguran Selatan 174-175 E 6
South Negril Point 88-89 G 5
South Ogden, UT 66-67 H 5
South Orkneys 31 C 32
South Ossetian Autonomous Region = 7 ◁ 142-143 H 7
South Pacific Basin 34-35 KL 6-7
South Padre Island 76-77 F 9
South Pageh = Pulau Pagai Selatan 174-175 CD 7
South Paris, ME 72-73 L 2
South Pasadena, CA 83 III cd 1
South Pass [USA, Louisiana] 58-59 J 6
South Pass [USA, Wyoming] 58-59 E 3
South Platte River 58-59 F 3
South Porcupine 50 L 2
Southport 116-117 H 7
Southport, NC 80-81 GH 3
South Portland, ME 72-73 LM 3
South River [CDN, place] 72-73 G 2
South River [CDN, river] 72-73 G 1-2
South Rona 116-117 EF 3
South Ronaldsay 116-117 J 2
South Saint Paul, MN 70-71 D 3
South Sandwich Islands 31 CD 34
South Sandwich Trench 31 D 34
South San Gabriel, CA 83 III d 1
South Saskatchewan River 46-47 OP 7
South Seal River 49 J 2
South Shetlands 31 C 30
South Shields 116-117 KL 6
South Shore, Blackpool- 116-117 H 7
South Shore, Chicago-, IL 83 II b 2
South Sioux City, NE 68-69 H 4
South Sulphur River 76-77 G 6
South Taranaki Bight 182-183 O 7
South Tent 74-75 H 3
South Tyrol 138-139 D 2
South Uist 116-117 D 3
South Umpqua River 66-67 B 4
South Wabasca Lake 48 L 2
Southwell 116-117 L 7
Southwest Cape [NZ] 182-183 N 9
Southwest Cay 58-59 KL 9
Southwest Indian Basin 26-27 MN 7
Southwest Miramichi River 51 CD 4
Southwest Museum 83 III c 1
Southwest Pass [USA, Mississippi River Delta] 58-59 J 6
Southwest Pass [USA, Vermillion Bay] 78-79 C 6
Southwick 116-117 L 10
South Williamsport, PA 72-73 H 4
Southwold 116-117 h 6
South Yorkshire = 3 ◁ 116-117 K 7
Soutpansberge 198 EF 6
Souzel 98-99 J 5
Sovetsk [SU, Kaliningradskaja Oblast'] 124 K 1
Sovetsk [SU, Kirovskaja Oblast'] 154-155 H 6
Sovetskaja Gavan' 154-155 ab 8
Soviet Union 154-155 E-b 5
Sowden Lake 70-71 E 1
Sōya [J, Hokkaidō] 170-171 b 1
Sōya-kaikyō 166-167 R 2
Sōya misaki 170-171 bc 1
Soyo 198 B 3
Soyopa 86-87 F 3
Sozopol 138-139 MN 4
Spafarief Bay 52-53 FG 3
Spain 132-133 E 7-F 9
Spalato = Split 138-139 G 4
Spalding 116-117 L 8
Spalding, ID 66-67 E 2
Spalding, NE 68-69 G 5
Spangle, WA 66-67 E 2
Spanish Fork, UT 66-67 H 5
Spanish Head 116-117 F 7-G 6
Spanish Peak = West Spanish Peak 68-69 D 7
Spanish Town 58-59 L 8
Spanta, Akrōtérion — 138-139 KL 8
Sparbu 114-115 D 6
Sparkman, AR 78-79 C 3-4
Sparks, GA 80-81 E 5
Sparks, NV 74-75 D 3
Sparta, GA 80-81 E 4
Sparta, IL 70-71 F 6
Sparta, MI 70-71 H 4
Sparta, NC 80-81 F 2
Sparta, TN 78-79 G 3
Sparta, WI 70-71 E 4
Sparta = Spártē 138-139 K 7
Spartanburg, SC 58-59 K 4-5
Spártē 138-139 K 7
Spartivento, Capo — [I, Calàbria] 138-139 G 7
Spartivento, Capo — [I, Sardegna] 138-139 G 6
Spassk = Kujbyšev 154-155 HJ 7
Spassk = Spassk-Dal'nij 154-155 Z 9
Spassk-Dal'nij 154-155 Z 9
Spatsizi River 52-53 X 8
Spean Bridge 116-117 G 4
Spearfish, SD 68-69 E 3
Spearhill 49 JK 5
Spearman, TX 76-77 D 4
Spearville, KS 68-69 G 7
Speke Gulf 198 F 2
Spenard, AK 52-53 N 6
Spencer, IA 70-71 C 4
Spencer, ID 66-67 G 3
Spencer, IN 70-71 G 6
Spencer, NC 80-81 F 3
Spencer, SD 68-69 H 4
Spencer, WI 70-71 E 3
Spencer, WV 72-73 F 5
Spencer, Cape — [AUS] 182-183 G 7
Spencer, Cape — [USA] 52-53 T 7
Spencer, Point — 52-53 D 4
Spencer Gulf 182-183 G 6
Spencerville, OH 70-71 HJ 5
Spences Bridge 48 G 4
Spennymoor 116-117 K 6
Sperling 68-69 H 1
Sperrin Mountains 116-117 DE 6
Spessart 124 D 3-4
Spétsai 138-139 K 7
Spey, River — 116-117 H 3
Speyer 124 D 4
Spèzia, La — 138-139 C 3
Spezzano Albanese 138-139 G 6
Sphakia = Chōra Sfakíōn 138-139 L 8
Spicer Islands 46-47 UV 4
Spike Mount 52-53 QR 3
Spilimbergo 138-139 E 2
Spillimacheen 48 J 4
Spin Bulgak 160-161 K 4
Spirit Lake, IA 70-71 C 4
Spirit Lake, ID 66-67 E 1-2
Spirit Lake, WA 66-67 BC 2
Spirit River 48 H 2
Spiritwood 49 E 4
Spiro, OK 76-77 G 5
Spithead 116-117 K 10
Spitsbergen 114-115 k 6-n 5
Spittal 124 F 5
Split 138-139 G 4
Split Lake [CDN, lake] 49 KL 2
Split Lake [CDN, place] 49 K 2
Split Rock, WY 68-69 C 4
Splügen 124 D 5
Spofford, TX 76-77 D 8
Spokane, WA 58-59 C 2
Spokane Indian Reservation 66-67 DE 2
Spokane River 66-67 DE 2
Spokojnyj 154-155 YZ 6
Špola 142-143 F 6
Spoleto 138-139 E 4
Spooner, MN 70-71 C 1
Spooner, WI 70-71 E 3
Spoon River 70-71 E 5
Sporades 138-139 M 6-7
Sportsmans Park Race Track 83 II a 1
Sporyj Navolok, mys — 154-155 M-O 2
Spotted Horse, WY 68-69 D 3
Spotted Range 74-75 F 4
Sprague, WA 66-67 DE 2
Sprague River 66-67 C 4
Sprague River, OR 66-67 C 4
Spranger, Mount — 48 G 3
Spratly Islands = Quân Đao Hoang Sa 174-175 F 5
Spray, OR 66-67 D 3
Spree 124 G 3
Spreewald 124 F 2-G 3
Spremberg 124 G 3
Sprengisandur 114-115 de 2
Spring, TX 76-77 G 7
Spring Bay 66-67 G 5
Springbok 198 C 7
Spring City, TN 78-79 G 3
Spring Creek Park 82 III c 3
Springdale, AR 76-77 GH 4
Springdale, MT 66-67 HJ 3
Springdale, NV 74-75 E 4
Springdale, UT 74-75 G 4
Springdale, WA 66-67 DE 1
Springer, NM 76-77 B 4
Springer, Mount — 50 O 2
Springerville, AZ 74-75 J 5
Springfield, CO 68-69 E 7
Springfield, GA 80-81 F 4
Springfield, ID 66-67 G 4
Springfield, IL 58-59 HJ 4
Springfield, KY 70-71 H 7
Springfield, MA 58-59 M 3
Springfield, MN 70-71 C 3
Springfield, MO 58-59 H 4
Springfield, OH 58-59 K 3-4
Springfield, OR 66-67 B 3
Springfield, SD 68-69 GH 4
Springfield, TN 78-79 F 2
Springfield, VA 82 II a 2
Springfield, VT 72-73 K 3
Springfield, New York-, NY 82 III d 2
Springhill, LA 78-79 C 4
Spring Hill, TN 78-79 F 3
Spring Hope, NC 80-81 GH 3
Springhouse 48 FG 4
Spring Mountains 74-75 F 4
Springs 198 E 7
Springsure 182-183 J 4
Spring Valley, IL 70-71 F 5
Spring Valley, MN 70-71 D 4
Spring Valley [USA] 74-75 F 3
Springview, NE 68-69 G 4
Springville, AL 78-79 F 4
Springville, NY 72-73 G 3
Springville, UT 66-67 H 5
Sproat Lake 66-67 A 1
Sprucedale 72-73 G 2
Spruce Grove 48 KL 3
Spruce Knob 58-59 KL 4
Spruce Mountain 66-67 F 5
Spruce Pine, NC 80-81 EF 2
Spry, UT 74-75 G 4
Spur, TX 76-77 D 6
Spur Lake, NM 74-75 J 5-6
Spurn Head 116-117 M 7
Spurr, Mount — 52-53 LM 6
Squamish 66-67 B 1
Squaw Harbor, AK 52-53 c 2
Squaw Rapids Dam 49 G 4
Squaw River 50 F 2
Squaw Valley, CA 58-59 BC 4
Squillace, Golfo di — 138-139 G 6
Squirrel River 52-53 G 3
Sráid na Cathrach 116-117 B 8
Sredinnyj chrebet 154-155 f 6-e 7
Sredna gora 138-139 L 4
Srednekolymsk 154-155 d 4
Sredne-Sibirskoje ploskogorje 154-155 R-W 4-5
Srednij Ural 154-155 KL 6
Sredsib 154-155 L 7-P 7
Srem 124 H 2
Sremska Mitrovica 138-139 H 3
Sremska Rača 138-139 H 3
Sretensk 154-155 W 7
Srê Umbell 174-175 D 4
Srīkākulam 160-161 M 7
Srī Lanka 160-161 N 9
Srīnagar 160-161 LM 4
Srīrangam 160-161 M 8
Srīvardhan 160-161 L 7
Środa Wielkopolski 124 HJ 2
Sseu-p'ing = Siping 166-167 N 3
Ssongea = Songea 198 G 4
Staaten River 182-183 H 3
Stachanov 142-143 G 6
Stackpool 50 L 3
Stack Skerry 116-117 G 1
Stade [CDN] 82 I b 1
Stade [D] 124 D 2
Stadium 82 II b 2
Städjan 114-115 E 7
Stadlandet 114-115 A 6
Staffa 116-117 E 4
Stafford 116-117 J 8
Stafford, KS 68-69 G 7
Stafford, NE 68-69 G 4
Stainland 116-117 JK 7
Staked Plain = Llano Estacado 58-59 F 5
Stalina, pik — = pik Kommunizma 160-161 L 3
Stalinabad = Dušanbe 160-161 K 3
Stalino = Ošarovo 154-155 S 5
Stalinsk = Novokuzneck 154-155 Q 7
Stallo, MS 78-79 E 4
Stalowa Wola 124 L 3
Stalwart 49 F 5
Stalybridge 116-117 JK 7
Stambul = İstanbul 160-161 BC 2
Stamford, CT 72-73 K 4
Stamford, TX 76-77 E 6
Stamford [AUS] 182-183 H 4
Stamford [GB] 116-117 L 8
Stampriet 198 C 6
Stamps, AR 78-79 C 4
Stamsund 114-115 EF 3
Stanberry, MO 70-71 C 5
Stanbury Mountains 66-67 G 5
Standerton 198 EF 7
Standing Rock Indian Reservation 68-69 F 2-3
Standish, MI 70-71 HJ 4
Stanford, KY 70-71 H 7
Stanford, MT 66-67 H 2
Stanislaus River 74-75 C 3-4
Stanke Dimitrov 138-139 K 4
Stanley, ID 66-67 F 3
Stanley, KY 70-71 G 7
Stanley, ND 68-69 E 1
Stanley, NM 76-77 AB 5
Stanley, WI 70-71 E 3
Stanley [CDN] 51 C 4
Stanley [Falkland Islands] 103 E 8
Stanley, Mount — 182-183 F 4
Stanley Mission 49 FG 3
Stanley Pool = Pool Malebo 198 C 2
Stanley Reservoir 160-161 M 8
Stanleyville = Kisangani 198 E 1
Stann Creek 58-59 J 8
Stanovoj chrebet 154-155 X-Z 6
Stanovoje nagorje 154-155 VW 6
Stanton, KY 72-73 E 6
Stanton, MI 70-71 H 4
Stanton, ND 68-69 F 2
Stanton, NE 68-69 H 5
Stanton, TX 76-77 CD 6
Stanwood, WA 66-67 B 1
Stapi 114-115 b 2
Staples, MN 70-71 C 2
Stapleton, NE 68-69 F 5
Star, MS 78-79 DE 4
Star, NC 80-81 G 3
Starachowice 124 K 3
Staraja Buchara = Buchara 160-161 JK 3
Staraja Russa 154-155 E 6
Stara Pazova 138-139 J 3
Stara Zagora 138-139 L 4
Starbuck [CDN] 49 JK 6
Starbuck [island] 34-35 K 5
Star City, AR 78-79 D 4
Stargard Szczeciński 124 G 2
Starigrad 138-139 F 3
Starke, FL 80-81 bc 2
Starkey, ID 66-67 E 3
Starkville, CO 68-69 D 7
Starkville, MS 78-79 E 4
Starkweather, ND 68-69 G 1
Starnberg 124 E 4-5
Starnberger See 124 E 5
Starobel'sk 142-143 G 6
Starogard Gdański 124 HJ 2
Starokonstantinov 142-143 E 6
Starominskaja 142-143 G 6
Starotitarovskaja 142-143 G 6-7
Start Bay 116-117 H 10
Start Point 116-117 H 10
Staryj Oskol 142-143 G 5
Stassfurt 124 E 3
Staszów 124 K 3
State College, PA 72-73 GH 4
State Line, MS 78-79 E 5
Staten Island 72-73 JK 4
Staten Island = Isla de los Estados 103 D 8
Staten Island Airport 82 III b 3
Statenville, GA 80-81 E 5
Statesboro, GA 80-81 F 4
Statesville, NC 58-59 K 4
Stathern 116-117 L 8
Statland = Stadland 114-115 A 6
Stauffer, OR 66-67 C 4
Staunton, IL 70-71 F 6
Staunton, VA 58-59 KL 4
Stavanger 114-115 A 8
Stavely 48 KL 4
Stavern 114-115 CD 8
Stavropol 142-143 H 6
Stavropol' = Togliatti 154-155 H 7
Stavropol, Kraj — 108-109 R 6-7
Stavrós 138-139 K 5
Stawell 182-183 H 7
Steamboat, NV 74-75 D 3
Steamboat Springs, CO 68-69 C 5
Stearns, KY 78-79 G 2
Stebbins, AK 52-53 F 5
Steel Creek, AK 52-53 R 4
Steele, AL 78-79 F 4
Steele, MO 78-79 E 2
Steele, ND 68-69 FG 2
Steele, Mount — 52-53 RS 6
Steele Island 31 B 30-31
Steelpoort 198 EF 6
Steel River 70-71 G 1
Steelton, PA 72-73 H 4
Steelville, MO 70-71 E 7
Steenkool 174-175 K 7
Steensby Inlet 46-47 V 3
Steens Mountain 66-67 D 4
Steenstrups Gletscher 46-47 Za 2
Steephill Lake 49 G 2-3
Steep Point 182-183 B 5
Steep Rock 49 J 5
Steep Rock Lake 70-71 DE 1

272 **Solončak**

Ştefăneşti 138-139 M 2
Stefansson Island 46-47 OP 3
Steflești 138-139 K 3
Stege 114-115 E 10
Steiermark 124 G 5
Steinbach 49 K 6
Steinen, Rio — 98-99 J 7
Steinhatchee, FL 80-81 b 2
Steinkjer 114-115 DE 5
Steinneset 114-115 m 6
Steins, NM 74-75 J 6
Stellaland 198 D 7
Stellarton 51 E 5
Stellenbosch 198 CD 8
Steller, Mount — 52-53 Q 6
Stendal 124 E 2
Stensele 114-115 G 5
Stepanakert 142-143 J 8
Stephanie, Lake — = Thew Bahir 194-195 M 8
Stephen, MN 68-69 H 1
Stephens, AR 78-79 C 4
Stephens Island 48 B 2
Stephenson, MI 70-71 G 3
Stephens Passage 52-53 U 7-V 8
Stephenville 46-47 YZ 8
Stephenville, TX 76-77 EF 6
Stephenville Crossing 51 GH 3
Stepn'ak 154-155 N 7
Stepovak Bay 52-53 cd 2
Sterkstroom 198 E 8
Sterley, TX 76-77 D 5
Sterling, AK 52-53 M 6
Sterling, CO 58-59 F 3
Sterling, IL 70-71 F 5
Sterling, KS 68-69 GH 6
Sterling, ND 68-69 FG 2
Sterling City, TX 76-77 D 7
Sterling Heights, MI 72-73 E 3
Sterling Landing, AK 52-53 K 5
Sterling Park, CA 83 I b 2
Sterlitamak 154-155 K 7
Stettler 49 B 4
Steuben, MI 70-71 G 2
Steubenville, OH 58-59 K 3
Stevenson, AL 78-79 FG 3
Stevenson, WA 66-67 BC 3
Stevenson Lake 50 A 1
Stevenson River 182-183 FG 5
Stevens Point, WI 70-71 F 3
Stevens Village, AK 52-53 N 3-4
Stevensville, MT 66-67 FG 2
Steveston 66-67 B 1
Stewart, AK 46-47 KL 6
Stewart, MN 70-71 C 3
Stewart, NV 74-75 D 3
Stewart, Isla — 103 B 8-9
Stewart Island 182-183 N 9
Stewart Islands 174-175 k 6
Stewart River [CDN, place] 46-47 J 5
Stewart River [CDN, river] 46-47 JK 5
Stewartsville, MO 70-71 CD 6
Stewart Valley 49 DE 5
Stewartville, MN 70-71 D 4
Steyr 124 G 4
Stickney, IL 83 II a 2
Stickney, SD 68-69 G 4
Stigler, OK 76-77 G 5
Stikine Mountains = Cassiar Mountains 46-47 KL 6
Stikine Plateau 46-47 K 6
Stikine River 46-47 KL 6
Stikine Strait 52-53 w 8
Stiles, TX 76-77 D 7
Stillwater, MN 70-71 D 3
Stillwater, OK 76-77 F 4
Stillwater Mountains 74-75 DE 3
Stilwell, OK 76-77 G 5
Stimson 50 L 2
Stimson, Mount — 66-67 G 1
Stinchar, River — 116-117 G 5
Stinear Nunataks 31 BC 7
Stinnett, TX 76-77 D 5
Štip 138-139 K 5
Stiperstones 116-117 HJ 8
Stirling [CDN] 66-67 G 1
Stirling [GB] 116-117 GH 4
Stirling City, CA 74-75 C 3
Stirling Range 182-183 C 6
Stites, ID 66-67 EF 2
Stjernøy 114-115 K 2
Stjørdalshalsen 114-115 D 6
Stobi 138-139 J 5
Stockbridge 116-117 K 9
Stockdale, TX 76-77 EF 8
Stockerau 124 H 4
Stockett, MT 66-67 H 2
Stockholm 114-115 GH 8
Stockholm, ME 72-73 MN 1
Stockholms län 114-115 GH 8
Stockport 116-117 JK 7
Stocks Seamount 98-99 N 7
Stockton 116-117 K 6
Stockton, CA 58-59 BC 4
Stockton, IL 70-71 EF 4
Stockton, KS 68-69 G 6
Stockton, MO 70-71 D 7
Stockton Island 70-71 E 2
Stockton Islands 52-53 OP 1
Stockton Plateau 76-77 C 7
Stockville, NE 68-69 FG 5
Stojba 154-155 Z 7
Stoke on Trent 116-117 JK 7
Stokkseyri 114-115 c 3
Stokksnes 114-115 f 2
Stolac 138-139 GH 4
Stolbcy 114-115 M 11
Stolbovoj, ostrov — 154-155 Za 3
Ston 138-139 G 4
Stone 116-117 J 8
Stone Canyon Reservoir 83 III b 1
Stone City, CO 68-69 D 6
Stonehaven 116-117 JK 4
Stonehenge [AUS] 182-183 H 4
Stonehenge [GB] 116-117 JK 9
Stonehouse 116-117 GH 5
Stone Mountains 80-81 F 2
Stoner, CO 74-75 J 4
Stonestown, San Francisco-, CA 83 I b 2
Stonewall 49 K 5
Stonewall, TX 76-77 E 7
Stonington 31 C 30
Stonington, ME 72-73 M 2-3
Stony Creek, VA 80-81 H 2
Stonyford, CA 74-75 B 3
Stony Point [CDN] 49 K 4-5
Stony Point [USA] 72-73 H 3
Stony River 46-47 EF 5
Stony River, AK 52-53 JK 6
Stony Tunguska = Podkamennaja Tunguska 154-155 R 5
Stopnica 124 K 3
Stóra Dímun 116-117 b 2
Stora Lulevatten 114-115 HJ 4
Stora Sjöfallet 114-115 H 4
Stora-Sjöfallets nationalpark 114-115 GH 4
Storavan 114-115 H 5
Stord 114-115 A 8
Store Bælt 114-115 D 10
Støren 114-115 CD 6
Storfjord 114-115 B 6
Storfjordbotn 114-115 LM 2
Storfjorden 114-115 k 6
Storlien 114-115 E 6
Storm Bay 182-183 J 8
Storm Lake, IA 70-71 C 4
Stormy Lake 50 CD 3
Stornorrfors 114-115 HJ 6
Stornoway 116-117 E 2
Storøya 114-115 n 4
Storoževsk 154-155 J 5
Storsjön 114-115 E 6
Storuman [S, lake] 114-115 G 5
Storuman [S, place] 114-115 G 5
Story City, IA 70-71 D 4
Stosch, Isla — 103 A 7
Stoughton 49 G 6
Stoughton, WI 70-71 F 4
Stour, River — 116-117 M 8-9
Stourbridge 116-117 J 8
Stourport on Severn 116-117 J 8
Stout Lake 50 B 1
Stowmarket 116-117 gh 6
Strabane 116-117 D 6
Straight Cliffs 74-75 H 4
Strakonice 124 FG 4
Stralsund 124 F 1
Strand 198 C 8
Stranda 114-115 c 1-2
Strangford Lough 116-117 F 6
Stranraer 116-117 FG 6
Strasbourg [CDN] 49 F 5
Strasbourg [F] 132-133 L 4
Strasburg, CO 68-69 D 6
Strasburg, ND 68-69 FG 2
Stratford, CA 74-75 D 4
Stratford, CT 72-73 K 4
Stratford, SD 68-69 GH 3
Stratford, TX 76-77 CD 4
Stratford, WI 70-71 EF 3
Stratford [CDN] 46-47 U 9
Stratford on Avon 116-117 K 8
Strathclyde 116-117 F 4-G 5
Strathcona Procincial Park 66-67 A 1
Strathcona Provincial Park 48 DE 5
Strathmore [CDN] 48 L 4
Strathmore [GB] 116-117 HJ 4
Strathnaver 48 FG 3
Strathroy 72-73 F 3
Strathy Point 116-117 G 2
Stratton, CO 68-69 E 6
Stratton, ME 72-73 L 2
Stratton, NE 68-69 F 5
Straubing 124 F 4
Straw, MT 68-69 AB 2
Strawberry Mountains 66-67 D 3
Strawberry Point, CA 83 I ab 1
Strawberry Point, IA 70-71 E 4
Strawberry River 66-67 H 5
Strawn, TX 76-77 E 6
Streachaill, Inis — 116-117 DE 5
Streaky Bay [AUS, bay] 182-183 F 6
Streaky Bay [AUS, place] 182-183 FG 6
Streator, IL 70-71 F 5
Street 116-117 J 9
Streeter, ND 68-69 G 2
Streetman, TX 76-77 FG 7
Streich Mound 182-183 D 6
Strelka-Čun'a 154-155 T 5
Strelna 142-143 G 2
Stresa 138-139 C 3
Stretford 116-117 J 7
Strevell, ID 66-67 G 4
Streymoy 116-117 a 1
Strickland River 174-175 M 8
Stringtown, OK 76-77 FG 5
Stroeder 103 D 6
Strofádes 138-139 J 7
Stroma 116-117 H 2
Strómboli 138-139 F 6
Stromeferry 116-117 F 3
Stromness 116-117 H 2
Strømø = Streymoy 116-117 a 1
Stromsburg, NE 68-69 H 5
Strömstad 114-115 D 8
Strömsund 114-115 F 6
Ströms Vattudal 114-115 F 5-6
Stroner, WY 68-69 D 3
Strong, AR 78-79 C 4
Strong City, KS 68-69 H 6
Stronsay 116-117 J 1
Stronsay Firth 116-117 J 1-2
Stroud 116-117 J 9
Stroud, OK 76-77 F 5
Stroudsburg, PA 72-73 J 4
Struer 114-115 C 9
Struma 138-139 K 5
Strumble Head 116-117 F 8
Strumica 138-139 K 5
Stryj 142-143 D 6
Strymón 138-139 K 5
Strzelno 124 HJ 2
Stuart, FL 80-81 c 3
Stuart, IA 70-71 C 5
Stuart, NE 68-69 G 4
Stuart, OK 76-77 FG 5
Stuart, VA 80-81 F 2
Stuart Island 46-47 D 5
Stuart Lake 46-47 M 7
Stuart Range 182-183 FG 5
Stubbenkammer 124 FG 1
Studenica 138-139 J 4
Stumpy Point, NC 80-81 J 3
Stung Treng 174-175 E 4
Stupino 142-143 G 4-5
Stura di Demonte 138-139 B 3
Sturge Island 31 C 17
Sturgeon Bay 49 JK 4
Sturgeon Bay, WI 70-71 G 3
Sturgeon Bay Canal 70-71 G 3
Sturgeon Falls [CDN, place] 72-73 FG 1
Sturgeon Falls [CDN, river] 50 L 2
Sturgeon Lake [CDN, Alberta] 48 J 2
Sturgeon Lake [CDN, Ontario] 50 D 3
Sturgeon Landing 49 H 3
Sturgeon River [CDN, Ontario] 72-73 F 1
Sturgeon River [CDN, Saskatchewan] 49 E 4
Sturgis, KY 70-71 G 7
Sturgis, MI 70-71 H 5
Sturgis, OK 76-77 C 4
Sturgis, SD 68-69 E 3
Sturminster Newton 116-117 J 10
Sturt, Mount — 182-183 H 5
Sturt Creek 182-183 E 3
Sturt Desert 182-183 H 5
Sturt Plain 182-183 F 3
Stutterheim 198 E 8
Stuttgart 124 D 4
Stuttgart, AR 78-79 D 3
Stykkisholm = Stykkishólmur 114-115 b 2
Stykkishólmur 114-115 b 2
Stylís 138-139 K 6
Styr' 142-143 E 5
Styria = Steiermark 124 G 5

Sūākin = Sawākin 194-195 M 5
Suan 170-171 F 3
Süanhua = Xuanhua 166-167 LM 3
Suanhwa = Xuanhua 166-167 LM 3
Suao 166-167 N 7
Su'ao = Suao 166-167 N 7
Šubarkuduk 154-155 K 8
Şūbāţ, As — 194-195 L 7
Subiaco 138-139 E 5
Sublett, ID 66-67 G 4
Sublette, KS 68-69 F 7
Subotica 138-139 HJ 2
Suca, An t- 116-117 C 7
Success 49 D 5
Suceava 138-139 LM 2
Suchaj nuur 166-167 GH 4
Suchana 154-155 W 4
Suchbaatar [Mongolia, administrative unit = 17] 166-167 L 2
Süchbaatar [Mongolia, place] 166-167 JK 1
Sucheng = Su Xian 166-167 M 5
Su-chia-t'un = Sujiatun 170-171 D 2
Su-ch'ien = Suqian 166-167 M 5
Suchiniči 142-143 FG 5
Suchona 154-155 G 6
Suchou = Xuzhou 166-167 M 5
Su-chou = Yibin 166-167 JK 6
Suchow = Xuzhou 166-167 M 5
Suchow = Yibin 166-167 JK 6
Suchumi 142-143 H 7
Suckling, Cape — 52-53 Q 7
Suck River = An tSuca 116-117 C 7
Sucre [BOL] 98-99 FG 8
Sucuaro 98-99 F 4
Sucunduri, Rio — 98-99 H 6
Sucuriú, Rio — 98-99 J 8
Sūd = As-Sudd 194-195 L 7
Sudan, TX 76-77 C 5
Sudan [landscape] 194-195 C-K 6
Sudan [Sudan, state] 194-195 J-L 6
Sudayr 160-161 EF 5
Sudbury 116-117 M 8
Sudbury [CDN] 46-47 U 8
Sudd, As — 194-195 L 7
Suddie 98-99 H 3
Súdhavík 114-115 b 1
Sudhur-Múla 114-115 f 2
Sudhuroy 116-117 ab 2
Sudhuroyarfjördhur 116-117 ab 2
Sudhur-Thingeyjar 114-115 ef 2
Sudirman, Pegunungan — 174-175 L 7
Sudong-ni = Changhang 170-171 F 4-5
Sudr = Rā's as-Sidr 199 C 3
Sudr, Wādī — = Wādī Sidr 199 C 3
Sue = Nahr Sūī 194-195 K 7
Sueca 132-133 G 9
Sueco, El — 86-87 GH 3
Suemez Island 52-53 w 9
Suez = As-Suways 194-195 L 3
Suez, Gulf of — = Khalīj as-Suways 194-195 L 3
Sūfeyān 142-143 J 8
Suffield 49 C 5
Suffolk 116-117 M 8
Suffolk, VA 80-81 H 2
Suflíon 138-139 LM 5
Şufu = Qāshqār 166-167 CD 4
Šuga 154-155 N 4
Sugar Island 70-71 H 2
Sugarloaf Mountain 72-73 LM 2
Suggi Lake 49 G 3
Sugiyasu 170-171 H 6
Sūhāj 194-195 L 3
Şuḩār 160-161 H 6
Suhelīpāḍ = Suheli Par 160-161 L 8
Suheli Par 160-161 L 8
Suhl 124 E 3
Su-hsien = Su Xian 166-167 M 5
Sūī, Nahr — 194-195 K 7
Suiá-Miçu, Rio — 98-99 M 10-11
Suichuan 166-167 L 6
Sui-chung = Suizhong 170-171 C 2
Suichwan = Suichuan 166-167 L 6
Suide 166-167 KL 4
Suifenhe 166-167 OP 3
Suihsien = Sui Xian [TJ, Hubei] 166-167 L 5
Suihua 166-167 O 2
Suihwa = Suihua 166-167 O 2
Suilai = Manaas 166-167 F 3
Súilighe, Loch — 116-117 D 5
Suir River = An tSiúir 116-117 D 8
Suiteh = Suide 166-167 KL 4
Suitland, MD 82 II b 2
Sui Xian [TJ, Hubei] 166-167 L 5
Suiyuan 166-167 K 4-L 3
Sui-yüan = Suiyuan 166-167 K 4-L 3
Suizhong 170-171 C 2
Šuja [SU, Ivanovo] 154-155 G 6
Sujiatun 170-171 D 2
Sukabumi 174-175 E 8
Sukadana 174-175 EF 7
Sukagawa 170-171 MN 4
Sukaraja 174-175 F 7
Sukch'ŏn 170-171 E 3
Sukhe Bator = Süchbaatar 166-167 JK 1
Sūki, As- 194-195 L 6
Sukkertoppen = Manîtsoq 46-47 Za 4
Sukkur = Sukkhur 160-161 KL 5
Sukses 198 C 6
Sukumo 170-171 J 6
Sukumo wan 170-171 J 6
Sul, Canal do — 98-99 K 4-5
Sula, MT 66-67 FG 3
Sula [Su, place] 142-143 K 2
Sula [SU, river] 142-143 F 6
Sula, Kepulauan — 174-175 HJ 7
Sulabesi, Pulau — 174-175 J 7
Sulaimān, Kohistān — 160-161 KL 4-5
Sulak 142-143 J 7
Sulan Cheer 166-167 K 3
Sula Sgeir 116-117 E 1
Sulatna Crossing, AK 52-53 JK 4
Sulatna River 52-53 K 4
Sulawesi 174-175 G 7-H 6
Sulawesi, Laut — 174-175 GH 6
Sulawesi Selatan = 21 ◁ 174-175 G 7
Sulawesi Tengah = 19 ◁ 174-175 H 6
Sulawesi Tenggara = 20 ◁ 174-175 H 7
Sulawesi Utara = 18 ◁ 174-175 H 6
Sulaymānīyah 160-161 EF 3
Sulaymīyah, As- 160-161 F 6
Sulayyil, As- 160-161 F 6
Şulb, Aş- 160-161 F 5
Sul'ca 142-143 J 3
Sule He 166-167 H 4
Sule Skerry 116-117 G 1
Sulet = Solta 138-139 G 4
Sulivan, IL 70-71 F 6
Sulima 194-195 B 7
Sulina 138-139 N 3
Sulina, Braţul — 138-139 N 3
Sulitjelma [N, mountain] 114-115 G 4
Sulitjelma [N, place] 114-115 FG 4
Šuljereckoje 142-143 F 3
Sullana 98-99 C 5
Sulligent, AL 78-79 E 4
Sullivan, IN 70-71 G 6
Sullivan, MO 70-71 E 6
Sullivan Bay 48 D 4
Sullivan Canyon 83 III a 1
Sullivan Island = Lambi Kyûn 174-175 C 4
Sullivan Lake 49 C 5
Šul'mak = Novabad 160-161 L 3
Sulmona 138-139 E 4-5
Su-lo Ho = Sule He 166-167 H 4
Sulphur, LA 78-79 C 5
Sulphur, NV 66-67 D 5
Sulphur, OK 76-77 F 5
Sulphurdale, UT 74-75 G 3
Sulphur River 76-77 GH 6
Sulphur Springs, TX 76-77 G 6
Sultanabad = Arāk 160-161 F 4
Sultānpur 160-161 N 5
Sulu Archipelago 174-175 H 5
Sulukna River 52-53 K 5
Sul'ukta 160-161 KL 3
Sulūq 194-195 J 2
Sulu Sea 174-175 GH 5
Sulusee 174-175 GH 5
Sulzberger Bay 31 B 21-22
Šumadija 138-139 J 3-4
Sumas, WA 66-67 BC 1
Sumatera = Sumatra 174-175 C 6-D 7
Sumatera Barat = 3 ◁ 174-175 D 7
Sumatera Selatan = 6 ◁ 174-175 D 7
Sumatera Tengah = Riau = 4 ◁ 174-175 D 6
Sumatera Utara = 2 ◁ 174-175 C 6
Sumatra 174-175 C 6-D 7
Sumatra, FL 78-79 G 5
Sumatra, MT 68-69 C 2
Sumaúma 98-99 G 6
Sumba 174-175 G 9
Sumba, Selat — 174-175 GH 8
Sumbawa 174-175 G 8
Sumbawa Besar 174-175 G 8
Sumbawanga 198 F 3
Sümber 166-167 K 2
Sumburgh Head 116-117 ef 4
Šumen 138-139 M 4
Šumerl'a 142-143 J 4
Sumgait 142-143 JK 7
Šumicha 154-155 L 6
Sumisu-jima 166-167 R 5
Sumisu zima = Sumisu-jima 166-167 R 5
Şummān, Aş- [Saudi Arabia ↑ Ar-Riyāḍ] 160-161 F 5
Şummān, Aş- [Saudi Arabia ↘ Ar-Riyāḍ] 160-161 F 6
Summer, Lake — 76-77 B 5
Summerfield, TX 76-77 C 5
Summer Island 70-71 G 3
Summer Lake 66-67 C 4
Summer Lake, OR 66-67 C 4
Summerland 66-67 CD 1
Summerside 50 E 4
Summertown, TN 78-79 F 3
Summerville, SC 80-81 FG 4
Summerville, WV 72-73 F 5
Summit 58-59 b 2
Summit, AK 52-53 N 5
Summit, CA 74-75 E 5
Summit, IL 83 II a 2
Summit, MS 78-79 D 5
Summit, OR 66-67 B 3
Summit, SD 68-69 H 3
Summit Lake [CDN] 48 FG 2
Summit Lake [USA] 52-53 P 5
Summit Lake Indian Reservation 66-67 D 5
Summit Mountain 74-75 E 3
Summit Peak 68-69 C 7
Sumner, IA 70-71 D 4
Sumner, MO 70-71 D 6
Sumner Strait 52-53 w 8
Sumoto 170-171 K 5
Šumperk 124 H 3-4
Sumprabum = Hsûmbārabûm 174-175 C 1
Sumpter, OR 66-67 DE 3
Sumrall, MS 78-79 E 5
Sumter, SC 58-59 KL 5
Sumy 142-143 FG 5
Sunagawa 170-171 b 2
Sunan 170-171 E 3
Sunburst, MT 66-67 H 1
Sunbury, OH 72-73 E 4
Sunbury, PA 72-73 H 4
Suncho Corral 103 D 3
Sunch'ŏn [North Korea] 170-171 E 3
Sunch'ŏn [ROK] 166-167 O 4-5
Sunchow = Guiping 166-167 KL 7
Suncook, NH 72-73 L 3
Sunda, Selat — 174-175 E 8
Sundance, WY 68-69 D 3
Sundar Ban = Sundarbans 160-161 OP 6
Sundarbans 160-161 OP 6
Sunda Trench 26-27 P 6
Sunday Islands = Raoul 178 J 5
Sunday Strait 182-183 D 3
Sundbyberg 114-115 G 8
Sunderbunds = Sundarbans 160-161 OP 6
Sunderland [CDN] 72-73 G 2
Sunderland [GB] 116-117 KL 6
Sundini 116-117 a 1
Sundown [AUS] 182-183 F 5
Sundown [CDN] 68-69 H 1
Sundre 48 K 4
Sundsvall 114-115 GH 6
Sungaidareh 174-175 D 7
Sungaipenuh 174-175 D 7
Sungari 166-167 N 2-O 3
Sungari Reservoir = Songhua Hu 166-167 O 3
Sung-chiang = Songjiang 166-167 N 5
Sungei Patani 174-175 CD 5
Sung hua Chiang = Songhua Jiang 166-167 N 2-O 3
Sŭngjibaegam 170-171 G 2
Sungkiang = Songjiang 166-167 N 5
Sungu 198 C 2
Sunhwa = Xunhua 166-167 J 4
Súnion, Atrōtḗrion — 138-139 KL 7
Sunke = Xunke 166-167 O 2
Sunnagyn, chrebet — 154-155 Y 6
Sunndalsøra 114-115 C 6
Sunniland, FL 80-81 c 3
Sunnūris = Sinnūris 199 B 3
Sunnyside, UT 74-75 H 3
Sunnyside, WA 66-67 CD 2
Sunnyvale, CA 74-75 B 4
Suno saki 170-171 M 5
Sunray, TX 76-77 D 4-5
Sunrise, AK 52-53 N 6
Sunrise, WY 68-69 D 4
Sun River 66-67 GH 2
Sunset, San Francisco-, CA 83 I b 2
Sunset House 48 J 2
Sunset Prairie 48 G 2
Sunstrum 50 C 2
Suntar 154-155 W 5
Suntar-Chajata, chrebet — 154-155 ab 5
Suntrana, AK 52-53 N 5
Suntsar 160-161 J 5
Sun Valley, ID 66-67 F 4
Sunyani 194-195 D 7
Suojarvi 154-155 E 5
Suojoki 142-143 F 3
Suokonmäki 114-115 KL 6
Suolahti 114-115 LM 6
Suomen selkä 114-115 K-N 6
Suomussalmi 114-115 N 5
Suō nada 170-171 H 6
Suonenjoki 114-115 M 6
Supai, AZ 74-75 G 4
Superb 49 D 5
Superior, AZ 74-75 H 6
Superior, MT 66-67 F 2
Superior, NE 68-69 GH 5
Superior, WI 58-59 H 2
Superior, WY 68-69 B 5
Superior, Lake — 58-59 HJ 2
Suphan Buri 174-175 CD 4
Süphan daği 142-143 H 8
Supiori, Pulau — 174-175 KL 7
Sup'ung-chŏsuji 170-171 E 2
Supung Hu 166-167 NO 3
Šupunskij, mys — 154-155 f 7
Sūq Ahrās 194-195 F 1
Suqian 166-167 M 5
Suquţrā' 160-161 G 8
Şūr, RL 142-143 FG 9
Şūr [Oman] 160-161 H 6
Sur, Point — 74-75 BC 4
Sura, Raas — 194-195 b 1
Šurab 160-161 L 2
Surabaia = Surabaya 174-175 F 8
Surabaya 174-175 F 8
Surakarta 174-175 F 8
Surat [AUS] 182-183 J 5
Surat [IND] 160-161 L 6
Surate = Surat 160-161 L 6
Surat Thani 174-175 CD 5
Surf, CA 74-75 C 5
Surf Inlet 48 C 3
Surgut [SU, Chanty-Mansijskij NO] 154-155 N 5
Surgut [SU, Kujbyšev] 154-155 J 7
Surguticha 154-155 PQ 5
Surigao 174-175 J 5
Surin 174-175 D 4
Suriname [SME, administrative unit] 98-99 L 2
Suriname [SME, state] 98-99 HJ 4
Suring, WI 70-71 F 3
Surnadalsøra 114-115 C 6
Surprêsa 98-99 F 10
Surprise, Lac de la — 50 O 2
Surprise Valley 66-67 CD 5
Surrey 116-117 L 9
Surrey, ND 68-69 F 1
Surt 194-195 H 2
Surt, As- 194-195 H 2-3
Surt, Khalīj as- 194-195 H 2
Surtsey 114-115 c 3
Surucucus, Serra dos — 98-99 G 3
Suruga wan 170-171 M 5
Surulangun 174-175 D 7
Surumú, Rio — 98-99 H 2-3
Suryškary 154-155 M 4
Susa [I] 138-139 B 3
Susa [J] 170-171 H 5

Tanana River 46-47 G 5
Tân Âp 174-175 E 3
Tana River 52-53 Q 6
Tànaro 138-139 B 3
Ţanburah 194-195 K 7
Tanchavur = Thanjāvar
160-161 MN 8
Tanchoj 154-155 TU 7
Tanch'ŏn 170-171 G 2
Tanchow = Dan Xian 166-167 K 8
Tancítaro, Pico de — 58-59 F 8
Tandag 174-175 J 5
Tandaho = Tendaho 194-195 N 6
Ţăndărei 138-139 M 3
Tanderagee 116-117 E 6
Tandil 103 E 5
Tanega-shima 166-167 P 5
Tanega sima = Tanega-shima
166-167 P 5
Tanew 124 L 3
Tanezrouft = Tānīzruft 194-195 DE 4
Tanga 198 G 3
Tangail = Ţangāyal 160-161 O 6
Tanga Islands 174-175 h 5
Tanganyika, Lake — 198 E 2-F 3
Tangar = Thangkar 166-167 J 4
Tangará 103 F 3
Tangāyal 160-161 O 6
T'ang-chan = Tangshan
166-167 M 4
Tanger = Ţanjah 194-195 C 1
Tanggela Youmu Hu = Thangra
Yumtsho 166-167 EF 5
Tanggu 166-167 M 4
Tangier 51 E 5
Tangiers = Ţanjah 194-195 C 1
Tangier Sound 72-73 HJ 5
Tangjin 170-171 F 4
Tang La [TJ, Himalaya pass]
166-167 F 6
Tang La [TJ, Tanglha] 166-167 G 5
Tangla = Tanglha 166-167 FG 5
Tanglha 166-167 FG 5
Tangshan 166-167 M 4
Tangshancheng 170-171 DE 2
Tanguj 154-155 T 6
Tangyuan 166-167 O 2
Tanhsien = Dan Xian 166-167 K 8
Tanimbar, Kepulauan — 174-175 K 8
Taninthāri 174-175 C 4
Taninthāri Taing 174-175 C 3-4
Tānīzruft 194-195 DE 4
Ţanjah 194-195 C 1
Tanjay 174-175 H 5
Tanjong Malim 174-175 D 6
Tanjor = Thanjāvar 160-161 MN 8
Tanjung 174-175 G 7
Tanjungbalai 174-175 CD 6
Tanjungkarang 174-175 DE 8
Tanjungkarang-Telukbetung
174-175 DE 8
Tanjungpandan 174-175 E 7
Tanjungpinang 174-175 DE 6
Tanjungpura 174-175 C 6
Tanjungredeb 174-175 G 6
Tankersly, TX 76-77 D 7
Tanlovo 154-155 NO 4
Tännäs 114-115 E 6
Tannin 70-71 E 1
Tannu-Ola 154-155 R 7
Tannu Tuva = Tuva Autonomous
Soviet Socialist Republic
154-155 RS 7
Tano 194-195 D 7
Tanout 194-195 F 6
Tanque, AZ 74-75 J 6
Tanque Alvarez 76-77 C 9
Tanshui 166-167 N 6
Tansīft, Wad — 194-195 C 2
Ţanţā 194-195 KL 2
Tantallon 49 GH 5
Tantoyuca 86-87 LM 7
Tanu 48 B 3
Tanunak, AK 52-53 E 6
Tanyang 170-171 G 4
Tanzania 198 FG 3
Tanzilla River 52-53 W 7
Taoan 166-167 N 2
Tao'an = Baicheng 166-167 N 2
T'ao-chou = Lintan 166-167 J 5
Taormina 138-139 F 7
Taos, NM 58-59 E 4
Taoudenni 194-195 D 4
Taourirt = Tāwrīrt 194-195 D 2
Tapa 142-143 E 4
Tapachula 58-59 H 9
Tapajós, Rio — 98-99 H 5
Tapaktuan 174-175 C 6
Tapanahony 98-99 L 3
Tapanatepec 86-87 NO 9
Tapara, Ilha Grande do 98-99 L 6
Tapará, Serra do 98-99 M 6
Ta-pa Shan = Daba Shan
166-167 KL 5
Tapat, Pulau — 174-175 J 7
Tapauá 98-99 FG 6
Tapauá, Rio — 98-99 F 6
Taperoá [BR, Bahia] 98-99 M 7
Tapeta = Tappita 194-195 C 7
Tāpī = Tāpti 160-161 M 6
Ta-pieh Shan = Dabie Shan
166-167 M 5
Tapini 174-175 N 8
Tapirapé, Serra do — 98-99 N 10
Tapirapecó, Sierra — 98-99 FG 4
Tapita = Tappita 194-195 C 7
Tappahannock, VA 72-73 H 5-6
Tappi-saki 170-171 MN 2
Tappita 194-195 C 7
Tāpti 160-161 M 6
Tapuaenuku 182-183 O 8
Ta-pu-hsün Hu = Dabas nuur
166-167 H 4
Tapuruquara 98-99 FG 5
Taquari Novo, Rio — 98-99 H 8
Tara [AUS] 182-183 K 5
Tara [SU, place] 154-155 N 6
Tara [SU, river] 154-155 O 6
Tara [YU] 138-139 H 4
Tara = Teamhair Breagh
116-117 E 7
Tarabillas, Laguna — 76-77 B 7
Tarabuco 98-99 FG 8
Ţarābulus 194-195 GH 2
Ţarābulus al-Gharb 194-195 G 2
Ţarābulus ash-Shām 160-161 CD 4
Tarahumar, Altos de — 86-87 G 4-5
Tarahumara, Sierra — 58-59 E 6
Tarāī = Terāi 160-161 NO 5
Taraika Bay = zaliv Terpenija
154-155 b 8
Tarakan 174-175 G 6
Taram Darya = Tarim darya
166-167 E 3
Taran, mys — 124 JK 1
Taransay 116-117 D 3
Tàranto 138-139 G 5
Tàranto, Golfo di — 138-139 G 5
Tarapoto 98-99 D 6
Taraquá 98-99 F 4
Tarare 132-133 K 6
Tarascon 132-133 K 7
Tarasovo 142-143 J 2
Tarat, Ouèd — = Wādī Tarāt
194-195 F 3
Tarāt, Wādī — 194-195 F 3
Tarauacá 98-99 E 6
Tarauacá, Rio — 98-99 E 6
Tarawa 178 H 2
Tarazona 132-133 G 8
Tarbagataij, chrebet — 154-155 PQ 8
Tarbagataj 166-167 EF 2
Tarbat Ness 116-117 H 3
Tarbert [GB, Isle of Lewis]
116-117 E 3
Tarbert [GB, Kintyre] 116-117 F 5
Tarbes 132-133 H 7
Tarboro, NC 80-81 H 3
Tarcoola 182-183 FG 6
Tardoire 132-133 H 6
Tardoki-Jani, gora — 154-155 a 8
Taree 182-183 K 6
Tareja 154-155 R 3
Tärendö 114-115 JK 4
Tareraimbu, Cachoeira — 98-99 J 6
Ţarfā', Wādī aţ- 199 B 3
Ţarfāyah [MA, place] 194-195 B 3
Tarfāyah, Rā's — 194-195 B 3
Targhee Pass 66-67 H 3
Târgovište 138-139 M 4
Tarhit = Tāghīt 194-195 D 2
Tarhūnah 194-195 G 2
Tarian Ganga = Dariganga
166-167 L 2
Tarīf 160-161 G 6
Tarifa 132-133 E 10
Tarifa, Punta de — 132-133 DE 11
Tarija [BOL, place] 98-99 G 9
Tarim 160-161 F 7
Tarim darya 166-167 E 3
Tarkio, MO 70-71 C 5
Tarkio, MT 66-67 F 2
Tarkio River 70-71 C 5
Tarko-Sale 154-155 O 5
Tarkwa 194-195 D 7
Tarlac 174-175 H 3
Tarn 132-133 H 7
Tärna 114-115 F 5
Tarnów 124 K 3
Ţārom 160-161 GH 5
Taroom 182-183 JK 5
Tāroūdânt = Tārūdānt 194-195 C 2
Tarpley, TX 76-77 E 8
Tarpon Springs, FL 80-81 b 2
Tarquinia 138-139 D 4
Tarragona 132-133 H 8
Tarrakoski 114-115 J 3
Tar River 80-81 H 3
Tarso Emissi = Kégueur Terbi
194-195 H 4
Tarsus 142-143 F 8
Tartagal [RA, Salta] 103 D 2
Tartas [SU] 154-155 O 6
Tartu 142-143 E 4
Ţarţūs 160-161 D 4
Tārūdānt 194-195 C 2
Tarumizu 170-171 H 7
Tarutung 174-175 C 6
Tarvisio 138-139 E 2
Tašauz 154-155 K 9
Tasāwah 194-195 G 3
Taschereau 50 M 2
Tascosa, TX 76-77 C 5
Tasejevo 154-155 RS 6
Taseko River 48 F 4
Tashichhö Dsong = Thimbu
160-161 OP 5
Tashigong = Zhaxigang
166-167 DE 5
Tashi Gonpa 166-167 G 5
Ta-shih-ch'iao = Dashiqiao
170-171 D 2
Tashijong Dsong 160-161 P 5
Tashilhumpo = Zhaxilhünbo
166-167 F 6
Ţashk, Daryācheh — 160-161 GH 5
Tashkent = Taškent 154-155 M 9
Tashota 50 F 2
Tash Qurghan 166-167 D 4
Tasikmalaja 174-175 E 8
Tāsīlī Wān Ahjār 194-195 F 3
Tasīlī Wān al-Hajjār 194-195 E 5-F 4
Taškent 154-155 M 9
Taš-Kumyr 160-161 L 2
Tas-Kystabyt 154-155 bc 5
Tasman Bay 182-183 O 8
Tasmania 182-183 HJ 8
Tasman Land 182-183 D 3-E 2
Tasman Rise 26-27 R 8
Tasman Sea 182-183 K-N 7
Tassili n'Ajjer = Tāsīlī Wān Ahjār
194-195 F 3
Taštagol 154-155 Q 7
Taštyp 154-155 Q 7
Tasu 48 B 3
Tata 124 J 5
Tatabánya 124 HJ 5
Tatar Autonomous Soviet Socialist
Republic = 6 ◁ 154-155 J 6
Tatarsk 154-155 NO 6
Tatarskaja Avtonomnaja Sovetskaja
Socialističeskaja Respublika =
Tatar Autonomous Soviet Socialist
Republic 154-155 J 6
Tatar Strait 154-155 b 7-a 8
Taţāwīn 194-195 G 2
Tateoka = Murayama 170-171 N 3
Tateyama 170-171 M 5
Tateyamahōjō = Tateyama
170-171 M 5
Tathlina Lake 46-47 N 5
Tathlīth 160-161 E 7
Tathlīth, Wādī — 160-161 E 6-7
Tatitlek, AK 52-53 O 6
Tatla Lake 48 E 4
Tatlawiksuk River 52-53 K 5-6
Tatlayoko Lake 48 E 4
Tatlīt = Tathlīth 160-161 E 7
Tatlmain Lake 52-53 TU 5
Tatlow, Mount — 48 F 4
Tatman Mountain 68-69 B 3
Tatnam, Cape — 46-47 ST 6
Tatonduk River 52-53 R 4
Ta-t'ong = Datong 166-167 L 3
Tatra = Tatry 124 JK 4
Tatran 166-167 EF 4
Tatry 124 JK 4
Tatsaitan = Tagalgan 166-167 H 4
Tatshenshini River 52-53 T 6-7
Tatsuno 170-171 K 5
Tatta = Ţhaţţha 160-161 K 6
Tatuk Lake 48 E 3
Tatum, NM 76-77 C 6
Tatum, TX 76-77 G 6
Tatums, OK 76-77 F 5
Tatung = Datong [TJ, Shanxi]
166-167 L 3
Ta-t'ung Ho = Datong He
166-167 J 4
Tatvan 142-143 H 8
Tau 114-115 AB 8
Tauá 98-99 L 6
Taubaté 98-99 KL 9
Tauberbischofsheim 124 DE 4
Tauini, Rio — 98-99 J 4
Taujskaja guba 154-155 cd 6
Taukum 154-155 O 9
Taumarunui 182-183 OP 7
Taumaturgo 98-99 E 6
Taum Sauk Mountain 70-71 E 7
Taungdwingyī 174-175 BC 2-3
Taunggyī 174-175 C 2
Taungngū 174-175 C 3
Taunton 116-117 HJ 9-10
Taunton, MA 72-73 L 4
Taunus 124 D 3
Taupo 182-183 P 7
Taupo, Lake — 182-183 P 7
Tauragė 142-143 D 4
Tauranga 182-183 P 7
Taureau, Lac — 72-73 K 1
Tauredu, Lac — 50 OP 3
Taurirt = Tāwrīrt 194-195 D 2
Taurovo 154-155 N 6
Taurus Mountains 160-161 C 3
Taushqan Darya = Kök shal
166-167 D 3
Tauz 142-143 J 7
Tavālesh, Kūhha-ye — 142-143 J 8
Tavan Bogd uul 166-167 F 2
Tavares, FL 80-81 c 2
Tavastehus = Hämeenlinna
114-115 L 7
Tavda [SU, place] 154-155 M 6
Tavda [SU, river] 154-155 L 6
Taveta 198 G 2
Taveuni 174-175 b 2
Tavira 132-133 D 10
Tavistock 116-117 G 10
Tavolara 138-139 CD 5
Tavoliere 138-139 F 5
Tavoy = Htāwei 174-175 C 4
Tavoy Island = Mali Kyûn
174-175 C 4
Tavua 174-175 a 2
Taw, River — 116-117 H 9-10
Ta-wa = Dawa 170-171 D 2
Ta-wang-chia Tao = Dawangjia Dao
170-171 D 3
Tawas City, MI 70-71 J 3
Tawau 174-175 G 6
Ţawīl, Bi'r — 194-195 L 4
Ţawīlah, Juzur — 199 CD 4
Tawile Island = Juzur Ţawīlah
199 CD 4
Tawi-tawi Island 174-175 GH 5
Ţawkar 194-195 M 5
Tāwrīrt 194-195 D 2
Ţāwurğā, Sabhat — 194-195 H 2
Tawzar 194-195 F 2
Taxco de Alarcón 58-59 FG 8
Tay, Firth of — 116-117 HJ 4
Tay, Loch — 116-117 G 4
Tay, River — 116-117 H 4
Tayabamba 98-99 D 6
Ta-yang Ho = Dayang He
170-171 D 2
Tayeegle 194-195 ab 3
Taÿgetos 138-139 K 7
Tayishan = Guanyun 166-167 MN 5
Taylor 48 G 1
Taylor, AK 52-53 E 4
Taylor, AR 78-79 C 4
Taylor, NE 68-69 G 5
Taylor, TX 76-77 F 7
Taylor, Mount — 76-77 A 5
Taylor Mountains 52-53 J 6
Taylor Ridge 78-79 G 3
Taylor River 48 C 1
Taylor Springs, NM 76-77 BC 4
Taylorsville, KY 70-71 H 6
Taylorsville, MS 78-79 E 5
Taylorsville, NC 80-81 F 2-3
Taylorville, IL 70-71 F 6
Taymā' 160-161 D 5
Tây Ninh 174-175 E 4
Tayoltita 86-87 GH 5
Tayport 116-117 J 4
Ţayr, Jabal aţ- 160-161 E 7
Tayside 116-117 GH 4
Taytay 174-175 GH 4
Ta-yü = Dayu 166-167 L 6
Tayung = Dayong 166-167 L 6
Taz 154-155 OP 4
Tazādīt 194-195 B 4
Tāzāh 194-195 D 2
Tazarbū 194-195 J 3
Tāzārīn 194-195 CD 2
Tazarine = Tāzārīn 194-195 CD 2
Tazawako 170-171 N 3
Tázerbó = Tazarbū 194-195 J 3
Tazewell, TN 80-81 E 2
Tazewell, VA 80-81 F 2
Tazimina Lakes 52-53 KL 6-7
Tazlina Lake 52-53 OP 6
Tazovskaja guba 154-155 NO 4
Tazovskij 154-155 OP 4
Tazovskij poluostrov 154-155 NO 4
Tbilisi 142-143 H 7
Tchad, Lac — 194-195 G 6
Tch'ang-cha = Changsha
166-167 L 6
Tchang-kia-k'eou = Zhangjiakou
166-167 L 3
Tch'ang-tch'ouen = Changchun
166-167 NO 3
Tchan-kiang = Zhanjiang
166-167 L 7
Tch'eng-tö = Chengde 166-167 M 3
Tch'eng-tou = Chengdu 166-167 J 5
Tchentlo Lake 48 E 2
Tchertchen = Chārchān 166-167 F 4
Tchibanga 198 B 2
Tchien 194-195 C 7
Tchin Tabaraden 194-195 F 5
Tchong King = Chongqing
166-167 K 6
Tchula, MS 78-79 D 4
Tczew 124 J 1
Tea, Rio — [BR] 98-99 EF 5
Teacapan 86-87 GH 6
Teague, TX 76-77 F 7
Teallach, An — 116-117 F 3
Teamhair Breagh 116-117 E 7
Teampall Mór 116-117 D 8
Te Anau, Lake — 182-183 N 9
Teaneck, NJ 82 III bc 1
Teano 138-139 F 5
Teapa 86-87 O 9
Teapot Dome 68-69 CD 4
Tea Tree Well 182-183 F 4
Te Awamutu 182-183 OP 7
Tebas = Thêbai [ET] 194-195 L 3
Tebessa = Tibissah 194-195 F 1
Tebingtinggi [RI, Sumatera Selatan]
174-175 D 7
Tebingtinggi [RI, Sumatera Utara]
174-175 CD 6
Tebingtinggi, Pulau — 174-175 D 6
Tebulosmta, gora — 142-143 J 7
Tecate 58-59 C 5
Techis 166-167 E 3
Tecka 103 B 6
Teckla, WY 68-69 D 4
Tecolote, NM 76-77 B 5-6
Tecomán 58-59 F 8
Tecoripa 86-87 EF 3
Tecozautla 86-87 L 7
Tecuala 58-59 E 7
Tecuci 138-139 M 3
Tecumseh, MI 70-71 HJ 4
Tecumseh, NE 70-71 BC 5
Tedžen 160-161 J 3
Teeswater 72-73 F 2-3
Tefé 98-99 G 5
Tefé, Lago de 98-99 F 6
Tefé, Rio — 98-99 F 5
Tefedest = Tafdasat 194-195 F 3-4
Tegal 174-175 E 8
Tégerhi = Tajarhī 194-195 G 4
Tegernsee 124 EF 5
Teguantepeque = Santo Domingo
Tehuantepec 58-59 G 8
Tegucigalpa 58-59 J 9
Tegul'det 154-155 Q 6
Tehachapi, CA 74-75 D 5
Tehachapi Mountains 74-75 D 5
Tehachapi Pass 74-75 D 5
Tehama, CA 66-67 B 5
Tehek Lake 46-47 R 4
Teheran = Tehrān 160-161 G 3
Tehrān 160-161 G 3
Tehuacán 58-59 G 8
Tehuantepec, Golfo de —
58-59 GH 8
Tehuantepec, Istmo de —
58-59 GH 8
Tehuantepec, Santo Domingo —
58-59 G 8
Teide, Pico de — 194-195 A 3
Teignmouth 116-117 H 10
Teixeira da Silva 198 C 4
Tejkovo 142-143 H 4
Tejo 132-133 C 9
Tejon Pass 58-59 C 4-5
Tekamah, NE 68-69 H 5
Te Kao 182-183 O 6
Tekax 86-87 Q 7
Tekeli 154-155 O 9
Tekirdağ 160-161 B 2
Tekoa, WA 66-67 E 2
Tekouiât, Ouèd — = Wādī Tākwayat
194-195 E 4
Te Kuiti 182-183 OP 7
Tel 160-161 N 6
Tela 58-59 J 8
Tēla = Tel 160-161 N 6
Telanaipura = Jambi 174-175 D 7
Telaquana, Lake — 52-53 L 6
Telavi 142-143 J 7
Telefomin 174-175 M 8
Telegraph Creek 46-47 K 6
Telegraph Range 48 F 3
Tel el-'Amarna = Tall al-'Amārinah
199 B 4
Telemark 114-115 BC 8
Telemsès = Tlemcès 194-195 EF 5
Teleno, El — 132-133 D 7
Telescope Peak 74-75 E 4
Teles Pires, Rio — 98-99 H 6
Telford 116-117 J 8
Telida, AK 52-53 L 5
Telig 194-195 D 4
Telijn nuur 166-167 F 2
Télimélé 194-195 B 6
Teljō, Jebel — = Jabal Talju
194-195 K 6
Telkwa 48 D 2
Tell, TX 76-77 D 5
Tell Atlas 194-195 D 2-E 1
Tell City, IN 70-71 G 6-7
Tell el-Amarna = Tall al-'Amārinah
199 B 4
Teller, AK 46-47 CD 4
Tellico Plains, TN 78-79 G 3
Telluride, CO 68-69 C 7
Telocaset, OR 66-67 E 3
Telok Anson 174-175 CD 6
Telok Betong = Tanjungkarang-
Telukbetung 174-175 DE 8
Teloloapan 58-59 FG 8
Tēlos 138-139 M 7
Tel'posiz, gora — 154-155 K 5
Telsen 103 C 6
Telšiai 142-143 D 4
Teluk Anson = Telok Anson
174-175 CD 6
Telukbetung = Tanjungkarang
174-175 DE 8
Telukdalam 174-175 C 6
Tema 194-195 DE 7
Temassinine = Burj 'Umar Idrīs
194-195 EF 3
Temax 86-87 Q 7
Temazcal, El — 86-87 LM 5
Tembellaga = Timboulaga
194-195 F 5
Tembenči 154-155 S 4
Tembilahan 174-175 D 7
Temblor Range 74-75 D 5
Temecula, CA 74-75 E 6
Temescal Canyon 83 III a 1
Temesvár = Timişoara 138-139 J 3
Téminos, Laguna de — 58-59 H 8
Temir 154-155 K 8
Temirtau [SU, Kazachskaja SSR]
154-155 N 7-8
Temirtau [SU, Rossijskaja SFSR]
154-155 Q 7
Témiscamie, Lac — 50 PQ 1
Témiscamie, Rivière — 50 P 1
Témiscaming 46-47 V 8
Temiscouata, Lac — 51 BC 4
Temnikov 154-155 G 7
Temora 182-183 J 6
Temosachic 86-87 G 3
Témpē 138-139 K 6
Tempe, AZ 74-75 GH 6
Tempe, Danau — 174-175 GH 7
Tèmpio Pausània 138-139 C 5
Temple, OK 76-77 E 5
Temple, TX 58-59 G 5
Temple Bay 182-183 H 2
Temple City, CA 83 III d 1
Temple Hills, MD 82 II b 2
Templemore = Teampall Mór
116-117 D 8
Templeton, IN 70-71 G 5
Tempoal de Sánchez 86-87 KL 6-7
Temporal, Cachoeira — 98-99 J 7
Temuco 103 B 5
Tena [CO] 98-99 D 5
Tenabo 86-87 P 7-8
Tenabo, NV 66-67 E 5
Tenabo, Mount — 66-67 E 5
Tenafly, NJ 82 III c 1
Tenaha, TX 76-77 G 7
Tenakee Springs, AK 52-53 U 8
Tenāli 160-161 N 7
Tenancingo 86-87 L 8
Tenasserim = Taninthāri
174-175 C 4
Tenasserim = Taninthāri Taing
174-175 C 3-4
Tenbury 116-117 J 8
Tenby 116-117 G 9
Tenda, Colle di — 138-139 B 3
Tendaho 194-195 N 6
Ten Degree Channel 160-161 P 8
Tendūf 194-195 C 3
Tendürek dağı 142-143 H 8
Ténéré 194-195 FG 4-5
Tenerife [E] 194-195 A 3
Ténès = Tanas 194-195 E 1
Tenessi = Tennessee River 78-79 F 3
Tenga, Kepulauan — 174-175 G 8
Tengchong 166-167 H 6-7
Tengchung = Tengchong
166-167 H 6-7
Tenggarong 174-175 G 7
Tenggeli Hai = Nam Tsho
166-167 G 5
Tenghsien = Teng Xian
166-167 M 4
Tengiz, ozero — 154-155 M 7
Tengrèla = Tingréla 194-195 C 6
Tengri Nuur = Nam Tsho
166-167 G 5
Teng Xian 166-167 M 4
Teniente, El — 103 BC 4
Teniente Matienzo 31 C 30-31
Tenimber Islands = Kepulauan
Tanimbar 174-175 K 8
Tenino, WA 66-67 B 2
Tenke 198 E 4
Tenkiller Ferry Lake 76-77 G 5
Tenkodogo 194-195 DE 6
Tenleytown, Washington-, DC 82 II a 1
Tennant, CA 66-67 C 5
Tennant Creek 182-183 FG 3
Tennessee 58-59 JK 4
Tennessee River 58-59 J 4-5
Tennille, GA 80-81 E 4
Tēnos 138-139 L 7
Tenryū gawa 170-171 L 5
Tensīft, Ouèd — = Wad Tansīft
194-195 C 2
Ten Sleep 66-67 K 3-4
Ten Sleep, WY 68-69 C 3-4
Tenstrike, MN 70-71 C 2
Tenterden 116-117 g 7
Tenterfield 182-183 K 5
Ten Thousand Islands 58-59 K 6
Tenyueh = Tengchong
166-167 H 6-7
Teocaltiche 58-59 F 7
Teófilo Otoni 98-99 L 8
Teotepec, Cerro — 58-59 FG 8
Teotihuacán 86-87 L 8
Teotitlán del Camino 86-87 M 8
Tepa 174-175 J 8
Tepasto 114-115 L 3-4
Tepatitlán de Morelos 58-59 F 7
Tepeji del Rio 86-87 L 8
Tepequem, Sierra — 98-99 GH 3
Tepic 58-59 EF 7
Teplice 124 E 3
Teques, Los — 98-99 F 2
Tequila 86-87 J 7
Ter 132-133 J 8
Tera [E] 132-133 D 8
Téra [RN] 194-195 E 6
Teradomari 170-171 M 4
Terai 160-161 NO 5
Terangan = Pulau Trangan
174-175 K 8
Terceira 188-189 E 5
Tercio, CO 68-69 D 7
Terek 142-143 H 7
Terence 49 HJ 6

Terence 275

Tochigi 170-171 MN 4
Tochio 170-171 M 4
Toch'o-do 170-171 E 5
Toco [RCH] 103 C 2
Tocopilla 103 B 2
Tocorpuri, Cerro de — 98-99 F 9
Tocqueville = Ra's al-Wād 194-195 E 1
Tocra = Tūkrah 194-195 HJ 2
Tocumen, Río — 58-59 c 2
Tocuyo, El — 98-99 F 3
Todatonten Lake 52-53 L 3
Todeli 174-175 H 7
Tödi [CH] 124 D 5
Todi [I] 138-139 E 4
Todmorden [AUS] 182-183 FG 5
Todmorden [GB] 116-117 JK 7
Todness 98-99 H 3
To-dong 170-171 H 4
Todo-saki 170-171 O 3
Todos os Santos, Baía de — 98-99 M 7
Todos Santos [BOL, Cochabamba] 98-99 F 8
Todos Santos [MEX] 58-59 D 7
Todos Santos, Bahía de — 86-87 B 2
Toejo 170-171 FG 3
Tofino 48 E 5
Tofte, MN 70-71 E 2
Tofty, AK 52-53 M 4
Tofua 178 J 4
Togi 170-171 L 4
Togiak, AK 52-53 GH 7
Togiak Bay 52-53 G 7
Togiak Lake 52-53 GH 7
Togiak River 52-53 GH 7
Togian, Kepulauan — 174-175 H 7
Togliatti 154-155 H 7
Togo 194-195 E 7
Togochale = Togotyalē 194-195 N 7
Togotyalē 194-195 N 7
Togtoh = Tugt 166-167 L 3-4
Togye-dong 170-171 G 4
Tōgyu-sen 170-171 FG 5
Tohatchi, NM 74-75 J 5
Tohoku 170-171 N 2-4
Toiama = Toyama 166-167 Q 4
Toijala 114-115 K 7
Toili 174-175 H 7
Toi-misaki 170-171 H 7
Toirc, Inis — 116-117 A 7
Toivola, MI 70-71 F 2
Toiyabe Range 74-75 E 3
Tokachi-dake 170-171 c 2
Tokachi-gawa 170-171 c 2
Tokai 170-171 LM 5
Tokaj 124 K 4
Tōkamachi 170-171 M 4
Ṭōkar = Ṭawkar 194-195 M 5
Tokara-kaikyō 166-167 O 5-P 6
Tokara-rettō 166-167 OP 6
Tokat 160-161 D 2
Tŏkchŏk-kundo 170-171 EF 4
Tŏkch'ŏn 170-171 F 3
Tokelau Islands 34-35 J 5
Toki 170-171 L 5
Tokio, TX 76-77 C 6
Tokio = Tōkyō 166-167 QR 4
Tokitsu = Toki 170-171 L 5
Tok Junction, AK 52-53 Q 5
Tokko 154-155 WX 6
Tok-kol 170-171 GH 2
Toklat, AK 52-53 MN 4
Tokmak [SU, Kirgizskaja SSR] 154-155 O 9
Tokolimbu 174-175 H 7
Tokoro 170-171 cd 1
Tokosun = Toksun 166-167 F 3
Tokra = Tūkrah 194-195 HJ 2
Toksun 166-167 F 3
Toktat River 52-53 MN 4
Tokuno-shima 166-167 O 6
Tokuno sima = Tokuno-shima 166-167 O 6
Tokushima 166-167 PQ 5
Tokusima = Tokushima 166-167 PQ 5
Tokuyama 170-171 HJ 5
Tōkyō 166-167 QR 4
Tōkyō wan 170-171 M 5
Tola, La — 98-99 D 4
Tolageak, AK 52-53 FG 1-2
Tolar, NM 76-77 C 5
Tolar Grande 103 C 2
Tolbuhin 138-139 MN 4
Tole 88-89 F 10
Toledo, OH 58-59 K 3
Toledo, OR 66-67 B 3
Toledo [E] 132-133 EF 9
Toledo [PE] 98-99 B 7
Toledo, Montes de — 132-133 E 9
Toledo Bend Reservoir 76-77 GH 7
Tolentino [MEX] 86-87 K 6
Toliara = Tūljā 194-195 EF 2
Toliary 198 H 6
Tolitoli 174-175 H 6
Toll'a, zaliv — 154-155 ST 2
Tolleson, AZ 74-75 G 6
Tolley, ND 68-69 EF 1
Tolloche 103 D 3
Tolo, Teluk — 174-175 H 7
Tolob 116-117 e 4
Tolono, IL 70-71 FG 6
Tolosa 132-133 FG 7
Tolovana, AK 52-53 N 4
Tolovana River 52-53 N 4
Tolox, Sierra de — 132-133 E 10
Tolsan-do 170-171 FG 5
Tolstoj, mys — 154-155 e 6
Toltén 103 B 5
Toluca, IL 70-71 F 5
Toluca, Nevado de — 58-59 FG 8
Toluca de Lerdo 58-59 FG 8
To-lun = Doloon Nuur 166-167 LM 3
Toma, La — 103 C 4
Tomah, WI 70-71 E 3-4
Tomahawk, WI 70-71 F 3
Tomakomai 166-167 R 3
Tomamae 170-171 b 1
Tomaniive 174-175 a 2
Tomar [BR] 98-99 G 5
Tomar [P] 132-133 C 9
Tomaszów Lubelski 124 L 3
Tomaszów Mazowiecki 124 K 3
Tomatlán 86-87 H 8
Tombador, Serra do — [BR, Mato Grosso] 98-99 H 7
Tomball, TX 76-77 G 7
Tombē 194-195 L 7
Tombetsu, Hama- 170-171 c 1
Tombetsu, Shō- 170-171 c 1
Tombigbee River 58-59 J 5
Tomboco 198 B 3
Tombouctou 194-195 D 5
Tombstone, AZ 74-75 HJ 7
Tomé 103 B 5
Tomé-Açu 98-99 OP 6
Tomelilla 114-115 EF 10
Tomelloso 132-133 F 9
Tomiko 72-73 G 1
Tomini 174-175 H 6
Tomini, Teluk — 174-175 H 7
Tomintoul 116-117 H 3
Tomioka 170-171 N 4
Tomkinson Ranges 182-183 E 5
Tommot 154-155 Y 6
Tomo 98-99 F 4
Tomo, Río — 98-99 F 3
Tomori, Teluk — 174-175 H 7
Tompkins 49 D 5
Tompkinsville, KY 78-79 G 2
Tompo 154-155 a 5
Tomra 114-115 B 6
Tomsk 154-155 PQ 6
Toms River, NJ 72-73 JK 5
Tomtabakken 114-115 EF 9
Tom White, Mount — 52-53 PQ 6
Tonalá 58-59 H 8
Tonalea, AZ 74-75 H 4
Tonami 170-171 L 4
Tonantins 98-99 F 5
Tonasket, WA 66-67 D 1
Tonate 98-99 M 2
Tonbai Shan 166-167 L 5
Tonbridge 116-117 M 9
Tonda 174-175 M 8
Tønder 114-115 C 10
Tondern 70-71 H 1
Tondi 160-161 M 9
Tone-gawa 170-171 N 5
Tonekābon 160-161 G 3
Tōngā [Sudan] 194-195 L 7
Tonga [Tonga] 174-175 bc 2
Tonga Islands 34-35 J 5-6
Tongaland 198 F 7
Tongatapu 178 J 5
Tonga Trench 174-175 c 2
Tongch'ang 170-171 EF 2
T'ongch'ŏn 170-171 FG 3
Tongchuan 166-167 K 4
Tongguan [TJ, Shaanxi] 166-167 L 5
Tonghan-man 166-167 O 4
Tonghua 166-167 O 3
Tongjosŏn-man = Tonghan-man 166-167 O 4
Tongliao 166-167 N 3
Tongling 166-167 M 5
Tonglu 166-167 M 5-6
Tongmun'gŏ-ri 170-171 F 2
Tongoy 103 B 4
Tongphu 166-167 H 5
Tongpu = Tongphu 166-167 H 5
Tongren 166-167 K 6
Tongue 116-117 G 2
Tongue River 68-69 CD 2
Tong Xian 166-167 M 3-4
Tongyang 170-171 F 3
T'ŏngyŏng = Ch'ungmu 170-171 G 5
Tongyu 166-167 N 3
Tonk 160-161 M 5
Tonkawa, OK 76-77 F 4
Tonki Cape 52-53 M 7
Tonkin 174-175 DE 2
Tonkin = Bắc Bộ 174-175 D 2
Tonkin, Gulf of — 174-175 E 2-3
Tonlé Sap 174-175 D 4
Tonneins 132-133 GH 6
Tonopah, NV 58-59 C 4
Tonorio, Volcán — 88-89 D 9
Tonosí 88-89 F 11
Tønsberg 114-115 CD 8
Tonsina, AK 52-53 P 6
Tonstad 114-115 B 8
Tonzona River 52-53 L 5
Tooele, UT 58-59 D 3
Toolik River 52-53 N 2
Toora-Chem 154-155 S 7
Toowoomba 182-183 K 5
Topagoruk River 52-53 JK 1
Topeka, KS 58-59 G 4
Topia 86-87 G 5
Topki 154-155 PQ 6
Topko, gora — 154-155 a 6
Toplița 138-139 L 2
Topcck, AZ 74-75 F 5
Topolobampo 58-59 E 6
Topolovgrad 138-139 M 4
Toponas, CO 68-69 C 5
Topozero 154-155 E 4
Toppenish, WA 66-67 C 2
Topsham 116-117 H 10
Ṭoqra = Tūkrah 194-195 HJ 2
Toqsun = Toksun 166-167 F 3
Toquepala 98-99 E 8
Toquerville, UT 74-75 G 4
Toquima Range 74-75 E 3
Toraigh 116-117 C 5
Torbat-e Heydarīyeh 160-161 HJ 3-4
Torbat-e Jām 160-161 J 3
Torbat-e Sheikh Jām = Torbat-e Jām 160-161 J 3
Torbay 116-117 H 10
Torbert, Mount — 52-53 LM 6
Torch Lake 70-71 H 3
Torch River 49 FG 4
Tordesillas 132-133 E 8
Töre 114-115 K 5
Torekov 114-115 E 9
Torellbreen 114-115 j 6
Torell land 114-115 k 6
Torgau 124 F 3
Tori 194-195 L 7
Toriñana, Cabo — 132-133 C 7
Torino 138-139 BC 3
Tōrīt = Tūrīt 194-195 L 8
Tormes 132-133 D 8
Tornado Peak 48 K 5
Torneå = Tornio 114-115 L 5
Torne älv 114-115 K 4
Torneträsk 114-115 H 3
Torngat Mountains 46-47 Y 6
Tornio 114-115 L 5
Torno Largo 98-99 G 9
Tornquist 103 D 5
Toro [E] 132-133 E 8
Toro, Cerro del — 103 C 3
Torodi 194-195 E 6
Torokina 174-175 hj 6
Toronto 46-47 UV 9
Toronto, KS 70-71 C 7
Toronto, Lago — 86-87 GH 4
Toro Peak 74-75 E 6
Toropec 142-143 F 4
Tororo 198 F 1
Toros dağları 160-161 C 3
Torpoint 116-117 G 10
Torrance, CA 74-75 D 6
Torrance Municipal Airport 83 III b 3
Torre del Greco 138-139 F 5
Torre de Moncorvo 132-133 D 8
Torrelaguna 132-133 F 8
Torrelavega 132-133 E 7
Torrens, Lake — 182-183 G 6
Torrens Creek 182-183 HJ 4
Torrente 132-133 G 9
Torreón 58-59 F 6
Torreón de Cañas 76-77 B 9
Torres 103 G 3
Torres Islands 182-183 N 2
Torres Martinez Indian Reservation 74-75 E 6
Torres Strait 182-183 H 2
Torres Vedras 132-133 C 9
Torrevieja 132-133 G 10
Torridon 116-117 F 3
Torridon, Loch — 116-117 EF 3
Torrijos 132-133 E 8-9
Torrington, CT 72-73 K 4
Torrington, WY 68-69 DE 4
Torsås 114-115 FG 9
Torsby 114-115 E 7
Tórshavn 110-111 G 3
Tortillas, Las — 76-77 E 9
Tortola 58-59 O 8
Tortolì 138-139 C 6
Tortona 138-139 C 3
Tortosa 132-133 H 8
Tortosa, Cabo de — 132-133 H 8
Tortue, Île de la — 58-59 M 7
Tortuguero 88-89 E 9
Ṭorūd 160-161 H 3
Torugart Davan 160-161 L 2
Toruń 124 J 2
Tory Hill 72-73 GH 2
Tory Island = Toraigh 116-117 C 5
Toržok 154-155 E 6
Torzym 124 G 2
Tosan = Chŭbu 170-171 L 5-M 4
Tosashimizu 170-171 J 6
Tosa-wan 170-171 J 6
Toscana 138-139 D 4
To-shima 170-171 M 5
Tosno 142-143 F 4
Tos nuur 166-167 H 4
To-so Hu = Tos nuur 166-167 H 4
Tosoncengel 166-167 H 2
Tostado 103 D 3
Toston, MT 66-67 H 2
Tosu 170-171 H 6
Tosya 160-161 C 2
Totana 132-133 G 10
Toteng 198 D 6
Tothill 49 C 6
Tot'ma 154-155 G 5-6
Totnes 116-117 H 10
Totogan Lake 50 E 1
Totonicapán 58-59 HJ 8-9
Totora [BOL, Cochabamba] 98-99 FG 8
Totoya 174-175 ab 2
Totson Mount 52-53 J 4
Totta 154-155 a 6
Tottan Range 31 B 35-36
Totten Glacier 31 C 12
Tottenham [AUS] 182-183 J 6
Tottenham [CDN] 72-73 FG 2
Tottenham, London- 116-117 LM 9
Tottenville, New York-, NY 82 III a 3
Tottori 166-167 P 4
Touat = At-Tuwāt 194-195 DE 3
Touba [CI] 194-195 C 7
Touba [SN] 194-195 A 6
Toubqâl, Jbel — = Jabal Tubqāl 194-195 C 2
Toudao Jiang 170-171 F 1-2
Tougan 194-195 D 6
Touggourt = Tughghūrt 194-195 EF 2
Touho 182-183 N 4
Toukoto 194-195 BC 6
Toul 132-133 K 4
Toulépleu 194-195 C 7
Toulon, IL 70-71 EF 5
Toulon [F] 132-133 KL 7
Toulouse 132-133 HJ 7
Toummo 194-195 G 4
Toumodi 194-195 CD 7
Toumotou, Îles — 34-35 K 5-L 6
Toungoo = Taungngū 174-175 C 3
Touṅis = Tūnis 194-195 FG 1
Touraine 132-133 H 5
Tourane = Đa Nẵng 174-175 E 3
Tourlaville 116-117 K 11
Tournai 132-133 J 3
Tournon 132-133 K 6
Touros 98-99 MN 5-6
Tours 132-133 H 5
Tourville 51 AB 4
Toussidé, Pic — 194-195 H 4
T'ou-tao Chiang = Toudao Jiang 170-171 F 1-2
Töv ◁ 166-167 K 2
Tovarkovskij 142-143 G 5
Tovqussaq 46-47 a 5
Towada 170-171 N 2
Towada-ko 170-171 N 2
Towanda, PA 72-73 H 4
Towcester 116-117 KL 8
Towdystan 48 E 3
Tower, MN 70-71 D 2
Towner, CO 68-69 E 6
Towner, ND 68-69 F 1
Townes Pass 74-75 E 4
Townley, NY 82 III a 2
Townsend, GA 80-81 F 5
Townsend, MT 66-67 H 2
Townshend Island 182-183 K 4
Townsville 182-183 J 3
Towot 194-195 L 7
Towson, MD 72-73 H 5
Towuti, Danau — 174-175 H 7
Towy, River — 116-117 H 8
Toyah, TX 76-77 C 7
Toyahvale, TX 76-77 BC 7
Tōya-ko 170-171 b 2
Toyama 166-167 Q 4
Toyama-wan 166-167 Q 4
Toyohara = Južno-Sachalinsk 154-155 bc 8
Toyohashi 166-167 Q 5
Toyohasi = Toyohashi 166-167 Q 5
Toyoma 170-171 N 3
Toyonaka 170-171 K 5
Toyooka 170-171 K 5
Toyota 170-171 L 5
Toyotama 170-171 G 5
Tōzeur = Tawzar 194-195 F 2
Tozitna River 52-53 LM 4
Trabzon 160-161 DE 2
Tracadie 51 D 4
Trachéia = Silifke 160-161 C 3
Tra Cu 174-175 E 5
Tracy 51 C 5
Tracy, CA 74-75 C 4
Tradum 166-167 E 6
Træna 114-115 DE 4
Traer, IA 70-71 D 4
Trafalgar, Cabo de — 132-133 D 10
Tráighlí 116-117 B 8
Tráigh Mhór, An — 116-117 D 8
Trail 58-59 N 8
Trail, MN 70-71 C 2
Trail City, SD 68-69 F 3
Trajanova vrata 138-139 L 4
Trakya 142-143 E 7
Tralee = Tráighlí 116-117 B 8
Tralee Bay = Bádh Thráighlí 116-117 AB 8
Trälleborg = Trelleborg 114-115 E 10
Tramore = An Tráigh Mhór 116-117 D 8
Tranås 114-115 F 8
Trancas 103 CD 3
Trangan, Pulau — 174-175 K 8
Trani 138-139 G 5
Trân Ninh, Cao Nguyên — 174-175 D 3
Transamazônica, Rodovia — 98-99 L 7
Trans Canada Highway 46-47 P 7
Transhimalaja = Transhimalaya 166-167 EF 5
Transhimalaya 166-167 EF 5
Transilvania 138-139 K-M 2
Transkasp 160-161 H 3
Transsib 154-155 L 6
Transturan 154-155 K 7
Transvaal 198 EF 6
Transylvanian Alps = Alpi Transilvaniei 138-139 KL 3
Trápani 138-139 E 6-7
Trapezûs = Trabzon 160-161 DE 2
Trapper Peak 66-67 F 3
Traralgon 182-183 J 7
Trarza = At-Trārzah 194-195 AB 5
Trārzah, At- 194-195 AB 5
Trasimeno, Lago — 138-139 DE 4
Trasna, Loch — 116-117 B 9
Trás-os-Montes 132-133 D 8
Trás-os-Montes = Cucumbi 198 C 4
Trat 174-175 D 4
Traunstein 124 F 5
Trava, Cachoeira — 98-99 H 5
Travá, Cachoeiro 98-99 K 5
Traverse, Lake — 68-69 H 3
Traverse City, MI 58-59 JK 2-3
Traverse Peak 52-53 GH 4
Tra Vingh 174-175 E 5
Tra Vinh = Phu Vinh 174-175 E 5
Travis, Lake — 76-77 EF 7
Travis, New York-, NY 82 III a 3
Trbovle 138-139 F 2
Treasure Island 83 I b 2
Treasure Island Naval Station 83 I b 2
Treasury = Mono Island 174-175 j 6
Treat Island 52-53 JK 3
Třebíč 124 G 4
Trebinje 138-139 H 4
Trebisonda = Trabzon 160-161 DE 2
Trechado, NM 74-75 J 5
Tredegar 116-117 H 9
Tregaron 116-117 H 8
Trego, MT 66-67 F 1
Tregoney 116-117 G 10
Trégorrois 132-133 F 4
Treherne 49 J 6
Treinta y Tres [ROU, place] 103 F 4
Trelew 103 C 6
Trelleborg 114-115 E 10
Tremadoc Bay 116-117 G 8
Trembleur Lake 48 E 2
Trémiti, Isole — 138-139 F 4
Tremonton, UT 66-67 G 5
Tremp 132-133 H 7
Trempealeau, WI 70-71 E 3-4
Trenary, MI 70-71 G 2
Trenčín 124 J 4
Trenque Lauquen 103 D 5
Trent = Trento 138-139 D 2
Trent, River — 116-117 L 7
Trente et un Milles, Lac des — 72-73 HJ 1
Trentino-Alto Adige 138-139 D 2
Trento 138-139 D 2
Trenton 72-73 H 2
Trenton, FL 80-81 b 2
Trenton, IA 70-71 D 5
Trenton, MI 72-73 E 3
Trenton, NE 68-69 F 5
Trenton, NJ 58-59 M 3-4
Trenton, TN 78-79 E 3
Trepassey 51 K 4
Tréport, le — 132-133 H 3
Tres Arroyos 103 DE 5
Tres Bôcas [BR] 98-99 C 7
Tresco 116-117 E 11
Três Corações 98-99 KL 9
Tres Esquinas 98-99 DE 4
Tres Forcas, Cap — = Rā's Wūruq 194-195 D 1
Treshnish Islands 116-117 E 4
Três Irmãos, Cachoeira 98-99 F 9
Tres Irmãos, Pontas dos — 98-99 M 6-N 5
Três Irmãos, Serra dos 98-99 F 9
Treska 138-139 J 5
Três Lagoas 98-99 J 9
Três Lagos 103 B 7
Tres Montes, Península — 103 A 7
Tres Picos, Cerro — 103 B 6
Tres Piedras, NM 76-77 B 4
Tres Puntas, Cabo — 103 CD 7
Três Rios 98-99 L 9
Tres Vírgenes, Las — 58-59 D 6
Treuer River = Macumba 182-183 G 5
Treungen 114-115 C 8
Trêve, Lac la — 50 O 2
Treviglio 138-139 C 3
Treviño 132-133 F 7
Treviso 138-139 E 3
Trevose Head 116-117 F 10
Treze Quedas 98-99 H 4
Triangle, ID 66-67 E 4
Triangulos, Arrecifes — 86-87 OP 7
Tribune 68-69 DE 1
Tribune, KS 68-69 F 6
Trichônis, Límnē — 138-139 J 6
Trichūr 160-161 M 8
Trida 182-183 HJ 6
Tridell, UT 66-67 J 5
Trident Peak 66-67 D 5
Trier 124 C 4
Trieste 138-139 E 3
Tríkala 138-139 JK 6
Trim = Áth Troim 116-117 E 7
Trinchera, CO 76-77 BC 4
Trincheras 86-87 E 2
Trincheras, Las — 98-99 FG 3
Trincomalee = Tirikuṇāmalaya 160-161 N 9
Trincomali = Tirikuṇāmalaya 160-161 N 9
Trindade [BR, Roraima] 98-99 H 4
Trindade = Trinidad [BOL] 98-99 G 7
Trindade = Trinidad [TT] 58-59 O 9
Trindade, Ilha da — 98-99 NO 9
Trinidad, CA 66-67 A 5
Trinidad, CO 58-59 F 4
Trinidad, TX 76-77 FG 6
Trinidad, WA 66-67 CD 2
Trinidad [BOL, Beni] 98-99 G 7
Trinidad [C] 58-59 KL 7
Trinidad [CO] 98-99 E 3
Trinidad [PY] 103 E 3
Trinidad [ROU] 103 E 4
Trinidad [TT] 58-59 O 9
Trinidad = Ilha da Trindade 98-99 NO 9
Trinidad, Bahía — 58-59 b 2
Trinidad, Isla — 103 D 5
Trinidad, Río — 58-59 b 3
Trinidad, Washington-, DC 82 II b 2
Trinité, Montagnes de la — 98-99 M 2
Trinity, TX 76-77 G 7
Trinity Bay 46-47 a 8
Trinity Center, CA 66-67 B 5
Trinity Islands 46-47 F 6
Trinity Mountains 66-67 B 5
Trinity Range 66-67 D 5
Trinity River [USA, California] 66-67 B 5
Trinity River [USA, Texas] 58-59 G 5
Trion, GA 78-79 G 3
Tripoli, WI 70-71 EF 3
Trípolis 138-139 K 7
Tripolis = Ṭarābulus al-Gharb 194-195 G 2
Tripolitania = Ṭarābulus 194-195 GH 2
Tripp, SD 68-69 GH 4
Tripps Run 82 II a 2
Tripura 160-161 P 6
Trishshivaperūr = Trichūr 160-161 M 8
Tristan da Cunha 188-189 FG 12
Triumph, MN 70-71 C 4
Triunfo [BOL] 98-99 E 9
Trivandrum 160-161 M 9
Trnava 124 H 4
Trobriand Islands 174-175 h 6
Trochu 48 L 4
Trofors 114-115 E 5
Trogir 138-139 FG 4
Troglav 138-139 G 4
Trōia [I] 138-139 F 5
Troia [TR] 160-161 B 3
Troick 154-155 L 7
Troickoje [SU, Rossijskaja SFSR] 154-155 a 8
Troicko-Pečorsk 154-155 K 5
Troickosavsk = K'achta 154-155 U 7
Trois-Pistoles 51 B 3
Trois-Rivières 46-47 W 8
Trojan 138-139 L 4
Trojanski prohod 138-139 L 4
Trollhättan 114-115 E 8
Trolltindan 114-115 B 6
Trombetas, Rio — 98-99 H 5
Tromelin 188-189 N 10
Troms 114-115 G-J 3
Tromsø 114-115 H 3
Tron 114-115 D 6
Trona, CA 74-75 E 5
Tronador, Monte — 103 B 6
Trondheim 114-115 D 6
Trondheimfjord 114-115 CD 6
Tróodos 160-161 C 4
Troon 116-117 G 5
Tropêço Grande, Cachoeira de — 98-99 OP 11
Tropic, UT 74-75 GH 4
Trosa 114-115 G 8
Trostan 116-117 E 5
Trotus 138-139 M 2
Troup, TX 76-77 G 6
Troup Head 116-117 J 3
Trout Creek 66-67 D 4
Trout Creek, MT 66-67 EF 2
Trout Creek, UT 74-75 G 3
Trout Lake, MI 70-71 H 2
Trout Lake [CDN, Alberta] 48 K 1
Trout Lake [CDN, Northwest Territories] 46-47 MN 5
Trout Lake [CDN, Ontario] 46-47 S 7
Trout Peak 68-69 B 3
Trout River 51 G 3
Trouwers Island = Pulau Tinjil 174-175 E 8
Trowbridge 116-117 JK 9

Trowbrid 277

Troy, AL 58-59 J 5
Troy, ID 66-67 E 2
Troy, KS 70-71 C 6
Troy, MO 70-71 E 6
Troy, MT 66-67 F 1
Troy, NC 80-81 G 3
Troy, NY 58-59 M 3
Troy, OH 70-71 H 5
Troy, OR 66-67 E 3
Troy, PA 72-73 H 4
Troyes 132-133 K 4
Trucará, Serra do — 98-99 N 7-O 6
Trucial Oman = United Arab Emirates 160-161 GH 6
Truckee, CA 74-75 CD 3
Truckee River 74-75 D 3
Trudante = Tārūdānt 194-195 C 2
Trujillo [E] 132-133 DE 9
Trujillo [Honduras] 58-59 J 8
Trujillo [PE] 98-99 CD 6
Trujillo [YV] 98-99 EF 3
Trujillo, Ciudad — = Santo Domingo 58-59 MN 8
Truk 178 F 2
Trumann, AR 78-79 D 3
Trumbull, Mount — 74-75 G 4
Trung Bô 174-175 D 3-E 4
Trung Phân, Cao Nguyên — 174-175 E 4
Trung Phân, Plateau de — = Cao Nguyên Trung Phân 174-175 E 4
Truro, IA 70-71 D 5
Truro [CDN] 46-47 Y 8
Truro [GB] 116-117 FG 10
Truscott, TX 76-77 E 6
Truth or Consequences, NM 76-77 A 6
Trutnov 124 GH 3
Truxilho = Trujillo 58-59 J 8
Tryon, NE 68-69 F 5
Trysil 114-115 DE 7
Trysilelv 114-115 DE 7

Tsabong 198 D 7
Tsaidam 166-167 GH 4
Tsai-Dam = Tsaidam 166-167 GH 4
Tsala Apopka Lake 80-81 bc 2
Tsamkong = Zhanjiang 166-167 L 7
Tsangpo 166-167 EF 6
Tsangwu = Wuzhou 166-167 L 7
Tsaratanana [RM, mountain] 198 J 4
Tsaratanana [RM, place] 198 J 5
Tsarskoye Selo = Puškin 154-155 DE 6
Tsau 198 D 6
Tsavo [EAK, place] 198 G 2
Tsavo National Park 198 G 2
Tschicoma Peak 76-77 AB 4
Tschida, Lake — 68-69 EF 2
Ts'ê-lo = Chira Bazar 166-167 DE 4
Tses 198 C 7
Tsethang 166-167 G 6
Tsetserlig = Cecerleg 166-167 J 2
Tshaidam 166-167 GH 4
Tshela 198 B 2-3
Tshikapa 198 CD 3
Tshing Hai = Chöch nuur 166-167 H 4
Tshipa = Katakumba 198 D 3
Tshofa 198 DE 3
Tsho Ngonpo = Chöch nuur 166-167 H 4
Tshopo 198 E 1
Tshuapa 198 D 2
Tshungu, Chutes — 198 DE 1
Tshwane 198 D 6
Tsiafajavona 198 J 5
Tsienkiang = Qianjiang 166-167 L 5
Tsihombe 198 HJ 7
Tsinan = Jinan 166-167 M 4
Tsincheng = Jincheng 166-167 L 4
Tsinchow = Tianshui 166-167 JK 5
Tsinghai = Qinghai 166-167 GH 4
Tsinghu = Jinghe 166-167 E 3
Tsingkiang = Qingjiang [TJ, Jiangsu] 166-167 M 5
Tsingkiang = Qingjiang [TJ, Jiangxi] 166-167 M 6
Tsingtau = Qingdao 166-167 N 4
Tsingyuan = Baoding 166-167 LM 4
Tsining = Jining 166-167 M 4
Tsining = Xining 166-167 J 4
Tsinyang = Qinyang 166-167 L 4
Tsiroanomandidy 198 J 5
Tsitsihar = Qiqihar 166-167 N 2
Tsivory 198 J 6
Tsu 166-167 Q 5
Tsubame 170-171 M 4
Tsuchiura 170-171 N 4
Tsugaru kaikyō 166-167 R 3
Tsukigata 170-171 b 2
Tsukumi 170-171 H 6
Tsuma = Saito 170-171 H 6
Tsumeb 198 C 5
Tsungming = Chongming 166-167 N 5
Tsuno-shima 170-171 H 5
Tsunyi = Zunyi 166-167 K 6
Tsuruga 170-171 KL 5
Tsurugi san 170-171 JK 6
Tsurumi-zaki 170-171 J 6
Tsuruoka 170-171 M 3
Tsurusaki 170-171 HJ 6
Tsushima 166-167 O 5
Tsushima-kaikyō 166-167 OP 5
Tsuyama 170-171 JK 5
Tsuyung = Chuxiong 166-167 J 7

Tu = Tibesti 194-195 H 4
Tu = Tsu 166-167 Q 5
Tua 132-133 D 8
Tuaim 116-117 C 7
Tuam = Tuaim 116-117 C 7
Tuamotu, Îles — 34-35 K 5-L 6
Tuamotu Basin 34-35 KL 6
Tuapse 142-143 G 7
Tuathail, Carn — 116-117 B 9
Tubac, AZ 74-75 H 7
Tuba City, AZ 74-75 H 4
Tuban 174-175 F 8
Tubarão 103 G 3
Tubau 174-175 F 6
Ṭubayq, Jabal aṭ- 160-161 D 5
Tübingen 124 D 4
Tub-Karagan, poluostrov — 142-143 K 7
Tubqāl, Jabal — 194-195 C 2
Ṭubruq 194-195 J 2
Tubuaï, Îles — 34-35 K 6
Tucacas 98-99 F 2
Tucano 98-99 M 7
Tucavaca 98-99 H 8
Tucholskie, Bory — 124 HJ 2
Tucho River 52-53 X 7
Tucker Bay 31 B 18
Tuckerman, AR 78-79 D 3
Tuckerton, NJ 72-73 JK 5
Tucson, AZ 58-59 D 5
Tucson Mountains 74-75 H 6
Tucumán = San Miguel de Tucumán 103 CD 3
Tucumán, San Miguel de — 103 CD 3
Tucumcari, NM 58-59 F 4
Tucumcari Mountain 76-77 C 5
Tucunuco 103 C 4
Tucuparé 98-99 L 7
Tucupita 98-99 G 3
Tucuruí 98-99 K 5
Tudela 132-133 G 7
Tuela 132-133 D 8
Tueré, Rio 98-99 N 6-7
Tufi 174-175 N 8
Tugaru kaikyō = Tsugaru-kaikyō 166-167 R 3
Tugela [ZA, river] 198 F 7
Tuggurt = Tughghūrt 194-195 EF 2
Tugh Fafan = Fafen 194-195 N 7
Tughghūrt 194-195 EF 2
Tugidak Island 52-53 f 1
Tugt 166-167 L 3-4
Tuguegarao 174-175 H 3
Tugur 154-155 a 7
Tuito, El — 86-87 H 7
Tujmazy 154-155 JK 7
Tukalinsk 154-155 N 6
Tukangbesi, Kepulauan — 174-175 H 8
Tuklung, AK 52-53 H 7
Tūkrah 194-195 HJ 2
Tuktoyaktuk 46-47 JK 4
Tukums 142-143 D 4
Tukuyu 198 F 3
Tula [MEX] 86-87 L 6
Tula [SU] 142-143 G 5
Tulach Mhór, An — 116-117 D 7
Tulach Ua bhFeidhlimidh 116-117 E 8
Tula de Allende 86-87 KL 6-7
Tulagi 174-175 jk 6
Tulameen 66-67 C 1
Tulancingo 58-59 G 7
Tulare, CA 58-59 C 4
Tulare, SD 68-69 G 3
Tulare Lake 58-59 C 4
Tulare Lake Area 74-75 D 5
Tularosa, NM 76-77 A 6
Tularosa Basin 76-77 A 6
Tularosa Mountains 74-75 J 6
Tulcán 98-99 D 4
Tulcea 138-139 N 3
Tul'čin 142-143 E 6
Tulcingo de Valle 86-87 LM 8-9
Tuléar = Toliary 198 H 6
Tulelake, CA 66-67 C 5
Tule River 74-75 D 4
Tule River Indian Reservation 74-75 D 4-5
Tul'gan 154-155 K 7
Tuli 198 E 6
Tulia, TX 76-77 D 5
Tūljā 194-195 EF 2
Tullahoma, TN 78-79 FG 3
Tullamore = An Tulach Mhór 116-117 D 7
Tulle 132-133 HJ 6
Tullow = Tulach Ua bhFeidhlimidh 116-117 E 8
Tully 182-183 J 3
Tuloma 142-143 F 2
Tulpan 154-155 K 5
Tulsa, OK 58-59 G 4
Tulsa = La Barge, WY 66-67 HJ 4
Tulsequah 52-53 V 7
Tuluá 98-99 D 4
Tulufan = Turpan 166-167 F 3
Tuluga River 52-53 M 2
Tuluksak, AK 52-53 G 6
Tulum 86-87 R 7
Tulun 154-155 ST 7
Tuma 142-143 H 4
Tumacacori National Monument 74-75 H 7
Tumaco 98-99 D 4
Tumaco, Rada de — 98-99 CD 4
Tuman-gang 170-171 G 1
Tumany 154-155 e 5
Tumba, Lac — 198 C 2
Tumbarumba 182-183 J 7
Tumbes [EC, place] 98-99 C 5
Tumboni 198 G 2
T'umen' [SU] 154-155 M 6
Tumen [TJ] 166-167 O 3
Tumen Jiang 170-171 G 1
Tumkūr 160-161 M 8
Tumkūru = Tumkūr 160-161 M 8
Ṭummō, Jabal — 194-195 G 4
Tumpat 174-175 D 5
Tumu 194-195 D 6
Tumucumaque, Reserva Florestal 98-99 L 3-4
Tumucumaque, Serra do — 98-99 HJ 4
Tumureng 98-99 G 3
Tunas, Las — [C] 88-89 H 4
Tunas, Victoria de las — 58-59 L 7
Tunceli 160-161 DE 3
Tünchel 166-167 K 2
Tundrino 154-155 N 5
Tunduma 198 F 3
Tunduru 198 G 4
Tundža 138-139 M 4
T'ung 154-155 W 4
Tungaru = Tunqarū 194-195 L 6
Tung-chou = Nantong 166-167 N 5
Tungchow = Nantong 166-167 N 5
T'ung-ch'uan = Tongchuan 166-167 K 4
Tungchwan = Huize 166-167 J 6
Tungchwan = Santai 166-167 JK 5
Tung-fang = Dongfang 166-167 K 8
Tung Hai = Dong Hai 166-167 NO 5-6
Tunghsien = Tong Xian 166-167 M 3-4
Tunghua = Tonghua 166-167 O 3
Tunghwa = Tonghua 166-167 O 3
Tungjen = Tongren 166-167 K 6
Tung-kuan = Dongguan 166-167 LM 7
Tungkuan = Dongguan 166-167 LM 7
T'ung-kuan = Tongguan 166-167 L 5
T'ung-liao = Tongliao 166-167 N 3
Tunglu = Tonglu 166-167 M 5-6
T'ung-p'u = Tongphu 166-167 H 5
Tungshan = Xuzhou 166-167 M 5
Tung-shêng = Dongsheng 166-167 K 4
Tungtai = Dongtai 166-167 N 5
Tung-t'ing Hu = Dongting Hu 166-167 L 6
Tun-hua = Dunhua 166-167 O 3
Tun-huang = Dunhuang 166-167 GH 3
Tunhwang = Dunhuang 166-167 GH 3
Tunica, MS 78-79 D 3
Tūnis 194-195 FG 1
Tunisi, Canale di — 138-139 D 7
Tunisia 194-195 F 1-2
Tunj 194-195 K 7
Tunja 98-99 E 3
Tunkhannock, PA 72-73 HJ 4
Tunki 88-89 D 8
Tunnsjø 114-115 E 5
Tunqarū 194-195 L 6
Tuntutuliak, AK 52-53 F 6
Tunuyan, Sierra de — 103 C 4
Tunxi 166-167 M 6
Tuoketuo = Tugt 166-167 L 3
Tuokexun = Toksun 166-167 F 3
Tuolumne, CA 74-75 CD 4
Tuolumne River 74-75 CD 4
Tuoppajärvi = Topozero 154-155 E 4
Tuosuo Hu = Tos nuur 166-167 H 4
Tupã 98-99 JK 9
Tupanciretã 103 F 3
Tupelo, MS 58-59 J 5
Tupelo, OK 76-77 F 5
Tupik [SU ↑ Mogoča] 154-155 WX 7
Tupik [SU, Smolensk ↗] 142-143 F 4
Tupinambaranas, Ilha — 98-99 H 5
Tupirama 98-99 O 9
Tupiza 98-99 F 9
Tupper Lake, NY 72-73 J 2
Tupungato, Cerro — 103 BC 4
Tuque, la — 46-47 W 8
Túquerres 98-99 D 4
Ṭūr, Aṭ- 194-195 L 3
Tura [SU, place] 154-155 ST 5
Tura [SU, river] 154-155 L 6
Turabah 160-161 E 6
Turan 154-155 R 7
Turan = Turanskaja nizmennost' 154-155 K 9-L 8
Turanian Plain = Turanskaja nizmennost' 154-155 K 9-L 8
Turanskaja nizmennost' 154-155 K 9-L 8
Ṭurayf 160-161 D 4
Turbat 160-161 J 5
Turbio, El — 103 B 8
Turbo 98-99 D 3
Turda 138-139 K 2
Turek 124 J 2
Turgaj [SU, place] 154-155 L 8
Turgaj [SU, river] 154-155 L 8
Turgajskaja ložbina 154-155 L 7
Türgen Echin uul 166-167 FG 2
Turgeon, Lac — 50 M 2
Turgeon, Rivière — 50 M 2
Turhal 142-143 G 7
Turia 132-133 G 9
Turiaçu 98-99 K 5
Turiaçu, Baía de — 98-99 KL 5
Turij Rog 154-155 Z 8
Turin 49 B 5-6
Turin = Torino 138-139 BC 3
Turinsk 154-155 L 6
Tūrīt 194-195 L 8
Turkana, Lake — 198 G 1
Turkestan 160-161 K-O 3
Turkey 160-161 B-E 3
Turkey, TX 76-77 D 5
Turkey River 70-71 E 4
Turkmen-Kala 160-161 J 3
Turkmenskaja guba 142-143 K 8
Turkmen Soviet Socialist Republic 160-161 HJ 2-5
Turks and Caicos Islands 88-89 KL 4
Turksib 154-155 P 7
Turks Islands 58-59 M 7
Turku 114-115 K 7
Turkwel 198 G 1
Turlock, CA 74-75 C 4
Turnberry 49 GH 4
Turneffe Islands 58-59 J 8
Turner, MT 68-69 B 1
Turner, WA 66-67 E 2
Turner Valley 48 K 4
Turnhout 132-133 K 3
Turnor Lake 49 D 2
Turnu Măgurele 138-139 L 4
Turnu Roşu, Pasul — 138-139 KL 3
Turon, KS 68-69 G 7
Turpan 166-167 F 3
Turqino, Pico — 58-59 L 8
Turquoise Lake 52-53 KL 6
Turrell, AR 78-79 D 3
Turriff 116-117 J 3
Turtkul' 154-155 L 9
Turtleford 49 D 4
Turtle Lake 49 D 4
Turtle Lake, ND 68-69 F 2
Turtle Lake, WI 70-71 D 3
Turtle Mountain 68-69 FG 1
Turtle Mountain Indian Reservation 68-69 G 1
Turton, SD 68-69 GH 3
Turuchansk 154-155 Q 4
Turugart = Torugart Davan 160-161 L 2
Turun ja Poorin lääni 114-115 K 6-7
Turut = Ṭorūd 160-161 H 3
Tuscaloosa, AL 58-59 J 5
Tuscany = Toscana 138-139 D 4
Tuscarora, NV 66-67 E 5
Tuscola, IL 70-71 F 6
Tuscola, TX 76-77 E 6
Tuscumbia, AL 78-79 EF 3
Tuscumbia, MO 70-71 D 6
Tusenøyane 114-115 l 6
Tu Shan = Du Shan [TJ, mountain] 170-171 B 2
Tuside = Pic Toussidé 194-195 H 4
Tusima = Tsushima 166-167 O 5
Tusima kaikyō = Tsushima-kaikyō 166-167 OP 5
Tuskegee, AL 78-79 G 4
Tussey Mountain 72-73 GH 4
Tustna 114-115 B 6
Tustumena Lake 52-53 MN 6
Tuticorin 160-161 M 9
Tutna Lake 52-53 K 6
Tutončana 154-155 R 4
Tutrakan 138-139 M 3-4
Tuttle, ND 68-69 FG 2
Tuttle, OK 76-77 F 5
Tuttle Creek Lake 68-69 H 6
Tuttle Lake 70-71 C 4
Tuttlingen 124 D 4-5
Tūttukkuḍi = Tuticorin 160-161 M 9
Tutuila 174-175 c 1
Tutupaca, Volcán — 98-99 E 8
Tutwiler, MS 78-79 D 3-4
Tuul gol 166-167 JK 2
Tuva Autonomous Soviet Socialist Republic 154-155 RS 7
Tuvalu 178 HJ 3
Tuwāt, At- 194-195 DE 3
Ṭuwayq, Jabal — 160-161 F 6
Ṭuwayshah, Aṭ- 194-195 K 6
Tuxedni Bay 52-53 L 6
Tuxedo, MD 82 II b 2
Tuxford [CDN] 49 EF 5
Tuxford [GB] 116-117 KL 7
Tuxpan [MEX, Jalisco] 86-87 J 8
Tuxpan [MEX, Nayarit] 58-59 E 7
Tuxpán de Rodriguez Cano 58-59 G 7
Tuxtepec 86-87 M 8
Túy 132-133 C 7
Tuy An 174-175 E 4
Tuya River 52-53 W 7
Tuy Hoa 174-175 EF 4
Tuyun = Duyun 166-167 K 6
Tuzgölü 160-161 C 3
Tuzla [YU] 138-139 H 3

Tvedestrand 114-115 C 8
Tver' = Kalinin 154-155 EF 6
Tvöroyri 116-117 ab 2

Tweed [CDN] 72-73 H 2
Tweed, River — 116-117 J 5
Tweedsmuir Hills 116-117 H 5
Tweedsmuir Provincial Park 46-47 L 7
Twelvemile Summit 52-53 OP 4
Twentieth Century Fox Studios 83 III b 1
Twentynine Palms, CA 74-75 EF 5
Twentytwo Mile Village, AK 52-53 PQ 3
Twerton 116-117 J 9
Twilight Cove 182-183 E 6
Twin Bridges, MT 66-67 GH 3
Twin Buttes Reservoir 76-77 D 7
Twin Falls, ID 58-59 CD 3
Twin Heads 182-183 E 4
Twin Islands 46-47 UV 7
Twin Lakes 52-53 KL 6
Twin Peaks [USA, Idaho] 66-67 F 3
Twin Peaks [USA, San Francisco] 83 I b 2
Twin Valley, MN 70-71 BC 2
Two Butte Creek 68-69 E 7
Two Buttes, CO 68-69 E 7
Twodot, MT 66-67 HJ 2
Two Harbors, MN 58-59 HJ 2
Two Hills 49 C 4
Two Rivers, WI 70-71 G 3

Tyamo 194-195 M 7
Tyborøn 114-115 BC 9
Tyencha 194-195 M 7
Tyew Bahir 194-195 M 8
Tygda 154-155 Y 7
Tygh Valley, OR 66-67 C 3
Tyler, MN 68-69 H 3
Tyler, TX 58-59 GH 5
Tyler Park, VA 82 II a 2
Tylertown, MS 78-79 DE 5
Tylösand 114-115 E 9
Tym 154-155 P 6
Tymfrēstós 138-139 JK 6
Tymovskoje 154-155 b 7
Tympákion 138-139 L 8
Tyndall, SD 68-69 H 4
Tyndinskij 154-155 XY 6
Tyndrum 116-117 G 4
Tynemouth 116-117 K 5
Tyne & Wear = 1 ◁ 116-117 K 6
Tynset 114-115 D 6
Tyonek, AK 52-53 M 6
Tyone River 52-53 O 5
Tyŏsen kaikyō = Chōsen-kaikyō 166-167 O 5
Tyrell, Lake — 182-183 H 7
Tyrifjord 114-115 CD 7
Tyrma 154-155 Z 7
Tyrol = Tirol 124 EF 5
Tyrone, OK 76-77 D 4
Tyrone, PA 72-73 G 4
Tyrrhenian Sea 110-111 L 7-8
Tysnesøy 114-115 A 7-8
Tyumen = T'umen' 154-155 M 6
Tywyn 116-117

Tzaneen 198 F 6
Tzechung = Zizhong 166-167 JK 5-6
Tzekung = Zigong 166-167 JK 6
Tzŭ-hu = Bajan Choto 166-167 JK 4
Tzŭ-kung = Zigong 166-167 JK 6

U

Uaçari, Serra — 98-99 H 4
Uachtair, Loch — 116-117 D 6
Uaco Cungo 198 C 4
Uacuru, Cachoeira — 98-99 HJ 10
Uaddân = Waddān 194-195 H 3
Uadi-Halfa = Wādī Ḥalfā 194-195 L 4
Uagadugu = Ouagadougou 194-195 D 6
Uaianary, Cachoeira — 98-99 FG 4
Uaimh, An — 116-117 DE 7
Ualega = Welega 194-195 LM 7
Ualik Lake 52-53 H 7
Uancheu = Wenzhou 166-167 N 6
Uanle Uen = Wanleweeyn 198 H 1
Uarangal = Warangal 160-161 MN 7
Uari 98-99 M 8
Uatumã, Rio — 98-99 H 5
Uauá 98-99 M 6
Uáu en-Nâmûs = Wāw an-Nāmūs 194-195 H 4
Uaupés 98-99 F 5
Uaupés, Rio — 98-99 F 4
Uaxactún 58-59 J 8

Ubá 98-99 L 9
Uba, Cachoeira do — 98-99 MN 9
Ubá, Salto do — 103 F 2
Ubaitaba 98-99 M 7
Ubangi 198 C 1
Ubari = Awbārī 194-195 G 3
'Ubārī, Edeien- = Ṣaḥrā' Awbārī 194-195 G 3
Ubaye 132-133 L 6
'Ubaylah, Al- 160-161 G 6
Ubayyiḍ, Al- 194-195 KL 6
Ube 166-167 P 5
Úbeda 132-133 F 9
Ubekendt Ø 46-47 a 3
Uberaba 98-99 K 8
Uberlândia 98-99 K 8
Ubiña, Peña — 132-133 DE 7
'Ubkayk, Jabal — 194-195 M 4
Ubsa Nur = Uvs nuur 166-167 G 1
Ubundu 198 DE 3

Učaly 142-143 LM 5
Ucami 154-155 S 5
Ucayali, Río — 98-99 D 6
Uchiko 170-171 J 6
Uchi Lake 50 C 2
Uchinoko = Uchiko 170-171 J 6
Uchinoura 170-171 H 7
Uchiura-wan 170-171 b 2
Uchta [SU, Komi ASSR] 154-155 J 5
Uchta = Kalevala 154-155 E 4
Üchturpan 166-167 DE 3
Uckfield 116-117 M 10
Ucluelet 48 E 5
Ucross, WY 68-69 C 3
Učur 154-155 Z 6

Uda [SU ◁ Čuna] 154-155 S 7
Uda [SU ◁ Selenga] 154-155 UV 7
Uda [SU ◁ Udskaja guba] 154-155 Z 7
Ūdah, Jabal — 194-195 M 4
Udaipur [IND ↗ Ahmadābād] 160-161 L 6
'Udaysāt, Al- 199 C 5
Udbina 138-139 FG 3
Uddevalla 114-115 DE 8
Uddjaur 114-115 H 5
Udine 138-139 E 2
Udipi 160-161 L 8
Uḍīsā = Orissa 160-161 N 7-O 6
Udjidji = Ujiji 198 E 2-3
Udmurt Autonomous Soviet Socialist Republic = 2 ◁ 154-155 J 6
Udmurtskaja Avtonomnaja Sovetskaja Socialističeskaja Respublika = Udmurt Autonomous Soviet Socialist Republic 154-155 J 6
U-do 170-171 F 6
Udon Thani 174-175 D 3
Udskaja guba 154-155 a 7
Uḍuppi = Udipi 160-161 L 8
Udža 154-155 W 3

Uebonti 174-175 H 7
Ueda 170-171 M 4
Uedineniya Island = ostrov Ujedinenija 154-155 OP 2
Uegit = Wajid 198 H 1
Uele 198 D 1
Uelen 46-47 BC 4
Uelzen 124 E 2
Uengan, mys — 154-155 LM 3
Ueno 170-171 L 5
Uere 198 E 1

Ufa [SU, place] 154-155 K 7
Ufa [SU, river] 154-155 K 6

Ugak Bay 52-53 g 1
Ugak Island 52-53 gh 1
Ugalla 198 F 3
Ugamak Island 52-53 o 3
Uganda 198 F 1
Uganik Island 52-53 K 8
Ugashik, AK 52-53 J 8
Ugashik Bay 52-53 HJ 8
Ugashik Lakes 52-53 J 8
Uglič 154-155 F 6
Ugljan 138-139 F 3
Ugogo 198 FG 3
Ugol'nyj = Beringovskij 154-155 j 5
Uguay 103 E 3

Uha 198 F 2
Uha-dong 166-167 O 3
Uhrichsville, OH 72-73 F 4

Ui-do 170-171 E 5
Uí Fáilghe 116-117 D 7
Uig 116-117 E 3
Uíge 198 BC 3
Uijŏngbu 170-171 F 4
Uiju 170-171 E 2
Uil [SU, place] 154-155 J 8
Uil [SU, river] 142-143 K 6
Uí Néid, Carn — 116-117 AB 9
Uintah and Ouray Indian Reservation [USA ↓ East Tavaputs Plateau] 74-75 J 3
Uintah and Ouray Indian Reservation [USA ↓ Uinta Mountains] 66-67 HJ 5
Uinta Mountains 58-59 DE 3
Uisŏng 170-171 G 4
Uitenhage 198 DE 8

Uj 154-155 L 7
Ujandina 154-155 b 4
Ujar 154-155 R 6
Ujda = Ujdah 194-195 D 2
Ujdah 194-195 D 2

Ujedinenija, ostrov — 154-155 OP 2
Uji-guntō 170-171 G 7
Ujiji 198 E 2-3
Ujjaen = Ujjain 160-161 M 6
Ujjain 160-161 M 6
Ujung Pandang 174-175 G 8

Ukerewe Island 198 F 2
Ukiah, CA 58-59 B 4
Ukiah, OR 66-67 D 3
Ukimbu 198 F 3
Ukonongo 198 F 3
Ukraine 110-111 O-Q 6
Ukrainian Soviet Socialist Republic 142-143 E-G 6
Ukumbi 198 F 3
Uku-shima 170-171 G 6

'Ulā', Al- 160-161 D 5
Ulaanbaatar 166-167 K 2
Ulaan Choto = Ulan Hot 166-167 N 2
Ulaangom 166-167 G 1-2
Ulaan mörön [TJ ◁ Dre Chhu] 166-167 G 5
Ulaan uul 166-167 G 5
Ulaidh = Ulster 116-117 DE 6
Ulak Island 52-53 t 7
Ulala = Gorno-Altajsk 154-155 Q 7
Ulamba 198 D 3
Ulan = Dulaan Chijd 166-167 H 4
Ulan Bator = Ulaanbaatar 166-167 K 2
Ulan Bator = Ulaan Bataar 166-167 K 2
Ulan-Burgasy, chrebet — 154-155 UV 7
Ulan Gom = Ulaangom 166-167 G 1-2
Ulan Hot 166-167 N 2
Ulankom = Ulaangom 166-167 G 1-2
Ulan-Udė 154-155 U 7
Ulapes 103 C 4
Ulastai = Uljastaj 166-167 H 2
Ulawa 174-175 k 6
Ul'ba 154-155 P 7
Ulchin 170-171 G 4
Ulcinj 138-139 H 5
Uldza = Bajan Uul 166-167 L 2
Üldzejt = Öldzijt 166-167 J 2
Uldz gol 166-167 L 2
Uleåborg = Oulu 114-115 L 5
Uleelheue 174-175 C 5
Ulen, MN 68-69 H 2
Ulete 198 G 3
Ulety 154-155 V 7
Ulge 198 BC 3
Ulhasnagar 160-161 L 7
Uliaga Island 52-53 m 4
Uliassutai = Uliastaj 166-167 H 2
Uliastaj 166-167 H 2
Ulijasutai = Uliastaj 166-167 H 2
Ulindi 198 E 2
Ulingan 174-175 N 7
Ulja 154-155 b 6
Uljanovsk 154-155 H 7
Uljinskij chrebet 154-155 ab 6
Ulkatcho 48 E 3
Ulladulla 182-183 K 7
Ullapool 116-117 FG 3
Ullin, IL 70-71 F 7
Ullsfjord 114-115 HJ 3
Ullswater 116-117 J 6
Ullŭng-do 166-167 P 4
Ullyul 170-171 E 3
Ulm 124 D 4
Ulm, AR 78-79 D 3
Ulm, MT 66-67 H 2
Ulm, WY 68-69 C 3
Uløy 114-115 J 3
Ulsan 166-167 OP 4
Ulster 116-117 DE 6
Ulster Canal 116-117 DE 6
Ulu 154-155 Y 5
Ulúa, Río — 58-59 J 8
Ulugh Muz tagh 166-167 F 4
Uluguru Mountains 198 G 3
Ulutau 154-155 M 8
Ulutau, gora — 154-155 M 8
Ulva 116-117 E 4
Ulverston 116-117 H 6
'Ulyā, Qaryat al- 160-161 F 5
Ulyastai = Uliastaj 166-167 H 2
Ulysses, KS 68-69 F 7
Ulysses, NE 68-69 H 5

Umala 98-99 F 8
Umal'tinskij 154-155 Z 7
Umán [MEX] 86-87 PQ 7
Uman' [SU] 142-143- F 6
Umanak = Umánaq 46-47 ab 3
Umanak Fjord 46-47 Za 3
Umánaq 46-47 ab 3
Umatilla Indian Reservation 66-67 D 3
Umatilla River 66-67 D 3
Umba = Lesnoj 154-155 EF 4
Umbarger, TX 76-77 C 5
Umboi 174-175 N 8
Úmbria 138-139 DE 4
Umbu [TJ] 166-167 F 5
Umeå 114-115 HJ 6
Ume älv 114-115 H 5
Umiat, AK 52-53 K 2
Umiris 98-99 J 7
Umm ad-Durūs, Sabkhat — 194-195 B 4
Umm al-Kataf, Khalīj — 199 D 6
Umm al-Qaywayn 160-161 GH 5
Umm ar-Rabīyah, Wād — 194-195 C 2
Umm aṭ-Ṭuyūr al-Fawqānī, Jabal — 199 D 6
Umm Badr 194-195 K 6
Umm Ball 194-195 K 6
Umm Bishtīt, Bi'r — 199 DE 6
Umm Bujmah 199 C 3
Umm Durmān 194-195 L 5
Umm el-'Abid 194-195 H 3
Umm Hagar = Om Hajer 194-195 M 6
Umm Hajer = Om Hajer 194-195 M 6
Umm Ḥibāl, Bi'r — 199 C 6
Umm 'Inab, Jabal — 199 C 5
Umm Kaddādah 194-195 K 6
Umm Keddāda = Umm Kaddādah 194-195 K 6
Umm Laǧǧ = Umm Lajj 160-161 D 5
Umm Lajj 160-161 D 5
Umm Naqqāṭ, Jabal — 199 CD 5
Umm Quṣur, Jazīrat — 199 D 3-4
Umm Rashrash = Ēlat 160-161 C 4
Umm Ruwābah 194-195 L 6
Umm Sa'īd, Bi'r — 199 CD 3
Umm Shāghir, Jabal — 199 B 6
Umnak Island 30 D 35-36
Umnak Pass 52-53 mn 4
Umniati 198 E 5
Umpqua River 66-67 AB 4
Ŭmsŏng 170-171 F 4
Umtali = Mutare 198 F 5
Umtata 198 E 8
Umvuma = Mvuma 198 F 5
Umzimvubu 198 EF 8

Una [BR] 98-99 M 8
Una [YU] 138-139 G 3
Unac 138-139 G 3
Unadilla, GA 80-81 DE 4
Unaí 98-99 K 8
'Unaizah = 'Unayzah 160-161 E 5
Unaka Mountains 80-81 DE 3
Unalakleet, AK 46-47 D 5
Unalakleet River 52-53 GH 5
Unalaska, AK 52-53 n 4
Unalaska Bay 52-53 n 3-4
Unalaska Island 30 D 35
Unalga Island [USA, Delarof Islands] 52-53 t 7
Unalga Island [USA, Unalaska Island] 52-53 no 4
'Unayzah [Saudi Arabia] 160-161 E 5
'Unayzah, Jabal — 160-161 DE 4
Uncía 98-99 F 8
Uncompahgre Peak 58-59 E 4
Uncompahgre Plateau 74-75 JK 3
Underwood, ND 68-69 F 2
Undurkhan = Öndörchaan 166-167 L 2
Uneča 142-143 F 5
Uneiuxi, Rio — 98-99 F 5
Unga, AK 52-53 c 2
Unga Island 46-47 D 6
Ungalik, AK 52-53 G 4
Ungalik River 52-53 GH 4
Unga Strait 52-53 c 2
Ungava 46-47 V-X 6
Ungava Bay 46-47 X 6
Ungava Crater = New Quebec Crater 46-47 VW 5
Ungava Peninsula 46-47 VW 5
Unggi 170-171 H 1
União 98-99 L 5
União dos Palmares 98-99 MN 6
Unib, Khawr — 199 D 7
Unije 138-139 EF 3
Unimak, AK 52-53 a 2
Unimak Bight 52-53 ab 2
Unimak Island 30 D 35
Unimak Pass 52-53 o 3
Unini, Rio — 98-99 G 5
Union, MO 70-71 E 6
Union, MS 78-79 E 4
Union, OR 66-67 E 3
Union, SC 80-81 F 3
Union, WV 80-81 F 2
Unión [RA] 103 C 5
Union [Saint Vincent] 88-89 Q 8
Unión, La — [E] 132-133 G 10
Unión, La — [ES] 58-59 J 9
Unión, La — [MEX] 86-87 K 9
Unión, La — [PE, Huánuco] 98-99 D 6-7
Unión, La — [RCH] 103 B 6
Union, Mount — 74-75 G 5
Union City, IN 70-71 H 5
Union City, NJ 82 III b 2
Union City, PA 72-73 FG 4
Union City, TN 78-79 E 2
Union Creek, OR 66-67 B 4
Unión de Tula 86-87 HJ 7
Union Pacific Railway 58-59 E 3
Union Point, GA 80-81 E 4
Union Springs, AL 78-79 G 4
Union Station [USA, Los Angeles] 83 III c 1
Uniontown, AL 78-79 F 4
Uniontown, KY 70-71 G 7
Uniontown, PA 72-73 G 5
Unionville, IA 70-71 D 5
Unionville, NV 66-67 DE 5
United Arab Emirates 160-161 GH 6
United Kingdom 116-117 C-E 5
United Nations-Headquarters 82 III c 2
United Provinces = Uttar Pradesh 160-161 MN 5
United Pueblos Indian Reservation 76-77 A 5
United States 58-59 C-K 4
United States Atomic Energy Commission Reservation = National Reactor Testing Station 66-67 G 4
Unity 49 D 4
Unity, ME 72-73 M 2
Universal City, TX 76-77 E 8
University City, MO 70-71 E 6
University Gardens, NY 82 III d 2
University Heights, OH 72-73 F 4
University Park, MD 82 II b 1
University Park, NM 76-77 A 6
Unjamwesi = Unyamwezi 198 F 2-3
Unsan 170-171 E 2-3
Unsan-ni 170-171 EF 3
Unst 116-117 f 3
Unstrut 124 E 3
Unuk River 48 B 1
Unyamwezi 198 F 2-3
Unža 142-143 H 4
Unže Pavinskaja 142-143 MN 4

Uolkitte = Welkītē 194-195 M 7
Uollega = Welega 194-195 LM 7
Uozu 170-171 L 4

Upanda, Serra — 198 BC 4
Upemba, Lac — 198 E 3
Upemba, Parc national de l' 198 E 3
Upernavik 46-47 Z 3
Upham, ND 68-69 F 1
Upham, NM 76-77 A 6
Upington 198 D 7
Upnuk Lake 52-53 H 6
Upolokša 114-115 O 4
Upolu 174-175 c 1
Upolu Point 78-79 de 2
Upper Arrow Lake 48 J 4
Upper Austria = Oberösterreich 124 F-H 4
Upper Bay 82 III b 2-3
Upper Darby, PA 72-73 J 4-5
Upper Egypt = Aṣ-Ṣa'īd 194-195 L 3
Upper Guinea 26-27 JK 5
Upper Humber River 51 H 3
Upper Klamath Lake 66-67 BC 4
Upper Laberge 52-53 U 6
Upper Lake 66-67 C 5
Upper Lake, CA 74-75 B 3
Upper Lough Erne 116-117 D 6
Upper Musquodoboit 51 E 5
Upper Nile = Aali an-Nīl 194-195 KL 7
Upper Peninsula 58-59 J 2
Upper Red Lake 70-71 C 1
Upper Sandusky, OH 72-73 E 4
Upper Seal Lake = Lac d'Iberville 46-47 W 6
Upper Volta = Burkina Faso 194-195 D 6
Uppingham 116-117 L 8
Uppland 114-115 G 7-H 8
Uppsala [S, administrative unit] 114-115 GH 7
Uppsala [S, place] 114-115 G 8
Upsala 70-71 E 1
Upsalquitch 51 C 4
Upstart Bay 182-183 J 3
Upton, KY 70-71 GH 7
Upton, WY 68-69 D 3
Uptown, Chicago-, IL 83 II ab 1

'Uqaylah, Al- 194-195 H 2
'Uqayr, Al- 160-161 FG 5
Uqṣur, Al- 194-195 L 3

Ur 160-161 F 4
Ur, Wādī — 199 B 6-7
Urabá, Golfo de — 98-99 D 3
Urabá, Isla — 58-59 bc 3
Uracas = Farallon de Pajaros 148-149 S 7
Urakawa 170-171 c 2
Ural 154-155 J 8
Ural, MT 66-67 F 1
Ural, Pol'arnyj — 154-155 LM 4
Ural, Pripol'arnyj — 154-155 KL 4-5
Ural, Severnyj — 154-155 K 5-6
Uralmed'stroj = Krasnoural'sk 154-155 L 6
Urals 154-155 K 5-7
Ural'sk 154-155 J 7
Urandangi 182-183 G 4
Urandi 98-99 L 7
Urania, LA 78-79 C 5
Uranium City 46-47 P 6
Uraricoera 98-99 H 3
Uraricoera, Rio — 98-99 G 4
Ura-Tube 160-161 K 3
Uravan, CO 74-75 J 3
Urawa 166-167 QR 4
'Uray'irah 160-161 F 5
'Urayyiḍah, Bi'r — 199 BC 3
Urbana, IL 70-71 FG 5
Urbana, OH 72-73 E 4
Urbana, La — 98-99 F 3
Urbino 138-139 E 4
Urbión, Picos de — 132-133 F 8
Urcos 98-99 E 7
Urda 142-143 J 6
Urdžar 154-155 P 8
Uren' 142-143 J 4
Ureparapara 182-183 N 2
Ures 58-59 DE 6
'Urf, Jabal al- 199 C 4
Urfa 160-161 D 3
'Urf Umm Rashīd 199 D 5
Urga 154-155 K 9
Urga = Ulaanbaatar 166-167 K 2
Urgenč 154-155 L 9
Uribe 98-99 E 4
Uribia 98-99 E 2
Urickoje 154-155 M 7
Urilia Bay 52-53 a 2
Urim = Ur 160-161 F 4
Urique, Río — 86-87 G 4
Urīsā = Orissa 160-161 N 7-O 6
Uriuaná, Rio — 98-99 N 6
Urla 160-161 B 3
Urla 142-143 E 8
Urmannyj 154-155 M 5
Urmia = Daryācheh Orūmīyeh 160-161 F 3
Urmia = Reḍā'īyeh 160-161 EF 3
Urmia, Daryācheh — = Daryācheh Orūmīyeh 160-161 F 3
Ursatjevskaja = Chavast 160-161 K 2
Ursine, NV 74-75 F 3-4
Urt Mörön = Chadzaar 166-167 G 4
Uruaçu 98-99 K 7
Uruana 98-99 JK 8
Uruapan del Progreso 58-59 F 8
Uruará, Rio — 98-99 M 6
Urubamba 98-99 E 7
Urubamba, Río — 98-99 E 7
Urubaxi, Rio — 98-99 F 5
Urubu, Cachoeira do — 98-99 OP 11
Urubu, Rio — 98-99 J 6
Urubu, Travessão do — 98-99 M 8
Urucará 98-99 H 5
Urucu, Rio — 98-99 FG 7
Uruçuí 98-99 L 6
Uruçuí, Serra do — 98-99 K 7-L 6
Urucurituba 98-99 H 5
Uruguai, Rio — 103 F 3
Uruguaiana 103 E 3
Uruguay 103 EF 4
Uruguay, Río — [RA ◁ Río de la Plata] 103 E 3
Uruguay, Salto Grande del — 103 F 3
Urumbi 98-99 F 4
Ürümchi 166-167 F 3
Urumchi = Ürümchi 166-167 F 3
Urundi = Burundi 198 EF 2
Ur'ung-Chaja 154-155 VW 3
Urup, ostrov — 154-155 cd 8
Urupa, Rio — 98-99 G 10
Uruppu = ostrov Urup 154-155 cd 8
'Urūq al-Mu'tariḍah, Al- 160-161 G 6-7
Uruša 154-155 X 7
Uruyén 98-99 G 3
Urville, Île d' 31 C 31
Urville, Mer d' 31 C 14-15
Urville, Tanjung d' 174-175 L 7
Urziceni 138-139 M 3
Uržum 154-155 HJ 6

Usa 154-155 K 4
Usagara 198 G 3
Uşak 160-161 B 3
Usakos 198 BC 6
Ušakova, ostrov — 154-155 OP 1
Usborne, Mount — 103 E 8
Usedom 124 F 1-G 2
Usetsu = Noto 170-171 L 4
'Usfān 160-161 D 6
Ushagat Island 52-53 L 7
Ushakova Island = ostrov Ušakova 154-155 OP 2
Ushakov Island = ostrov Ušakova 154-155 OP 1
Usherville 49 G 4
Ushibuka 170-171 GH 6
Ushuaia 103 C 8
Usk 48 C 2
Usk, WA 66-67 E 1
Usk, River — 116-117 H 9
Üsküdar, İstanbul- 160-161 BC 2
Üsküp = Skopje 138-139 J 4-5
Usman' 142-143 GH 5
Usolje = Usolje-Sibirskoje 154-155 T 7
Usolje-Sibirskoje 154-155 T 7
Usolje-Solikamskoje = Berezniki 154-155 JK 6
Usolye Sibirskoye = Usolje-Sibirskoje 154-155 T 7
Ussagara = Usagara 198 G 3
Ussuri = Wusuli Jiang 166-167 P 2
Ussurijsk 154-155 Z 9
Ussurijskij zaliv 170-171 HJ 1
Ust'-Abakanskoje = Abakan 154-155 R 7
Ust'-Barguzin 154-155 UV 7
Ust'-Bol'šereck 154-155 de 7
Ust'-Čaun 154-155 h 4
Ust'-Cil'ma 154-155 J 4
Ust'-Čižapka 154-155 OP 6
Ustica 138-139 E 6
Ust'-Ilimsk 154-155 T 6
Ust'-Ilyč 142-143 KL 3
Ústí nad Labem 124 FG 3
Ust'-Išim 154-155 N 6
Ustje-Agapy = Agapa 154-155 Q 3
Ust'-Juribej 154-155 MN 4
Ustka 124 H 1
Ust'-Kamčatsk 154-155 f 6
Ust Kamchatsk = Ust'-Kamčatsk 154-155 f 6
Ust'-Kamenogorsk 154-155 OP 7-8
Ust'-Kan 154-155 PQ 7
Ust'-Karabula 154-155 S 6
Ust'-Karsk 154-155 W 7
Ust'-Katav 142-143 L 5
Ust'-Kulom 154-155 JK 5
Ust'-Kut 154-155 U 6
Ust'-Luga 142-143 E 4
Ust'-Maja 154-155 Z 5
Ust'-Nem 142-143 KL 3
Ust'-Nera 154-155 b 5
Uštobe 154-155 O 8
Ust'-Orda = Ust'-Ordynskij 154-155 TU 7
Ust'-Ordynskij 154-155 TU 7
Ust-Ordynsky-Buryat Autonomous Area = 11 ◁ 154-155 T 7
Ust'-Oz'ornoje 154-155 Q 6
Ust'-Pinega 154-155 G 5
Ust'-Port 154-155 PQ 4
Ust'-Ščugor 154-155 K 5
Ust Sysolsk = Syktyvkar 154-155 J 5
Ust'-Tatta 154-155 Za 5
Ust'-Tym 154-155 OP 6
Ust'-Ulagan 154-155 Q 7
Ust'-Ura 142-143 HJ 3
Ust'urt, plato — 154-155 K 9
Ust'-Usa 154-155 K 4
Ust'-Vym' 142-143 K 3
Usu-dake 170-171 b 2
Usuki 170-171 HJ 6
Usuktuk River 52-53 J 1
Usulután 88-89 B 8
Usumacinta, Río — 58-59 H 8
Usumbura = Bujumbura 198 EF 2
Usuyŏng 170-171 EF 5
Usu zan 170-171 b 2

Utah 58-59 DE 4
Utah Lake 58-59 D 3
Utasinai 170-171 c 2
Ute, IA 70-71 C 4
Ute Creek 76-77 C 5
Ute Mountain Indian Reservation 74-75 J 4
Ute Peak 74-75 J 4
Utete 198 G 3
'Uthmānīyah, Al- 199 BC 4
U Thong 174-175 C 4
Utiariti 98-99 H 7
Utica, KS 68-69 F 6
Utica, MS 78-79 D 4
Utica, NY 58-59 LM 3
Utica, OH 72-73 E 4
Utiel 132-133 G 9
Utik Lake 49 KL 3
Utikuma Lake 48 K 2
Utiura-wan 166-167 R 3
Utopia, AK 52-53 L 3-4
Utopia, TX 76-77 E 8
Utopia, New York-, NY 82 III d 2
Utrecht [NL] 132-133 K 2
Utrera 132-133 E 10
Utrillas 132-133 G 8
Utsjoki 114-115 M 3
Utsunomiya 166-167 QR 4
Uttaradit 174-175 D 3
Uttar Andamān = North Andaman 160-161 P 8
Uttar Pradesh 160-161 MN 5
Uttoxeter 116-117 K 8
Utukok River 52-53 GH 2
Utunomiya = Utsunomiya 166-167 QR 4
Utupua 174-175 l 7

Uu = Wuhu 166-167 M 5
Uudenmaan lääni 114-115 K-M 7
Uusikaarlepyy = Nykarleby 114-115 K 6
Uusikaupunki 114-115 J 7
Uusimaa 114-115 KL 7

Uva 142-143 K 4
Uvalde, TX 58-59 G 6
Uvarovo 142-143 H 5
Uvat 154-155 M 6
Uvéa 174-175 b 1
Uvea = Île Ouvéa 182-183 N 4
Uvel'skij 142-143 M 5
Uvinza 198 F 2-3
Uvira 198 E 2
Uvs 166-167 G 2
Uvs nuur 166-167 G 1

Uwajima 166-167 P 5
'Uwayjā', Al- 160-161 G 6
Uwayl 194-195 K 7
'Uwaynāt, Jabal al- 194-195 K 4
'Uwaynidhīyah, Jazīrat al- 199 DE 4
'Uwayriḍ, Ḥarrat al- 160-161 D 5
Uwazima = Uwajima 166-167 P 5
Uwimbi 198 FG 3
Uwinsa = Uvinza 198 F 2-3

Uxbridge 72-73 G 2
Uxmal 58-59 J 7

Uyak Bay 52-53 KL 8
Uyuni 98-99 F 9
Uyuni, Salar de — 98-99 F 9

Už 142-143 E 5
Uzbek Soviet Socialist Republic 160-161 J 2-K 3
Uzboj 160-161 H 2-3
Uzen' 142-143 K 7
Uzgen 160-161 L 2
Užgorod 142-143 D 6
Uzinki = Ouzinkie, AK 52-53 LM 8
Uzlovaja 142-143 G 5
Užur 154-155 QR 6

V

Vääkiö 114-115 N 5
Vaala 114-115 M 5
Vaaldam 198 E 7
Vaal River = Vaalrivier 198 E 7
Vaalrivier 198 E 7
Vaalwater 198 E 6
Vaasa 114-115 J 6
Vác 124 J 5
Vacamonte, Punta — 58-59 b 3
Vacaria 103 F 3
Vacaville, CA 74-75 BC 3
Vach [SU] 154-155 O 5
Vachš 160-161 K 3
Vader, WA 66-67 B 2
Vadheim 114-115 A 7
Vaḍhvān = Wadhwān 160-161 L 6
Vadōdarā 160-161 L 6
Vadsø 114-115 NO 2
Vadstena 114-115 F 8
Vaduz 124 D 5
Værøy 114-115 E 4
Vaga 142-143 H 3
Vagaj 154-155 M 6
Vågåmo 114-115 C 7
Vágar 116-117 a 1
Vágarfjördhur 116-117 a 1-2
Vaggeryd 114-115 EF 9
Vágø = Vagar 116-117 a 1
Vågsfjord 114-115 G 3
Vágur 116-117 b 2
Váh 124 H 4
Vaiden, MS 78-79 E 4
Vaigach Island = ostrov Vajgač 154-155 KL 3
Vaigat 46-47 a 3
Vaila 116-117 e 3
Vaitupu lu 178 HJ 3
Vajdaguba 114-115 OP 3
Vajgač 142-143 LM 1
Vajgač, ostrov — 154-155 KL 3
Vakaga 194-195 J 7
Valachia 138-139 K-M 3
Valadim = Mavago 198 G 4
Valais 124 C 5
Val-Barrette 72-73 J 1
Valcheta 103 C 6
Valdagno 138-139 D 3
Valdajskaja vozvyšennosť 142-143 F 4
Val d'Aosta 138-139 B 3
Valdemarsvik 114-115 G 8
Valdepeñas 132-133 F 9
Valderaduey 132-133 E 7-8
Valders, WI 70-71 FG 3
Valdés, Península — 103 D 6
Valdesa, La — 58-59 b 3
Valdez, AK 46-47 G 5
Valdia = Weldya 194-195 M 6
Valdivia [RCH] 103 B 5
Val-d'Or 46-47 V 8
Valdosta, GA 58-59 K 5
Valdres 114-115 C 7
Vale, OR 66-67 E 3-4
Vale, SD 68-69 E 3
Valea-lui-Mihai 138-139 K 2
Vålebru 114-115 D 7
Valemont 48 H 3
Valença [BR, Bahia] 98-99 M 7
Valença [P] 132-133 C 7-8
Valença = Valencia [YV] 98-99 F 2
Valença do Piauí 98-99 L 6
Valence 132-133 K 6
Valencia [E, landscape] 132-133 G 8-9
Valencia [E, place] 132-133 GH 9
Valencia [YV] 98-99 F 2
Valencia, Golfo de — 132-133 H 9
Valencia, Lago de — 98-99 F 2
Valencia de Alcántara 132-133 D 9
Valencia de Don Juan 132-133 E 7
Valenciennes 132-133 J 3
Valentim, Serra do — 98-99 L 6
Valentin 154-155 Za 9
Valentine, MT 68-69 B 2
Valentine, NE 68-69 F 4
Valentine, TX 76-77 B 7
Valenza 138-139 C 3

Valenza 279

Valera 98-99 E 3
Valera, TX 76-77 E 7
Valga 142-143 E 4
Valhalla Mountains 66-67 DE 1
Valiente, Península — 88-89 F 10
Valier, MT 66-67 G 1
Valjevo 138-139 H 3
Valka 142-143 E 4
Valkeakoski 114-115 L 7
Valladolid [E] 132-133 E 8
Valladolid [MEX] 58-59 J 7
Valle, AZ 74-75 G 5
Vallecillo 76-77 DE 9
Vallecito Mountains 74-75 E 6
Vallecito Reservoir 68-69 C 7
Valle de Bandenas 86-87 H 7
Valle de la Pascua 98-99 FG 3
Valle del Rosario 86-87 GH 4
Valle de Zaragoza 76-77 B 9
Valledupar 98-99 E 2
Vallée-Jonction 51 A 4
Valle Grande [BOL] 98-99 G 8
Valle Hermoso [MEX] 58-59 G 6
Vallejo, CA 58-59 B 4
Vallenar 103 B 3
Valletta 138-139 F 8
Valley, NE 68-69 H 5
Valley, WY 66-67 J 3
Valley City, ND 68-69 GH 2
Valley Falls, KS 70-71 C 6
Valley Falls, OR 66-67 C 4
Valleyfield 46-47 VW 8
Valley Mills, TX 76-77 F 7
Valley of 10,000 Smokes 52-53 K 7
Valley of Willows, AK 52-53 JK 2
Valley Pass 66-67 FG 5
Valley River 49 H 5
Valley Stream, NY 82 III de 3
Valleyview 48 J 2
Valliant, OK 76-77 G 5-6
Vallican 48 J 5
Valls 132-133 H 8
Val Marie 68-69 C 1
Valmiera 142-143 DE 4
Valmont, NM 76-77 AB 6
Valmy, NV 66-67 E 5
Valnera 132-133 F 7
Valognes 116-117 K 11
Valparaiso, IN 70-71 G 5
Valparaiso, NE 68-69 H 5
Valparaíso [MEX] 86-87 HJ 6
Valparaíso [RCH] 103 B 4
Vals, Tanjung — 174-175 L 8
Valsbaai [ZA, Kaapland] 198 C 8
Valsch, Cape — = Tanjung Vals 174-175 L 8
Valsetz, OR 66-67 B 3
Valujki 142-143 G 5
Valverde [DOM] 88-89 L 5
Valverde [E] 194-195 A 3
Valverde del Camino 132-133 D 10
Vammala 114-115 K 7
Vamos Ver 98-99 OP 8
Van 160-161 E 3
Van Alstyne, TX 76-77 F 6
Vananda, MT 68-69 C 2
Van Asch van Wijck Gebergte 98-99 K 3-L 2
Vanavara 154-155 T 5
Van Buren, AR 76-77 G 5
Van Buren, ME 72-73 MN 1
Van Buren, MO 78-79 D 2
Vanceboro, ME 72-73 N 2
Vanceboro, NC 80-81 H 3
Vanceburg, KY 72-73 E 5
Van Cortlandt Park 82 III c 1
Vancouver 46-47 M 8
Vancouver, WA 58-59 B 2
Vancouver, Mount — 52-53 RS 6
Vancouver Island 46-47 L 8
Vandalia, IL 70-71 F 6
Vandalia, MO 70-71 E 6
Vandemere, NC 80-81 H 3
Vandenberg Air Force Base 74-75 C 5
Vanderbilt, TX 76-77 F 8
Vanderhoof 48 F 2
Vanderlin Island 182-183 G 3
Van Diemen, Cape — 182-183 EF 2
Van Diemen Gulf 182-183 F 2
Van Diemen Strait = Ōsumi-kaikyō 166-167 P 5
Vāndrā = Bāndra 160-161 L 7
Vandry 50 P 3
Vänern 114-115 E 8
Vänersborg 114-115 E 8
Vanga = Shimoni 198 GH 2
Vangaindrano 198 J 6
Van gölü 160-161 E 3
Vangunu 174-175 j 6
Van Horn, TX 76-77 B 7
Van Houten, NM 76-77 B 4
Vanikoro Islands 174-175 l 7
Vanimo 174-175 M 7
Vankarem 154-155 k 4
van Keulenfjord 114-115 jk 6
Vankleek Hill 72-73 J 2
van Mijenfjord 114-115 jk 6
Vännäs 114-115 HJ 6
Vannes 132-133 F 5
Van Norman, MT 68-69 C 2
Vannøy 114-115 HJ 2
Vanrhynsdorp 198 CD 8
Vanrook 182-183 H 3
Vansbro 114-115 EF 7
Vansittart Bay 182-183 E 2
Vansittart Island 46-47 U 4
Van Tassell, WY 68-69 D 4
Vanua Lava 182-183 N 2
Vanua Levu 174-175 b 2
Vanuatu 182-183 N 2-O 3
Van Wert, OH 70-71 H 5
Vanwyksvlei 198 D 8
Vanzevat 154-155 M 5
Vanžil'kynak 154-155 P 5
Vārānasi 160-161 N 5
Vārangal = Warangal 160-161 MN 7
Varangerbotn 114-115 N 2
Varangerfjord 114-115 NO 2-3
Varanger halvøya 114-115 NO 2
Varaždin 138-139 FG 2
Varazze 138-139 C 3
Varberg 114-115 DE 9
Vardar 138-139 K 5
Varde 114-115 C 10
Vardhā = Wardha [IND, place] 160-161 M 6
Vardhā = Wardha [IND, river] 160-161 M 6
Vardø 114-115 O 2
Varella, Cap — = Mui Diêu 174-175 EF 4
Varella, Cape — = Mui Diêu 174-175 EF 4
Vareš 138-139 H 3
Varese 138-139 C 3
Varfolomejevka 154-155 Z 9
Vargas Island 48 DE 5
Vargem Grande [BR, Amazonas] 98-99 DE 6
Varginha 98-99 K 9
Varillas 103 B 2
Varillas, Las — 103 D 4
Varjegan 154-155 O 5
Varkaus 114-115 MN 6
Värmland 114-115 E 8
Värmlandsnäs 114-115 E 8
Varna [BG] 138-139 MN 4
Varnado, LA 78-79 E 5
Värnamo 114-115 F 9
Varnek 154-155 KL 4
Varney, NM 76-77 B 5
Varnville, SC 80-81 F 4
Varsinais Suomi 114-115 JK 7
Varšipel'da 142-143 G 3
Várzea Alegre [BR, Goiás] 98-99 O 9
Varzuga 142-143 G 2
Vasa = Vaasa 114-115 J 6
Vaşcău 138-139 K 2
Vashon Island 66-67 B 2
Vaška 142-143 J 3
Vaskojoki 114-115 LM 3
Vaslui 138-139 MN 2
Vassar 72-73 E 3
Vassar, MI 72-73 E 3
Västerås 114-115 FG 8
Västerbotten [S, administrative unit] 114-115 F-J 5
Västerbotten [S, landscape] 114-115 H 6-J 5
Västerdalälven 114-115 EF 7
Västergötland 114-115 E 9-F 8
Västernorrland 114-115 GH 6
Västervik 114-115 G 9
Västmanland 114-115 FG 8
Vasto 138-139 F 4
Vas'ugan 154-155 O 6
Vas'uganje 154-155 N 5-O 6
Vasvár 124 H 5
Vasyugane Swamp = Vas'uganje 154-155 N 5-O 6
Vaté, Île — = Efate 182-183 N 3
Vatersay 116-117 D 4
Vatican City 138-139 DE 5
V'atka 154-155 H 6
V'atka = Kirov 154-155 HJ 6
Vatnajökull 114-115 e 2
Vatoa 178 J 4
Vatomandry 198 JK 5
Vatra Dornei 138-139 L 2
V'atskije Pol'any 154-155 HJ 6
Vättern 114-115 F 8
Vaughn, MT 66-67 H 2
Vaughn, NM 76-77 B 5
Vaupés, Río — 98-99 E 4
Vauxhall 49 BC 5
Vava'u Group 174-175 c 2
Växjö 114-115 F 9
V'azemskij 154-155 Za 8
V'az'ma 142-143 F 4
V. Carranza, Presa — 86-87 KL 4
Veadeiros, Chapada dos — 98-99 K 7-8
Veblen, SD 68-69 H 3
Vedea 138-139 L 3
Vedia 103 D 4
Veedersburg, IN 70-71 G 5
Vega 114-115 D 5
Vega, TX 76-77 C 5
Vega, La — [DOM] 58-59 MN 8
Vega Bay 52-53 r 7
Vega de Granada 132-133 EF 10
Vega Point 52-53 r 7
Veglio = Krk 138-139 J 5
Vegreville 46-47 O 7
Veimandu Channel 36 a 2
Veiros 98-99 MN 6
Vejer de la Frontera 132-133 DE 10
Vejle 114-115 C 10
Veka Vekalla = Vella Lavella 174-175 j 6
Vela, Cabo de la — 98-99 E 2
Vela de Coro, La — 98-99 F 2
Velay 132-133 JK 6
Velebit 138-139 F 3
Vélez-Málaga 132-133 EF 10
Velhas, Rio das — 98-99 L 8
Velho = Mágoè 198 F 5
Velikaja [SU ◁ Anadyrskij zaliv] 154-155 h 5
Velikaja [SU, Pskovskoje ozero ←] 142-143 E 4
Velikaja Ičinskaja sopka 154-155 e 6
Velikaja Kl'učevskaja sopka 154-155 f 6
Velikaja Kor'akskaja sopka 154-155 ef 7
Velikaja Kronockaja sopka 154-155 ef 7
Velikije Luki 142-143 EF 4
Velikij Ševeluč 154-155 f 6
Velikij Ust'ug 154-155 GH 5
Veliko Tărnovo 138-139 L 4
Velič 142-143 F 4
Velkomstpynten 114-115 j 5
Vella Lavella 174-175 j 6
Velletri 138-139 E 5
Vellore 160-161 M 8
Velluga 154-155 H 6
Velmerstot 124 D 3
Vel'sk 154-155 G 5
Velucá, Cerro — 88-89 D 7
Vēlūr = Vellore 160-161 M 8
Velva, ND 68-69 F 1-2
Vemdalen 114-115 EF 6
Venado, Isla — 58-59 b 3
Venado Tuerto 103 D 4
Venango, NE 68-69 EF 5
Venator, OR 66-67 DE 4
Vendas Novas 132-133 C 9
Vendée 132-133 G 5
Vendôme 132-133 H 5
Veneta, OR 66-67 B 3-4
Venetia = Vèneto 138-139 DE 3
Venetie, AK 46-47 G 4
Venetie Landing, AK 52-53 OP 3
Veneto 138-139 DE 3
Veneza 98-99 C 9
Venèzia 138-139 E 3
Venèzia, Golfo di — 138-139 E 3
Venèzia Tridentina = Trentino Alto Àdige 138-139 D 2
Venezuela 98-99 FG 3
Venezuela, Golfo de — 98-99 E 2
Vēngangā = Wainganga 160-161 MN 6-7
Vengerovo 154-155 O 6
Vengurlā 160-161 L 7
Vēnġurlēṅ = Vengurla 160-161 L 7
Veniaminof, Mount — 52-53 d 1
Venice, FL 80-81 b 3
Venice, LA 78-79 E 6
Venice = Venèzia 138-139 E 3
Venice, Los Angeles-, CA 83 III b 2
Venosa 138-139 F 5
Venta 142-143 D 4
Venta, La — 86-87 NO 8
Venta de Baños 132-133 E 8
Ventana, La — 86-87 KL 6
Ventana, Sierra de la — 103 D 5
Ventnor 116-117 K 10
Ventoux, Mont — 132-133 K 6
Ventspils 142-143 D 4
Ventuari, Río — 98-99 F 3
Ventura, CA 74-75 D 5
Ventura, La — 86-87 K 5
Venustiano Carranza 86-87 OP 9
Vera, TX 76-77 E 6
Vera [RA] 103 D 3
Vera, La — 132-133 E 8
Verá, Laguna — 103 E 3
Veracruz [MEX, administrative unit] 58-59 G 7-8
Veracruz [MEX, place] 58-59 GH 8
Veraguas 88-89 F 10
Veraguas, Escudo de — 88-89 F 10
Veranópolis 103 F 3
Verāval 160-161 KL 6
Verbena, AL 78-79 F 4
Vercelli 138-139 C 3
Verchn'aja Amga 154-155 Y 6
Verchn'aja Salda 142-143 M 4
Verchn'aja Tojma 154-155 GH 5
Verchn'aja Tura 142-143 L 4
Verchneimbatskoje 154-155 QR 5
Verchneje Adimi 170-171 H 1
Verchne Ozernaja 154-155 f 6
Verchneudinsk = Ulan-Udė 154-155 U 7
Verchneural'sk 154-155 KL 7
Verchneusinkoje 154-155 RS 7
Verchnevil'ujsk 154-155 X 5
Verchnij Baskunčak 142-143 J 6
Verchnij Ufalej 154-155 KL 6
Verchojansk 154-155 Za 4
Verchojanskij chrebet 154-155 Y 4-Z 5
Verdalsøyra 114-115 DE 6
Verden 124 D 2
Verde River 74-75 H 5
Verdi, NV 74-75 CD 3
Verdigre, NE 68-69 G 4
Verdon 132-133 L 7
Verdon-sur-Mer, le — 132-133 G 6
Verdun [CDN] 82 I b 2
Verdun [F] 132-133 K 4
Verdura 86-87 FG 5
Vereeniging 198 E 7
Vérendrye, Parc provincial de la — 46-47 V 8
Vereščagino [SU ↓ Igarka] 154-155 QR 5
Vereščagino [SU ← Krasnokamsk] 154-155 JK 6
Vergas, MN 70-71 BC 2
Verín 132-133 D 8
Veríssimo Sarmento 198 D 3
Verkhneudinsk = Ulan-Udė 154-155 U 7
Verkhoyansk = Verchojansk 154-155 Za 4
Verkhoyansk Mountains = Verchojanskij chrebet 154-155 Y 4-b 5
Verkola 142-143 J 3
Verlegenhuken 114-115 jk 4
Vermilion 46-47 O 7
Vermilion, OH 72-73 E 4
Vermilion Bay 78-79 CD 6
Vermilion Cliffs 74-75 G 4
Vermilion Lake 70-71 D 2
Vermilion Range 70-71 DE 2
Vermilion River 70-71 D 1-2
Vermilion River 49 C 4
Vermillion, OH 72-73 E 4
Vermillion, SD 68-69 H 4
Vermillion Bay 50 C 3
Vermillon, Rivière — 72-73 K 1
Vermont 58-59 M 3
Vermont, IL 70-71 E 5
Vernal, UT 66-67 J 5
Vernon, AZ 74-75 J 5
Vernon, CA 83 III c 1
Vernon, NV 66-67 D 5
Vernon, TX 58-59 FG 5
Vernon [CDN, British Colombia] 46-47 N 7
Vernon [CDN, Prince Edward I.] 51 E 4
Vernon [F] 132-133 H 4
Vernon = Onaqui, UT 66-67 G 5
Vernonia, OR 66-67 B 3
Vernyj = Alma-Ata 154-155 O 9
Vero Beach, FL 80-81 cd 3
Verona 138-139 D 3
Verrazano-Narrows Bridge 82 III b 3
Versailles 132-133 HJ 4
Versailles, IN 70-71 H 6
Versailles, KY 70-71 H 6
Versailles, MO 70-71 D 6
Versailles, OH 72-73 D 5
Veršino-Darasunskij 154-155 VW 7
Verte, Île de — 82 I bc 1
Vertientes 88-89 G 4
Verviers 132-133 KL 3
Vervins 132-133 JK 4
Verwood 68-69 D 1
Vescovato 138-139 C 4
Veselí nad Lužnicí 124 G 4
Vesjegonsk 154-155 F 6
Vesoul 132-133 KL 5
Vest-Agder 114-115 B 8
Vesterålen 114-115 FG 3
Vestfjorden 114-115 E 4-F 3
Vestfold 114-115 CD 8
Vestfonna 114-115 l 4
Vestmanna 116-117 a 1
Vestmannaeyjar 114-115 c 3
Vestspitsbergen 114-115 j-l 5
Vestur-Bardhastrandar 114-115 ab 2
Vestur-Húnavatn 114-115 cd 2
Vestur-Ísafjardhar 114-115 b 1-2
Vestur-Skaftafell 114-115 de 3
Vestvågøy 114-115 EF 3
Vesùvio 138-139 F 5
Vesuvius = Vesùvio 138-139 F 5
Veszprem 124 HJ 5
Vetlanda 114-115 F 9
Vetluga 142-143 HJ 4
Vetralla 138-139 DE 4
Vevay, IN 70-71 H 6
Vevay, OH 72-73 D 5
Veynes 132-133 K 6
Veyo, UT 74-75 G 4
Vézère 132-133 H 6
Viacha 98-99 F 8
Vian, OK 76-77 G 5
Viana [BR, Maranhão] 98-99 K 5
Viana del Bollo 132-133 D 7
Viana do Castelo 132-133 C 8
Vianópolis 98-99 K 8
Viarèggio 138-139 CD 4
Vibank 49 G 5
Víbora, La — 76-77 C 9
Viborg 114-115 C 9
Viborg, SD 68-69 H 4
Viborg = Vyborg 154-155 DE 5
Vibo Valentia 138-139 FG 6
Vic 132-133 J 8
Vicente, Point — 74-75 D 6
Vicente Guerrero [MEX, Baja California Norte] 86-87 BC 2
Vicente Guerrero [MEX, Durango] 86-87 HJ 6
Vicenza 138-139 D 3
Viceroy 68-69 D 1
Vichada, Río — 98-99 F 4
Vichy 132-133 J 5
Vici, OK 76-77 E 4
Vicksburg, AZ 74-75 FG 6
Vicksburg, MI 70-71 H 4
Vicksburg, MS 58-59 HJ 5
Victor, CO 68-69 D 6
Victor, ID 66-67 H 4
Victor, MT 66-67 F 2
Victor Harbor 182-183 G 7
Victoria, KS 68-69 G 6
Victoria, TX 58-59 G 6
Victoria [AUS] 182-183 HJ 7
Victoria [CDN] 46-47 M 8
Victoria [HK] 166-167 LM 7
Victoria [MAL] 174-175 FG 5
Victoria [RA] 103 DE 4
Victoria [RCH, Araucanía] 103 B 5
Victoria [SY] 188-189 N 9
Victoria [WAN] 194-195 F 8
Victoria [ZW] 198 F 6
Victoria, Ciudad — 58-59 G 7
Victoria, Île — ≈ Victoria Island 46-47 O-Q 3
Victoria, Lake — [lake] 198 F 2
Victoria, Mount — 174-175 N 8
Victoria, Mount — = Tomaniive 174-175 a 2
Victoria, Pont — 82 I b 2
Victoria and Albert Mountains 46-47 VW 1-2
Victoria Beach [CDN] 50 A 2
Victoria Cove 51 J 3
Victoria Hill 88-89 JK 2
Victoria Island [CDN] 46-47 O-Q 3
Victoria Lake [CDN] 51 H 3
Victoria Land 31 B 17-15
Victoria Peak 48 DE 4
Victoria Peak [USA] 76-77 B 7
Victoria Point = Kawthaung 174-175 C 4
Victoria River 182-183 EF 3
Victoria River Downs 182-183 F 3
Victoria Strait 46-47 QR 4
Victoriaville 72-73 KL 1
Victoria-Wes 198 D 8
Victoria West = Victoria-Wes 198 D 8
Victorica 103 C 5
Victorino 98-99 F 4
Victorville, CA 74-75 E 5
Vičuga 154-155 G 6
Vida, MT 68-69 D 2
Vidal, CA 74-75 F 5
Vidalia, GA 80-81 E 4
Vidalia, LA 78-79 D 5
Vidhareidhi 116-117 b 1
Vidhoy 116-117 b 1
Vidim 154-155 T 6
Vidin 138-139 K 3-4
Vidio, Cabo — 132-133 DE 7
Vidisha 160-161 M 6
Vidor, TX 76-77 GH 7
Vidra 138-139 M 3
Vidzeme 142-143 DE 4
Viedma 103 D 6
Viedma, Lago — 103 B 7
Vienchan = Vientiane 174-175 D 3
Vienna, GA 80-81 E 4
Vienna, IL 70-71 F 7
Vienna, MO 70-71 E 6
Vienna, SD 68-69 H 3
Vienna, WV 72-73 F 5
Vienna = Wien 124 H 4
Vienne [F, place] 132-133 K 6
Vienne [F, river] 132-133 H 5
Vientiane 174-175 D 3
Vientos, Los — 103 BC 2
Vientos, Paso de los — 58-59 M 7-8
Vieques 58-59 N 8
Vierwaldstätter See 124 D 5
Vierzon 132-133 J 5
Viesca 86-87 J 5
Vieste 138-139 G 5
Vietnam 174-175 D 2-E 4
Viêt Tri 174-175 E 2
Vieux Fort 88-89 Q 8
View, TX 76-77 E 6
View Park, CA 83 III bc 1
Vigan 174-175 GH 3
Vigia 98-99 K 5
Vigía, El — 98-99 E 3
Vigía Chico 86-87 R 8
Vignola 138-139 D 3
Vigo 132-133 C 7
Vigten Islands = Vikna 114-115 D 5
Vihren 138-139 K 5
Viipuri = Vyborg 154-155 DE 5
Viitasaari 114-115 LM 6
Vijāpur = Bijāpur 160-161 LM 7
Vijayanagaram = Vizianagaram 160-161 NO 7
Vijayawāda 160-161 N 7
Vik 114-115 d 3
Vika 114-115 M 4
Viking 46-47 O 7
Vikna 114-115 D 5
Vikøyri 114-115 B 7
Vila [Vanuatu] 182-183 N 3
Vila Arriaga = Bibala 198 B 4
Vila Artur de Paiva = Cubango 198 C 4
Vila Bittencourt 98-99 D 5
Vila Cabral = Lichinga 198 G 4
Vila Coutinho 198 F 4
Vila da Maganja 198 G 5
Vila de Aljustrel = Cangamba 198 C 4
Vila de Aviz = Oncócua 198 B 5
Vila de João Belo = Xai Xai 198 F 7
Vila de Manica = Manica 198 F 5
Vila de Sena 198 FG 5
Vila Fontes 198 G 5
Vila Fontes = Caia 198 G 5
Vila Franca de Xira 132-133 C 9
Vila General Machado = Coeli 198 C 4
Vila Gouveia = Catandica 198 F 5
Vila Henrique de Carvalho = Saurimo 198 D 3
Vilaine 132-133 F 5
Vila João de Almeida = Chibia 198 B 5
Vilaller 132-133 H 7
Vila Luso = Moxuco 198 CD 4
Vila Macedo do Cavaleiros = Andulo 198 C 4
Vila Marechal Carmona = Vige 198 C 3
Vila Mariano Machado = Ganda 198 B 4
Vilanculos 198 G 6
Vila Norton de Matos = Balombo 198 B 4
Vila Nova, Rio — 98-99 MN 4
Vila Nova do Seles 198 B 4
Vila Paiva Couceiro = Gambos 198 BC 4
Vila Pereira d'Eça = N'Giva 198 C 5
Vila Pery = Manica 198 F 5
Vila Real 132-133 D 8
Vila Real de Santo António 132-133 D 10
Vilar Formoso 132-133 D 8
Vila Roçadas = Roçadas 198 C 5
Vilas, SD 68-69 H 3
Vila Salazar = N'Dala Tando 198 BC 3
Vila Teixeira da Silva = Bailundo 198 C 4
Vila Teixeira de Sousa = Luau 198 CD 4
Vila Velha [BR, Amapá] 98-99 N 3
Vila Velha [BR, Espírito Santo] 98-99 LM 9
Vila Viçosa 132-133 D 9
Vilcabamba, Cordillera — 98-99 E 7
Vilejka 142-143 E 5
Vil'gort [SU, Syktyvkar] 154-155 HJ 5
Vilhelmina 114-115 G 5
Vilhena 98-99 G 7
Vilija 142-143 E 5
Viljandi 142-143 E 4
Vil'kickogo, ostrov — [SU, East Siberian Sea] 154-155 de 2
Vil'kickogo, ostrov — [SU, Kara Sea] 154-155 NO 3
Vil'kickogo, proliv — 154-155 S-U 2
Vilkitsky Island = ostrov Vil'kickogo 154-155 NO 3
Villa Abecia 98-99 FG 9
Villa Acuña, GA 78-79 G 3
Villa Ahumada 86-87 G 2
Villa Aldama 86-87 K 4
Villa Ángela 103 D 3
Villa Bella 98-99 F 7
Villablino 132-133 D 7
Villacañas [E] 132-133 F 9
Villacarillo 132-133 F 9
Villach 124 F 5
Villacidro 138-139 C 6
Villa Cisneros = Ad-Dakhlah 194-195 A 4
Villa Constitución [MEX] 86-87 E 5
Villa Coronado 86-87 H 4
Villada 132-133 E 7
Villa de Cos 86-87 J 6
Villa de Cura 98-99 F 2-3
Villa de María 103 D 3
Villa de Ramos 86-87 K 6
Villa Dolores 103 C 4
Villa Federal = Federal 103 E 4
Villa Flores 86-87 O 9
Villafranca del Bierzo 132-133 D 7
Villafranca de los Barros 132-133 DE 9
Villafranca del Penedès 132-133 H 8
Villa Frontera 58-59 F 6
Villagarcia de Arosa 132-133 C 7
Villàgio Duca degli Abruzzi = Joowhar 198 J 1
Villa Grove, IL 70-71 FG 6
Villaguay 103 E 4
Villahermosa [MEX] 58-59 H 8
Villa Hidalgo 86-87 H 4
Villajoyosa 132-133 GH 9
Villaldama 76-77 D 9
Villa López 76-77 B 9
Villa María 103 D 4
Villa Mazán 103 C 3
Villamil 98-99 A 5
Villa Montes 98-99 G 9
Villanova i la Geltrú 132-133 HJ 8
Villanueva, NM 76-77 B 5
Villanueva de Córdoba 132-133 E 9
Villanueva de la Serena 132-133 E 9

280 Valera

Villanveva 86-87 J 6
Villa Ocampo 103 DE 3
Villaodrid 132-133 D 7
Villa Ojo de Agua 103 D 3
Villa Quesada 88-89 D 9
Villarreal de los Infantes 132-133 GH 9
Villarrica [PY] 103 E 3
Villa San Martín 103 D 3
Villa Unión [MEX, Coahuila] 76-77 D 8
Villa Unión [MEX, Sinaloa] 86-87 GH 6
Villa Unión [RA, La Rioja] 103 C 3
Villa Valeria 103 CD 4
Villavicencio [CO] 98-99 E 4
Villaviciosa 132-133 E 7
Villa Victoria 86-87 J 8
Villavieja de Yeltes 132-133 D 8
Villefranche-sur-Saône 132-133 K 5-6
Ville-Marie 72-73 G 1
Villena 132-133 G 9
Villeneuve-Saint-Georges 132-133 J 4
Villeneuve-sur-Lot 132-133 H 6
Ville Platte, LA 78-79 C 5
Villeurbanne 132-133 K 6
Villingen-Schwenningen 124 D 4
Villisca, IA 70-71 C 5
Villmanstrand = Lappeenranta 114-115 N 7
Vilnius 142-143 DE 5
Vilos, Los — 103 B 4
Vil'uj 154-155 W 5
Vil'ujsk 154-155 X 5
Vilyui = Vil'uj 154-155 X 5
Vimmerby 114-115 FG 9
Vimont 82 I a 1
Vina, CA 74-75 BC 3
Viña, La — [PE] 98-99 D 6
Viña, La — [RA] 103 C 3
Viña del Mar 103 B 4
Vinalhaven, ME 72-73 M 2-3
Vinaroz 132-133 H 8
Vincennes, IN 58-59 J 4
Vincennes Bay 31 C 11
Vindelälven 114-115 H 5
Vindeln 114-115 HJ 5
Vindhya Range 160-161 L-N 6
Vineland, NJ 72-73 J 5
Vineyard Sound 72-73 L 4
Vinh = Xa-doai 174-175 E 3
Vinh Lo'i 174-175 E 5
Vinh Long 174-175 E 4
Vinho, País do — 132-133 CD 8
Vinita, OK 76-77 G 4
Vinje 114-115 B 8
Vinkovci 138-139 H 3
Vinnica 142-143 E 6
Vinson, Mount — 31 B 28
Vinsulla 48 GH 4
Vinte de Setembro 98-99 J 11
Vinton, IA 70-71 DE 4
Vinton, LA 78-79 C 5
Vinton, VA 80-81 G 2
Viola, KS 68-69 H 7
Virac 174-175 H 4
Viramgām 160-161 L 6
Viramgaon = Viramgām 160-161 L 6
Virden 49 H 6
Virden, IL 70-71 F 6
Virden, NM 74-75 J 6
Vire 132-133 G 4
Vírgenes, Cabo — 103 C 8
Virgina Hills, VA 82 II a 2
Virgin Gorda 88-89 OP 5
Virginia, IL 70-71 EF 6
Virginia, MN 58-59 H 2
Virginia [USA] 58-59 KL 4
Virginia Beach, VA 80-81 HJ 2
Virginia City, MT 66-67 GH 3
Virginia City, NV 74-75 D 3
Virginia Highlands, Arlington-, VA 82 II a 2
Virginia Mountains 74-75 D 3
Virginiatown 50 M 2
Virgin Islands 58-59 NO 8
Virgin Mountains 74-75 FG 4
Virgin River 74-75 FG 4
Virihaure 114-115 G 4
Viroqua, WI 70-71 E 4
Virovitica 138-139 G 3
Virtaniemi 114-115 MN 3
Virtsu 142-143 D 4
Virunga, Parc national — 198 E 1-2
Vis 138-139 G 4
Visagapatão = Vishākhapatnam 160-161 NO 7
Visakhapaṭṭaṇam = Vishākhapatnam 160-161 NO 7
Visalia, CA 74-75 D 4
Visayan Sea 174-175 H 4
Visby 114-115 GH 9
Viscount 49 F 4
Viscount Melville Sound 46-47 O-Q 3
Višegrad 138-139 H 4
Višera 142-143 L 3
Viseu [BR] 98-99 K 5
Viseu [P] 132-133 D 8
Vişeu-de-Sus 138-139 L 2
Vishākhapatnam 160-161 NO 7
Vishanpur = Bishenpur 160-161 P 6
Visitation, Île de la — 82 I b 1
Viso, Monte — 138-139 B 3
Vista Alegre [BR, Rio Amazonas] 98-99 H 4
Vista Alegre [BR, Rio Içana] 98-99 DE 4
Vista Reservoir 66-67 F 5
Vistula = Wisła 124 K 3
Vit 138-139 L 4
Vitebsk 142-143 EF 4
Viterbo 138-139 DE 4
Vitiaz Strait 174-175 N 8
Vitichi 98-99 F 9
Viti Levu 174-175 a 2
Vitim 154-155 V 6
Vitimskoje ploskogorje 154-155 V 7
Vitjaz Deep 166-167 S 3
Vitoria [BR, Espírito Santo] 98-99 LM 9
Vitória [BR, Pará] 98-99 MN 6
Vitoria [E] 132-133 F 7
Vitória da Conquista 98-99 L 7
Vitoša Planina 138-139 K 4
Vitré 132-133 G 4
Vitry-le-François 132-133 K 4
Vittangi 114-115 JK 4
Vittòrio d'Africa = Shalanbod 198 HJ 1
Vittòrio Vèneto 138-139 E 2
Vitu Islands 174-175 g 5
Vivarais, Monts du — 132-133 K 6
Vivario 138-139 C 4
Vivero 132-133 D 7
Vivi 154-155 S 4
Vivi, ozero — 154-155 R 4
Vivian 49 K 6
Vivian, LA 76-77 GH 6
Vivian, SD 68-69 F 4
Vivoratá 103 E 5
Vivsta 114-115 G 6
Vižajskij zavod = Krasnovišersk 154-155 K 5
Vižas 142-143 J 2
Vizcachas, Meseta de las — 103 B 8
Vizcaíno, Desierto de — 86-87 CD 4
Vizcaíno, Sierra — 58-59 D 6
Vize, ostrov — 154-155 O 2
Vizianagaram 160-161 NO 7
Vizinga 154-155 HJ 5

Vjatka = Kirov 154-155 HJ 6
Vjosë 138-139 HJ 5

Vlaanderen 132-133 J 3
Vladimir 154-155 FG 6
Vladivostok 154-155 Z 9
Vlasenica 138-139 H 3
Vlasotince 138-139 K 4
Vlissingen 132-133 J 3
Vlorë 138-139 H 5
Vltava 124 G 4

Vodla 142-143 G 3
Vodlozero 142-143 G 3
Vœune Sai 174-175 E 4
Vogelkop = Candravasih 174-175 K 7
Vogelsberg [D, mountain] 124 D 3
Voghera 138-139 C 3
Vohémar = Vohimarina 198 K 4
Vohibinany 198 JK 5
Vohimarina 198 K 4
Vohipeno 198 J 6
Voi [EAK, place] 198 G 2
Voinjama 194-195 BC 7
Voiron 132-133 K 6
Vojejkov šelfovyj lednik 31 C 12-13
Vojnica 142-143 EF 2
Vojvodina 138-139 HJ 3
Voj-Vož 142-143 KL 3
Volborg, MT 68-69 D 3
Volcano Bay = Uchiura-wan 170-171 b 2
Volcano Islands 148-149 RS 7
Volcán Viejo 88-89 C 8
Volchov [SU, place] 154-155 E 5-6
Volchov [SU, river] 142-143 F 4
Volchovstroj = Volchov 154-155 E 5-6
Volda 114-115 B 6
Volga [SU, river] 154-155 F 6
Volgo-Baltijskij vodnyj put' V.I. Lenina 142-143 F 3-G 4
Volgodonsk 142-143 H 6
Volgograd 142-143 H 6
Volgogradskoje vodochranilišče 142-143 J 5
Volin, SD 68-69 H 4
Volkovysk 142-143 D 5
Volnovacha 142-143 G 6
Voločanka 154-155 R 3
Volodarsk 142-143 H 4
Vologda 154-155 FG 6
Vol'sk 154-155 H 7
Volta [GH] 194-195 E 7
Volta, Black — 194-195 D 7
Volta, Lake — 194-195 DE 7
Volta, White — 194-195 D 7
Volta Noire [HV, river] 194-195 D 6
Voltera 138-139 D 4
Voltti 114-115 K 6
Volturino, Monte — 138-139 FG 5
Volturno 138-139 F 5
Volubilis 194-195 C 2
Volžsk 154-155 H 6
Volžskij 142-143 HJ 6
Von Frank Mount 52-53 K 5
Von Martius, Salto — 98-99 J 7
von Otterøya 114-115 I 5
Vopnafjördhur [IS, bay] 114-115 fg 2
Vopnafjördhur [IS, place] 114-115 f 2
Vorarlberg 124 DE 5
Vorderrhein 124 D 5
Vordingborg 114-115 D 10
Vorjapaul' 154-155 L 5
Vorkuta 154-155 L 4
Vorogovo 154-155 QR 5
Voroncovo [SU, Dudinka] 154-155 PQ 3
Voronež 142-143 GH 5
Voronino 142-143 HJ 4
Voronja 142-143 F 2
Vorošilov = Ussurijsk 154-155 Z 9
Vorošilovgrad 142-143 GH 6
Vorpommern 124 F 1-2
Vorskla 142-143 G 5
Võru 142-143 E 4
Vosges 132-133 L 4-5
Voss 114-115 B 7
Vostok [Antarctica] 31 B 11
Vostok [island] 34-35 K 5
Vostychoj = Jegyrjach 154-155 M 5
Votice 124 G 4
Votkinsk 154-155 J 6
Votkinskoje vodochranilišče 154-155 JK 6
Vouga 132-133 C 8
Vože, ozero — 142-143 G 3
Vožgora 142-143 J 3
Voznesensk 142-143 F 6
Vozroždenija, ostrov — 154-155 KL 9
Vozvraščenija, gora — 154-155 b 8

Vraca 138-139 K 4
Vranje 138-139 J 4
Vrbas [YU, place] 138-139 H 3
Vrbas [YU, river] 138-139 G 3
Vreed-en-Hoop 98-99 H 3
Vršac 138-139 J 3
Vryburg 198 D 7
Vryheid 198 F 7

Vsetín 124 J 4
Vsevidof, Mount — 52-53 m 4
Vsevidof Island 52-53 m 4

Vukovar 138-139 H 3
Vulcan 49 B 5
Vulcano, Ìsola — 138-139 F 6
Vùlture, Monte — 138-139 F 5
Vundik Lake 52-53 Q 3
Vuotso 114-115 M 3

Vyatka = Kirov 154-155 HJ 6
Vyborg 154-155 DE 5
Vyčegda 154-155 J 5
Vychegda = Vyčegda 154-155 J 5
Vyksa 154-155 G 6
Vyrica 142-143 F 4
Vyshniy Volochek = Vyšnij Voloček 154-155 EF 6
Vyšnij Voločʼok 154-155 EF 6
Vysokaja, gora — 154-155 a 8
Vysokogornyj 154-155 ab 7
Vytegra 154-155 F 5

W

W, Parcs National du — 194-195 E 6

Wa 194-195 D 6
Waajid 194-195 a 3
Waal 132-133 K 3
Waar, Mios — 174-175 KL 7
Wababimiga Lake 50 FG 2
Wabag 174-175 M 8
Wabamun 48 K 3
Wabana 46-47 a 8
Wabasca 48 L 1
Wabasca River 46-47 NO 6
Wabash, IN 70-71 H 5
Wabasha, MN 70-71 D 3
Wabash River 58-59 J 3
Wabassi River 50 F 1-2
Wabasso, MN 70-71 C 3
Wabeno, WI 70-71 F 3
Wabigoon 50 C 3
Wabimeig Lake 50 G 2
Wabowden 49 J 3
Wabuska, NV 74-75 D 3
Waccamaw, Lake — 80-81 G 3
Waccasassa Bay 80-81 b 2
Wachan = Wākhān 160-161 L 3
Waco 51 D 2
Waco, TX 58-59 G 5
Wād, Al- 194-195 F 2
Wadah, Al- 199 D 6
Wād an-Nayl 194-195 LM 6
Wadayama 170-171 K 5
Wād Bandah 194-195 K 6
Waddān 194-195 H 3
Waddington, Mount — 46-47 LM 7
Wadebridge 116-117 FG 10
Wadena 49 G 5
Wadena, MN 70-71 C 2
Wadesboro, NC 80-81 F 3
Wād Ḥāmid 194-195 L 5
Wadhwān 160-161 L 6
Wādī Ḥalfā 194-195 L 4
Wadi Jemal Island = Jazīrat Wādī Jimāl 199 D 5
Wādī Jimāl, Jazīrat — 199 D 5
Wadley, GA 80-81 E 4
Wād Madanī 194-195 L 6
Wadsworth, NV 74-75 D 3
Wadu Channel 36 a 2
Wād Zam 194-195 C 2
Waegwan 170-171 G 4-5
Waelder, TX 76-77 F 8
Wa-fang-tien = Fu Xian 166-167 N 4
Wagal-bong = Maengbu-san 170-171 F 2
Wageningen [SME] 98-99 H 3
Wager Bay 46-47 T 4
Wagga Wagga 182-183 J 7
Wagin 182-183 C 6
Wagina 174-175 j 6
Wagner, SD 68-69 G 4
Wagoner, OK 76-77 G 5
Wagon Mound, NM 76-77 B 4
Wagontire, OR 66-67 D 4
Wągrowiec 124 H 2
Wāḥah 194-195 H 3
Wahai 174-175 J 7
Wahlbergøya 114-115 k 5
Wahlenbergfjord 114-115 kl 5
Wahoo, NE 68-69 H 5
Wahpeton, ND 68-69 H 2
Wahrān 194-195 D 1
Wah Wah Mountains 74-75 G 3
Waialua, HI 78-79 c 2
Waianae, HI 78-79 c 2
Waidhofen an der Thaya 124 G 4
Waigama 174-175 JK 7
Waigeo, Pulau — 174-175 K 6
Waigev = Pulau Waigeo 174-175 K 6
Waikabubak 174-175 G 8
Waikerie 182-183 GH 6
Waimate 182-183 O 8
Waimea, HI [USA, Hawaii] 78-79 e 2-3
Waimea, HI [USA, Kanai] 78-79 c 2
Wainfleet All Saints 116-117 M 7
Wainganga 160-161 MN 6-7
Waingapu 174-175 GH 8
Waini Point 98-99 H 3
Wainwright 49 C 4
Wainwright, AK 46-47 DE 3
Waipahu, HI 78-79 c 2
Wairoa 182-183 P 7
Waitaki River 182-183 O 8
Waitara 182-183 OP 7
Waitsap = Huaiji 166-167 L 7
Waitsburg, WA 66-67 D 2
Waiyeung = Huiyang 166-167 LM 7
Wajh, Al- 160-161 D 5
Wajima 170-171 L 4
Wak, El — 198 H 1
Waka 198 D 2
Wakamatsu = Aizu-Wakamatsu 170-171 M 4
Wakamatsu-shima 170-171 G 6
Wakasa 170-171 K 5
Wakasa-wan 170-171 K 5
Wakaw 49 F 4
Wakayama 166-167 Q 5
Wake 34-35 H 4
Wa Keeney, KS 68-69 G 6
Wakefield 116-117 K 7
Wakefield, KS 68-69 H 6
Wakefield, MI 70-71 F 2
Wakefield, NE 68-69 H 4
Wakefield, New York-, NY 82 III cd 1
Wake Forest, NC 80-81 G 3
Wakeham = Maricourt 46-47 W 5
Wākhān 160-161 L 3
Wākhjīr, Koṭal — 160-161 LM 3
Wakinosawa 170-171 N 2
Wakkanai 166-167 R 2
Wakomata Lake 70-71 J 2
Wakunai 174-175 j 6
Wakwayowkastic River 50 L 1-2
Walakpa, AK 52-53 HJ 1
Wa'lan 194-195 E 4
Walapai, AZ 74-75 G 5
Walātah 194-195 C 5
Walātah, Ḍhar — 194-195 C 5
Wałbrzych 124 H 3
Walbury Hill 116-117 K 9
Walcheren 132-133 J 3
Walcott 48 D 2
Walcott, ND 68-69 H 2
Walcott, WY 68-69 C 5
Wałcz 124 H 2
Walden, CO 68-69 CD 5
Walden Ridge 78-79 G 3
Waldhofen an der Ybbs 124 G 5
Waldo, AR 78-79 C 4
Waldo, FL 80-81 bc 2
Waldport, OR 66-67 A 3
Waldron, AR 76-77 GH 5
Wales 116-117 H 8-9
Wales, AK 46-47 C 4
Wales, MN 70-71 E 2
Wales Island 46-47 T 4
Walgett 182-183 J 6
Walgreen Coast 31 B 26
Walhalla, MI 70-71 GH 3
Walhalla, ND 68-69 H 1
Walhalla, SC 80-81 E 3
Walikale 198 E 2
Walker, MN 70-71 C 2
Walker, SD 68-69 F 3
Walker Cove 52-53 x 9
Walker Lake [CDN] 49 K 3
Walker Lake [USA] 58-59 C 4
Walker Mountain 80-81 F 2
Walker Mountains 31 B 26-27
Walker River Indian Reservation 74-75 D 3
Walkerton 72-73 F 2
Walkerton, IN 70-71 G 5
Walkerville, MT 66-67 G 2
Walkite = Welkītē 194-195 M 7
Wall, SD 68-69 E 3-4
Wallace 72-73 GH 2
Wallace, ID 66-67 EF 2
Wallace, MI 70-71 G 3
Wallace, NC 80-81 GH 3
Wallace, NE 68-69 F 5
Wallaceburg 72-73 E 3
Wallal Downs 182-183 D 3-4
Wallaroo 182-183 G 6
Wallasey 116-117 H 7
Walla Walla, WA 58-59 C 2
Wallel = Tulu Welēl 194-195 LM 7
Wallingford 116-117 K 9
Wallingford, CT 72-73 K 4
Wallington, NJ 82 III b 1
Wallis, TX 76-77 F 8
Wallis, Îles — 174-175 b 1
Wall Lake, IA 70-71 C 4
Wallowa, OR 66-67 E 3
Wallowa Mountains 66-67 E 3
Wallowa River 66-67 E 3
Wallula, WA 66-67 D 2
Walney Island 116-117 H 6
Walnut, IL 70-71 F 5
Walnut, KS 70-71 C 7
Walnut, MS 78-79 E 3
Walnut Canyon National Monument 74-75 H 5
Walnut Cove, NC 80-81 F 2
Walnut Creek 68-69 F 6
Walnut Grove, MO 70-71 D 7
Walnut Grove, MS 78-79 E 4
Walnut Park, CA 83 III c 2
Walnut Ridge, AR 78-79 D 2
Walpole 182-183 NO 4
Walpole, NH 72-73 K 3
Walrus Islands 52-53 GH 7
Walsall 116-117 K 8
Walsenburg, CO 68-69 D 7
Walsh 182-183 K 5
Walsh, CO 68-69 E 7
Walsoken 116-117 M 8
Walterboro, SC 80-81 F 4
Walter Reed Army Medical Center 82 II ab 1
Walters, OK 76-77 E 5
Waltham 72-73 H 2
Walthill, NE 68-69 H 4
Waltman, WY 68-69 C 4
Walton, IN 70-71 G 5
Walton, KY 70-71 H 6
Walton, NY 72-73 J 3
Walton, Liverpool- 116-117 J 7
Walton le Dale 116-117 HJ 7
Walton on the Naze 116-117 h 7
Walvisbaai [ZA, place] 198 B 6
Walvis Bay = Walvisbaai [ZA, place] 198 B 6
Walvis Ridge 26-27 K 7
Wamba [WAN] 194-195 F 7
Wamba [ZRE, Bandundu] 198 C 3
Wamba [ZRE, Haut-Zaïre] 198 E 1
Wamego, KS 68-69 H 6
Wami 198 G 3
Wamlana 174-175 J 7
Wampú 88-89 D 7
Wanaaring 182-183 H 5
Wanapiri 174-175 L 7
Wanapitei Lake 72-73 F 1
Wanapitei River 72-73 F 1
Wanchuan = Zhangjiakou 166-167 L 3
Wanda Shan 166-167 P 2
Wandering River 48 L 2
Wan-do 170-171 F 5
Wandoan 182-183 JK 5
Wanfu 170-171 D 2
Wanganui 182-183 OP 7
Wangaratta 182-183 J 7
Wangpang Yang 166-167 N 5
Wangyemiao = Ulan Hot 166-167 N 2
Wanhsien = Wan Xian [TJ, Sichuan] 166-167 K 5
Wankie = Hwange 198 E 5
Wankie National Park 198 E 5
Wanleweeyn 194-195 NO 8
Wanning 166-167 L 8
Wantage 116-117 K 9
Wan-ta Shan-mo = Wanda Shan 166-167 P 2
Wantsai = Wanzai 166-167 LM 6
Wanzai 166-167 LM 6
Wapakoneta, OH 70-71 HJ 5
Wapanucka, OK 76-77 F 5
Wapato, WA 66-67 C 2
Wapawekka Lake 49 FG 3
Wapello, IA 70-71 E 5
Wapiti, WY 68-69 B 3
Wapiti River 48 GH 2
Wapsipinicon River 70-71 E 5
Waqf, Al- 199 C 4
Wāqif, Jabal al- 199 B 6
Waqooyi-Galbeed 194-195 a 1
War, WV 80-81 F 2
Warān 194-195 BC 4
Warangal 160-161 MN 7
Warba, MN 70-71 D 2
Warburton [AUS, river] 182-183 G 5
Wardān, Wādī — 199 C 3
Ward Cove, AK 52-53 x 9
Warden, WA 66-67 D 2
Wardere = Werdēr 194-195 O 7
Wardha [IND, place] 160-161 M 6
Wardha [IND, river] 160-161 M 6
Ward Hunt, Cape — 174-175 N 8
Wardlow 49 C 5
Ward's Stone 116-117 J 6-7
Ware 46-47 LM 6
Ware, MA 72-73 KL 3
Wareham 116-117 J 10
Waren [DDR] 124 F 2
Waren [RI] 174-175 L 7
Wari'ah, Al- 160-161 F 5
Warialda 182-183 K 5
Warin Chamrap 174-175 DE 3
Waring Mountains 52-53 GH 3
Warland, MT 66-67 F 1
Warley 116-117 J 8
Warman 49 E 4
Warmbad [Namibia, place] 198 C 7
Warmbad [ZA] 198 E 6-7
Warminster 116-117 J 9
Warmsprings, MT 66-67 G 2
Warm Springs, OR 66-67 C 3
Warm Springs, NV [USA ↓ Cherry Creek] 74-75 F 3
Warm Springs, NV [USA → Tonopah] 74-75 EF 3
Warm Springs Indian Reservation 66-67 C 3
Warm Springs Valley 66-67 C 5
Warnemünde, Rostock- 124 F 1
Warner 66-67 GH 1
Warner, SD 68-69 G 3
Warner Range 58-59 B 3
Warner Robins, GA 58-59 K 5
Warner Valley 66-67 CD 4
Warnes [BOL] 98-99 G 8
Waropko 174-175 LM 8
Warpath River 49 J 4
Warqlā 194-195 F 2
Wārqzīz, Jabal — 194-195 C 3
Warra 182-183 K 5
Warrego River 182-183 J 5
Warren, AR 78-79 CD 4
Warren, AZ 74-75 J 7
Warren, ID 66-67 F 3
Warren, IL 70-71 EF 4
Warren, IN 70-71 H 5
Warren, MI 72-73 E 3
Warren, MN 68-69 H 1
Warren, OH 58-59 K 3
Warren, PA 72-73 G 4
Warren, TX 76-77 G 7
Warren [CDN] 72-73 F 1
Warren Landing 49 J 4
Warrenpoint 116-117 E 6
Warrensburg, MO 70-71 CD 6
Warrenton 198 DE 7
Warrenton, GA 80-81 E 4
Warrenton, MO 70-71 E 6
Warrenton, NC 80-81 GH 2
Warrenton, OR 66-67 AB 2
Warrenton, VA 72-73 H 5
Warri 194-195 F 7
Warrington 116-117 J 7
Warrington, FL 78-79 F 5
Warrior, AL 78-79 F 4
Warrnambool 182-183 H 7
Warroad, MN 70-71 C 1
Warsaw, IL 70-71 E 5
Warsaw, IN 70-71 H 5
Warsaw, KY 70-71 H 6
Warsaw, MO 70-71 D 6
Warsaw, NC 80-81 GH 3
Warsaw, NY 72-73 GH 3
Warsaw = Warszawa 124 K 2
Warszawa 124 K 2
Warta 124 HJ 2
Wartrace, TN 78-79 F 3
Warwick, GA 80-81 DE 5
Warwick, RI 72-73 L 4
Warwick [AUS] 182-183 K 5
Warwick [GB] 116-117 K 8
Wasa 48 K 5
Wasatch, UT 66-67 H 5
Wasatch Range 58-59 D 3-4
Wascana Creek 49 F 5
Wasco, CA 74-75 D 5
Wasco, OR 66-67 C 3
Waseca, MN 70-71 D 3
Wash, The — 116-117 M 7-8
Washago 72-73 G 2
Washakie Needles 68-69 B 4
Washburn, ND 68-69 F 2
Washburn, TX 76-77 D 5
Washburn, WI 70-71 E 2
Washburn Lake 46-47 PQ 3
Washington, AK 52-53 vw 8
Washington, AR 76-77 GH 6
Washington, DC 58-59 LM 4
Washington, GA 80-81 E 4
Washington, IA 70-71 DE 5
Washington, IN 70-71 G 6

Washingt 281

Washington, KS 68-69 H 6
Washington, MO 70-71 E 6
Washington, NC 80-81 H 3
Washington, PA 72-73 F 4
Washington [USA] 58-59 BC 2
Washington, Mount — 58-59 M 3
Washington Island 70-71 G 3
Washington Monument 82 II a 2
Washington National Airport 82 II a 2
Washington Naval Station 82 II ab 2
Washington Park [USA, Chicago] 83 II b 2
Washington Virginia Airport 82 II a 2
Washita River 58-59 G 4-5
Washm, Al- 160-161 EF 5-6
Washow Bay 50 A 2
Wash Shahri 166-167 F 4
Wasilla, AK 52-53 N 6
Wasior 174-175 KL 7
Wāsiṭah, Al- 194-195 L 3
Waskada 68-69 F 1
Waskaiowaka Lake 49 K 2
Waskatenau 48 L 2
Waskesiu Lake 49 F 4
Waskish, MN 70-71 C 1
Waskom, TX 76-77 G 6
Wassamu 170-171 c 1-2
Wassuk Range 74-75 D 3
Wasta, SD 68-69 E 3
Wasum 174-175 g 6
Waswanipi 50 N 2
Waswanipi, Lac — 50 N 2
Watabeag Lake 50 L 2
Watampone 174-175 GH 7
Watansoppeng 174-175 G 7
Wataru Channel 36 a 2
Watchet 116-117 H 9
Watchung Mountain 82 III a 1
Watcomb 50 D 3
Waterberg 198 C 6
Waterbury, CT 72-73 K 4
Wateree River 80-81 F 3
Waterfall, AK 52-53 w 9
Waterford, CA 74-75 C 4
Waterford [CDN] 72-73 F 3
Waterford = Port Láirge 116-117 DE 8
Waterford Harbour = Cuan Phort Láirge 116-117 D 9-E 8
Waterhen Lake [CDN, Manitoba] 49 J 4
Waterhen Lake [CDN, Saskatchewan] 49 DE 3
Waterhen River 49 D 3
Waterloo, IA 58-59 H 3
Waterloo, IL 70-71 EF 6
Waterloo, MT 66-67 G 3
Waterloo, NY 72-73 H 3
Waterloo [AUS] 182-183 EF 3
Waterloo [B] 132-133 K 3
Waterloo [CDN, Ontario] 72-73 F 3
Waterloo [CDN, Quebec] 72-73 K 2
Waterproff, LA 78-79 D 5
Waters, MI 70-71 H 3
Watersmeet, MI 70-71 F 2
Waterton Lakes National Park 48 KL 5
Waterton Park 48 KL 5
Watertown, NY 58-59 LM 3
Watertown, SD 58-59 G 2
Watertown, WI 70-71 F 4
Water Valley, MS 78-79 E 3
Water Valley, TX 76-77 D 7
Waterville, KS 68-69 H 6
Waterville, ME 58-59 N 3
Waterville, MN 70-71 D 3
Waterville, WA 66-67 CD 2
Waterways 46-47 OP 6
Watford 116-117 L 9
Watford City, ND 68-69 E 2
Wathaman River 49 G 2
Watino 48 J 2
Watkins Glen, NY 72-73 H 3
Watkinsville, GA 80-81 E 4
Watlam = Yulin 166-167 L 7
Watling Island = San Salvador 58-59 M 7
Watlington 116-117 KL 9
Watonga, OK 76-77 E 5
Watrous 49 F 5
Watrous, NM 76-77 B 5
Watsa 198 E 1
Watseka, IL 70-71 G 5
Watson 49 F 4
Watson, AR 78-79 D 4
Watson, UT 74-75 J 3
Watson Lake 46-47 L 5
Watsonville, CA 74-75 BC 4
Watt, Mount — 182-183 E 5
Watton 116-117 M 8
Watts, Los Angeles-, CA 83 III c 2
Watts Bar Lake 78-79 G 3
Watubela, Pulau-pulau — 174-175 K 7
Watu Bella Islands = Pulau-pulau Watubela 174-175 K 7
Wau 174-175 N 8
Waubay, SD 68-69 H 3
Wauchula, FL 80-81 bc 3
Wau el Kebir = Wāw al-Kabīr 194-195 H 3
Wau en Namus = Wāw an-Nāmūs 194-195 H 4
Waugh 50 B 3
Waukarlycarly, Lake — 182-183 D 4
Waukeenah, FL 80-81 DE 5
Waukegan, IL 70-71 G 4
Waukesha, WI 70-71 F 4
Waukon, IA 70-71 E 4
Wauneta, NE 68-69 F 5
Waupaca, WI 70-71 F 3
Waupun, WI 70-71 F 4
Waurika, OK 76-77 F 5
Wausa, NE 68-69 H 4
Wausau, WI 58-59 J 2-3
Wausaukee, WI 70-71 FG 3
Wauseon, OH 70-71 HJ 5
Wautoma, WI 70-71 F 3
Wauwatosa, WI 70-71 F 4
Wave Hill 182-183 F 3
Waveney, River — 116-117 h 6
Waverly, IA 70-71 D 4
Waverly, NY 72-73 H 3
Waverly, OH 72-73 E 5
Waverly, SD 68-69 H 3
Waverly, TN 78-79 F 2
Waverly, VA 80-81 H 2
Waverly Hall, GA 78-79 G 4
Wāw [Sudan] 194-195 K 7
Wawa 70-71 H 1-2
Wawagosic, Rivière — 50 M 2
Wawaitin Falls 50 L 2
Wawina 88-89 D 7
Wawota 49 GH 6
Waxahachie, TX 76-77 F 6
Waxell Ridge 46-47 H 5
Way, Lake — 182-183 D 5
Wayan, ID 66-67 H 4
Waycross, GA 58-59 K 5
Wayland, KY 80-81 E 2
Wayland, MI 70-71 H 4
Wayne, NE 68-69 H 4
Wayne, WV 72-73 E 5
Waynesboro, GA 80-81 EF 4
Waynesboro, MS 78-79 E 5
Waynesboro, PA 72-73 H 5
Waynesboro, TN 78-79 F 3
Waynesboro, VA 72-73 G 5
Waynesburg, PA 72-73 FG 5
Waynesville, MO 70-71 DE 7
Waynesville, NC 80-81 E 3
Waynoka, OK 76-77 E 4
Wayside, TX 76-77 D 5
Waza 194-195 G 6
Wāza Khwā 160-161 K 4
Wāzīrābād = Balkh 160-161 K 3
Wazz, Al- 194-195 L 5
Wazzān 194-195 C 2

Weald, The — 116-117 LM 9
Weapons Range 49 D 3
Wear, River — 116-117 K 6
Wearhead 116-117 JK 6
Weatherford, OK 76-77 E 5
Weatherford, TX 76-77 F 6
Weaubleau, MO 70-71 D 7
Weaverville, CA 66-67 B 5
Webb 49 D 5
Webb, TX 76-77 E 9
Webbe Shibeli = Wābi Shebelē 194-195 N 7
Weber, Mount — 48 C 2
Webster 48 H 2
Webster, MA 72-73 KL 3
Webster, SD 68-69 H 3
Webster City, IA 70-71 D 4
Webster Reservoir 68-69 G 6
Webster Springs, WV 72-73 F 5
Weda 174-175 J 6
Weddell Island 103 D 8
Weddell Sea 34-35 PQ 8
Wedel Jarlsberg land 114-115 j 6
Wedgeport 51 C 6
Wedowee, AL 78-79 G 4
Wed Zem = Wād Zam 194-195 C 2
Weed, CA 66-67 B 5
Weedon Centre 72-73 L 2
Weedville, PA 72-73 G 4
Weeks, LA 78-79 D 6
Weeksbury, KY 80-81 E 2
Weenusk = Winisk 46-47 T 6
Weeping Water, NE 70-71 BC 5
Wee Waa 182-183 J 6
Wegener-Inlandeis 31 B 36-1
Weh, Pulau — 174-175 BC 5
Weichang 166-167 M 3
Weiden 124 EF 4
Weifang 166-167 MN 4
Weihai 166-167 N 4
Wei He [TJ ◁ Hai He] 166-167 M 4
Wei He [TJ ◁ Huang He] 166-167 K 5
Weimar 124 E 3
Weimar, TX 76-77 F 8
Weiner, AR 78-79 D 3
Weining 166-167 JK 6
Weipa 182-183 H 2
Weir River 49 L 2
Weirton, WV 72-73 F 4
Weiser, ID 66-67 E 3
Weiser River 66-67 E 3
Weisse Elster 124 F 3
Weissenfels 124 E 3
Weiss Knob 72-73 G 5
Weitzel Lake 49 E 2
Weiyang = Huiyang 166-167 LM 7
Wejh = Al-Wajh 160-161 D 5
Wekusko 49 J 3
Wekusko Lake 49 J 3
Welbourn Hill 182-183 F 5
Welch, TX 76-77 CD 6
Welch, WV 80-81 F 2
Weldon, NC 80-81 H 2
Weldona, CO 68-69 E 5
Weldon River 70-71 D 5
Weldya 194-195 M 6
Weleetka, OK 76-77 FG 5
Welega 194-195 LM 7
Welel, Tulu — 194-195 LM 7
Welkītē 194-195 M 7
Welkom 198 E 7
Welland 72-73 G 3
Welland, River — 116-117 LM 8
Welland Canal 72-73 G 3
Wellesbourne Montford 116-117 K 8
Wellesley Islands 182-183 GH 3
Wellesley Lake 52-53 RS 5
Wellingborough 116-117 L 8
Wellington 116-117 H 10
Wellington, CO 68-69 D 5
Wellington, KS 76-77 F 4
Wellington, NV 74-75 D 3
Wellington, OH 72-73 E 4
Wellington, TX 76-77 D 5
Wellington [AUS] 182-183 JK 6
Wellington [CDN] 72-73 H 3
Wellington [NZ, place] 182-183 OP 8
Wellington, Isla — 103 AB 7
Wellington Channel 46-47 S 2-3
Wellman, IA 70-71 E 5
Wellman, TX 76-77 C 6
Wells 48 G 3
Wells, MN 70-71 D 4
Wells, NE 68-69 F 4
Wells, NV 58-59 C 3
Wells, TX 76-77 G 7
Wells, Lake — 182-183 D 5
Wellsboro, PA 72-73 H 4
Wellsford 182-183 OP 7
Wells Gray Provincial Park 46-47 MN 7
Wells next the Sea 116-117 MN 7-8
Wellston, OH 72-73 E 5
Wellsville, KS 70-71 C 6
Wellsville, MO 70-71 E 6
Wellsville, NY 72-73 H 3
Wellton, AZ 74-75 FG 6
Welo 194-195 MN 6
Wels 124 FG 4
Welsford 51 C 5
Welshpool 116-117 H 8
Wem 116-117 J 8
Wembere 198 F 2-3
Wembley 48 H 2
Wenasaga River 50 C 2
Wenatchee, WA 58-59 BC 2
Wenatchee Mountains 66-67 C 2
Wenchow = Wenzhou 166-167 N 6
Wendel, CA 66-67 CD 5
Wendell, ID 66-67 F 4
Wendell, NC 80-81 G 3
Wenden, AZ 74-75 G 6
Wendling, OR 66-67 B 3
Wendover, UT 66-67 FG 5
Wendover, WY 68-69 D 4
Wendte, SD 68-69 F 3
Wener Lake = Vänern 114-115 E 8
Wenshan 166-167 JK 7
Wenshan Zhuangzu Miaozu Zizhizhou 166-167 JK 7
Wên-su = Aqsu 166-167 E 3
Wentworth 182-183 H 6
Wentworth, SD 68-69 H 3-4
Wentzville, MO 70-71 E 6
Wenzhou 166-167 N 6
Weobley 116-117 J 8
Wepener 198 E 7
Werdēr [ETH] 194-195 O 7
Wernecke Mountains 46-47 JK 5
Werner Lake 50 B 2
Wernigerode 124 E 3
Werra 124 D 3
Werris Creek 182-183 K 6
Wesel 124 C 3
Weser 124 D 2
Weserbergland 124 D 2-3
Weser Hills = Weserbergland 124 D 2-3
Weskan, KS 68-69 F 6
Wesleyville 51 K 3
Wesleyville, PA 72-73 FG 3
Wessel, Cape — 182-183 G 2
Wessel Islands 182-183 G 2
Wessington, SD 68-69 G 3
Wessington Hills 68-69 G 3
Wessington Springs, SD 68-69 G 3-4
Wesson, MS 78-79 D 5
West, MS 78-79 E 4
West, TX 76-77 F 7
West Allis, WI 70-71 FG 4
West Australian Basin 26-27 P 7
West Bay 78-79 E 6
West Bend, IA 70-71 C 4
West Bend, WI 70-71 FG 4
West Bengal 160-161 O 6
West Blocton, AL 78-79 F 4
Westboro, WI 70-71 E 3
Westbourne 49 J 5
West Branch, MI 70-71 HJ 3
Westbridge 66-67 D 1
West Bromwich 116-117 K 8
Westbrook, ME 72-73 L 3
Westbrook, TX 76-77 D 6
West Burra 116-117 e 3
West Butte 66-67 H 1
Westby, MT 68-69 D 1
Westby, WI 70-71 E 4
West Caicos Island 88-89 K 4
West Calder 116-117 H 5
West Caroline Basin 34-35 FG 4
West Carson, CA 83 III c 2
Westchester, Los Angeles-, CA 83 III b 2
Westchester, New York-, NY 82 III d 1
Westcliffe, CO 68-69 D 6
West Columbia, SC 80-81 F 4
West Columbia, TX 76-77 FG 8
West Des Moines, IA 70-71 CD 5
West End 88-89 G 1
Westerland 124 D 1
Westerly, RI 72-73 L 4
Western [EAK] 198 F 1
Western [Z] 198 D 4
Western Australia 182-183 C-E 4-5
Western Bank 51 E 6
Western Carpathians = Biele Karpaty 124 HJ 4
Western Isles 116-117 D 4-E 2
Western Isles = Açores 188-189 E 5
Western Peninsula 50 B 3
Western Port 182-183 HJ 7
Westernport, MD 72-73 G 5
Western Sahara 194-195 A 4-B 3
Western Sayan Mountains = Zapadnyj Sajan 154-155 Q-S 7
Western Shoshone Indian Reservation 66-67 E 4-5
Western Sierra Madre = Sierra Madre Occidental 58-59 E 5-F 7
Westerschelde 132-133 J 3
Westerville, OH 72-73 E 4
Westerwald 124 CD 3
West European Basin 26-27 HJ 3
West Falkland 103 D 8
Westfall, OR 66-67 E 3-4
Westfield 51 C 5
Westfield, MA 72-73 K 3
Westfield, NY 72-73 G 3
Westfield, PA 72-73 H 4
West Fork, AR 76-77 GH 5
West Frankfort, IL 70-71 F 7
West Frisian Islands 132-133 KL 2
Westgate 182-183 J 5
West Glamorgan 116-117 H 9
Westham, London- 116-117 M 9
West Haven, CT 72-73 K 4
Westhoff, TX 76-77 F 8
West Hollywood, CA 83 III b 1
Westhope, ND 68-69 F 1
West Ice Shelf 31 C 9
Westindien 58-59 LM 7
West Indies 58-59 L-O 7
West Irian 174-175 K 7-L 8
West Jefferson, NC 80-81 F 2
West Kirby 116-117 HJ 7
West Lafayette, IN 70-71 G 5
Westlake, LA 78-79 C 5
Westlake, OR 66-67 A 4
West Lanham Hills, MD 82 II b 1
West Liberty, IA 70-71 E 5
West Liberty, KY 72-73 E 6
West Linton 116-117 H 5
West Loch Tarbert 116-117 DE 3
Westlock 48 L 2
West Los Angeles, Los Angeles-, CA 83 III b 1
Westmeath = In Iarmhidhe 116-117 D 7
West Memphis, AR 58-59 H 4
West Mersea 116-117 gh 7
West Midlands = 6 ◁ 116-117 K 8
Westminster, CO 68-69 D 6
Westminster, MD 72-73 H 5
West Monroe, LA 78-79 C 4
Westmont, CA 83 III c 2
Westmoreland, KS 68-69 H 6
Westmorland, CA 74-75 F 6
Westmount 82 I b 2
West Mountain 72-73 JK 3
West New York, NJ 82 III b 2
West Nicholson 198 EF 6
Weston, CO 68-69 D 7
Weston, ID 66-67 GH 4
Weston, MO 70-71 C 6
Weston, OR 66-67 D 3
Weston, WV 72-73 F 5
Weston [CDN] 72-73 G 3
Weston [MAL] 174-175 G 5
Weston-super-Mare 116-117 HJ 9
Westover, TX 76-77 E 6
West Palm Beach, FL 58-59 KL 6
West Pass 78-79 G 6
West Plains, MO 78-79 CD 2
West Point, GA 78-79 G 4
West Point, KY 70-71 H 7
West Point, MS 78-79 E 4
West Point, NE 68-69 H 5
West Point, NY 72-73 K 4
West Point, VA 80-81 H 2
West Point [CDN] 51 D 3
West Point [USA] 52-53 P 4
Westport, CA 74-75 AB 3
Westport, OR 66-67 B 2
Westport [CDN] 51 C 5
Westport [NZ] 182-183 O 8
Westport = Cathair na Mart 116-117 B 7
West Pullman, Chicago-, IL 83 II b 2
Westray [CDN] 49 H 4
Westray [GB] 116-117 H 1
Westray Firth 116-117 H 1
Westree 50 L 3
West Road River 48 EF 3
West Scotia Basin 26-27 G 8
West Spanish Peak 68-69 D 7
West Spitsbergen = Vestspitsbergen 114-115 j-l 5
West Sussex 116-117 LM 9-10
West Union, IA 70-71 DE 4
West Union, OH 72-73 E 5
West Union, WV 72-73 F 5
West Unity, OH 70-71 H 5
Westville, IL 70-71 G 5-6
Westville, OK 76-77 G 4-5
West Virginia 58-59 KL 4
Westwater, UT 74-75 J 3
Westwego, LA 78-79 DE 6
West Whittier, CA 83 III d 2
Westwood, CA 66-67 C 5
Westwood, Los Angeles-, CA 83 III b 1
West Yellowstone, MT 66-67 H 3
West Yorkshire = 2 ◁ 150 116-117 K 7
Wetar, Pulau — 174-175 J 8
Wetaskiwin 46-47 NO 7
Wete 198 GH 3
Wetetnagani, Rivière — 50 N 2
Weti = Wete 198 GH 3
Wetmore, OR 66-67 D 3
Wet Mountains 68-69 D 6-7
Wetonka, SD 68-69 G 3
Wetter = Pulau Wetar 174-175 J 8
Wetter Lake = Vättern 114-115 E 8
Wetumpka, AL 78-79 FG 4
Wevok, AK 52-53 DE 2
Wewahitchka, FL 78-79 G 5-6
Wewak 174-175 M 7
Wewela, SD 68-69 G 4
Wewoka, OK 76-77 F 5
Wexford = Loch Garman 116-117 E 8
Wexford Harbour = Cuan Loch Garman 116-117 EF 8
Weyanoke, VA 82 II a 2
Weyb 194-195 N 7
Weyburn 46-47 Q 8
Weymouth [CDN] 51 CD 5
Weymouth [GB] 116-117 J 10
Weymouth, Cape — 182-183 HJ 2
Weymouth Bay 116-117 J 10
Weyprecht, Kapp — 114-115 l 5

Whakatane 182-183 P 7
Whaleback, Mount — 182-183 CD 4
Whale River 46-47 X 6
Whales, Bay of — 31 B 19-20
Whalsay 116-117 f 3
Whangarei 182-183 OP 7
Wharton, TX 76-77 FG 8
What Cheer, IA 70-71 D 5
Wheatland, CA 74-75 C 3
Wheatland, WY 68-69 D 4
Wheatley, AR 78-79 D 3
Wheaton, MN 68-69 H 3
Wheeler, OR 66-67 AB 3
Wheeler, TX 76-77 D 5
Wheeler Lake 78-79 F 3
Wheeler Peak [USA, Nevada] 58-59 CD 4
Wheeler Peak [USA, New Mexico] 58-59 E 4
Wheeler Ridge, CA 74-75 D 5
Wheeler River 49 F 2
Wheeling, WV 58-59 KL 4-5
Whelan 49 D 3-4
Whernside 116-117 J 6
Whewell, Mount — 31 B 17-18
Whichaway Nunataks 31 A 34-1
Whidbey Island 66-67 B 1
Whipple, Mount — 48 B 1
Whiskey Gap 66-67 G 1
Whitby [CDN] 72-73 G 3
Whitby [GB] 116-117 L 6
Whitchurch [GB, Hampshire] 116-117 K 9
Whitchurch [GB, Salop] 116-117 J 8
White, SD 68-69 H 3
White, Lake — 182-183 E 4
White Bay 46-47 Z 7
White Bear 49 DE 5
White Bear Lake, MN 70-71 D 3
White Bird, ID 66-67 EF 3
White Castle, LA 78-79 D 5
White City, FL 80-81 c 3
White City, KS 68-69 H 6
White Cliffs 182-183 H 6
White Cloud, MI 70-71 H 4
Whitecourt 48 K 2
White Deer, TX 76-77 D 5
White Earth, ND 68-69 E 1
White Earth Indian Reservation 70-71 C 2
White Eye, AK 52-53 O 3
Whiteface, TX 76-77 C 6
Whiteface Mountain 72-73 JK 2
Whitefish 50 L 3
Whitefish, MT 66-67 F 1
Whitefish Bay 70-71 H 2
Whitefish Bay, WI 70-71 G 4
Whitefish Falls 50 L 3
Whitefish Lake [CDN, Aleutian Range] 52-53 K 6
Whitefish Lake [CDN, Kilbuck Mts.] 52-53 GH 6
Whitefish Lake [CDN, Ontario] 70-71 F 1
Whitefish Lake [USA] 70-71 CD 2
Whitefish Point 70-71 H 2
Whitefish Point, MI 70-71 H 2
Whitefish Range 66-67 F 1
Whiteflat, TX 76-77 D 5
White Gull Lake 46-47 Y 6
White Hall, IL 70-71 EF 6
Whitehall, MI 70-71 G 4
Whitehall, MT 66-67 GH 3
Whitehall, NY 72-73 K 3
Whitehall, WI 70-71 E 3
Whitehaven 116-117 H 6
White Hills 52-53 N 2
Whitehorse 46-47 JK 5
White Horse, CA 66-67 C 5
White Horse Pass 66-67 FG 5
White House 82 II a 2
White Island = Kvitøya 30 AB 15
White Lake, SD 68-69 G 4
White Lake, WI 70-71 F 3
White Lake [CDN] 70-71 H 1
White Lake [USA] 78-79 C 6
Whiteland, TX 76-77 E 7
White Mountain, AK 46-47 D 5
White Mountains [USA, Alaska] 52-53 OP 4
White Mountains [USA, California] 74-75 D 4
White Mountains [USA, New Hampshire] 72-73 L 2
Whitemouth 49 KL 5-6
Whitemouth Lake 70-71 BC 1
White Nile = An-Nīl al-Abyaḍ 194-195 L 6
Whiteoak Swamp 80-81 H 3
White Otter Lake 50 CD 3
White Owl, SD 68-69 E 3
White Pass 52-53 U 7
White Pine, MT 66-67 F 2
White Pine Mountains 74-75 F 3
White Plains, NY 72-73 JK 4
White River, SD 68-69 F 4
White River [CDN, Ontario place] 70-71 H 1
White River [CDN, Ontario river] 70-71 GH 1
White River [CDN, Yukon Territory] 46-47 H 5
White River [USA, Alaska] 52-53 R 6
White River [USA, Arkansas] 58-59 H 4
White River [USA, California] 74-75 F 4
White River [USA, Colorado] 68-69 BC 5
White River [USA, Indiana] 70-71 G 6
White River [USA, South Dakota] 58-59 F 3
White River [USA, Texas] 76-77 D 6
White River, East Fork — 70-71 GH 6
White River, South Fork — 68-69 F 4
White River, West Fork — 70-71 G 6
White River Plateau 68-69 C 6
White River Valley 74-75 F 3
White Rock, SD 68-69 H 3
Whitesail Lake 48 D 3
White Salmon, WA 66-67 C 3
White Sands National Monument 76-77 A 6
Whites Brook 51 C 4
White Sea 154-155 FG 4
Whiteshell Forest Reserve 49 KL 6
Whiteshell Provincial Park 50 B 2-3
White Sox Park 83 II b 1-2
White Springs, FL 80-81 b 1
Whitestone, New York-, NY 82 III d 2
White Sulphur Springs, MT 66-67 H 2
White Swan, WA 66-67 C 2
Whitetail, MT 68-69 D 1
Whiteville, NC 80-81 G 3
Whiteville, TN 78-79 E 3
Whitewater, CO 68-69 B 6
Whitewater, KS 68-69 H 7
Whitewater, MT 68-69 C 1
Whitewater, WI 70-71 F 4
Whitewater Baldy 58-59 E 5
Whitewater Lake 50 DE 2
Whitewood, SD 68-69 DE 3
Whitewright, TX 76-77 F 6
Whithorn 116-117 G 6
Whiting, NJ 72-73 J 5
Whiting River 52-53 V 7
Whitla 49 C 6
Whitley Bay 116-117 K 5
Whitley City, KY 78-79 G 2
Whitman, ND 68-69 GH 1
Whitman, NE 68-69 F 4
Whitmire, SC 80-81 F 3
Whitmore Mountains 31 A
Whitney, NE 68-69 E 4
Whitney, OR 66-67 DE 3
Whitney, TX 76-77 F 7
Whitney, Mount — 58-59 C 4
Whitsett, TX 76-77 E 8
Whitstable 116-117 h 7
Whitsunday Island 182-183 JK 4
Whittier, AK 46-47 G 5
Whittier, CA 83 III d 2

282 **Washingt**

Whittier College 83 III d 2
Whittier Narrows Dam 83 III d 1
Whittington 116-117 K 7
Whittle, Cap de — 51 F 2
Whittlesey 116-117 L 8
Whitwell, TN 78-79 G 3
Wholdaia Lake 46-47 PQ 5
Whyalla 182-183 G 6

Wiang Phran = Mae Sai 174-175 CD 2
Wiarton 72-73 F 2
Wibaux, MT 68-69 D 2
Wichian Buri 174-175 D 3
Wichita, KS 58-59 G 4
Wichita Falls, TX 58-59 FG 5
Wichita Mountains 76-77 E 5
Wick 116-117 H 2
Wickenburg, AZ 74-75 G 5-6
Wickersham, WA 66-67 BC 1
Wickes, AR 76-77 G 5
Wickliffe, KY 78-79 E 2
Wicklow = Cill Mhanntáin 116-117 EF 7-8
Wicklow Head = Rinn Mhanntáin 116-117 F 8
Wicklow Mountains = Shléibhte Chill Mhanntáin 116-117 E 7-8
Wide Bay 52-53 ef 1
Widen, WV 72-73 F 5
Widgiemooltha 182-183 D 6
Widnes 116-117 J 7
Wi-do 170-171 F 5
Widyan, Al- 160-161 E 4
Więcbork 124 H 2
Wieluń 124 J 3
Wien [A, place] 124 G 4
Wiener Neustadt 124 GH 5
Wienerwald 124 GH 4
Wien Lake 52-53 M 4
Wieprz 124 L 3
Wiesbaden 124 CD 3
Wiese Island = ostrov Vize 154-155 O 2
Wigadēn 194-195 NO 7
Wigan 116-117 J 7
Wiggins, CO 68-69 D 5
Wiggins, MS 78-79 E 5
Wight, Isle of — 116-117 KL 10
Wigmore 116-117 J 8
Wigton 116-117 HJ 6
Wigtown 116-117 G 6
Wigtown Bay 116-117 G 6
Wijdefjorden 114-115 j 5
Wilber, NE 68-69 H 5
Wilborn, MT 66-67 G 2
Wilbur, WA 66-67 D 2
Wilburton, OK 76-77 G 5
Wilcannia 182-183 H 6
Wilcox, NE 68-69 G 5
Wilczek, zemľa — 154-155 L-N 1
Wilczek land = zemľa Wilczek 154-155 L-N 1
Wildcat Canyon Regional Park 83 I c 1
Wild Horse Reservoir 66-67 F 5
Wild Lake 52-53 M 3
Wild Rice River 70-71 BC 2
Wild River 52-53 M 3
Wildrose, ND 68-69 E 1
Wild Rose, WI 70-71 F 3
Wildwood, FL 80-81 bc 2
Wildwood, NJ 72-73 J 5
Wilhelm, Mount — 174-175 M 8
Wilhelmina Gebergte 98-99 H 4
Wilhelmøya 114-115 l 5
Wilhelmshaven 124 CD 2
Wilkes 31 C 12
Wilkes Land 31 BC 12-14
Wilkie 46-47 P 7
Wilkinsburg, PA 72-73 G 4
Wilkinson Lakes 182-183 F 5
Will, Mount — 52-53 X 8
Willacoochee, GA 80-81 E 5
Willamette River 58-59 B 3
Willapa Bay 66-67 AB 2
Willard, CO 68-69 E 5
Willard, MT 68-69 D 2
Willard, NM 76-77 AB 5
Willard, OH 72-73 E 4
Willard, UT 66-67 GH 5
Willcox, AZ 74-75 HJ 6
Willemstad [NA] 58-59 N 9
Willeroo 182-183 F 3
Willesborough 116-117 M 9
William Creek 182-183 G 5
William Lake 49 J 3-4
Williams, AZ 74-75 G 5
Williams, CA 74-75 B 3
Williams Bridge, New York-, NY 82 III c 1
Williamsburg, IA 70-71 DE 5
Williamsburg, KY 80-81 DE 2
Williamsburg, New York-, NY 82 III c 2
Williams Lake 46-47 M 7
Williamson, WV 80-81 E 2
Williamsport, IN 70-71 G 5
Williamsport, PA 58-59 L 3
Williamston, NC 80-81 H 2-3
Williamstown, KY 70-71 H 6
Williamsville, MO 78-79 D 2
Willibert, Mount — 48 B 1
Willimantic, CT 72-73 K 4
Willingdon 49 B 4
Willis, TX 76-77 G 7
Willis Group 182-183 K 3
Willis Island 51 K 3
Williston 198 D 8
Williston, FL 80-81 b 2
Williston, ND 58-59 F 2
Williston, SC 80-81 F 4
Williston Lake 48 F 1-2
Willits, CA 74-75 B 3
Willmar, MN 70-71 C 3
Willmar Station 68-69 E 1
Willmore Wilderness Provincial Park 48 H 3
Willoughby, OH 72-73 F 4
Willow 46-47 F 5
Willow Brook, CA 83 III c 2
Willow Bunch 68-69 D 1
Willow Creek, AK 52-53 P 6
Willow Creek [USA, California] 66-67 C 5
Willow Creek [USA, Oregon] 66-67 D 3
Willow Lake, SD 68-69 H 3
Willowlake River 46-47 MN 5
Willowmore 198 D 8
Willow Ranch, CA 66-67 C 5
Willow River 48 F 2
Willow River, MN 70-71 D 2
Willow Run, MI 72-73 E 3
Willows, CA 74-75 B 3
Willow Springs, MO 78-79 CD 2
Will Rogers State Historical Park 83 III a 1
Willsboro, NY 72-73 K 2
Wills Point, TX 76-77 FG 6
Wilmer, AL 78-79 E 5
Wilmington, DE 58-59 LM 4
Wilmington, IL 70-71 FG 5
Wilmington, NC 58-59 L 5
Wilmington, OH 72-73 E 5
Wilmot, AR 78-79 D 4
Wilmot, SD 68-69 H 3
Wilsall, MT 66-67 H 3
Wilson, AR 78-79 D 3
Wilson, NC 58-59 L 4
Wilson, NY 72-73 G 3
Wilson, OK 76-77 F 5
Wilson Bluff 182-183 EF 6
Wilson City 88-89 H 1
Wilson Creek, WA 66-67 D 2
Wilson Creek Range 74-75 F 3
Wilson Lake 78-79 F 3
Wilson River 182-183 H 5
Wilsons Promontory 182-183 J 7
Wilsonville, NE 68-69 FG 5
Wilton 116-117 JK 9
Wilton, ND 68-69 F 2
Wilton, WI 70-71 E 4
Wilton River 182-183 F 2
Wiltshire 116-117 JK 9
Wiluna 182-183 D 5
Wimbledon, ND 68-69 G 2
Wimbledon, London- 116-117 L 9
Wimborne 48 L 4
Wimborne Minster 116-117 JK 10
Wimmera 182-183 H 7
Wina = Ouina 194-195 G 7
Winamac, IN 70-71 G 5
Winburg 198 E 7
Wincanton 116-117 J 9
Winchcomb 116-117 K 9
Winchell, TX 76-77 E 7
Winchester, ID 66-67 E 2
Winchester, IL 70-71 EF 6
Winchester, IN 70-71 H 5
Winchester, KY 72-73 DE 5
Winchester, TN 78-79 F 3
Winchester, VA 58-59 L 4
Winchester, WY 68-69 BC 4
Winchester [CDN] 72-73 J 2
Winchester [GB] 116-117 K 9
Winchester Bay, OR 66-67 A 4
Windber, PA 72-73 G 4
Wind Cave National Park 68-69 E 4
Winder, GA 80-81 E 3-4
Windermere [GB, lake] 116-117 J 6
Windermere [GB, place] 116-117 J 6
Windesi 174-175 K 7
Windham, AK 52-53 V 8
Windhoek 198 C 6
Windigo Lake 50 D 1
Windigo River 50 D 1
Windom, MN 70-71 C 4
Windorah 182-183 H 5
Wind River, WY 68-69 B 4
Wind River [USA, Alaska] 52-53 O 2-3
Wind River [USA, Wyoming] 68-69 B 4
Wind River Indian Reservation 66-67 J 4
Wind River Range 58-59 DE 3
Windsor, CO 68-69 D 5
Windsor, MO 70-71 D 6
Windsor, NC 80-81 H 2
Windsor, ND 68-69 G 2
Windsor, VT 72-73 K 3
Windsor [CDN, Newfoundland] 51 HJ 3
Windsor [CDN, Nova Scotia] 51 D 5
Windsor [CDN, Ontario] 46-47 U 9
Windsor [CDN, Quebec] 72-73 KL 2
Windsor [GB] 116-117 L 9
Windsor Hills, CA 83 III bc 2
Windward Islands [West Indies] 58-59 O 9
Windy, AK 52-53 N 5
Winefred Lake 49 C 3
Winfield, AL 78-79 F 3-4
Winfield, IA 70-71 E 5
Winfield, KS 58-59 G 4
Winfred, SD 68-69 H 3-4
Wing, ND 68-69 F 2
Wingate 116-117 K 6
Wingham 72-73 F 3
Wingham Island 52-53 P 6
Wingo, KY 78-79 E 2
Winifred, MT 68-69 B 2
Winisk 46-47 T 6
Winisk Lake 46-47 T 7
Winisk River 46-47 T 7
Wink, TX 76-77 C 7
Winkelman, AZ 74-75 H 6
Winkler 68-69 H 1
Winlock, WA 66-67 B 2
Winneba 194-195 D 7
Winnebago, MN 70-71 CD 4
Winnebago, Lake — 70-71 F 3-4
Winnemucca, NV 58-59 C 3
Winnemucca Lake 66-67 D 5
Winner, SD 68-69 G 4
Winnetka, IL 70-71 G 4
Winnett, MT 68-69 B 2
Winnfield, LA 78-79 C 5
Winnibigoshish Lake 70-71 CD 2
Winnie, TX 76-77 G 8
Winning Pool 182-183 B 4
Winnipeg 46-47 R 7
Winnipeg, Lake — 46-47 R 7
Winnipeg Beach 50 A 2
Winnipegosis 49 HJ 5
Winnipegosis, Lake — 46-47 R 7
Winnipeg River 46-47 RS 7
Winnipesaukee, Lake — 72-73 L 3
Winnsboro, LA 78-79 D 4
Winnsboro, SC 80-81 F 3
Winnsboro, TX 76-77 G 6
Winona, AZ 74-75 H 5
Winona, KS 68-69 F 6
Winona, MI 70-71 F 2
Winona, MN 58-59 H 3
Winona, MO 78-79 D 2
Winona, MS 78-79 DE 4
Winona, TX 76-77 G 6
Winona, WA 66-67 DE 2
Winschoten 132-133 L 2
Winsford 116-117 J 7
Winslow 116-117 KL 9
Winslow, AR 76-77 G 5
Winslow, AZ 58-59 DE 4
Winslow, IN 70-71 G 6
Winslow, ME 72-73 M 2
Winsted, CT 72-73 K 4
Winston, MT 66-67 GH 2
Winston, OR 66-67 B 4
Winterberg [D] 124 D 3
Winter Garden, FL 80-81 c 2
Winter Harbour 48 C 4
Winterhaven, CA 74-75 F 6
Winter Haven, FL 80-81 c 2
Winter Park, CO 68-69 CD 6
Winter Park, FL 80-81 c 2
Winters, CA 74-75 C 3
Winters, TX 76-77 E 7
Winterset, IA 70-71 CD 5
Winterthur 124 D 5
Winterton [GB, Humberside] 116-117 L 7
Winterton [GB, Norfolk] 116-117 h 6
Winthrop, ME 72-73 LM 2
Winthrop, MN 70-71 C 3
Winthrop, WA 66-67 C 1
Winton, MN 70-71 E 2
Winton, WA 66-67 C 2
Winton, WY 66-67 J 5
Winton [AUS] 182-183 H 4
Winton [NZ] 182-183 N 9
Winyah Bay 80-81 G 4
Wirāj, Wādī al- 199 B 3
Wirksworth 116-117 K 7
Wirrulla 182-183 FG 6
Wisbech 116-117 M 8
Wiscasset, ME 72-73 M 2
Wisconsin 58-59 H 2-J 3
Wisconsin Dells, WI 70-71 F 4
Wisconsin Rapids, WI 70-71 EF 3
Wisconsin River 58-59 HJ 3
Wisdom, MT 66-67 G 3
Wiseman, AK 46-47 FG 4
Wishart 49 FG 5
Wishek, ND 68-69 G 2
Wisła 124 K 3
Wislana, Mierzeja — 124 J 1
Wislany, Zalew — 124 J 1
Wisłok 124 KL 4
Wisłoka 124 K 4
Wismar 124 E 2
Wisner, LA 78-79 D 4-5
Wisner, NE 68-69 H 4-5
Wissant 116-117 h 8
Wissel, Danau — 174-175 L 7
Wissembourg 132-133 LM 4
Wissmann, Chutes — 198 CD 3
Wistaria 48 D 3
Wister, OK 76-77 G 5
Witbank 198 EF 7
Witchekan Lake 49 E 4
Witham 116-117 M 9
Witham, River — 116-117 L 7
Witheridge 116-117 H 10
Withernsea 116-117 M 7
Witherspoon, Mount — 52-53 O 6
Witney 116-117 K 9
Witputs 198 C 7
Witten, SD 68-69 FG 4
Wittenberg 124 F 3
Wittenberg, WI 70-71 F 3
Wittenberge 124 EF 2
Wittenoom 182-183 C 4
Wittlich 124 C 4
Wittmann, AZ 74-75 G 6
Wittstock 124 F 2
Witu 198 GH 2
Witvlei 198 C 6
Wivenhoe 49 L 2
Wiwŏn 170-171 F 2

Wkra 124 JK 2

Włocławek 124 J 2
Włodawa 124 L 3

Woeonichi, Lac — 50 O 1
Wohlthatmassiv 31 B 2
Wokam, Pulau — 174-175 KL 8
Woking 48 H 2
Wolbach, NE 68-69 G 5
Wolcott, NY 72-73 H 3
Woleai 174-175 M 5
Wolf Creek, MT 66-67 G 2
Wolf Creek, OR 66-67 B 4
Wolf Creek Pass 68-69 C 7
Wolfe City, TX 76-77 F 6
Wolfenbüttel 124 E 2
Wolff, Chutes — 198 D 3
Wolfforth, TX 76-77 C 6
Wolf Mountains 68-69 C 3
Wolf Point, MT 68-69 D 1
Wolf River 70-71 F 3
Wolfsburg 124 E 2
Wolfville 51 DE 5
Wolin 124 G 2
Wolkitte = Welkītē 194-195 M 7
Wollaston 116-117 L 8
Wollaston, Islas — 103 C 9
Wollaston Lake 46-47 PQ 6
Wollaston Lake Post 49 FG 1
Wollaston Peninsula 46-47 NO 3-4
Wollega = Welega 194-195 LM 7
Wollo = Welo 194-195 MN 6
Wollogorang 182-183 G 3
Wollongong 182-183 K 6
Wołów 124 H 3
Wolseley [AUS] 182-183 GH 7
Wolseley [CDN] 49 G 5
Wolsey, SD 68-69 G 3
Wolstenholme 46-47 VW 5
Wolstenholme, Cape — 46-47 VW 5
Wolston 116-117 K 8
Wolsztyn 124 GH 2
Wolverhampton 116-117 J 8
Wolverine, MI 70-71 H 3
Woman River 50 K 3
Wombwell 116-117 K 7
Wonder, OR 66-67 B 4
Wŏngsŏng-dong 170-171 DE 3
Wŏnju 166-167 O 4
Wonosari 174-175 F 8
Wŏnsan 166-167 O 4
Wonthaggi 182-183 HJ 7
Wood, SD 68-69 F 4
Wood, Mount — [CDN] 52-53 R 6
Wood, Mount — [USA] 66-67 J 3
Wood Bay 31 B 17-18
Woodbine, GA 80-81 F 5
Woodbridge 116-117 h 6
Wood Buffalo National Park 46-47 O 6
Woodburn, OR 66-67 B 3
Woodbury, GA 78-79 G 4
Woodbury, NJ 72-73 J 5
Woodchopper, AK 52-53 PQ 4
Woodfjorden 114-115 j 5
Wood Green 116-117 L 9
Woodhall Spa 116-117 LM 7
Woodhaven, New York-, NY 82 III cd 2
Woodlake, CA 74-75 D 4
Wood Lake, NE 68-69 FG 4
Woodland, CA 74-75 BC 3
Woodland, WA 66-67 B 3
Woodland Park, CO 68-69 D 6
Woodlark Island 174-175 h 6
Woodlawn, Chicago-, IL 83 II b 2
Woodmere, NY 82 III d 3
Woodmont, MD 82 II a 1
Wood Mountain [CDN, mountain] 68-69 C 1
Wood Mountain [CDN, mountains] 49 E 6
Woodpecker 48 FG 3
Woodridge 70-71 BC 1
Wood-Ridge, NJ 82 III b 1
Wood River, IL 70-71 EF 6
Wood River, NE 68-69 G 5
Wood River [CDN] 49 E 5-6
Wood River [USA] 52-53 NO 4
Woodroffe, Mount — 182-183 F 5
Woodruff, SC 80-81 EF 3
Woodruff, UT 66-67 H 5
Woodruff, WI 70-71 F 3
Woods, Lake — 182-183 F 3
Woods, Lake of the — 46-47 R 8
Woodsboro, TX 76-77 F 8
Woodsfield, OH 72-73 F 5
Woodside 182-183 J 7
Woodside, UT 74-75 H 3
Woodside, Aberdeen- 116-117 J 3
Woodside, New York-, NY 82 III c 2
Woodson, AR 78-79 CD 3
Woodstock, IL 70-71 FG 4
Woodstock, VA 72-73 G 5
Woodstock, VT 72-73 K 3
Woodstock [AUS] 182-183 H 3
Woodstock [CDN, New Brunswick] 51 C 4
Woodstock [CDN, Ontario] 72-73 F 3
Woodsville, NH 72-73 KL 2
Woodville 182-183 P 8
Woodville, MS 78-79 D 5
Woodville, TX 76-77 G 7
Woodward, OK 58-59 G 4
Woody Island, AK 52-53 L 8
Wooler 116-117 JK 5
Woolgar, Lower — 182-183 H 3
Woollett, Lac — 50 P 1
Woolwich, London- 116-117 M 9
Woomera 182-183 G 6
Woonsocket, RI 72-73 KL 4
Woonsocket, SD 68-69 GH 3
Wooramel 182-183 BC 5
Wooramel River 182-183 C 5
Wooster, OH 72-73 F 4
Worcester, MA 58-59 M 3
Worcester [GB] 116-117 JK 8
Worcester [ZA] 198 CD 8
Worcester Range 31 B 17-15
Worden, OR 66-67 BC 4
Workington 116-117 H 6
Worksop 116-117 K 7
Worland, WY 68-69 C 3
Worms 124 CD 4
Worms Head 116-117 G 9
Worth, IL 83 II a 2
Wortham, TX 76-77 F 7
Worthing 116-117 L 10
Worthington, MN 70-71 C 4
Wosnesenski Island 52-53 c 2
Wotton under Edge 116-117 JK 9
Wou-han = Wuhan 166-167 L 5
Wou-hou = Wuhu 166-167 M 5
Wour 194-195 H 4
Wou-tcheou = Wuzhou 166-167 L 7
Wowoni, Pulau — 174-175 H 7

Wrangel, ostrov — 154-155 hj 3
Wrangell, AK 46-47 K 6
Wrangell, Mount — 52-53 P 5
Wrangell Island 52-53 w 8
Wrangell Mountains 46-47 H 5
Wrangle 116-117 M 7
Wrath, Cape — 116-117 F 2
Wray, CO 68-69 E 5
Wrens, GA 80-81 E 4
Wrexham 116-117 J 7
Wright 48 G 4
Wright, Lake — 182-183 EF 5
Wright City, OK 76-77 G 5
Wrightson, Mount — 74-75 H 7
Wrightsville, GA 80-81 E 4
Wrigley 46-47 M 5
Wrigley Gulf 31 B 24
Writing on Stone Provincial Park 66-67 H 1
Wrocław 124 H 3
Wrottesley, Mount — 66-67 B 1
Wroxton 49 GH 5
Września 124 HJ 2

Wschowa 124 H 3

Wubin 182-183 C 5-6
Wuchang 166-167 O 3
Wuchang, Wuhan- 166-167 LM 5
Wu Chiang = Wu Jiang [TJ, river] 166-167 K 6
Wu-chou = Wuzhou 166-167 L 7
Wuchow = Wuzhou 166-167 L 7
Wuchuan [TJ, Guizhou] 166-167 K 6
Wuchuan [TJ, Inner Mongolian Aut. Reg.] 166-167 L 3
Wu-chung-pao = Wuzhong 166-167 K 4
Wudaogou 170-171 EF 1
Wudi 166-167 M 4
Wudu 166-167 J 5
Wugang 166-167 L 6
Wuhan 166-167 L 5
Wu hei 166-167 K 4
Wu-hsi = Wuxi 166-167 MN 5
Wuhu 166-167 M 5
Wu-i Shan = Wuyi Shan 166-167 M 6
Wu Jiang [TJ, river] 166-167 K 6
Wujin = Changzhou 166-167 MN 5
Wukari 194-195 F 7
Wuli 166-167 K 7
Wuliang Shan 166-167 J 7
Wulik River 52-53 EF 3
Wuling He 166-167 P 2
Wulumuqi = Ürümchi 166-167 F 3
Wunnummin Lake 50 E 1
Wunstorf 124 D 2
Wupatki National Monument 74-75 GH 5
Wuppertal [D] 124 C 3
Wur = Wour 194-195 H 4
Wurno 194-195 EF 6
Wūruq, Rā's — 194-195 D 1
Würzburg 124 DE 4
Wushi [TJ ↓ Shaoguan] 166-167 L 7
Wushi = Üchturpan 166-167 DE 3
Wusi = Wuxi 166-167 MN 5
Wuskwatim Lake 49 J 3
Wusong 166-167 N 5
Wusu 166-167 EF 3
Wusuli Jiang 166-167 P 2
Wutai Shan 166-167 L 4
Wuti = Wudi 166-167 M 4
Wutongqiao 166-167 J 6
Wu-tu = Wudu 166-167 J 5
Wuvulu 174-175 M 7
Wuwei [TJ, Gansu] 166-167 J 4
Wuxi 166-167 MN 5
Wuxian = Suzhou 166-167 N 5
Wuxing 166-167 MN 5
Wuxue = Guangji 166-167 M 6
Wuyiling 166-167 OP 2
Wuying 166-167 OP 2
Wuyi Shan 166-167 M 6
Wuyuan [TJ, Inner Mongolian Aut. Reg.] 166-167 K 3
Wu-yüan = Wuyuan [TJ, Inner Mongolian Aut. Reg.] 166-167 K 3
Wuyun 166-167 O 2
Wu-yün = Wuyun 166-167 O 2
Wuz, El — = Al-Wazz 194-195 L 5
Wuzhang = Wuchang 166-167 O 3
Wuzhong 166-167 K 4
Wuzhou 166-167 L 7

Wyandotte, MI 72-73 E 3
Wyandra 182-183 HJ 5
Wyanet, IL 70-71 F 5
Wyangala Reservoir 182-183 J 6
Wyarno, WY 68-69 C 3
Wye, River — 116-117 J 8-9
Wymark 49 E 5
Wymondham 116-117 h 6
Wymore, NE 68-69 H 5
Wynbring 182-183 F 6
Wyndham 182-183 E 3
Wyndmere, ND 68-69 H 2
Wynne, AR 78-79 D 3
Wynne Wood, OK 76-77 F 5
Wynniatt Bay 46-47 O 3
Wynyard [AUS] 182-183 HJ 8
Wynyard [CDN] 49 FG 5
Wyola, MT 68-69 C 3
Wyoming 58-59 D-F 3
Wyoming, IL 70-71 F 5
Wyoming, MI 70-71 H 4
Wyoming Peak 66-67 H 4
Wyoming Range 66-67 H 4
Wytheville, VA 80-81 F 2

X

Xadded 194-195 b 1
Xa-doai 174-175 E 3
Xai Xai 198 F 7
Xalapa = Jalapa Enríquez 58-59 GH 8
Xalin 194-195 b 2
Xalisco = Jalisco 58-59 EF 7
Xamboiá 98-99 O 8
Xangongo 198 C 5
Xánthē 138-139 L 5
Xanxerê 103 F 3
Xaprui, Rio — 98-99 D 10
Xapuri 98-99 F 7
Xarardeere 194-195 b 3
Xar Moron He 166-167 MN 3
Xateturu, Cachoeira — 98-99 MN 8
Xauen = Shifshawn 194-195 CD 1
Xavantes, Serra dos — 98-99 K 7

Xcan 58-59 J 7

Xenia, IL 70-71 F 6
Xenia, OH 72-73 E 5
Xeriuini, Rio — 98-99 G 4

Xiachuan Dao 166-167 L 7
Xiadong 166-167 H 3
Xiaguan [TJ, Yunnan] 166-167 J 6
Xiahe 166-167 J 4
Xiamen 166-167 M 7
Xi'an 166-167 K 5
Xiangfan 166-167 L 5
Xianggang = Hong Kong 166-167 LM 7
Xiang Jiang 166-167 L 6
Xiangtan 166-167 L 6
Xiangxi Zizhizhou 166-167 KL 6
Xiangyang 166-167 L 5
Xiangyangzhen 170-171 E 1
Xianning 166-167 LM 6
Xian Xian 166-167 M 4
Xianyang 166-167 K 5
Xiaochangshan Dao 170-171 D 3
Xiao Hinggan Ling 166-167 O 1-2
Xiaoliangshan 170-171 D 1
Xiaoling He 170-171 C 2
Xiaomei Guan 166-167 LM 6
Xichang [TJ, Sichuan] 166-167 J 6
Xichū 86-87 K 7
Xichuan 166-167 L 5
Xicoco = Shikoku 166-167 P 5
Xicotepec de Juárez 86-87 LM 7
Xidachuan 170-171 FG 2

Xidachua 283

Xié, Rio — 98-99 E 4
Xiegar Zong = Shekhar Dsong 166-167 F 6
Xiêng Khouang 174-175 D 3
Xiengmai = Chiang Mai 174-175 C 3
Xifengkou 170-171 B 2
Xigezi = Zhigatse 166-167 F 6
Xiguit Qi 166-167 N 2
Xi Jiang 166-167 L 7
Xiliao He 166-167 N 3
Xilin Hot 166-167 M 3
Ximo = Kyūshū 166-167 P 5
Ximucheng 170-171 D 2
Xinbin 170-171 E 2
Xincai 166-167 LM 5
Xinchengbu 166-167 K 4
Xindi 170-171 B 2
Xindi = Honghu 166-167 L 6
Xindu 166-167 L 7
Xingang = Tanggu 166-167 M 4
Xingcheng 170-171 C 2
Xingning 166-167 M 7
Xingren 166-167 K 6
Xingtai 166-167 L 4
Xingu [BR, Amazonas] 98-99 F 6
Xingu [BR, Mato Grosso] 98-99 M 11
Xingu, Parque Nacional do — 98-99 M 10
Xingu, Rio — 98-99 J 6
Xinhua 166-167 L 6
Xining 166-167 J 4
Xinjiang [TJ, place] 166-167 L 4
Xinjiang = Xinjiang Uygur Zizhiqu 166-167 D-F 3
Xinjiang Uyghur Zizhiqu 166-167 D-G 3
Xinjiang Uygur Zizhiqu 166-167 D-F 3
Xinjin 170-171 CD 3
Xinkai He 166-167 N 3
Xinle 166-167 LM 4
Xinlitun 170-171 CD 1-2
Xinmin 166-167 N 3
Xinxian [TJ, Shanxi] 166-167 L 4
Xinxiang 166-167 LM 4
Xinyang 166-167 LM 5
Xinzhangzi 170-171 AB 2
Xinzhu = Hsinchu 166-167 N 7
Xiongyuecheng 170-171 CD 2
Xiquexique 98-99 L 7
Xiraz = Shīrāz 160-161 G 5
Xiriri, Lago — 98-99 L 5
Xiruá, Rio — 98-99 D 8
Xishuangbanna Daizu Zizhizhou 166-167 J 7
Xishuangbanna Zizhizhou ◁ 166-167 J 7
Xiuyan 170-171 D 2
Xi Xian [TJ, Shanxi] 166-167 L 4
Xizhong Dao 170-171 C 3

Xochistlahuaca 86-87 L 9
Xolapur = Sholāpur 160-161 M 7

Xpuhil 86-87 Q 8

Xuan'en 166-167 KL 5-6
Xuanhua 166-167 LM 3
Xuanwei 166-167 J 6
Xuchang 166-167 L 5
Xuddur 194-195 a 3
Xué 98-99 E 7
Xuguit Qi 166-167 N 2
Xunhua 166-167 J 4
Xunke 166-167 O 2
Xunyuecheng = Xiongyuecheng 170-171 CD 2
Xuyan = Xiuyan 170-171 D 2
Xuzhou 166-167 M 5

Y

Yaak, MT 66-67 F 1
Ya'an 166-167 J 6
Yaballo = Yabēlo 194-195 M 7-8
Yabēlo 194-195 M 7-8
Yablonovoi Mountains = Jablonovyj chrebet 154-155 U-W 7
Yabrīn 160-161 F 6
Yachats, OR 66-67 A 3
Yacheng 166-167 K 8
Ya-chou = Ya'an 166-167 J 6
Yachow = Ya'an 166-167 J 6
Yacolt, WA 66-67 B 3
Yacuiba 98-99 G 9
Yafi 174-175 M 7
Yafō, Tel Aviv- 160-161 C 4
Yahiko 170-171 M 4
Yahila 198 D 1
Yahk 66-67 EF 1
Yahuma 198 D 1
Yaichau = Ya Xian 166-167 KL 8
Yaizu 170-171 M 5
Yajalón 86-87 OP 9
Yakak, Cape — 52-53 u 7
Yakarta = Jakarta 174-175 E 8
Yakima, WA 58-59 BC 2
Yakima Indian Reservation 66-67 C 2
Yakima Ridge 66-67 CD 2
Yakima River 66-67 CD 2
Yakishiri-jima 170-171 b 1
Yako 194-195 D 6
Yakobi Island 52-53 T 8
Yakoko = Yapehe 198 DE 2
Yakt, MT 66-67 F 1
Yaku 170-171 H 7
Yakumo 170-171 b 2
Yaku-shima 166-167 P 5
Yaku sima = Yaku-shima 166-167 P 5
Yakutat, AK 46-47 HJ 6
Yakutat Bay 46-47 HJ 6
Yakut Autonomous Soviet Socialist Republic 154-155 U-b 4
Yakutsk = Jakutsk 154-155 Y 5
Yala [BUR] 174-175 D 5
Yale 66-67 C 1
Yale, MI 72-73 E 3
Yale, OK 76-77 F 4
Yale Point 74-75 J 4
Yalgoo 182-183 C 5
Yalinga 194-195 J 7
Yaloké 194-195 H 7
Yalong Jiang 166-167 J 6
Yalu 166-167 N 2
Yalu Cangpu Jiang = Tsangpo 166-167 EF 6
Ya-lu Chiang = Yalu Jiang 170-171 EF 2
Yalu He 166-167 N 2
Ya-lu Ho = Yalu He 166-167 N 2
Yalu Jiang 166-167 O 3
Ya-lung Chiang = Yalong Jiang 166-167 J 6
Yamada 170-171 NO 3
Yamada = Nankoku 170-171 JK 6
Yamaga 170-171 H 6
Yamagata 166-167 QR 4
Yamaguchi 170-171 HJ 5
Yamakuni 170-171 H 6
Yamalo-Nenets Autonomous Area 154-155 M-P 4
Yamal Peninsula = Jamal 154-155 MN 3
Yamanashi 170-171 M 5
Yamasaki 170-171 K 5
Yamato Bank 166-167 PQ 4
Yamato-sammyaku 31 B 4
Yambéring 194-195 B 6
Yambi, Mesa de — 98-99 E 4
Yāmbiū 194-195 K 8
Yambu = Kātmāndu 160-161 NO 5
Yamethin = Yamīthin 174-175 C 2
Yamīthin 174-175 C 2
Yamma Yamma, Lake — 182-183 H 5
Yammu = Jammu 160-161 LM 4
Yampa, CO 68-69 C 5
Yampa River 68-69 BC 5
Yampi Sound 182-183 D 3
Yamsay Mountain 66-67 C 4
Yamuduozuonake Hu = Ngamdo Tsonag Tsho 166-167 G 5
Yamuna 160-161 MN 5
Yanagawa 170-171 H 6
Yanai 170-171 HJ 6
Yanam 160-161 N 7
Yan'an 166-167 K 4
Yanaoca 98-99 E 7
Yanaon = Yanam 160-161 N 7
Yanbian 166-167 J 6
Yanbian Chaoxianzu Zizhizhou 166-167 OP 3
Yanbian Zizhizhou 170-171 GH 1
Yanbu' al-Baḥr 160-161 D 6
Yancheng [TJ, Jiangsu] 166-167 N 5
Yanchuan 166-167 KL 4
Yangambi 198 DE 1
Yangang-do = Ryanggang-do 170-171 FG 2
Yang-chiang = Yangjiang 166-167 L 7
Yangchuan = Yangquan 166-167 L 4
Yangdŏk 170-171 F 3
Yangdong Tsho 166-167 G 6
Yanggu [ROK] 170-171 FG 3
Yangi Hisar 166-167 CD 4
Yangjiang 166-167 L 7
Yangjŏng-ni 170-171 F 4
Yangkiang = Yangjiang 166-167 L 7
Yangku = Taiyuan 166-167 L 4
Yangp'yŏng 170-171 F 4
Yangquan 166-167 L 4
Yangsan 170-171 G 5
Yangshuling 170-171 B 2
Yangsi 170-171 E 3
Yangtze Kiang = Chang Jiang 166-167 K 5-6
Yangyang 166-167 O 4
Yangzhou 166-167 M 5
Yanina = Iōánnina 138-139 J 6
Yanji 166-167 O 3
Yanjing 166-167 H 6
Yankee Stadium 82 III c 2
Yankton, SD 58-59 G 3
Yanku = Taiyuan 166-167 L 4
Yanna 182-183 J 5
Yanonge 198 D 1
Yanqi = Qara Shahr 166-167 F 3
Yanskoi Bay = Janskij zaliv 154-155 Za 3
Yantai 166-167 N 4
Yanxi 166-167 L 6
Yao 194-195 H 6
Yaoganhutun = Yaoqianhu 170-171 D 2
Yaolo 198 D 1
Yaoqianhu 170-171 D 2
Yaoundé 194-195 G 8
Yap 148-149 R 9
Yāpanaya 160-161 MN 9
Yapehe 198 DE 2
Yapen, Pulau — 174-175 L 7
Yapen, Selat — 174-175 L 7
Yap Islands 174-175 L 5
Yaqui, Río — 58-59 E 6
Yaquina Head 66-67 A 3
Yaraka 182-183 H 4
Yarí, Río — 98-99 E 4
Yariga-take 166-167 Q 4
Yarkand 166-167 D 4
Yarkand darya 166-167 D 4-E 3
Yarmouth 46-47 X 9
Yarnell, AZ 74-75 G 5
Yaroslavl = Jaroslavl' 154-155 FG 6
Yarram 182-183 J 7
Yarraman 182-183 K 5
Yarumal 98-99 D 3
Yasanyama 194-195 J 8
Yasawa Group 174-175 a 2
Yashima 170-171 N 3
Yashiro-jima 170-171 J 6
Yass 182-183 J 6
Yasugi 170-171 J 5
Yatakala 194-195 E 6
Yates Center, KS 70-71 C 6-7
Yathkyed Lake 46-47 R 5
Yatsuga take 170-171 M 4-5
Yatsushiro 170-171 H 6
Yatsushiro-wan 170-171 H 6
Yauco 88-89 N 6
Yaunde = Yaoundé 194-195 G 8
Yautepec 86-87 L 8
Yauyos 98-99 D 7
Yavarí, Río — 98-99 E 5
Yavello = Yabēlo 194-195 M 7-8
Yaví, Cerro — 98-99 F 3
Yawatahama 170-171 J 6
Yaxchilán 58-59 H 8
Ya Xian 166-167 KL 8
Yayo 194-195 H 5
Yayuan 170-171 F 2
Yazd 160-161 G 4
Yazoo City, MS 78-79 D 4
Yazoo River 58-59 H 5

Ycliff 50 D 2

Ye 174-175 C 3
Ye-Buri midre Selate 194-195 N 5
Yecheng = Qarghaliq 166-167 D 4
Yech'ŏn 170-171 G 4
Yecla 132-133 G 9
Yécora 86-87 F 3
Yedo = Tōkyō 166-167 QR 4
Yeh-ch'êng = Qarghaliq 166-167 D 4
Yehsien = Ye Xian 166-167 MN 4
Yei [Sudan, place] 194-195 L 8
Yékia Sahal 194-195 H 5
Yélimané 194-195 BC 5-6
Yelizavety, Cape — = mys Jelizavety 154-155 b 7
Yell 116-117 e 3
Yellow Grass 49 FG 6
Yellowhead Highway 48 GH 3
Yellowhead Pass 46-47 N 7
Yellowknife 46-47 O 5
Yellow Medicine River 70-71 BC 3
Yellow Pine, ID 66-67 F 3
Yellow River 70-71 E 3
Yellow Sea 166-167 N 4
Yellowstone Lake 58-59 D 3
Yellowstone National Park 58-59 D 3
Yellowstone River 58-59 E 2
Yellowstone River, Clarks Fork — 68-69 B 3
Yellowtail Reservoir 66-67 JK 3
Yell Sound 116-117 ef 3
Yellville, AR 78-79 C 2
Yelwa 194-195 EF 6
Yemassee, SC 80-81 F 4
Yemen 160-161 E 7-8
Yemen, People's Democratic Republic of — 160-161 F 8-G 7
Yenangyaung 174-175 BC 2
Yên Bay 174-175 DE 2
Yencheng = Yancheng [TJ, Jiangsu] 166-167 N 5
Yen-ch'i = Qara Shahr 166-167 F 3
Yen-chi = Yanji 166-167 O 3
Yen-ching = Yanjing 166-167 H 6
Yen-ch'uan = Yanchuan 166-167 KL 4
Yendi 194-195 DE 7
Yeniceırmağı 142-143 G 8
Yenisei = Jenisej 154-155 Q 4
Yenisei Bay = Jenisejskij zaliv 154-155 OP 3
Yenki = Qara Shahr 166-167 F 3
Yenki = Yanji 166-167 O 3
Yenlo, Mount — 52-53 M 5
Yenpien = Yanbian 166-167 J 6
Yenping = Nanping 166-167 M 6
Yentai = Yantai 166-167 N 4
Yentna River 52-53 M 5
Yeo, Lake — 182-183 D 5
Yeovil 116-117 J 10
Yeppoon 182-183 K 4
Yerington, NV 74-75 D 3
Yermo 76-77 B 9
Yerna Tsho 166-167 F 5
Yerqiang = Yarkand 166-167 D 4
Yerupaja 98-99 D 7
Yĕrūshălayim 160-161 CD 4
Yesan 170-171 F 4
Yesilırmak 160-161 D 2
Yeso, NM 76-77 B 5
Yesso = Hokkaidō 166-167 RS 3
Yeste 132-133 F 9
Yeu, Île de — 132-133 F 5
Yeungkong = Yangjiang 166-167 L 7
Yew Mountain 72-73 F 5
Ye Xian [TJ, Shandong] 166-167 MN 4
Yezd = Yazd 160-161 G 4
Yezo = Hokkaidō 166-167 RS 3
Yezo Strait = Nemuro-kaikyō 170-171 d 1-2

Yhú 103 E 2

Yi'allaq, Gebel — = Jabal Yu'alliq 199 C 2
Yibin 166-167 JK 6
Yichang 166-167 L 5
Yicheng [TJ, Hubei] 166-167 L 5
Yichun [TJ, Heilongjiang] 166-167 O 2
Yichun [TJ, Jiangxi] 166-167 LM 6
Yidda = Jiddah 160-161 D 6
Yidu [TJ, Hubei] 166-167 L 5
Yidu [TJ, Shandong] 166-167 M 4
Yiershi 166-167 MN 2
Yilan 166-167 OP 2
Yilehuli Shan 166-167 NO 1
Yinchuan 166-167 JK 4
Yindu He = Sengge Khamba 166-167 E 5
Yingchuan 166-167 K 4
Yingde 166-167 L 7
Yingjisha = Yangi Hisar 166-167 CD 4
Yingkou 166-167 N 3
Ying-k'ou = Yingkou 166-167 N 3
Yingkow = Yingkou 170-171 CD 2
Yingpan 170-171 E 2
Yingshan [TJ → Nanchong] 166-167 K 5
Yingtan 166-167 M 6
Ying-tê = Yingde 166-167 L 7
Yining = Ghulja 166-167 E 3
Yinkow = Yingkou 166-167 N 3
Yinxian = Ningbo 166-167 N 6
Yi-pin = Yibin 166-167 JK 6
Yirga-Alam = Yirga Alem 194-195 M 7
Yirga 'Alem 194-195 M 7
Yirōl 194-195 L 7
Yishan [TJ, place] 166-167 K 7
Yi-tcheou = Linyi 166-167 M 4
Yitu = Yidu 166-167 M 4
Yi Xian [TJ, Liaoning] 166-167 N 3
Yixian = Ye Xian 166-167 LM 4
Yiyang [TJ, Hunan] 166-167 L 6

Yläne 114-115 K 7
Ylikita 114-115 N 4
Ylivieska 114-115 L 5
Yllästunturi 114-115 KL 4
Y Llethr 116-117 GH 8

Yoakum, TX 76-77 F 8
Yochow = Yueyang 166-167 L 6
Yoder, WY 68-69 D 5
Yodoe 170-171 J 5
Yogan, Cerro — 103 BC 8
Yogyakarta [RI, administrative unit = 13 ◁] 174-175 EF 8
Yogyakarta [RI, place] 174-175 EF 8
Yoho National Park 48 J 4
Yoichi 170-171 b 2
Yokadouma 194-195 H 8
Yōkaichiba 170-171 N 5
Yokchi-do 170-171 G 5
Yokkaichi 166-167 Q 5
Yokkaiti = Yokkaichi 166-167 Q 5
Yoko 194-195 G 7
Yokohama 166-167 QR 4
Yokosuka 166-167 QR 4
Yokote 166-167 QR 4
Yola 194-195 G 7
Yolaina, Cordillera de — 88-89 D 9
Yolombo 198 D 2
Yom, Mae Nam — 174-175 CD 3
Yonago 170-171 J 5
Yŏnan 170-171 EF 4
Yoncalla, OR 66-67 B 4
Yŏnch'ŏn 170-171 F 3
Yoneshiro-gawa 170-171 N 2
Yonezawa 166-167 QR 4
Yŏngam 170-171 F 5
Yongamp'o 170-171 E 3
Yong'an 166-167 M 6
Yŏngch'ŏn 170-171 G 5
Yongdeng 166-167 J 4
Yongdian 170-171 E 2
Yŏngdŏk 170-171 G 4
Yŏngdong 170-171 F 4
Yonggok-tang 170-171 E 2
Yŏnghae 170-171 G 4
Yongha-ri 170-171 F 3
Yonghŭng 170-171 F 3
Yŏnghŭng-do 170-171 EF 4
Yŏngil-man 170-171 G 4
Yongji 166-167 L 5
Yongjia = Wenzhou 166-167 N 6
Yŏngju 170-171 G 4
Yongling 170-171 E 2
Yongning 166-167 J 6
Yongning = Nanning 166-167 K 7
Yŏngsan 170-171 G 5
Yongtai 166-167 M 6
Yŏngwŏl 170-171 G 4
Yŏngwŏn 170-171 F 3
Yongxiu 166-167 LM 6
Yŏngyu 170-171 E 3
Yonker 49 CD 4
Yonkers, NY 58-59 M 3
Yonne 132-133 J 5
York, AL 78-79 E 4
York, ND 68-69 G 1
York, NE 68-69 H 5
York, PA 58-59 L 3-4
York, SC 80-81 F 3
York [AUS] 182-183 C 6
York [GB] 116-117 KL 6-7
York, Cape — 182-183 H 2
York, Kap — 46-47 X 2
York Dales 116-117 K 6
Yorke Peninsula 182-183 G 6
Yorketown 182-183 G 6-7
York Factory 46-47 S 6
York Harbour 51 G 3
York River 80-81 H 2
Yorkshire Wolds 116-117 L 6-7
York Sound 182-183 DE 2
Yorkton 46-47 Q 7
Yorktown, TX 76-77 F 8
Yorktown, VA 80-81 H 2
Yoro 88-89 C 7
Yosemite National Park 74-75 D 4
Yosemite National Park, CA 58-59 C 4
Yoshida 170-171 J 6
Yoshii-gawa 170-171 K 5
Yoshino-gawa 170-171 JK 5
Yoshioka = Taiwa 170-171 N 3
Yōsō-do 170-171 F 6
Yösön Bulag = Altaj 166-167 H 2
Yost, UT 66-67 G 5
Yŏsu 166-167 O 5
Yotaú 98-99 G 8
Yōtei-dake 170-171 b 2
Youanmi 182-183 C 5
Youghal = Eochaill 116-117 D 8-9
Youghal Harbour = Cuan Eochaille 116-117 D 9
Youkounkoun 194-195 B 6
Young, AZ 74-75 H 5
Young [AUS] 182-183 J 6
Young [CDN] 49 F 5
Young Island 31 C 16-17
Youngstown 49 C 5
Youngstown, FL 78-79 G 5
Youngstown, OH 58-59 KL 3
Younts Peak 66-67 J 4
Youville, Montréal- 82 I ab 1
Yowl Islands = Kepulauan Aju 174-175 K 6
Yoyang = Yueyang 166-167 L 6
Yŏyu 170-171 F 4
Yozgat 160-161 CD 3

Ypres = Ieper 132-133 J 3
Ypsilanti, MI 72-73 E 3
Ypsilanti, ND 68-69 G 2

Yreka, CA 66-67 B 5

Ysabel = Santa Isabel 174-175 jk 6
Ysabel Channel 174-175 NO 7
Ysleta, TX 76-77 A 7
Yssel Lake = IJsselmeer 132-133 K 2
Ystad 114-115 E 10
Ystalyfera 116-117 H 9

Yu'alliq, Jabal — 199 C 2
Yuan'an 166-167 L 5
Yüan-an = Yuan'an 166-167 L 5
Yüan Chiang = Hong He 166-167 J 7
Yüan Chiang = Yuan Jiang 166-167 L 6
Yüan-chou = Yichun 166-167 LM 6
Yuanchow = Zhijiang 166-167 KL 6
Yuan Jiang [TJ, river] 166-167 L 6
Yuanling 166-167 L 6
Yüan-ling = Yuanling 166-167 L 6
Yuanmou 166-167 J 6
Yuanping 166-167 L 4
Yuba City, CA 58-59 B 4
Yūbari 166-167 R 3
Yuba River 74-75 C 3
Yūbetsu 170-171 d 2
Yūbetsu, Shimo- 170-171 cd 1
Yūbetsu ↖ Kusiro 170-171 d 2
Yubo = Lī Yūbū 194-195 K 7
Yucatán 58-59 J 7
Yucatán, Peninsula de — 58-59 HJ 8
Yucatan Basin 58-59 JK 8
Yucatan Channel = Canal de Yucatán 58-59 J 7
Yucca, AZ 74-75 F 5
Yuci 166-167 L 4
Yudian = Keriya 166-167 E 4
Yüeh-yang = Yueyang 166-167 L 6
Yueqing 166-167 N 6
Yueyang 166-167 L 6
Yugor Strait = proliv Jugorskij Šar 154-155 L 4-M 3
Yugoslavia 138-139 F 3-J 5
Yuhuang 166-167 M 4
Yuhuang Ding 166-167 M 4
Yuki Mount 52-53 JK 4
Yuki River 52-53 J 4
Yukon, Territoire de — = Yukon Territory 46-47 JK 4-5
Yukon Crossing 52-53 T 5
Yukon Delta 52-53 EF 5
Yukon Plateau 46-47 J 5
Yukon River 46-47 H 4
Yukon Territory 46-47 JK 4-5
Yukuduma = Yokadouma 194-195 H 8
Yukuhashi 170-171 H 6
Yulee, FL 80-81 c 1
Yule River 182-183 C 4
Yulin [TJ, Guangxi Zhuangzu Zizhiqu] 166-167 L 7
Yulin [TJ, Shaanxi] 166-167 KL 4
Yü-lin = Yulin [TJ, Guangxi Zhuangzu Zizhiqu] 166-167 L 7
Yü-lin = Yulin [TJ, Shaanxi] 166-167 KL 4
Yulongxue Shan 166-167 J 6
Yü-lung Shan = Yulongxue Shan 166-167 J 6
Yuma, AZ 58-59 D 5
Yuma, CO 68-69 E 5
Yuma Desert 74-75 F 6
Yuma Indian Reservation 74-75 F 6
Yumari, Cerro — 98-99 F 4
Yumen 166-167 H 4
Yuna 182-183 BC 5
Yunaska Island 52-53 l 4
Yungan = Yong'an 166-167 M 6
Yungas 98-99 FG 8
Yungchang = Baoshan 166-167 HJ 6
Yung-chi = Yongji 166-167 L 5
Yung-chou = Lingling 166-167 L 6
Yungki = Jilin 166-167 O 3
Yung-ning = Yongning 166-167 J 6
Yungtai = Yongtai 166-167 M 6
Yung-têng = Yongdeng 166-167 J 4
Yung-tien-ch'êng = Yongdian 170-171 E 2
Yungxiao 166-167 M 7
Yunhe = Lishui 166-167 MN 6
Yünlin 166-167 MN 7
Yunnan 166-167 HJ 7
Yunnan = Kunming 166-167 J 6
Yunsiao = Yunxiao 166-167 M 7
Yunxiao 166-167 M 7
Yura-gawa 170-171 K 5
Yurimaguas 98-99 D 6
Yurung darya 166-167 DE 4
Yuscarán 88-89 C 8
Yûsef, Baḥr — = Baḥr Yusuf 199 B 3
Yu Shan [RC] 166-167 N 7
Yushu 166-167 O 3
Yushu = Chhergundo 166-167 H 5
Yushu Zangzu Zizhizhou 166-167 GH 5
Yusuf, Baḥr — 199 B 3
Yü-tien = Keriya 166-167 E 4
Yuty 103 E 3
Yutze = Yuci 166-167 L 4
Yuzawa [J, Akita] 170-171 N 3
Yuzawa [J, Niigata] 170-171 M 4

Z

Zaachila 86-87 M 9
Zaaltajn Gov' 166-167 H 3
Zaanstad 132-133 K 2
Zabajkal'sk 154-155 W 8
Zabarjad, Jazīrat — 199 DE 6
Zabīd 160-161 E 8
Žabljak 138-139 H 4
Zabok 138-139 FG 2
Zabol 160-161 J 4
Zaburunje 142-143 K 6
Zacapa 86-87 Q 10
Zacapu 86-87 K 8
Zacatecas 58-59 F 7
Zacatecas, Sierras de — 86-87 JK 6
Zacatecoluca 88-89 B 8
Zacatula, Río — 86-87 JK 8
Zacoalco de Torres 86-87 J 7
Zadar 138-139 F 3
Zădetkyī Kyūn 174-175 C 5
Ẓafār = Ẓufār 160-161 G 7
Za'farānah, Az- 199 C 3
Zafra 132-133 D 9
Žagań 124 G 3
Zagazig, Ez- = Az-Zaqāzīq 194-195 KL 2
Zaghūrah 194-195 C 2
Zagnanado 194-195 E 7
Zāgôrâ = Zaghūrah 194-195 C 2
Zagorsk 154-155 F 6
Zagreb 138-139 FG 3
Zāgros, Kūhhā-ye — 160-161 F 3-4
Zagros Mountains = Kūhhā-ye Zāgros 160-161 F 3-4

Žagubica 138-139 J 3
Zāhedān 160-161 J 5
Zahl, ND 68-69 E 1
Zahlah 142-143 G 9
Żahrān 160-161 E 7
Żahrān, Aż- 160-161 FG 5
Zaidam = Tshaidam 166-167 GH 4
Zaire [Angola] 198 B 3
Zaïre [ZRE, river] 198 C 2
Zaïre [ZRE, state] 198 C-E 2
Zaječar 138-139 JK 4
Zajsan 154-155 P 8
Zajsan, ozero — 154-155 P 8
Zakamensk 154-155 T 7
Zākhū 160-161 E 3
Zako 194-195 J 7
Zakopane 124 JK 4
Zakouma 194-195 HJ 6
Zakroczym 124 K 2
Zákynthos [GR, island] 138-139 J 7
Zákynthos [GR, place] 138-139 J 7
Zala 124 H 5
Zalaegerszeg 124 H 5
Zalău 138-139 K 2
Zālingei 194-195 J 6
Zalṭan 194-195 H 3
Žambaj 142-143 K 6
Zambeze, Rio — 198 F 5
Zambezi 198 EF 5
Zambézia 198 G 5
Zambia 198 E 5-F 4
Zamboanga 174-175 H 5
Zamboanga Peninsula 174-175 H 5
Zamfara 194-195 F 6
Zamora, CA 74-75 BC 3
Zamora [E] 132-133 E 8
Zamora [EC, place] 98-99 D 5
Zamora de Hidalgo 58-59 F 7-8
Zamość 124 L 3
Zamzam, Wādī — 194-195 G 2
Žanadarja 154-155 L 9
Zanaga 198 B 2
Žanatas 154-155 MN 9
Záncara 132-133 F 9
Zanderij 98-99 L 2
Zane Hills 52-53 JK 3
Zanesville, OH 58-59 K 4
Zang = Xizang Zizhiqu 166-167 EF 5
Zanjān 160-161 F 3
Zante = Zákynthos 138-139 J 7
Žanterek 142-143 K 6
Zanthus 182-183 D 6
Zanulje 142-143 J 3
Zanzibar 198 GH 3
Zanzibar and Pemba 198 GH 3
Zanzibar Island 198 GH 3
Zaouatallaz 194-195 F 3-4
Zaouia-el-Kahla = Burj 'Umar Idrîs
   194-195 EF 3
Zapadnaja Dvina 142-143 EF 4
Zapadna Morava 138-139 J 4
Zapadno-Sibirskaja ravnina
   154-155 L-Q 5-6
Zapala 103 BC 5
Zapaleri, Cerro — 103 C 2
Zapata, TX 76-77 E 9
Zapata, Península de — 88-89 F 3
Zapiga 103 BC 1
Zapokrovskij 154-155 W 7
Zapopan 86-87 J 7
Zaporožje 142-143 FG 6
Zaqāzīq, Az- 194-195 KL 2
Zara = Zadar 138-139 F 3
Zaragoza [E] 132-133 G 8
Zaragoza [MEX] 86-87 K 3
Zaragoza, Juchitán de — 58-59 GH 8
Zaragoza, Puebla de — 58-59 G 8
Zárate 103 E 4
Zaraza 98-99 F 3
Zarembo Island 52-53 w 8
Zaria 194-195 F 6
Zarisberge 198 C 6-7
Žarkamys 154-155 K 8
Žarkovskij 142-143 F 4
Žarma 154-155 OP 8
Žarmyš 142-143 K 7
Zarqat, Nā'am, Jabal — 199 D 6
Zarskoje Selo = Puškin
   154-155 DE 6
Żary 124 G 3
Žaryk 154-155 N 8
Žašejek [SU ✓ Kandalakša]
   114-115 O 4
Žašejek [SU ↑ Kandalakša]
   114-115 P 4
Žaškov 142-143 F 6
Zasla 114-115 M 10
Žataj 154-155 YZ 5
Žatec 124 F 3
Żatīr, Aż- 160-161 E 6-7
Zatoka 142-143 F 6
Záuiet el Beidá' = Al-Baydá'
   194-195 J 2
Zavalla, TX 76-77 G 7
Zavety Iljiča 154-155 ab 8
Zavia = Az-Zāwīyah 194-195 G 2
Zavidovići 138-139 GH 3
Zavitinsk 154-155 Y 7
Zavodoukovsk 154-155 M 6
Zavolžje 154-155 G 6
Zawi 198 EF 5
Zawia = Az-Zāwīyah 194-195 G 2
Zawîlah 194-195 H 3
Zāwīyah, Az- 194-195 G 2

Zaydūn, Wādī — 199 C 5

Zbąszyn 124 GH 2

Żdanov 142-143 G 6
Zdolbunov 142-143 E 5
Zduńska Wola 124 J 3

Zealand 51 C 4
Zealand = Sjælland 114-115 DE 10
Zeballos 48 D 4
Zeebrugge, Brugge- 132-133 J 3
Zeehan 182-183 HJ 8
Zeeland, MI 70-71 GH 4
Zeerust 198 E 7
Zēfat 160-161 D 4
Zeidūn, Wādī — = Wādī Zaydūn
   199 C 5
Zeila = Seyla' 194-195 N 6
Zeitz 124 EF 3
Zeja [SU, place] 154-155 Y 7
Zeja [SU, river] 154-155 Y 7
Zelenga 142-143 J 6
Zelenoborskij 114-115 P 4
Zelenodoľsk 154-155 HJ 6
Zelenogradsk 124 K 1
Železnik 138-139 J 3
Železnodorožnyj 154-155 J 5
Železnogorsk 142-143 G 5
Zelinograd = Celinograd
   154-155 MN 7
Zella = Zillah 194-195 H 3
Zembra, Djezîra — = Al-Jâmûr al-
   Kabîr 194-195 M 1
Zemcy 142-143 F 4
Zemio 194-195 JK 7
zemľa Aleksandra I 31 C 29
Zemlandskij poluostrov 124 K 1
Zémongo 194-195 J 7
Zempoala 86-87 M 8
Zempoaltepec, Cerro — 58-59 GH 8
Zemun, Beograd- 138-139 HJ 3
Zemzen, Uádī — = Wādī Zamzam
   194-195 G 2
Zenia, CA 66-67 B 5
Zenica 138-139 G 3
Zenshū = Chŏnju 166-167 O 4
Zephyrhills, FL 80-81 bc 2
Zeravšan 160-161 K 3
Zeravšanskij chrebet 160-161 K 3
Zerbst 124 F 2-3
Żerdevka 142-143 H 5
Zere, Gawd-e — 160-161 J 5
Zesfontein = Sesfontein 198 B 5
Zetland = Shetland 116-117 f 3
Zêzere 132-133 CD 9

Zgierz 124 J 3

Zhahang = Tsethang 166-167 G 6
Zhaling Hu = Kyaring Tsho
   166-167 F 5
Zhangguangcai Ling 166-167 O 2-3
Zhangjiakou 166-167 L 3
Zhangling 166-167 N 1
Zhangsanying 170-171 AB 2
Zhangye 166-167 J 4
Zhangzhou 166-167 M 7
Zhangzi Dao 170-171 D 3
Zhanjiang 166-167 L 7
Zhanjiang Gang 166-167 L 7
Zhaotong 166-167 J 6
Zhaxigang 166-167 DE 5
Zhaxilhünbo 166-167 F 6
Zhejiang 166-167 MN 6
Zheling Guan 166-167 L 6
Zhengzhou 166-167 LM 5
Zhenhai 166-167 N 5-6
Zhenjiang 166-167 M 5
Zhenxi = Bar Köl 166-167 G 3
Zhenyuan [TJ, Guizhou] 166-167 K 6
Zhenyuan [TJ, Yunnan] 166-167 J 7
Zhigatse 166-167 F 6
Zhijiang [TJ, Hunan] 166-167 KL 6
Zhikharkhunglung 166-167 F 5
Zhokhova Island = ostrov Žochova
   154-155 de 2
Zhongdian 166-167 HJ 6
Zhongshan 166-167 L 7
Zhongwei 166-167 JK 4
Zhongyang Shanmo = Chungyang
   Shanmo 166-167 N 7
Zhoujiakou = Zhoukou
   166-167 LM 5
Zhoukou 166-167 LM 5
Zhoushan Qundao 166-167 N 5
Zhuanghe 170-171 D 3
Zhucheng 166-167 MN 4
Zhuhe = Shangzhi 166-167 O 2
Zhuji 166-167 N 6
Zhushan 166-167 KL 5
Zhuzhou 166-167 L 6

Zibo 166-167 M 4
Zidani most 138-139 F 2
Ziel, Mount — 182-183 F 4
Zielona Góra 124 GH 2-3
Ziftá 199 B 2
Žigalovo 154-155 U 7
Žigansk 154-155 X 4
Zīghān 194-195 J 3
Zigong 166-167 JK 6
Ziguei 194-195 H 6
Ziguinchor 194-195 A 6
Zihu = Bajan Choto 166-167 JK 4
Zihuatanejo 86-87 JK 9

Zijin 166-167 M 7
Zilair 154-155 K 7
Zile 142-143 G 7
Žilina 124 J 4
Zillah 194-195 H 3
Zillah, WA 66-67 C 2
Ziltî, Az- 160-161 EF 5
Zima 154-155 T 7
Zimapán 86-87 KL 6-7
Zimbabwe [ZW, ruins] 198 F 6
Zimbabwe [ZW, state] 198 EF 5
Zimme = Chiang Mai 174-175 C 3
Zimnicea 138-139 L 4
Zinder 194-195 F 6
Zion, IL 70-71 G 4
Zion National Monument 74-75 G 4
Zion National Park 74-75 G 4
Zionsville, IN 70-71 GH 6
Zipaquirá 98-99 E 3-4
Žirje 138-139 F 4
Zirrāh, Gaud-e — = Gawd-e Zere
   160-161 J 5
Zi Shui 166-167 L 6
Zistersdorf 124 H 4
Žitomir 142-143 E 5
Zittau 124 G 3
Zitziana River 52-53 M 4
Ziway 194-195 M 7
Zizhong 166-167 JK 5-6
Zizó-zaki 170-171 J 5
Zlatica 138-139 KL 4
Zlatograd 138-139 L 5
Zlatoust 154-155 K 6
Zlatoustovsk 154-155 Za 7
Zlín = Gottwaldov 124 G 4
Žlītan 194-195 GH 2
Žlobin 142-143 EF 5
Złoczew 124 J 3
Złotów 124 H 2

Zmeinogorsk 154-155 P 7
Zmeinyj ostrov 142-143 F 6
Žmerinka 142-143 E 6

Znamenka 142-143 F 6
Znamensk 124 K 1
Znojmo 124 GH 4

Zóbuė 198 F 5
Žochova, ostrov — 154-155 de 2
Zohlaguna, Meseta de — 86-87 Q 8
Zoločev 142-143 DE 6
Zolotaja Gora 154-155 XY 7
Zomba 198 G 5
Zombo 198 F 5
Zongo 198 C 1
Zonguldak 160-161 C 2
Zoo [USA, Chicago] 83 II b 1
Zoo [USA, New York] 82 III c 1
Zorra, Isla — 58-59 b 2
Zortman, MT 68-69 B 2
Zorzor 194-195 C 7
Zouar 194-195 H 4
Zoutpansberge = Soutpansberge
   198 EF 6

Zrenjanin 138-139 J 3

Zuar = Zouar 194-195 H 4
Zubayr, Jabal — 199 C 4
Zubayr, Jazā'ir az- 160-161 E 7-8
Zubova Poľana 142-143 H 5
Zuénoula 194-195 C 7
Zuera 132-133 G 8
Żufār 160-161 G 7
Zug 124 D 5
Zugdidi 142-143 H 7
Zugspitze 124 E 5
Zuíla = Zawîlah 194-195 H 3
Zuishavane 198 F 6
Zújar 132-133 E 9
Zujevka 142-143 K 4
Zujevo, Orechovo- 154-155 FG 6
Žukovka 142-143 F 5
Zukur 194-195 N 6
Zumba 98-99 D 5
Zumbrota, MN 70-71 D 3
Zumpango 86-87 L 8
Zumūl, Umm az- 160-161 GH 6
Zungeru 194-195 F 7
Zuni, NM 74-75 J 5
Zuni Indian Reservation 74-75 J 5
Zuni Mountains 74-75 JK 5
Zunyi 166-167 K 6
Županja 138-139 H 3
Zūq, Ḥāssī — 194-195 B 4
Zuqar = Zukur 194-195 N 6
Zürich 124 D 5
Zürichsee 124 D 5
Zuru 194-195 F 6
Zuwārah 194-195 G 2

Zvolen 124 J 4
Zvornik 138-139 H 3

Zwai, Lake — = Ziway 194-195 M 7
Zweibrücken 124 C 4
Zwettl 124 G 4
Zwickau 124 F 3
Zwiesel 124 F 4
Zwolle 132-133 L 2
Zwolle, LA 78-79 C 5

Zyōhana 170-171 L 4
Zyōzankei 170-171 b 2
Zyr'anka 154-155 cd 4

Zyr'anovsk 154-155 PQ 8
Żyrardów 124 K 2